Women and Gender

A Feminist Psychology

SECOND EDITION

Women and Gender

A FEMINIST PSYCHOLOGY

Rhoda Unger
Montclair State University

Mary Crawford
West Chester University of Pennsylvania

THE McGRAW-HILL COMPANIES, INC.

New York St. Louis San Francisco Auckland Bogotá Caracas
Lisbon London Madrid Mexico City Milan Montreal New Delhi
San Juan Singapore Sydney Tokyo Toronto

McGraw-Hill

A Division of The ***McGraw-Hill*** *Companies*

WOMEN AND GENDER
A Feminist Psychology

Permissions Acknowledgments, appear on pages 663–664 and, on this page by reference.

This book is printed on acid-free paper.

7 8 9 0 FGR FGR 9 0 9

ISBN 0-07-065942-7

This book was set in Palatino by Ruttle, Shaw & Wetherill, Inc.
The editors were Beth Kaufman and Fred H. Burns;
the production supervisor was Kathryn Porzio.
The cover was designed by Christopher Brady.
The photo editor was Anne Manning.
Quebecor Printing/Fairfield was printer and binder.

Cover: Dennis Deloria (photographer), "The Dancers of Third Age," provided by Liz Lerman, Founder and Artistic Director of The Dance Exchange.

Library of Congress Catalog Card Number: 95.81568

About the Authors

RHODA UNGER is Professor of Psychology and Director of the Honors Program at Montclair State University in New Jersey. She received her Ph.D. in experimental psychology from Harvard University. Professor Unger was the first recipient of the Carolyn Wood Sherif Award from the Division on the Psychology of Women of the American Psychological Association. She is also the recipient of two distinguished publication awards and a recent distinguished career award from the Association for Women in Psychology. She has been active in various feminist organizations within psychology since 1972 and has lectured extensively in the United States and abroad. She is currently the North American editor of the international journal *Feminism & Psychology.* Professor Unger is the author or editor of five previous books, including *Representations: Social Constructions of Gender; Women, Gender, and Social Psychology;* and *Female and Male.*

MARY CRAWFORD is Professor of Psychology and Women's Studies at West Chester University of Pennsylvania. She has held the Jane W. Irwin Chair in Women's Studies at Hamilton College, served as Distinguished Visiting Teacher/Scholar at Trenton State College, and directed the graduate program in women's studies at the University of South Carolina. She received her Ph.D. in experimental psychology from the University of Delaware. Professor Crawford is active in the Division on the Psychology of Women of the American Psychological Association as well as many regional and national groups concerned with gender equity. Her publications include the books *Gender and Thought* and *Talking Difference: On Gender and Language.* In addition to her scholarly works, she has written on women's issues in popular periodicals such as MS. Magazine.

To our husbands
Burt Unger and Roger Chaffin
for always being there
and to our children:
Laurel and Rachel
Mary, Mark, and Ben
who represent our hopes
for the future.

Contents

Preface xi

1. Introduction to a Feminist Psychology of Women 1
2. Approaches to Understanding Girls and Women 28
3. The Meanings of Difference: Sex, Gender, and Cognitive Abilities 68
4. Images of Women 101
5. Doing Gender: Sex, Status, and Power 145
6. Biological Aspects of Sex and Gender 183
7. Becoming Gendered: Childhood 222
8. Becoming a Woman: Puberty and Adolescence 261
9. Sex, Love, and Romance 302
10. Commitments: Women and Long-Term Relationships 345
11. Mothering 383
12. Work and Achievement 427
13. Midlife and Beyond 471
14. Violence Against Women 513
15. Gender and Psychological Disorders 554

Afterword 595

References 597

Permissions Acknowledgments 663

Author Index 665

Subject Index 673

- *Women are a diverse group.* Perhaps the only appropriate response to a generalization about women is the question, "Which women?" Feminist scholars have become increasingly sensitive to the differences among women—in social class, ethnicity, age, sexual orientation, (dis)ability, and culture. Integrating diversity throughout each chapter of the book, we explore the ways that these differences affect women's experiences, including gender socialization, adult relationships, and the experience of psychological distress and disorder. We also make use of a great deal of cross-cultural data, because they help broaden psychological knowledge from its largely white, North American, middle-class perspective. Moreover, cross-cultural data provide powerful examples of our first theme, that gender is more than just sex. Even phenomena thought to have a strong biological base, such as hermaphrodism, menarche, and menopause, are shaped by culture.
- *Psychology should be related to social change.* Our feminist perspective implies that there are limits to the power of individual change. Many of the problems that confront girls and women today are the result of social structures that disadvantage them. While changes in individual attitudes and behaviors, traditionally a focus of psychological research and practice, are necessary, they must be linked with changes in societies as a whole. Women may view social change as more critical than men do because they suffer more from the oppressive aspects of societal structures. However, no social problem is "just" a woman's problem.

NEW IN THIS EDITION

New to this edition is a section headed "Connecting Themes." Each chapter ends with a summary of how the four themes are played out in the topics and issues of that particular chapter. This allows students to trace the themes throughout the book and see their importance and relevance across a wide range of topics.

The new edition incorporates more information about the diversity of women into each chapter. It expands the multicultural perspective of the previous edition by adding new findings about the interactions of ethnicity, sexual orientation, gender, and social class at many points in women's lives. It also pays more attention to the role of the media in defining and constructing girls and women of all ages. It continues and expands our concern with the *context* of women's lives both on the institutional level (for example, in schools and at work) and the interpersonal level (by analyzing the nature and structures of groups and the gendered behaviors produced within them). Of course, this edition is updated, with hundreds of new references to recent research. It has more (and livelier) illustrations and tables. And, through a long process of revision and refinement, the text is *shorter* than the first edition!

New topics in this edition include coverage and analysis of the backlash against feminism (Chapter 1); the role of sexism in the schools (Chapters 3 and 8); media images of women athletes; the representation of women in rap and music videos (both in Chapter 4); pornography, race, and hostility toward women (Chapters 4 and 14); factors influencing women's perception of their leadership abilities (Chapter 5); biological determinism in the media (Chapters 3 and 6); the "silencing" of adolescent girls (Chapter 8); differences among diverse groups of women in the meaning of sexuality and body image, and implications for therapeutic treatment (Chapters 9 and 15); the new reproductive technology and the medical, legal, and ethical issues it raises; woman-headed households; and socially created obstacles to mothering (all in Chapter 11); a new synthesis of the costs and benefits of juggling work, family, and relationship roles (Chapter 12); changing cultural views of menopause; and achievement in mid- and later life (both in Chapter 13).

Those who have used the first edition will also note expanded discussion of other topics, including cultural diversity and personality (Chapter 2); media portrayals of women (Chapters 3, 4, 6, 8, 9, 11, and 13); and cognitive mechanisms that maintain sexism (Chapters 3 and 5). Timely topics such as the "glass ceiling," the "mommy track," the politics of premenstrual syndrome, and the reported existence of a "gay gene" are introduced as well.

USING THIS BOOK

Women and Gender contains a great deal of information and a sophisticated analysis of the field. However, as the wide adoption of the first edition at very diverse institutions shows, it is an accessible text. It can be read by people who have the equivalent of one course in psychology and no previous exposure to women's studies. Students find the wealth of women's own accounts of their experiences compelling. And they like the touches of humor that lighten serious issues.

The book can be used in either a chronological developmental sequence, in social/personality/clinical clusters, or in groupings of topical issues. Each chapter can stand as a unit by itself, allowing maximum flexibility in combining them. Chapters 3, 6–8, 10, 11 and 13 have a developmental approach that covers the lifespan. Chapters 4, 5, and 12 are social psychologically oriented, and Chapters 2, 9, 14, and 15 form a clinical/personality cluster.

The Instructor's Manual for the new edition, by Mykol Hamilton, Amanda Durik, and Mary Crawford, is greatly expanded. It contains many more test items (multiple choice, short-answer, and essay), current film and video listings, new classroom demonstrations and other techniques for stimulating active involvement, sample syllabi, suggestions for using the internet and the world-wide web, course evaluation forms, and much more. We are grateful to Mykol and Amanda for taking on this sizeable task. Their superb work on the manual has made our commitment to fostering excellent teaching a reality.

ACKNOWLEDGMENTS

Like the previous edition, this book came about only because of the efforts of a large number of colleagues and friends. Most notable are Jackie White, Patricia Donat, and Barrie Bondurant, who contributed a compelling chapter on violence against girls and women to both editions. We are grateful to have their expertise and analysis on this vitally important topic.

We thank Lori Fitton, ace graduate assistant, for her help with references, illustrations, and manuscript preparation. Special thanks go to our editors at McGraw-Hill, Jane Vaicunas and Beth Kaufman, along with senior editing supervisor Fred Burns and photo editor Anne Manning. Their special brand of persistent patience got us through to the end; if we weren't exactly relaxed, at least we remained reasonably sane and (almost) on schedule.

We wish to thank all the students who read the first edition and responded to it in our classes, and the instructors and students around the United States and Canada who so generously gave us feedback on it. We thank, too, the reviewers for the second edition: Marlene Adelman, Norwalk Community Technical College; William B. Dragoin, Georgia Southwestern College; Karen G. Howe, Trenton State College; Korrel Kanoy, Peace College; Pat Lefler, Lexington Community College; Toby Silverman, William Patterson College of New Jersey; and Doris J. Wright, Georgia State University.

We consider this book to be truly a collaborative effort. Our families have only to read the dedication to know how important their contributions have been. Our colleagues, students and friends, too, should know that this book would not exist without your warm cooperation, insights, and support.

Rhoda Unger
Mary Crawford

Women and Gender

A Feminist Psychology

CHAPTER 1

Introduction to a Feminist Psychology of Women

BEGINNINGS
The Emergence of a Field
Voices from the Margins: A History
Feminist Perspectives
The Backlash Against Feminism
METHODS AND VALUES IN SCIENTIFIC INQUIRY
Nonsexist Research
Feminist Values in Research
THEMES OF THIS BOOK
Gender: More Than Just Sex
Language and the Power to Name
The Diversity of Women
Psychological Research and Social Change
OUR GOALS FOR OUR STUDENTS
SUGGESTED READINGS

BEGINNINGS

The Emergence of a Field

During the past thirty years, the science and practice of psychology have undergone a critical evaluation more intense and sustained than at any other time in their history. Here are a few of the critical voices:

> *Carolyn Sherif, 1964:* Ignorance about women pervades academic disciplines in higher education, where the requirements for the degree seldom include thoughtful inquiry into the status of women, as part of the total human condition (cited in Sherif, 1979, p. 93).

> *Mary Parlee, 1975:* The academic discipline (of psychology) . . . has distorted facts, omitted problems, and perpetuated pseudoscientific data relevant to women. Until recently, the body of "knowledge" developed by academic psychologists happened (apparently) to support stereotyped beliefs about the abilities and psychological characteristics of women and men, and such beliefs happen to support existing political, legal, and economic inequalities between the sexes (p. 124).

> *Kathleen Grady, 1981:* The promise of science cannot be realized if . . . certain questions are never asked, or they are asked of the wrong people and in the

wrong way, or they are not published because they do not fit accepted theories (p. 629).

Michelle Fine, 1985: Women who represent racial and ethnic minorities, working-class and poor women, and disabled women and lesbians, need to be involved in [psychological] research. The lives of these women need to be integrated into this literature, and the assumptions of psychological theories based on white middle-class experiences and beliefs that all persons are (should be?) heterosexual and nondisabled must be challenged (p. 178).

Rachel Hare-Mustin and Jeanne Marecek, 1990: We find it curious that psychological thought is still heavily influenced by such nineteenth-century theorists as Darwin, Marx, and Freud. As products of their era, they were primarily supportive of the status quo, of upper-class white male privilege with its limited knowledge of and marginal concern for women. If they were alive today, they would be astonished: What? You are still using those old books? Throw them away (p. 189).

And Naomi Weisstein (1968), in a now-classic paper titled "Psychology Constructs the Female," declared that psychology had nothing to say about what women are really like, what they need, and what they want because psychology did not know.

Moved by critical analyses of its limitations, the field of psychology began to examine the stereotypical thinking and sex bias that had characterized its knowledge about women. The more closely psychologists began to look at the ways psychology had thought about women, the more problems and inadequacies they saw. These have been summarized by Arnold Kahn and Paula Jean (1983):

> There was widespread agreement about [psychology's] faults: that women were infrequently studied; that theories were constructed from a male-as-normative viewpoint and that women's behavior was explained as deviation from the male standard; that the stereotype of women was considered an accurate portrayal of women's behavior; that women who fulfilled the dictates of the gender stereotype were viewed as healthy and happy; that differences in the behaviors of women and men were attributed to differences in anatomy and physiology; and that the social context which often shapes behavior was ignored in the case of women (p. 660).

Psychologists had begun to realize that psychological knowledge about women was *androcentric,* or male-centered. They began to rethink psychological concepts and methods and to produce new research with women as the focus of study. Moreover, they began to study topics of importance and concern to women and to develop ways of analyzing social relations between women and men. As a result, psychology has developed new ways of thinking about women, expanded its research methods, and developed new approaches to therapy and counseling.

The new psychology of women and gender is rich and varied. Virtually every intellectual framework from Freudian theory to cognitive psychology has been used in developing new theories and approaches, and virtually every area of psychology, from developmental to social, has been affected (Crawford &

Marecek, 1989). This book is an invitation to explore the knowledge and participate in the ongoing debates of psychology's reconstruction of the female.

The growth of the field can been seen in the number of psychology departments offering courses in the psychology of women or gender. Before 1968, there was virtually none. A recent survey that received responses from 503 psychology departments found that 51 percent listed undergraduate courses in the psychology of women. One hundred and seventy-two such courses are currently being taught at the graduate level in colleges and universities in the United States (Women's Programs Office, 1991). Psychology of women courses are often connected to, and have contributed to, the rapid growth of women's studies programs, which began about 1970. Only twenty years later, in 1990, the National Women's Studies Association reported 623 women's studies programs in the United States.

The new field has its own journals focusing on the psychology of women or gender: for example, *Sex Roles,* which began publishing in 1975; *Psychology of Women Quarterly,* published since 1977; and *Feminism & Psychology,* a recent addition from England. Psychological research on women and gender is also published in other psychology journals—such as *American Psychologist, Journal of Personality and Social Psychology,* and *Developmental Psychology*—and in such interdisciplinary women's studies journals as *Signs: The Journal of Women in Culture and Society, International Journal of Women's Studies,* and *Feminist Studies.*

The emergence of interest in women and gender took place in a social context of changing roles for women and the emergence of a feminist social movement in the late 1960s. Questioning psychology's representation of women was very much part of the more general questioning of "women's place" encouraged and led by women's liberation activists.

The women's movement of this era was not the first. A previous women's rights movement had reached its peak over a hundred years earlier with the Seneca Falls Declaration of 1848, which explicitly rejected the doctrine of female inferiority then taught by academics and clergy (Harris, 1984). However, the women's movement lost momentum in the 1920s, after women had won the vote, and psychology's interest in sex differences and gender waned. The area would not be a major part of psychology's research agenda until a social context of feminist activism again arose.

With the rebirth of the women's movement in the 1960s and with widespread voicing of feminist concerns once again a social force, researchers again became interested in the study of women and gender. Women psychologists and men who supported their goals also began to work toward an improved status for women within the field of psychology. They first formed the Association for Women in Psychology (AWP) in 1969, then lobbied the American Psychological Association (APA) to form a Division of the Psychology of Women. This division, officially approved in 1973, is now one of the larger divisions of APA, with more than 6,000 members. (Divisions on ethnic minority and gay/lesbian issues were established later.) Progress in incorporating women has also occurred among Canadian psychologists (Parlee, 1985) and, more recently, within the British Psychological Society. These organizational changes have acknowledged the presence of women in psychology and helped enhance their professional identity (Scarborough & Furumoto, 1987). And none too soon—women now earn 60 percent of Ph.D.s awarded in psychology (Trends in Education, 1995).

Voices from the Margins: A History

Throughout the history of psychology, there had been criticism of psychology's treatment of women and people of color, most often voiced by members of those groups. As early as 1876, Mary Putman Jacobi had completed a Harvard dissertation challenging the idea that women required special mental and bodily rest during menstruation, noting that

> An inquiry into the limits of activity and attainments that may be imposed by sex is very frequently carried on in the same spirit as that which hastens to ascribe to permanent differences in race all the peculiarities of a class, and this because the sex that is supposed to be limiting in its nature, is nearly always different from that of the person conducting the inquiry (cited in Sherif, 1979, p. 95).

Robert Guthrie's book *Even the Rat Was White* (Guthrie, 1976) has examined the history of racism in psychology and anthropology and documented the contributions of early African-American and Mexican-American psychologists in providing less biased views of human nature. In the early 1900s, some of the first scientifically trained women devoted much research effort to challenging accepted wisdom about the extent and nature of sex differences. Helen Thompson Wooley conducted the first experimental laboratory study of sex differences in mental traits, using a variety of innovative measures. In interpreting her results, she stressed the overall similarity of the sexes and the environmental determinants of observed differences, remarking daringly in a 1910 *Psychological Bulletin* article that "There is perhaps no field aspiring to be scientific where flagrant personal bias, logic martyred in the cause of supporting a prejudice, unfounded assertions, and even sentimental rot and drivel, have run riot to such an extent as here" (Wooley, 1910, p. 340). Among the women inspired by her work was Leta Stetter Hollingworth, who challenged the Darwinian view that women are innately less variable (and therefore less likely to be highly creative or intelligent) (Shields, 1982).

The work of a few early women psychologists opened the way for critical empirical research to replace unexamined assumptions about women's "natural" limitations (Rosenberg, 1982). Determined to demonstrate women's capacity to contribute to modern science on an equal basis with men, they chose to measure sex differences in order to challenge beliefs about women's limitations. In a sense, their research interests were dictated by questions chosen by others. Faced with the necessity of proving their very right to do research, these women labored to refute hypotheses that they themselves did not find credible and that they did not believe could account for the inferior social position of women (Unger, 1979a). Moreover, they worked in a social context that denied them opportunities because of their sex and forced them to make cruel choices between work and family relationships (Scarborough & Furumoto, 1987). Their story is one,

> in many ways, of failure—of women restricted by simple prejudice to the periphery of academe, who never had access to the professional chairs of the major universities, who never commanded the funds to direct large-scale research, who never trained the graduate students who might have spread their influence, and who, by the 1920s, no longer had the galvanizing support of a woman's movement to give political effect to their ideas (Rosenberg, 1982, p. xxi).

The challenges to psychology to develop knowledge about all humanity have been present throughout psychology's history. However, the efforts of women and minorities remained voices from the margins. It is only recently that an *Annual Review of Psychology* article could state that research on gender is an idea whose time has come (Deaux, 1985). The existence of an APA division on the psychology of women and dozens of feminist journals make it unlikely that it will "fade away" as it did in the 1920s. Because the new psychology of women and gender so clearly has developed in a social context of feminism, it is important to look closely at the relationship between the two.

Feminist Perspectives

The writer Rebecca West noted in 1913 that "I myself have never been able to find out precisely what feminism is: I only know that people call me a feminist whenever I express sentiments that differentiate me from a doormat" (quoted in Kramarae & Treichler, 1985). Exactly what is feminism and what does it mean to call oneself a feminist?

The Many Meanings of Feminism

Contemporary feminist theory has many variants. Each can be thought of as a different lens through which to view the experiences of women, and, like different lenses, each is useful for focusing perception on particular phenomena.

Feminism is most often conceptualized in terms of equality—an orientation that connects it to political liberalism. From this perspective, a feminist is a person who believes that women are entitled to full legal and social equality with men, and who favors changes in laws, customs, and values to achieve the goal of equality. This *liberal feminist* perspective has been especially useful in encouraging research on such topics as gender socialization (Chapter 7) and sex discrimination in employment (Chapter 12). It emphasizes the similarities between males and females, maintaining that given equal environments and opportunities they will behave similarly.

Another variant of feminism emphasizes differences but stresses that qualities characteristic of women have been devalued and should be honored and respected in society. This perspective, sometimes called *cultural feminism,* has been useful in understanding the importance of unpaid work contributed to society by women, such as child care (Chapter 11). It is often used in discussing sex differences in values and social behaviors—for example, the apparent tendency for women to be more nurturing, caring, and oriented toward others' needs (Chapter 2).

Still another feminist perspective emphasizes male control and domination of women throughout history. This perspective, sometimes termed *radical feminism,* views the control of women by men as the first and most fundamental form of oppression. Radical feminist theory has fostered much research on violence against women and on sexuality, seeking to understand the sources of males' greater power and to examine its consequences (Chapters 5, 9, and 14).

The diversity of frameworks and values in feminist thought may seem to be a source of confusion, but it is also healthy and productive. The lenses of cultural, radical, and liberal feminism can be used to develop and compare a variety of perspectives on women's experiences. In writing this book, we have drawn on a variety of feminist perspectives, using the lens of each as we thought it would help clarify a particular topic, sometimes comparing several feminist perspectives on an issue.

Feminism: Is There a Simple Definition?

Because of the plurality of definitions and viewpoints, it is perhaps more appropriate to speak of feminism*s* than feminism. However, feminist perspectives have two important themes in common, and these define feminism in its most general sense. First, feminism places a high value on women. Women are considered important and worthwhile human beings. (For feminist scholars, this means that women are worthy of study in their own right.) Second, feminism recognizes the need for social change if women are to lead secure and satisfying lives. Perhaps the simplest definition of a feminist is an individual who holds these basic beliefs: that women are valuable and that social change to benefit women is needed. And perhaps the simplest definition of feminism is one proposed by bell hooks (1984): it is a movement to end sexism and sexist oppression. These broad definitions allow feminists to work for political change together, while recognizing that ideas about how to reach their goals may differ.

Can men be feminists? Certainly! It should be clear that men can hold the values we have described as feminist; they can value women as worthwhile human beings and work for social change to reduce sexism and sex discrimination. Some men who share these values call themselves feminists. Others prefer to use *pro-feminist,* believing that this term acknowledges women's leadership of the feminist movement and expresses their understanding that women and men have different experiences of gender. Men, like women, take many different routes to becoming feminist (see Box 1.1).

The Backlash Against Feminism

Feminism, like other movements for social justice, has often met with resistance. This "backlash" has taken different forms at different times in history, but there are some characteristic patterns that seem to emerge repeatedly. These include stereotyping feminists and their ideas as crazy, outrageous, or trivial; insisting on immutable differences created by God or Nature that make social change impossible; and characterizing feminism as a mere quarrel among women. We will look at a few examples of each of these forms of "backlash."

Box 1.1 Why I Am a Feminist: One Man's Account

When the ideas of feminism first reached me about fifteen years ago, almost every detail of my life began to change, in ways I still don't fully comprehend. Since then I've been asked, probably hundreds of times, "What got you so interested in feminism anyway?" The question, or a version of it, is usually asked with bewilderment, though sometimes with frank suspicion—as if growing up a man and becoming a feminist (a radical one, at that) were off the map of human possibility.

I try to explain, as best I can, that beginning in 1974 I happened to be really challenged by some close women friends and some mind-blowing feminist books and hours and hours of intense discussion—all of which is true as far as it goes. But like so many men I've met across the country through profeminist activism over the past decade and a half, I count myself part of the struggle for women's equality for reasons that are intensely personal—so personal, sometimes, they can't be glibly declared.

I'm thinking of those men whose feminist convictions spring from loyalty to a particular woman in their lives—a mother, a lover, a cherished friend—someone who has brought them to an intimate, almost insider's view of what life for women is like under male supremacy. These men have made a vow to stand beside her and not abandon her, to wholeheartedly be her ally. For such men, loyalty to a woman's life is experienced as a profound form of intimacy (not a threat to selfhood, as it might be for other men).

I'm thinking also of those men whose commitment to feminism draws on their own experience of sexual violence or sexual abuse from other men, perhaps as a child or adolescent. Somehow such men have not paved over what happened to them; rather, they have recognized in it the same dimensions of violence and abuse that *women* were mobilizing to resist. So these men, for their own silent reasons, have cast their lot with the feminist struggle for freedom and bodily integrity—because they know full well it's what *everyone* should have.

I'm thinking also of those men who have become feminists in part because they have suffered the shame of growing up with a sexuality that was not "standard issue." It was a sexuality that longed for partnership and ardent tenderness; it did not stir at dominance and coercion. It was a sexuality that set them apart, whether with women or other men. These men have become, in a sense, dissidents from the sex-class hierarchy in intimacy; and they are gathering courage to defy that hierarchy beyond the bedroom as well.

I'm thinking also of those men whose advocacy of feminism derives from other sorts of principled political activism. Coming from the perspective of their pacifism, their antiracism, or their commitment to economic justice, for instance, these men have grasped the ideals of radical feminism with a seriousness and intellectual honesty such that they now regard feminism as logically consistent with—no, *integral to*—any human-rights struggle worthy of the name. Cerebral though it may seem at times, their commitment, in its own way, is also from the heart.

What would happen if we each told the deepest truth about why we are men who mean to be part of the feminist revolution—why we can't *not* be part of it—why its vision of full humanity for everyone so moves us? What would happen if we dared? As the poet Muriel Rukeyser once asked, I wonder sometimes: would the world split open?

Source: John Stoltenberg, 1989.

Negative Stereotypes of Feminists

When women began organizing to win the right to vote, political cartoonists depicted them in ways that will seem very familiar today. Figure 1.1 shows suffragists as ugly, cigar-smoking, angry women who foist their babies off on men. Their uncontrolled sexuality is represented by the women whose legs are exposed. The text tells us that they are brassy, sharp-tongued man-tamers.

FIGURE 1.1. An early example of backlash.
Source: Collection of The New-York Historical Society.

In the 1970s, the stereotypes that resurfaced were equally negative. Media studies professor Susan J. Douglas wittily sums up the image of the feminist circa 1975:

> The moment the women's movement emerged in 1970, feminism once again became a dirty word, with considerable help from the mainstream news media. News reports and opinion columnists created a new stereotype, of fanatics, "braless bubbleheads," Amazons, "the angries," and "a band of wild lesbians." The result is that we all know what feminists are. They are shrill, overly aggressive, man-hating, ball-busting, selfish, hairy, extremist, deliberately unattractive women with absolutely no sense of humor who see sexism at every turn. They make men's testicles shrivel up to the size of peas, they detest the family and think all children should be deported or drowned. Feminists are relentless, unforgiving, and unwilling to bend or compromise; they are singlehandedly responsible for the high divorce rate, the shortage of decent men and the unfortunate proliferation of Birkenstocks in America (p. 7).

By the 1980s, at least some women had made some gains toward equality. The media then turned to declaring feminism outdated, claiming that equal rights have been fully achieved, society is now in a "postfeminist" era, and women are abandoning feminism because it has proved to have terrible costs.

In the 1980s version of backlash, everything from infertility to the "breakdown of society" was blamed on feminism (Faludi, 1991).

Despite attempts to discredit the goals of the women's movement, the majority of women endorse many of these goals. Today, the stereotype of feminists has both positive and negative aspects. College women describe feminists as strong, caring, capable, open-minded, knowledgeable, and intelligent (Berryman-Fink & Verderber, 1985; Buhl, 1989). In one study, only 9 percent believed that sexism no longer exists in our society. However, they are very reluctant to label themselves feminists. They seem to be quite aware that "feminist" also connotes an angry woman who hates men, and "feminism" connotes an outdated ideology that is no longer necessary and possibly destructive. In Chapter 4, we will learn more about gender stereotypes and their effects.

Insisting on Differences

> If combat means living in a ditch, females have biological problems staying in a ditch for 30 days because they get infections and they don't have upper body strength. . . .On the other hand, men are basically little piglets. You drop them in the ditch, they roll around in it, it doesn't matter.

These words were spoken by the Speaker of the U.S. House of Representatives, Newt Gingrich, in 1995. Although it is disturbing to the authors that a person in high public office could profess such a simplistic stereotype (one that is insulting to both sexes), we are not surprised. The more women accomplish in realms formerly closed to them, the more loudly it is proclaimed that they cannot and should not be doing what they are doing. Today, women are astronauts, combat soldiers, coal miners, Supreme Court justices, and Nobel-prize–winning scientists, all the while continuing the traditional work of women: bearing and rearing children and caring for the needs of others. Yet theories and studies that purport to show that women are biologically inferior continue to receive press coverage and are used to "explain" women's disadvantaged status in society. Throughout this book we will critically examine theories and research claiming that women's minds (Chapter 3), brains (Chapter 6), and bodies (Chapters 8, 13, and 15) are so different from men's as to make women incapable of "male" achievements.

Women Against Women: Feminism as a Cat Fight

One of the ways that feminists and their ideas are trivialized is to portray women as fighting with each other (Douglas, 1994). Any woman who attacks the ideals and practices of feminism is almost guaranteed a hearing in the news media. It is even better if she claims to be a feminist, and it seems to matter little if her expertise on the issues is minimal. This prevents male social theorists and political analysts from having to study and consider feminist ideas themselves, and allows them to claim that "even women, at least the sensible ones, see through feminism and reject it."

In the 1970s, the media ignored the many groups of women working collectively for women's rights and the opposition they encountered from those in power. Instead, they focused on Gloria Steinem, an attractive feminist journalist and activist, versus Phyllis Schlafly, a conservative activist who called feminists a "bunch of bitter women seeking a constitutional cure for their personal problems." The debate over the Equal Rights Amendment to the U.S. Constitution was described, not as women versus entrenched male power, but as "women versus women." A 1977 network television special on the ERA was even titled "The War Between the Women!"

"The catfight remains an extremely popular way for the news media to represent women's struggles for equality and power" (Douglas, 1994, p. 243). In the 1992 presidential campaign, Barbara Bush and Hillary Rodham Clinton were portrayed as polar opposites—the good wife and mother versus the selfish career woman—and more recently, Newt Gingrich's mother gained headlines by quoting her son publicly insulting Ms. Clinton. Susan Douglas comments on current media practices:

> When it comes to portraying the multilayered complexities women have faced as they have negotiated through work, marriage, motherhood, and politics, the news media will opt for the simplistic yet coercive metaphor of woman-on-woman violence whenever possible. The reason Camille Paglia has become such a media darling, despite an ego the size of Australia and two books that don't make a lick of sense, is that she loves to trash feminists—or, at least, her particular caricature of feminists (1994, p. 244).

Attacks on women's studies, feminism, multiculturalism, "political correctness," and "feminazis" get far more publicity than feminist ideas ever did. The *Wall Street Journal*, not noted for reviewing feminist books or analyzing feminist theories, nevertheless featured a 1995 review of a book critical of feminism, claiming that it showed how feminism "has exhibited from the start a nasty streak of intolerance toward women who don't fall in with the party line," and uses "tactics more ruthless than those that feminists have accused men of using to oppress women." The review suggested that women's studies professors are just cruel and vicious little girls grown up who enforce conformity at the cost of academic integrity (Crittenden, 1995, p. A14). We were recently invited to attend a public lecture in which the speaker, a woman, promised to tell about the "vicious battle" that is "raging" among feminists. Asking "Has feminism become just another racket?" she accused other women of "hijacking" feminism and fabricating their research data.

We invite our readers to think critically about the ways that feminists and feminism are portrayed in our society. We think it is ironic that feminism, which originated in a challenge to stereotypical assumptions about women, should now have its own negative stereotype. It is absurd that, even as women break new ground, and do it in often hostile environments, they are increasingly labeled different and inferior. It is disturbing to us that the media focus on the ideas of feminism only through the distortions and attacks of antifeminists. (See Figure 1.2.) We ask our readers to consider whose interests it serves if a movement to end sexism is made to seem irrational, wrong, and futile.

Despite the attacks, feminism is a vital site of theory and research. Far from holding to an inflexible "party line," feminists have always encouraged debate and a plurality of viewpoints. In writing this book, we have tried to present a variety of feminist perspectives with the goal of encouraging critical thinking about them.

FIGURE 1.2. Sisterhood is complicated!

Source: ©1995 *Lynda Barry*. First printed in Newsweek; 1994.

METHODS AND VALUES IN SCIENTIFIC INQUIRY

Scientific research is often represented as a purely objective process in which a neutral, disinterested scientist investigates and reveals the secrets of nature. However, as some of the pioneering women psychologists realized, psychology has sometimes been anything but neutral when it came to understanding and explaining the behavior of women. The resurgence of interest in the psychology of women has led psychologists to identify a number of specific methodological flaws in traditional research on women. One major emphasis of feminist psychology has been to analyze sources of distortion in psychological research and propose ways to ensure nonsexist, or gender-fair, research.

Nonsexist Research

Let's look briefly at the research process. The researcher starts by generating a question to be answered by gathering information systematically. The question may originate in a theory, a personal experience, or an observation, or it may be raised by previous research. The next step is to develop a systematic strategy for answering the question—often called *designing* the research. In the design stage, a method is selected, such as experiment, survey, or case study. The research participants are chosen, materials such as questionnaires or laboratory setups are devised, and ways to measure the behaviors in question are decided on.

Next, the data are collected and analyzed so that patterns of results become clear. Statistical techniques are usually used for this task. The researcher then interprets the meaning of his or her results and draws conclusions from them. If reviewers and journal editors judge the research to be well conducted and important, the results are published in a scientific journal where they can influence future research and theory. Some research makes its way from journals into textbooks, influencing teachers and students as well as other researchers. Some even gets reported in the mass media, influencing perhaps millions of readers' and viewers' beliefs about such issues as racial differences in intelligence, sex differences in the brain, and the causes of social problems.

Biases can enter into the research process at any stage. In describing a few common types of bias at each stage, we will focus on gender-related examples. However, the principles of nonsexist research could also be applied to eliminating biases related to such characteristics as race/ethnicity, social class, or sexual orientation (Denmark, Russo, Frieze, & Sechzer, 1988).

Question Formulation

In the stage of choosing a research question, gender stereotypes related to the topic can bias the question and therefore the outcome of the study. For example, many studies of leadership have defined it in terms of dominance, aggression, and other stereotypically male attributes. A nonstereotypical definition of leadership might include the ability to negotiate, to be considerate of others, and to help others resolve conflicts without confrontation (Denmark et al., 1988). Another example of bias in question formulation is found in the large amount of research on mothers who work outside the home. Much of it focuses on the question of whether the mothers' work endangers their children's psychological welfare. There is much less research on whether fathers' commitment to their work endangers their children's welfare, or on whether mothers' employment might *benefit* mothers or children (Hare-Mustin & Marecek, 1990).

The process of creating research questions is perhaps the most neglected and undervalued part of the scientific enterprise. Psychology graduate students typically learn a great deal about how to test hypotheses using complex experimental designs and advanced statistics, but textbooks and research courses say very little about where hypotheses come from or how to decide if a question is worth studying (Wallston & Grady, 1985). It is not surprising, then, that unexamined personal biases and androcentric theories often lead to biased research questions.

Designing Research

In the design phase of research, one important aspect is deciding how to measure the behaviors under study. Pauline Bart (1971) described an extreme example of a biased measure in a study of women's sexuality. Participants' roles in sexual intercourse were assessed by their choice of one of the following responses: "passive," "responsive," "resistant," "aggressive," "deviant," or "other." The outcome of this research might have been very different if women had also been allowed to choose from alternatives such as "active," "initiating," "playful," and "joyous" (Wallston & Grady, 1985).

Another aspect of the design phase of research is the choice of an appropriate comparison group. The results and conclusions of a study can be very different depending on which groups are chosen for comparison with each other. For example, one group of researchers was involved in an ongoing study of aging among a selected group of college-educated professional men. When they decided to add a sample of women, the biomedical scientists on the research team suggested that they should add the sisters of the men already in the study. Because they had the same parents, these two groups would be similar in physiological characteristics. The social scientists on the research team, however, suggested that the appropriate sample would be college-educated professional women who would be similar in social status. Although one choice is not necessarily "right" and the other "wrong," the choice is a conceptually important one. The conclusions reached about sex differences in aging might be very different depending on which group of women was chosen, and the group chosen depends on assumptions about what kind of explanations (physiological or social) are most important (Parlee, 1981).

Choice of research participants is subject to many possible biases. Since the 1940s psychology has come to rely more and more on college student samples, creating biases of age, social class, and developmental stage (Sears, 1986). Moreover, males have been more likely to be studied than females. Several studies during the 1960s and 1970s found that males were greatly overrepresented in psychological research, perhaps because topics were sex-linked in the minds of researchers, and "male" topics were considered more important (Wallston & Grady, 1985).

The proportion of male-only studies has decreased since the 1970s (Gannon, Luchetta, Rhodes, Pardie, & Segrist, 1992). However, subtler kinds of sex bias persist. Nearly 30 percent of psychological journal articles still do not report the sex of the participants. When researchers use an all-female sample, they are more likely to state it in the article's title, to discuss their reasons for the single-sex sample, and to point out that their results cannot be generalized to the other sex (Ader & Johnson, 1994). It seems that psychologists feel it is important to indicate the limitations of an all-female sample, but they see nothing remarkable about an all-male sample—males are still the norm.

Research on ethnic minority people of both sexes is scarce except when they are seen as creating social problems (Reid & Kelly, 1994). There is abundant research on teen pregnancy among African-American women, for example, but little research on their leadership, creativity, or coping skills for dealing with racism.

Poor and working-class women, too, have been virtually ignored (Reid, 1993). Many well-known psychologists, both female and male, have pointed out that psychology, supposedly the science of human behavior, is in danger of becoming a science of the behavior of college sophomores, and white male college sophomores at that. Feminist psychology, with its valuing of women as worthy subjects of research and its recognition of the diversity of social groupings, is providing an important corrective to this type of bias.

Analyzing Data: A Focus on Differences

Psychologists have come to rely on statistical tests in data analysis. Over the past thirty years, both the number of articles using statistics and the number of statistical tests per article have increased. Statistics can be a useful tool, but they also can lead to many conceptual difficulties in research on sex and gender (Wallston & Grady, 1985).

Statistical models lead to a focus on differences rather than similarities. The logic of statistical analysis involves comparing two groups to see if the average difference between them is "statistically significant." Unfortunately, it is not easy to make meaningful statements about *similarities* using statistical reasoning (Unger, 1981). It is also unfortunate that statisticians choose the term *significant* to describe the outcome of a set of mathematical operations. As used by most people the word means *important,* but as used by statisticians it means only that the obtained difference between two groups is unlikely to be due to mere chance. A statistically significant difference does not necessarily have any practical or social significance. The meaning and interpretation of difference will be discussed in more detail in Chapter 3.

Interpreting and Publishing Research Results

Psychology's focus on group differences affects the ways that results are interpreted and conveyed to others. Bias is evident when sex differences in performing a specific task are interpreted as evidence of a sex difference in a more global characteristic, or when the performance style more typical of women is given a negative label. For example, men's better performance on a few (not all) types of spatial perception tasks was considered evidence of a sex difference in cognitive style. The "male style" was labeled *field independence,* and the "female style" *field dependence* (Denmark et al., 1988). The results would seem rather different if the two styles had been labeled *field insensitivity/sensitivity.* But rather than simply reverse the value connotation of the labels, it would probably have been better to recognize that performance on a few specialized tasks does not necessarily reflect a general cognitive style that is used in other situations. Furthermore, overinterpreting sex-related differences leads to thinking of men and women as two totally separate categories. Even when a statistically significant sex difference is found, there is always considerable overlap between the two groups.

Problems of interpretation are compounded by publication biases. Because of reliance on the logic of statistical analysis, studies that report differences between women and men are more likely to be published than those that report similarities. Moreover, the editorial boards of journals are predominantly made up of white men, who may perhaps see topics relevant to women and ethnic minorities as less important or of lower priority than topics relevant to people more like themselves (Denmark et al., 1988). This may be one reason, for example, that there has been little psychological research on pregnancy and mothering (see Chapter 11).

After they are published, some findings are noticed by the media and others are not. Television and the popular press often actively publicize the latest discoveries about sex-related differences, while sex similarities are not "news" (Crawford, 1989). "The fact that the sexes are more similar than they are different is not considered noteworthy either by psychology as a discipline or by society as a whole" (Unger, 1990, p. 104).

Nonsexist research is not value-free; that is, nonsexist research practices do not eliminate value judgments from the research process. Androcentric research is based on the value judgment that men and their concerns are more important and worthy of study than women and their concerns. In contrast, nonsexist research is based on the value judgment that women and men and their concerns are of equal worth and importance (Eichler, 1988).

Feminist Values in Research

Many feminist psychologists have asked whether feminist values can or should affect the research process in ways that go beyond eliminating sex biases in psychology's traditional methods. This issue has been the subject of lively debate among researchers and theorists. The controversy has centered around the following questions (Peplau & Conrad, 1989):

- *Are some methods of inquiry better than others for feminist research?* Feminist theorists have pointed out that methods are not neutral tools; the choice of method always shapes and constrains what can be found (Marecek, 1989). When Masters and Johnson decided to study women's sexual response by measuring physiological changes in the vagina during arousal and orgasm, they had already put limits on what they could discover. Had they chosen instead to interview women about their subjective experiences of arousal and orgasm, they would have had a very different set of discoveries about female sexuality (Tiefer, 1989).

  Traditionally, experimentation has been the most respected and valued psychological method. However, experimental methods have been criticized for at least two reasons. First, in an experiment, the researcher creates an artificial environment and manipulates the experience of the subjects. Experiments thus strip behavior from its social context (Parlee, 1979). Although laboratory studies isolate variables from the contaminating influence of real-life social processes, gender is played out in exactly those real-life processes (Crawford & Marecek, 1989). Therefore, behavior in the laboratory may not be representative of behavior in more naturalistic situations (Sherif, 1979). Second, experiments are inherently hierarchical, with "the powerful, all-knowing researcher instructing, observing, recording, and sometimes deceiving the subjects" (Peplau & Conrad, 1989). The inequality of the experimental situation may be particularly acute when the researcher is male and the subject is female, reflecting and reinforcing the dominance of male values and interests (McHugh, Koeske, & Frieze, 1986).

On the other hand, many important advances in understanding women and gender have come about because of experimental results. For example, in Chapter 4 you will learn about research that has clarified the nature and functioning of stereotypes about women. Research on perceptions of leadership (Chapter 5) and the evaluation of men's and women's performance (Chapter 12) has demonstrated in detail how sex discrimination occurs. Although psychology has perhaps used the experimental method too much and too unreflectively, it should not be rejected entirely.

- *Who can conduct feminist research?* Most feminist researchers in psychology are women. The membership of APA's Division 35 is more than 90 percent female, and "women have taken the lead in investigating topics relevant to women's lives and in developing new concepts and theories to explain women's experiences" (Peplau & Conrad, 1989, p. 391). However, it is important not to equate female with feminist and male with nonfeminist. Women who are psychologists work in every area from physiological, perception, and learning, to industrial and clinical psychology. Women psychologists may or may not personally identify as feminists, and even when they do, they may not bring a feminist perspective to their research. Also, male psychologists can identify as feminist. Men can and do conduct research on women and gender, and many conduct research on male gender roles. Of course, we would hope that all psychologists—male and female, feminist and nonfeminist—would, at a minimum, conduct their research in nonsexist ways and work to eliminate sexism from their professional practices and behaviors.
- *What values unite feminist psychologists?* Although feminist psychologists have been critical of psychology, they remain committed to it. The core beliefs that unite them have been summarized by Anne Peplau and Eva Conrad (1989):

Science can never be fully objective or value-neutral.

Science is done by human beings, all of whom bring their own perspectives to their work, based on their personal backgrounds. Personal experience sensitizes people to different aspects of problems (Unger, 1983). Because the values of dominant groups in a society are normative, they are not always recognized as values. When others—women and minorities, for example—question the assumptions of the dominant group, the underlying values are made more visible.

One of the most important insights of feminism is that research and the creation of knowledge do not occur in a social vacuum. Rather, each research project or theory is situated in a particular period in history and a particular social context. The psychology of women and gender is not unique in being affected by social currents such as feminism and liberalism. All of psychology is so affected. Moreover, psychology in its turn affects social issues and social policy through providing ways to interpret human behavior. Because psychology is a cultural institution, doing psychological research is inevitably a political act (Crawford & Marecek, 1989).

However, while the effects of values on the scientific process are inevitable, they need not be negative for women. We believe that psychology should admit values, not only as sources of bias, but as a means of evaluating all parts of the research process (Crawford & Marecek, 1989; Unger, 1983). An awareness of the politics of science can help feminist psychologists use science to foster social change and improve women's lives (Peplau & Conrad, 1989).

Empirical research is a worthwhile activity.

Although feminist psychologists recognize that science is far from perfect, they value its methods. Scientific methods are the most systematic way yet devised to answer questions about the natural and social world. Rather than abandon those methods or endlessly debate whether there is one perfect feminist way to do research, they go about their work using a rich variety of methods, theories, and approaches.

Just as any research method can be used in sexist ways, all methods can be used toward the goal of understanding women and gender. When the variety of methods is large, results based on different approaches can be compared to each other, and a richer and more complete picture of women's lives will emerge.

Human behavior is shaped by social, historical, and political forces.

Because feminists believe that gender equality is possible, although it has not yet been achieved, they are sensitive to the ways that social contexts and forces shape people's behavior and limit human potential. Feminist psychologists try to understand not only the effects of gender, but also the effects of other systems of social classification such as race, social class, and sexual orientation. They tend to be skeptical that psychology will ever discover universal laws of behavior. Rather, they prefer to try to clarify the ways that sociocultural forces, as well as biological and intrapsychic ones, affect behavior.

THEMES OF THIS BOOK

Because much of psychology's knowledge about women has historically been androcentric, one of the tasks of feminist psychology has been to *deconstruct* psychology by analyzing the implicit assumptions about women embedded in its theories and research practices. Throughout this book, you will find many examples of such critical analyses, in which feminist psychologists have exposed areas of neglect, androcentric concepts and research questions, and faulty reasoning in theory and research about women.

However, feminist psychology must go beyond criticizing androcentric psychology. In addition to deconstructing psychology's views of women, it is necessary to reconstruct, to create a more comprehensive and adequate psychology of women (Crawford & Marecek, 1989). This book draws on the work of hundreds of psychologists, both women and men, who have contributed to the ongoing process of revising—and transforming—psychology. It also draws on the work of feminist theorists and researchers in other disciplines, including philosophy, history, sociology, political science, and literary and cultural studies.

This book, then, provides both a critique of androcentric knowledge about women and a survey of emerging scholarship. Four broad themes are woven through the book. First, we distinguish between sex and gender, conceiving gender as a cultural construction. Second, we emphasize the importance of thinking critically about language and naming. Third, we recognize the diversity of women. Fourth, we emphasize that psychological knowledge about women can and should be used to foster social change that will benefit women. An overview of these themes follows.

Gender: More Than Just Sex

Researchers who study the psychology of women find it useful to distinguish between the concepts of sex and gender (Unger, 1979). *Sex* is defined as biological differences in genetic composition and reproductive anatomy and function. All mammalian species have two biological forms, female and male. Human infants are labeled as one sex or the other at birth, based on the appearance of their genitals. It sounds like a simple and straightforward matter (though in fact it can be surprisingly complex—see Chapter 6). Most important, the biology of sex is a very important *social* marker.

Gender is what culture makes out of the "raw material" of biological sex. All known societies recognize biological differentiation and use it as the basis for social distinctions. In our own society, the process of creating gendered human beings starts at birth. When a baby is born, the presence of a vagina or penis represents sex—but the pink or blue blanket that soon enfolds the baby represents gender. The blanket serves as a cue that this infant is to be treated as a boy or girl, not as a "generic human being," from the start.

Because gender is based on sex, the two terms have sometimes been used interchangeably. However, it is important to distinguish sex from gender for two reasons. First, equating them can lead to the belief that differences in the traits or behaviors of men and women are due directly to their biological differences, when the traits or behaviors actually may be shaped by culture. Second, keeping the concepts of sex and gender distinct can help us to analyze the complex ways they interact in our lives.

Gender distinctions occur at many levels in society. Their influence is so pervasive that, like fish in water, we may be unaware that it surrounds us. Gender-related processes influence behavior, thoughts, and feelings in individuals; they affect interactions among individuals; and they help determine the structure of social institutions. The processes by which differences are created and power is allocated can be understood by considering how gender is played out at three levels: societal, interpersonal, and individual.

The Social Structural Level: Gender as a System of Power Relations. We noted earlier that all known human societies make social distinctions based on gender. In the broadest sense, gender is a classification system that shapes the relations among women and men. Its influences are pervasive and multidimensional. Virtually all societies label some tasks as "men's" work and others as "women's" work. While there is a great deal of variability in the kinds of tasks assigned to each sex across societies, those labeled as "women's" work are usually seen as less important and less desirable (see Chapter 12). Not only women's work but women themselves are devalued. In our own society, for example, many kinds of violence against women are taken for granted (Chapter 14). Sexual harassment, rape, incest, and battering can be seen as culturally "useful" ways of controlling girls and women.

Thus, gender can be viewed as a system of social classification that influences access to power and resources. Men have more public power in most societies, controlling government, law, and public discourse. A quick check on the number of women in Congress and in the judiciary will illustrate that our own society is no exception. By and large, men make and enforce the laws that women and men must follow.

The Interpersonal Level: Gender as a Cue. Gender cues are used to tell us how to behave toward others in social interactions. Based on how a person appears and acts, we decide the person is either male or female, and we behave accordingly. Have you ever had the experience of seeing a person whose sex you could not readily identify? A long-haired person wearing jeans, one earring, and a loose sweatshirt can be very unsettling! A typical reaction is to search quickly for gender cues (Fly-front jeans? A trace of eye makeup?) that allow us to classify the person definitely as female or male. Why is it important to make that classification? Without it, we would not know whether to behave as though we were with a woman or with a man.

When people interact, the influences of sex and gender are intertwined. Not only do people use gender cues to make inferences about sex, they use perceived sex to make inferences about gender. When a man and a woman walk together into a car dealership, the salesperson is likely to direct the sales pitch to the man. Based on their appearance (gender), the salesperson decides that these two are a woman and a man (sex), assumes that they are a heterosexual couple, and acts according to his or her beliefs about which partner is more likely to make decisions about buying a car (gender). These kinds of interactions are so "normal" that they usually pass unnoticed. It is only when people "step out of line" that the gender forces shaping interaction become visible. A lone woman buying a car or a lone man selecting drapery fabric may feel quite uncomfortable as they violate the unwritten codes of gender.

Although much differential treatment of women and men (and boys and girls) happens outside awareness, research confirms that it is a reality. For example, observations in elementary school classrooms show that although teachers believe that they are treating boys and girls the same, boys receive more attention, both positive and negative, than girls do. Boys are yelled at and criticized more in front of their classmates. Moreover, in some classes a few boys are allowed to dominate class time by interacting constantly with the teacher, while most students remain silent (Eccles, 1989; Sadker & Sadker, 1994). Are teachers basing their behavior on perceived sex or gender? The answer is both.

Research shows that the behavior of men and boys is often evaluated more positively than the behavior of women and girls. Even when a woman and a man behave in identical ways, their behavior may be interpreted very differently. Moreover, sexual categorization is not simply a way of seeing differences, but a way of creating differences. When men and women are treated differently in ordinary daily interactions, they may come to behave differently in return. We will look more closely at gender influences in social interactions in Chapter 5.

The Individual Level: Gender as Masculinity and Femininity. To a greater or lesser extent, women and men come to accept gender distinctions visible at the structural level and enacted at the interpersonal level as part of the self-concept. They become *gender-typed,* ascribing to themselves the traits, behaviors, and roles normative for people of their sex in their culture. Women, moreover, internalize their devaluation and subordination. Feminist theories of personality development (see Chapter 2) stress that "feminine" characteristics such as passivity, excessive concern with pleasing others, lack of initiative, and dependency are psychological consequences of subordination. Members of subordinate social groups who adopt such characteristics are considered well adjusted; those who do not are controlled by psychiatric diagnosis, violence or the threat of violence, and social ostracism.

Much of the psychology of women and gender has consisted of documenting the effects of internalized subordination, and we will see many examples throughout this book. Laboratory and field research, as well as clinical experience, attest that, compared to boys and men, girls and women lack a sense of personal entitlement, expect less pay for comparable work, are equally satisfied with their employment even though they are paid significantly less than men, lose self-esteem and confidence in their academic ability, especially in mathematics and science, as they progress through the educational system, and are more likely to suffer from disturbances of body image, eating disorders, and depression. These differences are not "natural." They are shaped by differential opportunities and maintained in social interaction. They are the product of the gender system.

Related Concepts. People use gender to classify their social worlds in many ways. These processes have been studied and labeled by psychologists. Here, we will introduce some psychological terms related to sex and gender, returning to explain them in more detail later in the book.

Widely held beliefs about differences between males and females are termed *gender stereotypes.* (For example, it is widely believed in our society that women are more emotional than men.) In addition to such beliefs, all societies have *gender roles*—norms for acceptable behavior for females and males. (It is much more acceptable for a woman to cry in public than it is for a man.) As they grow up in gendered societies, girls and boys accept their culture's definitions of what is appropriate and normal for females and males as part of their own self-concepts. As we noted earlier, this process is termed "gender-typing." (Many, perhaps most, women believe that they themselves are more emotional than most men.) And people may develop negative attitudes and values about women as a group—the form of prejudice known as *sexism.* Learning sexist attitudes is made easier by the general devaluing of women and of characteristics associated with women. (In our society, being emotional is seen as a weakness or limitation, while being chronically cool and rational is seen as a virtue.) Sexist attitudes may lead to sexist behavior, or *sex discrimination,* against women and girls. (Would you vote for a candidate who you thought might respond emotionally in a crisis?)

Although the distinction between sex and gender is an important one, it is relatively new in psychology, and it is not always used consistently from one book or article to another (Deaux, 1993; Gentile, 1993; Unger & Crawford, 1993). Differing social behaviors in women and men, for example, should be referred to as *gender differences* or *gender-related differences,* because they are probably not directly caused by biological sex. However, by long tradition, they are often called *sex differences.* In contrast, differences in the behavior of male and female rats in a maze should be, and almost always are, referred to as sex differences. However, we once came across a study that referred to the rats' gender—perhaps they wore pink and blue hair ribbons as they ran the maze!

Language and the Power to Name

Controversies over terminology can sometimes seem like semantic hair-splitting. But language and naming are a source of power. Thinking critically about language can increase our understanding of how the system of social classification we call gender confers more power on males.

Aspects of reality that are named become "real" and can be talked about and thought about. Names allow people to share experiences and teach others to name their own experiences in the same way. Moreover, when certain aspects of reality are granted names, unnamed aspects become overshadowed and thus more difficult to think about and articulate. Unnamed experiences are less visible, and therefore, in a sense, less real to the social world (Berger & Luckmann, 1966). The idea that language shapes and constrains thought (sometimes called the Whorfian hypothesis) was proposed forty years ago by Benjamin Whorf and Edward Sapir. It still provides many unanswered and interesting questions for psychology (Henley, 1989).

The English language is, unfortunately, rich in linguistic sexism (Adams & Ware, 1989). One example is the traditional practice of using *he, his,* and *him* to represent both women and men—as in "Each student should bring his notebook." How are thinking and understanding affected by this androcentric naming? A great deal of psychological research has shown that the use of "generic" masculine language leads people of both sexes to think more about males.

The "generic he" is not the only way language treats males and females unequally. Language *devalues* women. For example, there is a tendency for words referring to females to acquire negative or debased meanings, while their counterparts referring to males retain their original meanings. A *governor* is still an important official, while a *governess* is little more than an educated nursemaid. Language also *stereotypes* women. For example, the traditional titles Mr., Miss, and Mrs. reveal the marital status of women but not men, indicating a difference in the social importance of marital status for the two groups (Henley, 1989). Perhaps even more revealing is a comparison of the connotations of the concepts *bachelor* and *old maid.*

Language also *omits* important aspects of female experience. The negative physical changes and feelings some women experience in conjunction with the menstrual cycle have the official and scientific-sounding label *premenstrual syndrome*—but the feelings of well-being and heightened competence that some women experience around the ovulation phase of the cycle have no label. Thus, PMS has become widely accepted as "real," is readily discussed everywhere from the Donahue show to the college classroom, and is a legitimate topic of research. Mid-cycle well-being is rarely a focus of research or discussion.

We will look at linguistic sexism more closely in Chapter 4. Throughout the book we will point out instances when linguistic categories make it easier to frame some questions and more difficult to conceptualize others.

Deconstructing language is not an easy task. Aspects of reality that are unnamed are obscured—made difficult to know and express. However, feminist scholars are analyzing language practices in depth to help understand how ideas about gender are perpetuated. Moreover, they are actively challenging sex bias in language use and have caused some important changes. Psychology as a profession has worked to change its biased language; the APA adopted guidelines for nonsexist language in 1977, and they are now part of the APA *Publication Manual.*

Language change as a result of feminist activism is evident outside psychology as well. One example is the widespread use of *Ms.* as a parallel title to *Mr.* When Ms. was first proposed, it was ridiculed; now it is the norm (Crawford & Stark, unpublished manuscript). The writer Gloria Steinem perhaps best expressed the importance of the power of naming—and the influence of feminist activism on language change:

> We have terms like "sexual harassment" and "battered women." A few years ago, they were just called "life" (Steinem, 1983, p. 149).

Until recently, the power to name a "problem" has been largely in the hands of men. Men controlled the institutions of knowledge, and even if women acquired expertise, they did not acquire legitimacy. History is full of stories about learned women whose work was attributed to their fathers, their brothers, or "anonymous." Such stories can be found in the history of psychology as well.

An excellent illustration of the distinction between expertise and legitimacy is the story of Mary Calkins, one of the first presidents of the American Psychological Association. She attended Harvard University during the latter part of the 19th century. But because Harvard was an all-male university, she was permitted to take courses only if she sat behind a curtain or was tutored individually. Despite completing an impressive Ph.D. dissertation with an important psychologist, she was denied a Ph.D. from Harvard because she was a woman.

Mary Calkins taught for many years at Wellesley College, established an experimental laboratory there, and made a number of important contributions to psychology. She was the first woman president of both the American Psychological Association and the American Philosophical Association. In 1927, toward the end of her life, a group of psychologists and philosophers, all Harvard degree holders, sent a letter to the president of Harvard requesting that Mary Calkins be awarded the degree that she had earned in the 1890s. Their request was refused (Scarborough & Furumoto, 1987).

Although Mary Calkins triumphed personally, her life illustrates the way even outstanding women may be marginalized. For example, she taught during her entire life at a women's college where she did not have doctoral students of her own. Under these conditions, her theories and research projects did not receive the continuity of investigation they deserved. Unlike many of her male peers, she did not found a "school" of psychology. Similar stories have been uncovered about other women in the group of early feminist psychologists of the 1920s, including Leta Hollingworth and Mary Jacobi (Scarborough & Furumoto, 1987). The ability to achieve continuity in the investigation of issues is part of "the power to name."

The Diversity of Women

Although gender is an important and universal dimension for classifying human beings and allocating power, it is not the only dimension. Social class, age, and race/ethnicity also serve as principles of social organization. Therefore, important though gender is, it would be a mistake to assume that all women necessarily have much in common with each other simply because they are women. A woman who is wealthy and privileged may, for example, have as much in common with wealthy and privileged men as she has with poor women. African-American and Latina women share with the men of their ethnic groups—and not with white women—the experiences of racism and racial stereotyping. Lesbians share the experience of being in a sexual minority with bisexuals and gay men, not with heterosexual women. The problems and concerns of older women and disabled women are not necessarily the same as those of young, able-bodied women.

Studies of different groups of women can help us to understand how biological, social, and cultural factors interact to influence behavior. Physical structure and physiology as well as the timing and form of physical development are, of course, biologically determined. On the other hand, the social reactions to and cultural meaning of physical structure have little to do with biology. It is important to look at different groups of women—both for their own sake and because their differences help us to test the limits of biological determination.

Yet creating a psychology of *all* women is not an easy task. If women of color are studied only in comparison to a mythical "generic" (white, privileged status) woman, researchers are implicitly making white women the norm, just as previous generations of psychologists made men the norm (Yoder & Kahn, 1992). It is important to study each group of women within their own cultural context. Fortunately, there are new writings by and about Latina, Native-American, African-American, Asian-American, lesbian, poor, older, and disabled women, to name just a few, that can guide understanding of the contexts of their lives. There is still a great need for more diversity in psychology itself: in 1993, 89.8 percent of doctoral degrees were awarded to whites, and only 4 percent to Hispanics, 3.7 percent to Asians and Asian Americans, 2.1 percent to African Americans, and .5 percent to Native Americans (Trends in Education, 1995).

In writing this book, we have tried to respect and express the diversity of women's experiences. As we worked on the book together, we noticed that feminists have often used metaphors of gender as a lens or prism through which to view the social structure (Bem, 1993; Crawford & Marecek, 1989; Unger, 1990). Viewing psychological and social phenomena through the "lens" of gender allows us to see aspects of social reality that are otherwise obscured. However, like any lens, gender can reveal only some features of the social landscape. Lenses such as race, class, and age reveal other, equally important features. Feminist psychologists do not wish to copy the limitations of androcentric psychology by replacing "male as norm" with "white-middle-class-heterosexual female as norm."

Psychological Research and Social Change

Traditionally, psychology has focused on changing individuals. Psychologists have developed new techniques to bring about attitude change, to increase insight and self-understanding, to teach new behavioral skills, and to reduce or eliminate self-defeating thinking and behaviors. These techniques are applied in a variety of educational and therapeutic settings. In this book we will discuss how feminist psychology has adapted and used the tools of traditional psychology.

However, the new scholarship on women and gender also suggests that there are definite limits to the power of individual change. Many of the issues and problems that confront women today are the result of social structures and practices that put women at a disadvantage and interfere with their living happy, productive lives. Social-structural problems cannot be solved through individual changes in attitudes and behavior; rather, the social institutions that permit the devaluation and victimization of women must be changed. Therefore, throughout this book we will discuss the implications of psychological research for changing institutions such as traditional marriage, language use, child rearing, the workplace, and, not least, the institution of psychology itself.

It is clear that personal change does not take place in a social vacuum. It is also clear that equality between women and men cannot occur in the absence of social justice for other marginalized groups. Social change is slow, but as more members of formerly powerless groups gain power in society, they should make further changes in it. They will be able to do so, however, only if they continue to identify with the marginalized groups from which they emerged. People who understand the role of both the individual and the group appear to be most effective in creating social change (Sherif, 1976).

Social changes are not always for the better. Sometimes policies that solve problems for one group create problems for others (McGrath, 1986). For example, the Communist regimes in Eastern Europe have been toppled. These regimes reduced the individual freedoms of everyone. New, more democratic regimes such as those in Poland, however, have voted to eliminate legal abortion and equal rights for women. Thus, women's freedoms will be curtailed in these new democracies. What will be defined as progress here? Of course, it will depend upon who is writing the definition.

Psychological research draws on the real world of people living in complex social contexts. It abstracts or isolates aspects of that world for systematic study. When researchers and textbook writers examine the implications of psychological research for changing women's social environments and opportunities, they return the isolated aspects to their context. Thus, a circle is closed, and psychological research is potentially more useful for women.

OUR GOALS FOR OUR STUDENTS

The authors of this book have changed, both personally and professionally, as a result of our involvement in the psychological study of women. Rhoda Unger has written:

> Once upon a time I was a confirmed behaviorist. In principle, this meant that I believed effects derived from orderly determinist causes, that the subjective aspects of behavior were irrelevant, and that the best studies required maximal distance between experimenter and subject. In practice, this meant that my first major research, my doctoral dissertation, involved making lesions in the caudate nucleus of rats and examining their effects upon temporal and spatial alternation by means of operant conditioning procedures. If I thought of sex professionally at all, I saw it as a variable which could neither be manipulated nor controlled and therefore of very little scientific interest. Even the rats were male (1989, p. 15).

Like Rhoda Unger, Mary Crawford started out as a psychologist believing that good science demanded a separation of personal or social concerns from scientific problem solving. Her dissertation was an analysis of species-specific reactions in rats and their effects on classical and operant conditioning. She writes:

> More and more, my research seemed like a series of intellectual puzzles that had no connection to the rest of my life. In the lab, I studied abstract theories of conditioning, accepting the assumption that the principles were similar for rats and humans. In the "real world," I became involved in feminist activism and began to see things I had never noticed before. I saw sex discrimination in my university and knew women who struggled to hold their families together in poverty. Trying to build an egalitarian marriage and bring up my children in nonsexist ways made me much more aware of social pressures to conform to traditional gender roles. I began to ask myself why I was doing a kind of psychology that had so little to say about the world as I knew it. I turned to the study of women and gender in order to make my personal and intellectual life congruent and to begin using my skills as a psychologist on behalf of social change.

Both of us have worked for social change on behalf of women. We have drawn on our skills and training as psychologists in activism on reproductive rights, gender equity in secondary and higher education, peace and nonviolent conflict resolution, nonsexist marriage and child raising, and gender-fair language. We have helped communicate psychology to the general public through speaking and writing on feminist issues. All these commitments have raised fresh questions and provided us with new insights on women and gender.

Today, we value our early research for teaching us how to go about scientific inquiry systematically and responsibly, but we have changed our views about what the important questions in psychology are and what theoretical frameworks are of most potential. We have chosen to specialize in the study of women and gender, and to write this book, in the hope that we may contribute to the creation of a new, transformed psychology.

A recent study suggests that our experience of professional and personal change through feminism is not unusual. Fifty-one distinguished members of APA's Psychology of Women Division were asked to describe their experience of feminism. Their replies indicated that, to them, feminism meant valuing women and their experiences, a concern with equality of power, the need for change and activism, and the idea of gender as a social construct. To these psychologists, a focus on women and gender in their research and teaching was part of a feminism whose meaning was "much more than the dictionary would suggest . . . a lived, conscious, changing experience" (Kimmel, 1989, p. 145). The researcher, Ellen Kimmel, noted the transformative power of feminist thought among her research participants and in her own life. Her summation can apply to the women who wrote this book as well:

> Feminism (whatever it is and all that it is) transformed my life by connecting it to my work and gathering the disparate parts of myself into a whole (Kimmel, 1989, p. 145).

Rhoda Unger has taught the psychology of women for twenty-five years and Mary Crawford for twenty years. Together, we have introduced thousands of students, both women and men, to feminist psychology. Our students have come from many different racial and ethnic backgrounds, including African-American, white, Asian-American, and Hispanic. In age and experience they have ranged from the traditional young-adult college student to postretirement. Some identified themselves, openly or privately, as gay, lesbian, or bisexual, others as heterosexual. Their personal beliefs and values about feminism, women, and gender varied a great deal. In short, our students have been a diverse group of people. We have welcomed that diversity, and in this book we try to reflect what we have learned from it. Whatever your own background, we welcome you, our newest students, to the study of women and gender.

Perhaps because of our own experience of change through learning about women and gender, our goals for our students involve changes in knowledge, thinking skills, and attitudes. We hope that you, like many of our students before you, will experience growth in at least some of the following areas as a result of your studies:

- *Critical thinking skills.* By studying the psychology of women, you can learn to evaluate psychological research critically and become a more astute, perceptive observer of human behavior.
- *Knowledge and understanding about the inequities faced by nondominant groups within our society.* Our primary focus is gender, but gender always interacts with other systems of domination.
- *Empathy for women.* You may come to appreciate the experiences and viewpoints of your mother, your sisters, and your women friends better. In addition, women students may experience a heightened sense of sisterhood with all women.
- *Desire to work toward social change that benefits women*—and a commitment to do so.

- *The ability to see the larger context of women's lives.* The psychology of women is linked to the biology, sociology, anthropology, and cultural representation of women.
- *The understanding that "women" is a complex category.* Women are a diverse group and must be studied in the context of other significant aspects of their lives, not as gendered beings alone.

There is one thing, however, that we cannot offer you as a consequence of studying women and gender: closure. A first course in women and gender, our students tell us, raises as many questions as it answers. Acquiring knowledge about human behavior is an ongoing process, and its outcome cannot be determined in advance. This is as true for professional researchers as it is for college students.

> Feminist psychology and feminism in general seem to be at the point of trying to piece together the individual parts of a quilt. The overall pattern of the quilt that we want to create is still emerging. No one knows what a feminist psychology will look like any more than we know what equality in a postpatriarchal world will look like. We are beginning to piece the separate parts together—to explore the kinds of stitching to use in connecting the pieces and how to place the separate pieces into the pattern. But we have not stopped questioning the process of quilting itself. . . .

Perhaps most important, the quilt is already useful, and "the conversations around the margins are vibrant and empowering" (Gentry, 1989, pp. 5–6).

SUGGESTED READINGS

EISENSTEIN, HESTER (1983). *Contemporary Feminist Thought.* Boston: G. K. Hall. A history and analysis of the development of feminist approaches to issues of gender and society in the United States, written for readers new to feminism.

HOOKS, BELL (1981). *Ain't I a Woman: Black Women and Feminism.* Boston: South End Press. An African-American feminist writes about the impact of sexism on black women during slavery, the devaluation of black women historically and in the present, racism among black men and white feminists, and black women's involvement with feminism.

SCARBOROUGH, ELIZABETH and LAUREL FURUMOTO (1987). *Untold Lives: The First Generation of American Women Psychologists.* New York: Columbia University Press. Documents the experiences of the first American women to earn Ph.D.s in psychology. Some of these women made important contributions to the field, while others, because of the social constraints imposed on them, were unable to fulfill their potential.

CHAPTER 2

Approaches to Understanding Girls and Women

TOWARD AN IDEAL THEORY OF WOMEN'S PERSONALITY
APPROACHES TO THE STUDY OF PERSONALITY
Psychoanalytic Theories
Social Learning Theory
Cognitive Developmental Theory
BEYOND GENDER TYPING
The Androgynous Personality
Transcending Gender Typing
PERSONALITY AND SOCIAL INFLUENCES IN WOMEN'S LIVES
Cultural Diversity and Personality
How Social Events Shape Personality
Interaction of Traits and Situations
Gender, Personality, and Power
Revaluing Women
THE IMPACT OF FEMINIST THOUGHT ON PERSONALITY RESEARCH AND THEORY
CONNECTING THEMES
SUGGESTED READINGS

In daily life, we often explain other people's behavior in terms of their personalities. We talk about their traits—"Keisha is shy and introverted" or "Nancy is domineering"—and make guesses about how they came to be their unique selves—"Luz doesn't trust anyone because of her relationship with her father." We routinely take other people's personalities into account in day-to-day interactions—"I would recommend Jan for that job because she's good at working with people." *Personality* has been defined as a pattern of characteristic thoughts, feelings, and behaviors that distinguishes one person from another and is consistent for each person over time and across situations (Phares, 1984). Understanding personality is a complex and difficult task. The personality theorist has to explain both the *uniqueness* of individuals and the *consistency* of their behavior patterns. Perhaps it's not surprising that when we try to specify the exact nature of personality, it "seems to evaporate before our eyes, leaving us frustrated and uncertain" (Maddi, 1989). Yet despite the difficulty of the task, many psychologists have tried to develop theories about human personality.

Somewhere in the first few years of life, virtually everyone develops a stable *gender identity*—a psychological sense of oneself as a female or male. No infant is born knowing her or his sex, yet gender identity becomes a central part of everyone's personality. How gender identity develops in the ordinary course of growing up is an important question within theories of personality.

Moreover, internalizing sex and gender as part of personality goes beyond merely knowing that we are female or male. People also undergo *gender typing*, the process of developing traits and behaviors that mirror their society's view of what is appropriate for a male or female and coming to hold these masculine/feminine traits and behaviors as part of one's self-concept.

Many people believe that men and women tend to have different sorts of personalities. It is widely believed that men are aggressive, self-reliant, and dominant, while women are yielding, nurturing, and emotional (see Chapter 4). Of course, *beliefs* or *stereotypes* about masculine and feminine personality differences may or may not be accurate. Important questions for any personality theory to address include, "To what extent is personality related to gender? When such relationships exist, how do they come about?"

Despite the importance of gender identity and gender typing in personality development, traditional theories of personality often have not developed satisfactory explanations of how they work. These theories usually focused on male development and men's lives. Because many influential thinkers and researchers in personality took men as the norm rather than thinking about men and women equally, they underemphasized or misunderstood the importance of gender influences. This androcentric bias is now being corrected, but tradition dies hard. For example, when we looked at two of the leading textbooks of personality theory, each of which covers every major theory from the 1890s to the present, we found that neither had a single listing in the index for sex, gender, sex/gender role, or gender identity! In this chapter we will focus on approaches to personality that have been influential in addressing questions of gender identity and gender typing. By starting with older theories and moving to more recent ones, we will illustrate a history of androcentric thought and the development of feminist alternatives. But before we turn to the already established theories, it will be useful to ask, What would an *ideal* theory of women's personality be like?"

TOWARD AN IDEAL THEORY OF WOMEN'S PERSONALITY

If many traditional theories of personality are androcentric, and therefore of limited usefulness in understanding women, what would the characteristics of a more adequate approach be? This is an intriguing—and difficult—question; after all, criticizing others' theories is always easier than inventing a better one. Hannah Lerman, a clinical psychologist, has clarified some of the issues involved by developing a set of criteria for a feminist personality theory (Lerman, 1986). Although her focus is on women, such a theory would not replace men with women but rather would encompass both.

Among the criteria Lerman proposes are these four:

1. An ideal theory of women's personality should *view women positively and centrally*. Women should be more than an afterthought to a theory based on

men's views of reality. Their experiences should not be viewed in terms of stereotypes or given negative connotations. Rather, women's lives should be equally important to men's in building a theory.

2. An ideal theory should *encompass the diversity of women.* Although it is sometimes useful to think of women as a single group, an adequate theory must apply to women who differ from each other in terms of race and ethnicity, religion, sexual orientation, and social class. With this criterion, Lerman is cautioning theorists and researchers not to move from a male norm to a different but still limited norm in their search to understand personality.
3. Ideally, *the concepts of the theory must remain close to the data of experience.* A good theory is one that has logical connections between its constructs and measurable behaviors. When the concepts of a theory are concretely and carefully specified, the theory can be tested against the behavior of real women. Testability is one of the most important scientific criteria for any theory. In contrast, theories that rely on abstract or vague theoretical concepts lead to overgeneralizing ("*All* women are X. . . .") and difficulty in determining whether the statement is valid or not.
4. An ideal personality theory should *recognize that the inner world of the individual is intertwined with the external world of society.* A theory must take some account of the inner processes of emotion, motivation, beliefs, values, and thoughts, and how they affect the person's interactions with society. But a good theory should not focus so much on the inner world of the psyche that it neglects to account for how the individual is shaped and constrained by external events. Societal forces such as poverty and sexism can and do affect individual personality.

These criteria are useful in two ways: They can help us envision a future approach to personality that encompasses women's experiences, and they can be used as yardsticks for judging the adequacy of the theories we already have. Keep them in mind as we turn to a review of several theoretical approaches to gender and personality.

APPROACHES TO THE STUDY OF PERSONALITY

Psychoanalytic Theories

Sigmund Freud

Freud was the first theorist to develop a comprehensive theory of personality, and the first to focus on the relationship between biological sex and personality development. Freudian theory has been very influential. Its ideas permeate our culture, appearing in our literature, media, and social sciences. Concepts such as death wish, sex object, ego, Freudian slip, the unconscious mind, and repression all have their origins in Freud's psychoanalytic theory. The Freudian approach to gender is largely a biologically based one with a focus on maturational stages.

Freud's stage theory of personality development is familiar to most psychology students, and we will not repeat it here. With respect to gender identity, he focused largely on boys, describing how they experience sexual desire for the mother and castration anxiety. The *Oedipal complex* is resolved when the boy identifies with his father, striving to be like him and accepting his values. This identification allows him to possess the mother vicariously. When identification takes place, the superego, the psychic site of conscience and moral ideals, develops.

The developmental story for girls unfolds differently. Freud believed that the girl's discovery that she lacks a penis is a turning point in her psychological development. She is "mortified by the comparison with the boy's far superior equipment . . . repudiates her love for her mother . . . with the discovery that her mother is castrated." The girl blames the mother for her own lack of a penis and transfers her love to her father, who has the organ she (and her "deficient" mother) can never possess:

> With the discovery that her mother is castrated it becomes possible to drop her as an object . . . as a result of the discovery of women's lack of a penis they are debased in value for girls just as they are for boys and later perhaps for men (Freud, 1933/1965, pp.126–127).

The girl's wish for a penis is not fully satisfied by turning to her father, however. It is translated into a wish for a baby from her father, and later into a wish to have children with her husband. According to Freud, a woman fulfills her femininity only by giving birth to a son, thus producing the longed-for penis at last.

Freud believed that, unlike boys, girls typically fail to resolve completely the Oedipal complex (sometimes called the Electra complex in girls), leading to a typically feminine personality characterized by passivity and intense desire to be a mother. Freud felt that the desire to be impregnated also indicates masochism, or the enjoyment of pain and suffering, since intercourse and childbirth may be painful. Narcissism, or vain self-love, forms the third component of femininity.

In addition, Freud believed that lifelong feelings of inferiority, as well as a tendency to jealousy, emerge as a consequence of penis envy. The superego is formed when the child identifies with the same-sex parent and internalizes society's moral standards. Since girls' identification with their mothers is incomplete and unsatisfactory, their internalization of social values is also less complete than boys':

> That they show less sense of justice than men, that they are less ready to submit to the great necessities of life, that they are more often influenced in their judgments by feelings of affection or hostility—all these would be amply accounted for by the modification in the formation of their superego which we have already inferred (Freud, 1948, pp. 196–197).

In summary, Freud explains the development of gender identity and gender typing in terms of events arising from biological (genital) differences—an "anatomy is destiny" orientation. When children resolve the Oedipal/Electra complex at about the age of six, their personalities are essentially formed. For boys, healthy masculinity in later life is determined by the strength of their identification with the father. By successfully resolving the Oedipal complex, the boy achieves his gender identity, accepts the moral values of his society, and lays the groundwork for gender typing. "Because I am male, like my father, I will try to be like him—strong, dominant, and masculine." For girls, the lesser resolution of the Electra complex determines a feminine personality orientation of passivity, masochism, narcissism, and feelings of inferiority.

Freud's Followers and Critics: Adler, Horney, Erikson. Freud's ideas about normal masculine and feminine personality were by no means universally accepted. Many of his own students took issue with his biological approach to gender identity and gender typing, and his theory served as the starting point for many reinterpretations and reformulations. Alfred Adler (1954), for example, believed that human beings are primarily social, not sexual, beings. He argued that "masculine dominance is not a natural thing" (p. 105) but rather an outcome of the conflicts among primitive people and the male role of warrior. Women learn quite early that the boys and men are the preferred and privileged members of the family and have the greater social value. Adler emphasized that a girl is born into a biased society that "robs her of her belief in her own value" (p. 110) and undermines her self-confidence.

Karen Horney (1926, 1966) believed that Freud's account of female development echoed a little boys' idea of female anatomy. Although a young boy may look at a girl and believe her to have "lost" her penis, there is no reason to believe that the girls perceive themselves as lacking anything. Horney did not see penis envy as an important part of normal female development. She speculated that some men's obsession with achievement really reflects feelings of inferiority over women's unique capacity to bring forth new life—in other words, men may suffer from womb envy!

Erik Erikson (1963, 1964) reformulated and extended Freudian theory to emphasize development across the lifespan. With respect to gender, Erikson emphasized the concept of *inner space.* Returning to Freud's emphasis on anatomical differences, Erikson believed that a woman's psychological development is governed by the fact that "her somatic design harbors an 'inner space' destined to bear the offspring of chosen men and, with it, a biological, psychological, and ethical commitment to take care of human infancy" (1964, p. 586).

Erikson's evidence that inner space affects gender identity came from his observations of the play behavior of ten- to twelve-year-old children. The children were provided with a variety of miniature figures of people, blocks, and animals and asked to build an exciting "movie scene." The typical girl's play construction was an interior scene with people and furniture inside a block enclosure, while the typical boy's was an exterior scene involving elaborate walls or facades with protrusions or high towers. The girls' scenes were peaceful and static, while the boys' were action-oriented. Erikson saw these gender differences in play constructions as parallel to the anatomical difference between the sexes: the internal, nurturing organs of females, and the external, active organs of males. However, other researchers have found no significant differences in the play constructions of girls and boys when they were rated by two neutral judges (McKay, Pyke, & Goranson, 1984).

Freud's theory attracted many more students, followers, and critics. Helene Deutsch elaborated on Freud's ideas of feminine narcissism, passivity, and masochism in her influential *Psychology of Women* (1944) and extended his analysis to development in adolescence and adulthood. Carl Jung (1971) stressed the integration of the masculine and feminine components of personality. Today, there are many derivatives and adaptations of psychoanalytic personality theory. Although few social scientists give much weight to concepts such as penis envy, some psychoanalysts still use them to interpret behavior, as this excerpt from a recent psychoanalytic case study of a two-year-old girl illustrates:

> Severe separation anxiety and excessive temper tantrums were the reason L.'s mother consulted me. L., a bright and verbally precocious child, was also responding to her parents' divorce six months earlier. . . . In her play, she was intrigued by broken crayons. She would take them to me and say, "Fix it." Another repetitive game was undoing her shoelaces and turning to her mother and me, saying "Fix it." It seemed clear that L. had experienced her lack of a penis as a punishment and persistently hoped for reparation. I interpreted to L. that she thought she had a penis and that it was broken because she had done something wrong (Chehrazi, 1986, pp. 29–30).

Nancy Chodorow: Psychoanalysis from a Feminist Perspective

Certain basic assumptions of the psychoanalytic perspective have been adopted by contemporary theorists who are concerned with explaining women's place in society. One of the most influential of these thinkers is Nancy Chodorow (1978, 1979). Chodorow accepts some of Freud's starting points, such as the idea that unconscious motivation and early life events determine personality. In contrast to Freud's emphasis on the phallic stage, however, she proposes that the crucial events underlying the development of gender identity and subsequent gender typing occur even earlier, in the first two years of life.

According to Chodorow's perspective, the infant has no "self"—it cannot distinguish between itself and its caretaker (usually the mother). Because the infant is totally helpless and dependent, it is psychologically merged with the mother as she meets its every need. Infants must go through a gradual process of *differentiation* in which they come to perceive boundaries between themselves and their primary love object. Developing a self is not automatic or invariable. It requires psychological and cognitive maturation (such as the ability to understand that objects exist independently of the child's presence). Most important, the self develops *in relation to the primary caretaker.* As the mother leaves and returns, meets (or fails to meet) the infant's needs, asserts her own needs, and responds to other people besides her infant, the infant comes to perceive her as separate, to make a "me/not me" distinction:

> Separateness, then, is not simply given from birth, nor does it emerge from the individual alone. Differentiation occurs in relationship, separateness is defined relationally: "I" am "not you" (Chodorow, 1979, p. 67).

Developing a separate sense of self is an essential task for every human infant. What does this process have to do with gender identity and gender typing? Because most child rearing is done by women, girl infants experience a caretaker who is like them in a very fundamental way. They can define them-

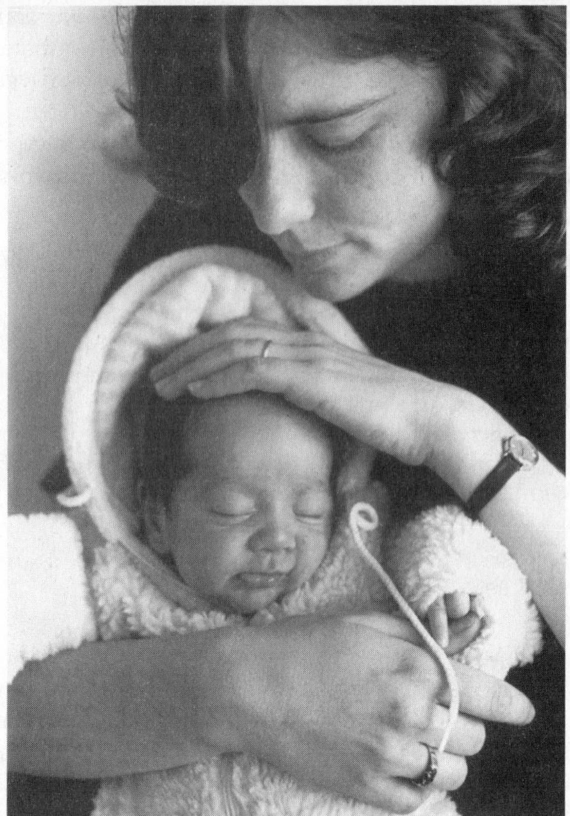

FIGURE 2.1. An infant's sense of self develops in relationship with a caring adult.

selves in terms of that similarity—they move from "I and you are one" to "I am like you." Their distinction between self and other ("me" and "not-me") is one of overlap and fluidity, built on their primary sense of oneness with the mother.

Girls grow up with a sense of similarity to and continuity with their mother, and a sense of connection to others in general. Boys, however, must learn the more difficult lesson that their gender identity is not-female, or not-mother. Because mother has been the first object of love, and because fathers are likely to be less available and emotionally involved with their infants, boys have a more precarious gender identity, an identity based on defining themselves as different. They are more concerned than girls with knowing what is "masculine" and "feminine" and drawing rigid boundaries between the two.

These gender differences in identity have important consequences for further personality development and adult roles. Boys who define masculinity as the opposite of femininity grow into men who devalue women and believe in the superiority of whatever qualities they define as masculine. They deny and repress their "feminine" needs for closeness and connection with others, which reduces their ability to be warm, loving fathers and leads them to be satisfied with less closeness in relationships. Women, on the other hand, do not see themselves as separate and independent from others in the way men do. On the contrary, they tend to define themselves in terms of their relationships with others and to feel a need for human connectedness. Their greater relational needs cannot be entirely satisfied by a man (especially one preoccupied with separateness and independence!). So women have babies, satisfying their needs for connectedness in the mother-infant bond.

The cycle is thus repeated as another generation of boys and girls defines gender in relation to female caretakers. Differences in social roles follow, for as long as women are responsible for children, their opportunities in the wider world will be curtailed. Chodorow titled her book *The Reproduction of Mothering* to indicate her thesis that masculine-feminine identities and roles are not biologically determined but are "reproduced" in every generation by social arrangements.

Psychoanalytic Theories: An Evaluation

We have looked at a variety of psychoanalytic approaches to personality. All of these approaches have been both influential and controversial. How do they fare as theories of *women's* development? To answer that question, we will compare them to the criteria we listed earlier.

In general, psychoanalytic approaches have failed to view women positively or centrally. Freud's theory, in particular, viewed women in terms of stereotypes of the upper class, late-Victorian women of his day—passivity, enjoyment of pain, and vanity. Freud's account of female development was an afterthought to a much better developed theory of male development. In it, girls and women are viewed almost entirely in relationship to boys and men. The stage where children become interested in their genitals was labeled the "phallic" stage, and women's personality was defined in terms of their "lack" of a penis rather than their possession of a uterus, ovaries, vagina, and clitoris. Freud did not devote attention to such central issues in female development as menstruation, childbirth, or orgasm, except to describe intercourse as masochistic and childbirth as an attempt to produce a penis.

Lerman (1986) concludes that Freud's writings provide ample evidence of his negative view of women. "Separated from the experience of women's lives in his youth as well as in his mature life, Freud built a theoretical structure permeated with the residue of his fears and negativity toward women" (p. 12). Other psychoanalytic theorists, building on Freud's foundation, also tended to take male development as the norm and female development as a deviation or afterthought. Karen Horney's concept of womb envy is an important exception.

Chodorow's theory is also exceptional among psychoanalytic approaches in its focus on women, perhaps because it is influenced as much by sociology and feminist social theory as by psychoanalysis. Women's experiences as mothers are central to her theory—indeed, she views the female phenomenon of mothering as the source of not only gendered personalities but the division of labor in society. Mothering is also viewed as a positive goal for women, one that satisfies important relational needs.

Psychoanalytic approaches have generally failed to encompass the diversity of women. Freud based his theory on his analysis of his patients, yet he believed the theory to be a universal account of human development. Moreover, he and all his psychoanalytic followers take the nuclear family as their unit of analysis, neglecting to ask how development might differ in other kinds of families. Cross-culturally and historically, an isolated nuclear family arrangement in which only the mother has extended contact with infants is the exception, not the rule. Chodorow acknowledges cross-cultural differences in the degree of father's involvement and nuclear family isolation but believes that these differences affect only the details and not the basic process of forming a self.

Another kind of diversity not addressed by psychoanalytic approaches is sexual orientation. In these theories, heterosexuality is the norm and the ideal outcome of feminine socialization. However, just as not all women are middle-class or white, not all are heterosexual (see Chapter 9). A good theory of personality should encompass diversity of sexuality in a way that does not label one orientation as necessarily better than another. Chodorow's theory that women have greater relational needs than men implies that women might tend to turn toward each other for friendship, connectedness, and sexual/affectional bonds, rather than to less satisfying relationships with men. Chodorow, however, glosses over this implication of her theory and, like other psychoanalytic theorists, sees heterosexuality as the only normal femininity (Rich, 1980).

Psychoanalytic approaches in general fail to meet our third criterion of being "testable" by remaining close to the data of observable experience. Psychoanalytic concepts are complex, abstract, and poorly tied to behavior. Empirical operations necessary for scientific evaluation are absent. The most important processes in personality development are assumed to take place at preverbal ages and/or outside conscious awareness. It is difficult or impossible to verify empirically whether an infant experiences itself as separate from its mother or whether young children suffer from penis envy and castration anxiety.

When analysts write that a woman has demonstrated penis envy, they usually do not say what specific behaviors or remarks of the woman led them to that conclusion (Lerman, 1986). Even when they do, their interpretations of behavior may seem far-fetched and not very systematic. As in the example quoted earlier, where a two-year-old girl's habit of breaking crayons was seen as indicating penis envy, other interpretations may be equally plausible. Another example of questionable interpretation comes from Erikson's research. Can you think of reasons other than "inner space" why 10-year-old girls and boys might build different play environments, or reasons why other researchers have obtained contradictory results in a similar study?

The final criterion is that a good personality theory should recognize social and cultural influences on development, in addition to intrapsychic influences. Many critics of Freud, including his own students Horney and Adler, have argued that he neglected important external forces, and have gone on to discuss how some of these forces affect personality. Chodorow also gives serious attention to the societal position of women. All these theorists agree that girls might well envy boys not because of their "superior anatomical equipment" but because of their greater privilege and social power.

Lerman (1986) sums up her own evaluation of psychoanalytic approaches as follows:

> I do not believe that Freud's original theories served women well. I also do not believe that the modern revisions of psychoanalytic theory further the health and well-being of the modern woman. After the initial feminist rejection of Freudian concepts in the early 1970s, some have reaccepted his ideas as having validity and applicability to women. I am not in that group because I see the theory as so fundamentally flawed in its thinking about women that it cannot be repaired, however extensive the tinkering with it. . . . Assumptions about the inherent inferiority of women are embedded in the very core of psychoanalytic theory. These are not readily changed and are also not very amenable to patchwork repair. I remind you too that every time people use a term such as Oedipal . . . they are implicitly accepting ideas whose validity has not been demonstrated despite years of trying. We need a theory that is likely to serve women's interests better . . . (p. 6).

Psychoanalytic approaches are (with some exceptions and variations) relatively weak as theories of women's development. They have serious shortcomings as scientific theories of men's development as well. Yet they are still taught to most beginning psychology students, and they continue to have enormous influence on our culture. People often talk about others' personalities as though there is an unconscious mind, that people act upon motives they are unaware of, that such things as an Oedipal complex and superego exist, that all women are passive and yearn for motherhood. All of these are *assumptions* of psychoanalytic theory.

No other psychological approach has attempted to explain so much of human nature and behavior. Indeed, psychoanalysis has been likened to a religious cult that offers a global account of all human nature—once you accept its basic assumptions (Brown, 1984; Lerman, 1986; Reiff, 1966).

Social Learning Theory

Almost everyone can remember childhood events that taught what a "good" girl or boy should—or shouldn't—do. We may have been spanked for getting a new dress dirty or rewarded for a good report card. Perhaps we were expected to do gender-specific household chores—boys may take out the trash, while girls set the table for dinner. We may have been encouraged to follow a same-gender example: "Susan doesn't talk back to *her* mother . . . ." When asked to explain how and why adult men and women seem so different from each other, students frequently remember events like these and express the idea that "we've all been conditioned by society." This way of thinking about gender is consistent with social learning theory, an approach that emphasizes how children learn gendered behavior from their environment (Mischel, 1966, 1970).

Learning Principles Applied to Gender Typing

Social learning theory is rooted in behaviorism and draws its terms and principles from experimental research on learning (Bandura & Walters, 1963). When an animal learns to do a task such as pressing a bar to obtain food, behaviorists say that the food is a reinforcer. Behavior that is not reinforced will extinguish, or gradually disappear. Punishment is another, faster way to suppress or eliminate behavior (although it has many drawbacks as a method of behavior change). According to social learning theory, people learn their characteristic behavior patterns in much the same way as nonhuman animals, except that reinforcers are not always as concrete as a morsel of food. Children's behavior is powerfully shaped by attention and approval from adults. Furthermore, unlike rats, people learn by observing others and imitating their behavior.

Reinforcement, punishment, and extinction of "sex-inappropriate" behavior are not always direct and obvious. Parents do not usually follow their little girl around feeding her candy when she picks up a doll and frowning at her when she picks up a toy bulldozer! But behavior shaping can be quite effective without being especially noticeable. If Dad merely glances up from his newspaper with a warm smile when little Debbie is coloring quietly in her coloring book but stays absorbed in his paper when she builds a block tower, she will, according to social learning theory, be more likely to color than to build with blocks in the future. The newly learned behavior may generalize to other situations—Debbie may begin to prefer coloring books to blocks at nursery school as well as at home. The lesson may also be quite broad—Debbie may learn that, in general, quiet play is "nicer" than active play.

The learning of gender-typed behavior is made easier when parents set up the environment in such a way that some activities are much more likely to occur (and thus be reinforced) than others. If a boy's room is filled with sports equipment and furnished in bright colors and sturdy furniture that can "take a beating," he is probably more likely to engage in rough-and-tumble play than is his sister, whose room is done in pink-and-white ruffles and furnished with a dressing table. Parents may then notice and reinforce the difference with comments about how "Boys will be boys," while "She's a real little lady."

An important point to remember about the effects of reinforcement, punishment, and extinction is that, according to social learning theory, they occur whether or not the parent is deliberately attempting to influence behavior. An adult need not *intend* to teach a lesson about gender for her or his behavior to serve as a reinforcer or punisher for a child. Teaching and learning about gender often seem "natural" and unremarkable to parent and child alike, and parents may sincerely believe that they treat their boys and girls similarly while they actually are reinforcing very different behaviors. In schools, too, a great deal of research has documented how well-meaning teachers inadvertently treat girls and boys differently, disadvantaging girls (Sadker & Sadker, 1994).

Imitation, or modeling, seems to be quite spontaneous in young children. They imitate mannerisms and postures. An extreme example was provided by a friend of ours whose 2-year-old daughter was cared for by a woman who wore a leg brace as a result of childhood polio. The child developed a style of walking that dragged one leg in imitation of her caretaker, and learned to walk more normally only when another adult also joined her day-care setting. Children also imitate speech, as many a parent has found to her dismay when a vivid curse word used in an unguarded moment is repeated by her toddler! And they imitate all sorts of other behaviors. A young boy "shaves" with a play razor

FIGURE 2.2. Children learn by imitating adults.

while his father does the real thing; a young girl plays with her dolls as her mother feeds the new baby. Imitation is often expressed in play, as children "drive to the store," "play house" or "play school." Figure 2.2 shows an everyday example of a child's imitative behavior.

Observational learning may not always be expressed in immediate imitation, but may be stored for later use. A small girl may observe her mother devoting much time to shopping for clothes, planning new outfits, applying makeup, doing her hair, and expressing concern about her weight. While she learns through these observations that attractiveness is a very important dimension for women, she might not express that knowledge very much until adolescence.

Of course, children have opportunities to see both men and women behaving in a variety of ways. Why, then, does behavior become gender typed? How do children learn that particular behaviors are acceptable for females but not males (and vice versa), and how do they apply that knowledge to themselves as girls and boys? To answer these questions, social learning theory has relied on the concept of identification, although this concept has a somewhat different meaning than in the psychodynamic approaches we discussed earlier.

To the social learning theorist, *identification* is a particular kind of imitation: the spontaneous copying of whole patterns of behavior, without specific training or direct reward, based on an intimate relationship with the person being imitated (Mussen, 1969). According to the theory, children identify with their same-sex parent, producing relatively stable aspects of personality that are resistant to change. They see themselves as like that parent in personality traits and feelings (Kagan, 1958). Identification is the source of gender identity, and gender typing follows when the child observes and imitates the parent with whom she identifies.

Observational learning of gender-typed behavior may be affected by other forces besides identification. Most young children see their mothers in largely gender-typed roles simply because mothers are more likely to be responsible for housework and child care, activities that a child can observe often and directly. If only women are seen cleaning house and changing diapers, both boys and girls may acquire the knowledge that these are "women's work." When mothers and fathers go to their jobs outside the home, their work is not directly observable by the small child. As with reinforcement, then, observational learning may be facilitated by environments that make gender-typed behavior frequent or salient.

Social Learning Theory: An Evaluation

Social learning theory fares very differently from psychoanalytic approaches as a theory of women's personality development. The biggest difference is with respect to the theory's emphasis on social and cultural forces affecting women. Social learning theory, of course, *is* a theory of social influences. It explains gender identity and gender typing as neither biologically determined nor inevitable, but as the result of moment-to-moment, day-to-day interactions between the developing child and her immediate social environment—her mother, father , and other caretakers; the media; school; and her playmates. Implicit in the theory is the idea that gender typing can be lessened or even eliminated if we as a society and as individuals choose to do so.

Women's experiences are also viewed more positively and centrally in social learning theory. Although the theory did not originate as an attempt to account for gender influences on personality, it has been extensively developed along those lines and has dealt centrally with gender (Mussen, 1969; Mischel, 1966, 1970). It views women positively in the sense that it does not see them as inherently inferior or view them in terms of negative stereotypes. However, social learning theory has sometimes been used to imply that women's socialization is necessarily limiting or deficient. As cultural feminists would point out, it is not necessarily a problem if some people are socialized to be gentle, nurturing, and attuned to others' needs! The problem is not gentle, nurturant behaviors but society's devaluation of them as "feminine" traits suitable only for girls and women.

Social learning theory has great potential for encompassing the diversity of women. Rather than viewing all women as essentially alike by virtue of biology, it assumes that what a child learns about femininity and masculinity will vary according to her social class, ethnic group, and family composition—indeed, any and all environmental factors are expected to influence gender identity and gender typing. This potential has not been fully developed; most research on social learning has focused on white, middle-class children. But in principle, the theory can be usefully applied not only to growing up female but also to growing up as a person who is black, Hispanic, disabled, or gay.

An important strength of social learning theory is that its concepts are clear, well defined, and easily put to the test. For these reasons, it has generated a tremendous amount of empirical research that has helped refine the theory and make it more useful. Much of what psychologists know about how gender becomes a social reality is based on research inspired by social learning theory (see Chapter 7). Here, we will focus on research evaluating two central theoretical claims of this approach—claims about gender typing and gender identity.

Social learning theory proposes that gender typing is learned through reinforcement, punishment, observation, and imitation. There is considerable evidence that parents do reward and punish some behaviors differently for girls and boys. We will review that evidence in detail in later chapters; meanwhile, you can probably think of examples from your own experience. Our students tell us that, in their families, boys were less likely to be punished for being messy or careless and more likely to be overtly rewarded for achievement in sports and school. Girls were rewarded for being thoughtful of others' feelings, looking pretty, and taking good care of their possessions and appearance. These students' memories are consistent with systematic research (Block, 1973).

There is also considerable research evidence to support the view that children learn by imitation. A classic study by Albert Bandura (1965) illustrates the operation of both reinforcement and imitation in learning to be aggressive. In Bandura's study, children were shown one of three films. In all the films, an adult behaved aggressively by hitting and kicking a large toy clown. In one film, the adult was rewarded; in another, the adult was punished; and in the third, no specific consequences followed the aggression. The children were then given the opportunity to play with the toy clown. Just as social learning theory would predict, children imitated the behavior most when it had been reinforced; that is, children who had seen the first film were more aggressive than those who had seen either of the other films. Overall, boys were more aggressive than girls.

In the next part of the experiment, children were offered small treats for performing as many of the adult model's aggressive behaviors as they could remember. Here, all children were more aggressive, and girls were, overall, nearly as aggressive as boys. Bandura's experiment shows that children do imitate adult models even when the children are not directly reinforced for doing so. In particular, they imitate models who are themselves reinforced. Furthermore, children may learn a behavior through observation but show no particular evidence of that learning until the behavior is reinforced—like the girls in the second part of the experiment.

The second major claim of social learning theory is that children identify with (and thus imitate) their same-sex parent in preference to the other parent. While it sounds intuitively reasonable, there is little evidence to support this idea (Maccoby & Jacklin, 1974). Children seem to imitate parents fairly indiscriminately, not on the basis of sex. Nor do children resemble their same-sex parent more in their personality attributes. Girls' scores on femininity scales are not related to the scores of their mothers, and boys' masculinity scores are not related to their fathers', nor are patterns of gender-role preferences similar in parents and their preschoolers (Hetherington, 1965; Mussen & Rutherford, 1963; Fling & Manosevitz, 1972).

The quality of the parent-child relationship seems to be more important than the parent's sex in influencing modeling (Lamb, 1976). Laboratory research on imitation shows that children are more likely to imitate adults who are warm, friendly, and attentive to the child (Bandura & Huston, 1961). They also imitate people they see as powerful (Bandura, Ross, & Ross, 1963; Mischel & Grusec, 1966). All these results suggest that either or both parents would normally be important models.

In an interesting study of the long-term effects of observational learning, college students who perceived their (homemaker) mothers as happy and successful tended to have traditional beliefs about women's roles, while those whose mothers had difficult lives or unhappy marriages were more liberal in their beliefs. The attitudes of male students were even more strongly affected than those of female students by observing their mothers' situations. Thus, both the male and female students had learned about gender roles from observing the outcomes attained by a female parent (Travis & Seipp, 1978). Others who have a close relationship with the child, such as caretakers, teachers, older siblings, and grandparents, could serve as models, too. One possibility is that children only imitate same-sex models when the specific behavior to be modeled is one that the children already know or believe to be gender typed (Bussey & Bandura, 1984; Perry & Bussey, 1979).

It is still an open question in social learning theory, then, precisely why children develop gender-typed patterns of behavior. If children show no particular tendency to identify only with their same-sex parent and readily learn by observing and imitating adult models of both sexes, how does gender typing occur? This question is given a different answer by the approach we turn to now.

Cognitive Developmental Theory

A Stage Theory of Cognitive Development

Cognitive developmental theory (Kohlberg, 1966) builds on the research of Jean Piaget, who observed that young children think in ways that are qualitatively different from older children and adults. Piaget believed that children move through a fixed series of stages in their cognitive development. He showed that particular concepts (such as the understanding that a quantity of liquid remains the same when it is poured from a short, wide container into a tall, narrow one) are impossible for children to grasp until they have reached the appropriate cognitive stage. Children's predictable errors in thinking indicate that they have different, less mature ways of thinking than adults—less sophisticated modes of cognitive organization. The child's understanding of gender, like her understanding of other cognitive concepts, changes at different stages.

Regardless of what stage they have reached, however, children actively strive to interpret and make sense of the world around them. According to Lawrence Kohlberg's cognitive developmental approach, gender identity and gender typing are the outcome of children's active structuring of their physical and social world.

Children understand some things about the concepts of sex and gender long before others. A 2- or 3-year-old child will answer correctly when asked if he or she is a boy or a girl. However, the child may believe that people can change sex by changing their hair styles or clothing. (At age 2 1/2, one of our own children maintained stubbornly that the "real" difference between boys and girls was that only girls wear barrettes!) The child may believe that boys can grow up to be mommies, as the following conversation between two young boys shows:

JOHNNY (age 4 1/2): I'm going to be an airplane builder when I grow up.
JIMMY (age 4): When I grow up, I'll be a mommy.
JOHNNY: No, you can't be a mommy. You have to be a daddy.
JIMMY: No, I'm going to be a mommy.
JOHNNY: No, you're not a girl, you can't be a mommy.
JIMMY: Yes, I can (Kohlberg, 1966, p. 95).

This conversation illustrates that children's understanding of gender is very concrete and limited. (It might also suggest that Jimmy suffers from womb envy!) Johnny, who is slightly older, understands gender constancy—he knows that gender is permanent—while Jimmy does not. By the age of 6 or 7, almost all children understand gender constancy, not as a result of learning through reinforcement and punishment but rather through cognitive maturation. And once children know that they are, and always will be, one sex or the other, they turn to the task of matching the cultural expectations for people of their sex.

Children come to value behaviors, objects, and attitudes that are consistent with their sex label. Girls want to do "girl things," wear gender-specific clothes such as ruffly dresses, and generally make a sharp distinction between girls and boys. Boys, too, behave as though they are thinking, "I am a boy; therefore I want to do boy things; therefore the opportunity to do boy things (and to gain approval for doing them) is rewarding" (Kohlberg, 1966, p. 89).

Children may begin to exaggerate gender roles at this age, with boys proclaiming anything remotely associated with girls as "yukky" and girls avoiding "boys'" activities like the plague. Even a child who has been cared for by a female physician may announce that "Only boys can be doctors." This exaggeration may be due to children's need to keep gender categories conceptually distinct (Maccoby, 1980).

According to Kohlberg, identification is an outcome, not a cause, of gender typing. The child tends to model those who are like himself and who are high in prestige and competence. "For the boy with masculine interests and values the activities of a male model are more interesting and hence more modeled" (Kohlberg, 1966, p. 129). The son's identification with his father thus progresses from identifying with a stereotyped masculine role to identifying with his father's own personification of that role. Feminine identification involves first identifying with a generalized female role, and then with the mother as an example of that role.

External rewards and punishments for gender-typed behavior are relatively unimportant from the cognitive developmental perspective. Children are not viewed as mere passive agents to be acted upon by reinforcement and punishment. Rather than being influenced by whatever reinforcers the social envi-

FIGURE 2.3. As cognitive-developmental theory predicts, this girl chooses "feminine" activities.

ronment sends their way, children actively try to fit their beliefs, values, and behaviors to their sex (see Figure 2.3). In their search to become the "best possible" girl (or boy), children rely on reinforcers only as a guide to how well they are doing. The cognitive developmental perspective does not deny social learning principles; rather, it adds to them by offering the intriguing idea that children willingly socialize themselves to be masculine or feminine.

The Cognitive Developmental Approach: An Evaluation

In general, the cognitive developmental approach treats women positively; it does not start with an assumption of female inferiority. However, women and their experiences have not been central to the development of the theory. Kohlberg's original research used results from male participants to generalize about male and female development. The limitations of this male-as-norm approach become clear when Kohlberg's analysis of gender typing is applied to girls.

According to the theory, once children achieve a stable gender identity, they should socialize themselves into "appropriate" gender roles because they are motivated to be prototypical girls or boys. For girls, this means that in order to want to be feminine they must first identify with femininity as a role. However, the feminine role is culturally less prestigious than the masculine role. As girls become aware of the categories of masculinity and femininity, they may also recognize the economic, occupational, and status advantages of men. How then do girls come to value their devalued role enough to want to follow it?

Perhaps because he thought primarily in terms of male socialization, Kohlberg did not give this question sufficient attention in building his theory. He suggested that girls may prefer the masculine role for a while—for example, many girls are "tomboys" throughout middle childhood (Hyde, Rosenberg, & Behrman, 1977). However, he did not completely account for how girls acquiesce to, as well as resist, gender typing. He proposed that girls eventually find the feminine role attractive enough to merit emulation. Certain aspects of it (such as nurturance) may be perceived as "nicer" than some aspects of the masculine role (such as aggression). Moreover, adult women have more power than girls, and that may provide a reason to identify with them. These suggestions seem almost afterthoughts to the theory. To be most useful as a theory of female development, the cognitive developmental approach must provide a more complete answer to the question of how girls come to adopt an orientation that is associated with low power and value.

The cognitive developmental approach can be criticized for paying insufficient attention to the gender-polarizing influences in children's environments. Why is sex the crucial category by which children classify themselves and others? Why do they divide the world conceptually by sex more readily and fundamentally than by other possible categories such as skin color, size, or eye color? It is not necessarily because the biological category of sex is naturally evident to them. Rather, they may be reacting to the *gender* distinctions made by everyone around them. Cognitive developmental theory has so completely ignored the social influences on children's gender learning that it "portrays early gender traditionalism as almost completely emerging from the mind of the child" (Bem, 1993, p. 112.)

Because it does not adequately address cultural influences on behavior, the theory says little about the diversity of women. Why are there wide individual variations in gender typing among women (and men) who have equally strong and stable gender identities? How do differences in ethnic group and social class affect the individual's motivation to become gender typed? Although in principle the theory could address these questions, it has not been used to do so in practice.

Testability is a strong point of the cognitive developmental approach. Because its concepts are clearly specified, their validity can be measured. Like social learning theory, it has generated a great deal of research (see Chapter 7). This research supports the idea that children's understanding of gender is related to their cognitive maturity (Fagot, 1985a). However, research does not support the idea that children become gender typed only after they acquire an understanding of gender constancy. On the contrary, children show a preference for gender-typed objects and activities by the age of 3 (Thompson, 1975), while they do not fully understand gender constancy before about the age of 5. In another study, children aged $1^1/_2$ to $4^1/_2$ showed the expected progression from understanding gender labels to understanding gender constancy. However, the children's level of understanding was not related to their adoption of gender-typed behaviors (Fagot, 1985b). Especially for girls, the relationship between understanding gender and becoming gender typed needs to be explored further in research.

Cognitive Development and Moral Thinking

Kohlberg's perspective suggests that the child's conception of right and wrong should depend on the child's stage of cognitive development, just as other kinds of reasoning and thinking do. He studied moral development in children and adults by posing hypothetical dilemmas like the one in Box 2.1 and carefully analyzing the answers people gave. For Kohlberg, the reasoning behind the solution was more important than the solution itself, because it revealed different levels of moral development.

According to Kohlberg, his research revealed three levels of moral reasoning, from least to most mature: *preconventional, conventional,* and *postconventional* morality. Within each level, there are two stages. As you can see from Box 2.2, children start out with a moral orientation based on avoiding punishment (for example, Heinz should not steal because he might get caught by the police). By the time they reach middle childhood, most people have moved to a conventional orientation based on gaining approval from others (that is, Heinz should not steal because it's not nice and people won't like him) and, later, on rules and laws (that is, Heinz should not steal because there are laws against stealing). Only a few people move beyond conventional morality to the postconventional level, where moral reasoning is based on internalized ethical principles. People at these stages may choose to break laws they believe to be unjust. People who deliberately chose to violate segregation laws during the civil rights movement provide examples of postconventional morality.

In Kohlberg's early research, boys and men tended to achieve at least stage 4 moral thinking, while girls and women were more likely to stop at stage 3. In other words, women seemed to have a less mature and less developed sense of morality. Carol Gilligan (1982) criticized this conclusion. First of all, she pointed

Box 2.1 How Would You Resolve This Dilemma?

In Europe, a woman was near death from a very bad disease, a special kind of cancer. There was one drug that the doctors thought might save her. It was a form of radium that a druggist in the same town had recently discovered. The drug was expensive to make, but the druggist was charging ten times what the drug cost him to make. He paid $200 for the radium and charged $2,000 for a small dose of the drug. The sick woman's husband, Heinz, went to everyone he knew to borrow the money, but he could get together only about $1,000, which was half of what it cost. He told the druggist that his wife was dying and asked him to sell it cheaper or let him pay later. But the druggist said, "No, I discovered the drug and I'm going to make money from it." Heinz got desperate and broke into the man's store to steal the drug for his wife.

Do you think that Heinz should have stolen the drug? Was his action right or wrong? Why?

Source: Excerpt from *Essays on Moral Development: The Philosophy of Moral Development* (Vol. 1) by Lawrence Kohlberg.

Box 2.2 Levels and Stages of Moral Development According to Lawrence Kohlberg and Carol G. Gilligan

I. Preconventional morality
Kohlberg:
Stage 1: Obeying rules in order to avoid punishment
Stage 2: Obeying rules to get rewards
Gilligan: Concern for oneself and survival

II. Conventional morality
Kohlberg:
Stage 3: "Good girl" orientation: obeying rules to gain approval
Stage 4: "Law and order" orientation: rigid conformity to society's laws and rules
Gilligan: concern for one's responsibilities; self-sacrifice and caring for others

III. Postconventional morality
Kohlberg:
Stage 5: Obeying rules because they are necessary for social order, but with understanding that rules can be changed
Stage 6: May violate society's rules or laws if necessary to meet one's own internalized standards of justice
Gilligan: Concern for responsibilities to others and to oneself; self and others as interdependent

Source: Kohlberg, 1981; Gilligan 1982.

out, Kohlberg's early research was conducted entirely with male participants and their responses became the norm by which girls and women were later evaluated. Second, the dilemmas posed by Kohlberg may have been easier for boys and men to relate to because they frequently involved men as the principal actor in the moral drama. The hypothetical dilemmas also might not reveal much about moral behavior in real-life situations. For all these reasons, Gilligan proposed, Kohlberg's theory may be an inadequate map of female development.

With this critique as a starting point, Gilligan went on to develop her own theory of women's moral development. In one study of real-life moral reasoning, Gilligan interviewed women who were pregnant and considering abortion. She chose the abortion situation because it is one area of decision making in which women make choices that are often framed as moral and ethical issues, and also an area that brings up a central conflict for women:

> While society may affirm publicly the woman's right to choose for herself, the exercise of such choice brings her privately into conflict with the conventions of femininity, particularly the moral equation of goodness with self-sacrifice. Although independent assertion in judgment and action is considered to be the hallmark of adulthood, it is rather in their care and concern for others that women have both judged themselves and been judged. . . . When a woman considers whether to continue or abort a pregnancy, she contemplates a decision that affects both self and others and engages directly the critical moral issue of hurting (1982, pp. 70–71).

Like Kohlberg, Gilligan also found preconventional, conventional, and postconventional levels of moral reasoning in the people she interviewed. However, the basis for each level is different (see Box 2.2). At level I, women are concerned with survival, and their immature responses, derived from their feelings of being alone and powerless, may seem selfish. One eighteen-year-old, for example, saw the decision only in terms of her own freedom. On the one hand, having a baby would provide "the perfect chance to get married and move away from home." On the other hand, it would restrict her freedom "to do a lot of things" (p. 75). At level II, women think primarily in terms of others' needs. The conventional morality of womanhood tells them that they should be prepared to sacrifice all for a lover or a potential baby. When their own and others' needs conflict, they may face seemingly impossible dilemmas. One 19-year-old, who did not want an abortion but whose partner and family wanted her to have one, posed the conflict:

> I don't know what choices are open to me. It is either to have it or the abortion; these are the choices open to me. I think what confuses me is it is a choice of either hurting myself or hurting other people around me. What is more important? If there could be a happy medium it would be fine, but there isn't. It is either hurting someone on this side or hurting myself (p. 80).

When women reach the final level of moral development, they resolve the conflicts between their own and others' needs not by conventional feminine self-sacrifice but by balancing care for others with healthy self-care. Because the woman is acting on internalized ethical principles that value relationships, caring is extended both to self and others. A 29-year-old married woman, already a mother, struggled to take into account the strain on herself and her family posed by her pregnancy and her desire to complete her education, and concluded:

> The decision has got to be, first of all, something that the woman can live with, a decision that the woman can live with, one way or another, or at least try to live with, and it must be based on where she is at and other significant people in her life are at (p. 96).

Gilligan's experiences in listening to what women said about moral issues convinced her that the type of morality studied by Kohlberg (and more common in men) is an ethic of rights, while the type she discovered (more common in women) is an ethic of responsibilities. Rather than judge women as "morally deficient" by a male norm, Gilligan believes researchers should recognize that women and men have different but equally valid approaches to moral issues. (For this reason, her book on moral development is titled *In a Different Voice.*) For both men and women, the highest levels of development should integrate the moralities of rights and responsibilities.

The Different Voice: An Evaluation

Carol Gilligan's ideas about moral development have generated a great deal of research and criticism. Some have questioned her use of the abortion dilemma. Comparing women's resolution of real-life abortion dilemmas to men's resolution of hypothetical Heinz-and-the-drug dilemmas may be an invalid "apples-and-oranges" method. Reasoning in the highly stressful abortion situation may not be generalizable even to women who haven't faced it, let alone to men (Code, 1983). Moreover, viewing this dilemma as only a woman's problem may fail to acknowledge that men should also be responsible for their sexual behavior and may distract attention from the evidence in Gilligan's interviews that many of the women were in exploitative and oppressive relationships (O'Laughlin, 1983).

At a minimum, these critics argue, the moral reasoning of women and men should be assessed in situations that are as comparable as possible. For example, the lovers and husbands of the pregnant women in Gilligan's study could have been interviewed on their moral conflicts about abortion (Colby & Damon, 1983). Other researchers have pointed out that Gilligan did not use well-defined measures or a standard scoring procedure and that she selected parts of the interviews to best illustrate her ideas rather than presenting her data systematically (Broughton, 1983; Nails, 1983).

Although Gilligan's research on women brings one kind of diversity to cognitive developmental theory, it did not systematically examine factors other than sex that could be related to differences in moral reasoning. It looked for the "different voice" only as a sex difference, ignoring the question of how a person's social class or religion might affect her moral orientation (Auerbach, Blum, Smith, & Williams, 1985). What appears to be a sex difference in moral reasoning could also reflect women's subordinate social position and lack of power; in other words, perhaps the "ethic of care and responsibility" is expressed by less powerful people generally rather than just by women (Hare-Mustin & Marecek, 1988; Tronto, 1987). Stimulated by Gilligan and Kohlberg's ideas, other psychologists have examined the existing research more systematically, showing that when women and men are compared directly and factors such as level of education are controlled, moral reasoning does not differ by sex (Ford & Lowery, 1986; Walker, 1984, 1986).

How large does a gender-related difference have to be before we stop calling it a similarity? How can we know that we have controlled all relevant variables (such as level of education)? Carol Gilligan's theory is too new for psychology to have definitive evaluations of its validity. She has eloquently described a "different voice"—a moral orientation that Kohlberg's research did not discover. Whether the different voice is a *woman's* voice is still being actively debated.

BEYOND GENDER TYPING

All the theories of personality that we have examined so far share some basic assumptions and values (Cook, 1985). First, they have conceptualized masculinity and femininity as opposite ends of a continuum (see Figure 2.4). A person may be masculine or feminine, but not both, because by definition, being more masculine means being less feminine. This assumption is built into many psychological tests of masculinity–femininity, which were constructed by giving a large number of items to both female and male research participants and then retaining those items that differentiate the two groups. Thus a masculinity–femininity test might have items such as "I prefer watching TV to going fishing" or "I want to make my mark in the world," not because these items reveal deep mysteries about gender typing but simply because men and women tend to answer them differently. An individual can score only as more or less masculine or feminine on these tests, never as a combination of both. Yet all of us know in-

I. As opposite ends of a single continuum or dimension.

II. As separate dimensions.

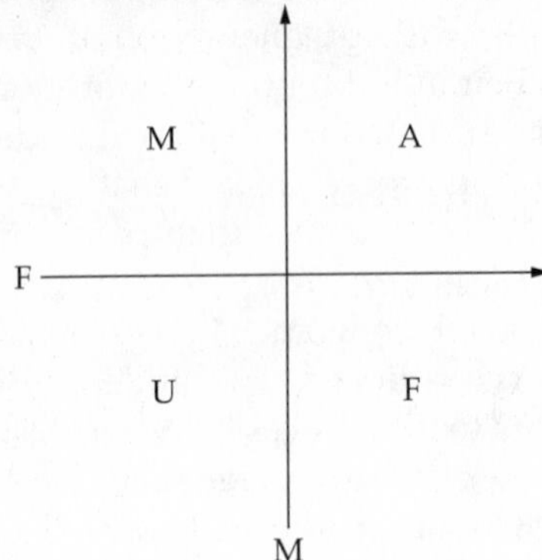

High F + high M = Androgynous or non-gender-typed (A)
High F + low M = Feminine gender-typed (F)
Low F + high M = Masculine gender-typed (M)
Low F + low M = Undifferentiated (U)

FIGURE 2.4. Two conceptualizations of masculinity/femininity.

dividuals who combine "masculine" and "feminine" traits and behaviors–for example, a woman who is both athletic and loves children, or a man who is both compassionate and a logical thinker. Conceptualizing masculinity and femininity as opposites may have interfered with psychology's understanding of gender typing (Constantinople, 1973).

Moreover, traditional personality theories share a value so universal that it has rarely been recognized as a value judgment at all: the idea that gender typing is desirable. Because of this value orientation, any child who did not behave in "appropriately" gender-typed ways was likely to be labeled deviant or maladjusted. Traditional psychological therapy and counseling often focused on helping people "adjust" by conforming to gender roles. However, the assumption that gender typing is all for the best is not borne out by research. On the contrary, highly feminine women (who theoretically should be better adjusted than less feminine women) frequently have been found to be anxious and low in self-esteem (for a review of these studies, see Forisha, 1978).

Finally, the personality theories we've described so far focus on early childhood as the crucial period in which gender identity is achieved and patterns of gender typing are laid down. (Although social learning theory suggests that behaviors could change at any time during the lifespan if reinforcement contingencies change, this possibility has not been much examined by social learning researchers.) All the theories imply that gender development is finished when the ideal of aggressive, dominant manhood, or yielding, nurturing womanhood is internalized. They view gender-typed behavior in adults as a direct consequence of early experience and an endpoint of development.

With the growth of the psychology of women in the last two decades, these assumptions and values have been questioned, alternative theories have been developed, and new empirical research has flourished. We turn now to some of these new approaches to personality.

The Androgynous Personality

Androgyny, a word that combines the Greek roots *andro* (male) and *gyn* (female), refers to a balance or blending of masculinity and femininity. The concept is a very old one, with roots in classical mythology, literature, and religion (Heilbrun, 1973; Kaplan & Sedney, 1980). In psychology, it was reflected in Jung's (1953, 1971) concepts of anima (feminine part of the self in men) and animus (masculine part of the self in women). Jung believed that the two must be integrated within each of us if the self is to be complete. As psychologists have used the term in recent research, psychological androgyny refers to the blending or balancing of *psychological traits* that are stereotyped masculine or feminine.

Before we discuss research on androgyny further, it will be helpful to discuss what psychological androgyny is *not* (Cook, 1985). Androgyny is not a synonym for liberal (or "liberated") attitudes about women's roles in society. A person may see himself or herself as less gender typed than others and at the same time have traditional beliefs about gender roles. Second, androgyny does not refer to sexual orientation. A homosexual or bisexual orientation is not related to androgyny or any other pattern of gender typing. Finally, androgyny does not refer to physical characteristics.

Psychologists Sandra Bem, Janet Spence, and Robert Helmreich have developed inventories that measure individual differences in androgyny (Bem, 1974; Spence, 1991; Spence & Helmreich, 1978). These inventories conceptualize masculinity and femininity as separate dimensions (see Figure 2.4). Persons score high in masculinity if they describe themselves by such stereotypically masculine traits as independent, aggressive, and unemotional; high in femininity by describing themselves in terms of stereotypically feminine traits such as empathy and nurturance; and androgynous if they see themselves as high in both sets of traits. A small number of people, labeled "undifferentiated," rate themselves as low in both kinds of traits. In research using large samples of college students, roughly one-third can be classified as androgynous.

Research on androgyny tells us that there is a great deal of individual variability in gender typing. Let's focus for now on the one-third of college students who see themselves as balancing the positive aspects of traditional masculinity and femininity. What are these androgynous women and men like, and how does their behavior differ from their more conventionally gender-typed peers? If androgyny is a meaningful personality dimension, it should predict a fairly wide range of behaviors, attitudes, and lifestyle choices (Worell, 1981).

One place to look for differences between gender-typed and androgynous people is in their behavioral flexibility (Bem, 1975; Bem & Lenney, 1976). Masculine-typed people should feel comfortable and be likely to excel when the situation draws on their abilities to be assertive, active, and independent, but not when the situation calls for tenderness, empathy, or emotional expressiveness. It is easy to imagine these people liking competitive sports, becoming hard-driving executives, and standing their ground in an argument—but becoming tongue-tied when it is time to say "I love you" or awkward when they attempt to comfort a child. Feminine-typed people, on the other hand, should excel and feel comfortable in situations that call for interpersonal skills, nurturing, and kindness, rather than in competitive and individualistic situations. It is easy to imagine these people liking cooperative games, becoming teachers or counselors, and being able to understand another person's point of view in an argument—but being unable to stand up to a bully or take charge in an emergency.

Sandra Bem hypothesized that only androgynous people can draw upon both sets of characteristics and therefore they should be comfortable (and able to excel) in a wider variety of situations. Unlike many earlier personality researchers, whose value judgments (that traditional masculinity and femininity are ideals for personality development) were unlabeled as values and left undiscussed in their theories, Bem was explicit in specifying her value orientation: androgyny is better. "It may well be—as the women's liberation movement has urged—that the androgynous individual will someday come to define a new and more human standard of psychological health" (1975, p. 643).

Predictions about the greater adaptability of androgynous people have been tested in a variety of situations. Androgynous people behaved like their masculine peers when put under pressure to conform (they resisted pressure and stuck to their own opinions). On the other hand, they behaved more like their feminine peers in "feminine" situations (they were good at playing with a kitten or listening to the problems of a lonely fellow student). People who were strongly gender typed were most competent only in situations that fit their gender type. Moreover, strongly gender-typed people were so uncomfortable engaging in ordinary activities they considered unsuitable for their gender that they chose not to participate in these activities even when the choice cost them money (Bem, 1975; Bem & Lenney, 1976; Bem, Martyna, & Watson, 1976).

These studies have frequently been taken as evidence that androgynous people are indeed more flexible in their behavior. However, in other studies, the expected differences have not appeared. Masculine people are sometimes more comfortable than all other groups in a variety of tasks, perhaps because self-confidence is part of what is measured as masculinity. In other studies, whether the individual is female or male often affects task performance more than his or her androgyny score does (see, for example, Helmreich, Spence, & Holahan, 1979). In addition, research on the behavioral flexibility of androgynous people has used different groups of participants for "masculine" and "feminine" tasks, so that flexibility in *the same individuals across situations* has yet to be proven (Taylor & Hall, 1982).

Nor do we yet know the relationship between the laboratory tasks devised by researchers and the "real-life" behavioral choices people make (Kaplan & Sedney, 1980). It is important not to overgeneralize the interpretation of psychological tests. Just because a person scores high on an androgyny scale does not mean that she or he will be generally androgynous in behavior (Spence &

Helmreich, 1980). After a careful review of research on behavioral flexibility and androgyny, Cook (1985) concluded that "the validity of this hypothesis about androgyny has not yet been demonstrated adequately" (p. 82).

If androgyny is to be a new ideal of psychological functioning (Bem, 1975; Kaplan & Bean, 1976), androgynous people should be higher in self-esteem and overall psychological adjustment than their more traditionally gender-typed peers. Masculinity and femininity should each make a positive (and relatively equal) contribution to a healthy personality. Unfortunately for this hypothesis, it is *masculinity*, not androgyny or femininity, that is correlated with self-esteem and psychological adjustment (Taylor & Hall, 1982; Basoff & Glass, 1982; O'Heron & Orlofsky, 1990; Whitley, 1983). In other words, people who possess the traits labeled masculine in our society are better adjusted and have higher self-esteem, according to their own reports and on a variety of behavioral measures.

These results, so puzzling and so in contradiction to the ideal of androgyny, hold across all samples of people studied, and regardless of how androgyny is measured (Cook, 1985). The most likely explanation lies in the fact that traits and behaviors associated with males are more valued overall in our society. Although our society praises an ideal of femininity, feminine attributes are often equated with weakness, while masculine attributes lead to social power and greater rewards (Cook, 1985; Locksley & Colten, 1979; Unger, 1976). According to this reasoning, if androgynous people sometimes appear to be better adjusted than gender-typed people, it is only because they have more masculine attributes.

Relationships between androgyny and behavior are complicated by measurement issues. When people score similarly to each other on a psychological inventory, the scores may not always mean the same thing. In one study, a sample of lesbians scored more like heterosexual college men than heterosexual college women on an androgyny scale. However, closer inspection showed that the lesbians' high "masculinity" score came largely from their self-ratings as independent, while the men's high scores reflected their self-ratings as competitive (Finlay & Scheltema, 1991). When white, African-American, Latina, and Asian-American college women rated themselves on gender-typed phrases ("I make decisions easily" or "I am passive," for example) the white women and the women of color did not differ. However, when the women were asked to say what they *meant* when they attributed these phrases to themselves, it became apparent that the same words meant very different things to the two groups. For women of color, "passive" meant not saying what one really thinks; to white women it meant easygoing and laid back. For women of color, assertive and passive were opposites, but for white women, the terms appeared unrelated (Landrine, Klonoff, & Brown-Collins, 1992).

Androgyny: An Evaluation

Perhaps psychology expected too much of the concept of androgyny. Because androgyny tests were easy to use and the concept was appealing, it generated an enormous number of studies. Many of these studies simply related scores on an androgyny scale with scores on some other measure or with presumably gender-typed behavior. Too often, there was no clear theoretical rationale for why a relationship should exist. If a relationship was found, no matter how weak, it was taken as evidence for the theory, although there was often no clear way to explain it. Contradictory and confusing results piled up.

Perhaps whatever is being measured by androgyny scales needs to be defined more precisely. Do androgyny scales really get at core features of personality or are they measures of stereotypes? To be considered androgynous, should a person merely need to report herself as possessing both sets of traits—or should androgyny mean integrating the two sets of traits, or transcending beliefs about masculinity and femininity altogether? Moreover, the concepts of masculinity and femininity encompass more than traits; they extend to physical appearance, occupations, roles, and statuses as well.

Questions about the meaning of masculinity, femininity, and androgyny are currently a source of lively debate among researchers (Morawski, 1987; Sedney, 1989). Because behavior is determined by many situational factors in addition to underlying predispositions (traits), there is little reason to expect that an androgyny score alone will predict behavior very accurately. In this respect, androgyny is like other traits—weakly related to behavior and not very consistent across situations (Mischel, 1968, 1984). Moreover, the more distantly related an attitude or behavior is to the actual items on the scale, the weaker the relationship will be. From this viewpoint, it is not surprising that androgyny scores do not predict attitudes toward women or preferences for gender-typed activities very accurately. The only strong relationships we should expect would be with behavior directly related to the specific traits on the scale (Spence & Helmreich, 1978, 1980).

A more fundamental criticism of the concept of androgyny is that it reinforces the widely held belief that behavior comes in two genders, masculine and feminine. Because androgyny scales label some behaviors "masculine" and others "feminine," they linguistically and cognitively "obscure the essential humanness of the behaviors" and "dull our appreciation of their fundamental teachability and modifiability" (Lott, 1981, p. 172). A woman who describes herself as self-reliant, ambitious, and analytical scores "masculine" on androgyny scales. But should this person be labeled "masculine"—or just self-reliant, ambitious, and analytical? Indeed, we have frequently given these scales to students in class demonstrations, and it is not uncommon for "masculine" women to disagree vehemently with their classification. As one older student wrote after scoring high on masculinity and low on femininity, "I am a wife, a mother of three healthy kids, and an ambitious, assertive college student on my way to my degree. I don't believe that wanting an education is 'masculine.' And whatever 'feminine' means, surely raising my family should cover it!" This student would agree with Bernice Lott's (1981) comment:

> Behavior, in fact, has no gender. . . . To label some behaviors as feminine and some as masculine, as androgyny researchers do, and then to put the two artificial pieces back together again . . . is to reinforce verbal habits which undermine the possibility of degenderizing behavior (p. 178).

Further, androgyny has been criticized as representing an unattainable ideal for most people. Few people, male or female, live in the kinds of supportive social environments that would allow them to develop both "feminine" and "masculine" capacities to their full potential. But the problem may be more acute for women, because the "masculine" traits are more highly valued overall and predict psychological adjustment better than the "feminine" ones. From a feminist perspective, androgyny may be a false ideal for women, one that would require them to accept the higher value accorded masculinity (Lott, 1981; Morawski, 1987).

Sandra Bem, who developed one of the most widely used androgyny scales, has recently concluded that the concept of androgyny has been used at too private and personal a level to be of value in encouraging social and political change. "By focusing on the person rather than the patriarchy, androgyny provides no conceptual or political analysis of gender inequality; in fact, it diverts attention away from such analysis" (Bem, 1993, p. 124).

Yet despite the many reasons to criticize the concept of androgyny, Bem feels that perhaps it should not be abandoned entirely. At the least, its historical importance should be recognized:

> At a certain historical moment for feminist theorists, and even today for many people confused about how to behave as a man or a woman, androgyny provides both a vision of utopia and a model of mental health that does not require the individual to banish from the self whatever attributes and behaviors the culture may have stereotypically defined as inappropriate for his or her sex. To my mind, that revolution in the discourse of the culture was—and is—a worthy political accomplishment (Bem, 1993, p. 124).

Androgyny was introduced to psychology because researchers believed that a single masculinity/femininity dimension did not adequately express the diversity of individual differences in gender typing or the costs of being highly gender typed. It gained attention and stimulated research because it provided a way of conceptualizing how people might go beyond gender typing in their personality development. The idea of gender-role transcendence remains an intriguing one to many personality theorists and researchers.

Transcending Gender Typing

Gender Typing as an Intermediate Stage

Perhaps thinking and behaving in gender-typed ways is only an intermediate developmental stage—inevitable but not an endpoint. According to this view, the initial stages of gender development, dependent on maturation and the development of logical thought, are similar to those described by Kohlberg's cognitive developmental approach. Children move from being unaware of gender (stage 1) to actively accepting the "appropriate" stereotyped gender role and rejecting the "inappropriate" one (stage 2). But gender development can continue to a third stage in which the gender learning from stage 2 is reorganized in a personal and unique way. The individual is no longer bound by the unwritten rules of masculinity and femininity but is able to express her or his unique characteristics (Rebecca, Hefner, & Oleshansky, 1976; for related theories of gender role transcendence, see Block, 1973; Pleck, 1975).

These intriguing theories view androgyny not as a balanced set of masculine

FIGURE 2.5. As people mature, they may become more flexible in their gender roles. This young woman's self-presentation is quite androgynous.

and feminine *traits* but as a *process* of becoming an individual, an orientation toward self-actualization (Forisha, 1978). Thus, a gender-role-transcendent person might score feminine, masculine, or androgynous on a personality scale, but the dimensions are actually irrelevant to her or his identity. Transcendence is

> a mature "none of the above" in response to the question, "Are you masculine or feminine?" Rather than incorporating some parts of traditional femininity and masculinity, the transcendent person is neither feminine nor masculine. Masculinity and femininity, alone or in combination, are simply not part of the transcendent person's world (Sedney, 1989, p. 129).

Transcendence, viewed as the highest stage of gender-role learning, involves a resynthesis and reintegration of the relationship between self and society. It is unlikely that a person could achieve the cognitive and emotional maturity of this stage before adulthood. Even children who are brought up by parents who themselves transcend traditional gender roles may not show evidence of their androgynous upbringing until they have passed through the strongly gender-typed stage 2 (Sedney, 1987). Moreover, the transition from stage 1 to stage 2 is bolstered by strong societal pressures, but there are few sources of support for the transition to stage 3. For this reason, not everyone succeeds in transcending gender-bound behavior and thinking. But for those who do, gender becomes irrelevant, and personality becomes fully human.

Gender Typing as a Cognitive Schema

Another approach to gender typing and gender-role transcendence is to examine the specific ways that people organize, categorize, and use gender-related information as they think and solve problems (Bem, 1981; Crawford & Chaffin, 1986; Markus, Crane, Bernstein, & Saladi, 1982). To understand this approach, we will look at gender as a cognitive category.

Even the simplest understanding of an event depends on having a great deal of organized knowledge in memory. For example, consider the sentence, "The little girl heard the ice cream man and rushed upstairs to get her piggy bank." In order to understand this sentence, you must bring to bear your knowledge of ice cream vending systems, taste preferences and financial resources of children, and purchasing norms in our society. The sentence itself says nothing about selling, liking ice cream, getting money, or buying; all this is supplied by you, the reader.

According to *schema theory*, your experience of ice cream buying is summarized in an organizing network of mental associations called a *schema*, which provides the framework necessary to understand the sentence. The schema provides a general outline of the main events (going to the van, choosing, buying, and eating) and of the acts that make up each event (paying, being handed the ice cream). The schema also specifies conditions (liking ice cream), roles (vendor, customer), props (money), and results (pleasure, having less money).

Understanding even a perfectly ordinary sentence requires mapping the information in the sentence onto the preexisting schema. Schemas can be very specific (college students usually have a "professor's office schema" and a "first-day-of-class schema") or relatively broad (a schema for "Japan" or "education"). According to schema theory, it is difficult or impossible to understand information when you cannot connect it to a schema or when you unintentionally connect it to the wrong schema (Crawford & Chaffin, 1986). See Box 2.3 and try it for yourself.

Like other schemas, the gender schema can be thought of as a network of mental associations representing general knowledge, which is used by the individual as an aid to thinking and understanding (Bem, 1981). According to this theory, learning of the gender schema begins very early, and the schema guides the individual in becoming gender typed. Gender typing occurs because the individual develops a generalized readiness to process information on the basis of the gender schema. Indeed, gender schema theory proposes that the self-concept itself gets assimilated into the gender schema.

As children learn the contents of the society's gender schema, they learn which attributes are to be linked with their own sex and, hence, with themselves. This does not simply entail learning where each sex is supposed to stand on each dimension or attribute—that boys are to be strong and girls weak, for example—but also imparts the deeper lesson that the dimensions themselves are differentially applicable to the two sexes (Bem, 1981, p. 355).

Gender schema theory, then, conceives of gender typing as a readiness to

Box 2.3 Schematic Processing: A Do-It-Yourself Demonstration and a Riddle

1. Read the following paragraph and then, without looking back at it, try to recall as much of it as possible. Write down every idea you remember from the paragraph.

   The procedure is actually quite simple. First, you arrange things into different groups. Of course, one pile may be sufficient, depending on how much there is to do. If you have to go somewhere else due to lack of facilities, that is the next step; otherwise you are pretty well set. It is important not to overdo things. That is, it is better to do too few things at once than too many. In the short run this may not seem important but complications can easily arise. A mistake can be expensive as well. At first the whole procedure will seem complicated. Soon, however, it will become just another facet of life. It is difficult to foresee any end to the necessity for this task in the immediate future, but then one never can tell. After the procedure is completed one arranges the materials into different groups again. Then they can be put into their appropriate places. Eventually they will be used once more and the whole cycle will then have to be repeated. However, that is part of life.

   Many students find that understanding and remembering this paragraph are very difficult. For an explanation, see Box 2.4.

2. Try to solve this riddle—and ask a few friends.

   A big Indian and a little Indian are sitting on a log. The big Indian points to the little Indian and says, "That Indian is my son." The little Indian points to the big Indian and says, "That Indian is not my father." Both are telling the truth. How is this possible?

For the answer, see Box 2.4.

Source: From J. D. Bransford and M. K. Johnson (1972). Contextual prerequisites for understanding: Some investigations of comprehension and recall, *Journal of Verbal Learning and Verbal Behavior, 11,* 722. Reprinted by permission of Academic Press.

organize the world in terms of gender and to process information in terms of a well-developed and salient network of gender associations. In other words, an important difference between people who are highly gender typed and those who are not is that gender-typed (gender-schematic) people have a well-developed gender schema and rely spontaneously on it in understanding and making sense of the world. They have "a readiness to look at reality through gender lenses" (Bem, 1987, p. 268). Less gender-typed (gender-aschematic) people have less developed gender schemas and rely more on other schemas. (Of course, the difference would be a matter of degree, since everyone in our society has developed some sort of schema for gender.)

For most people, the gender schema is enormously rich and diverse. Even concepts that are only metaphorically related to gender can become connected to the gender schema. (Why do poets personify the sun as male and the moon as female? Why are some colors "feminine" and others "masculine?") There may be no other pair of concepts in human experience with as many entities assimilated to it as the distinction between male and female (Bem, 1981).

Gender schema theory predicts that differences in cognitive processing of information will be observable between gender-typed and non-gender-typed people when they are placed in situations in which they are free to organize in-

Box 2.4 Schematic Processing: Answers and Explanations

1. Why is it so difficult to "make sense" of the paragraph in Box 2.3? The words are ordinary and the sentence structure is simple. Yet most people find it frustrating to read and difficult to remember the ideas in the paragraph for even a short time. The reason is that comprehension and memory depend on the activation of a schema. This paragraph does not activate any particular schema for most people, and thus it is vague, ambiguous, and difficult to understand.

   The title for the paragraph is "Washing Clothes." If you now look back at it, you will find that you read it with a new understanding and your memory for the ideas will be much better. The clothes-washing schema provides the structure that interrelates and explains all of the previously obscure details. Without the schema, the individual sentences are straightforward, but their relationship cannot be grasped.
2. The answer to the riddle is that the big Indian is the little Indian's mother.

   Why is this riddle difficult for many people to solve? Even the most ordinary sentences require the reader to go beyond the information given and use her own stores of information about the world—her schemas. For most North Americans, the schema for "Indian" is based on stereotypes from movies and stories about the Wild West. Therefore we automatically think "male" when we think "Indian." Because the schema activated by "Indian" assumes "male," the schema is not much help in solving the riddle (Crawford & Chaffin, 1986).

   Puzzles like this can help us understand aspects of our schemas that we are normally unaware of in everyday comprehension. If you had been asked directly "Can the word 'Indian' refer to a female?" you would no doubt answer yes. Yet if you found this riddle difficult, it is because your mental representation of "Indian" is primarily male. (Incidentally, does this riddle help you see why Native-American people prefer not to be called "Indians"?)

Source: From J. D. Bransford and M. K. Johnson (1972). Contextual prerequisites for understanding: Some investigations of comprehension and recall, *Journal of Verbal Learning and Verbal Behavior, 11,* 722. Reprinted by permission of Academic Press.

formation by gender or by some other schema. In one experiment, participants were first categorized as gender schematic or aschematic. They then listened to a group discussion and were later asked to remember who said what in the discussion. The researchers were not interested in overall memory accuracy, but in whether the participants confused males with other males, and females with other females, in remembering who said what. As predicted by gender schema theory, gender-schematic people were likely to mix up people of the same sex with each other. In other words, they were mentally sorting the people in the discussion into two classes, female and male. Gender-aschematic people showed no tendency to confuse people of the same sex with each other (Frable & Bem, 1985).

In contrast to stage theories of gender-role transcendence, gender schema theory does not view a high degree of gender typing as an inevitable part of the maturation process. Rather, the theory proposes that children become gender typed because adults teach them to differentiate the world in terms of gender. At home, girls, but never boys, are described as "pretty," and children learn to attach the dimension of attractiveness more to females. In school, boys are lined up on one side of the classroom and girls on the other, or a teacher asks for a strong boy to help move a desk, and children learn that gender is a useful way to categorize people and that strength is a more important attribute for males.

(It is hard to imagine a teacher asking for a strong blue-eyed person or lining children up by race.)

However, the theory suggests that children *can* be brought up in ways that minimize the development of a gender schema, and thus bypass gender-stereotyped thinking and behavior. If children were taught to use the concept of sex only in connection with physical (anatomical) differences, they would not assimilate irrelevant (gender) dimensions to the schema. They would differentiate where it matters (in sexual behavior and reproduction), but all other aspects of behavior would remain cognitively gender neutral (Bem, 1985; 1993).

Gender-Role Transcendence: An Evaluation

Theories that explore the possibilities of transcending gender typing are too new to be fully evaluated on the criteria we have used for judging more traditional theories. They appear to have considerable potential as theories about women in that they do not consider traditional gender typing to be necessarily adaptive or inevitable. In this respect, they reflect the diversity of people (both women and men). They are also open to encompassing cultural and social influences on personality; all agree that people become androgynous or role-transcendent through social learning and/or maturation. However, gender schema theory's emphasis on cognitive processing may neglect other important aspects of gender typing, and the theory as yet says little about how cognitive processing and behavior are related (Spence & Helmreich, 1981). Gender constancy, gender salience, gender knowledge, and memory for gender-related information are not always as closely related as the theory predicts (Bussey & Bandura, 1992; Hort, Leinbach, & Fagot, 1991).

Like androgyny theory, gender schema theory does not fully conceptualize gender at the social structural level. Thinking about gender in terms of individual differences in traits or cognitive processing does not fully reflect the fact that masculinity and femininity are not equally valued or rewarded in our society (Crawford & Chaffin, 1986; Morawski, 1987). These theories should both encourage and benefit from lifespan and cross-cultural research on gender identity and gender typing.

PERSONALITY AND SOCIAL INFLUENCES IN WOMEN'S LIVES

Cultural Diversity and Personality

Just as there is no "generic human being," there is no generic woman. Personality theories must account for how people incorporate not only gender but ethnicity and class into their identities (Bernal, Knight, Garja, Ocampo, & Cota, 1990; Espin & Gawelek, 1992; Ostrove & Stewart, 1994). For people who are in the minority because of their ethnic group or sexual orientation, the gender schema may be less important than other schemas. Images of the self may be negative because they are derived from cultural messages about (for example) the inferiority of black people or the sinfulness of gays and lesbians. Identity development involves questioning these messages, a developmental task that members of culturally valued groups do not encounter. The individual may experience much anger as she recognizes that she has believed in and accepted these messages. For members of oppressed groups, full identity development means going beyond the negative messages of the dominant culture to achieve self-esteem and a commitment to social change for one's group (Cass, 1979). The process may be similar to what white women do in transcending the negative aspects of gender roles (O'Neil, Egan, Owen, & Murry, 1993).

How Social Events Shape Personality

Personality does not develop in a social or historical vacuum. Social events and movements have lifelong meaning for people who experience them. This leads to *cohort effects.* Cohort refers to a group of people born in the same close time period—for example, within the same year or the same decade. Individuals of the same cohort will tend to be exposed to the same broad environmental events, which shape their personalities similarly. In general, social events experienced in childhood are likely to affect fundamental values, while events experienced in adolescence or early adulthood affect opportunities (Stewart & Healey, 1989). People who were children during the worldwide Great Depression of the 1930s, for example, tend to have different ideas about thrift and economic security than those of earlier or later cohorts, while those who were young adults at that time found their life choices (jobs, higher education) severely constrained by lack of money.

As part of an ongoing longitudinal study of women who graduated from Radcliffe College in 1964, the women (who were in their early forties at the time of this study) were asked to rate a series of social events in terms of their personal meaning at the time the events occurred and in the present. Events included Three Mile Island, Watergate, the civil rights movement, the Vietnam war, and the women's movement. The women's movement stood out for this group as particularly meaningful at the time and even more meaningful now. It seemed to validate their own thoughts, either at the time or later:

> I never could understand why people thought women would be happy to find their identification through their husbands and children. I thought, "That sounds stupid." I want people to be interested in me for me. . . .
>
> Up comes the women's movement with "women should not be satellites of their husbands, women should have freedom of choice whether or not to have children, women should have careers," and I thought this sounds good!

One woman expressed the sense of being part of a "cohort effect":

> I mean I couldn't explain how it happened. It's just as if everybody—you had the feeling other people were feeling the same thing. Why everybody should suddenly realize it then as opposed to earlier—I don't know what made the difference. But certainly you had the sense that there were other people, other women out there, you weren't alone (Stewart, 1994, pp. 242–244).

Higher levels of importance given to the women's movement were correlated with combining paid work and family life, choice of a nontraditional career, and staying in the work force after college. Thus, not only was the women's movement personally meaningful to this cohort of college graduates, but important life consequences were related to this meaningfulness (Stewart & Healey, 1989).

Interaction of Traits and Situations

Even among women who are similar in education, intelligence, and social class, there is great variability in life patterns. For example, some college-educated women achieve in high-prestige careers and others become homemakers. This variability has sometimes been explained in terms of external factors (such as whether the woman has children) and sometimes in terms of personality traits (such as the woman's sense of competence).

There are problems with both types of explanation. If external factors are emphasized, it is difficult to explain variability within a similar group. (Some mothers achieve in careers and others do not.) If personality factors are emphasized, it is difficult to decide cause and effect. (Does the woman achieve because she has higher feelings of competence, or does she have higher competence scores because of her history of work and achievement?) It would be simplistic to assume that either personality variables or life circumstances alone could predict life patterns in women. The best way to assess the relative contribution of the two types of influence is to study them longitudinally.

With first-year students at an elite women's college as her participants, Abby Stewart (1980) obtained personality measures of need for achievement and self-definition (defining oneself as capable of instrumental action). Both are stable personality traits that had been shown to be relevant to women's career behavior in previous research. Fourteen years later (ten years after they had graduated from college), the women were contacted and asked for information about their marital status, occupation, activities in the past ten years, and future goals.

Results showed that a woman's family situation set limits on her career activity. Both her type of career and her persistence in it were negatively affected by being married and having children. However, these external factors alone did not entirely determine her life pattern. When women were grouped by family circumstances, personality factors were also important. For example, if a woman was single, or married but without children, her need for achievement was positively related to her career persistence. Among married women with children, however, need for achievement had no relationship to career persistence—apparently, the external factors of marriage and motherhood overwhelmed individual differences. Stewart concluded that personality and social situations interact in complex ways: external factors such as a woman's child-care responsibilities set broad limits on her possible career behaviors, while personality factors may predict her choice of behaviors within those limits. In studying women's lives, we must recognize that they exercise active choice within social constraints (Stewart, 1994).

Of course, personality and life circumstances also interact in predicting men's behavior. However, it is important to focus on women as a separate group in such research because the kinds of constraints they face are different. Moreover, because of women's lower power as a group, external constraints are probably more severe for them. Do you think that a study of men might have

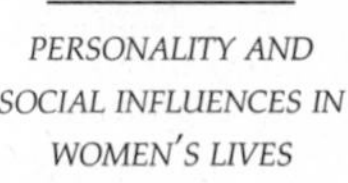

FIGURE 2.6. Anita Hill: The cost of taking action.

found different relationships among marriage, need for achievement, and career persistence?

Gender, Personality, and Power

Women's lower social power and status may do more than impose external constraints on life patterns. Power may determine personality in important ways. Jean Baker Miller (1976/1986) has proposed that because women are a subordinate group in society, they develop personality characteristics that reflect their subordination and enable them to cope with it.

Miller analyzes the effects of power differences on personality formation. Women have been socially defined as unequals, similar to other "second-class" groups, which are labeled as such because of their race, religion, or social class. Once a group is defined as inferior, the dominant group justifies its inferiority by labeling it as deficient. Just as blacks are seen as less intelligent and poor people are seen as lazy, women are seen as emotional, illogical, and so on.

Dominant groups define acceptable roles for subordinates, which usually involve services that the dominant group members do not want to perform for themselves. Thus, women, minorities, and poor people are relegated to low-status, low-paying jobs that often involve cleaning up the waste products of the dominant group or providing them with personal services. Roles and activities that are preferred in a given society are closed to subordinates. Subordinates are said to be unable to fill those roles, and the reasons given by the dominants usually involve subordinates' "deficiencies" of mind or body. As you learned in Chapter 1, whatever activities are considered "women's work" in a given society are usually considered the less important and valuable work. In our own society, the status and pay accorded nurses, teachers, homemakers, and child-care workers versus physicians, attorneys, carpenters, and auto mechanics reflect devaluation of "women's work," and it is easy to find people who believe that women are unsuited for certain prestigious or demanding jobs.

Since dominants control a culture's arts, philosophy, and science, they have the power to define "normal" personality and relationships. Dominants define inequality as normal and justify it in terms of the inferiority of subordinates.

> It then becomes "normal" to treat others destructively and to derogate them, to obscure the truth of what you are doing by creating false explanations, and to oppose actions toward equality. . . . Dominant groups generally do not like to be told about or even quietly reminded of the existence of inequality . . . if pressed a bit, the familiar rationalizations are offered: the home is "women's natural place," and "we know what's best for them anyhow" (Miller, 1976/1986, pp. 8–9).

When subordinates behave with intelligence, independence, or assertiveness—or even show potential for such behavior—they are defined as exceptions to the rule or abnormal. If women take direct action on their own behalf, they risk economic hardship, social ostracism, and psychological isolation. They may even be called "crazy." When Anita Hill reluctantly spoke out about sexual harassment, a powerful U. S. senator suggested she was a schizophrenic (see Figure 2.6). Moreover, women are controlled by violence and the threat of violence (see Chapter 14).

There are important psychological consequences of subordination, according to Miller. Subordinates are encouraged to develop psychological characteristics that are useful and pleasing to the dominant group, and the ideal subordinate is described in terms of these characteristics, which

> form a certain familiar cluster: submissiveness, passivity, docility, dependency, lack of initiative, inability to act, to decide, to think, and the like . . . qualities more characteristic of children than adults—immaturity, weakness, and helplessness. If subordinates adopt these characteristics they are considered well-adjusted (1976/1986, p. 7).

In order to survive, women become highly attuned to the dominants, able to "read" and respond to their smallest behaviors—perhaps the origins of "feminine intuition" and women's reputation for using manipulative "feminine wiles." As subordinates, women may know more about men than they know about themselves.

Another consequence of subordination is that women learn to monitor and worry about their relationships, to transmute anger into hurt feelings, chronic fatigue, or depression, and to try to influence others' behavior by indirect or extreme methods. Since direct assertive behavior toward a dominant may be dangerous, devious methods or emotional outbursts may seem preferable (Travis, 1988a). Moreover, women may come to accept the dominant group's untruths about women. According to Miller, there are a great many women who believe they are less important then men, just as there are blacks who feel inferior to whites. Finally, subordination sets up internal conflicts as women struggle to reconcile their own perceptions of reality with the interpretations imposed on them by men.

Revaluing Women

Miller and her colleagues argue that women and their characteristic activities must be reappraised (Jordan, Kaplan, Miller, Stiver, & Surrey, 1991). Women have been assigned the task of fostering others' development in relationships—of empowering others. In our society, women are expected to be nurturing, to take care of not only children but old people, ill people, and, of course, men. Women are expected to, and do, use their intellectual and emotional abilities to build other peoples' strength, resources, and well-being. Yet they have not been encouraged to value these interactions and activities, which are just "women's work."

Psychological theories of personality have failed women by devaluing their strengths. Many of the theories reviewed in this chapter focus on autonomy as the end point of development. That is, the ideal adult is seen as one whose sense of self is entirely separate from others, and who is independent and self-reliant. Within these theories, close relationships (for example, the infant-mother relationship) are characterized negatively in terms of dependency and lack of a differentiated self.

But very few people are truly autonomous, and when a person appears to be so, it is usually because many other people are quietly helping him to survive and function. The idea that psychological development is a process of separating from others may be an illusion fostered by dominant men.

Feminist theorists have articulated alternatives to the notion of the autonomous self, such as the notion of personality development within relationships (Jordan et al., 1991; Miller, 1984b), the self defined in terms of caring and responsibility (Gilligan, 1982), and fluidity in self-development (Kaplan & Surrey, 1984). Perhaps the most sophisticated of these alternative notions of the self is that of social individuality (Lykes, 1985). There is evidence that people who have experienced social relations of powerlessness and those who have engaged in collective social action have a notion of the self grounded in social individuality in contrast to one grounded in individual autonomy:

> Individuals from majority groups (e.g., white upper class males) whose material conditions and social relations are most likely to be consonant with individualism would be more likely to have a notion of the self as autonomous individualism. Persons in less powerful groups (e.g., women, people of color, working class people) are more likely to perceive contradictions between the assumptions of autonomous individualism and their social experiences. These individuals may also experience group solidarity or some sense of the "givenness" of "being-in-relation," for their survival as a group may seem possible only in relationship (Lykes, 1985, p. 364).

The criteria for personality development should include the ability to engage in relationships with others that empower others and oneself, with empathy, not autonomy, as the ideal (Jordan et al., 1991). By this measure, women would be revalued, and problems and deficiencies in men's development would become visible. The close study of women's experience may lead eventually to a new synthesis that will better encompass all experience.

THE IMPACT OF FEMINIST THOUGHT ON PERSONALITY RESEARCH AND THEORY

Our survey of approaches to personality shows that none fully satisfies criteria for an ideal theory. Instead of one approach that everyone can agree on, there is much debate on questions of gender and personality. Are psychoanalytic approaches useful in understanding women, or are they hopelessly sexist? Is androgyny a viable new ideal or a conceptual fad? Do women and men make moral decisions differently or are the "differences" the result of poor scientific methods? Do children inevitably go through a developmental stage in which they are highly gender typed or can they be brought up without gender-stereotyped beliefs and behaviors? These are a few examples of current questions touched on in this chapter (see Walsh, 1987, for these and other ongoing debates).

Feminist thought has led to the reform of existing theories—for example, Nancy Chodorow's and Carol Gilligan's contributions to personality development and moral reasoning—and to the development of new theories, such as Sandra Bem's research on androgyny and gender schema theory. It has encouraged researchers to use more diverse methods and study a greater variety of people (Brown & Ballou, 1992; Franz & Stewart, 1994; Stewart & Lykes, 1985). Perhaps most important, it has opened up ways to think about the effects of power, social status, and culture on the development of different personality orientations.

Personality theories are most useful when they are grounded in concrete experience. A person's biological sex may be relatively unimportant in determining personality, but gender-related influences leading to differential experiences in life can be crucial.

CONNECTING THEMES

1. Gender is what culture makes of biological sex. In this chapter, we have largely been concerned with gender at the individual level, describing theories of how children acquire a stable gender identity and become gender typed. These processes interact with gender at the social structural level. Children acquire a gender schema because they see the social world classified into "masculine" and "feminine" categories. Women acquire personality traits characteristic of subordinated people because they are placed in a gendered social structure.
2. When psychologists have named and classified personality dimensions, they have often used a male norm. Examples include penis envy, the ideal

of autonomy, and the idea that highly gender-typed people are well adjusted. Feminist personality theorists have developed new concepts about gender role transcendence, the self in relation to others, and the effect of social influences on personality. These concepts name and give voice to alternative conceptions of the healthy personality.

3. It is only in the past few decades that theories of gender development have been created to encompass women's experiences, replacing older, more androcentric theories. Little thought has been given to ethnic and cultural diversity, and theories of identity development for people of color, gay and lesbian people, and women of diverse social classes have yet to be fully articulated.
4. A woman's place in the social order powerfully affects her sense of self. For women, full identity development may mean transcending their culture's teachings about what is natural and good for their gender and making a commitment to political and social change. Cohorts of women influenced by the Women's Movement may be particularly ready to make that commitment.

SUGGESTED READINGS

FRANZ, CAROL and ABIGAIL STEWART (1994). *Women creating lives: Identities, resilience, and resistance.* San Francisco: Westview Press. New ways of studying how women construct their lives within social constraints, using a rich variety of methods, including case studies, longitudinal approaches, and cohort analyses.

GILLIGAN, CAROL (1982). *In a different voice.* Cambridge, MA: Harvard University Press. An account of women's moral development that shows how theories of human development have been based on a male norm and proposes that women rely on an ethic of care and responsibility in resolving moral dilemmas.

STEWART, ABIGAIL J., and M. BRINTON LYKES (Eds.) (1985). *Gender and personality: Current perspectives on theory and research.* Durham, NC: Duke University Press. In a collection of articles, a distinguished group of personality theorists and researchers evaluates how traditional and contemporary approaches to personality have conceptualized gender issues.

CHAPTER 3

The Meanings of Difference: Sex, Gender, and Cognitive Abilities

DEFINING DIFFERENCE
MEASURING GENDER-RELATED DIFFERENCES
Methods for Individual Studies: One Step at a Time
Methods for Summarizing Studies: The Big Picture
VALUES AND IDEOLOGY IN SEX DIFFERENCE RESEARCH: THE LESSONS OF HISTORY
GENDER AND COGNITIVE ABILITIES
Spatial Abilities
Mathematics Ability and Performance
Verbal Abilities and Communication Competence
COGNITIVE SIMILARITIES AND DIFFERENCES: SUMMARY AND IMPLICATIONS
Magnitude and Meaning
Origins
Cross-Cultural Effects
Psychological Research as Androcentric Knowledge
SOCIAL CONSEQUENCES
Social Uses of Difference Research
Gender-Related Differences and Social Policy
CONNECTING THEMES
SUGGESTED READINGS

Our language tells us that men and women are "opposite sexes." Most people believe that women and men differ in many important ways. Very often, students who have come to realize the pervasiveness of beliefs about differences feel angry and frustrated. They feel that people should not be judged on the basis of unfounded beliefs about how different the two sexes are. They demand to know what the "real" differences are between boys and girls or women and men in traits, abilities, and behaviors. They want "the facts—and just the facts," and they expect the science of psychology to be able to provide those facts.

Determining the facts sounds relatively easy. In principle, a psychologist could measure a group of women and a group of men for a trait or ability and compute the average difference between the groups. There is a long tradition of such sex-difference research in psychology. Between 1967 and 1985, for example, *Psychological Abstracts,* which lists published journal articles in psychology, indexed 16,416 articles on human sex differences (Myers, 1986). When females and males are shown to differ on a test of some ability or behavior, people are quick to "explain" the difference with unfounded ideas about women's natures. To discourage this sort of faulty reasoning, many feminist psychologists prefer to use the term *gender-related differences.*

Compiling the definitive list of sex/gender differences is a controversial goal. In fact, some feminist psychologists maintain that a good case can be made against studying such differences at all (Unger, 1979b). Their objections to a focus on difference are based on long-standing problems that include the lack of an agreed-upon *definition* of what constitutes a gender-related difference, problems in the *measurement* of difference, and issues of *values and interpretation* in understanding results. They have also looked back at psychology's past and found that, historically, women have been classified in terms of their difference from men in order to justify their inferior social status. Many feminist psychologists argue that the similarities between women and men far outweigh the differences, and that a focus on similarities is more likely to lead to legal and social equality for women. Moreover, simply finding a new difference between women and men tells little about how gender influences have produced that difference. A sex difference is a *description,* not an explanation.

Because of the influence of contemporary feminism, issues of sex, gender, and difference have been studied and debated with new intensity in the past two decades. In this chapter we will examine controversies in the definition, measurement, and interpretation of gender-related differences. We will then look closely at gender-related differences in cognition, including visual perception, verbal abilities, and mathematics achievement. Researchers in the psychology of women and gender are providing new ways of thinking about difference, important advances in research methods, and new answers to old questions about the "real" differences between women and men.

DEFINING DIFFERENCE

Although people frequently make assertions about differences in women's and men's abilities (see Figure 3.1), a closer look shows that the meaning of "difference" can be very ambiguous. Suppose you were at a social gathering where another guest, Mr. Peter Pompous, explained the underrepresentation of women in legal careers by saying, "Let's face it, women just don't reason like men. When it comes to reasoning ability, they just don't have what it takes." If you're like us, your first reaction would be anger and amazement. Your second reaction might be to ask yourself what psychological evidence could be brought to bear on this claim. Rather than accept opinions about human characteristics as self-evidently true, psychology students know that scientific research is the most systematic way to gather knowledge.

Pompous has asserted that there is a gender-related difference in reasoning, a cognitive ability. But before we examine the evidence, let's consider (using our reasoning ability!) what he might have meant. One interpretation is that all men and no women have the ability to reason—in other words, that reasoning ability is dichotomous by sex. If the entire population of men and women could be measured on a perfectly valid and reliable test of reasoning ability, the two

FIGURE 3.1. Calvin learns about sex differences in abstract reasoning.
Source: Calvin and Hobbs © Watterson. Distributed by Universal Press Syndicate. Reprinted by permission. All rights reserved.

sexes would form two nonoverlapping distributions, with the distribution for women being lower. This hypothetical situation is shown in Figure 3.2*a*. *Despite a hundred years of research on gender-related differences, no one has ever discovered a psychological trait or cognitive ability on which men and women are completely different.*

Since it would be ridiculous to argue that women are totally and categorically inferior, Pompous probably means something else when he talks about "difference." Perhaps he means that there is a mean, or *average* difference, such that the mean for women is slightly lower (Figure 3.2*b*) or very much lower (Figure 3.2*c*) than the mean for men. However, an average difference doesn't tell us very much if taken by itself. Sets of distributions can have the same differences in means but large differences in *variability*. Figure 3.2*d* shows males more variable than females and 3.2*e* shows females more variable than males. Looking at the areas in which males' and females' distributions do not overlap in each set shows that the meaning of "difference" is different for each. That is, the proportion of women who score below the lowest-scoring men and the proportion of men who score above the highest-scoring women differ greatly from one set of hypothetical distributions to the next.

Moreover, these are not the only possible population distributions. Women and men could be equal on average, but one sex could be more variable—as in Figure 3.2*f*. In other words, the difference between the lowest and highest scorer could be greater for one sex or the other. Try graphing other forms that a population difference might take: the possibilities are mind-boggling. The concept of "sex difference" has often been used loosely to cover all these possibilities.

Clearly, the sexes are more alike than different. On every cognitive trait or ability that has ever been measured, there is more similarity than difference—that is, the areas where females and males overlap are larger (usually much larger) than those where they do not.

Most research on gender-related differences reports a mean (average) difference between a sample of women and a sample of men, with statistical tests to determine whether the difference is *statistically significant* (unlikely to have occurred by chance). The concept of statistical significance is not the same as the ordinary meaning of "significant." A difference may be statistically significant

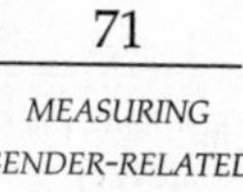

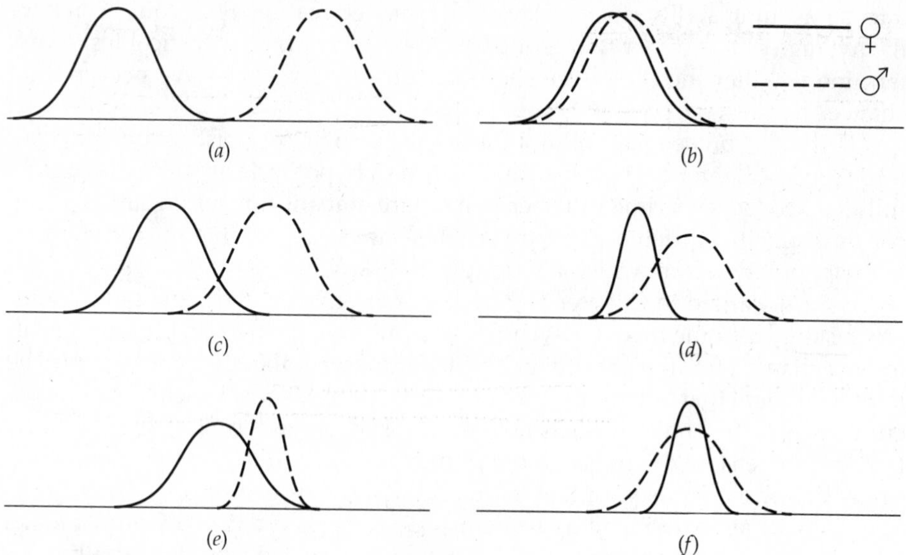

FIGURE 3.2. Some possible distributions of reasoning ability in females and males.

yet be trivially small and useless in predicting differential behavior in other experimental situations or in daily life. In other words, statistical significance is not the same as importance.

How large does a statistically significant difference have to be before we are justified in labeling men and women more different than similar? Should the importance of a difference be judged in terms of average scores for each sex or in terms of how much variability exists between scores for each sex, or in how much the distributions for women and men overlap? The answers to these questions involve value judgments about the meaning of difference. Value judgments are also involved when researchers attempt to see "the big picture" by comparing the results of several studies of the same trait or ability. How many studies are sufficient to settle a question? How consistent must the results be? Is it important to measure the trait or ability in people of different age groups, social classes, ethnic groups, and cultures—or is it safe to assume that what is true for North American college students is true for all people?

MEASURING GENDER-RELATED DIFFERENCES

Methods for Individual Studies: One Step at a Time

When an experimenter tests a hypothesis about a gender-related difference, she or he typically arranges to compare female and male performance on an appropriate task while attempting to match or balance any extraneous factors that could affect performance. Suppose a psychologist believed (contrary to Peter Pompous's claim) that women have higher reasoning ability than men. She might compare women and men on a standard test of reasoning, matching (or otherwise equating) her groups of participants on any other factors that might affect reasoning ability, such as level of formal education. She would compare the average scores of her two groups with an appropriate statistical test to determine whether the difference she obtained was likely to have occurred by chance.

This set of procedures follows the standard logic of statistical inference introduced in Chapter 1. The experimenter tests a hypothesis by setting up a carefully controlled experiment. If her results are statistically significant, she can conclude that the difference apparent in her sample represents a real difference in the population from which the sample was drawn.

As you learned in Chapter 1, the logic of experimental design and hypothesis testing leads the field of psychology to put more weight on findings of difference than on findings of similarity. Statistical tests allow psychologists to be fairly confident that when a difference is judged to exist the conclusion is an accurate one. When a difference is not found, psychologists cannot know for certain that there is no difference in the population—it could always be just a failure of this particular experiment to detect the difference.

Think of an experiment as a microscope for a moment. If a scientist looks through her microscope and sees what she expected to see, she usually concludes that her hypothesis was correct. If she sees nothing or sees only a blurred picture, she may conclude that her instrument or procedures were lacking, and that she should try again, rather than that her hypothesis was wrong. Relying on similar logic, professional journals are less likely to publish articles that report similarities between women and men (or boys and girls) than they are to publish reports of differences. This publication bias has been referred to as the *file-drawer problem.* For every journal article reporting gender-related differences, there may be an unknown number of comparable—but unpublishable—studies reporting gender-related similarities tucked away in researchers' file drawers.

The possibility of error is a built-in part of hypothesis testing. In addition, some errors are due to faulty experimental design. Many feminist psychologists believe that problems in research design are common (Deaux, 1984; Grady, 1981; Jacklin, 1981; Maccoby & Jacklin, 1974; Parlee, 1981; Unger, 1979b) and have charged that "psychology is replete with inconsequential, accidental, and incidental findings of 'sex differences'" that often are distorted, exaggerated, and miscited (Grady, 1981, pp. 632–633). Exaggeration of difference may occur because the concept of overlapping distributions is complex and difficult to keep in mind, or because gender is a dichotomous cognitive schema that encourages thinking in terms of opposites. Perhaps both reasons play a part.

There are several common methodological flaws in difference research (Jacklin, 1981). Some studies have measured behaviors of only one sex and erroneously drawn conclusions about differences between the sexes—for example, measuring the relationship between hormonal levels and mood only in women and concluding that only women show such relationships. Of course, it is impossible to demonstrate a sex/gender difference (or similarity) if only one sex is studied.

Other sources of bias include researchers' tendency to overgeneralize from their limited samples to all women and men and to conclude that a gender-related difference is due to innate or biological factors when such factors have not been measured in any way. Unfortunately, examples of these mistakes are easy to find. The eminent primatologist Harry Harlow explained the behavior of boys and girls in biological terms in discussing evidence that male rhesus monkeys are more aggressive than females:

> There is reason to believe that genetic variables condition similar differences in human primates. The gentle and relatively passive behavior of most little girls is a useful maternal attribute, and the more aggressive behavior of most little boys is useful preparation for the paternal function of protection (1971, p. 6).

When Harlow's own research showed that rearing female monkeys in abnormal environments caused them to be much more aggressive toward male monkeys, he was not convinced of the importance of environmental influences on aggression. Instead, his preexisting bias caused him to ignore the implications of his own data, and he resorted to stereotypes:

> Negative feedback, however, quickly suppresses this aggression. Females win their way into male hearts and minds through passive resistance and social sophistication. In our society females usually attempt to combine love and marriage with social security. . . Young males prefer action and young females prefer active attention (1971, pp. 90–91).

Not only had Harlow failed to study biological factors in aggression, but he hadn't even studied girls and boys. Instead, he generalized from his research on rhesus monkeys!

One of the most persistent methodological problems is the difficulty of separating sex from all the other factors it is related to in our society. The number of variables that interact with sex is probably the most pervasive problem in sex and gender research (Jacklin, 1981). These interactions lead to *confounding,* in which the effects of two or more variables are mixed, and it becomes impossible to decide which variable is causing experimental effects. Because sex is related to many differences in background and status, researchers can rarely know whether their female and male samples are really comparable.

Suppose we were matching participants for our imaginary experiment on reasoning ability. We would certainly not compare, say, male attorneys with their nonattorney spouses. Such a comparison would obviously be unfair because the different backgrounds and experience of the two groups, rather than the fact of their being male or female, could account for differences in reasoning ability. But even when a researcher attempts to measure comparable men and women (or boys and girls) it is often hard to decide what characteristics should be matched and which are irrelevant. Most researchers would assume that they had solved the comparability problem if they chose to compare, say, female and male college students. But although a sample of male and female college students can be matched on level of formal education, the women and men will have very different backgrounds in mathematics, science, and the humanities, starting in high school (Eccles, 1989), and will be concentrated in different courses of study in college. These differences may be irrelevant to some research questions but crucial to others.

Methods for Summarizing Studies: The Big Picture

As mentioned earlier, one difficulty in interpreting the research literature on gender-related differences is the sheer number of studies. When Eleanor Maccoby and Carol Jacklin reviewed the research in 1974, they compared the results of more than 1,600 studies published mostly between 1966 and 1973. Because they were aware of the file-drawer problem, they included not just published journal articles but dissertations and conference papers. (Their results will be discussed in detail later in this chapter.)

Maccoby and Jacklin found a great deal of inconsistency in research results. How can such inconsistency be interpreted? Suppose, for example, an equal number of studies in an area show an effect in favor of women and men. If you tried to settle the question of gender-related differences in reasoning ability by referring to all the studies cited by Maccoby and Jacklin (1974), you would find that, of twenty-nine studies, seven reported that males were higher, five reported that females were higher, and the remainder found no significant differences between females and males. What would you conclude about these results? Maccoby and Jacklin decided that, on balance, no gender-related difference in reasoning had been shown. This decision makes sense, given that there was no clear pattern favoring one sex. But inconsistency in the direction of differences is *not* the same as no differences. Such inconsistencies should not make us discard the question. Instead, they should lead us to look for variables that distinguish the two sets of studies from each other.

There are several possible reasons for inconsistent findings about gender-related differences (Block, 1976). In Maccoby and Jacklin's review, many studies in which similarities are found consist of samples of forty subjects or less. (Sample size affects the likelihood of finding statistically significant differences. In general, larger samples lead to finding more differences.) When small-sample studies are excluded from Maccoby and Jacklin's tally, the proportion of difference findings increases. This suggests that many gender-related differences are quite small and can only show up reliably with a large sample. Of course one may question whether small differences are of any conceptual or practical importance.

Gender-related differences also emerge with greater consistency as the age of the research participants increases (Block, 1976). Many studies are done on preschool children, the group that shows fewest differences. When Jeanne Block sorted studies according to the age of the participants, she found that significant differences had occurred in 37 percent of the studies of young children, 47 percent of the studies of older children, and 55 percent of the studies of teenagers and adults.

Maccoby and Jacklin produced a pioneering work that gathered all the information available about gender-related differences into one source and attempted to make sense of the patterns of results. But even such careful scholarly analysis of research does not eliminate value judgments. Whether or not a given difference is taken as "real" depends on how one evaluates available data. Many evaluation decisions depend on the reviewer's individual judgment, and even the most dedicated reviewer may not be entirely consistent or unbiased in making these decisions.

Recently, new methods for summarizing research data have been developed. Techniques for *meta-analysis* allow researchers to integrate the results of numerous studies on a single topic and to quantitatively (statistically) assess the magnitude and consistency of gender-related difference effects (Hyde & Linn, 1986). Meta-analysis has been used widely for only about the past ten years, but already many research areas have been reviewed. Many psychologists believe that meta-analysis can resolve some of the issues of definition and measurement in research on gender-related differences.

What is meta-analysis and how does it work? Basically, it uses quantitative methods to summarize the results of research studies (Hedges & Becker, 1986). Just as in traditional reviewing, the investigator first identifies all the relevant studies on a topic. The next step is to summarize the results of each study in a common unit of measurement. In traditional reviewing, any result is taken as equal to any other as long as they are both statistically significant. But there are different degrees of statistical significance, and the results of some studies may be stronger than others. In meta-analysis, studies can be reliably distinguished from one another in terms of the magnitude of the gender-related difference.

Finally, meta-analysis allows researchers to group studies by subcategory and thereby assess the influence of variables other than sex. For example, one might categorize studies of reasoning ability according to the type of task used or whether there was time pressure in the situation to see whether these *moderator variables* are playing a part.

It should be clear by now why many psychologists see meta-analysis as a real advance in techniques for studying sex and gender (Eagly, 1987; Hyde & Linn, 1986). It allows researchers to estimate the *size* of a gender-related difference. Its use of standard measurement units for describing and comparing studies makes it easier to interpret a body of research. It facilitates the study of other variables that interact with the participants' sex—especially important because sex almost always interacts with other factors (Hyde & Linn, 1986).

But these techniques should not be thought of as a panacea for the ills of traditional sex-difference research. Even though they provide improved ways of aggregating and interpreting data from large numbers of studies, they cannot wholly compensate for the biases in the original studies or ensure "objective" interpretation (Unger & Crawford, 1989). Reviewers must still rely on their own judgment in deciding which studies are relevant and whether several measures of the same construct (such as different tests of reasoning ability) are measuring the same thing. Moreover, an unrecognized source of bias common to all studies could lead to an overall assessment that is biased (Hedges & Becker, 1986). If all the tests of reasoning ability used in research happened to be sex-biased, a false "sex difference" might show up in a meta-analysis.

Nor does meta-analysis resolve all problems of interpreting differences. It can show which variables are correlated with the occurrence of gender-related differences, but it does not allow conclusions about the *causes* of the differences. Finally, there is still room for disagreement about how big a difference must be to count as an important one. We will return to these issues as we discuss gender-related cognitive differences later in this chapter.

VALUES AND IDEOLOGY IN SEX-DIFFERENCE RESEARCH: THE LESSONS OF HISTORY

It is not always easy to see the values and assumptions underlying our cultural practices. Much of what people believe about gender is learned and expressed at a nonconscious level (Bem & Bem, 1970). Students also learn that science is value-free and its practitioners objective, impartial seekers of truth. But values and beliefs related to gender have always affected scientific research (Crawford, 1978; Harding, 1986). A brief review of the history of gender and racial issues in science will help clarify the interconnectedness of values and practice.

Throughout most of Western history, the intellectual and moral inferiority of women was seen as self-evident. The first systematic empirical research on women conducted by scientists of the late nineteenth century took women's inferiority as a given and was aimed at uncovering its specific biological determinants (Gould, 1980; Hyde & Linn, 1986; Russett, 1989; Shields, 1975). Looking back at this period with the benefit of hindsight, it is relatively easy to see how the work of scientists was influenced by their beliefs and values about the inferiority of women and people of color. In an era of agitation over slavery and women's rights, members of the dominant social group needed to document the inferiority of other groups in order to defend the status quo. "You are women and hence different," was the message conveyed. "Your differences disqualify you for the worldly roles you seem, most unwisely, to wish to assume" (Russett, 1989, p. 23). Sometimes the scientists' antifeminist bias was expressed directly; one British anthropologist presented a "scientific" paper denouncing the "superficial, flat-chested, thin-voiced Amazons, who are pouring forth sickening prate about the tyranny of men and the slavery of women" (cited in Russett, 1989, p. 27).

Then (as well as now), sexism, racism, and class bias were often intertwined and the brain often was the battle site (Bleier, 1986). First, researchers asserted that the inferiority of women and people of color was due to their smaller brains. One prominent scientist asserted that many women's brains were closer in size to those of gorillas than to the brains of men (cited in Gould, 1981). Similarly, scientists measured cranial size in skulls representing various "races" and concluded that the races could be ranked on a scale of cranial capacity (and hence intelligence) with darker people such as Africans at the bottom, Asians intermediate, and white European men at the top. The brain-size hypothesis foundered when it occurred to scientists that, by this criterion, elephants and hippos should be much more intelligent than people. They then turned to the ratio of brain size to body weight as a measure of intellectual capacity. Little more was heard of this measure when it was discovered that women fared better than men by it.

Giving up on gross differences such as brain size, scientists turned to examining supposed differences in specific regions of the brain. When it was believed that the frontal lobe was the repository of the highest mental powers, the male frontal lobe was seen as larger and better developed. However, when the parietal lobe came to be seen as more important, a bit of historical revisionism occurred. Women were now seen as having similar frontal lobes but smaller parietal lobes than men (Shields, 1975).

When size differences in brain regions proved impossible to document, the debate shifted to the variability hypothesis. It was asserted that men, as a group, are more variable—in other words, that while men and women may be similar on average, there are more men at the extremes of human behavior. Variability was viewed as an advantageous characteristic that enabled species to evolve adaptively. The variability hypothesis was used to explain why there were so many more highly intelligent men than women. Only men could achieve the heights of genius. (It also predicted a greater incidence of mental deficiency among males, a prediction that was virtually ignored.)

The measurement of human abilities began in the nineteenth century with Sir Francis Galton's studies of physical variation and motor skills (cited in Hyde & Linn, 1986). Galton measured height, grip strength, and reaction time because he thought they reflected mental ability. Few questioned his view that these abilities were innate; those who suggested that experiences and opportunity might play a part were usually women, and their views had little impact. When physical abilities failed to correlate with intellectual functioning, the mental testing movement was born.

Although tests of mental ability failed to demonstrate sex differences, the belief in male intellectual superiority was not disrupted. Instead, scientists returned to the variability hypothesis to explain how apparent similarity reflected underlying difference, claiming that men and women might be equal on average, but only men appeared at the upper end of the distribution of mental ability (Hyde & Linn, 1986; Shields, 1982). Although Leta Hollingworth and Helen Montague laboriously examined the hospital records of 2,000 neonates for birth weight and length in order to test the variability hypothesis, and others of the first generation of women who became psychologists examined gender-related differences in emotionality and intelligence, few if any differences were found (Unger, 1979b). Widespread beliefs about sex differences in mental abilities thus persisted into the twentieth century, despite the lack of demonstrable differences in brain structures, variability, or overall performance on intelligence tests.

Today, the search for biological sex differences underlying intellectual functioning continues. For example, some researchers propose that women's brains are less specialized by hemisphere in processing information than men's brains, although the evidence is weak and contradictory (Bleier, 1986). We will examine contemporary theories and evidence about biological bases of gender in Chapter 6.

The history of attempts to find biologically based sex differences illustrates some important points about the study of group differences—points that should be kept in mind as we evaluate contemporary scientific research. Much of this history shows haphazard testing for a wide variety of differences. Of course, the number of possible group differences is infinite, and demonstrating the existence of one or many gives no information about their causes. Moreover, the "truth" discovered by science is historically and contextually limited. It is easy to see how the racist and sexist prejudices of past eras led researchers to search for justifications of the inferiority of women and people of color. It is less easy to see how personal values affect the work of contemporary scientists, but we can be sure that such influences exist. Although people could be grouped in any number of ways, in practice only a few—such as race and sex—are usually chosen. There seem to be no "separate but equal" classification schemes available. The traits attributed to women and minorities are less positive and socially desirable than the traits attributed to men. Because white men remain the norm by which others are judged, research is easily enlisted in support of the social status quo.

GENDER AND COGNITIVE ABILITIES

Ever since psychologists began testing mental abilities at around the turn of the century, male and female test-takers have shown a consistent pattern of overall intellectual similarity. This is due partly to the fact that the tests are carefully constructed so that there will be no average sex difference in overall IQ. Items that are more often answered correctly by one sex or the other are discarded in favor of items that are equally difficult for both (Halpern, 1992). This practice in itself reveals social and political influences on the scientific "truths" available. Perhaps the tests were balanced by sex because girls did better on them, an unthinkable event (Kimball, 1988).

If cognitive ability is measured in terms of school achievement, girls come out ahead. Girls get better grades than boys even in areas in which the boys score higher in ability tests (Eccles, 1989). Their higher academic achievement is rarely interpreted to mean that girls are more intelligent. Rather, it is argued that girls may get their higher grades by being quiet and neat, following directions, and trying hard to please their teachers. This may be an example of devaluing characteristics attributed to girls and women.

Because no one has ever defined a unitary concept of "intelligence" satisfactorily, it is more precise and scientifically fruitful to ask questions about specific cognitive skills and abilities. The general pattern in cognitive skills is one of sex similarity (Maccoby & Jacklin, 1974). In a few specific areas of cognition, small (but reasonably consistent) gender-related differences have been documented. Maccoby and Jacklin's pioneering review identified three such areas—spatial ability, mathematics performance, and verbal ability—setting the stage for further research. (Look ahead to Figure 3.5 for an overview.) In this section we will briefly describe each type of skill, summarize research comparing females and males, and discuss factors influencing the origin and development of gender-related differences in cognition.

Spatial Abilities

Spatial abilities involve perceiving and mentally manipulating shapes and images. They are useful in doing certain kinds of mathematics, in jobs such as architecture, and in everyday tasks such as sewing a dress or building a model from a pattern, doing jigsaw puzzles, or envisioning how furniture would fit into different arrangements in a room.

Reviews have generally concluded that there are gender-related differences in spatial ability, favoring males, which first emerge in adolescence (McGee, 1979; Maccoby & Jacklin, 1974; Meece, Parsons, Kaczala, Goff & Futterman, 1982). But this area, perhaps more than any other, illustrates the complexity of issues in research on gender-related differences. First, there is little agreement on a definition for the term *spatial ability*. While some researchers see it as a unitary construct, others argue that it is composed of varying numbers of subskills (Halpern, 1992) and still others argue that it is so ill-defined that it is useless as a psychological concept (Caplan, MacPherson, & Tobin, 1985). There are hundreds of tests that attempt to measure spatial ability, and it is not always clear how they can be grouped or compared with each other. On some tests, females' scores are more variable than males', and on others the reverse is true. To add to the confusion, there has been disagreement over the age at which differences first emerge and inconsistencies in the pattern and size of differences across age groups.

Today, the most reliable conclusions about gender-related differences in spatial abilities (as well as other cognitive abilities) can be drawn from two sources. The first is meta-analysis of the literature, which, as described earlier, is the state-of-the-art technique for interpreting large bodies of research.

The second is the norms for standardized psychometric tests. Large numbers of people take tests like the Differential Aptitude Test every year. Their norms are valuable to the researcher because they are based on representative samples and involve minimal publication bias, since both similarities and differences between male and female test-takers are published (Burnett, 1986). However, it should be noted that test norms use such enormous samples that even tiny differences are likely to be statistically significant.

Marcia Linn and Anne Petersen (1985, 1986) conducted a meta-analysis of spatial ability experiments, classifying tasks into three categories. In *spatial-perception* tasks, the test-taker must locate the horizontal or vertical in a visual field in spite of distracting information. One much-studied example is the rod-and-frame test (Witkin et al., 1962). *Mental-rotation* tasks involve the ability to imagine how a two- or three-dimensional figure would appear if rotated in space. Finally, *spatial-visualization* tasks require complex analysis of the relationships between different spatial representations. Examples include the embedded figures, hidden figures, and block design tests (Linn & Petersen, 1986). Items that measure spatial abilities are illustrated in Figures 3.3 to 3.5.

Linn and Petersen (1985) reported that starting in elementary school boys score higher on tests of spatial perception and mental rotation. The differences are larger for adults than for children and, for mental rotation, are highly task-dependent—in other words, some mental-rotation tasks reliably show large gender-related differences and others do not. On the more complex spatial-visualization tasks, which may require both mental rotation and spatial perception as well as analytic strategies for their solution, there were no gender-related differences at any age. The results of national standardized tests of spatial visualization still show a small gender-related difference, but it has declined by 59 percent in the past forty years (Feingold, 1988).

In the past, much weight was given to differences in performance on specialized spatial tasks. Performance on the rod-and-frame test was thought to measure a general cognitive style and personality dimension, labeled *field independence* (Witkin, Mednick, Schulsinger, Bakkestrom, Christiansen, Goodenough, Hirschhorn, Lundsteen, Owen, Philip, Rubin, & Stocking, 1976). *Field-dependent* individuals are overly affected by the context of a perceptual situation, and thus perform poorly on the rod-and-frame test; *field independent* individuals are able to ignore irrelevant cues in their surroundings. Females are

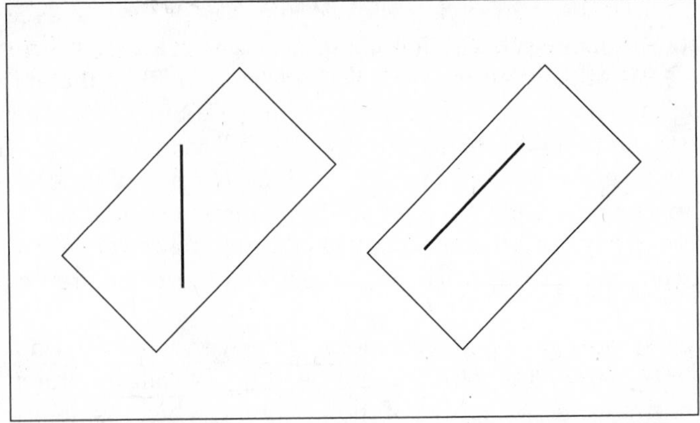

FIGURE 3.3. A spatial perception task. In the rod and frame test, the participant attempts to align a rod vertically within a tilted frame. The figure on the left is oriented correctly.
Source: From Halpern, Sex Differences in Cognitive Abilities, *2nd ed., p. 69. Copyright 1992 Laurence Erlbaum Associates, Inc. Reprinted by permission.*

more likely than males to be field-dependent, and this supposedly relates to "feminine" aspects of personality such as passivity, dependence, and conformity (Haaken, 1988; Halpern, 1992). McClelland (1964) even used the concept to explain why women go into nursing and social work while men enter occupations that "express their assertive interests, like selling, soldiering, engineering . . . and law" (p. 175). The values expressed in the concept of field dependence/independence are obviously sex-biased. Its originator, like the Victorian scientists discussed earlier, saw women's thought processes as childlike and similar to those of "primitive" people (Halpern, 1992).

Feminist researchers have challenged the characterization of women as field-dependent on many grounds. First, the term is much too general. Females and males perform similarly on nonvisual tasks that require separating stimuli from their context (Sherman, 1967). Field dependence may be no more than spatial perception by another name. Second, the term gives the impression of a stable trait. However, performance on spatial tasks is very responsive to training. The originator of research on field dependence observed this himself in a preliminary study, which he never followed up (Witkin, 1949). Finally, the term field-dependent is value-laden. A term such as *field sensitivity* would have very different connotations, implying a positive value for the ability to attend to one's surroundings. The ability to attend rigidly to one cue and screen out irrelevant ones may be valuable under some circumstances, while the ability to attend to context and modify one's response accordingly may be valuable under other circumstances. It seems unwise to characterize perceptual phenomena in terms of personality styles. Such overgeneralized conclusions are easily misapplied.

Factors Influencing Spatial Abilities

Sociocultural Experiences. Most of the gender-related difference in spatial abilities may be due to sociocultural factors. People in our society believe that

Hidden Patterns Test

How quickly can you recognize a figure that is hidden among other lines? This test contains many rows of patterns. In each pattern you are to look for the model shown below:

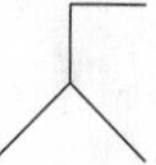

The model must always be in this position, not on its side or upside down.

In which patterns does the model appear?

Your task will be to place an X in the space below each pattern in which the model appears and an O below the pattern where the model does not appear.

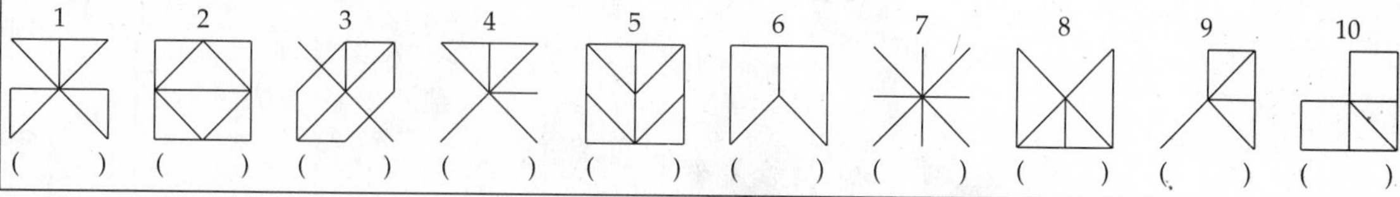

FIGURE 3.4A A spatial visualization task. Solution: X for 1, 3, 4, 6, 9; O for 2, 5, 7, 8, 10.
Source: From R. B. Ekstrom, J. W. French, H. H. Harmon, and D. Durman; *Manual for Kit of Factor– Referenced Cognitive Tests,* p. 22. Copyright © 1976 by Educational Testing Service. Adapted and reproduced under license.

Cube Comparisons Test

Imagine a set of cubical blocks with a different letter on each of the six faces (top, bottom, four sides). Each problem in this test consists of drawings of pairs of cubes or blocks of this kind. Remember, there is a different letter on each face of a given cube or block. Compare the two cubes in each pair below.

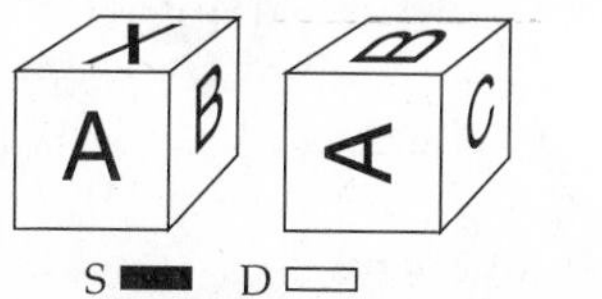

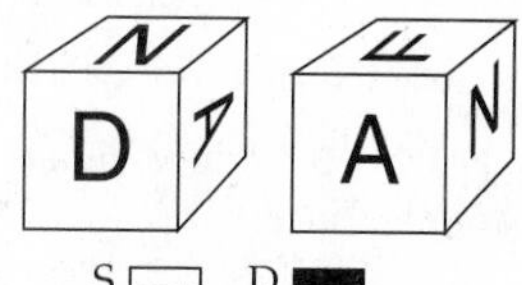

The first pair is marked S because the drawings could be of the same cube. That is, if the A is turned on its side, the X becomes hidden, the B is now on top, and the C (which was hidden) now appears. Thus the two drawings could be of the same cube.

The second pair is marked D because the drawings must be of *different* cubes. If the left cube is turned so that A is upright and facing you, the N would be to the left of the A and hidden, not to the right of the A, as shown on the right-hand member of the pair. Thus, the drawings must be of different cubes.

Note: No letters appear on more than one face of a given cube. Except for this rule, *any* letter can be on the hidden faces of a cube.

Work the three examples below.

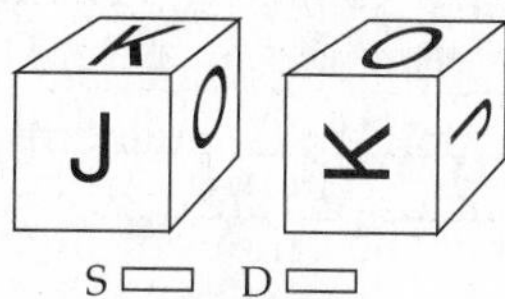

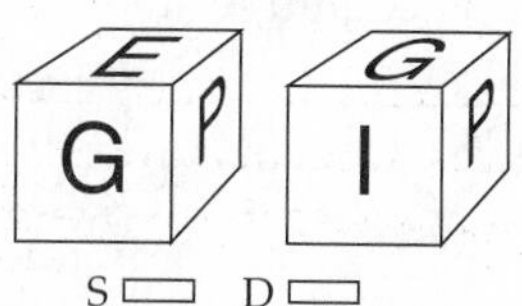

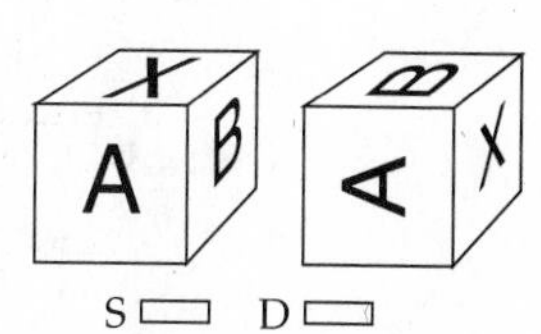

FIGURE 3.4B. A mental rotation task. Solution: left pair: S; center pair: D; right pair: D.
Source: From R. B. Ekstrom, J. W. French, H. H. Harmon, and D. Durman; *Manual for Kit of Factor–Referenced Cognitive Tests;* p. 152. Copyright © 1976 by Educational Testing Service. Adapted and reproduced under license.

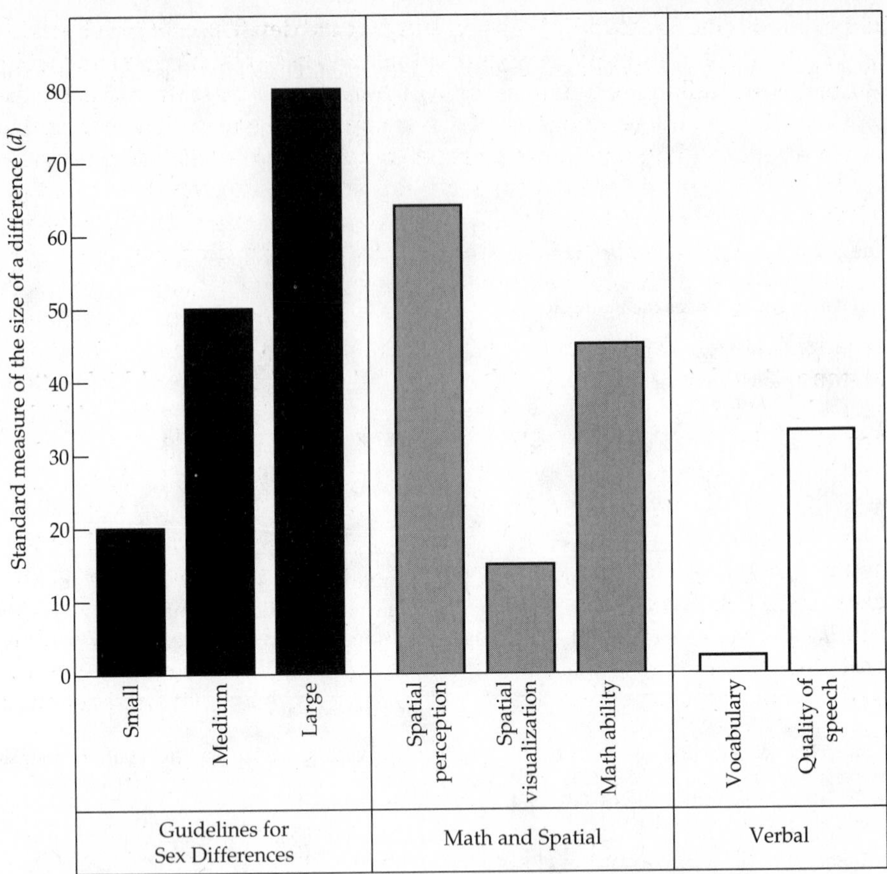

FIGURE 3.5. How big are gender-related differences? Some selected examples, based on meta-analysis.

large sex differences exist and that spatial skills are "masculine." For example, both college students and older men and women believe that men are better at remembering directions and locations (Crawford, Herrmann, Holdsworth, Randall, & Robbins, 1989). When college students were given an ambiguous set of directions for assembling an object (e.g., "First arrange all the parts in order according to the list. Work slowly and carefully."), men remembered the directions better when the task had a masculine gender-typed label ("Making a Workbench") and women remembered better when the task had a feminine gender-typed label ("Making a Shirt"). Thus, people's expectations about the gender typing of a cognitive task can affect their performance (Herrmann, Crawford, & Holdsworth, 1992). Simply changing the *name* of the task ("This is a test of how people think about objects" instead of "This is a test of spatial abilities") eliminated the sex difference in one study (Sharps, Welton, & Price, 1992). In another study, college students rated activities that they thought involved spatial skills as more masculine, and men said they participated in these activities more than women said they did (Newcombe, Bandura, & Taylor, 1983).

Beliefs about differences, along with a desire to appear appropriately masculine or feminine, create ample opportunity for the development of self-fulfilling prophecies. For example, if an individual who believes that men are better at directions is talking to a man and a woman who are together at a party, he may choose to give directions to a new restaurant to the man. The man in this couple thus gets more practice in a spatial-visualization/spatial-memory task, and the woman gets the message that she is unlikely to do well at such tasks.

There is further evidence for a relationship between gender-typed social roles and spatial visualization. Sharon Nash (1975) assessed gender performance by asking sixth- and ninth-grade boys and girls whether they preferred to be their own or the other sex, then measuring their performance on a spatial-visualization task. Male gender preference was positively related to spatial performance. In other words, boys who preferred to be boys scored higher than boys who preferred to be girls, and girls who preferred to be boys scored higher than girls who preferred to be girls.

There were few sixth-grade, and no ninth-grade, boys who preferred to be girls. Many girls, especially in the younger group, preferred to be boys. Children of both sexes who preferred to be boys did not differ in spatial performance. When asked to explain their preference for being a boy, children of both sexes referred to the desirability of male activities such as sports and the high value placed on male roles in our society. Nash's study indicates that masculine attributes and preferences are a better predictor of spatial performance than sex itself—perhaps because those who prefer to be boys act like boys and get more practice in spatial-skill–related play.

Children are encouraged to play with different toys and engage in different activities from a very early age. Boys are given vehicles and building equipment and encouraged to build models from diagrams, construct forts and playhouses, and take apart and reassemble objects. They are more likely to be provided with science-related toys such as microscopes and puzzles. These toys may help them learn more about manipulating movement and space than the dolls and miniature housekeeping equipment provided for girls. Table 3.1 shows the beliefs of a sample of 100 white middle-class college students about what toys are appropriate for boys and girls. Note that in addition to the gender typing of particular toys, there are fewer girls' toys than boys' toys.

These gender distinctions have been related to later differences in spatial ability. In a review of research on the play patterns of children aged 3 to 13, Dyanne Tracy concluded that boys and/or children with a masculine gender orientation play with a wider variety of toys and also develop better spatial and mathematics skills than girls and/or children with a feminine gender orientation (Tracy, 1987). In a study of preschoolers, girls and boys who preferred activities such as climbing, building with blocks, and playing with vehicles scored higher on a spatial-ability test than those who played with dolls and housekeeping toys (Serbin & Connor, 1979).

Other activities that may affect spatial skills distinguish boys' and girls' play. The permissible play space for boys is greater; girls are kept closer to home while boys learn to navigate a neighborhood "territory" (Bryant, 1985; Feiring & Lewis, 1987). Some sports have strong spatial-skills components. Computers are stereotyped as "masculine" (see Chapter 4). Boys dominate video arcades and computer clubs; both games and educational software are designed with

TABLE 3.1. Gender Typing of Toys

Girls' Toys	Boys' Toys	Neutral Toys
Tea set	Jack-in-the-box	Rocking horse
Raggedy Ann	Darts	Top
Picture books	Tricycle	Finger paints
Teddy bear	Tinkertoys	Chalkboard/chalk
Doll house	Model airplane	Play-Doh
Coloring book	Toy soldier	Stuffed dinosaur
Supermarket	Toy drum	Toy bank
Toy refrigerator	Dump truck	Water colors
Doll stroller	Wagon	Etch-a-Sketch
Hand puppet	Toy guns	
Toy telephone	Doctor's kit	
Doll	Football	
Jump rope	Tool bench	
Iron/ironing board	Space capsule	
Toy piano	Pogo stick	
Shopping basket	Water pistol	
	Remote control car	
	Matchbox cars	
	Electric train	
	Microscope	
	Tool kit	
	Blocks	
	Ride toy	

Source: From C. L. Miller, "Qualitative Defferences among Gender – Stereotyped Toys: Implications for Cognitive and Social Development in Boys and Girls;" *Sex Roles, 16*; 473–488. 1987 Plenum Publishing Company. Reprinted by permission.

boys in mind (Kiesler, Sproull, & Eccles, 1985). "Very few girls are found in the high school classes of mechanical drawing, analytical geometry, and shop. Spare-time activities of tinkering with the car, . . . direction finding, and map-reading are sex-typed and might also be sources of differential practice" (Sherman, 1967). Of course, a relationship between practice and skill does not prove that skill differences are caused by practice. It is possible that those with more aptitude or greater skill choose activities that allow them to practice spatial skills because they are enjoyable.

Training and Practice. If spatial abilities are strongly affected by experience, it follows that specific training on spatial tasks should improve performance. Although hundreds of studies have documented the existence of gender-related differences, surprisingly few have investigated the role of training and practice. Researchers have begun to fill the gap. A meta-analysis exploring the role of experience and training in spatial skills recently showed that both general experience and specialized training are associated with better performance on spatial tests for both sexes (Baenninger & Newcombe, 1989). In one study, first-grade boys performed better than girls on a hidden figures test. However, both sexes improved with training, and the girls improved more than the boys, so that the gender-related difference disappeared (Conner, Schackman, & Serbin, 1978). Junior high school students also showed benefits from training in some types of spatial skills (Conner & Serbin, 1985). When college students were trained to use mental imagery in performing a complex visual-spatial task, the women performed as well as the men after a mere eight training trials (Koslow, 1987). Even elderly (mean age=73 years) adults, with a lifetime of differential experience behind them, rapidly responded to training on a mental-rotation task. After five one-hour training sessions, women performed as well as men (Willis & Schaie, 1988).

Exposure to computer learning opportunities may be a big factor in spatial ability development. In a recent study, black and white children in the African nation of Zimbabwe were provided with the computer learning tool LOGO. Pretests and posttests showed that, compared with a group that was not exposed to computers, these children scored higher on a math scale of a standard intelligence test. In addition, black girls showed large gains in spatial reasoning. Clearly, the cognitive development of these 11- and 12-year-olds, especially the girls, was facilitated (Mundy-Castle, Wilson, Sibanda, & Sibanda, 1989).

These studies clearly indicate the role of experience and practice in spatial skills. They suggest that researchers who want to test for gender-related differences should first match their male and female research participants on relevant background experiences rather than just matching for age or grade in school. Otherwise, a "sex" difference simply reflects the fact that sex is correlated with particular experiences (Hyde, 1981). The studies also suggest that one way to help young girls develop their cognitive abilities is to provide them with computers and "boys' toys." "We may be shortchanging the intellectual development of girls by providing them with only traditional sex stereotyped toys" (Halpern, 1992, p. 215).

Mathematics Ability and Performance

Girls' mathematics performance is better than boys' in the elementary school years, but by high school they have lost their early advantage in computational skill and perform similarly to boys. In problem solving there are not consistent gender-related differences at any age (NAEP, 1983). Just a relatively short time ago, when standardized tests were first being normed in the 1940s to 1960s, the differences were much larger and favored boys. Today, however, boys and girls do not differ at all in basic math skills (Feingold, 1988). Contrary to beliefs that girls don't like math and are not good at it, many studies (summarized by Chipman and Wilson, 1985) show that girls like math just as much as boys do and, through the intermediate high school level, perform similarly.

There is, however, a well-documented difference favoring males in *advanced* mathematics performance. In recent years, boys have scored an average of about fifty points higher on the math portion of the SAT than girls. Among the very highest scorers in two recent test administrations, boys earned 96 percent of perfect 800 scores, 90 percent of scores between 780 and 790, 81 percent of scores between 750 and 770, and 56 percent of scores of 600 (Dorans & Livingston, 1987). In national math talent searches, far more boys than girls are identified as gifted, and the gifted boys score higher than the gifted girls (Benbow & Stanley, 1980).

The "gender gap" in math may be shrinking. In the most recent available data, the gap was forty-one points in favor of boys—still very large, but smaller than in previous years. Asian-American students now score as high on math as white students overall, while other ethnic groups still lag. Ethnic group differences are strongly related to social class: the lower a student's family income and parents' education, the less likely he or she is to do well on the SAT. However, the gender gap has diminished over time in every ethnic group (Shea, 1994).

What a puzzle for psychological research to unravel! Girls start out liking math and believing that girls are better at it than boys (Boswell, 1985). They actually do better than boys on standardized tests and get better grades in math (as well as in other subjects). Yet, by the time they are in high school, they score lower on advanced math skills. As you might expect, the development of this difference cannot be attributed to one or two isolated variables. Rather, there are many interacting factors that may be responsible for both gender and ethnic differences, especially social class background. Focusing on the gender gap, we will examine the possibility of sex bias in standardized tests, the effects of in-school and out-of-school opportunities to learn math, and girls' confidence in their math abilities. Implicated in all of these are beliefs about math as a male domain. Finally, we will consider hypotheses about biologically based differences in ability.

Factors Influencing Mathematics Performance

Sex Bias in Testing. The purpose of standardized tests like the SAT is to predict performance in college. But although women score lower on these tests, they get better grades than men in college. The tests thus "underpredict" women's performance (Rosser, 1987; Stricker, Rock, & Burton, 1992). Testing activists have charged that a test that underpredicts the performance of more than half the people who take it should be considered consumer fraud (Rosser, 1987; 1992). The consequences for women are serious. Nearly all four-year colleges and universities use test scores in admissions decisions. Because women's college grades are higher than their test scores predict, some women are probably being rejected in favor of male applicants who will do less well in college.

Moreover, women lose out on millions of dollars in scholarships based on test performance. More than 750 organizations use test scores in awarding scholarships. Only about one-third of National Merit scholarship finalists are female; proportions in other scholarship programs are similar (Sadker & Sadker, 1994). In New York State, students can win Regents scholarships for college. If these scholarships were awarded on the basis of grades, young women would win 55.5 percent of them; if SAT scores alone were used, young men would win 56.5 percent. When the state decided to change from SAT scores alone to both criteria in 1990, young women won a majority of the awards for the first time in the program's seventy-seven-year history. Boys continue to win more than 60 percent of the more prestigious Empire State scholarships, which require higher SAT scores (Verhovek, 1990). Young women also lose out on opportunities to participate in special programs for the gifted (we have already noted the overabundance of boys discovered in national talent searches in math). Finally, an individual's test scores affect her self-confidence and her future academic goals (Rosser, 1992; Sadker & Sadker, 1994). For all these reasons, sex bias in testing is an important issue.

Test publishers claim that the tests are not biased. But Selkow (1984), in a review of seventy-four psychological and educational tests, documented that girls and women were underrepresented and appeared in stereotyped roles. In math tests, items have tended to be set in contexts more familiar to boys, like sports (Dwyer, 1979). Along with measuring math ability, then, tests may be inadvertently reflecting a bias toward male interests. Although standardized tests are supposed to be objective, they are written by subjective human beings who reflect the values of their society. Furthermore, test-takers bring to the test different feelings about themselves and the test, and thus interpret items differently. There is no such thing as a value-free test (Teitelbaum, 1989). Given the importance of the decisions made on the basis of testing in our society, more research is needed on the tests themselves and how they produce similarities and differences among groups.

Gender in the Classroom. The single biggest influence on math performance is that girls take fewer math courses (Chipman & Thomas, 1985). Math performance diverges only in high school, when girls begin taking fewer math courses. When course-taking is controlled, the differences nearly disappear (Chipman, Brush & Wilson, 1985). Math course-taking is becoming more equal; girls now take algebra and geometry nearly as much as boys, but still avoid calculus (Sadker & Sadker, 1994).

Even when they take the same courses, boys and girls are experiencing different worlds in the classroom. Studies at all grade levels have shown that often a few males are allowed to dominate classroom interaction while other students are silent and ignored (Eccles, 1989) (see Figure 3.6). Gender interacts with race to determine who gets attention from teachers: White males get the most attention, followed by minority males and white females. Minority females get the least attention of any group. Classroom interaction studies show that African-American girls become less active, assertive, and visible in class as they move through the elementary grades (Sadker & Sadker, 1994).

Girls are praised for their appearance, boys for their performance. Girls experience sexual harassment from their peers and teachers far more often than boys. Twenty years of research on educational equity has shown such a dismal pattern of deeply ingrained sexism that researchers Myra Sadker and David Sadker titled their 1994 book *Failing at Fairness: How America's Schools Cheat Girls.* In the voices of the young women they interviewed, the sexism and its effects on bright girls are evident:

> In my science class the teacher never calls on me, and I feel like I don't exist. The other night I had a dream that I vanished.
>
> People are always surprised to learn that I have a 4.0 and I'm a National Merit Finalist. Their image of me is "that *blond* girl who used to go out with Scott." Why can't they understand there's more to me?
>
> I have a teacher who calls me "airhead" and "ditz." I used to think I was smart, but now I don't know. Maybe I'm not. What if he's right? The more he treats me like an airhead, the more I think maybe I am (p. 135).

Gender inequity that can affect math and science performance extends to out-of-school educational experiences as well. Boys are more likely to partici-

FIGURE 3.6 Sexism in the classroom.
Source: Doonesbury © 1992 G. B. Trudeau. Reprinted with permission of Universal Press Syndicate. All rights preserved.

pate in activities such as chess clubs, math clubs, summer computer courses, and science camps. In short, boys live in a math-enriched environment that encourages achievement, and girls in a math-impoverished one that encourages self-doubt.

Low Confidence, Low Self-Expectations. Girls' lower confidence about their abilities is a consistent finding in many studies (Chipman & Wilson, 1985), although meta-analysis shows that the difference is not large (Hyde, Fennema, Ryan, Frost, & Hopp, 1990). In 1992, the Mattel Corporation introduced Teen Talk Barbie, the first talking Barbie since the 1970s (see Figure 3.7). Among the words they put in her mouth: "Math class is tough." Myra and David Sadker noted:

> The national flap over Barbie's "Math class is tough" faux pas is a symptom of the inroads females have forged in this formerly male preserve. *The Washington Post* dubbed the doll "Foot-in-Mouth Barbie," and the American Association of University Women warned that this was precisely the kind of role model girls did not need. Math teachers around the country registered their dismay. "We've been working so hard at closing the gender gap and fighting math anxiety for girls," an Illinois teacher told us. "This is the last thing we need" (Sadker & Sadker, 1994, p. 122).

By the time they are in junior high, girls are losing their early confidence that they can do math as well as or better than boys, and their change in attitude is independent of their actual performance. Although their grades remain better than boys' grades, girls rate themselves lower in math ability, consider their math courses harder, and are less sure that they will succeed in future math courses (Eccles, Adler et al., 1985). For eighth-graders, math confidence and attitudes toward success in math are more important in determining whether girls will take college preparatory math than their actual math achievement scores are (Sherman, 1983). Among high school girls of equal ability, those who are less confident are more likely to discontinue math (Sherman, 1982). Female college students are also less confident that they can do well in computer courses, and this attitude affects their course enrollment (Miura, 1987). By the time they are in college, doing well in math is unrelated to women's (but not men's) feelings of overall competence (Singer & Stake, 1986). For many

FIGURE 3.7. Math may be tough, but if Barbie admits it, Ken should, too. During the 1993 holiday season, a group of parents and feminist activists calling itself the Barbie Liberation Organization switched the voice boxes on 300 GI Joe and Barbie dolls. This produced GI Joe dolls that said "Want to go shopping?" in high-pitched voices and Barbie dolls that threatened in gruff voices, "Dead men tell no lies." The BLO says that its goal is to reveal and correct harmful gender stereotyping in children's toys. Next, perhaps, a talking Ken who complains about his tough math class?

young women, math changes from a valued skill to something that is "just not me."

Parents of girls probably play a part in these attitude changes. Parents attribute a daughter's success in math to hard work and effort, and a son's success to natural talent. They view math as more difficult for daughters than for sons, and they believe that math, especially advanced math, is more important for sons. Parents provide an interpretive framework for their sons' and daughters' beliefs about their abilities (Eccles, 1989). Boys learn they have talent in an important area, and girls learn that hard work cannot wholly compensate for their lack of ability! One gifted woman told us that when she scored a 650 in SAT math and a 710 in verbal as a high school senior, her parents explained that her scores meant she was "not good in math compared to verbal." What these scores mean, of course, is that she is highly able in both areas.

Math as a Male Domain. Close your eyes and visualize a mathematician. Chances are your image is of a cerebral-looking middle-aged man with glasses and an intense but absentminded air—an Einstein, perhaps. Now visualize a woman mathematician. "Unattractive," "masculine," "cold/distant," and "unfeminine" are the negative stereotypes that women mathematicians perceive others to hold, along with "aggressive," "socially awkward," and "overly intellectual" (Boswell, 1985). When elementary and senior high school students were asked about their perceptions of people in math-related careers such as science, engineering, and physics, they described *men*—who were white-coated loners, isolated in laboratories, with no time for family or friends (Boswell, 1979). Children learn very early that math is a male domain. By the third grade, they believe that adult women are generally inferior to adult men in math (Boswell, 1985).

In the past, it was thought that the belief that "math is for men" was held largely by girls and women, and that it deterred them from choosing math courses and math-related activities. However, a meta-analysis of math attitudes has shown that *males* hold this belief much more strongly than girls and women do (Hyde et al., 1990). This finding is very interesting because it suggests that gender-related influences on math choices work at the interactional and social structural levels at least as much as at the individual level. In other words, we cannot explain the underrepresentation of girls and women in math courses and math careers by saying that they mistakenly believe that math is for men, an intrapsychic or individual "attitude problem." Rather, if this belief is affecting girls and women, it must be because boys and men hold it, and something in their behavior toward the girls and women they interact with puts subtle pressure on the girls not to achieve in math and science. In Chapter 5, we will examine more closely how gender pressures are conveyed in everyday interaction.

The gender incongruence of math for girls is heightened by a lack of role models. Beyond junior high, math and science teachers are predominantly men. Very few girls learn about great women mathematicians like Emmy Noether, who persisted in her research despite blatant sex discrimination and provided the mathematical basis for important aspects of relativity theory (Crawford, 1981). Few young girls have opportunities to offset negative influences through personal contact with women mathematicians and scientists.

Biological Influences. Some psychologists believe that the persistent differences in mathematics achievement reflect biological influences. As noted earlier, boys are much more likely than girls to be identified as gifted in national math talent searches. Based on this evidence, Camilla Benbow and Julian Stanley (1980) concluded that "Sex differences in achievement and in attitude toward mathematics result from superior male mathematical ability which may, in turn, be related to greater male ability in spatial tasks" (p. 1264). Although they had not investigated biological variables in any way, they suggested that biology was at the root of the difference because environmental factors were equated: their (junior high) boys and girls had taken the same number of formal math courses. As we have seen, overgeneralization and a rush to "biologize" results are unfortunately frequent in research on gender-related differences. We have described many sociocultural factors that have been shown to affect math attitudes and performance. As mathematics professors Alice Shafer and Mary Gray point out, environmental factors were not ruled out in Benbow and Stanley's study:

> Anyone who thinks that seventh-graders are free from environmental influences can hardly be living in the real world. While the formal training of all students may be essentially the same, the issues of who helps with mathematics, of

what sort of toys and games children are exposed to, of what the expectations of parents and teachers are, and of a multitude of other factors cannot lightly be set aside (1981, p. 231).

More recently, Benbow has reviewed evidence for environmental and biological factors and again concluded that "sex differences in extremely high mathematical reasoning ability may be, in part, physiologically determined" (1988, p. 182). Many other researchers have also suggested that biological differences in spatial ability are related to math performance. It seems plausible that some kinds of math—for example, geometry—require a spatial-skill component. But there is no conclusive evidence for a biological basis for gender-related differences in spatial skills. The existence of a sex-linked gene for math ability has been ruled out (Sherman & Fennema, 1978). Furthermore, several reviewers have concluded that there is no evidence that differences between girls and boys in spatial ability can account for their differences in math performance (Chipman, Brush, & Wilson, 1985; Linn & Petersen, 1986). And even among boys identified as gifted in math and science, the majority do not pursue math and science careers. Clearly, ability alone does not determine intellectual growth and career choice.

Possible connections between biological influences such as genetics or hormones and intellectual performance continue to be explored. One indication of the controversy and interest this line of research generates is that forty-two researchers chose to respond with written commentaries to Benbow's 1988 article, with a spectrum of opinions about the issues.

Ironically, Benbow and Stanley (1980) may have indirectly (and inadvertently) contributed to the sociocultural causes of math deficits in girls and women. Their article, published in the prestigious journal *Science,* was seized on by the popular press and reported in highly misleading stories and headlines (see Figure 3.8). Jacqueline Eccles and Janis Jacobs (1986) conducted a field study comparing the attitudes of parents who had heard about the article with those who had not. (Because Eccles's research on math attitudes and performance was under way at the time, she had a sample of parents whose attitudes toward their daughters' abilities she had already measured.) Reading about "scientific evidence" for a "math gene" favoring boys led mothers of daughters to lower their estimates of their daughter's abilities. We have already noted the importance of parents in providing an interpretational framework for their children's self-assessments.

Press coverage of research on gender-related differences in math performance is further documentation that theories about the meaning of difference are not value-neutral. The critical response to Benbow and Stanley's theorizing from the scientific community, such as the rebuttal by Alice Schafer and Mary Gray quoted earlier, received no press coverage. Gender-related biological influences on any human behavior are always a possibility (and a legitimate area of research). However, it must be recognized that, historically and in the present, "biological inferiority" is a frequently used justification for women's unequal position in society. It is encouraging to see recent press coverage presenting the research of Jacqueline Eccles, Janet Hyde, and Marcia Linn with these headlines: "Study: Male, Female Talent Equalizing," and "In Sum: Girls Are Not Bad at Math."

Do Males Have a Math Gene?

Can girls do math as well as boys? All sorts of recent tests have shown that they cannot. Most educators and feminists tude Test normally given to high-school seniors. In the results on the math portion of the SAT—there was no appreciable dif-

Newsweek, Dec. 15, 1980

The Gender Factor in Math

A new study says males may be naturally abler than females

Until about the seventh grade, boys and girls do equally well at math. In early high school, when the emphasis Julian C. Stanley of Johns Hopkins University, males inherently have more mathematical ability than females.

Time, Dec. 15, 1980

Male superiority

Are boys born superior to girls in mathematical ability? The answer is probably Yes, say Camilla Persson Benbow and Julian C. Stanley, researchers in the department of psychology at the Johns

The Chronicle of Higher Education, December, 1980

Are Boys Better At Math?

New York Times, Dec. 7, 1980

BOYS HAVE SUPERIOR MATH ABILITY, STUDY SAYS

Boys are inherently better at math than girls, according to an eight-year study of 10,000 gifted students. Coun-

Education U.S.A., Dec. 15, 1980

SEX + MATH = ?

Why do boys traditionally do better than girls in math? Many say it's because boys are encouraged to pursue

Family Weekly, Jan. 25, 1981

Study suggests boys may be better at math

WASHINGTON (UPI) – Two psychologists said Friday boys are better than girls in math reasoning, and they urged educators to accept the fact that something more than social factors is re-

Ann Arbor News, Dec. 6, 1980

FIGURE 3.8 Media messages: Biased reporting of a gender-based difference. *Source: From Eccles and Jacobs's, "Social Forces Shape Math Attitudes and Performance,"* Signs, 11, *pp. 367-389, 1986. University of Chicago Press. Reprinted by permission of Jacquelipine S. Eccles.*

Verbal Abilities and Communication Competence

The term *verbal ability* has been used almost as loosely as *spatial ability.* Verbal skills have been assessed in terms of a wide variety of measures, including vocabulary size, anagram-solving skill, spelling, language-acquisition rate, essay writing, verbal expressiveness, and analogy problem solving. For many years the general consensus among psychologists has been that females are superior to males in verbal performance. When Maccoby and Jacklin (1974) summarized the results of eighty-five studies of verbal ability, they concluded that girls' abilities probably mature somewhat more rapidly than boys' in early life. Overall, however, boys and girls were similar in verbal abilities until about age 11, when girls moved ahead of boys. This gender-related difference favoring girls increased through high school and perhaps beyond. It was evident on both lower-level skills such as simple verbal fluency and on high-level skills such as analogy solution and creative writing.

Maccoby and Jacklin's conclusions were consistent with other, earlier reviews and were not considered surprising. Their conclusions may also seem consistent with the stereotype of the talkative woman. It's important to remember that what is being measured in tests of verbal abilities is *quality* of speech, as well as the ability to comprehend and reason with words. Indeed, female superiority in verbal abilities is presented in textbooks as one of the best-established "facts" of psychology (Hyde & Linn, 1988), and people believe that women score higher than men on the verbal portion of the SAT (Matlin & Matkoski, 1985). We will see, however, that the evidence for a gender-related difference in verbal abilities is not as clear-cut as these generalizations imply.

Earlier, we noted that *spatial ability* is probably a too-general term for a number of separable skills, only some of which show gender-related differences. The same is true for *verbal ability.* When Janet Hyde and Marcia Linn (1988) performed a meta-analysis of verbal-ability studies, including both Maccoby and Jacklin's studies and a large sample of more recent ones, they found the *overall* difference to be so small that they concluded ". . . gender differences in verbal ability no longer exist" (p. 53). On some skills, there are no differences at all; on others, small but reliable differences (see Figure 3.5). The largest difference, although not large in absolute size, was for quality of speech production. This finding is consistent with Maccoby and Jacklin's conclusions about greater verbal fluency in females.

Gender-related differences in verbal abilities are now small or nonexistent on large-scale standardized tests such as the Differential Aptitude Test and the SAT. On the DAT, girls score slightly higher on spelling and English skills, but girls and boys do not differ in verbal reasoning scores. On recent administrations of the SAT, girls actually scored lower than boys on the verbal portion by about eleven points, reversing a longtime pattern of slightly better scores for girls (Feingold, 1988). Although this difference is small, it may have serious consequences for young women's career options when combined with the forty-to fifty-point advantage of boys in quantitative SAT scores and used in admissions and scholarship decisions. Furthermore, lower scores for girls and young women are incongruent with the fact that they get consistently higher grades in courses based on the abilities these tests measure (Rosser, 1987).

Assessing Verbal Abilities

Even though meta-analysis and standardized tests are useful tools, they cannot provide us with eternal truths about verbal (or any other) abilities. For example, meta-analysis cannot completely resolve problems related to the original studies. Hyde and Linn (1988) note that boys are much more likely to suffer from speech and language-processing disorders such as stuttering, dyslexia, and difficulty in learning to read. If more boys than girls are removed from regular classrooms for remedial reading and other special educational programs, the samples of children remaining in regular classrooms would be skewed; there would be fewer low-scoring boys available for testing in these classrooms, and the overall effect would be to raise the average score for boys, making boys and girls look more similar in verbal ability than they really are.

Another problem with tests of verbal abilities is that they test only a subset of such abilities. Most focus on verbal behavior in abstract tasks devoid of social meaning and context and fail to test *communication skills.* Yet a large part of the importance of language in daily life is the ability to communicate. Human beings use language to make our meaning understood to others, to convince others that they have been heard and understood, to persuade or influence others, to express feelings, and to exchange ideas. All these actions are social ones. It is not clear whether the sheer size of a person's vocabulary or her ability to solve verbal analogies is related to these communication skills.

It is interesting that the largest difference favoring girls and women found in research studies is in quality of speech production, an ability probably related to communication. In overall communication competence, females perform better than males (Wine, 1981; Wine, Moses, & Smye, 1980). Thus, while the definition of verbal ability encompasses a number of separable skills, it also "undertests" important abilities in which women excel. Neglecting "feminine" communication skills in the construct of verbal ability may be an example of how unrecognized values affect research agendas and results. Whether a "real" difference exists depends on the definition of the ability being studied.

Origins and Influences

Gender-related differences in verbal and communication skills have generated much less research aimed at finding causes and correlates than the other differences we have discussed—perhaps because they favor females. Maccoby and Jacklin (1974) evaluated the idea that girls may be talked to more as infants and young children, thus giving them an early advantage in verbal development. However, they concluded that other factors such as social class were more influential than the baby's sex in determining the amount and type of verbal interaction he or she received. There is a need for more research to learn how girls' and women's experiences encourage the development of verbal and communication abilities.

COGNITIVE SIMILARITIES AND DIFFERENCES: SUMMARY AND IMPLICATIONS

Magnitude and Meaning

We have seen that within a general pattern of similarity in cognitive abilities, there are a few reasonably consistent gender-related differences. Males score higher on some spatial skills and are more likely to achieve in advanced (but not elementary or intermediate) mathematics. Females score slightly better on some types of verbal abilities tests and have better verbal and communication skills. These generalizations refer to *average* differences. In every case, the overlap between females and males is much greater than the average difference.

We have also seen evidence that gender-related differences in cognition are decreasing. Girls and young women are increasingly claiming math and science as gender-equal territory. In the 1990 Westinghouse National Science Talent Search, 42 percent of the finalists were young women. Winner of first place and a $40,000 college scholarship was Ashley Melia Reiter, 17, who was inspired by her high school course on fractal geometry to design a project that found the dimensions of fractals generated by Pascal's triangle and its higher analogs (Cowen, 1991).

Given the unimpressive magnitude of gender-related differences and their place within an overall pattern of similarity, you may well wonder what all the fuss is about. Why have psychologists spent so much time and effort identifying and measuring small differences in the cognitive performance of women and men, developing theories about their causes, and emphasizing their importance? History tells us that "scientific evidence" about female inferiority has often been used to justify women's unequal position in society. Moreover, the methods of psychology are better suited for finding and interpreting differences than similarities among groups. Fortunately, psychology now has better tools than in the past for deciding whether a statistically significant difference between groups is large enough to be a focus of further research. The social meaning of a difference, however, can only be decided in terms of social values.

Origins

We are all so used to living in a gendered world that it is hard for us to appreciate the pervasiveness of gender differentiation. We grow up being given gender-typed toys: dolls and play jewelry for girls; microscopes, building sets, and computers for boys. We see pictures of boys on model train sets and pictures of girls on tea sets. We read jokes and stories that tell us that girls are talkative and boys are better at math, science, spatial directions, and reasoning. In Chapter 7 we will examine the process of becoming gendered—becoming "all boy" or "a real little girl"—in detail. With respect to cognitive skills, we have seen that the pattern of environmental influences has been most completely demonstrated for mathematics (Eccles, 1989). Similar patterns probably apply to other cognitive skills and abilities. Given the extent to which women and men live in different experiential worlds, it is surprising that cognitive differences are not larger and more general than they are.

The evidence for biological influences on gender-related differences in cognition is weak. Biological theories, in order to be viable, would have to explain areas of similarity as well as areas of difference. Why are females better at speech production but not vocabulary? Why are males better at mental rotation but not spatial visualization?

Cross-Cultural Effects

As you have seen from the growing similarity in girls' and boys' verbal skills over the past thirty years, gender differences in cognitive abilities are certainly not cast in stone. An exploration of situations in which such differences are either smaller or larger than those we've described can tell us much about the sources of differences usually attributed to gender. One area that has received little attention from psychologists is how different cultures may create, or at least exaggerate or minimize, various cognitive skills.

In Israel, for example, gender differences in cognitive abilities appear earlier than in the United States. Boys surpass girls on verbal as well as mathematical tests by the age of 13 (Lieblich, 1985). Almost identical patterns of performance have been found in both Jewish and Arab children. For both groups, however, socioeconomic class differences in test performance were larger than gender-related differences.

Why do gender differences appear earlier in Israel than in the United States? Marilyn Safir (1986), an Israeli psychologist, has hypothesized that these effects are mediated by the cultural context in which children are raised. Israeli society is more patriarchal than our own. For example, in orthodox Judaism, the only branch of Judaism officially recognized in Israel, only men can officiate at religious ceremonies, and only a husband can apply for a divorce. A male child is particularly important for religious families because only a son may say a prayer of mourning for his parents. Both Arab and Jewish parents in Israel have been found to value education more for their sons than for their daughters (Alazorov-Por, 1983).

Israel is, however, a young nation whose people continue to explore different ways of living in communities. Safir examined students' cognitive performance on standardized tests (similar to the SAT) for groups of young women and men who had been born and educated either in a city, a kibbutz (a communal settlement), or a moshav (an organization of individually owned farms that are worked cooperatively). Although the kibbutz movement has not completely fulfilled its goal of social and sexual equality, kibbutzim are relatively egalitarian. Moshavs, in contrast, are still patriarchal in nature; the father is the legal head of the household, and only he has the right to vote on community issues.

Safir found that men tended to score higher than women on both the mathematical and language subtests of these college entrance exams. Gender differences were, however, affected by the ideological conditions under which the students had been raised. Differences were largest between young men and women who had been born and raised in a moshav. Differences were smallest between young women and men who had been born and raised on a kibbutz. This group differed from the general Israeli norm in that it did not show sex-related differences in either English or Hebrew vocabulary.

This study demonstrates how sensitive cognitive abilities are to cultural context. We predict that as more cross-cultural comparisons are made, gender-related differences in cognitive abilities will be shown to be more sociocultural (and less biological) in origin. Even the variability hypothesis, which has been proposed for more than a hundred years as an explanation for women's lower achievement, does not hold cross-culturally. In the United States, males are more variable in math and spatial ability, and females in verbal ability. However, a review of studies in other countries showed that there are no consistent gender differences in these three abilities across cultures. Males are more variable in some countries and females in other countries (Feingold, 1994). Within our own culture, the gender-related difference in math performance is largely a white phenomenon: for African-American and Hispanic students, there is no difference by sex, and for Asian-Americans there is a very small difference favoring girls (Hyde, et al., 1990). Of course, these results do not support the notion that there is a purely biological basis for greater male variability or math achievement.

Psychological Research as Androcentric Knowledge

Most of the research on cognitive abilities has been based on standard research methods used in rigorous, nonsexist ways. But feminist theorists have questioned some assumptions of standard research methods, and many of their challenges are relevant to this research area. One criticism is that psychological research lacks ecological ("real-world") validity because it examines behavior outside its normal social context (Parlee, 1979; Fine & Gordon, 1989). Performance on a mental-rotation task or a rod-and-frame test, for example, may have little relevance to most jobs or everyday cognitive demands. If the importance of a task itself is unproven, the importance of a gender-related difference in the task becomes even more questionable. The belief that stripping behavior from its context results in greater objectivity of observation may be an illusion.

Another problem is the topics *not* defined as cognitive abilities by psychologists and test-makers. We have seen an example of this bias in the case of communication skills. At least one testing specialist, Phyllis Teitelbaum, maintains that, from a feminist perspective, standardized tests are deeply androcentric in this regard:

> Excluded are whole areas of human achievement that contribute to success in school and work. . . . Such characteristics and skills as intuition, motivation, self-understanding, conscientiousness, creativity, cooperativeness, supportiveness of others, sensitivity, nurturance, ability to create a pleasant environment, and ability to communicate verbally and nonverbally are excluded from standardized tests. By accepting and reflecting the androcentric model of knowledge, standardized tests reinforce value judgments that consider this model of knowledge more valid and important than other ways of viewing the world. Content that is not tested is judged less valuable than that included on tests (1989, p. 330).

SOCIAL CONSEQUENCES

Social Uses of Difference Research

If the only information you have about an individual is her or his sex, you know next to nothing about that individual's cognitive abilities. For every difference mentioned in this chapter, the overlap between the sexes is so great that the existence of an average difference cannot be used to predict individual abilities or behavior. Yet the tendency to do so seems irresistible. When the son of one of the authors was ready to enter kindergarten at a private school, the principal announced that he would have to spend two years in kindergarten because school policy prohibited boys from entering first grade before the age of 7. She explained that the policy was based on the well-established sex difference in verbal abilities: boys, on the average, were not ready to read before the age of 7. What would you do if your son were subjected to such a judgment—or if your daughter were discouraged from enrolling in a high school geometry class because girls, on average, have poorer spatial abilities?

Just as average group differences should not be used to predict individual performance, they should not be generalized to groups that have not been studied. Gender-related differences in mathematics achievement among highly gifted students do not hold for nonselected students. Gender-related differences among college students may not hold for the general population. Perhaps most important, there is strong evidence that the magnitude of differences in performance on standardized tests has grown much smaller over the past forty years, perhaps because of greater equality in educational opportunities and greater awareness of the harmful consequences of gender-role limitations (Feingold, 1988). Differences of the past cannot predict the future.

Gender-Related Differences and Social Policy

We have seen that research about gender-related differences is often distorted in press reports, and that these reports have very real effects on girls and their parents (Beckwith, 1984; Eccles & Jacobs, 1986). We have also seen that hypotheses about female inferiority, like the proverbial bad penny, seem to keep turning up, despite lack of evidence (Shields, 1982). We suggest that one useful way to review the material in this chapter is to imagine yourself picking up tomorrow morning's newspaper and reading the following headline: "Reasoning Ability: New Research Shows Boys May Have Genetic Advantage." Using what you have learned about the meaning and measurement of group differences, how would you evaluate this claim? This exercise is not merely academic. Although most readers of this book will not become psychologists, all of you will need to become critical thinkers when reading reports of scientific research.

Rather than focus further research effort on documenting differences, many feminist psychologists have proposed alternative approaches. These include suggestions that psychologists study exceptions to the average, such as girls with very high spatial abilities, and determine what experiences have influenced them and what cognitive strategies they use (Halpern, 1986); focus on how to equalize opportunity for girls (Hyde & Linn, 1986); or explore the social causes of differences (Unger, 1979).

Gender-difference issues are particularly difficult for psychology to deal with, since they depend more on interpretation of the evidence than on the evidence itself. The practice of drawing implications and making policy decisions on the basis of these data introduces further dangers. When a gender-related difference is thought to disadvantage boys, compensatory action is taken. This is less likely to occur when a difference is thought to disadvantage girls. Because it has been believed that boys' poorer verbal abilities make it more difficult for them to learn to read, most elementary textbooks and children's literature are specifically designed to appeal to boys and help them overcome their difficulties. Scott O'Dell, author of the prize-winning children's book *Island of the Blue Dolphins,* has described how he was asked by publishers to change his main character from a girl to a boy. A 1980 teacher education book suggests that the ratio of "boy books" to "girl books" in the elementary school classroom should be two to one (Segel, 1986). Standardized tests may also be designed to appeal to boys and men. In twenty-four recent SAT reading comprehension passages, thirty-four famous men and only one famous woman were named (Rosser, 1987).

Further, little research effort is expended in a search for a "verbal-abilities gene" or other biological determinants of the difference. Nor is the difference seen as a problem for boys in everyday life. There are few books for boys or men on "How to Improve Your Vocabulary and Get Ahead" or "How to Talk to Your Wife." Instead, *women* are encouraged to compensate for men's supposed inability to express themselves, by drawing them out in conversation and by accepting their limitations with grace and understanding. Finally, gender-related differences are not seen as limiting boys' and men's occupational options. It would seem ludicrous for a small average difference in verbal skills to imply that boys could not become successful writers, trial attorneys, English professors, politicians, or editors.

When a gender-related difference *favors* boys, however, a different story unfolds. Consider mathematics achievement. Textbooks and other learning and testing materials remain male-oriented, with problems more likely to have male characters and to be framed in terms of topics likely to interest more boys and men. One widely used test of problem-solving employs eight times as many male as female actors in the problems (Johnson, 1984). Further, there is a tendency to "biologize" the difference in spite of there being no evidence for a "math gene." Men are not encouraged to devise ways to help their women friends improve their mathematics abilities. Instead, women are encouraged to work at overcoming their own "math anxiety." Finally, the average difference is used to explain women's relative absence from certain math-related occupations such as engineering, even though the gender-related difference is much too small to account for the fact that only about 3 percent of engineers are women. Indeed, it seems that the social meaning of a group difference depends on the social position of the "deficient" group.

CONNECTING THEMES

1. What appears to be a "sex difference" may often be a *gender-related* difference. When differences in cognitive abilities and performance emerge, they are always preceded by differences in social environments and experiences. It is more important to analyze and explain the sociocultural (gender) differences than merely describe them as "sex" differences.
2. The concept of "sex difference" may encourage people to think in terms of opposites, although the two sexes are actually much more alike than different. The use of concepts such as field dependence/independence, defining scholastic ability in terms of test scores rather than grades, and defining verbal ability without including communication skills are examples of the power to name.

3. On every cognitive ability or skill ever studied, there is much more variability *within* sex than *between* the sexes. While small differences may exist between men and women on average, the differences among individual women (and men) are much greater. Comparisons of different ethnic and social groups within and across cultures suggest that cognitive diversity is strongly related to sociocultural factors.
4. "Sex differences" in ability and performance are matters of social controversy. History tells us that such differences have often been created and used to keep women "in their place." Some feminist psychologists believe that meta-analysis will allow us to finally answer long-disputed questions about sex differences. Others believe that the search for the definitive differences is futile and psychology should instead concentrate on achieving equity for girls and women in child rearing, education, and testing.

SUGGESTED READINGS

HARE-MUSTIN, RACHEL T., and JEANNE MARECEK (Eds.) (1990). *Making a difference.* New Haven: Yale University Press. A sophisticated analysis of how psychology has represented male and female as oppositions and an argument that it is time to move beyond conceptualizing gender as difference.

RUSSETT, CYNTHIA E. (1989). *Sexual science: The Victorian construct of womanhood.* Cambridge, MA: Harvard University Press. Gender and racial differences were twin obsessions of Victorian science. In a time when women and people of color were demanding civil rights, science was used to "prove" their biological inferiority. The history of this era is fascinating in itself—and also encourages analysis of the political aspects of contemporary sex difference research.

SADKER, MYRA, and DAVID SADKER (1994). *Failing at fairness: How America's schools cheat girls.* New York: Scribner. A very readable and powerful account of sexism in the classroom. The authors, distinguished educational researchers, show how gender bias makes it impossible for girls to receive an education equal to boys.

CHAPTER 4

Images of Women

RELIGIOUS IMAGES OF WOMEN
IMAGES OF WOMEN IN CROSS-CULTURAL PERSPECTIVE
AN INTRODUCTION TO STEREOTYPES
The Definition of Stereotypes
The Measurement of Stereotypes about Women and Men
Stereotypes as Cognitive Categories
Gender Stereotypes in the Mass Media
LANGUAGE AND WOMEN'S PLACE
Images of Women and Men
The Case of the Generic "He"
Disinformation and Sexist Language
STEREOTYPES AS SOCIAL DEMANDS
GENDER STEREOTYPES AND SOCIAL ATTRIBUTIONS
Physical Attractiveness and Social Deviance
Stereotypes about Sexual Orientation and their Implications
The Relationship between Occupational and Gender Stereotypes
Gender as an Attributional Variable
SEX AS A STIMULUS VARIABLE: SOME LIMITATIONS
GROUP DIFFERENCES IN STEREOTYPING
Sex of Subject Effects
Race-Related Differences
Cultural Differences
INDIVIDUAL DIFFERENCES IN SEX STEREOTYPING
THE PERSISTENCE OF STEREOTYPES
Have Stereotypes Changed over Time?
Cognitive Mechanisms in the Maintenance of Stereotypes
When Are Stereotypes Not Maintained?
The Cognitive Approach in Perspective
CONNECTING THEMES
SUGGESTED READINGS

As you can see from the range of pictures in Figure 4.1, womanhood—as well as manhood—is more than a biological or even a social category. Both are culturally imposed ideals by which women and men are measured, whether or not they find these images psychologically congenial. Images of women differ cross-culturally, and they vary within our own culture over time. At any given

FIGURE 4.1. Who is the *real* woman? As you can see, women come in all sizes, colors, and varieties.

point in time, however, the images are seen as having universal meaning. They are used as models by which women (and men) are judged as worthy members of their sex. These idealized images often become anchors for psychological identity and serve as a basis for self-perception and self-esteem (Gilmore, 1990).

Media images of women differ greatly from the pictures of real women that you have just seen. In the media women are portrayed in terms of their bodies much more than men are. They are also judged by more exacting physical and sexual standards. Women who are found deficient or deviant according to media standards may be criticized as immoral and subjected to social penalties. Women who "fail" to meet "minimal" standards of femininity (such as older or disabled women) may be denied a gender identity at all. They are invisible to our culture's images of women.

Although images of women are not constructed in the same way by all societies, you have seen in Chapter 1 that gender is a category that exists in virtually all cultures. Masculinity and femininity, based on easily observable characteristics, constrain the individual's behavior. Most societies tend to exaggerate biological differences by clearly differentiating gender roles and defining the proper behavior of women and men as opposite or complementary. Images of women convey cultural demands. The way a society pictures its women can never be considered trivial or meaningless. Indeed, the "media are the message."

RELIGIOUS IMAGES OF WOMEN

Images of the ideal woman have remained surprisingly consistent over time. For example, the goddesses of ancient Greece embodied qualities still sometimes suggested as desirable in modern women (see Table 4.1) Aphrodite, for example, was seen as every man's sexual fantasy—beautiful, sensual, and infi-

TABLE 4.1. Types of Women

Goddess	Role	Significant Other	Traits
Artemis	Sister Competitor Feminist	Companions (nymphs) Mother Brother	Goal-oriented Independent Forms friendships with women
Athena	Strategist	Father Chosen heroes	Problem-solver Forms strong alliances with men
Hera	Wife	Husband	Commitment Fidelity
Aphrodite	Sensual woman	Lovers	Sensuality Creativity

Source: Adapted from Jean Shinoda Bolen, M. D. 1984. *Goddesses in everywoman.* Copyright © 1984 by Jean Shinoda Bolen, M. D. Reprinted by permission of HarperCollins Publishers, Inc.

nitely available. Artemis, in contrast, was the chaste athlete—every man's "pal." Athena, the Greek goddess of wisdom, would seem to contradict modern conceptions of ideal femininity, and the Greeks appear to have been aware of this paradox: Athena did not have a normal birth or childhood but sprang full-grown from the head of Zeus, the chief god!

This kind of image of woman as part of man can also be found in the creation stories found in the Old Testament. For example, Eve is made from one of Adam's ribs. Interestingly, in Jewish folk tradition, God created Adam and Lilith at the same time, but Lilith refused to be subordinate to Adam and ran away. Lilith became a spirit of evil who seduced men from their wives (Reineke, 1989). In an effort to rehabilitate the image of Lilith as a spirit of independence, a major journal of Jewish feminist thought has been named for her.

Other major religions have also problematized women's sexuality. You are probably all familiar with the image of Mary, the virgin mother of Jesus, but you may be less familiar with Kuan-Yin, the Buddhist goddess of mercy. She became a goddess after earthly tragedies prevented her from becoming a wife and mother (Reineke, 1989). Feminine identity is seen by these religions as formed by childbearing, but female sexuality is seen as polluting. Images of virgin goddesses permit cultures to maintain their negative views of female sexuality and power (Sangren, 1983).

More negative views about women and sexuality are conveyed by Islamic imagery. The religion of Islam explicitly argues that social order depends on careful attention being paid to caste differences based on gender. Men live in the public sphere and worship in the mosque, whereas women remain in the private sphere—the home—where they also pray. If a woman finds that she must leave the seclusion of the home to enter the public sphere (such behavior is discouraged in traditional Islam), she must be veiled from head to toe so that no part of her body is exposed (Smith, 1987).

IMAGES OF WOMEN IN CROSS-CULTURAL PERSPECTIVE

These religious images of women parallel positive and negative values that are still found in different cultures today. In a twenty-five nation study of gender stereotypes, Williams and Best (1990) found that some adjectives were associated with women in all the countries studied. Women were seen as sentimental, submissive, and superstitious. Men were seen as adventurous, forceful, and independent. Stereotypes, however, differed in terms of the religious composition of the country studied. In countries with a high percentage of Catholics, women were viewed more favorably. They were seen as nurturant parents and sources of order. In Muslim countries, images of women and men were more different from each other and stereotypes about women were more unfavorable than those typically found elsewhere.

Cultural images of women may be internalized and used as sources for individual attitudes and beliefs. Images of women and men are conveyed by myths and fairy tales as well as by pictures and religious beliefs. They are acquired without consent or conscious awareness. In all the countries studied, a general developmental pattern was found. The acquisition of gender stereotypes typically begins before the age of 5, accelerates during the early school years, and is completed during adolescence (Williams & Best, 1990). You have probably been unaware of such stereotypes because they are so pervasive. There are few gender-fair or gender-free images with which to contrast them.

AN INTRODUCTION TO STEREOTYPES

Images are communicated in virtually every aspect of everyday life. We see or hear all kinds of depictions of women and men and girls and boys, but we pay little conscious attention to most of them. For example, there was a nursery rhyme that was popular in our childhood that declared:

What are little boys made of?
Sticks and snails and puppy dog tails.
That's what little boys are made of.

What are little girls made of?
Sugar and spice and everything nice.
That's what little girls are made of.

We rarely hear anything so explicitly sexist today, although comments about the physical characteristics of women are still more easily found than similar comments about men. When was the last time you heard remarks such as "Beautiful, but dumb!" or "You can never be too rich or too thin"? To which sex did the remarks refer?

Statements of this sort are stereotypes. Although the word *stereotype* has become part of our everyday language, it has some specific meanings when used by a psychologist. In this chapter we will focus on the cognitive aspects of stereotypes, and we will explore the way that stereotypes are measured and the way they are put together as cognitive constructs. In this connection we will explore the differences between stereotypes about women and men as general categories and stereotypes about various subcategories of men and women. We shall then look at some sources of stereotypes, particularly mass media and language.

Later in the chapter, you will learn about the connections between sex stereotypes and other forms of stereotypes involving physical attractiveness, occupation, race, ethnicity, and sexual preference. Interactions between gender and other kinds of stereotypes may be particularly important in influencing the way one thinks about particular groups of women in our society. In all of this material, the universality and consistency of stereotypes will be stressed.

Next, we will explore differences in gender stereotyping. We will look at how the race and class characteristics of women change stereotypes about them. We will also look at differences between individuals and social groups in the extent to which they stereotype. Last, we shall examine the issue of how stereotypes change. In this final section we will return to the cognitive perspective to explain the persistence of stereotypes and what it implies.

The Definition of Stereotypes

Surprisingly, the term *stereotype* was not invented by a psychologist. It was first used by Walter Lippmann (1922), a noted journalist of his day, to describe a kind of behavior. He defined stereotypes as mainly culturally determined pictures that intrude between an individual's cognitive faculties and his or her perceptions of the world. Lippmann appears to have borrowed the term from a kind of curved printing press in which the type had to be deformed to fit its structure. Stereotyping is still viewed today as a process that distorts reality. However, such distortions are now seen by most psychologists as part of the normal process of concept formation rather than as a form of irrational thought.

Stereotypes occur when individuals are classified by others as having something in common because they are members of a particular group or category of people. The earliest studies of stereotypes by social scientists involved the investigation of attitudes toward religious, racial, or ethnic groups. However, a number of early studies (Fernberger, 1948; Kirkpatrick, 1936; Sheriffs & McKee, 1957) demonstrated that gender stereotypes, defined as consensual beliefs about the different characteristics of men and women, were widely held, persistent, and highly traditional. Gender stereotypes, like other stereotypes, have the following characteristics:

1. Groups that are the targets of stereotypes are easily identified and relatively powerless.
2. It is unclear how much agreement there is between the composite picture of the group and the actual characteristics of members of that group.
3. The misperception appears to be the product of some form of bias in our information-processing mechanisms.
4. The misperception is difficult to modify, even though the people who hold the stereotype have encountered numerous disconfirming examples.
5. Stereotypes imply at least a covert comparison between groups, to the disadvantage of the stereotyped group.
6. People are largely unaware that they stereotype and will deny that they generalize about individuals. They are particularly likely to deny that stereotypes characteristic of their group apply to themselves.
7. Stereotypes are characterized by relatively little variability between individuals in terms of what characteristics they judge to fit the group in question.

Each of these points will be discussed more fully in this chapter. However, the last point is particularly important because it is the consistency and apparent universality of gender stereotypes that make them so dangerous. They are destructive because they influence perceptions independent of the individual characteristics of the stereotyped group. They weigh down these individuals, anchor interactions with them, and hold them back (Fiske, 1993).

Idiosyncratic beliefs are not the same thing as stereotypes. One of our colleagues, for example, believes that there is an inverse relationship between the length of a woman's fingernails and her grade-point average. Although he obviously has a negative bias against women with long nails, we would not consider this a stereotype because it is probably his eccentric perception—one that affects, at most, only some women in his classes.

In contrast, stereotypes are defined by their lack of variability. They are said to exist when the majority of people in a population choose a particular quality as characteristic of a particular group. For example, most people (including many professors) believe that women are less competent in math and science than men. The extent to which this belief influences the way people perceive and evaluate men and women differently may come to influence their relative abilities in these areas (see Chapter 3). Stereotypes appear to be more like forms of social consensus than individual attitudes. The way psychologists measure sex stereotypes illustrates their social nature.

The Measurement of Stereotypes about Women and Men

The classic studies of stereotypes about women and men were conducted in the late 1960s and early 1970s (Broverman, Vogel, Broverman, Clarkson, & Rosenkrantz, 1972). Inge Broverman and her colleagues developed a questionnaire made up of 122 pairs of adjectives that were antonyms—each member of the pair was opposite in meaning from the other. The pairs consisted of words that are commonly used to describe people's personality traits, such as sneaky/direct, passive/active, submissive/dominant, and so forth. Respondents were asked to indicate the extent to which each pair described a normal male, a normal female, and themselves, forcing them to choose between adjectives in describing the target individuals. This methodology is similar to that used in earlier studies of ethnic and religious stereotypes.

If no stereotypes exist, people should assign traits at random and no pattern will emerge. The researchers used a relatively conservative definition of whether or not a trait was gender stereotypic. Items were termed stereotypic only if at least 75 percent of individuals of each sex agreed that the adjective was more descriptive of the average man or woman. Nevertheless, they found high agreement on more than eighty traits about the differing characteristics of women and men. These beliefs were independent of the age, religion, education level, or marital status of the participants. People from a large variety of different groups, when forced to make a choice, select different traits for men and women.

Some patterns in the content of gender stereotypes also emerged. Broverman and her associates found two groups of traits that were highly associated with each other and with a particular sex—an *instrumental* dimension considered to be characteristic of typical males, and an *affective* dimension considered to be characteristic of typical females. Instrumentality included traits such as active, objective, independent, aggressive, direct, unemotional, dominant, and competent. These traits appear to describe a person who can manipulate the world effectively. Affective traits included warm, expressive, and sensitive. These traits appear to describe a person who is concerned about and nurturant of others and cares more for people than for things.

As you can see from the traits cited, there were more traits associated with typical males than with typical females, and a greater number of masculine traits were considered socially desirable. Typical feminine traits were also considered more childlike than typical masculine traits, whereas masculine and adult traits were seen as essentially identical in nature. This connection between femininity and immaturity reappears in a number of ways in studies on perceptions of women. It can have a negative impact when people make decisions about women's suitability for managerial careers (see Chapter 12).

Stereotypes as Cognitive Categories

These studies produced a great deal of discussion and criticism. First, they were criticized in terms of methodology. People may only stereotype when they are forced to; that is, the methodology used to measure stereotypes may actually produce them. This is because traditional methods of studying stereotypes require people to choose descriptive terms from a largely negative set of adjectives. Since respondents must make a choice, they may fall back on traditional cultural stereotypes in which they do not believe. They have no choice but to select one of the trait pairs as characteristic of males or females.

Second, gender-stereotype studies have been criticized in terms of their choice of descriptors. Trait stereotypes may be too narrow to define men and women. In other words, when we think about females and males we are thinking about more than their personality traits alone. Other characteristics such as roles, behaviors, and physical appearance are closely related to perceptions about gender in our society (Spence, Deaux, & Helmreich, 1985).

And, finally, early gender-stereotype studies have been criticized for using as referents only the terms *woman* and *man*. Stereotypes about all men and all women may be too general. More meaningful associations may be found when researchers examine perceptions about various subtypes of women and men. This criticism is particularly important because most of the target individuals used in such studies are white and middle-class. Thus, the studies assume not only that "male" and "female" are universal categories, but also that beliefs about white middle-class heterosexual women and men are the norm. Other groups of people have been rendered invisible. All of these criticisms led to further research on stereotypes.

Instead of forcing them to choose between two polar opposites in their characterization of men and women, Kay Deaux (Deaux & Lewis, 1984) asked college students to list all the characteristics they thought were pertinent to males and females. They found that people used role behaviors (financial provider, meal preparer), physical characteristics (sturdy, graceful), and occupations (construction worker, telephone operator) as well as personality traits. Perceptions in these different areas were closely associated with each other for a given sex. For example, women were seen as taking care of children and having small bones, as well as being warm and emotional. Stereotypes about females and males appear to consist of a tight network of associations that extends to virtually all aspects of human beings.

Suppose you were asked to list the attributes of *mother*. What would you say? In a subsequent study, Kay Deaux and her associates (Deaux, Winton, Crowley & Lewis, 1985) asked people to list attributes for various subtypes of women and men. Instead of views of men and women as general categories, the researchers were interested in perceptions of the sexes in terms of their different roles, such as *mother* and *father* or *grandmother* and *grandfather*. This kind of research can help to determine whether a particular component of the network of associations connected to sex is more important in the generation of sex stereotypes than sex as a global category is. In more specific terms, the kind of question asked is, Are women seen as warmer than men because they are perceived as mothers (a social role they occupy) rather than because they are women (the more global category)?

The researchers found that the same number of associations was generated for each label. No one category (sex, social role, etc.) appears to be more perceptually important than any other. By measuring the extent to which the same term appeared on lists with different labels, the researchers were able to calculate the degree of perceptual association between labels. For example, they found that the degree of overlap between *mother* and *parent* ($r = .64$) was significantly greater than that between *father* and *parent* ($r = .39$). Similarly, the description of *woman* was closer to descriptions of *mother* and *grandmother* than the description of *man* was to *father*. There was no relationship between the description of *man* and *grandfather*. In other words, the extent to which people use the same words to describe various aspects of women or men indicates what these words mean to them. These studies suggest that relational roles are very meaningful in conceptions of women but much less so for conceptions about men.

The same technique was also used to measure the beliefs about four subtypes of women and men who had frequently appeared in previous lists generated by college students. The four subtypes of women were housewife, athletic woman, businesswoman, and sexy woman. The four subtypes of men were athletic man, blue-collar working man, businessman, and macho man. Deaux and her associates found that the same number of terms was generated for each subcategory. The most frequent concepts generated for each type may be found in Table 4.2. Male targets were all viewed as equally unlikely to engage in female occupations or to have female physical characteristics. They were all seen as equally likely to perform masculine role behaviors and *not* to perform feminine role behaviors.

Each of the four female subtypes showed substantial variation from the generic *woman* and from each other. Businesswomen, for example, were viewed as more likely to engage in masculine roles and to have masculine traits. At the same time, they were seen as less likely to engage in feminine roles, to have female physical characteristics, or to have feminine traits. In contrast, housewives were seen as high in terms of their possession of feminine role behaviors and low for both male and female occupations and masculine traits. The housewife stereotype appears to bear the closest resemblance to people's global stereotypes about women in general (Eckes, 1994).

There are three important conclusions to be drawn from these data. First, stereotypes about particular types of women and men appear to be just as strong as stereotypes about men and women as global categories. Second, stereotypes about women appear to be more strongly differentiated than stereotypes about men. Men are like each other and not like women. Third, perceptions about the sexes appear to be conceived in terms of opposites. Men and

TABLE 4.2. Most Frequent Attributes Associated with Concepts

Woman	*Man*
Attractive	Strong
Feminine	Hides feelings
Smart	Acts macho
Sensitive	Sexy
Emotional	Muscular
Housewife	*Blue-collar working man*
Cleans things	Factories
Cooks	Hard worker
Takes care of kids	Middle-lower class
Motherly	Uneducated
Busy	Union member
Athletic woman	*Athletic man*
Muscular	Muscular
Good body	Healthy
Strong	Strong
Aggressive	In shape
Masculine	Good body
Sexy woman	*Macho man*
Good figure	Muscular
Long hair	Hairy chest
Good dresser	Moustache
Nail polish	Attractive
Pretty face	Self-centered
Businesswoman	*Businessman*
Smart	Wears suits
Nice clothes	Office with view
Unmarried	College education
Hard-working	Smart
Organized	Good appearance

Source: K. Deaux, W. Winston, M. Crowley, & L. L. Lewis (1985). Level of categorization and content of gender stereotypes. *Social Cognition*, 3, 145–167. Copyright © 1985. Reprinted by permission of Guilford Publications, Inc.

women are seen to have contrasting qualities even when respondents' choices are not constrained.

Because in real life women and men possess a number of characteristics that are not always consistent with each other, you may wonder when people abandon their stereotypes. In a final part of their study, Deaux and Lewis (1984) used the various characteristics generated in previous studies to determine how consistently stereotypical patterns were inferred. For example, they might state that a woman had a gender-characteristic role such as housewife and ask respondents to estimate how probable it was that she had a gender-related physical characteristic such as gracefulness. For other respondents, the relationship was reversed; for example, they might be given a physical label and asked to infer a social role. They found that if a man was described in terms of feminine traits such as emotional, kind, and helpful to others, people generally assumed that he engaged in feminine role behaviors and had feminine physical characteristics. Similarly, female athletes were assumed to have a more masculine appearance and masculine personality traits. In other words, gender stereotypes are "all of a piece."

Physical characteristics appear to be much more important than traits, roles, or behaviors in triggering stereotypes. This should not surprise you if you consider the fact that physical appearance is the first information people have when they meet a new person. Information about appearance is acquired within the first one-tenth of a second of seeing someone (Locher, Unger, Sociedade, & Wahl, 1993). The perception occurs so rapidly that people seem to be unaware of how much information they have acquired. Therefore, they tend to deny the extent to which physical appearance influences their perceptions of others. The importance of first impressions helps explain why there are few important differences among people in terms of the extent to which they stereotype the sexes (Wallston & O'Leary, 1981). Women and men appear to be remarkably similar in terms of the extent to which they see men and women as different.

In sum, current studies suggest that categorization based on gender is one of the main ways social reality is organized. Because of the network of associations linked by gender, a characteristic from one area may cue inferences in an apparently distinct conceptual arena. People have little awareness of the extent to which sex stereotypes influence their evaluations of others and little opportunity to disconfirm these beliefs because they are both unrecognized and universally shared.

Gender Stereotypes in the Mass Media

Since gender stereotypes appear to be internally coherent and consistently found despite the many ways in which people differ from each other, you may ask how we acquire such information. During the 1970s, researchers documented the existence of stereotypes in virtually every aspect of the communications media (Busby, 1975). Stereotypes were found in children's picture books, story books, and textbooks (see Chapter 7). They were found in the movies, on television, and in magazine fiction. Stereotypes were evident in the disproportionate number of males to females portrayed, the gender-specificity of the traits that individuals of each sex displayed, the limited behavioral roles of women compared with the roles of men, the smaller number of occupations in which women could be found, and the different physical characteristics associated with each sex (Unger, 1979a). Unfortunately, as you shall see next, it is still easy to document the existence of stereotypes in the media, and the forms they take are remarkably similar to those demonstrated in earlier studies.

Comic Strips

Sex stereotypes in the comics pages of newspapers may be particularly insidious. Because we do not take this kind of material seriously, we may be unaware of the sexist message we are receiving. Comics are also one aspect of the media easily accessible to young children. Images of men and women on the comics pages are still seriously distorted. Males appear more frequently as both central and minor characters. The most invisible women of all are ethnic minority women: Black women appear in less than 10 percent of Sunday comic

Adam® **by Brian Basset**

FIGURE 4.2. A recent example of sex stereotyping that shows how the funnies can offer a serious message.
Source: Adam © 1994 Universal Press Syndicate. Reprinted with permission. All rights reserved.

strips; when they do appear they speak little and/or in stereotypic ways (Etter-Lewis, 1988).

Only 4 percent of all women depicted in comic strips are in the labor force, as compared with 69 percent of the men (Chavez, 1985). A much larger number of occupations are shown for men. In an analysis of 100 randomly chosen comic strips, Chavez found the following occupations for men: travel guide, bartender, salesperson, general, information clerk, court jester, vicar, doctor, king, Viking, sergeant, cook, farmer, wizard, and flutist, as compared with two occupations for women: bank teller and secretary.

Another study by Sarah Brabant and Linda Mooney (1986) examined the same three Sunday comics ("Blondie," "The Born Loser," and "Dennis the Menace") that Brabant had examined ten years earlier. These strips were originally chosen because each included a married couple as central characters. As in the first study, women continued to appear less frequently (women or girls appeared in 59 percent of the comics and men or boys in 74.4 percent) and to remain in the home more often than men. There was no indication at either time that any of the women were employed outside the home. Passive behavior and home or child care were still the most frequently portrayed activities of women. Men were found in leisure activities 20 percent more frequently than women. The only major change over the ten-year period was that women were shown wearing aprons less often. Nevertheless, Alice of "Dennis the Menace" (the only protagonist with a young child) was shown wearing an apron 25 percent of the time.

The same two researchers (Mooney & Brabant, 1987) have also investigated more contemporary comic strips in which the wife is portrayed as working outside the home ("Hi and Lois," "For Better or for Worse," and "Sally Forth") to determine if these comics differed from more traditional strips in terms of activities, speaking appearances, and images portrayed. Even in these less traditional comic strips, husbands were more likely to be portrayed outside the home than wives were. Paradoxically, women characters who work outside the home were also *more* likely to be shown in both child and home care than full-time wives and mothers. Conversely, husbands of women who worked outside the home were shown less often in home care than husbands of nonemployed women and were never pictured taking care of the children. The image of career women in these comics was not favorable. They were shown as critical, worrying a great deal, and having stressful, sleepless nights.

Comics
News

Women in the News

Women are much less often featured in the news media than men are. One recent comprehensive survey looked at the front pages of ten major- and ten small-market newspapers in various parts of the United States (Hernandez, 1994). It found that men were referred to or solicited for comment on the newspapers' front pages 75 percent of the time (a decrease from the previous year's 85 percent). Women were referred to or quoted on the front pages only 25 percent of the time (the highest figure recorded during the six years that the survey has been conducted). Most of the front-page stories were written by men (67 percent, as were the op-ed or equivalent pieces (72 percent).

Women were portrayed negatively much more often than men in both small and large newspapers (30 percent versus 12 percent). Even the positive images of women and men were not equivalent. Nearly half (49 percent) of the positive portrayals of women in the major market papers (like the *New York Times* or the *Washington Post*) featured women as entertainers, whereas 82 percent of the positive portrayals of men were as authorities, experts, or opinion makers.

When mentioned at all, women's appearance is commented upon more frequently than that of comparable men. News articles treat males and females differently, mentioning the physical appearance and clothing of women much more often than those of men, no matter what the news story is about (Foreit et al., 1980). As examples of this kind of trivialization of women in the public sphere, the media discussed what length robes Sandra Day O'Connor would wear when she was selected for the Supreme Court and what kind of suits and haircut were appropriate for Geraldine Ferraro in her debates for the vice-presidency of the United States. More recently, the news media focused on Ruth Bader Ginsburg's diminutive stature in stories about her Supreme Court nomination. In contrast, it is difficult to recollect any physical feature possessed by the seven male members of the Court.

Images of women in sports are particularly likely to be distorted by the media when they can be found at all. In 1990, for example, stories on men's sports outnumbered those on women's sports twenty-three to one in four of the top-selling newspapers in the United States (Messner, Duncan, & Jensen, 1993). Messner and his colleagues also found that male and female athletes were even named differently in stories about them. Women athletes were most likely to be called by their first names, followed by black men athletes. Only white male athletics were routinely referred to by their last names.

Media images of men athletes tend to glorify their strength and power, even their violence. In contrast, media images of women athletes focus on feminine beauty and grace (so they are not really athletes; see Figure 4.3) or on their thin, small, wiry, androgynous bodies (so they are not really women) (Lorber, 1993).

In coverage of the Olympics, detailed attention is paid to women gymnasts,

FIGURE 4.3. Female athletes are not portrayed the same way male athletes are. Note how this photograph in a national news magazine highlights this young woman's weakness and emotional vulnerability.

figure skaters, swimmers, and divers rather than women's basketball, speed skating, or track and field. As Judith Lorber suggests:

> Extraordinary feats by women athletes who are presented as mature adults might force sports organizers and audiences to rethink their stereotypes of women's capabilities, the way elves, mermaids, and ice queens do not (p. 573).

When women athletes are powerful rather than sexy, they may not be treated well by either the media or sports viewers. Both Midori Ito and Tonya Harding were passed over by judges in the 1990 Olympics for more feminine but less powerful skaters. The media appear to have gone to extreme lengths to find photographs of Harding that showed her as unfeminine and unattractive (see Figure 4.4).

Women are stereotyped in American newspapers in terms of roles as well as physical appearance. Does the following newspaper item raise your eyebrows?

> Can a feisty 41-year-old father of four teenagers who has a master's degree from Harvard University restore the faded image of Norway's Labor Party government and win a general election in September?

FIGURE 4.4. When female athletes cannot be portrayed as weak, they may be portrayed as unattractive and unfeminine.

It appeared in the *Los Angeles Times* with only one word changed. (We don't think you will have much trouble figuring out which one.) The role of spouse or mother is still far more salient for women; in contrast, men appear in newspapers largely in terms of their sports activity or professional roles (Luebke, 1989).

There is some evidence to suggest that the way the media treat women candidates for public office influences perceptions about their suitability for these offices. When simulated newspaper descriptions of female candidates for various political offices were varied in terms of the degree to which they highlighted gender (e. g., words like "she" or "woman" were used rather than gender-neutral pronouns and the word "person"), women were more negatively evaluated for the positions of sheriff or town clerk (Dayhoff, 1983). The only position for which gendered language led to more positive evaluation of a female candidate was when she was seeking the presidency of the League of Women Voters.

Pictorial Images of Women and Men

Every time you turn on your TV you get a dose of sexism. It has been estimated that the average American adult watches about four hours of television per day (Comstock, 1991). Sexist biases in both children's and adult television programs have been demonstrated repeatedly (Davis, 1990; Signorielli, 1989). Biases take the usual form of a larger representation of men than women. A recent study found, for example, that 57 percent of all the characters on comedy shows are men, and this figure rises to 71 percent in action/adventure shows (Davis, 1990). Female characters are usually younger than male characters by an average of ten years. This age difference is dramatically illustrated in one of the findings of this study—men are four times more likely than women to have gray hair.

This double standard of aging, in which pictured women appear younger than men, has not decreased because of the women's movement (England, Kuhn, & Gardner, 1981). There was no change in the percentages of female models who were suggestively or partially clad, or nude, in magazine advertisements from 1964 to 1984 (Solely & Kurzbard, 1986). A look at current issues of magazines or an evening in front of your TV will show you how much sexism persists in spite of twenty years of modern feminism (see Figure 4.5). Contrast these images with those of the real women shown in the beginning of the chapter!

Women are less likely to be portrayed as working outside the home than men, yet few are housewives (Signorielli, 1989). Almost 40 percent of the women could not be classified by occupation as compared with 18 percent of the men. On the other hand, home, family, and marital status were much more likely to be developed in the characterization of women than men. These results are similar to those found in analyses of movies, where roles for women are also rigidly prescribed (Levy, 1990).

Compared with other TV genres, soap operas are more likely to include women characters who are normally excluded because of their age, appearance, or status. However, some groups of women are still excluded. Soap operas, because their plot lines often involve the family and community and close friendships among women based on their shared experiences, have difficulty incorporating both ethnic minority and lesbian characters (Geraghty, 1991).

Images of Attractiveness. Gender stereotyping on television commercials may be greater than in programming. For example, some form of attractiveness message was observed in one out of every 3.8 commercials (Downs & Harrison, 1985). Women were far more likely than men to be associated with attractiveness messages and with commercials involving a domestic setting. However, male voice-overs (more than 90 percent) continued to provide the voice of authority (Bretl & Cantor, 1988).

Women are about four times more likely to be provocatively dressed on television than men are (Davis, 1990). Women are particularly likely to be presented as sex objects in advertisements delivered during weekend afternoon sportscasts whose audience is primarily men (Craig, 1992). Women in these weekend ads are almost never shown without an accompanying man. When they are not models or sex objects, they are generally shown in roles subservient to men—as hotel receptionists, secretaries, or flight attendants.

One recent SONY commercial produced a large number of complaints from women viewers (Goldman, 1993). It was shown primarily on MTV and all-sports ESPN and featured an emotionless stud draped over a white convertible.

FIGURE 4.5. Another form of sex stereotyping in photographs is to focus on the sexuality of various parts of the female body.

As he punched a button on his disc player, the female names appeared—each accompanied by a scantily clad attractive woman. The final shot showed all of the women sitting in or lying on the car with a slogan "If you play it, they will come."

Similar images have been found in Australian, British, and Italian television advertisements. For example, 13 percent of the female central figures in the

TABLE 4.3. The Oscar-Winning Roles by Gender and Occupation

Men (Best and Supporting)			*Women (Best and Supporting)*		
Occupation	N	Percent	Occupation	N	Percent
Soldier	15	13.8	Actress	16	14.7
Sheriff	9	8.3	Prostitute	13	11.9
Criminal	9	8.3	Heiress	4	3.7
Politician	7	6.4	Teacher	4	3.7
Actor	7	6.4	Artist	4	3.7
Writer	7	6.4	Hotel proprietress	4	3.7
Laborer	7	6.4	Farmer's wife	4	3.7
Businessman	6	5.5	Secretary	4	3.7
Lawyer	5	4.5	Businesswoman	3	2.7
Journalist	5	4.5	Queen	3	2.7
Prizefighter	4	3.7	Politician	3	2.7
Priest	3	2.8	Nurse	2	1.8
Teacher	3	2.8	Seamstress	2	1.8
Scientist	2	1.8	Maid	2	1.8
King	1	0.9			
Other	15	13.8	Other	4	3.7
No gainful work	4	3.7	No gainful work	37	34.0
Total	109	100.0	Total	109	100.0

Source: From Emmanuel Levy, Stage, sex and suffering of women in American films, *Empirical Studies of the Arts, 8*, 53–76. Copyright © 1990 Baywood Publishing Company Incorporated. Reprinted with permission.

United States were sex objects (compared with 2 percent for men). In Australia, 91 percent of the voice-overs (sources of authority) were male (Mazzella, Durkin, Cerini, & Buralli, 1992). No change in gender stereotypes in British TV advertising has occurred over the past ten years (Furnham & Bitar, 1993).

Images of Power. Subtle interactions between the sex of central television figures and the roles they play are important. An early, classic study by Sarah Sternglanz and Lisa Serbin (1974) showed that major female characters in television shows popular with children were more likely than comparable male characters to be portrayed as having supernatural abilities. They suggested that this difference indicated an unwillingness to portray females as having direct power. Although some male figures have supernatural powers as well—like Superman—men are more likely to be portrayed as resolving situations through their strength or intelligence. What female hero is comparable to Dick Tracy or Indiana Jones?

Through the use of magic, women can be shown to manipulate others without them being aware of it. An examination of current television programming reveals that some shows like "Bewitched" and "I Dream of Jeannie" are still present on TV as reruns. Thus, children are still being exposed to unrealistic role models. If a woman cannot be a corporation president on TV, she can be a witch! Aside from the negative connotations of witchcraft in our society, "one can imagine the shock to the little girls at the age of 10 or so when they realize that witchcraft is not really a viable career" (Sternglanz & Serbin, 1974, p. 714).

Images of Sexuality. Probably the most overtly sexist images of women and men are presented on MTV. One recent study (Sommers-Flanagan, Sommers-Flanagan, & Davis, 1993) analyzed the characteristics of men and women on forty videos presented on music television. They found that men engaged in significantly more aggressive and dominant behavior; women engaged in significantly more implicitly sexual and subservient behavior; and women were more frequently the object of explicit, implicit, and aggressive sexual advances. They suggest that viewers are given the message that romance, sexual attraction, and sexually suggestive activity are central human activities.

Music videos aimed at predominately African-American rather than white audiences also feature men more than women. The situation may be slightly less dismal for black than for white women. For example, one group of researchers found only 11 percent of the featured singers or band leaders in videos aimed at a white audience were women, whereas 19 percent of the videos aired on Black Entertainment Television featured women (Brown & Campbell, 1986). It would be difficult to say, however, that blacks are less sexist in this area than whites. The level of sexual aggression and derogation aimed at women in gangsta rap music (which is more popular with African Americans) is enormous. Women are frequently called bitches or ho's and images of rape or assault are common. Many African Americans are furious about these kind of lyrics and are pressuring rap groups to "clean up their act."

Some of the worst images of women of color are found in pornography. Although pornography treats women in general as mere objects for male sexuality (see Chapter 14), women of color are treated even more negatively than white women. For example, white women are seen as objects, whereas black women are portrayed as animals. Animals may be treated more harshly than objects. They can be "economically exploited, worked, sold, killed, and consumed" (Collins, 1993b). In an analysis of X-rated videos, Gloria Cowan (1995) found that black women received a significantly greater number of acts of verbal and physical aggression than white women did. Asian-American women are also stereotyped in pornography, but their image is one of a "special sexuality" that is both more exotic and more subservient than that of women from other ethnic groups (Root, 1995). Over the past century there have been many portraits of Asian women as prostitutes, ranging from *Madame Butterfly* through *Suzy Wong* to today's *Miss Saigon.* The media exploit such images even when they purport to expose them. The *Time* cover in Figure 4.6 received a large number of letters objecting to this image of an Asian prostitute.

Magazines and Romantic Fiction

Subtle messages about gender roles are also present in both the fiction and nonfiction presented in women's magazines. Although a large number of the women profiled in established magazines such as *Harper's Bazaar, Ladies Home Journal, Vogue, Cosmopolitan, Redbook,* and *Woman's Day* work full-time for pay,

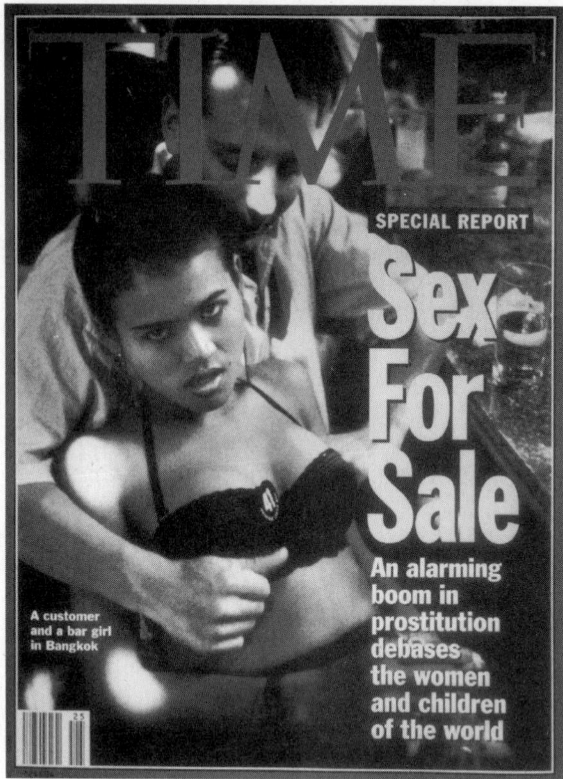

FIGURE 4.6. When photos depict women of color, they may be more brutal than photos of white women. *Time* magazine received many letters complaining about the racism and pornography in this cover photograph.

they are still more likely to be found in traditional occupations (Ruggiero & Weston, 1985). They are also less likely than women profiled in newer magazines (*Savvy, Ms, Working Woman,* and *New Woman*) to perceive themselves as having responsibility, power, or influence in relation to their jobs.

In her review of many studies of fiction in the mass media directed at women, Muriel Cantor (1987) found that the basic message is that sexual relationships are central and all-important in women's lives—more important than family, children, or career at the individual level and, of course, more important than politics, the economy, or war and peace at the societal level. This material is class- as well as sex-biased. Thus, in *True Story,* a women's magazine aimed at working-class readers, 35 percent of the stories are about sexuality. However, sexual drive is portrayed as male, not female, and rape and attempted rape are frequent themes. A contradiction that is presented in these stories is that although women must be careful of men's darker nature, they also need men to take care of them. Only one rape story appeared in *Redbook,* a magazine aimed at middle-class women. Cantor suggests that the fear of rape is used as a way of controlling the behavior of working-class women. In all the stories involving rape the woman was either in the "wrong place," had chosen not to accept advice, or had acted too independently.

These magazines even prescribe specific aspects of female attractiveness such as hair color. Researchers who examined the cover models for two women's magazines (*Ladies Home Journal* and *Vogue*) from the fifties through the eighties found many more blonds than would be found in the normal population (Rich & Cash, 1993). Blonds were even more common in *Playboy,* where they comprised 50 percent of the centerfold models. In this magazine blondness seems to be synonymous with sexuality as well as beauty. Of course, it is even more impossible for women of color to attain this standard of beauty than it is for most Caucasian women.

Face-ism and Body-ism

The pictures of women and men in magazines are even more sex biased than what is written about them. In a creative series of studies of visual representations of females and males, Dane Archer and his associates found ample evidence of a phenomenon that they have termed *face-ism* (Archer et al., 1983). They measured the distance from the top of the head to the lowest part of the chin as a numerator and the distance from the top of the head to the lowest visible part of the body shown as the denominator to produce an index of relative facial prominence in the representation of the two sexes. This index varied from .00 (no face shown) to 1.0 (only the face was shown). The higher this index, the greater the relative emphasis of the head versus the body. (Although they term the phenomenon face-ism, this term shows some androcentric bias. The "face-ism" of men actually reflects the "body-ism" of women.)

The face-ism index was used to examine 1,750 published photographs from at least twelve issues of each of five American periodicals: *Time, Newsweek, Ms,* the *San Francisco Chronicle,* and a small city newspaper, the *Santa Cruz Sentinel.* Of the eligible photos (they had to be of people by themselves, and not aimed at selling a particular product), with *Ms* excluded, more than 70 percent were of men. More women than men were found in ads than in news stories. The average facial index of men was .65, whereas for women it was only .45. The latter figure means that less than one-half of each photo was devoted to the woman's face. In contrast, two-thirds of each photo was devoted to the man's face.

A comparison of 3,500 photos in publications from eleven different countries also showed a greater amount of facial prominence in photographs of men. An analysis of paintings from the last six centuries indicated that sex-related differences in face-ism have been present from the seventeenth century and have increased over time. The greatest differences were found in twentieth-century artwork. When men and women students were asked to draw men and women, both sexes drew pictures in which the man's face was significantly more prominent than the woman's face (more facial detail was also provided in drawings of men). Finally, Archer and his associates asked students to rate stimulus photographs of men and women in one of two versions. Photos were identical except for variations in facial prominence. They found that photographs of either women or men with high facial prominence received more favorable ratings on intelligence, ambition, and physical appearance than the same photographs with low facial prominence.

Archer and his associates argue that visual representations may contribute to our conception of what is unique about the two sexes. Concepts of intellect, personality, and character are associated with the face, and the face is given more importance for men than for women. In contrast, qualities associated with the body are weight, physique, and emotion. Women's bodies are more salient than those of men. These images contribute to and perpetuate stereotypes about what is important about men and women.

Stereotypes in the images of women and men have not changed as a result of the women's movement. An examination of *Time, Newsweek, Ms,* and *Good Housekeeping* revealed that men still received greater facial prominence than women in photographs in these magazines (Nigro, Hill, Gelbein, & Clark, 1988). A recent study of photographs in various news magazines (*Time, Newsweek, Life,* and *U.S. News and World Report*) found higher face-ism scores for whites than blacks as well as for men as compared to women (Zuckerman & Kieffer, 1994). Black women had the lowest face-ism scores of all the groups. A similar effect for race was found in European news magazines (although there were not enough photos of black women to compare the effects of sex and race).

Face-ism was also found in portraits. Whites had significantly higher facial prominence scores than blacks. The facial prominence of American Indians was even lower than that of blacks. Although the researchers could not find enough portraits of women to analyze for effects, they did find significant facial prominence differences between women and men on postage stamps, despite the small sample of women portrayed.

The face-ism scores of women were lower than those of men even when differences in status were held constant. Although effects were not produced by status, they do contribute to people's perceptions about the relative importance of various groups. Targets were viewed as more dominant when depicted in high face-ism rather than low face-ism photographs. This effect was not moderated by any other factor. It is difficult to determine whether face-ism is a cause or an effect of gender stereotypes. For example, evaluations of women's attractiveness have been found to be based on both their faces and their bodies, whereas evaluations of men's attractiveness were based on their faces alone (Raines, Hechtman, & Rosenthal, 1990).

The Impact of Media Sexism

Stereotypes implicitly enacted but never explicitly articulated in TV commercials may inhibit women's achievement aspirations. Florence Geis and her associates tested this hypothesis by having college students of both sexes view replicas of four current gender-stereotypical commercials or four replicas that were identical except that gender roles were reversed (Geis, Brown, Jennings, & Porter, 1984). After viewing the commercials, all subjects wrote essays imagining their lives "ten years from now." Women who had viewed the traditional commercials de-emphasized achievement in favor of homemaking, more than men and more than women who had viewed the reversed role commercials.

Other studies have found a direct connection between TV viewing and acceptance of stereotypical roles. Heavy television viewers have been found to give more sexist responses to questions about the roles of men and women than people who watched less TV (Signorielli, 1989). People who watch a larger number of stereotyped programs also tend to describe themselves in more gender-stereotypic terms (Ross, Anderson & Wisocki, 1982). This relationship remained even when the frequency of television watching was taken into account.

What can we learn from all these studies of stereotypes in the mass media? Gaye Tuchman (1978) used the term *symbolic annihilation* to describe the media's portrayal of women. The term refers to their underrepresentation , their trivialization as adornments or ornaments, and the condemnation they receive when portrayed outside of rigidly prescribed roles. Some groups of women are more invisible than others. For example, women of color are virtually absent from magazine advertisements (see Table 4.4). Probably the most elaborate form of annihilation was found in the ultraorthodox Jewish press of Israel. One photograph of a woman politician was reported to have been altered to resemble that of a man (Jerusalem Report, 1993).

Negative biases against women in the visual media may be particularly effective both for creating and evoking stereotypes because people are less likely to monitor their responses to pictures than to words. After all, it's just entertainment!

The consistency and stability of images of women and men may lead people to believe that there is a social consensus about gender roles. The universality of these images may help to explain why (as you will see later in this chapter) relatively few individual differences in gender stereotyping have been found.

LANGUAGE AND WOMEN'S PLACE

Images of Women and Men

Analyses of the English language also demonstrate persistent negative biases against women. Various forms of debasement that have occurred in female-gender words have been traced (Schultz, 1975). The mildest form appears to be democratic leveling whereby the female member of a word pair that was previously reserved for people in high places comes to refer to people at any level of society. For example, the word *lord* still refers to the deity and a few Englishmen, while anyone may call herself a *lady*. Other examples of this process are *sir/madam* and *master/mistress*. In the last two examples, the female terms have been debased into words with sexual connotations. Whether a woman is a *madam* or a *mistress*, her identity is still based on her relationship with men as a sex object.

Terms of endearment addressed to females have also undergone debasement. Dolly and Tootsie, for example, began as pet names derived from nicknames but eventually acquired the meaning of mistress or prostitute. A *tart* was originally a small pie or pastry, then a term of endearment; next it became a term applied to young women who were sexually desirable, then to those who were deemed careless of their morals, and, finally, it is a word meaning women of the street. Words denoting boys and young men have failed to undergo the debasement that has commonly occurred in terms referring to girls or women.

Metaphors and labels are likely to have wide reference when applied to men and to be narrower, with sexual connotations, when applied to women (Lakoff, 1975). For example, if one states that a man is a professional, one is suggesting that he is a practitioner of a respected occupation. If one calls a woman a professional, one may be implying that she is practicing "the oldest profession." Other terms of the same sort include *tramp* (a male drifter but a female prostitute) and *game* (a male dupe but a female who is seducible).

To a surprising extent, terms referring to women resemble those referring to children. Excluding any negative connotations, words like *doll, honey, pussycat,* and *baby* can apply equally well to women or children (particularly girl children). Our language, like our culture, equates adulthood with manhood (Graham, 1975). The most popular image of women in popular songs is childlike (Cooper, 1985). There is a clear demarcation between the words *boy* and *man* that does not exist between *girl* and *woman.* A boy greatly increases his status when he becomes a man, while a girl is seen as losing status and bargaining power when her youth is lost. Language echoes gender stereotypes when it encourages females to cling to girlhood as long as possible. In the words of a popular cigarette ad, "You've come a long way, baby!" One could argue that if women had really "come a long way," the media would no longer be calling them "baby."

Power relationships between men and women are reflected in gender-specific slang vocabulary too. College-age men listed a far larger total number of sex-related slang expressions than comparable women did (Kutner & Brogan, 1974). They used many more words equating women with sexual objects. In fact, the score for female- versus male-related terms referring to sexuality was seventy-nine to five. Words that refer to women, such as *pussy, chick, cookie,* and *honey,* often emphasize their animal-like nature or their edibility. There are few similar words for men. If you find the results of this study outdated, ask your friends to generate some words. We believe your results will be similar to those found by professional researchers more than fifteen years ago.

Derogatory names are more likely to be aimed at women from ethnic outgroups. In a historical inventory of terms for women of various ethnic groups, seventy-three of ninety-six terms aimed at twenty different ethnic groups were interracial, and sixty-one of these interracial terms were directed at women of color (Allen, 1984). Negative terms alluded to stereotyped physical differences between the groups (in terms of color, hair texture, or shape of eyes), made derogatory sexual allusions, or used food and animal metaphors.

Some of the mechanisms that operate in the linguistic distortion of gender-specific words have been described (Graham, 1975):

1. Labeling of what is considered to be an exception to the rule—*woman doctor, male nurse, career girl.* The term *feminine logic* is a particularly sexist example of this process.
2. Trivializing female gender forms—*poetess, suffragette* (instead of suffragist), and, more recently, *libber.*
3. "His virtue is her vice"—*mannish attire* or *aggressive female.*
4. Exclusion, which may be the most pervasive mechanism of all. The use of *man* in its extended sense, as in *mankind* or "the child is father to the man," may be one of the major sources of the lack of relationship between perceptions of women and perceptions of adults.

The Case of the Generic "He"

One of the issues that have been raised about the English language by feminists is the extent to which the use of nouns such as *mankind* and "generic" pronouns such as *he* for both sexes perpetuates sex biases. It is clear that these supposedly neutral linguistic usages are not perceptually neutral. For example, when undergraduates read sentences aloud that used either *he, he/she,* or *they* and verbally described the images that came to mind, both sexes produced a disproportionate number of male images to the supposedly generic *he* (Gastil, 1990). Male students also gave male images when *he/she* was used. Only *they* appeared to function as a true generic pronoun.

Another study in this area (Wilson & Ng, 1988) had students read sentences using either masculine ("All men are created equal") or feminine ("The feminists protested outside the town hall") generic terms. Photographs of men's and women's faces were presented very quickly (just at the threshold of perception) while each sentence remained in constant view on the screen. The researchers found that use of the male generic sentences (but not the female ones) produced a significantly greater number of identifications of the ambiguous face as male.

Use of the generic pronoun "he" seems to make men and women think of males first, even when the context implies both sexes (Gastil, 1990; Moulton, Robinson, & Elias, 1978). However, all these studies refer to the generation of images rather than to some direct evidence of the effect of sex-biased language on behavior. Nancy Henley (1989) reviewed all the available evidence on the question of how well *he* and *man* perform their generic role and are interpreted as referring to women as well as men. After examining twenty studies in which people of various ages—from 6 years to adult—were presented with the masculine form used for both sexes, she concluded that the pictures selected or drawn, the names used for the persons referred to, the subjects of stories, the answers to questions about the sex of the people referred to in stories, or the imagery seen was predominantly, and often overwhelmingly, male. In all these studies females were excluded more easily than males when masculine grammatical forms were used.

All these studies indicate that we think of males as people. Mykol Hamilton (1991) has demonstrated that the inverse belief also exists—people equals males. She asked students to write a short paragraph about the most typical person they could imagine and then give that person the "perfect typical name." The instructions were gender neutral. Nevertheless, only 25 percent of the students in the study described and named a female.

You may ask whether any actual harm is done by masculine generic usage. After all, such usage may be a grammatical formality devoid of any actual influence on behavior. Newspaper columnists have been ridiculing criticisms of sex-biased language for their triviality for years. One favorite butt of humor is the "personhole cover."

Several studies have documented the behavioral effects of sexist language in a number of areas. In an early study, for example, Sandra and Daryl Bem (1973) found that women's interest in job positions was influenced by the wording of advertisements. Their research led to changes in job titles in a major telephone company. Other such changes in language are the shift from *mailman* to *mail carrier* and from *stewardess* to *flight attendant*. The sex composition of these occupations has changed as well.

Sex biases in language have also been found to influence comprehension and memory. For example, the number of correct answers given by women to questions about a science fiction story (presented out loud) was higher when it contained unbiased forms than when it contained masculine forms (Hamilton & Henley, 1982). In a study by Mary Crawford and Linda English (1984) women's recall of essays forty-eight hours later was worse when the essays were written with masculine generics than when they were written with unbiased grammatical forms. This effect was stronger for good learners than for poor ones and occurred despite the fact that participants did not notice which pronouns had been used.

Disinformation and Sexist Language

Differences in language can also influence expectations. In one study, undergraduates were exposed to one of three versions of the "Ethical Standards of Psychologists," each of which differed in sexist noun and pronoun usage (Briere and Lanktree, 1983). Students of both sexes exposed to an exclusively male version (in contrast to one that used "he or she" or no gender-specific words at all) rated a career in psychology as less attractive for women than for men.

A study that combined real-world and laboratory methodology illustrates how ambiguous language can influence our understanding in crucial areas. Mykol Hamilton (1988) conducted a content analysis of a sample of AIDS coverage in the *New York Times*, the *Los Angeles Times*, *Newsweek*, and *Time* during the period from 1983 to 1985. She found that 100 percent of the references in headlines or titles taken alone, and 75 percent of the text and headline references taken together, used the generic terms "homosexuals," "gays," or "bisexuals" without specifying men. Did this exposure lead readers to interpret the terms generically and thereby assume that lesbians and gays were at equally high risk for contracting AIDS?

To answer this question, Hamilton asked college students to rank in order various groups according to what they thought was each group's relative risk for AIDS. While nearly all the students accurately ranked homosexual men as the number-one risk group, 66 percent of the students incorrectly ranked homosexual women as of higher risk than either male or female heterosexuals. The truth is, of those named, lesbians are the *lowest* risk group.

Suspecting that her subjects' misinformation might have come from the media's failure to specify that the gays at risk are men, Hamilton conducted an experiment in which students read an informational paragraph on AIDS describing the risks associated with such factors as intravenous drug use, blood transfusions, and "homosexuality." In various versions of this paragraph, homosexuality was described in increasing degrees of specificity (from homosexual to homosexual men but *not* homosexual women). She found that the amount of perceived risk associated with being a lesbian decreased when the paragraphs were more specific. This study established a link between language practices similar to those used in the media and people's lack of understanding about a serious disease. The use of a generic word such as homosexual for men also reinforces the pervasive association between being male and being human.

New words acquire stereotypic assumptions similar to words that have been in the language longer. For example, Kenneth Dion (1987) has found that the title *Ms* conveys impressions about a woman who prefers this term of address. Women who prefer this title were seen by Canadian undergraduates as more achievement oriented, socially assertive, and dynamic, but less interpersonally warm than women who preferred the more traditional titles of *Miss* or *Mrs.* These attributions were more extreme if the students were informed that the woman chose Ms rather than simply being given her name with the title associated with it (Dion & Cota, 1991). The Ms stereotype overlapped the gender stereotype of men with its emphasis on competency and agency.

STEREOTYPES AS SOCIAL DEMANDS

One of the most remarkable features of sex stereotypes is their near-universal appearance even in contexts in which sex would seem to be totally irrelevant. One study, for example, found that men's bodies are more likely than women's bodies to appear as illustrations in medical school textbooks on anatomy (Giacomini, Rozee-Koker, & Pepitone-Arreola-Rockwell, 1986). In sections of the texts that dealt with standard anatomy that was not sex specific, men's bodies were shown 64 percent of the time, women's bodies were shown 11 percent of the time, and sex-neutral or equal representations were shown 25 percent of the time.

The researchers suggest that this practice results in the depiction of the male as the standard human body. Like so-called standard English grammatical

TABLE 4.4. Stereotypes or No Types*

Advertiser	Total ads	Ads with minorities	Percentage using minorities
Calvin Klein	156	0	0.0
Clairol	67	1	1.5
Cover Girl	226	1	0.4
Estee Lauder	114	0	0.0
Giorgio Armani	65	0	0.0
Gucci	69	0	0.0
L'Oreal	131	1	0.8
NordicTrack	168	0	0.0
Perry Ellis	78	0	0.0
Ralph Lauren	138	4	2.9
Toyota	135	24†	17.8

*More than 1,700 ads examined in 634 magazine issues revealed how seldom if at all African-Americans and other minorities were used by some of the nation's most prolific advertisers.
†Fourteen are "corporate message" ads.
Source: N.Y.C. Department of Consumer Affairs.

usage, it reflects the common societal view that male is normal and female is a special exceptional case. In fact, many text illustrations carried generic labels such as "*the* abdominal muscles" or "*the* human circulatory system" without qualifications of sex, despite the presence of male anatomical cues.

Stereotypes serve as the agents of social messages about the appropriate roles and behaviors of women and men. This aspect of stereotypes is most noticeable when there is no particular historical precedent for gender differences. For example, computers are a new invention. Nevertheless, stereotypes about who should use computers are already well established in popular computer magazines. Ware and Stuck (1985) analyzed the pictorial representation of men, women, boys, and girls in issues of three mass market computer magazines (a total of 2,637 pages were analyzed). Men appeared in illustrations almost twice as often as women. Women were overrepresented as clerical workers and sex objects while men were overrepresented as managers, experts, and repair technicians. In mixed-sex illustrations, men were more often shown in positions of authority. And only women were shown rejecting the computer. As you have seen in Chapter 3, there are considerable differences between males and females

FIGURE 4.7. A scene from *War Games* with a description of the movie that accompanied an article entitled "Female terror at the terminal." Although this photograph is more than twelve years old, men continue to outnumber women in computer use.

in the amount and kind of computer use. We may ask what role such stereotypic images have in the creation of gender-typed behavior (see Figure 4.7).

GENDER STEREOTYPES AND SOCIAL ATTRIBUTIONS

Earlier in this chapter we discussed how gender stereotypes consist of a network of associations involving personality traits, social roles, behaviors, and physical characteristics. In this part of the chapter we will discuss how various aspects of stereotypes influence assumptions about the behaviors of males and females in a variety of contexts. It is, in fact, difficult to find conditions in which the identical behavior of women and men is viewed similarly by observers. As you can see, gender-blind social judgments appear to be quite rare.

Stereotypes reflect the different perceptions people have about women and men. These perceptions involve the *descriptive* aspect of stereotypes. But sex stereotypes have a *prescriptive* as well as a descriptive function. They inform people about what behavior ought to be as much as they tell them what it is. The prescriptive aspect of stereotypes is conveyed primarily by the different *attributions* people make about others on the basis of their gender. Attributions are assumptions about why people behave the way they do. Beliefs about different causality lead to different expectations for men and women. It is through such attributions that stereotypes operate as mechanisms of social control.

You will see in Chapter 5 that different attributions about the behavior of men and women exist in a wide variety of behavioral areas and help form the basis for discrimination against women. In this section, we will focus on the way specific characteristics associated with gender influence attributions. These factors influence assumptions about the normality, social acceptability, and social deviance of women and men.

Physical Attractiveness and Social Deviance

As we discussed earlier in the chapter, physical attractiveness is one of the major sources of information that people use when they are making stereotypic judgments about the characteristics of men and women. So many positive social judgments are made about physically attractive people that Karen Dion coined the phrase "What is beautiful is good!" (Dion, Berscheid, & Walster, 1972). There is considerable evidence, however, that physical attractiveness is more salient in judgments about females than in judgments about males. Many of the studies you read earlier in the chapter stressed the disproportionate number of younger, attractive women as compared with men in the movies, on TV, and in magazines. They also stressed the differential emphasis on female bodies and male faces. The question we will address now is, What effect does this differential emphasis on women as symbols of beauty have on perceptions about women and men?

Despite the focus on male faces in the media, when people rated the attractiveness of men's and women's faces, they made more refined distinctions, offered more extreme positive and negative ratings, and showed more consensus for female than for male faces (Schulman & Hoskins, 1986). Facial expression also affected the ratings of women more than men. Women who smiled were seen as more attractive than those who did not. The absence of a smile had a greater effect on perceptions of women than of men. Nonsmiling women were rated as less happy, less warm, less relaxed, and less carefree than the average woman (Deutsch, LeBaron, & Fryer, 1987). These results support the view that facial appearance is more heavily weighted in the response to women than to men. They also illustrate the way even minor deviations from social expectations—that is, the belief that women should smile more than men—can result in negative social judgments.

In a series of studies, Rhoda Unger and her students investigated the effect of variations in physical attractiveness on perceptions about the social deviance of women and men (Unger, Hilderbrand, & Madar, 1982). As we had hypothesized, less attractive individuals of both sexes were sorted into the less socially desirable categories. Less attractive women were seen to be more likely to be involved in a radical student organization rather than in student government and were more likely to be viewed as lesbian than heterosexual. Less attractive men were also seen to be more likely to be involved in radical politics and to be more likely to be studying for a feminine-typed occupation such as that of nurse or librarian rather than a traditionally masculine field. Consistent with other studies of attributions related to sex, there were no important differences between the men and women who made these judgments. The respondents also appeared to be unaware that their judgments were based on the differential attractiveness of the people in the photographs.

Stereotypes about Sexual Orientation and Their Implications

Inferences of homosexuality are made more frequently about women who are perceived to be physically unattractive (Dew, 1985). Women who held conservative attitudes about gender roles were particularly likely to associate homosexuality with those women to whom they had given the worst evaluations concerning physical appearance. There is a high correspondence between perceived attractiveness and perceived gender. This relationship means that highly attractive women are seen as feminine and highly attractive men are seen as masculine (Gillen, 1981). Attractiveness serves as a mediator between perceptions about appropriate gender roles and assumptions about socially desirable behavior. Less attractive women are perceived as more masculine, and women who are described as masculine are perceived as more likely to be homosexual than women who are described as feminine (Storms, Stivers, Lambers, & Hill, 1981). As you saw in Chapter 1, a relationship between perceived feminism and perceived homosexuality also exists.

Mary Kite and Kay Deaux (1987) have conducted studies similar to those discussed earlier in this chapter to determine what attributes are associated with male and female homosexuality in our society. They asked participants to list all the attributes they thought appropriate for a specific kind of person and then used the frequency with which each attribute was mentioned as data by which to compare the similarities and differences in perceptions of various groups. Homosexual individuals of both sexes were most frequently described in terms of the stereotypic characteristics of the other sex.

The descriptions of homosexuals were more similar to heterosexual individuals of the other sex than they were to heterosexual individuals of the same biological sex as the homosexual. This effect was stronger for homosexual men. Gay men were seen as similar to heterosexual women. To a lesser extent, lesbians were seen as similar to heterosexual men.

As you will see in Chapters 9 and 10, this belief in the inversion of gender-related characteristics in gays and lesbians is, like most stereotypes, completely inaccurate. But this perceptual inversion is very strong. Although stereotypically masculine and feminine traits may exist independently within individuals (as is conceptualized in definitions of androgyny), perceptually these characteristics are organized as polar opposites that exist as indivisible wholes. It is difficult for people to recognize, for example, that a woman can feel sexual desire for another woman and still like makeup, work as a flight attendant, and be timid rather than prefer to wear overalls, work as a mechanic, and be assertive.

Attributions of homosexuality appear to be based on physical appearance cues similar to those that people use to make other inferences about gender. For example, undergraduates assigned higher homosexuality ratings to feminine male and masculine female faces as well as to unattractive female faces (Dunkle & Francis, 1990). Facial maturity affects attributions about a variety of other gender-related traits and roles as well. Atypical baby-faced males and mature-faced females were seen to be equal in warmth, masculinity, likelihood of caring for children, and being financial providers (Friedman & Zebrowitz, 1992). Baby-faced males were actually seen as lower in power than mature-faced females.

The Relationship between Occupational and Gender Stereotypes

As noted earlier, physically unattractive men are seen as more likely to be engaged in socially deviant occupations than more attractive men are (Unger et al., 1982). Occupation is one of the important dimensions by which gender attributes are categorized (Deaux & Lewis, 1984). Researches have now begun to ask the question: What underlies the connection between occupational and gender stereotypes?

In an extensive series of studies, Alice Eagly and Valerie Steffen (1984) varied descriptions of occupational roles for otherwise identical women and men. Students were asked to rate these individuals on various stereotypical masculine and feminine traits. The researchers hypothesized that the distribution of men and women into roles differing in status and authority underlies stereotypic perceptions of women as *communal* (caring about relationships) and affective and men as *agentic* (caring about getting things done) and instrumental.

Full-time homemakers, regardless of their sex, were perceived as more communal than those who were employed full time. When no occupational description was given, the traditional gender stereotype of the woman as more communal than the man was obtained. However, men and women employees were not perceived to differ in communion, nor were female and male homemakers. A similar effect was found for agency. Employees (regardless of their sex) were perceived as more agentic than homemakers. When occupational descriptions were not given, the more that raters inferred that the average woman or man was employed, the lower was her or his perceived communion and the higher was her or his perceived agency. These studies demonstrate that social roles, rather than sex, trigger some gender-stereotypic assumptions. Because men and women tend to be distributed in roles by sex, however, we tend to assume that sex is the causal variable.

In a second set of studies, these researchers used occupational descriptions involving part-time employment to test further their theory that stereotypes about the greater communion of women and the greater agency of men are associated with perceptions about their different life situations (Eagly & Steffen, 1986). They found that women who were employed part time were perceived to be more communal and less agentic than women who were full-time employees. Part-time employees were seen as less communal than homemakers. Men who were employed part time were perceived to be less agentic than fully employed men. They were also seen as less agentic and communal than both male homemakers and men with no occupational description. These sex-related differences may stem from different attributions about the reasons for part-time employment in women and men. For a woman this situation may be seen as due to her substantial commitment to domestic duties, whereas for a man it may be seen as due to difficulty in finding full-time employment.

Occupational stereotypes have both an informational component—this is the way things are—and an evaluative component—this is the way things should be. Some of the strength of occupational stereotypes may be due to the fact that they rather accurately reflect the reality of a sex-segregated occupational world. But, as you can see from the Price Waterhouse case, stereotypes also help to create sex inequality by confusing what is and what ought to be true. An individual who deviates from what is seen as her gender-appropriate role may be rated less positively than one who conforms to it even when her "deviant" behaviors are appropriate for a competent practitioner of that occupation (see Box 4.1 and Figure 4.8).

Gender as an Attributional Variable

Recently, stereotypes have been viewed by social psychologists as forms of bias based on errors in information processing. For example, people use different information to explain the sources of their own behavior than they do to explain the apparently identical behavior of others. They tend to make inference about the personality or character of another person (known as *dispositional attributions*) when explaining his or her behavior but explain their own behavior as due to *situational* factors. For example, when people explain why they failed a test, they usually say that it was because the test was hard or unfair. When, however, they explain why other people failed a test, they usually say that those people were uninterested or unprepared. This has been termed the *actor–observer difference.*

One explanation of this difference between actors and observers is that people have access to different amounts of information about themselves and oth-

Box 4.1 The Price Waterhouse Case

A recent Supreme Court case (*Hopkins* v. *Price Waterhouse*) demonstrates the biasing effect of stereotypes. When Ann Hopkins came up for review for promotion to partner in a major accounting firm, her aggressive (and very successful) strategies were interpreted as "overbearing, arrogant, self-centered, and abrasive." She was denied the promotion, despite the fact that she had brought more money to the company than any other person proposed for partner that year—$25 million (Fiske, Bersoff, Borgida, Deaux, & Heilman, 1991). She was denied the position because of "interpersonal skills problems" that could be corrected, a supporter told her, by walking, talking, and dressing more femininely. In contrast, an opponent suggested she needed to go to "charm school."

The American Psychological Association acted as an *amicus curiae* (friend of the court) in this trial and a group of researchers in cognitive social psychology served as expert witnesses. Social psychologist Susan Fiske's testimony (Fiske et al., 1991) stressed the circumstances under which stereotyping was most likely to occur. She testified that situations in which the target person is isolated or few of a kind in an otherwise homogeneous environment enhances stereotyping. (See the discus-

Ann Hopkins won a federal sex-discrimination case against Price Waterhouse (a major accounting firm). She was awarded the partnership that she had been denied on the basis that she was too macho, universally disliked, and in need of "a course at charm school." Do you think this description would have been applied to a man who had brought in a similarly large amount of business? One of Ms Hopkins's "problems" was that she does not wear makeup.

Box 4.1 Continued

sions of tokenism in Chapters 5 and 12.) Stereotyping is also more likely to occur when members of a previously omitted group move into jobs that are nontraditional for that group. Stereotyping increases when there is a perceived lack of fit between the person's social category and his or her occupation. And, finally, stereotypes are most likely to occur when evaluative criteria are ambiguous.

As of May 1990, Price Waterhouse had twenty-seven women partners out of a total of 900, or 3 percent (Fiske et al., 1991). Moreover, the attributes considered desirable in a manager—aggressive, competitive, driven, and masterful—are still not traits considered desirable in women (Heilman, Block, Martell, & Simon, 1989). In the Price Waterhouse partnership process, hearsay information was given equal weight with the opinions of people with more intensive contact with the candidate. There were no corporate policies prohibiting sex discrimination and no corporate awareness that sex discrimination was inappropriate (Fiske et al., 1991).

The Supreme Court decided in favor of Hopkins. Its ruling stated: "Nor . . . does it require expertise in psychology to know that if an employee's flawed interpersonal skills can be corrected by a soft-hued suit or a new shade of lipstick, perhaps it is the employee's sex and *not* her interpersonal skills that has drawn the criticism" (*Hopkins* v. *Price Waterhouse*, 1989, p. 1793, cited in Fiske et al., 1991). It also stated: "We sit not to determine whether Ms Hopkins is nice, but to decide whether the partners reacted negatively to her because she is a woman" (p. 1795). And, finally, their ruling pointed out the impossible dilemma for women that such stereotypes produce. "An employee who objects to aggressiveness in women but whose positions require this trait places women in an intolerable Catch-22: out of a job if they behave aggressively and out of a job if they don't" (p. 1791). We will discuss the social mechanisms that create such dilemmas (also known as *double binds*) further in Chapter 5.

ers. For example, they usually encounter others in particular situations (e.g., the classroom versus recreational activities) or roles (their mother, their boss, their teacher, etc.). They have, therefore, little information about how other people's behavior changes as a function of their different roles or social contexts. For example, both of the authors are professors, but our children probably have little idea about how we act in a college classroom. They would probably describe our personality traits quite differently than our students would. In contrast, people are well aware of the inconsistencies in their own behavior as it changes in response to others or to social demands.

Viewing gender as a basis for making attributions means changing our views about the causality of gender-related differences in traits and behaviors (Geis, Brown, Jennings, and Corrado-Taylor, 1984). Our prevailing cultural assumptions see biological sex as the origin of stereotypic personality traits and, hence, the cause of role and status differences. According to this view, women are biologically "programmed" to be nurturant, and this trait leads to occupational roles such as nurse or teacher. It is also possible, however, that historic factors and economic constraints have resulted in the sex segregation of occupations. The differential experience of women and men with different roles would then produce gender-related differences in personality traits. According to this view, people become doctors or nurses and then acquire the personality traits that "go with" these occupations.

This idea has been tested in an ingenious experiment by Hoffman and Hurst (1990). They told subjects to imagine a planet that had two kinds of people—Orinthians and Ackmians—who performed different jobs on the planet. Most of the members of one group worked in the industrial centers of the city. Most of the other groups were child raisers who stayed around the home. Subjects were then asked about the personality characteristics of the people in the two jobs. They were also asked why they thought there was an unequal distribution of the two group in these jobs. Subjects reported that they believed each group had personality characteristics which suited them for a particular kind of work.

The Orinthians and Ackmians are analogous to men and women. Because we have limited experience with men and women in the same roles, we tend to explain gender-related differences as dispositional in origin even though they may be a response to social constraints. This is why people are surprised when a woman executive or pro athlete acts like a man in the same role.

SEX AS A STIMULUS VARIABLE: SOME LIMITATIONS

While much of the research discussed in this chapter demonstrates remarkable consistency and coherency in our perceptions of women and men, there are some limitations to the understanding we can gain from it. The primary problem is that most of the studies discussed earlier used white middle-class men and women as stimulus persons for the perception of stereotypes. But there is evidence that stereotypes of women differ in terms of both race and class.

Hope Landrine (1985) provided undergraduates with the labels "white woman," "middle-class woman," "black woman," and "lower-class woman" and asked them to assign adjectives to each group in a "manner that best describes society's stereotypes of the group." Subjects offered different stereotypes for each group although all of the adjectives used were stereotypically feminine. White women were rated significantly higher than black women on dependent, emotional, and passive (traits that resemble those identified by Broverman and her associates in early studies). Lower-class women were rated significantly higher than middle-class women on confused, dirty, hostile, inconsiderate, and irresponsible. The stereotypes of white women and middle-class women were most similar to the traditional stereotypes of women in general.

Black women are evaluated considerably less positively than white women by white respondents. They are seen as louder and more talkative and aggressive than American women in general although they are also seen as more straightforward than Anglo-American women (Weitz & Gordon, 1993). Black women are rated as more masculine in traits and roles than white women and much more masculine in physical characteristics. There appears to be no difference between black and white women in ratings involving occupations. However, women of both races were seen as closer to each other than either racial group was to men of their own racial category (Deaux & Kite, 1985).

These studies provide evidence that both race and social class are implicit variables in gender stereotypes, but they are too preliminary and too few for us to do more than conjecture about the meaning of race–class interactions in gender stereotypes. It is important that such studies be continued and extended to include other ethnic groups for a number of reasons. First, the world is not simply white and middle class. Psychologists cannot assume that cognitive processes will be the same no matter what kind of stimulus person is used in their studies. Second, by not examining race and class variables, psychology ignores the extent to which these variables influence behavior. And, last, this kind of neglect makes members of minority groups invisible, with all of the psychological and social consequences that white middle-class women objected to when they were neglected.

GROUP DIFFERENCES IN STEREOTYPING

Sex of Subject Effects

As we noted several times during the course of this chapter, males and females are quite similar in their perceptions of the sexes and in the attributions that they make about them. This similarity between the sexes in their perception of difference appears even in children as young as 2 years of age (Cowan & Hoffman, 1986). These findings are consistent with a view of stereotypes as forms of social consensus. This means that stereotypes are not individual opinions, but collective agreements about what constitutes social reality.

Race-Related Differences

Judgments about gender are influenced by some aspects of group membership (different groups do, of course, encounter different versions of social reality). Blacks and whites, for example, appear to have different stereotypes about men and women. One large-scale open-ended survey studied more than 750 African-American and Anglo-American respondents in the Detroit area who differed widely in age, education, and economic status (Smith & Midlarsky, 1985). White respondents had more stereotypical views about women than black respondents did. For example, no black respondent characterized women as passive, although this trait appeared quite often in the responses of white subjects. White respondents also characterized men in terms of competency and aggressiveness more than black respondents did. Black respondents saw men more in terms of their roles—father, factory worker, basketball player, and so on—than white respondents did.

We need to be cautious about making statements about the similarities and differences between ethnic groups in gender stereotyping because culture influences both the way one sees and the way one describes social reality. For example, Hope Landrine and her colleagues (Landrine, Klonoff, & Brown-Collins, 1992) looked at ethnic differences in stereotyping using a number of gender-characteristic adjectives as cues. They examined several groups of undergraduate women who differed in ethnicity and found that although there were few differences between ethnic groups in self-evaluations, women from the various groups differed in terms of the meaning they attached to the adjectives they used. In other words, they appeared to be more similar than they actually were because they were using the same words with differing meanings. For example, women of color were most likely to define assertive as "Say whatever's on my mind" whereas white women were most likely to define it as "Stand up for myself." These differences would not be apparent if researchers look at self-rating of traits, but not their meaning.

Cultural Differences

In order to understand the processes that create stereotypes, it is important to explore societies where the meanings associated with maleness and femaleness are different from our own. This kind of cross-cultural exploration has been more the province of anthropology than of psychology. It is difficult to develop standardized instruments in different languages since stereotypes are, by definition, inextricably tied to the language we speak.

One solution to this problem is to use nonverbal or pictorial materials. As you saw earlier, *face-ism,* or the tendency to portray males as more facially prominent than females, was present in the published materials of all the countries studied (Archer et al., 1983). The greater importance or salience of female attractiveness also seems to be universally found in all the countries that have been studied (Buss, 1989). One large-scale study that surveyed attitudes toward men and women in more than twenty-five countries found similar perceptions about women and men in most of the countries surveyed, although some differences between cultures also existed (Williams & Best, 1990). No society examined was gender-blind.

It is important to keep in mind that differences in images of women and men can be much more extreme in some cultures than in the United States. Earlier in this chapter we spoke about the symbolic annihilation of women. Sometimes researchers find that representations of women simply do not exist. In an important ethnographic museum in Israel, for example, few women were found even in exhibits showing scenes from family life (Izraeli, 1993). One reproduction of a painting of holiday worship even erased the women who had originally stood in the balcony (see Figure 4.8). This exclusion of women from history had gone unnoticed by visitors because what is rendered invisible is rarely missed.

It is important to do more cross-cultural studies. But it is also clear that such studies may do little to tell us where the ultimate source of sex stereotypes is to be found. Thus, although women's roles are marginalized in Israel, they are also drafted into its army and hold major public policy positions. Similar contradictions between stereotypes and behavior can be found in other countries as well. For example, although women's bodies and attire are tightly controlled in many Moslem countries, both Pakistan and Bangladesh have had women prime ministers.

FIGURE 4.8. Women are sometimes made invisible. The painting on the right hangs in Israel's Diaspora Museum—a museum devoted to portraying Jewish life in many lands. The original painting by Gottlieb on the "Day of Atonement" (on the left) included women in the balcony. Museum officials have offered no explanation for their erasure.

INDIVIDUAL DIFFERENCES IN SEX STEREOTYPING

Some psychologists believe that stereotypes are motivationally based—that they serve to maintain a person's self-esteem or to help him or her cope with feelings of inadequacy. Although we have stressed the sociocultural and cognitive aspects of stereotypes, it is also important to recognize that people do differ in their degree of sex stereotyping, and these differences are related to other ways in which we differ from each other. Some of the areas of individual differences that have been explored are personality qualities such as self-esteem, the effect of the person's perception of his or her own gender identity, and conservative or egalitarian attitudes toward gender roles.

Few personality differences have been found between people who hold negative biases against women and those who do not (Goldberg, 1974). This may be because there are so few nonsexist people in our society. If most people agree that women are deficient as compared with men, this majority group will include people with all kinds of personality characteristics. Gender bias is more of a social norm than a reflection of personal inadequacy. However, a few studies have found that men who opposed the women's rights movement had lower self-esteem than those who did not (Miller, 1974).

The relationship between self-identity and the tendency to stereotype others is a controversial one. Sandra Bem (1985) has reported a number of studies showing a relationship between traditional gender typing of oneself and a tendency to view the world in gender-schematic terms. However, Janet Spence and Robert Helmreich (1978) have indicated that there is no relationship between either males' or females' scores on a questionnaire designed to measure a person's perception of his or her own gender-related traits and the extent to which the person stereotypes others in these same traits.

This controversy has not yet been resolved. It may depend on differences between scales used or on the fact that gender-schematic and -aschematic individuals appear in different numbers in different populations. We tend to believe that, as in other social arenas, there is little connection between the way men and women view their own gender-related traits and those of others (Spence & Sawin, 1985).

As you might expect, there is a connection between traditional or conservative attitudes about appropriate roles for women and men (other than oneself) and other aspects of sexism. Thus, both men and women who score as more traditional on the Attitudes toward Women Scale—a questionnaire that measures views about gender equality in the economic, political, and social spheres (Spence & Helmreich, 1978)—also rate sexist jokes as funnier than nonsexist jokes in contrast to those who score in a more egalitarian direction (Moore, Griffiths, & Payne, 1987). People who score in a more conservative direction on the AWS also have more negative views toward homosexuals (Whitley, 1987). There is some reason to believe that sexism, racism, and homophobia are related in some individuals (Henley & Pincus, 1978), but negative beliefs about one group or another may be modified by various special or personal circumstances (Galanis & Jones, 1986; Herek, 1987).

THE PERSISTENCE OF STEREOTYPES

Have Stereotypes Changed over Time?

You might expect that with the growth of the women's movement stereotypes about the sexes would have declined. The evidence suggests, however, that gender stereotypes have changed little over the past thirty years. One study by Werner and LaRussa (1985) replicated in 1978 a study of gender-role concepts that had first been published in 1957 (Sheriffs & McKee, 1957). The researchers used the same 200-item checklist with the same number of respondents at the same university (Berkeley) at which the earlier study had been conducted. They found that 62 percent of the adjectives that had been significantly assigned to men in 1957 were still part of the male stereotype in 1978. Of the adjectives that had been used to describe women in 1957, 77 percent were still part of the current stereotype. In no case did an adjective shift between men and women over the two decades between studies, although some adjectives dropped out as differentiators and some new ones appeared. The major difference between the two studies was that there are now fewer negative stereotypes about women. Roughly equal numbers of favorable and unfavorable adjectives are now ascribed to both sexes.

One reviewer of this book noted that the reduction in negative stereotypes about women should be a cause for joy. However, this change seems to be due to the ascription of positive communal qualities such as helpfulness, warmth, and understanding to women. Unfortunately, perceptions that women possess these qualities did not influence respondents' attitudes toward the equality of women and men. In other words, women are thought of as very good people but not as worthy as men of equal rights, roles, and privileges (Eagly & Mladinic, 1989). Cross-cultural studies also tend to show this distinction between goodness and other gender-related properties. Overall, neither sex is seen as better than the other, but men are viewed more favorably than women in dynamic terms such as activity and strength (Williams & Best, 1990). No change in the affective meaning of these adjectives has been found since the advent of the women's movement (Bergen & Williams, 1991).

Studies using other methods also indicate that gender stereotypes have not changed. For example, Thomas Ruble (1983) compared ratings by 128 college students of the typical (what people are really like) and the desirable (ideally, what people should be like) man or woman on fifty-four items taken from a gender-role inventory (see Table 4.5). Ratings of the typical man differed from those of the typical woman on fifty-three of the fifty-four traits used. The average level of agreement between men and women raters was more than 85 percent. In contrast, attitudes about what the desirable traits are for men and women were less sex differentiated. Ruble found significant differences on only twelve of the fifty-four items. Other studies have indicated that ideology about the social, economic, and political roles of men and women has become more egalitarian over time (Helmreich, Spence, & Gibson, 1982), but these data indicate that stereotypes about the sexes, as distinct from positive or negative attitudes about them, are still alive and well and existing in the United States.

Cognitive Mechanisms in the Maintenance of Stereotypes

At the very beginning of this chapter we introduced the idea of stereotypes as forms of information—cognitive categories that are used to simplify a complex social reality. In the final part of the chapter we shall discuss briefly some of the mechanisms that tend to perpetuate stereotypes despite the large number of disconfirming examples that people encounter every day. For example, don't you know women who are excellent athletes? What about men who are warm and sensitive? Do you think that you, yourself, possess characteristics that are perceived as stereotypically appropriate for people of the sex other than your own?

One of the mechanisms that helps to maintain stereotypes is the *subtyping* of social categories. When we encounter someone who disconfirms our beliefs about members of his or her category, it is easier for us to reclassify that person than to change our beliefs about a whole category. A person's response to a member of a social category will, therefore, depend on which subtype of that category is activated.

Subtyping helps to explain the rather puzzling findings that women may be evaluated more favorably than men (Eagly, Mladinic, & Otto, 1991). It all depends on the subtype aroused! A recent experiment by Haddock and Zanna

TABLE 4.5. Typical and Desirable Characteristics: Differences in Ratings of Male Versus Female Targets

Typical Man > Woman	Typical Woman > Man
Independent	Emotional
Aggressive*	Grateful
Not excitable in minor crises*	Home-oriented
Skilled in business	Strong conscience
Mechanical aptitude*	Kind*
Outspoken	Cries easily*
Acts as leader*	Creative
Self-confident	Understanding
Takes a stand	Considerate
Ambitious	Devotes self to others
Not easily influenced	Needs approval
Dominant*	Gentle*
Active	Aware of others' feelings
Knows ways of world	Excitable in a major crisis
Loud	Expresses tender feelings*
Interested in sex	Enjoys art and music
Makes decisions easily	Doesn't hide emotions
Doesn't give up easily	Tactful
Stands up under pressure	Feelings hurt
Not timid	Helpful to others
Good at sports*	Neat*
Likes math and science	Religious
Competitive*	Likes children
Adventurous	Warm to others
Sees self running show	Need for security
Outgoing	
Intellectual	
Feels superior	
Forward	

*Gender differences with asterisk were considered desirable as well as typical.
Source: Adapted from T. L. Ruble (1983). Sex stereotypes: Issues of change in the 1970s. *Sex Roles,* 9, 397–402. Plenum Publishing Company. Reprinted with permission.

(1994) illustrates the effect of subtypes. They examined the attitudes about women of different groups of men. They found that right-wing authoritarian men did not share the positive evaluations of women held by other groups of men. This was because the different groups constructed different images in response to the label "woman." Unlike other men, the term "woman" did not evoke the image of a "housewife" (the subtype most like the global concept) for authoritarian men. Instead, "woman" elicited an image of "feminist" and triggered negative evaluations. The authoritarian men had more negative beliefs about feminists and saw them as possessing a large number of values that they disliked.

Another cognitive mechanism called *priming* also helps to explain how stereotypes are maintained. Priming consists of apparently irrelevant information which evokes implicit stereotypes without the individual's awareness. In one study involving priming, for example, students unscrambled sentences describing neutral or gender-stereotypic behaviors involving dependence or aggression (the primes). Although ratings of male and female targets did not change after exposure to the neutral sentences, both female and male students exposed to dependency primes rated a female as more dependent than a male who performed identical behaviors. Similarly, they rated a male as more aggressive than a female after exposure to aggression primes (Banaji, Hardin, & Rothman, 1993). People appear to be able to ignore this kind of priming of stereotypes only when they are kept "cognitively busy" (e.g., forced to rehearse an eight-digit number while performing a task) before being asked to evaluate a target person (Gilbert & Hixon, 1991).

As you have seen in this chapter, gender stereotypes can be found everywhere. It is impossible, therefore, for people to avoid information which primes their implicit stereotypes about women and men. In fact, it is surprising that stereotypes can change at all.

When Are Stereotypes Not Maintained?

Stereotypes may be helpful to those who hold them by making it easier for them to make sense of a complex social world. If you "know" that all women are gossips or all men are aggressive, social decision making is simpler than if you had to treat each person as a unique individual. However, stereotypes produce harmful effects on those who are stereotyped by ignoring their distinctive personal qualities and their positive contributions to others and to society. It is, therefore, important to determine under what conditions stereotypes may be disconfirmed. After all, all of us have a personal stake in the matter, since we are all members of some group that is the target of negative stereotypes.

One of the areas in which social psychologists have focused recently is that of stereotype *disconfirmation.* In other words, what happens to a stereotype when a person meets someone of a group who does not fit the stereotype? As we discussed earlier, this can result in the formation of a subtype—considered atypical of their category—while the person retains his or her stereotype as describing typical members of the group (Johnston & Hewstone, 1992). This way they can keep their overall stereotypes intact.

Some disconfirming cases, however, are better than others. Change in stereotypes is promoted by examples of otherwise typical group members who engage in one atypical behavior. Change is also facilitated when the disconfirming behavior occurs repeatedly in many different settings. For example, women who are fighter pilots, rock climbers, and construction workers have undermined the stereotype that women cannot do tough, demanding work (Fiske & Stevens, 1993). Dispersed inconsistent information promotes more stereotype change than concentrated inconsistent information does.

Stereotype change is also influenced by the relative power of individuals. Susan Fiske (1993) has summarized a great deal of her own and others' research that clarifies this relationship. She finds three consistent and replicable results: (1) People pay attention to those who control their outcomes. When people's rewards or punishment depend on someone else, they increase their attention to stereotype-inconsistent information about their partner. (2) People make inferences about their partner on the basis of the inconsistent information they have gathered. They construct personality profiles of people on whom they depend, as if to increase their ability to predict their actions. (3) Interdependence decreases stereotyping regardless of whether it is the result of cooperation or competition. Attention to inconsistent information about the partner was even greater when their partner had more power than they did. When, however, no interdependence was involved, people discounted inconsistent information rather than used it.

Fiske points out that stereotyping is to some extent a matter of intent. People have alternative ways of thinking about others either as members of a category or as unique individuals. They can change the extent of stereotyping by how much attention they pay to others. Attentiveness can be modified by interdependence as well as self-interest. Therefore, less powerful people will be more likely to attend to the individual qualities of those with whom they interact. However, the attention and, therefore, the stereotyping of more powerful people can also be influenced by reminding them of their own responsibility and egalitarianism, by public accountability, or by fear of appearing to be a fraud.

The Cognitive Approach in Perspective

Although the cognitive approach has provided some very illuminating experiments that are helpful for our understanding of gender stereotypes, it does have some limitations. First, these cognitive mechanisms are assumed to work in all stereotypes. This is an important issue because all stereotyped groups are not alike. For example, unlike blacks and whites, women and men live in close proximity and should have ample opportunity to disconfirm each other's stereotypes. Yet gender stereotypes appear to be at least as strong as race stereotypes. Cognitive psychologists have just begun to give us some information about what forms disconfirming information must take and how many times it must be present in order for stereotypes to change.

Second, biases in our information generating, encoding, and memory processes are important for understanding stereotypes, but they do not explain everything about contemporary societal processes that discriminate against women. For example, although the structure of the work world has changed dramatically, sex segregation of occupations remains strong. If current societal arrangements underlie stereotypes, changes in cognitive biases will not occur (since the current biases are valid in terms of how the real world works). Thus, those interested in social change will have to look elsewhere than to cognitive biases.

Third, individual differences in the degree of stereotyping do exist. There is some evidence that categorization and prejudice are not the same processes, although the first must take place in order for the second to occur. If individual differences in bias are not due to cognitive differences in categorization, they must be looked for in motivational and social learning processes. In the framework of stereotypes as "normal" cognitive processes we must not forget to look at why some people stereotype more than others do.

Fourth, it is important to remember that some groups are more frequently the target of stereotypes than others. In his landmark book on prejudice, Gordon Allport (1954) attributed being a target to historical as well as psychological circumstances. The difference between believing in stereotypes and being the target of them is closely related to relative power. Groups do not exist in a social vacuum. The issue of power will be discussed more fully in Chapter 5, but it is important to emphasize here that an experimental laboratory perspective cannot tell us everything about how power works in the real world.

CONNECTING THEMES

1. Gender stereotypes exist inside people's heads as forms of cognitive bias. They are maintained through interactive processes involving both the person and society. The consistent and universal representation of women and men as different helps generate these biases. In turn, cultural images of the sexes are used to justify sexist perceptions.
2. Nothing in our culture can be regarded as trivial. Differences in the pictorial and linguistic representations of men and women influence the way both sexes perceive and think about the world. Reductions in stereotyping are facilitated by naming that brings previously invisible imagery to our attention.
3. The global stereotypes of "women" and "men" are too broad. Subtypes exist based on physical characteristics, roles, race/ethnicity, and class. It is important to investigate both the similarities and the differences between our views of different groups of women and men.
4. Stereotypes are almost "pure" forms of social construction. Cognitive social psychology can help us understand the psychological mechanisms underlying these constructions and how constructs are related to current social realities. However, cognitive social psychology can tell us little about how to bring about social change.

SUGGESTED READINGS

TUCHMAN, GAYE, ARLENE DANIELS, and JAMES BENET (Eds.) (1978). *Hearth and home: Images of women in the mass media.* New York: Oxford University Press. Although some of the information is slightly dated, this book provides an excellent framework by which to examine current stereotypes in the mass media.

WEISSTEIN, NAOMI (1971). Psychology constructs the female, or the fantasy life of the male psychologist. In M. H. Garskof (Ed.). *Roles women play: Readings toward women's liberation.* Belmont, CA: Brooks/Cole. This classic article shows how stereotypes about women affected psychologists as they created theories of human behavior.

FISKE, SUSAN, and LAURA STEVENS (1993). What's so special about sex? Gender stereotyping and discrimination. In S. Oskamp and M. Constanzo (Eds.). *Gender issues in contemporary society.* Newbury Park, CA: Sage (pp. 173–196). Well-written, up-to-date review of the social cognitive approach to stereotyping. It emphasizes the applicability of laboratory research to everyday life.

CHAPTER 5

Doing Gender: Sex, Status, and Power

WHAT DO WE MEAN BY DOING GENDER?
SEX AS A SOCIAL CATEGORY
The Importance of Sex as a Category
Cognitive Tricks We Use with Social Categories
Behavioral Confirmation and the Self-Fulfilling Prophecy
Sex and Self-Categorization
STATUS AND POWER
Some Definitions
The Relationship between Status and Power
GENDER DIFFERENCES AS STATUS DIFFERENCES
Gender-Related Differences in Nonverbal Behaviors
The Perception of Nonverbal Cues to Status
Gender and the Use of Social Power
THE ROLE OF GENDER IN BOUNDARY MAINTENANCE
Stigma
Deviance and the Power to Define
Dealing with Deviance in a Group Setting
The Token Woman
Group Dynamics: Gender, Status, and Roles
Gender and Leadership
Gender and Legitimacy
STATUS AND SOCIAL BEHAVIORS
The Impact of Roles: A Theoretical Framework
The Social Construction of Gender-Related Differences
The Construction of Social Behaviors: A Reprise
THE INTERNALIZATION OF GENDER NORMS
Women and Personal Entitlement
The Awareness of Categorical Bias
CONNECTING THEMES
SUGGESTED READINGS

WHAT DO WE MEAN BY DOING GENDER?

Recently, feminists have gone beyond counting, describing, and analyzing the origin and meaning of differences between men and women (as in Chapter 3). They have also moved beyond perceptions of difference and gender stereotypes (Chapter 4). They have begun to ask questions about the role gender differences play in society. This chapter will look at when and how cues about gender are noticed, how they organize perceptions about oneself and others, and how they structure behavioral interactions between people. In this chapter we want to show you how social practices elicit gender-related behaviors—even from people whose sex is not "appropriate" to these behaviors.

You have probably always thought of your gender as part of your identity—as something within yourself. But the material in the first chapters of this book may have led you to believe that you are not as different from people of the other sex as you might have thought. The focus of this chapter is the way in which interpersonal and social processes create gender. A question you may wish to think about as you read is, How much gender do women and men possess when they are alone and how much does gender emerge during interactions between people?

Gender and power are intimately connected. In this chapter we will also discuss how gender is used as a form of social control. As Nancy Henley and Jo Freeman (1989) state so eloquently:

> Social interaction is the battlefield on which the daily war between the sexes is fought. It is here that women are constantly reminded of what their "place" is and here that they are put back in their place, should they venture out. Thus, social interaction serves as the locus of the most common means of social control employed against women. By being continually reminded of their inferior status in their interactions with others, and continually compelled to acknowledge that status in their own patterns of behavior, women may internalize society's definition of them as inferior so thoroughly that they are often unaware of what their status is. Inferiority becomes habitual, and the inferior place assumes the familiarity—and even desirability—of home (Henley & Freeman, 1989, p. 457).

In this chapter, we will discuss in detail the social processes that maintain women's place.

You may wonder why we make so much use of experimental research in this chapter since we recognize that such methodology constrains what we can know about the richness of women's lives. We have done so because the social processes by which gender is constructed are complex. When women are not treated the same way as men, people can explain these distinctions on the basis of gender-related personality differences, skills, and roles. Experimental research allows us to disentangle the various factors involved. Paradoxically, these studies support the arguments of feminists. Interpersonal processes involving gender help to maintain a pattern of male dominance. Moreover, the large number of social mechanisms involved and people's relative unawareness of them help to convince both women and men that our androcentric reality has a substantive basis in the natural world.

The level of analysis that will be used most in this chapter is the interpersonal—gender as a process rather than as something that people possess. In this sense, gender is more a verb than a noun. Ongoing interactions between people construct the traits and behaviors linked to gender. The mechanisms for this construction involve social expectations and social demands. We will discuss such processes in some detail later in this chapter. This construction and maintenance of the behavior of women and men has been termed *doing gender* (West & Zimmerman, 1987).

SEX AS A SOCIAL CATEGORY

Gender may be viewed as a scheme for the social categorization of individuals (Sherif, 1982). It is a lens through which thought and behavior are framed. These thoughts and behaviors have been extensively studied by psychologists as forms of social cognition. As you will see, gender is one of our most important social categories. It is relevant even when it seems that it should be irrelevant—for example, when people use information about where people seat themselves to determine who the leader of a group is (see Figure 5.1).

As this example points out, gender as a social category is closely associated with other forms of social distinction. In particular, gender is closely tied to conceptions of power and status. Gender and status may be hopelessly confused in the way people organize social reality (Unger, 1978). Men behave and are behaved toward as high-status people in most situations, whereas women behave and are behaved toward as low-status people. These interpersonal relationships reproduce society's ideology about the greater worth of males.

The Importance of Sex as a Category

People frequently use the sex, race, and age of others as categories by which to organize their ideas about them. Of course, these are not the only categories available. Social psychologists have found that people construct social groups even when the rationale for doing so is either trivial or arbitrary. For example, students will put people into different groups on the basis of whether or not

FIGURE 5.1. Which of these people do you think is the strongest contributor to the group? College students usually guessed one of the two men, despite the fact that in same-sex groups the person at the head of the table is most commonly seen as the leader.

they liked abstract art or whether they consistently overestimated or underestimated the number of dots on a slide (Wilder, 1986).

Such groupings, however, differ from sex, race, and age in several important ways. First, we must find out something about these other people in order to use their behaviors in the construction of categories. Information about sex, race, and age is, however, immediately available. Second, these categories are relatively permanent. They cannot be changed as easily as one's preference in art can.

Perhaps because of these properties of externality and permanence, sex, race, and age appear to be particularly important cues for the categorization of others. Some early studies by Kathleen Grady (1979) demonstrated how important sex is for our identification of others. Her studies revealed that people almost always notice the sex of another person. They also have difficulty ignoring sex in favor of other aspects of the person that may be more useful to them.

To demonstrate that sex is a fundamental category in our identification of others, Grady chose a situation in which sex did not appear to have any functional value for the perceiver. She approached people who were waiting at a subway station and asked them if they had just purchased a token. If they had, they were told that a study on eyewitness reports was being conducted and would they please describe the token seller by listing characteristics for the purpose of identification. Of the characteristics mentioned, the sex of the token seller—in this case, female—was always included. It was given as a first or second characteristic 100 percent of the time. In fact, it was given first 75 percent of the time and was displaced to second position only by race—in this case, black.

"And they never varied—all respondents agreed on female for each of the token sellers. As if to underscore the prominence of sex as a characteristic, the one respondent who couldn't offer any description said 'I can't even remember whether it was a man or a woman'" (Grady, 1977, p. 4) Grady's informants apparently thought that sex was a very important characteristic to mention for purposes of identification. Of course it isn't important in any statistical sense. By naming sex, we only distinguish a person from about 50 percent of the population. Most people have many more individuating characteristics—glasses, blond hair, freckles, and so forth.

The major importance of sex as a social category has been documented by more recent studies too. These find that people are more likely to categorize others by their sex than by their race (Stangor, Lynch, Duan, & Glass, 1992). They are also more likely to confuse individuals of the same sex than individuals of the same age, race, role, or name (Fiske, Haslam, & Fiske, 1991). And they are more apt to notice when a person breaks a gender prescription than when he or she "fails to act his or her age" (Fiske & Stevens, 1993).

When sex is not available as a social category, people invent it. They infer sex on the basis of cues about gender. An ingenious study by Bertram John and Lori Sussman (1984–1985) illustrates the process by which people construct sex. They gave college students a story in which two individuals, "Brown Buttons" and "Gray Buttons," engaged in a dialogue in which they took turns furthering the progress of a relationship. At various points in the narrative, conversational dominance shifted from one protagonist to the other and back again. At each of these transitions respondents were asked to guess the sex of Gray and Brown Buttons. You can see some of this dialogue in Box 5.1. At each question mark, you may select the sex of the participants.

Box 5.1 Brown Buttons and Gray Buttons at a Singles Bar

The scene is a "singles" bar located in a middle-sized town. Some people are dancing in one section of the room. Others are sitting or standing around the bar drinking and socializing. An individual with brown shirt buttons (Brown Buttons) walks purposefully toward a person with gray shirt buttons (Gray Buttons) and begins a conversation. After a few minutes, Brown Buttons asks Gray Buttons to dance. Gray Buttons agrees, and they begin to move to the dancing area.

?

As they start to dance, Gray Buttons says to Brown Buttons, "You are a good dancer. I don't come across many people who dance this well."

"Thank you" says Brown Buttons with a slightly embarrassed smile. "I think you dance well too."

"What do you do for a living?" asks Gray Buttons.

"I'm a high school teacher," answers Brown Buttons. "And you?"

"I'm a research technician," says Gray Buttons, "but I'm thinking of getting into computers."

As the music comes to an end, Gray Buttons says, "You are a very interesting person. I'd like us to talk some more . . . why don't we sit over here?" motioning to a small table in the corner.

?

They've been sitting for quite a while. Brown Buttons orders drinks again, and they continue to talk. . . . "I'm really fascinated by your life; I'd like to get to know you better."

"That's interesting," says Gray Buttons. "I find you exciting too, but I'm not sure that I'm able to handle too much familiarity now. I'm really interested in pursuing my career. . . . "

?

"I understand your position," says Brown Buttons, "but I'd really like to see more of you."

"I'm going to think about it," says Gray Buttons. "Why don't we stop off at my place? Perhaps we'd both get some perspective over coffee and. . . ."

?

Source: From John and Sussman, "Initiative taking as a determinant of role reciprocal organization." In *Representations; Social Constructions of Gender;* edited by Rhoda Unger.

Did you think Gray Buttons was a man or a woman? How about Brown Buttons? At various points during this dialogue, people in the study changed back and forth between male and female labels as social dominance shifted from one character to the other. They changed sex labels even when this was at the expense of the logical continuity of the narrative; that is, they had to revise their previous labels and "re-sex" characters.

Many people seem to have difficulty accepting the idea that people can take turns engaging in gender-inconsistent behaviors during a social encounter. They see sex and gender as one indivisible whole. In addition, they perceive masculinity and femininity as complementary aspects of gender that reproduce sex. When one person was perceived as a man, the other was perceived as a woman. No one conceived of the actors as both of the same sex.

People's need for a secure sex identification has been made the subject of humor by the use of the character "Pat" in the television show "Saturday Night Live" (see Figure 5.2). Some of the episodes in this series illustrate the extent to which ordinary life is gendered. In one episode, for example, Pat gets his/her hair cut and the stylist cannot decide whether to charge for the male cut ($15) or the female cut ($18). In another, a druggist tries to figure out whether he should provide Pat with Mennen or Secret in response to a request for a deodorant.

FIGURE 5.2. Is Pat female or male? And, why do we care so much?

Pat's fellow employees go to great lengths to determine her/his sex, but are consistently foiled. Pat wins the game of "strip poker" and has an androgynous-looking significant other named "Terry." When asked questions such as "Who puts on the condom?" the response is similarly unhelpful—"Why we both do—as part of foreplay." The fact that audiences continue to find such a situation hilarious indicates how rigid gender categories are in our society.

Customary representations of reality do not leave any room for ambiguity of sex or gender. For example, in Ursula LeGuin's prize-winning science-fiction novel *The Left Hand of Darkness*—a story that takes place in a world in which people can alternate between sexes—one of her most startling lines is "The king was pregnant."

Cognitive Tricks We Use with Social Categories

Stereotypes describe what people think about members of various social categories. They constitute one form of cognitive bias. Such cognitive biases operate inside the head of the observer, and they would not be problematic if they would stay there. But biased beliefs based on social categories are communicated to others and influence their behavior.

People try to make the world an orderly, predictable place and use a variety of strategies to achieve that end. Popular strategies involve the use of social categories to explain the way people behave. Although often quite functional (they save the user time and energy in making decisions about the people he or she meets), such explanations are usually based on limited information and lead to broad generalizations that are wrong. Some of the strategies that people use to create and maintain categories include: selective attention, selective recall, selective interpretation, and selective causal attributions.

Selective Attention and Encoding Processes

People encode information about others on the basis of their race and sex. When asked to recall the speakers from a conversation they had heard, students were less accurate in distinguishing between members of the same social category (either race or sex) than they were between members of different categories (Taylor, Fiske, Etcoff, & Ruderman, 1978). All the women (or men) seemed to "look alike." The students did not intend to use race or sex as a strategy to remember particular people. In fact, the one student who admitted using race was very apologetic about having done so.

People tend to minimize differences within groups and exaggerate differences between them. Within-group characteristics are also exaggerated in inverse proportion to the size of the minority subgroup present. When few members of the minority subgroup are present, their characteristics are seen as more stereotypic of their social category. Thus, people saw women as more feminine and men as more masculine when there were few other members of their sex present in a group (Taylor et al., 1978). Women and blacks were just as likely to categorize and make social judgments about the minority group as men and whites. In other words, being a member of a subgroup does not necessarily influence how one sees others who are also part of that category.

Of course, social categories are not equivalent with respect to status and power. Low-status groups are often perceived as more homogeneous than higher-status groups (Messick & Mackie, 1989). High-status groups are also much more likely to receive favorable trait evaluations (Jost & Banaji, 1994).

Dominant group members perceive less variability between others than people do from subordinated groups. Men and women seem to agree about their relative place in the dominance hierarchy. When they were asked to identify different males and females in a group on the basis of what they had said (other cues were also varied—such as hair length and color of clothing), sex was the primary category they used. The mistakes they made using sexual categories were consistent with the relative status of men and women in our society. Men had more difficulty distinguishing between female target persons than between male target persons under all conditions. Women paid more attention to the environment in which the interactions took place, but still confused females more than males (Lorenzi-Cioldi, 1993). Thus, both sexes acknowledged the greater personal distinctiveness and individuality of males.

Selective Recall

When categorized as a group, people are thought to possess relatively similar beliefs and exhibit similar behaviors. People systematically distort their recollections about individuals from a particular category so as to make them resemble their stereotypes about members of that category. For example, when students who read a long story about the life of a woman named Betty K. were subsequently informed that she was currently living either a lesbian or heterosexual lifestyle, they "remembered" more events that supported their current interpretation of her sexual identity (Snyder & Uranowitz, 1978). Respondents who learned that Betty K. had a lesbian lifestyle recognized more events in her life that reflected stereotypic beliefs about lesbians; for example, that she had not dated in college. Similarly, people were more likely to recall having seen "librarian-like" qualities in the behavior of a stimulus person when she was portrayed as a librarian rather than as a waitress (Cohen, 1981)

Awareness of reconstructive processes in person perception should sensitize you to the powerful but often unnoticed consequences of our beliefs about other people. "In our quest to see others as stable and predictable creatures, we may cognitively create a world in which erroneous inferences about others can perpetuate themselves" (Snyder & Uranowitz, 1978, p. 949).

Selective Interpretation

A number of times throughout this book, you will find the statement that there is no such thing as a gender-blind reality. When men and women engage in identical behaviors, people perceive these behaviors differently. Many examples of selective inference can be found throughout this book. People do not seem to be aware of their biased assumptions. For example, both male and female college students unconsciously misattributed fame more to males than to females (Banaji & Greenwald, 1994). Their perceptions were unrelated to their conscious beliefs about gender equality. Such cognitive biases help explain why it is so difficult to change the gendered status quo.

Attributional Biases

Attributional biases occur when people try to infer the causes of behavior and take cognitive shortcuts that speed up the decision-making process. One major form of attributional bias is known as the *fundamental attribution error.* This term refers to the tendency to underestimate the impact of situations on other people's behavior and to overestimate the impact of their individual personalities. It is this error that leads people to believe that many behavioral differences between women and men are consistent and stable.

A number of attributional biases based on various aspects of gender have been found. For example, luck appears to be associated with the success of individuals for whom success is not expected. When respondents were asked to explain the rapid rise of attractive women or men as corporate executives, they viewed luck as more responsible for the success of attractive women than for the success of unattractive women. The reverse was true for men. Unattractive men were seen to have needed more luck to succeed (Heilman & Stopeck, 1985). Similarly, a white man with a successful banking career was seen as having greater ability and less luck than a comparable white woman, black man, or black woman (Yarkin, Town, & Wallston, 1982).

One particularly destructive bias is *blaming the victim.* Victim blame may be one form of the fundamental attribution error. Victims are seen as responsible for their misfortunes by people who do not wish to believe that the same random calamity could happen to them. As you will see in Chapter 14, blaming the victim is particularly likely to occur when women are raped.

Behavioral Confirmation and the Self-Fulfilling Prophecy

These cognitive biases are not just passive perceptions about others. When people interact with someone, they look for information that will confirm their beliefs about that person's social category. For example, when students were informed that they would be interviewing a person who was either an introvert or an extrovert, they chose questions that would confirm the social label they had been given (Snyder & Swann, 1978b). It is only a small step away from generating questions that confirm expectations to acting in such a way as to produce them. This process is part of a phenomenon known as the *self-fulfilling prophecy.*

There are really two aspects of self-fulfilling prophecies. One part of the process is the way people sometimes act to confirm the beliefs that others have about them. This process involves changes in *self-presentation.* One of the earliest studies that applied this concept to gender asked women students to describe themselves to a male partner whose stereotype of an ideal woman was said to conform closely to either a traditional or a nontraditional type (Zanna & Pack, 1975). The attitudes of these women had been measured on a previous occasion. When the partner was desirable (good-looking and attending an elite university), the women portrayed themselves more in terms of his ideal type regardless of their actual attitudes. The women performed better on tests of intellectual competence when the desirable partner was portrayed as having nonstereotypic views about women. Women also altered their self-presentation strategies when they believed they were to be interviewed by a male chauvinist rather than by a nonsexist potential employer (von Baeyer, Sherk, & Zanna, 1981). When women believed that they were to be interviewed by a chauvinist man, they wore more frilly clothing, more jewelry, and perfume to the interview.

It seems reasonable that people should choose to change their appearance in order to maximize the potential rewards in a social interaction. We believe, however, that this study demonstrates how sexism is maintained. Ask yourself the following questions: Did these women realize that they were altering their behavior? Are these shifts in self-presentation strategies sex symmetrical? That is, do men change to reflect what they perceive to be the desires of women with whom they are interacting?

These studies do not tell us whether the women were responding to the maleness or the status and power of the man with whom they interacted. Nevertheless, they tell us a great deal about the construction of social relationships between the sexes because neither we nor the participants know anything about the man's behavior. His behavior, in fact, exists only in the imagination of the women participants. These studies demonstrate that women will change their behavior to conform to what they believe to be the expectations of powerful or desirable men.

These studies also tell us nothing about the other part of the process by which self-fulfilling prophecies are created—how people's actions produce the behaviors they expect. This process is known as *behavioral confirmation.* Social psychologists have begun to clarify the processes by which people produce the behaviors they expect from others through their social interactions with them. Their studies show how many traits associated with men and women may be produced by social psychological mechanisms.

In the earliest study in this series, Mark Snyder and his associates demonstrated the existence of self-fulfilling prophecies in terms of physical attractiveness (Snyder, Tanke, & Berscheid, 1977). Male college students had a short conversation by telephone with women whom they had been led to believe were either physically attractive or unattractive. Photographs had, however, been assigned to their female partners at random. And the women were unaware that their male partners had received any false information about their physical appearance. Nevertheless, judges (who heard only the women's part of the conversation) rated those women who had been labeled as physically attractive as more friendly, sociable, and likable than those who had been labeled as less physically attractive. Presumably, the women were responding to subtle cues in the men's conversations with them.

Even in such a brief encounter, the perceivers created their own social reality. Such behaviors may have long-term effects on the behaviors of those who are categorized as attractive. For example, there is a widespread stereotype that "What is beautiful is good" (Dion, Berscheid, & Walster, 1972). Attractive people of both sexes have been rated as more socially skillful by people who have only had a telephone conversation with them (Goldman & Lewis, 1977).

Behavioral traits traditionally associated with either men or women can be influenced by the behavior of others who expect behaviors consistent with gender-traditional categories. For example, men who expected to interact in a competitive game with a man who had been labeled as hostile initiated more aggressive interactions with him (Snyder & Swann, 1978a). In turn, their behavior induced more aggression from him than from a supposedly nonhostile partner. Interestingly, if the target individuals in this study were led to believe that their aggressive behavior reflected their own *dispositional traits* (e.g., were indicative of their personality), they maintained this increased level of aggression in their subsequent competition with naive partners who had no prior knowledge about them. If, however, the targets were informed that their behavior in the game reflected their partner's behavior (a *situational attribution*), they did not continue this higher level of aggressive behavior with new partners.

This finding illustrates one of the most potent elements of the behavioral confirmation process. If a person internalizes the new behavior generated by the behavioral confirmation process, both that person and the perceiver may come to share perceptions about what he or she is like. "What began in the mind of the perceiver will have become reality not only in the behavior of the target but also in the mind of the target" (Snyder & Swann, 1978a, p. 151).

Self-fulfilling prophecies have been shown to contribute to the perpetuation of stereotypic beliefs about women (Skrypnek & Snyder, 1982). Unacquainted pairs of men and women were asked to negotiate a division of labor on a series of work-related tasks that differed in their gender-role connotations. Students were located in different rooms and communicated by means of a signaling system. Some of the men were told that they were interacting with a male partner, some with a female partner, and some were not informed about the sex of their partner. During the first part of the study, the men were given the opportunity to make the choices about how the tasks were to be divided between themselves and their partners.

The researchers found that men were more likely to choose the more masculine tasks when they believed their partner was a woman than when they believed she was a man or had no information about her sex. When both partners initially chose the same task, the men were much less willing to let their partner have the preferred task and switch to the alternative when they believed she was a woman.

As long as the men were the initiators in the situation, all their partners provided behavioral confirmation for their beliefs. The sex to which they were assigned rather than their actual sex influenced their behavior! "Male" partners chose more masculine tasks and "female" partners chose more feminine tasks. Even when the men no longer had the opportunity to guide the negotiations, many of their partners continued to manifest "gender-appropriate behaviors"—behaviors appropriate to the sex to which they had been assigned. This study clearly shows how one person's beliefs about the sex of another and the corresponding stereotypes associated with this belief actually channel the interaction so as to confirm stereotypical beliefs. At the same time, this experience probably confirms and strengthens the perceiver's stereotypes about women and men in general—stereotypes that he or she will then carry into new situations and act to confirm.

This study also reaffirms the idea discussed earlier in this chapter that people seem unable to tolerate ambiguity in their sexual categories. People whose sex was unlabeled behaved in a manner that was indistinguishable from those who were labeled as male. This is because perceivers adopted similar behavioral strategies for men and for people whose sex was unknown. These results are very consistent with other findings showing androcentric biases (as in Chapter 4). When sex is unspecified, people are assumed to be male. In other words, maleness is the normative condition.

Sex and Self-Categorization

The Effect of Dominance and Subordination

If sex is such an important stimulus for interactions with others, we would expect it to be an important label for ourselves as well. The use of sex as a self-label is so obvious that there have actually been few studies demonstrating it. One early study asked 156 male and female students to respond fifteen times to the question "Who am I?" (Gordon, 1968). The most frequent responses were age (82 percent) and sex (74 percent).

We all have many different social labels with which we can identify. Why did these students choose two of the many possibilities as an important source of self-identification? The social identities people choose appear to be partly a function of the relationship of their category to other societal distinctions. Individuals who are members of low-status or minority groups appear to identify more with those social categories that define their status. Thus, women mentioned their sexual category membership more than men did, blacks mentioned race more than whites did and Jews mentioned religion more than Christians did (Gordon, 1968). People who belonged to the normative group in the United States—white, Christian men—appeared to see no need to so identify themselves. In fact, they may not have been aware that these characteristics are also social categories.

Are these aspects of group identification a function of the status of a group? Although researchers cannot change a person's group membership at will, they can manipulate dominance/subordination relationships within a laboratory context. In one clever experiment, for example, a group was given the opportunity of making a choice of the place they wished to occupy. The other group did not have a choice (it was defined for them by the choices made by the first group). You can think of this as analogous to the last moves in the game of tic-tac-toe. When subjects were asked "Who am I?" choosers tended to make reference to general categories, such as person, whereas nonchoosers made more positional or relativistic choices (Deschamps, 1982). Dominant group members did not think of themselves as being determined by their group membership or their social affiliation. The social system is defined by them rather than the other way around.

The Effect of Distinctiveness

Recent studies suggest that group identification is also influenced by the distinctiveness of the category within its current social setting. For example, schoolchildren were much more likely to mention sex as an element of their self-concept when their sex comprised the minority in their classroom rather than the majority (McGuire & Padawer-Singer, 1976). Both boys and girls whose sex was, numerically speaking, the minority in their household were also more likely to mention sex as part of their self-identification (McGuire, McGuire, & Winton, 1979). For example, boys who had more sisters were more likely to mention being male than boys who had more brothers. Sex was also more salient for both college men and women when they were asked for self-identification in a just assembled group in which they were the minority (Cota & Dion, 1986). People focus on their own distinctive personal characteristics because of their value in distinguishing themselves from others.

In order to understand how gender creates as well as reflects the behavior of men and women, it is important to remember that gender categories are not symmetrical in our society. Women and men are seen not only as different but also as unequal. Men are dominant in our society and are valued more than women. In turn, they exert more power and influence and control cultural definitions that maintain women's subordination. Noted social psychologist Henri Tajfel (1984) argued in one of his last articles that it is not the difference that matters in our society, but the distinction. Distinction is the active social process that creates, expresses, and maintains differences. The first part of this chapter has focused on social mechanisms for making and maintaining distinctions between women and men. Power and status confer the ability to originate and diffuse powerful social myths. The next part of this chapter will discuss the nature of sex-related differences in status and power.

Some Definitions

In order to understand how gender functions to distinguish and stratify people, we must use terminology that has been considered to be more the province of sociologists than of psychologists. Some of these terms are *social power* (sometimes abbreviated as power), *ascribed status,* and *achieved status.* Before reading further, try to define these concepts in your own words.

Social power is not as easy to define as it first seems. There have been a large number of attempts to define it (c.f. Unger, 1978; Griscom, 1992). Power is an attribute of relationships, not individuals. It is determined by the control some people have over events or resources that others value (Molm & Hedley, 1992).

Social power differs from social influence in that it implies some form of implicit force. However, because it is often difficult to determine what sorts of rewards and punishments are operating in a relationship, psychologists use the terms social power and influence interchangeably. Part of the reason for this confusion of terminology is that power appears to represent a stabler quality than what psychologists investigate in the laboratory. Another reason is that personal power is not considered a desirable characteristic by many people in our society. For example, would you consider it a compliment if someone called you a "good politician"?

The term *status* is used to refer to a person's potential ability to influence others. Sociologists usually recognize two kinds of status: ascribed and achieved. *Achieved status* is based partly on the role one performs in an organization or a family—for example, boss versus secretary, father versus mother, or professor versus student. How well one performs one's role is also a component of achieved status, although this is often difficult to determine because many roles have no explicit criteria by which to evaluate a person. Good students are fairly easy to distinguish from poor ones, but within the general range of "normality" how does one distinguish "good" fathers from "poor" ones?

A more interesting form of status for those interested in gender is ascribed status. *Ascribed status* is based on the possession of characteristics with which someone is born. The degree of status conferred because of a particular characteristic depends on how valuable society defines it to be. In the United States, race, age, social class, and sex are all determinants of ascribed status. Although some of these characteristics can change, it is difficult or impossible for them to do so as a result of the person's efforts. Moreover, their relative value in society is determined by others' definitions rather than one's own.

Ascribed status is usually described in hierarchical terms—persons possess more or less status relative to others. Unlike achieved status, these differences are not based on functional roles. They are based on cultural norms. Ascribed status describes and predicts relations between categories of people in terms of the rewards, benefits, or compliance they give each other. In other words, ascribed status defines who is supposed to have more social power in a relationship.

You may find these distinctions clearer by the use of an example suggested by Cheryl Travis (personal communication). Think of a posh restaurant in New

York City. A tourist from the Midwest has difficulty getting a waiter's attention no matter how elaborately he gestures. A suave customer from Wall Street obtains obsequious service with the flick of a wrist. Obviously, the latter gentleman has ascribed status. A gender-relevant example from the real world is the tendency for women's suggestions and comments to be ignored until the same idea is proposed by a man. To get the same amount of recognition women often have to be more persistent and make repeated efforts, sometimes leading to the perception that successful women are "pushy," "mouthy," and "difficult."

The Relationship between Status and Power

As you can see from this example, people's actions and achievements are responded to differently, depending on who they are. Later in the chapter we will examine what happens to women when their achievements and social power clash with their ascribed status. Here we will examine some theoretical reasons people's behavior (which can alter their achieved status) has so little impact on ascribed status.

In a group or social system, individuals are typically differentiated from one another according to one or more dimensions involving ascribed or achieved characteristics. Sex, as an ascribed characteristic, conveys status and power. It has been argued that "maleness" is a diffuse status characteristic—associated with greater power, prestige, and social value than "femaleness" (Cohen, Berger, & Zelditch, 1972; Unger, 1976; 1978).

Because gender is an ascribed or diffuse status characteristic, it is not easily changed by the behavior of individuals. For example, if women lack power because of their roles as childbearers or child rearers, they will gain power as a result of changes in these roles (e.g., if men had an equal share in child care). If, however, their relative lack of power is a result of who they are, they will continue to lack power even in "male" roles.

GENDER DIFFERENCES AS STATUS DIFFERENCES

Gender-Related Differences in Nonverbal Behaviors

Nancy Henley (1977) pioneered the study of the relationship between nonverbal behaviors associated with status and the behaviors of women and men. In many aspects of nonverbal behavior women behave very much like men with low status and are treated by others as though they possess such subordinate status (see Table 5.1). Females' politeness, smiling, emotional responsiveness, smaller personal space, less frequent touching, and greater frequency of being interrupted may all reflect their subordinate status.

Recent studies continue to show gender-related differences in behavior that parallel the behaviors of people who differ in status. In one study, for example, pairs of men, pairs of women, and mixed-sex pairs interacted during a ten-minute task in which each pair constructed a domino structure for a contest (Lott, 1987). Under these laboratory conditions, women behaved the same way regardless of whether their partner was a man or another woman. Men, how-

TABLE 5.1. Gestures of Power and Privilege: Examples of Nonverbal Behaviors

	Between Status Nonequals		*Between Men and Women*	
Nonverbal Behavior	Used by Superior	Used by Subordinate	Used by Men	Used by Women
Demeanor	Informal	Circumspect	Informal	Circumspect
Posture	Relaxed	Tense	Relaxed	Tense
Personal space	Closeness (option)	Distance	Closeness	Distance
Touching	Touch (option)	Don't touch	Touch	Don't touch
Eye contact	Stare, ignore	Avert eyes, watch	Stare, ignore	Avert eyes, watch
Facial expression	Don't smile	Smile	Don't smile	Smile
Emotional expression	Hide	Show	Hide	Show
Self-disclosure	Don't disclose	Disclose	Don't disclose	Disclose

Source: Adapted from N. Henley (1977). *Body politics: power, sex, and nonverbal communication.* Copyright © 1977 by Simon & Schuster, Inc. Reprinted by permission of Simon & Schuster, Inc.

ever, distanced themselves more from female than male partners by turning their faces or bodies away and by placing the dominoes closer to themselves than to their partners. Among the seventeen mixed-sex pairs in which the structure was closer to one partner than to the other, in fourteen cases it was closer to the man than to the woman. Paper-and-pencil measures had not revealed any evidence of prejudice or gender stereotypes among these college students.

Since sex is highly related to ascribed status (the people with more social power are usually men), achieved status can be changed more readily. Researchers have manipulated assigned roles or levels of achievement to see if the way men customarily behave toward women is due to gender-typed behaviors or reflects their usually superior status in social settings. In one such study (Leffler, Gillespie, & Conaty, 1982), college women and men were assigned either the high-status position of teacher or the lower status of student. Statuses were reversed on the second trial so that teachers became students and vice versa. In general, high-status men and women claimed more direct space with their bodies, talked more, and attempted more interruptions than low-status men and women. By means of touching and pointing (to the partner and his or her possessions) they symbolically intruded on them.

In a similar study, Jack Dovidio and his associates manipulated the degree of expertise or reward power possessed by partners in mixed-sex interactions (Dovidio, Ellyson, Keating, Heltman, & Brown, 1988). Both men and women who were high in power displayed high visual dominance, defined as the ratio of looking while speaking to looking while listening. (Low-power individuals look more when they are listening than when they are speaking.) Under conditions in which women and men had not been given different levels of power, men behaved like those with high power and women exhibited visual behavior similar to patterns found in low-expertise and low-reward conditions. These studies show that in the absence of situation-specific status differences, maleness is a cue to higher status and power (Ellyson, Dovidio, & Brown, 1992).

Social expectations about gender and power are reflected in a number of nonverbal behaviors (see Table 5.1). The kinds of nonverbal behaviors in which men and women customarily engage in group settings not only reflect status and power differences but also help to perpetuate them. Women lean away from the group and smile when speaking significantly more than men do (Kennedy & Camden, 1983). People are more likely to be interrupted by others when they lean away, smile, or do not look at the turn-taker.

Recent studies on conversational dynamics illustrate the way beliefs about high male status reinforce traditional gender-linked patterns of behavior in mixed-sex groups. Interruptions, for example, are mechanisms through which higher-status individuals can gain the floor and restrict the contributions of lower-status group members. We noted earlier that men are likely to interrupt more than women in most groups. However, even in groups where men and women attempt to interrupt at roughly the same rate, researchers find that the men are more discriminating in their interruptions (they interrupt women more than men). Men are also more successful interrupting women than they are when they attempt to interrupt other men (Smith-Lovin & Brody, 1989).

These results show that the display of power by men is socially reinforced. Other studies have shown that those who feel most comfortable in social situations are more willing to interrupt others (Campbell, Kleim, & Olson, 1992). Women who interrupt others, however, cannot be so sure of social support. For example, Marianne LaFrance (1992) asked students to rate videotapes of interactions between two men, two women, or a man and a women that were identical in script features. They rated a woman who interrupted a man as ruder, more irritable, and more self-concerned than other interruptors (LaFrance, 1992). Interactions in which a woman interrupted a man tended to receive more negative ratings than any other pairing. Raters of both sexes agreed that there was something amiss about this situation. The woman appeared to have broken more than a conversational rule. She had violated an accepted social policy concerning appropriate behavior by those possessing less power. As you will see later in this chapter, such forms of social regulation decrease the probability that women will emerge as leaders of mixed-sex groups.

The Perception of Nonverbal Cues to Status

Women generally appear to be better at decoding nonverbal cues than men are (Hall, 1985). This difference is consistent with subordinate status, in which it is important for lower-power individuals to adapt their behaviors to the demands of more dominant individuals. When men communicate dominance, their female partners tend to respond with low-power gestures, although men do not show similar accommodation to dominant behaviors in women (Davis & Weitz, 1981).

Both women and men appear to have difficulty in perceiving when a woman is in a position of high power or leadership. The same nonverbal cues that communicate power for men may not work for women. Think back to the example we gave at the beginning of this chapter. Sitting at the head of the table in a mixed-sex setting is associated with being viewed as the leader of a group for men. But this same cue has no effect on the perception of women as leaders (Porter & Geis, 1981).

Under some conditions, nonverbal gestures of dominance may affect how others evaluate a woman's social power. Both men and women accurately interpreted different levels of visual dominance displayed by a woman who was interacting with either a man or another woman (Ellyson, Dovidio, & Fehr, 1981). They rated her as more powerful when her use of visual dominance cues was high. Thus, it may be possible to change perceptions of status by changing nonverbal behaviors. However, much more research on how nonverbal cues communicate power is necessary. We do not know why some cues, such as visual dominance, can enhance perceptions of women's authority while others, such as where she sits at a table, have no effect.

It is important to keep in mind, moreover, that women are not expected to possess power and authority in our society. For example, Paula Johnson (1974, 1976) found that subjects of both sexes believed that messages from an unseen partner communicating *expert, legitimate* (conferred by a socially sanctioned authority), and *informational* power were more likely to have been sent by a man than by a woman. In contrast, messages communicating *referent* (in support of one's group), *helpless,* and *indirect* power were seen as more likely to have been sent by a woman.

Gender and the Use of Social Power

The use of masculine forms of power may be less effective for women than for men. In a recent study, Linda Carli (1990) found that women speak more tentatively when interacting with men with whom they disagree than when interacting with other women under the same circumstances. This use of tentative speech appeared to be functional for women. Men were influenced to a greater degree by women who spoke tentatively than by those who spoke assertively. Women who spoke tentatively were less effective with other women. Both men and women judged a woman who spoke tentatively to be less competent and knowledgeable than a woman who spoke assertively. The kind of language used, however, had no effect on their judgments of male speakers.

This study illustrates a classic double bind. If women use tentative language as a subtle influence strategy, it compromises their perceived competence and makes it difficult for them to persuade other women. If they use more assertive language, however, they will find it difficult to influence men. Since most influence attempts in the real world take place in mixed-sex situations, there is no behavior by which a woman can "win." This study was circulated widely on e-mail (electronic computer networks) and sent to one of the authors by her daughter, who was very dismayed at the findings. We find them distressing too!

One reason women in mixed-sex interactions use indirect power strategies may be that women anticipate unfavorable reactions from men. These assumptions are not unfounded. In a study of emergent leaders in mixed-sex groups, female leaders were found to receive more negative emotional responses when they made the same contributions as male leaders. Negative responses included furrowed brows, tightening of the mouth, and nods of disagreement. Women's contributions to the group also received fewer positive responses such as smiles and nods of agreement (Butler & Geis, 1990).

It is not surprising, therefore, that it is difficult to induce women to behave in a dominant manner in group situations. Steve Ellyson and his colleagues (1992), for example, formed groups of two men and two women with a group leader who received three times as much credit for class participation than the other members of the group. Groups were either (1) told that the leader had received the unanimous vote of everyone in the group; (2) told that the leader had received more votes than others, but the vote was split; or (3) given no information about leadership selection. They found that women leaders displayed lower levels of visual dominance except when their leadership was securely mandated (e.g., the result of a unanimous vote). Men, in contrast, displayed high visual dominance even when their position was not secure. The women leaders appeared to underestimate their own power and/or question their own legitimacy.

By behaving in a nondominant manner, the women created a self-fulfilling prophecy. Observers who were not aware of the leadership conditions in the study rated the women in insecure leadership positions as significantly less powerful than comparable men. Only the women who were unanimously authorized in their leadership displayed high visual dominance and were perceived to be as powerful and competent as the men.

Women's choice of indirect influence strategies appears to be a function of their lower power rather than their personality differences from men. Women and men have been found to prefer the same order of influence strategies (White & Roufail, 1989). Both sexes also choose more direct influence tactics when they are powerful and more indirect strategies when they have less power (Sagrestano, 1992). Cross-culturally, power predicts what kind of influence tactic is used more than sex does (Steil & Hillman, 1993).

Women's customary use of indirect power in groups as well as their more subordinate nonverbal behaviors appear to be a response to the double standard for men's and women's identical behaviors. For example, the form of social power men use has no impact on their ability to influence either women or other men. As you will see in chapter 7, both boys and girls learn the differential use of power and status to influence others early.

The effects of gender on social influence are not limited to public groups or workplace settings. Studies among romantic couples show, for example, that the more dominant or powerful person of either sex is more likely to interrupt and to be successful at it, whereas the less powerful individual uses more tentative language (Kollock, Blumstein, & Schwartz, 1985). The more dominant partner is likely to be a man. In your own relationships, who determines most of the topics of conversation?

Women who exert power over men may even be punished for it. Women directing men received less positive evaluations and were seen as acting out of role when compared to men directing either women or men, or women directing only women (Jacobson, Antonelli, Winning, & Opeil, 1977). Experienced managers rated men who were portrayed as influential in a corporate setting as significantly more powerful, as higher in position, and as warmer than women in identical situations (Wiley & Eskilson, 1982). The men were seen as particularly effective and active when they used expert power. When women used expert power, they were seen as far colder than the men.

THE ROLE OF GENDER IN BOUNDARY MAINTENANCE

Stigma

It should be clear from the material discussed earlier in this chapter that gender does far more than tell us about the behavior of women and men. Gender also prescribes the way women and men ought to behave. People who do not conform to our perceptions about the way typical and "normal" individuals of their sex behave are likely to be punished for their nonconformity. The mechanisms by which such nonconformity is socially defined and punished are often described by social scientists in terms of two processes—*stigma* and *deviance.* These processes impose social control. Those who have the power to define acceptable behavior in others benefit by labeling others as deviant.

Deviance and stigma are related concepts, although they are not exactly the same. Stigmatization refers to the process of responding to a person in terms of some physically negative or socially undesirable characteristic she or he possesses. Erving Goffman (1963) defines a stigma as a trait that intrudes itself on our attention and prevents the person who possesses it from engaging in normal relationships with others. We react to the characteristic rather than to the person. It is difficult, for example, for us to ignore the fact that someone is in a wheelchair, is blind, or has an unattractive scar.

We tend to avoid stigmatized people or to deal with them only in terms of their "handicaps" (Asch & Fine, 1988). We react to them in terms of their stigma rather than in terms of other human qualities they possess. In daily life, women are often perceived and responded to in terms of their categorical membership—as females, first and foremost. Such a response carries with it a certain degree of social stigma because, relatively speaking, femaleness appears to be a devalued status.

People who fall into a devalued category are typically thought of as comprising a unitary or homogeneous group. A variety of evidence discussed in Chapter 4 demonstrates that women are a devalued group in our society. For example, women in groups "look more alike" than men do. Women are also objectified more than men are and are denigrated in cultural symbolism, for example, the pervasive negative stereotypes found in the mass media, pornography, and language itself. Chapter 12 will document the existence of sex inequality within our social and economic system. Highly valued persons are not systematically relegated to the lower echelons of the socioeconomic and occupational prestige ladder. Occupying these positions, in turn, tends to be a basis for evaluating women unfavorably.

Deviance and the Power to Define

Women's vulnerability to stigmatization is due to their general social subordination and relatively poor power position. They are not in a good position to define the rules that evaluate their own behavior. Some sociologists (c.f. Schur, 1983) have argued that women's social subordination is maintained by defining many of their characteristics and behaviors as deviant. "Social groups create deviance by making the rules whose infraction constitutes deviance, and by applying these rules to particular people and labeling them as outsiders" (Becker, 1963, p. 9).

Women's deviance is, like any deviance, a social construct. What most counts socially is how people perceive and react to a given behavior or condition. The very same behavior or condition may be defined or responded to differently when it is associated with a woman rather than with a man. For example, we have very different names for an unmarried woman or man who has an active and varied sex life. Depending on our values, such an unmarried woman may be considered "promiscuous" or "liberated." You will notice that the behavior being described is not different, but our labels are. You may also notice that the same categories do not apply to men. What level or kind of sexual behavior is defined as promiscuity for a man?

Dealing with Deviance in a Group Setting

Several studies illustrate the way a woman may be defined as deviant within a group setting. One important study by Carol Wolman and Hal Frank (1975) examined the role of the lone woman within small groups designed to enhance interpersonal communication. All participants were of equal status. They were, in fact, peer groups of graduate students or psychiatric residents who participated in these groups as part of their professional training. In five of the six groups studied, the lone woman became a deviant or isolated member of the group. In one group she was able to acquire low-status regular membership.

The researchers provide an illuminating description of the techniques used by groups of men to deal with a woman who is "out of place." They found that when the group members started to interact, women were not allowed to compete freely for status. Attempts by a woman to influence the group were ignored, while similar attempts made by a man were heeded and credited to him. A woman who persisted in trying to influence the group after having been ignored received either coordinated reaction against her or further instances of no reaction. Men labeled assertiveness as bitchiness or manipulation and appeared to be more threatened by competition with a woman than with each other. When a woman showed feelings or advocated their expression, emotionality became identified with feminine behavior. The sex of the woman was either virtually ignored or joked about. When the women tried to escape their role as isolates or deviants by increasing their interactions with others, they were increasingly ignored.

Many coping mechanisms carry contradictory sex-role labels in our culture (see Figure 5.3). If she acted friendly, she was thought to be flirting. If she acted weak, the men tried to infantilize her, treating her as a "little sister" rather than a peer. If she apologized for alienating the group, she was seen as a submissive woman knowing her place. If she asked for help, she earned a "needy female" label. If she became angry or tried to point out rationally what the group process was doing to her, she was seen as competitive, in a bitchy, unfeminine way. "Feminine" coping mechanisms increased her perceived differences; "masculine" ones threatened the men so that they isolated her even more. Any internal ambivalence about her sexual role was rekindled by these labels, and increased

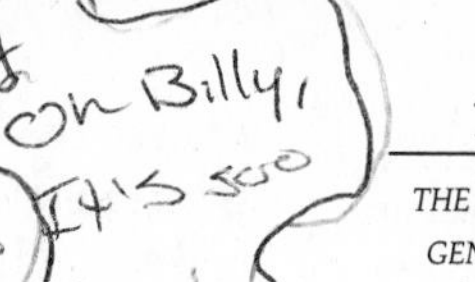

FIGURE 5.3. The contradictory treatment of Hillary Clinton by the media. Is she the high-powered lawyer or the motherly cookie baker?

her anxiety, which increased her coping behavior, which further increased her deviance (Wolman & Frank, 1975, p. 168)!

Men who supported the lone woman in these groups risked being identified with her and sharing her deviance. Recently, studies in the laboratory have found similar effects for whites who associated with blacks and for heterosexual men who associated with gay men (Neuberg, Smith, Hoffman, & Russell, 1994). The negative qualities associated with those who supported members of stigmatized groups persisted even after attempts to make the heterosexual target seem similar to the respondents and to present him as a person with high achieved status. This generalization of stigma makes it more difficult for those who wish to change the group process to do so.

Since they had been led to expect that the professions were a male sanctuary, the men presumably resented the presence of a woman and acted to prevent her from becoming a regular member so that they could have an almost all-male group. The women tended to give up their efforts after a while, becoming depressed instead. We could almost consider them group casualties. The single characteristic that these women shared and that was presumably the rationale for group hostility was the fact of being female.

Women who have attained high professional status may also be excluded. Here are some examples in their own words:

> I've attended several dean's conferences where about six out of the seventy participants are women. Women are usually ignored—during panels and informal discussions—because men think they have nothing to learn from women (woman vice president at a university).
>
> Several times, my male colleagues used my records of my patients to do research. It's never occurred to them to ask me to participate on these projects or to ask my opinion about diagnoses. I know I'm doing a good job, but I feel very isolated professionally (woman physician at a major medical school).
>
> When a team of engineers presented a study, they avoided eye contact with me and spoke directly to the men on the board. It was so obvious that they were presenting their findings "over my head" that I decided to take action in order to demonstrate I had an understanding of the project. I asked a technical question. . . . It made some difference, but I can see that I have to be ever alert to dealing with subtle discrimination constantly and that I am not being paranoid (only woman on the board of trustees of an electric cooperative).
> (From Benokraitis & Feagin, 1986, pp. 92–94)

A person's sex greatly affects how his or her violation of procedural rules in a group setting is perceived. In one set of studies (Wahrman & Pugh, 1972, 1974), a man or woman (who were confederates of the experimenter) violated rules about turn-taking and reward allocation at various times during a series of trials involving problem-solving. Early nonconformity by a man led coworkers to consider him more influential and desirable, although the nonconformist was disliked more than one who went along with the group. In contrast, the earlier a woman violated the rules, the less she influenced the group and the more disliked and less desirable as a coworker she became. The best liked of all the confederates was the conforming woman.

A nonconforming woman was least acceptable in these otherwise all-male groups. Even her ability to solve problems well did not affect men's negative evaluations of her. Competent nonconforming women were preferred less than incompetent nonconforming men—even though the group as a whole benefited from competent performance. These findings about the negative evaluations of competent women are similar to those involving assertiveness and influence discussed earlier in the chapter.

The Token Woman

Obviously, a woman is much more likely to be seen as a representative of the social category "female" when she is the single person of her sex present in a group. This situation has been studied extensively in the past few years in terms of a phenomenon that has become known as *tokenism* (see Chapter 12). Token women are more visible and isolated than the men who, because of their numerical dominance, determine the culture of the group. They are likely to be defined in stereotypically feminine terms, and they are likely to be seen by themselves and others as representing women's issues rather than the interests of the group as a whole (Izraeli, 1983).

The consequences of having solo status are markedly different for women and men. Solo women were unlikely to be selected as group leaders; overall group satisfaction was lowest when a lone woman was present; and gender-related issues were most likely to be raised in groups that included only one woman (Crocker & McGraw, 1984). Solo men, on the other hand, tended to be integrated into their groups as leader, resulting in smoother group functioning.

Men were seen by others in the group as more masculine when they had solo status, whereas women were perceived to be least feminine when they had solo status. Such gender-stereotypical expectancies could account for why the lone men were likely to be chosen as group leaders. There was no room in these groups, however, for a solo with low status. For example, there were no "assistant" roles available.

These studies demonstrate that tokenism is not simply a result of numerical dominance. Numerical dominance is situationally dependent (based, for example, on who might be available to serve on a committee). Tokenism, however, exerts its effects through cultural dominance, which is a constant. Those who dominate a field of action over time come to determine the rules of interaction for strangers who chance to penetrate the boundaries. Neither their culture nor their power is neutralized by numerical reshuffling (Izraeli, 1983).

Group Dynamics: Gender, Status, and Roles

The impact of gender-related variables in groups is extremely complex (see the extensive review by Dion, 1985). The extent to which women are discriminated against depends not only on the percentage of each sex present in the group, but also on such factors as the task in which the group is engaged, whether leaders are elected or emerge, and the position of the group within the more general institutional framework. In this part of the chapter we shall focus on group processes. We shall review briefly a number of recent studies that demonstrate how the perceptions and behaviors of both women and men interact to maintain male dominance.

As you saw earlier in this chapter, experimental manipulations of the relative status of women and men can change the nonverbal behaviors customarily displayed by each sex. Manipulations of perceived competence can also change the way men and women usually perform in groups. For example, researchers observed students interacting in four-person mixed-sex groups (Wood & Karten, 1986). When they were given information only about each other's name and sex, men were perceived by themselves and by other group members to be more competent than women. Men also engaged in a greater amount of active task behavior (giving information and opinions), whereas women showed more positive social behaviors (agreeing and acting friendly).

Within such groups women and men also responded differently to the positive and negative behaviors of others. When a positive act occurred, women were more likely to respond with another positive act (especially if the initiator of the action was another woman), whereas men used the positive action as a cue to begin task-related behavior (Wood & Rhodes, 1992). If, on the other hand, someone behaved negatively within the group, men were much more likely to respond negatively, especially when the initiator was another man. Women rarely responded at all to negative actions. The consequence of these gender-related differences was that the men tended to elevate the level of conflict within a group whereas the women did not build on conflict and sought to avoid it.

Normative beliefs about greater male competence and social power are difficult to change. Men, for example, did not change their beliefs about their own ability even when they were told that they had less ability than their partner. Women, in contrast, formed either weak or strong expectations about their own ability depending on the experimenters' manipulations (Foschi & Freeman, 1991). The men appeared to be unwilling to accept the authority of others when it conflicted with their standards for themselves.

The perceptions of women are also difficult to change. One set of researchers attempted a large number of interventions designed to reduce men's influence in group decisions involving spatial judgments (Pugh & Wahrman, 1983). When no experimental intervention took place, women deferred to men significantly more often than men deferred to women. Both sexes agreed that men were more competent than women.

The only way that the experimenters were able to change this traditional pattern was to rig the task so that women performed better than men. Under these circumstances, women became more influential and men became less. However, these supposedly superior women still did not gain a significant advantage over their male partners. Instead, a woman had to perform much better than a man in order to be seen as just as good!

Traditional perceptions about men and women sometimes disappear when people are reminded about their egalitarian gender-related beliefs (Porter, Geis, Cooper, & Newman, 1985). But messages conveying traditional gender roles can have the opposite effect. As indicated in Chapter 4, sexist messages in the media have a particularly strong effect on women's behavior. Women who were exposed to advertisements that portrayed women in their traditional role as homemakers subsequently reported less favorable attitudes toward political participation than women who were not exposed to such advertisements (Swarz, Wagner, Bannert, & Mathes, 1987). Similarly, women who were exposed to traditional television commercials de-emphasized achievement in

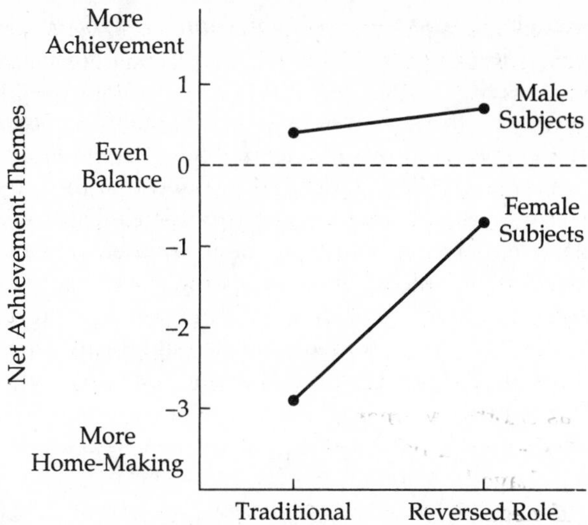

FIGURE 5.4. Differences in women's use of achievement themes after exposure to traditional or role-reversed commercials.

Source: From F. L. Geis et al., "Sex versus status in sex-associated stereotypes," Sex Roles, 11, *1984. Plenum Publishing Corporation. Reprinted with permission.*

favor of homemaking in images of their future lives (Geis, Brown, Jennings, & Porter, 1984). Women who had been exposed to role-reversed commercials were more autonomous in their visions of the future (see Figure 5.4).

Gender and Leadership

Since women are seen to be less competent than men, it is not surprising that they emerge as leaders of groups far less often than men (Eagly & Karau, 1991). The reluctance to select women as leaders is particularly strong in U.S. politics. There are only seven women in the Senate and fewer than fifty women in the House of Representatives (about 10 percent of all the legislators in Congress). And, despite the existence of women prime ministers in such diverse countries as India, Pakistan, Israel, and Great Britain, there has never been a serious woman candidate for the presidency of the United States. The scarcity of women in positions of political leadership extends downward to state and local levels. How many women on your campus hold offices other than that of secretary in your student government?

It has sometimes been argued that women are not elected to leadership positions because they lack necessary experience and skills. Of course, it will be difficult for them to learn skills if they are not given the opportunity to acquire them. Experimental studies of the voting process also indicate that men will be elected over women who possess the same qualifications for office. In a simulated mayoral election, a black man, a white woman, an older white man, and a younger white man, all with equivalent qualifications, were each pitted in two-candidate races against the same candidate, a middle-aged white man. He was able to win four of the five contests—only the younger white man was able to beat him (Sigelman & Sigelman, 1982).

In another study by the same researchers (Sigelman, Thomas, Sigelman, & Ribich, 1986), undergraduates evaluated six challengers to an incumbent in either a mayoral or a county clerk's race. They found that men, but not women, consistently discriminated against women candidates. Discrimination against women candidates appears to be independent of other indicators of social or racial awareness. For example, liberals were found to be more likely than conservatives to vote for a black candidate but not for a woman (Hedlund, Freeman, Hamm, & Stein, 1979). Black men were also significantly less likely to vote for a woman candidate than were black women or white women and men (Sigelman & Welch, 1984).

As we discussed earlier in this chapter, women who assert themselves in mixed-sex groups are likely to be penalized for their behavior. Both men and women associate effective leadership with an authoritarian style (Linimon, Barron, & Falbo, 1984). Such a style is inconsistent with stereotypes prescribing femininity. Men are also more stressed by threats to their status (see Figure 5.5) than women are (Brinkerhoff & Booth, 1984). They appear to be even more threatened by a woman's authority than by her competence. When a woman is portrayed as having authority over men of the same age and social class, she is seen as reducing their status rather than enhancing her own (Denmark, 1980).

The ability to be effective as a leader is influenced greatly by expectations based on gender roles. Although men and women leaders appear to be equally effective overall, women did particularly poorly in settings such as the military in which leadership was defined in highly masculine terms. Men did slightly less well than women in educational settings and governmental and social service organizations (Eagly, Karau, & Makhijani, 1995). Both sexes appear to have more difficulty with task effectiveness when they are in a context that is more congenial to the other sex. Until recently, of course, public settings were much more congenial to men than to women.

Gender and Legitimacy

It should not be surprising, therefore, that women who have attained high positions of leadership in government and industry have been found to question their own legitimacy. Erika Apfelbaum (1993) interviewed fifty women leaders in France and Norway and found that they rarely described their accomplishments in terms of their own intrinsic qualities even though they knew how competent they were. Instead, they explained their positions in terms of extrinsic and external circumstances.

Many of the older French women leaders mentioned their feeling of being a "token woman" who had achieved power as a result of some male authority. Their loneliness was highlighted by the absence of any mention of family in their lives. Their narratives stressed their marginality and sense of lack of control over their destiny. As we will discuss later in this chapter, women often seem to have less sense of *entitlement* than men do.

The second generation of French women leaders (who had had the first group as role models) and the Norwegian women leaders (who comprised a

FIGURE 5.5. Equality depends on one's point of view.

much larger percentage of the leadership in their country) had a much greater sense of their own legitimacy. They seem to have experienced much less conflict than the earlier leaders had. Of course, cultural norms about women in leadership had also changed.

These findings demonstrate how issues of gender involve a complex interplay of cultural, interpersonal, and intrapersonal factors. Even two apparently similar Western European democracies have different conceptions about the division between the public and the private which influence the number of women who enter public life. These norms, in turn, affect the way women resolve career/family conflicts. And, finally, they influence how apparently similarly situated women experience their lives. The positive side of this picture is clearer. Changes in historical/situational circumstances can produce rather rapid changes in women's lives.

STATUS AND SOCIAL BEHAVIORS

The Impact of Roles: A Theoretical Framework

Earlier in this chapter we reviewed the evidence that both men and women see men as having more power and status in groups than women do. There is evidence, moreover, that beliefs about the relative status of the two sexes extend beyond differences in competence and leadership skills. Status appears to influence our beliefs about many characteristics of women and men more than sex does. In other words, gender stereotypes may actually be status and role stereotypes. In contemporary culture, at least, gender and role are intertwined. Roles conferring authority and power are played by men, while women occupy subordinate positions.

A clever experiment by Alice Eagly and Wendy Wood (1982) demonstrates how people use gender to infer information about status. Students were given written scenarios set in either a bank or a supermarket where either a man was said to be trying to influence a woman or a woman was said to be trying to influence a man. In some of these scenarios, the students were informed about the sex of the people portrayed but lacked any more valid information for judging their relative status. These respondents inferred that the man held a higher status job than the woman. They believed that he would be more successful in his attempts to influence her than a woman would be in influencing a man under comparable conditions. When job titles such as bank vice president and bank teller were added to denote relative status, students used status rather than gender cues to predict compliance. This study found that people believed that men and women who had equal status had equal influence.

Beliefs about the personality traits of women and men may also be influenced by their relative status. For example, Florence Geis and her associates (Geis, Brown, Jennings, & Corrado-Taylor, 1984) showed women and men TV commercials that encoded the unequal status of men and women as tacit assumptions. Some undergraduates saw videotapes of reenactments of three originals of such commercials. Other students were exposed to reenactments of these same commercials in which the male and female actors switched roles. The students made personality attributions about each character on five sex-stereotypic dimensions.

The three traditional scenarios, which showed men treated as important authorities and women as subordinate helpmates, produced traditional stereotypes. The men were described as dominant, rational, independent, ambitious leaders, and the women were seen as submissive, emotional, dependent, contented followers. When, however, the same men and women actors switched roles in the same scenarios, the personality attributions also reversed.

Other studies also demonstrate this confusion of status, roles, and traits. For example, many studies indicate that women are more interpersonally sensitive than men (Hall, 1985). Studies that separate sex from roles and status, however, show that it is subordinates who are more sensitive than dominant individuals to the feelings of other group members (Deutsch, 1990; Snodgrass, 1985; 1992). As in the studies on competence, sex had no effect independent of role or status (e.g., women who were given higher status or social power by the experimenters were no more sensitive than comparable men were. These findings suggest that when status is not specified, traditional gender differences occur because of the belief that men are more likely to occupy high-status leadership roles (Eagly, 1983).

People may be unaware of the extent to which many gender-related characteristics actually reflect socially mediated role demands because most social roles are largely confined to one sex. This is why we have discussed laboratory manipulations designed to separate roles and gender so extensively. It is difficult to find real-world examples where gender, status, and roles function independently. When men violate their gender roles they usually lose status (What do you think about a man who is unemployed or a househusband?). Women do not necessarily gain status when they violate gender roles. Instead, they become subject to allegations about their deficiencies in femininity (see Chapters 4 and 12). In the next part of this chapter we will examine how many gender-related differences in social behavior usually attributed to personality may actually be constructed by role demands.

Conformity and Compliance

Meta-analyses have shown a small but consistent tendency for women to be more easily influenced than men (Eagly, 1987). The tendency for men to be more resistant to influence than women is clearest in group-pressure conformity studies. The presence of an audience heightens self-presentational concerns and encourages gender-role-consistent behavior. Women have been found to show little difference in their tendency to conform between public and private conditions. Their behavior is not influenced by whether they respond privately on a written questionnaire or publicly in a group contest. Men, on the other hand, are much more nonconforming in public than they are in private (Eagly, Wood, & Fishbaugh, 1981). Resisting the influence of others is, of course, a component of the normative male role in our society.

People also ascribe more highly communal qualities to conforming than to nonconforming people (Santee & Jackson, 1982). Thus, a tendency for women to agree more readily with others may be a product of the demand for communal traits in women as well as the demand for independence in men. In sum, gender differences in conformity appear to be due to a confusion between sex and status in our society as well as people's need to conform to societal images of masculinity and femininity.

Helping and Being Helped

It is possible to apply this form of analysis to other areas of social behavior besides conformity and compliance. Helping is a particularly rich area to explore in terms of gender because it is a form of behavior that can be studied unobtrusively. There are a large number of field studies on helping that have been conducted outside of the laboratory without the participants' awareness. It is easy to do such studies because helping is a relatively easy behavior to define, and it is not considered unethical to ask people for help or examine whether some people are helped more readily than others.

When a large number of studies of helping are examined, a small but consistent difference between men and women has been found (Eagly, 1987). One aspect of this gender-related difference, however, is not in the direction of our traditional stereotypes. Men are only somewhat more helpful than women, although women are, indeed, more likely to be the recipients of help. These effects, however, are not simply a function of helper and recipient sex. Helping, like many other social behaviors, reflects and maintains gender distinctions in our society.

Women are not always helped more than men. Many studies show little difference in the way women and men are treated, and some studies show clear discrimination against women. For example, college students of both sexes worked less hard in a card-sorting task when they were told that the quota had been set by a woman rather than a man (Sanders & Schmidt, 1980). Several studies (Stead & Zinkhan, 1986; Zinkhan & Stoiadin, 1984) have found that men receive service priority in department stores even when they arrive at the same time as a woman customer. The men were assisted first twice as often as the women were. When the salesclerks (mostly women) were asked about this difference, they gave answers that reflected gender stereotypes such as "Women shop around more," "Men are more serious buyers," "Men need more help than women," or "Men are easier to deal with."

Women tend to be helped more than men in situations where norms about female dependency are evoked. For example, the field studies that show the clearest differences are those that involve travel away from home (Piliavin & Unger, 1985). Women are helped more than men when they require a flat tire to be changed, when they have had a car break down on the highway and need someone to relay a call for them, or when they need travel directions. Men also help women more than men when there is some potential danger for the helper, such as assistance with a supposed theft. Such conditions are consistent with definitions of help in terms of heroism and chivalry—both aspects of the normative masculine role. Men do not help more than women when the situation calls for empathy or less active social support.

These findings all suggest that helping between women and men is influenced by social norms involving gender. Women are more likely to be helped if they are perceived to be needy or dependent on the goodwill of others. Women, however, are also likely to be regarded as more dependent than men even if no other information is available.

Helping between men and women involves more than empty gestures of courtesy or chivalry. Implicit social demands are uncovered when people violate customary norms for such everyday behavior as door opening. When women opened the doors for men, what has been described as deference confrontations occurred (Walum, 1974). There were delays and confusion about who should do what to whom. The amount of emotion and discussion generated by this apparently slight deviation from routine indicates that more than a violation of the rules of Emily Post was occurring.

Laurel Walum compared sex differences in door opening to encounters between individuals possessing differing amounts of authority: "The doctor ushers in his patient, the mother—her children, and the Dean—his faculty, the young and able facilitate the old and infirm. Even reference to the 'gatekeepers of knowledge' symbolically acknowledges the role of authority vested in those responsible for the door" (1974, p. 509). She suggests that opening a door is a political act, one that affirms patriarchal ideology.

You may feel that a study conducted more than twenty years ago is too out-of-date to tell you anything about current ideology about gender. This is an investigation you can easily do for yourself. One of us has done it as a class project several times over the last five years and has found behaviors similar to those described by Walum. One aspect of men's behavior after a door has been opened for them (not found in the written studies) has been described by students. Men tend to touch the door after they have passed through it. This behavior is remarkably similar to that described by Nancy Henley (1977) in public encounters between women and men in which the woman touches the man first. Under these conditions, men reciprocate the touch much more frequently than women do. "Touch privilege" appears to be a mark of the dominant group.

Upsetting Hierarchical Relationships

If helping and being helped are related to status, what happens when the woman needing assistance has higher status than the man? An interesting study by Jack Dovidio and Samuel Gaertner (1983) examined what happens when the customary relationship between sex and status is upset. In their experiment, men and women college students interacted with a man or woman who was introduced as either their supervisor or their subordinate. They were told that this individual (actually a confederate) was either higher or lower in ability than themselves. Before the students worked with this person on the task that was supposedly to be the object of the research, he or she "accidentally" knocked a container of pencils to the ground. The researchers unobtrusively measured helping by the extent to which the students helped the confederate to pick up the pencils.

Status but not ability influenced the frequency with which women were helped, whereas ability, not status, primarily influenced the degree to which men were helped (see Table 5.2). Men and women helped their high- and low-ability women partners equally as often, but they helped high-ability men more than those with low ability. In contrast, both women and men helped women supervisors less than women subordinates but did not discriminate between men who were supervisors and those who were subordinates. Dovidio and Gaertner (1981) had previously found a similar reluctance by white men to help black men who were supposedly supervising them. Relative ability also had no effect on helpfulness toward black men, although the high-ability white confederate was helped significantly more than his low-ability counterpart.

We have discussed these studies in great detail because they illustrate a number of important points about how sex and race function as status variables in our society. First, people in a higher-status group appear to be unwilling to recognize ability differences in individuals with a lower status than their own. White men helped other white men whose abilities were supposedly greater than their own but did not appear to notice superiority of abilities in either

TABLE 5.2. The Effects of Role and Described Ability on Subjects' Helping Behavior toward White Male and White Female Partners and toward White and Black Male Partners

	Effects of Sex	*Effects of Race*
Role and Ability	Percent Helping	
	Male (white)	*White (male)*
Supervisor		
High ability	80.0%	75.0%
Low ability	30.0%	33.3%
Subordinate		
High ability	80.0%	58.3%
Low ability	20.0%	25.0%
	Female (white)	*Black (male)*
Supervisor		
High ability	50.0%	58.3%
Low ability	50.0%	58.3%
Subordinate		
High ability	87.5%	83.3%
Low ability	75.0%	83.3%

Source: J. F. Dovidio & Gaertner (1983). The effect of sex, status, and ability on helping behavior, *Journal of Applied Social Psychology, 13*, 191–205. Copyright © 1983 V. H. Winston & Son, Inc. Reprinted by permission.

white women or black men. Second, when traditional role relationships were threatened (by the experimenters conferring supervisory rank on a woman or a black man), helping declined. And, third, these studies illustrate that the potential for discrimination may be greater than people believe because it is frequently masked by people's desire to behave in a socially desirable manner. Studies such as these, which use indirect and unobtrusive measures, indicate a level of sexism and racism of which the subjects themselves may be unaware.

The Effects of Being Helped

Help-seeking is also related to conceptions about roles and status. Women and men with high self-confidence are particularly reluctant to seek help from others (Fisher, Nadler, & Whitcher-Alagna, 1982). They resist being helped by people who have greater resources or power than their own and prefer to be helped by someone who expects to be repaid. Being helped seems to reduce self-esteem, whereas being helpful raises it (Nadler & Fisher, 1986). Men who received unsolicited help from another student actually performed less well on a subsequent task than men who received no such help (Daubman & Lehman, 1993). Both men and women even prefer help from a computer than from another human being (Karabenick & Knapp, 1988). These studies indicate that people are aware of the negative aspects of receiving help.

Individuals who habitually seek help from others appear to trade a short-term gain for a long-term loss. Being helped lowers their self-esteem and increases their sense of dependency, making them more likely to seek help yet again. Learned helplessness has been associated with depression—a disorder that is more common among women than among men. Although we are not suggesting that depression is the consequence of having a car door opened for you or having someone help you with a coat, such "courtesies" help to define and maintain traditional gender roles in our society. Women are socialized into perceiving themselves as helpless and dependent. They are more likely to be helped than men under some circumstances, and this reinforces their belief that they need such help. The long-term consequences of such social processes may create gender-biased vulnerability to some forms of emotional distress.

Aggression

Because a discussion on violence against women will appear in Chapter 14, we will limit ourselves here to a relatively brief comment about how aggression also acts as a form of social control to maintain social constructions of gender. As you can see in Figure 5.6, it is socially acceptable to picture men behaving aggressively against women. Female targets are not chosen at random. Women who are "out of place" are more likely to be the targets of male aggression. For example, highly placed women like Margaret Thatcher (the former prime minister of Great Britain), Leona Helmsley (a wealthy hotel owner and tax evader), and Hillary Rodham Clinton have all been the recipients of a number of vicious attacks disguised as "humor."

The willingness to aggress is influenced by the social context. Men are likely to behave more aggressively than women when they are observed by an experimenter or by a single peer or when the aggression is required rather than a matter of choice (Eagly, 1987). Aggressive behavior appears to be very sensitive to

FIGURE 5.6. Women as targets. Would you expect so much aggression in an advertisement in a popular magazine if the sex of the two individuals shown here were reversed?

the presence of social sanctions. It appears or disappears, depending on whether the societal script says it is "O.K." or "against the rules" (Richardson, Bernstein, & Taylor, 1979).

The Construction of Social Behaviors: A Reprise

Studies on helping and aggression indicate that women are particularly likely to be the target of sexist behaviors when they violate norms about women's inferior status. There are a large number of ways in which women can violate such norms. Direct violations include having a position that confers power over men, behaving aggressively, or telling men what to do. All of these violations involve women being in positions of authority. It is the subordinate's claim to authority rather than her competence that may be most potent in evoking discrimination against her.

These studies also indicate that situational cues can either enhance or reduce helping and aggression. Such cues are often associated with assumptions about appropriate gender roles. Thus, women are helped more when they enter traditional masculine domains that involve travel away from home. In contrast, their involvement in aggressive sports such as wrestling appears to make aggression against women more acceptable to some men.

Finally, these studies demonstrate how traditional gender-related differences may be constructed and maintained by social interactions. People believe that women and men are good at different things. They also perceive identical behavior in women and men differently. These beliefs and perceptions affect behavior toward women and men and confirm people's gender-related beliefs about themselves. The relative ease with which such behaviors can be altered by social context argues against gender-related differences as primarily due to biological causes, the long-term consequences of socialization, or personality differences between men and women. As you have seen and will see in later chapters, all of these factors do play a role. But until gender ceases to be a central organizing factor in our social relationships, it will be difficult to determine how much of an individual's behavior is due to such internal causes.

THE INTERNALIZATION OF GENDER NORMS

This chapter has shown that many gender-related differences in social behaviors are constructed by means of behavioral interactions. However, people continue to believe in innate sex differences. One could call beliefs about differences *social myths.* The power of deeply entrenched social myths resides in their ability to protect the individual from cognitive conflicts. Members of both the dominant and the subordinate group share these cultural beliefs. Such myths determine views of the world that are conceived to be objectively "true." They are maintained because each person does not create his or her social reality anew but must use cultural beliefs to understand and justify all the forms of inequality in which he or she is involved (Tajfel, 1984).

Women and Personal Entitlement

One of the paradoxes in the study of women is the extent to which they accept beliefs and behaviors that are detrimental to themselves as members of a subordinated social category. For example, women deny the extent to which they are discriminated against. Faye Crosby (1982) conducted a large-scale survey of 400 adults in a Boston suburb. She found no significant differences between employed women and men in measures of job-related grievances, satisfaction, or deservedness. This subjective equality existed despite the fact that the employed women made significantly less money than employed men with equivalent jobs. The women felt no sense of personal discrimination even though they were keenly aware of sex discrimination in general. In other words, they knew that discrimination against women existed, but only against *other* women.

There are a number of different explanations for women's denial of discrimination against themselves, but none of them is totally satisfactory. For example, women sometimes lack information with which to make group comparisons (Crosby, 1984). (It is sometimes more difficult to get information about the salaries of one's coworkers than about their sexual habits!) People also make more favorable judgments about themselves than about others even when they are using the same information (Unger & Sussman, 1986).

Some of this denial, however, may be a function of women's acceptance of general social myths involving their differences from and inferiority to men. When interviewed in depth, even very powerful women leaders in national and international business and politics indicated a lack of a sense of entitlement (Apfelbaum, 1993). This was distinctly different from feelings of lack of competence, which was never in question in their minds. They questioned the legitimacy of their own authority.

This sense of undeservedness may reflect women's awareness of their membership in a subordinate category. In an ingenious experiment, Madeline Heilman and her associates distributed to both men and women rewards that they were told were based either on their performance or on their sex (Heilman, Simon, & Repper, 1987). Women's, but not men's, self-perceptions were negatively affected by selection based on sex in comparison to selection based on merit. When given rewards based on sex, women devalued their leadership performance, took less credit for successful outcomes, and reported less interest in remaining as leader of their group. They also characterized themselves as more deficient in general leadership skills.

Categorical reward had no effect on men's view of themselves or their own worth (perhaps because it is a meaningless distinction for them since they are in the normative category). This study has obvious implications in terms of affirmative action programs in which members of subordinate groups are told that they have received their positions because of their sexual or racial category.

Women's devaluation of their own worth appears to be a common response to sexual categorization. Women who attributed their selection as managers mainly to the fact of being a woman were dissatisfied with their work in general and experienced a great deal of work-related role conflict (Chacko, 1982). The term *procedural stigma* has been used to describe how being selected by way of procedures perceived as unfair leaves the person selected feeling stigmatized. These women's perceptions appear to reflect similar perceptions in others. For example, when women undergraduates read a story in which a woman protagonist received a research award, they expected poorer subsequent evaluations when they believed that the selection criteria had included preferential treatment based on sex (Nacoste & Lehman, 1987).

Feelings of lack of entitlement extend to monetary rewards as well as acceptance of personal power. Studies have consistently found that women pay themselves less than men do when allocating rewards between themselves and others (see review by Major, 1994). In the absence of social comparison information, women perceived less money as fair pay for their work and paid themselves less money than men did. They gave themselves lower rewards even though they recognized that their work input was similar to that of men (Major, McFarlin, & Gagnon, 1984). Actually, they had worked longer, did more work, did more correct work, and were more efficient than men for the same amount of pay.

Gender differences in personal entitlement do not appear to be related to differences in personal history. Women's willingness to give themselves lower pay for work that is identical to that of men is more consistent with a model of cultural sexism. Both men and women are responding to cultural norms about the relative lower worth of women.

The Awareness of Categorical Bias

The information contained in this chapter makes for dismal reading. Women students have sometimes told us that they would rather not know so much about how things are stacked against their own sex. However, awareness of the sexist bias of others appears to reduce its negative effects. For example, Kenneth Dion (1975) performed an experiment in which women students believed they were competing against several unseen opponents (who were said to be either men or women). They were informed that they had either failed mildly or severely in this competition. The women's self-esteem was more adversely affected by men's than women's judgments, especially when severe failure was experienced. However, women who attributed their severe failure at the hands of male opponents to prejudice had stronger self-esteem and more positive feminine identification than women who did not attribute their failure to men's sexist bias.

Similar effects have been found in other groups. For example, Dion has reported similar findings with Asian and French-Canadian minorities (Dion, Earn, & Yee, 1978). And Jennifer Crocker and her colleagues (Crocker, Voelkl, Testa, & Major, 1991) have found that when black students received negative feedback from supposedly prejudiced white evaluators of their own sex, their self-esteem decreased only when they believed the evaluator could not see them. These findings suggest that the awareness of social stigma can be self-protective, because it provides an explanation for negative outcomes.

These results are related to those discussed earlier involving the internalization of beliefs about the causes of one's own behavior (Snyder & Swann, 1978a). People who believe that their behavior is internally based may be more likely to maintain it in the absence of social cues to do so than those who understand that their behaviors are situationally caused. Women of all ages appear to have acquired a more external locus of control between the late 1960s and late 1970s (Doherty & Baldwin, 1985). A similar change has not occurred in men.

Some clinical psychologists have argued that external locus of control represents a deficiency in recognizing the relationship between one's behavior and its outcomes. It can also be argued, however, that external locus of control represents a realistic appraisal of environmental contingencies for groups with lower power and status in our society (Furby, 1979). The change in women's belief patterns may be the beginning of a cultural shift in ideology about the self. Because of the rise of the feminist movement, women have become more aware of the external constraints on their ability to meet their personal goals.

An understanding of systemic and contextual factors has been linked with group identification and militancy in both blacks (Forward & Williams, 1970) and women (Sanger & Alker, 1972). It is important, however, to distinguish between our explanations of control for ourselves and for the world in general. Feminist activists, for example, appear to believe both that many structural factors are beyond the individual's control and that individuals can change social systems (Unger, 1984–1985). Such a contradictory belief pattern may be particularly adaptive in an ambiguous reality.

We believe that the material examined in this chapter gives us reasons for both negative and positive emotions. On the negative side of the ledger, women share cultural assumptions about the lesser worth of women to an astonishing degree. Cultural ideology about gender is conveyed to women by the attitudes and behaviors directed toward them in everyday life situations. Women are stigmatized because of their membership in the social category "female." It is not surprising that women come to internalize the belief that they are less important than men. "All things being equal, the greater the consistency, duration, and intensity with which a definition is promoted by others about an actor, the greater the likelihood the actor will embrace that definition as truly applicable to himself" (Lofland, 1969, p. 122). Systematic devaluation implies a strong likelihood of impaired self-esteem.

The findings discussed in this chapter are also cause for hope. People are not totally at the mercy of external constraints. Self-perceptions are clearly influenced by both the perceptions of others and by what one believes the causes of such perceptions to be. You might think of this in terms of how people look at people looking at them. People are less likely to confirm gender-stereotypic expectations or to be influenced by others' judgments about their worth if they attribute their perceptions to external structural factors rather than internal causes.

Feminists are particularly likely to have a socially constructionist view of reality (Unger, 1984–1985). They are able to understand that gender-differentiated behavior is constructed by themselves and others. They do not see it as just existing naturally. But this does not change the fact that sexist practices also reflect real-world distinctions. Real social change will take place only when there are changes in both inner and outer reality.

CONNECTING THEMES

1. This chapter emphasizes how sex as a category is used to construct gender differences and distinctions. This process begins with perceptual and cognitive biases that lead individuals to expect different behaviors from women and men. People act to confirm these expectations, which are, indeed, often confirmed by others' self-presentational strategies. These behaviors, in turn, reinforce gender-biased views about the differing characteristics of men and women.
2. "Naming" (in the sense of deviance and stigma) can be used to delegitimize women who exercise social power or possess public authority. However, "naming" (in the sense of conscious awareness) can also reduce the extent to which gender-biased views of the self are internalized.

3. Sex is not the only social category that is used to produce and maintain distinctions between groups of people. Other categories with similar effects are race, age, and disability. It is important to remember that most of the effect of these categories on behavior is a result of normal cognitive and social psychological processes rather than conscious discrimination.
4. A social construction model of gender is a positive step in the movement for social change. This model argues that gender-related traits and behaviors are situationally constructed. It also suggests that changes in the relationship of sex to power and status will have a major impact in creating an egalitarian society.

SUGGESTED READINGS

HENLEY, NANCY, and JO FREEMAN (1989). The sexual politics of interpersonal behavior. In J. Freeman (Ed.). *Women: A feminist perspective* (4th ed.). Mountainview, CA: Mayfield Publishing Co. This article presents an excellent review of studies on the relationship between the micropolitics of interpersonal behavior and structural inequalities between women and men.

KANTER, ROSABETH MOSS (1977). *Women and men of the corporation.* New York: Basic Books. A classic work in the field, this book shows how some of the processes discussed in this chapter play out in the workplace.

RIDGEWAY, CECILIA L. (Ed.) (1992). *Gender, interaction, and inequality.* New York: Springer-Verlag. Although the contributions to this book are rather technical in nature, they provide an up-to-date review of the theories and findings of the major sociologists and social psychologists who work in the area of status, power, and gender.

CHAPTER 6

Biological Aspects of Sex and Gender

WHAT IS SEX?
- Is Sex Immutable?
- Are There Always Two Sexes?
- Are The Sexes Always Separate?
- Breaking Up a Unitary Category: The Many Components of Sex

NORMAL PRENATAL DEVELOPMENT
- Chromosomal Sex
- Gonadal and Hormonal Sex
- Genital Sex
- Sexual Differentiation of the Central Nervous System

THE QUESTION OF BIOLOGICAL DETERMINISM
- Prenatal Hormones
- Social Factors
- The Findings from Studies of Human Beings: The Inconsistent Relationship between Hormones and Behavior

DOES THE HUMAN BRAIN HAVE A SEX?
- A Brief History of the Construction of Female Inferiority
- The Case of Neural Laterality
- The Construction of Neurological Differences

ANOMALIES OF HUMAN SEXUAL DEVELOPMENT AND WHAT THEY TELL US
- Conceptual and Methodological Issues
- Chromosomal Anomalies
- Prenatal Hormones and Sex Differentiation

IS THERE A CRITICAL PERIOD FOR GENDER IDENTITY?
- Cross-Sex Rearing in a Prenatally Normal Male
- The Role of Body Image

CHANGING IDENTITY
- Transsexualism
- Gender Bending and Body Image

CULTURAL CONSTRUCTIONS OF GENDER

CONNECTING THEMES

SUGGESTED READINGS

The biology—or "plumbing"—chapter of a book on sex and gender is probably the one that most readers decide ahead of time they are not going to like. This is because medical jargon seems mysterious to people interested in the social sciences or humanities. The language of physical and natural science sometimes seems designed to mystify. Its difficulty not only affects understanding but also makes scientific concepts and methodology difficult to criticize. We hope to make biological research accessible by providing more definitions and explanations here than in other chapters. We do so in the hope that you will learn how to think critically about science.

People in social science are often not especially interested in biological issues. Natural science is, however, an important part of our current world. Biologists make many statements about social issues having to do with gender. These statements are given much weight because science seems to many people to have a unique path to "truth." Scientific research is often judged as more relevant and important than other kinds of research. Because of the high value placed on science in our society news about scientific breakthroughs are likely to be featured in the news media (see Figure 6.1). You are less likely to find a cover story in a news magazine exclaiming that boys and girls are given different kinds of toys!

Things that are biological are also viewed as more permanent, inevitable, and less variable than things that are not biological. This is what we mean when we refer to theories as *determinist* later in this chapter. Such theories imply that differences between females and males are "hard-wired" into human genes, brains, or hormones.

FIGURE 6.1. The article inside this magazine is more balanced than its cover would indicate. However, the cover is far from balanced in its stress on scientific validity. One might wonder also if the connection between the cover and the banner advertising another story on affirmative action is truly accidental.

Science has a kind of privilege in our society that is not conferred on other forms of scholarship. It is assumed to be objective and to some extent to be removed from the influence of current social and political beliefs. As you have seen in Chapter 1 and will see in other chapters throughout this book, scientific theories about women have been far from objective. And, as you will see in this chapter, scientific theories about sex as a biological variable have been influenced by implicit assumptions and ideology about the roles of women and men. These theories have stressed the idea of two separate sexes with little overlap between them. They have focused on biological determinants while frequently ignoring the role of the environment in inducing sex-related differences. In the interest of maintaining the concept of two naturally different sexes, biological theories have oversimplified the concept of sex and ignored its many interacting components.

WHAT IS SEX?

Despite the fact that everyone talks about sex, very few people try to define it. Examination of a number of articles and books on the subject has led us to conclude that researchers feel that sex is either too self-evident to require an explanation or so complicated that they feel justified in devoting an entire book to the subject. About all they agree on is that sex represents a division of reproductive labor into specialized cells, organs, and organisms (Bermant & Davidson, 1974).

Most definitions of sex stress the separateness and incompleteness of the sexes. They also equate sex with reproduction. As you will see later in this chapter, this confusion of the ability to reproduce with other aspects of sex and gender has led to some medical decisions about sexually anomalous individuals that have had tragic consequences.

Sociobiologists have also focused on the reproductive aspects of sex. They see organisms as the egg and sperm's way to create other eggs and sperm. Some sociobiologists have attempted to reduce almost all complex human social behaviors to reproductive strategies (c.f. Konner, 1983). They generalize freely between insects, lower mammals, primates, and human beings. However, different species differ in their reproductive arrangements. There are no clear theories available to help us to determine when a particular animal is a useful model for human reproduction.

Some exceptions to the usual "rules" demonstrate that even the most basic aspects of sex are neither fixed nor universal. Some of the rules that may be challenged are:

1. If an organism has a sex (and some lower organisms do not), it must be either male or female.
2. There are always two sexes.
3. Within a single individual, sex is always permanent.
4. There are strong and consistent relationships between anatomy, physiology, and sex-related behaviors across species.

Is Sex Immutable?

Although evolutionary biologists see two sexes as useful for increasing the genetic variability of a species, two separate sexes do not always exist. Many invertebrate organisms (for example, earthworms and oysters) have both kinds of *gonads* (the organs that make either eggs or sperm), either at the same time or in sequence. Even among species that have two sexes, sex is not always fixed at birth. Some fish and birds can be made to change sex. These animals produce viable eggs or sperm after a period of maturity during which they have produced the kind of germ cells consistent with the other sex (Diamond, 1993). Some fish change spontaneously from fertile female to fertile male in the absence of any males of the species. This transformation is inhibited by the sight of a male even if he cannot be reached by any of the females.

Are There Always Two Sexes?

Not all vertebrates have two sexes. Recently, researchers have begun to examine the reproductive physiology and behavior of an all-female species of whiptail lizards (Crews, 1987a). In this species, there are no males and the females reproduce from unfertilized eggs that contain the same genes as those of their single parent (this process is sometimes known as *cloning*). This species has separated reproductive biology from reproductive behavior. Although male individuals and their sperm have been lost, courting behaviors supposedly characteristic of males have been retained. The extent to which both male-like and female-like behaviors are exhibited is influenced by ovarian hormones. The pseudo-male behaviors encourage reproduction much as male courtship behavior does in species with two sexes.

These species are not simply interesting scientific curiosities. The study of such species allows us to ask how fundamental the relationship is between various biological components of sex and sex-related behaviors. Our separation of behaviors into "male" and "female" may be a false dichotomy. It is created by ignoring all the exceptions to the rules. And, as you will see later, this separation may have more political and social than scientific usefulness.

Are The Sexes Always Separate?

Females in at least one all-female species show the complete range of behaviors associated with males in related species. This kind of evidence suggests that categorizing sex-related behaviors as *dimorphic*—characteristic of two forms or bodies—may be misleading. No single behavior appears to be found exclusively in either males or females. The only sex-irreducible dimorphisms found among primates are that males impregnate and females ovulate, menstruate, and lactate (Money, 1987).

As you will see later in this chapter, other supposedly dimorphic behaviors such as nurturance or aggression are best expressed in probabilistic terms. These behaviors are more easily elicited or expressed in one sex or the other but may be found in either sex under some conditions. Like sex differences (see Chapter 3), sexual dimorphism is a term based on a judgment call that is not always free of bias.

Even the so-called male and female hormones are not found only in one sex. Nevertheless, many scientists appear to share the biases of the culture as a whole in terms of absolute distinctions between the sexes. For example,

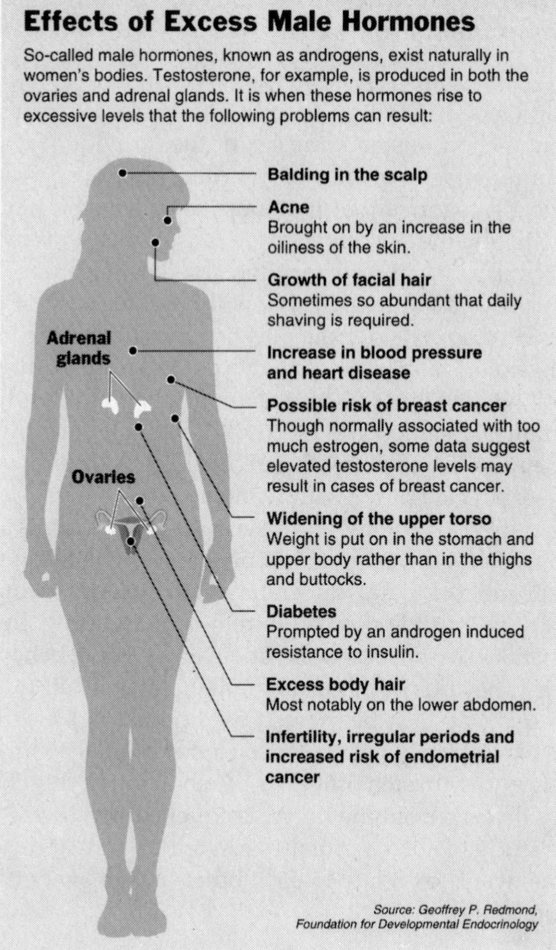

FIGURE 6.2. Even when the media indicate that women and men may be more alike physiologically than medical experts used to believe, they still stress the harmful rather than the normative effects of male hormones in women's bodies.
Source: From ''Male Hormone Molds Women as Well, in Mind and Body.'' The New York Times, *May 3, 1994. Copyright © 1994 by The New York Times Company. Reprinted by permission.*

throughout the nineteenth century, estrogen was known as the female hormone despite the fact that the substance was isolated from the urine of male horses (Laqueur, 1990). The brain and pituitary gland appear to be able to transform the major sex hormones into each other rather easily (McEwen, 1981), but it is only recently that researchers have noted that "male" hormones have normative influences on women's bodies too (Angier, 1994). However, even within the article that announced this research, the popular press stressed the negative effects on women of excess "male" hormones (see Figure 6.2).

Breaking Up a Unitary Category: The Many Components of Sex

Just as animal species are not necessarily composed of two discrete subgroups—male and female—the sex of individual members of a species is not an all-or-none phenomenon. Instead, the sex of the individual may be viewed as the result of a cumulative sequence of interdependent processes. At least five separate biological categories that make up an organism's sex may be distinguished. These include the *sex chromosomes,* the *gonads, hormones,* sex of the *internal accessory organs,* and sex as determined by the appearance and function of the *external genitalia* (see Figure 6.3). We will consider each of these aspects of sex shortly. We will also consider the question of whether the brain has a sex—produced by physiological processes that operate before birth.

In human beings we must also consider social variables: the sex to which the newborn infant is assigned and the sex with which the individual identifies (these are more appropriately termed aspects of gender). And we must consider the meaning of sexual categories within and across cultures. Under normal circumstances, all of these biological and psychological variables are highly correlated with one another. However, experiments on animals and studies of disorders of prenatal and postnatal development in human beings suggest that considering sex as indivisible may be extremely misleading. Even though eggs or sperm production, sex-hormone secretion, and mating behavior coincide for many vertebrates, they do not coincide for all (Crews, 1987b).

A person's sex may best be viewed as the result of a series of events or stages that take place largely before birth. Under normal conditions all of these events are consistent with each other. As we shall see in this chapter, however, later stages may diverge from the normal sequence, producing an "experiment of nature." The study of such anomalies can tell us a great deal about how the various components of sex relate to each other and to gender identity and behavior in human beings.

NORMAL PRENATAL DEVELOPMENT

Chromosomal Sex

The first stage in the determination of sex in mammals is the presence of either two Xs or an X and a Y chromosome in the fertilized egg. As you probably remember from high school biology, human beings have twenty-three pairs of chromosomes, with one of each pair inherited from each parent. Twenty-two pairs of these chromosomes (the *autosomes*) are roughly identical in size and shape. The *sex chromosomes* differ, however, in that females have two x chromosomes that are comparable in size and shape to the autosomal chromosomes, whereas males have one X chromosome and a Y chromosome that is only a fraction of the size of the other chromosomes.

In mammals the Y chromosome contains genes that cause the formation of a testis (Gordon & Ruddle, 1981). This regulatory function appears to be associated with the presence of H-Y antigen—a male-specific protein associated with

Stages in normal female and male sex differentiation

	Female	**Male**
Stage 1 Chromosomes	XX	XY Male gonad differentiates faster and earlier
Stage 2 Gonads	Ovaries	Testes
Stage 3 Gonadal hormones	Estrogens	Androgens
Stage 4 Internal accessory organs	Fallopian tubes Uterus	Vas deferens Seminal vesicles
Stage 5 External genitalia	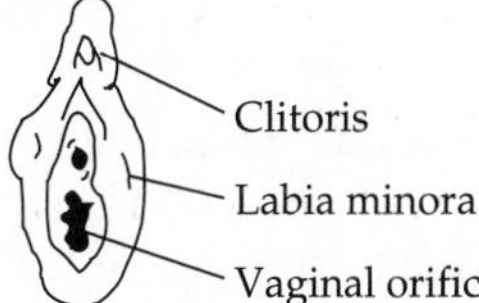	Penis Scrotum
Stage 6 Sex label	Female	Male
Stage 7 (Humans) Gender of rearing	 Feminine	Masculine

FIGURE 6.3. The many stages of sex determination: (1) chromosomal sex; (2) gonadal sex; (3) hormonal sex; (4) sex of the internal accessory organs; (5) sex of the external genitalia. In human beings, the sex of assignment and that of socialization are also very important for gender identity.
Drawing by Alina Wilczynski.

testicular development. The chromosomal bases for sexual differentiation are by no means universal—even among vertebrates. In birds, for example, it is the female who has two different-sized sex chromosomes and the male who has two the same size.

Why is it important to know that sex determination in birds is not the same as it is in mammals? Findings about sex-related behaviors such as nurturance and dominance are often generalized across species. They are seen to have important implications for human social roles. For example, because male ducks sometimes jump on a female's back and force her to mate with them, some sociobiologists argue that rape has an evolutionary advantage. Such behaviors are widely considered to have a genetic basis. If, however, species are not always comparable in the genetic mechanisms that create sex, why should one assume that they will be comparable in the genetic underpinnings of behavior?

Gonadal and Hormonal Sex

All vertebrate embryos, whatever their sex chromosome constitution, originally develop the beginning of both male and female sex organs (Mittwoch, 1973). Immediately after being formed, the gonads pass through an apparently undifferentiated state and contain the forerunners of both ovarian and testicular tissue. The process of sex *differentiation* (the change from general to more specialized structures during development) may be regarded as a change from a bipotential condition to the progressive development of the organs of one sex at the expense of the other (see Figure 6.4).

Male and female human embryos develop identically during the first few weeks of gestation. If a Y chromosome is present, however, the gonads begin to grow faster and to develop into *testes.* Testicular development does not appear to depend on the presence of *androgens;* in fact, it precedes the presence of these hormones.

Shortly after the testes differentiate they begin to secrete a number of hormones that are collectively called androgens. These hormones act on the internal and external genital structures to produce what are considered to be male structures, such as a penis and scrotum. One androgen inhibits the development of female accessory organs (the uterus and Fallopian tubes). *Testosterone* is responsible for the masculinization of the male internal genital tract and its derivative *dihydrotestosterone* causes development of the male external genitalia—fusion of the scrotum and growth of the penis (Wilson, George, & Griffin, 1981). All three of these substances must be present prenatally to produce an anatomically normal male.

Predictably, there has been much more investigation of male than female differentiation (Fausto-Sterling, 1989). Although many developmental biologists state that the embryo develops in a female direction if the Y chromosome is absent, this model has been criticized as androcentric. A more balanced model of sex determination argues that parallel genetic pathways for gonadal development exist—one for testis formation and the other for ovarian formation. In fact, a female-determining gene has recently been located on the X chromosome (Angier, 1994).

The *ovaries* and their hormonal products—collectively known as *estrogens*—play little role in the development of a female appearance. In fact, ovarian differentiation takes place after female external structures are far advanced in de-

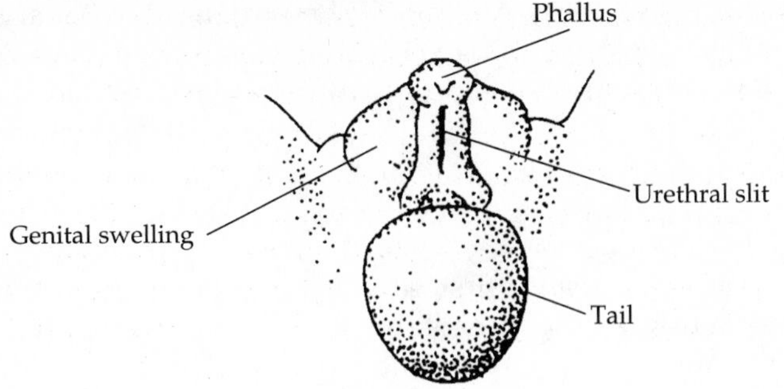

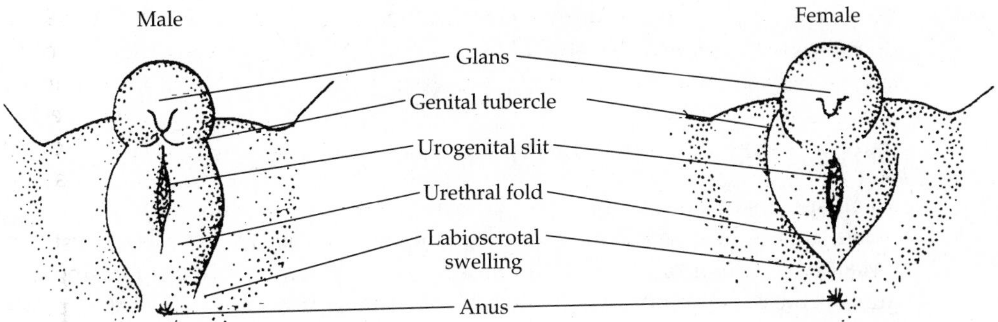

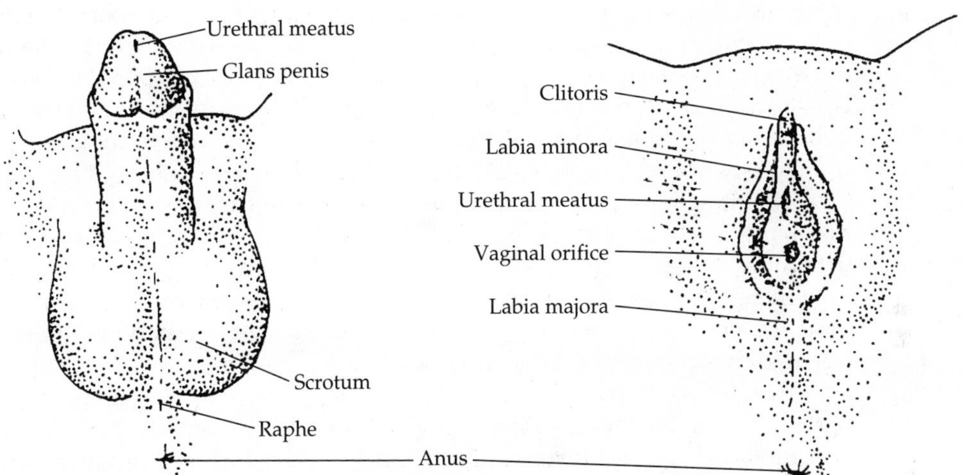

FIGURE 6.4. The development of the female and male genitalia from the undifferentiated or bipotential gonad during early fetal development.
Drawing by Alina Wilczynski.

velopment (Wilson et al., 1981). A second X chromosome is necessary, however, for female fertility. Those who lack this chromosome have nonfunctional gonads and no uterus despite their superficially female external appearance.

Genital Sex

The external genitals are also, at first, sexually undifferentiated. Even after the fetal gonads begin to be distinguishable by the second month of pregnancy, several more weeks are necessary for the more distinctive development of the external genitals. Since the reproductive systems of females and males develop from the same embryonic origins, each part has its developmental counterpart, or *homologue,* in the other sex. You can easily identify some of these homologous structures by comparing the male and female internal and external reproductive systems in Figures 6.3 and 6.4.

Sexual Differentiation of the Central Nervous System

In all species examined there is a critical period during which the central nervous system is sensitive to the organizing effects of gonadal hormones (MacLusky & Naftolin, 1981). In human beings, this period is around the same time as the differentiation of the external genitals. As in other mammals, neural differentiation is under the control of androgens. Prenatal exposure to these hormones suppresses cyclic fluctuation of pituitary hormones in adult females.

In lower mammals prenatal hormones change the threshold of sex-related reproductive behaviors such as *mounting* (in which an animal climbs onto the back of another and engages in pelvic thrusts) and *lordosis* (in which an animal arches its back and permits another to mount). The former behavior is more likely to be found in males and the latter in females, but instances of both kinds of behavior are found in both sexes. One of us once had two female dogs that tried to mount each other frequently, to the consternation of our young daughters. Mounting is an expression of dominance as well as of sexuality.

In many species, the capacity for both male and female behaviors is retained in both sexes. Only their threshold of activation is altered by prenatal hormones. In higher species, such as primates and human beings, other factors such as experience also play a role. Thus, sexually experienced men who have been castrated may continue to engage in sexual activity.

For the most part, it remains impossible even to state where in the central nervous system hormones act to bring about sexual differentiation (MacLusky & Naftolin, 1981). Few structural differences in the brains of male and female animals have been found. Even fewer connections between structure and function have been established.

Sometimes the connections that are found are understandable, but not terribly enlightening. For example, one of the authors recently participated in a NATO-sponsored conference on the development of sex differences and similarities in behavior. The conference was dominated by neurophysiologists and biologically oriented psychologists (Haug, Whalen, Aron, & Olsen, 1993). A number of these scientists were very excited by findings showing that one particular structure in the hypothalamus (the *dimorphic nucleus*) was larger in males than in females in a number of animal species, including human beings. When the author asked what this nucleus controlled, she was told that it regulated penile thrusting. But does this difference in the brain tell us any more than a more overt anatomical finding? We all know that males have a penis with which to thrust and females do not!

Despite the limited data on structural differences between male and female brains in mammals, a large literature on human central nervous system differences has accumulated. These kinds of investigations are currently being extended to neural differences between heterosexual and homosexual individuals of the same sex. Several investigators have claimed to have found differences in various parts of the brain between gay and straight men (Allen & Gorski, 1992; LeVay, 1991; Swaab & Hofman, 1990). These studies have been criticized for their small sample size, lack of replicability, and the fact that many of the homosexual subjects had died of AIDS (Fausto-Sterling, 1992). They are, however, achieving the same kind of media attention that purported sex differences in math genes have received (see Chapter 3). Below is a sample of the headlines that followed the publication of LeVay's article.

> The Biology of What it Means to be Gay
>
> —*New York Times*
>
> Zone of Brain Linked to Men's Sexual Orientation
>
> —*New York Times*
>
> What Causes People to be Homosexual? Study Pinpoints a Difference in the Brain
>
> —*Newsweek*
>
> Are Gay Men Born That Way?
>
> —*Time*
>
> Homosexuality and Biology
>
> —*Atlantic Monthly*

The media's enthusiastic response demonstrates the popularity of biologically determinist explanations for any kind of sex-related difference. It also shows the continued assumption that being male equals being human. Although none of the researchers found a difference in the brains of lesbian and heterosexual women (indeed, few have looked for one), several of the headlines generalized the results from males to homosexuals in general.

Science still does not have a good definition of sexual orientation. Still, researchers are now looking for evidence of a gay gene. Evidence for a genetic contribution to homosexuality includes studies showing that homosexuality can be traced within families. Other findings indicate that if one of a pair of identical twins of either sex is homosexual, the other is also likely to be homosexual about 50 percent of the time (Diamond, 1993; Hamer, Hu, Magnuson, Hu, & Pattatucci, 1993). Since identical twins are genetic duplicates, these findings also indicate that other factors must play an important role. However, it does not appear likely that we will locate news headlines proclaiming "Environment modifies sexual orientation!"

FIGURE 6.5. Magazine cover with baby heralding the existence of the "gay gene." Another example of the media's emphasis on biological determinism. The finding that some twins are both gay does not explain the many sets of twins who differ in sexual orientation.

THE QUESTION OF BIOLOGICAL DETERMINISM

To what degree are sex-related differences biologically determined? Surprisingly, this is not as easy a question to answer as you might believe. In most cases, both sexes behave the same way. It is the relative difference in frequency, intensity, or context associated with the display of a particular behavior pattern that is termed a sex difference. In other words, although individuals may display the behavior of the other sex, it is much more likely that they will display behaviors characteristic of their own sex. It might be fair to say, therefore, that behavior has no sex.

Nevertheless, researchers continue to be interested in the biological determinants of differences between the sexes. These researchers have concentrated on two major areas of investigation. One is studies of human beings with anomalous biological properties (to be discussed later in this chapter). The other area is studies of animals, especially primates, because they are most like human beings. Researchers have focused on three major categories of primate behavior: aggression, rough-and-tumble play (both more characteristic of males), and nurturance (more characteristic of females).

Prenatal Hormones

Animal studies indicate that prenatal hormones and social factors both play a role in influencing these behaviors. For example, female rhesus monkeys whose mothers had been injected with testosterone during pregnancy showed levels of play intermediate between that of normal males and normal females (Goy, 1970). They also showed more chasing and threat behavior than normal females did. Prenatal exposure to androgens appears to induce higher levels of physical activity in both primate and human females.

Social Factors

Activity levels have also been shown to be influenced by social factors. For example, David Goldfoot and Deborah Neff (1987) investigated the level of rough-and-tumble play exhibited by juvenile female rhesus monkeys living in five-member groups. This form of play is rare among females living in all-female groups. However, it is considerably more common in females in one-male, four-female groups and lower again in females living in two-male, three-female groups. The researchers suggested that males initiate the activity and select male partners for it. When no male partner is available, they engage a female in rough-and-tumble play and she reciprocates. This pattern is startlingly similar to play patterns among groups of human children (see Chapter 7).

Another study (Gibber, 1981) looked at sex-related differences in the parenting of rhesus monkeys. She found that male and female monkeys looked at, approached, and picked up "stranded" newborn monkeys in an adjacent cage with an attached passageway to an equal extent when they were alone. However, when both a male and a female were in the testing cage, females displayed virtually all the parenting behavior observed. Many of the males who had showed nurturant responses when alone did not do so in the presence of an adult female. If these animals had been tested only in mixed-sex pairs, the researchers might have concluded a much greater sex-related difference in the tendency to take care of infants.

These studies indicate that monkeys of both sexes are capable of a wide variety of behaviors that have been linked with only one sex. In social situations, however, they appear to "take the easy way out" and let the more experienced sex get involved. You may prefer to think about this behavior in terms of a human analogy. Most women probably find it easier than most men to change a baby's diaper. Most men will wait for a woman to do the dirty work. However, no one believes that a man would refuse to do so if it were necessary and no women were available or would volunteer.

The Findings from Studies of Human Beings: The Inconsistent Relationship between Hormones and Behavior

The effect of yet unknown factors may underlie individual differences in human behaviors where the connection between physiological events and behavior is relatively strong. For example, young women who (because of genetic disorders or medical treatment of their mothers) were exposed to masculinizing hormones before birth were not found to be significantly more aggressive than other young women (Ehrhardt & Meyer-Bahlburg, 1981). Moreover, no consistent correlation between the level of circulating testosterone and various measures of hostility or aggression in normal male volunteers has been found (Rubin, Reinisch, & Haskett, 1981). In contrast, studies of plasma testosterone in overtly assaultive, aggressive, and violent male prisoners have shown somewhat more consistent relationships. For example, groups of prisoners with long and vivid histories of violent and aggressive crimes in adolescence or before incarceration (such as rapist-murderers) have been found to have higher average levels of circulating testosterones than prisoners without such histories.

We do not yet know how to explain correlations between behaviors and hormonal levels. A good example in human beings is the finding that testosterone is correlated with the occupational status of women. In a study of fifty-five normal women, it was found that independent of age, women in professional, managerial, and technical occupations had higher levels of all androgens than clerical workers and homemakers did (Purifoy & Koopmans, 1980).

There are at least two possible explanations for this effect. Higher levels of androgen could have predisposed these girls to higher activity levels; higher activity levels could have caused them to seek out boys as friends; and greater contact with boys might have increased their opportunities for rehearsal of a larger variety of adult roles as well as for the acquisition of instrumental traits. (As you will see in Chapter 7, activity level does appear to play a role in the gender socialization of boys and girls.) It is also possible that social rewards associated with high-status professional careers include less stress. Stress has been found to play a role in the depression of androgen in both sexes.

These studies demonstrate how interactions between physiological and environmental factors influence many sex-related behaviors. One must be cautious about inferring similar causal mechanisms across different species. The role of social factors may be quite different for rats, monkeys, and human beings.

Differences between individuals as well as between species are important in animals as well as human beings. For example, prenatal hormones can affect the probability of some behaviors in primates. However, the probability that an individual female monkey will display the so-called male behavior of mounting ranges from near 0 percent to 67 percent, depending on the social conditions of rearing and testing, quite independent of hormonal considerations (Goldfoot & Neff, 1987).

It would be a mistake to ignore the possibility of biological involvement in sex-related behaviors in human beings. The studies discussed earlier, however, also demonstrate the important role of the environment. The extent to which the social environment affects behavior is likely to be overlooked or de-emphasized in most animal studies (Fausto-Sterling, 1992). Researchers may be all too ready to generalize from animals to human beings when linking biological mechanisms with behavioral effects. When the animal species is a primate, the tendency to assume analogous mechanisms is even greater because of the genetic relatedness of these species and the similarity of their appearance to ourselves.

A Brief History of the Construction of Female Inferiority

Probably the most controversial issue in this area is the extent to which gonadal hormones influence the structure and function of the human brain. As you have seen, this question extends beyond mere scientific interest. A number of researchers have argued that differences between the male and female brain account for cognitive differences between the sexes—in particular, differences between their verbal, spatial, and mathematical skills (see Chapter 3).

Attempts to demonstrate differences between male and female brains have been popular since the mid-nineteenth century. For example, some researchers were convinced that they could distinguish between male and female brains in gross structure. They disagreed only on where such differences were to be found. The location of the differences varied according to the theoretical framework that was in vogue at that particular time. As you read in Chapter 3, when a particular part of the brain was seen as more important, it was also seen as larger in males. Supposed sex differences in the brain shifted from the frontal to the parietal lobes when the latter came to be viewed as the site of higher mental capacities (Shields, 1975). In case you are wondering, no reliable relationship between brain size and intelligence has ever been found (Gould, 1981).

Other theories about sex-related differences centered around the size of the brain as a whole (Broca, 1861, cited in Gould, 1981). However, these theories took no account of differences between men and women in terms of height and general body build. Broca's data were used by Le Bon (1879), a founder of social psychology, as the basis for a vicious attack on women.

> In the most intelligent races, as among the Parisians, there are a large number of women whose brains are closer in size to those of gorillas than to the most developed male brains. This inferiority is so obvious that no one can contest it for a moment, only its degree is worth discussion. All psychologists who have studied the intelligence of women, as well as poets and novelists, recognize today that they represent the most inferior forms of human evolution and that they are closer to children and savages than to an adult, civilized man. They excel in fickleness, inconstancy, absence of thought and logic, and incapacity to reason. Without doubt there exist some distinguished women, very superior to the average man, but they are as exceptional as the birth of any monstrosity, as, for example, a gorilla with two heads; consequently, we may neglect them entirely (Le Bon, 1879, pp. 60–61, cited by Gould, 1981, pp. 104–105).

These data were used to draw social conclusions. Le Bon was horrified by the proposal of some American educators to grant women access to higher education on the same basis as men.

There is still no agreement today about how to measure brain size. Stephen Jay Gould (1981) concludes that, correcting for body size, there is no significant difference between the brains of women and men. However, arguments about sex-related differences in the brain have simply moved to a different arena.

The Case of Neural Laterality

Today, the search for biological sex differences underlying intellectual functioning continues. For example, a number of researchers have proposed that female brains are less lateralized than those of males. *Lateralization* refers to the degree to which brain functions are specialized in the right or left hemisphere. In right-handed people, the left hemisphere is usually dominant for language skills as well as motor control. The right hemisphere, on the other hand, is more dominant in spatial activities. The brains of left-handed people appear to be less specialized.

Although lateralization differences between males and females are much smaller and more elusive than differences between left- and right-handed people, they are often used to "explain" sex-related differences in cognitive abilities such as mathematics. This "explanation" is a clear example of how processes associated with females are defined as inferior (Unger, 1979b). This point may be made clearer by looking at the cognitive skills of left- versus right-handed people instead of those of women and men.

In normal populations, there is no evidence that left-handers have any more difficulty in acquiring mathematical skills than right-handers. In a large-scale study of more than 3,000 individuals, no significant differences in any cognitive factor between right- and left-handed men or between right- and left-handed women were found (Kocel, 1977). This finding strongly suggests that it is a mistake to reason that less lateralization leads to lower innate math ability in females. The idea that a "left brain/right brain" distinction is importantly related to intellectual abilities and personality is selectively used to "explain" the behavior of normal women but not normal left-handed people. Of course, handedness, unlike sex, is not a distinction of great social and political importance in contemporary American culture.

Another indication of the politicization of this research area is the language used to make distinctions about laterality. People whose brain functioning is spread more evenly over the two hemispheres are described in the literature as "less well-lateralized" or "less specialized." Being lateralized is in the process of being defined as good for people (Unger, 1979b), despite the well-documented fact that women recover from strokes better than men do. Why, for example, do we not define "less lateralized" people as "more balanced?" Instead, "(m)en are specialized to the right hemisphere, and we know that to be specialized is to be better" (Bleier, 1986, p. 154). The careless (or perhaps misogynist) use of language not only makes greater lateralization seem more desirable, but also obscures the fact that there is no evidence for a relationship between lateralization and cognitive ability.

At least five recent reviews have documented in great detail the flaws in research on sex-related differences in spatial ability (c.f. Caplan, MacPherson, & Tobin, 1985). At the end of a book reviewing the literature on sex differences in hemispheric laterality, M. P. Bryden, a respected leader in the field, wrote: "The literature on sex-related differences in lateralization is rife with inconsistencies. . . . To a large extent, one's conclusions rest on the choice of which studies to emphasize and which to ignore" (1982, p. 238).

Despite weak research support, respected scientists and important institutions of scholarship have continued to proclaim the existence of sex differences in neural laterality. Ruth Bleier (1988), a distinguished physician and neuroscientist, documented one such example of the construction of meaning in the neurosciences.

In 1982, Norman Geschwind, a well-known neurologist at Harvard, published a study reporting an association between left-handedness, certain disorders of the immune system, and some developmental learning disabilities, such as dyslexia and stuttering, a complex more common in boys than girls (Geschwind & Behan, 1982). The researchers argued that these disorders were linked by the prenatal effects of testosterone, which slowed down the development of the left hemisphere, resulting in right-hemispheric dominance in males. An important part of their evidence was a study of human fetal brains that reported that two convolutions of the right hemisphere appear one or two weeks earlier during fetal development than their counterparts on the left (Chi, Dooling, & Gilles, 1977). They failed to mention, however, that this study of more than 500 fetal brains failed to find any sex differences (Bleier, 1988). This result completely undermined Geschwind's theory, since testosterone should certainly have had some differential effect on male versus female brains.

Science, one of the most important journals of scholarly research, hailed Geschwind's theory as an elegant explanation of a variety of sex differences. The bold headline "Math Genius May Have Hormonal Basis" prefaced an interview with Geschwind in which he stated that testosterone effects on the fetal brain can produce "superior right hemisphere talents, such as artistic, musical, or mathematical talent" (Kolata, 1983, p. 1312). Another study using Geschwind's theory (that had not examined any physiological variables) received banner headlines such as "Study Shows Male Hormones Multiply Boys' Math Skills" (Bleier, 1988, p. 96). *Science,* however, rejected Bleier's paper showing no differences between the size of the corpus callosum (the structure connecting the two hemispheres) and has, in general, paid little attention to findings that contradict the idea of biological determinism.

Headlines in the science section of the *New York Times* proclaimed still other, subtle sex differences in the brain. One article reported recent findings discussed at a meeting of the New York Academy of Sciences (Goleman, 1989). One study, for example, indicated that women have larger corpus callosums than men. Another study reported that the size of the corpus callosum in women was related to their verbal abilities. No such relationship was found between the size of the corpus callosum and women's spatial abilities, although this structure connects the brain's spatial centers as well as its verbal ones. No mention was made in the article about any relationships found in men. Nor were researchers able to explain why left-handed men had a bigger connection between the hemispheres than right-handed men although there was no relationship between the size of the callosum and handedness in women.

Still other studies reported structural differences in the brains of male and female rats. In fact, despite the headline stating "Subtle and Intriguing Differences Found in the Brain Anatomy of Men and Women," only one of the papers reported in the article directly compared the brains of male and female human beings. And this finding was about an area of the brain (the corpus callosum) in which other negative results have also been reported.

We have gone into great detail in this area for several reasons. First, people tend to believe evidence in the "hard" sciences such as physiology and biology more than evidence from the "soft" sciences such as psychology or sociology. Structures are seen as having more of a real existence than processes do. Second, we tend to think of biological effects as being more irreversible than social effects. This belief has major consequences for the way people think about others and the kinds of social policies they espouse. Beliefs in biological determinism, political conservatism, and the inequality of the sexes are associated even at the present time (Unger, Draper, & Pendergrass, 1986). Last, although researchers interested in neurology and physiology are aware of the major effects of the environment on biological processes, reports in the popular and professional media de-emphasize the importance of learning. Such biases perpetuate sexist beliefs that, in turn, lead to practices that produce the "evidence" that supports these beliefs.

ANOMALIES OF HUMAN SEXUAL DEVELOPMENT AND WHAT THEY TELL US

Conceptual and Methodological Issues

We have argued that one must be wary of overgeneralizing from animal to human studies. It is unethical, however, to do experimental studies of human sexual differentiation. Therefore, clinical cases in which the various components of sex are not consistent with each other appear to be the only way to explore the nature of the relationships between biological sex and psychological aspects of gender in human beings. As you shall see, the use of clinical case material carries with it additional problems, and researchers need to be as careful in generalizing between anomalous and normal development as they are in generalizing between animals and people.

You are probably interested in learning about people with sexual anomalies to see how individuals who do not conform perfectly to dualistic sexual categories deal with our gender-divided world. The major reason for scientists' interest in anomalies of sexual differentiation is, however, the clues they can provide to the bases of gender identity and the determinants of other kinds of gender-related behaviors in normal human beings. By looking at people for whom the various components that make up one's sex are inconsistent, researchers can figure out what factors must be present in order for a particular behavior to occur. They can then eliminate those variables that may be present but do not appear necessary for that behavior. They can ask questions such as: What is the effect of absent or additional sex chromosomes on sex-related behaviors? Are sex hormones necessary for an individual to identify strongly as a male or female? And what happens to an individual whose external sex is different from that of his or her internal structures?

Examination of human beings is important because of the major role that culture and learning play in our gender-related behavior. It is possible, of course, to check whether the findings from human case studies are comparable to findings from experimental studies done on animals. As you will see, some of these comparisons indicate that human beings and animals are very much alike and others indicate that they are very different.

It is important to be cautious in generalizing from human beings with sexual anomalies to other human beings. People for whom the multiple determinants of sex do not coincide may be more sexually flexible or plastic than other people (Diamond, 1965). It may be easier for them to shift their gender identities than it is for people whose sex is consistent. Individuals who come for clinical treatment may not even be a representative sample of people with the same anomalies. People who seek or are sent for clinical treatment are often more adversely affected than others with the same characteristics. It is impossible to know how many people in the "normal" population also possess unusual biological properties.

Finally, it is important to remember that biological and environmental variables may affect different kinds of gender-related behaviors in different ways. Susan Baker (1980) has proposed that gender-role behavior (such as aggression or nurturance), gender identity (whether the person perceives himself or herself to be male or female), and sexual orientation may all be influenced by a different mix of biological and social variables. Look at each of these categories as you examine different patterns of sexual discordance.

Chromosomal Anomalies

Turner's Syndrome: Can One Be a Female without Estrogen?

Under normal circumstances human beings possess forty-six chromosomes—twenty-two pairs of autosomes and one set of sex chromosomes. During the development of the egg or sperm, however, it is possible for one of these chromosomes to be deleted or for an extra one to be added. One of the most interesting of the chromosomal abnormalities that affect sexual development produces what is known as *Turner's syndrome.* Individuals with this disorder usually have only one unmatched X chromosome. Turner's syndrome is rather rare—it occurs in fewer than one in 10,000 live births (Hartl, 1983). Although there is considerable variation in structural characteristics, individuals with Turner's syndrome are unusually short (rarely reaching more than four and a half feet as adults) and do not become sexually mature.

Although the missing chromosome could have been either an X or a Y (in genetic terminology, people with Turner's syndrome are classified as 45, XO), these individuals are always identified as "female" on the basis of their external genitalia, which are completely female although they remain immature. Breasts fail to develop and pubic hair does not grow at adolescence. Their internal reproductive structures are undeveloped, with ovaries represented only by fibrous streaks of tissue. They do not menstruate and, of course, they are completely sterile.

People with Turner's syndrome are particularly interesting because they represent how development occurs in the absence of any sex hormones except those produced by the mother before birth. Findings about these people parallel those found in animal experiments—in the absence of any gonadal influences differentiation will take a female direction. However, people with Turner's syndrome are not simply aberrant females. They are essentially neuter individuals whose external genitalia are similar to those of females. They are defined as females simply because of the inadequacy of our binary classification system for sex.

Individuals with Turner's syndrome provide researchers with an opportunity to examine the psychological effects of the sex of assignment and rearing independent of the biological influences usually associated with that sex. A number of studies have been done comparing their psychological and behavioral responses to those of normal females (Money & Ehrhardt, 1972). People with Turner's syndrome have often been described as being slightly retarded. Their verbal IQs are in the normal range, however, and it is only their nonverbal performance that is significantly below normal. The discrepancy seems to derive from their relative inability to understand space–form relationships. This defect is sometimes known as space–form blindness. To a lesser extent, XO individuals have difficulty orienting themselves in terms of direction and performing numerical calculations.

The basis for this deficiency is unknown, although it has sometimes been ascribed to the lack of a Y chromosome. The Y chromosome, however, is not known to carry any genes besides those for male sex determination except, possibly, a gene for hairy ears (Hartl, 1983). It is also difficult to consider the problem as comparable to "similar" difficulties found in normal females (and attributed to their biology), since the two groups are comparable only in terms of their sex of assignment and rearing.

Although their central nervous systems have not been exposed to any gonadal hormones during gestation, individuals with Turner's syndrome identify themselves as female. As children they appear even more feminine than girls with whom they are compared. They show less interest and skill in athletics, fight less, and have a greater interest in personal adornment.

Despite the handicap of their stature and infertility, which all of the older Turner girls knew about, all but one explicitly hoped to get married one day. They all reported daydreams and fantasies of being pregnant and wanted to have a baby to care for. All but one had played with dolls exclusively and the exception preferred dolls even though she played with boys' toys occasionally (Money & Ehrhardt, 1972). These findings suggest that a feminine gender identity can develop without any help from prenatal gonadal hormones that might influence the brain.

Do we need to bring in gonadal hormones to explain these results? The only obvious physical difference, and sometimes the only external sign, of XO children is their small size. Other aspects of their physical immaturity do not become obvious until adolescence. It is probable that these children will not be reinforced for their skill in athletics or fighting. Size is also a cue for status and power among children (Garn, 1966). Since children with Turner's syndrome tend to be consistently much smaller than their peers, they probably have low status and power as well.

Individuals with Turner's syndrome scored lower in enthusiasm and impulsiveness than comparable ninth-grade girls (Shaffer, 1963). They also scored lower in generalized activity, energy, and masculinity on temperament scales and higher in personal relationships and cooperativeness. There was more uniformity in these traditionally feminine traits among children with Turner's syndrome than among comparable girls. In fact, the degree of overcompliance that the XO individuals showed would be considered a clinical problem in chromosomally normal females.

There is no clear evidence that the personality and behavioral differences between XX and XO individuals are socially determined. But the lack of a second X chromosome may not be directly responsible for these effects either. Factors such as activity level and body image and its social consequences should be taken into consideration in addition to biological variables.

XYY and XXY Males: What Is the Power of the Y Chromosome?

Both scientists and ordinary people tend to overestimate the extent to which biological variables determine our behavior. An excellent example of the tendency to overgeneralize biological determinants may be found in the case of the so-called criminality syndrome. Individuals with an extra Y chromosome (47, XYY) were first reported in 1965 among the inmates of institutions for violent, dangerous, and aggressive patients. No physical abnormality was reported except for excessive height. XYY males tend to be tall, averaging over six feet.

More than fifty similar studies have now been carried out in prisons in Europe and the United States, and it has held true that the frequency of XYY males confined for crimes of violence is about ten times greater than the percentage of XYY males found among a sample of newborn infants. This result led a number of investigators to conclude that the extra Y chromosome predisposed these men toward excessive aggression and violence. Such conclusions are an example of an extreme form of biological determinism.

These studies were biased by the fact that they took place in an institutional setting. They had, therefore, no information about the XYY men who are not societal problems (the greater number). Chromosomal factors, moreover, do not rule out social influences as well. Since XYY men tend to be taller than the average, it is possible that their extra height imposes psychosocial stresses that makes violent aggressive behavior more likely. Their height may also make any aggression more effective and reinforcing.

One Danish study of criminality among XYY males is particularly important because it is free of many of the biases found in other studies. The study was possible because of the excellent records kept in the small country of Denmark. The researchers (Witkin et al., 1976) examined *all* available records on almost all men 28 to 32 years of age born in Copenhagen whose height was within the top 15 percent of the height distribution of Danish males. Eventually, sex-chromosome determination was done on 4,139 males who made up more than 90 percent of the starting group. The researchers also obtained information on any crimes committed by these men, the educational level they had attained, and the results of an intelligence test used to screen army recruits.

Among these men, twelve XYY and thirteen XXY individuals were identified. The individuals with an XXY chromosomal composition (also known as *Klinefelter's syndrome*) served as a comparison group for the XYY males. This group is also taller than average, but the presence of an extra X chromosome produces a smaller penis and testes and feminization of the hips, with some breast development. The testes fail to enlarge at puberty, the voice remains rather high-pitched, and pubic and facial hair remain sparse. Because of the feminizing effects of an extra X chromosome, the researchers expected such men to engage in fewer violent aggressive acts than either XY or XYY males.

Chromosomal composition, by itself, was not highly related to the probability that a man would be convicted of a crime. Height was also not related to the probability of being convicted of a crime (criminals were actually shorter than their noncriminal counterparts). Those of low socioeconomic status—irrespective of their chromosomal composition—were more likely to have been convicted.

The most important findings of this study were that both XXY and XYY males had significantly lower army intelligence test scores and lower educational levels than XY males did. For each group, men with criminal records were substantially lower in both measures of intellectual function than men without criminal records. These findings seem to imply that the somewhat higher rate of criminality among XYY males may be due to their moderately impaired mental function. The hypothesis about the relationship of an extra Y chromosome and aggression was definitely not supported. In fact, the only violent crime committed by any man with extra chromosomes was the physical attack on a woman committed by an XXY male.

The case of the so-called criminality syndrome illustrates the danger of overestimating biological causality. At about the time of the first discovery of XYY males among exceptionally violent criminals, a pathological killer, Richard Speck, sneaked into a nurses' dormitory in Chicago and brutally murdered several student nurses. A newspaper claimed that he had been "born to kill" because he was XYY. This turned out to be untrue—he was XY—but the false report was widely disseminated and believed. Several proposals were made for the mass screening of newborn boys to detect those with XYY and to provide them with special education and psychological counseling to counteract their supposed "killer instinct." This could have produced a self-fulfilling prophecy and created problems for individuals because those with whom they interacted believed them to have severe problems with aggression. The results of the Danish study indicate, however, that the rate of criminality is related more to income level and the level of intellectual functioning than to sex-chromosomal composition.

Do the Chromosomes Determine Sex?

Perhaps because the X and Y chromosomes carry relatively little genetic information, missing and extra sex chromosomes appear to be the most common form of chromosomal abnormality in human beings. Extra chromosomes may be accompanied by lower intelligence, but many people with them may be completely unaware of their unusual chromosomal nature.

The ignorance of chromosomal status can have tragic results for women who compete in world-class athletic events like the Olympics. Women who are found to have a Y chromosome in some of their cells (this is common enough that several such women are usually identified at most major international sports events) are routinely denied the opportunity to participate (Lorber, 1993). Only women are tested to see if they are "female enough" to compete. Men are not tested. The purpose is to prevent women from having to compete unfairly with individuals who have male advantages in size and strength. However, there is no evidence that chromosomes affect sports prowess (Birrell & Cole, 1990). And, recently, the prestigious International Amateur Athletic Federation has urged that sex be determined by simple genital inspection (Kolata, 1992).

Chromosomal composition also appears to have little direct effect on gender identity or sexual orientation. Instead, gender identity is related to the appearance of the external genitalia, which, in turn, determines the sex to which children are assigned and raised. There is no clear evidence that links chromosomes with sexual orientation in either sex. Men with Klinefelter's syndrome are somewhat more likely to evidence homosexual behavior than XY males, but this could be because other men respond to their ambiguous female appearance by treating them like women rather than because of a direct effect of their chromosomes on their brains.

In sum, studies of human beings with missing or extra sex chromosomes indicate few direct effects of sex chromosomes on behavior. Many of the differences found appear to be due to the impact of physical characteristics and/or intellectual deficits that, in turn, influence the way people treat the affected individual. In view of the extreme belief in genetic determinism of some sociobiologists, it is surprising how few differences from normative patterns have been found.

Prenatal Hormones and Sex Differentiation

Pseudohermaphrodism: What Is Sex Anyway?

As noted earlier in this chapter, sex is actually the result of a number of stages in the development process. If something goes wrong during the developmental sequence, individuals are produced who are neither entirely male nor entirely female; that is, their sex is ambiguous. Such individuals have been known as *hermaphrodites* after the mythical offspring of the Greek god Hermes and the goddess Aphrodite who had the attributes of both sexes.

The term hermaphrodite, however, is currently only applied to organisms that are capable of producing both functional sperm and functional eggs. Human beings who have a mixture of male and female sex organs are usually termed *pseudohermaphrodites* because they usually produce neither functional eggs nor sperm. The terms pseudo (or false) hermaphroditism and *intersexuality* are often used interchangeably to describe various kinds of disorders that result from discrepancies between the sex of the chromosomes, gonadal and/or hormonal sex, the sex of the reproductive organs, and the external genitalia. Like those with chromosomal anomalies, people with such conditions are studied because of what they may tell us about the causality of sex-related behaviors in normal human beings.

The Andrenogenital Syndrome: How Do We Determine Sex?

The *andrenogenital syndrome* is a form of pseudohermaphroditism caused in some cases by a hereditary defect in the adrenal glands. In these individuals, there is a buildup of *progesterone*—a hormone characteristic of pregnancy—that is broken down by the body into a series of substances that have an action similar to that of testosterone. The testosterone-like effects of the breakdown products cause varying degrees of masculinization in affected females (Hartl, 1983). There have been a number of studies of these individuals as well as of a population of females whose mothers received doses of progesterone during pregnancy to prevent a threatened miscarriage. The two groups seem to be similar, suggesting that any behavioral effects are due to prenatal androgens, since the masculinized daughters of progesterone-treated mothers need no treatment after birth except for the surgical correction of an enlarged clitoris in some cases.

Females with adrenogenital syndrome have two normal X chromosomes, normal ovaries, uterus, and fallopian tubes. However, the external genitalia of affected infants bear varying degrees of resemblance to those of male infants (see Figure 6.6). There is usually an enlarged clitoris and a fusion of the labioscrotal folds, producing a picture of sexual ambiguity. Some individuals have complete closure of the urethral groove and a penis that is capable of becoming erect.

Until rather recently, sex was assigned to newborn infants on the basis of inspection of their genitalia. Thus, two individuals with equivalent ambiguities might have been classified differently. In the United States, at least, this kind of misassignment no longer occurs for individuals with the adrenogenital syndrome. Advances in knowledge about gonadal structure and chromosomal composition have led to most such individuals being correctly raised as females. Since their internal structures tend to be normally female and many of them are fertile, a relatively small amount of cosmetic surgery is all that is required to make their external appearance consistent with the other components of their sexual category. If these girls receive proper replacement therapy with other hormones, they experience pubertal development spontaneously at the normal age, and their sexual functioning and fertility do not appear to be impaired in adulthood (Ehrhardt & Meyer-Bahlburg, 1981).

Since such females have received a heavy dose of masculinizing hormones during fetal life, questions about their gender identity, gender-related behaviors, and sexual orientation are of great interest. Girls with the adrenogenital syndrome (the inherited form is also known as congenital adrenal hyperplasia, or CAH) have been found to identify firmly as girls and women. However, they differed from comparison groups (either matched normal females, unaffected siblings, or individuals with other clinical disorders) in that they typically showed more intense active outdoor play, increased association with male peers, and

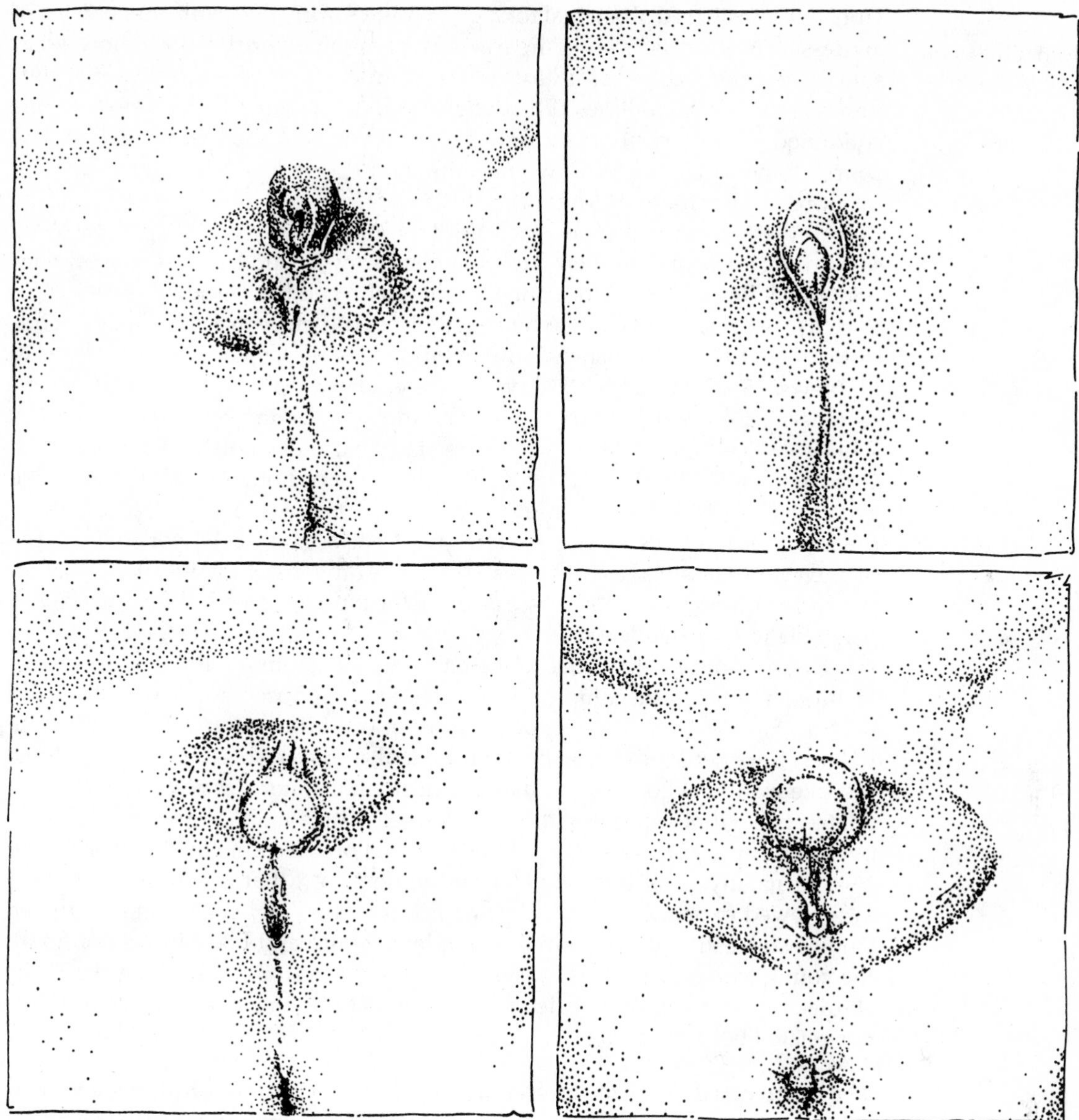

FIGURE 6.6. Genitals are not always clearly "male" or "female." Here are examples of the external genitalia of several pseudohermaphroditic or intersexed infants. *Drawing by Alina Wilczynski.*

long-term identification as a "tomboy" by themselves and others. They preferred "masculine" toys to "feminine" ones beginning in their nursery school years (Berenbaum & Hines, 1992). All of these behavioral differences are probably related to the higher activity levels that they also show from an early age.

They also differed from comparison girls by displaying a lower level of parenting concerns in terms of doll play or baby care and less interest in rehearsal of the roles of wife and mother versus having a career. None of their behaviors would be considered abnormal for a girl in our culture. They were not any more aggressive than girls from comparison populations, nor did they show what some researchers consider a "male-like" cognitive profile—better spatial-perceptual than verbal abilities (Ehrhardt & Meyer-Bahlburg, 1981). Despite their childhood characterization as tomboys and their avid interest in high school sports, none of these young women pursued sports as a career or even as a major pastime (Money & Mathews, 1982).

As these young women reach adulthood, however, there appears to be some disagreement over their feminine identification and heterosexual orientation. In a follow-up study of young women who had been studied during adolescence, none of these women had a history of difficulty in establishing friendships or dating relationships with men and four were married (Money & Mathews, 1982). In another study of nine young women with CAH, other researchers reported a consistent pattern of delay in dating and sexual relations (Hurtig & Rosenthal, 1987). Still others state that the majority of women with CAH are heterosexual, although several bisexual or homosexual women have been identified (Ehrhardt & Meyer-Bahlburg, 1981). When classified by erotic dreams and fantasies as opposed to overt sociosexual behavior, half of the women were classified as heterosexual and the other half bisexual; none was exclusively homosexual. This was true even for those women whose adrenal hyperplasia was treated late.

These studies suggest that the effects of prenatal masculinizing hormones on human females are complex. Gender identity is closely related to the sex of rearing. Sexual orientation appears to be more idiosyncratic. Some of these women were heterosexual, some homosexual, and some bisexual in orientation just like women who have not had any hormonal abnormalities. Some gender-related behaviors, especially those associated with a high degree of energy expenditure, appear to be influenced by the level of masculinizing hormones present prenatally. It is important to stress, however, that most of the women interviewed expressed satisfaction with themselves as females and that even studies suggesting disturbances in gender identity and body image found all the young women with CAH to be within the norms for adolescent girls. These studies rule out any rigidly deterministic effect of prenatal androgens on gender-related behaviors.

The Testicular-Feminization Syndrome: What Does the Y Chromosome Do?

The *testicular-feminization syndrome* (also sometimes known as *androgen insensitivity*) is an inherited condition of chromosomally XY individuals. It is apparently caused by the inability of the embryonic tissues to respond to testosterone. Affected individuals have female external genitalia and an incompletely developed vagina but no uterus or fallopian tubes. Their internal reproductive apparatus is similar to that of a normal male in appearance, although the testes contain unusual cells and are present in the abdominal cavity rather than the scrotum. They are usually unquestioningly classified as female at birth and diagnosed as having the testicular-feminization syndrome only after the discovery of a hernia (a gap in the abdominal wall through which the internal organs bulge) that turns out to be a testis.

These individuals appear to be totally irresponsive to testosterone. However, their bodies (like those of other males) produce estrogens whose effects are not canceled out by the presence of testosterones. These estrogens induce breast development and feminine contours at puberty and individuals with testicular feminization often appear to be very attractive women. They are unambiguously raised as females and little or no medical treatment is necessary. Of course, such individuals, having no uterus, do not menstruate and are sterile.

Since this is a rare disorder, there have been relatively few studies of the behavior of people with testicular feminization syndrome. Money and Ehrhardt (1972) surveyed the clinical data on ten such individuals and reported that they show a high preference for a traditionally feminine role. Eighty percent preferred the role of homemaker over an outside job; 100 percent reported having dreams and fantasies of raising a family; 80 percent reported playing primarily with dolls and other girls' toys. They rated themselves as high in affectionateness and fully content with the feminine role. Adults with this syndrome tend to be found in occupations that put a high premium on an attractive feminine appearance and behavior, such as modeling, acting, and prostitution.

It has been suggested that people with this syndrome present an unusually attractive appearance. The Y chromosome carries information that is not completely mediated by testosterone. Thus, they tend to have male height. Their breast development is normal and appears to result from the action of estrogens produced by their testes (if they are still present) and their adrenal glands. Pubic and axillary hair tends to be sparse or absent. It is disconcerting to find that the most attractive female body may be that of a genetic male. In any case, the socially mediated effects of personal attractiveness must be considered before the feminine identity of these individuals can be attributed to the lack of testosterone in their central nervous systems.

5 Alpha-Reductase Deficiency: When Is Culture Important for Understanding Biology?

The newest syndrome in which biological determinist theories may be examined is *5 alpha-reductase deficiency.* Like testicular feminization, it is an inherited condition due to a recessive gene. Affected individuals lack an enzyme that aids in the conversion of testosterone to *dihydrotestosterone.* This androgen induces fusion of the scrotum and the growth of the penis. Thus, these people are born with normal testes and male internal structures combined with a clitoris-like penis and an incomplete or absent scrotum that resembles the *labia* of females. In brief, their external genitalia are quite similar to the ambiguous structures of girls who have been exposed to prenatal androgens (see Figure 6.6). When modern scientific methods for determining sex are unavailable, they may be identified and raised as girls.

Males with 5 alpha-reductase deficiency are, however, masculinized at puberty, when their normal testes pour large amounts of testosterone into their systems. This testosterone produces deepening of the voice, enlargement of the penis and testicles, erections, and ejaculation from a urethral orifice at the base of the penis (Imperato-McGinley & Peterson, 1976; Peterson, Imperato-McGinley, Gautier, & Sturla, 1977). Such individuals would appear to provide a perfect test case for examining the effect of socialization versus biological factors in gender identity since they are biological males who have been raised as females throughout childhood. The interesting question is, What happens to their gender identity when their sex of rearing and their physical properties become different at this relatively late point in their lives? Or, how reversible is gender identity?

This issue has received a great deal of attention as a result of the work of Julianne Imperato-McGinley and her colleagues (Imperato-McGinley, Peterson, Gautier, & Sturla, 1979). They studied a group of thirty-eight related individuals with the disorder in a rural region of the Dominican Republic. In this isolated group, 5 alpha-reductase deficiency is so common that it has a name: *guevedoce,* or "penis at twelve." The researchers claim that the first nineteen cases of this disorder were reared unambiguously as girls, but more recent cases have been recognized early and treated as special. What is surprising is their reports of the striking ease with which these people shifted gender at puberty. The researchers state that seventeen successfully assumed a masculine identity and fifteen were married. Their findings suggest a much later capacity for gender identity reversal than studies on other sexual anomalies would indicate is possible. These researchers believe that the shift was made possible by the prenatal masculinization of the brain in these individuals; that is, their "male" brains were able to overcome easily many years of feminine socialization.

As you can see, "nature versus nurture" arguments are still alive and well in the area of sexual development and behavior. Some researchers have challenged that a more intensive analysis of Imperato-McGinley's own data suggests that the shift from feminine to masculine identity was not as simple as it first appeared. For example, these individuals are described as realizing that they were different from other girls sometime between the ages of 7 and 12 (Rubin, Reinisch, & Haskett, 1981). This realization took place shortly after the age at which children in this culture are encouraged to segregate by sex for play and domestic tasks. They shifted their gender identity over several years and initiated sexual intercourse with young women at the same age as those affected males who had been raised as boys.

It is also not clear whether these individuals had indeed been raised unambiguously as females. Their genitalia, while not masculine, were certainly not like those of normal girls. Photographs of the external genitalia of three of the prepubescent children revealed marked fusion of the labia and scrotum in two cases; absent labia in all three cases; and phallic structures ranging in size from an enlarged abnormal clitoris to a small penis. "Even cursory inspection of the genitalia should have revealed the abnormal configuration of these organs to any observer, especially to the mother" (Rubin et al., 1981, p. 1322). However, no one asked about whether anything was noticed or what others thought it meant, despite the fact that there was little individual privacy in this society and any physical abnormality would be likely to be noticed by many people in a relatively small, isolated society.

We have discussed this case in some detail because it illustrates how we cannot ignore the role of culture in the differentiation of gender identity even in situations where development differs drastically from the norm. Anthropological investigations of this population have, for example, indicated a social class effect in affected individuals' acquisition of an adult male role. Individuals from poor families are likely to drift into marginal occupations, including prostitution, whereas similarly affected individuals from well-to-do families marry and purportedly "father" children with their wives (Tobach, personal communication).

A recent study of another isolated population—in New Guinea—with 5 alpha-reductase deficiency (Herdt & Davidson, 1988) also illustrates how cultural categories may influence gender identification. As in the Dominican Republic, the genetic abnormality is common enough to have received a colloquial name. In fact, this society actually has three linguistic terms for sex: male, female, and an ambiguous compound word that emphasizes the quality of change or transformation. This belief in the modifiability of sex is also indicated by the local word used to describe hermaphroditic individuals, "Turnim-man."

Herdt and Davidson argue that male pseudohermaphrodites represent a third sex in this society. They are usually recognized at birth because of anomalies in their genitals. Their data on fourteen individuals with the disorder indicate that nine were reared ambiguously as males (they were not given all the initiation rites available to normal boys in this society) and five as females.

Those raised as females changed to a masculine role at adulthood, but under circumstances of social trauma. For example, two such individuals were rejected after marriage by their husband when he discovered they had small penises. None of them was initiated into the men's cults. They switched roles to "pass" as men under a great deal of external public pressure because there was no place in this small rigid society to hide or to be a woman. The shift was facilitated by the availability of a third sexual category.

The researchers ask, "How do we interpret this scandal-induced halting outcome twenty years after birth?" It is hard to see strong support for the suggestion that either male hormones or a brain masculinized before birth led to the change in gender identity. A number of these individuals shifted to manhood after they had failed to live successfully as women. Many of them moved away to larger towns. They tended to opt out of a confining village situation because there was no place for exposed unmarried female-like individuals. It is understandable that they would switch to the masculine role to adapt better to a male-dominated society once their defects were known. Such considerations may also have played a role in the masculine identity switch found within gender-traditional rural Dominican society.

The ability to shift gender may depend on factors other than purely biological ones. For example, eight such individuals in the United States who were raised as females and who experienced testosterone-induced activation at puberty prior to medical intervention apparently maintained feminine gender identity despite disfiguring pubertal virilization (Rubin et al., 1981). Similar results have been found for females with adrenogenital syndrome who were misassigned as males at birth (Money & Ehrhardt, 1972). Once gender identity is formed (usually in the first few years of life), it cannot easily be reversed, despite coarsening of features and beard growth in a "girl" at puberty or breast development and erectile inadequacy in a "boy."

IS THERE A CRITICAL PERIOD FOR GENDER IDENTITY?

Conclusions about the critical importance of the early years of socialization in the development of permanent gender identity are based largely on studies of clinical populations. To resolve the controversy over whether the gender assignment at birth and during the first few years of life is of paramount importance in the gender identification of normal human beings, it is necessary to find biologically normal individuals who have been reared as members of the other sex. Obviously, such cross-rearing would usually be related to a peculiar and probably pathological family situation. Milton Diamond (1965) states that people who were subjected to such attempts have always reverted to their "proper" chromosomal sex as soon as they were offered the opportunity to do so.

Attempts to induce cross-sex identification in a normal child would be complicated by the child's having genitalia consistent with his or her biological sex. However, examination of the early lives of *transsexuals* (individuals who manifest a gender-identity pattern opposite to that of their biological sex) reveals little in the way of overt, consistent, or long-term familial imposition of a cross-sex identification. These findings suggest a complex relationship between genital anatomy and gender identity.

Cross-Sex Rearing in a Prenatally Normal Male

John Money (1974) has provided information about a case whose bizarre aspects seem more suited to a science-fiction story than to scientific annals. The case involves a set of identical twins whose development before birth was normally male. In infancy, however, an accident during circumcision resulted in near-total destruction of the tissue of one twin's penis. After much professional and parental agonizing, it was decided to reclassify the child as female. This was formally done at the age of 17 months. The sex reassignment was based on the opinion that a child without a penis will be able to function more adequately as a female than as a maimed male. It was also based on findings from clinical studies of hermaphrodites suggesting that children identify with the gender in which they are reared if the assignment occurs within the first two or three years of life and the child is treated consistently as either a male or a female from then on.

Think about both the conceptual bases and the ethical implications of such a sexual reassignment. First, it reflects our cultural bias about the primacy of the penis. Anyone without a functional penis is not considered to be truly male. Experts were willing to subject this child to additional surgery (including castration or removal of the testes as well as construction of a vagina) and lifelong hormonal replacement therapy because they believed he could not function as a male without a penis. The experts also did not question whether this individual would have sexual pleasure as a woman or whether she would consider herself a "normal" female without menstruation or the capacity to bear children.

Second, although such treatment is medically feasible and the procedures well worked out for male-to-female transsexuals, it is done with their consent. This child was not old enough to give his informed consent and, in fact, as of age

13, had not yet been informed about the sex reassignment. Given the higher status of males in our society, it is possible the child might have preferred to remain a male even without a penis. On the other hand, perhaps he would have preferred to be a functional female rather than a maimed male since he/she would be sterile in any event. It is easy to have 20/20 hindsight in this case, but what would you have done?

These children were followed extensively throughout childhood. The ways in which the parents distinguished between this child and her previously identical twin brother are noteworthy. The first items to be changed were clothes and hairdo. The mother reported: "I started dressing her not in dresses but, you know, in little pink slacks and frilly blouses . . . and letting her hair grow. . . . I even made all her nightwear into granny gowns and she wears bracelets and hair ribbons" (Money & Ehrhardt, 1972, p. 119). By the age of four she was reported as preferring dresses over slacks, taking pride in her long hair, and being much neater and cleaner than her brother. She had been taught to sit while urinating and to be modest about exposing her genital parts (the latter in contrast to her brother, for whom an incident of public urination was described with amusement by the mother). The child was also encouraged to help her mother with housework, again in contrast to her brother who "could not care less about it" (p. 121). "She" was described as having feminine toy and occupational preferences, while at the age of 5 the boy preferred such traditionally masculine careers as being a fireman or a policeman. Although it is stated that the "girl" had many tomboyish (a peculiar word to use with reference to this child) traits, she had been encouraged to be less rough-and-tumble than her brother and to be quieter and more "ladylike." The boy was reported as responding by being physically protective of his "sister."

During the childhood of these twins, stereotypically masculine and feminine characteristics seemed to be more under the control of socially mediated factors than biological ones. This case and two other cases of sex reassignment reported by Money (1974) appeared to provide strong evidence that most traditional gender differences are socially learned. However, when the twin was seen at age 13 by a new set of psychiatrists, she was said to be beset by problems (Diamond, 1982). The reports stated:

> At the present time the child refuses to draw a female figure and when asked to draw a female, refuses, saying it's easier to draw a man.
>
> The child . . . has a very masculine gait, er, looks quite masculine, and is being teased by each group that she attempts to make overtures toward . . . they will call her cavewoman and they make reference to the fact that she is not particularly feminine.
>
> At the present time, she feels that boys have a better life. That it's easier to be a boy than it is to be a girl. She aspires to masculine occupations, wants to be a mechanic (Diamond, 1982, p. 183).

This latter statement might be made by many untreated adolescent girls (see Chapter 8).

At 18 years of age this individual sought and received surgery to reconstruct a penis and scrotum. As a mature adult, he now lives as a male and seeks females as sexual partners (Diamond, 1993). This case study no longer supports the thesis that gender identity is primarily dependent on social learning during a critical period of early childhood.

The Role of Body Image

This case, however, also does not prove that gender identity is dependent on prenatal factors. One of the more obvious (but frequently neglected) truisms in the study of the biological bases of behavior is that one cannot remove the organism from his or her environment. The organism's body structure (and in the case of human beings, social reactions to that structure) forms part of that environment.

The studies on various types of pseudohermaphroditism summarized earlier suggest that some individuals may have difficulty in maintaining a gender identity that conflicts with bodily norms that are considered desirable for a member of that sex within a society. Lack of attractiveness is a major stigma for females in our society. It is significant that girls with CAH who were virilized showed higher masculinity scores than their nonvirilized counterparts (Hurtig & Rosenthal, 1987). It should not be surprising, therefore, that this relatively unattractive twin would reject her feminine role. It is a simple fact of binary logic that if you feel everything is wrong the way you are, maybe the correct way is the other way.

Stoller (1985) reported a similar case of an individual with 5 alpha-reductase deficiency who was raised as a girl, but switched at age 14. Stoller remarked, ". . . it was a bad masquerade . . . it was clear that this child was living an impossible existence as a girl" (p. 67). The child had been a "model tomboy" until she reached puberty. As you will see in Chapter 8, puberty is the period during which standards of attractiveness and femininity (which are closely associated in our society) are strongly imposed.

CHANGING IDENTITY

Transsexualism

One way to examine the effect of body image on gender identity is to look at a group of people who firmly believe that they were born with the bodies of the wrong sex. This phenomenon is known as *transsexualism.* The transsexual has somehow acquired the "wrong" gender identity and, once acquired, this identity appears to be unchangeable. Many transsexuals maintain that they have been discontented with their identity from earliest childhood. Their belief is not easily influenced by any form of psychological therapy.

These people are not, however, psychotic. They are not confused about the actual biological condition of their bodies, but believe that their psyches are consistent with the body of the other sex. A number of transsexuals have had successful careers before seeking gender reassignment. One such individual is Jan Morris, a well-known writer, who was James Morris and who wrote the story of her transition from male to female in the best-selling book called *Conundrum* (1974). Another such individual is René Richards (previously Richard Raskin), an eye surgeon who made headlines when she attempted (unsuccessfully) to play on the women's professional tennis circuit after having played on the men's circuit.

It has been estimated that there are 30,000 transsexuals worldwide, 10,000 of whom are believed to live in the United States (Grimm, 1987). Male-to-female transsexuals outnumber female-to-male transsexuals by at least four to one, perhaps by as much as eight to one. Many researchers believe that the reason for this disparity is that primarily androcentric cultures are less accepting of variant masculine role behaviors. Thus, men who deviate in some ways may come to feel that they are not men at all. For example, it is perfectly acceptable for women to wear pants, carry briefcases, and enjoy sports, but what do you think about a man who wears dresses, carries a purse, and enjoys needlepoint?

Adults who decide to pass as members of the other sex may range from those who simply dress in that sex's attire in the privacy of their homes (usually called *transvestites*) to those who undergo extensive surgery to make their bodies consistent with the sex with which they identify. Clinics that perform such surgery usually require the individual to live successfully as a member of the other sex for at least a year. Passing as a member of a particular gender category seems to be more a matter of attire, hairstyle, voice, mannerisms, and gestures than of any extensive physiological change. In fact, two-thirds of the transsexual population have not gone as far as surgery but are nonetheless living as members of the other sex on a full-time basis (Grimm, 1987). They typically take years to change sex and go through a gradual readjustment to their changing body image and societal reactions to it (Ehrhardt & Meyer-Bahlburg, 1981).

Transsexuals do not transcend traditional masculine-feminine dichotomies. Male-to-female transsexuals in particular often adopt an exaggerated stereotypical version of feminine dress and behavior. They wear more elaborate clothing and makeup than most women. In *Conundrum,* Jan Morris (an ex-war correspondent) recounts feeling pleased to be helped on and off trains with her luggage following sex-change surgery. The medical establishment appears to encourage such stereotyping since the more feminine the appearance and behavior of the applicant, the more likely his request for surgery will be granted (Raymond, 1979).

Surgical treatment of transsexuals actually confirms traditional social constructions of masculinity and femininity. It opts for massive, permanent changes in the body rather than acceptance of the idea that roles and bodies may be independent and that the connection is imposed by the cultural standards for each sex.

> This group of people would—potentially—be the most potent group of people pressing for changes in the sex structure because their aversion to their "sex appropriateness" roles is apparently insurmountable. By declaring them by surgical fiat, as members of the other sex, this change potential is diverted and becomes as conservative as it could have been revolutionary (Eichler, 1980, p. 88).

The outcome of such surgery is currently a matter of great controversy. Some studies of postoperative transsexuals have found high levels of satisfaction with the surgery and the new life (Blanchard, Steiner, & Clemmensen, 1985). But not all studies report such positive outcomes. For example, one study, which followed up patients an average of twelve years after surgery, found that the majority were judged to be unchanged in sexual or psychosocial adjustment (Lindemalm, Korlin, & Uddenberg, 1986). Another study, which compared male heterosexuals, transvestites, and preoperative and postoperative transsexuals (Beatrice, 1985), found no differences between the groups in self-concept but found that postoperative transsexuals were significantly higher than the other groups on the paranoia and schizophrenic subscales of the MMPI. This researcher argued that his study supports recent literature indicating that sex-reassignment surgery for transsexuals is not the treatment of choice.

We cannot separate the outcome of such drastic changes in gender identity from the social meaning of gender in our society. For example, one interesting outcome of gender reassignment may be a change in economic status. Taking on the masculine role was correlated with higher economic status for women, whereas the change to a feminine role was associated with lower economic status for men (Blanchard, 1985). Even for the same person, being a man no matter how it is achieved, is associated with a higher income.

Gender Bending and Body Image

An interesting study of women who are sometimes mistaken for men (Devor, 1987) also illustrates how maleness is more highly valued in our society. These women do not pass as men in a consistent or purposeful fashion. They have clear feminine identities, but because of their height, body build, and nonverbal behaviors are often mistaken for men or boys during brief encounters of an impersonal and public nature (see Figure 6.7). The kinds of male advantages most frequently reported by these women had to do with freedom of movement. They cited the feeling of safety on the streets at night or safety from the threat of rape as a very valuable result of their masculine appearance.

> I was walking down the street and men were looking me straight in the eye with this incredible amount of respect. I didn't know what the fuck was going on. . . . Like it was totally different . . . this feels like being in another world, it was like being a human being, I couldn't believe the sensation. What a power trip, it was wonderful, so I started to learn, hey, if I looked like a guy no one is going to hassle me.

A number of women also reported that they received more "respect" as men than they did as women.

> It's awful to be treated like a girl by the general public. . . . They think you're dumb, they think you don't know anything.
>
> I guess a lot of it is that men are so in control of the world, and this is an awful thing to say. . . . I'm shocked that I even think it . . . men, in this world, are so dominant that everything seems to go towards them, like sometimes to be mistaken, to look like a man, can be an advantage . . . (Devor, 1987, p. 28).

These women are unusual in that they have regular experiences of being either "male" or "female." They are in an excellent position to report on the dichotomous response to the two sexes in our society. They also show us how, in everyday life, sex may be irrelevant to the ascription of gender. Assumptions

FIGURE 6.7. Gender-bender.

about the separateness of the sexes permit people to explain away any lingering misaligned bodily cues. For example, a prominent chest on a women who is identified as a man may be seen as large pectoral muscles or simply fat on the upper body.

Although these women are not transsexuals, they may tell us something about the social pressures that produce ambivalences about gender in our society. All of them reported that as girls they enjoyed physical activity and that they were tomboys throughout their early years. The majority played mostly with boys or were loners. About half came from homes where their fathers acted as though they would have preferred them to be sons. Many of these women were tall . . . only one was smaller than the average North American woman. This combination of behavioral preferences and physical characteristics appears to have led them to become "gender benders."

Body image may play a greater role in the development of gender identity than we had previously believed. For example, Richard Green and his associates (Green, Williams, & Goodman, 1982) found virtually no differences in familial characteristics between fifty traditional and forty-nine nontraditional girls ages 4 to 12. The mothers of nontraditional girls, however, reported more than the other mothers that adults comment that their daughters would make handsome boys. Physical attractiveness in childhood is sometimes associated with the development of a feminine gender identity in boys (Green, 1974).

CULTURAL CONSTRUCTIONS OF GENDER

There is no clear evidence of a biological basis for cross-gender identity (Bolin, 1987). Recently, feminist scholars have begun to look at transsexualism as a violation of the rules by which sex and gender are constructed in our society. Transsexualism tests the extent to which cultural definitions of sex and gender are taken for granted.

Suzanne Kessler and Wendy McKenna (1978), for example, argue that gender is constructed and maintained by social interactions. As you can see from the preceding discussion on transsexualism and other forms of gender-bending, aspects of gender identity can be learned relatively easily. In fact, as we noted above, transsexuals do not undergo surgical manipulations to change their sex until they have satisfied their physicians that they have successfully "passed" as a member of the other sex for at least a year. In most encounters, the gender by which one presents oneself is accepted by others. Since the "natural" connection between sex and gender is rarely questioned, people assume that the signals associated with gender in our society (such as clothing, hairstyle, and nonverbal behaviors) also define biological sex. The presence of sex-appropriate genitalia is assumed.

Recently, Suzanne Kessler (1990) has conducted interviews with physicians who deal with intersexed infants. These physicians, like everyone else in our society, cannot deal with gender ambiguity. They assign sexually ambiguous infants to a gender category based largely on how well they can construct an adequate genital appearance and function for a member of that category. While these physicians recognize that they are assigning and constructing gender, they attempt to make the categorization nonproblematic for both parents and, eventually, for the affected individuals themselves. They do so by informing their clients that medical science has uncovered the child's real sex and that their manipulations will "improve" this fundamental design. This (mis)information reinstates the male–female distinction considered normal in our society and reinforces our ideology that sex and gender are natural and overlapping categories.

Almost no one in this society questions assumptions about sex and gender. However, not all cultures agree with Western society's notion that all people are either men or women. Earlier in this chapter we discussed some alternative sexual categories such as "Turnim-man" associated with biological anomalies. However, the idea that various societies can and do construct alternative genders, independent of a person's physical body, is difficult to conceive. One such category used by some northwestern Native American societies is called the *Berdache.* A similar category known as the *Xanith* exists in some traditional Arab societies (Wikan, 1977). These individuals are biological males who have adopted the clothes and some of the roles of the other sex and who have sexual relations with other men. They may, however, revert back to the masculine role without sanction or switch back and forth between roles.

Attempts to classify such individuals as hermaphrodites, homosexuals, transvestites, or transsexuals fail because their behavior fits none of these ethnocentric norms (Williams, 1987). Difficulties arise because scholars cannot agree whether sexual orientation, dress, gender role, or even identity is a core characteristic. For example, the Berdache do not appear to question their biological maleness, and they do not invariably cross-dress. Homosexuality in their society is not always associated with being a member of this social category. Moreover, Berdache are not expected to have sex with each other, but only with "normal" males.

Walter Williams (1986) has published a book based on an extensive participant-observer study of the Berdache. He concludes that some traditional Native American societies are neither as biologically reductionist nor as bipolar in their gender system as current Western cultures are. He sees the Berdache as a third, alternative gender.

Williams also interprets the Berdache role as integrated within a broader gender system of male and female status disparity. In Native American societies in which a positive valuation of the Berdache exists, women are also of high status. Men who become Berdache have an enhanced status. Because women are valued, androgyny is allowed to men. In contrast, if women are devalued by the society, feminine characteristics in men are denied.

Although Williams's analysis is very interesting, it is instructive that there seems to be no room for a fourth gender category in these societies—one for women who act out some aspects of the masculine role. This omission may also be related to status. Even when women are valued, only men have enough status to act out the devalued feminine role.

This kind of analysis of alternative cultural arrangements attempts to deconstruct our conceptions of sex and gender. It provides an alternative to assumptions about a stable core to which one simply adds deviations to broaden the picture. Instead, it argues that the margin is itself culturally specific. Other societies validate the gender variance that our society denigrates as deviance (Brod, 1987).

As you finish reading this chapter you should appreciate more than when you began it the great complexity of the apparently simple word *sex.* Sex is used to refer to our reproductive category, physiological properties, reproductive and nonreproductive behaviors, and, in human beings, our sense of who we are. It also refers to a system of categorization that differs from one culture to another. As you have seen in Chapter 1, some of these meanings are more appropriately assigned to gender.

But even if we limit our discussion to the biological aspects of sex, we will probably never be able to determine what causes a person to be male or female. Instead, no one is entirely and permanently male or female, and the sexes are certainly not opposite to each other. Sexual dichotomies are a result of both androcentric and ethnocentric bias. It may sound strange, but try thinking about *all* the sexes rather than the two sexes for a while!

CONNECTING THEMES

1. Just as gender is more than just sex, "sex" is more than just sex too. Studies of various animal species and of sexually anomalous human beings indicate that an individual's sex is a composite of biological and social factors. Probably no one single factor determines maleness or femaleness.
2. The assumption that males and females are "opposite" sexes is a good example of the "power to name." Beliefs about biologically determined differences between the sexes are maintained by the media's attention to findings about the anatomical bases for such differences and its lack of attention to social and environmental factors.
3. All cultures do not think about sex and gender the same way we do. Human beings with the same biologically induced anomalies may have different experiences based on their culture's beliefs about sex and gender. The connections between biology, physical appearance, social roles, and sexual orientation may not be as stable as we had once assumed.
4. Biology is a double-edged sword when one wishes to use it to facilitate social change. For example, biological arguments can be used to define homosexuality as morally acceptable (because it is not a matter of choice) or as a reason to commit mass murder (homosexuals were routinely killed by the Nazis because of their biological deficiency). It is probably better to consider social rationales sufficient reasons for making societal changes.

SUGGESTED READINGS

HARDING, SANDRA (1986). *The science question in feminism.* Ithaca: Cornell University Press. This book explores from a philosophical perspective the question of whether science can be useful in analyzing questions about gender.

LeGuin, Ursula (1969). *The left hand of darkness.* New York: Ace Books. This award-winning science fiction novel takes place in a world in which the same person can be either male or female. It challenges our assumptions about the relationship between sex and gender.

Tavris, Carol (1992). *The mismeasure of woman.* New York: Simon & Schuster. A very clear and readable feminist analysis of some of the myths about women's similarities to and differences from men.

CHAPTER 7

Becoming Gendered: Childhood

INTRODUCTION
BEFORE BIRTH
- The Preference for Sons
- Selective Mortality: The Missing Girls

THE NEWBORN CHILD
INFANTS AND TODDLERS
- The Role of Parents
- Attributions about Little Girls and Boys
- Children's Environments: The Fostering of Gender Typing
- Stories and the Communication of Gender Roles
- Individual Differences in Parental Behavior and Its Consequences

THE NURSERY SCHOOL YEARS
- Gender-Related Differences in Play
- Gender-Related Preferences in Toys

THE EARLY SCHOOL YEARS: SEX SEGREGATION
- The Formation of Social Networks
- Differential Reinforcement by Peers
- Unlearning the Traits and Behaviors of the Other Sex
- Group Dynamics and Sex-Related Differences
- Social Mechanisms for Maintaining Boundaries
- Social Dominance and Social Influence
- The Socialization of Aggression

THE MIDDLE SCHOOL YEARS
- Gender Differences In Instrumentality
- Stages in the Development of Gender Understanding
- Resisting Gender
- The Case for Positive Social Deviance

CONNECTING THEMES
SUGGESTED READINGS

Early one midsummer's night, Daddy Sam settled on the plush gold carpet in the nursery to play with Baby while the evening bath was being prepared. Reaching for Baby's teddy bear, he slowly and rhythmically bounced it toward Baby, softly saying, "Here comes Teddy! Teddy's coming to see you! Look, look at Teddy. He's coming to play with Baby." Giggling in delight, Baby opens her arms to hug the oncoming teddy bear. Next door, a different Daddy and a dif-

> ferent Baby played on the nursery floor. Holding Baby's teddy bear, Daddy John marched the bear resolutely toward Baby in a series of quick, controlled movements, mock growling, "Here comes Teddy! Teddy's coming to *get* you! Better get Teddy, before *he* gets *you!*" Screeching at the challenge, Baby reaches out and tumbles on his now captive Teddy (Brooks-Gunn & Mathews, 1979, pp. 5–6).

What does this scenario tell us? It tells us that fathers play with their babies. But it also tells us that parents can treat infant boys and girls differently even when they are apparently engaged in the same games. And it shows how babies respond to the behaviors of their parents. This anecdote illustrates that gender does not exist in a social vacuum. In this chapter we will show how gender is constructed rather than innate.

How do babies become boys or girls? At first glance the commonsense answer to this question is obvious—infants are born either male or female. That is, they are born not only with the biology of their sex, but also with behavioral tendencies that are considered characteristic of that sex. But is this true? Certainly we are able to assign most children to an unambiguous sex at birth on the basis of their anatomy (although there are more exceptions than one might expect; see Chapter 6). It is much more difficult, however, to make the same case for behavioral sex differences. There is only weak documentation for behavioral differences during the first weeks of life, and few consistent sex-related differences appear during the first year. It takes a long time before a child acquires his or her gender.

INTRODUCTION

It is the purpose of this chapter to discuss the nature of the processes that lead to the establishment of gender. Contrary to our commonsense beliefs, various aspects of gender are *not* highly correlated with sex, nor do they emerge at birth as a seamless whole. Gender may be thought of as a jigsaw puzzle that is put together over time. As you will see, the establishment of gender in children appears to require a great deal of work and commitment by the people who come into contact with them as well as by the social system as a whole.

Gender is molded by means of a complicated interaction of cognitive factors and social learning processes. These processes are truly developmental in nature; that is, both the age of the child and the social environment to which he or she is exposed must be taken into account. Seemingly identical social messages do not have the same meaning at different ages. The child changes as a consequence of these messages and, consequently, interprets them differently. In this sense, the meaning of gender is a function of the cognitive level of the child. In other words, what the child thinks makes a person male or female changes as he or she grows.

Societal definitions of appropriate gender roles also change as the child grows older. For example, we do not expect little girls to wear makeup and high heels (although we think it is "cute" when they do so). However, adolescent girls who refuse to do so may be labeled as unfeminine. The process by which gender is constructed is called *interactive* by psychologists. This means that there is continuing interplay between the child and the environment, with no predominant control of development from within the organism or from the environment.

Although gender is complex, studies show a surprising amount of consistency with which our society informs children about gender-related aspects of behavior. Much of the information about gender is a product of *social learning*, similar to the way children learn about other aspects of the physical and social world. We discussed this theoretical framework in Chapter 2. As you will see in this chapter, boys and girls are treated differently even before birth. This differential treatment produces behavioral differences that, in turn, lead to different social consequences (rewards and punishments) for the two sexes, making them still more different. You may think of the process of constructing gender in terms of the saying "As the twig is bent, so the tree will grow." Little differences become larger as the child grows, until we forget that the sexes were originally not very different at all.

For the sake of clarity, we will explore the development of gender chronologically. Different cognitive and social-learning processes operate for the newborn, the toddler, and the school-age child. However, some recurring themes operate throughout childhood. These include the following:

1. Males are the more valued sex, even in our own society.
2. Pressure for conformity to gender roles occurs earlier for boys and is stronger than that on girls throughout the childhood years.
3. Parents appear to be largely unaware of the extent to which they treat their young sons and daughters differently.
4. Differential treatment of boys and girls appears to be consistent with producing a pattern of independence and efficacy in boys and a pattern of emotional sensitivity, nurturance, and helplessness in girls.
5. The child is not a passive recipient of gender socialization, but actively participates in this socialization by way of his or her views of self, expectations, and behavioral choices.
6. People are largely unaware of how the culture as a whole mandates dichotomies based on sex and punishes those who do not conform to social expectations.

Although the particular phenomena associated with gender change as the child matures, the themes noted above seem to remain. Look for these patterns as we trace the development of gender from birth through the middle years of childhood. Children are different at these various stages because of the operation of such mechanisms. Thus, the meaning of gender changes as the child grows. You must be careful not to assume that all such changes represent progress. As you will see, children show more and more sex biases—similar to those of adults—as they mature. The majority of children become increasingly sexist and, thus, fit "better" into a sexist world.

Since this chapter uses a chronological framework, the various processes that contribute to the construction of gender will be highlighted during the age/stage at which they become important to most children. We shall explore differential expectations and treatment based on sex from birth through the middle-school years. We shall also examine the effect these differential processes have on children's views of themselves, and how they view others and behave toward them. As you will see, it takes time to make a "boy" or "girl."

After a few years of gender socialization, adults become less important and gender socialization becomes the responsibility of peers. It is very difficult to ignore the disapproval of one's friends. Nevertheless, some individuals resist becoming entirely polarized in terms of gender. An examination of such individuals can tell us a great deal about the forces that shape gender. These people also help us to celebrate the idea that dichotomies based on gender are neither necessary nor socially desirable.

BEFORE BIRTH

The Preference for Sons

We began this chapter with an allusion to commonsense beliefs about sex because beliefs and expectations play an important role in the formation of gender in the young child. Beliefs about the usefulness of sex for predicting behavior are present even before the child is born. For example, Jeanne Brooks-Gunn and Wendy Mathews (1979) offer a list of recipes for determining whether a pregnant woman is carrying a boy or a girl. Some of the most common are as follows:

> The man and woman each take hold of one end of a wishbone and pull it apart. If the longest part comes away in the man's hand, the baby will be a boy.
>
> If you suddenly ask a pregnant woman what she has in her hand and she looks at her right hand first, she will have a boy. If she looks at her left hand it will be a girl.
>
> If the mother's belly is bigger on the right-hand side a boy will be born, and, also, if her right breast is bigger than her left, or if her right foot is more restless.
>
> If a woman is placid during pregnancy she will have a boy, but if she is bad-tempered or cries a lot, she will have a girl.
>
> If her complexion is rosy, she will have a son; if she is pale a daughter.
>
> If her looks improve, she is expecting a boy; if they worsen, a girl.
>
> If the fetal heartbeat is fast, it is a boy; if it is slow, it is a girl.
>
> If the fetus has started to move by the 40th day it will be a boy and the birth will be easy, but if it doesn't move until the 90th day it will be a girl (pp. 74–75).

You will probably have noticed that girls are symbolized by negative or less desirable characteristics.

The preference for males is not limited to predictions about the pregnant woman. There is still a clear preference for male children in the United States and Canada, although this is beginning to change among women at least. In the late 1960s, 90 percent of the male college students and 78 percent of the female students questioned stated that they would prefer a boy if they could have only one child (Hammer, 1970). A more recent study of 1,045 Canadian women

(Krishnan, 1987) found some preference for sons, although the women generally preferred to have children of both sexes. The most recent study of college students (Pooler, 1991) found that the preference for sons was due primarily to men's responses. In 1988, 86 percent of the male students surveyed said they would prefer a son if they could only have one child, while only 42 percent of the female students had such a preference.

Preference for boys is most extreme in Asian countries like Korea and Taiwan. A common Korean saying is "a girl lets you down twice, once at birth and the second time when she marries." Daughters are described as "water spilled on the ground" in Taiwan and as "maggots in the rice" in China. In some Arab cultures, an unexpected pause in the conversation might be followed by the comment "Why the silence? Has a girl been born?" (Sohoni, 1994). The reasons given for the preference for sons were similar in all the countries investigated: continuation of the family name, economic reasons (including support of parents in old age), and as companions for fathers. In all the countries surveyed men showed a greater preference for boys than women did (Arnold & Kuo, 1984).

Using behavioral rather than attitudinal measures, researchers have found that when the first child is a boy, the interval before the next birth is, on the average, three months longer than it is when the child is a girl (Westoff, Potter, & Sagi, 1963). Having a girl rather than a boy has been found to be associated with postpartum emotional distress (Gordon & Gordon, 1967). It has even been found that women who are pregnant for the first time dream about boy babies twice as often as about girl babies (Gillman, 1968).

Selective Mortality: The Missing Girls

Probably the most compelling evidence demonstrating the preference for sons are data on voluntary abortion. Because of recent advances in sex determination, parents can be informed about the sex of their prospective offspring during the first few months of pregnancy. In Asian societies, where the preference for sons is most extreme, selective abortion of female fetuses is also extreme. In one study published in the British journal *Nature,* which used statistics provided by an Indian social worker, out of a sample of 8,000 abortions, 7,997 were on female fetuses (Hrdy, 1988). Sex-selective abortion is not officially sanctioned. In fact, more than one state in India has banned prenatal sex determination.

Sex-selective abortion is consistent with cultural practices permitting female infanticide. It has been estimated that sex-biased infanticide has been practiced by about 9 percent of the world's cultures, and more often than not, the unwanted sex has been female (Hrdy, 1988).

Discrimination can also be indirect (see Figure 7.1). In a number of cultures, for example, there is evidence that boys are breast fed twice as long as girls. In many societies, men and boys eat first, and whatever is left is then distributed to the women and girls. Invariably, women and girls eat less food which is of inferior quality and nutritive value (United Nations, 1991b). Historical records indicate that among some south Asian groups, four times as many boys survive as girls (Hrdy, 1988). Although more girls survive when agricultural, urban,

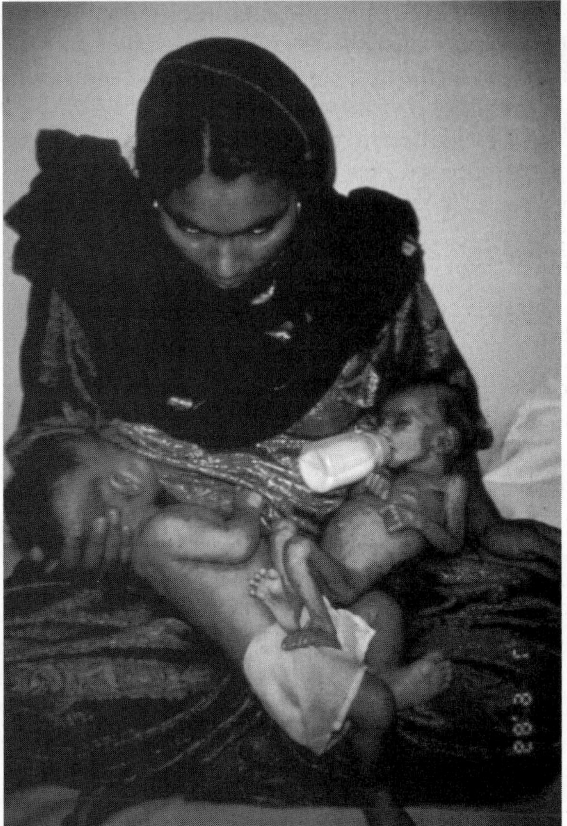

FIGURE 7.1. A mother's grief: This picture from Islamabad, Pakistan, tells a poignant story about the age-old bias in favor of the male child. The child being bottle-fed is a girl. Her twin brother was breast-fed. The woman was told by the mother-in-law that she did not have enough milk for both the children, so she should breast feed the boy. The infant girl died the next day.

and industrial development increase, the survival rate of girls does not improve relative to that of boys (Kishor, 1993). Based on demographic information, the United Nations has estimated that more than 100 million females are missing from the world's population (Sen, 1990).

You may believe that this kind of selective killing of unwanted girls occurs only in "primitive" groups. There is, however, some evidence from our own society that prenatal information about sex can influence the decision about whether or not to abort a fetus. In an article in *Harvard Magazine* about the ethical issues involved in the ability to evaluate one's children before birth, John Lauerman (1990) related the following incident:

> A genetic counselor at Brigham's and Women's Hospital, Bieber ruefully recalls a seeming lack of communication between two of his clients. Although the ex-

> pectant father never mentioned the fetus's sex in counseling sessions, he made private efforts to find out whether it was female. It became apparent that the husband would pressure the wife to abort a female fetus. Bieber decided to inform the parents that the fetus was, in fact, female. The couple subsequently decided on an abortion (p. 46).

It is obvious that if this girl had been permitted to be born, she would not have entered a gender-blind family.

THE NEWBORN CHILD

As you might expect, the sex of a child is his or her most conspicuous feature as soon as he or she is born. For example, one study conducted in English delivery rooms found that 82 percent of the parents' comments within 20 minutes of the baby's birth were made about the infant's sex (Woollett, White, & Lyon, 1982). Fathers appear to be more likely to differentiate between their newborn sons and daughters than mothers are (Parke, 1976). One review of the literature on parental interaction with infants (Power, 1981) showed that in sixteen studies involving mothers, seven found that they treated boys and girls differently. In fifteen studies involving fathers, fourteen showed patterns of gender distinction.

Popular culture mandates attention to the sex of the newborn. When one of the authors had her first child, she found it impossible to locate a gender-neutral birth announcement. There are many other characteristics besides sex that could be used to describe an infant, such as its size, its coloring, the presence or absence of hair, and so forth. One innovative birth announcement we have seen compared the baby to a new model car. Nevertheless, even this relatively ungendered birth announcement was pink and proclaimed "It's a girl!" rather than "It's a beautiful baby!"

Birth congratulations cards also remain sexist. One recent study looked at girl and boy cards selected from eighteen stores in four municipalities that varied in size, ethnicity, and social class (Bridges, 1993). It found that visual images of activity were more commonly shown on boy cards, while verbal messages of sweetness and sharing were more likely to be present on girl cards. A few of the cards displayed clear gender stereotypic messages. For example, two apparently comparable cards (one for girls and one for boys) stated: "Soon she'll be able to say simple two-syllable words: 'ma-ma, da-da, . . . vi-sa'" or "Soon he'll be able to say simple two-syllable words: 'ma-ma, da-da, hon-da, . . . toyo-ta'."

Despite differential responses to boys and girls, young infants show few, if any, consistent sex-related differences. The differences found are often complex and hard to interpret. For example, differences between boys and girls found at two days after delivery disappeared at four days (Lewis, 1987). Significant gender-related differences in young infants are more likely to be reported in countries where circumcision rates are high (Richards, Bernal, & Brackbill, 1975). Thus, it is difficult to determine whether reports from the United States of greater activity and irritability among infant boys than among infant girls can be attributed to their gender or the impact of early medical intervention.

The Role of Parents

Although behavioral differences between baby boys and girls are minimal, evidence is accumulating that parents treat their sons and daughters differently from the earliest days of life. One expert on child development, Aletha Huston (1983), concluded that the evidence for gender-differentiated socialization is stronger today that it was ten years ago. Parents consistently promote differences in activities and interests in their sons and daughters. The evidence for differential responses to boys' and girls' emotional and social behaviors is, however, less strong (Lytton & Romney, 1991).

One of the reasons that evidence for parental socialization of gender-typing has increased in recent years is the greater attention of researchers to the role of fathers. Examination of a large number of studies indicated that fathers differentiate between their sons and daughters much more than mothers do (Lytton & Romney, 1991). For example, in a sample of parents of 2-year-olds in Great Britain, fathers more than mothers saw their children as conforming to gender stereotypes (McGuire, 1988). Boys, in particular, were stereotyped by their fathers. More than two-thirds of the boys' fathers saw them as very masculine, while only 40 percent of the girls' fathers saw them as very feminine. Even for these very young children, the commonest masculine attribution was physical ability or athletic skill. Feminine attributes for girls usually involved comments about physical attractiveness or appearance (mothers) or nurturant doll play, gentleness, and doing housework (fathers). These 2-year-olds appeared to be receiving some fairly clear information from their parents about how they were supposed to behave.

This study also illustrates two other major themes in the socialization of gender. First, it indicates yet again the different content of stereotypes about males and females. Not only are little boys seen as athletic and little girls as gentle, but appearance is stressed for females and actions for males. The greater rigidity of appropriate roles for males is also seen in this study. Other studies also emphasize fathers' concerns about the early gender socialization of boys. For example, fathers have been found to be especially critical of doll play in sons (Fagot, 1978).

Attributions about Little Girls and Boys

Gender-differentiated patterns of communication with young infants and toddlers are also consistent with the themes discussed earlier in this chapter. For example, parents treat their sons as though they are more valuable than their daughters. Within the hospital environment, both mothers and fathers touch their newborn sons more than their newborn daughters (Parke, 1976). At home, mothers touch, hold, rock, and kiss sons during the first three months of life more than they do daughters (Lewis, 1972). Although mothers talk to their infant daughters more than to sons, they appear to be more sensitive to the mood of their sons (Tronick & Cohn, 1989).

Consistent with gender-stereotypic beliefs, parents have been found to emphasize different emotions when they talk to their daughters and sons. Parents used a greater number and variety of emotion words when talking to their 40-month-old daughters than when they spoke to sons of the same age. They also mentioned the sad aspects of events more with girls than boys (Kuebli & Fivush, 1992).

Children acquire beliefs about emotions that are consistent with this pattern of parental socialization. Preschoolers of both sexes believe that females are much more likely to feel sad than males and that men are particularly incapable of expressing this emotion (Karbon, Fabes, Carlo, & Martin, 1992). They see adults of both sexes as capable of becoming angry, but believe that men become angry more frequently and intensely than women do.

Beliefs about differences in the emotional responses of boys and girls may lead to different adult responses to identical behaviors. For example, a videotaped snowball fight between two boys was viewed by adults as less aggressive than the same behavior described as being between a boy and a girl or two girls (Condry & Ross, 1985). Those who do not approve of aggression in children might well stop the "girls" from "fighting" while permitting the "boys" to "horse around."

Both parents and other adults appear to believe that girls require more help (as contrasted to responsiveness) than boys. Studies in the home have found that fathers are more likely to hold their year-old daughters in contrast to their sons and to give them toys (Snow, Jacklin, & Maccoby, 1983). An observational study made of families visiting a zoo, an amusement park, or a nursery rhyme theme park found that male toddlers were more likely to be allowed to walk alone than female toddlers were (Mitchell, Obradovich, Herring, Tromborg, & Burns, 1992).

Gender-differentiated beliefs associated with little girls' greater need of help are dramatically illustrated by a clever laboratory experiment entitled "Sex differences: A study of the ear of the beholder" (Condry, Condry, & Pogatshnik, 1983). While performing an unrelated task, young men and women heard a tape-recording of an infant awakening next door. The infant had previously been labeled a boy or a girl. Although they denied any belief about differences in fragility between girls and boys, the young women responded more quickly to a "girl" than to a "boy." Young men responded equally slowly to both sexes.

Such differential responses to young children may subtly reinforce the distinction between the sexes by means of self-fulfilling prophecies. For example, girls are seen as more fearful than boys (Condry & Condry, 1976). They are helped more quickly and more often—especially by their fathers. By being taken care of more, girls learn that they are needier than boys. Greater adult assistance confirms their belief in their own helplessness.

This kind of socialization into helplessness may be exaggerated when the toddler is an attractive girl. A recent study found that adults (mothers, fathers, and caretakers) were more likely to interact with attractive girls aged 12–38 months by helping them, telling them what to do and how to do it, and stimulating their interest in the object at hand. These behaviors were not directed toward attractive boys or toward unattractive children of either sex (Leinbach & Fagot, 1991). The adult help seemed to foster attractive girls' communication skills, but giving them help when they did not need it may also make them less competent and more dependent.

Children's Environments: The Fostering of Gender Typing

Obviously, the greater tendency to pick up and carry little girls than little boys restricts their ability to acquire the skills needed for independence. From the age of 6 months on, demands for socially distant behavior are stricter for boys than for girls (Lewis, 1972). Differences in parental responses to little girls and boys are only a small part of the factors that encourage male independence and female dependence. Other aspects of differential socialization patterns that have been documented include clothing, toys, and the kind of custodial care given young children.

Clothing

Without making the request explicit, it is virtually impossible to get parents to provide a neutral environment when dressing their young child. An anecdote from a child development textbook recounts the frustration of one researcher who encountered this problem:

> One investigator who was studying sex differences in infancy and did not want her observers to know whether they were watching boys or girls complained that even in the first few days of life some infant girls were brought to the laboratory with pink bows tied to their wisps of hair or taped to their little bald heads. Later, when another attempt at concealment of sex was made by asking mothers to dress their infants in overalls, girls appeared in pink and boys in blue overalls, and as the frustrated experimenter said, "Would you believe overalls with ruffles?" (Hetherington & Parke, 1975, pp. 354–355).

Another investigator made a similar point more recently: ". . . in our laboratory, ruffles on girls' overalls are common, and we have even seen beruffled jogging suits!" (Fagot & Leinbach, 1987, p. 93). Girls' more delicate and restrictive attire can inhibit play and promote gender-stereotypic behavior. A similar point can be made about the ruffles and white furniture found in girls' rooms as compared with the sturdy brown pine found in boys' rooms.

One study demonstrated clearly how young children are "color coded" (Shakin, Shakin, & Sternglanz, 1985). The researchers categorized the clothing found on infants in shopping malls. Baby girls were dressed in pink, puffed sleeves, ruffles, and lace (even on tiny socks), while boys were dressed in blue or sometimes red, but nothing ruffled or pink. Similar sex-related differences in clothing colors have also been found among young children in French-speaking Canada (Pomerleau, Bloduc, Malcuit, & Cossette, 1990). Gender-typed clothing ensures gender-appropriate treatment from strangers. If you wish to see for yourself just how important this aspect of appropriate identification is, deliberately "mis-sex" an infant the next time you are in a public place. At the very least, you can expect a firm correction.

Appropriate distinctions are very important if two genders are to be constructed. Gender-appropriate behaviors must be elicited from the infant and reinforced when they occur. As noted earlier, infant girls and boys have few, if any, behaviors that distinguish between them. In neutral clothing it would be difficult to tell them apart. Knowledge of their sex may not be sufficient to guarantee that strangers react differentially to them. A recent review of studies involving neutrally clothed infants who were labeled either "male" or "female" indicated that knowledge of the label did not consistently influence adults' reaction to them (Stern & Karraker, 1989).

Toys

Many parents explicitly deny any intention to distinguish between their sons and daughters (Fagot, 1978). In one study of parents of 6-month-old infants, 87.5 percent stated that it was important for infant boys and girls to play with *all* toys (Culp, Cook, & Housley, 1983). Only two adults (members of the same couple) said there should be different types of toys for girls and boys.

Behavioral measures tell a different story. The earliest study that graphically demonstrated that gender stereotyping in toy selection can take place without parental awareness was conducted by Harriet Rheingold and Kaye Cook (1975). The furnishings and toys found in the rooms of forty-eight boys and forty-eight girls under the age of 6 were examined on the assumption that whatever differences were found would indicate parental ideology regarding gender suitability. The researchers assumed that children under 6 do not control much of their own toy selection (although studies on toy requests would suggest older children exert control through their preferences). The children in this study were from a highly selected, highly educated university setting in which one might expect that gender differentiation was at a minimum. In fact, the parents denied in a questionnaire that they made any distinctions between sons and daughters.

The investigators found that there were no gender differences in the number of books, musical objects, or stuffed toys found in the children's rooms. However, gender differences in several categories of toys were impressive. Summed over age, the number of vehicles for the boys was 375 versus 17 for the girls. No girl's room contained a wagon, boat, kiddie car, motorcycle, snowmobile, or trailer. Conversely, only 8 of the boys' rooms contained a female doll, compared to 41 of the girls' rooms.

A study conducted fifteen years later (Pomerleau et al., 1990) found similar although somewhat less dramatic sex-related differences in these two categories of toys. This study used a sample of younger children ranging from 5 through 25 months of age. Girls had 3.9 dolls as compared with an average of 1.2 for boys. Boys, in contrast, had an average of 10.3 small vehicles each, whereas girls had 3.5. There were no differences between the sexes in terms of the number and variety of toys.

Dolls provide very different cues for play than vehicles do. Girls are provided with toys that encourage nurturance (by 2 years of age they have more kitchen appliances and utensils than boys do) and/or concern with fashion. On the other hand, masculine toys such as vehicles quite literally promote motor activity (Liss, 1983; O'Brien & Huston, 1985b).

A large number of toys have gender-stereotypic labels (see Chapter 3). Many children display gender-stereotyped toy preferences and behaviors by 18 to 24 months of age at home and in group settings (Huston, 1983; O'Brien & Huston, 1985a; Perry, White, & Perry, 1984). By the age of 10 months girls already showed a preference for dolls and were more likely than boys to offer dolls to their parents (Roopnarine, 1986). At this age, boys and girls were equally likely to play with trucks, blocks, and kitchen utensils. But parental responses to this play are already gender differentiated. Both mothers and fathers were found to be more likely to attend to the block play of their sons than of their daughters.

Parents clearly encourage involvement with toys stereotyped as gender-appropriate and avoidance of toys that have cross-gender connotations (see Figure 7.2). One study (Caldera, Huston, & O'Brien, 1989) videotaped forty parent–child toddler pairs playing with six different sets of toys for four minutes each. The parents' initial nonverbal responses to the toys were more positive when the toys were stereotyped for the child's and parent's sex than when they were not. Children showed greater involvement when playing with stereotypically gender-appropriate toys even when parental behavior was statistically controlled. They were less interested in toys stereotyped for the other sex even when no alternative toys were available.

It is interesting that some parents were reported to have had difficulty complying with the instructions to play with all the toys. "As an extreme example, one father with his daughter opened a box of trucks, said 'Oh, they must have boys in this study,' closed the box, and returned to playing with dolls" (Caldera et al., p. 75). It is also interesting that different types of toys elicited different kinds of play regardless of the sex of either parent or child. Stereotypically masculine toys evoked high levels of activity and low physical proximity whereas feminine toys elicited close physical proximity and more verbal interaction.

By the time they are 3 years of age children are well aware of the socially prescribed nature of the kind of toys with which they play. In keeping with the more rigid demands for gender-role conformity from boys than from girls, three-fourths of all the 3- to 5-year-old boys studied requested gender-stereotypic toys for Christmas (Robinson & Morris, 1986). In contrast, girls' choices became gradually more stereotypic as they got older. Only 29 percent of the

FIGURE 7.2. No comment.

girls requested stereotypically feminine toys at age 3 versus 73 percent at age 5. It is difficult to determine whether gender-typing in toy preference among young children is a cause of or a response to parental gift-giving behavior. However, children were less likely to receive toys they requested for Christmas when the toys were atypical for their sex (Etaugh & Liss, 1992).

Play

It has been suggested that play is the work of children. Different kinds of toys provide children with different opportunities for the rehearsal of adult roles. Play preferences that become rigidly stereotyped at an early age limit the kinds of experience that children have. Children do not seem inclined to challenge these limits. Toy preferences become increasingly more stereotypic with age. By age 6, 75 percent of the children studied refused to alter their stereotypic toy choices even after being informed and shown toys that were appropriate for both sexes (Frasher, Nurss, & Brogan, 1980).

Toy preferences do not appear to be much influenced by the child's own inclinations either. When forced to choose between the activity level required by a toy and its gender category, (for example, an active boy being forced to choose between a jump rope and an erector set) almost 80 percent of the 3- to 6-year-old children studied based their preferences on the gender appropriateness of the toy (Eaton, von Bargen, & Keats, 1981). Children are clearly informed about the gender appropriateness of toys by advertisements (Schwartz & Markham, 1985) as well as by the relative frequency in which they are found in their homes.

Different kinds of toys encourage different kinds of play. Play with stereotypically feminine toys appears to involve more structure and less use of physical space than place with stereotypically masculine toys. As you will see, the behavioral consequences of toy and play preferences have a great deal of importance when the child enters the school environment. The most important consequence of the gender typing of toy and play preferences may be the limits set on the sex of the children with whom a child customarily plays.

Stories and the Communication of Gender Roles

Traditional fairy tales as well as more modern stories written for children also inform them about their proper gender roles. In many fairy tales, women are especially desirable when they are passive. In some, like "Snow White" or "Sleeping Beauty," they are most desirable when they are comatose (Dworkin, 1974). Disney's recent feature cartoons for children, like *The Little Mermaid, Beauty and the Beast,* and *Aladdin,* would appear to provide more positive roles for females. A closer scrutiny, however, reveals a repetition of the old narrative that selfless, beautiful girls are rewarded by the love of a prince they barely know (Douglas, 1994).

Analyze some of your favorite fairy tales from a feminist perspective. You may find yourself asking whether anyone in her right mind could possibly want to be a fairy-tale princess. They are either passive victims, decorative figures, or must die in order to be loved. If they resist these roles, they are punished or portrayed as evil or mad (Sapiro, 1994).

Readers designed for the early school years have improved in the rate at which boys versus girls are portrayed as main characters, but many gender-appropriate roles have been retained. As in traditional fairy tales, a common theme in stories with a female main character is that of rescue. When not rescued by boys or men, the protagonist is shown being rescued by a pet or an animal. Boys, in contrast, almost never have to depend on animals. "Girls are shown as being very brave while waiting for rescue, but they still cannot help themselves out of trouble" (Purcell & Stewart, 1990, p. 184).

Similar to stereotypes about adults discussed in Chapter 4, these stories seldom show boys engaged in any form of domestic activity. While women are now shown in what were once primarily male-dominated fields, only men are shown in more adventurous arenas. Women doctors are now common, but women explorers and big-game hunters are still few and far between (Purcell & Stewart, 1990).

Sexism reveals itself in ways other than in frequency counts. It occurs when disparaging statements are made about women or when traits are characterized as different for the two sexes. A recent analysis of award-winning picture books for children found, for example, that girls are portrayed as passive dependent as often as they were fifty years ago and boys are portrayed as no less instrumental (Kortenhaus & Demarest, 1993). Young girls are still valued for their beauty while older women are denigrated as hags or witches or given barely visible domestic roles. With such social messages, you should not be surprised to read below that boys and girls engage in different kinds of fantasy play. The universal presence of such images also helps to explain why parental attitudes about gender roles have so little impact on children's behavior.

Individual Differences in Parental Behavior and Its Consequences

One of the most remarkable aspects of gender socialization is the limited extent to which individual differences in gender-role ideology influence parents' treatment of their child. Parental ideology may have less effect than one would expect because it has little impact upon parental behavior. For example, it has been found that parents who held highly stereotypic beliefs about sex and gender and those who did not behaved similarly: both groups talked to their sons differently than to their daughters (Fagot, 1974; Weitzman, Birns, & Friend, 1985). Even ideologically egalitarian mothers gave their sons more stimulation than their daughters on a number of language variables considered likely to facilitate cognitive development. Sons were taught more and given more action verbs, questions, explicit directions, and so forth.

A mother's behavior rather than her attitudes may have some impact on her child. For example, mothers who held egalitarian beliefs about the rights and roles of women did not appear to influence their preschoolers' degree of gender stereotyping (Barak, Feldman, & Noy, 1991). But mothers in nontraditional occupations seemed to foster nontraditional aspirations in both their preschool daughters and sons. Mothers who have stereotypic beliefs about gender differences have been found to discourage active toy play in their daughters but not in their sons (Brooks-Gunn, 1986). More alarmingly, daughters of mothers who had strong gender-typed beliefs had lower IQ scores at 24 months than did those with less rigidly gender-typed mothers.

THE NURSERY SCHOOL YEARS

Gender-Related Differences in Play

By the time children have reached the age of 3 they have acquired preferences for toys and play based on their experience during their early years. Observations conducted in preschool classrooms have found that boys use the block area much more frequently than girls, whereas girls use the art area much more than boys (Pellegrini & Perlmutter, 1989). Such choices do not reflect an inability to deal with unfamiliar materials. When children are assigned to play areas, they play according to the theme inherent to the properties of the area.

Little girls and boys also engage in different kinds of fantasy play. One study found that 4-year-old girls spent 73 percent of their fantasy activities engaged in domestic activities, as compared with 31 percent of boys' fantasy play (Mathews, 1977). Boys' fantasy play frequently involved interesting and unusual adult roles, such as marching bands, parades, and fireworks displays (none of the girls' play was in these categories). Fantasies with exotic themes such as witches and magic, adventure, spies, ghosts, and wild animals occupied 11 percent of the boys' fantasy play, in contrast to only 1 percent of the girls'. If we think of play as a rehearsal for adult roles, what do these gender-related differences in fantasy play tell us about children's idea of men's versus women's worlds?

Although we tend to think of the games of little boys as more active than those of little girls, research suggests that the difference is more one of style than of activity. For example, Eleanor Maccoby (1988) and her colleagues have observed groups of children at play throughout the nursery school years. They studied the activities of trios of same-sex playmates in a mobile laboratory equipped with a thick carpet, a child-size trampoline, and a beach ball. As Table 7.1 shows, girls spent more time than boys jumping on the trampoline. Thus, the girls' play style was not a passive, inactive one. However, a girl would almost never throw herself on top of another girl who was jumping on the trampoline, whereas some boys did so. Boys' play often ended up in bouts of wrestling or mock fighting. Rough play of this sort was seldom seen among trios of girls.

Gender-Related Preferences in Toys

Although the preschool-age child has not yet become completely gendered, most children have developed preferences for gender-typed toys and play by this age. Girls spend significantly more time playing with stereotypically feminine toys and less with stereotypically masculine toys, whereas the reverse pattern is found in boys (Powlishta, Serbin, & Moller, 1993). There is, however, considerable within-sex variability and between-sex overlap in these play patterns. For example, girls spent 5 to 22 percent of the observed time intervals playing with masculine toys, compared with 5 to 71 percent for boys. In contrast, boys

TABLE 7.1. Percentage of Intervals in Which Target Child Engaged in Each Behavior by Sex of Child and Cohort

	Cohorts 1 and 2			Cohort 3		
Behavior	Boys (n = 30)	Girls (n = 22)	t	Boys (n = 25)	Girls (n = 16)	t
Aggressive physical assault	.10	.00	1.79	.40	.00	1.66
Rough-and-tumble play[a]	14.30	4.70	2.79‡	20.00	3.30	3.14‡
Jumping (trampoline)	9.20	15.20	-1.88*	11.50	19.00	-2.20†

[a]DiPietro (1981) reported data on rough-and-tumble play and jumping for Cohorts 1 and 2. The remaining data are reported for the first time here.

*$p<.10$. †$p<.05$. ‡$p<.01$.

Source: From E. E. Maccoby (1988). Gender as a social category. *Developmental Psychology, 24,* 755–765.

spent 0 to 47 percent of their time playing with feminine toys, compared with 18 to 54 percent for girls.

Current research indicates that children are influenced by the gender labels conferred by adults on various objects. For example, one study exposed preschoolers to three boxes of gadgets that were labeled as for the same sex, for the other sex, or for both sexes by the researcher (Bradbard & Endsley, 1983). Children explored the gadgets less, asked fewer questions about them, and recalled their names less frequently when they were labeled for the other sex rather than for their own sex or for both sexes. The children remembered the objects they had seen and how they had been labeled for at least a week.

Children appear to avoid objects labeled as appropriate for the sex other than their own. Comments by the researchers who conducted the study described in the previous paragraph are instructive. "Two boys and six girls overtly reacted to the treatments by (1) seeking reassurance that they could play with the other-sex labeled objects; (2) making negative statements about the other-sex labeled objects ("Yuk, girls!"); and/or (3) refusing to look at, repeat the names of, or move near the table containing the other-sex labeled objects" (Bradbard & Endsley, p. 257). Such behaviors obviously limit these children's opportunities to learn about all the aspects of their world.

Boys who engage in cross-gender play are particularly likely to receive less positive attention and more criticism from their peers. They are often ignored and left to play alone. An example of how extreme this isolation can be is provided by an anecdote from another group of researchers on child development:

> . . . case of a boy who spent many hours in his preschool class playing with the doll house and furniture. He played alone. Because of parental concern, the teacher inquired what he was doing, only to learn that he was playing "moving man." No one—children, teachers, or parents—could see the sex-appropriate truck for the sex-inappropriate doll house and furniture (Wynn & Fletcher, 1987, p. 84).

It is important to stress that not all aspects of gender typing increase at the same rate for all children. Because the focus of research has been on conventional gender-role development, gender-neutral behavior may be underrepresented. For example, preschoolers have been observed to spend a greater proportion of time with neutral toys than with gender-typed ones (Cameron, Eisenberg, & Tyron, 1985). Parents also offer more neutral and masculine toys when playing with their children, even though they claim to prefer gender-typed toys (Idle, Wood, & Desmarais, 1993). Only one study found peer pressure to conform and play with gender-typed toys and only among 4-year-old boys (Roopnarine, 1984).

Children rarely come together to do nothing. Rather, they interact for the purpose of play and games. Observations of very young children in daycare indicate that preferences for play with same-sex children begin to develop at about 27 months of age (La Freniere, Strayer, & Gauthier, 1984). At this age girls begin to direct affiliative responses to other girls at a level above that of chance. Boys show same-sex preferences about a year later. These same-sex preferences increase steadily with age during the preschool years (Feiring & Lewis, 1987).

Although preferences for same-sex playmates are clearly present in some children by 3 years of age, no relationship has been found between peer preferences and other measures of gender-typing such as preference for masculine or feminine toys or proximity to a teacher (Powlishta, Serbin, & Moller, 1993). In this age group, the choice of toy determines the sex of one's playmate rather than the other way around (Eisenberg, Tryon, & Cameron, 1984). Boys and girls who choose gender-appropriate toys are more likely to find other children of the same sex who will play with them. The children themselves are the social arbiters.

As you can see, evidence is accumulating that apparently independent processes combine to produce strong behavioral effects by the time the child is 3 or 4 years of age. In review, children are taught gender-appropriate labels for objects in their environment by both their parents and the media. They are also accustomed to different play objects by the kind of toys they are given. Thus, they come to prefer certain activities and to avoid others. The choice of activities influences both the behaviors that we attribute to masculine and feminine personality traits and the sex of the children with whom a child is likely to play. By the time the child has reached school age, he or she is likely to have become part of a single-sex network that maintains gender roles.

THE EARLY SCHOOL YEARS: SEX SEGREGATION

The Formation of Social Networks

The social networks of young girls and boys show properties that emphasize stereotypic assumptions about the sexes. Boys are socialized to play with larger groups of children and at distances farther from home (Feirling & Lewis, 1987). They are more likely to use space and visit settings outside the home than girls are (Bryant, 1985). Lesser surveillance by adults and greater opportunity to explore alternative environments contribute to the development of greater independence by boys than by girls.

The foundation for sex segregation is laid before children reach elementary school. The ages between 4 and 6 appear to be critical in the development of same-sex social networks. Ask parents of children in this age group to describe what one might term the "birthday party effect." During the nursery school years, playmates of both sexes are invited to birthday parties with equal frequency. At some point between ages 4 and 6, however, children of the other sex begin to be excluded. Both children and mothers report that, by age 6, more same-sex than opposite-sex friends would be invited by the child to a birthday party (Feiring & Lewis, 1987).

In a longitudinal study, Eleanor Maccoby and Carol Jacklin (1987) found that among nursery school children 4½ years of age, children spent three times as much time playing with same-sex playmates as they did with cross-sex playmates, although some play did occur in mixed groups. By the time the children had reached the age of 6½, the ratio of same-sex to other-sex play had increased to eleven to one. Similar results have been found cross-culturally (Edwards & Whiting, 1988). As in the United States, sex segregation increases from early to middle childhood. It is greater when many children are available as potential playmates and when children are in same-age versus mixed-age groups. The segregation is greatest in situations that have not been structured by adults (Thorne, 1986).

> Gender segregation—the separation of girls and boys in friendships and casual encounters—is central to daily life in elementary schools. A series of snapshots taken in varied school settings would reveal extensive spatial separation between girls and boys. When they choose seats, select companions for work or play, or arrange themselves in line, elementary school children frequently cluster into same-sex groups. At lunchtime, boys and girls often sit separately and talk matter-of-factly about "girls' tables" and boys' tables." Playgrounds have gendered spaces: boys control some areas and activities, such as large playing fields and basketball courts; and girls control smaller enclaves, such as jungle-gym areas and concrete spaces for hopscotch and jump rope (Thorne & Luria, 1986, p. 178).

Sex segregation in elementary and middle schools has been found to account for more separation than race (Schofield, 1982).

By the time children reach the first grade, boys and girls are socialized into two virtually nonoverlapping groups of peers. Preference for same-sex companions no longer needs to be supported by adults; it has become part of the group processes of the children themselves. Preference for same-sex peers is associated both with a devaluation of the other sex and an avoidance of activities associated with that sex.

Differential Reinforcement by Peers

Sex-segregation of activities and friendships is maintained partly by differential reinforcement of gender-typed activities. Same-sex peers appear to be the most potent agents of gender segregation (Fagot, 1985a). Here, again, we find a difference in the behavior of boys and girls. Beverly Fagot found that girls responded positively to other girls about twice as often as to boys independent of the kind of activity in which they were engaged. Boys responded positively to other boys more than twice as often as to girls, except when the boys were engaged in girl-preferred activities.

When the continuation of the activity was used as the criterion for the effectiveness of the social reinforcement, girls were found to be influenced by other girls and by teachers, but less by boys. Boys were influenced by other boys, but less by girls or by teachers. Boys were not influenced at all by girls or teachers if they were engaged in male-preferred activities (defined from previous studies as rough-and-tumble play, or play with transportation toys, large blocks, or carpentry tools, whereas female-preferred play was defined as doll play, dress-up, art activities, or dance). In other words, boys engaged in male-preferred activities appear to have developed a group structure that is impervious to the social demands of anyone except other boys.

Unlearning the Traits and Behaviors of the Other Sex

There is a considerable body of evidence suggesting that children (especially boys) actively unlearn those traits and behaviors stereotypically associated with the other sex. Some particularly compelling evidence has been collected by Phyllis Berman (1980) on age-related changes in children's nurturant responses. Berman placed either a young infant or a kitten or puppy in a playpen in various day-care facilities and observed children's behavior toward these young creatures. She found that at age 3, both boys and girls approached the baby human being or baby animal equally closely and were equally affectionate toward it. By age 5, however, boys showed a much greater interest in the animals than in the infant, whereas girls' behavior was unchanged. These data suggest that nurturant impulses are present in boys and girls at an early age, but boys learn to withhold responsiveness to young infants because they perceive this behavior to be incompatible with masculine roles.

Sometime between 4 and 6 years of age, both black and white children learn what the "correct" gender-appropriate responses toward infants are. Studies show that when 5-year-olds were asked to pose for photographs with a same-sex peer and with an infant, girls stood significantly closer, smiled more, and touched the baby more often than boys did (Reid, Tate, & Berman, 1989). The gender differences that appeared when children were asked to enact the same-sex parental role may be even more interesting. Girls asked to act as "mommy" moved closer to the infant, while boys asked to act as "daddy" actually stood further from the infant than when they had posed with the infant without any instructions. This study illustrates the strength of the perceived penalties for boys of deviating from stereotypically appropriate roles. They affect not only children's everyday behavior, but also the way in which they visualize their adult roles.

Group Dynamics and Sex-Related Differences

Children develop social behaviors that support sex segregation. For example, male bonding is enhanced by transgressions of adult rules, especially those involving the use of words with an obscene or sexual connotation. Barrie Thorne and Zella Luria (1986) observed groups of boys playing a "Mad Lib" game in which their rules required filling in the blanks with "dirty" words. The boys were visibly excited when they broke rules together—they were flushed as they played, they wiped their hands on their jeans, and some looked guilty. The investigators never found groups of girls playing a game of this sort, although some of their young women students recalled having done so in grade school, but giving it up either after being caught by teachers or out of fear of being caught. Both boys and girls may acquire knowledge of the game, but boys repeatedly perform it because their peer group gives them support. The boys play for an audience of other boys.

By the time they are in third or fourth grade children have developed gender-differentiated speech styles. Boys brag and insult their opponents more during both mixed- and same-sex competition (checkers). They have also been found to be more verbally aggressive during collaborative play with puppets (Leaper, 1991). Girls talk off-topic, interrupt, and laugh more in same-sex dyads than they do in mixed-sex dyads or boys do under any condition. Boys make more demands and use more self-promoting speech in their interactions with girls. Although boys do not appear to dominate their conversations, girls seem to be less happy and less engaged when they are interacting with boys than with other girls (McCloskey & Coleman, 1992).

Social Mechanisms for Maintaining Boundaries

The avoidance of other-sex playmates is closely controlled by group processes, especially among boys. Marginal or isolated boys are verbally taunted with such terms as "sissy" or "fag." Elementary school children may not be completely aware of the adult meaning of the latter term (which is used essentially as a synonym for "nerd"), but sexual idioms are a major resource that children draw on to maintain sex segregation (Thorne & Luria, 1986). In a context of teasing, the charge that a particular boy "likes" a particular girl (or vice versa) may be hurled as an insult. Children have great difficulty countering such accusations. Here is an example from a conversation with an adult observer in a Michigan school:

> Susan asked me what I was doing, and I said that I was observing the things children do and play. Nicole volunteered, "I like running, boys chase all the girls. See Tim over there? Judy chases him all around the school. She likes him." Judy, sitting across the table, quickly responded, "I hate him. I like him for a friend." "Tim loves Judy," Nicole said in a loud sing-song voice (Thorne & Luria, 1986, p. 186).

Sexual and romantic teasing mark social hierarchies. The most popular children and the pariahs—the lowest status, most excluded children—are most frequently mentioned as targets of "linking." Linking someone with a pariah suggests shared contamination and is an especially vicious tease.

Boundaries between boys and girls are also emphasized and maintained by rituals such as cross-sex chasing. When boys and girls chase each other, they become, by definition, separate teams. Gender labels override individual identities: "Help, a girl's chasing me!" "C'mon, Sarah, let's get that boy." "Tony, help save me from the girls" (Thorne & Luria, 1986, p. 187). Cross-sex chasing is sometimes structured around rituals of pollution, such as "cooties," when individuals or groups are treated as contaminating or carrying germs. Cooties usually originate from girls. Although "cooties" may be framed as play, it may have serious implications. Female pariahs—the ultimate school untouchables because of their sex and some added stigma such as being overweight or from a very poor family—are sometimes called "cootie queens" or "cootie girls." On the other hand, "cootie kings" or "cootie boys" do not seem to exist (Thorne & Luria, 1986).

> Gender-marked rituals of teasing, chasing, and pollution heighten the boundaries between boys and girls. They also convey assumptions which get worked into later sexual scripts: (1) that boys and girls are members of distinctive, opposing, and sometimes antagonistic groups; (2) that cross-gender contact is potentially sexual and contaminating, fraught with both pleasure and danger; and (3) that girls are more sexually-defined (and polluting) than boys (pp. 187–188).

With such social mechanisms operating it is hardly surprising that friendships between girls and boys among 7-year-olds are reported to be very rare (Gottman & Parker, 1987). These rare friendships had been maintained over several years—most commonly since about the age of 3. Of special interest is the fact that by age 7 such friendships had gone underground. The boys and girls seldom acknowledged one another at school, but continued to play together mainly in the privacy of their own homes. At what age did you stop associating with the other sex on a regular and public basis?

Social Dominance and Social Influence

As you saw in Chapter 5, gender differences are also status differences. By the second or third grade children are well aware of the social hierarchy that exists in their classroom and in their school. In one early study in this area, 70 percent of the children agreed on a dominance hierarchy (Edelson & Omark, 1973). Boys were nominated for the top 40 percent of the positions in the hierarchy, while girls were generally in the bottom 40 percent. Girls agreed with boys on these judgments of peer status.

The characteristics of boys' play appear to promote their dominance in group situations. For example, researchers examined dominance behavior in groups of four children (two boys and two girls) playing with a movie viewer that was designed to allow only one child at a time to see the movie (Charlesworth & La Freniere, 1983). In these groups, boys generally achieved the dominant position. On the average, boys spent three times as much time in the viewing position as the girls.

Another study on all-boy and all-girl groups showed that the tactics used to attain dominance varied for the two sexes. Boys usually obtained dominance by shouldering other children out of the way, whereas dominant girls usually managed by greater use of verbal persuasion (Charlesworth & Dzur, 1987). The implication of these two studies taken together is that the techniques adopted by dominant girls for gaining control of resources in all-girl groups do not work very well with boys.

Working with a somewhat younger age group (children aged 3½ to 5½), Lisa Serbin and her colleagues (Serbin, Sprafkin, Elman, & Doyle, 1984) found that both boys and girls make increased attempts to influence their playmates as they grow older. Among girls, however, these attempts took the form of an increased number of polite suggestions. Among boys, the attempts took the form of an increased number of direct demands. Over this age range, boys became less and less responsive to polite suggestions. Thus, the girls were developing a style of influence that worked with one another but that was progressively more ineffective with boys. It should not be surprising, therefore, that researchers consistently find that boys are more influential over group decisions than girls (Lockheed, 1985).

What does all this mean? Although some researchers have suggested that sex segregation of boys and girls is due to incompatibility between their interactional styles (Maccoby, 1988), it may be more useful to look at the role of status and power in the creation of so-called boys' and girls' cultures. These cultures are actually social categories. The major problem is, therefore, the cultural system that supports the existence of these categories (Thorne, 1993). A little later in this chapter we will discuss the way children learn these categories and the different values associated with them.

Our culture permits boys and girls to have distinctive social behaviors which have implications for interactions between them. Boys in all-boy groups are more likely to interrupt one another; use commands, threats, and boasts of authority; refuse to comply with another child's demands; heckle a speaker; and call another child names than girls in all-girl groups are (Maltz & Borker, 1983). Boys use at least some of these forms of covert aggression when they play with girls, too. Researchers may have underestimated the extent to which covert forms of aggression regulate male–female contact as well as contact between males.

The Socialization of Aggression

Social learning from earliest childhood may facilitate the greater use of all forms of aggression by males. Studies on children show how the level of aggression that is expressed by an individual is influenced by social cues about the acceptability of such aggression. For example, by the age of 10, boys are reported to expect less parental disapproval for aggression than girls of the same age do (Perry, Perry, & Weiss, 1989). Adolescent boys have also been found to believe more than girls that aggression increases self-esteem and that victims do not suffer (Slaby & Guerra, 1988).

Successful aggression may serve as its own reward. Children who are successful in an aggressive encounter will tend to repeat it (Unger, 1979a). Exposure to violence also increases aggression. When various forms of aggressive play are made available to children—for example, violent videogames—both boys and girls who played such games showed more aggression in subsequent observations (Schutte, Malouff, Post-Gorden, & Rodasta, 1988). These findings suggest that social learning plays a major role in gender-related differences in aggression (see Figure 7.3).

Both boys and girls were affected the same way by violence on TV at age 3, but other factors inhibited aggression in girls in later childhood (Eron, 1980).

FIGURE 7.3. The socialization of aggression. What are the consequences for the development of gender-typed traits in boys and girls who are given either guns or dolls?

One possible explanation for this gender-related difference may be that male models of successful aggression are much more available. For example, when men engage in violence on television they are equally likely to hurt others as to be hurt themselves. For every ten women who hurt others, sixteen women are hurt (Signorielli, 1989).

Findings about sex-related differences in children's aggression are, however, limited by the narrow range of populations that have been studied—almost entirely white middle-class children in the United States. In a recent paper, Kaj Bjorkqvist from Finland (1994) argued that we have underestimated levels of female aggression by using the wrong measures as well as the wrong populations. He notes that physical aggression is replaced by verbal aggression among children as their social skills develop. He also notes that anthropological investigations of many societies suggest that adult women use many indirect aggressive strategies such as locking their husbands out of the house for the night or singing mocking songs about them.

Intensive studies of children outside of the laboratory also reveal a more limited number of sex-related differences. For example, nursery school boys and girls in Brazil differed only in the amount of bullying (dominant aggression) found. Bullying was, however, more class- than sex-related. Middle-class boys engaged in significantly more acts of bullying than boys from the slums or girls of either social class (Frey & Hoppe-Graff, 1994). Barrie Thorne (1993), who has conducted several intensive ethnographic studies of children in the United States, is also reluctant to stress sex-related differences in aggression. She found a number of acts of aggression instigated by girls on school playgrounds, including name calling, teasing, and chasing, as well as occasional physical fights. All of these studies suggest that the social context is even more important in studies of aggression than in other areas.

THE MIDDLE SCHOOL YEARS

Gender Differences in Instrumentality

By the time children reach the middle school years, girls' incorporation of stereotypic gender roles limits their ability to explore both the physical and the intellectual world. At age 11, for example, girls were found to be less likely than boys to use buses for leisure journeys on their own, to go into city centers, or to travel by bus alone for more than one-half hour (Newson & Newson, 1987). Such sex-related differences are probably partly a result of the greater amount of adult supervision given to girls of all ages as well as their realistic (see Chapter 14) and unrealistic fears of sexual aggression.

Computers are a new technological development, and one might expect that gender would play little part here. However, boys dominate school computers. In one elementary school observed by researchers, boys monopolized the school computers and actively prevented the girls' access to the machines (Kiesler, Sproull, & Eccles, 1985). When teachers instituted time-sharing rules and, thus, gave the girls "permission" to use the computers, they used them enthusiastically. Apparently, girls can enjoy the computer and do like to use it, but not if they have to fight with boys in order to get a turn. Even if girls do not have to compete for the use of a computer, games oriented around masculine interests such as wars, battles, crimes, and destruction lead girls to see computing as a male domain (see Figure 7.4).

Gender differences in instrumentality may also be enhanced by the kinds of chores boys and girls are asked to do around the home. Researchers who examined a large age-range of children (from below 6 years of age through 18) found that, on average, boys had fifty minutes more of leisure time per day than girls did (Mauldin & Meeks, 1990). This difference was largely due to the fact that from the age of 10, girls spent more time doing household chores than boys did.

FIGURE 7.4. Advertisements for computer games stress sports and adventure, but look who the adventurer is and who the prize is!

These tasks also differed in terms of the skills involved. Girls spent more time in meal preparation and cleanup, whereas boys were more likely to do miscellaneous tasks, including repairs and home improvements.

A study of 279 Australian families containing a 9- to 11-year-old found similar large gender differences in the construction and repair of objects (Burns & Homel, 1989). Some of the figures given illustrate the extent of these differences: 79 percent of the boys versus 33 percent of the girls made models; 81 percent of the boys versus 33 percent of the girls built something of wood; and 71 percent of the boys versus 23 percent of the girls fixed possessions such as bicycles. These differences illustrate how differential experiences build differences in skill which, in turn, lead to differential abilities to influence the world. Girls who were given stereotypically feminine chores and toys were found to have more traditional feminine occupational preferences than both girls and boys who were assigned stereotypically masculine chores (Etaugh & Liss, 1992). The physical world promotes active problem-solving and mastery because its laws are generally orderly and discoverable (Block, 1983). As you shall see in Chapter 8, issues involving mastery and control make the transition into adolescence more difficult for girls than for boys.

Stages in the Development of Gender Understanding

Cognitions about Gender

Obviously, gender affects children greatly, but what kind of ideas do children acquire about gender and gender roles? A number of different concepts need to be learned. Some consistency between children has been found in terms of the sequence in which various concepts are acquired. This sequence of gender understanding appears to be the same in different cultures, although the age at which each stage is achieved is influenced by the culture (Munroe, Shimmin, & Monroe, 1984). These findings suggest that there is a strong cognitive component underlying gender understanding.

It is clear that the first things children learn are *gender labels.* This concept is defined as having been acquired when the child knows how to categorize correctly his or her own sex or that of another person. This ability is present in the majority of children by the time they are 26 to 31 months of age (Weinraub, Clemens, Sockloff, Ethridge, Gracely, & Myers, 1984). Children are able to make gender distinctions almost as soon as they can use enough language to show that they understand the question. In fact, the distinction between "good" and "bad" and between "boy" and "girl" appear to be the first categories that children learn (Thompson, 1975).

Next, children learn various kinds of *gender schema.* In their simplest forms these schema involve linking gender labels to objects, traits, and behaviors. When a child learns to "know" that dolls are "girls' toys" or that "boys like to play rough," he or she is using a simple gender schema. As you have seen, such schema can be used to organize the child's own preferences for play, toys, and even playmates. By the time children are between 35 and 65 months of age, they show a great deal of knowledge about gender-appropriate toys and clothes and have high preferences for such toys as well as for same-sex playmates (Martin & Little, 1990).

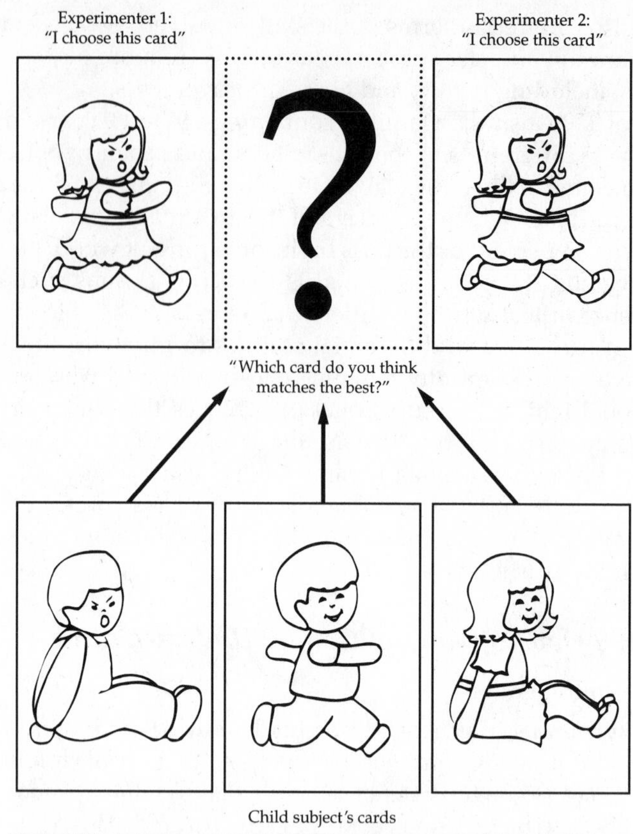

A

FIGURE 7.5. Examples of materials to test young children's conceptions of gender. Figure A tests whether a child categorizes drawings on the basis of mood, activity, or gender. Figure B tests how well a child remembers pictures of girls and boys engaged in gender-appropriate or -inappropriate activities.

Source: From B. Hort, et al., "Is there coherence among the cognitive components of gender acquisition?" Sex Roles, 24, *pp. 195–207. 1991 Plenum Publishing Corp. Reprinted with permission.*

These preferences are present before children have acquired a sophisticated understanding of the meaning of gender. For example, they show a great deal of gender-typing before they understand concepts like *gender stability* and *gender constancy. Gender stability* is defined as having been achieved when children recognize that gender is a relatively stable attribute over time. It is usually evaluated in terms of questions like "When you were a little baby, were you a little boy or a little girl?" or "Are you going to be a mommy/daddy when you are older?" Children appear to understand that gender is relatively stable by the time they are 4 to 5 years old (Smith, 1987).

Complete *gender constancy* is said to be attained when the child realizes that

B

gender is constant and invariant despite changes in appearance, clothes, or activity. It is tested by questions such as "If Janie really wants to be a boy, can she be?"; "If Jim put on girls' clothes, what would he be?"; or "Suppose a child like this (picture of a boy) lets his hair grow very long, is the child a boy or a girl?" Gender constancy is usually achieved between 7 and 9 years of age (Smith, 1987). Below this stage of cognitive development, children cannot understand that a person will remain a member of a particular gender category (1) whether he or she likes it or not, (2) no matter what kind of activities she or he engages in, and (3) no matter what he wears or how she looks (see Figure 7.5).

Studies have repeatedly found that the child's level of gender understanding does not appear to be well related to his or her degree of gender typing

(Hort et al., 1991; Golombok & Fivush, 1994). This lack of relationship between the cognitive and social aspects of gender has been found in several ethnic groups. For example, among both black and white children ages 4 through 9, gender-stereotypical preferences are highly developed prior to the period when gender constancy is fully formed (Emmerich & Shepard, 1984). Although individual differences in gender schemas exist (and will be discussed later in this chapter), gender typing appears to be largely independent of how particular children are socialized.

The Impact of Gender Stereotypes

We have discussed in great detail the gender stereotypes found in our culture as a whole as well as in materials for children in particular. It should not be surprising, therefore, that there is evidence that children possess some knowledge of gender stereotypes as early as 2 to 3 years of age. Preschool girls and boys have been found to object to stories with characters of their own sex engaging in gender-inappropriate behavior (Kropp & Halverson, 1983). The researchers reported frequent comments such as: "He's a boy and boys don't play with dolls" or "She's a girl and girls don't play with trains." Almost half the children referred to Jane (a character in a story who played with a train) as "he."

As discussed in Chapter 4, TV is a major source of gender stereotypes. There is evidence that children are more likely to avoid a gender-neutral toy if they are shown a child of the other sex playing with it on a TV toy commercial (Ruble, Balaban, & Cooper, 1981). Children who watched the most TV (four or more hours per day) had the most stereotypical views about what household chores should be performed by girls and boys. Their beliefs were not related to the chores they actually did perform (Signorielli & Lears, 1992).

Evidence of Greater Stereotyping among Boys than Girls

A number of studies have indicated that boys show a greater number of gender stereotypes at an earlier age than girls do. White middle-class boys showed a greater level of such stereotyping than either black middle-class or white working-class boys (Bardwell, Cochran, & Walker, 1986). Boys more than girls have also been found to choose gender-stereotypical jobs for themselves (O'Keefe & Hyde, 1983) and to show greater sex typing in activities when playing in mixed-sex groups (Smetana & Letourneau, 1984). Peer acceptance appears to become more closely tied to gender-appropriate play for boys than for girls as they move into the later elementary school years (Moller, Hymel, & Rubin, 1992).

Boys show stronger gender-typed preferences than girls at every age. Older girls become more flexible and older boys less flexible than their younger counterparts (Katz & Boswell, 1986). As we discussed earlier in this chapter, part of the reason for this sex-related difference is that little girls are permitted more latitude in their attire, toy preferences, and behaviors than little boys are.

Ironically, girls and women are probably permitted more latitude because boys and men are seen as the more valuable sex (thus, requiring greater attention to their socialization) and because masculine activities are regarded as having higher status than feminine ones (Feinman, 1981). For example, both girls and boys assigned more positive attributes to males than to females (Urberg, 1982). People can understand why a little girl might prefer to engage in stereotypically masculine activities, but a boy who prefers stereotypically feminine activities is regarded as doubly deviant. He is engaged in behavior that is not only considered inappropriate for an individual of his sex but that is also of lower status than masculine behavior.

Such findings are also consistent with evidence suggesting that there is more pressure on little boys than on little girls to conform to gender-stereotypic demands. We have already discussed gender-related differences in adult treatment of little boys who violate gender norms in toy preference or behavior. Here is one more such story from a man who excelled in high school and college athletics.

> Later, at home, my father informs me that two boys on the team throw like girls, and that I, unfortunately, am one of them! By the next practice, he tells me, we will have corrected that problem. That evening, with glove and cap securely in place, I anxiously face my father on the front lawn. And we play catch, for quite a while. I am concentrating, working hard to throw correctly ("like a man"), pulling my arm back as far as I can and snapping the ball overhand, just past my ear. When I do this, it feels very strange—I really have very little control over the flight of the ball, and it hurts my shoulder a bit—but I am rewarded with the knowledge *that this is how men throw the ball.* If I learn this, I won't embarrass either myself or my father. When at times I inadvertently revert to what feels like a more natural and more easily controllable throwing style (more of a shot-put style, with hand and ball starting just behind the ear and elbow leading the way), I am immediately rewarded with a return throw that sails far over my head and lands two or three houses down. "Run! Run after that ball! You won't have to chase it anymore when you quit throwing like a girl!"
>
> Simple behavior modification, actually. And it worked—I learned very rapidly how to throw properly. But it wasn't really having to run after the ball that taught me; it was the threat to my very fragile sense of masculinity. The fear—oh, the *fear* of being thought a sissy, a *girl* (Messner, 1994, pp. 29–30)!

Children appear to acquire information about the greater importance of gender conformity for boys at an early age. In a recent experiment examining the effect of sex, gender typing of interests, and labels such as "tomboy" or "sissy," Carol Martin (1989) found that 4-year-olds ignored the target child's interests and used his or her sex to determine whether they would like him or her as a playmate. By 7 years of age, however, children used interests, labels, and sex to determine a playmate's desirability. Older children disliked children described as sissies more than any other group of potential playmates.

When college students were given information about children who played with toys and had personality traits considered more appropriate for the other sex, they also gave more negative evaluations to nonconforming boys than girls (Martin, 1990). They expected such boys to be less well adjusted and more likely to be homosexual when they grew up, but expected tomboys to convert to more traditional behavior when they got older.

Children's understanding of the flexibility of rules about gender does not seem to be related to their attitudes about those who violate such rules. By the age of 10, children appear to have reached an adult level of understanding that gender norms are subject to exception. At the same time, however, they show a greater intolerance of peers who violate the norms for gender-typed behavior (Carter & McCloskey, 1984).

The Role of Genital Knowledge

It is clear from all these studies that children are given abundant amounts of information about gender, but what information are they given that connects gender to sex? It is possible to imagine a scenario in which children are given no such information and acquire a gender-blind relationship with the world. Such a scenario was devised by Lois Gould (1972) in a fable about *Baby X.* She imagines what would happen when other people are uninformed about a child's sex. From the dilemmas presented by pseudohermaphroditic individuals discussed in Chapter 6, we can imagine that the social problems encountered by Baby X would be even greater for children who didn't know than for children who weren't telling.

Few studies have examined the link between children's biological knowledge and their understanding of the meaning of gender. From the little that has been done, it is clear that young children have little idea about the link between genital structure and gender as a social category. For example, one researcher used a "gender jigsaw puzzle" that displayed schematic line drawings of two nude children who had no facial features and who differed only with respect to hair length, clothing, and genitalia (McConaghy, 1979). She found that 0 percent of 4-year-old children and only 34 percent of 8-year-olds appeared to understand that the male and female figures in her puzzle would remain male and female even if their (transparent) clothing or their hair underwent a gender transformation. Similarly, Suzanne Kessler and Wendy McKenna (1978) found that young children appeared to be more influenced by the length of hair of children in assigning their sex than they were by anatomical information.

These studies demonstrate the important role that social labels play in children's understanding of gender. Children are not given much information about the genital structure of individuals other than themselves. One could argue that

> . . . it is this very lack of intimate access that underlies our culture's insistence on sexual dimorphism in attire, hair length, and preferred behaviors. Children's gender label is their major descriptor at birth and one of the earliest labels they are taught. Chris and Terry are not told that they are tall or short, fat or thin, black or white, Catholic or atheist, rich or poor nearly as repeatedly as their sex is labeled for or to them. In fact we are vaguely embarrassed by many of the other labels and may even request children not to use them (Unger, 1979a, p. 132).

If human sexuality is kept shrouded in mystery for the young child, stereotyped characteristics are all that remain for the identification of gender. As noted in Chapter 2, Sandra Bem (1989) has suggested that teaching children that sex is a narrowly constructed biological category that need not matter much outside of the domain of reproduction might reduce gender traditionalism. Such a message would simplify the meaning of gender. Right now, sex matters very much indeed in virtually all domains of human activity. The emphasis on sex as a biological property could make children "less disposed to believe that every arbitrary gender rule is a moral absolute, every violation a disturbing redefinition of one's maleness or femaleness" (Bem, 1989, p. 661).

Box 7.1 Excerpts from the Story of X

Once upon a time, a Baby named X was born, it was named X so that nobody could tell whether it was a boy or a girl.

The parents could tell, of course, but they couldn't tell anybody else. They couldn't even tell Baby X—at least not until much, much later.

You see, it was all part of a very important Secret Scientific Xperiment, known officially as Project Baby X. . . .

These parents had to be selected very carefully. Thousands of people volunteered to take thousands of tests, with thousands of tricky questions.

Almost everyone failed because, it turned out, almost everybody wanted a boy or a girl, and not a Baby X at all. . . .

Nobody in X's class had ever known an X. Nobody had ever heard grown-ups say, "Some of my best friends are Xes."

What would other children think? Would they make Xist jokes? Or would they make friends?

You couldn't tell what X was by its clothes. Overalls don't even button right to left, like girls' clothes, or left to right, like boys' clothes.

And did X have a girl's short haircut or a boy's long haircut?

As for the games X liked, either X played ball very well for a girl, or else played house very well for a boy. . . .

When X said its favorite toy was a doll, everyone decided that X must be a girl. But then X said the doll was really a robot, and that X had computerized it, and that it was programmed to bake fudge and then clean up the kitchen.

After X told them that, they gave up guessing what X was. All they knew was they'd sure like to see X's doll.

After school, X wanted to play with the other children. "How about shooting some baskets in the gym?" X asked the girls. But all they did was giggle and make faces behind X's back.

"Boy, is *he* weird," whispered Jim to Joe.

"How about weaving some baskets in the arts and crafts room?" X asked the boys. But they all made faces and giggled behind X's back too.

"Boy, is *she* weird," whispered Susie to Peggy . . . X won the spelling bee. X also won the relay race.

And X almost won the baking contest. Xcept it forgot to light the oven. (Remember, nobody's perfect.)

One of the Other Children noticed something else, too. He said: "X doesn't care about winning. X just thinks it's fun playing boys' stuff and girls' stuff."

"Come to think of it," said another one of the Other Children, "X is having twice as much fun as we are!"

The end of this story is that the children began to use each others' toys and play each others' games. Their parents objected on the basis that X had an identity problem and would mix up all their children as well. We recommend that you find the story to see what happened. Do you think this fable has a happy ending?

Source: Excerpted from Lois Gould (1972). The Story of Baby X. *Ms Magazine*.

Resisting Gender

So far, we have discussed the processes through which children become gendered in a way that seems to make such an outcome inevitable. It is clear that gender is socially programmed. However, we do have some information about what factors lead children to "deviate" from socially approved masculine and feminine rules. Some of these factors have been discussed earlier in this chapter, but we will remind you of them one more time in terms of how they may help us understand the processes through which gender is incorporated.

Tomboyism

You can see the difference in social approval of masculine versus feminine activities by the different words that we use to describe children who habitually engage in cross-gender behaviors. The word "tomboy" does not have the same negative connotations that the word "sissy" does. Tomboys are girls who wear jeans, climb trees, and play baseball. Sissies are boys who are absent from these activities. They are defined as much by what they do not do as by what they do. In other words, it is not necessary for a boy to play with dolls to be called a sissy. It may be enough if he does not engage in rough-and-tumble games or verbally aggressive horseplay.

There are many more tomboys than sissies. In fact, tomboyism may be a "normal" aspect of girls' development. In a questionnaire given to women college students, junior high school students, and a sample of adult women contacted in a nearby shopping mall, Janet Hyde and her colleagues found that more than half of their respondents reported having been tomboys in childhood (Hyde, Rosenberg, & Behrman, 1977). The percentages ranged from 78 percent of those in a Psychology of Women course to 51 percent of randomly sampled women. A high proportion of tomboyism is not limited to retrospective reports. More than half the girls surveyed in grades four, six, eight, and ten identified themselves as tomboys (Plumb & Cowan, 1984).

Tomboyism is characterized by a positive preference for boys' attire, male playmates, and boys' games. Young girls who have been identified as tomboys appear to show a more varied set of traits and behaviors than girls who conform to gender-stereotypic norms. For example, they were more likely to have been selected as popular and having leadership skills (Hemmer & Kleiber, 1981) and were found to be more creative than other girls in a test of the uses for everyday objects (Lott, 1978). Considering the status conferred by our society on masculine activities versus feminine ones, what is surprising is that more girls and women do not report such preferences.

Girls who have been tomboys as young children are more likely to continue their interest in sports in later childhood. Researchers find large differences in the sports participation of boys and girls by the time they are 11 years of age. One study in England found that 57 percent of boys versus 24 percent of girls had active sports interests in addition to those at school or in organized associations (Newson & Newson, 1987). In the United States, it has been estimated that 80 percent of young people withdraw from all levels of organized sport between ages 12 and 17 (Brown, Frankel, & Fennell, 1989). Young women withdraw at an earlier age than young men, often before they reach their peak learning and performance potential.

Girls who continued their involvement in sports reported that they received parental encouragement for doing so (Brown, Frankel, & Fennell, 1989). The encouragement of fathers was reported as more important than that of mothers. However, the active involvement of mothers in physical activity was also an important determinant of girls' continued involvement. The presence of a physically active mother legitimized participation in serious norm-violating forms of activity such as competitive sports.

Family Factors

As we discussed earlier, parents, particularly fathers, emphasize different behaviors for their sons and daughters. Parental differentiation occurs not only in terms of toy selection and play with children, but also in terms of the kinds of tasks that children are assigned in the home. In almost all cultures surveyed, including our own, girls are more likely to be assigned tasks that involve domestic and child-care responsibilities. In less developed countries both boys and girls are under the supervision of women who use children's labor to assist them in their often heavy work (Bradley, 1993). As they reach middle childhood, however, the boys usually leave home to perform tasks that often involve other boys (Whiting & Edwards, 1973). For example, boys in rural cultures do more of the care and feeding of animals. In urban cultures, they are more likely than girls to run errands or deliver goods and services.

Gender-related differences in task assignment obviously cannot occur if there is only one child in a family or all the siblings are of one sex. Thus, girls who were only children showed a higher preference for masculine activities than other girls, although their level of performance was still well below that of the average boy (Burns and Homel, 1989). Women who achieved a high degree of prominence in professions considered nontraditional for women were more likely to have been only children or to have had only female siblings than less prominent women (Anderson, 1973). This effect has been extended to younger women who choose nontraditional careers. A study in England found that young women's choice of science 0 levels (roughly equivalent to the selection of majors in U.S. colleges) declined as their number of brothers increased (Abrams, Sparkes, & Hogg, 1985).

Involvement in cross-gender activities appears to influence the characteristics of boys as well as girls. For example, boys who have had the task of caring for their younger siblings (because there is no appropriately aged girl available to do so) have been found to be less aggressive in encounters with their peers than boys who have not had such responsibilities (Ember, 1973; Whiting & Edwards, 1973). Nurturance and aggression may be incompatible. If this is true, it is easy to understand why a culture that values aggression—like our own—would stress gender-differentiated patterns of socialization of children in these areas from an early age.

Cultural Factors: Race and Class Effects

As noted earlier, peers may have a stronger impact than parents on children's perceptions of and behaviors associated with gender once the early years of childhood are over. Thus, it should not be surprising if studies examining cultural effects within the family—as indicated by race, social class, ethnicity, or other variables—might be confusing. However, some general trends appear to be emerging.

One set of data from a large cross-national study of 3,944 adults in the United States indicated that men, older persons, and poor persons were more gender-traditional in their assignment of household chores to children (Lackey, 1989). Studies in Australia (Burns & Homel, 1989) also indicated that children in homes with a higher socioeconomic level were less gender typed in terms of chores.

These data are consistent with older findings indicating that working-class children showed more gender-stereotypical behaviors than middle- or upper-class children did (Unger, 1979a). Girls are, however, less influenced by the social class of their parents than boys are. For working-class girls, perhaps, resisting gender may also mean resisting other undesirable aspects of their class. It may be of some interest to you that both authors of this textbook are from working-class families.

Studies on ethnic differences in gender typing are more inconsistent. Studies have reported that black children are both less stereotyped (Bardwell, Cochran, & Walker, 1986) and more stereotyped than white children (Price-Bonham & Skeen, 1982). These inconsistencies may be due to the content of the questions asked. There is, for example, a considerable amount of evidence that working outside the home has been more a part of the expected feminine role for black than for white women (McGoldrick, Garcia-Preto, Hines, & Lee, 1989). Black girls have been found to give less stereotyped responses to questions about adult work roles than white girls do (Gold & St. Ange, 1974). African-American men are also less hostile to this aspect of cross-gender behavior than they are about some other aspects of women in nontraditional roles (see Chapter 5).

It is also possible that some of these apparent ethnic differences are due to other factors. For example, Pamela Reid and Katherine Trotter (1993) found gender differences between 8- to 10-year-old white American boys and girls in their responsiveness to infants that they did not find among African-American children of the same age. When asked to pose for a photograph with an infant, white boys did not stand as close as white girls and African-American children of both sexes did. Interestingly, the researchers had previously found that 4- to 6-year-old white boys interacted with infants as closely as white girls did and more than black children of either sex (Reid, Tate, & Berman, 1989). These findings suggest that white boys are actively unlearning their attraction to infants as they mature and that preferences for infants are not necessarily linked to gender.

We must take into account the way gender, ethnicity, and class braid together in our society. People of color and people from working-class origins in general are less successful in obtaining societal rewards. These limits may, however, cause them to be less rigidly defined than individuals from mainstream society. White middle- and upper-class males, in particular, may have the most to gain by identifying with normative prescriptions about gender.

The School Environment and Manipulations Designed to Create Social Change

Studies designed to change gender-stereotypical behaviors in children have shown only a limited effect. For example, Jan Carpenter and her colleagues assigned preschool children to high- or low-structured activities during their first fifteen minutes of free play (Carpenter, Huston, & Holt, 1986). High-structured activities have been found to elicit stereotypically feminine behaviors (high bids for recognition from adults and requests for help from them) from children of both sexes. In contrast, low-structured activities enhance peer interactions and leadership skills irrespective of sex. The researchers found that the kind of activity did structure the children's behaviors in the expected ways but did not change the children's subsequent free choice of activities or alter their gender-stereotypic social behaviors.

Another study (Lockheed, 1986) attempted to manipulate children's sex segregation by encouraging teachers to utilize small, mixed-sex instructional groups. Students in experimental classrooms engaged in more cross-gender interactions than students in other classrooms. However, all the students continued to rate their same-sex classmates more positively than classmates of the other sex, with no treatment effect on the ratings.

Manipulations by adults appear to have little lasting impact on children's behavior (Katz, 1986). Such short-term maneuvers are ineffective in changing the cultural context that maintains sex segregation. Children who defy societal pressures for gender conformity appear to have had support from a variety of sources over a long period of time. They must also be able to ignore a considerable amount of pressure exerted against them because of their "social deviance."

The Case for Positive Social Deviance

As we shall see in Chapter 8, girls who resist becoming gendered continue to take math and science courses and to compete in sports. Such activities help to maintain the high self-esteem needed by girls to fight pressures toward conformity that become stronger as adolescence approaches. It is important, therefore, to reinforce what we know about the factors that help to produce young women who resist becoming gendered.

The research in this area is limited, but we know that highly creative and achieving women must have a high ability to tolerate deviance (Helson, 1978). It was helpful if they did not have brothers. But anything that encourages fathers not to gender type is important in the production of independent, self-actualizing girls.

Strong women role models may also be important but, until recently, few models of high-achieving women were available to most girls (see Chapter 12). Girls can, however, find meaningful role models in the most improbable places. For example, one of the authors (Unger, 1988) conducted a study examining the childhood heroes of those women who are considered leaders in Division 35 of the American Psychological Association. These women have been recognized for both their professional achievements and their feminism. The role model that was most frequently reported (by almost 50 percent of those surveyed) as an important influence in their childhood was *Nancy Drew.* It seems surprising that such an intelligent and independent group of women would select a series that had such little intellectual merit (the books were written by formula). As a number of these women pointed out, however, Nancy drove her own car, had adventures, and solved mysteries. And, anyway, who else was available?

Obviously, the kind of books and toys available to children influences their behaviors. It is more difficult to engage in active, adventurous play if one's only toys are dolls. We should not, however, overlook the capacity to subvert gender-appropriate toys that is shown by some girls. The following is a true story that happened to one of the authors of this text. Her 4-year-old daughter demanded a Barbie doll. Since her feminist mother did not want to frustrate her, she reluctantly acceded to the request. You can imagine her delighted surprise when she found her daughter and two friends in the backyard playing with their dolls—they had taken off all the dolls' clothing and were tossing them like darts at a target they had made from a cardboard box.

A series of statements from a group of women writers, artists, scientists, and scholars who were invited to talk about their lives and work (Ruddick & Daniels, 1977) brings life to these issues:

> The journey begins, as usual, with my parents—one an attorney and one a teacher. Both were exceptionally able to hand on their experience, their enthusiasms, and their intellectual curiosity. However, they were also "bridge-builders." Firmly committed to the ideal of equality, they did not see a chasm between those who worked with their heads and those who worked with their hands (or between intellectuality and action). "Oh, for goodness sake," my mother used to say, "life is not only in books! Put that down, go outside, and look at the world!" My father said, "You will be narrow-minded if you don't work" (Kay Hamod, historian, p. 12 in Ruddick & Daniels).
>
> The family member who most consistently sustained me was my mother. Though she burdened me with some of her fantasies and expectations about my future, she also freed me from a debilitating pressure to accept the dictates of femininity as usual. She urged me to have a more intellectually gratifying life than she felt she had had. I need not imitate her life, she said, as long as I did something that was both respectable and excellent. If she encouraged me, my father did not discourage me. Indeed, he paid the bills for the ambiguously supportive and straightforwardedly expensive women's college I attended (Catherine Stimpson, literary scholar, p. 74).
>
> My mother and father never doubted my ability to take care of myself. I had been a loved and trusted child. I was a successful and much-admired student. I was not in the habit of asking for help. The realm of art and ideas, a mystery to my parents, was respected, but not basic. I would build my life on these things, but I would take care of the practical side of living, too (May Stevens, artist, p. 104).
>
> I rejected "women's work," but I rarely considered "men's work"—professional work. Although I imagined future families, I had no comparable fantasy career. When I was already nearly adolescent, I was greatly taken with *Sally Wins Her Wings*—the story of a pilot who, though glamorously attractive, rejects immediate love for the disciplines and adventures of flying. About the same time I cut out advertisements for writers' school, realizing, I suppose, that any wings I might acquire would be far less challenging to health and home than those of the braver Sally. From grade school on I wrote—stories, then poems, then essays—and took my writing fairly seriously (Sara Ruddick, college professor, p. 132).
>
> As I mentioned, I was not prepared for the discovery that women were not welcome in science, primarily because nobody had told me. In fact, I was supported in thinking—even encouraged to think—that my aspirations were perfectly legitimate. I graduated from the Bronx High School of Science in New York City where gender did not enter very much into intellectual pursuits; the place was a nightmare for everybody. We were all, boys and girls alike, equal contestants; all of us were competing for that thousandth of a percentage point in our grade average that would allow us entry into one of those high-class, out-of-town schools, where we would go, get smart, and lose our New York accents (Naomi Weisstein, experimental psychologist, pp. 242–243).

As you can see, these women were encouraged by their parents, and their gender-inappropriate traits and behaviors were taken seriously by others, and,

FIGURE 7.6. A rare photo showing positive gender deviance in girls. These girls are portrayed as being both good at science and enjoying themselves.

thus, by themselves (see Figure 7.6). One highly achieving psychologist of our acquaintance used to say that she had been improperly socialized. As this chapter indicates, however, the penalties for girls of "proper" socialization may be severe.

It is important to stress by way of conclusion that not all aspects of boys' socialization are good while all aspects of girls' socialization are bad. As you will see in Chapter 15, internalization of rigid gender roles can lead to psychological distress for both men and women. Psychological disorders appear to be highly gender-specific in our society. While girls are socialized for dependence and passivity, boys are socialized for overindependence and a lack of close ties. Women's problems with achievement (Chapter 12) are paralleled by men's problems with relationships (Chapters 9 and 10). Women's problems may actually be easier to "cure" because they are largely structurally induced.

It should also be clear to you from this chapter that there is a limit to the amount of change that any one individual can effect. If you choose to become parents, you will (we hope) make every effort to minimize gender typing of both your daughters and your sons. But as long as socialization takes place in a sexist society, boys and girls will have difficulty escaping gender categories. As the number of people who are exceptions to the "rules" continues to increase, however, they may serve as reinforcers of further gender nonconformity in their peers.

CONNECTING THEMES

1. Gender appears to be much more important than sex in the construction of girls and boys. Gender takes various forms for children, including self and other labels, typing of toys and play, and, somewhat later, a basis for the segregation of boys and girls into largely separate "cultures." These effects are largely independent of children's cognitions about the basis of sex and gender.
2. What is impressive about gender socialization is the lack of awareness of both children and adults of the processes involved. The lack of relationship between gender typing and most individual difference measures of gender understanding is also impressive. This lack of relationship indicates that gender socialization is primarily the acquisition of societal norms.
3. Social class seems to affect gender typing in boys and girls. Those who have the most to gain from the cultural status quo (white middle-class boys) seem to be most rigidly bound by social norms mandating the separation of the sexes.
4. This chapter lays out the framework for the social construction of gender in girls and boys. Although the first steps in this process are produced through social learning, children soon take an active part in maintaining gender categories and supporting stereotypically appropriate behaviors for both sexes. Once a sex-segregated social system is established, it is difficult to provide short-term interventions that alter gender distinctions.

SUGGESTED READINGS

EDWARDS, CAROL, and BEATRICE WHITING (1987). *Children of different worlds.* Cambridge, MA: Harvard University Press. This book reminds us that our culture's concepts about appropriate gender roles for children are not universal.

GOLOMBOK, SUSAN, and ROBIN FIVUSH (1994). *Gender development.* New York: Cambridge University Press. An up-to-date integrative review of gender development with a topical organization. The material on cognitions about gender is especially clear.

THORNE, BARRIE (1993). *Gender play: Girls and boys in school.* New Brunswick, NJ: Rutgers University Press. This book is an engaging and thoughtful account of a series of ethnographic studies on children during their unstructured activities in school. It gathers all the author's previously published material in one place and offers us insightful ideas from outside the laboratory.

CHAPTER 8

Becoming a Woman: Puberty and Adolescence

GENERAL OVERVIEW
WHAT IS PUBERTY?
- Distinguishing Puberty from Adolescence
- Puberty in Girls and Boys
- The Boundaries of Puberty
- Individual Variability
- The Pubertal "Fat Spurt" and Its Implications

MENARCHE
- Historical Changes in the Age of Menarche and Their Significance
- The Personal and Social Significance of Menarche
- Menstruation and Our Cultural Conspiracy of Silence
- Menarche, Menstruation, and Popular Culture
- Reactions to Menstruation

OTHER ASPECTS OF THE MATURING FEMALE BODY
- Breast Development
- Weight and Body Image
- Early versus Late Menstruation

RACE AND CLASS AND THE RESPONSE TO PUBERTY
AN EXAMINATION OF VARIOUS THEORIES ABOUT THE IMPACT OF PUBERTY
- Factors That Make Early Adolescence A Unique Life Phase
- Psychodynamic Theories, Femininity, and Self-Esteem
- The Individual as a Social Stimulus
- Social Power Issues
- The Role of Peer Culture

FACTORS IMPEDING GENDER EQUALITY
THE EARLY TEENAGE YEARS: AN INTEGRATION
SEXUALITY
- The Demographics of Teenage Sexual Behavior
- Negative Attitudes toward Teenage Sexuality and Their Consequences
- The Antecedents of Sexuality

CONTRACEPTIVE USE
- Contraceptive Use and Sexual Activity
- Factors Associated with Not Using Contraception
- Parental Communication and Contraceptive Use
- The Role of the Media
- Unmarried Childbearing: An Alternative Perspective

SEXUALITY IN THE AGE OF AIDS
SOCIAL CONSTRUCTIONS AND DILEMMAS INVOLVING PERSONAL CHANGE
CONNECTING THEMES
SUGGESTED READINGS

In previous chapters we discussed developmental trends in the socialization of differences between girls and boys. Our major conclusion is that it takes a great deal of input from family, friends, various social institutions, and, finally, from children themselves, to produce a relatively small amount of behavioral differences between the sexes. Part of the reason gender socialization is slow to have an impact is that during childhood there are no great differences between girls and boys either biologically or in terms of social rules.

GENERAL OVERVIEW

As children move toward their teenage years, however, differences between boys and girls appear to increase. Many of the explanations for this increase have tended to focus on hormonal events that begin during late childhood and accelerate during early adolescence. These hormonal processes induce major internal and external bodily changes in both males and females. Biological changes are, indeed, important. They cannot, however, be examined independently of their social meaning as well as their meaning for each individual adolescent.

This chapter will focus on the complex interactions between biological, psychological, and social processes that operate in the transition from girlhood to womanhood in our society. We will look at the hormonal events that produce what is known as puberty, the significance of various pubertal events in our society, the meaning pubertal events have for individual girls, and the interaction of these events with other social milestones, such as the transition from elementary to junior/senior high school.

One cannot discuss the transition to maturity without discussing the implications of pressures for sexuality and the ability to reproduce. Therefore, the latter part of this chapter will focus on the development of sexuality in girls and boys, the effects of sexuality on the interactions between boys and girls, the implications of adult sexuality for their families and other social institutions such as schools, and differences in sexual norms between various subgroups within our society. The consequences of teenage sexuality will also be discussed.

Finally, this chapter will end with a discussion of how causal explanations lead us to focus on particular aspects of important social issues. For example, teenage pregnancy may be viewed as a personal or a social problem. Views have shifted in the direction of defining it as a social problem as increasing numbers of white teenagers have become pregnant and have not married. Views of pregnancy also differ depending on whether it is seen primarily as a failure of sexual control or as a failure of contraception. What is defined as normative behavior is an important issue in this area. But views of what is "normal" vary widely with historical and cultural circumstances. Therefore, the behaviors of subgroups of adolescents in our society will be examined in terms of sociostructural factors rather than as forms of social deviance.

In this chapter we will argue that the physical, sexual, and social changes that occur during early and middle adolescence for girls are so great as to constitute a discontinuity in their development. In particular, different views of the self emerge between girls and boys that could not be predicted from events that occur during childhood. These self-perceptions come both from the different biological events that occur during puberty in boys and girls and from the different social meanings attached to these events. In particular, contradictory social messages are much more likely to be applied to the mature female than to the mature male body.

WHAT IS PUBERTY?

Distinguishing Puberty from Adolescence

Puberty is the period of most rapid physical growth that human beings experience. The only period in which we grow faster is during prenatal and the early months of postnatal life. And, of course, we are not aware of our growth during this early part of our lives.

The word *puberty* is derived from the Latin word *pubescere,* which means "to become hairy." In contrast, the word *adolescence* is derived from the Latin word meaning "to grow up" (Brooks-Gunn & Petersen, 1983a). The derivation of these two words emphasizes their difference in meaning. Puberty involves physical events such as the growth spurt, changes in body composition, and the development of secondary sexual characteristics. (We will discuss each of these physical changes and its personal and social significance in detail later in this chapter.) Every normal individual in every society experiences puberty at some time between their late childhood and middle teenage years.

Puberty is easier to define than adolescence because its definition depends on biological events. Adolescence, on the other hand, is a socially defined phenomenon. In our society, it is defined as the period between childhood and maturity. Adolescents are a relatively recently created social group: the product of an affluent mid-eighteenth-century society where a falling infant mortality rate, a corresponding growing population, and the need for a smaller work force resulted in a surplus of young people (Hollin, 1987).

This period has become more important as the age at which one is able to take on adult roles and the age at which one is permitted or expected to do so have diverged. In societies where one is expected to do adult work as soon as one is physically able to do so, there is no such stage as adolescence. Some subcultures, even in our own society, do not recognize adolescence. Without adolescence, as we shall see later in this chapter, there is also no such "social problem" as adolescent pregnancy.

Puberty in Girls and Boys

Puberty differs for girls and boys in a number of important ways. First, the timing of pubertal changes is different. On the average, girls begin and complete puberty two years before boys. Second, the quantity and quality of change are different for girls and boys. During puberty differences in height, body composition, and physical configuration between males and females increase. Teenagers' bodies become increasingly *sexually dimorphic* (two-bodied) in comparison to children's bodies, for whom it is sometimes difficult to distinguish sex without inspecting the genital area.

The most important physiological difference between girls and boys that occurs during puberty is *menarche*—the onset of menstruation. Although this is a relatively late event in the process of girls' physical maturation, it possesses a great deal of personal and social meaning. In purely physical terms, menarche conveys the information that a girl is sexually mature and able to bear children. In many societies, menarcheal rites are designed to publicize this information in order to obtain the greatest amount of economic benefit for a girl's family (Paige & Paige, 1981). Our culture pays little overt attention to the onset of menstruation. However, this does not mean that it is of little personal or social importance.

The Boundaries of Puberty

The ages at which puberty begins and ends differ, depending on which physiological measure we observe. By any measure, however, puberty takes a long time. Some physiological changes begin in the bodies of girls and boys long before they can be seen. For example, the level of *gonadotropins* (hormones produced by the pituitary gland that stimulate the ovaries or testes) in the bloodstream begins to rise around the time children are 7 or 8 years of age. The end of puberty is marked by a stabilization of gonadal hormone levels in the mid to late teens. Thus, in endocrinological terms, puberty lasts about ten years.

Puberty is more typically defined in terms of external changes. For girls, the *growth spurt* (produced by the stimulating effect of gonadal hormones on growth centers in the long bones) may begin as early as age 9. Most girls reach their adult height by 14 to 16 years of age. Boys, in contrast, usually start their growth spurt after age 11 and may continue to grow until their late teen years.

Individual Variability

There is a great deal of variation between individuals in terms of the timing of various changes associated with puberty. Girls, in particular, differ greatly in terms of the age at which their external appearance begins to change and the length of time it takes for the changes to be completed. For example, in some early-maturing girls, the beginning stages of secondary sexual characteristics such as breast buds and pubic and axillary hair may appear as early as 8 years of age. However, the average age at which breast buds appear for American girls is 11 and may be as late as 13 years (Brooks-Gunn, 1988).

It takes approximately four and a half years for an average girl to progress from breast budding to complete breast development, but some girls do so in less than a year and a half (see Figure 8.1). Moreover, some girls never reach what is considered the final stage of breast development (large, well-defined, fatty breasts). Given the importance of breasts in our culture, it is difficult to view puberty as *only* a physiological process. As we shall see later in this chapter, puberty has very different implications for early-maturing versus later-maturing girls.

The timing, sequence, and duration of pubertal changes may influence

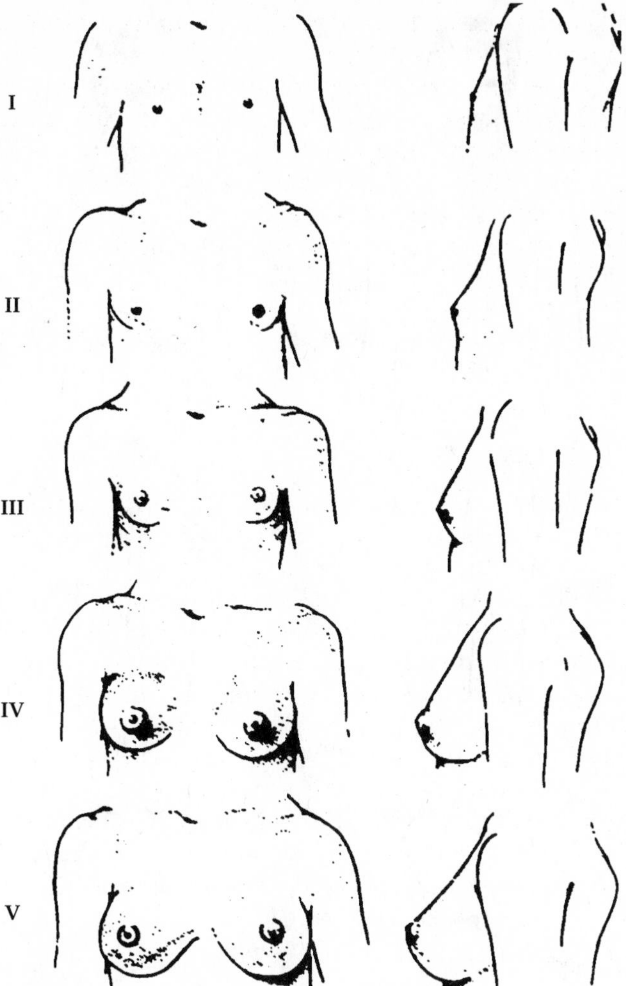

FIGURE 8.1. Breast stages during adolescence.

teenagers' views of themselves as compared with others of the same age. It is important in this regard to remember that girls' and boys' progression through puberty is different in timing as well as in terms of specific events. As we noted earlier, girls usually experience their growth spurt and onset of secondary sexual characteristics earlier than boys. Thus, an early-maturing girl is not only different from other girls but is also way ahead of her male classmates. By contrast, a late-maturing girl is "in synchrony" with her male peers (Brooks-Gunn, 1988).

The Pubertal "Fat Spurt" and Its Implications

Girls experience a rapid gain in fat as well as height around puberty. They experience an average weight gain of twenty-four pounds, which is deposited largely in the breasts, hips, and buttocks (Figure 8.2). Prepubescent boys and

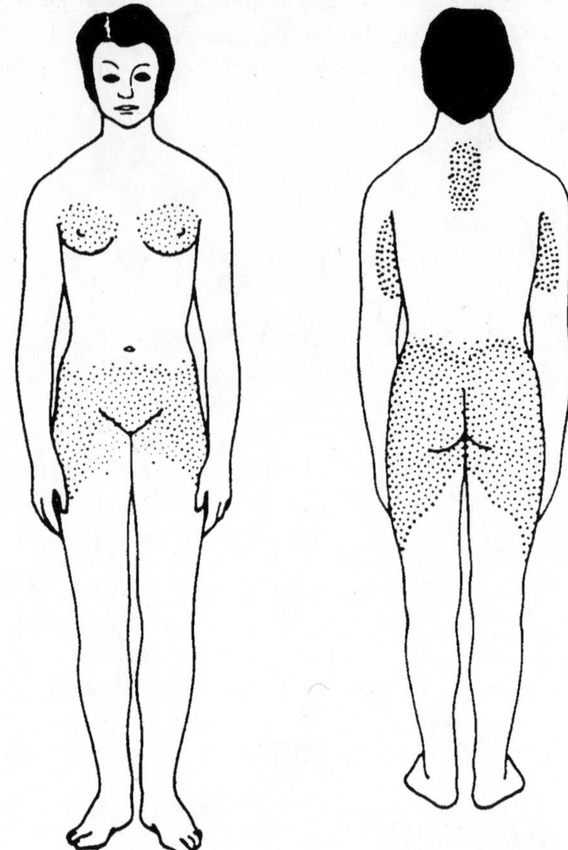

FIGURE 8.2. The places on a girl's body where fat is most likely to be deposited.

girls are similar to each other with respect to lean body mass, skeletal mass, and body fat. By maturity, however, females have twice as much body fat as males (Warren, 1983).

Fatty tissue appears to be necessary for sexual maturation. Menarche usually occurs when about 24 percent of the body mass is composed of fat (Frisch, 1983a). Sexual maturation depends on factors other than simple chronological age. For example, undernutrition delays sexual development in both boys and girls as well as in other mammals. Rose Frisch (1983b) has argued that girls require a critical amount of body fat in order for menarche to occur. During their adolescent growth spurt, girls' body fat increases 120 percent, compared with a 44 percent increase in lean body weight. (In contrast, boys increase in the amount of muscular tissue.) This increase represents a relative as well as an absolute increase in fatty tissue. As age 18 fat is 27 percent of total body weight.

A number of researchers believe that the tendency for menarche to occur earlier over the past century is due to better nutrition during childhood. Girls simply reach the critical weight sooner. Weight gain is, of course, one of the few pubertal changes over which the teenager has some control. It is possible, therefore, to test the hypothesis that a critical amount of body fat is necessary for menstruation to occur. Severe dieting or intense athletic activity can delay menarche. Nevertheless, almost every young woman reaches menarche by the age of 16 (Frisch, 1983b).

MENARCHE

Historical Changes in the Age of Menarche and Their Significance

The age at which girls began to menstruate is often noted in diaries, letters, and medical records, so it is possible to document the fact that the average age of menarche has declined over the last 100 years. The average age of menarche in mid-nineteenth-century Britain was 15½ to 16½ years. Menarcheal age also differed by social class. Upper-class women began to menstruate six months to a year earlier on average than working-class women. The delay among working-class women was explained as due to undernutrition and hard living (Frisch, 1983a).

What is probably more interesting is the fact that girls in the United States in 1871 who began to menstruate at 11½ to 12½ years of age were considered to be cases of precocious puberty (Frisch, 1983a). The average age of menarche today is 12½ years. If we consider menarche the end of childhood and/or the beginning of sexual maturity, this change over the past century represents a significant shortening of childhood for girls.

The Personal and Social Significance of Menarche

Menarche is actually only a late step in a long series of changes. It typically occurs after girls have stopped growing at their peak velocity and after their breast development is nearly complete. As is obvious from our previous discussion, menarche also occurs after a great deal of body fat has been gained. All of these bodily changes are important determinants of how a girl is viewed by others and, therefore, of the way she feels about herself. However, menarche carries particularly important messages for the individual and society because it is the most sudden and dramatic event that occurs during sexual maturation. The meaning of menarche in our society is both positive and negative. The messages girls receive and convey are quite contradictory.

When girls write about their own menarche, the emotional impact of these messages is evident.

> When I discovered it . . . (my mother) told me to come with her, and we went into the living room to tell my father. She just looked at me and then at him and said, "Well, your little girl is a young lady now!" My dad gave me a hug and congratulated me and I felt grown up and proud that I was a lady at last (Shipman, 1971, p. 331).

> I had no information whatsoever, no hint that anything was going to happen to me. . . . I thought I was on the point of death from internal hemorrhage. . . . What did my highly educated mother do? She read me a furious lecture about what

a bad, evil, immoral thing I was to start menstruating at the age of eleven! So young and so vile! Even after thirty years, I can feel the shock of hearing her condemn me for "doing" something I had no idea occurred (Weidiger, 1975, p. 169).

More structured methods underline the extent to which young women are ambivalent about the onset of menstruation. Anne Petersen (1983), for example, presented a group of seventh-graders with the beginnings of stories based on passages from Judy Blume's book *Are you there, God? It's me, Margaret,* a book that is popular with teenage girls and that focuses on puberty. The story about menarche was:

"Mom—hey, Mom—come quick!" When Nancy's mother got to the bathroom she said: "What is it? What's the matter?" "I got it," Nancy told her. "Got what?" said her mother.

Virtually all the girls recognized that "it" was Nancy's period.

More revealing was their response to the question "How did Nancy feel?" Half of the girls ranked "scared" first, while 39 percent ranked "happy" first, and no girl ranked "sad" first. Happy and scared were also the most popular second choices. Their responses suggest that girls feel both happy and frightened about menstruation. They were expressing ambivalence to the extent to which the measure was permitting them to do so.

Despite their anxiety about menarche, girls also engage in a certain amount of menarcheal competition. This competition is mentioned in fiction as well as in girls' anecdotal accounts of their experiences. The basis for this competition is the status that girls gain when they attain "womanhood." As we have discussed throughout this text, womanhood carries more mixed messages than manhood. Thus, girls are more ambivalent about maturation than boys are.

Retrospective accounts of menarche given by adult women indicate the same kind of ambivalent feelings displayed by pubertal girls (Woods, Dery, & Most, 1983). A majority of adult women reported positive emotions, such as happiness, pride, or excitement. Most, however, also recalled negative emotions, such as upset, embarrassment, fear, and anger. Eighty percent reported feeling surprised. Age at menarche was not related to any current menstrual attitudes.

The personal importance of menarche—in contrast to our society's silence on the subject—is evident from girls' reluctance to discuss menstruation immediately following menarche. The majority do not discuss it with anyone except their mothers (Brooks-Gunn & Ruble, 1983). Only after several periods do they begin to discuss feelings, symptoms, and practical problems with friends.

Menarche appears to focus the adolescent girl's attention on her body. One example of this change in body image comes from the work of Elissa Koff and her colleagues (Koff, Rierdan, & Silverstone, 1978). They collected human figure drawings from girls at two points in time—in sixth and eighth grades. Most of the girls had not reached menarche when they made their first drawings. Some had done so by the time the second drawings were completed. Thus, the researchers were able to compare drawings from comparably aged girls, some of whom had begun menstruating and some of whom had not, but all of whom had experienced the same passage of time. The researchers were interested in the shift in body image reflected by these figure drawings.

They found that postmenarcheal girls, as a group, produced significantly more sexually differentiated drawings than their premenarcheal peers (Figure 8.3). Among those girls who had begun to menstruate during the course of the study, there was a significant increase in the sexual characteristics noted in their drawings from the first to the second occasion. Those girls who had not yet begun to menstruate did not show this change.

Additional studies by these researchers (Koff, 1983; Koff, Rierdan, & Jacobson, 1981) indicated that young adolescent girls actively believe that menarche will produce a sudden and momentous transformation into mature womanhood. For example, seventh and eighth graders responded to the open-ended sentence cue: "Ann just got her period for the first time. When Ann looked at herself in the mirror that night. . . ." with statements such as:

> She saw herself in a different way.
> She thought she had changed.
> She felt very grown-up.
> She felt mature.
> She thought she looked older (Koff, 1983, p. 81).

Physical maturity for females in our society carries mixed messages. It is desirable to become an adult, but, as you have seen in Chapter 4, youthful bodies are more valued for women than for men. And, as you will see later in this chapter, physical maturity can provoke parental fears about premature sexuality and consequent restrictions of girls' behavior. It should be no surprise, therefore, that girls are ambivalent about an event they see as the symbol of womanhood.

Menstruation and Our Cultural Conspiracy of Silence

Although women spend as much as 25 percent of their adult years menstruating, both menarche and menstruation are still largely taboo as subjects of public discussion. As one group of authors who have written a book entitled *The Curse: A Cultural History of Menstruation* wittily pointed out:

> We live in a greeting card culture where, for twenty-five cents, we purchase socially approved statements about childbirth, marriage, or death. But Hallmark manufactures no cards that say, "Best Wishes on Becoming a Woman." Rather than celebrate the coming-of-age in America, we hide the fact of the menarche, just as we are advised to deodorize, sanitize, and remove the evidence (Delaney, Lupton, & Toth, 1988. p. 107).

Would you be willing to send such a card?

A survey conducted by Tampax in 1981 found that two-thirds of Americans believed that menstruation should not be talked about at social gatherings or in the office and one-fourth think it is an unacceptable topic even for the family at home (Delaney et al., 1988). Even the booklets distributed by the manufacturers of menstrual care products include a confusing blend of messages (Whisnant, Brett, & Zegans, 1975). Menstruation is characterized not only as a normal, natural part of life, but also as an embarrassing event, one that needs to be con-

FIGURE 8.3. Stage, not age. Girls exaggerate secondary sexual characteristics when they draw female figures after menarche in contrast to their premenarcheal drawings. Drawings 1a and 1b were produced by a girl who was premenarcheal both times. Drawings 2a and 2b were produced by a girl who was postmenarcheal both times. Drawings 3a and 3b were produced by a girl who was premenarcheal at time 1 and postmenarcheal at time 2.

Source: From Koff, E. (1983), Through the looking glass of menarche: What the adolescent girl sees. In S. Golub (ed.), Menarche *(pp. 77–86). Lexington, MA: Lexington Books. Reprinted with permission.*

cealed; and as a hygienic crisis, one that needs to be combated by frequent bathing and napkin changing.

Until 1972, ads for sanitary protection products were banned from TV and radio (Delaney et al., 1988). Advertisers are still restricted about what they can say on the air and when they can say it. They tend to make generalized statements relating to grooming, femininity, and freshness. Only in 1985 did Tampax break the ultimate taboo and use the word "period" in a TV ad.

Despite the caution with which menstruation is treated, some people still feel the need for a menstrual taboo. A letter written to "Dear Abby" in 1984 illustrates this view:

> Please tell me what can be done to stop the advertising of personal feminine products on television. . . . I find such commercials embarrassing in mixed company, and degrading to women. Is nothing sacred anymore? My daughter says it is impossible to watch TV with her boy friend because of these commercials. . . . DISGUSTED (Delaney et al., 1988, p. 136).

The absence of specific information about menstrual products can be hazardous to young women's health. For example, many were unaware of the connection between tampons and toxic shock syndrome (a sometimes fatal disease that can be caused by the buildup of toxin-producing bacteria in tampons).

Secrecy also heightens young women's suspicion that menstruation is *not* a normal event. For example, one large-scale retrospective study looked at college women's memories of menarche. This age group was selected because the researcher believed they were distanced enough from menarche to be able to reflect thoughtfully and dispassionately on the event but were close enough to reconstruct their experiences reliably. It found that the young women believed that they had received enough abstract information about the biological aspects of menstruation (Rierdan, 1983). They felt, however, that they had received insufficient preparation for menstruation as a personal event. Menstruation, they felt, needed to be distinguished from disease, injury, and uncleanliness. They were very much aware of such associations, but taboos prevented them from acknowledging their feelings of fright and embarrassment.

Girls who mature much earlier than most of their friends appear to have a particularly difficult time coming to terms with menarche. One investigator (Petersen, 1983) found that 43 percent of girls in her sample who had menstruated at age 11 denied that menarche had occurred. The mothers of these girls reported the most negative experiences of all mothers of menarcheal girls. For example, one of these mothers said:

> When she got her first period, I found her pants. She was eleven and a half. She wouldn't tell me—she denied it the first two times. I saw it as denying her femininity. She would hide her pants. I finally told her she had to use the stuff or she couldn't go on a ski trip (Petersen, 1983, p.72).

The girl denied menstruating in both sixth and seventh grade. Her responses on a TAT test (a projective measure designed to get at nonconscious motivations) indicated that she was afraid of growing up.

Menarche, Menstruation, and Popular Culture

Neither menarche nor menstruation has received much attention in American literature. Not surprisingly, what we know about initiation into maturity we know from men writing about the male experience. One of the first explicit references to menarche may be found in *A Tree Grows in Brooklyn,* a novel published in 1943 about growing up Irish, female, and poor in New York City in the early twentieth century. (One of the authors remembers sneaking this novel out of an aunt's bureau drawer a few years after it was published.) The passage exemplifies many of the issues already discussed, such as instant transition to womanhood, pain, secrecy, and the consequences of female sexuality.

> She went upstairs to the flat and looked into the mirror. Her eyes had dark shadows beneath them and her head was aching. She lay on the old leather couch in the kitchen and waited for Mama to come home.
>
> She told Mama what had happened to her in the cellar. She said nothing about Joanna. Katie sighed and said, "So soon? You're just thirteen. I didn't think it would come for another year yet. I was fifteen."
>
> "Then . . . then . . . this is all right what's happening?"
>
> "It's a natural thing that comes to all women."
>
> "I'm not a woman."
>
> "It means you're changing from a girl into a woman."
>
> "Do you think it will go away?"
>
> "In a few days. But it will come back again in a month."
>
> "For how long?"
>
> "For a long time. Until you're forty or even fifty." She mused awhile. "My mother was fifty when I was born."
>
> "Oh, it has something to do with having babies."
>
> "Yes. Remember to always be a good girl because you can have a baby now." Joanna and her baby flashed through Francie's mind. "You musn't let the boys kiss you," said Mama (Smith, 1943, p. 212).

This scene is very benign compared with the menarche scene in *Carrie,* written by Stephen King more than thirty years later. King's menarcheal counter-ceremony is part of a horror story. Carrie White, the butt of all jokes—the scapegoat—is standing dazed in the shower in the girls' locker room when the book opens. She grunts a "strangely froggy sound," and turns off the water. "It wasn't until she stepped out that they all saw the blood running down her leg" (King, 1974, p. 5).

> "*Per*-iod!"
>
> The catcall came first from Chris Hargensen. It struck the tiled walls, rebounded, and struck again.
>
> "*PER*-iod!"
>
> It was becoming a chant, an incantation. Someone in the background . . . was yelling, "*Plug it up!*" with hoarse, uninhibited abandon.
>
> "*PER*-iod, *PER*-iod, *PER*-iod!"
>
> Carrie stood dumbly in the center of a forming circle, . . . like a patient ox, aware that the joke was on her (as always), dumbly embarrassed but unsurprised.
>
> Sue felt welling disgust as the first dark drops of menstrual blood struck the tile in dime-sized drops. "For God's sake, Carrie, you got your period!" she cried. "Clean yourself up!"

> Carrie looked down at herself.
>
> She shrieked.
>
> The sound was very loud in the humid locker room.
>
> A tampon suddenly struck her in the chest and fell with a plop at her feet. A red flower stained the absorbent cotton and spread.
>
> Then the laughter, disgusted, contemptuous, horrified, seemed to rise and bloom into something jagged and ugly, and the girls were bombarding her with tampons and sanitary napkins, some from purses, some from the broken dispenser on the wall . . . the chant became: "Plug it *up*, plug it *up*, plug it. . . ."
>
> The gym teacher . . . slapped Carrie smartly across the face. She hardly would have admitted the pleasure the act gave her, and she certainly would have denied that she regarded Carrie as a fat, whiny bag of lard.

King (1974) emphasizes the fear of blood and of the power that menstruating women were once supposed to possess. Superstitions included the belief that menstruating women could blight green plants, curdle milk or other dairy products, and sour wine (Maddux, 1975). The similarity between the characteristics of menstruating women and those of traditional witches is quite striking.

Men appear to have more negative views of menstruation than women do. Among the large number of euphemisms used for the event, only one has been found to be used more by males than by females (Ernster, 1975). This term is "on the rag." Men interpret the phrase in very negative ways. It is said to imply lack of attractiveness in personality and even in looks. It is sometimes used by men to describe moodiness, easy anger, or irritability in other men.

Reactions to Menstruation

Reports of Subjective Experience

Reactions to menstruation are usually more negative than reactions to menarche. Many women view it as a secret and, at worst, as a curse. One of the most frequently quoted self-revelations about menstruation is the one found in Anne Frank's diary:

> Each time I have a period . . . and that has been only three times—I have the feeling that in spite of all the pain, unpleasantness, nastiness, I have a sweet secret and that is why, although it is nothing but a nuisance to me in a way, I always long for the time that I shall feel that secret within me again (1952, p. 143).

Most women, however, are less lyrical about menstruation. One quote from a group of women asked, "How would you explain menstruation to a young girl who didn't know anything about it?" illustrates a more negative viewpoint.

> I would tell her that her menstrual is like one of the worst nightmares. . . . I would tell her it is something that she had to go through. With it comes displeasure because one, your period makes me sick because the blood, it ain't got the best odor in the world and I would tell her to check with the pharmacist for the best thing to use. Because tampons can give you toxic syndrome or something. But the Kotex is very uncomfortable. It is like a big bulk. And you feel it close to you and it is an icky feeling. Just like having sex and not going to wash up. And if she has sex she could get pregnant if she wasn't using some kind of protection (Martin, 1987, pp. 108–109).

Although this may be a more hostile picture of menstruation than most, in-depth interviews with women about their menstrual care practices (Patterson & Hale, 1985) revealed that the central core of their experience involved "making sure." The women reported that they had to make sure that they didn't leak, that they were close enough to a bathroom, that they didn't stain, and that they didn't have an odor. In other words, they were concerned about making sure that there was no evidence of menstruation.

The problems of making sure are even greater for adolescents who have to deal with menstruation. In junior or senior high school, how does a young woman find time and private space to change pads or tampons so she won't "show?" Here are accounts of some of these problems.

> In school it's hard: teachers don't want to let you out of the classroom, they're upset if you're late and give you a hard time.
>
> In seventh grade I didn't carry a pocketbook or anything—wow!—How do you stash a maxipad in your notebook and try to get to the bathroom between classes to change? It was like a whole procedure, to make sure nobody saw, that none of the guys saw. From your notebook and into your pocket or take your whole notebook to the ladies' room which looks absolutely ridiculous (Martin, 1987, pp. 93–94)!

Strategies for dealing with menstruation in school included putting the maxi-pad up a sleeve; tucking it into a sweatshirt; or slipping a tampon into a sock.

Girls' Attitudes about Menstruation

Given these hassles, it should not be surprising that even before they begin to menstruate, young girls have a variety of erroneous or negative views about menstruation. One survey of elementary school girls found, for example, that 89 percent believed that increased emotionality was associated with menstruation and 68 percent believed that menstrual blood had a bad odor (Williams, 1983). Most believed that menstruation was not a subject for discussion with boys, fathers, or in public, and that it should be kept as unnoticeable as possible. Indeed, when such girls began to menstruate, 85 percent told their mothers, while only a few told their fathers (Brooks-Gunn & Ruble, 1983). No girls told their brothers or boyfriends—indicating again their feeling that menstruation is a taboo topic.

Younger and premenstrual girls appear to have the most negative expectations about menstruation. For example, premenarcheal girls expected to experience more pain than their postmenarcheal counterparts (Brooks-Gunn & Ruble, 1983). They expected significantly more severe symptomology in terms of water retention, negative mood, and poorer concentration than their postmenarcheal peers reported experiencing. Adolescent girls, in general, appear to view menstruation considerably more negatively than their mothers do (Stoltzman, 1986). They also appear to get more information about menstruation from the media and their peers than from mothers. These data suggest that even if a mother has a positive, healthy attitude toward menstruation, she might be stymied in her attempts to communicate the idea of a "friendly monthly nuisance" to her daughter.

OTHER ASPECTS OF THE MATURING FEMALE BODY

Breast Development

Unlike menarche, which can be hidden or denied, breast development is easily observed by others. Over one-half of elementary or junior high school girls who were in the middle of their breast development reported having been teased about it (Brooks-Gunn, 1987b). The most frequent teasers were mothers, fathers, and girlfriends. When asked to indicate how they felt when teased, 8 percent reported being upset, 22 percent embarrassed, and 22 percent angry. None of the girls reported being pleased!

Some of the teasing about breasts has a ritual quality. Barrie Thorne (1993) in her observations of school culture reports that "Once in a classroom and several times on the playground I saw a girl or boy reach over and pull on the elastic back of a bra, letting it go with a loud snap followed by laughter" (p. 142). Sometimes this shaming ritual may be followed by little jokes such as "I see you're wearing a Band-Aid!" The adult staff at these schools generally ignored bra snapping.

Pubertal girls are embarrassed or angered by parental discussion of their breast growth or purchase of a bra. In one study, girls were shown a picture of an adult female pulling a bra out of a shopping bag in front of a teenage girl and an adult man (Brooks-Gunn & Zahaykevich, 1989). The stories told by these pubescent girls focused on anger at the "mother" and embarrassment that such an event would be discussed in front of the "father" (Table 8.1).

One director of a private elementary school for girls has speculated that fourth and fifth graders are much more disturbed about the loss of their childish bodies than grownups think (Delaney et al., 1988). She cited the sloppy big shirts and sweaters common to this age group—no matter what the prevailing style—as evidence of their anxieties.

As in other areas having to do with the body, girls' physical maturation puts them into a double bind. Breasts are viewed as a necessary part of an attractive woman's body, but there seems to be no such thing as "perfect breasts." A recent magazine advertisement illustrates this point clearly. It states "Your breasts may be too big, too saggy, too pert, too flat, too full, too far apart, too close together, too A cup, too lopsided, too jiggly, too pale, too padded, too pointy, too pendulous, or just two mosquito bites." With the advertiser's product, however, young women are assured "at least you can have your hair the way you want it." Other advertisements for cosmetic breast surgery show a beautiful small-breasted woman standing naked at a mirror covering her breasts with her hands and saying: "It was the one area in my life where I always felt deprived. . . ." With such messages it should not be surprising that some adolescent girls would prefer that the matter not be discussed.

Weight and Body Image

Baggy styles not only hide developing breasts, but they also mask the fact that girls' bodies are becoming increasingly different from those of boys. As noted

TABLE 8.1. THREE STORIES OF EARLY ADOLESCENT GIRLS: THE FIRST BRA

Story 1

The parents are probably saying that she needs a bra now, and she's probably embarrassed because of her father. And her mother went out and bought it for her.

Story 2

The mother just went out and bought her daughter a new bra.

And the daughter's probably feeling a little embarrassed that the father is standing right there, as well as maybe a little excited. I mean, it's her first bra.

And the mother is feeling, doesn't feel as, is rather neutral about the whole thing.

She doesn't see why her daughter or her daughter's father, or her husband, should be so embarrassed about it. Probably rather proud of her daughter.

The father's probably feeling a little embarrassed, and maybe a little down that his daughter's growing up so fast.

And the story ends, the daughter gets the bra, and everybody lives happily ever after.

Story 3

She like went shopping with her mom or something, she got a bra.

Her dad is wondering what they got.

She doesn't want her dad to see.

Her mom took it out, and she was totally humiliated and embarrassed.

Her dad understood and stuff like that, but um, she thought it was really rude of her mother to do that, because her mother was sort of teasing her and joking her and so was the dad.

And she was very embarrassed.

Source: From J. Brooks-Gunn & S. Zahaykevich (1989). Parent–daughter relationships in early adolescence: A developmental perspective. In K. Krepper & R. Lerner (Eds.). *Family systems and lifespan development.* Hillsdale, NJ: Erlbaum.

earlier in this chapter, puberty involves a considerable increase in fatty tissue in girls both in relative and absolute terms. Although such changes in body composition appear to be necessary to maintain normal reproductive functioning, weight gain cannot be viewed merely as a physiological matter. An increase in weight has severe negative consequences in current society. First, it accentuates female difference from the "normative" lean male body. Second, it causes the young woman to deviate from the "ideal" thin female body. Being fat has acquired a greater cost as our society has steadily reduced its weight standards for attractive women (see Chapters 9 and 15).

Beliefs about what is attractive, gender-appropriate, or erotic vary enormously from one culture to another and from one historical era to another. The "long lithe look" is considered to be the epitome of female beauty today, and it has been so for several decades. Fashion-model sketches and photographs of the female form accentuate the leg length of women and girls more so than that of men and boys (Faust, 1983). This is especially the case in high-fashion illustrations. Margaret Faust conducted a spot check of women's magazines and fashion advertisements in daily newspapers. She found that women were depicted with significantly longer legs than men (see Figure 8.4). This portrayal is contrary to actual differences between women and men. It is characteristic of girls only in the earliest phases of puberty.

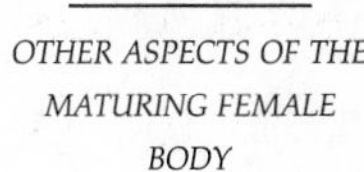

FIGURE 8.4. People in pants suits: apparently similar outfits, but look at the different body proportions of women and men!

You may ask, "What are the consequences for young women of setting up an ideal of beauty that few of them can attain?" Puberty is the period in which differences in self-esteem between girls and boys begin to emerge. Dissatisfaction with how one looks begins during puberty and is linked to rapid and *normal* weight gain that is part of growing up (Attie & Brooks-Gunn, 1989).

These gender-related differences are related to differences in the social meaning of weight for boys and girls (see Figure 8.5). Boys are less likely to be defined by their physical self than girls are. Boys, moreover, gain muscle rather than fat during puberty. The consequences of defining a normal physiological change as unattractive are major in their effects on girls' satisfaction with themselves. For example, in both seventh and eighth grade, the more physically mature girls were found to be generally less satisfied with their weight (Crockett & Petersen, 1987). Boys with greater physical maturity tended to be *more* satisfied with their weight. They also reported less desire to change their appearance than less mature boys did.

Boys perceive their bodies significantly more positively than girls in terms of overall body image (Tobin-Richards, Boxer, & Petersen, 1983). Pubertal girls were less proud of their bodies than boys, felt more poorly developed, and wished they were thinner. Perceptions about weight produced the largest gender-related differences of any measure and were more salient for girls than for boys. For girls, perceiving oneself as underweight was associated with the greatest amount of satisfaction, followed closely by average weight. A large dip in satisfaction occurred with perceptions of being overweight.

FIGURE 8.5. The different sources of self-esteem for girls and boys: doing versus being.

Early versus Late Maturation

Because there is a great deal of individual variation in the timing of the events of puberty, it is possible to use these individual differences to examine the impact of social beliefs on psychological functioning. For example, the "long lithe look" is more attainable by girls who enter puberty later than the average age. Early-maturing girls, on the other hand, weigh more and are slightly shorter than their late-maturing peers even when pubertal growth is complete (Brooks-Gunn, 1987a). As you might expect, early maturers have poorer body images related to weight and are more concerned about dieting than late maturers (Attie & Brooks-Gunn, 1989). In contrast, boys who mature early tend to perceive themselves more positively than boys who are either on time or late (Tobin-Richards et al., 1983).

Early-maturing girls have been found to date more than late-maturing girls in middle and junior high school (Brooks-Gunn, 1988). Early-maturing eighth-grade girls were more likely to report having a boyfriend, talking with boys on the phone, dating, and "making out" than their less mature peers (Crockett & Petersen, 1987). They may also engage in "adult behaviors" such as smoking, drinking, and sexual intercourse at an earlier age (Magnusson, Strattin, & Allen, 1985). These effects appear to be due to the chronologically older friends with whom they associate.

There is also some evidence that early puberty has negative implications for girls' academic performance. In a large-scale longitudinal study of students in sixth through tenth grade conduced in Milwaukee, researchers found that pubertal girls performed less well in both sixth and seventh grade (Simmons & Blyth, 1987). They had significantly lower grade-point averages and poorer reading and math achievement scores than later-maturing girls. These effects are the flip side of these girls' greater popularity and social acceptance. Researchers have found, for example, that the number of contacts with boyfriends was negatively related to academic performance for early adolescent girls (Feiring & Lewis, 1991).

The effects of the timing of maturation for girls are complex. This complexity probably reflects the mixed nature of womanhood as constructed by our society. The clear positive social response to the physical maturation of boys does not occur for girls. Becoming an adult in our society does not bring with it the same social advantages for a woman as it does for a man. The social advantages for the maturing boy include athletic prowess, an opportunity for leadership roles, and expectations of occupational success. Physical maturation for girls may carry more explicit sexualized meanings. The premature sexualization of early-maturing girls puts them at risk in terms of involvement in activities with peers who are socially more experienced than they are themselves. The difficulties of the early-maturing girl in comparison with comparably aged boys and later-maturing girls illuminate the contradictions implicit in being a mature woman in our society.

RACE AND CLASS AND THE RESPONSE TO PUBERTY

Weight concerns among adolescent girls in the United States appear to be virtually universal. Far more women than men diet. In every social class the majority of young women, upon reaching full sexual maturity, wish that they were thinner (Dornbusch, Gross, Duncan, & Ritter, 1987). More than 70 percent of white women within normal weight ranges have been on a diet (Thornberry, Wilson, & Golden, 1986). However, young women from the higher social classes appear to have bought the belief that one "cannot be too rich or too thin" more than other teenage girls. Researchers have found that young women from higher social classes are more likely to wish to be thinner—even after the actual level of fatness of each individual has been controlled for statistically (Dornbusch et al., 1987).

Unfortunately, most of the studies of the impact of puberty on girls and boys have been done on white middle-class populations. A few studies suggest, however, that unrealistic standards of weight have had less of an impact on black than on white women. For example, a survey of 55 white and 11 black female dancers in nine regional and national ballet companies in the United States and western Europe (Hamilton, Brooks-Gunn, Warren, & Hamilton, 1987) found that 15 percent of the white and none of the black American dancers were anorexic. None of the black dancers reported binging or purging, whereas 19 percent of the white dancers reported having done so.

Although, as you will see in Chapter 15, the incidence of eating disorders in women of color has probably been underreported and is increasing, these women have probably been somewhat protected from the effects of unrealistic weight standards by a racist paradox. The current American standard of thinness applies mainly to white upper-class women (Chapter 9). This management of weight is designed to position women within an elite class location (Bordo, 1993). The tight, svelte body reflects material and moral comfort.

Body control may take different forms for adolescents who are neither white nor middle-class. Michelle Fine and Pat Macpherson (1992) reported that the four teenagers with whom they had extensive dinner conversations (two African-American, one Korean, and one Anglo-American) had received unsolicited advice on "having too many pimples," "being too chocolate," "looking chubby," "becoming too thin," "looking like a boy,", or, in the case of a sister, dressing "very butch." While the elite young women in this group were very familiar with eating disorders, the African-American women were bewildered at the image of a young woman binging on food and then purging.

White adolescent girls have been found to have higher self-consciousness, more instability of self-image, and lower self-esteem than black girls of the same age and social class (Simmons & Rosenberg, 1975). Recent studies also suggest that black pubertal girls are less disrupted by moving between elementary and junior high school than white girls are (Simmons, Burgeson, & Reef, 1988). Unlike white girls, whose pubertal status had no effect on the difficulty they had with school transitions, black girls who had recently reached menarche showed significantly fewer problem behaviors following a school transition. No one has yet offered a satisfactory explanation for these racial differences.

There is also some evidence that attitudes about menstruation are different for middle-class versus working-class women regardless of race (Martin, 1987). When middle-class women were asked: "What is your own understanding of menstruation?" they tended to give explanations based on what might be described as the "failed production" model. That is, their explanations focused on scientific models involving the rejection of an egg that had not been fertilized. Working-class women, in contrast, focused on their subjective experience and the meaning of the process in terms of life change. They did this even when the interviewer gave them a number of opportunities to use a medical model and even though they had all been exposed to such a model in school. Their responses suggested either that the medical model was not meaningful to them or that it was offensive because it is phrased in such negative terms.

This fragmentary information indicates the great need for more diversity in our study of the meaning of reproductive phenomena for individual women. We need to look at a greater range of populations as well as to give respondents more room to construct their own responses.

AN EXAMINATION OF VARIOUS THEORIES ABOUT THE IMPACT OF PUBERTY

Factors that Make Early Adolescence a Unique Life Phase

Puberty is unique and important, especially in the lives of women, for a number of reasons:

1. It is the period of most rapid growth that human beings consciously experience.

2. Most of the physical changes that occur are not under the control of the individual, with the exception of weight and, under extreme conditions, timing of maturation.

3. Rapid changes in gonadotropic hormones may affect mood directly.
4. It is a period during which various developmental processes are not in synchrony. Thus, an individual may have a chronological age (age as dated from one's birth day) that differs from his or her biological age (stage of physical maturation). Pubertal stage may, in turn, differ from cognitive age and/or grade in school. This kind of variation within and between individuals allows researchers to disentangle partially some explanatory factors—for example, by comparing the psychological functioning of early- versus late-maturing girls.
5. People do not develop in a social vacuum. Puberty is a period during which one can examine the role of the peer group, and it may be the last period of a person's life in which to examine reciprocal interactions between parent and child while the child is still in the home.

Many theories have been developed to account for pubertal change. We shall focus on those that attempt to explain the greater amount of psychological difference between males and females after puberty as compared with childhood. As you can see from the number of factors that make puberty unique, such theories are able to draw on virtually every aspect of an individual's biological, psychological, and social reality.

Psychodynamic Theories, Femininity, and Self-Esteem

As you have seen in Chapter 2, Freud and other personality theorists have not had much to say about the psychodynamics of gender differences after early childhood. They proposed that females are more narcissistic than males, especially after they reach sexual maturity, but they have paid little attention to the cultural importance of female attractiveness in constructing such differences between women and men.

As noted earlier, the events of puberty seem to focus the child's attention on his or her changing body as well as the body maturity of others (Greene & Adams-Price, 1990). The effects are stronger for girls than for boys. Studies involving human figure drawings, reviewed earlier in this chapter, suggest that puberty produces a reconstruction of a young woman's identity. After menarche young women are more apt to draw more sexually explicit female bodies and are more likely to draw a woman before a man when asked to draw a person. In terms of psychodynamic theories, these behaviors suggest an increase in identification with mature femininity (Koff, 1983).

The effects of puberty do not influence all areas of behavior. For example, they do not appear to be related to cognitive functioning (Petersen, 1987). Behaviors that are most affected by maturational timing appear to be those in which cultural standards play a role. Of all the psychological factors studied, body image is most affected by maturation (Brooks-Gunn, 1988).

The decline in self-esteem among girls after puberty is partially related to their perceptions about their attractiveness. However, a relationship between perceived attractiveness and self-esteem has been found only in white adolescents (Tashakkori, 1993). Beliefs about parental closeness were a better predictor of self-esteem for African-American adolescents. Clearly, the demand for thinness contributes to the potential difficulties faced by girls entering puberty. Recent studies (Powell & Kahn, 1995) suggest that such demands are stronger in the white than in the African-American community.

A longitudinal study that followed girls and boys from the fourth through the twelfth grade indicates that the decline in self-esteem among young women is also related to the declining importance of relationality for their image of themselves (Allgood-Merten & Stockard, 1991). The researchers found that although self-esteem was significantly associated with perceptions of self-efficacy and relationality for girls in the fourth grade, by the twelfth grade only self-efficacy contributed to their self-esteem. It appears as though only stereotypically masculine traits are valued in the world of adolescents.

The devaluation of traits such as expressiveness and relationality contributes to the conflicts for girls entering adolescence. They are coming of age as women while, at the same time, the traits considered characteristic of women decline in importance. It is important to keep this kind of social construction in mind when evaluating psychodynamic theories about the female personality.

The Individual as a Social Stimulus

Gender Intensification

John Hill and Mary Ellen Lynch (1983) have proposed a theory of intensification of gender roles at puberty that takes into account social pressures from both peers and parents. They note that changes in physical appearance may lead to changes in self-views and in the expectations of others. Within each sex, for example, greater height has been found to be associated with higher aspirations and higher expectations in both parents and the young people themselves (Dornbusch et al., 1987). Teachers' assessments of intellectual ability and academic achievement were also associated with height. This effect was actually larger than that for physical maturation.

For boys, early sexual maturation was associated with greater independence in decision making and late maturation with a lower level of independence. The relationship was much weaker in girls. This difference may be due to adult perceptions that early development in girls is more of a problem in terms of sexuality and less a prologue to greater independence and achievement in adulthood. Since girls also mature, on the average, two years earlier than boys, their chronological status may interfere with the degree of independence their apparent physical maturity confers on them.

Physical development in girls exposes them to dating pressures from older boys. Early dating activity may affect relations with other girls. For example, girls tend to choose best friends who are at the same level of physical maturation as themselves (Brooks-Gunn, Samelson, Warren, & Fox, 1986). Attention from older boys may also intensify self-consciousness and concern about being liked among 12- to 14-year-old girls (Rosenberg & Simmons, 1975). Junior high school girls who were physically mature and who had started dating were found to have the lowest self-esteem of all the girls studied (Simmons, Blyth, Van Cleave, & Bush, 1979). We will discuss the important role of male–female relationships later in this chapter.

Both girls and boys show trends in the direction of gender-role intensification from grades seven through nine. Not acting like the other sex becomes more important (Simmons & Blyth, 1987). Girls in the higher school grades were much less likely than girls in sixth grade to admit that they could ever act like boys. There was little room for boys to change in this measure since even in childhood they are unwilling to admit that they could ever act like a girl.

Changes in Parent–Child Relationships

Findings suggest that postmenarcheal girls both perceive themselves and are perceived by their parents to be more mature than girls who have not yet reached menarche. Postmenarcheal girls were allowed to set more limits on their own, had fewer restrictions on their time, and slept less on school nights (Danza, 1983). They were also more likely to wear makeup and a bra and to date than their premenarcheal peers. These effects were related to menarcheal status—not to age.

Puberty serves as a pivotal point for changes in familial relationships. Time spent with parents and yielding to parents in decision making decrease for both girls and boys from early to middle adolescence (Montemayor & Hanson, 1985). Emotional distance between parents and children increases during this period. Conflict between parents and children appears to be highest in early adolescence. Although such conflicts are mild in most cases, both parents and children agree that these conflicts are significant. Adolescents perceive them as more frequent than parents do.

In white middle-class families, mother–daughter conflict is pronounced during early puberty (Brooks-Gunn & Zahaykevich, 1989). These conflicts appear to be due more to social than to physiological factors. For example, negative emotions about menarche and pubertal change are common in girls, and girls may attribute them to parents, particularly the mother, who is perceived as not being sensitive to their desire for secrecy. Menarche appears to produce a particularly intense, although temporary, period of family turmoil. Daughters reported more parental control in the first six months after menarche than either premenstrual girls or those whose menarche had occurred more than six to twelve months in the past (Hill & Holmbeck, 1987).

Mother–daughter relationships appear to remain close after puberty in African-American families (Fine & Macpherson, 1992). Black girls spoke frequently about how much they learned from their mothers. In contrast to the individualistic focus of white adolescents, black adolescent girls expressed respect for their mothers in terms of their strength, honesty, ability to overcome difficulties, and ability to survive (Joseph & Lewis, 1981).

Fathers were largely absent from black adolescent girls' discourse. White fathers were figuratively rather than literally absent. They reported not wishing to talk about body changes or sexuality with their daughters. Hill (1988) has found that fathers become more assertive or brusque with their postmenarcheal daughters. This may be a way of physically distancing themselves, given cultural strictures about father–daughter incest. Did those of you who are female notice any changes in parental behavior during this period?

Puberty appears to be a conflictual time for mother–son relationships as well. Mothers reported the highest levels of opposition from their sons and the lowest levels of parental satisfaction and child involvement in family activities during this period (Hill & Holmbeck, 1987). Fewer changes appear to occur in father–son relationships. This may be due to the fact that the father–son hierarchy remains unchanged, whereas mothers appear to lose influence to their sons during adolescence (Steinberg, 1981).

Most of these studies suggest that the changing physical bodies of teenagers serve as a social stimulus to which their parents respond. Pubertal change is also likely to affect relationships between parents and adolescents indirectly by way of altered self-definitions, changes in parents' expectations of the emerging adult, and multiple social role changes occurring at the same time. Demands for autonomy must be negotiated (especially in upper- and middle-class families) and are experienced as conflictual in most cases. Only one mother–daughter dyad in more than 100 seen by one team ever informed researchers that they had no disagreements (Brooks-Gunn & Zahaykevich, 1989).

Change and the Social Environment

Most of the studies already discussed in this chapter indicate that girls are at much greater psychological risk during puberty than boys are. Their increased risk during puberty over childhood probably has two major causes: (1) unrealistic standards of attractiveness for women as compared with standards for men and (2) the ambiguous meaning of mature femininity. Maturity carries with it contradictory messages for girls in our society. The fact that it is bodily maturity rather than other factors that put adolescent girls at risk is evident from our earlier comparisons of early- versus late-maturing girls.

As you are aware, however, many things affect how a person reacts to a particular life event. For example, the rate at which a girl physically matured had less impact on her ability to function in tenth grade than it had in sixth or seventh grade. The effects of pubertal timing appear to dissipate over time. Other events in the lives of teenage girls and boys may become more important.

Social Power Issues

The Silencing of Young Women

As girls move into their teenage years, they appear to become silenced in a variety of ways. Lyn Mikel Brown and Carol Gilligan (1993) illustrate one aspect of this phenomenon in their repeated interviews with girls from an elite private girls' high school. They note that these girls appeared to lose their ability to take seriously their own experience, feelings, and thoughts. One girl, for example, used the phrase "I don't know" 112 times in her eighth-grade transcript—more than three times more frequently than in the previous year, although the interviews were of the same length. These girls appear to be struggling with the conflict between authenticity and relatedness. To stay true to themselves they risk being seen as neither "nice" nor "normal" by others.

It is difficult to assess how general such silencing may be. The two adolescent girls that Brown and Gilligan focused on, Anna and Neeti, both differed from their classmates in important ways. Anna was a working-class scholarship student and Neeti was from an Asian Indian background. Their perceived need to "fit in" may have had class and ethnic components in addition to problems in making the transition to adulthood. Silencing must also be viewed in a more multicultural perspective. In more communal cultures, for example, it would not be considered undesirable for someone (male or female) to submerge their own feelings for the good of the group.

Brown and Gilligan also suggest that silencing represents a form of resistance by young women. But this is not the only form of resistance possible. Young black women may resist silencing by becoming "loud" and oppositional in order to counter their invisibility in largely white schools (Fordham, 1993). However, this form of resistance (which is more collectivist than individualistic in nature) can also result in their disengagement from education and the loss of an opportunity to acquire power in white society.

Social Power and Schools

Girls as a group appear to be much more permanently affected than boys by school transitions during their pubertal years. Large-scale longitudinal studies conducted in both Baltimore and Milwaukee have shown that the shift from elementary to junior high school and then to high school has a particularly strong impact in lowering the self-esteem of girls (Simmons & Blyth, 1987). Girls drop in both school participation and leadership after the transition into a large junior high school. The effect occurs again in high school. Girls who have made two such changes remain impaired when compared with boys and girls who have made one transition from a K–8 elementary to high school.

These effects are inconsistent with beliefs about the greater social maturity of girls. It is important to understand why the transition to a large impersonal environment at an early age has such a great impact on them. One possibility is that when they make a school transition after sixth grade they are being thrust into a social environment for which they are emotionally unprepared. They come into contact with older boys and, as noted earlier in this chapter, the opportunity to date decreases rather than enhances girls' self-esteem.

As we have stated over and over in this text, evaluations based on physical attractiveness are more salient for women and girls than for men and boys. Examples of this kind of evaluation occurring in a school setting have been graphically described by some of the Canadian high school students interviewed by June Larkin and Katherine Popaleni (1994).

> This guy and his brother went on in their sick way of having fun by rating young women as they passed by in the hallway. I told the guy he was sexist and by rating young women as they passed by . . . he was making them uncomfortable. He said "Just for saying that, I give you a zero."

> I came across a stack of boards in the corner of the art classroom with graffiti written all other them. I expected to read "So and so, 100% true love" or the names of people's favorite bands, but as I looked at the graffiti I saw a picture of a naked woman (no arms, head, calves, or knees) with her legs wide open

> showing her vagina, anal opening and breasts. I was shocked to see such explicit graffiti in my favorite class. I never thought anyone from our school could draw such violent pictures of women in the classroom and not have anyone say or do anything about it. Other people must have seen it because the room is used by three other classes. [To me] that picture says "Rape is OK, sexual abuse is OK, and this is what I'm scared of the most (Larkin & Popaleni, 1994, p. 220).

Evaluations have the greatest impact when an individual enters a new setting (Lerner, Lerner, & Tubman, 1989). Valuation based on looks is problematic for any individual. It involves subjective and unstable criteria. And it places the person at the mercy of outside judges. These judgments may be harder to control in a new school with lesser known peers.

The Role of Peer Culture

During the teenage years, peer groups increase in size and complexity. Both girls and boys spend more time with their peers than children do. Peer groups can develop a social system that affects the behavior of all their members regardless of the individual's level of physical maturity. For example, an entire group may begin to engage in "pubertal behavior," such as increases in talking on the telephone, frequency of showers, and time spent in front of the mirror (Petersen, 1987). Such group effects may precede individual change at least for some late-maturing adolescents. Grade-in-school effects are often much stronger than maturational timing effects (Brooks-Gunn, 1988). Because the adolescents' social world is organized by school grade rather than pubertal development, the importance of the former should not surprise you.

Some recent ethnographic and observational studies of behavior in the school environment suggest that relationships between the sexes can be quite hostile during adolescence. We already discussed how girls' appearance can be a source of public embarrassment for them. Sue Lees (1993) has done extensive work in English schools and reports a great deal of verbal abuse of girls by boys. A double standard of terminology referring to girls' and boys' sexuality is used to maintain male dominance. The word that illustrates this asymmetry more clearly than any other term is "slag." Although the term is supposed to refer to sexual promiscuity, it is used in many situations that are not related to a girl's actual sexual behavior. Thus, a girl may be called a slag if she wears too much makeup, if her skirt is slit too high, or if her clothes are too tight (see Figure 8.6). On the other hand, unattractive or unfashionably dressed girls are never called slags, although other pejorative terms are available for them. The term is ambiguous—it implies that the woman is both contemptible and sexually desirable. It is used by both boys and girls as a form of sexual and social control.

African-American adolescent girls have been found to be more family oriented than either white girls or African-American boys (Coates, 1987). Their reliance on family as a source of support may help them resist some of the more negative aspects of "teen culture." It is interesting, for example, that researchers (Simmons et al., 1988) have found that black girls were protected from the negative effects of school transitions if they transferred to schools with a group of thirty or more peers. The size of the peer network had no impact on the negative consequences of school transition for white girls.

FIGURE 8.6. The "slut look" in teenage fashions. Fashions for teenage girls stress their sexuality. The negative consequences of premature sexualization include sexual harassment and the possibility of pregnancy.

FACTORS IMPEDING GENDER EQUALITY

The cultural factors that make adolescent girls more vulnerable to social stress do not appear to have changed as a result of the feminist movement. The studies on the more negative impact of school transitions for girls than for boys were conducted in the late 1970s—well after the feminist movement was under way. Other researchers (Lewin & Tragos, 1987) have found that gender-role stereotyping among boys and girls was not significantly less in 1982 than in 1956.

Boys emphasized gender-role differentiation and symbols of male dominance more than girls did. They also had more traditional attitudes toward the social, economic, and political rights of women than girls did (Galambos, Petersen, Richards, & Gitelson, 1985). It is noteworthy that boys appear to be more traditional than girls in all national groups sampled in a recent cross-cultural study (Gibbons, Stiles, & Shkodriani, 1991). However, an unusual pattern has been found for African-American adolescent males. They appear to have more traditional attitudes about male gender roles combined with less conservative attitudes about female gender roles than white male adolescents (Pleck, Sonenstein, & Lu, 1994). They are more likely to disagree, for example, with the statement that it is better for everyone if the man earns money and the woman takes care of home and family.

Beliefs about women and men can be affected by the social environment. For instance, rural adolescents endorse significantly more traditional attitudes than urban adolescents do. Beliefs are related to individual characteristics as well. Thus, less traditional attitudes toward women were related to higher self-esteem in girls and in one sample of boys (Galambos et al., 1985). Beliefs will not change readily, however, unless significant social change takes place both in adolescent peer groups and in society as a whole. There is little to indicate that such changes are taking place. In fact, one study (Plumb & Cowan, 1984) has indicated that tenth graders stereotyped various boys' and girls' activities more than children in fourth, sixth, or eighth grades did.

The popular media to which young women are exposed certainly do not present images of equality to them. One study examined the number of pages of *Seventeen* magazine that were devoted to various themes for the years 1961, 1972, and 1985 (see Table 8.2). Although the number of pages on male–female relationships decreased and the number of pages on self-development increased in 1972 (possibly as a result of the feminist movement of the late 1960s), by 1985 the percentage had returned to the 1961 figures (Peirce, 1990).

A further analysis of *Seventeen* by the same researcher (Peirce, 1993) found that more than 60 percent of the articles in each issue were on fashion, beauty, food, and decorating. Most of the fiction showed males and females in gender-traditional occupations. Below is Peirce's example of a story from *Seventeen* in which the heroine, a high school sophomore, suddenly finds herself with a boyfriend.

> Now I was someone with a future. . . . Until now I'd been a kid, stumbling along. . . . A few weeks ago I'd been a zero and now I had a boyfriend!

When it turns out that the boy is involved with someone else, the protagonist comments:

> Now I didn't have a boyfriend anymore, an Ivy-League, advanced math, possible husband-in-a-big-modern-house boyfriend (Peirce, 1993, p. 64).

"Fortunately" for this young woman, there is another boy waiting in the wings. One could hardly call these images self-actualizing!

We have discussed most aspects of the stereotyping of women in Chapter 4. Here we stress only those parts of the media that target adolescents. For example, 12- to 17-year-olds are the primary listeners to radio programs during certain parts of the day. Males dominate this programming as DJs, newscasters, voice-overs in advertisements, sportscasters, and weather forecasters. Females are more likely to be found as traffic reporters and audience participants (Lont, 1990). The terms used to identify males and females in these broadcasts also dif-

TABLE 8.2. Percentages of Editorial Pages Given to Selected Topics in *Seventeen*

	1961	1972	1985
Appearance	48.0	52.0	46.0
Home	9.0	10.0	11.0
Male–female relations	7.0	2.7	6.5
Self-development	7.5	16.6	6.8

fer. Women are referred to primarily by family roles such as wife, mother, daughter, or sister (or, sometimes, as ladies). Men are usually referred to as guys, sir, or Mr.

Even so-called slasher films (which also appeal primarily to adolescents) have a sexist component. Although female and male victims are portrayed equally frequently and are as likely to die in an attack, female nonsurvivors wore significantly more revealing and provocative clothing, were more likely to be shown undressing, nude, or engaging in sexual activity, and were rated as promiscuous more than females who survived (Cowan & O'Brien, 1990). Other studies have shown that women who wear heavy makeup are rated as more immoral and more likely to be sexually harassed than those who use less makeup (Workman & Johnson, 1991). However, these women are also seen as more attractive and feminine than women who do not use cosmetics. These images construct a double bind similar to the one found in the use of the term "slag" discussed earlier in this chapter. Adolescent girls are being told simultaneously that they should appeal to the sexual fantasies of men, but also that such appeal is dangerous. How can this dilemma be resolved?

THE EARLY TEENAGE YEARS: AN INTEGRATION

Psychological changes during puberty appear to be the result of a complex interaction of physiological, interpersonal, and social processes. Despite belief in the major impact of raging hormone effects during this period, hormone changes only accounted for about 4 percent of the variance in negative affect found in young teenage girls (Brooks-Gunn & Warren, 1989). Social factors accounted for more than three times as much variance.

A girl's level of physical maturity appears to be a very important influence on behavior during her early teenage years. Physical maturity effects are mediated by self-perceptions and the perceptions of parents and peers. Timing and extent of pubertal maturation influence behavior indirectly by way of social pressures to engage in "adultlike" heterosexual behaviors such as dating and (for middle-class white girls) struggles with parents involving conflictual views of autonomy and independence. Puberty is more conflictual for girls than for boys because of our culture's ambivalent views about the mature female body and about the role of sexuality in women's lives.

Pubertal effects can either be maximized or minimized, depending on other aspects of the girl's environment. Girls, for example, have more problems than boys in large impersonal school environments. Involvement in some sports such as figure skating may heighten a young woman's probability of eating disorders, but sports involvement, in general, seems to be correlated with higher self-esteem for adolescent girls (Butcher, 1989; Cate & Sugawara, 1986).

Pubertal effects are most marked in some emotional and social areas such as body image and social relationships, but have little influence on cognition or on global self-esteem. Due to the absence of longitudinal studies past puberty, it is also difficult to determine how long such effects persist. Most appear to be small and transient, but at least one study suggests that amount of body fat and a negative body image at age 14 are predictive of eating disorders two years later (Attie & Brooks-Gunn, 1989).

SEXUALITY

Physical maturation is closely related to sexual development in both women and men. Of course, only one sex bears the overwhelming majority of the consequences of sexual behavior. Virtually all societies attempt to manage sexual behavior in order to regulate fertility and its economic benefits (Paige & Paige, 1981). Almost all such fertility regulation focuses on the postpubertal girl rather than her male partner.

Earlier menarche and a lengthening of dependence of children on their parents have created a long period in our society during which teenagers are physically capable of reproduction, but reproduction is considered disadvantageous for their future adult goals. Nevertheless, almost one-half of all teenage girls report having intercourse during their teenage years (Brooks-Gunn, 1988). Control of their fertility has come to be seen as a major social problem. Adolescent sexuality is still much more problematic for girls than for boys. This is because of society's belief that sexual control is more the responsibility of women than men, as well as our society's double standards about women's and men's sexual activity and pregnancy as the woman's burden.

The Demographics of Teenage Sexual Behavior

Ethnic and Gender Differences in Levels of Sexual Intercourse

Until fairly recently, young women who engaged in premarital intercourse were regarded as quite deviant from the norm. Early intercourse was also regarded as a working-class phenomenon and/or one found mostly in the inner cities rather than in mostly white suburbs. If these beliefs were ever true, they certainly are not today. Levels of sexual activity among teenage girls increased dramatically during the 1970s. Today approximately 45 percent of girls ages 15 to 19 are sexually active before marriage, and an estimated 36 percent of them become pregnant within two years after beginning sexual activity (Hayes, 1987).

The gap between the sexual activity rates of young men and women has narrowed as more and more girls have become sexually active. For example, a study in 1982 found that 60 percent of white boys had had intercourse by age 18 and the same percentage of white girls had done so by age 19 (Hayes, 1987). Black adolescents had significantly higher rates of teenage intercourse than white adolescents, although the difference had dropped to only 13 percent by 1982. In fact, the rate of sexual intercourse among black girls has declined relative to that of white girls in recent years and is at the lowest it has been since such data have been available.

Ethnic Differences in Other Forms of Sexual Activity

We cannot equate sexual behavior and intercourse (see Chapter 9). Until recently, studies showed that most white adolescents, especially young women, advanced through various stages of sexual intimacy from kissing, necking (touching above the waist), heavy petting (touching below the waist), to intercourse (Chilman, 1986). Among black adolescents, however, unclothed petting occurs less frequently than intercourse does (Smith, 1989). Differences in sexual behavior between the two racial groups do not appear to be related to differences in intellectual ability or socioeconomic status.

Researchers may not be asking the right questions. They are particularly ignorant about the meaning of eroticism in adolescents' sex lives and about the influence of social contexts on the regulation and expression of sexual behaviors. The initiation of sexual behavior and the form it takes are highly associated with what is perceived as normative in one's peer group (Furstenberg, Moore, & Peterson, 1986). For both boys and girls, the strongest predictor of sexual activity was the perceived level of sexual activity of the adolescent's best friends (DiBlasio & Benda, 1992).

The Relationship between Sexual Intercourse and Childbearing

The level of sexual intercourse among teenagers in the United States is comparable to that found in many western European countries. However, in the United States, girls under the age of 15 are five times more likely to give birth than young adolescents in any developed country for which data are available (Hayes, 1987). The birth rate differences are due to differences in the use of contraception. Contraceptive use is, in turn, influenced by cultural attitudes toward sexuality. Attitudes about sexuality are more negative in the United States than in most western European countries. Unfortunately, while sex-negative attitudes do not discourage sexual activity, they do discourage responsible use of contraception (Fisher, Byrne, & White, 1983).

Negative Attitudes toward Teenage Sexuality and Their Consequences

The Suppression of Women's Sexual Desire

Michele Fine (1988) has written an excellent critique of American attitudes toward sexuality and their consequences for adolescent girls. She points out, for example, that today's sex education curriculum suppresses the idea that women might feel sexual desire. When sex is presented in schools, it is often highly anatomical, overly didactic, and of little practical use (Hamburg, 1986). Many schools continue to avoid sex education because of some parents' conviction that presenting this material will encourage promiscuity.

The kind of instruction provided does not allow young women to come to terms with their own feelings of sexuality. Instead, it promotes the view that women are sexually victimized by men's drives and needs. Almost magically, a young girl's male companions, with whom she previously may have played freely, are transformed into slightly dangerous strangers. The neighborhood itself is no longer safe for her. bell hooks (1989) has poignantly described the consequences of this fear.

> I no longer felt the intimate sweet companionship with strange black men and even the old familiar faces. They were the enemies of one's virginity. They had

> the power to transform women's reality—to turn her from a good woman into a bad woman, to make her a whore, a slut. Even "good" women suffered, were somehow always at the mercy of men, who could judge us unfit, unworthy of love, kindness, tenderness, who could, if they chose to do so, destroy us (hooks, 1989, p. 149).

The conditions under which it is acceptable for a girl to become sexually active are narrowly prescribed in our society. It must be done to please her partner (certainly not herself), must be because she is "in love," and must be unexpected (Cusick, 1987). Ironically, both men and women expect the woman to be responsible for contraception, yet she is not permitted to anticipate the possibility of sexual intercourse. This expectation is particularly unfair to teenage girls, since the majority of teen mothers are not impregnated by teen fathers (Press, 1988).

Contrary to popular belief, early sexuality in girls appears to be related to acceptance of feminine socialization rather than rebellion from it. For example, adolescents who hold traditional attitudes about gender were found to be *more* likely to become sexually active and less likely to employ effective contraception on a regular basis (Jorgensen & Alexander, 1983). Nonpregnant teenagers described themselves as having more "masculine" characteristics than similarly sexually active teenagers who have become pregnant (Crovitz & Hayes, 1979). Black pregnant teenagers were found to have the most traditional ideas about feminine roles of all the groups studied (Blum & Resnick, 1982).

Michele Fine's (Fine & Zane, 1988) observations during her one-year ethnographic study of public high schools in New York City indicated that many of the girls who got pregnant were not those whose bodies, dress, and manner evoked sensuality and experience. The pregnant girls were more likely to be those who were quite passive and relatively quiet in their classes. Traditional notions of what it means to be a woman did little to empower them or to evoke a sense of entitlement.

The relationship between the acceptance of feminine socialization and early sexuality and pregnancy should not be surprising. As Cusick (1987) eloquently phrased it:

> From childhood up, women are socialized to become mothers, which requires participation in a sexual act, but they are not socialized to accept their own sexuality. The ideal woman is sexually attractive, but asexual. Her sexuality does not exist except as a device to entice males (Cusick, 1987, p. 119).

Low-income women who subscribe to traditional views of gender roles are more likely to drop out of high school. Sophomores who were nongraduates were five times more likely than those who did graduate to anticipate being a mother by age 19 and twice as likely to expect to be a wife (Fine & Zane, 1988).

The Privileging of Married Heterosexuality

Sex education also privileges married heterosexuality over other forms of sexual behavior. Even a teenage girl's pregnancy may not be considered a problem if it occurs in the context of marriage. As one high school administrator told Fine:

> Don't worry. She's dropping out, but it's a good case. She's fifteen, pregnant, but getting married. She'll go for a G.E.D. (Fine & Zane, 1988, p. 20).

The birthrate among Latina teenagers appears to be regarded as less of a social problem than that of other ethnic minorities, because they tend to marry at a younger age than other North American teenagers. In 1985, more than 25 percent of Latina girls aged 15 to 19 were married—usually to considerably older men (Lopez, 1987). Marriage does not, however, protect Latinas from the academic consequences of teenage pregnancy. In 1982, only 26 percent of Latina teenage mothers had completed high school, as compared with 41 percent of white and 36 percent of black teenage mothers (Cusick, 1987).

In order to avoid being victimized, young women are taught to defend themselves against disease, pregnancy, and "being used." They are also taught that the victimization of women occurs in the context of unmarried, heterosexual involvement. They are not taught about victimization due to pervasive male dominance and existing gender, class, and racial arrangements. The only protections from victimization by men offered are sexual abstinence or marriage.

Homosexuality among Teenage Girls

One alternative to sexual abstinence or marriage is sexuality with members of one's own sex. We do not yet understand what causes same-sex attraction, just as we do not understand why people are attracted to individuals of the other sex. The development of sexuality among lesbians is particularly unclear both because little attention has been paid to the issue by researchers and because many lesbians appear to identify their sexual preference relatively late in life (see Chapter 9).

Lesbians who had their initial same-sex experience in their teenage years have been found to be more open to their own sexual desires than those who did not engage in same-sex relations prior to age 20. They were more likely to define themselves as exclusively homosexual than the latter group and were more sexually active at an earlier age (Vance & Green, 1984). They also reported examining their sexual parts at an earlier age and having learned about masturbation from their friends. The majority of both groups reported that they had had some sexual involvement with men, but 62 percent of those who had done so reported that the experience was not pleasurable.

Teenage lesbians may have particular difficulty in managing their sexuality. Here is the recollection of one woman:

> When I entered adolescence I encountered even greater risk of exposure, because adolescence is a time when knowledge and following the rules of sexual interplay between boys and girls becomes increasingly important. . . . Sex role invisibility was necessary in order to avoid isolation. I achieved this invisibility in two ways. First, I wore feminine camouflage: makeup, seamed stockings, starched crinolines, and endless curlers. I took on feminine habits; I spoke in deliberate tones and flirted with the boys. This created problems for my Italian male persona, who although now underground always felt that he was in drag. I could never figure out if I wanted Lennie Nulett because he was boy or because I craved his leather jacket (Zevy, 1987, pp. 85–86).

Heterosexual adolescents can also have male personae, but may be less concerned about them because their heterosexuality protects them from identity issues. Many lesbians also report moving back and forth between same- and other-sex relationships. It is not clear whether they do so because of changes in erotic needs or because of pressures for compulsory heterosexuality in our society. The same woman wittily summarized her dilemma:

> Like all of us who grew up in the fifties and sixties, I had received the American Dream as gospel. In our minds, the fantasies were reality. One day a prince would come and take care of me, and even if I didn't want a prince, I still wanted to be taken care of. A princess is not a prince, not the kind I had seen in my storybooks and later in the movies, nor the kind my parents had in mind for me (Zevy, 1987, pp. 86–87).

Adolescent lesbians have even less opportunity than their heterosexual peers to explore their feelings of sexuality in comparison with other needs, like dependency, that have been socialized as normative for girls and women in our society.

Ironically, Fine (1988) found that the only students who had the opportunity for an in-school critical discussion of sexuality in the company of peers were those few who had organized a gay and lesbian association at their high school. Very few such individuals "come out," because of widespread prejudice against homosexuality. It has been estimated that homophobia accounts for the disproportionate number of gay and lesbian students who drop out of high school (Grayson, 1987).

The Antecedents of Sexuality

Biological Factors

The factors that influence girls' initiation into sexual behavior appear to be complex. An earlier age of menarche has been associated with earlier sexual activity among both black and white adolescents (Smith, 1989; Zelnick, Kantner, & Ford, 1981). Androgen level (as measured by pubic hair stage) and estrogen level (as estimated by menarche and level of breast development) are both positively related to girls' sexual behavior (Smith, 1989). These hormonal influences appear to act independently of each other.

Hormonal levels have been found to have a strong effect on the level of a girl's sexual interests but only weak effects on her sexual behaviors (Udry, Talbert, & Morris, 1986). Age at menarche, for example, has no relationship to the frequency with which a girl reports masturbating (Gagnon, 1983). The relationship between age at menarche and sexual intercourse may be due to dating frequency. Girls with high rates of dating have been found to be equally likely to report having intercourse, regardless of their age of menarche.

Social Factors

Findings showing a connection between early dating and early intercourse are consistent with our belief that sexual intercourse is controlled by social factors more for girls than for boys. As we noted earlier, social norms mandate that girls engage in sexual intercourse in order to fulfill the needs of their male partner rather than their own. To avoid pressures to engage in sexual activities,

African-American teenage girls who are educationally ambitious tend to seclude themselves socially, backed by strong, achievement-oriented mothers (Chilman, 1983).

Late-developing girls are more likely to become sexually active sooner after menarche than earlier developing girls (Cusick, 1987). Although both groups of girls are presumably at the same level of hormonal development at menarche, late-developing girls are in a social environment in which sexual activity has already become normative for girls of their age.

These findings illustrate the importance of peer pressures on the sexual behavior of girls. Boys' sexual behavior is proportionately more influenced by hormonal levels (Udry, Billy, Morris, Groff, & Raj, 1985), although peers' behavior plays a role in their sexual involvement as well. Perceptions about what one's peers are doing or what is normative in one's peer group are more strongly associated with adolescent sexual behavior than the peers' actual behavior (Brooks-Gunn & Furstenberg, 1989). Adolescents have, of course, no way of determining directly what their peers are really doing sexually.

Although it has been found that girls who felt closer to their parents engaged in less heterosexual physical involvement than those who felt less close to them (Westney et al., 1983), parents have much less influence than peers on an adolescent's sexual involvement. Good parent–child communication may even have different effects, depending on whether the teenager is a boy or a girl. For example, one study found that while mothers' ability to communicate with sons and daughters was associated with later intercourse, sons' discussions with their fathers were related to earlier sexuality (Kahn, Smith, & Roberts, 1984). This effect may be due to the double standard for sexuality in our society. Fathers may encourage sexual activity in their sons in response to sexual scripts endorsing masculinity and potency. In one study conducted in Cleveland, 70 percent of the fathers surveyed wanted their sons to feel that premarital sex was acceptable (Beckstein, Dahlin, & Wiley, 1986). Only 2 percent, however, had ever mentioned contraception to their sons.

Cultural Factors

Low socioeconomic status is associated with an early age of intercourse for adolescent girls (Zelnik et al., 1981). This is especially true for African-American teenagers. However, it is difficult to distinguish between the economic and cultural factors associated with such differences in sexual activity. Black and white adolescents, for example, still mostly attend racially segregated schools with their own peer cultures. School segregation is an indirect measure of low socioeconomic status among many blacks and reflects the pervasive conditions of disadvantage that characterize the neighborhoods in which they live. When social class is controlled in local studies, little variation in the sexual behavior of black and white adolescents has been found (Nettles & Scott-Jones, 1987).

The belief that low-income black women are sexually promiscuous is a racist assumption. African-American teenagers are, in fact, less likely than Anglo teenagers to have had a number of sex partners, and they report having intercourse less frequently (Chilman, 1983). A majority of adolescent mothers are white. Black adolescents have been the target of social programs because of their higher birthrate and the lower probability that they will marry because of a pregnancy.

Contraceptive Use and Sexual Activity

About half of all teenagers did not use contraception the first time they had sexual intercourse (Zelnik & Shah, 1983). Younger teenagers were much less likely to use contraception than older adolescents were. More whites than blacks reported having used birth control the first time they had intercourse, but this difference largely disappears when the age of first intercourse is controlled (Zelnik et al., 1981). Among both races, more boys than girls reported not using contraception during their first intercourse.

When contraception was used, male methods were preferred (Brooks-Gunn & Furstenberg, 1989). Those who had planned the first intercourse were much more likely to have used contraception than those who had not. However, when young adolescent girls begin having intercourse, it is generally infrequent and unpredictable. They often report the need to be "spontaneous." Societal norms that are unwilling to acknowledge the sexuality of teenage girls—and make them unwilling to acknowledge it themselves—certainly contribute to the high pregnancy rate of teenagers in the United States. Research from other developed countries shows that even young sexually active teenagers can effectively avoid pregnancy (Hayes, 1987).

A majority of adolescent boys seem to be markedly inconsistent and unconcerned about contraceptive use (Chilman, 1983). One survey of black, white, and Hispanic adolescents, ages 13 to 19, found that among the 69 percent who were sexually active, only 15 percent always used an effective form of contraception, and only 35 percent sometimes did. "Among the 72 percent who indicated that they had taken no precaution during their latest coital experience, less than 20 percent said that they believed their partner could not conceive. Their rationale more simply was that they really did not care . . ." (Philpps-Yonas, 1980, p. 410). Adolescent boys who had the most traditional attitudes about the male role have been found to be less likely to use condoms than more liberal adolescents (Pleck, Sonenstein, & Lu, 1991).

Some teenage fathers never acknowledge parenthood. In a study conducted in Baltimore, a much lower proportion of male teenagers reported they had ever impregnated a woman than female teenagers reported ever having been pregnant (Furstenberg, Brooks-Gunn, & Chase-Lansdale, 1989). Of course, part of this difference is due to the fact that at least half of all children born to teenage girls were fathered by men over the age of 20.

Factors Associated with Not Using Contraception

The most frequent reason given by sexually active teenage girls for not using contraception is, "I thought I would be lucky and not get pregnant" (Chilman, 1983). A number of researchers have found that failure by girls to use contraception effectively is associated with a feeling of lack of control over their lives that probably contributes to a fatalistic viewpoint.

This kind of attitude is only one of many factors that contribute to unreliable contraceptive techniques. It should not surprise you that being young, poor, and uneducated is associated with failure to use contraception effectively. Structural variables such as sporadic and unplanned intercourse and lack of access to a free, confidential family planning service also play a role, as do various psychological factors, including desiring a pregnancy or putting a high value on fertility (Chilman, 1987). These factors are all correlated with each other. Researchers do not know which combination, if any, causes young women to avoid effective contraception.

Cognitive factors are probably also important. For example, almost all girls report being surprised at finding themselves pregnant. What accounts for their surprise? Reasons include the belief that they could not become pregnant because of cycle phase (although the majority of adolescents cannot identify the time at which ovulation occurs); the misperception that they had not had sex often enough or had not had an orgasm or were too young; belief that they would not get "caught"; and procrastination or forgetting to use birth control (Brooks-Gunn & Furstenberg, 1989). Many of these reasons appear to indicate an unwillingness to take personal responsibility for their pregnancy.

Parental Communication and Contraceptive Use

Conservative policymakers argue that discussions about sexuality and birth control should remain within the family. Recent studies of the effect of parent–child communication on contraceptive use, however, indicate that it has little effect. Even when parents were aware that their child had visited a family planning clinic, the amount of discussion about birth control did not increase, nor did adolescents use contraception more effectively (Furstenberg, Herceg-Baron, Shea, & Webb, 1986.)

Why parental communication has so little effect on teenagers' contraceptive behavior is not yet clear. There may be several reasons (Furstenberg et al., 1986). First, it appears that most parents do not wish to get directly involved in the sexual activity of their children, and most teenagers discourage such involvement as well. Second, most parents would prefer that their teenagers postpone sexual activity but seem to be resigned to the fact that their view is not likely to be a major determinant of their child's decision. And, finally, recognizing that sexual activity is taking place, parents want to be sure that their daughters avoid pregnancy. They are relieved to discover that their teenager has received contraception. Beyond that, they are either willing or prefer to respect the adolescent's privacy.

The Role of the Media

The media have helped to make sexual activity more attractive to teenagers. For example, soap operas—a favorite form of entertainment of this age group—contain a higher incidence of implied or explicit sexual acts than any other type of television program (Hayes, 1987). In them, sex is made to seem particularly romantic and desirable when it is illicit. Contraception is almost never mentioned or referred to, and the negative consequences of an unintended pregnancy are rarely portrayed.

The advertisement of nonprescriptive contraceptives—until the age of

AIDS—was virtually banned. Thus, TV programming and advertising provided young people with lots of clues about how to be sexy, but little information about how to be sexually responsible. Even today, TV advertisements about condoms emphasize physical security rather than fertility control.

Unmarried Childbearing: An Alternative Perspective

Concern about teenage contraception reflects two demographic changes: the rising rates of sexual activity among teenagers, especially younger girls, and the falling rates of teen marriages. It is interesting that the rate of births to adolescents was higher in the mid-1950s than it was in the 1980s (Nettles & Scott-Jones, 1987) (see Figure 8.7). The major difference was that then they married and created apparently stable families. What has increased today is the birthrate of *unwed* adolescents, especially among white teenagers! More unmarried teenage mothers are white than black. However, the rate of pregnancy outside of marriage is still higher among black than among white teenagers (Furstenberg et al., 1989).

The fact that marriage rather than pregnancy is the primary impetus for societal action is illustrated from the treatment of teenage pregnancy among Latina women. The birthrate among Hispanic teenagers does not appear to be a matter of public concern. Few studies have been conducted on Latina populations, although their birthrate is higher than that of white teenagers (Lopez,

FIGURE 8.7. Birthrates in the United States of white and nonwhite teenagers. Although the rate has actually declined over the past twenty-five years, the relative share of births to teenagers as compared with adult women has increased from 12 percent in 1955 to 29 percent in 1979.
Source: From J. Brooks-Gunn and F. F. Furstenberg, Jr., "Adolescent Sexual Behavior," American Psychologist, 44, *pp. 249-257. 1986 American Psychological Association.*

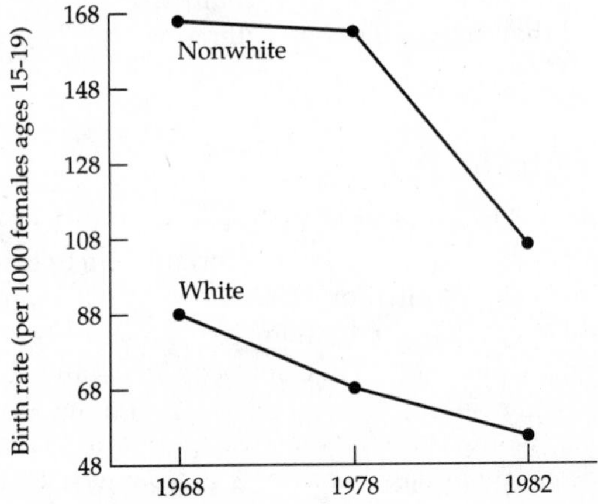

1987). As we pointed out earlier in the chapter, this is because they tend to marry at a younger age than their other American counterparts and tend to marry older men.

African-American teenagers, lacking a legacy of forced marriage, often expect to bear children before they marry (Cusick, 1987). They are likely to report an expected age at parenthood that is less than or equal to their expected marriage age (Furstenberg et al., 1986).

Cooperation between generations appears to be a norm among black women. Most teenage mothers in minority populations remain within their extended families (Field, Widmayer, Stoller, & de Cubas, 1986). The family members provide support, companionship, and role models for them. Later on, daughters provide domestic support for their mother when she is employed outside the home. Girls as young as 9 may have primary responsibility for taking care of younger siblings (Reid, 1982).

For white women, early childbearing is associated with a large number of children. Age of first child and completed family size are not related for black women. And, although adolescent mothers experience major disadvantages in terms of educational attainment and economic well-being, the differences between early and late childbearing appear to dissipate over time, especially for African Americans (Furstenberg et al., 1989). Most early childbearers manage to stage a recovery in later life.

We are not arguing that early childbearing is desirable. But you should not view it only as a consequence of personal inadequacy. Sociostructural factors that are different from those of the dominant culture must be taken into account. Among some Latino cultures, for example, the concept of adolescence as a stage between girlhood and womanhood is not accepted. "Chicano girls, in particular, argue for a close temporal relation between the generations and against the concept of adolescent development. Adolescence, they have guessed, is a construct, a notion that seems to them synonymous with a waste of ripe time" (Thompson, 1986, p. 33).

SEXUALITY IN THE AGE OF AIDS

One of the authors of this text is the mother of two young women—only a few years past their teenage years. The following is her account of the dilemma produced for concerned parents in this age of AIDS.

> As a liberal and "liberated" parent I always believed that my responsibility was to teach my daughters to engage in sexual activity because they wanted to and how to use contraception to avoid getting pregnant. As a feminist I was also committed to the use of female methods of contraception because they put control of fertility in a young woman's own hands. How, then, am I to convey concerns about communication with sexual partners in a situation where, as one writer put it: "when you have sex with one man you are having sex with all the other people he as ever slept with"?

HIV infection is growing among women largely due to infection through heterosexual contact. Although currently the number of reported cases of AIDS in adolescents is low, it is doubling every year (Brooks-Gunn, Boyer, & Hein, 1988). Moreover, a greater proportion of female adolescents than female adults are becoming infected (14 percent versus 7 percent); of minority group members than majority group members (53 percent versus 38 percent); and from heterosexual rather than homosexual transmission. Heterosexual contact accounted for 46 percent of all AIDS cases in adolescent women. The other cases were largely accounted for by intravenous drug use.

Condoms are the most effective means of preventing HIV infection during heterosexual contact. But lack of information about contraception and/or the unwillingness to use it puts minority women at particular risk. One study of 233 adolescent Latinas experiencing their first birth found that 20 percent did not know that condoms were an effective means of birth control (Mays & Cochran, 1988). In another study of ninety-eight sexually active African-American women college students, only 50 percent used birth control on a regular basis. Seventeen percent had never used condoms, and 48 percent only rarely. Less than one-fourth insisted on using condoms as a means of reducing their risks for sexually transmitted diseases like AIDS, despite the fact that they knew about condom effectiveness.

Why are these young women unwilling to protect themselves? Condom use is resisted by many men. Fine (1988) notes that adolescent black women are aware of the way institutional racism and the economy have adversely affected black men and often view self-protection as taking something away from them. "If I asked him to use a condom, he won't feel like a man" (p. 36).

SOCIAL CONSTRUCTIONS AND DILEMMAS INVOLVING PERSONAL CHANGE

The problem of sex education and the prevention of AIDS, while important in itself, also illustrates some of the dilemmas encountered when psychologists attempt to change people's behavior. Techniques that stress "just say no," for example, assume that people behave as autonomous individuals who are influenced only by rational beliefs. They fail to take fully into account people's emotional needs as well as their response to the needs of others around them. We are particularly unlikely to pay attention to the emotional needs of individuals with low power in our society, such as children and adolescents, women in general, and lesbians in particular.

Theories that stress personal responsibility are also particularly likely to be incorrect for people who both lack personal power and are members of groups with little collective power in our society. Adolescent women of color exemplify the kind of people who lack both personal and social power. One should be careful not to interpret their "failure" to act the way our majority society demands as the result of moral or intellectual deficiencies.

The major lesson we hope you learn from this chapter is that a person's behavior is a response to a complex mix of biological, psychological, and sociocultural forces. Adolescence is a life stage at which many such forces converge and conflict for young women. Contradictory cultural constructions of womanhood are imposed during a period when both girls and boys are negotiating for adulthood. Very few women report that they wish to return to their teenage years. Men appear to have found them more satisfactory. How would you like to be 13 again?

CONNECTING THEMES

1. Adolescence is an excellent example of the way biological sex and the many social aspects of gender interact. The difference in the life experiences of early- versus late-maturing girls shows how perceptions about a young woman's body can influence her in ways that seem largely beyond her control.
2. Adolescence involves both naming and not naming. Recent observational studies demonstrate that the relationships between boys and girls during this period may have a larger power dimension and be much more verbally abusive than researchers had previously thought. Young women may respond to the ambivalence of being a mature woman in a society that devalues women by becoming silenced.
3. Because adolescence is a socially constructed category (in distinction to puberty, which is a biological event), it is expressed quite differently by young women from different social classes and racial/ethnic groupings in our society. White middle- and upper-class girls appear to be most vulnerable to the stresses produced by normative definitions of mature femininity. For example, they are more affected by school transitions, are more likely to suffer from eating disorders, and may be more likely to be silenced by the contradictions they encounter.
4. Societal responses to teenage sexuality and pregnancy are also social constructions. Because young women are not supposed to be sexual, they are denied the opportunity to protect themselves effectively from pregnancy and, more recently, from AIDS. Data from societies other than the United States demonstrate that sexual activity and pregnancy can be quite independent of each other.

SUGGESTED READINGS

BROOKS-GUNN, JEANNE, and ANNE PETERSEN (Eds.) (1983). *Girls at puberty: Biological and psychological perspectives.* New York: Plenum Press. Good selection of readings on all aspects of puberty written by some of the best-known and most productive researchers in the field.

MARTIN, EMILY (1987). *The woman in the body.* Boston: Beacon Press. An excellent introduction to the personal and cultural meaning of various aspects of the body and reproductive system as described by women in their own words.

PHOENIX, ANN (1991). *Young mothers?* Cambridge, England: Polity Press and Basil Blackwell. This book looks at both the positive and negative aspects of the experience of teenage motherhood.

CHAPTER 9

Sex, Love, and Romance

SEXUALITY: SHAPED BY CULTURE
- Sexual Scripts

PSYCHOLOGY STUDIES SEXUALITY: SOCIAL CONTEXTS OF RESEARCH
- A Brief History of Sex Research
- Sex Research: A Critical Evaluation

SEXUALITY IN SOCIAL CONTEXTS
- The Experience of Orgasm
- Masturbation
- Romantic Love
- Women's Quest for Beauty
- Learning to Be Ambivalent
- Desire and Pleasure

LESBIAN AND BISEXUAL WOMEN
- A Social History of Lesbianism
- Stereotypes of Lesbian and Bisexual Women
- Research on Bisexual Women and Lesbians
- Developing a Lesbian or Bisexual Identity

RELATIONSHIP DYNAMICS
- Heterosexual Relationships
- Lesbian Relationships
- Date Rape and Dating Violence

WHAT DO WOMEN WANT? SATISFACTION IN CLOSE RELATIONSHIPS

CONNECTING THEMES

SUGGESTED READINGS

homage to my hips

these hips are big hips.
they need space to
move around in.
they don't fit into little
petty places. these hips
are free hips.
they don't like to be held back.
these hips have never been enslaved,
they go where they want to go
they do what they want to do.
these hips are mighty hips.
these hips are magic hips.
i have known them
to put a spell on a man and
spin him like a top!

—LUCILLE CLIFTON *(1980).*

The Homely War

When another year turns over
compost in the pile
last year's feast breeding knots of juicy worms,
I do not want to be indicting
new accusations to another ex-lover
who has thrown off the scarlet cloak of desire to reveal
the same skeletal coldness, the need to control
crouching like an adding machine in his eyes,
the same damp doggy hatred of women,
the eggshell ego and the sandpaper touch,
the boyish murderer spitting mommy on his bayonet.
I am tired of finding my enemy in my bed.

—MARGE PIERCY *(1976).*

In these poems, women speak of their sexuality and relationships. Lucille Clifton expresses pleasure and delight in her sexual power. Marge Piercy compares sex to warfare. As the contrasting voices of these two poets suggest, women's sexuality is characterized by a tension between pleasure and danger (Joseph & Lewis, 1981; Vance, 1984).

SEXUALITY: SHAPED BY CULTURE

Sexuality, the most intimate aspect of the self and the most private of experiences, "is clearly shaped by a social order where issues of status, dominance and power prevail in a political way on that which is personal" (Travis, 1990). In Chapter 8, we saw that social forces were clearly operating in girls' decision making about sexual activity and contraception. In order to understand more about how women's sexuality is learned and how sexual limits are enforced in everyday beliefs and interactions, it is necessary to think of sexuality as a social construct. Each individual develops her or his own sense of sexual identity and desire in the context of a particular time in history, social class and ethnic group, religion, and prevailing set of gender roles (Foucalt, 1978; Rubin, 1984).

As we noted in Chapter 6, human sexuality is not understandable in purely biological terms. Sexual behavior, like food-related behavior, is based on human biological potential and depends on particular body parts, both internal and external. But understanding the hunger drive and the eating-related body parts explains little about the complex and varied rules by which different cultures regulate what counts as food and nonfood, who is entitled to eat what, methods of preparing food, and the etiquette of eating.

> The belly's hunger gives no clues as to the complexities of cuisine. The body, the brain, the genitalia, and the capacity for language are all necessary for human sexuality. But they do not determine its content, its experiences, or its institutional forms. Moreover, we never encounter the body unmediated by the meanings that cultures give to it (Rubin, 1984, pp. 276–277).

Sexual Scripts

Each individual has a biological capacity for sexual arousal and physiological limits to the sexual response. But, rather than being "naturally" sexual, people learn rules that tell them how to have sex, with whom they may have it, what activities will be pleasurable, and when the individual is—and is not—allowed to take advantage of the biological potential for sexual enjoyment (Gagnon & Simon, 1973; Radlove, 1983). Together, the repertoire of sexual acts that is recognized by a particular social group, the rules or guidelines for expected behavior, and the expected punishments for violating the rules form the basis of sexual scripts (Laws & Schwartz, 1977).

The sexual scripts women (and men) learn can be thought of as schemas for sexual concepts and events. They represent *ways of understanding and interpreting* potentially sex-relevant situations and *plans for action* that people bring to such situations. Scripts operate at both a social and a personal level. They are part of cultural institutions (for example, sexual behaviors are regulated by law and religion), and they are also internalized by individuals (some behaviors come to be seen as exciting and others as disgusting). Table 9.1 shows a familiar script: the first date. Throughout this chapter, the psychology of women's sexuality and intimate relationships will be considered in terms of both biological potentials and the influences of society's sexual scripts.

PSYCHOLOGY STUDIES SEXUALITY: SOCIAL CONTEXTS OF RESEARCH

For most of human history, people learned about their own and others' sexual behavior only through religious teachings and family regulation. Starting about 100 years ago, sex came to be seen as an acceptable topic for scientific study. For better or worse, educated people in Western societies can now compare their own sexual behavior with what the "experts" say is normal (see Figure 9.1). Science has changed society even more profoundly by developing effective methods of contraception. For the first time in human history, sexual intercourse can be separated from reproduction. The rise of the mass media has also had important effects. People in much of the world now learn about sex from books, television, magazines, and films, as well as from the more traditional sources. With these social changes, it is not surprising that sexual attitudes and behaviors have changed markedly in the past century.

A Brief History of Sex Research

Nineteenth-century research on sexuality was conducted mainly by physicians, who frequently reported case studies of people with sexual problems or "pathologies." Some of these pioneer researchers were social reformers who wanted to make society more tolerant of sexual variation; others were judgmental, condemning "deviant" sexual practices. By the early twentieth century, anthropologists like Margaret Mead began to study sexual behavior in other cultures. Evidence of the enormous cross-cultural variability in sexual norms and practices helped create an understanding that there is no single way of being sexual that is "natural" for human beings.

TABLE 9.1. Characteristics of a Potential Partner: First-Date Scripts Based on Actions Mentioned by 25 Percent or More of Participants—Per Script[a]

First-Date Scripts Courtship and dating are scripted activities. People know what to expect in dating situations because they have been exposed to many examples of standard practices and norms.

What should one expect to do and feel on a first date? When asked to list the typical behaviors they expected from a woman and a man, college students emphasized concerns about appearance, conversation, and controlling sexuality for the female script, and control of planning, paying for, and organizing the date for the male script. The behaviors listed in this table were mentioned by 25 percent or more of those asked.

SCRIPT	
A Woman's First Date	A Man's First Date
Tell friends and family.	Ask for a date.
Groom and dress.[b]	Decide what to do.
Be nervous.	*Groom and dress.*
Worry about or change appearance.	*Be nervous.*
Check appearance.	*Worry about or change appearance.*
Wait for date.	Prepare car, apartment.
Welcome date to home.	Check money.
Introduce parents or roommates.	Go to date's house.
Leave.	Meet parents or roommates.
Confirm plans.	*Leave.*
Get to know date.	Open car door.
Compliment date.	*Confirm plans.*
Joke, laugh, and talk.	*Get to know date.*
Try to impress date.	*Compliment date.*
Go to movies, show, or party.	*Joke, laugh, and talk.*
Eat.	*Try to impress date.*
Go home.	*Go to movies, show, or party.*
Tell date she had a good time.	*Eat.*
Kiss goodnight.	Pay.
	Be polite.
	Initiate physical contact.
	Take date home.
	Tell date he had a good time.
	Ask for another date.
	Tell date will be in touch.
	Kiss goodnight.
	Go home.

[a] N = 58 women, 39 men.

[b] Italics indicate the action was mentioned for both scripts.

Source: Rose and Frieze, "Young Singles' Script for a First Date," *Gender and Society*, 3, 258–268.

Another important method of studying sexual behavior has been the survey. The first survey of women's sexual behavior was done in the Victorian era of the late 1800s by an American physician, Dr. Clelia Mosher. The forty-seven

Copyright 1987 by Nicole Hollander.

FIGURE 9.1. What it takes to be average.

women Mosher sampled (her patients and other women she knew) were educated and upper middle class. She asked them about their experiences of orgasm (seventy-two percent of the women were orgasmic) and their use of birth control (sixty-four percent used some form). She also asked them about marital conflict over sexual issues such as the length of time required to reach orgasm. Mosher's survey is often overlooked in histories of sex research. Although the sample was small and nonrepresentative, hers is the only sex survey of Victorian women known to exist, and it shows that although the Victorian norms for women's sexual behavior were very restrictive, at least some women did experience satisfying sex lives (Jacob, 1981, cited in Hyde, 1990).

When Alfred Kinsey and his colleagues conducted surveys of male and female sexual behavior (Kinsey, Pomeroy, & Martin, 1948; Kinsey, Pomeroy, Martin, & Gebhard, 1953), sex became a matter for public discussion. "Whether bought, read, debated, or attacked, the Kinsey reports stimulated a nationwide examination of America's sexual habits and values" (D'Emilio & Freedman,

1988, p. 285). Kinsey (a zoologist whose previous research was on insect behavior) even appeared on the cover of *Time* magazine.

Although Kinsey's books were written in a dry academic style, they created a furor because his findings were in conflict with traditional moral values:

> The study of the male revealed that masturbation and heterosexual petting were nearly universal, that almost 90 percent had engaged in premarital intercourse and half in extramarital sex, and that over a third of adult males had had homosexual experiences. . . . More than three-fifths [of American women] had engaged in masturbation, 90 percent had participated in petting, half in premarital intercourse, and a quarter in extramarital relations. Taken together, Kinsey's statistics pointed to a vast hidden world of sexual experience sharply at odds with publicly espoused norms (D'Emilio & Freedman, 1988, p. 286).

Kinsey also found that masturbation was the most reliable method for obtaining an orgasm in women (perhaps partly because sexual intercourse was reported to have an average duration of less than two minutes), and that some women experienced multiple orgasms. This last result was widely disbelieved and ridiculed.

Religious leaders disapproved of Kinsey's research—one book, *I Accuse Kinsey*, even claimed that the results must be fraudulent because no decent American woman would take part in such a survey. However, the majority of the public approved of scientific research on sexuality, and other surveys followed.

Kinsey's studies used large (though not random) samples of the American population—5,300 males and 5,940 females. His samples were all white, disproportionately young, and well educated. Other surveys share this problem. Clearly, questionnaires published in magazines like *Psychology Today* and *Redbook* and answered by their readers do not provide information about the population in general, even if the number of respondents is large. Obtaining representative samples in sex research is a problem that has no simple solution.

By the 1960s researchers had added another method for gaining information about sexuality: direct observation. In the 1950s, William Masters, a physician, began laboratory research on the physiology of sexual arousal. His first participants were heterosexual female and homosexual male prostitutes. Masters devised ways of measuring physiological changes during sexual activity—using instruments to measure heart rate, muscular contractions, vaginal lubrication and acidity—and a laboratory procedure for observing sexual behavior. With Virginia Johnson, he continued the research, using medical and graduate students, his own former patients, and women and men of all ages, both single and married, who volunteered because they needed to earn money or wanted to contribute to medical research (Masters & Johnson, 1966). A later study (Masters & Johnson, 1979) used similar procedures with gay men and lesbians as volunteers. In both studies, the participants were mostly white and well educated. And, of course, people who would feel uncomfortable about having sex under observation in a laboratory were not studied. Masters and Johnson, however, did not consider the representativeness of the sample important, because they believed that the basic physiology of sexual behavior is similar in all human beings (Hyde, 1990).

Sex Research: A Critical Evaluation

Sex surveys and observational research provide two different kinds of information about sexuality. Surveys describe normative or typical practices, while direct observation yields descriptions of individual physiological responses to sexual stimulation. Both kinds of knowledge can be useful, but both have their drawbacks.

With surveys, it is difficult to obtain representative samples, and participants may misremember or distort their accounts. There is also a danger that people who read the results of surveys will interpret their own behavior in terms of the supposedly normal behavior reported by others. It is important to remember that no survey is ideologically neutral; the questions asked and the people chosen as respondents can bias toward a particular social construction of sexuality. Kinsey, for example, used a biological-drive model. He thought of sexuality as an instinctual urge demanding satisfaction and maintained that rape and child sexual abuse were the result of denying men the sexual release they needed (Jackson, 1987). Feminists, of course, have developed different explanations of these occurrences, often in terms of power (see Chapter 14).

In laboratory studies using direct observation, sex is conceptualized as a set of biological responses to stimulation. But desire and arousal are not simply or directly reducible to blood pressure changes and muscle contractions. An emphasis on biology to the exclusion of subjective experience and social context may imply that biology is (and should be) the primary determinant of social arrangements.

Perhaps the biological approach to sexuality has prevailed because of sexology's need to present itself as an objective, rational science despite its not-too-respectable subject matter. From this viewpoint, laboratory research has come to dominate the field, not because it is necessarily the best way to understand human sexuality but because connecting sexology to the more prestigious biological sciences helps to bring it legitimacy (Tiefer, 1991).

Ideally, sex research should use participants' subjective experiences and perceptions, as well as more "objective" measures, to understand sexual activity in social and cultural contexts (see Figure 9.2). Leonore Tiefer, a feminist psychologist and sexologist, has articulated a vision for the future:

> Feminist research on sexuality would begin by adopting a collaborative stance, using participants' subjective perceptions to enrich objective measurements, and planning research to benefit the participants as well as the researchers. Research would be contextualized to as great a degree as possible, since no understanding of sexuality can emerge from any study that ignores the social, demographic, and cultural features of participants' lives. . . . The assumption would be that we are studying *sexualities*, and looking for ways that all women are alike would play no part (Tiefer, 1988, p. 24).

SEXUALITY IN SOCIAL CONTEXTS

The Experience of Orgasm

Describing orgasm (and other aspects of sexual response) in terms of frequency or physiology hardly gives a complete picture. The subjective, emotional re-

© Martha F. Campbell.

FIGURE 9.2. A subjective measure of sex?

sponse is equally important. Women who do not have a great deal of sexual experience are sometimes unsure about whether they have had an orgasm because they do not know how it is supposed to feel. Men, with their visible erections and obvious ejaculatory response at orgasm, need have no doubt when the event occurs.

One way to get an idea of the subjective experience of orgasm is to ask women to describe their own behaviors and sensations. Shere Hite (1976) collected lengthy surveys from more than 3,000 women. Although this is a large sample, it represents only about three percent of the questionnaires she distributed, and there is no way to know how accurately the women who chose to respond represent all women. The major strength of Hite's work is that she used open-ended questions. Many of her respondents wrote lengthy, detailed answers that give a picture of the experience of sexuality, at least for the individual writers. A few sample descriptions of orgasm are given in Box. 9.1.

Is the experience of orgasm different for women and men? Asking this question would seem to require comparisons of apples and oranges! However, research suggests that the experiences are similar. In a study in which college students were asked to write descriptions of their orgasms, judges (psychologists and physicians) could not reliably distinguish women's and men's descriptions (Vance & Wagner, 1976). In another study, students chose adjectives from a list to describe their experiences of orgasm (Wiest, 1977). Again, there were no significant differences in responses by women and men. These similar-

Box 9.1 Women's Accounts of Orgasms

"There are a few faint sparks, coming up to orgasm, and then I suddenly realize that it is going to catch fire, and then I concentrate all my energies, both physical and mental, to quickly bring on the climax—which turns out to be a moment suspended in time, a hot rush—a sudden breathtaking dousing of all the nerves of my body in Pleasure—I try to make the moment last—disappointment when it doesn't."

"Before, I feel a tremendous surge of tension and a kind of delicious feeling I can't describe. Then orgasm is like the excitement and stimulation I have been feeling, increased, for an *instant*, a hundred-fold."

"It starts down deep, somewhere in the 'core,' gets bigger, stronger, better, and more beautiful, until I'm just four square inches of ecstatic crotch area!!"

"The physical sensation is beautifully excruciating. It begins in the clitoris, and also surges into my whole vaginal area."

"It's a peak of almost, almost, ALMOST, ALMOSTTTT. The only way I can describe it is to say it is like riding the 'Tilt-a-Whirl.'"

"Just before orgasm, the area around my clitoris suddenly comes alive and, I can't think of any better description, seems to sparkle and send bright dancing sensations all around. Then it becomes focused like a point of intense light. Like a bright blip on a radar screen, and that's the orgasm."

"There is an almost frantic itch-pain-pleasure in my vagina and clitoral area that seems almost insatiable, it is also extremely hot and I lose control of everything, then there is an explosion of unbelievable warmth and relief to the itch-pain-pleasure! It is really indescribable and what I've just written doesn't explain it at all!!! WORDS!"

Source: Hite, *The Hite Report*, pp. 149–150, 1976 Macmillan.

ities fit well with Masters and Johnson's (1966) emphasis on male–female similarities in the physical sexual response cycle.

Masturbation

Stimulating one's own genitals is a very common sexual practice (Hyde, 1990). Although traditionally masturbation was thought to cause everything from dark circles under the eyes to insanity, the majority of young people today believe that it is neither harmful nor wrong (Hunt, 1974). Women usually masturbate by stimulating the clitoris, either by hand or with a vibrator. Other methods include pressing the clitoral area against a pillow or using a stream of water while in the bath or shower. Most women who masturbate engage in sexual fantasies while doing so (Hunt, 1974; Hite, 1976). Hite's survey respondents described both their techniques and their fantasies (see Box. 9.2).

There is a persistent sex difference in masturbation experience. Kinsey's survey showed that virtually all males, but only about 60 percent of females, reported having masturbated to orgasm. Not only were women less likely to have masturbated, but also those who did began at a later age than the men. A recent meta-analysis has confirmed that this difference persists. Curiously, women do not report more negative attitudes toward masturbation, but they are definitely less likely to do it (Oliver & Hyde, 1993).

Women's relative lack of experience with self-pleasuring has effects on other aspects of sexuality. For example, Kinsey et al. (1953) found that women who had masturbated to orgasm before marriage were more likely to enjoy or-

Box 9.2 Women's Accounts of Masturbation

"To masturbate, I almost always need to be turned on by something like pornographic literature (and believe me it's hard to find anything even halfway decent). I lie in bed, on my back, slide out of my panties or pajama bottoms because I like to be free to move. I rub my two middle fingers up and down and around the clitoral area. Sometimes I put two fingers of my other hand into my vagina. I rub for a few seconds and tense up my body. I can usually feel a definite fuzzy feeling when I know the orgasm is coming on and then I rub harder, mostly up and down. My legs are apart. The vaginal area is usually moistened as a result of my pornographic reading, otherwise I use spit or, very rarely, cold cream. I usually arch my back slightly when I am really turned on, at which point I take the fingers of my other hand out of my vagina and I push down on the uterine area just above the pubis."

"I lie down and begin to fantasize in my mind my favorite fantasy, which is a party where everyone is nude and engaging in group sex, lovely, lovely sex, all positions, kissing, caressing, cunnilingus, and intercourse. After about five minutes of this I am ready, very lubricated. I lift one knee slightly and move my leg to one side, put my middle finger on or around the clitoris and gently massage in a circular motion. Then I dream of being invited to this party and all those delicious things are happening to me. I try to hold out as long as possible, but in just a minute or two I have an orgasm. It is very simple, all in the mind. After the first orgasm I do not fantasize any longer, but concentrate entirely on the delicious feeling in my vagina and surrounding areas, continuing the same movement of my finger, but slightly faster and in about one minute I have another orgasm. I am very quiet, but do moan some during each orgasm. After several orgasms in this manner I start thinking of what's for dinner and the party is over."

"I don't masturbate like anybody else I ever heard of. I make a clump in the bedding about the size of a fist (I used to use the head of my poor teddy bear, but since I became too old to sleep with a teddy bear, a wad of the sheets has to suffice) and then lie on my stomach on top of it so that it exerts pressure on my clitoris. I then move my hips in a circular motion until I climax—very simple. It works with legs apart or together—either one, although when I am in a particularly frenzied state, together sometimes feels better. I usually end up sort of with my weight on my knees and elbows, so I can't do too much else with my hands."

Source: Hite, *The Hite Report*, pp. 89, 98–99, 113–114, 1976 Macmillan.

gasm during intercourse in the first years of marriage than those who had not. In a recent study of married women aged 18–30, those who had experienced orgasm through masturbation had more orgasms with their partners, greater sexual desire, more rapid arousal, higher self-esteem, and greater marital satisfaction than women who had never masturbated (Hurlbert & Whittaker, 1991).

Masturbating can be an important way for a woman to learn about her own pattern of sexual arousal and satisfaction. Through practice, she can learn what fantasies are most arousing, what kinds and amounts of stimulation are most enjoyable, and what to expect from her body. For these reasons, sex therapists frequently use a program of masturbation education (and "homework") for women who are unable to experience orgasm with a partner (LoPiccolo & Stock, 1986). If a woman has learned to know and love her own body and her own sexual impulses, she is better prepared to help her partner learn about her. Equally important, feminist writers have encouraged women to use masturbation as a route to erotic skill and sexual independence (Dodson, 1987). The woman who can enjoy solo orgasms is not dependent on a partner for sexual pleasure and can enjoy sexual satisfaction without risk of pregnancy.

Romantic Love

Love as a Cultural Script

In virtually every drugstore, supermarket, and shopping mall bookstore in America a rack of romance novels is prominently displayed. Each of their covers features a woman (always young, always white, always beautiful) gazing rapturously up into the eyes of a tall, strong, handsome man. Their titles and their plots tell women that "Love Is Everything."

Romance novels are read by more than 22 million American women. They account for 25 percent of all paperback sales in the United States, forming a $250 million industry each year, with 120 new titles published every month. Many readers subscribe to their favorite series (Harlequin, Candlelight Ecstasy, Second Chance at Love) by mail so that they can be sure to get every new volume (Brown, 1989).

No one would claim that these novels are great literature. They follow a predictable formula: "Woman meets (perfect) stranger, thinks he's a rogue but wants him anyway, runs into conflicts that keep them apart, and ends up happily in his arms forever" (Brown, 1989, p. 13). But their enduring popularity and appeal suggest that many women still believe (or want to believe) that love conquers all.

In romance novels, the heroine attracts the hero without planning or plotting on her part. In fact, she often fights her attraction, which she experiences as overwhelming, both physically and emotionally—her knees go weak, her head spins, her heart pounds, and her pulse quickens. The hero is often cold, insensitive, and rejecting, but by the end of the novel the reader learns that his coldness has merely been a cover for his love. The independent, rebellious heroine is swept away and finally acquiesces to the power of love and desire.

Why do so many women enjoy these fantasies? They provide an escape from humdrum reality and a time when hardworking wives and mothers can treat themselves to solitude and leisure. They also provide a reassuring fable of women transforming men. Although the hero is initially cold, patronizing, sometimes even brutal, he actually loves the heroine, and it is the power of her love that transforms him into a sensitive, passionate, and caring lover. In reading the romance, women may learn to interpret the insensitivity of their own boyfriends and lovers as "evidence" that underneath the gruff exterior is a manly heart of gold, and thus to make the limitations of their (un) romantic relationships more bearable (Radway, 1984).

Some feminist scholars believe that by escaping into romances women are encouraged to learn to tolerate oppressive aspects of gender relations. However, other feminists point out that one should not blame the novels or their readers:

> An understanding of Harlequin romances should lead one to condemn not the novels but the conditions which have made them necessary. Even though the novels can be said to intensify female tensions and conflicts, on balance the contradictions in women's lives are more responsible for the existence of Harlequins than Harlequins are for the contradictions (Modleski, 1980, p. 448).

Romance novels are one of the many ways that women learn the cultural script that love defines and redeems a woman's existence. From earliest child-

Copyright 1987 by Nicole Hollander.

FIGURE 9.3. Not what she bargained for.

hood, girls are encouraged to identify with heroines who are rescued by a handsome prince from poverty and the cruelty of other women ("Cinderella"), who are awakened from the coma of nonbeing by the love of a good man ("Sleeping Beauty"), or who transform an extremely unpromising prospect into a handsome prince through their unselfish devotion ("Beauty and the Beast"). As teenagers, they may read *Cosmopolitan*, where articles tell them to buy a St. Bernard in order to attract the attention of that handsome man who walks his dog in front of their apartment building or to choose a city in which to live on the basis of its "prospects"—meaning marriageable men, not careers. College students' sexual ideas stem largely from mass consumer culture: movies, popular music, advertising, TV; Dr. Ruth and sex manuals; *Playboy, Penthouse, Playgirl*, etc.; and Harlequin romances (Moffat, 1989).

Moreover, romantic love is seen as sufficient reason for sexual activity. Regardless of race, religion, socioeconomic class, and urban or rural background, teenagers believe that love makes sexual activity more permissible. One study showed that although only 3 percent approved of a teenage girl having sex with a stranger, and 10 percent with a date, 41 percent approved if the girl was "in love"—and about two-thirds of the teens interviewed said they had been "in love" at some time, including 52 percent of 13-year-old girls (Coles, 1985).

The Experience of Love

Given that the ideology of romance is directed largely at women, it might be expected that women are more romantic in their beliefs about relationships than men. The opposite seems to be true (see Figure 9.3). Studies (reviewed by Peplau and Gordon, 1985) show that, at least among the young, predominantly white college students studied by most researchers, men are more likely to believe that true love comes only once, lasts forever, and overcomes obstacles such as race or religious differences. They are more likely to believe in love at first sight and to be "game players," enjoying flirtation and pursuit. Consistent with their beliefs, men report falling in love earlier in a new relationship. They also feel more depressed, lonely, and unhappy after a breakup, and are less likely to initiate the breakup than their female partners.

Women, on the other hand, report more emotional symptoms of falling in love—feeling giddy and carefree, "floating on a cloud," and being unable to concentrate. And once a relationship has moved beyond its first stages, they may become more emotionally involved in it than their male partners.

The reasons for these differences in the experience of romantic love are unclear (Peplau & Gordon, 1985). Men may fall in love more readily because they rely more on physical attractiveness to decide whom to love—a characteristic that is easy to ascertain at the start of a relationship. They may also react more quickly because the cultural script says that men should initiate a dating relationship. Women traditionally may have been more pragmatic because, in choosing a mate, they were choosing a provider as well as a romantic partner. Yet they may be more "emotional" because cultural norms allow them to admit to having feelings. Gender-related differences in the experience of romantic love are not large, and there is a great deal of overlap in the beliefs and self-reported behaviors of the two sexes. But the differences are interesting because they do not always fit stereotypical expectations. Perhaps future researchers will examine them in more detail.

Intercultural Differences: The Diversity of Love

Because almost all psychological research on romantic beliefs and behavior has relied on white heterosexual college students, the experiences of other groups of people can be described only sketchily. There is much more to learn.

Western (European) ideals of love are not shared by all cultures. Do people from Asian cultures experience love in the same way as people from Anglo-European backgrounds? Recent research suggests that there are some differences. Canadian college students of Chinese and other Asian backgrounds held a more friendship- and companionship-based view of love than students from European backgrounds, perhaps because their cultures stress the interdependence of all group members. However, the gender-related differences observed in white U.S. students held in this ethnically diverse Canadian group: Women were more oriented toward friendship, more pragmatic, and less likely to view love as a game (Dion & Dion, 1993). Both gender and cultural factors must be considered in understanding the psychology of love.

Religion and social class separate cultural groups even within the United States. Like their white peers, African-American girls learn different lessons about sex and love, depending on their social class and religion. They may be brought up in strict homes, receiving explicit warnings from their mothers about men and sex, or in quite permissive ones where sexual activity is regarded as good, pleasurable, and expected (Joseph & Lewis, 1981). Some writers have suggested that black women may be less likely than their white counterparts to believe in romantic love as a woman's reason for living and more likely to maintain strong feelings of autonomy and independence.

Like black women, Latinas in the United States are a diverse group with respect to social class. In addition, their families come from many different countries, including Cuba, Puerto Rico, Guatemala, and Mexico. Despite this diversity, there are some commonalities affecting romantic and sexual attitudes and behaviors (Espin, 1986). Because of historical influences and the Catholic religion, virginity is an important concept. In Hispanic cultures, the honor of a family depends on the sexual purity of its women. The Virgin Mary is presented as an important model for young women. Traditionally, an unmarried woman who had "lost" her virginity was automatically perceived as promiscuous and evaluated very negatively. Hispanic women who immigrate to the United States soon encounter the idea that all American women are sexually free; to become "Americanized" is to become sexually promiscuous.

The traditional Hispanic ideal for men is one of *machismo*—men are expected to show their manhood by being strong, demonstrating sexual prowess, and asserting their authority and control over women. Women's complementary role of *marianismo* (named after the Virgin Mary) is to be not only sexually pure and controlled but submissive and subservient. Of course, not all Latino men endorse the values of machismo, and when they do it may be at least partly in response to the oppression they themselves suffer from white society. And Latinas do have some sources of power, especially in their roles as mothers and among other women. Nevertheless, the cultural imperatives of virginity, martyrdom, and subordination continue to exert influence over the experience of love for Hispanic women (Espin, 1986).

Women's Quest for Beauty

Attractiveness and Sexual Desirability

In earlier chapters, we discussed how physical attractiveness is important in triggering stereotypical thinking and affecting attributions about others. Attractiveness is an important factor in relationships as well. Good looks are more important to men than to women in evaluating a potential date, and especially important in a prospective sexual partner (Nevid, 1984) (see Table 9.2). The male emphasis on looks starts early in adolescence. In a study of 11- to 15-year olds in Iceland and the United States, boys and girls ranked ten characteristics of their "perfect woman" or "perfect man." Both Icelandic and American girls ranked kindness and honesty as most important, while boys from both countries ranked good looks highest (Stiles, Gibbons, Hardardottir, & Schnellman, 1987). Similar results have been found in a great many other research studies using a variety of methods.

The relative importance of attractiveness for women and men is shown in the personal ads that people use to meet new partners. In a 1970s study, women more often mentioned their physical attractiveness in their ads, while men's ads advertised their financial resources. Women who described themselves as attractive in their ads more often mentioned looking for financial security in a mate, and men who described themselves as well-off more often mentioned looking for an attractive mate—the researchers titled their study "Let's make a deal" (Harrison & Saeed, 1977)! Men's emphasis on looks had not changed much during the 1980s, when Kay Deaux and Randel Hanna (1984) analyzed 800 personal ads for same- and other-sex romantic partners. Men were more concerned with physical characteristics, while women were more interested in psychological factors.

Beauty may represent a kind of power for women (Unger, 1979a). As the personal ads suggest, women may be able to barter their looks for financial security or other material resources. A study of dating on a southern U.S. campus found that attractive women are perceived by both women and men as deserv-

TABLE 9.2. Top Ten Relationship Characteristics According to Males and Females

When college students were asked to rate physical, personal, and background characteristics they considered important in a sexual relationship, males emphasized their partners' physical characteristics, and females emphasized personal qualities. However, when rating characteristics they considered important in a long-term, "meaningful" relationship, both men and women emphasized personal qualities more than looks.

Ratings were on a five-point scale. Numbers represent mean ratings by 238 males and 307 females.

Males, $\overline{X}$		Females, $\overline{X}$	
Sexual relationship		Sexual relationship	
Build/figure	4.53	Attractiveness	4.51
Sexuality	4.36	Sexuality	4.46
Attractiveness	4.31	Warmth	4.42
Facial features	4.25	Personality	4.41
Buttocks	4.09	Tenderness	4.39
Weight	4.07	Gentleness	4.36
Legs	4.02	Sensitivity	4.24
Breath	3.94	Kindness	4.23
Skin	3.92	Build/figure	4.22
Chest/breasts	3.79	Character	4.20
Meaningful relationship		Meaningful relationship	
Honesty	4.68	Honesty	4.89
Personality	4.65	Fidelity	4.83
Fidelity	4.60	Personality	4.82
Sensitivity	4.51	Warmth	4.80
Warmth	4.49	Kindness	4.79
Kindness	4.47	Tenderness	4.77
Character	4.41	Sensitivity	4.75
Tenderness	4.36	Gentleness	4.73
Patience	4.34	Character	4.70
Gentleness	4.31	Patience	4.56

Source: Nevid, "Sex differences in factors of romantic attractions," *Sex Roles, 11,* 401–411. 1984 Plenum Publishing Corporation. Reprinted with permission.

ing better treatment by their romantic partners. Usually, partners are fairly evenly matched on attractiveness. The less attractive the woman is compared with the man, the more likely she is to give him her loyalty and affection without his doing anything to "earn" it. Conversely, the more attractive she is in comparison to his attractiveness or social prestige, the more he must compensate by efforts to treat her well. When a man treats a woman well, "her attractiveness is validated and she gains prestige in her social group" (Holland & Skinner, 1987, p. 89).

Attractive women raise the prestige of men. Men are evaluated more highly when they are presented as the boyfriends of attractive rather than unattractive women. Curiously, men paired with attractive women are not necessarily seen as more physically attractive—instead, they are seen as "better" people. People seem to infer that these men must have something going for them in order to win such an attractive "prize."

This was seen most clearly in a study in which college students were asked to evaluate characteristics of women and men from their photographs (Bar-Tal & Saxe, 1976). Some students, told that the photos were of married couples, evaluated them in pairs. Others evaluated them as individuals. Evaluations of the women did not change under these two conditions. However, ratings of the men were affected by the attractiveness of the woman with whom they were paired. Unattractive men married to attractive women were seen as having the highest income, the most prestigious occupation, and the most professional stature. Apparently, since women's beauty is such a valued commodity, people assume that an unattractive man who manages to marry a good-looking woman must have something else to offer her.

Learning to Care about Looks

Girls and women cannot escape the cultural message that a woman's worth is to be judged by her appearance. In terms of gender-schema theory (discussed in Chapter 2), attractiveness becomes a central dimension of the schema for femininity and sexual desirability, and girls become motivated to strive toward beauty.

Learning to care about looks is a lifelong process. As discussed in earlier chapters, parents of newborns see their daughters as cuter, prettier, softer, and more delicate than their sons, and treat their babies accordingly. Currently, elasticized pink ruffled headbands are the height of fashion for bald female infants. Many girls have their ears pierced and wear nail polish before they enter kindergarten. They listen to stories of princesses whose beauty drives men to slay dragons; they play with Barbie dolls and watch Miss America pageants. Throughout elementary school, girls receive more compliments on their appearance than boys do. Their wardrobes are bigger and more elaborate, and girls are especially noticed and admired when they wear dresses (Freedman, 1986). Images of females in popular magazines also contribute to girls' learned obsession with appearance. Photographs of women and girls are usually subjected to computer retouching, leaving readers with the impression that such flawlessness is real and attainable. Photographs of males, however, tend to show their stubble, scars, and facial lines (Tannen, 1994).

Makeup sets are sold for girls as young as 3, advertised as "the fun way to learn beauty secrets." They include rollers, styling combs, curling irons, hairpieces, and dye for the hair; paint, gloss, shadow, and mascara for the face; and lotions, polish, and decals for the hands and nails (Freedman, 1986). Recently, a "workout kit" (jumprope, leotard, exercise mat) was nationally advertised "for girls ages 5 and up," not as a means of developing coordination, fitness, or athletic skill but as a way to "work off that extra chocolate chip cookie." From toys like these, girls learn that feminine beauty requires many faces, that they should impersonate grown-up women by disguising themselves, and that parents approve of spending much time and money on appearance (see Figure 9.4). Perhaps most important, each girl learns that her own face and body are inadequate and need to be improved (Freedman, 1986).

Coupled with the attention given to girls' ornamentation and "improve-

FIGURE 9.4. Little girls learn to disguise their looks with makeup in order to be "glamorous."

ment" of face and body is a relative silence about the normal physical aspects of being a girl or woman. Nearly three-quarters of the African-American and white women participating in one community study reported that they had wanted more sex education when they were growing up (Wyatt & Riedele, 1994). Parents mislabel sexually important parts of the body or simply give them no names at all—especially for girls. Mothers are more reluctant to name the sexual parts of their daughters' anatomy than their sons' and do it at a later age. Few girls know they have a clitoris or that it is a separate organ from the vagina; many confuse the urinary opening with the vagina, thus associating sexuality with the taboos and shame surrounding elimination. In contrast, the more visible and more readily named organs of boys are a source of pride. Boys learn to personify their penises with names like *peter* or *dick,* to ascribe power and strength with names like *cock* and *tool,* or to make everyday comparisons (testicles are *nuts, balls,* or, in Spanish, *eggs*). Girls learn to talk about their genitals, if at all, with terms such as *down there, privates, between your legs, nasty,* or *bottom.* In sum, "Boys learn to perceive their genitals as a source of pride and pleasure, girls mainly develop a sense of shame, disgust and humiliation about theirs" (Ussher, 1989, p. 19). It is not surprising that after years of societal attention to their looks and shamed silence about their sexual embodiment, many young women are far more prepared to *look sexy* than to *be sexual.*

Impossible Standards of Weight

As you learned in Chapter 4, women in Western cultures are bombarded with images of "ideal women." Women are also exposed to far more media messages about staying slim and keeping in shape than men are. A content analysis of forty-eight issues each of women's and men's magazines found sixty-three ads for diet foods in the women's magazines—and only one in the men's. At the same time, women were receiving many more messages about eating—the women's magazines contained 359 ads for sweets and snacks, while the men's magazines contained exactly one. Overall, there were 1,179 food ads in women's magazines and 10 in men's magazines. The message for women, then, is that they should stay slim while at the same time thinking constantly about food (Silverstein, Perdue, Peterson, & Kelly, 1986). Women are expected to nurture others, but not themselves, by preparing and serving food.

Girls and women learn that no matter how hard they try, they can never measure up. The definition of what is beautiful has gotten more restrictive over the past few decades. For example, the ideal body shape has (literally) narrowed. An analysis of measurements of Miss America contestants and *Playboy* centerfold models showed that they became steadily thinner after 1960 (Garner, Garfinkel, Schwartz, & Thompson, 1980). The curvaceousness of movie actresses and models in women's magazines has been declining since about 1950 (Silverstein et al., 1986), until many models look as though they are starving. Advertisers call this the "waif look." Even Barbie is thinner now than when the doll was introduced in 1959 (Freedman, 1986).

Negative messages about women's bodies can cause psychological distress, low self-esteem, and an alienation from one's physical and sexual self. Research (reviewed by Jackson, Sullivan, & Rostker, 1988) shows that women evaluate their bodies less favorably, express more dissatisfaction with their bodies (particularly their weight), and perceive a greater discrepancy between their own body image and their ideal than men do.

Many adolescent girls and women develop distorted perceptions of their bodies. They may believe themselves to be wider or fatter than they really are, exaggerating descriptions of their "huge" thighs, breasts, or stomachs. Increasingly, cosmetic surgery is sold as an acceptable response to normal aging and variation in body shapes (see Figure 9.5).

People who evaluate their bodies less favorably have lower self-esteem than those who view their bodies more positively (Jackson et al., 1988). For women, especially, low self-esteem may be tied to body image. Being overweight, for example, affects the self-attitudes of women more than men (Stake & Lauer, 1987). One woman with a history of being overweight wrote about her adolescent sexual development:

> I felt imprisoned by my body, somewhere between childhood and adulthood, living mostly in a fantasy about how life could be if only my body were improved. Little experience, much fantasy—fantasy about being attractive, looked at, sought after and admired (Munter, 1984, p. 226).

The fantasy this woman describes is one of self-realization through the perfection of the body. "If only I were thin, or if only my body were different in whatever way, then everything would be fine" (Munter, 1984, p. 227).

There is only one other time in this century (the 1920s) when standards of thinness were as extreme as they are now; during that decade, an epidemic of eating disorders appeared among women (Silverstein, Peterson, & Perdue, 1986). Is history repeating itself? Eating disorders among women will be discussed further in Chapter 15.

Minority Women and White Standards of Beauty

In a working-class, predominantly black neighborhood in Philadelphia, a large billboard pictures three glamorous African-American women. All are very light-skinned, thin, and young, with dainty noses and soft-looking hair. The words underneath the picture are "Philadelphia's Faded Beauties"; the billboard advertises skin bleach.

From fairy-tale princesses to movie stars, the idealized image of feminine

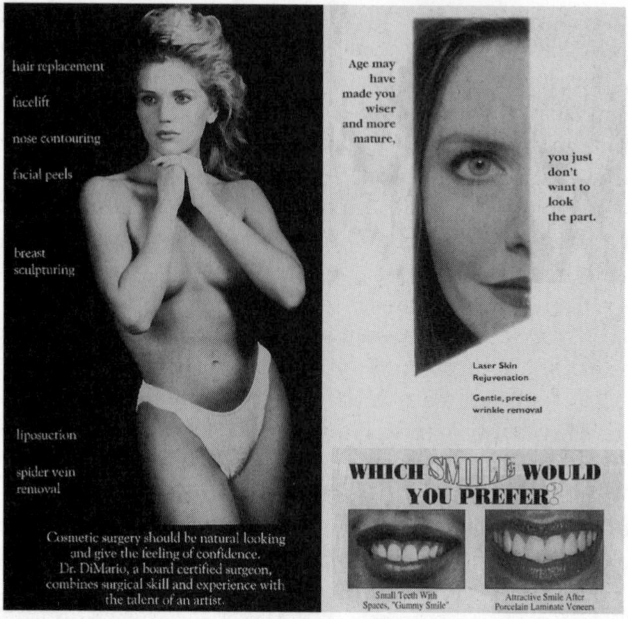

FIGURE 9.5. Media messages: The ideal woman is made, not born, with a little help from the surgeon's scalpel.

beauty in Western societies has traditionally been a Caucasian one. Women of color bear a greater burden than their white counterparts as looks-ism combines with sexism and racism to stigmatize them as unattractive. Black women, even more than white women, describe feeling ugly. In the 1960s, the message that "black is beautiful" began to influence the African-American community, and the white beauty image was displaced by Afro, corn row, and dreadlock hairstyles, along with African-influenced jewelry and clothing. Yet despite these changes, women of color describe being rejected because of their dark skin or curly hair. In one recent study, 70 percent of black women believed that black men prefer very light-skinned women (Bond & Cash, 1992). For some African Americans, marrying a lighter-skinned partner is still a mark of status—a legacy of adapting to a racist culture (Freedman, 1986).

On the other hand, the ideal of waif-like slimness seems to be applied more to white women. Within the African-American community, heavier women are not necessarily considered unattractive, and a wider range of body shape and size is accepted. This ethnic-related difference may be related to social class as well. In one study, African-American women of higher social status valued thinness as much as white women, while those of lower social status perceived a heavier body size as attractive. They did not judge themselves "overweight" unless they were much heavier than the weight that would have triggered such a judgment in the other groups of women (Allan, Mayo, & Michel, 1993). Cultural norms may help protect at least some African-American women from excessive dieting and eating disorders (see Chapter 15).

African Americans are not the only women of color judged by white standards. As North-American movies, television programs, magazines, and commercial beauty products are increasingly marketed throughout the world, the North-American beauty ideal is becoming an international one, part of a "global culture machine," where each woman is encouraged to aim to be "whiter, more Western, more upper-class." Women factory workers in Malaysia are provided with makeup classes by their employers, and Asian women undergo eyelid surgery to Westernize their eyes (Chapkis, 1986, pp. 37–38).

There is virtually no systematic psychological research on the effects of inappropriate standards of beauty on women of color. At present the effects may only be hypothesized. Oliva Espin, in discussing sources of oppression common to Hispanic and other women of color, suggests that "the inability of most non-white women to achieve prescribed standards of beauty may be devastating for self-esteem" (Espin, 1986, p. 276). In the absence of psychological research, perhaps the best way to understand the oppression of appearances (and how that oppression is internalized by people of color) is to attend to descriptions and analyses by members of the oppressed groups. In Maxine Hong Kingston's book *Tripmaster Monkey*, Asian-American characters discuss eyelid surgery. The African-American novelist Toni Morrison has provided a moving example of a black girl who prays daily for blue eyes and blond hair in her tragic novel *The Bluest Eye*. In his film *School Daze*, Spike Lee analyzes the effects of blacks' internalized racism on young black women's relationships with each other and with black men.

Disability, Attractiveness, and Sexuality

Despite the presence of some 36 million people with disabilities in American society, such people tend to be socially invisible. Moreover, studies have rarely considered gender as a factor in the experience of disability. Michelle Fine and Adrienne Asch (1981, 1988), among the first researchers to consider these issues, concluded that women with disabilities experience "sexism without the pedestal."

Disabled girls and women, like nondisabled women, are judged by their attractiveness. Additionally, they are judged against an ideal of the physically perfect person who is free from weakness, pain, and physical limitations. Women who are "less than perfect" may be seen as not entitled to be sexual (Galler, 1984). In a recent study of attitudes about the sexuality of disabled and nondisabled women, Australian college students expressed much more negative attitudes about the disabled women's sexuality, and men were more negative than women (Chandani et al., 1989).

Among the stereotypes women with disabilities confront are beliefs that sexual activity is "not appropriate" for them; that people with disabilities need caretakers, not lovers; that they cannot cope with sexual relationships; that they are all heterosexual and should feel grateful if they find any man who wants them; and that they are too fragile to have a sex life. When people around them express these stereotypical beliefs, it is difficult for women with disabilities to see themselves as potential sexual and romantic partners. Many are concerned that they will not find loving relationships or will be forced into restrictive roles (Corbett, 1987). Indeed, disabled women are less likely to be married than disabled men, and ongoing relationships frequently end with the onset of the disability (Fine & Asch, 1988).

Parental attitudes and expectations for daughters with disabilities can have important effects on daughters' sexual development. In a study of forty-three women with physical and sensory disabilities (including cerebral palsy and spinal cord injury), many of the parents had low expectations of heterosexual involvement for their daughters because they saw them as unable to fulfill the typical role of wife and mother. Some of these daughters became sexually active partly out of rebellion and a desire to prove their parents wrong, while others remained sexually and socially isolated. In contrast, other parents saw their daughters as normal young women, with the disability only one of many unique characteristics. These young women became socially and sexually active as a matter of normal growing up. One interviewee reported:

> In childhood, I was led to believe that the same social performance was expected of me as of my cousins who had no disabilities. I was a social success in part because my mother expected me to succeed. In fact, she gave me no choice (Rousso, 1988, p. 156).

Learning to Be Ambivalent

The Sexist Language of Sex

A negative evaluation of female sexuality is deeply embedded in language. An analysis of terms for "prostitute" found more than 200 in English novels (Stanley, 1977). Linguists agree that languages develop an abundance of terms for concepts that are of particular interest or importance to a society. The fact that English has many terms describing women in specifically sexual ways, and that most of these are negative, leaves women in the position of being defined in terms of a sexuality that is considered ugly and distasteful (Adams & Ware, 1989).

Absences in language are also revealing. For men, *virile* and *potent* connote positive masculine sexuality, as do other, more colloquial terms such as *stud, macho man,* and *hunk.* However, there is no English word for a sexually active woman that is not negative in connotation. Words such as *nympho, whore, tramp,* and *slut,* when applied to women who are sexually assertive or choose many partners, function as a means of social control.

Slang words for sexual intercourse (hump, bang, nail, lay) suggest that it is something violent and mechanical done to women rather than an equal and reciprocal act. The same verb can even be used to describe harm and sex—as in "she got screwed." It is not difficult to see how women might become ambivalent about sexual pleasure when the very language of sex suggests that the female role is synonymous with being exploited, cheated, or harmed.

Michael Moffat, an anthropologist who studied college students in their "natural habitat" (the dorm), reported that about one-third of the young men he studied talked of women, among themselves, as "chicks, broads, and sluts." Their "locker-room style" was characterized by "its vulgar Anglo-Saxon vocabulary, by its focus on the starkest physicalities of sex itself, stripped of any stereotypically feminine sensibilities such as romance, and by its objectifying, often predatory attitudes toward women" (Moffat, 1989, p. 183).

The Whorfian hypothesis, discussed in Chapter 1, asserts that language reinforces, as well as reflects, social reality. Talking in negative ways about women and women's part in sexual acts probably encourages both women and men to view women and their sexuality in these ways. By making it hard to imagine alternatives, sexist language also inhibits social change.

The Double Standard: Studs and Sluts

Traditionally, a double standard of sexual behavior was widely endorsed: Women were severely sanctioned for any sexual activity outside of heterosexual marriage, while for men such activity was expected and tolerated. Boys had to "sow their wild oats," while girls were warned that a future husband "won't buy the cow if he can get the milk for free." Because sexual activity before marriage was viewed as wrong for women, its incidence varied greatly by sex. For example, a 1959 study (cited in DeLamater & MacCorquodale, 1979) found that 59 percent of men and only 14 percent of women had engaged in premarital intercourse. Moreover, men were most likely to have sex with casual acquaintances, and women with men they expected to marry.

For women, the double standard was often connected with a madonna/whore dichotomy. Women were either "the pure, virginal, 'good' woman on her pedestal, unspoiled by sex or sin" or "her counterpart, the whore . . . consumed by desires of the flesh . . . dangerous and inherently bad" (Ussher, 1989, p. 14). A woman could not belong to both categories, and women who sought out or enjoyed sex were relegated to the "bad." Oliva Espin describes this dichotomy in Latin culture:

> To enjoy sexual pleasure, even in marriage, may indicate lack of virtue. To shun sexual pleasure and to regard sexual behavior exclusively as an unwelcome obligation toward her husband and a necessary evil in order to have children may be seen as a manifestation of virtue. In fact, some women even express pride at their own lack of sexual pleasure or desire (1986, p. 279).

By the 1970s, sex researchers announced the death of the double standard (Coles, 1985). Teenagers, college students, and young adults had come to hold virtually the same sexual standard for men and women. Young people judged it equally acceptable for a girl or for a boy to engage in sex if they were going with each other (24 percent), in love (46 percent), or planning marriage (61 percent). While sex with affection was the new norm, a substantial minority of young adults thought that casual sex without affection was also acceptable (DeLamater & MacCorquodale, 1979).

However, the death announcement for the double standard was premature. Although today people are about equally accepting of sexual activity for females and males generally, subtler measures of attitudes toward women, men, and sexuality suggest that a modified double standard still exists.

The modified double standard can be seen in attitudes about having sex with many partners. As one 16-year-old woman put it, "Guys can go around and screw a lot of girls, and they look macho, but when a girl does it, she looks like a slut" (Coles, 1985, p. 168). In Moffat's study of college students, over half the women and about half the men believed that women and men should follow different moralities. They thought of sex as a bargain, a game, or a battle, between (aggressive) men and (reluctant) women. Women and men agreed that women came in two types: "good women" and "sluts." (There were no corresponding categories for men.) Moffat summed up the men's attitudes:

> I am a man and I need sex. Most women want it more than they admit. Men have the right to experiment sexually for a few years. There are a lot of female sluts out there with whom to so experiment. And once I have gotten this out of my system, I will then look for a good woman for a long term relationship (or for a wife) (Moffat, 1989, p. 204).

In a recent study, simply asking students to judge the sexual behavior of a woman versus that of a man produced little evidence of a double standard. However, when given more information about the type of relationship (monogamous or multiple partners) and amount of sexual activity, evidence of a double standard emerged. Highly sexually active men were seen as more attractive than other men, suggesting that the "stud" is a valued type. Highly sexually active women, on the other hand, were less attractive than other women, suggesting that "too much" sexual behavior in a woman lowers her desirability (Breay & Gentry, 1990). Shere Hite's surveys of college students reveal similar sentiments among men (see Box 9.3).

Attitudes toward extramarital sex among married people also reflect a bias toward a double standard. Research (reviewed by Margolin, 1989) shows that men have more opportunities for sexual infidelity than their wives, are more likely to take advantage of the opportunities, feel more justified in doing so, and show less guilt and remorse. When college students were asked to read scenarios involving extramarital involvement, men were more tolerant of infidelity in male than in female characters (Margolin, 1989).

All in all, the new sexual freedom for women seems to have rather definite limits. Rather than being a gender-neutral freedom, it is freedom with a male bias (Moffat, 1989). It is easy to see how a modern double standard may create ambivalence in women. On the one hand, sex is good and everyone is entitled to sexual pleasure. On the other hand, "too much" interest or experience in sex earns the label "slut."

Desire and Pleasure

Romantic Ideals and Women's Experience of Their Sexuality

Young women, especially those of the dominant white culture, are exposed to many messages that tell them "love is everything to a woman." At the same time, they learn that finding fulfillment and self in the love of a man is outside their control. In the romantic script, it is always the man who actively initiates and pursues; the woman passively offers token resistance but finally gives in to his desire.

These beliefs inform the sexual scripts of contemporary young adults. College students stereotype men as using interpersonal strategies in dating situations to *have* sex and women as strategizing to *avoid* sex. Moreover, when asked their own strategies, they reported that they behaved according to stereotype: Men said they tried to influence their dates to have sex and women said they tried to control their "turned on" dates (LaPlante, McCormick, & Brannigan, 1980). This finding is consistent with other research on dating couples and marital partners, showing that men are more likely to initiate sex. People are especially vulnerable in sexual encounters; the woman who wants to initiate sex and the man who wants to say

Box 9.3 College Men Vote on the Double Standard

Between 1983 and 1987, more than 2,500 college men were asked the following series of questions by sex researcher Shere Hite, with the following responses:

1. Do you believe the double standard is fair? *No, according to 92 percent of men.*
2. If you met a woman you liked and wanted to date, but then found out she had had sex with ten to twenty men during the preceding year, would you still like her and take her seriously? *Most men were quite doubtful they could take her seriously; only 35 percent could.*
3. If one of your best male friends had sex with ten to twenty women in one year, would you stop taking him seriously and see it as a character flaw? *Definitely not—according to 95 percent of the men.*
4. Isn't this a double standard? And to equalize it, what should be done? Do you believe (a) men should stop being so "promiscuous" or (b) women should have as much sex as men do, with no negative feedback?

Most men found this a very difficult choice, but could see the logic of the question; the majority, approximately two-thirds, voted for (b), preferring giving women "equal rights" to changing their own view regarding sex. But many men also commented that of course the woman they would marry would probably not be one of those women who had chosen to have sex with that many men!

Source: From *Women and Love: A Cultural Revolution in Progress* by Shere Hite.

"no" may fear being rejected as future dates and labeled as deviants. It feels more comfortable and secure to follow familiar patterns.

When the woman in a dating situation wants to respond positively to a man's sexual initiative, she may still feel that she ought to offer token resistance to his advances. In a questionnaire study of more than 600 undergraduate women, 39 percent had engaged in token resistance at least once. Given societal scripts for female passivity and sexual limit-setting, token resistance may be an adaptive behavior on the part of the women. If resistance is expected, the woman who does not follow the script risks being seen as promiscuous. Resistance may enhance her desirability (Muehlenhard & McCoy, 1991). On the other hand, saying "no" when they really mean "yes" may have serious negative consequences for women. It discourages honest communication and perpetuates restrictive gender stereotypes. Most important, it may teach men to disregard women's refusals. If men learn from experience that "no" is often only a prelude to "yes," they may become more aggressive with dates. Token resistance may provide a context of ambiguity that encourages date and acquaintance rape (Muehlenhard & Hollabough, 1988). Of course, some men are sexually aggressive despite a woman's clear, unambiguous "No" (see Chapter 14).

Romantic scripts also encourage people to think of lovemaking as something that "just happens." However, although sex may seem "perfectly natural," it is not naturally perfect (Tevlin & Leiblum, 1983). Women who take responsibility for their own pleasure and who take an active role in sex are much more likely to experience pleasure than those who are passive. Satisfying sex depends on communication, learning, and initiative on the part of both partners.

Women are encouraged to view sex in rosy, romantic terms, focusing on candlelight dinners, courtship, and soft caresses, rather than to incorporate images of genital sex into their fantasies. Since many men do not require a romantic context for arousal, they may initiate intercourse with little romantic prologue. Romance novels portray men as the "experts" who make "their" women come alive sexually. But men are likely to be expert only in the techniques and behaviors that bring *them* pleasure. Though men could benefit from learning about women's desires, sexual scripts can impede their development. Women who have not learned to acknowledge their own arousal and who do not feel entitled to initiate or direct sex are not in a good position to teach their male partners how to give them pleasure.

North American culture is more ambivalent and restrictive about women's sexuality than some European cultures, and this may affect the ways American young women experience their first sexual encounter. In a study of more than 400 American and Swedish college women, the Americans expressed significantly more negative reactions to their first experience of sexual intercourse (Schwartz, 1993). Little research has been done on discrepancies between romantic expectations and actual sexual encounters or how women may reconcile them in their own minds. The gap between the ideal and the real is highlighted in the following two accounts. The first is from a Harlequin romance novel. The second is from a sexual autobiography written by a college sophomore, reproduced here exactly as she wrote it.

> For a long timeless moment Roddy gazed down at the sleeping figure, watching the soft play of moonlight on her features. The expression on his own face was unreadable as he slipped the towelling robe from his shoulders, letting it fall unheeded to the floor. Gently he pulled back the blankets and lay down beside the motionless girl. She turned in her sleep, one hand flung out towards him. Tenderly he stroked a dark strand of hair from her face, then pulled her into his arms. . . . Still half drugged from brandy and sleep, she found herself stroking his hair. "Such a perfect dream," she murmured, her eyes already beginning to close again.
>
> "No dream, my lady," and Roddy's mouth found hers, silencing her words. Tenderly he slipped the ribbon straps of her nightdress over her shoulders, and her body arched up towards him as his fingers traced a burning path across her breast. A groan vibrated deep in her throat as he threw her nightdress to the floor. Then his body was pressed along hers and she gasped at the feeling of skin on naked skin, the soft hair on his chest raising her sensitivity to such a pitch she felt she couldn't bear it any longer . . . his hands played across her skin, turning her into a creature of pure feeling. It all seemed so real, so right, as though all those other memories of the cold contempt in his eyes and his voice were in reality the bad dreams.
>
> Driven now only by pure instinct, she moved against him, raining kisses down on his hair-roughened skin, tracing her fingers down the hard strength of his muscled chest. His breathing became ever more ragged, his hands slipping under her to pull her closer still, and she gave a tiny cry of surrender as he finally claimed her body, her fingers digging his shoulders as they moved together in frenzied rhythm. A vast well seemed to surge up within her, and as the room exploded into fragmented light she heard a voice crying "I love you"—but never knew which one of them had spoken.
>
> Afterwards they lay in silence . . . she felt herself slipping back into sleep, secure in the knowledge that his arms were holding her close (Elliot, 1989, pp. 116–118).

> I don't think I will ever forget the night that I did lose my virginity. It was this

past September (September 7th to be exact). My boyfriend and I had been going out for six months. I met him at a party late that night, but, by the time I had gotten there, he was extremely drunk. We came back to my room because my roommate was not going to be there. We always slept together without making love so, it wasn't like we had those intentions on that night. Well, my boyfriend was very drunk and very amorous to say the least. Once we got into bed, I knew exactly what he had in mind, he was all hands and lips. I figured that we might as well have sex. . . . So, I made the decision to let him do whatever he wanted.

For the actual act of sex itself, I hated it the first time. Not only was it painful but, it made a mess on my comforter. I hated my boyfriend at that time. I actually kicked him out of my room and sent him home. I was upset for a lot of reasons: My boyfriend was too drunk to remember the night so, I had made the wrong decision in letting him do whatever he wanted; there had been no feelings involved; I hadn't enjoyed it in the slightest; my comforter had to be washed at three o'clock in the morning; I had lost my virginity and betrayed my parents. I was upset for just a couple of days.

After that first night, the sex between my boyfriend and myself has been great (Moffat, 1989, pp. 191–192).

Sexual Scripts and Sexual Dysfunction

Because our society does not give women the same permission to be fully sexual that it gives men, women may learn to repress sexual desire and need (Radlove, 1983). A meta-analysis of studies of self-reported sexual attitudes and behavior showed that women express somewhat more anxiety, fear, and guilt about sex than men, and are less accepting of casual and extramarital sex (Oliver & Hyde, 1993). However, the women and men did not report any overall difference in sexual satisfaction. Most of the participants in these studies were college-age students. Other research suggests that adult women in heterosexual relationships experience less pleasure in sexual activity than their partners. Survey data show that more than 50 percent of women are dissatisfied with some aspect of their sexual lives (Morokoff, 1990). Many women have orgasms only rarely during heterosexual intercourse, because they do not get the sexual stimulation they need (Radlove, 1983). In a study of couples, 35 percent of the women (and only 16 percent of the men) reported difficulty in experiencing sexual desire. Moreover, 47 percent of the wives (and 12 percent of husbands) said they had trouble relaxing during sex (Frank, Anderson, & Rubenstein, 1978).

Acceptance of traditional sexual scripts is implicated in women's sexual dysfunction and suppression of desire. One scripted message is that the "good" woman experiences no desire of her own. However, sexual pleasure and orgasm require an awareness of one's own needs plus a feeling that one is entitled to express those needs and have them met. Women's recognition of themselves as sexual beings is blocked in many ways, related to the cultural influences described earlier in this chapter. Women are more likely to feel guilty and ashamed about their bodies ("I look too fat in this position"; "I shouldn't ask my partner for oral sex or to touch my 'dirty' genitals"; "I don't smell good"). They may feel guilty about having needs and fear their partners' disapproval if they express their needs ("I shouldn't be taking so long to climax"; "He'll get angry if I suggest a new position") (Tevlin & Leiblum, 1983, p. 134). Guilt, fear, and shame inhibit and even extinguish sexual arousal.

Another script is that women are sexually passive, men sexually aggressive. As noted earlier, adolescents and college students believe that males almost always want to have sex and females almost always want to avoid it. The effect of accepting this script is that sexual behaviors may proceed on "his," not "her," timetable, and the woman's pleasure is reduced. Because both sexes believe that it is "natural" for the man to initiate a sexual encounter and take the lead throughout, it is he who decides what activities the couple will (and will not) try, the duration of intercourse, and the sequence of events. With such little control, it is unlikely that the woman will have her needs met. If the man prefers only brief "foreplay," the couple may proceed to penile penetration before the woman is aroused, making intercourse painful and unpleasant for her. (The term "foreplay" itself implies that penis-in-vagina is the main event, with hugging, kissing, talking, genital touching, and all other sexual activities merely a prologue.) Women typically need more stimulation to have an orgasm than men do. If intercourse seems to be over almost before it has begun, the woman who has accepted a passive role may be reluctant to ask for more stimulation. Repeatedly engaging in sex when one is not aroused and not satisfied may lead to clinical sexual problems (Tevlin & Leiblum, 1983).

That passivity is a learned script rather than a "natural" mode for women is shown by comparing the behavior of the same women with both female and male partners. When bisexual women were with a male partner, they were much less active and initiating than when they were with a female partner (Masters & Johnson, 1979). Women who take an active, autonomous, and assertive part in sexual expression are more likely to be orgasmic (and multiorgasmic) (Radlove, 1983).

Another aspect of sexual scripts is the idea that women should be oriented primarily toward their partner's pleasure. Among best-selling sex manuals, some have advocated that women should fake orgasm in order to gratify their male partners. *The Sensual Woman*, purportedly written anonymously by a woman, "instructs the reader in great detail how to fake an orgasm convincingly" and states that no woman would refuse to make love to a man she cares about just because she doesn't feel like it (cited in Altman, 1984). Some sex manuals instruct women to "act like prostitutes" or perform specific acts (such as strip routines or oral sex) in order to arouse and please their partners. Faking arousal, pleasure, and orgasm may become so ingrained that the woman may not be able to distinguish between her own sexual desire and her desire to please, and her sex life may come to feel like a part she is acting rather than an expression of herself (Morokoff, 1990).

Sexual Scripts and Women's Health

Because traditional sexual scripts focus on male pleasure and male control, women often may be unable to assert a claim to safety during sexual activity. The consequence is an increased risk of sexually transmitted diseases and unwanted pregnancy.

As noted in Chapter 8, the number of women being infected with AIDS is rising rapidly. In parts of Africa, as many women as men carry the virus. In the United States, the most common means of transmission for women is intravenous drug use, but the second most common and the fastest growing is sexual intercourse with infected men. Black and Hispanic women who have sex with men are at greater risk than white women because of the higher rates of infection among men of these groups (Hyde, 1990).

There is no completely risk-free set of sexual practices (except perhaps computer sex on the Internet!). However, there are ways to minimize the risk of AIDS and other sexually transmitted diseases. Having sex only in a stable, monogamous relationship is one. Unfortunately, the double standard gives men greater freedom to have sex with many partners and encourages less guilt about doing so. They and their partners are both exposed to health risks, and the female partners of high-risk men may have no accurate way to judge their own risk.

The next best alternative is always to use condoms for intercourse. Despite educational campaigns that urge condom use, studies show that large proportions of young heterosexuals still engage in unprotected sex, and the main reason seems to be an emotional one: "safer sex" is inconsistent with the romantic, spontaneous sex of scripted fantasies. In one study of American college students, 38 percent never used condoms, while 42 percent said they always or almost always did (Boyd & Wandersman, 1991). In a study of 162 Australian students, 39 percent never used condoms even for casual sex with new partners, although they rated this activity as high risk. The strongest factors determining both men's and women's condom use were their concern that it would destroy the romance and their fear of negative implications ("What will he/she think of me if I start talking about condoms?") (Galligan & Terry, 1993).

The Missing Discourse of Desire

As we learned in Chapter 8, American attitudes toward girls' sexuality are mixed. Many schools avoid sex education because of pressures from some parents and conservative religious groups who believe that knowledge about sexuality encourages "immoral" behavior. At best, girls are taught that they should avoid being victims—of teen pregnancy, sexually transmitted diseases, or selfish males. They also learn that "good girls just say no" to sex. But nowhere do they hear the suggestion that girls and women might like, want, need, seek out, or enjoy sexual activity (outside of heterosexual marriage). While boys are seeing educational films about wet dreams, erections, and penis size, girls see films about menstruation.

This kind of sex education does not allow young women to come to terms with their own feelings of sexuality. By emphasizing to girls the many ways that they can be victimized, it may convey the idea that women are always weak and vulnerable, undermining their self-confidence and sense of their own power (Marecek, 1986).

"In the public school arena, this construction of what is called sexuality allows girls one primary decision—to say yes or no—to a question not necessarily their own" (Fine, 1988, p. 34). This social construction of sexuality gives young women little opportunity to learn how to say "no" at whatever stage of sexual activity suits them, and no chance to learn when they would rather say "yes." And it leaves no room for them to become initiators of sexual activity. By assuming that girls and women are not active agents in their own sexuality, sex education contributes to muting women's desires:

> The naming of desire, pleasure, or sexual entitlement, particularly for females, barely exists in the formal agenda of public schooling on sexuality. When spo-

> ken, it is tagged with reminders of "consequences"—emotional, physical, moral, reproductive, and/or financial. . . . A genuine discourse of desire would invite adolescents to explore what feels good and bad, desirable and undesirable, grounded in experiences, needs, and limits (Fine, 1988, p. 33).

Fine found resistance to this silencing among some black and Puerto Rican girls, whose discourses on sexuality defy easy classification. They often combine a sense of danger and desire. As one of them explained to Fine:

> Boys always be trying to get into my panties. . . . I don't be needin' a man who won't give me no pleasure but takes my money and expect me to take care of him (Fine, 1988, p. 35).

Women's sexual agency and desire also have been relatively invisible in "sex ed" materials for adults. The sex manuals of the first half of this century constructed a model of sexuality that "purported to be objective and scientific but in fact reflected and promoted the interests of men in a sexually divided society" (Jackson, 1987, p. 52). Female sexuality was defined as passive or even as nonexistent outside the actions of men. Thus, women were characterized as slow to become aroused, needing to be "given" orgasms, and capable of being sexually awakened only by the skill of their husbands in the security of marriage. Musical metaphors abounded, with women characterized as harps or violins that the male master musician could cause to give forth beautiful melodies. The sex manuals of the 1960s and 1970s sexual revolution urged women to be sexually free, but still on others' terms. After analyzing their contents, one feminist researcher asked, "Clearly, the new liberated woman is 'sensuous' and sexy—but is she sexual, on her own behalf?" (Altman, 1984, p. 123).

Even in feminist theorizing, it is hard to find positive accounts of erotic experiences. A large proportion of feminist writing about sexuality has come from a radical perspective that views men (and heterosexuality) as oppressive. These writers explore sexual domination by focusing on graphic depictions of sexual violence against women and making connections among forms of violence from pornography to rape. At the extreme, heterosexual intercourse is seen as inherently coercive, the prototype of male domination (Dworkin, 1987). This approach implies that women who experience heterosexual desire and pleasure are suffering a kind of false consciousness (Joseph & Lewis, 1981).

In the midst of the pressures to experience sex on others' terms, it is well to remember that in spite of social pressures from all sides, some women, some of the time, do manage to have good sex! Where can the missing discourse of women's sexual desire, action, and pleasure be found? Women's accounts of their sexual experiences, relationships, adventures, and fantasies offer possibilities (Friday, 1973; Hite, 1976, 1987; Vida, 1978). New guides to women's bodily health and sexual functioning such as *Our Bodies, Ourselves* have been written by women. Works of fiction and poetry by women, such as the Lucille Clifton poem that began this chapter, explore their naming and claiming of desire. Powerful and playful voices emerge from women's music. Ida Cox, a star blues singer of the 1920s, recorded Porter Grainger's "One Hour Mama" at the age of 43 (Box 9.4). These lyrics represented a woman's statement of sexual independence and assertiveness. Unfortunately, the record was never released (we wonder why!) and has only recently been rediscovered. Ida Cox's recording can now be heard on *Mean Mothers: Independent Women's Blues* (Rosetta Records).

Box 9.4 One Hour Mama

I've always heard that haste makes waste,
So I believe in takin my time.
The highest mountain can't be raced,
It's something you must slowly climb.

I want a slow and easy man;
He needn't ever take the lead,
Cause I work on that long time plan
And I ain't alookin for no speed.

I'm a one hour mama, so no one minute papa
Ain't the kind of man for me.
Set your alarm clock papa, one hour that's
proper, Then love me like I like to be.

I don't want no lame excuses,
Bout my lovin being so good,
That you couldn't wait no longer
Now I hope I'm understood.

I'm a one hour mama, so no one minute papa
Ain't the kind of man for me.

I can't stand no greenhorn lover
Like a rookie goin to war
With a load of big artillery
But don't know what it's for
He's got to bring me reference
With a great long pedigree
And must prove he's got endurance
Or he don't mean snap to me.

I can't stand no crowing rooster
What just likes a hit or two.
Action is the only booster
Of just what my man can do.

I don't want no imitation.
My requirements ain't no joke
Cause I got pure indignation
For a guy what's lost his stroke.

I'm a one hour mama, so no one minute papa
Ain't the kind of man for me.
Set your alarm clock papa, one hour that's proper,
Then love me like I like to be.
I may want love for one hour
Then decide to make it two,
Takes an hour fore I get started
Maybe three fore I'm through.

I'm a one hour mama, so no one minute papa
Ain't the kind of man for me!

—VANCE, 1984, pp. 415–416.

Source: From Porter Grainger, "One Hour Mama." In C. Vance (ed.) *Pleasure and $109.81 Danger: Exploring Female Sexuality.*

Researchers can also explore how women act on their own sexual choices within gender constraints—for example, how they use "feminine" flirting behaviors to choose a partner (McCormick & Jones, 1989). Such records of women's experiences remind us that the terms of sexual attraction and erotic arousal are not merely programmed into us. Often, they may even be contradictory to the cultural stereotypes that surround us. Future research on female (and male) sexuality needs to develop ways of understanding how, "in spite of the patriarchal contours separating and opposing men and women, women do still desire and even celebrate sexual pleasure with men, and men still can renounce some of the . . . oppressive sexual practices which the sexual power divisions of our society produce and encourage in them" (Joseph & Lewis, 1981, pp. 238–239).

LESBIAN AND BISEXUAL WOMEN

A Social History of Lesbianism

The term *homosexual* was coined in the mid-nineteenth century. Although the term was applied to both women and men, it was defined as the inability to have a "normal" erection—a notable example of androcentrism in scientific thinking (Money, 1987)!

Throughout the nineteenth century, many women in North American society had intense friendships, in which they spent weeks at each others' homes, slept in the same beds, and wrote passionate and tender letters to each other describing the joys of perfect loving harmony and the agonies of parting. These relationships sometimes were part of a lifelong commitment. Yet no one labeled these women homosexuals or lesbians (Faderman, 1981; Smith-Rosenberg, 1975). Of course, we have no way of knowing how many of these relationships involved genital sex. They certainly involved romance, attachment, and intimacy.

By the early twentieth century, lesbianism came to be seen as a serious form of pathology. The lesbian was "sick" with a grave "disease." The change in attitude may have come about because women were beginning to demand political and social equality with men. The first wave of feminists were campaigning for women's education and the vote, and more women were entering the work force. When women's friendships and attachments to other women had the possibility of leading to real alternatives to heterosexual marriage and dependence on men, they were stigmatized and controlled. Feminists in particular were likely to be diagnosed as suffering from the newly invented disease of lesbianism (Kitzinger, 1987). One writer (cited in D'Emilio & Freedman, 1988) claimed that "The driving force in many agitators and militant women who are always after their rights is often an unsatisfied sex impulse, with a homosexual aim" (p. 193).

The medical and psychiatric establishment continued to evaluate lesbianism as pathological until the second wave of feminism in the late 1960s. Responding to pressure from women's liberation and gay liberation activists, the American Psychiatric Association conceded that there is no evidence that homosexuality in itself is a disorder and removed this "sexual deviation" from its official manual of psychiatric diagnoses in 1973. Overnight, millions of people who had had a psychiatric disorder became normal—a compelling example of the power of social institutions to construct—and reconstruct—reality.

Contemporary definitions of *lesbianism* reflect the political and social complexities of the category. Some definitions focus on lesbianism as a refusal to accept male dominance:

> Lesbian is a label invented by the Man to throw at any woman who dares to be his equal, who dares to challenge his prerogatives . . . , who dares to assert the primacy of her own needs (Radicalesbians, 1969, cited in Kitzinger, 1987, p. 43).

> A Lesbian is the rage of all women condensed to the point of explosion (Radicalesbians, 1973, cited in Golden, 1987).

Others focus on behaviors showing intimacy and attachment:

> . . . a woman who loves women, who chooses women to nurture and support and to create a living environment in which to work creatively and independently, whether or not her relations with these women are sexual (Cook, quoted in Golden, 1987, p. 20).

Still others emphasize the individual's self-definition, as well as her behavior:

> . . . a woman who has sexual and erotic-emotional ties primarily with women or who sees herself as centrally involved with a community of self-identified lesbians whose sexual and erotic-emotional ties are primarily with women and who is herself a self-identified lesbian (Ferguson, quoted in Golden, 1987, p. 21).

The poet and essayist Adrienne Rich has proposed that lesbianism should be thought of as a continuum rather than a category. Sexual relationships are only one point on the continuum, which encompasses "women's passion for women," as well as "women's choice of women as allies, life companions, and community" (Rich, 1980, p. 232).

Definitions of *bisexuality* are equally complex. A bisexual woman is capable of emotional and sexual attachment to both women and men. However, traditionally some researchers and clinicians have maintained that there is no such thing as a "true" bisexual, implying that they are just confused or indecisive and will eventually decide to be either gay or straight.

Bisexuals may feel that they fit in with neither gay nor straight culture. They may have been accused by the gay community of wanting to avoid the stigma of the homosexual label and of using cross-sex relationships to hide from their own homosexuality (Blumstein & Schwartz, 1993; Rust, 1993). The heterosexual community devalues both bisexual and lesbian women: "Heterosexist society defines bisexuals based on their lesbianism. They are not 50 percent oppressed" (Shuster, 1987, p. 59).

Bisexual women seem to resist easy labeling:

> [They] make individual, contextual decisions to love and make love with women and men in their lives. They make complex choices within and across different periods of their lives. By definition, bisexuals defy categorization. Some of them, sometimes, are contemporaneous bisexuals in intimate relationships with both a woman and a man. Some of them, sometimes, are sequential bisexuals in a series of relationships with people of both genders. Others are in-

definitely monogamous or sexually involved with a series of people of one gender; they define themselves as bisexuals on a theoretical basis. There is no bisexual prototype; that is the center of both their significance and their challenge (Shuster, 1987, p. 57).

Stereotypes of Lesbian and Bisexual Women

Women who are sexually and emotionally oriented toward other women form a largely invisible minority and have been described as a "subculture in hiding" (Lewis, 1979). Invisibility allows stereotypes to flourish. One stereotype is that all lesbians are "butch" or mannish in appearance. Many people believe that they can "spot" a lesbian by dress or appearance. However, most lesbians look just like other women. The "butch" stereotype is probably related to the belief, common among heterosexuals, that lesbians are women who want to be men. This belief confuses gender identity and affectional orientation. The affectional orientation of lesbians is toward other women, but their gender identity, like the gender identity of heterosexual women, is usually unambiguously female. The lesbian "is quite definitely a woman and typically has no desire to be a man" (Hyde, 1990, p. 420).

Although the medical and psychiatric professions now officially regard lesbianism and bisexuality as normal variations, sex "experts" may still show negative stereotyping and heterosexual bias. Such bias is evident in some recent best-selling sex manuals, even though they are marketed as liberating and educational for women. For example, the title *The Joy of Sex* suggests that the book is inclusive (it is not, after all, called "The Joy of Heterosexual Sex"). However, it never mentions homosexuality, and the only reference to bisexuality is under "Problems." Dr. David Reuben's 1969 best-seller *Everything You Always Wanted to Know about Sex (But Were Afraid to Ask)* discusses lesbians in the chapter on prostitution. Lesbian sex is characterized as promiscuous, lacking in love, and unsatisfying: "One vagina plus another vagina still equals zero" (Altman, 1984). As you will see, Reuben's ugly stereotypes are contradicted by research on lesbian sexuality and relationships. .

Societal attitudes about gays and lesbians are generally negative. About three-fourths of all Americans believe that sexual relations between two same-sex adults are always wrong, and the percentage expressing that opinion has not changed since 1973 (Hyde, 1990). At the extreme, some people endorse the death penalty for lesbian and gay sexual acts (Lewis, 1979). The ideology that denies or denigrates any nonheterosexual behavior has been termed *heterosexism* (Herek, 1993). Just as racist ideology is used to justify prejudice and discrimination against people of color, heterosexist ideology is used to justify antigay prejudice and discrimination and to discourage lesbians and gay men from becoming socially visible.

Research on Bisexual Women and Lesbians

Research has tended to echo society's model of lesbianism and bisexuality. When lesbianism was labeled a form of pathology, professional research by physicians, psychiatrists, sexologists, and psychologists supported that view not only by lending it the weight of professional authority but also by focusing on theories of causes (note that there is little research on the causes of heterosexuality), on juicy details of the deviant behaviors, and on various approaches to "curing" the disorder (Kitzinger, 1987).

In this context, it is not difficult to see why the results of the first survey and experimental research on lesbians were controversial and shocking. Kinsey et al. (1953) found that 28 percent of the women he interviewed had engaged in some sort of lesbian sexual activity at some time in their lives. As adults, 13 percent had had at least one sexual experience with another woman leading to orgasm. About 3 percent had had sexual relationships *only* with other women. This is quite a lot of "pathological" women.

Kinsey argued that researchers should think of individuals' sexual behaviors on a continuum from exclusively heterosexual to exclusively homosexual rather than in terms of "normal" and "pathological" categories. This approach, which emphasizes that every human being has the capacity to respond sexually in both heterosexual and homosexual ways, was strengthened by laboratory research showing that the pattern of physiological changes in the sexual-response cycle is the same regardless of whether one's partner is a woman or a man (Masters & Johnson, 1979). No longer a deviant and inherently unsatisfying act, lesbian sex now came to be seen as more satisfying than heterosexual sex. Kinsey noted that his respondents reported greater consistency in having orgasms in lesbian sex than in heterosexual sex. Masters and Johnson (1979) suggested that women are better at making love to women than men are, and that lesbians have more satisfying relationships.

The effects on individuals of these rapid changes in the social construction of lesbianism can only be guessed at. Women born in the first decades of the twentieth century have seen lesbianism transformed from an official psychiatric disorder to a "lifestyle choice" in their own lifetime.

Developing a Lesbian or Bisexual Identity

Despite Kinsey's concept of a sexual continuum, most people still assume that the sexual orientation of others can be placed neatly in categories—"straight" or "gay," with bisexual and asexual for the leftovers. Assuming that others' behavior consistently fits these tidy categories, they assume that there is always a sexual identity that matches the behavior. It seems logical to assume that a person who has sex with both male and female partners *is* a bisexual, and one who has sex only with same-sex partners *is* a homosexual, and that they will apply these labels to themselves as part of their identity. But sexual identity and sexual behavior are not always so simple (Golden, 1987).

The process of *coming out,* or accepting lesbianism as a part of one's identity, may be slow and erratic. It has been likened to a "second adolescence"—however, it is an adolescence that can take place at any time from middle childhood to late middle or old age. One woman, who came out as a 56-year-old grandmother, explained that "I simply did not know there was any other way to live than heterosexual. I knew I was pretty miserable, but I just accepted that as part of the way things had to be" (Lewis, 1979, p. 19).

Women may first come into contact with lesbians or the idea of lesbianism in many ways. They may read about the topic or hear it discussed in the media and connect it with their own feelings even though they have had no actual sexual contact with other women. They may discover the existence of a lesbian community, perhaps through a friend or perhaps by being interested in gay activism or politics. Or they may engage in same-sex activity, perhaps starting in adolescence, without at first labeling it as lesbian:

> I think . . . I was 16 when I first got sexually involved for about four years on and off. . . . Then she came to college, we were in different sororities. . . . It really tapered off because she got interested in a guy who she married. . . . Our sexual relationship we kept to ourselves, and I was more excited about it than anything else. I just thought it was a delicious secret. And at the same time, I had a mad crush on a guy. I didn't think of it as being anything weird. I just thought of it as being neat, really something terrific. . . . I thought it was a unique thing we were doing (Ponse, 1978, p. 187).

Accepting a stigmatized social identity may occur in stages (Cass, 1979). The woman may move from identity confusion and uncertainty (when she initially realizes that she is unlike the heterosexuals around her) through a stage of feeling alienated and alone, to an increasing tolerance of her orientation. She gradually comes to accept her lesbian identity, making contacts with others like herself, and then to take pride in her identity. Finally, she may develop a network of lesbian friends, patronize women-owned businesses, attend a gay and lesbian religious congregation, join civil-rights groups for lesbian and gay people, and so forth, finding her place in a lesbian community.

However, the stage theory of lesbian identity may oversimplify matters. There seems to be no inevitable or "correct" process or outcome in matters of sexual identity. Rather, women's sexual identity seems to be (at least potentially) very fluid and changeable (Golden, 1987; Rust, 1993). Some women identify first as heterosexual, then as lesbian, later as bisexual. Others go through these "stages" in reverse. And labels and behaviors don't necessarily match. Some women say they are lesbians although their actual behavior is heterosexual or bisexual; still others say they are heterosexual although their behavior is lesbian or bisexual. Some women experience their sexual orientation as freely chosen, while others see it as beyond their control. Women's racial or ethnic identification is also intertwined with their development of a sexual identity.

Recent research has begun to explore these differences in women's labeling and understanding of their sexual orientation. In interviews with women college students, Carla Golden (1987) found that "Every possible permutation of feelings and activities existed within each sexual identification category" (p. 30). Among women who identified themselves to the researcher as lesbians, there were some who were sexually inexperienced, some whose sexual behavior was exclusively with other women, some with heterosexual experience, and some with bisexual experience. In response to an anonymous in-class survey of ninety-five psychology-of-women students, 65 percent identified as heterosexual, 26 percent as bisexual, and 9 percent as lesbians. However, their actual sexual experiences were 72 percent exclusively heterosexual, 20 percent bisexual, 4 percent lesbian, and 4 percent inexperienced. These results show that sexual identity is not perfectly congruent with sexual experience. They also suggest that bisexuals are a larger, yet more hidden, group than lesbians. The researcher noted that while lesbian issues were frequently discussed in class, bisexual identities and issues were not, because bisexuals felt less comfortable about revealing their orientation than lesbians did.

Like those who identify as lesbian, women who identify themselves as bisexual show a diversity of actual experience. In a poll of members of a bisexual organization, about 4 percent described their sexual behavior as exclusively with other women, 7 percent as mostly with other women, 23 percent as more with women than men, 38 percent as both equally, 7 percent as mostly with men, and none as exclusively with men (Shuster, 1987).

It is clear that women do not always mean the same things when they say "I am a lesbian" (or bisexual). A recent study done in England compared the accounts—explanations or stories about the woman's subjective experience of her lesbianism—given by a sample of forty-one self-identified lesbians ranging in age from 17 to 58 (Kitzinger, 1987). Five viewpoints emerged from a close comparison of the accounts. The first was the idea of lesbianism as personal fulfillment. Women who viewed themselves primarily in this way were sure of being lesbians, were unashamed of their orientation, and thought of themselves as happy, healthy individuals:

> I have never stopped feeling relief and happiness about discovering myself and, you know, accepting about myself and finding all these other women, and it means that I'm happy almost every day of my life. . . . I've never regretted being a lesbian, or becoming a lesbian, if you want to put it that way, or coming out, or whatever. I mean, at least one was alive, you know, and doing things one was meant to do, doing things that were natural to one (Kitzinger, 1987, p. 99).

A second viewpoint defined sexual preferences in terms of love: lesbianism was seen as the result of falling in love with a particular person, who just happened to be a woman. Though defining themselves as lesbian, these women felt that they could or would have a heterosexual relationship if they fell in love with a man. A third viewpoint had to do with the feeling of being "born that way," yet resisting sexual labeling:

> I'm me. I'm . . . a social worker; I'm a mother. I've been married. I like Tschaikowsky; I like Bach; I like Beethoven; I like ballet. I enjoy doing a thousand and one things, and oh yes, in amongst all that, I happen to be a lesbian; I love a woman very deeply. But that's just a *part* of me. So many other lesbians seem to have let it overtake them, and they are lesbians first and foremost (p. 110).

The fourth view identified women who came to lesbianism through being radical feminists:

> It was only through feminism, through learning about the oppression of women by men and the part that the enforcement of heterosexuality, the conditioning of girls into heterosexuality plays in that oppression, it was through that I decided that whatever happens I will never go back to being fucked by men. My resolution to choose sexual partners from among women only, that decision was made because I'm a feminist, not because I'm a lesbian. I take the label "lesbian" as part of the strategy of the feminist struggle (Kitzinger, p. 113).

A final view identified women who saw their sexual orientation as a sin or weakness—a "cross to bear." These women were sometimes ashamed of being lesbians, said they would not have chosen it, and would be happier if they were heterosexual.

Celia Kitzinger's study explores the multiple meanings women give to their sexuality and the relationship they see it as having to the rest of their lives, including their political beliefs. Each of the ways these women subjectively experience their sexuality has both costs and benefits for the woman's understanding of who she is and where she fits into her society.

Almost all the research on lesbian and bisexual women has relied on all-white or predominantly white samples. How does identity development differ for women of different ethnic and racial backgrounds? Focusing on Latina lesbians, Oliva Espin (1987) noted that

> coming out to self and others in the context of a sexist and heterosexist American society is compounded by coming out in the context of a heterosexist and sexist Latin culture immersed in racist society. Because as a Latina she is an ethnic minority person, she must be bicultural in American society. Because she is a lesbian, she has to be polycultural among her own people. The dilemma for Latina lesbians is how to integrate who they are culturally, racially, and religiously with their identity as lesbians and women (Espin, 1987, p. 35).

Latina lesbians are perhaps more likely to remain *in the closet,* keeping their orientation secret from family and friends, than white lesbians because most members of their ethnic group strongly reject and disapprove of lesbians. However, families who become aware of a daughter's lesbianism are unlikely to openly reject or disown her. They will remain silent, tolerating but never openly accepting the situation.

Espin used an open-ended questionnaire to study sixteen Latina (Cuban-born) lesbians. Like white participants in previous research, her respondents showed a wide range of subjective understandings of their lesbianism. They also wrote eloquently about the difficulty of integrating their ethnic and sexual identities. This woman had earlier said that being a Cuban and being a lesbian were equally important to her:

> I guess that if the choice were absolute, I would choose living among lesbians . . . but I want to point out that I would be extremely unhappy if all my Latin culture were taken out of my lesbian life. I had a hard time with all the questions that made me choose between Cuban and lesbian, or at least, made me feel as if I had to choose . . . it is a very painful position because I feel that I am both, and I don't want to have to choose . . . (p. 47).

In interview studies, African-American lesbians also have described issues of integrating multiple identities and group memberships: as lesbians, as members of the black community, and as part of the larger culture with its racism, sexism, and heterosexism:

> Diane (hesitated) to discuss her lesbian feelings while in college. The college she attended was predominantly White, and Diane relied a great deal on the Black community there for support. She considered that coming out to these individuals might jeopardize her acceptance in this group. Although Diane continued to explore her lesbian feelings internally, she also continued to date men. Sev-

eral years later, as she did begin to come out to others, she feared that identification as a lesbian might pull her away from what she considered her primary reference group—Black Americans (Loiacano, 1993, pp. 369–370).

Some writers have speculated that lesbianism is even more invisible in black communities than white ones (Joseph & Lewis, 1981). This may be due to the strong influence of organized religion, with the black church keeping silence on issues of sexual orientation, as well as to community values that emphasize childbearing as a central role for women (Hatton, 1994). The very small samples used in interview research to date make it difficult to generalize about African-American lesbians, and underscore the need for more study of homosexuality in the black community (Hatton, 1994).

Asian-American lesbians, too, face issues of multiple identity. Within Asian cultures, being a lesbian is viewed as a rejection of women's most important role, that of wife and mother. Moreover, the implication is that the lesbians' parents have failed and that the child is rejecting not only family values but Asian culture. In a study of nineteen Asian-American lesbians, the majority felt more comfortable in the lesbian community than the Asian-American one, and reported that they had experienced more frequent discrimination as Asians than as lesbians. The researcher speculated that perhaps the stereotype of the passive but exotic Asian woman is so strong that the possibility that an Asian woman could be a lesbian is rarely considered; therefore Asian lesbians experience more discrimination as women and Asians than as lesbians (Chan, 1993).

More research is needed on how women—especially minority women—integrate sexual identity with other aspects of their sense of self. Psychological research that takes women's own accounts of their development seriously is a start in this direction, and should be extended to more diverse groups of women. Such research also has implications for the social construction of heterosexuality. It suggests that woman cannot be categorized neatly into "straight, gay, or bi" because the labels do not mean the same things to everyone and because women's sexual behavior and identity are changeable across the lifespan and in changing circumstances.

RELATIONSHIP DYNAMICS

Regardless of the sex of the partners, every couple believes that its relationship is unique and that love is its central motivation. However, relationships involve power and influence as well as love and intimacy. Because the normative script for relationships is a heterosexual one, the patterns of power can be seen most clearly in heterosexual dating and courtship. Recent research has also examined power and influence in lesbian couples, providing a basis for comparison and new information about the dynamics of being a couple.

Heterosexual Relationships

Power

The traditional script for a date says that the man should take the lead. He should ask the woman out, offer her a selection of activities, provide transportation, and pay the bills (Peplau & Campbell, 1989). Today, the traditional date, with its clear spheres of power, is disappearing. Along with changes in dating patterns have come changes in power relationships. Actively indicating interest in a man and even taking the sexual initiative are not as frowned on as in the past (McCormick & Jesser, 1983). However, as shown in Table 9.1, people are still very much aware of the traditional script. Expectations of male control can affect perceptions of behavior. For example, male college students perceived women who asked for a date as more flexible and agreeable, more of a casual dater, and more sexually active than women who did not ask for a date (Muehlenhard & Scardino, 1985).

Gender-related power differentials continue to affect dating relationships. In a large study of predominantly white college students, both partners in more than 200 heterosexual dating couples independently completed a questionnaire about their relationship three times over a two-year period. (The average couple had been dating for about eight months at the start of the study.) The couples held a strong belief in egalitarian relationships: When asked which partner should have more say in the relationship, 95 percent of women and 87 percent of men felt that each partner should have "exactly equal" power. However, when asked specific questions about decision-making power (e.g., who has more say in what the partners do together), a less egalitarian pattern emerged. Fewer than half the students reported equal-power relationships. In the unequal ones, it was usually the man who had more power. The large difference between the proportion of people who felt that power *should* be equal and those who felt their relationship *was* equal suggests that many couples who want equality do not achieve it.

What factors predict a balance of power in dating relationships? Not surprisingly, couples with less traditional attitudes toward male–female roles tended to have more egalitarian relationships. The woman's career goals were especially relevant. The higher her educational aspirations, the less likely she was to be in a male-dominant relationship (Rubin, Peplau, & Hill, cited in Peplau & Campbell, 1989).

Equality is also more likely if the partners are about equally involved. If one partner is deeply in love or dependent on the relationship for self-esteem and the other is only casually interested, the balance of power tips toward the least involved partner. This factor seems to be especially important for women: The less they love relative to their partners, the more power they see themselves as having (Sprecher, 1985).

Influence Strategies

Gender stereotypes about how to get one's way in a relationship are very clear. Women are believed to use indirect and manipulative strategies—pouting, crying, sulking, and accusing the partner of being insensitive. Men are believed to express anger directly, to call for a logical, unemotional assessment of the problem, and to avoid exploring feelings. Dating partners not only express these beliefs but say that their own behavior fits the stereotypes (Kelley et al., 1978). These results reflect the power structure of heterosexual relationships. Since men have more power, they may have little to gain by displaying and exploring feelings and may retain their power edge by avoidance. Since women have less power, they may have more to gain from negotiation and manipulation of feelings (Peplau & Gordon, 1985).

Indirect power strategies are gentler and less confrontive. They are also the strategies of the weak. The "woman's" strategies of silence, withdrawal, and sulking are "last resort" tactics used by people of both sexes when they perceive themselves as less powerful than their partner. Cross-cultural research shows that women from the United States use more direct interactional ("men's") influence tactics than women from Mexico, who have relatively less economic power and more restrictive gender roles (Belk, Garcia-Falconi, Hernandez-Sanchez, & Snell, 1988).

Lesbian Relationships

In general, most lesbians (like most heterosexuals) desire egalitarian relationships. In a study using matched samples of lesbians, gay men, and heterosexuals, all groups (and especially women, both lesbian and heterosexual) said that having an equal-power relationship was very important. However, only 59 percent of lesbians reported that their current relationship was exactly equal—a higher proportion than among the heterosexual women but still short of their expressed desires (Peplau & Cochran, 1990).

Lesbian relationships are similar to heterosexual ones in that if partners are equally interested, committed, or in love, power tends to be equal. However, when one partner is more dependent, committed, or involved than the other, the less involved person tends to have more power (Caldwell & Peplau, 1984).

In discussing influence strategies among heterosexual couples, we noted that "weak" influence tactics are stereotyped as typical of women and "strong" tactics as typical of men. This stereotype would suggest that both partners in lesbian couples would use similar tactics of withdrawal and emotionality. However, it was also noted that "women's" strategies are the strategies of low-power partners. This analysis would suggest that strategies used by lesbian (and gay male) couples would be related less to their sex than to the power differential within the particular couple. Research tends to support the importance of power rather than sex. In a study comparing self-reported influence strategies used by lesbians, gay men, and heterosexuals in their relationships, sex affected the type of strategy only among heterosexuals. Heterosexual women expressed negative emotions or withdrew; heterosexual men bargained or appealed to reason. Gay men and lesbians did not use gender-differentiated strategies. Regardless of whether they were gay or straight, people who saw themselves as the more powerful partner in their relationship used direct, interactive strategies (the prototypical heterosexual male strategies) and low-power partners used indirect and noninteractional tactics (Falbo & Peplau, 1980).

Research on the dynamics of lesbian relationships is still in its infancy. Because of the fluidity of sexual identity and the variability of sexual relationships, future research should also study more of a variety of woman–woman *and* woman–man relationships, including those in which partners express passion and commitment without genital sexual activity and those in which one or both partners identify as bisexual (Peplau & Cochran, 1990).

Date Rape and Dating Violence

Sexual aggression and violence are quite common in close relationships (see Chapter 14). In a study of more than 300 heterosexual college students, 15 percent of the women had been victims of date rape, and 78 percent had been the recipient of some form of sexual coercion, most often unwanted touching of the woman's breasts, buttocks, or genitals (Muehlenhard & Linton, 1987). Studies of high school and college students confirm that up to 90 percent of women report having experienced at least one incident of dating violence. The most common forms are verbal aggression (yelling and name-calling), followed by slapping, grabbing, pushing, hitting, restraining, and shoving. Punching, throwing objects, threatening with weapons, and severe physical attack also occur.

Men who endorse traditional sex roles and a "battle-of-the-sexes" attitude about relationships are more likely to use sexual coercion and physical aggression against their dates. Coercive men are most often those who endorse the traditional script in which women's role is to be passive and coy, offer token resistance, and eventually give in, while the man's role is to initiate, persevere, and prevail until she has been "conquered" (Muehlenhard & Linton, 1987; Russell, 1984b). Feminist analyses of violence against women often emphasize the relationship between all forms of violence and the oppression of women as a class (Yllo & Bograd, 1988). Sexual assault and violence in relationships is an abuse of power.

WHAT DO WOMEN WANT? SATISFACTION IN CLOSE RELATIONSHIPS

Bookstores are flooded with advice manuals aimed at teaching women how to have satisfying relationships with men. These books—with titles such as *Women Who Love Too Much; Women Men Love, Women Men Leave;* and *Smart Women, Foolish Choices*—carry a clear message that women are responsible for their relationships and have only themselves to blame if they are unhappy or unsatisfied.

Judith Worell, a counseling psychologist, has analyzed "pop psych" books aimed at heterosexual women. In these books, women are portrayed as ignorant in relationships—as not knowing what they want or what they need to be happy. They are also shown as incompetent—lacking the skills or techniques that would allow them to initiate or maintain satisfying relationships. Are women really ignorant and incompetent about relationships? Worell (1988) surveyed a large body of research on close relationships. She demonstrated that this research shows that women know very well what they want and need in a relationship: intimacy and equality. However, they may have difficulty meeting those needs within heterosexual relationships and may settle for less than they would prefer.

Nor are women (as a group) in any way deficient in relationship skills. On the contrary, they often give much more social support to others, especially boys and men, than they receive in return. They are named as confidant, friend, or intimate more often than men by children, friends, spouses, and kin. Another important aspect of interpersonal functioning is the ability to communicate clearly and understand others' attempts at communication, both verbal and nonverbal. As discussed in earlier chapters, where gender-related differences in communication skills exist, they are in favor of women. Nevertheless, each of the pop psych books "recognizes a valid relationship issue for women, and then places the blame on the woman for having allowed herself to become involved in this painful situation" (Worell, 1988, p. 480). Such books foster illusions by dichotomizing women and men—portraying them as fundamentally different and opposed in their personalities and needs.

The demands of providing social support to many people may be a significant source of stress for women, and one of the reasons they turn to psychological counseling. Moreover, women are often expected to use their communication skills to help lovers and partners understand themselves and to mediate among other people. Pop psych books that tell women they are incompetent may compound stress and add to women's belief that they are to blame when their own and their friends' relationships are unhappy.

CONNECTING THEMES

1. In the study of sexuality and relationships, it is important to view the "facts of life" as socially and politically constructed. What appears to be natural and normal—female passivity, male aggression, the suppression of female desire, power differentials in relationships—may be neither. At the social structural, interactional, and intraindividual levels, sexuality is constructed by the gender system.
2. Women are defined by their sexuality, and the definition is a negative one. The language of sex portrays women as objects and sexual activity as something aggressive done to a female. Women are viewed in terms of a "madonna/whore" dichotomy. Their sexual body parts and their sexual agency remain unnamed, leading to shame and suppression of desire. But names can change. One of the clearest examples of the power of a label is the reclassification of lesbianism from a psychiatric disorder to a normal sexual orientation.
3. Sexuality and relationship norms are shaped by culture. How important is virginity before marriage? Will unrealistic standards of weight lead a woman to excessive dieting and low self-esteem? How will a family react to a daughter "coming out" as a lesbian? What is a woman's risk of HIV infection? The answers to all these questions depend on the social class, ethnicity, religious background, and disability status of individual women. Moreover, women's sexual identity is fluid and changeable across the lifespan, adding to the diversity of ways that women experience their sexual selves.
4. Women of the past few generations of Western societies have lived through an era of rapidly changing ideas about sexuality. Reliable contraception and the increasing acceptance of same-sex and extramarital sexual behavior have been "liberating" in some ways, but a sexual double standard remains, and women's sexuality is still controlled and suppressed. Social change efforts for the future should focus on developing nonsexist sex education, en-

larging cultural images of beauty and romance, and empowering women to make sexual choices without coercion and shame.

SUGGESTED READINGS

D'EMILIO, JOHN, and ESTELLE B. FRIEDMAN (1988). *Intimate Matters: A History of Sexuality in America.* New York: Harper & Row. Changing values and practices throughout the history of American society. Reading about the meanings of sexuality (including homosexuality) over time shows how individual desire and social judgment interact.

HYDE, JANET, S. (1990). *Understanding Human Sexuality* (4th ed.) New York: McGraw-Hill. A matter-of-fact, nonsexist college text on human sexuality. This book, written with wisdom and humor by a well-known feminist psychologist, provides a great deal of factual information.

VANCE, CAROL S. (Ed.) (1984). *Pleasure and Danger: Exploring Female Sexuality.* Boston: Routledge and Kegan Paul. A rich collection of essays reflecting feminist views from sociology, anthropology, psychology, and literary and cultural studies. The diversity of women's sexual identities and expression is evidenced here.

CHAPTER 10

Commitments: Women and Long-Term Relationships

MARRIAGE
- Life in an Institution
- Who Marries and When?
- Who Marries Whom?
- "Marrying Up" and "Marrying Down": The Marriage Gradient
- Varieties of Marriage
- Biases in Research on Marriage
- Power in Marriage
- Happily Ever After? Marital Satisfaction and Psychological Adjustment

LESBIAN COUPLES
- Stereotypes
- Who Are Lesbian Couples?
- Relationship Characteristics
- Power in Lesbian Relationships
- Satisfaction in Lesbian Relationships
- Limitations of Research

"POSSLQS": COHABITING COUPLES
- Who Cohabits and Why?
- Relationship Characteristics
- Living Together and Marital Choices

NEVER-MARRIED WOMEN
- Stereotypes and Social Judgments
- Who Stays Single and Why?

ENDING THE COMMITMENT: DIVORCE AND SEPARATION
- Divorce Rates
- Correlates of Divorce
- Consequences of Divorce
- Breaking Up
- Countering Biases in Research on Divorce

REMARRIAGE

EQUALITY AND COMMITMENT: INCOMPATIBLE IDEALS?

CONNECTING THEMES

SUGGESTED READINGS

She gave a gasp as he slid her underneath him. . . . By now Merril didn't want to talk any more. She simply wanted to fly, wherever Torrin chose to pilot her into the upper reaches of the seventh heaven.

But he lifted his head one last time. "Now will you tell me what it is I haven't asked you yet?"

"It's all right, I think you already have—" she breathed.

"And will you? Marry me, I mean?" he asked tenderly.

"Torrin, what are you doing?"

His voice was husky. "I'm giving you a lesson in love."

"Let it last forever, my dream lover," she whispered, moving sensually beneath his touch. "Like our marriage."

"And like my love for you," he murmured in velvet tones beside her head.

And as she moved against him, all notion of holding back now gone, she knew that, like love, their dream would last forever—because it was the real thing.

—*The ending of* FANTASY LOVER, *a Harlequin Romance* (HEYWOOD, *1989, p. 187*).

Happy endings like this one appeal to women's hopes of finding the "real thing" and settling down to a lifetime of happiness. The romantic relationships that we discussed in Chapter 9 lead—at least sometimes—to a desire to make a commitment to one partner. In our society that commitment usually leads to marriage, and when people marry they almost always hope it will last a lifetime. Not all enduring commitments to a partner take the form of marriage. Some lesbian couples choose long-term commitment, although they do not have the right to legal marriage. Some heterosexual couples choose to live together without formal marriage. The desire to be part of a couple is so strong that when marriages (or other long-term relationships) fail, most partners try again with someone else.

In spite of the importance of committed relationships in people's lives, the study of relationships is a relatively new research focus in psychology. For many years, psychologists tended to leave the study of long-term relationships to sociologists. Social changes such as the rising divorce rate have challenged traditional views of marriage, however, and made the study of long-term relationships more relevant. Moreover, the emergence of feminist psychology has encouraged researchers to question common assumptions about marriage and love relationships (Peplau & Gordon, 1985). Psychologists are increasingly interested in studying enduring relationships, and feminist psychologists in particular have studied their effects on women's lives. In this chapter we will explore the kinds of commitments couples make to each other and the consequences of these commitments for women.

MARRIAGE

Life in an Institution

As a very old joke puts it, "Marriage is an institution—but who wants to live in an institution?" This joke recognizes that marriage is the way that societies legalize and regulate private relationships between couples. Laws and statutes stipulate who may marry whom—for example, same-sex couples and some biological relatives are prohibited from marrying, and in the past, interracial marriages have been prohibited. Laws also regulate the minimum age for marriage, the division of property when marriages dissolve (indeed, whether they are permitted to dissolve), and the responsibilities of each partner within the marriage (for example, what behaviors constitute grounds for divorce).

In cultures in which written law is less important, religious codes or powerful social norms may serve the same regulatory function. For example, cross-cultural studies of preindustrial hunter-gatherer societies show that 79 percent of these societies allow men to have more than one wife. Few prohibit divorce and remarriage, but most punish married people for having sexual relations outside the marriage (Gough, 1984).

Although people in Western societies are aware that marriage is a legal contract subject to regulation by the state, they rarely think of it that way in relation to themselves. Rather, they choose their partners as individuals and expect to live out their married lives according to their own needs and wishes. Nevertheless, the formal definitions of rights and responsibilities imposed by the state may have consequences for both partners—especially when the marriage ends, with divorce or the death of a spouse.

Behaviors and attitudes are importantly shaped by the institutional aspects of marriage. Because the definition of marriage is an institutional one, there are cultural scripts that inevitably affect individuals:

> An institution is a way of life that is very resistant to change. People know about it; they can describe it; and they have spent a lifetime learning how to react to it. The *idea* of marriage is larger than any individual marriage. The *role* of husband or wife is greater than any individual who takes on that role (Blumstein & Schwartz, 1983, p. 318).

Marriage, then, is both a personal relationship and a scripted social institution.

Who Marries and When?

The vast majority of people in Western societies will marry at some time in their lives. About 90 percent of American women marry by the age of 30; the proportion has remained fairly constant for the past 100 years. However, marital patterns for white and black women are diverging. The marriage rate among African Americans is declining. At present, about 35 percent of African-American women have not yet married by the age of 34, and it is estimated that about 25 percent will never marry (Dickson, 1993). Over all ethnic groups, the timing of marriage has changed. Both women and men are waiting longer to marry. In the 1990s, the typical first-time bride is three and a half years older than her 1970s counterpart. A similar trend is occurring in other industrialized countries. Teenage marriages are becoming much less common, and at least half of all women have not yet married by the age of 24. Scandinavian countries lead the way in the trend to delaying marriage; for example, only 15 percent of 24-year-old Swedish women are married (Bianchi & Spain, 1986; Norton & Moorman, 1987). In contrast, women in developing areas of the world marry very young. In many parts of Africa and Asia, the average age at first marriage is under 18 (United Nations, 1991a).

What is the cause of these changes? There are probably several. In the United States, many young women have been influenced by feminism's emphasis on choices for women. Even though not all young women label themselves feminists, the idea that women should have aspirations other than wife and mother has been widely accepted. Advances in contraceptive methods have made premarital sex and living-together arrangements more practical, and these practices have become more acceptable to many. For black women, there is a shortage of men, due to a number of socioeconomic forces. In the African-American community, marriageable men are a scarce resource (Dickson, 1993) (see Chapter 11 for more on African-American family patterns). Economic factors may play a part, too, as young people find it difficult to become financially independent of their parents and to afford separate housing (Bianchi & Spain, 1986).

Whatever the causes, the tendency to marry later has important implications for women because the increased time between high school and marriage offers opportunities to broaden experience. A woman who enters her first marriage at an older age is less likely to exchange dependence on her parents for dependence on a husband. She is likely to have had some experience of independent living; has probably held paid jobs and perhaps has supported herself with her work; and has had time to get more education, which exposes her to a variety of viewpoints and experiences and also increases her employment opportunities. All in all, she is more likely than a younger woman to enter marriage with a well-developed sense of self and broad horizons for her life.

Who Marries Whom?

In recent cross-cultural study, more than 9,000 people from thirty-seven nations representing every part of the world were asked to assess the importance of thirty-one characteristics in a potential mate (Buss et al., 1990). The diverse characteristics included good health, chastity, dependability, intelligence, social status, religious background, neatness, ambition, and sociability. The participants in this study were young (their average age was 23) and typically urban, well educated, and prosperous—in other words, they are not representative samples from their countries. Nevertheless, their answers give an interesting picture of what women and men from diverse cultures look for in a potential marriage partner.

No two samples ordered the characteristics in exactly the same way. The biggest difference across cultures was in a cluster of characteristics that reflect traditional values such as chastity (the potential husband or wife should not have had previous sexual intercourse), being a good cook and housekeeper, and desire for a home and children. Samples from China, Indonesia, India, and Iran, for example, placed great importance on chastity, while samples from Scandinavia considered it irrelevant.

Overall, cultural differences were much more important than gender differences. Men and women from the same culture were more similar in their mate preferences than men to other men, or women to other women, from different cultures. In fact, men's and women's rankings were virtually identical overall, with a correlation of +.95. This gender similarity suggests that each culture—whether Bulgarian, Irish, Japanese, Zambian, Venezuelan, or whatever—socializes men and women to know and accept its particular script for the institution of marriage. Of course, such scripts may include different marital goals for women and men. In this study, women were similar to each other across cultures in being slightly more likely to emphasize a mate's earning capacity and ambition, and men in emphasizing good looks and physical attractiveness.

When all thirty-seven cultures were considered together, an overall picture of an ideal mate emerged. Women and men agreed, rating mutual attraction and love, dependable character, emotional stability and maturity, and pleasing disposition as the four most important characteristics in a potential marriage partner. In the United States sample, women and men also agreed on the importance of education and intelligence.

Many other studies have focused on spouse choices in the United States, providing a detailed picture of who marries whom in America (reviewed by Peplau & Gordon, 1985). In general, these studies, like the cross-cultural one described above, show that the desires of men and women are more similar than different. For example, when husbands and wives ranked the overall importance of both task-oriented and interpersonal aspects of marriage, both emphasized affection and companionship most (Levinger, 1964).

However, some differences in Americans' marital expectations and desires are related to sex and social class. The high value that women of all social classes place on affection and companionship is shared more by middle-class than by working-class men. The partner's capacity for self-disclosure in a relationship appears to be more important to women than to men across all social classes. And middle-class women express concerns about keeping their independence and autonomy in relationships more than men or working-class women do (Peplau & Gordon, 1985).

Men tend to be somewhat more traditional in their thinking about marital scripts and roles. They are more likely than their wives to believe that traditional gender roles are innate and unchangeable (Mirowsky & Ross, 1987). Several studies in the 1970s and 1980s (reviewed by Peplau & Gordon, 1985) have shown that men are more likely to believe husbands should be the primary family wage earner and women should be in charge of home and family. In a 1980 study of students entering college, 35 percent of the men—and only 19 percent of the women—believed that "women's activities should be confined to the home" (Astin, King, & Richardson, 1980). Overall, women appear to expect and desire more flexible marital patterns than men.

"Marrying Up" and "Marrying Down": The Marriage Gradient

Individual couples usually end up being fairly closely matched on social class and ethnic/racial group as well as on characteristics such as height, SAT scores, attractiveness, and age. Couples are similar in values, too: Religious people tend to marry other religious people, traditionalists marry other traditionalists, and feminists marry other feminists. When there are differences within a couple, it is usually the man who is older, is better educated, and has a more prestigious occupation (Peplau & Gordon, 1985), and this is true cross-culturally (United Nations, 1991a).

The tendency for women to "marry up" and men to "marry down" by sorting themselves into couples in which the man has higher prestige and income potential is called the *marriage gradient* (Bernard, 1972). Historically, the mar-

riage gradient probably came about because women had little access to education and high-status occupations in their own right and could best achieve economic security through marriage. In the United States, women's tendency to "marry up" has decreased as women have become more equal to men in earning power and educational opportunity. It also varies among groups of women. Black women, for example, are less likely than white women to "marry up" with respect to education (Schoen & Wooldredge, 1989). The marriage gradient has important implications for power in marriage, which will be discussed later in this chapter.

Varieties of Marriage

In twentieth-century America, many different marriage patterns coexist, from the most traditional to the most experimental (Blumstein & Schwartz, 1983). We will classify marriage patterns in terms of three important characteristics: the division of authority, how spousal roles are defined, and the amount of companionship and shared activities they provide (Peplau & Gordon, 1985; Peplau, 1983; Scanzoni & Scanzoni, 1976; Schwartz, 1994).

Traditional Marriage

In traditional marriage, both husband and wife agree that the husband has (and should have) greater authority; he is "the head of the family," or "the boss." Even in areas in which the wife has some decision-making responsibility (for example, household shopping), he retains veto power over her decisions. In traditional marriages, the wife is a full-time homemaker who does not work for pay. Clear distinctions are made between the husband's and wife's responsibilities. She is responsible for home and child care, and he is the breadwinner (see Figure 10.1). Couples in these marriages may not expect to be "best friends"; rather, the wife finds companionship with other women—neighbors, sisters and other kin, or members of her church. The husband's friendship networks are with male kin and coworkers, and his leisure activities take place apart from his wife.

Most studies of traditional couples have focused on working-class families, and traditional marriage may be more common in this group. However, it is not confined to one social class. In middle- and upper-class families, traditional wives may serve as hostesses for elaborate social functions or become active in community volunteer work. However, they do not work for pay, and husbands' authority outweighs theirs.

The value placed on traditional marriage has changed a great deal in the past few decades. A comparison of national opinion polls over the years (cited in Bianchi & Spain, 1986) shows that in 1937 only 18 percent of the population approved of a married woman working for pay if her husband was capable of supporting her; by 1982, the proportion had risen to 75 percent. Married women's actual economic dependency has changed in an equally striking way. In 1940, the vast majority of married white women were completely dependent on their husbands for money. Today, such wives are a minority (Sorenson & McLanahan, 1987).

Throughout this century, black women have been less economically depen-

FIGURE 10.1. Every mother is a working mother!

dent and more likely to work for pay than white women. Black women and men in general have more liberal views about women's appropriate roles, and there is less of a gap between men's and women's views than there is among whites. Attitudes in the black community, like those of the population in general, have grown more liberal over time (Crovitz & Steinmann, 1980). However, these changes do not mean that marriages based on traditional beliefs and values are entirely a thing of the past. As discussed earlier, a significant proportion of people (more men than women) still expressed traditional views about marriage in studies conducted in the 1970s and 1980s.

Modern Marriage

In modern marriage, the spouses have a "senior partner—junior partner" or "near-peer" relationship. Modern wives work outside the home, but, by mutual agreement, the wife's job is less important than the husband's—he is the breadwinner, and she is working to "help out" or to provide "extras." Moreover, it is expected that her paid employment will not interfere with her responsibilities for housework and child care. She may leave her paid job with the birth of her first child, returning to work when the children are in school or leave home. Modern couples emphasize companionship and expect to share leisure time activities. They value "togetherness" and may discuss husband/wife roles rather than taking them for granted as more traditional couples do.

Modern marriage may seem to be a relationship of equality when compared with traditional marriage, but the equality is relative (see Box 10.1). Husbands still have more financial responsibility, and women have more responsibility for the home and the children (Steil, in press). This work, along with their jobs, means that modern wives do a "second shift" every day (Hochschild, 1989). As one marital researcher put it, "males support female equality but only up to the point it collides with their privilege" (Schwartz, 1994, p. 9).

Egalitarian Marriage

Egalitarian marriage, once relatively rare, is becoming more common (Schwartz, 1994). In egalitarian marriages, the partners attempt to have equal

Box 10.1 Equality or Inequality? The Role-Reversal Test

Read the following paragraph about modern marriage:

> Both my wife and I earned Ph.D. degrees in our respective disciplines. I turned down a superior academic post in Oregon and accepted a slightly less desirable position in New York where my wife could obtain a part-time teaching job and do research at one of the several other colleges in the area. Although I would have preferred to live in a suburb, we purchased a home near my wife's college so that she could have an office at home where she would be when the children returned from school. Because my wife earns a good salary, she can easily afford to pay a maid to do her major household chores. My wife and I share all other tasks around the house equally. For example, she cooks the meals, but I do the laundry for her and help her with many of her other household tasks.

Sandra Bem and Daryl Bem have suggested that gender is a largely unconscious ideology of inequality. Both women and men are socialized to believe that equality exists where it does not, and inequality is hard to recognize. If it represents a truly gender-neutral arrangement, the paragraph you just read should have the same tone and implications when the roles are reversed. As a test for hidden inequality, here is the paragraph with the roles reversed:

> Both my husband and I earned Ph.D. degrees in our respective disciplines. I turned down a superior academic post in Oregon and accepted a slightly less desirable position in New York where my husband could obtain a part-time teaching job and do research at one of the several other colleges in the area. Although I would have preferred to live in a suburb, we purchased a home near my husband's college so that he could have an office at home where he would be when the children returned from school. Because my husband earns a good salary, he can easily afford to pay a maid to do his major household chores. My husband and I share all other tasks around the house equally. For example, he cooks the meals, but I do the laundry for him and help him with many of his other household tasks.

Source: Bem & Bem "Training the woman to know her place: The power of a nonconscious ideology." In M. H. Garskof (Ed.); *Roles Women Play: Readings toward women's liberation*, pp. 84–94. 1971 Brooks Cole. Reprinted by permission of the authors.

power and authority. They also attempt to share responsibilities equally without respect to gender roles. For example, one partner's paid job is not allowed to take precedence over the other's. In practical terms, this would mean that either the husband or the wife might relocate to accommodate the other's promotion; either would be equally likely to miss work to care for a sick child or to work part time to accommodate household responsibilities. The ever-present tasks of running a household—housework, bill paying, errands—would ideally be allocated by interest and ability, not because certain jobs are "women's work" and others are "men's work."

Egalitarian marriage is much more than just a fifty–fifty division of labor, however. More than any other type of marriage, it provides the couple with profound intimacy, intense companionship, and mutual respect. Egalitarian couples put their relationship first, ahead of work and other relationships (even family and children). Because they share a great deal (housework, financial responsibility, child care) they understand each other, communicate well, and choose to spend a lot of time together. Often, each believes that the other is irreplaceable and their relationship is unique (Schwartz, 1994).

Biases in Research on Marriage

Marriages in which both spouses work for pay have been around for a long time, especially among black, immigrant, and rural couples, for whom two jobs were often necessary for economic survival. Farm wives sold butter, eggs, and homemade foods; immigrant women earned money in garment factories and textile mills, or worked alongside their husbands in small "Mom-and-Pop" stores and businesses. Wives also took in boarders and did laundry, sewing, and cleaning for wealthier families (Aldous, 1982). During World War II, women held factory and industrial jobs of all kinds. These patterns are not just a matter of history; rural, immigrant, and working-class women continue to contribute to their families' economic survival in these ways.

However, working-class dual-earner families have not been studied systematically by social scientists; neither have Asian-American, Puerto Rican immigrant, or African-American dual-earner families. Instead, research has focused on white, upper-middle-class professional couples. There is a need for research on the lives of working couples who do not have high-prestige careers, especially since the number of such couples is increasing rapidly (Pleck, 1987). For the present, however, most of psychology's insight into dual-worker marriage comes from studies of professional couples.

One reason dual-career couples have been considered more interesting and important than dual-earner couples may be that the values of both partners resemble the male ideal in our society. Also, many researchers who study dual-career couples are themselves part of a dual-career marriage (Aldous, 1982). These observations serve as a reminder of how social norms and values can influence a research agenda.

Thinking about marriage in terms of distinct types may oversimplify the varieties that exist. But it helps to illustrate the importance of the dimensions of role differentiation, companionship, and authority. Different marriage types reflect different beliefs about what the duties of husband and wife should be and how they should view each other. In traditional, modern, and dual-career marriages, men have more power and authority. Completely egalitarian marriages are still relatively rare. Although Americans like to think of marriage as an equal partnership, men end up having more say. We will now take a closer look at the power dimension. Why is it that the end result of a stroll down the aisle and the words "I do" is often a long-term state of inequality?

Power in Marriage

Studying marriages in terms of power is not an easy task. Many people do not like to think or talk about their relationships in such "crass" terms. Marital privacy makes it difficult for researchers to see the power dynamics involved in a couple's life together. In addition, it is not always clear just what the word *power* means in a marriage. In spite of these difficulties, psychologists and sociologists have conducted studies of marital power for at least the past thirty years.

One way to define power is as "the ability to get one's way, to influence important decisions" (Blumstein & Schwartz, 1983, p. 62). Accordingly, researchers have often compiled lists of the sorts of decisions that must be made in families and asked one or both partners who usually makes the final decision about each type of issue. In the best known of these studies (Blood & Wolfe, 1960), more than 900 urban, suburban, and rural wives were asked who had the final say on whether the husband should change jobs (90 percent said husbands always did) and on how much to spend on food (41 percent reported that wives always did). Only 39 percent of the wives had decision-making power over whether or not they themselves should hold a paying job. Of course, some decisions are much more important to the family's welfare than others. Note that the decision with the most far-reaching consequences, the husband's job, is one where husbands had virtually uncontested power.

Another approach is to ask couples who the "real boss" is in the family or who usually "wins out" when there's a really important decision on which the spouses disagree. In a sample of 336 Canadian households, 76 percent of wives said that the husband was the boss and only 13 percent said both had equal power (Turk & Bell, 1972). More recent research confirms that the norm has not changed. Even in dual-career marriages, which are often claimed to be the most egalitarian marriage form and the vanguard of future trends, there is a consistent pattern of inequality; the roles and responsibilities are more balanced than in traditional marriages, but "despite an essentially supportive orientation, both partners seem to endorse some level of male dominance" (Steil, 1983, p. 53).

Sources of Power

Many factors are associated with husband dominance in marriage (Steil, 1983). Social class and ethnicity make a difference: Black and working-class couples have less of a power differential than white middle- and upper-class couples. Wives who are employed have more power than those who work only at home. White middle-class women in traditional marriages may have less power in their marriages than any other group of women.

One reason the power balance in marriage is weighted in favor of men is the influence of traditional beliefs and social norms (Steil, 1994). In a major study of American couples, Phillip Blumstein & Pepper Schwartz (1983) asked couples whether they agreed or disagreed that it is better if the man works to support the household and the woman stays home. In couples where either spouse agreed, the husband was more powerful, regardless of how much money each partner actually earned. Husbands and wives described the power difference in their own words. For example, Marlene and Art have been married for thirty years. She is an executive with the telephone company and he is a farm-equipment dealer; their incomes are about equal, although sometimes she earns more:

MARLENE: Art makes the major economic decisions in our household. We are as consulting of one another as possible, but I realize that in the final push comes to shove that he is the one who shoulders the responsibility for this family. . .

ART: I would say that I make the decision when it comes to money and I guess I would also say that if there is an argument and we cannot totally work it out so that we both agree, then I have more to say . . . someone has to finally make a decision and we have always done it this way (Blumstein & Schwartz, 1983, pp. 57–58).

Another explanation for greater male power in marriage comes from *social exchange theory* (Thibault & Kelley, 1959). This theory proposes that the partner who brings greater outside resources to the relationship will have the greater influence in it. The partner who has less to offer, be it status, money, or knowledge, will inevitably take a back seat. Blumstein and Schwartz (1983), for example, noted that their research had clearly shown that money establishes the balance of power in heterosexual relationships. They pointed out that their conclusion seemed a rather cynical one that does not fit American beliefs about equality:

> Most people like to think that the right to affect decisions is based on the demands of daily events, on which partner is wiser on a certain issue, or on special gifts of persuasion. They do not like to think that income, something that comes into the relationship from the outside, imposes a hierarchy on the couple. But it does (Blumstein & Schwartz, 1983, p. 53).

Do Two Incomes Lead to Equality?

Dual-career marriages often contain unrecognized inequalities. For example, housework is not a mutual and equal responsibility. In a study of a national sample of more than 1,500 dual-career, dual-earner, and traditional couples, it was found that wives in all three categories spent considerably more time in housework each week than their husbands. Dual-career husbands did not spend any more time each week doing housework than other men (Berardo, Shehan, & Leslie, 1987).

Another way in which dual-career marriages often fall short of being truly egalitarian is in the relative importance attached to each partner's career. Imagine a situation in which one partner is a psychologist and the other is also engaged in a demanding career. Which spouse would be more likely to move to a different location to advance the career—husband or wife? Which would be more likely to relocate because the spouse had a job offer in a different place? When male and female members of the American Psychological Association were asked about their own choices, 42 percent of the men and only 19 percent of the women said they had moved for an increase in salary. However, 25 percent of the women and only 7 percent of the men had moved because of their partners' relocation. (Incidentally, these couples also said that the women spent more time on housework and child care. The researcher (Gutek, 1989) noted that gender typing seems to be alive and well among psychologists!).

In American marriages, husbands usually bring more of three very important resources: money, education, and prestige. Husbands usually earn more than wives, even when both are employed full time, and are likely to have higher status jobs. (This is true for a variety of reasons that we will look at more closely in Chapter 12.) As noted above, wives who have no income or employment of their own have the least power of any group of women. Moreover, because of the marriage gradient, the husband in most marriages has a higher level of education than the wife. In American society, educational attainment brings status and prestige in itself and is also associated with higher income.

When the husband earns more, couples agree that he automatically has the right to make important financial decisions for the family. But it frequently happens that the money he brings in also gives the husband the right to make other important decisions that have nothing to do with money. One wife described how a husband can dominate family decision making by appealing to his earning power. Gordon and Leanna have been married twelve years. He is a highway patrol officer and she works in a delicatessen:

> Gordon is aggressive, and me I'm somewhat passive. And while that has equalized some over the years, Gordon still has to have the last word on everything. We get annoyed with each other over that, but when I start to push back, he reminds me just who supports me and the children. He doesn't always bring that up, but if I start to win an argument or to make more sense about something we should do, I think he gets frustrated and so he gives me his big final line which is something like, "If you're so smart, why don't you earn more money?" or how dumb I am 'cause if I had to go out and support myself I'd be a big fizzle . . . He's only lousy like that when he thinks I'm winning and he gets threatened (Blumstein & Schwartz, p. 59).

Social-exchange theory implies that if husband and wife have equal external resources, marital interaction will also be equal. But we have noted that even in dual-career families, where the resources are fairly well matched, husbands still have more weight. Social-exchange theory may also have to take into account that specific resources acquire their exchange value because of social norms—for example, the "good provider" expectation for men means that their capacity to earn money is more highly valued than their capacity to nurture children. For women, on the other hand, "being there" to provide emotional nurturance to husband and children is a central expectation. Even if a wife brings in as much money as her husband, she may not have equal power because her success is seen as undermining his provider role and interfering with her nurturing role. In other words, the same resource (in this case, earned income) may function differently for husband and wife (Steil, 1994; Steil & Weltman, 1991).

Just how central is earning power to marital equality? And does its influence work the same way for husbands and wives? To answer these questions it is necessary to study couples in which the wives have achieved incomes equal to or greater than those of their husbands. These couples are "rare birds," indeed. However, one intriguing study (Steil & Weltman, 1991) managed to find thirty couples in which the wife earned at least 33 percent more than the husband and matched them with an equal number of couples in which the husbands earned at least 33 percent more than the wives. All partners were employed full time, all couples were white, and family incomes ranged from $25,000 to more than $75,000 annually.

Respondents were asked questions about the relative importance of careers ("Whose career is more important in the relationship?") and decision-making power ("Who has more say about household/financial issues?). Consistent with social-exchange theory, spouses who earned more saw their careers as more important and also had more say at home than spouses who earned less. Nevertheless, wives overall had less say in financial decisions, had more responsibility for children and housework, and felt that their husbands' careers were more important than their own. In other words, equal access to money can be an equalizer of power in marriage—but even when wives earn more money than their husbands, beliefs about the appropriate roles of women and men still in-

Reprinted by permission of Nicole Hollander for *Getting in Touch with Your Inner Bitch* by Elizabeth Hilts. Hysteria Publications.

FIGURE 10.2. Let's make a deal . . .

fluence the balance of power in favor of men. Social resources and social norms are both important.

Happily Ever After? Marital Satisfaction and Psychological Adjustment

"Happily ever after," as romance novels remind us, is our society's romantic ideal of marriage. However, in her influential book *The Future of Marriage* (1972), Jessie Bernard maintained that marriage is not good for women. She suggested that every marriage is really two marriages, "his" and "hers"—and "his" is much more advantageous. Which is closer to reality, the romantic ideal or the social scientists' seemingly cynical view? Does marriage bring happiness and fulfillment (see Figure 10.2)? We can examine the issue by looking at research on whether women (and men) are generally satisfied with the marriages they make, and whether marriage has any relationship to psychological adjustment.

The Life Cycle and Marital Happiness

The happiness and satisfaction of married women (and men) varies greatly across the life course of a marriage. Almost all studies of marital satisfaction over time show an initial "honeymoon period" followed by a substantial decline in happiness with the birth of the first child. Satisfaction often hits its lowest point when the children are school-aged or adolescents. Some studies have shown that the happiness of the early years is regained or even surpassed in later life, when the children have grown and left home. In other studies, the happiness trend has been all downhill (Feeney, Peterson, & Noller, 1994; Schlesinger, 1982; Steinberg & Silverberg, 1987).

Women may experience changes in marital satisfaction across the life of the marriage more than men do. In one study of 700 middle- and upper-middle-class couples, women's satisfaction declined more than their husbands' when they became parents and rebounded more at the "empty-nest" stage (Rollins & Feldman, 1970). Altogether, the rather depressing findings on satisfaction across the life course of a marriage recall Bernard's (1972) distinction between "his" and "her" marriage and suggest that, in marriage, the first twenty years are the hardest!

What accounts for the changes in marital happiness over time? And why are the changes more pronounced for women? One possibility is that the birth of children ends the happy honeymoon for women because of the increased work and responsibility children bring. As we discussed earlier, even in relatively nontraditional marriages, women do more child care than their partners. However, it seems that it is not the increased workload itself but rather the increased inequality that makes mothers less satisfied with their marriages than nonmothers. When more than 700 women were studied during pregnancy and three months after the birth of their first child, they reported doing much more of the housework and child care than they had expected. Their negative feelings about their marriages were related to the violation of their expectancies of equal sharing. In other words, it was not the tedious domestic chores that made these new mothers less happy than they had been earlier, but their feeling that the new division of labor was unfair. The more they had expected equality, the more dissatisfied they were (Ruble, Fleming, Hackel, & Stangor, 1988).

Even when couples have been married thirty years or more, they look back at the child-rearing years as their least happy (Finkel & Hansen, 1992). When children leave home, couples have fewer demands on their money and time. Many couples experience the postchildren stage of their marriage as a time of greater freedom and flexibility, and therefore of increased marital happiness (Schlesinger, 1982).

Marriage and Psychological Well-Being

Married women are more likely than married men to have psychological disorders and problems. Single women, on the other hand, have fewer disorders and problems than single men. In fact, for every type of unmarried person (ever-single, divorced, and widowed), most studies show higher rates of psychological adjustment disorders for men than women. Only married women have more disorders than their male counterparts (Bernard, 1972; Gove, 1972; Steil & Turetsky, 1987b). This pattern was one reason Bernard (1972) made the "his and her" marriage distinction; it seems to show that marriage is not good for women's mental health. Indeed, recent research continues to show that men are more satisfied than women with their marriages, and receive greater mental health benefits from being married (Fowers, 1991).

Why do husbands enjoy better psychological adjustment and well-being than wives? To answer this question we need to consider the different types of marriage. Several studies have shown that full-time homemakers have the poorest psychological adjustment, employed husbands have the best, and employed wives are intermediate (Steil & Turetsky, 1987b)—suggesting that something about being a homemaker contributes to the occurrence of psychological disorders.

We will look at women's work in homemaking and child care more closely in Chapters 11 and 12 and at psychological disorders in Chapter 15. For now, it is important to note that some of the unpaid work that women do in marriage is low status and boring. It may provide valuable social and emotional resources for others, while the woman herself has less support (Peplau & Gordon, 1985). Wives usually keep up contacts with friends and relatives, care for family members when they are ill, and encourage their husbands and children to take good care of themselves. They are likely to be available to listen to their husbands' troubles and problems.

In one study of more than 4,000 married persons aged 55 and over, husbands said they were most likely to confide in their wives, while wives were less likely to confide in their spouse and more likely to turn to a friend, sister, or daughter. Those who confided in their spouses, regardless of sex, had markedly higher marital satisfaction and overall psychological well-being than those who did not (Lee, 1988). The work of caring and emotional support that married women do is an important resource for others' well-being and may partly account for their husbands' better psychological adjustment.

The homemaker role seems to be only part of the problem. Note that employed husbands have fewer disorders than employed wives. In marriages, wives' problems may be related to husbands' unwillingness to do a fair share of housework and child care. In other words, differences in psychological adjustment may be related to power and equality in the marriage. Couples who see their marriage as equal are more satisfied than more traditional couples, report better sexual adjustment and communication, and are less likely to use manipulative and indirect influence tactics with each other (Aida & Falbo, 1991; Steil, 1994). Perhaps it is not marriage *per se* that is bad for women's mental health but marriages in which women have little power and status (Steil, 1983). Inequalities of power and status are also related to physical and sexual abuse in marriage (see Chapter 14).

In a study of more than 800 dual-career professional couples, Janice Steil and Beth Turetsky (1987a) set out to test the hypothesis that marital power is related to psychological well-being. They gathered information on each woman's earned income, her influence and responsibilities within the marriage, and her symptoms of psychological disorders. Because of earlier research connecting the presence of children to lowered marital happiness, they also compared childless women and mothers.

For childless women, the more equal a woman's marital relationship, the more satisfied she was with her marriage—and marital satisfaction was an important factor in overall psychological well-being. The mothers experienced their marriages as significantly less equal than the childless women did, and the perceived inequality was directly related to psychological well-being. Although the dual-career professional couples in this sample are not representative of all married couples (the power differences between husbands and wives were smaller than most), this study suggests that relative power and equality play an important role in married women's well-being, one that future research on marriage and psychological adjustment should take into account.

Lifelong Marriages

What are the "secrets of success" of husbands and wives in enduring marriages? Despite the importance of marriage in people's lives, there is very little research on marriages that last for twenty, thirty, or more years. In a study of 129 Canadian couples who had been married an average of twenty-five years and had parented at least one child, more than half the women said that they had started out their married lives with traditional expectations; only 23 percent had expected to share domestic and workforce responsibilities. However, only 20 percent still had traditional expectations at the time of the study; over the course of their marriages their expectations had evolved to an ideal of shared responsibilities and more independence for themselves. Wives and husbands were asked to indicate the factors that had contributed to their staying together. Although they were interviewed separately, spouses agreed almost perfectly (Schlesinger, 1982). More recently, 147 U.S. couples who had been married at least twenty years were asked similar questions (Fenell, 1993). The factors both sets of couples thought were most important are shown in Table 10.1.

Of course, not all marriages that last a long time are happy marriages. In the Canadian study, about 10 percent of women and men indicated dissatisfactions with their relationships; for women, the dissatisfactions centered around sexual relations, finances, the husband's workload, and children (Schlesinger, 1982). Chronic marital dissatisfaction is related to problems of mental and physical health for older women (Levenson, Carstensen, & Gottman, 1993). Because marriage is an institution supported by the society as a whole, some marriages endure despite unhappiness and lack of fulfillment. Long-term marriages may involve a lifetime of accumulated inequalities and set patterns of male dominance that are difficult to renegotiate even if the couple enters therapy (Siegel, 1983).

TABLE 10.1 Long-Time Married Couples Cite Factors That Make Marriage Last

Canadian Couples	U.S. Couples
Respect for each other	Lifetime commitment to marriage
Trusting each other	Loyalty to spouse
Loyalty	Strong moral values
Loving each other	Respect spouse as best friend
Counting on each other	Commitment to sexual fidelity
Considering each others' needs	Desire to be a good parent
Providing each other with emotional support	Faith in God and spiritual commitment
Commitment to make marriage last	Desire to please and support spouse
Fidelity	Good companion to spouse
Give and take in marriage	Willingness to forgive and be forgiven

Source: Fenell, 1993; Schlesinger, 1982.

Blumstein and Schwartz (1983) found that couples who were living together (but not legally married) were more likely to break up when there was a pattern of inequality in the relationship; however, for married couples, inequality had no effect on whether the couple stayed together. Although marital inequality may lower marital satisfaction and fulfillment for women, social norms may keep unhappy marriages together.

Psychological research on happiness in marriage points up some interesting discrepancies between the romantic ideal and the psychological and sociological realities. Our society tells us that marriage and parenthood are more important routes to fulfillment for women than for men. Women are thought to be eager to "catch" a husband and men are thought to be "caught" reluctantly. Women may invest a great deal of energy in planning their weddings and their married lives—have you ever met a man with a "hope chest" or seen a "Grooms" magazine on the newsstand? Yet research on marital satisfaction and the psychological adjustment of married people suggests that Jessie Bernard was right when she proposed that there are two marriages in every marital union, his and hers, and that his is better than hers. Perhaps it would make more sense for men than for women to be investing their time in dreaming and planning for the day they will find their "one and only" mate and begin to live "happily ever after" (see Figure 10.3).

LESBIAN COUPLES

Stereotypes

In the same way that individual lesbian and bisexual women form an "invisible minority" of the population (Chapter 9), lesbian couples form a largely invisible minority of people in long-term committed relationships. This lack of visibility allows stereotypes about lesbians to flourish. One popular stereotype is that lesbian couples mimic (white middle-class) heterosexual roles, with one partner being the "husband" ("butch") and the other the "wife" ("femme"). This stereotype, which applies a heterosexual script to the relationships of lesbians, has been described as the single most persistent and inaccurate myth about lesbian relationships (Peplau & Gordon, 1983).

Why does the stereotype of "butch/femme" lesbian couples persist? One reason may be that the few lesbians who do play these roles are much more visible to the public than the majority who do not.

Movies and television also perpetuate the stereotype. Finally, heterosexual marriage models provide such a powerful script for love relationships in our culture that it is difficult for most people to imagine a committed, intimate relationship that does not conform to that script (Peplau & Gordon, 1983).

Who Are Lesbian Couples?

In surveys of lesbians conducted over the last two decades, about 75 percent of respondents were currently in a steady relationship, with the range between 45 percent and 80 percent in different samples. Not all steady relationships in-

FIGURE 10.3. No Comment

volved living with the partner. Women not currently in committed relationships were unattached for a variety of reasons—some had been through a recent breakup or the death of a partner, others were actively looking, and others did not want a relationship (Peplau & Gordon, 1983).

When two women make a commitment to live together as lovers and friends, their relationship has some similarities to conventional marriage—but without the institutional aspects or the label. Lesbians (and gay men) do not have access to the predictable features of marriage that make it seem desirable to become a couple and difficult to break up. For example, there is no standard way for them to have an engagement ritual or public wedding ceremony or to establish reciprocal legal rights and responsibilities. There are no tax advantages or spousal insurance benefits. Lesbian partners may even be legally forbidden to see each other in the event of serious accident or hospitalization if their families of origin do not approve. Ending the relationship is not hampered by complicated laws regulating divorce but can be very difficult if property and finances are contested. Nor does society urge gay couples to work at their relationships and remain loyal through the hard times.

This lack of institutional and societal support can give people a feeling of freedom to make their own rules, but it can also lead to a feeling of instability. Some lesbian couples have written their own wedding ceremonies; occasionally one partner legally adopts the other or the other's children. Many include each other in their wills and insurance policies, buy homes together, or draw up contracts delineating rights and responsibilities to each other. All these are ways of giving the relationship some institutional and legal status (Blumstein & Schwartz, 1983).

Relationship Characteristics

What are the characteristics of enduring lesbian relationships and how do they compare to heterosexual marriages? These questions have been the subject of a great deal of research by psychologists and sociologists. Lesbian relationships can be compared on the same dimensions as heterosexual marriages: roles and the division of labor, companionship and communication, power and authority, and satisfaction.

As we noted above, few lesbian couples mimic "husband" and "wife" roles in their lives together. In fact, most lesbians (and gay men) actively reject these roles (Peplau & Gordon, 1983). In one study of more than 1,500 lesbian couples, 75 percent expressed the belief that both should work for pay (Blumstein & Schwartz, 1983). Fewer than 1 percent of these couples actually lived in a one-earner situation. Because same-sex couples cannot assign the "breadwinner" role on the basis of sex and because they tend to value independence in their relationships, the importance of the work or career interests of each partner is much more likely to be fairly equal than in heterosexual marriages.

Just as they balance work roles, lesbians are highly likely to share household duties (Kurdek, 1993). Perhaps because they resist being defined in terms of traditional (and low-status) "women's" work, they assign housekeeping chores on the basis of preference and ability, with each partner adjusting her responsibilities to fit her paid-work schedule. The basic principle is fairness, and couples negotiate changes in work and home responsibilities. In one couple interviewed, the speaker is an investment officer at a bank and her partner is a medical student:

> She feels very strongly about having an equitable situation and I think that comes from her having lived with men and feeling taken advantage of in the past, so she definitely feels it ought to be equitable. It's easy to slip into something where she does more because I am the only one working full time . . . but we see the dangers of that and we are keeping things in line so she doesn't get stuck with too much (Blumstein & Schwartz, 1983, p. 150).

Same-sex couples tend to share more leisure activities than heterosexual couples. They are more likely to socialize with friends together, belong to the same clubs, and share hobbies and sports interests. There are probably several reasons for this. Perhaps, due to socialization, two women are more likely to have interests in common than a woman and a man; or perhaps most people need same-sex "best friends," and only lesbians and gay men can find a same-sex friend and a spouse in the same person. Whatever their sexual orientation, women are more likely than men to say that they value emotional expressiveness, sharing feelings, and having egalitarian relationships (Peplau & Cochran, 1980). The majority of lesbian couples are relationship-centered: they want their relationship to be central to their lives, and they value companionship and communication (Blumstein & Schwartz, 1983).

Power in Lesbian Relationships

When there are power differences in a lesbian relationship, they are usually due to the same factors that influence power in heterosexual relationships, such as one partner having greater resources of money, status, or education, or one partner being more committed than the other (Peplau & Gordon, 1983). However, the egalitarian ideal may be more important than status and money in determining power relations among lesbians. In one study of seventy couples, power sharing was *un*related to age, income, and education of the partners (Reilly & Lynch, 1990).

Many of the other factors that influence power, such as traditional beliefs, are much less likely to be present in lesbian relationships. Therefore, we might expect that lesbian couples will typically have a more equal balance of power—more egalitarian relationships—than heterosexual married couples. Research bears out this expectation. Unlike heterosexual couples, many of whom believe that the man should be the head of the family, the lesbian ideal is a relationship "where two strong women come together in total equality" (Blumstein & Schwartz, 1983, p. 310). In one study of seventy-seven women currently involved in lesbian relationships, seventy-five thought that both partners should have exactly equal power (Caldwell & Peplau, 1984).

Satisfaction in Lesbian Relationships

Several studies have compared the self-reported satisfaction and happiness of lesbian and heterosexual committed couples. In general, these studies show that there are few differences between the two types of couples in scores on marital adjustment measures (Cardell, Finn, & Marecek, 1981; Peplau & Gordon, 1983). When matched samples of lesbians and heterosexuals were compared on liking and loving scales, the lesbians, like the heterosexual women, reported that they both loved and liked their partners—in other words, were high in attachment, caring, and intimacy, as well as affection and respect (Peplau & Cochran, 1980). Like heterosexual women, lesbians are likely to be more satisfied if the relationship is egalitarian (Caldwell & Peplau, 1984). If the two partners have different levels of career commitment, satisfaction is lower (Eldridge & Gilbert, 1990). However, lesbians may be more likely to establish egalitarian relationships than heterosexual women (Caldwell & Peplau, 1984; Schneider, 1986; Steil, 1994); therefore, their relationship satisfaction may be greater on the average.

Conflicts in lesbian relationships may come from the high value both partners place on both independence and connectedness (Blumstein & Schwartz, 1983) or echoes of the mother–daughter relationship (Burch, 1987). External pressures can affect relationships, too. Women who love women have to cope with being labeled deviant and with having heterosexist behavior directed at their relationship. This may include rejection or "disowning" by a woman's parents, removing the lesbian child from a will or denying her an inheritance, refusing to acknowledge the partner or the relationship, exclusion from family gatherings, active encouragement to break up, and forbidding all contact between partners. One important determinant of relationship satisfaction for lesbians is having a social support network. Women who are "out" (identified as homosexual) to significant others in their lives (parents, best friends, siblings, employees) report more satisfaction with their partners. Receiving social support from friends and family is related to individual psychological adjustment as well as happiness in the relationship for both lesbians and gay male couples (Berger, 1990; Kurdek, 1988).

Limitations of Research

Although psychology has come a long way in the past twenty years in studying love relationships among both heterosexuals and homosexuals, research on relationships is limited in several important ways. It frequently relies on self reports (interviews or questionnaires), which may be biased because people want to look well-adjusted to researchers or because they lack insight into their relationships. For example, some heterosexual couples may not recognize inequality when it exists because it is the norm. Some lesbians may want to present a rosy picture of their own relationships because of political views about women's oppression in heterosexual marriage.

Research has also depended heavily on samples of volunteers that are not representative of the general popuiation, especially the population of gay and lesbian people, many of whom would probably not volunteer for research. Lesbians who have volunteered for research tend to be young, white, and middle class. Therefore, comparisons of gay and heterosexual couples may have built-in race, class, and age biases that are not easily uncovered. Much more research is needed on older couples, women of color, and relationships that cross barriers of class, color, and ethnicity (Garcia, Kennedy, Pearlman, & Perez, 1987). Yet it may be all but impossible to study a truly representative sample of lesbians as long as the dominant culture stigmatizes lesbianism (Peplau & Gordon, 1983).

POSSLQS: COHABITING COUPLES

No, the heading above is not a misprint. Today many heterosexual couples choose to live together without being legally married. Sociologists give this arrangement the unromantic name *cohabitation.* The U.S. Department of the Census uses the descriptive term *persons of the opposite sex sharing living quarters*—POSSLQs, for short (we pronounce it *possel-cues*). Couples who do it usually call it "living together"—not a very good distinguishing term since room-

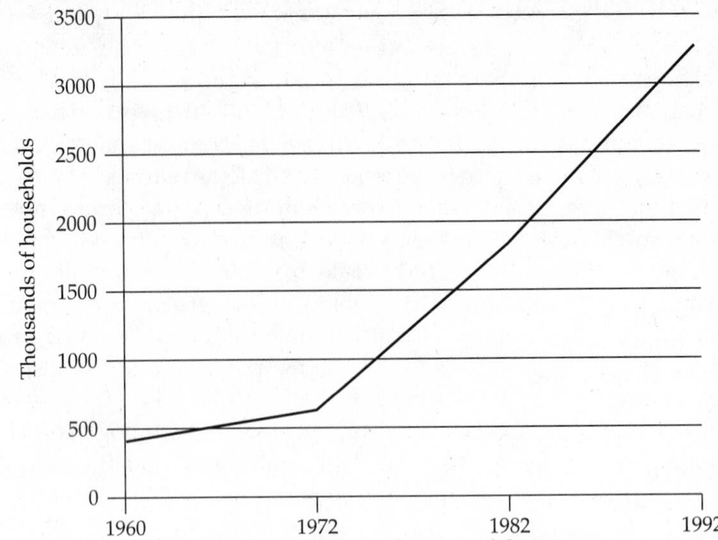

FIGURE 10.4. Cohabitation trends in the United States.
Source: Adapted from *Bianchi & Spain, 1986, Figure 1.1, p. 20;* Costello & Stone, Table 1.4, p. 260.

mates or parents and children can be said to "live together," too. A generation ago, the extreme social disapproval directed at cohabitation was expressed in the term "shacking up." None of the tags seems quite right ("Hello, I'm June, and this is my posslq, Duane" lacks a certain flair). The absence of a suitable everyday term is one clue that the cohabitation relationship is not yet an institution in society. (A similar problem exists in naming the living-together relationships and roles of gay men and lesbians. "Marriage" implies a legally sanctioned unit, "husband" and "wife" aren't quite right, "lover" is too sexual, "significant other" is too formal, and "partner" can sound too much like a law firm.)

Who Cohabits and Why?

Whatever the label, the practice of heterosexual couples living together without being officially married is more popular than ever in the United States (see Figure 10.4). Black women are more likely than white women to cohabit. Cohabiting women are generally young: Nearly 40 percent are under the age of 25. Living together is especially popular among college students: About 25 percent of undergraduates have cohabited, and another 50 percent say they would if the situation were right; only 25 percent object on moral or religious grounds (Bianchi & Spain, 1986; Spanier, 1983).

Although the increase in cohabitation is a dramatic social trend, the United States still has a lower proportion (about 4 percent of all couples) than many other industrialized countries. Estimates for France are about 13 percent; for the Netherlands, 7 percent; and for Sweden, about 25 percent. Cohabitation in Sweden is almost as much an institution as conventional marriage. Virtually all

Swedes cohabit before marriage, and a growing number never marry at all. Cohabitation is regarded both legally and morally as an accepted alternative to marriage even for couples who have children (Popenoe, 1987). One couple recounted the following "marital history" to a researcher:

> They met in 1967, moved in together in 1969, exchanged rings in 1973 (this was around the time their first child was born and was for the purpose of "showing others that they were attached"), and married in 1977. When asked what anniversary they celebrated they responded, "The day we met" (Popenoe, 1987, p. 176).

Swedes believe that cohabitation is a way of liberating oneself from oppressive traditions about marriage and from state control of a private relationship. A common attitude is, "Why marry? It's our love that counts" (Popenoe, 1987).

In the United States, people choose to cohabit for a great variety of reasons (Murstein, 1986). For some, it is a prelude to marriage or a "trial marriage" in which the couple assesses its compatibility. Some cohabitants have previously been married and divorced. They may cohabitate because they are not yet ready to remarry or because they feel soured on marriage. Some young people cohabit to show that they are emancipated when they leave their parents' home for college. Some cohabiting arrangements are more a matter of convenience or dependency than deep commitment. Some are monogamous, others not.

People who choose cohabitation tend to be more sexually experienced and active than those who do not. They are also more liberal in attitudes about gender roles. Cohabiting women generally value their independence and autonomy; they say they prefer to be thought of as an individual rather than half of a couple. Their desire for independence and equality in the relationship sometimes hits a stumbling block when they cannot contribute what they consider a "fair share" financially because they earn much less than their partners (Blumstein & Schwartz, 1983; Murstein, 1986).

Relationship Characteristics

Cohabiting couples usually have a nontraditional division of labor similar to modern marriage. They almost always expect that both partners will work outside the home. In one study, 78 percent of cohabiting women believed that both partners should work, compared with only 39 percent of married women. Cohabiting men (66 percent agreed) were slightly more traditional. (Married men were the most conservative group on this issue; only 31 percent believed that both partners should work.) However, as with married couples, the division of labor at home is still more or less traditional, with women doing much more housework than men (Blumstein & Schwartz, 1983). Liberal attitudes about gender roles do not always lead to role-free behavior.

Though many cohabiting women have egalitarian ideals (and choose to cohabit rather than marry partly because of those ideals), their goals of independence and autonomy within a relationship are usually only partly fulfilled. As with married couples, issues of money, power, and the division of labor inside and outside the home can be sources of conflict. Nevertheless, most cohabitants report high satisfaction with their arrangement, and the vast majority plan to marry someday, though not necessarily their current partner (Murstein, 1986).

Living Together and Marital Choices

Does cohabitation affect later marital satisfaction? It would seem that if people use living together as a trial marriage, those who do go on to marry should be better adjusted and less likely to divorce. However, in the United States, Sweden, and Canada, research studies show a greater tendency for former cohabitants to divorce, though their total time together is as long as the average married couple spends before divorcing (Teachman & Polenko, 1990). There may be ethnic and racial differences, too. In a study of about 200 black and 175 white couples in their first year of marriage, living together before marriage was unrelated to marital happiness for whites, but negatively related for blacks (Crohan & Veroff, 1989). Of course, a higher divorce rate for people who had previously cohabited is not necessarily an indication that cohabitation is a social problem. Part of the reason may be that women who cohabit (and their partners) are more unconventional, independent, and autonomous than those who do not; therefore they may be more likely to leave a marriage that does not meet their expectations (Murstein, 1986).

NEVER-MARRIED WOMEN

At any given time, about one-third of the adult women in the United States are single. Most of these are women under 25, cohabitants, or older women who have been divorced or widowed. An unknown proportion are lesbians, living alone or with other women. Many are mothers. Widows, divorced women, and single mothers are discussed elsewhere; here we will focus on never-married women without children.

The number of women who remain single throughout their lives is probably increasing, although exact statistics are not available. The majority of never-married women maintain their own independent households (Bequaert, 1976; Bianchi & Spain, 1986).

Stereotypes and Social Judgments

Women who do not marry are "often judged but seldom studied" (Simon, 1987). Negative judgments of never-married women are certainly easy to document. The goal of a perennial children's card game is to avoid being stuck with the "Old Maid" card. Poets and authors write of "maidens withering on the stalk" or "the tasteless dry embrace of a stale virgin with a winter face"; or they belittle a male character by comparing him to a fussy old maid. In advertising, spinsters are symbols of penny-pinching, prissiness, timidity, and overly proper behavior. Barbara Levy Simon (from whose 1987 book these examples are taken) concludes that "In Anglo-American culture, the never-married old woman is a stock character, a bundle of negative personal characteristics, and a metaphor for barrenness, ugliness, and death" (p. 2). Never-married men, or bachelors, are rarely the targets of such negative assessments.

Classical clinical psychology and psychiatry have reinforced the notion that for women, remaining unmarried is evidence of a serious psychological flaw. The orthodox view is that being able to form long-term committed relationships is a mark of emotional maturity and healthy personality. This view assumes that unmarried women do not have close relationships and that being unmarried is not due to the woman's own choice. It supports the harmful fallacy that there is one psychological norm that exemplifies good adjustment and social value. Because of such societal stigma, unmarried women must cope with judgments about their supposedly deficient psyches that may lower their self-esteem. They also are subjected to psychological tactics that question their motives. For example, when an unmarried woman asserts that she is single by choice, she may be accused of rationalization or denial due to unconscious conflicts and pent-up sexual energy (Adams, 1976).

Who Stays Single and Why?

In contrast to these stereotypes and social judgments, it is generally true that women who remain unmarried have better physical health and greater economic resources than those who marry. Earlier, we discussed research showing that unmarried women have fewer serious psychological disorders than married women. Single women are better educated, are more intelligent, and achieve greater occupational success than their married counterparts. The lower marriage rate of highly capable women has been explained in terms of the marriage gradient we discussed earlier in this chapter. Because men prefer to marry women who are slightly below them in education, occupational status, and income (and women prefer to "marry up"), the women who are at the top of the social scale are likely to be the "leftovers," with nobody sufficiently "superior" to them to want to marry them! (The marriage gradient idea also implies that men who do not marry are more likely to be those at the very bottom of the social scale.) However, it is important to remember that data about who marries whom are correlational, and causation cannot be determined. Whether highly educated, intelligent women are unattractive to men, whether they are less likely to marry because they have alternatives that are more appealing, or whether other factors not yet analyzed are involved is an open question (Unger, 1979a). Moreover, the marriage gradient is less prevalent in black communities.

Rewards of the Single Life

What are the advantages and disadvantages of a permanently single way of life? Because never-married women have seldom been studied, the evidence is scarce. However, a few researchers have completed interview studies, and their results give a descriptive picture of a single woman's life (Bequaert, 1976; Simon, 1987). In the largest of these studies, fifty elderly women reflected on their lives in in-depth interviews in their homes (Simon, 1987). All these women had supported themselves, and many had helped support their parents in old age. Work and financial independence were important aspects of their lives.

Sixty-eight percent of the women stressed the importance of autonomy and freedom from the role expectations of marriage: "You see, dear, it's *marriage* I avoid, not men. Why would I ever want to be a wife? . . . A wife is someone's servant; a woman is someone's friend" (Simon, 1987, pp. 31–32).

More than three-fourths of the group had consciously and deliberately chosen to be single:

> I dated four men over the years who wanted me as a wife. They were darlings, each of them. I spent huge amounts of time with them. But I never for a moment considered marrying one. Well, why would I? I had their company and their attention without all the headaches a wife bears. I knew all about birth control from the time I was a girl, so I didn't worry about getting pregnant. . . . (Simon, 1987, pp. 41–42).

Rather than being socially isolated, the women were closely involved with their families and had many friendships with coworkers and neighbors, both women and men. The women in this study were of an age group and era that did not tolerate discussion of sexuality, and they refused to answer interview questions about lesbianism. However, many spontaneously described their friendships with women as especially rewarding, and some had intimate relationships with female life partners:

> There is nothing I did that Joyce didn't know about . . . I shared everything with her. She did the same with me. We got to be friends in high school . . . We stayed roommates for fifty-seven years, until her heart gave out suddenly six years ago . . . I'm still reeling from that loss. She leaned on me all those years just like I relied on her. In selfish moments, I wish that I had gone before her. Now I come home to silence and to memories (Simon, 1987, p. 92).

Of course, people looking back on their lives in retrospect may remember selectively. Nevertheless, the voices of the never-married women in these studies give reason to challenge the stereotype of the frustrated, unfulfilled "old maid."

ENDING THE COMMITMENT: DIVORCE AND SEPARATION

The rise in divorces has probably gained more attention and caused more concern than any other social trend of our times. While psychologists and sociologists analyze causes and consequences, marital conflicts, separation, divorce, and their effects are dramatized in movies (*When a Man Loves a Woman, War of the Roses, The Favor*) and TV shows ("Civil Wars," "Grace under Fire"), and corporations market greeting cards that proclaim "Congratulations on your divorce."

Divorce Rates

The United States has the highest divorce rate of any industrialized nation, a rate that more than doubled between 1960 and 1980 and has only recently begun to level off at an all-time high (Costello & Stone, 1994). By the 1970s, for the first time in American history a marriage was more likely to end in divorce than in

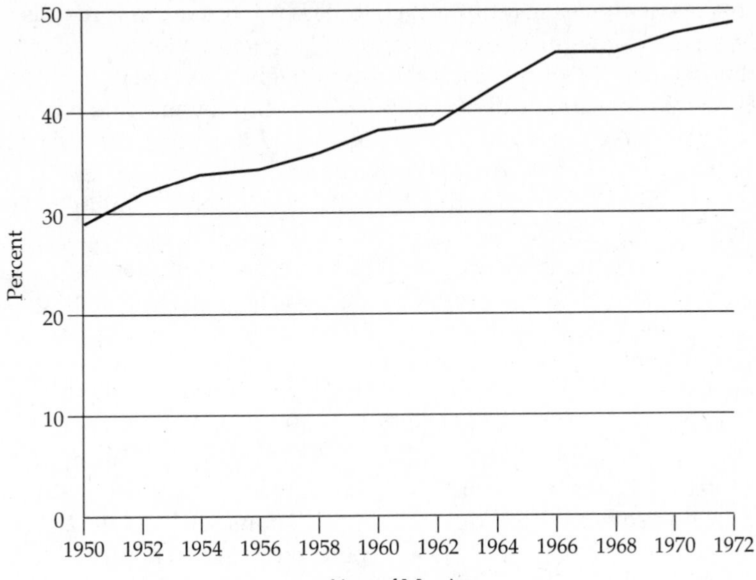

FIGURE 10.5. Divorce rates in the United States.
Source: Bianchi & Spain, 1986, Figure 1.3, p. 23.

the death of a spouse. Black women are considerably more likely than white women to end a marriage through divorce or prolonged separation. Based on earlier age groups, it is projected that between 40 percent and 50 percent of Americans born during the 1970s who marry will proceed to divorce. Figure 10.5 shows this trend. Other countries have experienced similar increases in divorce rate, though none as extreme as the United States (Bianchi & Spain, 1986; Norton & Moorman, 1987; Price & McKenry, 1988).

In terms of the number of people involved, the impact of divorce trends is striking. Each year since 1972, more than 1 million children have been involved in a parental divorce. Currently, there are more than 17 million divorced women in the United States. What are the causes and consequences of divorce for women?

Correlates of Divorce

At the societal level, several factors have been correlated with rising divorce rates. Divorce rates rise along with women's participation in the paid work force, both in the United States and in many other countries (Trent & South, 1989). Wives' paid employment is not usually a direct cause of divorce; rather, it seems that when women have alternatives for economic survival other than dependence on a husband's income, they are less likely to stay in unsatisfactory marriages (Bianchi & Spain, 1986; Price & McKenry, 1988). Age at first marriage is also highly correlated with later separation and divorce: The younger the man and woman are when they marry, the more likely they are to divorce. As of 1985, for example, more than 12 percent of teenage marriages ended in divorce within five years (Norton & Moorman, 1987). Another factor related to the rising divorce rate is changing attitudes: Divorce is no longer the social disgrace it once was.

At the personal level, people who divorce give a variety of reasons. Of course, these reasons are hardly "objective"; rather, they indicate how women and men try to make sense of what has happened to their dreams of a happy marriage. Interview studies of divorcing women in the 1940s and 1950s generally showed that their reasons had to do with their husbands failing to support the family or being excessively authoritarian. In contrast, lack of communication and companionship is more common reasons given in recent studies (Price & McKenry, 1988). This suggests that the "ideal" marriage that divorcing women are using as a yardstick by which to judge their own marriages has changed over time and is now closer to the modern than the traditional type.

Women and men tend to give somewhat different reasons for the breakup of their marriages. In one study (Cleek & Pearson, 1985), more than 600 divorcing persons were asked to indicate which of eighteen possible causes of divorce were applicable to their own situation. (The eighteen causes had been derived from counseling sessions with other divorcing spouses.) Table 10.2 shows the causes and the percentage of people who perceived each as applicable. Women were more likely than men to stress basic unhappiness, incompatibility, emotional and physical abuse, and their husbands' alcohol abuse and infidelity as

TABLE 10.2 Causes of Divorce

Perceived Divorce Cause	Females	Males
Indicated significantly more often by females:		
Basic unhappiness	59.9%	46.9%
Incompatibility	56.4	44.7
Emotional abuse	55.5	24.7
Alcohol abuse—spouse	30.0	5.8
Infidelity—spouse	25.2	10.5
Physical abuse	21.7	3.6
Children	8.9	4.4
Indicated significantly more often by males:		
Women's lib	3.0	14.5
Alcohol abuse—self	.9	9.4
No significant difference between males and females:		
Communication problems	69.7	59.3
Financial problems	32.9	28.7
Sexual problems	32.1	30.2
In-laws	10.7	11.6
Religious differences	8.6	6.5
Mental illness	5.0	6.9
Drug abuse—spouse	3.9	1.4
Infidelity—self	3.9	6.2
Drug abuse—self	.3	1.1

Source: From Margaret Cleek and T. Allan Pearson, "Perceived causes of divorce: An analysis of interrelationships," *Journal of Marriage and Family, 47*, Table 3, p.181. Copyright 1985 by the National Council on Family Relations, 3989 Central Avenue, N.E., Suite 550, Minneapolis, MN 55421. Reprinted by permission.

causes of their divorce. Men were more likely to indicate that their own alcohol abuse and "women's lib" were responsible for their divorce. It would be interesting to explore the different meanings that women and men in this sample gave to the term "women's lib," a negative term for feminism, since men considered it to be more of a contributor to marital breakdown.

Consequences of Divorce

Whatever the reasons for its occurrence, divorce has serious and long-lasting consequences for women. Three types of consequences can be distinguished, each intertwined with the others in its effects. We will examine, in turn, psychological adjustment, economic effects, and responsibility for children.

Psychological Adjustment Following Divorce

A considerable number of divorcing women (from 17 percent to 33 percent in different samples) describe their divorces as causing little or no psychological disturbance or pain. These women view their divorces as ending a stressful or unbearable situation (for example, physical or emotional abuse) and leading to increased feelings of freedom and competence. For most women, however, adjustment to divorce includes feelings of anger, helplessness, and ambivalence. Stress during divorce is related to a variety of physical health problems. (As with all correlational research, it is not possible to determine cause and effect in these studies.) Compared with married people, divorced people of both sexes have higher rates of illness and death, alcoholism, and serious accidents.

The adjustment to divorce seems to be more difficult for men than women. While both divorced men and women are more likely to commit suicide than their married counterparts, divorced men are 50 percent more likely to do so than divorced women. They are also more likely to show serious psychological disturbances (Price & McKenry, 1988). Women appear to be better at building and maintaining networks of close friends and family during and following divorce (Gerstel, 1988), and men may miss their partner's caretaking more (see Figure 10.6). However, women and men are quite similar in their responses to divorce in many other ways (Gove & Shin, 1989). The question of whose divorce is worse, "his" or "hers," is not easily resolved. Some researchers have suggested that men are more negatively affected in the short term, while women have more long-term problems to resolve (Price & McKenry, 1988).

Women whose marriages and personal values are traditional may have a more difficult time adjusting to divorce than those whose values and marriages are more egalitarian. Women who have devoted themselves to nurturing others and furthering their husbands' careers may find that their life's work is devalued when they must seek paid employment. Many of these women are over 40—20 percent of divorces involve marriages of more than fifteen years' duration (Weitzman, 1985)—and entered marriage with the expectation that they would be lifelong homemakers, their husbands the family providers. When these *displaced homemakers* lose their source of financial support, they have few marketable skills and "face triple jeopardy of discrimination; because they are women, because they have been homemakers, and because they are older" (Greenwood-Audant, 1984, p. 265). Moreover, they are likely to suffer from low

"That's right, Phil. A separation will mean—among other things—watching your own cholesterol."

FIGURE 10.6. "No comment."

self-esteem because their sense of self is heavily invested in being a good wife and mother. The displaced homemaker is especially likely to view her divorce as a personal failure and a negation of all she has worked for.

Economic Effects of Divorce

Divorce in the United States has been characterized as an economic disaster for women. It has been documented repeatedly that the economic status of men improves upon divorce, while the economic status of women deteriorates (Price & McKenry, 1988). Moreover, modern "no-fault" divorce laws, designed in part to ensure equitable division of assets, have actually made the situation worse for women (Weitzman, 1985).

Why do women lose out financially with divorce? There are several reasons. Counselors and psychologists often emphasize emotional aspects to the neglect of financial considerations when counseling divorcing couples. Women's sense of guilt and failure during the breaking-up period may prevent them from asserting financial needs. However, structural factors are probably more important than individual ones. The majority of state property laws assume that property belongs to the spouse who earned it. As you have seen, husbands usually have had greater earning power during the marriage; therefore, these laws result in men being awarded more of the couple's assets. The economic value of the wife's unpaid labor may not be considered. When courts decide what an equitable share is, the divorcing wife usually receives only about one-third of the couple's property (Price & McKenry, 1988).

In other states, attempts to make divorce fairer for women have led to laws that order equal division of property. However, most divorcing couples (especially younger ones) have very little in the way of valuable property—perhaps a car (complete with loan payments), household furnishings, and a modest bank account, offset by credit card debt. Fewer than half have equity in a house. The biggest assets for the large majority of couples are the husband's education, pension benefits, and future earning power. As we discussed earlier, the husband's career usually takes priority in both single-earner and dual-earner marriages. Couples invest their time, money, and energy in his advancement; frequently the wife will postpone her education or career plans in order to put him through school, and she will do the unpaid work at home that allows him to concentrate on his paid job. Courts have been slow to recognize that the benefits husbands gain from traditional and modern marriage patterns translate into economic advantages upon divorce (Weitzman, 1985).

Contrary to the stereotype of the ex-wife leading a life of ease on alimony payments, only 15 percent of all divorced women in the United States in 1982 had ever been awarded spousal support (alimony). The average amount awarded was about $3,000 a year; most awards were for a period of about two years; and less than half of the men ordered to provide such support actually complied (Price & McKenry, 1988)

Children: Women's Responsibility

The presence or absence of children is an important factor in adjustment to divorce for women. This is because women of all social classes and marriage types are likely to be left with the financial responsibility and the day-to-day care of children when a marriage ends. The benefit of awarding custody to women is that most divorced women stay connected with their children and receive the emotional rewards of parenting more than most divorced men do. However, current custody arrangements also have costs for women.

Most divorces involve children; about 71 percent of divorcing women have one or more children at home (Norton & Moorman, 1987). Being a single parent is not easy. The single mother may feel overwhelmed with responsibility, guilty at having separated the children from their father, and compelled to be a "supermom" (L'Hommedieu, 1984).

While social scientists have concentrated on the emotional effects on children of growing up in a "fatherless family" it seems likely that "the most detrimental aspect of the absence of fathers . . . is not the lack of a male presence but the lack of a male income" (Cherlin, 1981, p. 81). About 80 percent of divorced mothers with custody of their children are awarded child support. However, the average award is only about $2,500 a year (Bianchi & Spain, 1986). The U.S. government estimated in 1985 that the cost of raising one child in a moderate-income family is $96,000; other estimates that take inflation into account range up to $175,000. Child support payments, therefore, clearly do not cover the actual costs of bringing up a child.

Moreover, the majority of women entitled to child support do not receive it. A 1978 U.S. Census Bureau survey documented that only about half of men ordered to pay child support did so; 25 percent paid some but not all of the amount ordered; and 25 percent made no payments at all. In other national studies, only about 25 to 35 percent of women were receiving the support due them. Black women are half as likely as white women to receive support (Costello & Stone, 1994), and the poorest, least educated women are the least likely of all. Only 10 percent of welfare clients receive child support (Price & McKenry, 1988). In an important analysis of the effects of divorce on women and children, Lenore Weitzman (1985) pointed out that no study has ever found that more than half of the fathers complied with child support orders; many who comply do it irregularly; and one-fourth to one-third of fathers never make a single payment despite court orders.

Thus, divorced women and their children must adjust to a lower standard of living even before they complete their emotional adjustment to divorce. A woman's standard of living declines by about 30 to 40 percent on average (Duncan & Hoffman, 1991; Morgan, 1991). In some samples, the decline has been as large as 73 percent (Weitzman, 1985). Nearly half of all woman-headed families with children live in poverty (Costello & Stone, 1994). More than 25 percent of divorced women fall into poverty for some time within five years of divorce. In addition to those who are below official poverty levels, there are many who "balance on the brink of poverty" (Morgan, 1991, p. 96).

Breaking Up

In contrast to the large amount of research on divorce, few studies have examined the process or consequences when cohabiting men and women or lesbian couples end a relationship, perhaps because these arrangements lack the institutional and legal status of marriage. As we discussed earlier, heterosexual cohabiting couples are more variable in their degree of commitment than married couples. Overall, then, one would expect that the breakup rate for cohabitors would be higher than the divorce rate for married couples, and this is true cross-culturally—for example, in Australia (Sarantakos, 1991) and Sweden. One study of Swedish couples attempted to sample only highly committed cohabiting couples by selecting only those who had had a child. Still, their breakup rate was three times the rate for comparable married couples (Popenoe, 1987).

For a U.S. sample of couples, the best comparisons of breakup rates come from Blumstein and Schwartz's (1983) study. A year and a half after participating in the original study, couples were contacted again and asked if they were still together. Figure 10.7 shows the percentage of married, cohabiting, and lesbian couples who had separated. The data show that lesbians were the most likely to break up, a surprising finding given the lesbian couples' emphasis on commitment and equality, but not so surprising when lack of social support for lesbian relationships is considered. People rarely talked about a breakup without sadness, anger, or regrets. Whether the relationship is (socially approved) heterosexual marriage, (stigmatized) living with a man, or (doubly stigmatized) living with another woman, the emotional consequences are probably similar.

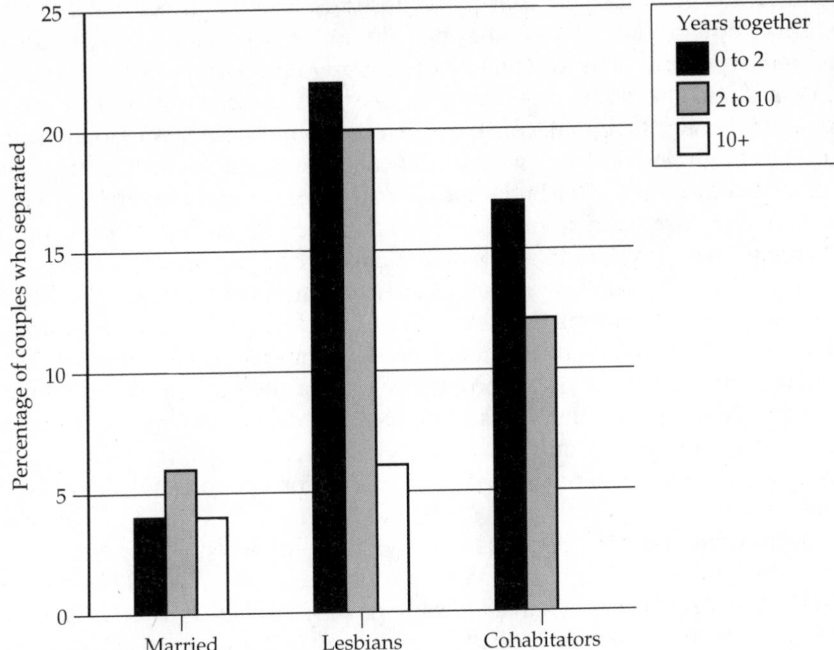

FIGURE 10.7. Percentage of couples who separated.
Source: Blumstein & Schwartz, 1983. Adapted from Figure 53, p. 308, and Figure 54, p. 315.

Countering Biases in Research on Divorce

Research on divorce usually treats it as a personal and social tragedy; "broken" families are stigmatized. This perspective reflects an androcentric bias in which the only "normal" family is a traditional, patriarchal nuclear unit. From a feminist perspective, resistance to marriage can be positive for women, and divorce may be an important way that women counter marital inequality. As we have seen, women are likelier to divorce when they can earn a living on their own; they cite abuse and unhappiness as major causes; and they adjust to divorce better than men, despite reduced income and increased responsibility for children. Despite its costs, divorce, as a way out of an oppressive situation, may be an affirmative choice for many women (Rice, 1994). In a study of successful egalitarian marriages, almost half were not first marriages, and most of the women said they had left their first marriage because of inequitable treatment (Schwartz, 1994).

REMARRIAGE

Most women who get divorced remarry, about half of them within three years of the divorce (Ihinger-Tallman & Pasley, 1987). Today, more than one-fourth of all brides are previously divorced. A cynic might say that remarriages represent a triumph of belief over experience; women (and men, who are even more likely to remarry) do not question the institution of marriage after they have been divorced. Rather, they believe that they chose the wrong partner last time and now know how to choose the right one. Women may remarry partly to escape divorce-induced poverty. Research shows that women with lower levels of education and income are more likely to remarry than those with more economic options. However, given all you have learned about power relations in marriage, you might suspect (as we do) that the consequences of entering a new marriage from an impoverished "one-down" position are unlikely to be positive. Economic discrepancies may be related to the higher rate of spouse abuse in remarried families (Crosbie-Burnett & Giles-Sims, 1991).

Are second marriages more successful? In general, the level of satisfaction in second marriages is about the same as in first marriages; as in first marriages, husbands are more satisfied than their wives (Ihinger-Tallman & Pasley, 1987). However, self-reported satisfaction is only part of the picture. Several studies have shown that second marriages are somewhat more likely to end in divorce than first marriages (Cherlin, 1981). Researchers predict that over half of women in their thirties who remarry will experience a second divorce (Dolan & Lown, 1985).

The complex family structures and dynamics of second marriages ("his," "hers," and "their" children, stepparents, ex-spouses, in-laws, and ex-in-laws) may be a source of stress. Financial problems may be increased by lack of support payments from former husbands, and many families have conflicts over how to allocate money to various household members (Ihinger-Tallman & Pasley, 1987). (Who should pay Tiffany's medical bills or college tuition—mother, father, or stepparent?) Second marriages may also be less stable because, once having violated the societal and religious ideal of lifelong marriage, people are even less inclined to stay in unsatisfying relationships.

Some of the special problems of remarried couples—and the unshaken belief in the ideal—can be seen in the words of one couple, married less than two years at the time of the interview. She is a homemaker and he is a carpenter:

WIFE: I feel anyone thinking about marrying a person who has been previously married should think very seriously about it. There are definitely special problems that accompany this type of marriage. I feel the couple should have counseling before and not marry until *all* doubts about the marriage are gone. I feel my husband and I will always have his previous marriage overshadowing our marriage. My husband also feels guilty for not having his children with him. I in turn feel guilty and feel if it wasn't for me, maybe my husband would get back with his ex-wife and kids and live happily ever after.

HUSBAND: I think everyone should find the right spouse the first time. I found mine the second time and the only thing that stops it from being perfect is my previous marriage (Ihinger-Tallman & Pasley, 1987, p. 60).

EQUALITY AND COMMITMENT: INCOMPATIBLE IDEALS?

Throughout this chapter we have focused on women in long-term relationships with men and with other women. A recurrent theme has been patterns of equality and inequality. We have seen that women in relationships with men almost always have less power than their partners. Even when both partners believe in equality and want to work toward it, and even when both take on the "male" role of paid employment, the division of labor in the home remains relatively traditional, his job or career is given more importance than hers, and he has greater decision-making power.

This pattern seems to suggest that commitment and equality are incompatible, at least in heterosexual relationships. But egalitarian marriage and cohabitation are not impossible. Studies of power in marriage have consistently found that a small number of couples do manage to have long-term egalitarian relationships. Although their numbers may be small, their existence tells us that the ideal is not beyond human power to achieve. Egalitarian marriage may be emerging as a new way to be married—a life pattern of the future (Scanzoni & Scanzoni, 1976; Schwartz, 1994). The voices of women and men in relatively egalitarian relationships tell us that these relationships can work. Here, the speaker is a man married for sixteen years.:

> I started out pretty traditional. But over the years it made sense to change. We both work, and so we had to help each other with the kids, and pretty soon they start asking for you—so only you will do, so you do some of that. And we worked together at church, and we both went whole hog into the peace program. So that got shared. I don't know; you can't design these things. You play fair, and you do what needs doing, and pretty soon you find the old ways don't work and the new ways do (Schwartz, 1994, p. 31).

It is tempting to believe that equality in marriage or long-term cohabitation can be achieved simply by being willing to work at it. This belief is related to the ideology of romantic love we discussed in Chapter 9, a variation of "Love conquers all." How many times have you heard people express the belief that "If two people love each other enough, and if they're both willing to compromise, they can have a good marriage"? A related belief is that if the husband does not *intend* to oppress or dominate the wife, oppression and domination will not occur. Happy marriage, then, should be mainly (or entirely) a matter of picking the right person. But one major conclusion that can be drawn from the research reviewed in this chapter is that power differentials between husbands and wives are *not* solely the result of individual differences. Rather, they are strongly related to social-structural aspects of gender. The single biggest obstacle to egalitarian marriage is men's greater earning power, which steers couples into investing in his career and leaving the family to her (Schwartz, 1994).

The institution of marriage has been organized around gender inequality and "attempts to change this framework have not yet been very successful. . . . Even couples who willingly try to change traditional male and female behavior have difficulty doing so" (Blumstein & Schwartz, 1983, pp. 323–324). In order to understand how equality in marriage might become the rule rather than the exception, we will need to look at both personal and structural factors.

To have an egalitarian marriage, both wife and husband must be willing to integrate their work and family responsibilities despite social pressures to conform to more traditional roles (Gilbert, 1987). Women who openly value their work outside the home and set limits on the sacrifices they make for husbands and children may be perceived as cold, unfeminine, and selfish; men who do housework and child care and set limits on their career involvement may be perceived as weak and unmasculine, or even gay. (One of our children once asked his father not to wear an apron in front of the child's friends!) Fortunately for the future of egalitarian marriage, attitudes toward the work and family roles of women and men have changed a great deal in the past twenty years and continue to become more flexible. A large majority of women express nontraditional, pro-feminist attitudes about gender roles, and the popularity of these views is increasing over time. Though men remain more conservative than women, they also have become considerably more liberal across time (Mason & Lu, 1988). Blacks are slightly more liberal than whites on family issues.

The fact that women have more pro-feminist attitudes suggests that they will be more likely than men to take the lead in initiating change within their families. Moreover, women must lead the way to more egalitarian relationships because men are unlikely to fight a status quo that gives them many benefits. However, only when women perceive gender roles in marriage as unequal and unjust can they begin to change them. In order to recognize their position as unjust, women must be aware that other possibilities exist, must want such possibilities for themselves, must believe they are entitled to them, and must not feel personally to blame for not having them (Crosby, 1982; Steil, 1994).

Change involves negotiation. Roles are not engraved in stone, nor are they totally defined by society. Rather, they are expressed in day-to-day activities and can be negotiated between partners:

> Human beings are not just robots programmed by society. They are also willful actors, capable of choosing nonconformity and altering social structure if they so wish. . . . Role expectations are not as clear, consensual, rigid, and monolithic as an oversocialized approach implicitly assumes . . . (there are) enormous possibilities for negotiation, compromise, and innovation. Individuals can construct their own realities to a surprising extent (Thoits, 1987, p. 12).

When we think of roles as negotiable, we can ask what social factors give women more negotiating power in relationships with men. If the wider society allows for more flexible commitments to paid work by both women and men, there will be less likelihood that the man's job or career will "naturally" take precedence. It is encouraging that many social critics are calling for corporations to be more flexible and adaptable to the needs of dual-worker couples (Guinn & Russell, 1987). In Norway, the women's movement has endorsed the idea of a universal six-hour workday as a way to reduce marital inequity (Haavind, 1983), based on the idea that work within the home is unlikely to be shared equally if one or both partners have an excessive commitment to paid work. The interaction of work and family life will be discussed further in Chapter 12.

Economic power is a key social factor. We have seen that equality is most likely when the partners' economic resources are most balanced. This is partly because money buys freedom from structural constraints. Couples may be less likely to allocate housework unfairly if they can buy out of some responsibilities; they may not choose his job over hers if they can afford good child care (Thoits, 1987).

One important factor in achieving egalitarian relationships combines the personal and the social-structural. It is important for couples who are trying to find new "unscripted" ways to live together to provide social support for themselves by building networks of like-minded people. Couples who spend time with other nontraditional couples can learn from each other, provide havens from the criticism that more traditional people may aim their way, and provide role models of healthy alternatives to male dominance for themselves and their children. As the number of couples who are consciously trying to build egalitarian relationships increases, it should be easier for them to find each other and build such supportive networks. "Subcultures of consensus" will arise, in which nontraditional arrangements are seen as legitimate, normal, and even routine (Thoits, 1987). Similar needs can be met for lesbian couples by being part of a lesbian community (Krieger, 1982). Although the heterosexual world may not value and support their relationships, other lesbians can.

At present, change in the roles of spouse, parent, and worker is "essentially a grass-roots movement, originating at the interpersonal level and generalizing only gradually to the societal level" (Thoits, 1987, p. 21). The grass-roots movement toward egalitarian relationships will bring benefits for both women and men. Men will be relieved of some of the economic burdens of traditional marriage and be freer to become involved with their children's growth and development. For women, the benefits of equality are even greater: more satisfying relationships and better psychological adjustment (Schwartz, 1994; Steil & Turetsky, 1987b). For both, equality and role flexibility in committed long-term relationships offer a chance to become more fully human.

CONNECTING THEMES

1. When women and men are in enduring relationships, they often have "his" and "her" experiences, such as differential workloads and roles, relationship satisfaction, and psychological adjustment. This is not because women and men are fundamentally different in needs and goals, but because differences in power and status structure different roles for them.

2. Marriage is an institution with a name and a script. The life paths of lesbians, unmarried women, and heterosexual cohabitants are either not named or given negative labels. Within marriage, inequality is so much the norm that it may be invisible.

3. Women who do not enter heterosexual marriages are a diverse group. Lesbian couples form a largely invisible minority, and ever-single women are rarely studied. Even within heterosexual marriage, there is great diversity along lines of ethnicity, social class, and marriage type (traditional, modern, egalitarian).

4. The disadvantages women suffer in long-term relationships—and when those relationships end through death or divorce—cannot be remedied by individual efforts. Restructuring the gendered domain of relationships requires restructuring the domains of work and public power that support it. However, individual couples can develop strategies to support egalitarian relationships.

SUGGESTED READINGS

BOSTON LESBIAN PSYCHOLOGIES COLLECTIVE (Eds.) (1987). *Lesbian psychologies: Explorations and challenges.* Urbana: University of Illinois Press. This book, winner of an award from the Association for Women in Psychology, has sections on lesbian identity, psychological adjustment, and community. Of special interest to this chapter is a section on lesbian relationships and families.

LERNER, HARRIET G. (1985). *The dance of anger.* New York: Harper & Row. Subtitled "A Woman's Guide to Changing the Patterns of Intimate Relationships," this book encourages the reader to recognize that anger and dissatisfaction are signals that something is wrong in a relationship and can provide a starting point for the renegotiation of roles.

SCHWARTZ, P. (1994). *Peer marriage: How love between equals really works.* New York: Free Press. A sociologist reports on interviews with couples in egalitarian marriages and suggests that this kind of relationship is becoming more widespread.

CHAPTER 11

Mothering

IMAGES OF MOTHERS AND MOTHERHOOD
- "Mother" and "Parent" as Cognitive Categories
- The Motherhood Mystique

THE DECISION TO HAVE A CHILD
- Women's Reasons for Having Children
- The Motherhood Mandate
- Childless by Choice
- Restrictions on Women's Choices
- Technology and Choice

THE TRANSITION TO MOTHERHOOD
- Changes in Work and Marital Roles
- Impossible Expectations
- Sexuality and Motherhood
- Bodily Changes and Body Image
- Social Reactions to Pregnant Women
- Identity Change and Loss

THE EVENT OF CHILDBIRTH
- Childbirth and the Social Construction of Meaning
- The Medical Model of Birth
- Toward Family-Centered Childbirth
- Postpartum Depression

EXPERIENCES OF MOTHERING
- Woman-Headed Households
- Black Mothers and the Matriarchal Myth
- Lesbian Mothers
- Socially Created Obstacles
- Commonalities

MOTHERING, RESPONSIBILITY, AND BLAME

CONNECTING THEMES

SUGGESTED READINGS

God could not be everywhere, so He invented Mothers.

The hand that rocks the cradle rules the world.

A mother is only brought unlimited satisfaction by her relation to a son; this is altogether the most perfect, the most free from ambivalence of all human relationships. A mother can transfer to her son the ambition which she has been obliged to suppress in herself. . . . Even a marriage is not made secure until the wife has succeeded in making her husband her child as well and in acting as a mother to him.

—FREUD, 1933/1965, pp. 133–134.

The very fact that a woman cannot tolerate pregnancy, or is in intense con-

flict about it, or about giving birth to a child, is an indication that the pre-pregnant personality of this woman was immature and in that sense can be labeled as psychopathological . . . . pregnancy and birth are the overt proofs of femininity.

—FROMM, 1967, cited in Ussher, 1989, p. 79.

Mother is one of the most fundamental archetypes of woman. The voices of Western society, expressed in proverbs, religious teachings, and the writings of psychiatrists and psychologists, tell us that motherhood is women's ultimate source of power and fulfillment.

Like marriage, motherhood is an institution. Its meaning goes beyond the biological processes of reproduction, encompassing "customs, traditions, conventions, beliefs, attitudes, mores, rules, laws, precepts, and the host of other rational and non-rational norms which deal with the care and rearing of children. It has also, like other institutions, a powerful symbolic component as well" (Bernard, 1974, p. vii). Yet women who become mothers, though they mother in the context of the social and symbolic meanings of Motherhood, are individuals. As Jessie Bernard pointed out, "Mother is a role; women are human beings" (1974, p. 7).

In this chapter we will look at the institution of motherhood and the experiences of women who mother. What are the images and scripts that define mothers and motherhood? How do women go about choosing whether or not to have children—and to what extent are they allowed to choose? How does the transition to motherhood change women? What are women's experiences of birth and mothering? How does motherhood combine with other roles in women's lives? We will also examine power, responsibility, guilt, and blame in the lives of women who mother.

IMAGES OF MOTHERS AND MOTHERHOOD

"Mother" and "Parent" as Cognitive Categories

It would seem that defining *mother* is fairly simple—for example, "a mother is a woman who has given birth to a child." However, this definition does not cover the range of cases to which people ordinarily apply the word mother; there are different facets of motherhood that allow people to mean different things when they use the word. The definition above reflects the principle that the mother is the woman who gives birth. A person who said, "I am adopted and I don't know my real mother's name" would be relying on the birth principle. Other facets include the genetic principle, in which the female who contributes the genetic material is seen as the mother. For example, given today's radical new birth technologies, we can imagine someone saying "My real mother died when I was an embryo, and I was frozen and implanted in the uterus of another woman." Or motherhood could be defined in terms of nurturance, as in, "I am adopted, and my real mother is the person who raised me." It could even be defined in terms of legal or family roles, such as "The woman who married my father last year is now my mother" (Lakoff, 1987).

There is little agreement, even among makers of dictionaries, about which definition of motherhood is primary. Yet the idea that every individual has one and only one "real mother" is compelling. It would seem very strange for someone to say, "I have four real mothers: the woman who contributed my genes, the woman who gave birth to me, the woman who raised me, and my father's current wife" (Lakoff, p. 75). Indeed, in the prototypical case of motherhood all the different facets are combined in a single person. The cognitive prototype of a mother is a person who is and always has been female, who gave birth to the child, supplied half the child's genes, nurtured the child, is married to the father, is one generation older than the child, and is the child's legal guardian (Lakoff, p. 83). This is very close to the stereotypical "housewife" in traditional heterosexual marriage; thus, the prototypical mother is a "housewife-mother." Mothers who do not conform to the prototype are marked by language indicating their deviance: "single mother," "foster mother" "stepmother," "surrogate mother," and "working mother" are a few examples.

The prototype of a parent for white North Americans seems to be the middle-class stereotype that we see in grade-school readers and TV sitcoms: stable heterosexual marriage, conventional sex life, planned pregnancy, and traditional gender roles (Chaffin & Winston, 1991). Of course, most parents do not have all the attributes of the prototype. In a recent study, college students were given typical and atypical scenarios about situations that resulted in the birth of a child, from the prototypical planned pregnancy in a heterosexual marriage to unmarried partners, stepparents, adoptions, pregnancies resulting from rape, and situations involving medical technology and contract motherhood. They were asked to evaluate whether each of the characters in the scenario had a right to be considered the "parent" of the child. As expected, characters who were most similar to the prototype of parent were seen as having the strongest claim to parenthood.

There were some gender-related differences in judgments about parenting. Women and men agreed that the most important attributes of a parent are intention to raise the child, gestation (for the female parent), genetic contribution, and nurturing. However, women gave more weight to intending to raise the child, especially when judging female characters, perhaps because child care is mainly women's responsibility in our society. Men gave more weight to genetic contribution and providing material and financial support, especially when judging male characters. These differences reflect stereotypes of middle-class mothers and fathers, suggesting that despite the recent popularity of the word *parenting*, people do not really see *parent* as a gender-neutral concept (Chaffin & Winston, 1991).

The Motherhood Mystique

In our society, motherhood is viewed as central to a woman's life and identity, a natural and unchanging aspect of being a woman. As we have learned with other topics in this book, often those aspects of society that seem most natural are the ones most in need of critical examination (see Figure 11.1). What are our cultural images of ideal motherhood and good mothers?

The ideology of motherhood has been termed the *motherhood mystique*.

FIGURE 11.1. The motherhood mystique internalized!
Source: Copyright © 1989. Reprinted with special permission of King Features Syndicate.

Michelle Hoffnung (1989) and Ann Oakley (1974) have analyzed these myths of the motherhood mystique:

> 1. Ultimate fulfillment *as a woman* is achieved through motherhood. Motherhood is a natural and necessary experience for all women. Those who do not want to mother are psychologically disturbed, and those who want to but cannot are fundamentally deprived.
> 2. Women are naturally good at caregiving, and should be responsible for infants, children, elderly parents, home and husband. A woman who experiences conflicts among these demands is maladjusted or poorly organized.
> 3. The role of mother is defined in terms of infinite patience, nurturing, and self-sacrifice. A woman who does not put her own needs last is an inadequate mother.
> 4. A woman's intense, full-time devotion to mothering is best for her children; children need their mother's exclusive attention in order to develop normally. Women who work for pay, whether out of financial need or to use their skills and talents, are inferior mothers.

Although Western society is in the process of rewriting the script for motherhood (Bernard, 1974), the motherhood mystique lives on. During the 1990 Gulf war, a *People* magazine cover story, "Mom Goes to War," featured a woman in uniform embracing her sad-eyed toddler, with the question, "Mommy, what if you die?" Though the U.S. military is 89 percent male, there were no heartrending stories of "Dad Goes to War." Media representations such as these reinforce the view that motherhood is the sole important aspect of women's identity (Flander, 1992). You will easily be able to find other examples of the mystique in "experts'" advice to mothers, advertising portrayals of mothers, and the attitudes of people around you (see Figure 11.2).

The mystique persists because it has important functions for *men*. Assigning caretaking to women creates economic dependence on men and is used to justify women's lower status and pay at work. "The social order that elevates men over women is legitimated by women's devotion to child care, since it takes them out of the running for top-level jobs and political positions and defuses their consciousness of oppression" (Lorber, 1993, p. 170).

FIGURE 11.2. A mother's work.
Source: Calvin and Hobbes © 1990 Watterson. Dist. by Universal Press Syndicate. Reprinted with permission. All rights reserved.

THE DECISION TO HAVE A CHILD

Women's Reasons for Having Children

Reasons for having children in our society differ from those in more traditional societies. In the latter, children are necessary as a source of family income, as domestic workers, as a path for passing on property and a traditional way of life, and sometimes as a form of personal immortality. In postcolonial and underdeveloped societies, a high birthrate is considered essential because many children are lost to disease and malnutrition in infancy and childhood. Five or more children may have to be conceived for two to live to adulthood; these children may provide the only form of economic support available for their parents' old age.

As third world countries adopt Western industrialized ways of life, the birthrate drops. The best predictor of smaller families is not modernization itself, but attitude toward modern science and medicine. As people begin to believe that science and medicine can deal with social problems, they may feel that it is not necessary to bear many children in order to have a few grow up. Nevertheless, attitudes change more slowly than material conditions, so that there is a considerable lag between the development of better medical conditions and smaller family size.

In our society, children are more a liability than an asset in material terms. They are not expected to produce much useful work or income for their parents or to support them financially in their old age. The cost of bringing up even one child is very great (see Chapter 10). Why, then, do the great majority of women choose to have children?

The sociologist Jessie Bernard has discussed one traditional explanation, a "maternal instinct" (Bernard, 1974). If wanting children is instinctive, she asks, why are so many powerful socialization forces directed at instilling this "instinct" in girls? And why have abortion and infanticide been features of so many human societies throughout history? At the species level, it is necessary for women and men to reproduce. At the individual level, there are no inherent physiological benefits of motherhood for women, and no instinctive drive for pregnancy.

One theory is that women have a psychological need to mother and men do not. In Chapter 2, we discussed the approach of Nancy Chodorow (1978), who stresses the importance of psychological differentiation in infancy. Because girls' separation from their mothers differs from boys', they grow up defining the self in terms of relationship and connectedness. Having babies satisfies deep relational needs. Unfortunately, it also leads to dependence on and subordination to men.

Chodorow's theory has been criticized along several dimensions. First, it takes white middle-class family patterns as the norm. African-American girls follow a different pattern, being brought up to expect that they will be mothers *and* possibly head their own households. Only white norms regard love and economic self-sufficiency as incompatible (Joseph, 1991). Second, even among white middle-class mothers, many women feel isolated and unfulfilled by mothering. In a qualitative interview study, these mothers were aware of their own needs for autonomy, but found little social support (Kaplan, 1992). Other research has revealed the importance of social structural factors: A parent who cares for a child experiences more emotional closeness with the child regardless of whether that parent is male or female; and a sample of single fathers reported more "feminine" personality traits than dual-career or traditional fathers, even though they were not single-parenting by choice (Risman, 1987). Biological theories assume that women are "programmed" to care for children; socialization theories assume that women are more nurturing because of early learning—but it is just as likely that a "nurturing personality" is created by being put into a nurturing role as an adult.

Among the reasons our students mention when we discuss motherhood in our classes are the desire to experience pregnancy and birth, to participate in the growth of another human being, to please a husband or partner, to have the love given by a child, to strengthen a relationship, to prove oneself an adult to one's own mother, to be needed and loved by someone who is helpless and dependent, and to pass on a family name, or one's genes, or one's values. Which of these reasons for parenthood seems most compelling to you? What do you think your own mother's answer would be?

The Motherhood Mandate

The motherhood mystique asserts that being a mother is the ultimate fulfillment for a woman. In contrast, men are viewed as being fulfilled not merely by becoming fathers but by having varied experiences and achievements. Given the influence of this ideology, there is considerable social pressure on all women to have children. Moreover, one child is not enough. "Real" women have at least two children, make sure they are properly brought up, and keep employment, public life, and creative activities secondary to their mothering. This pervasive social pressure to have children has been called the *motherhood mandate* (Russo, 1979).

The motherhood mandate has a long tradition in American society. More than seventy-five years ago, one of the first women psychologists, Leta Hollingworth, analyzed the social techniques used to persuade women to have babies (see Box 11.1). Americans surveyed in the 1950s showed overwhelming approval of motherhood for married women, describing childless people as "selfish" and "bad" (Baruch, Barnett, & Rivers, 1983). Studies during the 1960s and 1970s (reviewed in Unger, 1979a) also showed a strong social norm against childlessness and one-child families. Deliberately choosing not to have children was viewed as a sign of psychological maladjustment in women; stereotypes of the woman who declined to be a mother represented her as selfish and neurotic. Stereotypes of the "only child" represented him or her as maladjusted, socially inadequate, self-centered, unhappy, and unlikable. (There is no evidence that only children actually possess these characteristics.)

Do you think the motherhood mandate has decreased because of the influence of feminism? We know of no definitive research. Surveys in the late 1970s showed an increased tolerance for people who chose not to have families. This change may have reflected the influence of the women's movement or increasing concerns with the environment and overpopulation. However, in the 1980s, the media rediscovered motherhood, announcing all of the following (sometimes contradictory) "trends":

- Women's chances of marrying decrease drastically each year.
- There is an infertility epidemic, and women's careers are to blame.
- There is a "baby boomlet," as women rediscover motherhood.
- Women are fleeing the work force and abandoning career paths to devote themselves to full-time motherhood.
- Employed mothers and full-time mothers are enemies.
- Married and single women are enemies; single women are so desperate to marry and have children that they are stealing husbands by the millions.
- Day-care centers are dangerous, and women are afraid to leave their children in them.
- Women have achieved equality, but at a terrible cost (home and family).

These "trend stories" claimed to show huge shifts in women's attitudes and behavior. However, they were based on biased anecdotes and sweeping generalizations, and had little basis in reality. Pulitzer prize–winning journalist Susan Faludi, in her important book, *Backlash* (1991), documented their inaccuracies and showed how each "trend" was a way of telling women that they must return to traditional roles or suffer dire consequences. "For women, the trend story was no news report; it was a moral reproach" (Faludi, 1991, p. 80).

In this social context, the decision to have a child may not represent a free choice as much as an inability to escape the pressure to conform. Adrienne Rich has remembered her own decision in these words: "I had no idea of what *I* wanted, what *I* could or could not choose. I only knew that to have a child was to assume adult womanhood to the full, to prove myself, to be 'like other women'" (Rich, 1976, p. 25).

Childless by Choice

Throughout history, the childless woman has been regarded as a failed woman (Phoenix, Woollett, & Lloyd, 1991; Rich, 1976). Our language provides no ready positive term for her. Traditionally, she was labeled *barren*. The more neutral term *childless* still defines her in terms of a lack. Only very recently has the term

Box 11.1 Mothers Are Made, Not Born

In 1916, Leta Hollingworth wrote a powerful article entitled "Social Devices for Impelling Women to Bear and Rear Children." Asserting that it is necessary to "clear our minds of the sentimental conception of motherhood and to look at facts," she went on:

> The facts, shorn of sentiment, then, are: (1) The bearing and rearing of children is necessary for tribal or national existence and aggrandizement. (2) The bearing and rearing of children is painful, dangerous to life, and involves long years of exacting labor and self-sacrifice. (3) There is no verifiable evidence to show that a maternal instinct exists in women of such all-consuming strength and fervor as to impel them voluntarily to seek the pain, danger, and exacting labor involved in maintaining a high birth rate.

Hollingworth described ways in which societies ensure that women will choose to have and care for children.

Leta Hollingworth

Personal Ideals. The "normal," or "womanly," woman is proclaimed by experts to be one who enthusiastically engages in maternity. Citing medical and psychological authorities, Hollingworth shows how women are told that "only abnormal women want no babies."

Law. Childrearing is ensured by restrictions on abortion. "There could be no better proof of the insufficiency of maternal instinct as a guaranty of population than the drastic laws which we have against birth control, abortion, infanticide, and infant desertion."

Belief. Religions, for example, may "regard family limitation as a sin, punishable in the hereafter."

Art. "The mother, with children at her breast, is the favorite theme of artists. Poetry abounds in allusion to the sacredness and charm of motherhood . . . fiction is replete with happy and adoring mothers. Art holds up to view only the compensations of motherhood, leaving the other half of the theme in obscurity."

Illusion. "One of the most effective ways of creating the desired illusion about any matter is by concealing and tabooing the mention of all the painful and disagreeable circumstances connected with it. Thus there is a very stern social taboo on conversation about the processes of birth. . . . The drudgery, the monotonous labor . . . are minimized."

Education. Women's education is aimed at making them better wives and mothers, not at enabling them to achieve independence or public achievement.

"Bugaboos." Women are told by experts that they must have their children before the age of 30 or they are highly likely to face grave complications. They are told that motherhood increases happiness and longevity. Finally, it is claimed that only children grow up selfish and disturbed.

Are the social devices described by Hollingworth valid today?

Source: Hollingworth, 1916.

child-free been suggested as a more positive alternative. Why do some women choose not to have children, and what effects does this choice have on their psychological development and adjustment?

Studies comparing women who express a preference for remaining childless with those who express a preference for having children suggest that there are factors in personality and attitudes that distinguish the two groups. Women who want to be child-free are more individualistic, more independent of their families during adolescence, more inclined to identify with the women's movement, more interested in vocational success, and more aware of the disadvantages of motherhood. They are high in autonomy, androgyny, and achievement orientation (Houseknecht, 1979; Gerson, 1980; Landa, 1990; Unger, 1979a).

Some women make the decision not to be mothers at an early age, even before they marry. Others decide through a process of repeated postponement, finally realizing that there probably never will be a "right time" for them. Women's reasons include financial considerations, a desire to pursue their education or career, the dangers of childbirth and the possibility of bearing a defective child, concerns about overpopulation, and a belief that they are not personally suited to nurturing and the work of caring for children (Landa, 1990). Regardless of when the decision is made, the choice to remain child-free is definitely a minority choice, and it is important for the woman to have a supportive social environment. Like couples trying to create egalitarian marriages (Chapter 10), women who are childless by choice need to know that they are not the only ones making this "deviant" decision (Houseknecht, 1979).

Does choosing not to have children lead to unhappiness? We learned in Chapter 10 that marital satisfaction drops with the birth of the first child and, in some studies, does not return to its original level until children leave home. When advice columnist Ann Landers asked her readers whether they would have children if they had the choice to make over again, 70 percent said "no." Of course, readers who were disillusioned about parenthood may have been more likely to answer Ms. Landers' question than others.

What does research tell us about the outcomes of women's choices about motherhood? In Grace Baruch and Rosalind Barnett's study of women at midlife, they found that whether a woman had children had no relationship to her psychological well-being. Baruch and Barnett point out that the group they studied had grown up in an era when the motherhood mandate was in full force: If these women could attain well-being at midlife with or without children, today's young women should be able to look forward to outcomes at least as positive. Noting that their results contradict the belief that children are central to a woman's happiness, they concluded that "many supposed truths about women are based simply on myth and misinformation. . . . There is an urgent need to build a new vision about women's lives that is based on reality, not on stereotypes, assumptions, or wishful thinking" (Baruch, Barnett, and Rivers, 1983, p. 107).

Restrictions on Women's Choices

Women's choices about child rearing do not take place in a social vacuum. Most societies concern themselves with regulating women's rights to have—and choose not to have—children. Moreover, practical and economic factors restrict women's options. The feminist concept of *reproductive freedom* includes a range of issues, such as the right to comprehensive and unbiased sex education; access to safe and reliable contraception; an end to forced sterilization and birth control for poor and minority women; and access to safe and legal abortion (Baber & Allen, 1992; Bishop, 1989). Issues of reproductive freedom are of concern to all women in their reproductive years, but especially for poor and minority women, who often experience more coercive efforts to control their childbearing choices.

At the heart of the concept of reproductive freedom is the idea that all choices about reproduction should be made by the woman herself: It is her body and her right to choose. For this reason, feminist perspectives on reproductive freedom are often termed *pro-choice*. Reproductive freedom is connected to other issues of women's rights; every woman should be free to plan her own life, and she cannot plan a fulfilling life with the fear of unwanted, unmanageable pregnancies (Bishop, 1989).

Contraception

Accidental pregnancies can be the result of a number of factors: contraceptive failure, lack of contraceptive knowledge or skill, lack of access to contraceptives, failure to use contraception, and unplanned or coerced sexual activity. Moreover, we learned in Chapter 9 that although women are expected to take most of the responsibility for contraception, psychological factors, lack of power within heterosexual relationships, and sexual scripts make it difficult for many women, particularly young and inexperienced ones, to take control in this area.

Every form of contraception has drawbacks. Some methods are messy, inconvenient, and awkward, and interfere with spontaneity (foam, condoms, diaphragms). They may be painful or cause vaginal bleeding (IUDs). They may cause nausea and weight gain, require daily remembering, or have the potential for long-term side effects (the pill).

Most recently, hormonal contraceptives that can be implanted under the skin to ensure infertility for up to five years have been developed. This is the first contraceptive method (other than sterilization) that does not require the use of contraception to be connected to the act of intercourse or remembered and acted upon daily. By separating contraception from both sexual encounters and daily behavior patterns, the implant method provides important new psychological advantages. A major drawback at present is its high cost. Like other hormonal methods, it may have possible long-term side effects as yet undetermined (Hardon, 1992). Even more important, this type of contraceptive can be implanted without the woman's consent (see Box 11.2). Already, six states have proposed mandatory Norplant implantation for some women. The National Black Women's Health Project and the American Medical Association have both denounced the punitive use of birth control on poor women and women of color (Long-Scott & Southworth, 1992).

Abortion

Abortion is a reproductive option that many women find necessary at some time in their lives. In the United States, 30 percent of pregnancies are terminated by abortion; 91 percent of these abortions take place within the first three months of pregnancy. Women choosing abortion tend to be young: 57 percent

Box 11.2 Reproductive control in the news: Coerced contraception

JUDGE ORDERS NORPLANT IN A CHILD-ABUSE CASE

A California judge has ordered a woman convicted of beating her children to have the recently approved Norplant birth-control device implanted in her arm for three years. . . . Darlene Johnson, a 27-year-old pregnant mother of four, was found guilty of beating her children with a belt. As part of a plea bargain with her court-appointed attorney on Wednesday, Broadman sentenced Johnson to one year in county jail and three years of probation.

But on the day of sentencing, Broadman also ordered Johnson to have six plastic Norplant tubes inserted into her upper arm by June. Johnson agreed to the conditions, but her attorney now says that Johnson did not understand that Norplant must be surgically implanted.

"She had a gun to her head. She was told she agrees or she goes to state prison" instead of county prison, said Johnson's attorney. "She didn't understand what was involved. She had never heard of this procedure before. I had never heard of this procedure before."

The enforced contraception marks the first time a judge has ordered a woman to use the implantable device.

. . . Johnson is black and Judge Broadman is white.

"The use of Norplant for any kind of a coercive purpose is something I am totally against," said Sheldon Segal of the Rockefeller Foundation, the originator of implantable contraceptives and the driving force behind the development of Norplant. "I consider it a gross misuse of the method."

"I told you so," said Arthur Caplan, director of the center for biomedical ethics at the University of Minnesota. "I am not surprised by this, but I find it troubling when reproductive capacity is manipulated as a form of punishment. It sure didn't take long."

. . . Segal and others agreed that ordering Norplant would set a dangerous precedent because Norplant is a prescription drug with possible side effects, such as headaches and irregular menstrual bleeding, and could be wrong for some women.

"The judge really appears to be going beyond his expertise," Segal said.

[Ms. Johnson's attorney] said his client, who has diabetes and a heart ailment, may not even be an appropriate candidate for Norplant. He said he will try to overturn the order.

"I think it is an effort by government to say to certain people, 'You shouldn't have children,'" he said.

Source: From William Booth, "Judge Orders Norplant in a Child-Abuse Case," © 1991 *The Washington Post*. Reprinted with permission.

are under 24 years of age, and girls under 15 are the most likely of any age group to end a pregnancy through abortion. The great majority (81 percent) of those having abortions are unmarried. Minority women comprise approximately one-third of those choosing to have an abortion (Albert, 1993; Bishop, 1989).

Abortion has been legal in the United States since 1973, when the Supreme Court, ruling in *Roe v. Wade*, affirmed that women have a right to decide whether to terminate their pregnancies on the basis of the constitutional right to privacy. Abortion, the Court ruled, is a matter to be decided between a woman and her physician. Although the principle of choice was affirmed by this ruling, in practice there are many limitations and legal restrictions on women's choices with respect to ending unwanted pregnancies.

In 1976, Congress passed the Hyde Amendment, which prohibited the use of federal Medicaid money to pay for abortions except in the few cases in which the mother's life is (medically) endangered. Since Medicaid provides health care for low-income families, poor women were left with the bitter choice of paying for an abortion out of their own inadequate incomes or carrying an unwanted fetus to term. The Medicaid restriction has resulted in some women delaying abortion until they can afford to pay for it, so that more poor women have their abortions later in the pregnancy, when there is more risk of complications (Bishop, 1989). In 1994, a law was passed ordering states to pay for abortions for poor women who were victims of incest or rape. However, this law met with immediate protest from six states that had laws prohibiting the use of state Medicaid funds for abortions (Hall, 1994). Since 99 percent of the money spent annually on abortions for poor women comes from state (rather than federal) funds, state compliance with the 1994 law will be necessary for the law to have any beneficial effect on poor women (Daley & Gold, 1993).

Recent Supreme Court decisions give more power to individual states to set abortion regulations, and many states have responded with very restrictive laws. For example, a 1980s Pennsylvania law required that women seeking abortion be given information about the availability of agencies to help women who bear unwanted children, and that they be educated about the growth and development of the fetus every two weeks during gestation and about the "psychological effects" of abortion (Bishop, 1989). In this case, the Supreme Court struck down the law, ruling that states are not free to intimidate women into continuing pregnancies under the guise of protecting their health. However, various states continue to pass restrictive laws requiring the consent of a husband or partner, parental consent for young women, mandatory waiting periods, and "educational" requirements that are designed to discourage women from seeking abortions. Additionally, the number of doctors who perform abortions has dropped 18 percent since 1982 (Vobejda, 1994). Violence at abortion clinics, including murders of physicians and clinic staff, has wide societal impact.

Women in some European countries face even greater restrictions on their abortion option (see Box 11.3) Poland had a highly available abortion policy until 1994, when the legislature passed one of the most restrictive policies in Europe. This complete reversal came largely from pressure from Polish Catholic Church leaders who believe abortion should be prohibited under any circumstances. Although 95 percent of the population report being Catholic, public opinion polls indicate that the populace wants a freer abortion policy.

Other European countries have implemented high fees, waiting periods, and requirements for women to have two doctors' opinions before obtaining an abortion (Darnton, 1993). Ireland has a complete ban on abortions. In Germany, a liberal law providing free abortions with few limitations was declared invalid. Counseling is strongly anti-abortion, similar to the recent "gag rule" in America (Kinzer, 1993). Women in these countries who cannot afford to travel to neighboring countries with more liberal policies find themselves with few options regarding their pregnancies. More than 200,000 women die each year from illegal abortions; most of these deaths occur in Asia, Africa, and Latin America (United Nations, 1991a).

However, the abortion debate does not center solely around countries that prohibit or restrict availability. A proposed law in China advocates abortion and sterilization to prevent the birth of children with mental or physical disabilities. Although the government claims to offer women the final decision regarding their fetuses with abnormalities, prenatal counseling for these women gives strong persuasion for abortion. Chinese officials wish to prevent the birth

Box 11.3 Reproductive Control in the News: The Uterus Inspectors

A UNITED GERMANY IS DIVIDED OVER ABORTION

BERLIN—From the start, Kathrin K. was suspect to the federal German border police. She was female, she was young, and she and her husband were driving back to Germany from the Netherlands, where each year thousands of West German women seek the abortions their own land outlaws.

So the police searched her car. They searched her bag.

And finally, when she wouldn't answer to interrogation, they searched her womb: They forced the 22-year-old mother of one to submit to a vaginal exam by a doctor at a nearby hospital.

Kathrin now stands charged with obtaining a first-trimester abortion abroad, a crime punishable by a year in prison.

. . . Abortion inquisitions are standard practice at the border crossing at Gronau, where Kathrin was stopped.

In one earlier case, a woman was prosecuted after a car search turned up a bill from an abortion clinic. Another became a criminal suspect because she was bleeding and asked police for help. Some women made themselves vulnerable to prosecution by volunteering information about their abortions after police accused them of traveling to the Netherlands to buy drugs. . . . For Kathrin K., a nightgown and two sanitary napkins packed in an overnight bag were considered enough evidence of crime for police to follow through with the forced gynecological exam. . . . The West German law forbids abortion except when the woman's life is endangered, the fetus is deformed, or the woman can prove to medical counselors that the abortion is necessary because of "extraordinary social circumstances." In former East Germany, abortion in the first trimester remains legal and unrestricted.

Source: Nina Bernstein, Staff Writer, "Germany Still Divided on Abortion," *Newsday,* March 11, 1991. New York Newsday, Inc., copyright 1991.

of children of "inferior quality" (World Wire, 1993). Because China restricts the number of children a woman may have to one, most women abort the abnormal child in hopes of carrying a healthier child in a later pregnancy. In the United States, federal guidelines encourage routine HIV testing for "at-risk" pregnant women. The potential for coercing these women, most of whom are poor women of color, to have abortions or to be sterilized is a major concern for feminist health-care activists (Amaro, 1993).

Psychological Effects of Abortion

Women making reproductive decisions today are living in a sociocultural environment of lesser power and status, and in a society in which many people condemn abortion. The conflicts many women feel over sexuality and their right to make decisions on the basis of their own needs complicate decision making. Add to these factors the fact that the decision to bear a child has irrevocable, long-term effects for women, and it is easy to see why ambivalence is the norm. "There is no painless way to deal with either an unwanted pregnancy or an intended pregnancy and the knowledge that one is carrying a genetically defective fetus. Abortion is rarely a decision taken lightly, even by pro-choice women" (Lemkau, 1988, p. 461).

One of the arguments used in legal and social efforts to restrict abortion is that it has harmful psychological consequences for women. While psychology cannot resolve moral or ethical differences of opinion about abortion, empirical research can readily be used to answer questions of psychological well-being.

Does abortion cause psychological damage and decreased psychological well-being for women?

To determine the effects of abortion on women's mental health, the American Psychological Association commissioned a study of all the scientific research published in the United States since abortion was legalized in 1973. This research review established that the legal termination of an unwanted pregnancy does not have major negative effects on most women. Measurements of psychological distress usually drop immediately following the abortion and remain low in follow-ups after several weeks (Public Interest Directorate, 1987). Jeanne Lemkau (1988), in her own review of the research, concludes that when a woman *freely* chooses a *legal* abortion, negative emotional aftereffects are very rare. "The typical emotion of a woman who freely chooses abortion is one of relief" (p. 462).

Research studies assessing psychological problems over a range from one week to ten years following abortion show such effects for anywhere between 0.5 percent and 15 percent of clients. Several risk factors, both internal and external, have been identified. A woman is more likely to have postabortion psychological problems if she has a history of prior emotional problems, has received little support from her family or friends, felt pressured into the abortion decision, has strong religious beliefs that abortion is immoral, or believed in advance that she would have problems in coping (Public Interest Directorate, 1987). When a woman obtaining an abortion had a partner who did not support her choice, her likelihood of psychological problems was higher only if she did not firmly believe in the integrity of her own decision (Major, Cozzarelli, Testa, & Mueller, 1992).

Women who experience severe distress following abortion may want to obtain psychological counseling. However, women should not have to deny their conflicts for fear of being labeled emotionally disturbed:

> Women may (and are entitled to) have many conflicting feelings about abortion, including guilt and grief as well as relief, either at the time or later in their lives. Abortion, like other moral dilemmas, does cause suffering in the individuals whose lives are impacted. That suffering does not make the choice wrong or harmful to the individual who must make the choice, nor should the individual be pathologized for having feelings of distress. In fact, the shouldering of such suffering and of responsibility for moral choices contributes to psychological growth (Elkind, 1991:3).

Choices about whether, when, and how often to bear children are complex ones. Although our society expects women to accept most of the responsibility for caring for children, it has been less willing to entrust them with the freedom to make responsible reproductive choices. Steeped in the motherhood mystique, many people still view reproductive rights as unnatural and maternal sacrifice as women's lot in life.

Technology and Choice

Our discussion of contraception and abortion made it clear that the development of new technology to intervene in the biology of reproduction does not always result in increased choice for women. Although each technological change is presented as an "advance" in "scientific progress" to benefit women, the reality is that the new reproductive technologies have introduced many troublesome questions of ethics, morality, power, and choice. Indeed, the body may be the major battleground of women's rights for decades to come. The most difficult issues include the following:

- *Selective abortion.* Blood tests, amniocentesis, and other new technologies allow selective abortion of "defective" fetuses. The great majority of women who find that they are carrying a Down syndrome fetus, for example, choose to abort, and a majority of Americans endorse that choice (Wertz, 1992). Is abortion justified for disorders that cause mental retardation? What about those that may cause social (but not cognitive) problems, such as the sex chromosomal variations discussed in Chapter 6—XXY, Turner's syndrome, and so on? Some women feel that they do not have the right to end a potential life simply because the child will be less than the perfect one they envisioned (Rothman, 1988). On the other hand, it is women who bear the burden of child rearing. People with disabilities argue that disability is in large part socially constructed. If social supports were available, parenting a disabled child would not involve the sacrifices it now does. And what counts as a "disability?" In Chapter 7 we discussed the misuse of amniocentesis so that female fetuses could be aborted.
- *Fetal "rights."* The monitoring of women's behavior during pregnancy is a current issue (Baber & Allen, 1992). In at least seventeen states, women have been charged with child abuse for using drugs or alcohol during pregnancy. This form of social control falls more heavily on poor women—those who can afford private health care are not monitored or tested against their will. Feminist health-care activists are concerned about the "slippery slope"—will women soon be jailed for smoking, failing to take their medication, or not getting enough exercise during pregnancy? Medical resources should be used to help ensure healthy babies without treating women as though they were only vessels for fetal development. The best way to foster infant health is to help pregnant women by providing low-cost prenatal care, drug treatment programs, and social support services—not by punishing women for being less than perfect incubators.
- *Infertility technology.* Couples who are unable to conceive a child can now make use of new technologies such as *in vitro fertilization*, or IVF, commonly known as the "test-tube baby" procedure. A woman's ovaries are stimulated with strong fertility drugs so that they produce multiple eggs, which are then surgically removed. Her partner's sperm (obtained by masturbation) are combined with the eggs in a glass dish. If fertilization occurs, the embryos are inserted into the woman's uterus to develop into full-term fetuses (Williams, 1992). Many feminists argue that women are at risk for exploitation by this revolutionary change in the reproductive process. Men control the technology, but it is women's bodies that are manipulated and experimented on. More than ever, women may be viewed solely as egg providers and incubators (Baber & Allen, 1992; Raymond, 1993).

  IVF carries many risks. The fertility drugs and surgeries can lead to unpleasant and dangerous side effects and complications. The emotional costs are high, as women put their lives and careers on hold to concentrate on getting pregnant, and the attempt can fail at any time. The success rate is low (less than 10 percent per attempt), the procedure is very expensive ($3,000 to $7,000 per attempt), and most couples make several attempts (Baber & Allen, 1992).

Women who choose to undergo IVF describe themselves as desperate to have children at any cost. Their strong desire to become biological mothers is usually seen as "natural," and is taken for granted by physicians and the general public alike. The popular press frequently features heartrending stories of a woman's quest for a child, with physicians as techno-heroes who can fulfill her deepest needs. Rarely do these stories analyze how the need to have children is socially constructed. "To what extent does our society *create* a market for IVF by placing so many important meanings on fertility that to be infertile indeed becomes an unbearable problem?" (Williams, 1992, p. 262).

Recent studies exploring women's motivations for seeking IVF suggest that these women have been strongly influenced by the motherhood mandate: the majority believe that having children is natural and instinctive and that parenthood is an essential part of marriage and women's roles in life. Moreover, they report having experienced strong external pressures to bear children (Williams, 1992). Indeed, some women may undergo IVF in part because it "proves" how much they desire to bear children. Only after IVF fails can they be accorded the socially acceptable identity of a woman who is *involuntarily* childless (Koch, 1990).

- *Contract motherhood.* Because new reproductive technologies separate genetic and physiological aspects of pregnancy, it is now possible for people to pay for the services of others who will breed "their" children. Many feminists believe that these practices exploit women physically, emotionally, and economically (Baber & Allen, 1992; Raymond, 1993). Others argue that contract pregnancy can have substantial benefits to all parties, but only if it is stringently regulated to protect women's interests (Purdy, 1992). As currently practiced, contract pregnancy raises seemingly insoluble ethical dilemmas. The following are descriptions of actual cases:

> Robert M. contracts for a baby with Elvira J. without telling her that he is considering divorcing his wife Cynthia M. On learning of the coming divorce, Elvira refuses to give up the baby for adoption, although she allows the M.'s to take the baby home with them on the condition that they seek marriage counseling. Six months later, Robert M. files for divorce, triggering a three-way custody battle between biological father, biological mother, and social mother. Who is being exploited here? Does the fact that Elvira is a Latina with only a seventh-grade education make a difference? (Nelson, 1992).
>
> Mark C. and Cristina C. hire Anna J. to gestate an embryo grown from their sperm and egg. Finding herself attached to the child, Anna seeks visitation rights. A judge rules that Anna is not the child's mother (although it is she who has given birth) but merely a temporary foster mother, and denies her request. Anna is a black single mother; the C.'s are white and Asian-American, respectively (Purdy, 1992).

Cases such as these, along with the notorious "Baby M" case, illustrate the ethical and social dilemmas created by reproductive technologies, dilemmas involving fetuses, women, couples, biomedical researchers, and health-care providers. In these conflicts, who will represent the needs of women?

- *Brave new families.* Scientific knowledge about reproduction is not inevitably a source of oppression for women. Women (and men) are using novel reproductive methods in ways that increase their options for parenthood, creating unconventional new families. In one case, two long-time lesbian partners, D. and B., were approached by a cousin of B.'s with a request that she bear a child for her and her husband. (The cousin was unable to conceive.) Although B. was sympathetic and believed that the couple would be loving parents, she already had adult children from an earlier heterosexual marriage and did not wish to become pregnant again. However, B.'s partner, D., decided to bear the child. Using sperm donated by B.'s adult son, D. became pregnant and gave birth to a healthy baby daughter. B. had the opportunity to support her partner during the pregnancy and throughout the birth of B.'s (genetic) grandchild, and the cousins were able to bring up a child that was genetically related to them. D. described the process as deeply satisfying (see Box 11.4).

  In another case, a lesbian couple had a child with sperm donated by one partner's father to the other partner. Both genetic and social ties of grandparent to grandchild were thus created. In many such cases, the methods are decidedly "low tech," with the kitchen turkey-baster the favored means of insemination. Most important, the couples themselves are in control of the technology and its outcome.

THE TRANSITION TO MOTHERHOOD

Becoming a mother changes a woman's life perhaps more than any other single event. Yet surprisingly, there has been little research on the psychology of pregnancy and the transition to motherhood. Prior to recent feminist work, the little that had been done was based either on a psychoanalytic model, focusing on the "pathological" nature of the woman who does not react positively to pregnancy and birth, or on the medical model, which treats pregnancy as an illness requiring medical management. It is as though psychology has been indifferent to this major life transition that affects women: "Women are supposed to get pregnant; it is their lot; why make a fuss about it?"

The changes that come about with pregnancy, birth, and the transition to motherhood include both biological and social events. These events interact to produce changes in life circumstances, lifestyle, and involvement in paid work, as well as changes in relationships with significant others such as partner and parents. Each additional child also has further effects, as a new pregnancy is added to caring for young children. Once a woman becomes a mother, the role is hers for life, and she will be defined by society largely through that role, much more than men are defined through their roles as fathers. It is not surprising that motherhood profoundly affects a woman's sense of self (Ussher, 1989). Let's

Box 11.4 Live ! A Poem by Dale Gray

(or How a Shade of Gray Made Me a Surrogate Mother, Step-Grandmother and Step-Aunt)
Dedicated to all of my soul mates from USC's first graduate Psychology of Women class.

Surviving your first delivery (transcontinental UPS)
Southern hospitality claimed you
with a little red ticket stub
(see page five of your baby book)
the airport filled with Operation Rescue
two skin-heads from Fort Gordon, warm welcome.

Mom-Bette (Nana) and I bounced you
back and forth on our knees
mid-May all the way home
past every cop to keep you frozen.

On the back porch low fat frozen micro-meals
line the freezer where Bette once stored
twin Himalayan kitties—who didn't make it—
in a gray shoe box we hid you behind ten gallons
of frozen chocolate and blueberry yogurt.
In June, Nana-Bette rescued you from the cold void
of spermatozoan incompleteness.

From hands as potent and lived as Vita's and Virginia's
you received your first commission to swim
thru vinegar to the double helix of our dreams
Winner that you are of the golden egg you reached the prize
first combined replicated parasitically nestled
into my womb and there we kept you safe
warmed loved nourished and secret for 3 months.

Bette's and Dale's little girl
whom we talked to, talked of, sang to, wrote for and felt.
You moved in September at my hairline under my scar.

On page six of your baby book there's a sonogram.
Not a bad black and white for a shade of gray
all a flutter in primordial water swishing around.
By October we shocked everyone with news of you—
you had shock value even then—
mimicking all five of your sisters and brothers
something I dare say they thieved from their two moms.

And so you grew more now they knew until most unexpectedly
in full tradition of your parents who hate being constricted
you demanded super prematurely
to be given your independent life
your freedom to move
and your true mommy and daddy.
None could stop you/thus
we helped see you through
your entrance with a flair
in two hours of wimmin born
so tiny in the center of my palm
3 pounds and 14 inches strong
we took turns holding you
between our breasts
singing their names
a lullaby of survivors:

Virginia and Vita and Violet, Maya & Alice, Adrienne & Audre, Kay and Marge, and Nana and Sue. Elizabeth and Phoebe, Linda & Sandra, Deborah and Bette, and Gertrude and Alice. Elizabeth and Sandy, Judith and Mary, Keri & Beth, Elaine & Sally, Sue and Hillary, Kitty and Peg, and Judy & Julie. Barbara & Trudy, Faye & Janie, Janis & Tami, and Umbra and Tamala. Connie & Gretchen, Betty & Ethel, Velvet & Lyndie, and Donna & Levonne. Ann Adelle and Dog, Chris and Tret, Charlon & Maria, and Dawn & Kelly. Tina and Beverly, Lea and Lita, Nina and Barbara, and Peggy and Michele. Becky and Bobbie, Donnis and Sue, Alretta and Joan, Nancy and Shirley, George & George, Charlotte & Sylvia, Djuna & Natalie, and Radclyffe & Lillian. Germain & Gloria, Eleanor & Victoria, Toni & Jane and Thelma and Louise LIVE!

Source: Reprinted by permission of Dale Gray.

look more closely at some of the changes that occur with pregnancy and motherhood and their effects on women's identities.

Changes in Work and Marital Roles

The motherhood mystique suggests that children need full-time care provided by their biological mothers and that women are uniquely suited to provide such care. Traditionally, middle-class women have been expected to end their paid work when their first child is born. Today full-time mothering is less common than in the past, though there is great variability; the new mother may make housework and child care her full-time job for periods ranging from a few weeks following the birth to twenty years or more. Many women experience the change from paid worker to unpaid at-home mother as stressful. The changes from a nine-to-five schedule to being on call twenty-four hours a day, from adult company to isolation with an infant, from feeling competent to feeling overwhelmed with new tasks, all require difficult adjustments. The difficulties may be offset by the rewards of getting to know one's growing baby, the belief that caring for one's children is a worthwhile and important job, and the sense of mastery that comes from learning how to do it well. Nevertheless, conflicts occur.

A major source of conflict is that women's expectations of their partners' involvement do not coincide with men's actual behavior once the child is born. Studies suggest that although many men are positive about the idea of becoming a father, they do not follow through with a fair share of the work (Nicolson, 1990). In one study, new mothers kept time-use diaries and were also interviewed twice. Their workdays ranged from eleven to seventeen and a half hours a day, and they spent an average of six hours a day alone with their babies. Although they cited the babies' fathers as their main source of support, fathers actually contributed only zero to two hours a day of primary care (Croghan, 1991).

In another study of eighty-six new mothers, 77 percent said that their partners were their single biggest source of help. However, husbands definitely did not contribute equally, as evidenced by the women's descriptions of the kinds of help they received: "If I'm at the end of the rope, he'll step in and take over." "At dinner time he pitches in . . . entertains the baby." Husbands expressed understanding, but did not offer to change the situation: "He doesn't make me feel there's something wrong with me if I can't cope perfectly." (Rhoades, 1989, pp. 131–141).

These studies suggest that new mothers are stressed by inequality in marital roles. Women may enter motherhood with expectations of equality in parenting, but these expectations collide with reality (Ruble, Fleming, Hackel, & Stangor, 1988). It is difficult for women to express frustrations over these violated expectations or to change parenting relationships. Myths of motherhood still imply that women should be happy and fulfilled when they are selfless mothers. A partner's contribution is an optional extra for which they should be grateful, however small it is (Croghan, 1991).

Impossible Expectations

If motherhood is women's natural fulfillment, it should make women blissfully happy. Women are encouraged to evaluate themselves as mothers against images of the "ideal mother" whose nurturance is infinite, the radiant, serene "madonna," and the "superwoman" who juggles the demands of house, children, male partner, and full-time job, while providing her children with unfailing love and plenty of "quality time" (Ussher, 1989). Women often are not prepared for negative and ambivalent feelings and may feel like failures when these feelings occur. The proportion of women who experience decreased emotional well-being during pregnancy and early motherhood is probably a majority (Condon, 1987; Ruble et al., 1988; Ussher, 1989).

Women who report their experiences to researchers or in writing about motherhood often describe the conflicts that come from experiencing negative feelings they knew did not live up to the ideals:

> Motherhood wasn't what I expected—unadulterated wonder. The shock of the isolation and much of the sheer slog and boredom were exacerbated by the fact that I felt I wasn't supposed to feel dissatisfied (Wandor, 1980, cited in Ussher, 1989, p. 84).

> I was haunted by the stereotype of the mother whose love was "unconditional"; and by the visual and literary images of motherhood as a single-minded identity. If I knew parts of myself existed that would never cohere to these images, weren't those parts then abnormal, monstrous? (poet Adrienne Rich, 1976, p. 23).

> I needed money and I needed it fast. A friend of mine told me about baby-sitting jobs at the large hotels. . . . The problem was, I had to be available night and day. When a call came, I had to leave or miss the job. (The oldest child) helped me with the other children, and I learned to be more comfortable with the idea of leaving my home to work. Being brought up in the traditional way, I always feared something terrible would happen if I went away, like the house would burn down. I felt I would be punished for leaving the children, even to go to work. Especially to go to work (a single mother, Nancy Hall, 1984, pp. 17–18).

> I couldn't seem to do anything right; I felt so tired, the baby kept crying, and I kept thinking that this was supposed to be the most fulfilling experience of my whole life. It felt like the most lonely, miserable experience (a mother three weeks after the birth of her first child, cited in Ussher, 1989, p. 82).

Sexuality and Motherhood

"During pregnancy and motherhood, one of the fundamental aspects of a woman's identity which is oppressed is sexuality" (Ussher, 1989, p. 92). When women become pregnant, they are confronted with many of the contradictions about sexuality that characterize Western society. The image of the madonna, who is pure, serene, and asexual, is at odds with the adult woman's own sense of herself as a sexual being. "Defining sexuality as linked to reproduction, yet simultaneously denying the existence of sexuality in the pregnant woman or the mother, perpetuates the split between body and self. . . ." (Ussher, 1989, p. 92).

One example of this split is the disconnection between sexual desire and behavior during pregnancy. Many women experience increased sexual desire during pregnancy, especially in the middle three months (Kitzinger, 1983). This desire may reflect physical changes such as an increased blood supply to the pelvic area, as well as psychological factors. (For one thing, the woman and her partner needn't worry about contraception!) Yet women may engage in sexual activities less often, out of fear of harming the fetus, feelings of being unattractive, or physical awkwardness.

Research has shown that in a normal pregnancy, intercourse and orgasm are safe until four weeks before the due date; these activities do not harm the fetus or cause miscarriage (Masters & Johnson, 1966). When women were surveyed about their physicians' advice, however, 60 percent had received no information at all, and another 10 percent were told they should not have intercourse after their seventh month (Gauna-Trujillo & Higgins, 1989). Feminist writers have suggested that the medical profession perpetuates the myth of the asexual mother because doctors, themselves influenced by the myth, are reluctant and embarrassed to discuss sex with pregnant women (Ussher, 1989).

Bodily Changes and Body Image

The hormonal changes of pregnancy are much greater than those of the menstrual cycle. The levels of the hormones progesterone and estrogen in pregnant women are many times higher than in nonpregnant women, and drop precipitously after birth.

Besides these major changes in gonadal hormones, there are other alterations in levels of substances that may be associated with the functioning of the central nervous system. The level of the neurotransmitter norepinephrine is lower during pregnancy, while the levels of stress-associated adrenal cortical hormones increase (Treadway, Kane, Jarrahi-Zadeh, & Lipton, 1969). Norepinephrine and progesterone have both been related to depression in nonpregnant people. Although there have been few studies of the relationships between hormones and mood during pregnancy, the effects of oral contraceptives provide a parallel situation. Substances in birth-control pills mimic the actions of estrogen and progesterone during early pregnancy. Many of the "side effects" of the pill are similar to the symptoms of early pregnancy: weight gain, nausea, fluid retention, headache, loss of sexual desire, and so on. A number of researchers have also reported an increase in negative mood states in women who use the pill (e.g., Paige, 1971).

Pregnancy has been characterized both as a time of psychological well-being and a time of emotional upheaval. Estimates of the incidence of depression in pregnant women range from below the rate in the nonpregnant population to as high as 38 percent. Because researchers have never systematically charted the normal course of mood changes during pregnancy, little is known about exactly what is abnormal. Many of the bodily changes and mood changes experienced by pregnant women are similar to those used to diagnose clinical depression: change in appetite or weight, change in sleep patterns, loss of energy, increased worries about health, and mood fluctuation. Are pregnant

Box 11.5 "A Brand New Body": One Woman's Account of Pregnancy

Suzanne Arms (1973) kept a journal during her first pregnancy. Her reactions to her changing body are captured in these journal entries, ranging from early to late in her pregnancy.

> I have the feeling that I brought a brand new body home from the doctor's office. I'm a new me. Nobody else would look at me and call me pregnant, but it's wonderful to know that I really am, and I look for every tiny sign to prove it's true. My developing breasts are encouraging, and my nipples have become much larger. My nipples stand erect at times, and they're at least three shades darker (p. 13).
>
> I have never felt beautiful but I've always liked my face and filled-out body. . . . But looking at pictures of me crying last week really hurt. They're so un-me. Just a pudgy woman. Today I don't feel like that at all. I've tied my hair back, vowed not to wear those baggy farmer jeans till after the baby comes, and put on a dress; I really do feel beautiful. In fact, I feel like I'm a pretty good place for a baby to stay and grow in. Nice, round, firm, with just enough fat all over to make it really soft and safe for the baby (p. 29).
>
> . . . I've been getting more and more pleasure from my sensual feelings. There's some old tightness in me that seems to be losing its hold at last, and I feel all of me expanding (p. 35).
>
> I rub cocoa butter on my tummy and breasts every morning after showering. The skin has become pink and smooth and I can't help feeling it all the time. The other day we were in the bookstore, and I was absent-mindedly rubbing myself and staring into space. A young woman with a child called to me from across the store, "That's a lovely belly you have there!" (p. 40).
>
> . . . I've begun to feel huge. I remember hearing other pregnant women hassle themselves about getting fat. I never could figure it out. To me they looked beautiful, round and blooming. I assured myself that I would never feel that way, and I would love my tummy and all the extra pounds. Well, that's great in theory—but suddenly the day comes when I look in the mirror and my face is round and I really do look like an orange! even holding my stomach in. So yesterday I spent the whole day feeling fat, ugly, and unlovable. Despite every nice thing John has said, I knew he would soon see how unappealing I am (p. 44).
>
> A very full feeling today. I'm thick and stuffed like a bulging cabbage (p. 59).
>
> I never thought it would come to this. I can't reach over my stomach to get to my feet. John has to lace up my hiking boots! (p. 63).
>
> Sometimes it seems as though I've been pregnant all my life. I can't remember being unpregnant (p. 64).

Suzanne Arms' pregnancy was planned and wanted, and she was in a stable relationship with a supportive male partner. How might the reactions of women to their changing bodies differ in differing social circumstances?

Source: Arms, 1973.

women who have these "symptoms" depressed, or are the symptoms of true depression distinguishable from those of pregnancy? It is difficult to separate the two, because "pregnancy is a complex biological process occurring in a significant psychosocial context" (Kaplan, 1986, p. 45).

Labeling common changes associated with pregnancy as depression may lead pregnant women to misdiagnose themselves as depressed; on the other hand, a depressed woman could mislabel her symptoms as due to her pregnancy and fail to ask for help. Research is needed to chart the normal state of mood and emotion during pregnancy. This research could "debunk the cultural stereotype of happy placid pregnant women and provide women with

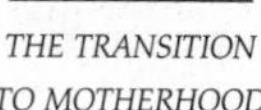

FIGURE 11.3. Suzanne Arms, pregnant.

more realistic expectations of the mood changes in pregnancy" (Kaplan, 1986, p. 46).

If psychologists have neglected the effects of hormonal changes accompanying pregnancy, they have virtually ignored the role of the social changes. Throughout this book we have discussed the social importance of slimness and attractiveness in evaluating women. Pregnancy may be viewed as a progressive loss of these valued attributes. It should not be surprising that pregnant women feel unfeminine or that they react with negative mood states, even apart from hormonal causes.

Many women feel extremely ambivalent about the dramatic changes in body shape and size that accompany pregnancy (Ussher, 1989). Reactions include feeling temporarily free from cultural demands to be slim, feeling awe and wonder, feeling afraid and disgusted by their size, and feeling alienated and out of control (see Box 11.5). In a study of more than 200 women, changes in body image were among the most frequently reported stressors of pregnancy and early motherhood, second only to physical symptoms (Affonso & Mayberry, 1989).

Indeed, pregnancy can be viewed as a time of loss of control over one's body. Changes will occur to the pregnant woman no matter what she does or does not do. She is helpless (short of terminating the pregnancy) to govern her own body, and yet she remains defined to society largely through her body. Moreover, society encourages a more general helplessness. Pregnant women (at least those who are white and middle class) are thought to be delicate, incapable of working, and frail. Until quite recently, pregnant women were expected to remain secluded within the home, and they may still be forced to leave paid work. If a woman comes to view herself merely as a vessel for the forthcoming generation, it would be surprising if she did not experience depression!

Social Reactions to Pregnant Women

Pregnant women are powerful stimuli for the behavior of others. "A woman begins to assume the identity of mother in the eyes of society almost as soon as she is visibly pregnant, ceasing to be a single unit long before the birth of her child" (Ussher, 1989, p. 81). On the one hand, her body symbolizes the eternal power of women:

> As soon as I was visibly and clearly pregnant, I felt, for the first time in my adolescent and adult life, not-guilty. The atmosphere of approval in which I was bathed—even by strangers on the street, it seemed—was like an aura I carried with me, in which doubts, fears, misgivings, met with absolute denial. *This is what women have always done* (Rich, 1976, p. 26).

On the other hand, pregnancy is a kind of stigma: people react very differently to pregnant and nonpregnant women, and their reactions may lead to changes in the women's behavior in return. Shelley Taylor and Ellen Langer (1977) illustrated such differential treatment in an intriguing experiment. They used two female stimulus persons who alternated between appearing pregnant (with the help of a little padding) or carrying a box the same size as the "pregnancy." The women stood in elevators and measured the distance that other passengers stood from them. Both men and women stood closer to the "nonpregnant" woman. Men, especially, avoided the "pregnant" woman. She was also stared at more; both men and women spent considerable time furtively looking at her stomach, so much so that both experimenters felt very uncomfortable when playing the pregnant role. Differences in treatment could be quite extreme:

> A large curious dog was wrenched away from the pregnant confederate by his master so abruptly and so far that he spent the remainder of the ride sitting on the feet of the nonpregnant experimenter, a fact completely unnoticed by his owner, who was still apologizing to the pregnant experimenter (Taylor & Langer, 1977, p. 30).

In another part of the study, people were given the chance to interact in a laboratory situation with either a pregnant or a nonpregnant woman. Women preferred the pregnant woman more if she had been passive, rather than assertive, in a previous group discussion. However, they also preferred not to interact with the passive pregnant woman in the future.

How can we explain these results? We suggest that the social encouragement for pregnant women to withdraw from their usual public activities makes them a novelty. People then react to them both by unwarranted attention to the novelty (staring) and by avoiding contact. Both responses can make the pregnant woman uncomfortable, which further increases her social isolation.

Of course, Taylor and Langer's study was done in the 1970s. Since then, the public presence of pregnant women may have become more acceptable. One indication of attitude change is changes in maternity clothing styles. Until quite recently, maternity clothes were tentlike and infantilizing, aimed at both concealing the pregnancy and making the woman look as childlike as possible, with ruffles, bows, and polka dots. Today, one can buy maternity T-shirts with a bold BABY logo and an arrow pointing to the protruding abdomen, maternity tights and sweaters, and business clothes for the pregnant executive. And actress Demi Moore appeared nude and very pregnant on the cover of *Vanity Fair* in 1991. Do you think pregnant women are still stigmatized? With the help of a little padding, perhaps some intrepid female researchers will conduct another study.

Identity Change and Loss

The transition to motherhood involves losses. The woman ceases to be seen as an autonomous individual and is instead viewed as an "expectant mother" and then "mother." It is not surprising that feelings of loss are experienced. It is hard to change from being "Joy Williams, secretary/jogger/painter/daughter/spouse and more" to being "Timmy's mom." One of the authors remembers her feelings of sadness and loneliness when the nurses in the hospital following the birth of her first child referred to all the women in the obstetric unit as "Mother" ("Mother, are you ready for your lunch tray?") rather than by our names. It seemed as if everything that had gone before—education, work, individual life history—was now to be put aside for the all-encompassing identity and job of Mother. One of the ways our cultural constructions of motherhood may oppress women is that they are not allowed to mourn or grieve the old, lost self (Nicolson, 1993; Ussher, 1989).

These feelings of loss of identity are not easily reconciled with the motherhood mystique, which tells us that women should enjoy and be fulfilled by everything about motherhood. Women may come to understand their experiences as wrong, labeling themselves as ill or abnormal, or believing that "baby blues" are inevitable and biologically determined. Rather than pathologize women's experiences, feminist psychology looks for explanations in the sociopolitical context of mothering (Ussher, 1989).

Jonathan Smith (1991) conducted an intensive case study of one woman's pregnancy. Clare's identity change during early pregnancy involved imagining the child-to-be:

> In one respect, it's—it's a person, a whole person that just happens to be in there, and in another way, it's something different (p. 231).

In the middle phase, Clare experienced a growing sense of psychological relatedness with others—partner, mother, sister. In defining herself and the child-to-be, Clare sought social confirmation; the process of constructing a family was beginning. Near the end of the pregnancy, Clare sees herself as very changed:

> I'm one of two and I'm also one of three. . . . An irrevocable decision, the steps have been made that mean that my other identities, if you like as a mother and a partner, make up that essential me now (p. 236).

So far, we have been talking about the transition to motherhood mainly as it has been constructed for white, middle-class women. Women of color and poor women, in contrast, have less often been exposed to the extremes of the motherhood mystique. They have been expected to bear and bring up children while struggling for survival; for them, the identity of mother has a different meaning. One of the most eloquent expressions of class and color differences in ideals of womanhood and motherhood comes from a famous speech by Sojourner Truth, a crusader for abolition and suffrage and an ex-slave, to the Akron Convention for women's rights in 1851:

> That man over there says that women need to be helped into carriages, and lifted over ditches and have the best place everywhere. Nobody ever helps me into carriages, or over mud puddles or gives me any best place, and ain't I a woman? Look at me! Look at my arm! I have ploughed, and planted, and gathered into barns, and no man could head me! And ain't I a woman? I could work as much and eat as much as a man—when I could get it—and bear the lash as well! And ain't I a woman? I have borne thirteen children, and seen them most all sold off to slavery, and when I cried out with my mother's grief, none but Jesus heard me. And ain't I a woman? (adapted from Ruth, 1990, pp. 463–464).

As in Sojourner Truth's day, the realities of motherhood for poor women are even more distant from the motherhood mystique than those of affluent women. Attitudes toward pregnant women, and women's perceptions of themselves, still vary by social class in today's society. Middle-class women in heterosexual marriage may be treated as delicate and special, but poor single mothers are labeled "welfare moms," undeserving of respect.

The psychological and biological events of pregnancy are not inherently negative. Outcomes are related to many social influences. Women who are least influenced by the mystique of motherhood seem to adjust better (Breene, 1975). In a carefully controlled study, women who received social support during pregnancy showed many beneficial physical and psychological outcomes that persisted through the first year of motherhood (Oakley, 1992).

THE EVENT OF CHILDBIRTH

Childbirth and the Social Construction of Meaning

Like pregnancy, childbirth is not a neutral event socially or psychologically. In virtually all cultures, the event of birth is associated with fear, pain, awe, and wonder; it is viewed as both "the worst pain anyone could suffer" and as "peak experience." Yet there are surprisingly few accounts of childbirth *by women*. Instead, birth is described in the words of men. When male anthropologists visit preindustrial cultures, they are rarely allowed to see the "women's work" of attending birth and instead rely on men to tell them about the group's customs. Margaret Mead noted that "I have seen male informants writhe on the floor, in magnificent pantomime of painful delivery, who have never themselves seen or heard a woman in labor" (cited in Rich, 1976, p. 156).

Young women in industrialized countries receive little direct information about birth in the normal course of growing up. Adrienne Rich has written that "As a girl of twelve or thirteen, I read and reread passages in novels which recounted births, trying to imagine what actually happened. I had no films, no photographs of childbirth to enlighten me. . ." (Rich, 1976, p. 164). Unfortunately, it seems that in novels, writers often feature childbirth when they want to punish or kill off a female character! (For an exception, see Box 11.6.)

Women's experience of childbirth is even more invisible in the visual arts. Artist Judy Chicago has noted that images of war and death are innumerable in Western art, but images of birth are nonexistent (Chicago, 1990). Instead, there

Box 11.6 Takver Gives Birth

In this passage from her novel *The Dispossessed*, acclaimed science-fiction writer Ursula LeGuin movingly describes the work and the triumph of giving birth.

> Takver got very big in the belly and walked like a person carrying a large, heavy basket of laundry. She stayed at work at the fish labs till she had found and trained an adequate replacement for herself, then she came home and began labor. Shevek arrived home in midafternoon. "You might go fetch the midwife," Takver said. "Tell her the contractions are four or five minutes apart, but they're not speeding up much, so don't hurry very much."
>
> He ran to the block clinic, arriving so out of breath and unsteady on his legs that they thought he was having a heart attack. He explained. They sent a message off to another midwife and told him to go home, the partner would be wanting company. He went home, and at every stride the panic in him grew, the terror, the certainty of loss. . . .
>
> Takver had no time for emotional scenes; she was busy. She had cleared the bed platform except for a clean sheet, and she was at work bearing a child. She did not howl or scream, as she was not in pain, but when each contraction came she managed it by muscle and breath control, and then let out a great *houff* of breath, like one who makes a terrific effort to lift a heavy weight. Shevek had never seen any work that so used all the strength of the body.
>
> He could not look on such work without trying to help in it. He could serve as handhold and brace when she needed leverage. They found this arrangement very quickly by trial and error, and kept to it after the midwife had come in. Takver gave birth afoot, squatting, her face against Shevek's thigh, her hands gripping his braced arms. "There you are," the midwife said quietly under the hard, engine-like pounding of Takver's breathing, and she took the slimy but recognizably human creature that had appeared. A gush of blood followed, and an amorphous mass of something not human, not alive. The terror he had forgotten came back into Shevek redoubled. It was death he saw. Takver had let go his arms and was huddled down quite limp at his feet. He bent over her, stiff with horror and grief.
>
> "That's it," said the midwife, "help her move aside so I can clean this up."
>
> "I want to wash," Takver said feebly.
>
> "Here, help her wash up. Those are sterile cloths—there."
>
> "Waw, waw, waw," said another voice.
>
> The room seemed to be full of people. . . .
>
> Somehow in this extreme rush of events the midwife had found time to clean the infant and even put a gown on it, so that it was not so fishlike and slippery as when he had seen it first. The afternoon had got dark, with the same peculiar rapidity and lack of time lapse. The lamp was on. Shevek picked up the baby to take it to Takver. Its face was incredibly small, with large, fragile-looking, closed eyelids. "Give it here," Takver was saying. "Oh, do hurry up, please give it to me."
>
> He brought it across the room and very cautiously lowered it onto Takver's stomach. "Ah!" she said softly, a call of pure triumph.
>
> "What is it?" she asked after a while, sleepily.
>
> Shevek was sitting beside her on the edge of the bed platform. He carefully investigated, somewhat taken aback by the length of gown as contrasted with the extreme shortness of limb. "Girl."
>
> The midwife came back, went around putting things to rights. "You did a first-rate job," she remarked, to both of them. They assented mildly. "I'll look in in the morning," she said leaving. The baby and Takver were already asleep. Shevek put his head down near Takver's. He was accustomed to the pleasant musky smell of her skin. This had changed; it had become a perfume, heavy and faint, heavy with sleep. Very gently he put one arm over her as she lay on her side with the baby against her breast. In the room heavy with life he slept.

are images of the blissful Madonna or virgin with child. Chicago's Birth Project is a collective effort by women artists and crafters to represent images of birth (see Figure 11.4).

FIGURE 11.4. Judy Chicago's image "Crowning" represents the moment the baby's head first becomes visible at the vaginal opening. The work is needlepoint over hand-painted canvas, 40.5 inches by 61 inches.

If a woman were training to run a marathon, climb a mountain, or go on an "Outward Bound" trek, she would probably think of the event to come as a challenge. She would acknowledge that her body would be worked hard and stressed, her courage tested, and her life at some risk. Yet she could feel in control of the event, prepared and accepting of the challenge. She might undertake such an experience as a way of knowing her own psychological and physical self or of developing her strengths and resources. Childbirth is a normal physical process with some of the same potential for testing and growth, yet women are rarely encouraged to think of it in this way (Rich, 1976). Instead, they are taught to think of it as an event in which they will be dependent, passive, subject to authority, and in need of expert medical intervention.

The Medical Model of Birth

In some countries, birth is considered a natural phenomenon that in the majority of cases needs no medical interference at all. For example, in the Netherlands the dominant obstetrical philosophy is that the laboring woman needs only "close observation, moral support, and protection against human meddling." A healthy woman can best accomplish her task of birthing her baby if she is self-confident, in familiar surroundings—preferably her own home—and attended by a birth specialist such as a midwife. Physicians believe that they can reliably identify the small number of women who are likely to require medical resources, and they hospitalize people in the high-risk group. However, the majority of babies are born at home (MacFarlane, 1977, p. 29).

In contrast, virtually all U.S. births take place in hospitals. This trend is very recent. As late as 1935, the majority of babies were born at home. By the end of the 1970s, 99 percent of births took place in hospitals attended by physicians (Shorter, 1982). Even the language of childbirth has come to reflect the centrality of the physician: People routinely speak of babies being *delivered* by doctors instead of *birthed* by women. Is the medical model of birth best for women?

Many of the customary procedures surrounding birth in the United States are virtually unknown in other societies and are not necessarily in the best interest of mother or baby. For example, in hospital births the woman lies on her back during delivery, while in most cultures women give birth in a squatting or semi-seated position. The supine position puts pressure on the spine, may slow labor, works against gravity, increases the risk of vaginal tearing, and makes it more difficult for the woman to push actively during the process. Why, then, do hospitals insist on this position? It is easier for the physician, who can view the birth more conveniently.

American women have experienced childbirth with feet in the air, drugged, shaved, purged with an enema, denied food and water, hooked up to machines and sensors, and psychologically isolated to a degree that is virtually unknown in other parts of the world. Research shows that giving birth in an unfamiliar environment, being surrounded by strangers, and being moved from one room to another late in labor adversely affect the birth process even in nonhuman animals; yet these practices have been routine features of medicalized childbirth (Newton, 1970; MacFarlane, 1977).

In the United States women have also been routinely taught that they will need relief from pain during normal birth. When anesthetics were first introduced in the mid-nineteenth century, clergymen opposed their use in childbirth on the grounds that the Bible prescribed that women *should* suffer while giving birth, and physicians claimed that they were unnatural. Queen Victoria endorsed the practice of pain relief during childbirth by using an anesthetic for the birth of one of her own children in 1853, thus silencing religious opposition (Hyde, 1990). Today, the use of drugs during childbirth is routine. They include tranquilizers, barbiturates, and regional and local anesthetics. (An example of the latter is an injection near the spinal cord that numbs the abdomen and thighs.)

The almost universal use of drugs in childbirth is controversial. On the one hand, it is argued that modern technology can spare women unnecessary pain. On the other hand, there are "a number of well-documented dangerous effects on both mother and infant" (Hyde, 1990, p. 139). For example, anesthetics may prolong labor by inhibiting contractions and making the mother unable to help in the process of actively pushing the baby through the birth canal. Perhaps more important psychologically, they reduce the woman's awareness of and ability to control one of the most challenging and awesome events of her life.

The medical model of birth encourages physicians and pregnant women to focus on possible complications and emergencies and may cause them to react to even remote possibilities with drastic medical interventions. In the past twenty-five years, there has been a dramatic increase in the number of Caesarean births in the United States, from about 4 percent to 24 percent of all births (U.S. Bureau of the Census, 1989). One of every four babies is now surgically removed from its mother's body. This rate is much higher than in comparable countries such as Great Britain and is *not* associated with lower infant mortality.

The reasons for the epidemic of surgical intervention are unclear. Some critics have rather cynically suggested that scheduled surgical births are more convenient and profitable for physicians. Others have attributed the increase to physicians' fear of malpractice suits. When birth is defined as a medical event, helping and supporting the laboring woman seems inadequate, and heroic medical measures seem desirable. It has also been suggested that the high rate of surgical deliveries is an attempt by the medical profession to keep its dominant role in childbirth, despite women's increasing insistence on viewing birth as a normal process.

Toward Family-Centered Childbirth

The medicalization of birth probably reached its height in the United States in the 1950s and 1960s. After undergoing male-managed childbirth, many women began to write about their experiences and work toward more woman-centered birthing practices. Women organizers founded the International Childbirth Education Association in 1960. Widely read books such as *Our Bodies, Ourselves; Immaculate Deception; Of Woman Born;* and *The Great American Birth Rite* helped change public attitudes in the 1970s.

At about the same time, methods of *prepared* or *natural childbirth* were introduced to the American public. The most popular type of prepared childbirth is the Lamaze method, named after a French obstetrician. Women who use this approach learn techniques of relaxation and controlled breathing. Relaxation helps to reduce tension and the perception of pain and conserves energy during labor. Controlled breathing helps the woman work with, not against, the strength of each uterine contraction. The Lamaze method does not rule out the use of pain-relieving drugs, but it emphasizes that with proper preparation they may not be needed, and it leaves the choice to the laboring woman.

Another important part of the Lamaze technique is the presence of a "coach," or trusted partner—usually the baby's father—during labor and birth. Men had been banished from the delivery room at the heyday of the medical model, regarded as unhygienic, superfluous, and likely to get in the way of the physician (MacFarlane, 1977). The coach helps the mother with relaxation and controlled breathing and provides emotional support and encouragement. Research shows benefits of the father's presence to the mother, including a more positive emotional reaction to the birth (MacFarlane, 1977). Many men feel that participating in the birth of their child is a privilege and an important part of being a father (Hyde, 1990).

Studies comparing women who used Lamaze and other methods of childbirth education and training with women who had no special preparation have shown that there are definite benefits associated with prepared childbirth. These include shorter labor, fewer complications, less use of anesthetics, more positive attitudes after birth about the experience, less reported pain, and increased feelings of self-esteem and control (Hyde, 1990). These studies, while they do suggest that childbirth education and preparation are important, must be interpreted carefully. Perhaps women who choose to take control over their birth experiences by signing up for Lamaze training are largely those who are motivated to experience childbirth positively under any circumstances. In other words, the studies do not rule out self-selection.

One recent study of support during the birth process does rule out self-selection effects (Kennell, Klaus, McGrath, Robertson, & Hinkley, 1991). More than 600 pregnant women, mostly Hispanic, poor, and unmarried, were randomly assigned to one of three groups. One group received emotional support during labor from a specially trained woman helper. The helpers, who were recruited from the local community, stayed with the laboring women to provide encouragement, explain the birth process, and offer soothing touch and hand-holding. A second group had a noninteractive female observer present, and the third group had standard hospital care.

Women in the emotional support group had a Caesarean rate of 8 percent, compared with 13 percent in the observed group and 18 percent in the standard procedure group. They experienced less pain in labor: the standard group were almost 7 times as likely to need anesthesia as the emotional support group. Moreover, their labor time was shorter and they and their babies spent less time in the hospital. Clearly, emotional support made a large difference. The study's director estimated that investing small amounts of money in training "mother's helpers" would save $2 billion a year in costs of high-tech interventions. However, we suspect that hospitals will continue to invest in "advanced" technology more than the helping wisdom of women.

Women's efforts to regain control of the event of birth have resulted in many changes from the extreme medical model of thirty years ago. Today, fathers are more likely to be with the birthing woman. More births are taking place in homelike birth centers, attended by nurse-midwives. Women and their partners are far more likely to be educated about the normal processes and events in pregnancy and birth. Such knowledge reduces fear and helplessness, and thus reduces discomfort. Learning techniques to use during labor can replace passive suffering with active involvement and coping. However, new technology is continually being introduced, and each new intervention can readily be overused.

The movement toward care by nurse-midwives, drug-free birth, and the involvement of the woman's partner and family continues to grow. Women's struggle for choice and control in childbirth parallels women's struggle for self-determination in general, and is part of a social revolution that is not yet complete. Issues involving childbearing, an exclusively female function, are still subject to rigid social control. The medical model of birth illustrates the way social institutions can decrease the power of women. When real control is lacking, women perceive themselves as helpless and passive, and this perception in turn contributes to their continued powerlessness. Women in our "advanced" society have been taught that they should be dependent on experts and authorities. Treating birth as a normal, woman-centered event, rather than a medical one, could prove very beneficial to women, their partners, and their children.

Postpartum Depression

The first weeks following childbirth (*postpartum* literally means "after birth") have often been characterized as a time of mood swings and depression. Women learn from friends, magazine articles, and physicians that they can expect to suffer the "baby blues," a period of irritability, disappointment, sadness, crying spells, and ambivalence toward the new baby.

What are the causes of postpartum mood changes, and how common is postpartum depression? Researchers have not always agreed about the defining symptoms of a postpartum depressive state or even about the defined length of the postpartum period. Many older studies lack comparison groups, use inappropriate groups for assessing the likelihood of depression (for example, generalizing from women who seek psychiatric care to all women), or use memories of events in the past as data. In various studies, the proportion of women classified as mildly clinically depressed at some time within the first six weeks following childbirth has ranged from 10 to 20 percent (Mercer, 1986).

The most popular explanation of postpregnancy mood disorders is that they are due directly to hormonal changes. The event of birth is followed by dramatic decreases in the high levels of estrogen and progesterone that characterize pregnancy. However, hormone changes have not been shown to be the *cause* of depression; in fact, there is no direct link between hormone levels and mood (Hopkins, Marcus, & Campbell, 1984). In one study of hormonal state and mood state, for example, pregnant women were assessed six weeks before their due date and during the postpartum period. Compared with a matched sample of women who had not been pregnant, the new mothers were more depressed and cognitively slower. However, although these women showed postpartum hormone changes, there was no relationship between hormonal state and mood; some women with progesterone-related changes reported depressed feelings and some did not (Treadway et al., 1969).

The hormonal changes of pregnancy and the postpartum period are real; like the smaller changes of a normal menstrual cycle, they give rise to bodily changes and sensations that must be interpreted by the woman who is experiencing them. Growing up in a society that expects new mothers to be depressed encourages women to label emotions and bodily sensations experienced at this time as the "baby blues." However, little or no research has examined the effects of this cognitive labeling process.

The social situation of the new mother has been almost completely ignored in explaining postpartum mood shifts. Many factors involved in the transition to motherhood may contribute to depression and mood swings among new mothers: dissatisfaction with body size and shape, feelings of not being competent at one's "natural" task of caring for a newborn, a sense that one's real self is lost in the role of mother, disappointment with a partner's lack of support, and so on.

One factor obvious to the authors of this book, both mothers, but often overlooked by researchers distanced from the experience of birth, is sleep deprivation. During the last weeks of pregnancy, a woman may not sleep well due to the discomfort caused by the heavy, restless fetus. Next, the hard physical work and stress of birthing a child are followed by many consecutive nights of disturbed sleep. Babies rarely sleep for an unbroken six to seven hour period before they are 6 weeks old, and some take much longer to "settle down." We know of no studies of postpartum depression that have examined sleep deprivation as a factor or compared moodiness in new mothers with moodiness in sleep-deprived nonmothers. The lack of attention to this possibility is a striking example of how socially influenced variables are often overlooked in studying women's lives.

EXPERIENCES OF MOTHERING

The realities of mothering are as different as the social circumstances of women who mother. In this section we will look at what motherhood involves for diverse groups of women.

Woman-Headed Households

The number of families that consist of a woman and her children is increasing dramatically. The main reason for this increase is the high separation and divorce rate (documented in Chapter 10). A secondary reason is a rise in births to single women, which now make up nearly one-fourth of U.S. births (Sapiro, 1994). Minority children are more likely to grow up in single-parent families; 16 percent of white, 27 percent of Hispanic, and 50 percent of African-American children are in women-headed households (Sapiro, 1994).

Families headed by women are far more likely to be poor than families with a male wage-earner; in 1989 they were 52 percent of all poor families, up from 23 percent forty years ago. The link between single motherhood and poverty is especially strong for minority families. In 1992, 30.2 percent of white, 53.7 percent of black, and 51.2 percent of Hispanic woman-headed families were living in poverty. Poverty among women and children is one of the most serious social problems in the United States today (Polakow, 1993).

Why are woman-headed households so likely to be poor? Some of the reasons for women's poverty are the same as men's: They may lack education or job skills, live in an area in which there are few jobs, or belong to minority groups that are discriminated against. But women are poor for gender-related reasons as well: because they are expected to both care for and provide for their children, and because they are underpaid and discriminated against in the job market (see Chapter 12) (Polakow, 1993). Perhaps most important of all, public policy does not reflect the needs of women and children.

Even women who are able to find full-time employment may not be able to earn enough to keep themselves and their families out of poverty. Of the 4.7 million workers who earned the minimum wage or less in 1987, 65 percent were women, employed primarily as salesclerks and service workers (Stout, 1988). The story of one single working mother illustrates the dilemmas of being both nurturer and provider. Lori P. worked full time as a secretary at a university, earning about $800 a month. When her partner left her and their 4-year-old son, she was unable to pay her monthly bills, which included $500 for child care. Although Lori started out with advantages—health care coverage, good child care, safe housing, occasional child support contributions from the absent partner, and middle-class respectability—she barely managed to survive on her own with her young son:

> I don't know what I'm going to do. My dad helped last month, but rent's due next Wednesday and I don't have any money. I mean I don't. I just paid all my bills. It's the end of the month now and I don't get paid for two more weeks. I have $2.50 in my account; two dollars and fifty cents! Rent's $545—I get paid in two weeks again, but that will only be $400. . .I need help—I feel like I'm sinking (Polakow, 1993, pp. 82–83).

Ashamed to be "on welfare," Lori wants to get her college degree so that she can get a better job, but she cannot afford extra hours of child care while she attends night classes. For now, she is relying on another poor single mother, who babysits for $2.00 an hour.

As you learned in Chapter 10, the failure of divorced men to provide child support is a major source of single mothers' economic burdens. Nor do they appear to provide other kinds of support. In a recent interview study of the social networks of long-term single mothers, ex-partners were most often reported as absent or harmful (Malo, 1994). In addition, the lack of publicly subsidized child care makes it impossible for a mother to "get ahead." Even if she works full time at minimum wage, child care for one child will consume between 37 percent and 78 percent of her income (Polakow, 1993). Of all the Western industrialized nations, only the United States fails to provide family support benefits as a matter of public policy (Lorber, 1993).

The primary response to the feminization of poverty in the United States seems to be to blame the victims. Women who accept benefits are castigated as "welfare moms" and accused of causing the very problems they are trying to cope with. In President Ronald Reagan's 1986 State of the Union address, he blamed the "welfare culture" for the breakdown of the family, child abandonment, women and children's poverty, crime, and the deterioration of the public schools (Polakow, 1993). Throughout the 1980s, public aid programs to help people help themselves out of poverty were repeatedly cut (Polakow, 1993; Sapiro, 1994), and the current political climate is even more harsh.

Black Mothers and the Matriarchal Myth

African women were brought to the United States to work as slaves and to produce more slaves, sometimes through rape and forced breeding. If they were given a few days off from slave labor after childbirth, it was more to protect the owner's investment than to allow them to rest and recover. They were able to care for their own children only after all their other work was done and, as Sojourner Truth eloquently testified, were likely to see their children sold away from them (Almquist, 1989).

African-Americans are the only minority group in the United States to have had the experience of systematic, widespread destruction of their family units. In addition to this legacy of slavery, there has since been a scarcity of black men able to fill roles as providers and husbands. The causes for this scarcity include migration from the South, heavy casualty rates of black men in various wars, high death rates from poor health care, and the effects of poverty and discrimination, leading to drug use, crime, and violent death. Thus, black women have been (and still are) more likely than white women to be bringing up families without a resident father/husband. For African-American women, motherhood is not equated with being dependent on a man (Collins, 1991). (See Box 11.7.)

Black women have coped with oppression in many ways. They often form extended households, with two or three generations living together and sharing resources. Grandmothers, sisters, cousins, and aunts care for the children of young mothers. Black families are more likely than white ones to informally adopt the children of friends and relatives whose families are stressed. In the

Box 11.7 Mamawoman

Wait a minute. I've got something to say.

First of all. I ain't all of ya'll's mamma, so you can just forget that.

I've got two children, Jamilah and LeRoy.
I named him after his father.
That's the last favor I'll do for that guy.
We didn't get along.

I'm Jamilah and LeRoy's Mamawoman.

See this here, that's me flying over the projects, over all that junk in the street and all those livin' dead folks down there. There I am bringing the groceries home with no hassles. Look, there, that's Jamilah and LeRoy looking out the window waving at me.

Jamilah is very talented and smart.
And so is Leroy of course!
But that girl is a real artist.
She made this card herself, see.
She drew this blue outfit for me with the word
MAMAWOMAN written on it.

'Mamawoman'
Jamilah and LeRoy started calling me that after I had to knock a young man in the head because he tried to take my purse.

The kids and I were walking home from the food stamp office when these two young guys come walking up behind me and tried to snatch my purse.

Jamilah and LeRoy just stood there like they were frozen to the ground. They were too small to help anyhow.

But I just flipped! I grabbed one of those guys before he could get away and started beating him with my bare hands.

I didn't even think about what I was doing.
All I could think about was
that they were trying to take food from me and my kids.

I threw that dude on the ground
and before he know what was happenin'
I was kicking his butt, his head
and everything else I could kick.

Then Jamilah and LeRoy was
pickin' up rocks for me to hit him with,
and jumpin' up and down hollerin'
"Get 'em mama, git 'em."

I mean rock and feet were flyin' at that fool.
And he was pleadin' "I'm sorry ma'am I'm sorry! I swear
to god I'm sorry."

And I was kickin' and preachin'

continued

Box 11.7 Continued

"Are you a fool! Tryin' to take food from my children?
Don't you know I'm just as poor as you with two children to feed?
You should be ashamed of yourself!"

When I saw blood on his hands
I realized I was really hurtin' the guy.

So I kicked him in the butt one more time
And I told him to get the hell out of there
And that he was lucky I didn't shoot him.

I had to tell LeRoy
a hundred times after that that I was bluffing
that I just said that to scare the guy.
I don't really have a gun.

Anyhow, the kids started callin' me Mamawoman after that.
They told all the kids in the neighborhood
and talked about it for weeks.

I want them to fight for themselves when they have to
cause nobody out in that mean world
is goin' to love 'em like their mama

So I teach them to be strong in mind and body
like my mama taught me.

—Ardena Shankar

Source: Taylor, D. (Ed.) *Feminist Parenting: Struggles, Triumphs, and Comic Interludes,* Freedom, CA: Crossing Press 1994, pp. 63– 65.

black community, these informal adoptions are seen as better than stranger adoption, because they allow continued contact with the child's mother, and the child is with people she knows and trusts (Almquist, 1989). This collective, co-operative child rearing may reflect a West African heritage (Collins, 1991; Greene, 1990).

Unfortunately, the strengths and coping strategies of black mothers have often been interpreted negatively (Greene, 1990). Black women have been judged against a white middle-class norm of female submission and traditional marriage arrangements (Collins, 1991). Sociologists and psychiatrists have accused them of "castrating" their husbands and sons by being "unfeminine" (Giddings, 1984). The infamous *Moynihan Report* (Moynihan, 1965) attributed the problems of the urban black ghetto to the "matriarchal" social organization of black families. While the white community has often criticized black women for bearing "too many" children in poverty, some male advocates of the 1970s Black Power movement have claimed that black women's control over their own bodies through birth control and abortion was selfish and misguided and contributed to "black genocide" (Almquist, 1989).

Black mothers' extended households and woman-centered child rearing appear to be problems only if the implicit norm is traditional (white) middle-class marriage. Blaming black women for the social problems they have had to adapt to and labeling their resourcefulness and strength as "dominance" are a way of avoiding confrontation of the real problems of racism and sexism. Moreover, it obscures the unique social contributions of African-American family patterns. Black women's involvement in social activism often stems from their definition of motherhood: a good mother does not just take care of her own biological offspring, she works to meet the needs of her entire community (Collins, 1991; Naples, 1992).

Lesbian Mothers

Most research on motherhood assumes that all mothers are heterosexual. However, about one lesbian in six is a mother (Strommen, 1993). As we learned in Chapter 9, the *coming out* process is a gradual one for many women. Some women who marry or cohabit with men and have children within these relationships later identify as lesbian and bring their children up in lesbian households. Other lesbians, both single and in lesbian relationships, choose to have a child through adoption or artificial insemination. What are the special issues and stresses that confront lesbian mothers? According to Sally Crawford (1987), a clinical psychologist, there are several common sources of psychosocial stress in the clients who come to her for counseling.

One of the biggest potential problems is the reaction of others. The lesbian couple's own parents may react negatively, providing a painful contrast with their celebration of the grandchildren provided by their "straight" daughters and sons. Although there is increasing acceptance of lesbians, we still live in a heterosexist culture in which many people consider a lesbian family to be unnatural;

> Vicky's parents had a party to introduce their grandchild to the family, but they refused to acknowledge me as the other parent; rather, they chose to identify me as a very good friend who is helping Vicky raise the baby. I wept for hours and knew that I would never again hide the nature of our relationship. At a particularly vulnerable time in our union, the birth of our child, I was asked to deny my identity, connection, and contribution. It would have been easier if I had not been there (Mercer, 1990, p. 233).

Economic problems and strains exist. Like single mothers, lesbian mothers have to manage both paid work and child care without a man's greater earning power. The income of one or two female parents is often so low that lack of money is a source of daily stress. If the mother has to deal with a welfare department, there is the added stress of a state agency making judgments about her lesbian lifestyle.

Lesbian families often experience isolation. Children must operate in the larger heterosexual world, but their lesbian mothers may feel little in common with the heterosexual families of their children's friends. Turning to the lesbian community for support, they may find that the lives of their lesbian friends who do not have children are very different from their own on a practical, day-to-day level. As more lesbians decide to have children, support groups and networks of lesbian families are growing.

Finally, lesbian mothers may confront problems of internalized homophobia:

> Lesbians should not be surprised or ashamed to find themselves grappling with questions such as: Is this natural? Is it okay for lesbians to have kids? Am I hurting my children . . . is it unfair to bring them into a homophobic world? Am I a woman who is able to mother like other women? These old questions are important to take seriously; they are questions that have been answered in positive ways by many lesbian mothers over the years (Crawford, 1987, p. 197).

Do lesbians raise children differently than heterosexual mothers, and do their children turn out differently? There is very little research to guide us in answering these questions. What is available suggests that there are some differences in child raising but that the children of lesbian families are remarkably similar to those of heterosexual families.

Marjorie Hill (1987) compared the attitudes of a sample of twenty-six heterosexual and twenty-six lesbian mothers, all black women, to assess similarities and differences in their approaches to child-raising. The two groups were similar in the value they placed on independence and self-sufficiency for their children, and how open and candid they saw themselves as being in general. The lesbian mothers, however, were more tolerant about rules and more accepting of children's sexuality (less restrictive of sex play, less concerned with modesty, and more open in providing sex education and information to children). They also viewed boys and girls as more similar to each other than the heterosexual mothers did and expected more traditionally masculine activities from their daughters. (Given the costs of feminine socialization for girls, these latter differences can be seen as strengths.) In general, research on the attitudes and behaviors of lesbian and heterosexual mothers shows that they are more alike than different (Falk, 1993).

On the whole, it seems that lesbian family life produces children who are very much like the children from heterosexual families, with the full range of adjustment problems and strengths. A recent review of research (Falk, 1993) found no detrimental effects of lesbian parenting on children's psychological adjustment or gender-role development. It seems that the power of the larger society to create gender-role conformity in children (in combination with children's own cognitive-developmental needs) is scarcely affected by growing up in a "deviant" household.

Lesbian (and gay men) are at high risk of losing their children in custody disputes. Courts have often assumed that lesbians are "unfit mothers" who are liable to molest their children, interfere with their becoming "appropriately" gender typed, or cause them to become homosexual. None of these assumptions is supported by research evidence (Falk, 1993; Pollack, 1990).

In 1993, the American Psychological Association, the national Association of Social Workers, and other professional organizations argued in a Virginia court case that there is no specific evidence that lesbians are worse parents than heterosexuals or that the children of lesbians are at risk for psychological disorders. The court had awarded custody of a 2-year-old boy to his grandmother solely because his mother is a lesbian. There was no evidence that Sharon Bottoms was a poor mother or that her son Tyler was suffering any problems; her relationship with another woman was the only custody issue. This case is not atypical; "admitted" lesbians stand a fifty-fifty chance of losing their children in custody disputes (Falk, 1993). In a 1975 case, Mary Jo Risher—a college graduate, nurse, Sunday school teacher, and PTA president—lost custody of her 9-year-old son to her ex-husband and his new wife. There was no question that Mary Jo Risher was demonstrably a "good mother"; yet as a lesbian she was deemed unfit (Pollack, 1990). In Sharon and Tyler Bottoms' case, an appeals court, influenced by the APA brief and psychologists' expert testimony, overturned the earlier verdict and returned Tyler to his mother and her partner (Sleek, 1994).

Socially Created Obstacles

Women are more vulnerable to the life stresses associated with parenthood than men, because they are assigned primary responsibility for child rearing and are given little support from society to make their job easier. Instead, we have seen that the stresses associated with childbirth and the transition to motherhood are increased by many women's isolation within nuclear families, by a loss of control during pregnancy and childbirth, and by a lack of governmental commitment to child and maternal well-being. Although American society gives lip service to the sanctity of motherhood, recent decades have seen a decrease in government spending on prenatal care and nutritional programs for poor mothers and children, as well as a continuing refusal to recognize parents' needs for child care.

In addition, there is little planning for the presence of children outside their homes. Public spaces and public transport are designed without regard to the safety and comfort of children or their caretakers. Food and clothing stores, which depend on the business provided by women who shop for their families, rarely provide play areas for children. Commuter trains and airplanes make special provisions for smoking and dining but provide no facilities for children's play. Although women's breasts can be seen exposed on magazine covers at every newsstand, there are very few places where women can comfortably nurse their babies outside their homes, and seeing women breastfeed in public is widely considered disgusting (see Figure 11.5). Public institutions plan schedules as though all women were available for full-time child care—for example, nursery schools and kindergartens with half-day programs assume a mother will be free at midday to retrieve her child, and the hours of service provided by day-care centers frequently are inadequate for women on shift work. These are just a few examples of socially created obstacles that make motherhood into a kind of disability. If you try to view the world from the perspective of someone who has full-time responsibility for one or more children, you will surely be able to think of others.

Commonalities

With the experiences of women who mother being shaped by social class, sexual orientation, economic status, and many other factors, are there any overall similarities? Do most mothers have at least some things in common? In writing this chapter, we read many accounts by mothers of their feelings and thoughts about motherhood. Several themes emerged in these accounts. Here, we will illustrate each of five themes we perceived with the words of some of the women

FIGURE 11.5. After security guards ordered a woman to leave the premises when she was discovered discreetly nursing her baby, mothers staged a "nurse-in" at a New York shopping mall.

who chose to write their stories in *Balancing Acts,* a book edited by Katherine Gieve (1989).

1. *Becoming a mother results in large, significant, and permanent changes in identity and life circumstances.*

   Daniel is seven, Matthew, five, and when I think about the past seven years I feel like a person watching the dust begin to settle after an earthquake. Seismic tremors still shoot through my life, but perhaps not so frequently nor quite so catastrophically as they did in earlier years (p. 41).

   I did not imagine the force or the excitement—nor how I would willingly be taken over by my children. . . . I look at the world with different eyes and inward with a new vision. I feel riven, torn apart, and made again (p. 51).

   I am not where I was before—not in a single detail. I have learned to pride myself on new abilities, some I had never considered of value. I was blown wide open by motherhood and by the emotions that came with it. . . . I had no idea that I could love that well. . . . Conversely, other abilities by which I had set great store, producing words on time, selling an idea, keeping myself fired up . . . seem useful but little more than that (pp. 127–128).

2. *Motherhood can involve feelings of intense love, competence, and achievement.*

   The rewards of motherhood were immediate and lasting. I have established a relaxed physical intimacy with both my children which tolerates anger and laughter, built up over a decade of washing them, reading to them, and tumbling about with them. The relationship I have with my children is the single most important part of my present life (p. 114).

   Pregnancy had suited me, I enjoyed giving birth, but nothing prepared me for the reality of the new baby. I was almost paralyzed by the joy that shot through me as I looked through the plastic (hospital crib) that morning . . . and caught a glimpse from the bright little eyes which, wide open, were waiting to engage mine. I have never felt emotion like it . . . it's just impossible to put into words . . . I was transported (p. 124).

My mother was proud and confident of her role and people came to her for advice. The kitchen was always full of the children of neighbors and aunts, and, by the time of my own adolescence, the children of my own older sisters. My mother has an ample bosom and a sense of rhythm which can reduce any infant to a coma within minutes. She knows nursery rhymes you have never heard and old wives' tales that would make your hair stand on end. . . . I absorbed from her an overwhelming sense that childbirth was miraculous, that having children was at the core of being a woman. . . . I was left in no doubt that I, too, wanted children. I wanted the experience which had made her life so worthwhile and I wanted, like her, to be good at it (pp. 1–2).

She's brought into a room. . . . Not much hair, toothless, a fat bald child in a scratchy pink dress. It is love at first sight. . . . I feel as if I've been waiting all my life for this moment, for this child. . . . The "I" who adopts this four-month-old baby is forced to recognize that, physically and symbolically, she is another being, formed by other bodies, in relationships I know nothing of. But in my imagination, she is the missing part of myself, at last returned. I am complete. . . . There is gratitude, passion, absorption—above all gratitude—to the birth mother whose child I swear to love and cherish, to my own mother who gave me existence, to my newly found daughter who has given me this feeling (pp. 138–139).

3. *Motherhood is a constantly changing relationship, as both child and mother grow and develop. Mothers and children move from a relationship of profound inequality, with the child literally dependent on the mother for life itself, to one of (ideally) equality. Throughout the process, the mother moves from meeting physical needs to meeting intellectual ones; yet, emotional demands remain a constant.*

It was not the hard work of child care that I found so difficult (probably because I shared it with others) but the constantly changing relationship which continued in terms not chosen by me at an unpredictable and changeable pace. It required constant reassessment and with it pain, anger, and remorse, as well as excitement and pleasure. Daniel elicited from me both my greatest love and generosity and my darkest anger and frustration (p. 45).

As our children grow and change, and new pleasures, new battles, take the place of the early ones, I feel I live in a constant state of surprise and suspense. It is like reading the best of novels, combined with being in love; I want things to stand still yet can't wait to see what will happen next. And, above all, I don't want the story to end (p. 159).

4. *Both child and mother must confront the limitations of love and care.*

To be kissed better is the child's expectation of the mother and to kiss better is the mothers' hope of herself; to take away the pain and bring peace in its place is to be a good mother. Why do all those baby care manuals not tell us how difficult it is? We cannot kiss better all the suffering even in our own homes (p. 46).

My (adopted) daughter came from a white mother and a black father. I can be a white mother to her but I cannot represent either that maleness or that blackness. . . . With all my love, I cannot be everything she wants and needs any more than I can shield her from pain . . . indeed I must add to her pain. . . . My fantasy, that if I love her enough nothing else matters, has to give way. I see that it matters to her, being black, to have two white parents and that I am not powerful enough in the real world, where black is different from white, to undo this. This is one of the things I cannot change (p. 140).

"You are not my real mother," says my daughter to me. I did not feel either that my mother was my real mother, perhaps every daughter, every child, has this doubt. . . . The gap between the ideal Mother, and the mother we actually have, is perhaps always there. If the Mother is the fixed perfect image of the ideal, a mother (small m) is always what falls short of that image (pp. 143–144).

5. *Mothers and children must adapt to a society that is structured as through children did not exist and does not provide necessary social arrangements for those who care for the young.*

The world suddenly became a much more dangerous place once I had a baby dependent on me for his very life. For the first time I was thrown into a world that did not recognize my physical, emotional, social, and political needs. This applied to design, architecture, roads, public transport, dangerous machinery; not to mention lack of community child care facilities. . . . it isn't the child that makes your life hard, it is the response of the adult world and the powers that be. Usually, it is the very people who sentimentalize and idealize motherhood who stop listening (pp. 53–54).

Motherhood . . . has made me aware of time in many different ways. In particular how women's time is taken for granted so that there is little concordance between the way time is structured in the so-called public world and the rhythm of time associated with caring for a young child (p. 77).

If men had to travel with children in buggies on public transport as often as they had to carry briefcases, I suspect they would have devised a rather different transport system and invented escalators and steps on which it was possible to take children in buggies easily (p. 87).

These five commonalities emerged for us as we read the writings of diverse women about their experiences of motherhood; they are more intuitive than systematic. Perhaps you can think of others?

MOTHERING, RESPONSIBILITY, AND BLAME

Our society has myths about both the Perfect Mother and the Bad Mother (Caplan, 1989) (see Figure 11.6). The Perfect Mother is an endless fount of nurturance, naturally knows how to raise children, and never gets angry. The measure of her success is a "perfect" child; a "bad" (less than perfect or atypical) child is seen as proof of a "bad" mother. Perfect Mother myths establish standards that every woman fails to meet. Bad Mother myths exaggerate mothers' limitations or faults and transform them into monstrous flaws. They include beliefs that mothers are bottomless pits of neediness, mothers are dangerous when they're powerful, and closeness between mother and daughter is unhealthy.

"Mother-blaming is like air pollution"—so pervasive that it often goes unnoticed (Caplan, 1989, p. 39). The societal tendency to scapegoat mothers extends to mental health researchers and practitioners. Paula Caplan and Ian Hall-McCorquodale (1985) reviewed articles published in major mental health journals between 1970 and 1982. They found that among psychoanalysts, psy-

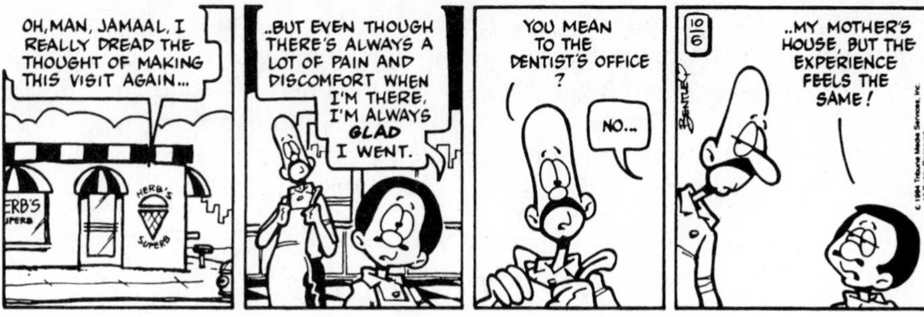

FIGURE 11.6. Mixed feelings about Mom.
Source: Reprinted by permission. Tribune Media Services.

chiatrists, psychologists, and social workers (both female and male), there was a strong tendency to blame mothers for clients' problems. In fact, in the 125 articles reviewed, mothers were blamed for seventy-two different kinds of problems in their offspring. The list included aggressiveness, agoraphobia, anorexia, anxiety, arson, bad dreams, bedwetting, chronic vomiting, delinquency, delusions, depression, frigidity, hyperactivity, incest, loneliness, minimal brain damage, marijuana use, moodiness, schizophrenia, sexual dysfunction, sibling jealousy, sleepwalking, tantrums, truancy, inability to deal with color blindness, and self-induced television epilepsy!

Where are the fathers when blame is handed out? They seem to be invisible. In popular advice books about parenting, mothers are represented as being dangerously emotional, and their (inevitable) failure to control their emotions is claimed to cause their children's problems. Even when the books are focusing on single fathers, however, they are not blamed. Rather, the problems are presented as outside their control. Emotional expressiveness, which is part of women's caregiving roles, is portrayed as inherently dangerous (Shields, Steinke, & Koster, 1995). Even when fathers or other male family members sexually abuse their children, women are held responsible. In correspondence with the sexual scripts discussed in Chapter 9, mothers are blamed for failing to control and regulate their partners' sexuality. Men are represented as unable to control themselves. Of course, women often lack resources to protect their children—they are in positions of "powerless responsibility" (Hooper, 1992; Rich, 1976).

Psychology has contributed more than its share to the father-invisibility problem. A recent review of 544 empirical research studies of children's psychological disorders published between 1984 and 1991 found that only 1 percent focused exclusively on fathers, while 48 percent focused exclusively on mothers. Another 25 percent included both parents but did not analyze for sex differences or interactions (Phares & Compas, 1993). When the studies including fathers were examined separately, clear effects were found: Fathers do play a role in children's psychopathology. The evidence is clearest in children whose fathers sexually molest them, abuse alcohol, or are depressed.

Our society has assigned mothers responsibility not only for their children's physical care but also for their psychological well-being to an extent that few other cultures around the world or throughout history have done. It has asked them to fulfill their responsibilities in relative isolation, and often without the material and social support they need. Moreover, it has created myths that disguise the realities of parenting. Perhaps, for each of us, one task of growing up is to look beyond the myths of motherhood at the human being who is our mother, to see her as a complex, multifaceted individual, and to stop blaming her for being only human (Howe, 1989; Caplan, 1989).

CONNECTING THEMES

1. The ability to bear children is a biological capacity unique to women. However, birth, child rearing, and motherhood occur within a gender system that controls and regulates women's sexuality and fertility. Sexual biology becomes a gendered experience.
2. The motherhood mandate decrees that all women should be mothers, and the motherhood mystique defines the approved way to do it. "Deviant" mothers are stigmatized by labels such as "working mother" and "welfare mom." Accounts of motherhood in women's own language and images have been conspicuously absent from art, literature, and history.
3. Experiences of mothering are shaped by social class, ethnicity, sexual orientation, and many other factors that define a women's social position. Rather than generalize about a mythical motherhood, we should recognize the diverse experiences of women who mother.
4. The United States is virtually alone among industrialized nations in its failure to develop public policy that recognizes the needs of today's families. Poverty among women and children is a major social issue. Women's reproductive rights are contested, and new medical technologies complicate issues of ethics, choice, and power.

SUGGESTED READINGS

BELL-SCOTT, PATRICIA, BEVERLY GUY-SHEFTALL, JACQUELINE JONES ROYSTER, JANET SIMS-WOOD, MIRIAM DECOSTA-WILLIS, and LUCILLE P. FULTZ (1991). *Double Stitch: Black Women Write about Mothers and Daughters.* New York: HarperCollins. This rich collection of poems, stories, and essays explores and analyzes black mother–daughter relationships through a beautifully developed quilt-making metaphor.

CAPLAN, PAULA J. (1989). *Don't Blame Mother.* New York: Harper & Row. Written by a feminist clinical psychologist, this book not only documents the pervasiveness of mother-blaming but encourages the reader to examine her own tendency to expect perfection from her mother and gives thought-provoking and practical suggestions for mending the mother–daughter relationship (useful for sons, too).

COLE, JOHNETTA B. (Ed.) (1986). *All American Women: Lines That Divide, Ties That Bind.* New York: Macmillan. This collection, edited by a noted African-American sociologist, contains nine articles describing the experiences of diverse women (Jewish, Hispanic, lesbian, black, white, middle class and working class) as mothers in nuclear and nontraditional families.

CHAPTER 12

Work and Achievement

WOMEN'S PAID AND UNPAID WORK
The Invisible Work of Women
Working Hard for a Living: Women in the Paid Work Force
SOCIOCULTURAL FACTORS: "DOING GENDER" IN THE WORKPLACE
Attributions for Success and Failure
Devaluing Women's Performance
Discrimination in Hiring and Promotion
Social Reactions to "Uppity Women"
Mentors and Role Models
Sexual Harassment from Nine to Five
OBSTACLES FROM WITHIN
Socialized Differences
Achievement Motivation
Do Women Fear Success?
EXCEPTIONAL WORK LIVES
Achievement in the Professions: From Pink Collar to White
Nontraditional Occupations: From Pink Collar to Blue
PUTTING IT ALL TOGETHER: WORK AND FAMILY
Costs of the Balancing Act
Benefits of the Balancing Act
WOMEN, WORK, AND SOCIAL POLICY: MODELS FOR CHANGE
CONNECTING THEMES
SUGGESTED READINGS

Work of one kind or another is a part of virtually every woman's life. In this chapter we will examine the unpaid and paid work of women, women's values about work and achievement, explanations for the differing work patterns of women and men, and factors affecting women's achievement in both traditional and nontraditional professions and trades. We will listen to the voices of women as they talk about their work: its problems, its satisfactions, and its place in their lives.

All human beings are motivated to work in order to provide for physiological survival, to obtain the built-in or intrinsic satisfactions of their work tasks, to be useful to society, and to obtain recognition (Astin, 1984). But the opportunities to meet these needs differ greatly for men and women. The world of work is a gendered world; the differences between women and men are mainly in the *kinds* of work done by each, the *obstacles* to satisfaction and achievement, and the *rewards* provided to them.

The Invisible Work of Women

"Just a Housewife"

The phrases *working woman* and *working mother* suggest that a woman is not really a worker unless she is in the paid work force. Much of the work women do is unpaid and therefore often not formally defined as work. Listen to one full-time homemaker talking with a psychologist conducting a study of adult identity:

Q: What is your current employment status?
A: Do you mean am I working? No, I'm just a housewife.
Q: Do you consider yourself to be a full-time homemaker?
A: Yes.
Q: How important to you is your work as a homemaker?
A: Very important. It's all I do (Whitbourne, 1986, p. 161).

This conversation captures some of the contradictions of the homemaker role. The homemaker works full time in an unpaid job that is low in status, especially in comparison to the idealized image of the "career woman." Scrubbing floors and toilets; shopping for food and cooking meals; changing beds; washing, ironing, and mending clothes; doing household planning, scheduling, and recordkeeping—all the chores required to keep a household functioning—certainly qualify as work. She may justifiably feel that her work is necessary and important, yet she labels herself "just a housewife."

Feminist scholars and researchers are examining the experiences and activities hidden behind the phrase "just a housewife" (e.g., Oakley, 1974). Because it is invisible to the larger society, there are misconceptions about women's work in the home (Vanek, 1984). For example, some people believe that couples today share housework equally, that labor-saving appliances and modern conveniences have made housework easy, and that housework is trivial, with little monetary value. Let's look at each of these beliefs more closely.

Is Housework Shared? You have already learned in Chapters 10 and 11 that equality in the domestic realm is rare. Although gender roles are changing in many ways, housework and child care remain largely the responsibility of women (Baber & Allen, 1992; Ferree, 1987; Lorber, 1993). For example, a recent study of more than 3,000 U.S. couples showed that women worked more than twice as many hours per week (33.10) than men (14.44) on household chores. Even in families in which men contributed more than average, chores were highly sex-segregated: women cooked and cleaned, men worked outdoors (Blair & Lichter, 1991).

When wives work outside the home, some studies show that husbands' participation in housework changes little. The *proportion* of total housework they do goes up, but this is because wives are doing less. Other studies suggest an emerging pattern of women doing less and men doing somewhat more (Baber & Allen, 1992; Dancer & Gilbert, 1993).

The prevailing pattern, however, is one of overworked women and resistant to moderately involved men (Baber & Allen, 1992; Hochschild, 1989), and the pattern is quite consistent across cultures and ethnic groups. In a study of sixty-three dual-earner African-American families, husbands spent about half as much time as wives on household labor—they were involved, but hardly egalitarian (Hoosain & Roopmarine, 1993). In Mexican-American families, women do more housework even when they are professionally employed, and, especially in working-class families, traditional roles prevail (Hartzler & Franco, 1985; Williams, 1990). Comparisons of couples in Indonesia, the Philippines, Taiwan, South Korea, and the United States showed that women did more housework regardless of their own income or their country's level of economic development (Sanchez, 1993).

Is Housework Easy? Surprisingly, women today spend as many hours each week in housework as their grandmothers did in 1900—between fifty-one and fifty-six hours a week for married women with no employment outside the home (Vanek, 1984). Housework demands more hours each day than many paid jobs. Labor-saving devices such as automatic washers and technological advances such as household electricity and running water have made the work less dirty and arduous than it used to be, and the smaller size of modern families means less work, but new tasks have taken the place of old ones. Travel for errands, shopping, and transporting children takes up many hours each week. Household equipment must be maintained and serviced. Moreover, the modern middle-class homemaker is much less likely to have paid help than her grandmother.

But perhaps the most important factor in keeping housework a full-time job is that our standards of housekeeping have risen. Today's homemakers are encouraged to go far beyond past standards in providing a spotless and stylishly decorated home, gourmet food preparation, and a warm, welcoming emotional climate for husband and children (see Figure 12.1). Laundry may be done daily rather than weekly; thorough cleaning, weekly rather than seasonally. Homemakers often take pride in their high standards; for example, one told an interviewer that her children "don't know what it is to eat store-bought cookies. They won't eat them. Because they're so used to me doing it" (Whitbourne, 1986, p. 164). Another described her duties as follows:

> I know every day when I get up that I have "x" amount of things to do in the house, and I just do 'em . . . . They like a clean house. You know, they like it vacuumed, picked up, cleaned . . . clothes, they like their clothes washed and things like that . . . They like decent meals every night. It's not Burger King. Or, you know, Kentucky Fried Chicken. They like to eat at home, they like a good meal. . . . I have a lot of conveniences, too . . . microwave oven . . . so, it's not really that hard a task (laughs) (Whitbourne, 1986, p. 171).

Today, housework has higher standards of achievement than our grandmothers could have imagined, and it is just as time-consuming as it was in their day.

Is Housework Trivial? What is the value to society of the unpaid domestic work of women? Within individual families it is often accorded very little value:

FIGURE 12.1. Superwoman.
Source: Copyright 1993 by Nicole Hollander.

> The garbage could overflow and no one would dump it, or the dog may need to be fed . . . and everybody relies on mother to do it . . . some days I feel that they're taking me for granted. They know I'm not going out into the work force, and every once in a while I hear one of my sons say, "Well, you don't do anything all day long." . . . If they didn't have clean clothes or their beds weren't changed or something like that they might realize that their mother does do something. But most of the time they don't. I don't think men feel that a woman does a day's work (Whitbourne, 1986, p. 165).

The devaluation of housework is also apparent at the societal level. Unpaid housework is not listed in the U.S. Department of Labor's *Dictionary of Occupational Titles.* Its monetary value is not computed into the Gross National Product—an example of androcentrism and an "official denial that this work is socially necessary" (Ciancanelli & Berch, 1987). One official Labor Department ranking put *homemaker* at the same level of complexity and skill as parking lot attendant (Baruch, Barnett, & Rivers, 1983).

Obviously, families could not live as comfortably and cheaply without the services of a homemaker. But exactly how much is her work "worth"? It is difficult to compute the monetary value of women's work in the home. One way is to estimate the cost of replacing her services with paid workers—cook, chauffeur, babysitter, dishwasher, janitor, and so forth. Another is to calculate the wages the homemaker loses by staying at home. If she could earn $250 a week as a bank clerk, for example, that is the value of her housework. But neither method really captures the unique characteristics of homemaking.

Many women feel that their services could not be replaced with paid workers because the work demands loving care and an intimate knowledge of the family. Who could calculate the appropriate pay for planning a small child's birthday party—or the "overtime" involved when a woman cooks and serves an elegant dinner for her husband's boss? These tasks require organizing, scheduling, shopping, cooking, and so forth, plus loving personal involvement. Calculating lost wages from a paid job also presents problems. By this method, housework done by a woman who could earn $80 an hour as an attorney is worth twenty times as much as the identical chores done by a woman who could only earn $4 an hour as a food server (Vanek, 1984). Because housework does not fit a definition of work derived from male experience, it resists classification.

Once we begin to think of the homemaker's job as work rather than as "doing nothing all day," contrasts with paid work become even more apparent. Imagine how a "help wanted" ad for a homemaker might look:

> WANTED: Full-time employee for small family firm. DUTIES: Including but not limited to general cleaning, cooking, gardening, laundry, ironing and mending, purchasing, bookkeeping, and money management. Child care may also be required. HOURS: Avg. 55/wk but standby duty required 24 hours/day, 7 days/wk. Extra workload on holidays. SALARY AND BENEFITS: No salary, but food, clothing, and shelter provided at employer's discretion; job security and benefits depend on continued good will of employer. No vacation. No retirement plan. No opportunities for advancement. REQUIREMENTS: No previous experience necessary, can learn on the job. Only women need apply.

The homemaker's job looks unattractive indeed in this description. Women do find it unsatisfying in many ways. They dislike the boring, repetitive, and unchallenging nature of much of the work. They frequently feel lonely and isolated from others—unlike paid employment, household work is performed without the companionship of coworkers, and there is no built-in source of feedback on how well you are doing. Women also express concern about not bringing in income:

> I never wanted to be a helpless person economically—and I'm probably about as helpless now as I could be in that respect, because I'm not making anything and don't really have many ideas about a lucrative job that I could go and get. If anything happened to my husband I'd be very worried. . . . The family is completely dependent on him (Baruch et al., 1983, p. 199).

On the other hand, full-time homemakers appreciate the freedom to make their own schedules rather than to punch a time clock or answer to a supervisor. They like having time to pursue interests and hobbies and to do creative tasks such as decorating. (If this seems unrealistic given a fifty-five-hour workweek, remember that the homemaker is comparing herself to employed women, who usually work at both housework and their paid jobs.) And they enjoy the rewards that come from being emotionally and physically available to their children and husbands (Baruch et al., 1983). In the rare cases in which men take primary responsibility for housework and child care, their feelings about the job are similar to women's. Interviews with sixteen "househusbands" showed that they rated increased involvement with their children as the best aspect of their unusual situations—and doing housework as the worst (Rosenwasser & Patterson, 1984–1985).

Relational Work

Once researchers began to study housework as *work* rather than as women's natural fulfillment, other aspects of women's unpaid activities also became more visible. Women are largely responsible for caring for others' emotional needs. Keeping harmony in the family has long been defined as women's work (Parsons & Bales, 1955). The time and energy necessary for this work may be considerable, as everyone relies on "Mom" to smooth emotional crises:

> The hardest part of my life is having to deal with two college-age kids and a husband who has professional needs and an eighty-year-old mother who is going through great difficulties. . . . I sometimes feel put upon by all the demands made on me by others, that's all. And I think that's a difficulty, but being a concerned mother, that may not change (a 51-year-old homemaker, quoted in Baruch et al., 1983, p. 190).

Relational work goes beyond a woman's immediate family to a wider network of relatives (Baruch et al., 1983; Di Leonardo, 1987). Women are in charge of visits, letters, and phone calls to distant family members. They buy the presents and remember to send the card for Aunt Anna's birthday. They organize family reunions and holiday celebrations, negotiating conflicts and deciding who will host the dinner. Although the specifics of the family rituals vary according to social class and ethnic group, families' dependence on women's labor is similar, whether they are upper-class Mexican, working-class African American, middle-class Italian American, migrant Chicano farm workers, or immigrants to America from rural Japan (research reviewed in Di Leonardo, 1987). Like housework, the relational work of women is largely ignored in traditional definitions of work. But it requires time, energy, and skill, and it has economic and social value. Exchanging outgrown children's clothes with a sister-in-law or sending potential customers to a cousin's business firm as a family "favor" is a way of strengthening family relationships that also helps families maximize financial resources (Di Leonardo, 1987).

The Two-Person Career

Women's unpaid work also benefits the career development of their husbands. Hanna Papanek (1973) coined the term *two-person career* to describe situations in which wives serve as unofficial (and often unacknowledged) contributors to their husbands' work. The two-person career has been studied most extensively in the case of the corporate wife (e.g., Kanter, 1977), but it is not limited to couples in which the husband is a business executive. The male graduate student whose wife supports him by working for pay, typing his papers, and keeping mundane household problems out of his way so he can study is receiving the benefits of a two-person career (see Figure 12.2). So is the politician, whose wife must be able to "give the speech when he can't make it but to shut her mouth and listen adoringly when he is there" (Kanter, 1977, p. 122). The clergyman's wife and the college president's wife are highly visible examples.

When the role is public, it may be quite rewarding. But at the same time, the woman's freedom of action is strictly controlled (Kanter, 1977). The furor over Hillary Rodham Clinton illustrates the implicit expectations for the wife of a prominent man. A graduate of Yale law school, she was still expected to engage in a cookie recipe contest with Barbara Bush. And, at times, it seemed that the press was more interested in her hairstyle than her health care plan.

What kinds of work do women do in the service of their husbands' careers? The specific tasks vary, depending on the husband's job and career stage (Kanter, 1977). She may serve as a hostess, entertaining clients or customers in her home; make friends with and socialize with people who can be useful in advancing her husband; and engage in other aspects of image building for him. She is expected to be available at any time for complete care of their children, so

FIGURE 12.2. No comment!
Source: "For Better or For Worse" © Lynn Johnston Prod., Inc. Reprinted with permission. All rights reserved.

that he can travel or work evenings and weekends. She often participates in volunteer or community service related to his position—the faculty wives' club raises money for scholarships, and the ladies' auxiliary at the hospital raises money for equipment for their physician husbands. She may also contribute direct services in place of a paid employee—typing, taking business or sales calls, keeping books or tax records for his small business, or scheduling his travel arrangements. Finally, she provides emotional support. She is expected to listen to his complaints, help him work through problems at work, cheerfully accept his absences and work pressures, avoid burdening him with domestic trivia, and motivate him to achieve to his fullest potential. She is, indeed, "the woman behind the man."

The Benefits and Costs of Invisible Work Roles

Obviously, housework, relational work, and the ladies' auxiliary do not provide a paycheck. The traditional homemaker is expected to be rewarded for her services indirectly, through a sense of vicarious achievement (Lipman-Blumen & Leavitt, 1976). In other words, she is supposed to identify with her husband and feel rewarded and gratified by his successes. Many women do report this kind of gratification; they are glad to be "the woman behind the man." Others feel exploited and powerless to change the system. One corporate wife complained to an interviewer, "I am paid neither in job satisfaction nor in cash for my work. I did not choose the job of executive wife, and I am heartily sick of it" (Kanter, 1977, p. 111).

One risk for women who achieve through their husbands is vulnerability. If the marriage ends through the husband's death or divorce, or if despite her efforts he does not achieve fame and glory, she may have little to put on a résumé and few skills that prospective employers would regard as valuable. As discussed in Chapter 10, such women may become displaced homemakers, lacking the protection of a successful man and without marketable skills.

The availability of some women as unofficial employees for their husbands' companies also has implications for women who are employed and competing with men. There is no "corporate husband" position to match that of the corporate wife. The female employee may appear less talented and motivated than her male colleague because she lacks his invisible support staff and therefore cannot accomplish as much. If she is married, her husband is unlikely to invest his future in vicarious achievements. Gay men and lesbians also are disadvantaged in the workplace by the expectation that everyone has a wife at home. A gay friend of ours in graduate school shared the feelings of many career-oriented women both lesbian and heterosexual, single and married, when he observed, "I need a wife!"

Working Hard for a Living: Women in the Paid Work Force

It is no secret that more women are working outside the home than ever before, a worldwide social change (United Nations, 1991a). About 95 percent of young American women expect to combine paid work and marriage (e.g., Rand & Miller, 1972), and 95 percent do work outside the home at some time in their adult lives. The U.S. Department of Labor predicts that the average woman can expect to spend 29.3 years in the labor force (Betz & Fitzgerald, 1987). A majority of American women, including most mothers of young children, now work for a living (see Table 12.1).

In the United States, women from minority ethnic groups have historically been much more likely to work outside the home than white women; women's increasing trend to paid employment is one of white women "catching up" to other women (Almquist, 1979; Betz & Fitzgerald, 1987; Bose, 1987; Kim, 1986). Employment patterns differ by ethnic subgroup. For example, women of Puerto Rican background had the highest employment rate of any group of women in the 1950s (39 percent, compared with 37 percent for black and 28 percent for white women), but opportunities in the garment industry, where many urban-dwelling Puerto Rican women worked, have declined; now, they are less likely than other groups of women to be employed. Nearly two-thirds of all Asian-American women are in the paid work force (Kim, 1986). Filipino-American women have the highest employment rate for any ethnic group and are frequently found in medical professional roles, while Chinese- and Japanese-American women are concentrated in clerical jobs and food service (Bose, 1987; Kim, 1986).

Sex Segregation and Sex Stratification

In 1900 the three main occupations available to women were schoolteacher, factory worker, and domestic servant (Perun & Bielby, 1981). Though women's job options have expanded a great deal since 1900, the American workplace is

TABLE 12.1 Percentage of Women in the Labor Force by Race

	1993	Projected, 2000
White	58%	62%
Black	57%	61%
Hispanic	52%	56%

Source: U.S. Bureau of Labor Statistics.

still *sex segregated:* There are few occupations in which the proportion of women and men is about equal. Instead, there are women's jobs and men's jobs (Lorber, 1993). The gender labels attached to particular occupations have changed little—nursing is still "feminine" and engineering is still "masculine"—and the proportion of workers in these occupations who are women has also changed relatively little (see Figure 12.3).

Women are more than six times as likely as men to do clerical work and twice as likely to be in service occupations. Men are about six times as likely to be in skilled trades like carpentry (Ciancanelli & Berch, 1987). Some occupations have an overall equal ratio of women and men but remain segregated at the level of the individual workplace or task (England & McCreary, 1987; Lorber, 1993; Nieva & Gutek, 1981). For example, men sell appliances, cars, and men's clothing, while women sell other clothing items. Women prepare and serve fast food, but men are more likely to be waiters and chefs in expensive restaurants.

Sex segregation has begun to decline as more women are entering formerly male jobs. This change is happening for both black and white women, at all job levels—women are now more likely to be bus drivers, bartenders, janitors, and insurance agents than they were in 1970. However, sex segregation at the level of specific jobs does not seem to be decreasing. Women bus drivers are more likely to hold part-time school bus employment and men to hold more lucrative intercity routes; women pharmacists tend to work in hospitals and men in higher-paying retail stores (England & McCreary, 1987).

There is also a great deal of *sex stratification* within general occupational categories: Men tend to occupy more advantageous positions (Lorber, 1993). In the field of education, women are 51 percent of college instructors (the lowest rank) and only 5 percent of full professors; 86 percent of elementary school teachers and only 26 percent of school administrators (Betz & Fitzgerald, 1987). In health care professions, women are nurses' aides, abortion clinic workers, social workers, laboratory technicians, and nurses, while men are much more likely to be physicians and hospital administrators. Men are twice as likely as same-aged women to hold supervisory jobs; women workers who have authority are disproportionately white and usually supervise only a small number of other women. Only 9 percent of women have decision-making power over others' pay or promotions (D'Amico, 1986). It is difficult to think of any jobs or professions in which women typically hold the authority to determine overall work conditions and policies (Needleman & Nelson, 1988). Sex segregation and stratification are worldwide phenomena (United Nations, 1991a).

As more women enter traditionally male occupations, it would seem that sex stratification would decrease. However, the path to the top of a professional hierarchy is not always a smooth one. Although women are not totally excluded, they find it difficult to move past mid-level positions in business and the professions. The pervasive phenomenon of women being blocked from advancement has been termed the *glass ceiling:* The woman can see her goal, but she bumps into a barrier that is both invisible and impenetrable (Lorber, 1993).

Women's Work as Extension of Family Roles: "It's Only Natural"

The qualities valued in women—service, empathy, caretaking, sexual and intellectual flattery of men—keep women out of the top ranks of business, gov-

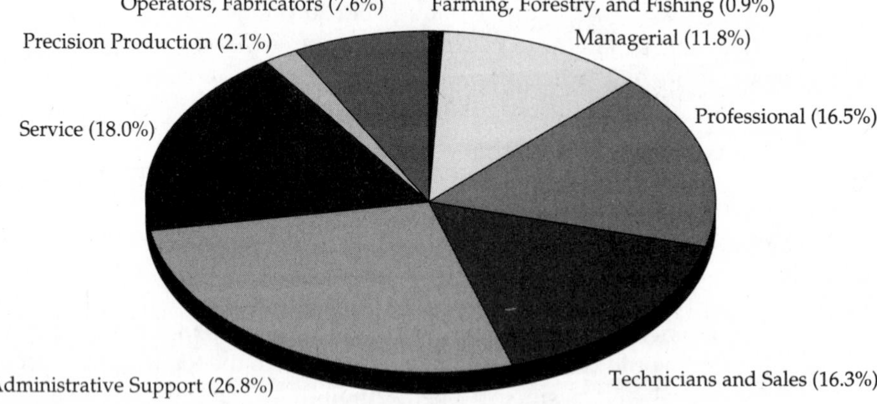

FIGURE 12.3. Although professional women are more visible than in the past, most women still work in clerical, sales, and service jobs. The pie chart here shows the percentage of women in eight occupations (1993 figures).
Source: Chart reprinted by permission of the National Committee on Pay Equity.

ernment, and professional life. These characteristics are "feminine," but they are also subordinating (Miller, 1986; Lorber, 1993). Many women's paid jobs are characterized by service to others in ways that are extensions of the unpaid work wives and mothers do (Nieva & Gutek, 1981). Secretaries have traditionally been expected to provide personal services (such as serving coffee) for the supervisor. Their status depends on the status of the individual man to whom they are assigned, and they are rewarded for loyalty. Indeed, secretaries may be treated like "office wives" (Kanter, 1977). Many secretarial and clerical workers have begun to protest employers' expectations of service and to insist that their jobs be defined in terms of skills.

Other jobs dominated by women also have strong service components. Women provide food and cleaning services as waitresses and as staff in hotels, restaurants, and hospitals. Nurses are expected to provide tender loving care to patients, manage the unit like good housekeepers, and serve as handmaidens to physicians (Corley & Mauksch, 1988). Teachers provide emotional nurturance to young children, and social workers care for the poor and needy. The caring required in these jobs is usually stressed more than the skills (Nieva & Gutek, 1981). Because caring fits into a feminine stereotype, it is often seen as a natural by-product of being female rather than an aspect of job competence. This contributes to the devaluation of women's work: If women perform certain functions "naturally," the reasoning goes, virtually any woman can do them, and they need not be noticed or rewarded by employers (Needleman & Nelson, 1988).

People who take care of zoo animals earn, on average, $2,500 a year more than those who take care of children in child-care centers. In 1993, the *highest* paid teachers at these centers, most of whom have college-level training in early childhood education, earned $15,488 a year. Ninety-eight percent of these workers are women, and 33 percent are women of color. (The average wage for men with some college training in 1992 was $33,161) (Noble, 1993). One researcher who studied women in social work, nursing, and education noted societal indifference to women's caring functions and asked about the future of these professions, "How much do we care about caring? And are we willing, as a society, to offer respect and a living wage to those who do it for us?" (Collins, 1988).

Differential Earnings

Women earn less money than men. This generalization holds for full- and part-time workers and white, African-American, Asian-American, and Hispanic women (Betz & Fitzgerald, 1987; England & McCreary, 1987; Kim, 1986; Nieva & Gutek, 1981; Russo & Denmark, 1984). Indeed, as Figure 12.4 shows, no group of women has a median income that comes close to the median income of white men. The difference holds for every level of education. Although young people are urged to get a college education in order to increase lifetime earnings, the financial "payoff" of education is much greater for men. Overall women college graduates earn about $11,667 less annually than college-educated white men (National Committee on Pay Equity, 1994).

The gender gap in wages has remained fairly constant over the past forty years (see Figure 12.5). In general, women have earned about 60 percent of men's earnings. The bright part of this picture is that the most recent trends in-

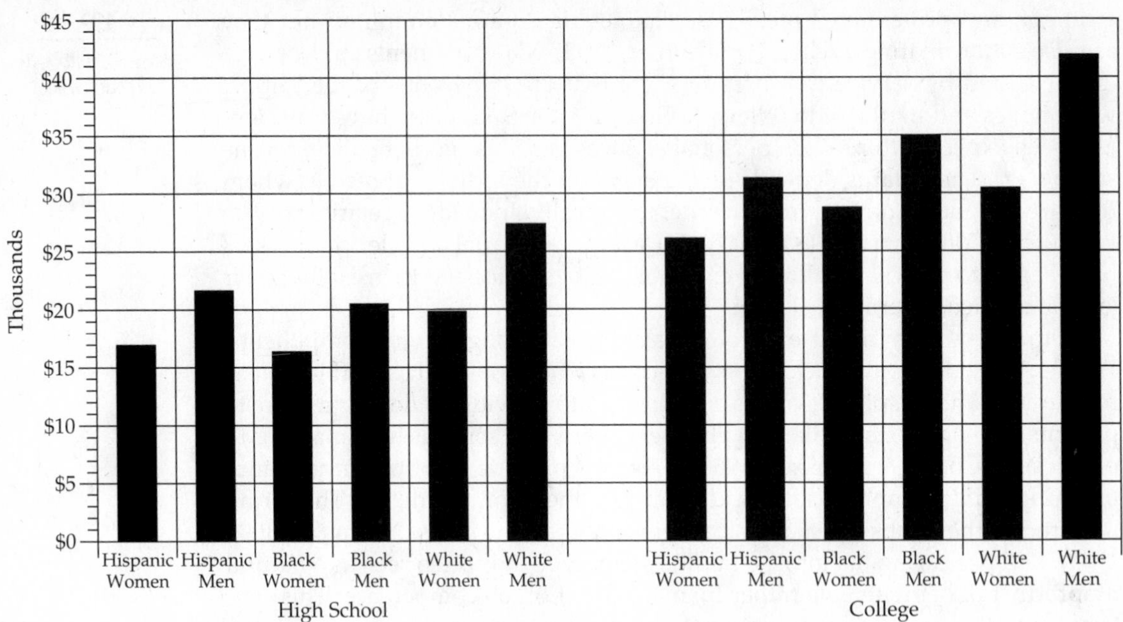

FIGURE 12.4. Annual salary of women and men by race and education: 1993 Median Annual Earnings.
Source: Reprinted by permission of the National Committee on Pay Equity.

dicate that the earnings of African-American women are catching up to those of white women, and that the gender gap has decreased slightly. But although these gains are encouraging, the gap between all women's earnings and those of white men is still very large (England & McCreary, 1987; National Committee on Pay Equity, 1994).

Why this large and persistent inequity in earnings? Many possible causes have been suggested. One traditional explanation is that women invest less in their work roles than men—they are less committed to their work, less likely to obtain extra training and education, more likely to be absent or to quit a job. However, there is little evidence to support these claims. On the contrary, the gender gap in earnings remains substantial when a number of variables such as education, absences, and years on the job are controlled (Betz & Fitzgerald, 1987; England & McCreary, 1987; Nieva & Gutek, 1981). The individual investment hypothesis also does not explain why women's jobs that require high levels of education and skill pay less than men's jobs with lower requirements (Betz & Fitzgerald, 1987).

Another explanation focuses on the jobs rather than the sex of the worker—secretaries and clerks are paid less than electricians and truck drivers, and since more women choose the former jobs, they earn less on average. It is certainly true that women are clustered in a few low-paying job sectors, but it is unclear whether women choose these jobs or whether they are the only ones available to most women. Moreover, there are substantial wage differences when women and men do exactly the same jobs. Women who are engineers and chemists earn

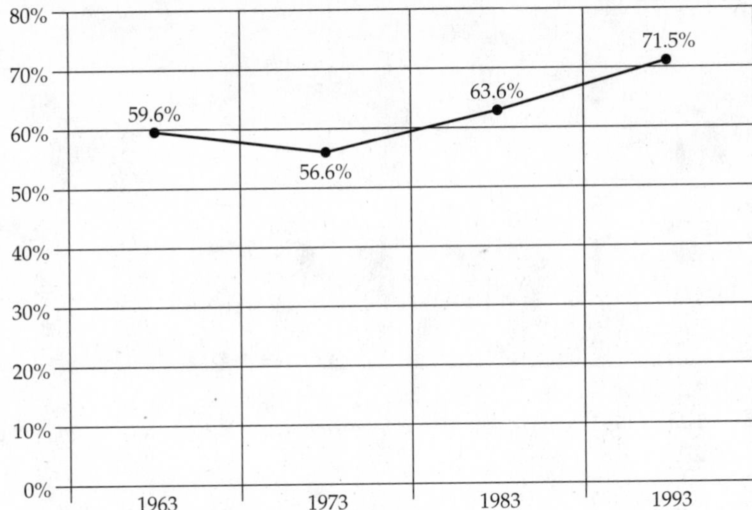

FIGURE 12.5. Wage Gap through the Years: Women's Earnings as a Percent of Men's Earnings, 1963, 1973, 1983, 1993.
Source: Reprinted by permission of National Committee on Pay Equity.

less than men who are engineers and chemists (Nieva & Gutek, 1981); women social workers earn less than men in the same positions (Kim & Johnson, 1984).

According to Nancy Betz and Louis Fitzgerald (1987, pp. 175–176), specialists in women's career development, "It is difficult to escape the conclusion that men are paid more for what they do quite simply because they are men." The income discrepancy between women and men is part of a larger pattern of overvaluing whatever is male and undervaluing whatever is female (see Figure 12.6).

Unemployment and Underemployment

Workers are classified as *unemployed* when they want to work but cannot find a job, and *underemployed* when they are in jobs that do not fully use their skills and qualifications. Women are more likely to be unemployed than men (Nieva & Gutek, 1981). Unemployment creates significant stresses for the individual and her family, including financial worries, loss of self-esteem, and depression (Dew, Penkower, & Bromet, 1991; Dew, Bromet, & Penkower, 1992).

In a study of 114 Hispanic women laid off from jobs in a canning factory, the women reported several kinds of stresses due to the job loss. These included family-based stress (life conditions became inadequate for raising a family; children could not understand the job loss and deprivation), occupational stress (feelings of sadness remembering the lost job and coworkers; worry about finding another job) and financial stress (90 percent reported difficulty in providing basic food and clothing for their families) (Romero, Castro, & Cervantes, 1988). The importance of financial security to psychological well-being is underscored by a study of white middle-class women in which total family income proved strongly related to overall psychological well-being (Baruch et al., 1983). While

FIGURE 12.6. Sex discrimination—the power of a good allegory.
Source: Copyright © 1993. Reprinted with special permission of King Features Syndicate, Inc.

the old saying that "money can't buy happiness" may be true, lack of money and job security brings stress and unhappiness to women and their families.

Underemployment in women has been little studied, although it is widespread (Nieva & Gutek, 1981). The sex-segregated and sex-stratified world of women clerical and service workers has been termed *pink-collar* employment (Howe, 1977). Most of the top ten occupations for women are low in status, are poorly paid, and offer few opportunities for advancement. Their low pay has long-term effects on social security and other benefits.

Pink-collar work is frequently monotonous and unchallenging. Moreover, the worker has little decision-making power or autonomy; her task is to follow directions and complete her work to a supervisor's satisfaction. Pink-collar jobs do have some compensations or positive aspects. Many women report that they enjoy the company of coworkers and develop close friendships with them. Office birthday parties and sharing of family news and photographs are among the ways that women humanize the workplace and create solidarity with each other (Ferree, 1987).

The "women's professions" of nursing, social work, and teaching are very important to society and require both skill and dedication. More than most other jobs held by women, they offer intellectual challenge and the rewards of doing socially valued work. However, their educational requirements do not lead to high pay; rather, they are characterized by "learning without earning." Moreover, like other occupations with a high proportion of women they tend to lack clear avenues for advancement and autonomous working conditions (Betz & Fitzgerald, 1987).

When women (and people of color) are channeled into a narrow range of occupations that do not allow the full development of their unique skills or abilities, there is loss both to individuals and to society (Betz & Fitzgerald, 1987). Individuals may come to believe that the job they are "stuck" in is all they deserve and to suffer from decreased motivation to work (Kanter, 1977). Society in general accepts the "homogenization" of women into a few occupations as natural and inevitable, making future change difficult (Bem & Bem, 1971). And society loses much needed talent.

One of the most poignant examples of societal loss associated with underemployment of women comes from a well-known study of gifted children (Terman & Oden, 1959). More than 1,500 children with measured IQs over 135 were followed as they grew into adulthood. The boys almost invariably became prominent, respected professionals—as adults, they were scientists, authors, and college professors. The girls were most likely to become full-time homemakers; only about half held paid jobs, and the greatest number of these were schoolteachers and secretaries.

Lewis Terman came to recognize the waste of talent that his results demonstrated, remarking of the gifted women in his study that "After marriage they fall into the domestic role. . . . The woman who is a potential poet, novelist, lawyer, physician, or scientist usually gives up any professional ambition she may have had and devotes herself to home, husband, and children . . . [robbing] the arts and sciences of a large fraction of the genius that might otherwise be dedicated to them. My data strongly suggest that this loss must be debited to motivational causes and limited opportunity rather than to lack of ability" (Seagoe, 1975). Terman's sample reached adulthood in the 1950s. It is interesting to speculate whether gifted girls growing up today would still be less likely than gifted boys to achieve their fullest potential. What do you think?

SOCIOCULTURAL FACTORS: "DOING GENDER" IN THE WORKPLACE

Women's position in the workplace is not just a static aspect of social structure. Rather, it is continually enacted and remade as people make workplace decisions influenced by gender. Sexism in the world of work operates in many ways, both subtle and overt. Psychological research contributes to our understanding of the dynamics of gender in the workplace by providing experiments and field studies that identify the conditions and circumstances of sex discrimination.

In Chapter 5 we learned that judgments about other people are affected by gender in many ways, and affect others' behavior in turn:

- *Attributional biases* lead to different explanations of women's and men's behavior.
- Gender functions as a *status cue,* with men being accorded higher status.
- Gender distinctions maintain social boundaries.

We turn now to a look at how these cognitive and social processes affect working women.

Attributions for Success and Failure

When faced with an example of a woman or man who has succeeded at some achievement, people very often come up with different reasons to explain her or his success. As described in Chapter 5, men's success is more likely to be seen as the result of high ability—"He succeeded because he's talented or smart." Women's success is more likely to be attributed to luck (Deaux & Emswiller,

1974). When the task is one that cannot reasonably be attributed entirely to luck (for example, becoming a successful physician), people are still reluctant to judge women equal to men in ability. Instead, they attribute the woman's success more to hard work (Feldman-Summers & Kiesler, 1974) (see Box 12.1).

If people tend to view women's success as due to luck or effort and men's success as due to ability, how do they explain situations in which a male or female attempts achievement but fails? Several studies show that they are likely to blame a woman's failure on lack of ability and a man's failure on bad luck or the quirks of the situation, such as an unusually difficult task (Cash, Gillen, & Burns, 1977; Etaugh & Brown, 1975). Sexism seems to interact with racism when people make judgments about others' success (Yarkin, Town, & Wallston, 1982).

Sexism and racism in explaining others' achievements are not universal. Managers (both female and male) who have more positive attitudes toward women in business generally are less likely to make attributions based on stereotypes (Garland, Hale, & Burnson, 1982). Nevertheless, it is easy to see how the typical pattern of attributing males' successes to ability and females' to luck disadvantages women in the workplace. A manager is probably far more likely to hire or promote someone who is perceived as highly able than someone who just got lucky. Similarly, an employer might view an isolated failure as a confirmation of a woman's lack of ability but as only a temporary setback for a man. The assumption behind the typical pattern of attribution seems to be that men are basically competent; whether they succeed or fail, that belief remains intact. Women and blacks, on the other hand, are basically incompetent, and that belief, too, can be maintained whether they succeed or fail.

Devaluing Women's Performance

"Are women prejudiced against women?" is a question first asked by Philip Goldberg (1968) in a study that set off a wave of research on how people judge the performance of women versus men. Goldberg asked female college students to rate several professional articles on their quality and importance to their field. Some of the articles were from stereotypically female professions, such as dietetics; others from stereotypically male professions, such as city planning; and others from relatively gender-neutral areas. Each article was prepared in two versions, as though written either by "John MacKay" or "Joan MacKay." Except for the authors' names, the two versions of each article were identical.

Goldberg found that the students rated the articles more highly when they thought they had been written by a man. Even articles from "feminine" fields were seen as better when written by a man. Other researchers extended Goldberg's study to male raters, with similar results (Paludi & Bauer, 1983; Paludi & Strayer, 1985). Sex bias isn't always found—it interacts with other factors people use in making judgments about others' work, and sometimes the work of women and men ends up being evaluated similarly (Wallston & O'Leary, 1981; Nieva & Gutek, 1981).

There are also a few studies reporting that highly competent performance by a woman may actually be evaluated more positively than comparable performance by a man—as though being out of role and unexpected gives female competence greater value (Abramson, Goldberg, Greenberg, & Abramson,

Box 12.1 Impressions from an Office

The family picture is on HIS desk.
  Ah, a solid, responsible family man.
The family picture is on HER desk.
  Um, her family will come before her career.

HIS desk is cluttered.
  He's obviously a hard worker and a busy man.
HER desk is cluttered.
  She's obviously a disorganized scatterbrain.

HE is talking with his coworkers.
  He must be discussing the latest deal.
SHE is talking with her coworkers.
  She must be gossiping.

HE's not at his desk.
  He must be at a meeting.
SHE's not at her desk.
  She must be in the ladies' room.

HE's not in the office.
  He's meeting customers.
SHE's not in the office.
  She must be out shopping.

HE's having lunch with the boss.
  He's on his way up.
SHE's having lunch with the boss.
  They must be having an affair.

The boss criticized HIM.
  He'll improve his performance.
The boss criticized HER.
  She'll be very upset.

HE got an unfair deal.
  Did he get angry?
SHE got an unfair deal.
  Did she cry?

HE's getting married.
  He'll get more settled.
SHE's getting married.
  She'll get pregnant and leave.

HE's having a baby.
  He'll need a raise.
SHE's having a baby.
  She'll cost the company money in maternity benefits.

HE's going on a business trip.
  It's good for his career.
SHE's going on a business trip.
  What does her husband say?

HE's leaving for a better job.
  He knows how to recognize a good opportunity.
SHE's leaving for a better job.
  Women are not dependable.

Natasha Josefowitz

Source: Reprinted by permission of Warner Books. N. Josefowitz (1983), New York from *Is This Where I Was Going?*

1977). (This has been called the talking platypus phenomenon. The platypus is not judged by how well it talks, but by the fact that it can talk at all.) In general, research from the 1960s through the 1980s (reviewed by Lott, 1985) presents a convincing case that devaluation of work attributed to a woman is a fairly general problem that can have large effects in the workplace.

Discrimination in Hiring and Promotion

Sex discrimination in employment has been illegal since 1964, when the Civil Rights Act was passed. Before that time, many employers discriminated as a matter of policy. For example, AT&T allowed women to work only up to certain levels and in a limited range of tasks (Gutek & Larwood, 1987). Prestigious Vassar College denied tenure to every married woman professor in the sciences for thirty years. A recent court ruling stated that the tenure decisions were the result of prejudice based on the stereotype that women with families cannot be productive scientists (Kelly & Sanchez, 1994). Although employers may no longer refuse to hire or promote applicants because of race or sex, a great deal of informal discrimination still occurs. For example, 37 percent of women in a recent Australian study said they had been discriminated against in promotion decisions (Snizek & Neil, 1992).

A classic study of sex bias in hiring used psychologists themselves as the subjects. Linda Fidell (1970) composed and sent fictitious sets of credentials for psychologists to psychology department chairpersons, asking them to indicate how likely they would be to hire the individual described and what level of job they might offer. Although the chairpersons were not aware of it (each saw only one set), the fictitious credentials were identical except for the sex of the applicant. When the chairpersons thought they were evaluating a female psychologist, "she" was rated less favorably and considered qualified for a lower-level position than when "he" was evaluated. Many other studies have shown similar biases; equally qualified women are less likely to be hired or are offered lower-paying, less desirable jobs (Betz & Fitzgerald, 1987; Fitzgerald & Betz, 1983; Nieva & Gutek, 1981).

In general, sex bias in hiring and promotion is most likely to occur under the following conditions:

1. When the situation is ambiguous and judgments must be made on the basis of criteria that may or may not be relevant. People are generally most likely to rely on stereotypes when little specific information is available. If the situation has clear-cut cues for competence—for example, a woman who is already in a position of established high status—a sex-biased judgment is less likely (Isaacs, 1981). Specific rather than vague performance criteria also reduce sex bias (Lenney, Mitchell, & Browning, 1983). These results suggest that a woman is most likely to be harmed by discrimination at the beginning of her career, when employers are making global predictions about future performance on the basis of a relatively small amount of information. Unfortunately, early discrimination may prevent women from reaching levels at which their work might be evaluated more fairly.

2. When the job in question is highly gender stereotyped and the applicant is of the "wrong" sex. In one study, male and female researchers posing as applicants telephoned to inquire about jobs selected from classified advertisements in urban newspapers. In more than one-third of the cases, men applying for female-typed jobs and women applying for male-typed jobs were told the job was filled. When an applicant of the "right" sex for the job called immediately afterward, that applicant was invited to come for an interview (Levinson, 1975). Of course, discrimination on the basis of gender appropriateness affects women more than men. Relatively few men are striving to gain access to low-paying clerical and service jobs, while many women might hope to improve their status and pay by moving to male-typed jobs.

3. When personal values and organizational factors support discrimination. Sex discrimination in hiring is more likely to occur if the potential employer

has strongly stereotyped views about males and females (Sharp & Post, 1980) and if there are few women already in the organization (Yoder, Crumpton, & Zipp, 1989). But discrimination is not solely the result of personal prejudices. Even people who do not have strong negative opinions about the competence of women and minorities may discriminate against them if they feel that those in power expect or approve of such behavior, or if the organizational climate is one in which discrimination is the norm (Katz, 1987; Larwood, Szwajkowski, & Rose, 1988). These results suggest that strong messages that fair play is expected could lessen race and sex discrimination in organizations.

In addition to sex discrimination, lesbians may also face discrimination on the basis of sexual orientation. They may be fired, not hired, or not promoted due to stereotypes about lesbians being maladjusted, mentally ill, or child molesters. In a survey of 203 lesbians in a metropolitan area (mainly white-collar, middle class, and highly educated), 25 percent reported specific instances of formal or informal discrimination, including being fired or forced to resign when their personal life became known. Others were denied raises or promotions. Informal discrimination included taunts, gossip, ridicule, social rejection, and even physical violence (Levine & Leonard, 1984).

Because of heterosexism, the majority of lesbians remain "in the closet" at work (Levine & Leonard, 1984). This limits their ability to lobby for an end to heterosexual privilege in the workplace. A few progressive employers (including the American Psychological Association) now provide health insurance and other benefits for same-sex couples, but gay and lesbian civil rights and workplace equity are by no means assured (Babar & Allen, 1992).

Unfortunately, patterns of discrimination are often very hard to see. For example, if you are a woman with a bachelor's degree who has been with a company for five years and you are not promoted, you might compare yourself with a male coworker who was promoted. Suppose this man has been with the company for only three years but he has a master's degree: It's hard to decide whether or not you have been discriminated against. But suppose you look further in the company and find a man who was promoted with only a high school diploma and ten years of service and a woman who was not promoted with two years of college and eight years of service. A pattern begins to form. But that pattern is apparent only when many cases are averaged, and discrimination is usually examined one case at a time (Crosby, 1994; Crosby, Clayton, Alksnis, & Hemker, 1986).

Even when people know that their group as a whole is discriminated against, they often persist in believing that they themselves have never been affected. This is true not only for women in general but for other disadvantaged groups like lesbians and working-class people. Like ostriches who keep their heads in the sand, people often deny that sex bias and discrimination affect them (Crosby, Pufall, Snyder, O'Connell, & Whalen, 1989).

Discrimination is not inevitable or invariable. It depends on a complex set of influences that can be studied systematically and *can* be changed. By showing how discrimination works, psychological research can help point the way to change.

Social Reactions to "Uppity Women"

Women who choose occupations other than teaching, pink-collar work, and nursing are likely to work mostly with men. In her study of a large corporation in the mid-1970s, Rosabeth Moss Kanter (1977) found only twenty women in a 300-person sales force scattered over fourteen offices. These women's coworkers, managers, and customers were nearly all men. What is it like to be virtually the only woman on the job?

As you learned in Chapter 5, the ways women are treated in male-dominated work settings may have as much to do with their rarity as their sex. The "odd person," whether black, Hispanic, disabled, or female, encounters a predictable set of problems. She or he becomes a *token,* a symbol of all members of her group.

Marian Pour-El, a mathematician, described her reception as a graduate student in the math department at Harvard:

> I recall very vividly my first day in class: three seats in front of me, three seats in back of me, and two seats on either side were left vacant. I was a complete pariah in that social setting. . . .
>
> My first colloquium at Harvard University was a memorable event. The tea, which preceded the actual lecture, was held in the library and was a rather formal affair. As I entered, all eyes sank lower into the teacups in a great effort not to seem to notice me. Needless to say, no one talked to me at all. At the end of the tea the chairman . . . turned to me and said with a twinkle in his eye, "Your presence is noted here" (Pour-El, 1974, p. 36).

Because tokens are highly visible in the organization, they feel a great deal of performance pressure. The token woman or black management trainee may be deliberately and publicly displayed to prove that the company is complying with affirmative-action policies or asked to give speeches about the progress made by women and blacks in industry. One woman commented about this treatment, "If it seems good to be noticed, wait until you make your first major mistake" (Kanter, 1977, p. 213).

When a white male employee makes a mistake, it is interpreted as an individual error and no more; if the token woman or minority makes a similar mistake, it is taken as evidence that "those people" should not have been hired and are bound to fail. Paradoxically, tokens must also worry about being too successful. Since all eyes are on the token, if she performs well enough to "show up" members of the dominant group she will be criticized for being a workaholic or "too aggressive." Tokens are usually very eager to "fit in," so they do not challenge the values and practices of the men in power—indeed, they may outdo the men in enforcing the status quo, becoming "queen bees" who reject other women (Lorber, 1993). To sum up, the token position is a highly stressful and ambivalent one (see Box 12.2).

Kanter's theory of tokenism suggests that token status should be equally stressful for any group and that increasing the number of women in a job or profession will eliminate tokenism problems. Recent research has examined both these questions.

Women and minorities are much more likely than white men to experience token status. However, as noted in Chapter 5, when white men are the tokens,

Box 12.2 The Effects of Tokenism: A Case Study

Social psychologist Janice Yoder has written a moving description of her experiences as a visiting faculty member at a U.S. military academy. Yoder's token status was extreme on several dimensions: She was one of sixteen women among 545 faculty members, 97 percent of whom were military officers. Her visibility, isolation, and relegation to negative roles were correspondingly extreme:

> My differences as a civilian, a researcher, and a woman created uncertainty among my colleagues and threatened to disrupt the team . . . I frequently was isolated from group discussions . . . One subgroup (of the department) dubbed itself the "Wolf Gang," used "We eat sheep!" as their motto, and howled when called upon to make group presentations. The departmental theme song chosen was "Macho Man," hardly appropriate for an academic department that included two female officers and myself. The gossip about my sexuality ranged from lesbian to heterosexually promiscuous. . . .
>
> I was assigned to one of two female roles: "wife" or "feminist/libber." In the former role, I was invited to a luncheon for wives. . . . While this was mildly amusing, the effects of my second label as "feminist/libber" were not. . . . I watched as my colleagues began to get restless when I raise my hand, rolled their eyes as I spoke, and concluded by ignoring. . . . I became totally ineffectual, yet unwilling to keep quiet and thus implicitly condone these actions. My role as a deviate became predictable, unwelcome, and ignored (pp. 64–65).

Yoder described the psychological effects of token treatment in a journal entry made after only three months of such treatment:

> What does happen to the deviate? The deviate can convert, but short of a sex-change operation . . . and a personality overhaul, conversion seems out of the question for me. . . . What can I do? Yet, the failure is placed squarely on my shoulders. "What's wrong with you?" "Why can't you get along?" These questions haunt me, undermining my self-image to a point where I am reduced to crying at home alone at night. . . . I feel impotent, I can't sleep, but I am never clear-headed and fully awake. I have an eye infection. Daily problems have become insurmountable difficulties. . . . I can't work. I can't go out and have fun. . . . I have become bad in my eyes; the attributions of blame have been internalized (p. 66).

Janice Yoder resigned from her visiting professorship after one semester.

Source: From Yoder, "An academic woman as a token: A case study," *Journal of Social Issues, 41,* 61–72. 1985 Plenum Publishing Corporation. Reprinted with permission.

they do not encounter negative treatment. Male nursing students did not differ from females on measures of social isolation, performance pressure, and so on (Snavely & Fairhurst, 1984). In a field study of work groups in an amusement park, only female tokens were negatively evaluated. In fact, male tokens advanced more quickly than nontokens (Yoder & Sinnett, 1985). These results are intriguing—is there a double standard even for tokenism?

Would balancing the number of women and men in organizations bring an end to tokenism? Unfortunately, as the percentage of women increases to 15 percent, they are more isolated than ever. Research suggests that this is a form of organizational "backlash." While the dominant group may tolerate one or two tokens, the appearance of more women (or minorities) threatens their control and leads to more open and aggressive discrimination (Lorber, 1993).

Mentors and Role Models

Role models are members of one's own reference group who are visibly successful (Yoder, Adams, Grove, & Priest, 1985). Just knowing that other women have managed to overcome the obstacles to success may help the newcomer deal with her conflicts and prepare for the challenges to come (Basow & Howe, 1980; O'Connell & Russo, 1980). For example, female graduate students who had female professors as role models described themselves as more career oriented, confident, instrumental, and satisfied with their student role than those who had male role models (Gilbert, Galessich, & Evans, 1983).

While white men are exposed to many role models, women and minority men have had few. Lack of role models probably contributes to loneliness and feelings of deviance. Adding a few token women to the workplace does not solve the role model problem. In fact, pressures to be role models for others add to the other pressures on the token:

> Linda (the only female faculty member in a 50-member university department of economics) puts the dilemma clearly: "I feel I can't do anything wrong because it will be attributed to my sex and not to me. I know that in schools where there are women economists on the faculty, more women major in economics and more go on to graduate school. But I can't be a role model for everybody, and I can't do it alone."
>
> Like 19th-century country schoolteachers, academic women are expected to be living illustrations of competence, moral rectitude, and self-discipline. Because their male colleagues can distribute role demands among many more people, a man's personal life may be in shambles, his teaching atrocious, or his research 30 years out of date, yet it occurs to no one to question the quality of his role modeling (Crawford, 1978, p. 93).

Role models may be admired from afar, while *mentors* are people who take a personal interest in the newcomer (Yoder et al., 1985). Knowing the formal rules in a workplace is rarely enough. Whether you are working in a corporation, factory, hospital, or small office, there is inside knowledge about how to get ahead that is never written down in the employee manual. Instead, workers rely on informal social networks to work "the system" to their advantage (Lorber, 1993). Successful older men frequently serve as mentors to young men on their way up, providing them with introductions to important people, special training, and hints on how to bypass the bureaucracy. They may also stand up for the young man if he makes a controversial decision and empower him simply by associating with him.

Women workers lack access to this "old-boy network," with its "bands of brothers" who look out for each other's interests (Lorber, 1993). High-status men are reluctant to sponsor women. Quite simply, these men feel more comfortable with people they perceive as similar to themselves. Also, young women may not always have realized the importance of finding mentors, believing instead that hard work and playing by the rules will guarantee success (Kanter, 1977; Nieva & Gutek, 1981). However, a study of 171 female attorneys showed that those who had had mentors were more successful and satisfied in their careers than those who had not (Riley & Wrench, 1985).

What about women mentoring other women? In the past, only a few women were in positions that would allow them to be mentors for other women, and the pressures of their own token status may have prevented them from reaching out (Yoder et al., 1985). The scarcity of mentors is probably easing, as "old-girl networks" have grown to provide women with advantages traditionally available to men. For example, the Psychology of Women Division of the American Psychological Association has a volunteer program that matches beginning researchers with accomplished ones for mentoring and encouragement. Female and male mentors may provide much the same practical benefits and advantages to women (Gaskill, 1991). However, women may be better mentors for women in the areas of creating a professional self-image, empowerment, and supportive personal counseling (Gaskill, 1991; Gilbert & Rossman, 1992).

Sexual Harassment from Nine to Five

Sexual harassment is any deliberate or repeated sexual behavior that is unwelcome and unwanted by the target. It is a form of abuse that includes obscene remarks, dirty jokes, or suggestive comments about one's sexual habits or personal life—behaviors that create a hostile working environment. It may also include threats and coercion to "put out or lose your job," being grabbed and fondled, and even being raped (Fitzgerald, 1993).

In the past fifteen years, since sexual harassment was first legally defined, both large-scale surveys and studies of particular job settings have shown that one of every two women is sexually harassed at some point during her education or working life (Fitzgerald, 1993). Recent legal cases and public events have increased awareness of this issue (Feldman, 1994; Fitzgerald, 1993):

- A bank employee, Michele Vinson, was raped forty to fifty times by her employer.
- A shipyard worker, Lois Robinson, was subjected to pornographic pictures and graffiti at work, including a dart board with a drawing of a woman's breast, complete with nipple "bull's eye".
- A judge assaulted five women employees and forced another woman to perform oral sex during a job interview.
- The "Tailhook Scandal," in which scores of women officers were assaulted during a naval aviators' convention, led the U.S. Navy to publish a harassment prevention manual.
- Law professor Anita Hill testified that Supreme Court nominee Clarence Thomas had repeatedly harassed her. Despite her testimony, Thomas's appointment was confirmed.

Women frequently describe the experience of harassment as degrading, disgusting, and humiliating. They feel shamed and helpless. Women in Barbara Gutek's (1985) study described their experiences as follows:

> He was a gross man. That was his manner toward everyone in the office. He thought it was cute that he could have every woman in the office. He was executive vice president and he thought this would give him special privileges. I thought it was disgusting how he acted. He acted real macho, like he was God's gift to women. I quit (p 80).

> . . . This man went after every girl in the office and he went after me. Every female who worked in the office was subjected to this guy. We got fired if we did not go out with him (p. 82).

> He was a creep. He was my supervisor. He was just one of those people. That's all that's on his mind. It happened to other women, too. Thank God there aren't that many like him. I fixed him. I spilled hot soup all over his lap later (p. 82).

So far we have discussed only heterosexual harassment. Lesbian workers may face harassment based on their sexual orientation (Gelwick, 1984; Levine & Leonard, 1984). Accusations of lesbianism are also used to keep heterosexual women "in line":

> I worked with some very chauvinistic men. They thought women were sex objects. They would make sexual jokes and I was expected to respond to the jokes in a favorable way or else they would call me a dyke or a lesbian (Gutek, 1985, p. 89).

Sexual harassment can happen to any woman, young or old, lesbian or heterosexual, feminist or not, in any kind of job. It even happens to clergywomen; 70 percent of a sample of 140 female rabbis had been sexually harassed (Cowen, 1993). Young women and women who are unattached to men (lesbians, single women, and divorced women) are more likely to be harassed than married women. (Perhaps married women are seen as being protected or possessed by men, while other women are "fair game.") In about half the cases, the harasser is a supervisor but he may also be a coworker or client (Gutek, 1985; Maypole, 1986; Maypole & Skaine, 1983; Rosenberg, Perlstadt, & Phillips, 1993).

More than 20 percent of women have quit a job, been transferred, been fired, or quit trying to get a job because of harassment (Gutek, 1985). Women who are harassed may also suffer from lowered self-esteem, self-blame, impaired social relationships, and overall lowered satisfaction with their lives (Gruber & Bjorn, 1982; Maypole, 1986). Psychological consequences include anxiety, depression, and sexual dysfunction (Fitzgerald, 1993). Organizations also have costs when the morale of women workers is low and when they quit because of harassment.

Sexual harassment can be seen as an abuse of power, a reflection of the low status of women, and a means of social control (Fitzgerald, 1993; MacKinnon, 1979). Because men have greater authority, status, and material power in the workplace, they are able to force their sexual attentions on women. They justify their behavior by claiming that women invite harassment or use it to "sleep their way to the top." Male-dominated organizations legitimize harassment by claiming that it is a minor problem and treating women who complain as though they were crazy (for example, a U.S. senator suggested that Anita Hill was schizophrenic).

Sexual harassment is not inevitable or natural. Organizations can reduce it by educating people about the problem, sending clear messages to employees that harassment will not be tolerated, rewarding nonsexist managers and spotlighting them as role models for other men, and punishing harassers (Gutek, 1985). Women can join with other women to name harassment, to bring it into the open, and to convey the message that it will not be tolerated. As a poster in our university's Women's Center states, "Sexual harassment is not a compliment. It's offensive and illegal."

OBSTACLES FROM WITHIN

So far our discussion of obstacles to women's job and career satisfaction has focused on forces in the social environment that can affect any woman. We now turn to psychological factors—individual differences in beliefs, values, motives, and choices.

Socialized Differences

Limited Expectations

Starting at an early age, girls see their career options as limited. When first- and second-grade children were asked "What would you like to be when you grow up?" the thirty-three boys named eighteen different occupations and the thirty-three girls named only eight. Boys' aspirations included football player (the top choice), policeman, doctor, dentist, scientist, pilot, and astronaut. Girls' top choices were nurse and teacher—chosen by twenty-five of the girls—followed by mother, flight attendant, and sales clerk. One girl wanted to be a doctor.

The researcher (Looft, 1971) went on to ask the children, "Now what do you think you *really* will do when you grow up?" Girls were more likely than boys to stick with their first choice—they saw themselves not only as having fewer options than the boys but as having a lower possibility of changing options. The response of the only girl who expressed a desire to be a doctor poignantly illustrates these limited expectations. When asked what she "really" would do as an adult, she replied, "I'll probably have to be something else—maybe a store lady" (p. 366).

In Chapter 5, we noted that women often do not feel *entitled* to equality. They know that sex discrimination is pervasive but deny that it has ever happened to them (Crosby, 1984). They pay themselves less than men in laboratory experiments, even though they do better work (Major, 1994). When they achieve positions of power, they continue to question the legitimacy of their authority even though they know they are competent (Apfelbaum, 1993).

Why do women have low expectations for their career options? The answer may lie partly in women's awareness of the social obstacles described earlier. If a woman suspects that her attempt at a career may lead to devaluation of her competence, the stresses of being a token, sexual harassment, discrimination, and social rejection, she may think it pointless to hold high aspirations. Women's low expectations may also reflect the fact that people learn to expect and aspire to what they see around them. With abundant role models of nurses and teachers, and few for most other professional occupations, girls and women may find it difficult to imagine alternatives (England & McCreary, 1987). If women do not feel entitled to equality, it is because they are responding to pervasive cultural norms.

Values and Interests

Perhaps women and men differ in their work roles because they have different values. Do women workers want and need different rewards than men? Do they end up in "feminine" occupations because these occupations fit with their personal values? A great deal of research (reviewed by Betz & Fitzgerald, 1987; Nieva & Gutek, 1981) has attempted to answer these questions.

In general, women and men in similar jobs do not differ in their need for *intrinsic* rewards (those that come from actually doing the job, such as a sense of accomplishment and feeling that the work is interesting and important). Both women and men, especially those employed in high-status occupations such as medicine, report that it is important that their careers meet these needs. However, when women and men are compared on *extrinsic* rewards (those that come after the job is done or as a by-product of the job), there are some differences. Men are more likely to say that pay and promotion are important, while women place higher value on a pleasant working environment—friendly coworkers, comfortable surroundings, ease of transportation, and so forth. We have already seen that women frequently create a work environment of interpersonal caring and involvement by sharing aspects of their personal lives with coworkers (Ferree, 1987). Perhaps women value comfort and friendliness on the job more than men because many women leave paid work at the end of the day for a second full-time job of homemaking and child care. A comfortable and pleasant day in paid work may help them stretch their energy for the second shift.

Women's and men's values, already somewhat similar, seem to be becoming even less gender differentiated. In a recent study of more than 200 advanced business students, both women and men valued such aspects as job security, respect from others, and a feeling of mastery. Contrary to past research, however, men reported higher needs than women for security and leisure time, while women reported higher needs than men for achievement and continued growth in skills and knowledge (Beutell & Brenner, 1986).

While values may help determine one's occupational setting, the occupational setting may also affect one's values. When a person is given opportunities to advance he or she is likely to develop attitudes and values that help propel a worker to the top, such as a strong work commitment and high aspirations for promotions and raises. A person placed in a job with little upward mobility tends to become indifferent, to complain, and to look for extrinsic satisfactions. Thus, the social structure of the workplace is a powerful force in shaping values and behavior. But its effects are often overlooked. Rosabeth Kanter (1977), in studying women and men in a large corporation, noted that when women in dead-end jobs developed poor attitudes, these attitudes were seen as characteristic of women as a group instead of a human response to blocked opportunities. As Kanter put it, "What the clerical worker with low motivation to be promoted might need is a promotion; what the chronic complainer might need is a growthful challenge. But who would be likely to give it to them?" (p. 158).

Math: A Critical Filter

Many of the best career opportunities in American society today require a background in mathematics. These include jobs in engineering, science and medicine, computer science, business, technical fields, and skilled trades (Betz & Fitzgerald, 1987). As we discussed in Chapter 3, math is stereotyped as a male domain, and girls lose confidence and interest in doing it. As soon as the educational system allows them to, girls choose to take fewer math courses than boys. Thus, choices made in high school limit girls' options later. Lacking a math background, they are limited to a small range of potential career fields. Possible remedies for this problem include educating girls to understand that math is necessary to many careers, including ones that offer high pay and challenging work; requiring four years of math in high school for all students; special math/science conferences for junior high and high school girls to stimulate interest; educating girls in single-sex schools; providing girls with stories and pictures of female role models in math; and helping teachers create a positive classroom climate for girls (Betz & Fitzgerald, 1987; Eccles, 1989; Sadker & Sadker, 1994).

Achievement Motivation

For more than thirty years, psychologists have explored the question of why some people strive for success in situations involving a standard of excellence (McClelland, Atkinson, Clark, & Lowell, 1953). The individual high in achievement motivation will strive to excel when the motivation is aroused. Achievement behaviors of any sort—from running a marathon to making the best pickles at the county fair—could theoretically be predicted by one's score on an achievement-motivation measure. For research purposes, however, scores were used to predict performance in academic settings and competitive games in the laboratory.

Achievement motivation has traditionally been measured using the Thematic Apperception Test (TAT). Research participants are shown pictures and asked to make up stories about them. The pictures are deliberately ambiguous—there is no clear-cut message or plot. Theoretically, people will project their own motives onto the characters in the picture. Responses are scored as high in achievement motivation if the story features themes of hard work, prolonged striving, and a "happy ending" of outstanding performance being rewarded.

Does this description sound a great deal like the (middle-class white male) American dream? One criticism of achievement-motivation research is that it defines achievement in stereotypically male terms. Becoming president of the firm or the top student in the class is defined as achievement, but accomplishments that might have meaning to more women, working-class people, and people of color are not.

Early research showed that TAT scores were able to predict the achievement behavior of men but not women. The researchers' response to the inability of their measure to predict the behavior of half the human race was a single footnote in their immense tome. Reflecting the strong masculinist bias of research at that time, the intriguing question of why women behaved less predictably than men was not explored further; instead, researchers moved on to concentrate on boys and men in other cultures (Unger, 1979a).

Do women and men really differ in achievement motivation? Although the different response patterns of women were interpreted as a lack of motivation (Veroff, Wilcox, & Atkinson, 1953), the issue is more complex. In early research women actually had higher achievement scores under relaxed, noncompetitive conditions. Also, both women and men created more achievement-related stories for pictures with men in them (Veroff, Wilcox, & Atkinson, 1953), perhaps because both considered achievement and success to be masculine. More recent research shows women behaving more similarly to men (Chusmir, 1985; Gama, 1985).

Achievement motivation probably has more dimensions than were originally measured (Spence & Helmreich, 1983). Robert Helmreich and Janet Spence (1978) have developed a three-dimensioned measure of achievement motivation, the Work and Family Orientation Questionnaire. By their definition, achievement motivation is composed of *mastery,* or liking challenge; *work,* liking to work hard; and *competitiveness.*

Using this measure, both women and men who are instrumentally oriented score higher on all dimensions, especially competitiveness. In other words, people of both sexes whose backgrounds lead them to be oriented toward acting on the environment tend to be higher in all aspects of achievement motivation (Spence & Helmreich, 1983). This sort of background is, of course, more often provided for males in our society, so it is not surprising that overall, men score higher on mastery and competitiveness. (Women score higher on the desire to work hard.) These differences are small, however, compared with the differences between people in different occupational groups.

Today, researchers in achievement motivation recognize that men and women have similar motives overall. However, the ways those motives are channeled and expressed are influenced by gender-role socialization. Rather than showing that women are less motivated to achieve than men, the research has shown that the complexities of motivation cannot be understood without considering gender socialization in both women and men (Canter, 1982; Sutherland & Veroff, 1985).

Do Women Fear Success?

Imagine that you were asked to write a story about a fictional character, "Ann," with the following beginning:

> After first-term finals, Ann finds herself at the top of her medical school class.

When Matina Horner (1972) analyzed stories written to this cue by male and female college students, she found a large difference in their responses. About two-thirds of women characterized Ann in negative terms. She was seen as physically unattractive, unpopular, unlovable, and unhappy. Her future was miserable: she got pregnant and dropped out of medical school, or her boyfriend left her, or she ended up a lonely spinster. In some stories, her success was denied (medical school was changed to nursing school in the story, or her grades were a "computer error"). For the women who wrote these stories, unusual achievement in women was clearly associated with loss of femininity, social rejection, and long-term unhappiness. In contrast, men (who wrote about "John" using the same cue) described negative consequences of achievement in only 9 percent of their stories.

Horner believed that the story cue provided an ambiguous situation similar to TAT pictures, and that students projected their own motives into their stories. Therefore, she reasoned, these stories provided evidence that many bright and academically able women are motivated to avoid success because it puts them in danger of social rejection. If valid, this theory could explain why women's behavior in situations designed to arouse achievement motivation seemed erratic and unpredictable. Interestingly, it predicted that the brightest and most able women would be most handicapped in competitive situations, since success is actually within their grasp.

Horner's research generated more than 200 other studies and received a great deal of publicity under the label "fear of success" (Unger, 1979a; Walsh, 1987). To many, the idea that most women fear success and undermine their own achievement strivings seemed to explain why women rarely "make it" in the most prestigious occupations. The theory seemed intuitively "right," and people did not always look closely at its scientific basis. Like assertiveness training, it became popular by calling for women to change themselves, not society, in order to succeed (Crawford, 1995; Crawford & Marecek, 1989; Paludi, 1984; Paludi & Fankell-Hauser, 1986). Further research showed many problems with the fear-of-success construct.

Rather than an internalized motive, people's stories seem to reflect their knowledge of cultural stereotypes about what happens to socially deviant people. When both women and men were asked to write about Ann and John (rather than women writing only about Ann and men only about John, as in earlier research), both men and women wrote more negatively about Ann than John (Monahan, Kuhn, & Shaver, 1974). Other studies show that the more deviant Ann or John is portrayed as being in the cue, the more likely the cue is to elicit "fear-of-success" imagery (Bremer & Wittig, 1980). For example, when Ann and John were described as either the top student or in the top 5 percent, 15 percent, or 25 percent of their medical school class, the more successful Ann was portrayed as being, the more negatively she was portrayed by both female and male college students (Paludi, 1979). When Ann was presented as being in a medical school class with equal numbers of men and women, high school students wrote fewer negative stories than when Ann was the lone woman (Olsen & Willemson, 1978).

When writing about Ann and medical school versus John and medical school, research participants were writing about a nontraditional type of success for Ann and a conventional type of success for John. When the occupation referred to in the cue was changed to ballet, there was significantly less fear-of-success imagery from females and more from males (Shapiro, 1979). In a similar study, males produced more fear-of-success imagery to a nurse cue and females to an engineering cue (Janda, O'Grady, & Capps, 1978). Changing "medical school" to "nursing school" demonstrated that both female and male college students wrote more fear-of-success stories for the sex-inappropriate conditions (Cherry & Deaux, 1978). These studies suggest that people's stories may reflect their stereotypes about social deviance and "sex-inappropriate" success.

Fear of success as a "woman's problem" seems to have a "now-you-see-it, now-you-don't" quality that detracts from its scientific usefulness (Alper, 1974). When Michelle Paludi reviewed sixty-four studies, she found that the percentage of women categorized as high in fear of success ranged from 6 percent to 93 percent, while the percentage of men so classified ranged from 7 percent to 95 percent. The median for males was 46 percent; for females, 49 percent (cited in Paludi & Fankell-Hauser, 1986). Black women are less likely to show fear of success than white women (Weston & Mednick, 1970). Thus, social class and racial group may be as important as sex in predicting whether an individual will foresee negative consequences of success.

Fear of success has probably been overemphasized as an important determinant of women's behavior. It seems that story cues measure mainly beliefs or stereotypes about achievement; moreover, there is little evidence that the stories people write are related to their actual achievement behavior.

An alternative way to study motivation is to interview people in depth about their goals and their efforts to achieve them. This approach has the advantage of allowing research participants to define achievement in their own terms, rather than imposing an arbitrary definition such as success in medical school. Women's and men's own definitions of achievement are much broader than academic success (Gravenkemper & Paludi, 1983). In one study using biographical interviews of women ranging in age from their twenties to their eighties, the women's goals reflected their age and life stage. In addition to academic success, many mentioned "being independent" and "having successful relationships." When asked if they had ever been in a situation in which they were about to succeed and had feared success, 91 percent said no. However, 96 percent of women reported that they had wondered whether their achievements were worth the costs to themselves and their families (Paludi & Fankell-Hauser, 1986).

EXCEPTIONAL WORK LIVES

Achievement in the Professions: From Pink Collar to White

Current Status of Women in the Professions

Until recently, women professionals were largely found in the "women's professions" of education, social work, and nursing. One woman remembered that "It never occurred to me to be anything but a teacher; medicine and law were not for girls. But I have often wondered why I did not consider medicine. I remember being in the top of the class in physiology and anatomy, competing with boys who later became M.D.s" (Peterson, 1974, p. 78). Like this woman, who later became a university teacher and consumer specialist, many women have built careers of distinction after being channeled into "women's" professions (Collins, 1988). Today most career-oriented women continue to enter these professions. In 1985, 96 percent of all nurses and 84 percent of elementary school teachers were women (Ferree, 1987). Meanwhile, others are entering "male" professions—law, medicine, psychology, college teaching, science and engineering, the military, and business management (Jacobs, 1992; Stevens & Gardner, 1987). There is no doubt that we are living in an era of expanding options for women in corporate and professional roles. The most dramatic increase is in the number of African-American women in white-collar and professional cor-

TABLE 12.2 Proportion of Women in Nontraditional Occupations

Occupation	1975	1988
Airplane pilot, navigator	—	3.1
Architect	4.3	14.6
Auto mechanic	0.5	0.7
Bartender	35.2	49.6
Carpenter	0.6	1.5
Computer systems analyst	14.8	29.5
Dentist	1.8	9.3
Firefighter	—	2.1
Lawyer, judge	7.1	19.5
Physician	13.0	20.0
Police officer	2.7	13.4
Telephone installer, repairer	4.8	12.1
Welder	4.4	4.9

Source: Adapted from Rix (1990), Table 19, based on U.S. Bureau of Labor Statistics data.

porate jobs. They are entering management at almost twice the rate of African-American men (Gaiter, 1994). Table 12.2 shows changes in the proportion of women in some nontraditional professions and trades since 1975. Although some of the changes are dramatic, they also illustrate that women have yet to achieve equity.

Developmental Factors

Reviewing the obstacles to achievement described in this chapter can give us an appreciation of why so few women have achieved professional success. Yet, despite the odds, some women do. How are these women different? What factors in their personalities and backgrounds make the difference between them and their nonachieving peers? Researchers have been interested in answering these questions. Although high-achieving women are few in number, they are an important group. They provide potential role models for other women. Their backgrounds suggest ways to bring up girls without limiting their aspirations and development, and their achievements represent the possibility of breaking down sex segregation and sex stratification in the workplace. If a few women can "make it," a world of equal power and status for all women and men becomes easier to imagine.

In general, high-achieving women come from backgrounds that provide them with a relatively unconstricted sense of self and an enriched view of women's capabilities (Lemkau, 1979, 1983). Their families and their upbringing are unusual in positive ways, as shown in Table 12.3. As social-learning theory would predict, girls who are exposed to less gender-stereotyped expectations are more likely to become high achievers. Attending all-girls' schools and women's colleges can provide role models, opportunities for leadership, and a woman-centered learning environment. Not surprisingly, parents play an important role. Employed mothers—especially when they enjoy their work and are successful at it—provide an important model for achievement. Since fathers

TABLE 12.3 Characteristics Associated with Achievement in Women

Individual variables	*Background variables*
High ability	Working mother
Liberated sex role values	Supportive father
Instrumentality	Highly educated parents
Androgynous personality	Female role models
High self-esteem	Work experience as adolescent
Strong academic self-concept	Androgynous upbringing
Educational variables	*Adult lifestyle variables*
Higher education	Late marriage or single
Continuation in mathematics	No or few children
Girls' schools and women's colleges	

Source: From Betz & Fitzgerald, *The Career Psychology of Women*, p. 143. 1987 Academic Press. Reprinted by permission.

usually encourage gender typing in their children more than mothers do and usually have more family power, a father who supports and encourages his daughter's achievements may be especially influential (Weitzman, 1979). One black woman who became a distinguished physician has provided an eloquent description of her parents' belief in her:

> As a woman, I was told, I would be able to do whatever I wanted. I was taught that my skin had a beautiful color. This constant, implicit reinforcement of positive self-image was my parents' most valuable gift to me. I grew up loving my color and enjoying the fact that I was a woman . . . In school, I performed well because my mother and father expected it of me. When I entered high school, I elected the college preparatory program as a matter of course.
>
> What happened next is, tragically even today, all too familiar to blacks. A faculty adviser called me in. In her hand was the (college prep course schedule). The courses I had elected were crossed out, and substituted with a Home Economics curriculum. I took the paper home . . . When my mother saw it she was outraged. Together, we went back to the school to face the adviser . . . (who) attempted to placate my mother. "Mrs. Texiera," she pleaded, "what is a colored girl going to do with college? If she learns cooking and sewing, she can always get a good job." But when we left the office, I was enrolled in the college course (Hunter, 1974, pp. 58–59).

The personalities and values of high-achieving women are nontraditional. They have a high and healthy level of self-esteem and liberal opinions about women's roles. They describe themselves as independent, assertive, and rational. The latter traits, of course, are labeled "masculine" in our society. But these women do not fit the stereotype of the desexed, aggressive masculine woman who sacrifices femininity for success. They also see themselves as warm, expressive, and nurturing—in other words, as androgynous.

The research summarized in Table 12.3 has been very useful in helping psychologists understand the dynamics of achievement in women, but it does have limitations. Obviously, all these characteristics are not true of all high-achieving women. Some women who do not have any of them manage to succeed anyway, and some even report having been spurred on by a disapproving parent or an attempt to hold them back (Weitzman, 1979). In one recent study, black and white women who came from poor families where neither parent had finished high school were extensively interviewed. Despite their disadvantaged backgrounds, these women had achieved extraordinary success in business, academia, or government service. The biggest difference between them and a comparison group of women from middle-class backgrounds with similar achievement levels was that the "odds-defying" achievers had an unusually strong belief in their ability to control their lives. They believed that "You can do anything if you put your mind to it" (Boardman, Harrington, & Horowitz, 1987).

Studying the factors leading to success by looking at successful women is an example of *retrospective* research in which participants look back at factors influencing them at an earlier time. It can show us what characteristics successful women tend to share. However, it can also lead us to assume that we know the *causes* of success when we may be observing its *results.* In other words, women who—for whatever reason—have the opportunity to test themselves in a demanding career may develop high self-esteem, assertiveness, independence, and achievement motivation as a *consequence* of their success. From this perspective, opportunity creates a "successful" personality, rather than vice versa (Kanter, 1977). Retrospective memory is not always accurate, either. Successful women may remember more achievement emphasis in their backgrounds than nonachieving women simply because this dimension is relevant to them as adults (Nieva & Gutek, 1981).

As they are growing up, girls and young women continually make choices, both consciously and unconsciously, about how they will spend their time and efforts. Achievement-related choices are made in a complex social context. They are affected by many factors, from outright discrimination to gender socialization. One of the best models of how various influences interact has been developed by Jacqueline Eccles and her colleagues (Eccles, 1994). The individual's *expectations of success* (If I take this math course, will I pass?) and the *subjective value* of various options (Do I enjoy English more than math? Will I really need math for my chosen career?) strongly affect decision making. In a series of studies, Eccles has shown that such expectancies and values are shaped by parental attributions (My daughter got an A in math because she works hard, my son because he's bright), gender-role beliefs (scientists are nerdy guys), and self-perceptions (I can't do physics). Because gender-role socialization affects values, definitions of success, and the kinds of activities seen as crucial to one's identity, it affects virtually every aspect of achievement-related decision making.

It will be fascinating to see the results of future studies as researchers attempt to find out more about how some women resist or rebel against socialization pressures. The growing number of mid-life women returning to college and taking up new careers provides a chance for researchers to study factors affecting achievement across the life span (Weitzman, 1979). Nontraditional students often experience increased self-esteem and life satisfaction with their commitment to academic achievement (Astin, 1976).

Research on high-achieving women has been done mostly on white women. Racial and ethnic differences in family background and gender socialization probably affect Hispanic, Asian-American, and African-American women differently. For example, black women generally grow up expecting to support themselves rather than to rely on a male breadwinner, while traditional Asian-American culture discourages women from independence and rewards subservience. In a cross section of 161 employed Asian-American women, those who were more instrumentally oriented or androgynous had higher self-esteem, had higher status jobs, and were more satisfied with their work than their more traditional peers (Chow, 1987). More research is needed on diverse groups of women achievers to give a complete profile of successful women.

It is likely that racism and sexism interact to impede the career development of women of color. Black women, for example, have higher aspirations than black men or white women during high school, but, like white women, their career goals decline during college. Black women are more likely than black men, but less likely than white women, to achieve success in a profession. In comparison to white women in the professions, they are even more likely to be in a traditional "woman's" profession, especially teaching (Betz & Fitzgerald, 1987). More than 82 percent of the highly educated and productive Hispanic women professionals in one survey reported that they had experienced discrimination (Amaro, Russo, & Johnson, 1987).

Nontraditional Occupations: From Pink Collar to Blue

Like professional women, women who work in traditionally male blue-collar occupations are few in number. Overall, only about 13 percent of all white women and 18 percent of all black women employed in 1990 were in blue-collar jobs; most of these were traditionally female trades such as sewing in garment factories. Increasingly, however, women are entering "men's" blue-collar fields. They are enrolling in apprentice programs in the skilled trades and taking jobs as coal miners, police officers, truck drivers, welders, carpenters, and steelworkers (Braden, 1986; Deaux & Ullman, 1983; Hammond & Mahoney, 1983; Martin, 1988). Employers have responded to federal affirmative-action guidelines, sex-discrimination suits from workers, and union pressure by opening up opportunities for women in these fields (Harlan & O'Farrell, 1982) (see Table 12.2).

Who are these women and why do they choose these particular kinds of "men's work"? How do they feel about their unusual way of making a living, and how well do they perform in their jobs? They are an important group to study because they challenge stereotypes and because their choices represent one way of breaking out of the pattern of lower earnings for women. However, there is relatively little research on blue-collar women, and conclusions about them are necessarily more tentative than about professional women.

Most women who become skilled blue-collar workers in male-dominated areas did not specifically plan to do so (Deaux & Ullman, 1983; Martin, 1988). Rather, they often started out in other occupations and changed to meet perceived opportunities. Those who pioneered in entering the trades before affirmative-action mandates have been described by themselves and their coworkers as "fighters": brave, rugged, tough, aggressive, confident, and willing to take risks (Harlan & O'Farrell, 1982).

In one study of 470 women (Houser & Garvey, 1985), African-American, white, and Hispanic women who entered programs in which more than 80 percent of the students were male were compared with women who entered programs with a preponderance of female students. The biggest difference between the two groups of students was that women in the nontraditional group (regardless of ethnic background) had received more support and encouragement from female and male friends, family, teachers, and counselors. They were also more instrumentally oriented. These factors, interestingly, correspond to background and personality factors influencing professional women. Another recent study of 325 white and black workers showed that economic need was the biggest factor in women's decision to move from traditionally female (white-collar) to traditionally male (blue-collar) jobs, and this was especially true for black women (Padavic, 1991). Thus, individual background, personality factors, and current contexts may interact to influence women's employment choices.

Blue-collar women generally report a high level of satisfaction with their jobs. They like the high pay and the variety and challenge of the work. They take pride in feelings of competence and autonomy, have high levels of self-esteem, and often aspire to promotion and advancement (Deaux & Ullman, 1983; Ferree, 1987; Hammond & Mahoney, 1983; O'Farrell & Harlan, 1982). Being well paid may be a particularly important component of satisfaction because it enables women to provide well for their families. In one study, two-thirds of a sample of black, white, and Hispanic women steelworkers had children at home, and 61 percent of these were the sole wage earners for their families (Deaux & Ullman, 1983). In a study of twenty-five women coal miners, twenty-two were the primary or sole breadwinners for their families. The miners were aware that they could always get low-status, low-paying "women's" jobs but rejected them. One woman remembered her experience as a waitress: "I thought there must be a better way—here I am making $1.45 an hour and $1.00 an hour in tips. Jesus, there's gotta be another way." She described her decision to become a coal miner to support her family in vivid terms: "I can wash off coal black but I can't wash off those damn bill collectors" (Hammond & Mahoney, 1983, p. 19).

Of course, we have no way of knowing whether the woman shapes the job or the job shapes the woman—a problem with retrospective research discussed earlier. It does seem that proving oneself in a job that requires physical strength and endurance is empowering. One woman mechanic/shipfitter described her early fears but also reported how she learned to deal with "static" from male coworkers, one of whom told her "This is no place for a woman, you ought to be outside taking care of your kids."

> I got angry one day, and I told one of the guys that I had to feed my damn kids just like he did, that's why I was there, and I never had too much trouble after that (Braden, 1986, p. 75).

Blue-collar women do face some disadvantages in their jobs. As the foregoing example illustrates, male coworkers and supervisors may feel threatened by their presence. Physical strength, endurance, and courage are central components of manhood. If mere women can handle their jobs, how are these men to distinguish themselves as men? Because blue-collar women are a very small minority numerically—for example, they constitute only about 6 percent of police officers and less than 1 percent of miners—they suffer the high visibility and isolation of tokens (Martin, 1988). Sexual harassment is particularly prevalent in blue-collar jobs (Gruber & Bjorn, 1982; Lembright & Riemer, 1982; O'Farrell & Harlan, 1982). Women may be taunted and ridiculed, subjected to physical hazing, threatened with physical injury, deliberately given unsafe equipment, and exposed to hostile, violent pornography on the job (Fitzgerald, 1993).

A survey of blue-collar women (compared with school secretaries) showed that they experienced more sexual harassment and sex discrimination, more adverse working conditions, higher stress levels, and lower satisfaction. The black women in the sample also reported more racial discrimination than their counterparts who were secretaries (Mansfield, Koch, Henderson, Vicary, Kohn, & Young, 1991). Clearly, the satisfaction of doing a tough job and getting paid well for it can be offset by the burden of working in a hostile environment.

Other job disadvantages include the often dirty and dangerous working conditions and the fact that, as the "last hired, first fired" employee group, women are subject to layoffs and plant closings (Deaux & Ullman, 1983; Ferree, 1987). Despite these obstacles, research suggests that women perform similarly to men. In the sample of steelworkers studied by Deaux and Ullman (1983), the women, although they had a higher rate of absenteeism (probably due to child-care responsibilities), were no more likely than the men to quit their jobs.

PUTTING IT ALL TOGETHER: WORK AND FAMILY

Despite society's efforts to keep work and family roles separate (for example, when we say that "you shouldn't bring your work home from the office" or that "you shouldn't let personal problems affect your work"), they do affect each other. Men's and women's work and family roles function as a system, with each component affecting every other (Lorber, 1993; Pleck, 1977). A woman's involvement in her paid work may depend not only on whether she has young children but also on whether she has a partner. If so, how flexible is her partner's work role (can he/she stay home with a sick child?) and how do both partners define housework responsibilities? Each partner's involvement in paid work depends on the other. If one earns a high salary, the other may feel less tied to a particular job; if one job is only part time, the other may put in overtime.

Today, women are highly likely to combine mothering with paid work. As we have seen, many mothers are unmarried or divorced and must provide all or most of the financial support of their children. Even married mothers, however, increasingly work outside the home as well as in it. According to U.S. Census data, 52 percent of married women who had children under 1 year old were working in 1988, and 71 percent of those with school-age children were working (Sapiro, 1994).

Unlike most research on work, which focuses on men, research on the problems of combining work and family has focused almost exclusively on women, especially on white, upper-middle-class women who are pursuing "male" careers in business and the professions. It has emphasized the social and personal costs of multiple roles, rather than their rewards (Crawford, 1982; Gilbert, 1994). For example, researchers have frequently investigated whether women's work involvement is detrimental to their mental health or their marriages. They have been much less likely to ask whether family involvement or a happy marriage may make one a better and more productive worker.

In a way, focusing on women (and on costs) is a rational research strategy, because multiple roles have different consequences for women and men. Men's main family responsibility, to be a "good provider," is compatible with being heavily involved in work roles (Bernard, 1981), while women's many responsibilities as primary parent, emotional nurturer, and housekeeper are not. However, the research emphasis on women may lead to seeing working women as a social problem and leave important questions unexamined.

There is a need for more research on how family and personal life affect work for women *and* men, on benefits to women *and* men of juggling dual roles, and on role issues among women who are not heterosexual, financially privileged, or white. It is interesting that women's dual roles became a research issue only in the 1970s, when middle-class white women began entering the work force in greater numbers. The fact that working-class, black, and some groups of Hispanic women had always held both types of roles had not been considered worthy of psychological research. Fortunately, researchers are now examining work and family from a broader perspective.

Combining the multiple obligations of spouse, parent, and worker has often been described as a "balancing act" for women. Here we will look at some costs and benefits of the balancing act for working women and their families.

Costs of the Balancing Act

There is no doubt that the combination of paid and unpaid work done by many women is difficult and demanding. *Role conflict* refers to the psychological effects of being faced with two or more sets of incompatible expectations or demands; *role overload* describes the difficulties of meeting these expectations. The secretary who is asked to work overtime on short notice and must scramble to find child care may experience both conflict (feeling guilty and torn between her two obligations) and overload (as she calls babysitters while typing the overdue report). Because her mother and worker roles are incompatible, there is no really satisfactory resolution of the conflict, and it may lead to guilt, anxiety, and depression. Chronic overload may lead to fatigue, short temper, and lowered resistance to physical illness.

Research has consistently shown that most women workers experience role conflict (Crosby, 1991; Gilbert, 1993). In one study of twenty-eight professional couples, every woman reported major career–family conflicts (Johnson & Johnson, 1977). In a study of more than 200 married couples (both partners psychologists), 58 percent mentioned such conflicts as significant problems (Heckman, Bryson, & Bryson, 1977). Similarly, the majority of a group of 232 married women who were doctors, lawyers, and professors said that they often experienced strains between work and family (Gray, 1983). Black women, both professionals and those in more typical women's jobs such as clerical and service work, reported using a variety of strategies to cope with conflicts as wife/worker, mother/worker, and mother/wife (Harrison & Minor, 1978). Compared with women who were not in paid employment, married women workers in a variety of jobs experienced more irritating or frustrating "hassles" in everyday life (Alpert & Culbertson, 1987). In a study of more than 300 Hispanic women professionals, managers, and business owners, on-the-job stress and the amount of support provided by the spouse were important factors influencing the stress of balancing work and family roles. Having young children led to less satisfaction with one's professional life, and high income was related to less stress and more satisfaction (Amaro, Russo, & Johnson, 1987).

Although working lesbians engage in the same roles as heterosexual women and experience similar conflicts and strains, the very fact of being a lesbian can become an issue at work, providing an added source of conflict. In a study of seventy lesbians, most of whom currently had a relationship with a partner, 41 percent reported conflicts between their relationship and work roles—usually problems in allocating time and energy to each. Moreover, 33 percent reported conflicts at work in feeling socially unacceptable in a heterosexist and male-dominated work environment. They felt unable to "be themselves" or to discuss their partner or home life, and they reported pressure to dress and act in stereotyped heterosexual ways (Shachar & Gilbert, 1983). In another recent study, lesbians reported less satisfaction with their interpersonal relationships at work than heterosexual women did (Peters & Cantrell, 1993).

Benefits of the Balancing Act

Effects on Women

Side by side with research showing widespread problems with role conflict and overload is a great deal of research showing *benefits* associated with multiple roles (reviewed in Betz & Fitzgerald, 1987; Crosby, 1991; Gilbert, 1993; Gutek, Repetti, & Silver, 1988; Nieva & Gutek, 1981). Working women have fewer psychological problems than homemakers (Bernard, 1972). Married women consistently report higher job satisfaction than single women (see, e.g., Bersoff & Crosby, 1984). In a recent study of 300 dual-career couples, higher job quality was related to lower psychological distress in both women and men (Burnett, Marshall, Raudenbush, & Brennen, 1993). In other words, being satisfied in one's work is as important in overall psychological adjustment for women as for men—at least among middle-class dual-career couples.

People who are happier at home also tend to be happier on the job and experience less job stress. In a systematic study of more than 200 middle-aged women, having both a job and a family was related to feelings of greater competence, mastery, and pleasure. In fact, the women who had the overall best psychological adjustment were those who had husbands, children, *and* high-prestige, demanding jobs (Baruch et al., 1983). Other studies show comparable results: Handling more roles is related to higher self-esteem, happiness, and job satisfaction (Miller, Moen, & Dempster-McClain, 1991; Pietromonaco, Manis, & Frohart-Lane, 1986).

Why does involvement in many roles benefit psychological well-being? One reason may be that success in one domain may help people keep a sense of perspective about the others (Crosby, 1982, 1991). In a recent study of more than 200 managers, both women and men believed that their roles as parents and active members of their community had more positive than negative effects on their performance at work (Kirchmeyer, 1993). Being passed over for promotion might seem less of a disaster if one is happily involved in leading a Girl Scout troop; dealing with a difficult teenager at home may be made easier by being in charge and well rewarded at the office. Women who "juggle" home and work develop good coping strategies, such as choosing the most rewarding aspects of each job and delegating the others. Having a paid job can provide a handy excuse for a woman not to do things she didn't want to do in the first place (Baruch et al., 1983). Employment also increases women's power in the family, especially in financial decision making (Nieva & Gutek, 1981).

There are limitations to the research in this area, however. Research samples are *self-selected*—people have sorted themselves into employed and nonemployed groups before being studied. It is possible that multiple roles and happiness go together simply because better adjusted people are more likely to attempt multiple roles in the first place. Furthermore, most of the research on the benefits of multiple roles has been done on women who have the advantages of high income and professional status. Role conflict and overload may contribute to "burnout" in less prestigious women's jobs such as nursing and teaching (Greenglass & Burke, 1988; Statham, Miller, & Mauksch, 1988). And virtually no one has asked blue-collar or poor women their opinions about the "balancing act." A West Indian domestic servant who works a fifty-hour week in New York without overtime or medical benefits to support her family in the islands might express very different views (Colen, 1986). As Baruch et al. (1983, p. 180) summed it up, "For women, it's not having a job that's bad for your health, it's having a lousy job with inadequate support for at-home responsibilities."

Effects on Children

What about the children? Do they suffer when both parents work outside the home? When Claire Etaugh (1980) reviewed articles in the popular press on day care versus home care for children, she found that they were largely negative about nonmaternal care, presenting mothers' work as a problem for children. And employed mothers are still viewed as second-class mothers. After reading a brief description of a mother of an infant who was either employed or not, college students gave the employed mother lower approval ratings and saw her as lower in communal ("feminine") traits. She was especially seen as less communal if her motive for working was personal fulfillment rather than financial necessity (Bridges & Orza, 1992).

However, research does not confirm the popular wisdom. The effects of mothers' paid work on children are generally neutral or positive. When the outcomes have been negative, they are often explainable by other factors: social class, family attitudes toward working women, reasons for working, full-time versus part-time work, and so on (Farel, 1980; Silverstein, 1991). In general, children in day care do not suffer from disruption of their affectional bond with their mothers; they may actually experience increased intellectual growth and development, especially if they come from low-income homes where families cannot provide an enriched environment; and they are at least as socially skilled as home-care children (O'Connell, 1983; Scarr, Phillips, & McCartney, 1990).

Because researchers have most often chosen to ask questions about possible problems or pathologies created by mothers working, they may have overlooked potential benefits—an example of bias in the framing of research questions. We noted earlier that some studies show more rapid intellectual development in children who have day-care experience, especially when they come from poorer homes. Moreover, comparisons of day care versus maternal care have often treated "day care" and "home care" as if all day-care settings, and all homes, are alike. Of course, child-care settings vary enormously, and family settings do, too. Child care can provide enrichment and foster intellectual and social development, while family care can be neglectful and abusive (Scarr et al., 1990; Silverstein, 1991). One benefit of maternal employment that has rarely been considered by researchers is that in many families, mothers' incomes are a matter of necessity. For fathers, but not mothers, providing money to keep a family out of poverty has been viewed as being a good enough parent.

Employed mothers also provide alternative role models for their children. The benefits of a mother who models many areas of competence may be especially great for girls. Adolescent daughters of women who work outside the home were more likely to name their mother as the person they most admire and resemble. These girls tend to be autonomous, independent, and active, and have higher occupational goals than daughters of homemakers (Hoffman, 1974). As adults, they are more likely to become high achievers (Betz & Fitzgerald, 1987).

It is time for a new agenda in child-care research (Scarr et al., 1990; Silverstein, 1991). Instead of starting with the assumption that "mother care is good and other care is bad," researchers should acknowledge that most mothers *do* work outside the home, and that the risks involved in child care are small compared with the damage caused by the unavailability of the kinds of child-care support today's families desperately need (see Figure 12.7). "We must tie research on child care to the negative consequences of the lack of affordable, government subsidized, high-quality programs" (Silverstein, 1991, p. 1030).

WOMEN, WORK, AND SOCIAL POLICY: MODELS FOR CHANGE

Clearly, the world of work presents women with many problems. Alexis Herman, chair of the National Commission on Working Women, has eloquently expressed some of them:

> The 34 million women who are in the pink- and blue-collar work force—sales workers, service workers, factory and clerical workers—have a simple agenda. They want decent wages and benefits; they want affordable child care . . . ; they want training and education for advancement in their jobs; and they want decent and dignified working conditions. They have said it over and over again—with different accents and in different ways, but it is always the same. As Bella Abzug says, "It is shocking that as women, we have to beg to contribute our labor to society. We have to beg for family support systems, decent wages, and the dignity to do what men have always done" (Herman, 1988, p. x).

The problems may seem large and unsolvable, but equity for women workers, whether pink collar, blue collar, or professional, is not an impossible dream.

FIGURE 12.7. Day-care fantasies and realities.
Source: Doonesbury © 1987 (Sunday) G. B. Trudeau. Reprinted by permission of Universal Press Syndicate. All rights reserved.

How to go about achieving that dream is, however, an open question. Different ideas about the causes of inequity lead to different proposed solutions. Some researchers and policymakers focus on the individual level, others on the interpersonal or intergroup level, and still others on the structural level (Nieva & Gutek, 1981).

At the individual level, there is an emphasis on problems within women themselves: women fail to achieve because they lack achievement motivation, fear success, or are socialized early in life to value vicarious achievement and nurturing rather than autonomy. According to this model, the best way to change women's work situation is to provide self-improvement and training programs to help women overcome their deficiencies. An example is the popular assertiveness training courses for women. Individual change efforts may be helpful for the small minority of women with psychological problems, but, as we have seen, there is little evidence that women as a *group* lack achievement motivation, have an internalized fear of success, or lack instrumental abilities. The individual-deficit model runs the risk of blaming the victim (Ryan, 1971; Henley, 1985) and ignores social factors that are beyond the control of the individual. How helpful can assertiveness training be when the assertive woman is judged less likable than the equally assertive man (Gervasio & Crawford, 1989)?

More recently, a "mommy track" for corporate women has been proposed (and highly publicized in the popular media) (Schwartz, 1989). The idea is that corporations should identify "fast track" women—those whose career is primary—early in their careers and treat them just like men. Other women would be placed on a "mommy track" of lower job prestige in return for such advantages as parental leave, flexible schedules, and so on.

The idea created a great deal of controversy. What do you think of the advantages and disadvantages of classifying women workers into two "tracks"? Objections raised by feminists are that this solution presents women (but not men) with an impossible choice between sacrificing a family life for success on the one hand and having a family but underachieving on the other (Lorber, 1993; Makosky, 1989). It leaves the "choice" at the individual level, without questioning the male values of corporate culture or the assumption that only women are part of a family.

A structural-level approach focuses on the impact that organizations have on the people in them. It proposes that the situation a person is placed in shapes and determines her or his behavior. Thus, when women are discriminated against in hiring and promotion and confined to dead-end, unrewarding jobs, they will not display initiative or ambition. When a few women are made into tokens, their performance will be negatively affected by the stresses of high visibility and isolation.

From this perspective, women's low expectations and "lack of ambition" are adaptive adjustments to reality and will change if real opportunities for advancement become available. This approach implies that the system, not the individual, must change in order for equity to be achieved. Rather than viewing women as unique, it sees their problems as similar to problems faced by other disadvantaged groups such as racial and ethnic minorities. Legislation for equal opportunity and affirmative action is one route to change. Evaluating jobs on the basis of comparable worth is another (Lowe & Wittig, 1989). According to this approach, equal opportunity leads to equal performance.

A final approach is based on intergroup power. From this perspective, when men have more social power, women inevitably become the "out group." This model explains why women's work is devalued, why male career patterns and definitions of work and achievement are taken as the norm, and why occupations so frequently end up in a pattern of sex stratification, with women at the bottom. Sexual harassment in the workplace is seen as an exercise of power. Stereotypes about differences between women and men serve to reinforce the in group–out group distinction. The intergroup power model has been stressed throughout this book and is the focus of Chapter 5.

The intergroup perspective views change in the workplace as dependent on societal change. Educating people about stereotyping might help in the short run, but fundamental change would depend on altering the power structure of society. Power-oriented strategies include passing and enforcing equal-opportunity legislation, increasing women's political power, and forming women's organizations and networks to exert pressure for social change. Many women today are engaged in these strategies.

As you think back over the information and analysis in Chapters 10, 11, and 12, it will become increasingly apparent that women's experiences in relationships, families, and workplaces are braided and interdependent. Much recent feminist analysis recognizes these interrelationships (Baber & Allen, 1992; Lorber, 1993). Women who cannot achieve economic parity at work are disadvantaged by having less power in their marriages. Much of the work women do is unpaid and undervalued. Sexual harassment at work or school has an impact on work productivity and quality of life. If women are to have the same career opportunities as men, they must be able to decide if and when they will bear children. Families suffer when social policy is based on myths of motherhood instead of the realities of contemporary life. These are just a few examples of the complex relationships among family roles and workplace issues. Models of change that focus on gendered social structures and power inequities are more useful than those that stress changing women's attitudes and values.

CONNECTING THEMES

1. Women and men have very different experiences in the workplace, and these differences both reflect and perpetuate the gender system. The gendered world of work encompasses structural factors (such as sex segregation and stratification), interactional factors (such as tokenism), and individual-level differences (such as feelings of entitlement).

2. Because work has been defined in terms of a male norm, much of the work that women do—housework, child care, emotional maintenance of families, and building the careers of their male partners—has remained largely invisible. A feminist perspective places women's paid work in a larger context that recognizes the complexities of multiple roles and obligations.

3. Most research on women and work has focused on upper-middle-class women who have professional careers. However, the majority of women are underemployed in low-paying clerical and service jobs. Discrimination and harassment are based not only on sex but also on race/ethnicity, age, and sexual orientation.

4. Women are engaged in a complex "balancing act" in trying to integrate work and family roles. However, solutions depend not only on individual efforts but also on developing public policy that recognizes the realities of women in the work force. Women and their families need social supports such as child-care options, paid parental leave, wage equity, and effective sanctions against sex discrimination and harassment.

SUGGESTED READINGS

GILBERT, LUCIA ALBINO (1993). *Two careers/one family: The promise of gender equality.* London: Sage. An exploration of today's societal gender expectations as they affect young dual-career couples. Current changes in the workplace that affect employed parents balancing work and family are discussed and predictions about future challenges are presented.

HASLETT, BETH J., FLORENCE L. GEIS, and MAE R. CARTER (1992). *The organizational woman: Power and paradox.* Norwood, NJ: Ablex. This compilation of research from the social psychology literature argues that gender stereotypes and self-fulfilling prophecies interact with power, verbal and nonverbal behavior, and leadership to lead to sex discrimination in the workplace. Chapter summaries and hypothetical case studies clarify theoretical points made in the chapters.

STATHAM, ANNE, E. M. MILLER, and H. O. MAUKSCH (Eds.) (1988). *The worth of women's work: A qualitative synthesis.* Albany: State University of New York Press. A close look at the experience and working conditions of women who work in traditional occupations (teaching, nursing, social work) and less traditional ones (policewoman).

CHAPTER 13

Midlife and Beyond

THE SOCIAL CONTEXT OF AGING
- Images of Age and Aging
- Sexism and Ageism: Some Comparisons
- The Double Standard of Aging
- The Social Invisibility of Older Women
- The Meanings of Midlife

MENOPAUSE
- The Aging Woman's Body and Its Social Meaning
- Biology and Culture
- Health Risks and Menopause
- The Medicalization of Menopause
- Estrogen Replacement Therapy
- Language about Menopause and Popular Consciousness
- Alternative Views of Menopause
- Correlates of Positive and Negative Menopausal Transitions
- Attitudes about Menopause in Relation to Power and Status
- The Meaning of Menopause: A Brief Integratory Summary

ROLE TRANSITIONS OF MIDLIFE AND OF LATER LIFE
- Cultural Context and Midlife Transitions
- The Complex Nature of Midlife Role Transitions
- Retirement
- Other Caregiver Roles

PSYCHOLOGICAL WELL-BEING IN THE SECOND HALF OF LIFE
- Older Women and Poverty
- Friendship and Social Support

ACTIVISM AND FEMINISM AMONG OLDER WOMEN

CONNECTING THEMES

SUGGESTED READINGS

Though not occasioned/to mirror watching/I stopped/and saw delightedly/star streaks, grey lights/moving through my hair./I was mother-reflection/then, my mother watching me/becoming old as she had not/lived to do./I cannot know/what she would have felt/as age came on in silence,/but I dance elated on seeing/touches of silver/appearing unasked/but earned by living/as widely as I dare.

—KATHIAN POULTON (1986)

What do women feel "as age comes on in silence"? Kathian Poulton's poem suggests a joyful welcoming of the physical changes of aging, the "star streaks" of graying hair a reward for meeting life's challenges. In this chapter we will explore the meanings of growing older for women, examining aging as both a set of biological changes and a social phenomenon.

THE SOCIAL CONTEXT OF AGING

Research on aging has traditionally compared people of different chronological ages on measures of physical health or emotional adjustment. This approach, which treats "age" as a simple biological variable, can be thought of as analogous to the traditional study of sex differences. In both cases, people are chosen for study on the basis of their membership in a (biologically defined) group. Like gender, however, age is a social classification system that organizes access to resources: Age is connected to differences in power, prestige, and opportunities (Markides, 1989). To the extent that age is a source of inequality, it affects people over and above any biological realities. Therefore, to understand the effects of age and aging, we must consider both biological and social factors. Because age is confounded with many other variables, it is not easy to separate the biological from the sociocultural. Not only do biological events affect social ones, but causation also goes in the other direction: Social factors affect biological events as well.

A society's beliefs and attitudes about aging provide a powerful cultural context for growing older. In a society where the old are seen as wise elders or keepers of valued traditions, the stress of aging is less than in a society where they are seen as mentally slow and socially useless. To understand the meaning of age and aging for women in contemporary Western societies, we will start by examining stereotypes about the old in general and old women in particular. We will assess the social visibility of old people as well as their images in our own and other societies.

Images of Age and Aging

In Western cultures, aging has long been viewed negatively or at best ambivalently (Kimmel, 1988). Even the word *old* is avoided, as though to be old is so terrible that it should not be mentioned in polite company. Instead, people use a variety of euphemisms, such as *senior citizen,* or *golden ager.* One woman wrote that when she mentioned the activist group OWL, the Older Women's League, to a friend, the friend's immediate response was, "What an awful name!" (Healy, 1986, p. 59).

Language researchers have noted the ambivalence and negativity expressed in terms of older people. Viewed through slang, old people are debilitated, foolish, and pathetic (see Table 13.1). Although some terms for old men connote respect (an *old salt,* for example, refers to an experienced sailor), terms for old women have almost always focused on evil powers, repulsiveness, and disagreeableness (Covey, 1988). Stereotypes about old women portray them as "sick, sexless, uninvolved except for church work, and alone" (Payne & Whittington, 1976).

In a recent study (Kite, Deaux, & Miele, 1991), college students and adults were asked to list the characteristics of 35-year-old and 65-year-old women and men. Age stereotypes were more pronounced than gender stereotypes—for example, same-age persons were seen as more similar to each other than same-sex persons. But, the stereotype of 65-year-olds was not uniformly negative. They were seen as experienced, interesting, physically active, and friendly, as well as

TABLE 13.1. Terms for Old People from the Late Eighteenth Century to the Present

Male or Gender-Neutral	Female
Old buzzard	Little old lady
Old coot	Granny
Old salt	Old hag
Old duffer	Old maid
Gay old dog	Old bag
Old crock	Old biddy
Old fogey	Old crow
Dirty old man	Old cow
Gramps	Old bird
Grandpa	Crone
Old codger	Old hen
Fuddy-duddy	
Fossil	

Source: From Covey, "Historical terminology used to represent older people," *Gerontologist, 28,* 291–297. Copyright 1988 The Gerontological Society of America.

wrinkled, hard of hearing, rigid, grouchy, and lonely. Perhaps age stereotypes are becoming more positive as old people become more visible in society. This study also found that 65-year-old women and men were evaluated similarly. In contrast, other research in which college students and older persons evaluated photographs of young, middle-aged, and old women and men found that women's femininity was believed to decrease with age, but men's masculinity was unaffected by age (Deutsch, Zalenski, & Clark, 1986).

Negative attitudes toward the aged as a group have been labeled *ageism.* Ageism, like sexism, includes not only beliefs and attitudes but the discriminatory practices that follow from such prejudices (Butler, 1980). There is evidence that ageism is a common prejudice (Kimmel, 1988). Both younger and older research participants evaluated identical behavior differently, depending on the age of the actor: For example, an episode of forgetfulness was viewed more negatively in a 75-year-old than in a 35-year-old (Rodin & Langer, 1980). Psychologists are not exempt from ageism either! One research study found that clinical psychologists evaluated a case study more negatively and were more likely to diagnose psychosis when the client was older (Settin, 1982).

Sexism and Ageism: Some Comparisons

Several parallels can be drawn between ageism and sexism. Both involve categorizing people on the basis of their membership in a group, resulting in negative stereotypes. Both are reflected and perpetuated in language about the devalued groups. Both are pervasive in our society. Finally, they are prejudices that are frequently shared by members of the devalued groups themselves. Can you think of other similarities?

Feminists have argued that the stereotype of the old woman, which is sometimes more negative than that of the old man, is a "logical extension" of the sexist belief that "women are only valuable when they are attractive and useful to men" (Healy, 1986, p. 59). Discrimination based on sex may add to discrimination based on age to put older women in double jeopardy. For those who are also from minority cultural groups, such as Latinas, Asian-American women, or African-American women, and who are also economically deprived, the situation has been labeled "quadruple jeopardy." If being female is a devalued status in itself, to be female, black, old, and poor is to be multiply devalued (Padgett, 1988).

Because women live longer than men, the majority of old persons are women. In 1990, for example, there were 149 women for every 100 men over age 65 and 259 women for every 100 men over age 85 (Hatch, 1995). As you will see later in this chapter, the majority of those caring for old persons are also women. The effects of ageism on older men are often cushioned by the women who care for them. However, older women may have no such cushion (Kimmel, 1988). Though our society does not reward or honor older people generally, the costs of ageism seem to be greater for women.

The Double Standard of Aging

A double standard of aging can be seen in many ways. For example, the physical changes of age are viewed very differently in men and women: The middle-aged man's wrinkles and gray hair are seen as evidence of character and distinction, while the middle-aged woman is urged to conceal all signs of growing older with makeup, hair dye, and cosmetic surgery. The ideal woman's face shows no signs that she has lived a life of experience and emotion; it is supposed to remain unblemished and childlike (Sontag, 1979).

Men are not perceived as losing their sexual attractiveness until a later age than women. Their sexual value is defined mainly in terms of personality, intelligence, and social status, while for women sexual value is defined almost entirely as physical attractiveness. One of the most overt ways in which this double standard is conveyed to women is that when middle-aged and older men remarry following divorce or widowhood, they show an increasing tendency to choose women younger than themselves. It is socially acceptable for men to marry women as much as twenty years younger than themselves, while older women–younger men combinations are rare (Bell, 1989).

Ageism and Sexism in the Media

This double standard about aging in women and men is particularly apparent in the movies and on TV, where male actors (e.g., Robert Redford, Paul Newman) play romantic leads into their fifties and sixties, often paired with females a generation younger. Romantic leading roles for middle-aged women are almost nonexistent. At 40, Jane Fonda told an interviewer that she could find no good roles because "Who wants to look at a 40-year-old woman?" Other middle-aged actresses opt to play older parts. Sally Field was Tom Hanks's lover in *Punchline* in 1988 and his mother in *Forrest Gump* six years later (Weinraub, 1994). Film is an insidiously powerful tool for telling us what we aren't as women and what we should be.

So conditioned for shame about our bodies as they age, we watch portraits of once-vital women degenerate before our eyes while the men they support, each his own Dorian Gray, retain supernatural youthfulness (Kozlowski, 1993, p. 7).

An analysis of the Academy Awards illustrates the differential impact of aging on women and men. From 1927 through 1990, women over the age of 39 accounted for 27 percent of the nominations for best actress, whereas men over the age of 39 accounted for 67 percent of the nominations for best actor (Markson & Taylor, 1993). Katherine Hepburn, who won three Oscars for best actress, accounted for half the awards made to women over 60.

A recent content analysis of prime-time TV found that older people made up only 3 percent of the characters and that older men were generally portrayed more positively than older women (Vernon, Williams, Phillips, & Wilson, 1991). Among the "Golden Girls," only two had gray hair (Gerike, 1990). Even *Lear's*—a now defunct magazine that portrayed itself as being "for the woman who wasn't born yesterday"—rarely published photographs of gray-haired women (see Figure 13.1).

Editors of women's magazines admit that signs of age are routinely airbrushed from photographs through computer imaging so that 60-year-old women can be made to look 45 (Chrisler & Ghiz, 1993). The absence of women over 40 in advertising is striking. Unless their images are used to sell laxatives or denture adhesives or to give homey advice about cooking, older women are usually ignored.

Cultural Images of the Aging Woman

It is not surprising that women more than men are concerned about growing older, since ageism is much more of an issue for them. Older women were uncommon figures in society until the mid-nineteenth century. Between 10,000 B.C. and A.D. 1640, the average woman's life expectancy increased only about four years: from 28 to 32 (Low, 1983). By 1800, a woman's life expectancy was still only 50 years, the age at which she would typically enter menopause. Until the late nineteenth century, fewer than 30 percent of all women reached the menopausal age of 50 to 51 years (Edman, 1983).

Early images of middle-aged women, such as those found in the Old and New Testament, focused on their ability to bear children. In the biblical story of Sarah, for example, a woman is celebrated for her ability to conceive a child long past her normal time. A similar story is told about Saint Elizabeth, the mother of John the Baptist. Both women were stigmatized by their society for their "barrenness" and honored for their belated fertility. They symbolize motherhood as the highest calling for a woman (see Chapter 11). Age was seen as no barrier to a woman with enough faith. Medical scientists have recently announced a breakthrough that allows less exalted postmenopausal women to bear children. Do you think this "advance" indicates any cultural continuity between biblical and current views on women and reproduction?

Barren and/or powerful old women were likely to be transformed into witches by way of a false logic that argued that because good power is fertile, unfertile power must be evil (Kincaid-Ehlers, 1982). Older female archetypes in

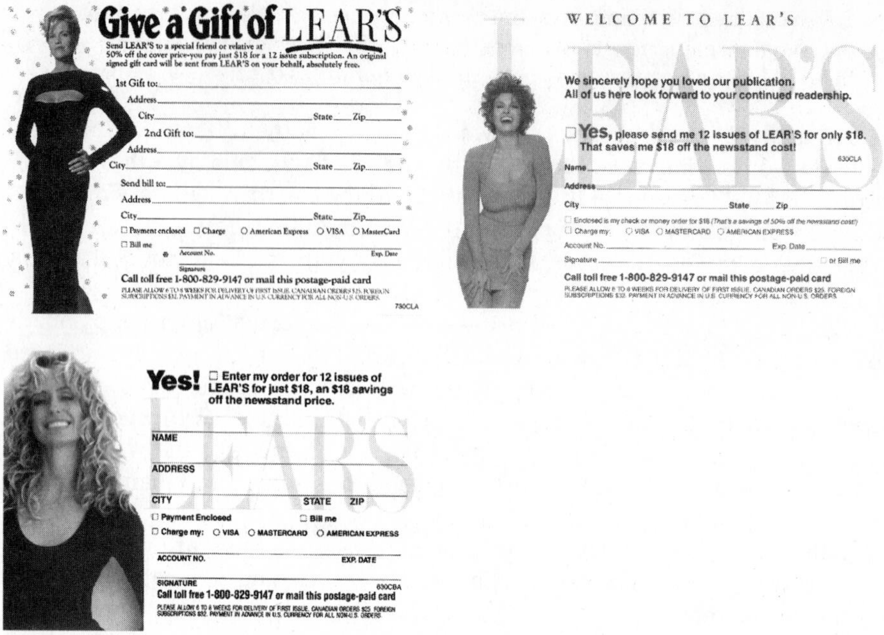

FIGURE 13.1. Do you know many women over 40 who look like these women?

various cultures have also been recast in a similar way. For example, the term "crone" once meant a wise elder woman, but was changed to mean a malevolent old woman (Mantecon, 1993). The goddess Kali in India was once seen as a source of transformation. Although her image implied both creation and destruction, she is generally portrayed as an image of chaos and death.

Normal, middle-aged women are especially unlikely to be depicted. There were few, if any, literary representatives of the *process* of female aging. Little was said about the continuity of female life from birth to death. Kincaid-Ehlers (1982) points out that the word *menopause* did not even exist in English until the last quarter of the nineteenth century. The "change of life" was considered the "end of life." Since people tend to ignore aspects of life that frighten them, it is perhaps not surprising that so few images of old women can be found. Even birthday cards for older women cite few causes for celebration. They allude to failing memory, decreased sexual abilities, and diminished vigor and attractiveness, all in the guise of humor (Adolph, 1993). Clearly our culture views getting older to be a cause for mourning.

The double standard of aging encourages women to deny their age to themselves and others. Even professional women, for whom age represents professional experience and maturity, are rarely candid about it. In the official membership directory of the American Psychological Association, women are ten times as likely as men not to list their age (Bell, 1989).

The double standard may, however, be less relevant to lesbians. In a comparison of "personals" advertisements written by lesbians and heterosexual women, 98 percent of the lesbians and 76 percent of the heterosexuals specified their age in their ad. Heterosexual women were *more* likely than lesbians to specify the desired age of a prospective partner. These results suggest that age is less of a stigma and a less important dimension in choosing a romantic partner among lesbians than among heterosexuals (Laner, 1979).

The Social Invisibility of Older Women

Throughout this book we have emphasized that women as a class have a lower status than men. The difference persists and may even increase as women and men grow older. When older women are no longer seen as sexually desirable, they become socially invisible (Bell, 1989).

Women have also been largely invisible in psychological research on aging. Much research on older people has either used all-male samples or failed to analyze results by sex, so that possible differences between men and women are obscured. Moreover, biases based on stereotypes of women have affected researchers' choice of participants. For example, researchers have equated aging for women with the end of the childbearing years, while for men it is conceptualized in terms of retirement from paid work; thus the importance of work in women's lives is often underestimated (Bumagin, 1982). In one major study of the effects of menopause, women who worked outside the home were excluded, apparently because they were "deviant." In an important study of retirement, married women were excluded on the grounds that their husbands' retirement, and not their own, was the most important influence (cited in Barnett & Baruch, 1978). Omissions and biases such as these result in research that has little validity for understanding the lives of today's aging women.

The bias against including women and gender is widespread and slow to change. For example, two widely respected research handbooks on aging published in the 1980s list no index entries for "women," "men," "sex differences," or "gender." Omitting women and gender from the study of aging seems to be based on the assumption that the older the people being studied, the less important gender is. However, gender is as important a lens for understanding midlife and elderly people as it is for any other age group. The omission of women is especially ironic since women make up a majority of the aging population (Grambs, 1989).

The Meanings of Midlife

Especially little attention has been paid to the years from ages 45 to 65, when women are deemed to have passed from middle to old age. This period is obviously not socially neutral, but there has been relatively little research on individual and societal responses to growing old. Even less attention has been paid to developmental changes that normally occur for both men and women during this time period. These changes include reassessment of past goals and ambitions and examination of the future with anticipation and dread.

Because physical appearance is more important for social judgments about women and because women "age" sooner than men, the midlife transition can be particularly problematic for women. From her experiences in clinical practice, Sarah Pearlman (1993) has described a phenomenon she termed "late midlife astonishment." She found that between the ages of 50 and 60, many women suddenly become aware of an acceleration of aging and an increasing stigmatization based on its visible signs. "Passing" as younger is no longer possible for them. They fear being discriminated against in the workplace and rejected or abandoned by romantic partners or mates. These fears produce a sense of heightened vulnerability, shame, and loss of self-esteem.

Such fears are a realistic product of the combination of sexism and ageism of our society, which focuses on women's bodies more than those of men. Women appear to have a shorter period of presentability in the labor market than men do. For example, one manager was quoted as saying "We have two good secretaries with first-rate skills who cannot move up because they dress like grandmothers. . . (Rodeheaver, 1990, p. 57). The most frequent compliment given to older women is "You don't look your age." Think about the unstated assumptions in this remark! "If you looked your age, you would look ugly" (Healy, 1993).

MENOPAUSE

The Aging Woman's Body and Its Social Meaning

There is one glaring exception to the omission of women from the study of aging. Menopause has been the subject of great attention from both the medical profession and the media. In fact, aging and menopause are treated as almost synonymous in women. As we have discussed in a number of earlier chapters, women are defined by their reproductive functions more than men are. This is especially true for the phases of life that appear to have no parallels for males, such as menarche, pregnancy, and menopause. Many researchers in these areas believe that women's behavior during these life stages is determined by the direct influences of hormones on their brains. Beliefs about biological causality have led to the neglect of other psychological and social events that occur at the same stage of life.

Since biological and physiological explanations are usually viewed as primary, *menopause*—physiologically, the end of menstruation and, therefore, fertility—has been used to explain much of women's behavior at midlife. Menopause—or what is sometimes known as the "change of life"—occurs in most women between the ages of 45 and 55. The average age of menopause—around 50—has not changed since the medieval period. This average age seems to be relatively constant across cultures despite a wide range in levels of nutrition and health.

These facts would seem to indicate that menopause is a purely biological phenomenon. Indeed, menopause is biologically caused by a decrease in the production of estrogen and progesterone by the ovaries. Natural menopause is a gradual process. It is defined as having occurred when a woman has not menstruated in a year.

Menopause is not, however, treated as a normal life event in our society. Instead it is used as a metaphor for disparaging the aging female body. Menopause coincides with many other life events such as children leaving home; changes in domestic, social, and personal relationships; changes in identity and body image; possible divorce or widowhood; new experiences of retirement; and increasing anxiety about aging, dying, and losing friends, loved ones, and financial security. Rather than analyzing women's responses to these events, however, people portray menopause as a fundamental cause of women's loss of prestige, status, visibility, and value during their last quarter century of life (Zita, 1993).

Media descriptions of menopause illustrate our culture's view that the end of reproductive life is a disease that renders women sexless and useless (Chrisler, Torrey, & Matthes, 1990). Descriptions have changed over the past three decades, although they continue to "accentuate the negative." The symptoms stressed during each decade document changes in cultural attitudes toward women. In the 1960s, for example, the focus of the articles in popular magazines was on beauty and femininity. Symptoms such as weight gain, sagging breasts, wrinkles, loss of femininity, and loss of sexuality were noted more frequently in this decade. In succeeding years, the number of emotional symptoms and psychiatric conditions mentioned also declined. The 1980s woman was not warned to fear for her sanity. Instead, she was told to worry about such health issues as osteoporosis and heart disease.

Despite these extensive lists, there are few consistent signs of menopause. The only symptom that is found in *all* women is the end of menstruation. Other signals of the end of menstrual life are, however, found in some women. Although all of these effects have been attributed to a decline in ovarian hormones, no relationship has been found between hormone levels and the number and severity of symptoms. Moreover, only hot flashes and vaginal changes are successfully treated by hormone therapy in most women (Gannon, 1985). Despite the evidence that no definitive menopausal syndrome exists, studies continue to appear in professional journals. We will discuss a few of the more important areas below to show you biological and medical views of the aging female body and feminist and social constructionist critiques of this perspective.

Biology and Culture

The Hot Flash

The most consistently found symptom during menopause is the *hot flash.* Hot flashes are usually described as sensations of heat, often limited to the face and upper torso, that persist for some minutes. Hot flashes are now considered physiological phenomena, although they were at one time considered to be "all in a woman's head" (Travis, 1988b). They usually begin during the years before menopause and gradually decline after menopause has occurred. Researchers believe that hot flashes are caused by a reduction in estrogen that influences the temperature regulation centers of the hypothalamus. Hot flashes are among the few menopausal symptoms that are successfully treated by estrogen replacement (Gannon, 1985).

Evidence suggests, however, that hot flashes are not completely controlled by hormones. For example, hot flashes begin before menopause in many women—frequently before their level of estrogen has declined to a critical level

(Kronenberg, 1990). Moreover, although women vary enormously in the severity of this symptom, no relationship has been found between hormone levels and the number or intensity of hot flashes reported (Gannon, 1985). Researchers do not know why hot flashes last only a few months in some women, while in others they persist for years or never occur at all. They are unrelated to employment status, social class, age, marital status, domestic workload, and number of children (Kronenberg, 1990).

The percentage of women who report having hot flashes around menopause varies widely. Different studies have found a prevalence rate ranging from 24 to 93 percent of the women surveyed. The prevalence also varies widely from culture to culture. For instance, Japanese and Indonesian women report far fewer than women from Western societies do (Flint & Samil, 1990; Goodman, 1982; Kaufert, 1990). One study, using comparable data-gathering techniques, found that 69.2 percent of Caucasian women reported having experienced a hot flash at some time, while only 20 percent of a sample of Japanese women reported having had one (Lock, 1986). In the most extreme case, Mayan women in the Yucatan did not report any symptoms at menopause except menstrual-cycle irregularities (Beyene, 1989).

These cross-cultural findings illustrate how biological determinism can produce overly simplistic causal explanations. Hot flashes may be partly a function of a reduction in female hormones during menopause. But other factors also play a role. For example, cultural standards differ on the ideal weight for women; norms vary in terms of the age at which a woman has her last child; diets vary in terms of the amount of animal fat eaten; and so on. All of these factors illustrate the interaction between biological and social variables. There is no good way to separate purely "physical" aspects of hot flashes from their social and cultural context.

Psychological Responses to the Hot Flash

Most women do not find hot flashes incapacitating, but many women do find them embarrassing.

> I can remember being very embarrassed talking with a fellow worker and my face turned very red. I was sure it was written all over my face what the cause of that redness was and there was nothing for me to be blushing about, nothing in the conversation that was embarrassing, so I remember those little embarrassing episodes (Martin, 1987, p. 168).

When asked what she did about this incident, the woman replied, "Nothing, just prayed he wouldn't notice it."

Many women are unable to explain why they are embarrassed by hot flashes. They associate them with situations in which they are "nervous" or especially want to make a good impression (Martin, 1987). Emily Martin suggests that hot flashes may be embarrassing because they are an outward public sign of an inner body process associated with the uterus and ovaries, which is supposed to be kept private and concealed. They reveal indisputably that a woman is of a "certain age." They also reveal a woman's difference from men, with a focus on her reproductive system—a system that may be devalued even more because it is now "failing." Nevertheless, only a small percentage of women (perhaps 10 to 15 percent) report being seriously bothered by hot flashes.

Health Risks and Menopause

Osteoporosis

Osteoporosis is characterized by a decrease in skeletal mass or in the quantity of bone. This reduction in bone mass is regarded as a major factor in the bone fractures found in older people. It is generally believed that menopause is at least a contributing factor, and possibly the primary factor, in the development of osteoporosis. The characterization of this disorder as menopausal may, however, be another example of the confusion between menopause and the normal processes of aging.

Loss of skeletal mass with age is not found only in women. People of both sexes reach their peak bone mass at around age 35 and begin to lose bone mass thereafter. Women are, however, more prone to fractures because of thinning of their bones since they have less massive skeletons to begin with. Men who live long enough for their skeletons to reach a critically thin level are also prone to osteoporotic fractures.

There is also no evidence that loss of estrogen is directly associated with the development of osteoporosis. Loss of bone mass in women normally begins during the fourth decade of life, or well before menopause. No difference has been found in the level of estrogen in the blood between postmenopausal women with osteoporotic fractures and age-matched women without fractures (Edman, 1983).

Factors other than menopause have been implicated in osteoporosis. Diet and exercise appear to be extremely important. For example, the risk of osteoporosis is five times greater in thin than obese women (Gannon, 1985). Women who have been anorexic are particularly prone to this problem. Some interesting ethnic differences have also been found. Black and Puerto Rican women in the United States were found to have a lower incidence of vertebral atrophy and fractures than white women (Gannon, 1985). The less affected women had a higher level of calcium in their diet. Asian women also appear to have a lower rate of osteoporosis than white North American women. In fact, risk for this disorder appears to be related to skin color—the fairer the complexion, the greater the risk (Doress-Worters & Siegal, 1994).

Less affected women were also from a lower socioeconomic bracket, with jobs that were more physically demanding. Exercise has been found to reduce the loss of bone mass (Doress-Worters & Siegal, 1994). It is possible that the traditional gender-role difference in levels of physical activity accounts for the greater risk of osteoporosis in women. The connection between osteoporosis and menopause may also be mediated by traditional gender roles. For example, men begin to lose bone mass in their sixties rather than in their forties. This is the age at which men retire and drastically reduce their level of physical activity. An equivalent reduction in physical activity for women may take place in their forties, when their children leave home (Gannon, 1985).

The idea that osteoporosis is related only to sex is also called into question by an examination of sex-by-race interactions. Thus, there are no clear sex differences among African Americans (black women and men have the same risk of this disorder) and no clear race differences for men (black and white men are equally at risk) (Doress et al., 1987). Osteoporosis seems to be primarily a disease of affluent white women. Among the factors that may contribute to this disorder are a calcium-poor diet, lack of exercise, and/or maintenance of an excessively thin body weight.

The effectiveness of estrogen-replacement therapy for osteoporosis is quite controversial. There is no consensus about how estrogen works, what the mechanisms are, and even the reliability and validity of the measures used to evaluate bone loss (MacPherson, 1985). Not *all* postmenopausal women need long-term estrogen therapy. The individuals most at risk are thin, small-framed, white women who smoke and who weigh less than 120 pounds (Edman, 1983). It does not appear to be good medical practice to place all menopausal women on medication to protect 25 percent to 30 percent of the population. Calcium supplements and daily exercise are less risky alternatives.

Coronary Heart Disease

Loss of female hormones is also assumed to increase the risk of coronary heart disease. The argument is that because death from coronary heart disease is rare in premenopausal women and relatively high in men under 50, estrogens must protect premenopausal women. The incidence of cardiovascular disease appears to increase disproportionately in women following menopause. For example, the ratio of male to female deaths from heart disease decreases from eight to one at age 45 to one to one at age 85.

The logic of this argument is faulty, however. The shift is not due to a rapid acceleration of death from this cause among women after menopause, but to a decline in male deaths with age. The drop may be due, in part, to a high incidence of early death in men who are genetically predisposed to fatal coronary heart disease (Edman, 1983). In fact, women never "catch up" to men in risk for coronary heart disease. Women in their forties and fifties have disease rates approximately 45 percent lower than men of the same age. This same 45 percent difference is found for people in their sixties and seventies as well.

It would seem to be a contradiction that more women die from coronary heart disease than men although they have a lower rate of risk. The contradiction is explained by the fact that women, on the average, develop the disease seven to eight years later than men. Since there are substantially more older women than men, more women actually die of coronary heart disease, but always at a lower rate (Bush, 1990).

The erroneous connection between hormones and heart disease in women is a good example of the extent to which health problems in women are overly attributed to their reproductive functions. This emphasis on reproductive events leads researchers to ignore important social and cultural factors. For example, the sex ratios in deaths from coronary heart disease in individuals ages 45 to 54 are two to one in Italy and one to one in Japan (Edman, 1983). Sex-related differences are also smaller among blacks in the United States than among whites.

Excessive attention to biology also leads to less attention to other important risk factors. For example, smoking increases the rate of coronary heart disease for women as much as it does for men. It has been said that "women who smoke like men die like men who smoke" (Bush, 1990, p. 266). Smoking may also contribute to an earlier menopause, but its effects on heart disease appear to be quite egalitarian.

The Myth of Emotional Instability

There is little evidence to support a connection between menopause and psychoneurotic disorders (Doress et al., 1987; Edman, 1983). There is also little evidence that postmenopausal women are more depressed than younger women. Two large-scale community surveys, for example, have failed to find a higher rate of depression among menopausal women (Lennon, 1987).

Part of the reason for the perceived association between menopause and depression may be an emphasis on women who seek treatment for psychological problems during menopause. One recent study found that estrogens were significantly lower among depressed women attending a menopause clinic (Ballinger, 1990). This decrease in estrogens may, however, have been a result rather than a cause of their depression. This group of women had more environmental stressors and coped less well with them than a comparable nonclinical population. They were also more prone to depression *before* menopause as well as during it. A British study also found a relationship between premenopausal and postmenopausal mood (Hunter, 1990). Premenopausal depression, holding a negative stereotype about menopause, and being unemployed (combined with a low socioeconomic status) accounted for more than half the variance in postmenopausal depression. There was no relationship between measures of mood and the level of gonadotropic hormones.

The midlife woman's attempts to take control of her life may also be interpreted by others as a form of "menopausal madness." A poem by former Ann Arbor City Councilwoman Kathy Kozachenko illustrates how such attributional processes can act as a form of social control (see Box 13.1).

The Medicalization of Menopause

There is evidence that physicians and nurses see menopausal symptoms as more severe and pathological than menopausal women see them (Cowan, Warren, & Young, 1985). This is probably because medical personnel encounter only the 10 percent to 30 percent of all menopausal women who seek treatment. Such women probably have more severe symptomology than most.

Women who seek treatment have more negative attitudes about menopause than other women. They complain about its unpredictability, their inability to control symptomology, and the loss of a sense of continuity in their lives. In one study conducted in England, it was reported that women patients at menopausal clinics saw themselves as having completely changed with the onset of menopause—both physically and in terms of their personalities. They viewed their symptoms as some sort of mystery over which they had little control (Ussher, 1989).

Physiological signs and symptoms can be interpreted in a number of ways. Symptoms can also be experienced differently, depending on how medical authorities react to them. Physicians do not create actual physiological symptoms but can define which symptoms are important, which are to be disregarded,

Box 13.1 Mid-Point

She stored up the anger
for twenty-five years,
then she laid it on the table
like a casserole for dinner.

"I have stolen back
my life," she said.
"I have taken possession
of the rain and the sun
and the grasses," she said.

"You are talking
like a madwoman,"
he said.

"My hands are rocks
my teeth are bullets,"
she said.

"You are
my wife,"
he said.

"My throat is an eagle,
my breasts
are two white hurricanes," she said.

"Stop!" he said.
"Stop or I shall call
a doctor."

"My hair
is a hornet's nest.
My lips
are thin snakes
waiting for their victim."

He cooked his own dinners,
after that.

The doctors diagnosed it
as common change of life.

She, too, diagnosed
it change of life.
And on leaving the hospital
she said to her woman-friend
"My cheeks
are the wings
of a young
virgin dove.
Kiss them."

Source: Poem by Kathy Kozochenko. From Bart and Grossman, "Menopause." In M. T. Notman and C. C. Nadelson (Eds.), *The Woman Patient: Medical and Psychological Interfaces*, pp. 351–352. 1978 Plenum Publishing Corporation. Reprinted with permission.

which should be treated, and which should not (Zimmerman, 1987). The creation of a diagnostic category such as "involutional depression" or "menopausal syndrome" can lead physicians as well as women themselves to assign symptoms of stress to menopause rather than social causes (see Figure 13.2).

Many women express a strong sense of dissatisfaction with their physicians and the medical advice that they have been offered (Logothetis, 1993). Physicians tend to view women's health problems, whatever their type, location, or symptoms, in terms of reproductive function. This preoccupation of physicians with the menopausal status of their patients has persisted for more than a century.

> Women are treated for diseases of the stomach, liver, kidneys, heart, lungs, etc.; yet, in most instances, these diseases will be found on due investigation, to be, in reality, no diseases at all, but merely the sympathetic reactions or the symptoms of one disease, namely, a disease of the womb (Dirix, 1869; cited in Zimmerman, 1987, p. 448).

For Better or For Worse® **by Lynn Johnston**

FIGURE 13.2. The link between hormones and emotions at both ends of the reproductive cycle.

> A woman is a uterus surrounded by a supporting organism and a directing personality. In advancing this proposition I am neither facetious nor deprecatory of womankind. I am biologically objective (Galdston, 1958; cited in Zimmerman, 1987, p. 448).

The definition of women's reproductive system as a source of illness and disability has ignored findings about poor women and women of color. These groups are absent from most of the studies on the medical risks of menopause. For example, Patricia Kaufert (1990) reviewed 108 papers cited in an important review article on menopause and found that only two looked at ethnicity as a variable. When populations that are *not* middle-class white Americans are taken into account, they often contradict hypotheses about the direct relationship between hormones and symptomology. The lack of a difference between black women and men in susceptibility to osteoporosis (discussed earlier in this chapter) is an example of one such contradiction.

Medicalizing the normal changes of midlife has serious consequences for women. Patricia Kaufert and Penny Gilbert (1986) have found a tremendous gap in health care for midlife women. They stay away from available health care providers because they find their experience medicalized in ways that they cannot tolerate. One large-scale study (Goodman, 1982) found that more than 50 percent of the women in her sample had undergone some form of surgery in relation to their menopause and 66 percent were taking some kind of medication (not necessarily estrogen). This is an astonishing number in view of the fact that only 28 percent reported symptoms of menopause on their medical history forms.

Recent investigations by anthropologists in Japan (Lock & Kaufert, 1988) have uncovered the development of a belief in a menopausal "syndrome" comparable to that found in the United States, even though Japanese women show few symptoms during this period. Physicians described women who complained of menopausal symptoms as middle-class urban housewives whose complaints were a reflection of increasing leisure and the loss of traditional values. The investigators found, however, no difference in symptom patterns by whether a woman was urban or rural, or whether she was a housewife from a middle-class area in Kyoto or a worker in one of Kyoto's factories. This study illustrates how little evidence is required for the invention of a medical "phenomenon."

Estrogen Replacement Therapy

There is fairly good evidence that estrogen replacement is helpful in treating such effects of menopause as hot flashes and vaginal thinning. It is more controversial as a treatment for osteoporosis—where other factors, such as poor nutrition, lack of exercise, and smoking, may contribute as much to bone loss as hormones do. There is no good evidence that the risk of cardiovascular disease in women is linked to menopausal hormonal changes. And, finally, estrogens are only as helpful as a placebo in dealing with anxiety, irritability, and so on.

It should be clear from this summary that estrogens should be thought of as a treatment for a specific set of symptoms suffered by a minority of women. These symptoms, moreover, usually disappear gradually after menopause or can be treated by less potent medications. Nevertheless, beginning in the early 1960s, estrogens were used liberally in an attempt to perpetuate youth for menopausal women. Physicians' enthusiasm for estrogen replacement is illustrated in the following quote:

> Estrogen has remarkably beneficial effects as an energizer, a tranquilizer, and an antidepressant. It stimulates and maintains mental capacity, memory and concentration with the concomitant effect of restoring a zest for living, and giving a youthful appearance and outlook on life (Jern, 1975, quoted in Travis, 1988a, p. 92).

By 1975, Premarin (a brand name for synthetic estrogen) was the fourth or fifth most popular drug sold in the United States and was used by 6 million women (MacPherson, 1993). The "feminine forever" ideology was challenged in the mid-1970s when several investigators noted an increased incidence of endometrial cancer in the United States (Edman, 1983). It has been estimated that 15,000 cases of endometrial cancer over a five-year period could be attributed to the use of replacement estrogen. A decline in the incidence of this cancer began when sales of estrogen began to decline (Travis, 1988a).

Physicians and drug companies promised women a safe, symptom-free menopause. Currently, hormone replacement therapy is marketed with the promise of escape from chronic diseases. The problem here again is the confusion between menopause and aging. For example, Kathleen MacPherson (1993) notes that although 95 percent of all women have undergone menopause by age 55, less than 11 percent develop cardiovascular disease by this age. The mortality rate for women for this disease does not reach one in 100 until after age 70. By this age the average woman has been postmenopausal for fifteen to twenty years.

Today, feminists charge that the majority of doctors are more likely to prescribe hormones to menopausal women than to consider any other form of advice, supplement, or intervention. This excessive use of hormones continues despite a recent report of the World Health Organization that challenged the use of estrogens in treating menopausal symptoms. This report stated that in 70 percent to 80 percent of postmenopausal women the level of circulating estrogens is sufficient (Ussher, 1989).

There is some evidence that the use of hormone replacement therapy is more a function of a woman's general attitudes about menopause than her level of menopausal distress. Mary Lou Logothetis (1991) found that when the level of distress was controlled, users and nonusers of hormone replacement therapy had significantly different beliefs about susceptibility, seriousness, the benefits and barriers of hormone use, and philosophical orientation to menopause.

By the year 2000 there will be 20 million women over the age of 65 who represent a potentially lucrative market for hormones if women and their physicians can be convinced that hormones are a way of treating the ills of aging and staying feminine forever. It seems advisable, in the light of the lack of information about the long-term effects of hormone therapy, to look at these claims with a healthy degree of skepticism (Doress et al., 1987).

Language about Menopause and Popular Consciousness

It is not surprising that women will seek drugs to stave off aging at any cost. The equation of aging and menopause has no parallel in men. The language used to describe menopause is particularly hostile. It is in sharp contrast to the language used to describe changes men experience during this part of the life cycle:

> We do not have "testicular insufficiency" to match "ovarian insufficiency" or "senile scrotum" to match "senile ovaries." In the *Merck Manual of Diagnosis and Therapy,* the common physician's handbook, in describing premature menopause, specific medical directions are given for "preservation of a serviceable vagina." Do you think there is equal discussion of a "serviceable penis?" . . . Of course there isn't. When a doctor injects testosterone into a man, it isn't for the purpose of preserving or creating a "serviceable penis" . . . men do not serve. Women do. The purpose is to increase his libido, to raise his hormone level (Reitz, 1981, p. 73).

The language of loss leads some women to believe that all midlife changes are negative, inevitable, and debilitating (Ussher, 1989). The following quotes are representative of the comments of the many women who dread the approach of menopause.

> I look at every new wrinkle, every grey hair and think of the time when I won't be able to cope with anything: when I'll probably finally go mad. Isn't it true that women who are going through the change are out of their minds for most of the time? (Melanie, aged 30, in Ussher, 1989, p. 109).

> I guess it's more of a fear, not of post-menopause, just the actual process. You're not really in control of your body. That much is not predictable, that's what scares me about it (Tania Parrish, aged 20, in Martin, 1987, p. 174).

> My grandmother almost went insane, she almost didn't make it through menopause at all (Marcia Robbins, aged 19, in Martin, 1987, p. 174).

These comments were all made by women who were far from the age of menopause. As you have seen, they are in sharp disagreement with the comments of older women who see menopause as "no big deal." The comments of the younger women, however, echo the views of some physicians:

> I cannot help feeling that the reason so few women being (sic) found in leading positions is to be at least partly explained by the mental imbalance in these years around the time of the menopause. It is around the age of 50 that men take the final step to the top, a step that women with equal intellectual capacities rarely take. I know that many aspects are involved, but the climacteric may well be an important one (cited in Martin, 1987, p. 175).

> . . . is the trigger for the powder keg of emotions slowly smoldering somewhere in the hypothalamus (Dunlop, 1968, p. 45).

> The assumption has been put forward that women's ability to work reduces to a quarter of the normal by menopause (Achte, 1970, p. 13).

One gynecologist even described menopausal women as "a caricature of their younger selves at their emotional worst" (Bart & Grossman, 1978).

It should not be surprising to you that negative images about menopause abound. What is surprising is the number of women who reject the model of menopause as illness.

Alternative Views of Menopause

Methodological Biases

There are a great many methodological biases in research on menopause. Some of the most glaring problems will be discussed briefly. First, many studies examine only those women who come to doctors or medical clinics for treatment. We do not know how representative such women are of similarly aged women in the general population who do not seek treatment. Second, many studies on menopause combine groups of women whose menopause has been prematurely caused by surgery (hysterectomy, or removal of the uterus, is the most frequent major surgical procedure performed in the United States) with those who have reached menopause naturally. Surgical menopause appears to produce more physical symptoms than natural menopause (Gannon, 1985). Last, many studies of menopause use symptom checklists with only negative symptoms listed. (This bias is found in studies of premenstrual syndrome as well.) Respondents are allowed no opportunity to offer alternative views of the phenomenon.

Other Voices: Nonclinical Views of the Menopausal Experience

Studies that examine women's accounts of their experiences find relatively little distress. Over and over, women described menopause by saying, "It was nothing." "Nothing. Never had any problem. It just stopped, it slowed up." and "Nothing. Just stopped and that's about it" (Martin, 1987, p. 173). The vast majority of older women respondents saw menopause in a positive light. They felt pleasure at avoiding whatever discomfort they had felt during menstruation and relief from the nuisance of dealing with bleeding, pads, or tampons. For those women who were sexually active with men, menopause meant delight in freedom from the fear of pregnancy.

A more recent study that asked women between the ages of 40 and 60 to write about menopause found similar results. The women's unconstrained responses were overwhelmingly positive (Logothetis, 1993). Most of them placed menopause in the overall context of their reproductive lives. Here are some of their remarks (Logothetis, 1993, pp. 128–129):

> It's like your period—it's what you make of it, good or bad.
>
> I had more discomfort from periods than from menopause.
>
> No more fear of getting pregnant.

There was no indication of the "empty nest syndrome" among these women. Instead, they frequently communicated a sense of freedom from the responsibility of bearing and nurturing children.

Emily Martin notes that women do not appear to experience menopause as if it were a separate episode in life akin to a major illness. Her interviewers reported, in fact, that they had difficulty keeping older women respondents on the topic because they wanted to wander off from menopause to talk about many other aspects of their lives.

The difference in the contexts in which questions are asked may be another form of methodological bias in the study of menopause. A recent study creatively illustrates how both women and men may be influenced by context in this area. Linda Gannon and Bonnie Ekstrom (1993) looked at attitudes toward menopause in the context of medical problems, life transitions, or symbols of aging. For example, one group of people expressed their attitudes toward a broken leg, a stomach ulcer, and menopause. Another group expressed their attitudes about menopause in the context of puberty and leaving the parental home, and a third group responded to questions that included attitudes toward gray hair and retirement. The researchers found that the medical context elicited significantly more negative attitudes than the other two contexts. In general, women's attitudes were more positive than those of men and their attitudes became increasingly positive with age and experience.

Attitudes about menopause have many similarities to other gender-related stereotypes. For example, women believe others have more problems than they themselves do. Like another reproductive milestone, menarche, attitudes are most negative among those women who have not yet experienced the event. The negative emotional status associated with menopause may be, therefore, a response to popular stereotypes—to what is perceived as the expectations of others about this life stage.

Correlates of Positive and Negative Menopausal Transitions

The emotional states supposedly associated with menopause have been found to vary with women's level of education and their social class. Upper-middle-class women, in particular, minimized the importance of menopause (Bart & Grossman, 1978). A similar social-class effect was found in an analysis of a large representative sample of 922 married women in Belgium who ranged from 46 to 55 years of age (Severne, 1982). Those women who worked outside the home reported the least impact on them. In a smaller U.S. study, researchers examining the attitudes of women and their families also found that the women's level of education had an effect. For women who had completed high school and their families, the changes of menopause were seen as a part of a time of life when things were getting better (Dege & Gretzinger, 1982). For example, the midlife period was seen as a time when there was more opportunity for outside employment. These data on the impact of education and social class demonstrate that we cannot separate the emotional responses associated with menopause from other aspects of women's lives.

Psychologists must be wary of class bias in analyses of the effects of menopause. Paid employment probably cushions the effects of menopause for middle- and upper-class women because their jobs are both physically less exacting and socially more rewarding than those of working-class women. The effect of new freedom at midlife presupposes that women have both the time and resources for the exploration of new roles (Perlmutter & Bart, 1982). For working-class women, physical problems at midlife may combine with the long-term consequences of unemployment, intermittent employment, and/or poor salary.

Attitudes about Menopause in Relation to Power and Status

Women who have the most positive attitudes about menopause perceive that it has given them more power to direct their own lives. As we noted earlier in this chapter, when people age in our society they often lose power and status. Many feminist researchers have argued, therefore, that the negative consequences of middle age for women are a result of American society's attitude toward aging rather than the menopause per se. Since women in all societies go through menopause but cultures vary in their response to aging women, it is possible to infer whether there is a relationship between menopausal symptomology and the status and power of aging women by examining a number of cultures.

Certain structural arrangements and cultural values appear to be associated with an increase in women's status after the childbearing years (Bart & Grossman, 1978). (See Table 13.2.) These arrangements have major consequences in the lives of middle-aged women in many non-Western societies. For example, the end of fertility and/or responsibility for childrearing may give them greater opportunity for geographic mobility; the right to exert authority over certain members of the younger generation (usually daughters or daughters-in-law); and recognition beyond the household unit (Brown, 1982). In contrast, relatively weak bonds between women and their adult children, minimal menstrual taboos (giving women no more freedom after menopause than before it), and the high value placed on youth and sexual attractiveness decrease the power of middle-aged women in our society.

A number of studies have indicated that women in non-Western societies suffer fewer physical and psychological problems during menopause than women in our society do. Kyra Kaiser (1990), for example, examined fifteen non-Western cultures and found no evidence of depression in menopausal women. Women in these societies enjoyed enhanced social status and political power. They were freed from taboos involving menstrual pollution; they had

TABLE 13.2. The Structural Arrangements and Cultural Values Associated with Increases and Decreases in Women's Status after Childbearing Years

Increased Status	Decreased Status
Strong tie to family of orientation (origin) and kin	Marital tie stronger than tie to family of orientation (origin)
Extended family system	Nuclear family system
Reproduction important	Sex an end in itself
Strong mother–child relationship reciprocal in later life	Weak maternal bond; adult-oriented culture
Institutionalized grandmother role	Noninstitutionalized grandmother role; grandmother role not important
Institutionalized mother-in-law role	Noninstitutionalized mother-in-law role; mother-in-law doesn't train daughter-in-law
Extensive menstrual taboos	Minimal menstrual taboos
Age valued over youth	Youth valued over age

Source: From P. B. Bart & M. Grossman (1978). Menopause. In M. T. Notman & C. C. Nadelson (Eds.). *The Woman Patient: Medical and Psychological Interfaces,* pp. 351–352. 1978 Plenum Publishing Corporation. Reprinted with permission.

seniority in their domestic unit, new role opportunities, permission to participate in traditional male domains of power, greater decision-making authority, and the respect and responsibility accorded to the elderly. Thus, Arab women in Israel appear to gain power as they grow older (Friedman & Pines, 1992), although a similar shift with age is not found among poor women in either the United States or Kenya (Todd, Friedman, & Kariuki, 1990).

The Meaning of Menopause: A Brief Integratory Summary

What should you learn from all this information about menopause? It is clear that menopause involves a great many physiological, psychological, and cultural factors that cannot be considered in isolation from each other. It should also be clear that the kinds of questions asked and the solutions sought differ, depending on which of these factors is considered primary. In fact, whether or not menopause is seen as a problematic time for women is strongly influenced by its cultural meaning.

In mainstream U.S. society, menopause is especially problematized. Many physicians and clinicians assume that the biological changes of menopause are among the most salient aspects of the life experience and physical well-being of women who are middle-aged or older. This presumption is revealed in language use. Women are typically identified by an adjective referring to the menopause—"menopausal," "postmenopausal," or "premenopausal"—rather than by a reference to their social situation, such as "widowed," "newly promoted," or "empty nester" (Parlee, 1990). Physical symptomology is stressed, but women's experiential accounts are ignored.

The reliance on biomedical causality leads researchers to ignore the social context of menopause and to exaggerate differences between women and men.

Sex differences are seen as important because other differences, such as ethnicity, class, and culture, are ignored (Unger, 1990; 1992). Cultural factors seem to be very important in determining the valuation and importance of midlife transitions. Indeed, they are important determinants of physical symptomology as well. For example, researchers have found that women and men who live in kibbutzim (where there is less division of labor and other roles based on sex than in other social contexts) have similar life expectancies and levels of illness (Anson, Levenson, & Bonneh, 1990). Studies such as this one argue that "social facts," such as group norms that minimize gender differences, can have an impact.

ROLE TRANSITIONS OF MIDLIFE AND OF LATER LIFE

Cultural Context and Midlife Transitions

Psychologists are only beginning to recognize the extent to which culture shapes the context of women's lives in middle age:

> Irrevocable decisions of childhood, adolescence, and young adulthood shape the social context of middle age determining whether a woman will be surrounded by many children or one or two; whether she will be surrounded by grandchildren while she still has small children of her own at home; whether her family will be her primary concern or if she is likely to seek an outside job; if she does seek work outside the home whether she can hope for white-collar work or will be restricted by illiteracy to menial jobs (Datan, Antonovsky, & Maoz, 1981, pp. 2–3).

In a pioneering study of midlife transitions for women, Nancy Datan and her colleagues examined aging in five subcultures in Israel. The participants ranged from a modern city-living population, similar to most women in the United States, to women living in an extremely traditional nomadic tribal society. Other groups of women in the study were in various stages of the process of modernization; that is, they had been born or raised in a traditional society but were now living in a more modern cultural situation. The basic question asked by the researchers was, "How is a woman's response to the changes of middle age shaped by the culture in which she has grown?"

The researchers had expected that attitudes about the end of fertility would be shaped by the value placed on childbearing in a woman's cultural group. They hypothesized that middle age would be perceived most negatively by women in the most traditional groups since their cultural role is defined largely by their reproductive and mothering roles. Surprisingly, the study found that few of the women in any of the groups mourned their loss of fertility. Menopause was welcomed by women of all five subcultures, regardless of whether they had borne fifteen children (as was likely in the most traditional group) or one or two (as was probable in the most modern subculture).

Psychological well-being at middle age was found to be highest for the most modern and the most traditional subcultures. Women in the transitional groups were least satisfied because they saw no choices for themselves among possible roles, although they recognized the broadened horizons open to other women.

Women in the most traditional group appeared to gain power after menopause. The researchers suggested that Western biases may have led some previous researchers to confuse tradition for passivity. For example, one traditional Arab woman described the measures she took to deal with menopause: She made use of free medical help in Israeli clinics, traveled to a gynecologist for the sake of the excursion, and consulted a faith healer.

> Through her response we were helped to remember that what our culture identifies as magic and witchcraft are simply ritual practices which we now know to be ineffective, while scientific measures are those which, as far as we can tell, *do* work—or at least have not yet been proven ineffective (Datan et al., 1981, pp. 144–145).

The stress on reproductive status had led researchers to ignore other social aspects of women's roles in our society. In the next part of this chapter, we shall discuss some of the changes in social roles that occur at midlife. We will discuss, in particular, the "empty-nest syndrome," the addition and subtraction of other familial roles (for example, that of grandmother), and the place of work and friendship in older women's lives. All of these roles are influenced by culture and ethnicity as well as gender.

Cohort Effects

It is necessary to account for *cohort* effects in explaining role changes and aging. Cohort refers to a group of persons born in the same close time period—for example, within the same year or the same decade. Individuals of the same cohort will tend to be exposed to the same broad environmental events, which shape their life prospects and values similarly. People who were young adults during the worldwide Great Depression of the 1930s, for example, tend to have different ideas about thrift and economic security than those of earlier or later cohorts.

A person's cohort provides a better prediction of her beliefs, values, and behavior than her chronological age does. A 40-year-old woman in 1940 cannot be readily compared with a 40-year-old woman of 1990. Research on women is particularly influenced by cohort effects, because women's roles in the past few generations have changed more dramatically than men's roles. Old age is also not an isolated stage of life. The resources available to older women derive from the opportunities and constraints they have experienced over a lifetime. In the United States, for example, women now in their middle years were the first cohort legally able to control childbearing through effective contraception and legal abortion. Thus, they are the first generation of women who could plan a career without a high probability that it would be disrupted by an unplanned pregnancy (Grambs, 1989).

Because of increased life expectancy, our society currently has cohorts of women whose life experiences have been "worlds apart" (Hagestad, 1987). To illustrate the impact of cohort differences, we can compare women currently aged 85 and older, the very old of our society, with the postwar "baby boom" cohort now approaching midlife.

Many of those who are currently very old probably never expected to live as long as they have. When they were born, life expectancy was 49. Death was a part of life for all age groups; a majority of this cohort had lost a parent, brother, or sister by the time they were 15. They grew up with a constant fear of killer childhood diseases, and they survived an influenza epidemic in 1917 to 1918 that killed millions of people. The great majority of people in this cohort did not finish high school.

In contrast, members of the current middle-age cohort usually have both parents living and may also have grandparents. Medical advances have made direct experience with death rare in their lives. The great majority are high school graduates, and a substantial number have college degrees. For women of the earlier cohort, divorce was a shame and a scandal; today it is an acceptable personal decision. They were also much less likely to have lived alone or been financially independent as young adults than today's women. The importance of all these differences in cohort experiences should demonstrate why it is impossible to generalize about aging across cohorts. People experience aging differently, depending on the beliefs, values, and important experiences of the earlier parts of their lives (Grambs, 1989; Hagestad, 1987).

Race and Ethnicity

The paragraph you have just read, however, may not apply to older women from ethnic minority groups. Members of such groups have shorter life spans and may be functionally old well before age 65. The burden of poverty is also greater for aging women of color. Eighty percent of older black women and 50 percent of older Latinas live in poverty compared with 20 percent of older women as a whole (Padgett, 1988).

Although older women of color suffer a greater relative decline in health as they age than Anglo-American women, their relative deprivation in income and health is not necessarily linked to less satisfaction in life. Blacks actually report greater life satisfaction than whites during their late middle age (Carlson & Videka-Sherman, 1990). African-American women have consistently been found to have the lowest rate of suicide of all age/ethnic categories (Padgett, 1988). Despite a lifetime of racism and poverty, they seem to view old age as a reward. Older women of color may be "survivors" who expect less than older women from more privileged groups.

These ethnic differences are, however, more than just the effect of selection bias. Social networks within minority communities play an important role in life satisfaction that has largely been overlooked by mainstream researchers. Investigators conducting an in-depth examination of aging African Americans living in low-income high-rise public housing found, for example, that almost everyone had received help from family, friends, and/or neighbors (Faulkner & Heisel, 1987). Women were significantly more likely to both give and receive favors than men. Much of this support occurred in the context of religious activity. Older Native-American women were also more likely to attend church and perform volunteer activities than either Anglo or Latina women (Harris, Begay, & Page, 1989).

Ethnic minority families place great importance on interdependence and the needs of the family over the needs of the individual. These values mean that increasing dependency in old age is not viewed as negatively as it is within dominant cultures (Yee, 1990). Such values may also contribute to a feeling of entitlement among older individuals so that they do not lose their sense of self-worth when their needs are met by others (Faulkner & Heisel, 1987). This sharing of limited economic and social resources is a positive adaptation to the pressures of poverty.

Gender-Related Differences

Just as it is a mistake to overlook cohort differences in developmental patterns, it is a mistake to overlook gender-related differences. Unfortunately, most of the best-known theories of adult development across the life span are androcentric, relying on a male norm of development and describing a "universal" sequence of life stages derived from male experience. The life-span developmental theory of Erik Erikson, for example, proposes that identity formation is achieved in late adolescence and early adulthood. However, for many women, issues of personal identity ("Who am I? What do I want from my life?") are more critical in their thirties and forties, when child-care responsibilities lessen.

Similarly, the theory of Daniel Levinson, which was the basis for the popular book *Passages* (Sheehy, 1974), views life stages in terms of chronological age. The twenties are a time for entering marriage and deciding on work; the thirties, for becoming established, and, later, for "becoming one's own man" by achieving independence from one's mentor. As its masculine language suggests, Levinson's theory was developed through studying only men. Women are much less likely to have an uninterrupted pattern of work achievement in their thirties because these are the prime childbearing years. They are far less likely to have mentors to emulate, and their commitment to paid work may increase in their late forties, fifties, and beyond as their earlier focus on the family is phased out. Both Erikson's and Levinson's models reflect male experience. For women, they are simply inappropriate (Barnett & Baruch, 1978).

Keeping in mind these important cautions about research on midlife and older women—that cohort is more meaningful than chronological age, that cultural and ethnic factors impinge on women and men differently, and that androcentric theories rarely fit the life patterns of women—we turn now to an examination of role patterns in middle and later life.

The Complex Nature of Midlife Role Transitions

Although a number of biological events occur during midlife, it is also characterized by a series of role transitions. As you may remember, roles are clusters of expectations placed on people who occupy a position in the social structure. Most of us have many roles. These roles may be relational, such as the role of daughter, mother, wife, or grandmother, or they may be work related, such as the role of nurse, truckdriver, or salesperson. As is obvious from these examples, many roles carry with them assumptions about the sex of the person occupying them as well as about his or her gender-related properties.

During midlife, many roles begin to be redefined, resulting in permanent changes in an individual's life. Although every individual is embedded in many roles, researchers have focused on different midlife transitions in women and men. Changes in women's relational roles have been examined much more than changes in their work roles, whereas the opposite is true for men. The different numbers of studies are due largely to unexamined assumptions about what roles are important for each sex. They tell us what concerns are considered normative for women and men.

When one role is singled out for attention, other roles may be neglected. Roles are not, however, acted out in isolation from each other. For the midlife woman, the departure of her last child from home; loss of a spouse or other longtime companion; entry into, reentry into, or departure from the labor market; or acquisition of a college degree is not an isolated event. Although we will examine each of these role transitions separately, you should keep in mind that they all influence each other. These transitions also interact with other events that are likely to occur in middle age, such as the aging of one's parents, the birth of grandchildren, and the new freedom offered by retirement to explore alternative lifestyles.

It is important to remember that the consequences of life transitions are also influenced by their timing. Individuals are judged as being "on time" if their role behavior accords with cultural prescriptions for their age/sex category and "off time" if it does not.

> Ironically, for a midlife woman, a lifetime of "on-time" events such as marriage and childbearing in early adulthood means being vulnerable to economic declines throughout the latter half of the life span. Being "off-time," for women, as in completing a college degree, entering an occupation early in the work life, and postponing marriage and childbearing so as to advance in the career, usually predicts economic security in later years (Long & Porter, 1984, p. 142).

Since psychologists have tended to focus on women who are "on time" in their roles, they may have developed an overly negative image of women at midlife. These misperceptions have not been corrected because theories about women at midlife tend to be based on Freudian tradition. Such theories focus on reproductive heterosexual womanhood. Thus, work on older women represents them as mourning the loss of reproductive and sexual functions (Gergen, 1990). Little attention has been paid to older women in general and even less to women in deviant "off-time" roles.

In this section of the chapter we will discuss briefly some traditional as well as some nontraditional midlife transitions. First, we will discuss relational roles—both because much research has focused on such roles and because this research illustrates the way women's lives are constructed in terms of their reproductive functions. As you have seen in many other areas, the realities of midlife for women are quite different from what you may have believed.

The "Empty-Nest Syndrome": Myths and Realities

For women who have followed a traditional lifestyle of early marriage and childbearing, midlife is usually the period when their last child leaves home. This period has been thought to be characterized by depression. A combination of unrealistic fears, loneliness, and crying bouts was even named "Mama Portnoy's complaint" by one researcher (Bart, 1970). Other psychologists and sociologists have labeled the phenomenon the *empty-nest syndrome.* It is considered to be related to the arrival at adulthood of a woman's youngest child and her sense that she is no longer needed by her family. Such depressive reactions are said to be more common among women in ethnic groups that traditionally place great value on motherhood and the family (e.g., Jewish- and Italian-Americans).

In considering the empty nest as a cause of middle-age depression it is important to remember that when the empty nest is experienced it appears to be quite idiosyncratic. One woman reported that she felt the strongest impact when her youngest child went to kindergarten, others when their first or last child went to college, and still others reported sadness when their child moved his or her personal belongings out of the family home after college (Black & Hill, 1984).

The majority of midlife women who have developed other interests do not experience severe trauma when their last child departs from the home. On the contrary, most mothers positively anticipate freedom from childrearing responsibilities and look forward to the opportunity to pursue their own interests and to spend more time with their peers (Black & Hill, 1984; Long & Porter, 1984). These mothers appear to view motherhood more as an episode than a lifelong occupation.

The concept of an empty-nest syndrome seems to have been the result of psychologists' focus on women who have been socialized in traditional beliefs of motherhood. An interesting recent study by Patricia Adelmann and her associates (Adelmann, Antonucci, Crohan, & Coleman, 1989) illustrates how changes in early socialization patterns can influence role transitions much later in life. They found that the empty nest was more likely to be a negative experience among a cohort of women who had reached adulthood during a period of strong societal emphasis on women's maternal role. Those women who had come of age in the 1950s (during the height of the so-called feminine mystique) reacted more negatively to the empty nest than women who had come of age during World War II (when women were encouraged to enter the labor market).

These comparisons were done on successive twenty-year samples so that the women were the same age when they were surveyed. They demonstrate that the empty-nest syndrome is more an effect of socialization during young adulthood than an inevitable response to maternal loss. In fact, the researchers argue that the current group of midlife women—who reached their young adulthood during the feminist movement—should experience the departure of their last child from home as positively as their grandmothers did!

It seems likely that the empty-nest syndrome is class based as well as time bound. For example, in two successive samples of the alumnae of a private women's college in California, women in their early fifties often described their lives as "first-rate" and rated their quality of life as high (Mitchell & Helson, 1990). The conditions that were positively associated with quality of life were more empty nests, better health, and higher incomes. These respondents reported that after the children left home, life at home became simpler, and the energy that went to children was redirected to the partner, work, the community, or self-development. The women reported a greater sense of control over their lives than they had had previously.

These women, however, were in an excellent position to make use of the life opportunities that became open to them when their children left home. For example, 43 percent of the older cohort and 78 percent of the younger cohort in this study were in the work force at least part time. Studies conducted in Israel, Kenya, and the United States (Todd, Friedman, & Kariuki, 1990) have indicated that only women with higher economic and social status gain greater power with age.

The departure of children from home may result in major economic losses for some women. For example, eligibility for public assistance such as Aid to Families with Dependent Children or survivor's benefits (if the woman is a widow with dependent children) ceases when children reach age 18 (Long & Porter, 1984). At this time of a woman's life, opportunities for job training and career placement are few.

Another factor that has been neglected in research on the empty nest is the circumstances under which children leave home. For example, one study found that mothers who found the event traumatic also reported such negative circumstances as a too-early marriage or a child who had to be asked to leave because he or she was acting out (Black & Hill, 1984).

There is no evidence that being a mother enhances a woman's well-being. In a study of women over 50, researchers found no difference in happiness or satisfaction between mothers and childless women once income and employment status were controlled (Glenn & McLanahan, 1981). Attitudes about the gains and losses of retirement have been found to be unrelated to the presence or absence of children (Anson, Antonovsky, Sagy, & Adler, 1989). Even for widows aged 60 to 75, who would seem to be most in need of children, children had only very slight effects on measures of life satisfaction (Beckman & Houser, 1982). One pair of researchers concluded:

> Best evidence now available indicates that the present young adult should not choose to have children on the basis of expectations that parenthood will lead to psychological rewards in the later stages of life. The prospects of such rewards seem rather dim at best (Glenn & McLanahan, 1981).

As we shall see in subsequent parts of this chapter, other sources of social support can make up for a lack of children.

Retirement

Retirement is a major life transition and a salient marker of age. Stereotypes of retired people include both positive images—of freedom, travel, hobbies, and leisure—and negative ones of boredom, withdrawal, and feelings of uselessness. As with other developmental stages, the norm has been a male one; when people think of retirement, it is the stereotypical male pattern of leaving the pinnacle of a lifelong career climb that comes to mind. For women, whose work patterns and life goals may be different, the stereotype does not always fit.

There has been little research on women's adjustment to retirement or its meaning in women's lives. In keeping with the tendency to biologize aging more for women than for men, researchers have concentrated on menopause and the empty nest rather than on exploring women's patterns of paid work and their consequences for the retirement years (Barnett & Baruch, 1978).

In many countries, the standard retirement age is lower for women than for men—for example, in the USSR, Italy, and Japan women retire at age 55 and men at age 60. It seems ironic to require women to leave the work force before men do when they are likely to live several years longer after retirement. Moreover, such patterns disadvantage women economically, allowing them less time to accumulate pension benefits (Grambs, 1989).

In general, the limited data comparing women and men's experiences of retirement suggest that "women do it differently" (Grambs, 1989). Women's planning for and adjustments to retirement are complex, and not parallel to men's. A common pattern among women currently near retirement was to view their homemaker role as primary and their paid work as secondary. When these women retire from paid work, they expand the familiar role of homemaker. The transition is more abrupt for men of their cohort.

The experiences of women who have had more years in the work force is also different. Older women who chose the dual role labels of homemaker and retiree had higher self-esteem and less depression than those who labeled themselves either homemaker or retiree (Adelmann, 1993). However, those women who identified themselves with both roles were less likely to be married and had more education than women in the other groups. Most women retire from low-paid, low-status, and relatively unrewarding jobs, not from "careers."

As might be expected, income is an important factor in retirement satisfaction. Women who earned more in their paid work are happier with their retirement than those who earned less (Grambs, 1989). Poverty in old age remains a critical issue for women (see Figure 13.3). In 1990, the median annual income for women over age 65 was $8,044 versus $14,183 for men of the same age (Noble, 1994). The median income for black women was even lower, at $5,938. These figures include social security benefits, other pensions, and the income from investments. Income differentials are the consequence of lifetime inequalities. Few women or African Americans of either sex have the same number of work years at the same pay level as white men. And few have held jobs in industries that provide additional pensions (Hess, 1990).

Other Caregiver Roles

Being a Grandmother

Becoming a grandmother in her fifties is a probable event for a woman who has led a traditional "on-time" lifestyle of early marriage and motherhood. This is a positive event for most women, who may look forward to having a less stressful relationship with their grandchildren than they had with their own children.

> Being a grandmother is one of the great experiences of life, especially today, when we don't take the miracle for granted. There is no question that having a grandchild come to visit is demanding physically, mentally, and emotionally, especially when the grandmother is also working. Our three-year-old granddaughter has just left after a four-week visit. As the wildflowers in the juice glass fade, I try to decide which of the twenty-one crayon and watercolor pictures to keep taped to the banister. I rescue a 1950 miniature trailer truck her father used to play with from under the bed and hear her say proudly, "I'm bigging!" I see the world anew through her eyes and hope I'm still bigging too (a woman in her seventies, in Doress et al., 1987, p. 133).

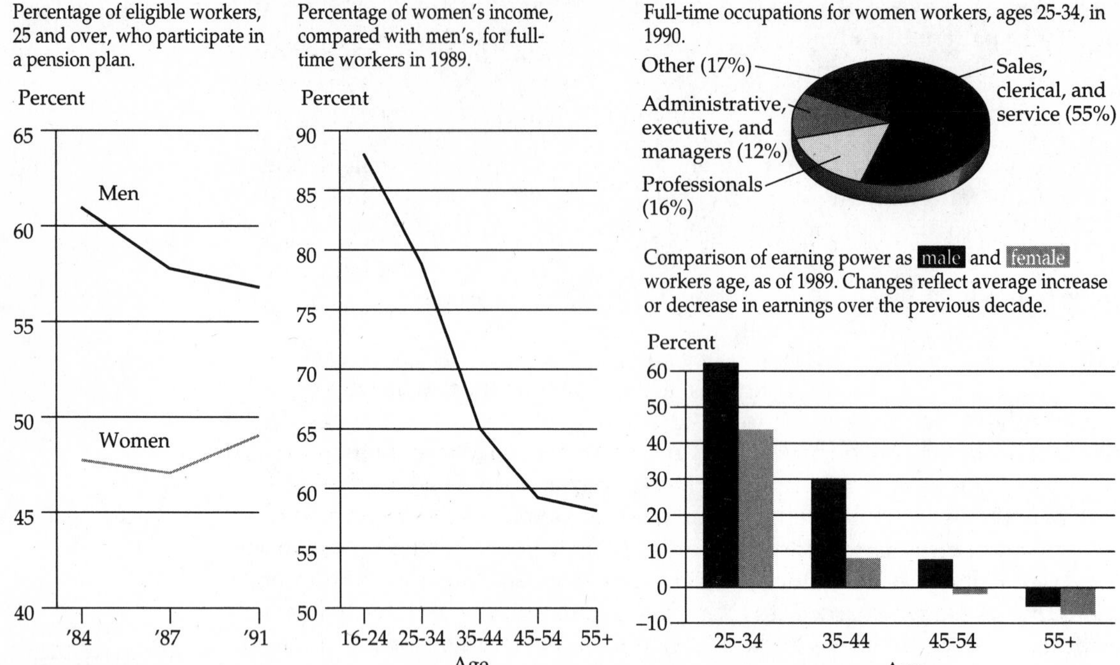

FIGURE 13.3. Women's financial well-being declines more than men's with age.
Source: From The New York Times, *February 6, 1994, p. F29. Copyright © 1994 by the New York Times Company.*

Today's grandmothers want to define for themselves the specific relationship they have with their grandchildren (Doress et al., 1987). Few want to babysit regularly or be responsible for child care.

> I have an unwritten understanding with my children. I do not babysit my grandchildren, I entertain them. I invite them—but I am not called in as a babysitter. I think babysitting damages the relationship. They know when I'm with them I'm there because I want to be and because I enjoy their company. And I invite them on that basis too. I don't want to be considered a babysitter because that's not the relationship I want to establish with my grandchildren (a 74-year-old woman, in Doress et al., 1987, p. 135).

For some women, however, being a grandmother involves more than a short-term commitment. Economic factors may limit their ability to make choices. Many midlife women take on substantial responsibility for the care of grandchildren. Current economic conditions make it necessary for many young adults who have left home to return (Long & Porter, 1984).

Some women also care for their grandchildren because of the illness, incapacity, or death of the child's parents. In some ethnic groups, active grandmothering is common and considered normative. Black women, for example, commonly experience raising their children's children, whether as their own or as their grandchildren. Grandmothers often play a positive role in single-parent families. Researchers have found that preschoolers whose mothers were adolescents performed at a higher level when their relatives (especially their maternal grandmother) participated in child rearing (Spurlock, 1984).

Lack of involvement in an extended family appears to be peculiar to white middle-class culture. In one survey of women over 60 in the American Southwest, 50 percent of the Native-American and 32 percent of Latina respondents reported taking care of children versus only 14 percent of the Anglo respondents (Harris, Begay, & Page, 1989). Black women tend to report significant familial networks even when they are single and living alone (Spurlock, 1984). In fact, having a spouse had little influence on the number of socially supportive relationships or the most important sources of financial assistance reported (Brown & Gary, 1985). Unmarried black mothers reported visiting and maintaining contact with relatives more than married mothers did (McAdoo, 1980). However, they reported no difference in the amount of help that they received.

Care for Aging Parents

The impact of sexism. In our culture, women are expected to tend to their elderly parents when they are ill, provide transportation to the doctor's office, and be on call for any emergency (Stueve & O'Donnell, 1984). In a phone survey of 315 adults living in western Alabama, such gender-stereotypic assumptions were confirmed. Both women and men agreed that it was more appropriate for an employed son to help his infirm parent with yard work, whereas it was more appropriate for a similarly employed daughter to assist with housework and to bring meals to her mother's home (Roff & Klemmack, 1986). Consider the amount of time and effort that will have to be expended by daughters versus sons in their "gender-appropriate" caretaking tasks!

Daughters provide more support to older parents than sons do. They help by running errands, giving custodial care, and taking older parents into their home. In a study in Quebec, daughters also had more contact with formal authorities on behalf of the elderly. For these women, other obligations did not reduce their amount of assistance although it did reduce the amount of time that they spent providing it. Employed women provided as much care as unemployed women. For men, in contrast, other obligations reduced both helping and time. The group that spent the least time on caregiving were single men with children and married men without children (Jutras & Veilleux, 1991).

When there are no daughters, sons do not necessarily step in. Daughters who were only children were found to be twice as likely as only sons to become caregivers (Coward & Dwyer, 1990). When sons did involve themselves in the care of their elderly parents, they were likely to wind up as "care managers" (Montgomery & Kamo, 1989). Widows without daughters tended to receive such support from daughters-in-law, sisters, female kin, or friends and neighbors (O'Bryant, 1988). These gender differences probably stem from the lower expectation of involvement by both the sons themselves and by others.

The Impact of Class. Daughters from working-class backgrounds are more likely to live with or near parents and to have built up patterns of interdependence and helping out. By contrast, middle-class daughters, particularly those women who left home to attend college, are more likely to draw strict boundaries between their own nuclear families and those of their parents and to have constructed lives that are separate from those of parents and siblings (Stueve & O'Donnell, 1984). For working-class women, parents are seen as part of the immediate family, and their needs are seen as part of the fabric of daily life. The extent to which they are unaware of providing care is illustrated by the following case study.

> Nora Dubchek lives two miles away from her widowed father. She works part time as a hairdresser, and her husband is a self-employed gardener. When she was first asked if her father had come to rely on her, she replied, "No, no. Only when he doesn't feel well. You know, I will sometimes take him to the post office, or drive him here, or go over and do a few things in the house." When asked how often she saw her father, however, she went on to say, "Oh, I see him every day. I was there this morning. This morning I did the dishes for him because he has a bad hand. And I just talked to him." Later in the conversation, it came out that Mrs. Dubchek did many other things for her father—she tends to home repairs, makes sure his house is properly cleaned, takes him places in bad weather, and nudges her brothers and children to make regular visits. She has thought about her father's advancing age and the possibility that at some point he may not be able to live alone. She anticipates becoming more involved in his life, even to the point of establishing a joint residence (Stueve & O'Donnell, 1984, p. 217).

Middle-class parents and daughters believed more than those from the working class that parents can be taken care of by people other than family members. Parents were seen as having the financial resources to purchase needed services and were also perceived as being accustomed to making arrangements without the help of their children. Among daughters who lived within an hour's drive of parents, full-time employed women provided less assistance and visited less often (Stueve & O'Donnell, 1984).

The Woman in the Middle: Myths and Realities. Demographic changes involving fewer children and longer life spans have increased the possibility that women in their fifties will have living parents. Because of smaller families, the number of daughters per mother decreased from 1.8 per mother in 1930 to 1.2 in 1970 (O'Bryant, 1988). A new version of the problems associated with women's involvement in multiple roles is the conception of "the woman in the middle" (Brody, 1981). This label describes the middle-aged woman who must cope simultaneously with the needs of elderly parents and teenaged children. Her burdens have been richly detailed by the popular media (see Figure 13.4).

This concept of the "woman in the middle" may be a construction of mainstream society's preoccupation with autonomy and independence. As we mentioned earlier in this chapter, ethnic minority groups seem to have a more interdependent view of relationships between the generations. Black women take relatives into their homes at twice the rate of their white age peers (Beck & Beck, 1989). Black middle-age women provide both economic and social support for both older and younger relatives. While these practices are probably partly a result of economic necessity, they also provide psychological benefits for the elderly that help explain why older African Americans are more satisfied with their lives than older white peers.

Periods of simultaneous heavy demands appear to be relatively rare

FIGURE 13.4. An example of negative images of the caretaking role.

"Your husband is lucky to have you to take care of him at home, Mrs. Jacobs."

FIGURE 13.5. No comment.

(Baruch, 1984). Our assumption that elderly parents are typically needy and dependent is also not correct. The majority of older people are in good health. In a survey conducted in 1975, almost 70 percent of people over 65 rated their health as excellent or good (Stueve & O'Donnell, 1984). Moreover, women—who comprise the largest part of the population over 65—report sizeable networks of women their own age who provide mutual support (O'Bryant, 1988). Little attention has been paid to how this "society of women" functions to facilitate adjustment to the problems of aging.

Women constitute 71 percent of family caregivers; they are "the invisible laborers without whom neither the health care system nor the patient could survive" (Polansky, 1975–1975). Caregiving results in isolation as well as loss of freedom and privacy. This is especially true for those women who take on the care of their partners who have become incapacitated or chronically ill (Doress et al., 1987). Former friends and children may withdraw their support because they cannot deal with the changes illness has wrought.

Our society assumes that wives will care for their incapacitated husbands (see Figure 13.5). Indeed, they may have little choice about the matter, and little attention has been paid to their emotional or physical needs.

> I cry a lot because I never thought it would be this way. I didn't expect to be mopping up the bathroom, changing him, doing laundry all the time. I was taking care of babies at twenty; now I'm taking care of my husband.
>
> People tell me he deserves all the care I can give him because he's such a nice person and was always so good to me. Well, I'm a nice person and have always been good to him—what do I deserve? (Doress et al., 1987, pp. 199–200).

Caregiving when a woman resents it or is overwhelmed by economic and social responsibilities is a great burden—one that our society has preferred to ignore.

On the other hand, some women find satisfaction in caring for someone they love.

> My mother never had any joy, only hard work and struggle. I tried to make it up to her, to do things for her and to give her things, and felt guilty because I couldn't take away the old pains and troubles and make her into a happy person. But at least I was able to take care of her in her old age. I have no guilt about that. And she died at home, in my house, where I could say goodbye to her in my own way and in my own space. That was five years ago, and as I get older I see more and more of my mother in myself, and that's okay because she was a wonderful woman and I love her (a woman in her fifties, in Doress et al., 1987, p. 203).

Caring for and losing a parent when a woman is older can seem like a part of the natural timing of events. Women who are "on time" with respect to the age of their parents when they were born may find such transitions as the aging and death of their parents easier. They have friends and acquaintances who have had similar experiences (Stueve & O'Donnell, 1984).

Feelings about the personal costs of caregiving are very different from one woman to another. It is important that society permit women to have as many choices as possible. These include the availability of full- and part-time support systems to relieve the primary caregiver. Pressures on women who are not employed outside the home are particularly intense. They often feel they must be endlessly available to others, and when they do feel resentful or overwhelmed about their obligations, they feel they have failed (Baruch, 1984). These feelings result from societal assumptions that only women should and can provide care.

Loss of a Significant Other

Widowhood. Differences in the life expectancy of women and men, combined with a marital pattern in which women marry men older than themselves, mean that women are more likely to become widowed than men. The average widow lives for eighteen years after her husband's death (Silverman, 1981). Men who lose their wives are more apt to remarry than women who lose their husbands.

The experience of widowhood varies according to the time of life when it occurs. Younger women usually recover from their loss better than older women do. The older women may be in ill health themselves or in economically straitened circumstances. One study of 226 women between the ages of 60 and 89 who had been widowed from seven to twenty-one months found that positive feelings were associated with greater religious involvement, a larger number of siblings, and support from children and families (McGloshen & O'Bryant, 1988). Negative feelings were associated with additional deaths among family or friends, housing dissatisfaction, and a history of employment outside the home during marriage. No explanation was given for the latter finding.

We might expect black women and women from other groups with close relational networks to be less devastated by widowhood, but little attention has been paid to race and class differences in this area. Spousal relationships appear to play a comparatively less important role in black women's than in white women's lives (Brown & Gary, 1985). Black women may rely less on male support because the greater vulnerability of black men to poor health makes it likely that these women will face middle age as a widow or with the added responsibilities of a chronically ill spouse (Spurlock, 1984).

Ethnicity and class differences are, of course, intertwined with economic need. Social security pays a widow with dependent children a caretaker's allowance, but only until the children reach age 18. This system does not supplement a widow's income again until she reaches age 60 (50 if she is disabled). Private pensions and life insurance contribute to widows' economic well-being in only a small percentage of cases. Moreover, if a woman has followed a traditional life path, the time she has spent out of the labor force reduces the number of years used to compute her retirement benefits (Long & Porter, 1984). Forty percent of widows fall into poverty for at least some time during the first five years after their husbands die (Morgan, 1989).

Nevertheless, women cope better with the loss of a spouse than men do (Gove & Shin, 1989). Widowed women have higher levels of happiness, life satisfaction, and home life satisfaction than widowed men. These data are consistent with findings showing that widowhood is a much higher predictor of suicide for older men than for older women (Canetto, 1992). Older men depend on their wives for emotional support, personal care, and running of the home. These losses appear to be psychologically more devastating than the economic losses sustained by women who have lost their husbands.

Loss of Lesbian Life-Partner. Lesbians who have lost their companions may suffer additional stresses because the relationship is not publicly acknowledged. Women who have lost a lover may have to carry on without the usual social supports offered to widows. Even when the relationship is an open one, friends may not be aware of the depth of the loss. As one woman recounted:

> Recently, I vacationed with friends who had been friends also with my deceased partner-in-life. A guest arrived with slides of earlier vacations, including pictures of my lover. I objected that if I had been a man who had been recently widowed, they surely would have asked if I would object to showing the pictures. One friend responded that she wanted very much to see them. She blanched when I suggested she might feel differently after the death of her husband. Clearly, she thought that my relationship with Karen differed from her marriage; she evidently also thought my love differed from her friendship with Karen only by degree. Heterosexuals really do not understand what lesbians feel for their partners, even when they know us well. All of these friends had

known Karen and me as lovers and had sent me bereavement condolences when Karen died (in Doress et al., 1987, p. 139).

The loss of a significant other of either sex to whom a woman has not been married is multiplied by the lack of legal acknowledgment of such relationships. The lover of the departed person may find herself deprived of economic resources she has long shared. And, of course, she receives no spousal benefits of any kind.

The Reentry Woman

Life at midlife and beyond should not be considered merely a catalog of losses. "Women's history is filled with stories about women for whom life began at 40—or thereabouts. Grandma Moses's late start was somewhat excessive—at age 78—but the fact that her serious work began late is not atypical for her sex" (Alington & Troll, 1984, p. 196). In some cases, personal misfortune serves as a catalyst for new kinds of achievement. For example, divorced women are disproportionately represented among the ranks of adult students, and they are noticeably more committed, both as students and workers, than any other group (Alington & Troll, 1984).

Midlife achievement may be due to a reduction in family responsibilities or because the woman did not have an opportunity to indulge her passions for personal achievement earlier in life. Two-thirds of all adults who have returned to school (the majority of whom are women) reported that they had wanted to enroll sooner than they actually did (Schlossberg, 1984). They were impeded by institutional barriers, such as requirements that students take at least twelve credits or the lack of evening courses.

Contrary to assumptions that an older life stage is one of limited choice and few opportunities, many women choose to do new things and expose themselves to new experiences. Rachel Siegel (1993) listed an exciting catalog of achievements provided by a group of fifty-six women between the ages of 60 and 70.

> Emalu has published a book of her newly written poems; Betty and Laura took a study tour to Antarctica; Charlotte and her husband attend a different Elder Hostel every year; Bev gave herself a cruise in Norwegian waters for her 60th birthday; Laci is taking piano lessons and has given two recitals; Carol learned Italian before taking a sabbatical year in Rome. . . .
>
> Shevy Healy and Vera Martin took on leadership roles in creating the Old Lesbians Organizing Committee. Lydia Peyton tutors children in her granddaughter's elementary school. Lucille Parker, an African-American civil service retiree, helped create new projects at her senior center . . . (Siegel, p. 181).

Midlife achievement may also be a result of a personality change in the direction of assertive independence that occurs in midlife women. There is evidence that women who attend college at a nontraditional age are more assertive, and their assertiveness leads them to expect and receive more spousal support (De Groot, 1980).

As life expectancies continue to increase and health care helps women to live healthier lives in their fifties and beyond, we can expect that the ranks of those who are "off time" in their years of peak achievement will continue to grow. Already we are finding such women as the deans of law schools (Barbara Aronstein Black, Columbia University), the authors of best-selling books (Belva Plain), and at the forefront of organizations for social change (Maggie Kuhn). One recent study has found that more women in their early fifties rated their lives as first-rate than either younger or older women in their sample (Mitchell & Helson, 1990). For economically advantaged women, midlife may indeed be prime time.

PSYCHOLOGICAL WELL-BEING IN THE SECOND HALF OF LIFE

Older Women and Poverty

Whether a woman is able to lead a satisfying and rewarding life in her middle and later years depends on a combination of material and psychological factors. Not surprisingly, money is an important material factor. Today's older women are nearly twice as likely to be existing on incomes below the poverty level as same-age men, and black and Latina women are worse off than white women. Overall, more than one elderly woman in six is poor. According to U.S. census data, 82 percent of elderly black women are in "poor" or "near-poor" categories (Grambs, 1989).

The most important single factor pushing older women into poverty is widowhood. A husband's pension usually ends with his death, and the couple may have exhausted their savings during his final illness. Women who have earned their own incomes do not necessarily fare better, however. The cumulative effect of a lifetime of low-paying, low-status work—the pattern documented in Chapter 12—results in low social security benefits and inadequate pension coverage for retired women. In 1984, only 20 percent of women over 65 had pensions, and the median amount was $233 a month (Grambs, 1989) (see Box 13.2).

Younger cohorts of women will have had more years of work experience than the currently retired; you might expect that poverty in old age will be less likely for them. However, the income gap for retired men and women has actually widened in the last decade. "Midlife women need to be vigilant lest when they reach old age they will be no better off than their mothers and grandmothers before them" (Grambs, 1989, p. 179).

Friendship and Social Support

Perhaps the most important psychological factor in satisfaction during later life is connections with other people. Loneliness is one of the most feared consequences of aging. Women seem to be at an advantage over men in creating and sustaining networks of friends. Women's support networks are a valuable resource in aging. Their friendships help to maintain physical health, increase psychological adjustment and satisfaction, and contribute to continued psychological growth in old age.

Box 13.2 Social Security

She knows a cashier who
blushes and lets her use
food stamps to buy tulip
bulbs and rose bushes.

We smile each morning as I
pass her—her hand always
married to some stick
or hoe, or rake.

One morning I shout,
"I'm not skinny like
you so I've gotta run
two miles each day."

She begs me closer, whispers
to my flesh, "All you need,
honey, is to be on welfare
and love roses."

Poem by Barbara Bolz. Source: Martz, 1987. Reprinted with permission.

Many research studies have shown that women of all ages are more likely to have close friends, to confide intimate matters to their friends, and to have a varied circle of friends than men are (Grambs, 1989; Lewittes, 1988). In a study of more than 400 elderly widows, contact with their adult children was unrelated to morale, while contact with friends and neighbors was correlated with decreased loneliness, less worrying, and feeling useful and respected. Relationships with friends seem to be more important than family contacts because they are voluntarily chosen and based on common interests. Interacting with friends is a boost to one's sense of efficacy and self-esteem in old age.

Women maintain and widen their friendship networks even when they are limited in their mobility. In a study of elderly residents in a retirement home, it was found that the women relied on the telephone to "keep in touch" with old friends and made new friends in nearby rooms (Hochschild, 1978). Women are probably being socialized for affiliation no less today than they ever were. We can predict that younger cohorts of women will continue to rely on their connectedness with friends as they grow older, and we can speculate that they will find "keeping in touch" easier with advances in communication technology. If it seems farfetched to imagine Great-Grandma logging onto her international computer network from her bedside chair in a retirement home, remember that future cohorts of elderly women will have grown up with such technology.

ACTIVISM AND FEMINISM AMONG OLDER WOMEN

Midlife is a time when many women feel freed from the constraints of femininity. We have already pointed out that the "empty nest" is usually experienced with relief and joy, and that menopause is rarely a major concern. Just as they outgrow their early roles and definitions, midlife women may also outgrow a need to conform to social pressures to be passive and self-sacrificing. In general, older people give less gender-typed descriptions of themselves to researchers than younger people (Sinnott, 1984). Women are more likely to describe themselves as competent and autonomous, and men to describe themselves as expressive (Fischer & Narus, 1981).

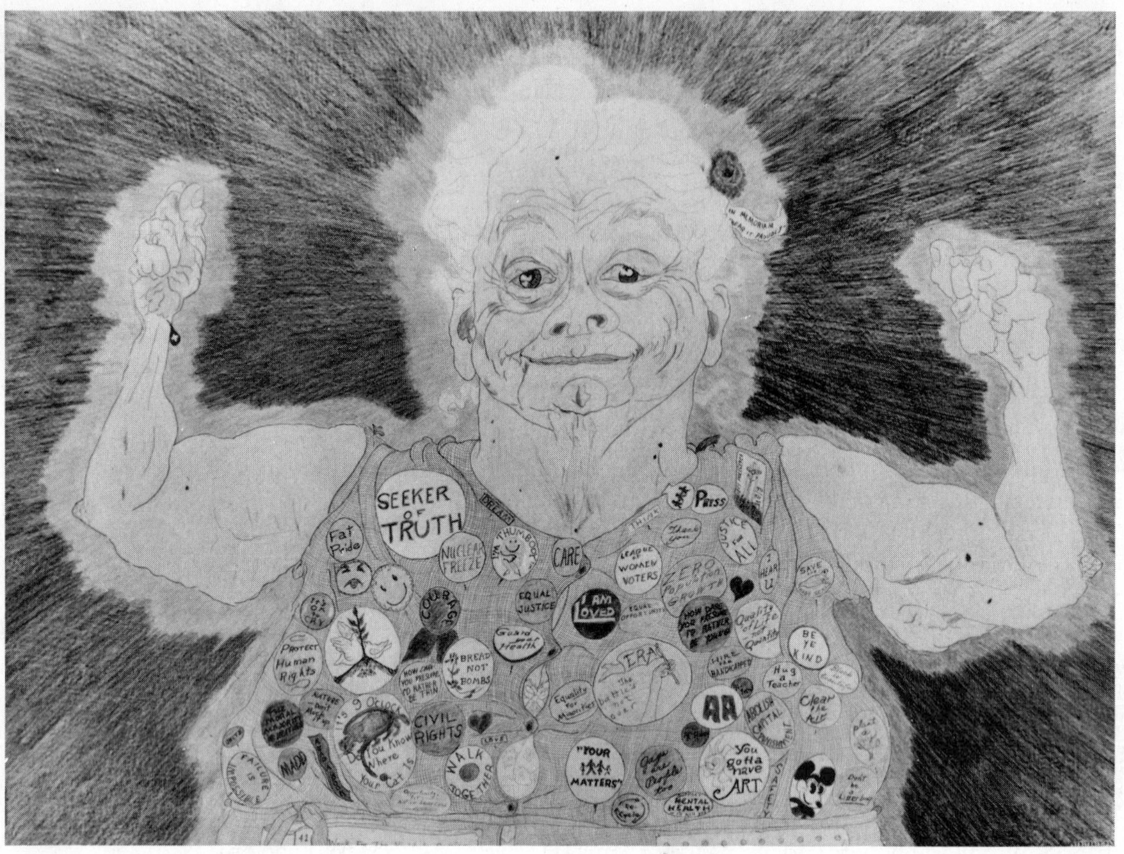

FIGURE 13.6. Older women as activists: An alternative view.

Another view of the freedom of middle and later life for women is shown in Figure 13.6. Elizabeth Layton began her life as an artist in 1977 at the age of 68. Her work, exhibited nationally since 1980, has won many honors. Although depicting aging is taboo in the art world, "Layton is able to tackle such difficult content because she doesn't give a damn about the art world. She has unselfconsciously mastered the fusion of personal and political that so many progressive artists strive for." In this radiant self-portrait, *Her Strength Is in Her Convictions,* Layton shows off a chestful of political buttons (Lippard, 1986).

As family and job pressures recede for midlife women, activism and political involvement of all kinds may increase. This will probably be especially true of cohorts of women now entering middle and later life, because they have grown up with important social movements like the civil rights movement, the women's movement, the antinuclear and antiwar movements, and environmental activism.

People aged 55 to 64 are now more likely to exercise political power by voting than any other segment of the population. The percentage of elderly in the American population is larger than at any other time in history and is still increasing (Grambs, 1989). Thus, simple demographics suggest an increasingly important role in public life for older women.

The political activism of older people is often focused on the position of the elderly in society. Activist Maggie Kuhn founded the Gray Panthers after she was forced to retire at the age of 65. Her organization is now a strong national advocacy group for the elderly. The Older Women's League (OWL) lobbies effectively on policy issues affecting older women. The American Association of Retired Persons, another powerful lobbying group, has a special program on women's concerns. SAGE (Senior Action in a Gay Environment) provides services and information for older gay men and lesbians (Macdonald & Rich, 1983). "As women become more sensitive to their vulnerability in old age and more educated in public affairs, we can expect both more participation and more leadership from older women" (Grambs, 1989, p. 101).

Among women who become activists against social injustice, many see their activism as connected to their feminism. A recent interview study has chronicled the activism of fourteen women leaders on issues such as toxic waste, neighborhood community life, education for disadvantaged children, auto safety, and nuclear weapons. These women are a diverse group ranging from well-to-do white Jewish suburbanites to a former Catholic nun working in Appalachia and the black daughter of a Virginia sharecropper. They conceived of their feminism broadly, believing that "everything is connected," and that social activism is a form of nurturing others. One reported that she had started seeing the nuclear issue in terms of her children; another said that she had never thought of herself as a feminist, but

> when I have to fight for my children, I do, and I guess I've always been a feminist in my own way; I've always fought for what I think is important. To me, that's what it means to be a feminist—being able to fight for your rights, your community, your children, and other women (Garland, 1988, p. xxi).

Though psychologists are beginning to view midlife as a time of growth and expansion of roles for women, rather than a time of loss and decline, there is virtually no psychological research on the political consciousness and activism of midlife women. In order to begin understanding the meaning that political and social events have for women, feminist psychologists Abigail Stewart and Sharon Gold-Steinberg (1990) have recommended the use of intensive case studies. In their own study of three women who had graduated from college in 1964, they found several factors that seemed to have influenced political consciousness in later life. These included growing up in a politically aware family; political activity in adolescence and young adulthood; the desire to make a contribution to the world; experiences as a parent; and access at midlife to time, energy, and resources. Interviews and case studies can help researchers conceptualize this new area of research in ways that are meaningful to women.

In a powerful message to feminists of all ages who want to be active on behalf of older women, Barbara Macdonald cautions that our activism must be based on a real knowledge of women in all their diversity, not on stereotypes or our own fears of aging (Macdonald & Rich, 1983). She advises each of us not to talk about "the woman's movement" until all the invisible women are present—all races and cultures, and *all ages* of all races and cultures. And she reminds us that an old woman has not always been old. She is in the process of discovering what 70, 80, and 90 mean. As more and more old women talk and write about the reality of this process, in a world that negates them, we will all discover how revolutionary that is.

CONNECTING THEMES

1. Women's and men's lives are different because of sexism rather than sex. The consequences of these differences are clear when we look at the roles and role transitions of middle and later life. Both the timing and nature of roles differ greatly, so that aging has very different implications for women and men.
2. The power to name is particularly clear in the identification of menopause as synonymous for aging. This has made aging appear to be more destructive for women than for men and has put women at risk for many medical procedures that cannot "cure" aging.
3. Models of aging are based almost entirely on white middle-class women in the United States. Cross-ethnic and cross-cultural studies indicate that consequences of aging are not determined by biology.
4. Social change is impeded by U.S. views of individualism and autonomy. Successful transitions from midlife to beyond are facilitated by social support systems and collectivistic philosophies. However, little research has been done in this area.

SUGGESTED READINGS

DATAN, NANCY, A. ANTONOVSKY, and B. MAOZ, (1981). *A time to reap: The middle age of women in five Israeli subcultures.* Baltimore: Johns Hopkins. In analyzing how the meaning of the "empty nest" is socially and culturally constructed, this book goes beyond the particular cultures studied to show how researchers' beliefs about women influence the questions they can ask and the answers they can find. A wise blend of anthropology, sociology, and psychology.

DORESS-WORTERS, P. B., and D. N. SIEGAL, (1994). *The new ourselves growing older.* New York: Simon & Schuster. A new edition of the popular book by and for women, this work relies on an excellent base of scholarship and research, yet avoids jargon. It has many excellent and practical suggestions for understanding and coping with the physical and social changes of the second half of life.

GRAMBS, JEAN D., (1989). *Women over forty: Visions and realities.* New York: Springer. A readable book on normal aging in women. Recent research in psychology, sociology, anthropology, gerontology, medicine, and other fields is thoroughly covered, yet the author also analyzes critically the gaps and biases in existing research. The effects of cohort and situational influences on older women are given full weight.

CHAPTER 14

Violence Against Women

PORNOGRAPHY
- Defining Pornography
- Negative Effects of Pornography
- Social Implications

INCEST
- Defining Incest
- Frequency of Incest
- Characteristics of Incest
- Who Commits Incest?
- Who Are the Victims?
- Consequences for the Survivor
- Steps to Protect Children and Treat Victims

COURTSHIP VIOLENCE
- Defining Courtship Violence
- Frequency of Courtship Violence
- Inflicting and Sustaining Courtship Violence
- When Is Courtship Violence Committed?
- Consequences of Courtship Violence
- Steps to Take

ACQUAINTANCE SEXUAL ASSAULT AND RAPE
- Defining Sexual Assault
- Frequency of Sexual Assault
- Who Is at Risk?
- Who Commits Sexual Assaults?
- When is a Sexual Assault Likely?
- Consequences for the Victim
- Steps to Take

WIFE ABUSE
- Wife Abuse versus Spouse Abuse
- Frequency of Wife Abuse
- Who Commits Wife Abuse?
- Who Are the Victims?
- Consequences for the Victim
- Steps to Take

CONCLUSION

CONNECTING THEMES

SUGGESTED READINGS

every 3 minutes a woman is beaten
every five minutes a
woman is raped/every ten minutes
a lil girl is molested
yet i rode the subway today
i sat next to an old man who may have beaten his old wife
3 minutes ago or 3 days/30 years ago
he might have sodomized his
daughter but i sat there

This chapter was contributed by Jacquelyn Weygandt White, Patricia L. N. Donat, and Barrie Bondurant.

cuz the young men on the train
might beat some young women
later in the day or tomorrow
I might not shut my door fast
enuf/push hard enuf
every 3 minutes it happens...
every three minutes
every five minutes
every ten minutes
every day

—NTOZAKE SHANGE, *1978, pp. 114, 117.*

There is no difference between being raped
and being pushed down a flight of cement steps
except that the wounds also bleed inside.

There is no difference between being raped
and being run over by a truck
except that afterward men ask if you enjoyed it.

There is no difference between being raped
and being bitten on the ankle by a rattlesnake
except that people ask if your skirt was short
and why were you out alone anyhow.

There is no difference between being raped
and going head first through a windshield
except that afterward you are afraid
not of cars
but of half the human race.

—MARGE PIERCY, *1976; In* Living in the open, *88–89, New York: Knopf.*

One of the most, if not the most, devastating consequences of gender inequality is violence toward women. Women are victimized by nonintimate violence (i.e., robbery, burglary, aggravated assault, forcible rape, and murder) and intimate violence (i.e., child abuse, incest, courtship violence, acquaintance rape, battering, marital rape, and elder abuse). For many reasons, which we will discuss in this chapter, the risk of intimate victimization is significantly greater for women than for men. Violence takes many forms, from psychological intimidation and coercion through name calling, moderate physical violence (pushing, shoving, slapping), to severe physical violence (beating, using weapons) and sexual assault. Women are victimized by strangers, acquaintances, friends, and relatives, including fathers, brothers, and husbands. The consequences are psychological and physical, short term and long term. (See Table 14.1.) In all analyses of violence against women a disturbing conclusion is unavoidable: We live in a society that tolerates and even sanctions men's authority and entitlement to subdue and control a woman against her will. Until quite recently, women were reluctant to report, and society failed to acknowledge, the extent of intimate victimization.

Although most intimate violence qualifies as crime, a historical tradition that has condoned violence within the family has created strong forces toward secrecy that oppose disclosure of such incidents into public record. . . . Coverup may be facilitated by the forced secrecy that is almost uniformly demanded by perpetrators of abuse. That victims were silent is attested by the small proportion of victims who informed authorities. In fact, only 2% of intrafamilial child sexual abuse, 6% of extrafamilial sexual abuse, and 5% to 8% of adult sexual assault cases were reported to police according to recent victimization studies. By comparison, 61.5% of the robberies and 82.5% of the burglaries were reported (Koss, 1990, pp. 374–375).

The evidence documenting violence against women is so compelling that many experts have suggested that the United States is experiencing an epidemic. Experts also suggest that the largest single group of posttraumatic stress disorder sufferers are female sexual abuse and assault victims (Foa, Olasov, & Steketee, 1987). Taken together it is not surprising that violence against women is one of the top three priorities identified in a report establishing a national mental health agenda for women (Russo, 1985). In response to this agenda, the American Psychological Association appointed a task force on violence against women, which has published *No Safe Haven*, the most comprehensive review of the research to date (Koss, Goodman, Fitzgerald, Russo, Keita, & Browne, 1994).

As previous chapters have shown, messages that teach and reinforce gender stereotypes and roles come from many sources. The same is true regarding

TABLE 14.1. Effects of Crime on Women

	Had Nervous Breakdown	Thought Seriously about Suicide	Attempted Suicide
Nonvictims	3.3%	6.8%	2.2%
Victims of:			
Attempted robbery	0.0%	9.1%	12.1%
Completed robbery	7.7%	10.8%	3.1%
Aggravated assault	2.1%	14.9%	4.3%
Attempted sexual molestation	5.4%	32.4%	8.1%
Completed sexual molestation	1.8%	21.8%	3.6%
Attempted rape	8.9%	29.1%	8.9%
Completed rape	16.0%	44.0%	19.2%

Source: From Dean Kilpatrick et al., "Mental health correlates of criminal victimization: A random survey," *Journal of Consulting and Clinical Psychology, 53,* 866–873. Copyright © 1985 by the American Psychological Association. Reprinted with permission.

messages about men's right to dominate and control women using intimidating, coercive, and physically forceful tactics, and women's obligation to acquiesce. These messages are learned at a very young age and reinforced as children grow to adulthood and begin to form intimate relationships of their own. The home is where children learn how to perceive and treat themselves, others, and the world. Children both observe and experience violence in the home—they learn that people who love each other also hurt each other. Themes of male domination are reinforced further, and frequently romanticized, in the media—books, movies, television programs. In this context, pornography plays a particularly insidious role in socially sanctioning messages that condone the objectification and domination of women.

As children grow to adolescence, society provides a dating script that offers a blueprint for developing and rehearsing heterosexual skills that they will subsequently take into their own marriages and model for their children. In this chapter we suggest that intimate violence is learned and maintained within a broader social context that has tolerated violence against women. We begin our discussion with an examination of media images, especially in pornography and its influences on consumers. Given our developmental perspective, we then discuss, in turn, child sexual abuse—incest in particular—dating violence, acquaintance rape, and wife battering.

During this discussion, please keep in mind that obtaining accurate information on violence against women is not always easy. The types of violence we are discussing in this chapter cannot be studied in the laboratory using the traditional methods of experimental psychology. Rather, researchers must depend on various sources, each with its own limitations. One source, crime statistics, does not include episodes of violence that are not reported to the police. Another source, large-scale surveys, depends on who is sampled, how questions are asked, and respondents' willingness to disclose. Samples of convenience, such as women who go to shelters, call crisis hot lines, or seek mental health services, provide another source of information regarding victimization experiences; again, the information obtained depends on who was interviewed and what they are willing to reveal about their past experiences. In general, we believe that crime statistics underestimate the incidence and prevalence, whereas samples of convenience may result in inflated estimates because women without victimization histories are less likely to be included in these studies. On the other hand, large-scale surveys, based on random samples of women, probably yield more accurate estimates, though these too are probably on the conservative side due to possible denial or memory loss.

When we describe the characteristics that distinguish victims from nonvictims and perpetrators from nonperpetrators we are not talking about static sex differences (as discussed in Chapter 3). Rather, as with the discussion of power in Chapter 5, we believe that gender-related patterns in intimate violence strongly reflect status differences between women and men. Cultural norms that prescribe men as more powerful than women and power differences in individual relationships contribute to the dynamic gendering process that can result in violence by the more powerful individual toward the less powerful.

PORNOGRAPHY

Nowhere is the victimization of women in the media more obvious than in the pornographic literature that is prevalent in our society. "Pornography is a media equivalent to the crime of rape. It is the sexual expression of power and anger" (Groth & Birnbaum, 1979). Pornography is readily available in most bookstores and convenience stores across the nation and grosses millions of dollars as a business annually. *Playboy, Penthouse,* and *Hustler* are just a few of the widely read magazines available. Video pornography also is available on cable television and in video stores.

Some men first show an interest in these types of magazines at a very young age and continue to consume this material as they grow older. The average boy is first exposed to pornography before the age of 12 (Check & Maxwell, 1992). Furthermore, by junior high school, 87 percent of boys report that they have viewed video pornography (Check & Maxwell, 1992). Now, with the advent of computer pornography and internet bulletin boards, pornographic images are increasingly accessible. Although the typical patriarchal view states that looking at pornography is just "boys being boys," research on pornography suggests it may be harmful to the observer and the women it portrays.

Defining Pornography

Before going any further it may be helpful to clarify what is meant by the word "pornography." Not all sexually explicit material is pornographic. When talking about sexually explicit material that is not pornographic, we will use the word "erotica." Erotica means "sexual representations that are premised on equality" (Leidholdt & Russell, 1989). Pornography, however, is "material that combines sex and/or the exposure of genitals with *abuse* or *degradation* in a manner that appears to endorse, condone, or encourage such behavior" (Russell, 1993, pp. 2–3). This distinction between erotica and pornography is an important one and has been supported empirically (Saunders & Naus, 1993).

Indeed, pornography doesn't just illustrate women being degraded or abused—the filming or photographing of pornography itself may involve women being forced, abused, or mutilated (Russell, 1993). At a commission hearing in Los Angeles, one witness testified about "how women and young girls were tortured and suffered permanent physical injuries to answer publisher demands for photographs depicting sadomasochistic abuse" (Attorney General's Commission, 1986, p. 787). Linda Marchiano, a former star of pornographic movies like *Deep Throat*, has written two books, *Ordeal* (1980) and *Out of Bondage* (1986), that document her rape during the filming of the movie. Linda Marchiano has testified that she was virtually held prisoner and forced either to participate in the filming or to face severe beatings. "So many people say that in *Deep Throat* I have a smile on my face and look as though I'm really enjoying myself. No one ever asked me how those bruises got on my body. . . . Every time someone sees *Deep Throat*, they're seeing me being raped" (in Blakely, 1985, p. 231).

Negative Effects of Pornography

Even erotic materials may have a negative effect on the consumer. Erotic and pornographic materials often idealize sexual relationships. These idealized depictions may decrease the consumer's sexual satisfaction in his or her own relationships. Viewing erotic material in general makes people more dissatisfied with their own sexuality and that of their partner (Weaver, Masland, & Zillmann, 1984). In addition, Dolf Zillmann and Jennings Bryant (1986) found that exposure to nonviolent pornography "arouses an interest in and creates a taste for pornography that portrays less commonly practiced sexual activities, including those involving the infliction of pain" (p. 578). This finding was replicated by Clive Davis and Robert Bauserman (1993). Repeated exposure to sexually explicit materials tended to make the types of behavior, beliefs, and attitudes that were depicted more accepted among participants in their study.

Pornography not only influences dissatisfaction with oneself and one's partner, but it can also have an influence on the way men view women in general. Men who view violent and degrading pornography tend to show a decreased sensitivity to women, particularly women portrayed as being the victims of a sexual assault. The woman is dehumanized and is viewed more as an object than as a person with feelings, needs, and desires. James Check and Neil Malamuth (1985) found that college men exposed to pornography prior to being shown a scene from a rape trial were more likely to perceive the rape victim as having experienced less trauma and as having enjoyed the experience more than men who were not exposed to pornography. Women come to be viewed as less human and as objects for male pleasure rather than active agents in their own sexuality.

> Even the "softest" pornographic materials could not be defined as benignly as "two naked people caressing each other." No, sex or nudity alone is not violence, but the continual stereotyping of women as sex objects, as the always willing, vulnerable, and youthful sexual playthings of men, is violence, and it is this stereotype that the majority of pornography promotes. Pornography is just one link in the chain of a patriarchal culture that subordinates women, just one interdependent element in a society where one in four women are sexually assaulted, a society where women are more likely than professional soldiers to live lives of violence (Jensen, 1991).

Pornography also exploits the history of racism in this country by depicting stereotypic images of men and women of color. Asian women are portrayed as malleable dolls; Latin women as sexually insatiable yet submissive; black women as savage sexual animals (Leidholdt, 1981). Similarly, black men are portrayed as dehumanized, well-endowed sexual predators (Cowan & Campbell, 1994). Many of these images are grounded in this country's history of slavery. In fact, historical depictions of African-American women parallel pornographic images and may very well have served as the foundation upon which contemporary pornography's objectification, domination, and control of women's images are based (Collins, 1993). This type of pornography only

FIGURE 14.1. Women unite to fight pornography in their neighborhood.

serves to perpetuate racist–sexist stereotypes and behavior; yet, little has been done to curb its dissemination (Mayall & Russell, 1993).

Steady use of pornography may lead to the development of and/or intensification of rape fantasies that have been shown in turn to influence behavior. Neil Malamuth (1981) found that exposure to violent pornography increased violent rape fantasies. Moreover, some rapists report that they did not have violent rape fantasies until they began viewing pornography (Beneke, 1982). One of the rapists interviewed by Timothy Beneke reported that fantasies of rape, prompted by pornography, provided the impetus for his sexual violence.

Men who view pornography may become more likely to believe rape myths such as "women secretly desire to be raped" and "many women may enjoy rape and other forced sex acts" (Check & Malamuth, 1985). Pornography often reinforces these rape myths and encourages men to fantasize or actually enact the behavior being portrayed. Through pornography's depictions, men may become aroused by sexual violence. Karen Rapaport and C. Dale Posey (1991) found that rapists and sexually coercive men (men who admit using manipulation or threats to engage in sexual activity) are more likely to be aroused by sexually explicit material, including depictions of rape, than men who report only engaging in consensual sexual behavior.

Pornography, then, may condition sexual arousal to depictions of sexually violent acts through repeated association. The more a person sees violence and sexually arousing acts paired, the more likely the person is to become aroused by violent acts in the future. This pairing is typical in pornographic material. Malamuth (1981) reported that college men may become sexually aroused when exposed to scenarios describing a rape. This association is especially dangerous if men become sexually aroused not only by depictions of violent pornography but also by imitating these violent interactions with their partners. Eventually the men may have difficulty achieving peak arousal unless violence and sexuality are paired. Ed Donnerstein (1983) found that 57 percent of college men, following exposure to violent pornographic images, stated some likelihood of raping a woman if they knew they would not be caught. When not previously exposed to pornography, 25–30 percent of college men report a likelihood of raping (Briere & Malamuth, 1983). These findings suggest that a man's perception of his likelihood to rape approximately doubles following exposure to sexually explicit scenes of a woman enjoying a rape.

After viewing pornography, men may imitate the general sexual behavior that they see pictured. Women enjoying sadomasochistic acts and anal intercourse are common in pornographic materials despite the fact that most women do not enjoy such sexual contact. In addition, having men urinate or ejaculate in women's faces is common in pornographic materials, thus emphasizing the degrading images that are prevalent. In some pornographic materials, violence against women appears to be legitimized by the media that portray it and by the society that allows it. As a result, men may feel that the sexually aggressive behaviors that are illustrated are appropriate and sanctioned by society.

Although no studies have been conducted testing whether men imitate sexually aggressive behavior that they see in pornography, the victims of sexual assault have reported being forced to engage in behavior that their attacker had previously viewed. For example, one woman reported,

> I was sexually abused by my foster father from the time I was seven until I was thirteen. He had stacks and stacks of *Playboys*. He would take me to his bedroom or his workshop, show me the pictures, and say "This is what big girls do. If you want to be a big girl, you have to do this, but you can never tell anybody." Then I would have to pose like the woman in the pictures. I also remember being shown a *Playboy* cartoon of a man having sex with a child (Attorney General's Commission, 1986, p. 783).

Social Implications

Women's opinions about pornography's influence on sexually aggressive behavior vary widely. Some women feel that "pornography sexualizes inequality and the hatred of women" (Dworkin & MacKinnon, 1993) and should be censored. Andrea Dworkin and Catharine MacKinnon drafted a model antipornography statute in the early 1980s that stated that pornography was a violation of women's civil rights. The statute, however, was declared unconstitutional by the Supreme Court in 1986 because it was ruled to violate First Amendment rights of freedom of speech.

Other women feel that pornography is a reflection of societal values (Russell, 1988). The restriction of pornography will not be enough to promote change. If society is to eradicate violence against women, attitudes and cultural beliefs about women and sexuality need to change as well. Still other women acknowledge that pornography can be a source of erotic pleasure for many men and women (D'Emilio & Freedman, 1988). These women fear that the antipornography movement once again places women in the position of setting the limits on acceptable images of sexuality. Rather than freeing women to express themselves sexually, they will again be restricted sexually and oppressed if censorship is allowed to occur.

As has been described, pornography may contribute to an increase in the incidents of rape and sexual assault. Indeed, pornography appears to legitimize violence toward women in our culture.

> We live in a society where themes of dominance and submission characterize the essence of maleness and femaleness. The image of a strong, powerful man dominating a female, forcing her to submit sexually, is a powerful erotic image that is probably arousing to most men and women. Rape and sexual assaults are perceived as a logical extension of this culturally ingrained theme (Morokoff, 1983, p. 133).

Even if pornography does *not* lead to sexual aggression, it is still likely to influence the behavior and expectations of men on dates or in marriage. When violence does occur, media images may influence the decisions of police officers, doctors, lawyers, jurors, and judges.

INCEST

In the United States researchers are finding that child sexual abuse is more prevalent than once thought. The sexual abuse of children occurs across all ethnic groups and economic classes. The children who are victimized are not flirtatious or provocative. They do not asked to be abused. What makes the statistics you are about to read even more frightening is the fact that most children are molested by people whom they know and trust. In fact, approximately 75 percent of child molesters are actually family members to whom the child looks for nurturance and protection (Russell, 1986).

Defining Incest

Any exploitive sexual behavior occurring between relatives is labeled incest. This behavior is illegal in the United States, but the law varies from state to state as to what behavior (fondling, oral sex, sexual intercourse, etc.) and what relationships (parent–child, uncle–niece, cousin–cousin, etc.) meet the criteria of incest. In general, incest is considered to be one possible form of child sexual abuse. Abusive incest occurs "when a child of any age is exploited by an older person for his [the perpetrator's] own satisfaction while disregarding the child's own developmental immaturity and inability to understand the sexual behavior" (Steele, 1986, p. 284).

Box 14.1 Recovery of Repressed Memories

Recently controversy has flared in the media regarding whether repressed memories of childhood sexual abuse can be recovered years after the abuse. On one side of the debate, reports of childhood sexual abuse uncovered during the course of psychotherapy are accepted as truth. On the other side of the debate, accused abusers are claiming that these recovered memories are, in fact, false memories created by highly suggestive therapeutic techniques, such as hypnotism and age regression, and that the clients of therapists who used these techniques are suffering from a false memory syndrome.

Unfortunately, there has not been enough research to date to resolve the controversy. Moreover, real cases of childhood sexual abuse may be discounted amidst the controversy. Laboratory studies show that, depending on the circumstances, memories can be recalled accurately, memories can be distorted, or memories can be created. However, for ethical reasons laboratory research cannot deal with memories of the same traumatic nature as childhood sexual abuse. Before the possibility of false memory syndrome can be accepted, further research is needed to:

- Determine whether a distinction between repression and ordinary forgetting is meaningful, and what the nature of the differences are
- Clarify the diagnostic criteria for a "false memory syndrome" and determine its clinical usefulness; at present such a syndrome does not exist in the Diagnostic and Statistical Manual of the American Psychiatric Association
- Evaluate the legal criteria for establishing the validity of repressed memories; for example, a therapist may be more interested in how a person interprets what has happened, whereas the legal system is more interested in observable, verifiable behaviors
- Explore repression and ordinary forgetting in accused perpetrators as well as abuse survivors
- Explore the effects of an unequal distribution of power in child abuse relationships on memory

Frequency of Incest

In recent years, society has become more aware of child sexual abuse, including incest. "Social and personal denial and suppression of such abuse have begun to give way to acknowledgement and validation" of victimization (Courtois, 1988, p. 5). This increased awareness and concern have prompted research efforts to learn more about the frequency, characteristics, and patterns of child sexual abuse (see Box 14.1).

Based on a national sample, David Finkelhor and his colleagues found that 27 percent of women and 16 percent of men had been the victims of child sexual abuse (Finkelhor, Hotaling, Lewis, & Smith, 1990). These percentages translate to approximately 34 million female and 19 million male victims of child sexual abuse in the United States alone.

In her study of incidence and prevalence of sexual abuse among female children, Diana Russell (1986) interviewed 930 women living in San Francisco. Approximately 38 percent of all women in her sample were sexually victimized by the age of 18. Twenty-eight percent were sexually victimized by their own family members. The average duration of the incestuous abuse was four years, with approximately twenty incidents occurring during that time. The abuse began for most women when they were between the ages of 8 and 12, with 41 percent reporting onset of the abuse between the ages of 10 and 13. Similar rates were found by Dean Kilpatrick and Connie Best (1990). They interviewed women on the telephone using random-digit selection of telephone numbers across the country. Kilpatrick and Best found that 25 percent of all women reported being victimized before age 11 and 36 percent between ages 11 and 17. These figures translate to a conservative estimate that one in four women has experienced some form of incestuous abuse.

White and black women are at equal risk for becoming a victim of incest. Gail Wyatt (1985) found that there were no statistical differences between the percentages of black and white women reporting incestuous victimization. Of her sample, 57 percent of black women and 67 percent of white women reported at least one incident of sexual abuse prior to the age of 18 (Wyatt, 1985). Her data, however, revealed that white women were more likely to have experienced sexual abuse earlier in their childhood (Wyatt, 1985).

Characteristics of Incest

Children who are victimized often feel powerless to stop the abuse and feel they have nowhere to turn for help, comfort, and support. The following are accounts of women who shared their experiences as survivors of child sexual abuse in the book, *I Never Told Anyone: Writings by Women Survivors of Child Sexual Abuse* (Bass & Thornton, 1983). Maggie Hoyal recalled this in the story of her experiences, "These Are the Things I Remember":

> He pulled his hand out of my pants and spit on his fingers and rubbed them together. He didn't even seem aware of me. The sound of his spitting made me sick. Then he put his hand back down my pants and started to say something in that singing voice he used. . . . The front door slammed and his hand ripped out of my pants like it was burned. Then he turned on me and whispered harshly, "Don't you say anything to your mother ever. If you do, you'll be sorrier than you've ever been in your life."

Karen Asherah recalled a similar experience in "Daddy Kanagy":

> Then one afternoon when I was just waking up from a nap, he sat next to me on the side of the bed. He put his big heavy fingers in my pants and began rubbing my clitoris. I had no idea what he was trying to do. He asked, yet sort of told me, "It feels good, doesn't it?" All I knew was I couldn't say no. I felt powerless to move. I said Yes.

Most incestuous relationships involve no physical force (68 percent), but some physical restraint or pressure is used in a significant minority of cases (29 percent). Two percent of incestuous relationships involve more serious physical force, such as hitting, and 1 percent of cases involve severe violence, such as beating or hitting forcefully. As described in the previous accounts, however, the child's ability to confront and refuse sexual contact is overwhelmed by the feelings of loyalty and trust that the child may have developed for the perpetrator. The adult is in a position of authority (and often one of trust as well) and communicates to the child that the behavior is acceptable. The adult uses the exclusive, secretive, special relationship to coerce the child into sexual contact, describing the contact as a special time. For children who may otherwise be neglected and emotionally isolated, the special attention and inappropriate sexual contact with the adult may be confusing because of the associated positive feelings.

Who Commits Incest?

Most sexual abuse is perpetrated by men, with female children as the victims. A small percentage, approximately 5 percent, of all sexual abuse of girls and 20 percent of all sexual abuse of boys, however, involves women either as co-perpetrators or sole perpetrators (Russell, 1986). In these cases the women either are observers of the abuse or are directed by men to participate (Finkelhor & Hotaling, 1984) and do not control the extent and duration of the abuse.

Abuse may also be perpetrated by fathers/mothers, uncles/aunts, grandparents, siblings, cousins, and in-laws. In a study by Diana Russell (1986) the prevalence of sexual abuse perpetrated by uncles with their nieces was somewhat more prevalent (4.9 percent of surveyed women) than father–daughter abuse (4.5 percent of women). The prevalence of other forms of incestuous contact has also been documented. Russell (1986) found that 3 percent of the women in her sample were abused by a first cousin, 2 percent were abused by a brother, and almost 1 percent were abused by a grandfather.

Parent–child incest has been the most studied of all forms of incest, particularly father–daughter incest. Although mother–child and father–son abuse occur and are serious violations to the young victim, few data have been collected about these forms of abuse primarily because of their relatively low incidence rates. Therefore, our discussion of incest focuses on father–daughter incest only.

Parent–child incest has been considered the most harmful not only because the child is exposed to age-inappropriate sexual behavior, but also because the parental role of protector and nurturer is violated (Courtois, 1988; Roth & Lebowitz, 1988). In addition, given that the children usually live in the same home as their parents, the privacy of the home provides greater opportunity for incestuous contact to be of longer duration, greater frequency, and greater severity (Courtois, 1988). Given these circumstances, the child is more likely to be entrapped in a continuing cycle of abuse if her or his abuser is a parent (Summit, 1983). Most parental abuse is perpetrated by the father or stepfather, with stepfathers being reported as more likely to abuse than natural fathers (Russell, 1984b).

Adult survivors of parent–child incest typically describe their fathers as authoritarian, punitive, and threatening. The victim of incestuous abuse tends to feel overwhelmed by her father's authority and feels unable to resist his advances. Although she may feel repulsed and ashamed, her father's sexual attention may be the only form of intimacy and love that she is given. This conflict often results in a conspiracy within the family to keep the abuse a secret. The family refuses to see the abuse, and the daughter often feels she cannot talk about the abuse for fear of betraying the family secret. The perpetrator may also convince the child that awful things will happen if she tells: Her mother will be angry with her or will not believe her. The perpetrator may even convince the child that the abuse is her fault.

Who Are the Victims?

Although specific intrapersonal characteristics of the perpetrator have been identified by researchers, the risk factors for who will be victimized are situational ones, outside the child's control, rather than victim characteristics. Any child may be victimized by an adult family member, but some factors have been identified that increase the child's risk of incestuous abuse. Even though incest is found in all socioeconomic groups, it is more common in low-income families (income less than $10,000 a year) and in families living in rural areas (Finkelhor, 1980; 1984). The higher proportion of victims within lower-income families, however, may be due to the greater involvement of social services and therefore greater likelihood of discovery of abuse within these families. In addition, Finkelhor (1984) suggested that the reason for the higher portion of sexual abuse in rural areas may be greater social isolation.

Incest is also more common in families in which the parents are unhappily married and there is little mutual affection between them. In addition, the incestuous family members typically are isolated and depend on each other for support and comfort. The children may act as caretakers in the family. The families often are emotionally distant and do not demonstrate affection with physical touch. The families also tend to have a low tolerance for conflict and anger, to be overly moralistic, and to have little humor and a large amount of sarcasm in their interactions (Calof, 1987).

In addition, if the father displays little affection toward the child and has conservative family values, the risk of incestuous abuse is increased (Finkelhor, 1984). Conservative family values in Finkelhor's study were defined as a belief in the subordination of women and the obedience of children. Children living without a father or with a stepfather are also likely to become the victims of incest (Finkelhor, 1984). David Finkelhor (1984) noted that not only are girls who have stepfathers more likely to be abused by the stepfather himself, but they are also more vulnerable to abuse perpetrated by other men. They have greater exposure and potentially greater risk from a variety of unfamiliar men prior to the mother's remarriage, during her dating, and following the remarriage as the new spouse introduces his friends to the family.

Distance from the mother, either physically (through death, illness, divorce, etc.) or emotionally, represents a significant risk factor for the child (Finkelhor, 1984). The mother's distance may provide the opportunity for abuse to occur, therefore leaving the child vulnerable. In addition, if the mother has little education (less than a high school diploma), the child is at greater risk for incestuous abuse. A mother's limited education may reflect a women's relative power within the marital relationship (Finkelhor, 1984). The wife may be more dependent on her husband financially and emotionally when she is poorly educated, as she is unable in many cases to leave an incestuous mate and support herself.

Consequences for the Survivor

The responses to sexual abuse vary as the children develop strategies to cope with their abuse. Some children develop highly successful strategies for isolating the abuse; other children develop self-destructive strategies to cope with their pain. Children who are victims of sexual abuse may have difficulty in school. They may wet the bed, may fear going to bed at night, and may have nightmares. They may fear being alone and may cry hysterically when left with the perpetrator. They may demonstrate regressed, babyish behavior. They may show a precocious interest in sexual contact and behave in a seductive manner when trying to get their way.

Often children do not report the abuse because of fear. Children may feel responsible for keeping the family going and avoiding conflict and pain.

> The daughter may gain a semblance of power in the family through bargaining with the father for things she wants. But her main experience is shame and guilt, isolation, and an oppressive, disproportionate sense of responsibility for holding the family together, which she accomplishes in part by keeping her secret (Breines & Gordon, 1983, p. 526).

Although survivors may remain silent as children, the abuse may resurface in adulthood. Adult survivors may be reminded of their abuse when seeing a family member again, looking at pictures, watching a movie about incest, being sexually victimized again, or having children reach the same age they were when they were abused. "Abuse is not destiny, but it does make progress toward successful social, interpersonal, and intrapsychic functioning in adult life more difficult" (Mullen, 1993, p. 431).

Approximately 40 percent of all survivors suffer aftereffects serious enough to require therapy in adulthood (Browne & Finkelhor, 1986). These aftereffects include depression, low self-esteem, sexual dysfunctions, posttraumatic stress disorder (PTSD) symptoms, and symptoms of dissociation (Roesler & McKenzie, 1994). Adult survivors also may have difficulty trusting others, may experience feelings of powerlessness, may have difficulty expressing their emotions, may have an increased risk of drug and/or alcohol abuse, and may have a fear of intimacy (Bass & Davis, 1988). Although the abuse was in the past, these effects for some survivors are a daily part of their lives.

> People have said to me, "Why are you dragging this up now?" Why? WHY? Because it has controlled every facet of my life. It has damaged me in every possible way. It has destroyed everything in my life that has been of value. It has prevented me from living a comfortable emotional life. It's prevented me from being able to love clearly. It took my childhood away from me. I haven't been able to succeed in the world. If I had a comfortable childhood, I could be anything today. I know that everything I don't deal with now is one more burden I have to carry for the rest of my life. I don't care if it happened 500 years ago! It's influenced me all the time, and it does matter. It matters very much (Lavender in Bass & Davis, 1988, p. 33)

Although the adult psychological impact of incest can be very serious, many victims are able to use coping and adaptation strategies that allow them to protect their personal integrity (DiPalma, 1994). In her in-depth interviews with incest survivors, Linda DiPalma found that many survivors demonstrated great inner strength and determination. As child victims, these women used realistic, future-oriented fantasies to find relief from their pain and to escape their identity as a victim. Some focused their energy toward academic achievements, finding validation and personal affirmation through their educational pursuits. Others used creative outlets (e.g., writing, drama, music, dance) to enhance their ability to cope. Together, these strategies suggest a holistic view of incest survivors, acknowledging survivor strengths as well as vulnerabilities.

Steps to Protect Children and Treat Victims

Protection of children from abuse is a focus of national attention in recent years. The schools are beginning to educate teachers about the signs of physical and sexual abuse. The schools are also beginning to teach children what is appropriate touch, to teach children that their body is their property and they have the right to say no to someone who is abusive, and to encourage children to tell a teacher, parent, or adult friend when someone touches them inappropriately (Crewdson, 1988). Doctors also are being trained to identify signs of child sexual abuse in their patients and to conduct the necessary tests to verify sexual abuse.

Many adult survivors also are becoming aware of their victimization and are seeking help from private therapists, support groups of other survivors, and books. Even though the memory of the abuse may not be completely forgotten, many women have found ways to heal and to come to terms with their history.

> I don't know if I will ever be completely healed. It's like there was a wound and it healed over, but it was still infected in there. It needed to be lanced and cleaned out so that a good healthy scar tissue could grow over it. I knew that once that scar tissue grew, it wouldn't be very pleasant to look at, but it wouldn't hurt anymore. It would be raised, and you would know it was there, but you could touch it and it wouldn't be painful. And I think that's how it is. I have scars, but they don't hurt. They're cleaned out now (Bass & Davis, 1988, p. 167).

COURTSHIP VIOLENCE

Young people usually begin dating in high school, though children as young as kindergartners talk about having boyfriends and girlfriends. The idea of being paired with a member of the other sex is pervasive in our society. Traditionally, it has been assumed that children's "playing house," and later, dating, provides a context for socialization into later marital roles. Roles that are important in marriage, such as wife, lover, and confidante, can be explored and rehearsed in these situations (Rice, 1984). Unfortunately, these roles prescribe and reinforce power inequalities that can lead to the gendering of violence.

Dating also offers opportunities for companionship, status, sexual experimentation, and conflict resolution. Inevitably, as a relationship develops, conflicts arise. No two people are always going to agree on everything. How do young people deal with conflicts? Unfortunately, the research evidence is clear. Violence is a failure to resolve conflict constructively (Billingham & Sack, 1986). It is a frequent reaction to the confusion and anger young people experience in heterosexual conflicts. Violence is also a tactic used to gain control in a relationship (see Box 14.2).

Defining Courtship Violence

Courtship violence, dating violence, and premarital violence are all terms researchers have used to refer to acts of aggression occurring between young un-

Box 14.2 Example of High School Courtship Violence

When I was 16 my boyfriend of two years began to hit me. . . . I spent most of my time covering up for him—putting make-up on my bruises, going into the hospital under an assumed name (for a cracked rib). I was afraid to tell my friends because I was embarrassed. I didn't want to tell my father because I knew he would fight violence with violence. I couldn't tell my mother because she was beaten by my father when she was younger. I felt helpless and alone. Finally, I was too worn out to hide anymore. My grades were suffering. My family relationships were suffering. My social relationships were suffering. I felt I would 'go crazy' if I didn't talk to someone. First I tried to talk to his mother. Her reply was that if he was hitting me it was my own fault. This set me back a little since this was the idea hiding in the back of my mind. The turning point came when he hit me in front of a group of people—friends, parents, teacher. I was humiliated that they viewed this but I was also elated because I knew I was saved. For a few years afterwards I was extremely insecure and unwilling to trust anyone, male or female. . . . The only remaining effect is that I flinch when a man makes any sudden movements toward me.

Source: Anonymous student, 1991.

married women and men. Researchers have studied the gamut of aggression, from verbal aggression, such as screaming, yelling, name calling, and threatening, to severe physical violence involving the use of weapons. Depending on which measure of aggression one uses, rates of courtship violence range from a low of 6 percent to a high of almost 90 percent. Not surprisingly, when the definition of courtship violence focuses exclusively on severe forms of physical aggression, the rates are lower than when definitions of verbal aggression also are used.

Several researchers have found that violence is more likely to occur in serious than in casual relationships (Pedersen & Thomas, 1992), suggesting that violence in more committed relationships may reflect the acceptance of violence as a legitimate mode of conflict resolution (Billingham, 1987). On the other hand, violence in a developing relationship may be a way of "testing the relative safety of a relationship before movement to greater commitment is risked" (Billingham, 1983, p. 288). In a large percentage of committed, violent relationships, the violence occurs more than once, the couples stay together, and some even feel the relationship improved as a result of the violence—some interpret violence as a sign of love (Cate, Henton, Koval, Christopher, & Lloyd, 1982). Many students believe dating violence is more acceptable in serious relationships (Bethke & DeJoy, 1993), and not sufficient grounds for ending the relationship (O'Keeffe, Brockopp, & Chew, 1986). (See Box 14.3.)

Frequency of Courtship Violence

A national survey of approximately 2,600 college women and 2,100 college men revealed that within the year prior to the survey 81 percent of the men and 88 percent of the women had engaged in some form of verbal aggression, either as perpetrator or victim (White & Koss, 1991). Approximately 37 percent of the men and 35 percent of the women inflicted some form of physical aggression and about 39 percent of the men and 32 percent of the women sustained some

Box 14.3 Teenager glad she's rid of abusive boyfriend

Dear Ann Landers: I know you've written a lot about battered women, but most people aren't aware that teenage girls can be battered, too.

I began dating a terrific-looking guy when I was 16. He was really cool and had his own car. A year later I was scared to death of him. I didn't dare tell my family for fear they'd make me stop seeing him and I didn't want to. If I broke one of his rules, he would beat me up. Once, when I wore my jeans too tight (according to him) he locked me in the trunk of his car. I thought I would suffocate to death. It was a horrible experience.

My family knew nothing of the hell he put me through. He made an effort to put the bruises where no one would see them. On the rare occasion when they were visible (like a black eye), I would tell people I had had an accident.

I was the ideal child—I had straight As, got home on time, did all my household chores and never gave my parents any trouble. It wasn't until I attempted suicide at the age of 18, and then got some great counseling, that I began to understand how he had taken control of my life.

Ann, please print this letter and alert teenage girls and their parents to this potentially dangerous situation. No one would have guessed such a thing was going on in my life. I realized that I wasn't alone when I met other girls in the support group who were just like me. — Lucky to Be Out of It.

Dear Lucky: This is not the first letter I've printed from a teenager who was battered by her boyfriend. My advice has been to get out at once. No guy is worth it.

There is no national support group for battered teenage girls, but they can call the Domestic Violence Hotline for help. The number is 1-800-333-SAFE.

Source: Permission granted by Ann Landers and Creators Syndicate.

physical aggression. In this survey all types of heterosexual relationships were included, from the most casual to the most serious, thus providing a comprehensive estimate of the scope of courtship violence. The measures of verbal aggressin included arguing heatedly, yelling, sulking, and stomping. Physical aggression included throwing something at someone, pushing, grabbing, shoving, or hitting.

Studies also indicate that courtship violence during the teen years is common, with as many as 35 percent of female and male students surveyed reporting at least one episode (O'Keeffe et al., 1986), although fewer experienced recurring violence (Burcky, Reuterman, & Kopsky, 1988). As with college students, fewer high school students experience physical violence (15.7 percent of female students and 7.8 percent male students, according to Bergman, 1992).

Inflicting and Sustaining Courtship Violence

The ubiquity of courtship violence among college students is apparent in that comparable rates of violence have been observed across gender, ethnic group, and type of institution of higher learning, such as private or public, religious or secular. All the evidence to date suggests that it would be unusual to find a high school or college student who had not been involved in some form of verbal aggression. Significant correlations between inflicting and sustaining both verbal and physical forms of aggression were found in heterosexual couples. The same people who reported inflicting some form of violence reported sustaining violence. Clearly, violence begets violence.

The finding that women and men do not appear to differ in the frequency with which they engage in aggressive acts should not be taken to mean that there are no gender-related differences in aggression. On the contrary, when the motives for violence and the consequences are considered, gender-related differences are clear. Most data suggest that women are more likely to engage in aggression for self-defense, whereas men report that they aggress to instill fear and to intimidate. For example, Mary Laner (1989) found that women who believed that their partner was using socially undesirable tactics to gain and/or maintain control were more likely to be aggressive than women who did not.

However, some data suggest that at least for dating relationships, women are often the initiator (DeMaris, 1992), though these findings are difficult to interpret. These studies tend to have small samples and do not control for gender-related differences in the perceived meaning of terms such as "slap," "push," or "shove," and differences in willingness to report aggressive behavior (see White & Kowalski, 1994, for a discussion of these issues in the study of female aggression). Even if women do initiate some instances of courtship violence, it is clear that they are more likely than men to sustain serious injury.

Finally, the underlying processes involved in courtship violence for women and for men appear different. Several studies have been conducted to identify factors that predict who is most likely to be aggressive in an intimate relationship. The results of these studies are quite consistent. Although the best predictor of being aggressive is having an aggressive partner (Bookwala, Frieze, Smith, & Ryan, 1992), other predictors are different for women and men. For men the prior use of aggression in a variety of interpersonal situations is the best predictor of courtship violence, followed by various impulsive/aggressive personality characteristics, including hostility toward women and psychopathic tendencies. Men who are quick to react to anger and who have successfully used violence in other situations are likely to do so again (White, Koss, & Kissling, 1991). For men, drug use, divorced parents, the belief that violence between intimates is justifiable, and less traditional sex role attitudes also have been identified as predictors (Bookwala, Frieze, Smith, & Ryan, 1992; Tontodonato & Crew, 1992).

For women, on the other hand, anxiety and depression have been found to be good predictors of courtship violence, followed by prior use of aggression and parental aggression. Women with personality characteristics reflecting an extreme concern for others, combined with low levels of self-assuredness, were less likely to be involved in courtship violence. It is possible that these women may accommodate to the needs of others at the expense of their own needs, thereby reducing the likelihood that their partners would resort to violence to get their way (White, Koss, & Kissling, 1991). Diane Follingstad and her colleagues (1992) compared women who had experienced one incident of dating violence to women who reported ongoing victimization. These latter women showed a tendency to allow their partner to control them, were more committed and in love with their partner, and less likely to end the relationship because of the abuse. These women also reported more traditional attitudes toward women's roles, justified their abuse, and tended to romanticize relationships and love.

Gwartney-Gibbs and her colleagues (1983) have suggested that learning violence in the home and associating with peers who endorse the use of violence provide a backdrop of social norms that legitimate violence, thereby increasing the probability of being involved in courtship violence. However, factors more distant in time and place (i.e., parental influences) have less influence on courtship violence than more immediate factors (i.e., peer influences). For example, Denise Worth and her colleagues (1990) found that fraternity and sorority affiliation were significant factors in involvement in abusive dating relationships. Nevertheless, witnessing and experiencing violence in the home increase the likelihood of experiencing courtship violence, probably through the learning of violence as a tactic of dealing with interpersonal conflict (Reuterman & Burcky, 1989; Thompson, 1991; Worth, Matthews, & Coleman, 1990).

When Is Courtship Violence Committed?

Courtship violence is most likely to occur in private settings (Laner, 1983; Roscoe & Kelsey, 1986), on weekends (Olday & Wesley, 1983), in disputes involving jealousy, disagreements about drinking, or sexual denial (Roscoe & Kelsey, 1986). These are the conflicts young people report most frequently leading to feelings of confusion and anger, and resulting in violence (Sugarman & Hotaling, 1989).

Furthermore, violence is typically reciprocal—i.e., one person initiates, the other reacts—often provoking an even more intense response. Thus, it is easy to see why someone who reports sustaining aggression also reports inflicting it. It is also easy to imagine a verbal conflict escalating into physical aggression. Indeed, significant correlations have been reported between inflicting verbal and physical aggression, and between sustaining verbal and physical aggression. Ninety-seven percent of the women and men in one survey who reported inflicting physical aggression also used verbal aggression (White & Koss, 1991). On the other hand, 44 percent of the men and 39 percent of the women who said they were verbally aggressive also reported physical aggression. Thus, if you hit you probably yell too, but if you yell you do not necessarily hit.

Consequences of Courtship Violence

Most victims and offenders experience at least some mild emotional trauma, and as many as half may experience physical injury (Makepeace, 1984). The consequences tend to be more severe for the women involved. Women are three times as likely as men to experience a major emotional trauma (Makepeace, 1986). Victims are most likely to experience, anger, fear and/or surprise (Matthews, 1984), whereas offenders experience sorrow. Although few victims (only 4 percent) seek professional help in resolving their feelings, most tell a friend about the incident. Other factors associated with dating violence include disciplinary problems in school, lower grade averages, and not attending college, as well as frequent dating and drug use (Reuterman & Burcky, 1989).

A further serious consequence of courtship violence is a possible increased risk of marital violence either with the same or with a different partner. Little systematic research on this has been conducted. For example, it is not known what percentage of women who were victimized during courtship are also victimized in marriage, but for women who are victimized in marriage there is evidence that some were victimized during courtship. In 25 percent of the violent marriages, the violence began before marriage (Gayford, 1975). More recently, interviews with eighty-two clients at domestic violence shelters found that 51 percent of the clients had experienced previous physical abuse in a dating relationship (Roscoe & Benaske, 1985).

Steps to Take

Courtship violence has not received the public attention that other forms of violence against women have—in particular, incest, rape, and wife battering. Given the current climate of concern about violence in the school and in youth in general, interpersonal violence is receiving more attention than in the past, although we are not aware of many prevention programs. However, it is encouraging to know that students who are involved in courtship violence will turn to community resources in the absence of campus resources (Bogal-Allbritten & Allbritten, 1987). A recent program for Canadian secondary school children was successful in altering attitudes, knowledge, and behavioral intentions after six weeks. The program consisted of a large group presentation followed by classroom discussion led by community professionals (Jaffe et al., 1992).

At present it appears that the prevalence of courtship violence and its consequences are not seen widely as the real problems they are. It may be that young people are so accustomed to witnessing and experiencing behaviors such as arguing, yelling, pushing, and slapping that these actions seem normal. They do not label these experiences as problems. It appears that a major educational effort to change attitudes toward courtship violence is needed to sensitize persons to the consequences of their aggressive interactions with others.

ACQUAINTANCE SEXUAL ASSAULT AND RAPE

> At age 17 I lost my virginity on a squeaky hotel bed—against my will. It scared the hell out of me. I didn't want to be touched by any man for months. Worse yet, it was my boyfriend—someone I had trusted. I got pregnant—a scared 17-year-old who couldn't even afford a pregnancy test. I confided in only one person, my best friend. I told her that if I really was pregnant I was going to kill myself. My period was about one month and a half late already—a week later I miscarried (anonymous student, 1990).

Approximately 85 percent of all sexual assaults are perpetrated by someone at least casually known to the victim. Romantic partners commit as many as 57 percent of all assaults (Koss, 1990).

Defining Sexual Assault

Sexual assault, sexual coercion, and sexual aggression are all terms used to refer to instances in which one person engages in sexual behavior against another's will. These terms encompass acts that range from unwanted sexual contact,

Box 14.4 Like Incest, Sexual Assaults Can Mean a Violation of Trust by Powerful Authority Figures

I had a very upsetting encounter as a youth. I was fifteen and off on a church camp-out. My sister was with me and we were the only young people there. The others were a lot older and then there was the minister who was recently widowed. I had never met him before but had no reason to doubt his sincerity when I told him I was freezing at night. My sleeping bag wasn't warm enough. Well, he told me the less clothes I wore the warmer I would be in the sleeping bag. That night while in my bag, away from the men, I took my shirt and shorts off and went to sleep. It did seem toastier in my bag, but I was petrified when a hand came into my bag and held onto my breast. I couldn't move; I was so scared. I pretended I was asleep, but remember hearing him almost quiver as he held on. It seemed like an eternity but I'm sure it was only seconds. His hand slid out of the bag and he was gone. I didn't go back to sleep that night and have never forgotten that night. Someone I trusted, who held such a meaningful position, betrayed me. That incident has left its scar on me forever. I told my sister the next day and we were like Siamese twins from then on until we ended that nightmare camp-out.

That week I lost something. A part of me that was young and innocent and a man in a high position took it. A man of God whom we are all taught to trust and put our faith in. I have never been that trusting again.

Source: Anonymous student, 1990.

such as forced kissing or the fondling of breasts and/or genitals, to attempted rape and rape (see Box 14.4). Forcible rape is defined as ". . . the carnal knowledge of a female forcibly and against her will" (Federal Bureau of Investigation, 1989). In research, the term sexual assault often is used rather than rape. An inclusive term such as sexual assault reminds us of the various ways that a man may force himself on a woman. A man's tactics may range from psychological pressure (i.e., threatening to end the relationship; saying things he does not mean, such as falsely professing love), verbal persuasion ("if you loved me, you'd let me"; "you owe it to me"), verbal threats of harm, use of alcohol and drugs, physical intimidation, mild physical force (pushing, slapping, holding down), severe physical force (beating, choking), to displaying or using a weapon. The term sexual aggression also reminds us that sexual activity falls on a continuum ranging from consensual sexual contact at one end to violent rape at the other.

Although the legal definition of rape appears straightforward, it is a label some are reluctant to apply to some acts of forced sexual intercourse. Numerous researchers have documented people's hesitancy to label forced sex between acquaintances as rape, particularly if any of the following circumstances were present: The man initiated the date; he spent a great deal of money; the couple went to his place; there had been drinking, kissing, and petting; the couple had been sexually intimate on previous occasions; the woman had sex with other men (Goodchilds, Zellman, Johnson, & Giarrusso, 1988).

This reluctance is apparent in recent criticisms appearing in the popular press (i.e., trade books, newspaper articles, and magazine features) questioning the veracity of rape statistics. These critics suggest that if young women do not label their experiences as rape, they are not victims. Of course, this is illogical. While a woman may not realize that forced sexual intercourse by an acquain-

FIGURE 14.2. Information table at the Port Authority Bus Terminal in New York City, educating the public about violence against women.

tance during a date is rape, this does not change the legal definition of the act as rape, nor does it reduce the culpability of the perpetrator. Furthermore, whether or not a sexual assault is labeled rape does not alter the consequences (discussed below). There is clearly an incongruity between legal and social definitions of what constitutes "real rape." Susan Brownmiller (1975), in her ground-breaking book *Against Our Will*, noted,

> . . . it is evident that the social definition of rape is quite incongruous with the legal definition and displays a characteristic set of biases primarily reflecting . . . the rape-supportive belief system. Thus the question of "What is a rape?" is not answered by a powerful legal litmus test but through a system of beliefs that derive from a misogynistic social context, the "rape culture" (p. 436).

Frequency of Sexual Assault

Recent research has shown that rape is the crime least likely to be reported and, if reported, the least likely to result in a conviction, particularly if the rape was committed by an acquaintance. Not only do many women not report their assault to the authorities, many never tell anyone. Thus, crime statistics grossly underestimate the frequency of rape. Researchers must rely on large surveys of women to obtain accurate estimates of victimization rates. Women are asked about a number of sexual experiences that may have involved force or threat of force, some of which meet the legal criteria for rape, rather than being asked directly "Have you ever been raped?" This is important because many victimized women (73 percent) never label the forced sexual intercourse as rape. This approach has suggested that the actual rape victimization rate is ten to fifteen times greater than corresponding FBI estimates (Koss, 1992). Because most of these unlabeled, unreported rape experiences are perpetrated by acquaintances, Koss (1985) has labeled acquaintance rape a "hidden" crime.

The most comprehensive survey of women's sexual assault experiences asked more than 3,000 college women from thirty-two institutions of higher education across the United States about sexual experiences since the age of 14 (Koss et al., 1987). This is an extremely important study because it distinguished clearly between different forms of sexual assault, reducing the possibility that cases of unpleasant sex or regrettable sex (i.e., consent was given, but subsequently regretted) would be counted as a form of sexual assault. Of those surveyed, more than half (53.7 percent) had experienced some form of sexual victimization; 15.4 percent had experienced acts by a man that met the legal definition of rape (though only 27 percent labeled the experience rape), and 12.1 percent, attempted rape. An additional 11.9 percent had been verbally pressured into sexual intercourse, and the remaining 14.4 percent had experienced some other form of unwanted sexual contact, such as forced kissing or fondling with no attempted penetration.

It appears that women in many segments of society are at risk for sexual assault. Community-based surveys have found that 25 percent of African-American women, 20 percent of white women (Wyatt, 1991), and 8 percent of Hispanic women (Sorenson & Siegel, 1992) reported at least one sexual assault experience in their lifetime. High school women also appear to be at greater risk for rape than previously thought. In a recent survey of 834 entering college students, Jacquelyn White and John Humphrey (1990a) found that 13 percent reported being raped between the ages of 14 and 18, and an additional 15 percent reported being victims of an attempted rape.

Who Is at Risk?

Numerous studies have been conducted to identify risk factors for sexual victimization, most with little success. One risk factor is being a college student; sexual victimization rates are about three times higher among college students than in the general population (Aizenman & Kelley, 1988; Koss et al., 1987). Other risk factors have been difficult to determine. For example, Mary Koss and Thomas Dinero (1989) examined fourteen different potential risk factors. Considering all the variables together, they found that childhood sexual abuse combined with higher than average alcohol use (which itself could be a response to the childhood victimization) was the best predictor. Though their results may be disappointing in that they do not tell us a great deal about what type of person is at greatest risk for sexual assault, their study has done a great deal to dispel some of the prevalent myths regarding the kind of woman likely to get raped. They concluded,

> In short, rape vulnerability was either linked to earlier experiences beyond a victim's control or was not predictable. Both circumstances constitute justification for clinicians to use the most therapeutic sentence: "It wasn't your fault" (p. 249).

Box 14.5 Gang Rape

Most research on acquaintance rape has focused on instances involving a single attacker. However, gang rape is a phenomenon that is beginning to receive attention (O'Sullivan, 1991). Looking at police records, Amir (1971) found that 26 percent of the reported rapes had involved three or more perpetrators, and that 55 percent of convicted rapists had been part of a gang rape. The rate of conviction for gang rape is probably higher than the rate for rapes by single perpetrators because a victim of a gang rape is more likely to label the rape as a crime and report it than a victim of a single perpetrator, especially if he is an acquaintance. However, because not all gang rapes are reported, we need to consider data sources that assess unreported gang rapes. On the Koss survey described earlier (Koss et al., 1987), data revealed that multiple offenders were involved for 5 percent of the women who had been raped. The survey also revealed that for 16 percent of the men who reported having committed rape, at least one other male was involved. O'Sullivan (1991) noted that "Of the twenty-three documented cases of alleged gang-rape by college students in the last ten years, thirteen were perpetrated by fraternity men, four by groups of basketball players, four by groups of football players, and only two by men unaffiliated by a formal organization" (p. 11). She feels that the cohesiveness of all-male groups that promote macho values of sex as adventure may challenge men to perform in a group situation to prove they belong. According to O'Sullivan, victims of gang rape are usually first-year students who are naive, but have a reputation among the men for being promiscuous.

Since Koss and Dinero's study, several others have confirmed that the best predictor of victimization is past victimization. As a matter of fact, the results are so consistent that it is safe to say that victimization is a consistent predictor of future victimization (Gidycz, Coble, Latham, & Layman, 1992; Mills & Granoff, 1992; White & Humphrey, 1992; Wyatt, Guthrie, & Notgrass, 1992). Research has not identified the ways in which victimization acts on an individual to increase her vulnerability to further assaults. (See Box 14.5.)

Who Commits Sexual Assaults?

The Koss survey (Koss et al., 1987) described above also examined the sexual experiences of more than 2,900 college men. Of this group, 4.4 percent admitted to behaviors meeting the legal definition of rape, 3.3 percent admitted to attempted rape, 7.2 percent to sexual coercion, and 10.2 percent to forced or coerced sexual contact, indicating that 25.1 percent of the college men admit to some form of sexual aggression. The White and Humphrey survey (1990b) noted that of 329 men, 6 percent admitted to behaviors that meet the legal definition of rape, and another 7 percent admitted to committing attempted rape between the ages of 14 and 18.

Recent research indicates that the typical acquaintance rapist appears to be a "normal" guy. He is not a crazed psychopath. However, there are a number of characteristics that appear to distinguish him from others. Among college students, alcohol use (Koss & Gaines, 1993; White & Humphrey, 1994b) and athletic affiliation (Jackson, 1991; Koss & Gaines, 1993) are associated with sexual aggression toward women. Other significant correlates include a history of family violence, an early and varied sexual history, including many sexual partners, acceptance of rape myths, an impulsive personality, hedonistic and dominance motives for sex, lower than average sense of self-worth, and lower religiosity, as well as peers who condone and encourage sexual conquests (see White & Koss, 1993, for a review). Sexually aggressive men also feel that if they initiate a date, pay all the expenses, and drive the car, they are entitled to sex by any means as a return on their investment (Goodchilds et al., 1988). Finally, sexually aggressive men are more likely to perceive a wider range of behaviors as indicative of sexual interest than nonsexually aggressive men do (see Box 14.6).

Recently Neil Malamuth and Mary Koss, along with two of their colleagues, developed a model to explain sexual aggression. They demonstrated that two sets of attributes, sexual promiscuity and hostile attitudes, characterize aggressive men. According to the model, childhood experiences involving family violence lead to delinquency, which, in sexually promiscuous men who have a hostile personality, leads to aggression toward women (Malamuth, Sockloskie, Koss, & Tanaka, 1991).

In other research, Neil Malamuth and Nancy Thornhill (1994) found that sexually aggressive men were more domineering in an unstructured, five-minute get-to-know-each-other conversation with a female confederate than with a male confederate. These men used "one up" messages aimed at "gaining control of the exchange" (e.g., bragging about oneself and criticizing the other person). They concluded, "This may be the result of learning that women are 'safer targets' due to their size and physical strength . . . [being domineering] is an intrinsically aggressive act that is meant to convey authority and dominance" (p. 191). They speculate that being domineering in conversation may be a test sexually aggressive men use to identify vulnerable targets. A woman who resists the domination may be seen as unavailable, whereas a subordinate response from a woman may indicate that she is a potential target.

When Is a Sexual Assault Likely?

Sexual assault is most likely to occur in circumstances of privacy, when the opportunity of detection and likelihood of victim escape are lowest. According to Janice Belknap (1989), the riskiest season for acquaintance rape is summer (31 percent) and the riskiest time of day is six p.m. to midnight. Assaults most frequently occur in the victim's home (42.5 percent), followed by the assaulter's home or car, or any other secluded place. The presence of others, however, does not prevent a rape from occurring. Women have reported assaults at parties.

Frequently alcohol and drugs are present. One-third to two-thirds of rapists and many rape victims report having consumed alcohol prior to the assault (Richardson & Hammock, 1991). Alcohol can disinhibit the man, provide him with an excuse for his behavior after the fact, and/or be used to reduce the victim's resistance. Alcohol may also function as a cue to men for sexual access; women who drink may be perceived as "loose" or more interested in sex.

Rape can occur at any stage in a relationship (Shotland, 1989). However, sexual assaults between couples who have engaged in sex previously often are

Box 14.6 Is Acquaintance Sexual Assault a Result of Miscommunication?

Miscommunicaton has been put forth as a way of understanding the social process that results in a young woman being forced into sexual activity by her date. The term "miscommunication" implies that the problem lies in the communication skills of the two people involved, particularly the woman. Many young women on college campuses across the nation are admonished in freshman "rape awareness workshops" to communicate more clearly their refusal to have sex; the implication is that if the woman believes she has communicated her nonconsent and sexual intercourse occurs, the failure is hers. This way of thinking about sexual aggression has led a host of researchers to study women's verbal and nonverbal cues that may suggest sexual interest. This line of reasoning presumes that the man's motive is sexual, and he is looking for cues from the woman that may communicate sexual interest. This work also assumes that if these cues are present, any man would interpret them as indicators of a woman's willingness to engage in sex with him. However, these assumptions are incorrect.

Men who self-report sexually aggressive behaviors have been found to perceive nonverbal cues, especially cues that others perceive as reflecting little sexual interest, as connoting more sexual interest than sexually nonaggressive men (Bondurant, 1994). Furthermore, sexually aggressive men claim that their victims were more sexually interested in them than sexually nonaggressive men involved in consensual sex do, and they base this perception on the presence of behaviors that previous research has found to indicate low sexual interest (Kowalski, 1992). These behaviors include eye contact, smiling, accepting a date, and slow dancing. In contrast, sexually nonaggressive men base their inferences of their partners' sexual interest on the presence of behaviors such as kissing the man, undressing him, removing her top, and suggesting they spend the night (White & Humphrey, 1994a).

Whereas the language of miscommunication suggests that a sexual assault occurs because a normal guy understandably misunderstands his date's intentions on the basis of how she looks or what she does, the language of aggression and violence suggests a more negative view of men who commit acts of sexual aggression. It is sexually aggressive men's perception rather than a woman's actions that drives the inference of sexual interest. The language of miscommunication tends to reduce the culpability of the perpetrator, and diverts attention from a study of perpetrator characteristics and factors that contribute to perpetrators' attitudes and behaviors, such as sexism and the glorification of violence in the media.

not acknowledged as rape (Shotland & Goldstein, 1992). College students believe that sexual precedence (i.e., a past history of sexual intercourse) reduces the legitimacy of sexual refusal. However, in any sexual assault, the man apparently believes that the use of force to obtain sex is justified. That this force is not perceived as aggression or rape indicates an acknowledgment of rape as socially acceptable.

Consequences for the Victim

In spite of the tendency for the public to consider stranger rape as "real rape" and acquaintance rape as something less serious, mental health data clearly suggest otherwise. Several studies have shown that the psychological impact of nonstranger rape may be worse than that of stranger rape (Katz, 1991); however, people persist in their belief that stranger rape is much worse (Stacy, Prisbell, & Tollefsrud, 1992), and are more likely to hold the victim responsible for the acquaintance rape (Kanekar & Seksaria, 1993). Susan Roth and her colleagues (Roth, Wayland, & Woolsey, 1990) found that victims of a single assault by a date were more distressed than victims of stranger, acquaintance (i.e., known to the victim, but not a date), or husband rape. They suggested that the strong negative psychological reactions to date rape were due to feelings of betrayal and self-blame, i.e., uncertainty about their role in the assault.

Many victims are unable to acknowledge their victimization for months to years following the assault. A recent survey by Roberta Ogletree (1993) of women at three midwestern universities found that only 28 percent of the sexual assault victims sought any type of help, and of those who did, 75 percent turned to a friend. Acknowledged or not, symptoms develop, with 31 to 48 percent of rape victims eventually seeking professional help (Koss & Burkhart, 1989). Unfortunately, rapid recovery is not likely for the majority of victims. Interviews with rape victims four to six years after the sexual assault revealed that only 37 percent felt they had recovered within a few months of the assault; 26 percent did not yet feel recovered. Although recovery is often slow, the good news is that recovery is possible.

The reactions of sexual assault victims are many. Recently, clinical psychologists have argued that rape victims suffer from posttraumatic stress disorder (PTSD) (Roth, Dye, & Lebowitz, 1988). In their review of the literature on rape-related PTSD, Karlee Hoecker and Jacquelyn White (in press) concluded that approximately 25 percent of those sexually victimized develop symptoms serious enough to receive the PTSD diagnosis. Dean Kilpatrick and his colleagues (1992) estimate that approximately 1.3 million women in this country currently have rape-related PTSD. Such a diagnosis summarizes and amplifies the long-lasting and pervasive consequences of rape.

Emotional reactions to the assault include persistent fear and anxiety, phobias, depression, diminished self-esteem, sexual dysfunctions, and posttraumatic stress disorder. Behavioral reactions can include alcohol/drug use and dependency and behavioral deviancy, including sexual promiscuity, and an increased risk of future victimization. Physical difficulties, including psychosomatic symptoms, can arise from injuries associated with the assault itself and the attendant violence, as well as from the emotional trauma. Risk of contracting any one of several sexually transmitted diseases, including AIDS, and/or pregnancy is also associated with rape. Finally, for many rape victims their relationships with family members, friends, and intimate partners—i.e., husbands or boyfriends—frequently become severely strained. In some instances, the victim is blamed; in others, the assault is often trivialized—often with the well-meaning intention of trying to make the victim feel better.

Victims may not experience all of these symptoms, and they may not experience them all at the same time. Features of the assault, including the victim–assailant relationship, where the assault occurred, and the amount of force used affect the victim's reactions. Various family characteristics, prior sexual victimization, personality attributes, and the support received from family, friends, and the medical and legal communities also affect the victim's reactions to the rape and the extent and speed of recovery.

Victims go through various phases during their recovery. According to

Taylor (1983) they struggle initially with the meaning of the assault. Subsequently, they attempt to gain a sense of control, which can include self-blame, i.e., "What did I do wrong?" "How could I have avoided this situation?" Following this phase, victims may tend to minimize the seriousness of the experience as a means of self-enhancement; for example, they are grateful they lived though the attack. Mary Koss and Barry Burkhart (1989) suggest that as victims go through this process of redefining the meaning of the assault and their lives, and as they develop a greater sense of mastery, positive outcomes emerge. The victim progresses from being a victim to being a survivor.

Steps to Take

There are two types of responses to the question, "What can be done?" First, we must respond to the victim's trauma. Second, we must work to prevent sexual assault.

Most larger communities now have twenty-four-hour hotlines and rape crisis centers. Law enforcement, medical, mental health, and judicial personnel increasingly are receiving training to facilitate treatment of the victim and adjudication of the perpetrator.

Beginning in the mid-1970s most states began to revise their rape laws. It was hoped that changes in (a) the definition of rape as assault, (b) statutory age offenses, and (c) evidentiary reforms (such as ruling a woman's past sexual history or manner of dress inadmissible evidence) would result in increases in the reportage, prosecution, and conviction of rape cases, and improvement in the treatment of rape victims by the criminal justice system (Searles & Berger, 1987). However, analyses of the effects of these legal reforms provide little optimism that the plight of victimized women has improved. The gains to date are piecemeal.

> Rape law reform has removed many of the law's most sexist provisions and has helped to legitimate increasingly varied and independent roles and styles of behavior for women. Much progress remains to be made for women, both generally and in legal reform (Searles & Berger, 1987, p. 30).

The most recent legal innovations are focusing on the trial itself, with the aim of correcting jurors' misconceptions about rape and its sequelae (Ambrose-Goldberg, 1992). In particular, expert testimony on rape trauma syndrome and societal rape myths now is allowed as part of the prosecution in some states.

These recent legal efforts to alter society's understanding of sexual assault are reflective of most feminists' belief that the key to sexual assault prevention is change in societal attitudes.

> As long as sex and rape are seen in traditional ways, the likelihood is that a woman (or man) who is raped by an acquaintance is at the mercy of the whole legal system's interpretation as to whether a crime was committed. There is much less need to change the law in the area of rape, and especially acquaintance rape, than there is to change the way we view sexual behavior (Bohmer, 1991, p. 332).

At issue is how best to change societal attitudes. Because society is a collection of individuals, we must use methods that ultimately change the individual. The methods must challenge factors that encourage and enable the enactment of male-female status differences which contribute to the gendered nature of violence. Rape prevention techniques aimed at individuals and institutions have been offered.

At the institutional level, experts encourage schools and universities to espouse a philosophy condemning sexual assault, to develop policies, and to offer services congruent with their policies (i.e., escort services, rape prevention programming for students, faculty, and staff, counseling/treatment services, strict judicial procedures, and punitive consequences).

Several types of rape prevention programs have been aimed at the individual. These programs may be for women only, men only, or mixed sex groups, and involve videos and films depicting acquaintance rapes, group discussions, consciousness-raising activities, and education about counseling services available.

Programs for women, in addition to providing general information about sexual assault, especially acquaintance rape, offer tips for day-to-day conduct that may help reduce one's risk for sexual assault, and may teach self-defense (Cummings, 1992). Unfortunately, these recommendations result in a life full of restrictions (e.g., don't go out alone; watch what you wear; don't drink on dates; don't take any man for granted) and precautionary behaviors (e.g., walk with a friend or a dog; take a flashlight, whistle, and/or mace; dress for easy escape; learn self-defense).

All these restrictions, while obviously contributing to one's safety, may interfere with the quality of one's life, such as missing a beautiful sunrise on the beach, or forgoing a nighttime run in the park, or freely setting the limits on one's sexual activity, such as wanting to kiss and pet, without engaging in intercourse. However, rape prevention programs may not work equally well for all women. For example, Kimberly Hanson and Chris Gidycz (1993) developed a state-of-the-art prevention program at Ohio University, and assessed its effectiveness in actually reducing the likelihood of sexual victimization. They found that the program reduced the incidence of sexual assault among women with no prior history of sexual assault, but it was ineffective for women with a history of sexual assault.

Aiming rape prevention programs at women places the responsibility for rape prevention solely on women. However, the recognition that men are ultimately responsible for their aggressive behavior has led some to direct educational efforts at men.

Other rape prevention programs have targeted all-male groups such as fraternities and/or athletic teams. In some instances, national fraternities, like Pi Kappa Phi, are taking the initiative to develop their own programs. In other instances, local fraternities or athletic teams are forming associations to combat male violence against women. Finally, men are organizing their own campaigns to stop sexual assault, such as the Men Stopping Rape group in Madison, Wisconsin, and the Dialogue About Men at Haverford College near Philadelphia. In all these cases, the leaders are men. "With males conducting such sessions, information about date rape and acquaintance rape that some men might resist

Box 14.7 Fraternity Violence Education Project

A Statement by West Chester Fraternity Men Against Violence Against Women

We believe that it is important for men to struggle against the sexism in themselves and other men. Our goal is to challenge the attitudes amd dispel the myths that perpetuate sexism and violence against women. This requires taking risks, being willing to listen and speaking out.

Violence against women is often viewed as a woman's problem. Women are told to take self-defense classes, not to walk alone at night and to dress conservatively. We feel that restricting the behavior of women ignores the responsibility of some men to not only accept their role as perpetrators but for all men to be spokespersons against it. We believe that violence against women is an issue that both men and women must confront.

It is a common belief that women bring violence on themselves, while in fact, we live in a culture that permits violence toward women. Men are socialized through their upbringing, the media and the educational system to assume a more dominant role in relation to women. This leads to the belief that men can control women though physical means and that these actions are justifiable.

To date, women have provided the leadership and direction to stop violence against women. Since men are the perpetrators of these acts of violence, *we feel that men must also take action.*

Source: From D. Mahlstedt and K. Kohat (August 1991), Fraternity violence education project: When men take action. Paper presented at the American Psychological Association convention, San Francisco. Reprinted by permission of Dr. Deborah Mahlstedt.

accepting from women is often more successfully transmitted and believed" (Warshaw, 1988, pp. 164–165). (See Boxes 14.7 and 14.8.)

Initially, many of these programs were implemented without an effort to evaluate their effectiveness. This is changing, fortunately, because it has become apparent that some types of programs may produce a boomerang effect. In par-

Box 14.8 What You Can Do to Help Stop Violence against Women

- Attend events that raise your consciousness about violence against women.
- Confront men who use sexist language or make jokes degrading to women.
- Be aware of your own behavior which may be threatening to women. (For example, on a quiet street at night, realize that walking behind a woman may be threatening to her. Crossing to the other side of the street would relieve this threat.)
- Be willing to examine your defensiveness when listening to the expression of feminist ideas.
- Do not confuse mere friendliness with sexual invitation.
- Discuss issues related to sexism and violence with your male and female friends.
- Be aware of sexism in advertising and the media that depicts women in degrading ways.
- Be responsible for your actions when drinking. Do not use alcohol as an excuse or reason for acting violently.
- If you suspect or directly experience physical or verbal abuse directed toward a woman (or man) take appropriate action.

Source: Compiled by West Chester University (WCU) Fraternity Violence Education Project and Seattle Men Against Rape.

ticular, some men who have deeply entrenched hostile attitudes about women and who accept rape myths may actually have their attitudes strengthened as a result of a rape awareness program. For example, Barbara Wilson, along with Daniel Linz, Ed Donnerstein, and Horst Stipp (1992), found that older men exposed to a TV movie about acquaintance rape actually attributed more blame to women in date rape situations after viewing the film than before, whereas women and younger viewers showed an increased sensitivity to date rape as a result of viewing the film. They suggested that the impact of an intervention must be based on a consideration of one's emotional involvement and selective perception processes.

WIFE ABUSE

Spouse abuse is usually defined as the use of physical force by one partner in an intimate relationship against the other. Physical force can range from a slap or push to the use of a weapon. Partner abuse can also include psychological abuse, such as intimidation, threats, public humiliation, and intense criticism. For many battered women, the psychological abuse is more harmful than the physical. Although physical abuse rarely occurs without psychological abuse (Tolman, 1989), they are usually considered separately for two reasons. First, although psychological abuse can be extremely painful, erode a person's self-esteem, and deeply scar a person emotionally, it does not result in permanent bodily damage or death, while physical abuse can and does. Second, physical abuse is easier to measure and study; a broken rib or bloody nose is easier to determine and record than emotional abuse that humiliates and demeans a person. Although physical violence is the focus of this section, the effects of psychological abuse cannot be minimized and is usually present in violent couples.

Wife Abuse versus Spouse Abuse

Partner abuse occurs between married and unmarried partners, including lesbian (see Box 14.9) and gay couples (Brand & Kidd, 1986; Lie & Gentlewarrior, 1991). The majority of cases, however, involve heterosexual couples where the woman is at greater risk of physical harm (Straus, 1993). In addition, abusive men sometimes batter their partners when they are pregnant. Not only are pregnant women more vulnerable personally, but their unborn child can also be harmed (Gelles, 1988; McFarlane, Parker, Soeken, & Bullock, 1992). For these reasons women are usually the victims of more severe partner abuse by their male partners than are men by their female partners.

Although women often engage in aggressive acts toward their partners, in many of the cases they act in self-defense (Saunders, 1988) and are less likely to harm their partner (Straus, 1993). Thus, the evidence suggests that wife abuse is a much more frequent and serious social problem than husband abuse. In fact, it has been argued that terms such as "spouse abuse" obscure the central issue in wife abuse—men physically harming women in intimate relationships (Bograd, 1988). "Wife abuse" is a more specific term that raises questions about the social, political, psychological, and economic context in which violence against women occurs.

Box 14.9 Lesbians and Battery

Relationship abuse is not limited to heterosexual relationships. For lesbian women, the rate of relationship abuse is not significantly different from that for heterosexuals (27 percent and 25 percent, respectively) (Brand & Kidd, 1986). Other studies have found 32 to 37 percent of lesbians have been in a physically or sexually abusive relationship (Lie & Gentlewarrior, 1991; Schilit, Lie, & Montagne, 1990). In sum, it appears that spouse abuse is a problem that occurs with similar frequencies in heterosexual and lesbian relationships. Gay male couples report slightly less sexual abuse than lesbian couples, but have more violence associated with abusive acts (Waterman, Dawson, & Bologna, 1989). Apparently, violence in committed relationships is not simply a gender issue. Issues of power and control arise in all relationships, and provide the basis for abuse. Spouse abuse has been associated with issues of power and dependency in both lesbian (Hart, 1986; Renzetti, 1992) and heterosexual couples (Finkelhor, 1983).

When seeking help, lesbians face discrimination from police, counselors, and shelters that assume a battered women is a heterosexual. Many counselors and police officers have homophobic reactions to victims of lesbian battering (Renzetti, 1992). Shelters and organizations are slowly beginning to assimilate information on the issue and some states, like Minnesota, now have a full-time staff person specifically to deal with lesbian battering (Suh, 1990).

For instance, it has been argued that a woman's second-class status in society makes her more likely to be economically dependent and unable to leave an abusive situation (Bograd, 1988; Browne, 1993). A woman with a college degree still earns less, on the average, than a man with a college degree (U.S. Department of Labor, 1993). By leaving the relationship, a woman may lose her house, car, and insurance. She may need to relocate and find new employment. If she has been out of the job market raising a family, she may lack needed skills. Furthermore, if children are involved, day care and the economic demands of single parenthood must be faced. Poverty is not an unrealistic consequence for a single mother. One out of every three female-headed households is poor; for African-American and Hispanic women the rate is one out of two (Hagan & Davis, 1992).

Also, social acceptance of wife beating has been common until recent years (Goldstein, 1983). Seventy percent of college university men report some likelihood that they would hit a hypothetical wife (Briere, 1987). People with more traditional attitudes toward male and female roles tend to blame the victim more and the perpetrator less for wife assault (Hillier & Foddy, 1993). Moreover, clergy who counsel women often hold traditional attitudes that blame women for their abuse (Wood & McHugh, 1994). Jokes about "needing to beat one's wife" are another example of the lingering social acceptance of wife abuse. All of these economic, social, and psychological factors may not be addressed in a discussion of "spouse" abuse, but become obvious when the topic is defined as "wife" abuse.

Frequency of Wife Abuse

> A Burlington woman and her daughter were killed, police say, after the daughter's estranged husband walked into their home Thursday morning and shot them (Swinson, 1994).

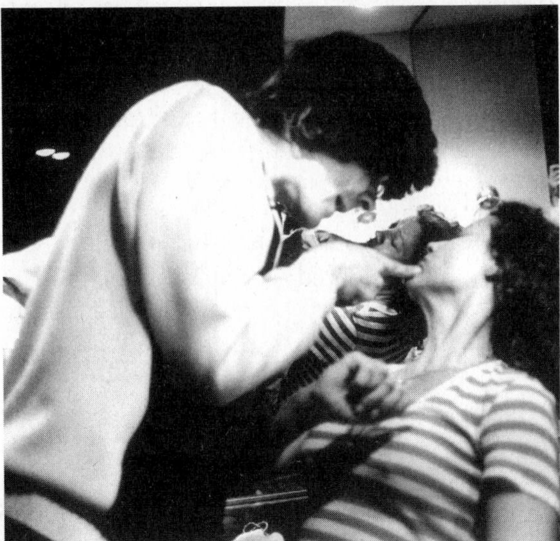

FIGURE 14.3. This photo, from a series taken by Donna Ferrato, shows one of many actual abusive episodes between Garth and Lisa. Their marriage, which had the appearance of being ideal, ended after many bouts of violence when Lisa divorced Garth and moved away with their children. Garth continued to deny that he ever hit Lisa (Ferrato, 1991).

Incidents like the one described above can be found in the news frequently. In fact, one of the most common causes of injury for women in the United States is wife abuse. It is estimated that one-third of all women will be battered at sometime in their lives (Straus & Gelles, 1990). In one study, more than 33 percent of the female patients admitted to an urban emergency room were suspected victims of spouse abuse and 22.5 percent were confirmed victims (Stark, Flitcraft, & Frazier, 1979). In a study of women at a community-based family practice clinic, 25 percent of 351 women reported physical injuries inflicted by their partner and 15 percent reported injuries in the past year (Hamberger, Saunders, & Hovey, 1992).

Wife abuse may result in homicide; sometimes a woman's death is the result of a severe beating; other times her death is the result of wounds inflicted by a gun or other weapon. Two-thirds of partner homicides are women killed by their male partners and more than one-half of all murders of women are committed by current or former partners (Browne & Williams, 1993; Walker, 1989). In contrast, only 6 percent of male murder victims are killed by wives or girlfriends (Federal Bureau of Investigation, 1985).

Most researchers agree that spouse abuse is probably underreported due to shame, guilt, and the belief that wife-beating is a normal part of marriage (Browne, 1993; Dutton, 1988). Reported rates for wife abuse in two large surveys were 28 percent (Straus et al., 1980) and 21 percent (Schulman, 1979). These surveys consisted of a random sample of all homes in the United States and Kentucky, respectively. These couples reported that the wives were assaulted with a gun or knife, threatened with a gun or knife, beaten up, hit with objects, hit with a fist, kicked, bitten, slapped, pushed, or shoved. Schulman found that 63 percent of the assaults were likely to occur more than once. Murray Straus and Richard Gelles (1986) compared survey results for 1975 and 1985 and found no statistically significant change in wife abuse across time, which suggests that these results are stable.

Altogether, these data suggest that wife abuse is a serious social problem. The image of the family and home as a refuge of safety and love for many crumbles when these facts are considered. For at least one-third of the women in America, the home is a dangerous place where physical assault by their mates will occur at least once.

Who Commits Wife Abuse?

Wife abuse is a complex phenomenon; there do not appear to be any easy explanations or solutions. Some social factors that may contribute to wife abuse are a general societal acceptance of violence, devaluation of women, and acceptance of men's right to dominate women. Removal of these three factors from our society perhaps would eradicate wife abuse. However, every man in our society does not batter his wife; therefore, factors other than culture should be examined.

Unemployed and lower-income men report abusing their wives more than employed and higher-income men (Howell & Pugliesi, 1988). Frustration or stress might explain why these men engage in higher levels of marital violence than other men (Howell & Pugliesi, 1988). Spouse abuse occurs, however, in all social classes (Gelles & Straus, 1988). As the narrative below indicates, wealthy people and public figures may engage in wife abuse.

> Sometimes I even like the glare of public life. Certainly it forces Walter to pay a little attention to me when others are around. But shut off the TV cameras and he's mean and nasty and ignores me as usual. I don't know how much longer I can go on. Alcohol doesn't help nor do pills. I've tried them and just got put away in a fancy hospital. I can scream and shout for attention, but all I get is more sneers, more verbal abuse, and more pity. Now that we're public figures, Walter rarely hits me anymore, but his cruelty remains. He'd die if he knew I was here talking with you (Walker, 1979, p. 166).

This particular woman, like many abused women, felt trapped in her abusive marriage. Due to her high social status and role as a public figure, she and her husband were careful to hide the abuse.

Social scientists have looked for differences between men who batter and men who do not. Men who engage in wife abuse are more likely to have a history of alcohol abuse (Barnett & Fagan, 1993), to have witnessed physical abuse in the family as children (Russell, Lipov, Phillips, & White, 1989), to have experienced physical violence as children (Barnett & Fagan, 1993), to have more life stress (Barnett & Fagan, 1993), and to have had more childhood conflict with their fathers (Beasley & Stoltenberg, 1992). Men who batter also are more likely to be socially isolated (Dutton, 1988). Other characteristics of abusive men are lack of coping skills, low self-esteem, a need to dominate, depression, dependency on others to meet emotional needs (Hale, Duckworth, Zimostrad, & Nicholas, 1988), and hostility toward women (Dewhurst, Moore, & Alfano, 1992). Abusive men are more likely than nonviolent men to attribute negative intentions, selfish motivations, and blame to their wives, especially in marital situations involving jealousy or rejection by the wife (Holtzworth-Munroe & Hutchinson, 1993).

The above characteristics, although related to wife abuse, cannot be assumed to cause wife abuse. For instance, alcohol use may simply be a man's excuse to beat his wife. He may dismiss his responsibility for the battering by saying that he can't control himself when he's drinking. Furthermore, all men do not violently attack their spouses when they drink. It may be that mediating factors, such as poor coping skills and low self-esteem, could lead a man to both drinking and battering. Therefore, caution should be used in interpreting characteristics associated with battering.

Who Are the Victims?

When the phenomenon of wife abuse first became widely publicized, the masochism theory, which states that women who enjoy pain are likely to seek out and stay in abusive relationships, was offered as an explanation for wife abuse (Goldstein, 1983). This theory has found no support and is now seen as a mechanism for blaming the victim. Contrary to the masochism theory, it is now believed that the majority of women who suffer from wife abuse do not remain in the relationship because they enjoy the pain of battering (Walker, 1983; Kuhl, 1984). Furthermore, studies of abusive couples have found little evidence that battered women have certain personalities that put them at risk (Russell, Lipov, Phillips, & White, 1989).

Battered women have been reported to display low self-esteem and a feeling of helplessness (Walker, 1984), but both of these characteristics may *result* from battering rather than cause the abuse (Aguilar & Nightingale, 1994). Martin Schwartz (1989) argues that asking why women stay in abusive relationships assumes that women are weak and unable to protect themselves. He suggests that research has focused on women who are married or in relationships with abusers. Thus, women who *do* leave abusive relationships often are not studied. A recent follow-up study of fifty-one battered women found that after 2.5 years only 25 percent of the previously battered women were still in a violent relationship. However, 23 percent of those who were in a nonviolent relationship at time one were in a violent relationship at time two. A variety of factors, including depression, self-esteem, education, and childhood abuse, *failed* to distinguish women in battering relationships from other women (Campbell, Miller, Cardwell, & Belknap, 1994). Future research is needed to investigate the many ways women respond to abusive incidents, including leaving the relationship.

Contrary to expectation, abused women do not usually blame themselves for their husbands' violence against them (Cantos, Neidig, & O'Leary, 1993; Holtzworth-Munroe, 1988). Abused women are most likely to cite external unstable causes for the battering, such as his having a bad day at work (see Box 14.10). The fact that unstable forces (forces that can change at any time) are seen as the cause of abuse can help explain why an abused woman may stay or re-

Box 14.10 Example of Battered Spouse

Stacey was a sweet little baby. She rarely cried except, it seemed, when Vic was having problems of his own. One night Vic came home in a horrid mood. I knew there would be trouble, so I fed Stacey and put her to bed a little earlier than usual. She was real good and played in her crib for a while until we fell asleep. I managed to keep things calm and thought I was about to avert an explosion, when later on that night, Stacey got up and was crying. I got out of bed and went into her room to hold her and calm her down, and decided that maybe she was hungry and that I needed to give her another bottle. At that point, Vic came in the room and started screaming and yelling at me. I had just had oral surgery and my gums were feeling pretty badly, but Vic started beating me on the head with the castanets that we had brought back from one of our trips. He banged one of them so hard across my mouth and across my head that the beads flew all over. As soon as he started coming at me, I went to sit on the bed with the baby and rolled up so he couldn't reach my face, so he was banging more on my back and head. Once the castanet broke, he then took off his shoe and started beating me with it, all over my legs, head, and my back. The baby started crying because the bottle was knocked out of her mouth. He pulled me off the bed, with the baby in my arms, by my feet. I had to protect that baby. I landed on the floor and I took all the bruises. He didn't say a word while he was beating me. He seemed to be so calm, no rage. I was so scared he'd hit the baby, or he'd do something to the stitches in my mouth. I didn't think he was going to beat me to death this time, but I thought he'd do it to that baby. I protected her that time. I don't know why he stopped, but all of a sudden and almost as fast as it started, it was over.

Source: Excerpt from *The Battered Woman* by Lenore E. Walker.

turn to the relationship. It is often the victim's belief that her spouse or the external situations can and will change: "as soon as he gets a good job," "when the stress of his work is reduced," "if he would just give up drinking," or "when the children get older." However, as the abuse increases in frequency and severity the woman becomes more likely to attribute blame to stable forces within her husband (Cantos, Neidig, & O'Leary, 1993; Holtzworth-Munroe, 1988). Women who feel the abuse is caused by stable forces in their husbands are more likely to leave the relationship (Frieze, 1979). Thus, it may be that it takes abused women time to realize and accept that their mates will not change their behavior.

Consequences for the Victim

Lenore Walker summarizes the consequences of abuse for 120 women she interviewed:

> Major physical assaults included: Slaps and punches to the face and head; kicking, stomping, and punching all over the body; choking to the point of consciousness loss; pushing and throwing across a room, down the stairs, or against object; severe shaking; arms twisted or broken; burns from irons, cigarettes, and scalding liquids; injuries from thrown objects; forced shaving of pubic hair; forced violent sexual acts; stabbing and mutilation with a variety of objects, including knives and hatchets; and gunshot wounds. The most common physical injuries reported are those inflicted by the man's hands and feet to the head, face, back, and rib areas. Broken ribs and broken arms, resulting from the woman's raising her arm to defend herself, are the most common bro-

> ken bones. Several women in this sample have suffered broken necks and backs, one after the man stomped on her back, others after being flung against objects in the room. One woman suffered the loss of a kidney and severe injury to her second kidney when she was thrown against a stove. Others suffered serious internal bleeding and bruises. Swollen eyes and nose, lost teeth and concussions were all reported (Walker, 1979).

A person who lives with someone who physically and emotionally abuses them develops a stress response when attacked. If the attack is repeated or the threat of attack is present, a chronic set of symptoms develops. Posttraumatic stress disorder (Koss, 1988) and the battered woman's syndrome (Walker, 1984), a subcategory of posttraumatic stress disorder (Walker, 1993), are diagnoses sometimes used to characterize the psychological effects of battering.

From extensive interviews with battered wives, Walker (1979, 1984) has developed the battered woman's syndrome to explain why women remain in relationships with abusive men, and why these women may sometimes see murdering their husbands as the only solution. The victims may feel helpless to make changes in their relationships with their husbands. This learned helplessness occurs when women are battered repeatedly and feel they have no way to protect themselves or escape. Often women's perceptions of helplessness are accurate; social and economic pressures can prevent them from leaving. It is not unusual for abused women to be blamed for their husbands' behavior or have their stories discounted. Women are often told to "try and be a better wife" or to "be thankful for what you have." Furthermore, many women are economically dependent on their husbands, lacking money or job skills to provide for themselves and their children. Without financial and social supports women may be very accurate in feeling that they have nowhere to go.

It is common for battered women to say they are afraid to leave their husbands because they fear that their husbands may kill them if they try. This can be an accurate perception; sometimes when battered women try to leave, their husbands do threaten to kill them. Indeed, Walker (1984) reports that leaving an abusive husband may result in an attempted or successful murder.

Walker explains how the psychological consequences of abuse further increase feelings of helplessness. When repeatedly degraded and ridiculed by their husbands over a period of time, wives can come to believe the husbands' accusations. Women's self-esteem and confidence erode. They may actually come to believe that they deserve their husbands' abuse and that they are incapable of caring for themselves and their children.

Steps to Take

One view of wife abuse examines the structure of society in which wife abuse occurs (Dobash & Dobash, 1992). Historically, women had fewer rights than men (Steil, 1989). Prior to the Civil War, husbands had the right to control their wives' property, collect and spend their wages, and punish their wives for transgressions. The abuse of women was tolerated, if not accepted, by many men and women (Gordon, 1988). Although women have gained many rights in the last 130 years, it is thought that many people still hold values that support the abuse of women by men.

Not only may some people still consider wife abuse a normal and acceptable behavior, but it is suggested that our society supports wife abuse with a male-dominated family structure and economic system. Husbands usually have more power than wives in a society in which men make most of the money and many of the important family decisions. This unequal distribution of power leads men to feel entitled to dominate and leads women to feel vulnerable. Battering has been linked with other social problems: "Battering is rooted in a culture of domination, a culture that does not celebrate our differences in race, age, sexual preference, physical and mental abilities, and gender, but instead uses these differences to exploit and dehumanize" (Pence & Shepard, 1988, p. 296).

From this perspective, the way to end battering is to change our social structure. The battered women's movement over the past two decades has begun this process through public education, legal reform, and programs designed to aid battered women. The first battered women's shelter opened in 1974, largely in response to the growing awareness of battered women's needs. Now there are shelters in most large cities in America. These shelters, largely through volunteer effort, provide temporary emergency housing, emotional support, and information about legal and social services for which battered women may qualify. Shelters also work to educate the public about the difficulties of battered women. Education programs can be successful in educating young people about the seriousness of wife abuse (Tulloch & Tulloch, 1992).

In many states, police departments are now trained in how to deal with men who batter. Police have been reluctant to arrest male batterers and have discouraged women from pressing charges. Due to education programs, officers are now more likely to respond to calls and make an arrest. Some localities have adopted programs to arrest an abusive person without waiting for the abused person to press charges. Acknowledging that a woman may have trouble pressing charges against her partner, the police take the decision away from her. Although arresting the abuser has not been found to remedy battering, its merits still are being debated (Berk, 1993; Buzawa & Buzawa, 1993). In many states, such as North Carolina and Rhode Island, women can now get temporary restraining orders against their abusers without having to hire a lawyer. Although it is unclear how effective these orders may be, at least some states are taking steps to acknowledge women's fears and increase their safety.

Psychologists have designed programs targeted toward the men in our society who batter their wives (Dutton, 1988). These programs aim to help men learn other ways to deal with anger and other emotions besides abusing their spouse. The men have to want to change and be willing to undergo lengthy counseling. The success of these programs has yet to be fully evaluated but appears promising.

Although these steps have not changed society enough to eradicate wife abuse, it is obvious that some movement has been made. Unfortunately, many areas of the country still do not have shelters for battered women and many shelters suffer from lack of funds and space to meet the volume of battered women needing help. In addition, programs that treat male batterers are still in their infancy and it is difficult to solicit participants unless under court order. Clearly, the battle to end wife abuse is not over.

CONCLUSION

Reading this chapter may have been a distressing experience for many of you. Some of you may have realized, perhaps for the first time, that you are a victim of one of the forms of violence we discussed. Feelings of despair and anger may arise. This is natural. We too have experienced despair, sadness, and anger while researching and teaching this material. It is indeed a sad commentary on women's place in society that violence, most often at the hands of an acquaintance or loved one, is one of the major mental health issues facing women today. But we are learning to turn our emotions into activism. You can learn to do likewise.

Though the magnitude of violence against women is alarming, awareness of the problem is the first step toward prevention. We cannot stop something we cannot see. Once named, violence against women in its various forms is no longer socially and culturally invisible. As noted in Chapter 1, naming is power.

Violence against women is inextricably bound to the social context of male domination and control. The patriarchal view of society gives men a higher value than women. It is taken for granted that men should dominate in politics, economics, and the social world, including family life and interpersonal relationships. This is seen as normal and natural. Violence against women is an assertion of the power and control men have over women. Today feminists are challenging this power, through scholarship and activism.

Analyses of violence against women from a feminist perspective help us understand the double-edged sword a patriarchal society presents to women. Dominance and aggression are rewarded in men while submission and humbleness are rewarded in women. This submission, however, makes women more vulnerable to male violence. Our culture teaches men to protect women and women to look to others for safety and security. Ironically, in a chivalrous society, men are both those who commit violence and those who protect. "In the system of chivalry, men protect women against men . . . chivalry is an age-old protection racket" (Griffin, 1971, p. 30) that depends on male violence for its very existence. Chivalry promotes the man as the protector and the woman as the protected; the man as the aggressor and the woman as the victim.

A key aspect of chivalrous behavior in men is to protect women's chastity and vulnerability from involuntary defilement and violent attacks. The protection, however, has its own costs for women in our culture by prescribing a code of appropriate behavior called femininity. The characteristics of traditional femininity may make women perfect victims and vulnerable to attack. Women are not taught how to protect and defend themselves. Women are not encouraged to develop their bodies and increase their strength. They are encouraged to wear clothing and shoes that restrict movement and prevent escape. Women are encouraged to look to men for economic support.

If a woman is attacked, she may be accused of noncompliance with the traditional codes for feminine behavior and blamed for her victimization. The culture in general, and men specifically, may accuse her of teasing and dressing provocatively in a sexual attack or of nagging and being disrespectful in a physical attack. Within the patriarchal system, a woman is both bound by rules for feminine behavior and accused when she is attacked and cannot protect herself, even though it is the culture that discouraged her from learning how to defend herself.

"Each girl as she grows into womanhood is taught fear. Fear is the form in which the female internalizes both chivalry and the double standard" (Griffin, 1971, p. 33). Her fear results in a passive rather than active response to male aggression. She may become paralyzed with fear, restrict her behavior (i.e., not go out alone, not do anything without her partner's permission), try to appease her attacker, and worry about how *she* can prevent a future attack. "The passive woman is taught to regard herself as impotent, unable to act, unable even to perceive, in no way self-sufficient" (Griffin, 1971, p. 33). In order for women to confront violence in our patriarchal society, women must use their own strength as an energy source for reform.

> Social movements, feminism included, move toward a vision; they cannot operate solely on fear. It is not enough to move women away from danger and oppression; it is necessary to move toward something: toward pleasure, agency, self-definition. Feminism must increase women's pleasure and joy, not just decrease our misery (Vance, 1984, p. 24).

In addition, men must be included in the fight to end violence against women. Men are secondary victims as their girlfriends, sisters, wives, mothers, and daughters face the threat of attack. Men are also the victims of the chivalric codes that demand accountability for protecting women in a society in which it may be difficult to do so. By recognizing women as equals, refusing patriarchal demands for men to be dominant and aggressive, and fighting for legal and societal reforms, men will be liberated and our society transformed.

Feminist analyses of patriarchy and violence have given women and men a basis for combating violence against women. Though the evidence of violence against women is distressing, documentation of the problem provides the first step toward eradication. Public demand for treatment facilities, legal reforms, explicit institutional policies condemning sexual misconduct of all forms, and educational programs for students signal hope that future generations of women, in equal partnership with men, will enjoy a life free from the fear of violence.

CONNECTING THEMES

1. The pattern of intimate violence, where women are the victims and men are the perpetrators, is not due to biological destiny. Women are not born victims and men are not biologically predetermined to be aggressors. Rather, stereotypes of how women and men are supposed to behave, experiences that reinforce stereotypical behaviors, and a social structure that supports power inequities between women and men all contribute to violence against women.
2. Traditionally, secrecy and myths regarding male-female relationships trivialized and/or justified male violence against women. The women's movement has done much to bring to public awareness the extent of the harm

done to women by men and has prompted redefinitions that acknowledge the violence. Thus, for example, no longer is rape defined as a sexual act and wife-abuse viewed as a legitimate way to "show the little woman who is boss"; rather, each is seen as male efforts to dominate and control women.

3. Violence against women is influenced by social and cultural factors. Social class, ethnic group membership, sexual orientation, and age are some of the factors that can affect the occurrence of and responses to intimate violence. While this chapter focused on the United States, violence against women is a problem throughout the world. The incidence of aggression, the forms that the violence takes, and societal attitudes can vary greatly across cultures.
4. Violence against women, in its various forms, is now recognized as a public health and social problem. Hence, research has moved from focusing on individual psychopathology to identifying the sociocultural factors that contribute to such violence. Also, communities, institutions, and organizations are combating violence against women by developing interventions that not only help individuals but also promote change in values and attitudes at the societal level.

SUGGESTED READINGS

KOSS, MARY, LISA GOODMAN, LOUISE FITZGERALD, NANCY RUSSO, GWENDOLYN KEITA, and ANGELA BROWNE (1994). *No safe haven.* Washington, DC: American Psychological Association.

RUSSELL, DIANA E. H. (1993). *Making violence sexy: Feminist views on pornography.* New York: Teachers College Press.

RUSSELL, DIANA E. H. (1986). *The secret trauma: Incest in the lives of girls and women.* New York: Basic Books.

WALKER, ALICE, (1982). *The color purple.* New York: Washington Square Press.

WARSHAW, ROBIN (1988). *I never called it rape: The Ms. report on recognizing, fighting, and surviving date and acquaintance rape.* New York: Harper & Row.

CHAPTER 15

Gender and Psychological Disorders

INTRODUCTION
PROBLEMS OF PSYCHOLOGICAL DIAGNOSIS: AN ILLUSTRATION
SEX-RELATED DIFFERENCES: A REVIEW OF EXPLANATIONS
- The Medical Model
- Stereotypes
- The Social Construction of Symptoms
- Power Issues

DEPRESSION
- Roles, Power, and Depression
- Blaming Women: Reproductive Function as a Source of Depression

THE SOCIAL CONSTRUCTION OF FEMALE DISORDERS: THE VIEW FROM HISTORY
CULTURAL DETERMINATION OF SYMPTOMOLOGY
- Eating Disorders
- Agoraphobia

ISSUES IN TREATMENT
- Sex Bias in Diagnosis: The Politics of Labeling
- Sex Bias in Practitioner Attitudes
- Sex Biases in Treatment: The Use of Medication
- Institutional Biases in the Treatment of Women and Men

GENDER AND THERAPY
- The Feminist Critique of Traditional Treatment Methods
- Feminist Therapy
- Some Principles of Feminist Therapy
- The Difference between Nonsexist and Feminist Therapy
- The Impact of Therapist Characteristics
- Therapy with Marginalized Populations

ISSUES OF DIVERSITY
CONNECTING THEMES
SUGGESTED READINGS

The issue of gender is central to any discussion of mental illness and health. Unlike many areas in the field, clinical psychology has never ignored women. Most of Freud's patients were women. Even today, more women than men seek treatment for psychological distress. *Women and madness* has been a common theme in Western literature and art (c.f. Gilbert & Gubar, 1978). This thematic relationship was illustrated by Elaine Showalter (1987) in her discussion of a nineteenth-century French painting showing the freeing during the French Revolution of the insane men and women who had been imprisoned in the Bastille.

> In the painting that commemorates this historic occasion, Robert-Fleury depicts "the insane" as madwomen of different ages, from youth to senility. Some are crouched in melancholia, others crying out in hysterical fits, while one gracefully kisses the hand of Pinel. The representatives of sanity in the painting are all men, and this division between feminine madness and masculine rationality is further emphasized by the three figures in the center. In the foreground is a lovely, passive and disheveled young woman, her eyes modestly cast down, upon whose exposed bosom an erect and dignified Pinel gazes with ambiguous interest. (Showalter, 1987, p. 2).

Both men and women had been freed by Pinel. However, this representation of mental disorders as feminine was not simply one artist's fantasy. We are sure you can think of many examples from your literature courses.

INTRODUCTION

As you will see in this chapter, women are more frequently diagnosed as having psychological problems than men and are more likely to be treated for psychological disorders. Women and men are also seen to have different disorders. Since sex and gender influence every aspect of people's lives, it would be surprising if they did not affect the number and kind of psychological symptoms exhibited by women and men.

But why do women show more signs of psychological distress? The topic of psychological disorders has produced a greater range of unresolved questions than virtually any other area of the psychology of women. These questions include: "Do women and men manifest different kinds of psychological disorders or do they show different symptoms of the same disorders?" "If some disorders are found to be more prevalent in one sex, are differences related to biological sex, gender, or social roles?" "What is the role of the situational context in influencing the signs of psychological distress that women and men exhibit?" "Can a person's social environment create psychological disorders as well as influence their expression?" "Are psychological diagnosis and treatment intrinsically sexist?" "And, finally, how can aspects of psychotherapy related to gender be improved?" These questions and others will be explored in this chapter.

We take a *social constructionist* perspective on mental illness. This means that we view psychological distress as a social as well as a personal event. Social norms define what traits and behaviors are considered desirable and undesirable. Norms are social constructions and, as such, they may change over time. As norms change, our ideas about what a mentally healthy person is change too. As you will see, forms of mental illness in women have also changed over time.

However, norms are not applied equitably. People who have lower amounts of power are more likely to be punished for engaging in undesirable behaviors than more powerful people. This is because the less powerful do not have the ability to define themselves. Feminist psychotherapists are very concerned about how the politics of gender intersect with those of class and ethnicity (Brown, 1994). How psychological diagnoses are created, applied, and treated is greatly influenced by power. The power to name is also the power to control.

PROBLEMS OF PSYCHOLOGICAL DIAGNOSIS: AN ILLUSTRATION

In order to deal with some of these issues, it is important to understand how a psychological disorder is diagnosed. This is much more problematic than diagnosing a physical illness because there are few objective standards that can be applied. How, for example, do we take a psychological temperature or do a psychological blood test? The therapist is usually limited to information given by the client and/or the observations of others with whom the client is in close contact. From this limited information, he or she must infer causes and offer a psychological label.

The capsule descriptions in Box 15.1 are examples of the kinds of information that clinical practitioners (usually psychiatrists, clinical psychologists, and psychiatric social workers) have used to diagnose an individual's problems.

What kind of people do these descriptions remind you of? Do you think they are male or female? Young or old? Rich or poor? The answers to these kinds of questions demonstrate that psychological symptoms are not evaluated in a social vacuum. In a series of interesting studies, Hope Landrine (1988, 1989) showed such descriptions to students of various ages. Person A is a description of a mild depression. When students were asked who such a person was likely to be, a large majority of them rated the stimulus person as white, middle-class, and female (Landrine, 1988). They rated Person B (dependent personality disorder) as significantly more likely to be a married, middle-class, white woman, and Person C (antisocial personality disorder) as significantly more likely to be a young lower-class man (Landrine, 1989).

These studies illustrate that perceptions of psychological symptoms are inextricably associated with social characteristics. They involve assumptions about social roles (married or single) as well as about class, race, age, and sex. Although it is impossible to do a similar study with professionals (who are familiar with these diagnostic categories), Landrine (1987) found that clinicians also show a strong connection between gender stereotypes and diagnostic labels. For example, they labeled a stereotypical description of a single, middle-class white woman as an hysterical personality, whereas these same practitioners labeled the stereotype of a married, middle-class woman as depressed. The therapists' sex and clinical orientation had no effect on their labels.

Studies such as these show that there is a connection between gender stereotypes and psychological diagnoses. They do not tell us, however, why such a connection exists. The range of theoretical viewpoints in this area is enormous. For example, some people conclude that such beliefs reflect actual differences in the incidence of various disorders. Others argue that some disorders are identified in some people just because they are members of a particular gender, race, or class category (Chesler, 1972; Kaplan, 1983). In other words, under some circumstances, simply being a woman is a sufficient reason to be considered "mad."

Psychological symptomology probably has a multitude of causes. Individual, social, and cultural factors all play a role. Some disorders considered characteristic of women may be induced by the demands placed on them by their social circumstances. However, not every woman shows the "appropriate"

Box 15.1 Capsule Descriptions of Clinical Symptoms

PERSON A

This person is depressed most of the time, tending to feel sad, blue, down in the dumps, and "low." The person doesn't seem to be interested in his/her usual activities, and doesn't get pleasure out of them anymore. This person isn't depressed all the time, however. Instead, the person has periods of a couple of days or weeks of being in a normal mood and being interested in things . . . always tired, and shows a general lack of energy. The person feels inadequate, or feels worthless, and has a very low opinion of himself/herself. The person doesn't really seem to pay attention, and has difficulty concentrating and thinking straight. The individual doesn't show any real interest in doing things with other people, and doesn't respond to compliments with pleasure. The person broods, and cries a lot, also sleeps a lot (through things he/she is expected to do). . . . (Note: This is a description of a mild depression.)

PERSON B

This person passively allows others to assume responsibility for major areas of his/her life because of a lack of self-confidence and an inability to function independently. This person subordinates his/her own needs to those of others on whom he/she is dependent in order to avoid any possibility of having to be self-reliant. This person leaves major decisions to others. For example, this person will typically assume a passive role and allow the spouse to decide where they should live, what kind of job he/she should have, and with which neighbors they should be friendly. This person is unwilling to make demands on the people he/she depends on for fear of jeopardizing the relationships and being forced to rely on himself/herself. This person lacks self-confidence. This person tends to belittle his/her abilities and assets by constantly referring to himself/herself as "stupid." (Note: This person has a dependent personality disorder.)

PERSON C

This person habitually violates the rights of others. In childhood, this person engaged in frequent lying, stealing, fighting, truancy, and resisting of authority. In adolescence, this person showed unusually early or aggressive sexual behavior, excessive drinking, and use of illicit drugs. Now in adulthood, this behavior continues, with the addition of an inability to maintain consistent work performance or to function as a responsible parent and a failure to obey the law. This person shows signs of personal distress, including complaints of tension, inability to tolerate boredom, and the conviction (often correct) that others are hostile toward him/her. This person is unable to sustain lasting, close, warm, and responsible relationships with family, friends, or sexual partners. (Note: This is an antisocial personality disorder.)

symptomology. A weaker version of the idea that society creates madness is the view that society shapes symptomology, but other, more individual factors, determine who is most susceptible to these social forces. This point of view allows us to recognize that men's symptomology is also shaped by gender stereotypes.

It is also important to recognize that the identification and treatment of gender-characteristic disorders are not value-free. Many symptoms of psychological distress are both vague and highly subjective in nature. Stereotypic beliefs can lead to different labels being attached to the same symptoms, different opinions about the severity of such symptoms, and different views about the nature of effective treatment for women and men. Women and men may internalize these beliefs so that they themselves view their symptoms differently and seek treatment at differing rates. Ironically, sexist assumptions about symptoms can either increase or decrease a person's possibility of receiving help. Some women may be treated needlessly whereas others (both women and men) may not receive the help and support they need.

SEX-RELATED DIFFERENCES: A REVIEW OF EXPLANATIONS

There appears to be general agreement among clinical researchers that three categories of mental illness are much more likely to be found in women than in men. These psychological disorders are depression, agoraphobia, and anorexia. Most mental health surveys indicate a two to two and a half times greater incidence of depression among women than men. It has also been estimated that 85 percent of all agoraphobic individuals and 95 percent of those suffering from anorexia are women (Franks, 1986).

Although it is easy to give statistics about the different incidence of various disorders in men and women, it is not easy to explain why such differences exist. We will briefly review some of the major explanatory theories. Some of these theories appear to explain some disorders better than others. We will refer to them again when we discuss specific sex-related disorders a little later in this chapter.

The Medical Model

Medical models assert that women are biologically more vulnerable to certain disorders, especially depression. As you have seen in Chapters 8, 11, and 13, women are regarded as being particularly at risk during periods of hormonal change such as menstruation, following childbirth, and at menopause. A major problem with such medical models is that they define women almost entirely in terms of their reproductive functions. In effect, they see a direct connection between the uterus and the mind!

A higher rate of mental illness in women appears to be a recent phenomenon in the United States. Before World War II more men than women were admitted to mental hospitals. Moreover, while more recent surveys report a higher incidence of psychological symptoms among women than among men, the converse was true in earlier studies (Unger, 1979a). In developing countries, such as India, Iraq, New Guinea, and Rhodesia, more men than women are diagnosed as being depressed (Rothblum, 1983). A recent study that explored the rates of mental disorders among various ethnic groups in Los Angeles County found no gender differences in depression for Asian Americans (Root, 1995). Asian-American men had higher depression rates than men from other ethnic groups, including African Americans, Latinos, and Anglo Americans. Such historical trends and ethnic/cultural differences suggest that biological vulnerability is too simplistic an explanation for gender differences.

Stereotypes

An alternative explanation for sex differences in the prevalence of some psychological disorders is the idea that gender-appropriate roles increase the risk for one sex. In other words, behaving like a woman increases a woman's chance of developing depression, agoraphobia, or some form of eating disorder. All of these disorders show an astonishing degree of overlap between symptomology and stereotypes about women. They are characterized by passivity, dependence, and concern for pleasing others. In contrast, disorders that appear to be

more prevalent among men, such as alcoholism and aggressive acting-out behavior, are more consistent with stereotypes about men (see Table 15.1). There is good reason to believe that exaggerated stereotypes are pathological for both sexes.

Women who have internalized characteristics considered appropriately feminine by our society seem to be at risk for so-called feminine disorders. For example, learned helplessness (a belief that nothing you can do will matter) has been associated with depression (Blechman, 1984) and dependency with agoraphobia (Chambless & Goldstein, 1980). This kind of linkage, however, tends to place the blame for an illness within the woman. She is expected to use therapy to assist her to change her maladaptive characteristics. Little attention is paid to the role of her family and society as a whole in rewarding these same characteristics.

The Social Construction of Symptoms

It is also possible that stereotypes function more as prescriptions for women's behavior rather than accurate descriptions of that behavior. Social systems may create many so-called maladaptive behaviors. A major mechanism in this constructive process is the *double bind* (also discussed in Chapter 5). A double bind exists when mutually contradictory assumptions exist within the same social context. For example, it is almost impossible for a woman to be seen as feminine and instrumentally competent at the same time because our society's definition of competence excludes so-called feminine characteristics such as sensitivity, dependence, or even physical attractiveness. In order for a woman to gain the rewards of femininity she must forgo rewards for competence and vice versa. No such dilemma exists for men because the definitions of masculinity and competence coincide.

Double binds are the result of social definitions. They are more likely to be imposed on individuals who are relatively powerless. But they are not merely a consequence of that person's life choices. Because of contradictory demands, a woman is likely to incur some social penalty no matter how she behaves. You

TABLE 15.1. DSM III Disorders Grouped by Prevalent Sex

Women Predominate	Men Predominate
Depression	Alcoholism
Agoraphobia	Drug abuse
Sexual dysfunction	Antisocial behavior
Simple phobias	Transsexualism
Anxiety states	Pathological gambling
Somatization disorder	Pyromania
Multiple personality	Intermittent explosive disorder
Histrionic personality disorder	Paranoid personality disorder
Borderline personality disorder	Antisocial personality disorder
Dependent personality disorder	Compulsive personality disorder

Source: From Fodor & Rothblum, "Strategies for dealing with sex-role stereotypes." In C. M. Brody (ed.), *Women Therapists Working with Women: New Theory and Process of Feminist Therapy*, pp. 86–95. 1984 Springer Publishing Company, Inc., New York 10012. Used by permission.

have all heard the phrase "Out of the frying pan into the fire." You can probably think of many examples in your own lives. For example, what is the appropriate reaction of a woman who is the target of street remarks? Or, what does a woman do when her promotion is assumed to be a result of "sleeping with the boss"?

Many so-called female disorders may be a response to covert control mechanisms like the double bind combined with a lack of socially acceptable behavioral options. Whatever a woman does under such circumstances may be labeled "sick." Socially defined feminine illness may be the only way that some women can find to rebel against social constraints. Conversely, the label of psychological disorder can serve to control rebellious women as well.

Social constructionist views force us to look at the situational context of women's lives. They help us to understand some of the trends and changes in women's mental health. They do not, however, assist us in understanding why some women acquiesce in their roles, others develop effective coping mechanisms, and still others develop maladaptive behavioral patterns.

Power Issues

The Case of Dora

Some of these unresolved issues can be understood by means of analyses based on power. In general, women possess less power than men do. The lack of specific criteria for psychological disorders is a great problem for individuals in a society who are marginal. Throughout the history of clinical psychology, women have been the patients and men the practitioners. Examples of the effect of power differentials on clinical diagnosis and treatment may be found from the earliest psychoanalytic annals. One case (see Box 15.2) that has been reconstructed by feminist scholars is that of Dora (Hare-Mustin, 1983; Lakoff, 1990).

This case history shows various forms of abuse of power. First, Freud did not see himself as his patient's advocate or agent, but as her father's (who was paying for the therapy). He did not see as his task to make Dora happy or productive, but to "bring her to reason"—to make her stop pestering her father and his friends. Second, Freud and his followers (mostly men) were able to define Dora's view of her reality as a form of fantasy. She, rather than her family, was seen as the source of her problems. Freud, of course, wrote the case history. Until recently, women have had little power to define themselves.

Robin Lakoff (1990) has pointed out that Freud's analysis of Dora represented therapy in its most adversarial form. In his notes, for example, he indicated that he "forced her to acknowledge" certain truths; she "confessed that she had masturbated"; and that her objections to his interpretations were "easy to brush aside." In case histories with male patients, Freud noted that they "discovered" such facts together, or that he "explained" his hypothesis. With Dora, in contrast, Freud's interpretations were used as weapons to convince her to submit.

Personal Consequences and Social Circumstances

It is important to remember that the impact of power in therapy is not limited to issues involving gender. Psychologists' perceptions of people's situa-

Box 15.2 The Dora Case

In 1899, an acquaintance and former patient brought his 18-year-old daughter, known as Dora, to Freud. She suffered from a number of hysterical symptoms, which were making life annoying for her family and, in particular, for her father. The father requested that Freud "bring her to reason." Freud was acting on the father's behalf. He saw it as his job to persuade Dora that—however correctly she may have analyzed her family's situation—she had to admit that her neurosis was self-induced and that, in order to be "cured," she must renounce her own perceptions in favor of those of her father's and Freud's.

For many years, Dora's family had been friends with another family, the K's. Herr K. was like Dora's father (and Freud): an ambitious and successful man in his forties. Frau K. and Dora, not yet out of childhood, became confidantes and Dora came to realize that her father and Frau K. were having an affair and that the families were making vacation plans to facilitate it. Since no one wanted Dora's mother, Herr K. was the odd man out.

From the time Dora was 7 or 8, Herr K., the busy, successful businessman, found the time to take long walks with her and to buy her expensive gifts. At the age of 14, Dora went by invitation to Herr K's office to watch a festival from the window. Herr K's family was supposed to be there too. When she arrived, Herr K. was alone and the curtains were drawn. He grabbed the child when she went up the stairs and gave her a deep kiss. She felt his erection and pulled away in horror and disgust. Her symptoms began with this incident. There were a couple of similar, but more serious, incidents and after each, her symptoms increased. Dora eventually tried to tell her father about the incidents. He confronted Herr K., who denied everything, and Dora was accused of creating fantasies in order to make trouble. Dora ultimately came to the conclusion that the two men were using her as an item of barter: my wife for your daughter. The only problem with the arrangement was that, although the other three were consenting adults, Dora's preferences were never consulted. Freud acknowledged that Dora's perceptions had validity, but felt that it would be an error for him to tell her because it would just encourage her in her willful and disruptive ("neurotic") behavior.

Dora remained in analysis with Freud for only three months. Freud offered several reasons for her ending treatment. She was taking revenge on him for not responding sexually to her or she was incapable of relating to him because of her homosexual attraction to Frau K. There is no explicit evidence for either argument in Dora's own recollections or associations.

Source: Lakoff, 1990, pp. 59–61.

tions are influenced by their own ethnicity, class, and relatively affluent circumstances. Clinicians may be unaware of culturally diverse coping strategies as well as insensitive to the negative consequences of so-called healthy coping strategies under some circumstances. Michele Fine (1983–1984) has provided an excellent example of the way such biases can affect therapy in her candid account of a rape-counseling session with a black woman, Altamese Thomas. Altamese did not want to prosecute her attackers or talk with social workers or counselors. She disrupted Fine's middle-class views about taking control in the face of injustice.

Here is an excerpt from their dialogue:

FINE: Altamese, the police will be here to speak with you. Are you interested in prosecuting? Do you want to take these guys to court?

THOMAS: No, I don't want to do nothin' but get over this. . . . When I'm pickin' the guy out of some line, who knows who's messing around with my momma, or my baby. Anyway nobody would believe me. . . .

FINE: Do you think maybe you would like to talk with a counselor, in a few days, about some of your feelings?

THOMAS: I've been to one of them. It just made it worse. I just kept thinking about my problems too much. You feel better when you are talking, but then you got to go back home and they're still there. No good just talking when things ain't no better (Fine, 1983–1984, pp. 253–254).

Altamese Thomas has little power to change the causes of her problems—racism, poverty, and violence. Individualistic strategies could make matters worse for others in her family. They do little to improve oppressive economic and social arrangements.

We can, of course, argue that Altamese Thomas's passivity represents a form of psychological surrender. It is obvious that her behavioral patterns cause her great pain. They will not help her, nor will they help others like her in a similar situation. But if we do not take her social circumstances into account, we may blame her for her own victimization. Self-knowledge without power will do little for her.

This discussion of coping and power illustrates the dilemmas produced by limitations in the range of options available. It helps explain why psychological distress is expressed in gender-specific ways. It may also help put the question of whether one sex is "sicker" than the other in perspective. We cannot look at individual behavior in isolation from sociocultural circumstances. Psychological symptomology is closely tied to what normative roles are available. Because of the general inequality between women and men, it is inevitable that their psychological concerns will be acted out differently.

DEPRESSION

The disorder that has received the most attention in terms of sex and gender issues is depression. This is because mild to severe depression is a common problem in American society today. Superficially, depression appears to be an exaggeration of normal sadness. Depressed individuals describe their emotional state in highly negative terms, they may have a sad facial expression, and they may experience loss of appetite, insomnia, and fatigue. Other symptoms include stooped posture, slow speech, indecisiveness, hopelessness, and feelings of inadequacy and guilt. It has been estimated that 2 to 12 percent of American men and 5 to 26 percent of American women will suffer from depression at some time in their lives (Rothblum, 1983).

This variability in risk estimates illustrates some of the difficulties associated with clinical diagnoses of women and men. Diagnosis is an attempt to classify illnesses in discrete, mutually exclusive categories, each with a common origin, common course, and similar outcome. However, diagnosis is susceptible to sexist biases in a variety of ways (e.g., Worell & Remer, 1992).

Roles, Power, and Depression

Do gender roles affect how women and men experience depression? Are some life paths more likely to lead to depression than others? Is depression in women related to lack of power? The answer to these questions seems to be "yes." Let's look at the evidence.

Research suggests that women are expected to be more depressed than men, and men are judged more harshly when they act depressed. Depressive behavior in a man leads to more social rejection by peers than the same behavior does in a woman (Hammen & Peters, 1977). When college students interacted by phone with someone enacting a depressed or nondepressed role, depressed men were more strongly rejected than depressed women (Hammen & Peters, 1978). They were also seen as having more feminine traits than nondepressed men. Thus, a man who acts depressed may be doubly rejected—both because of his negative characteristics and because these characteristics are considered gender inappropriate.

It may take some time before males realize that depressive behavior is socially unacceptable for them. Girls and boys begin to express depression differently during the early teenage years (Webb & VanDevere, 1985). And, although they reported the same levels of subjective depression in college, young men stated that they would need to be more depressed to talk about it to a friend or to seek help than young women indicated (Padesky & Hammen, 1981). These self-appraisals were consistent with their actual behavior. Fewer men than women reported having talked to friends or having sought therapy for depression.

Gender may be more important than sex in affecting behaviors associated with depression. One recent study, for example, found no sex-related difference in overall depression. However, male and female college students with the same level of depression reported symptoms consistent with gender stereotypes. Depressed men reported physical symptoms such as sleep disturbances and loss of sexual drive. They also reported more social withdrawal and suicidal thoughts. Depressed women tended to report more emotional symptoms such as crying, sadness, and a sense of failure (Oliver & Toner, 1990). Similar gender-stereotypic differences have also been reported in patients who have been hospitalized for severe depression (Vredenburg, Krames, & Flett, 1986).

The degree of identification with traditional gender roles also influenced the way depression was expressed. Gender-typed individuals of either sex showed symptoms of depression that were consistent with traditional gender roles. For example, depressed feminine-identified women reported more self-dislike and weight loss and less insomnia than equally depressed but less gender-typed women. Depressed gender-typed men reported more withdrawal than other depressed men (Oliver & Toner, 1990).

Instrumental traits (associated with traditional masculinity) may protect both men and women from depression. On the basis of a meta-analysis of thirty-two studies of the relationship between gender-role orientation, depression, and general adjustment, Bernard Whitley (1985) has concluded that there is support for what he calls a masculinity model of adjustment. As discussed in Chapter 2, "masculine" people of either sex show higher adjustment and less depression than "feminine" people. Mental health is *not* associated with a gender orientation traditionally considered appropriate for one's sex.

On the other hand, emotionality (stereotypically associated with traditional femininity) may prolong depression and/or make it more severe. Women in whom a depressed mood had been induced were found to be more likely to think about emotions than similarly treated men, even though this prolonged their depressed mood. Cognitive style rather than biological sex actually predicted depressive outcomes. Once the tendency to dwell on particular thoughts was controlled, sex-related differences in the length or severity of the depressed mood disappeared (Butler & Nolen-Hoeksema, 1994).

Before you decide we would all be better adjusted if "a woman was just like a man," it is important to recognize the role that self-esteem plays in the relationship between traditional masculinity and mental health. The relationship between masculinity and adjustment disappears when level of self-esteem is taken into account (Feather, 1985; Whitley, 1985). High self-esteem protects individuals against depression. Of course, self-esteem reflects the values considered important by the culture as a whole. In Western society these values are androcentric and their expression is controlled by gender categorization. Signs of psychological disturbance may occur whenever people are denied an opportunity to engage in behaviors that enhance their self-esteem.

Life paths are also related to depression. As you learned in Chapters 10 and 12, married women consistently report more depression than married men, even when they are matched on age, income, and number of children. Single women report less depression than single men (Radloff, 1975). Full-time homemakers are particularly at risk for depression because of the low value that society places on their life path.

Contrary to the opinion that modern women are "stressed out" and depressed by juggling work, family, and relationships, research reviewed in Chapter 12 indicates that multiple roles are good for women's physical and mental health. Employment gives women more power, and power is linked to psychological well-being for both sexes. In fact, a great deal of the "sex difference" in depression may actually be attributable to power differences. Individuals who are younger, less educated, have lower incomes, or are unemployed are at high risk for depression regardless of their sex (Golding, 1988). Many of these factors are associated with being female. When they are all taken into account, "sex differences" may be insignificant.

A recent report of a Task Force on Women and Depression of the American Psychological Association (McGrath, Keita, Strickland, & Russo, 1990) highlights the extent to which their place in the social structure depresses women. It found, for example, that the most commonly found depressed individual was a woman with a young child who was living in poverty. It also found that the sexual and physical abuse of women was much greater than suspected and that victims were very vulnerable to depression. (See Chapter 14.) When we look at social context, it is difficult to view depression as an indicator of psychopathology unless it is the psychopathology of society rather than that of individual women.

Blaming Women: Reproductive Function as a Source of Depression

Despite the considerable body of evidence suggesting social causes for depression, explanations based on women's body chemistry still have an important place in medical texts. Women are regarded as being particularly vulnerable during critical points in their reproductive cycle: Three *syndromes* have been identified with stages in this cycle: the *premenstrual syndrome* or PMS, *postpartum depression*, and the *menopausal syndrome*. We will discuss them in some detail because they illustrate the power that social constructions have to define women's experience.

A syndrome is a constellation of symptoms associated with a particular cause. However, syndromes associated with women's reproductive lives appear to be particularly poorly defined. For example, no single symptom or pattern of signs is required for a diagnosis of PMS. There is also no agreed-upon standardized test to determine its existence or its cure (Ussher, 1989). Nevertheless, estimates have claimed that from 25 to 100 percent of women suffer from some form of premenstrual or menstrual emotional disturbance (Laws, 1983).

Medical and pharmaceutical interests helped to create PMS (Parlee, 1989). Careful research has produced little evidence to support the idea that most women have a negative premenstrual phase. In fact, the percentage of women in one study who said they had PMS (about 50 percent) was the same for those who did not actually meet the criteria for such a diagnosis as for those who did (about 10 percent of each group) (McFarlane & Williams, 1994). Since the researchers found that most participants (men as well as women) experienced a cyclic fluctuation of moods, they suggested that those women who believe they have PMS are attending to actual physiological changes, but mislabeling them.

Social labels have an important impact on the way women view their bodily changes. In another recent study, female college students completed either a "Menstrual Joy Questionnaire" or a "Menstrual Distress Questionnaire" before responding to a measure of menstrual attitudes. Those who first encountered "menstrual joy" reported more positive attitudes and cyclic changes (Chrisler, Johnston, Champagne, & Preston, 1994). Participants also reported that they were surprised by these findings because they had never before considered positive aspects of the menstrual cycle.

Postpartum depression is said to affect between 3 and 25 percent of women (Elliot, 1984). Like PMS, it is difficult to find a consistent description of this disorder, as there is little agreement between different researchers and practitioners (Ussher, 1989). A similar situation exists for menopausal depression (discussed in Chapter 13). There is a lack of agreement about what symptoms are required for diagnosis, no medical tests that differentiate sufferers from nonsufferers, and no effective medical treatment.

Feminists have charged that biologically determinist causes are being used to ignore the historical and political context of women's reproductive experiences (Brown, 1994; Ussher, 1989). As you have seen in Chapters 8 and 13, menstruation and menopause carry many negative values in our society. Pregnancy is a more mixed event. Thus, it is the postpartum period that is seen as dangerous.

The vagueness of what constitutes the risk period after birth makes it easy to confuse depressive responses to child rearing with those to childbearing. For example, a substantial percentage of women with children under the age of 5 years have been diagnosed as depressed (Oakley, 1986). The role of a parent with young children may be particularly stressful. In fact, men who are the primary caregivers for young children have been shown to suffer more severely from depression than their female counterparts (Jenkins, 1985).

The existence of so-called reproductive syndromes helps to justify beliefs in the biological inferiority of women. The view that their reproductive cycle makes women vulnerable to psychological problems helps to limit women, to define them as dangerous and deviant, and to exclude them from a role in society equal to that of men. Biological determinism—or anatomy as destiny—causes people to neglect other, more social, sources of women's unhappiness. Rather than social change, unhappy women are offered chemicals in the form of hormones or psychotropic drugs. At best, these substances are ineffective and, at worst, they may be habit forming and/or medically harmful. Although there is little evidence to support the existence of hormonal imbalance syndromes, they support a thriving industry of physicians, psychiatrists, and drug companies.

THE SOCIAL CONSTRUCTION OF FEMALE DISORDERS: THE VIEW FROM HISTORY

This is not the first time that scientific classification has been used to legitimate internal explanations for women's distress. Beginning in the mid-nineteenth century, an epidemic of nervous disorders labeled anorexia nervosa, hysteria, and neurasthenia raged in England and the United States.

The first of the female nervous disorders to be labeled during this period was *anorexia nervosa*—identified in 1873 as a new clinical syndrome among adolescent girls in both England and France. It was characterized by extreme emaciation, loss of appetite, lack of menstruation, and restless activity (Showalter, 1987).

The years between 1870 and World War I were also the "golden age" of *hysteria*. Classic hysteria had two defining characteristics—seizures or fits and sensations of choking (the latter was believed to be caused by the rising of the uterus within the body). However, attention soon moved from fits, paralyses, and anesthesias to traits, moods, and personality. By the end of the nineteenth century, "hysterical" had become almost interchangeable with "feminine" (Showalter, 1987). Hysterical women were described as highly impressionable, suggestible, and narcissistic (Smith-Rosenberg, 1985).

Neurasthenia, like hysteria, had a wide range of symptoms, from blushing, vertigo, and headaches to insomnia, depression, and uterine irritability. It was seen to be caused by increased mental activity in women, which sapped their strength (Showalter, 1987). All of these disorders were especially frequent among well-to-do, intellectual women, including those in the professions.

Physicians attributed these nervous conditions to the weakness of the female reproductive system and the strains put upon that system by women's ambition. As late as 1900, one physician pictured the female reproductive cycle in the following melodramatic terms:

> Many a young life is battered and forever crippled in the breakers of puberty; if it crosses these unharmed and is still not dashed to pieces on the rock of childbirth, it may still ground on the ever-recurring shallows of menstruation, and lastly, upon the final bar of the menopause ere protection is found in the unruffled waters of the harbor beyond the reach of sexual storms (Smith-Rosenberg, 1985, p. 184).

Others declared that mental breakdown would occur when women defied their "nature" by competing with men instead of serving them or by seeking alternatives or even additions to their maternal functions. One physician "concerned about 'the danger of solitary work' for girls 'of nervous family' studying at home, forbade the fifteen-year-old Virginia Woolf to continue her lessons and ordered her to spend four hours a day gardening" (Showalter, 1987, p. 126).

Many well-known women suffered from these disorders. Alice James, the sister of Henry and William James, began her career as an invalid at the age of 19. There is no way to know if Alice James's lifelong illness had a "real" organic basis. We do know, however, that unlike her brothers, she was never encouraged to go to college or to develop her gift for writing (Ehrenreich & English, 1979).

Psychiatric treatment of nervous women has been described as ruthless. Physicians assumed that patients were shamming. Their goal "was to isolate the patient from her family support systems, unmask her deceitful stratagems, coerce her into surrendering her symptoms, and finally overcome her self-centeredness" (Showalter, 1987, p. 137). The standard treatment was a "rest cure" developed by a noted American neurologist named Silas Weir Mitchell. During this treatment the patient was isolated from her family and friends for six weeks, confined to bed, and forbidden to sit up, sew, read, write, or do any intellectual work.

One of Mitchell's patients was Charlotte Perkins Gilman, who wrote a fictionalized account of her experiences in "The Yellow Wallpaper." Gilman's heroine went mad, although Gilman herself recognized that she was being brainwashed and left treatment. Among Mitchell's other patients were Jane Addams and Edith Wharton. These women were exceptions in that they went on to live full and active lives. Most cases were more like those of Alice James—neither fatal nor curable (Ehrenreich & English, 1979).

Feminist scholars have attempted to explain this epidemic of nervous diseases. They emphasize the limited roles that upper-class women were permitted during the Victorian era. These women had no serious productive work in the home, and tasks such as housework, cooking, and minding the children were left as much as possible to domestic servants. In general, they were expected to exchange sexual and reproductive duties for financial support (Ehrenreich & English, 1979).

Nervous disorders such as neurasthenia and hysteria provided a socially acceptable way for a woman to remove herself from her self-sacrificing role as a wife or mother. This escape from emotional and sexual demands was, however, purchased at the personal cost of pain and disability, and the social cost of an intensification of stereotypes about women's passivity and dependence (Smith-Rosenberg, 1985). This behavior also contributed to Victorian images of madwomen and to the idea that to be female was to be unstable.

The diagnosis of hysteria was limited to women, and when large numbers of men began to suffer from "shell shock" in response to the intolerable conditions of World War I, their "hysterical" behavior was labeled a functional neurosis (Showalter, 1987). This kind of attributional pattern of labeling women's characteristics as internally caused and men's as situationally induced can be found in discussions of gender-related differences in achievement as well as distress (see Chapter 12). Society's different view of social deviance in women and men is also found in the tendency to label men as "bad" and women as "mad." The relative distribution of men and women in prisons versus mental institutions reflects these assumptions (Burns, 1992).

The differential labeling of similar symptoms for women and men is an example of the social construction of psychological disorders. Disorders were also constructed in terms of social class. Working-class women did not have the time or money to support a cult of invalidism. Because they were not potential patients, nineteenth-century experts ignored their health. These experts blamed education for the greater weakness of affluent women. As you can see from the quotation below, their arguments were both sexist and racist:

> At war, at work, or at play, the white man is superior to the savage, and his culture has continually improved his condition. But with woman the rule is reversed. Her squaw sister will endure effort, exposure, and hardship which will kill the white woman. Education which has resulted in developing and strengthening the physical nature of man has been perverted through folly and fashion to render women weaker and weaker (Dr. Sylvanus Stall, in Ehrenreich & English, 1979, p. 114).

Social constructionism does not deny the reality of women's suffering. It does, however, point out the way in which some parts of women's experience may be expressed while others may not. In the nineteenth century, for example, educated women were permitted to be sick or mad, but they were not allowed to be angry or to protest their limited choices. It is possible to argue that some of our twentieth-century female disorders, such as anorexia and PMS, involve similar forms of social construction. For example, if the unacceptable parts of one's personality can be labeled PMS and be seen as the result of a pitiable hormonal imbalance, one can retain one's self-definition as a good woman (Laws, 1983). PMS can be used to deny responsibility for one's actions; for example, *women* are never violent, aggressive, and antisocial, but women with PMS are.

The issue here is not whether or not women make up their symptoms. Clearly so-called female disorders refer to real experiences. What is important is how we are taught to describe and label these experiences and how these labels fit socially acceptable roles. Sophie Laws (1983) argues that it is plausible to tie the recent boom in PMS to the second wave of feminism. Like nineteenth-century nervous disorders, PMS attempts to define women's consciousness of discontent in medical terms.

CULTURAL DETERMINATION OF SYMPTOMOLOGY

Eating Disorders

Hysteria and neurasthenia probably seem like quaint old-fashioned diseases. Anorexia, another major nineteenth-century female malady, is alive and well today. Professional journals and the popular press have proclaimed the existence and growth of an epidemic of eating disorders. Estimates of the incidence of eating disorders vary widely, but it is clear that the vast majority of people with anorexia and bulimia are women. In fact, the extent of dieting and concerns about weight control among women is so high today that it has been deemed a "normative discontent" (Rodin, Silberstein, & Striegel-Moore, 1984).

The "Normal" Desire For Thinness

Differential standards for weight in women and men have been discussed in Chapters 4 and 9 in terms of stereotypes and ideals of attractiveness. The results of one survey of college students illustrate the extent of sex-related differences in satisfaction with body weight. The researchers (McCaulay, Mintz, & Glenn, 1988) surveyed 176 undergraduates from several midwestern colleges. They found that a similar percentage of college men and women were in the normal weight category. Fifty percent of the male students perceived themselves to be of normal weight, compared with 40 percent of the female students. The other 50 percent of men were equally divided in perceiving themselves as either overweight or underweight, whereas the majority of women perceived themselves as overweight. The women wanted to *lose* an average of 8.4 pounds, while men wanted to *gain* an average of 2.9 pounds. Sex-related differences were even larger in the slightly overweight category. In this group, men wanted to lose an average of 5.5 pounds, whereas women wanted to lose 24 pounds. Even slightly underweight women wanted to lose an average of 1.4 pounds (see Figure 15.2).

Prejudice and Discrimination Against Overweight Women

Social factors seem to be more helpful in explaining weight disorders than individual differences are. The importance of thinness for feminine attractiveness is not merely a stereotype. Overweight children of both sexes are stigmatized. As adults, however, women are much more harshly punished than men for failing to achieve slenderness. Overweight high school girls are less likely to be accepted to college than their thinner peers with comparable credentials. Obese women, but not men, have lower academic and economic attainments than their parents (Wooley & Wooley, 1980). Overweight women frequently report that they have been subjected to job discrimination and feel that they have been the butt of unsavory jokes because of their weight (Snow & Harris, 1985). Overweight men more frequently mention that they were not asked to join social clubs and sports activities.

Media insults to the obese usually choose women as their targets. For example, many articles about Roseanne mention her weight as much as her personal crudity. Overweight women are also symbolically annihilated by the media (see Chapter 4). They have virtually disappeared as models in women's magazines over the last thirty-five years (Snow & Harris, 1986).

Although concerns about weight are justified on the basis of health, most of the data relating mortality and health risks to weight refer to men!

> Weight is of greatest concern to and weight loss is pursued most avidly by women, who are actually least affected in terms of health and survival. Among women the actual/expected mortality ratio rises negligibly from underweight women to women who are markedly obese. . . . Among women with marked overweight (average height 5′3″ to 5′6″ and weights 195 to 254 lbs.) the mortal-

FIGURE 15.1. Dying to be thin.

> ity rates are still lower than among men in the most favorable build category, i.e., underweight . . . (Gubner, 1974, in Wooley & Wooley, 1980, p. 140).

As indicated in Chapter 9, cultural standards about weight have become more demanding in recent years. It is probably worth noting that even the word *obesity* is a twentieth-century word. (See Figure 15.2.)

Social control of weight in women even involves control of their eating behavior. In one intriguing study, entitled "Women, but not men, are what they eat," male and female undergraduates read a food diary and rated the person who had written it (Chaikin & Pliner, 1987). In the diary, either a young woman or young man was portrayed as eating either a small breakfast and lunch or a large breakfast and lunch. Ratings of the man were not affected by the size of the meals he ate. In contrast, individuals of both sexes saw a woman who ate smaller meals as significantly more feminine and more expressive (emotional, kind, and understanding of others) than a woman who ate larger meals. They also saw the woman who ate less as more concerned about her appearance and significantly better looking than the woman who ate more.

Susan Basow and Diane Kobrynowicz (1993) conducted a similar study recently using videotapes of college women and men consuming the same large or small meal. Both women and men rated the female who ate the smallest "feminine" meal (a salad) as more socially appealing than the same woman when she ate the larger "masculine" meal (a hoagie).

College-age women appear to be aware of the effect that eating less has on perceptions of their femininity. They have been found to eat a smaller snack during a "get-acquainted" study when they interacted with a desirable male confederate than when they interacted with an undesirable male or any female (Mori, Chaikin, & Pliner, 1987). Their behavior indicates that they are aware of stereotypes that label overweight people as low in self-esteem, unlikely to be dating, unerotic, and more deserving of a fatter, uglier partner than normal-weight individuals (Harris, 1990).

Disordered Eating as Pathology

It is unclear at what point this desire for thinness translates into the pathological behaviors associated with *anorexia* (dieting to skeletal weight, fasting,

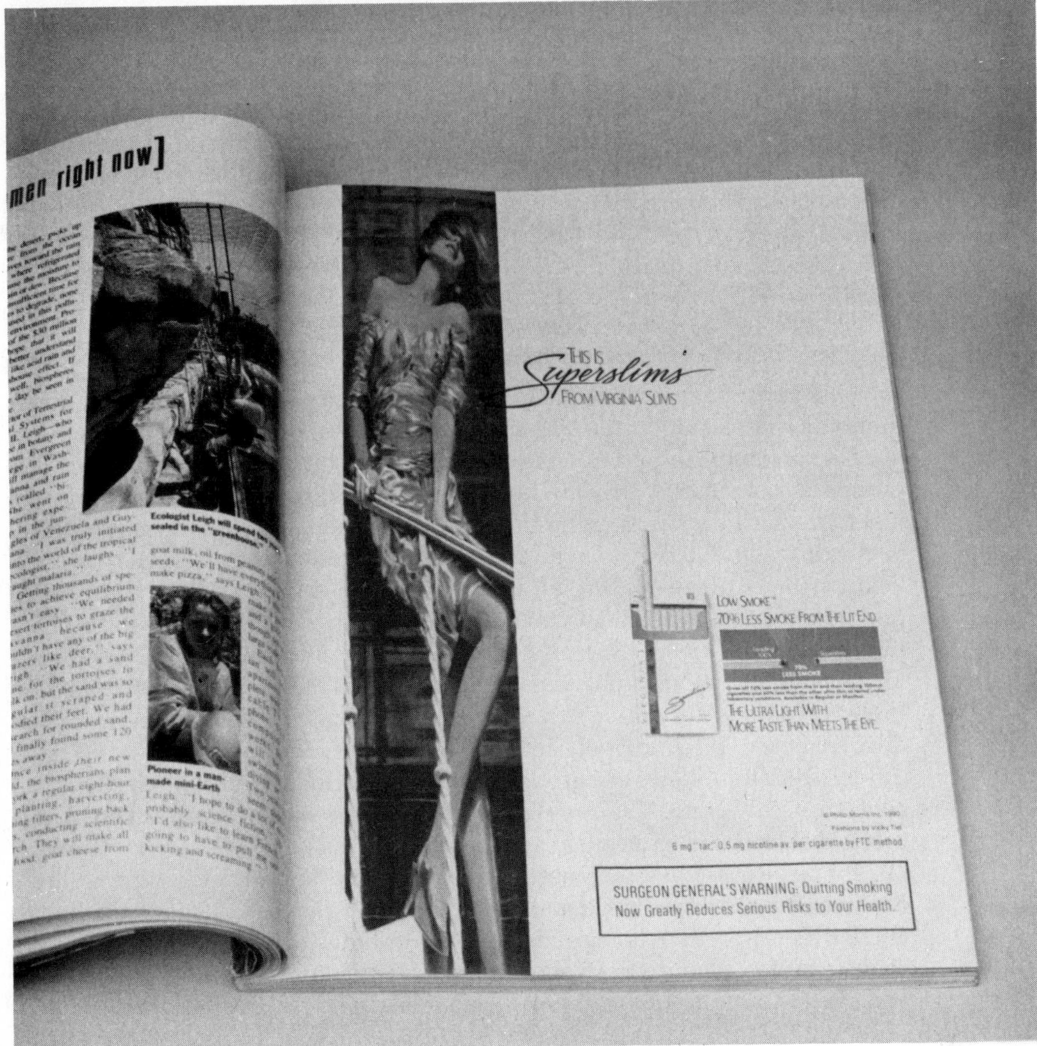

FIGURE 15.2. This advertisement illustrates normative pressures for extreme thinness in women.

and purging combined with rigorous exercise) and *bulimia* (bingeing combined with purging in which normal weight may be maintained). Women have been found repeatedly to score higher than men on scales assessing disordered eating (Hesse-Biber, 1989; Silberstein et al., 1988). For women, exercise for weight control is also associated with disordered eating.

Large-scale surveys of college populations have found many more women than men who are obsessed with the need to be thin. In one such study, for example, 21.4 percent of the women and only 1.8 percent of the men scored in the abnormal range of an eating disorder scale (Hesse-Biber, 1989). Studies that have used the DSM III diagnostic criteria for bulimia find prevalence rates from 5 to 19 percent for women and 0 to 4 percent for men in various college samples.

Most of these women appear to be able to function reasonably well despite their extreme preoccupation with weight. It is difficult to determine their actual health status, however, because most anorexic women deny that they have any problem at all. Bulimic women are also unwilling to disclose their "disgusting and wasteful" food practices. Since our culture so highly values thinness, excessively low weight may be ignored or even socially rewarded. Women in treatment are often those who still reside within the parental home, where their abnormal food habits and excessive exercise cannot escape notice. Nevertheless, anorexia is a serious illness that can result in death. Psychological treatment of anorexic women is notably ineffective and relapses are frequent (Bemis, 1978). (See Figure 15.3.)

The Demography of Eating Disorders

The "typical" anorexic woman has been portrayed as postadolescent, upper or middle class, and white. Recent evidence suggests, however, that this disorder is extending itself into younger age groups, some male groups, and some groups of women of color. One study found that fourth graders are joining the diet craze and risk stunting their growth to maintain a very thin body (Mellin, Scully, & Irwin, 1986). Another found that 11 percent of the girls in a rural public high school primarily serving a low-income Hispanic and Native-American population reported eating habits consistent with clinical criteria for bulimia (Snow & Harris, 1989). Other researchers have found there is an increased risk for developing eating problems among gay men, some of whom stress a thin body type and are attentive to fashion and appearance (Herzog, Norman, Gordon, & Pepose, 1984; Striegel-Moore, Silberstein, & Rodin, 1986).

In-depth interviews of a group of high school girls reveals the extent of their concern with weight. The girls engaged in a form of discourse among themselves that has been termed "fat talk" (Nichter & Vuckovic, 1994). The statement "I'm so fat" was frequently repeated throughout the school day. It was not used, however, by girls who are actually overweight or those who had attempted to change their weight over sustained periods of time. The phrase appears to be a request for reassurance from one's peers rather than an actual statement about weight. At least one 14-year-old informant seemed to be aware of this.

> Interviewer: What usually happens when someone says I'm so fat?
>
> Jamie: About six or seven girls go "No, you're not!" Probably it's just because, you know, you like to hear that people don't think you're fat. And it's mostly like in gym, cuz when you change into your gym clothes those are so bunchy anyway they make you look fat. And, uh, but I'd say, I'd say that not very many of them mean that, mean it when they say it. They just want to hear "Oh no you're not" (Nichter & Vuckovic, 1994, p. 114).

A confusion between thinness and a perfect life appears to be characteristic of many white female adolescents. Researchers report being struck by the uniformity of teenage girls' descriptions of the ideal girl (tall, thin, and usually with long blond hair) regardless of the girls' own physical characteristics (Nichter & Vuckovic, 1994). The responses of African-American adolescents were much more varied. Their descriptions often began with a list of personality traits rather than physical attributes (Parker, Nichter, Nichter, Vuckovic, Sims, & Ritenbaugh (1995). In terms of physical attributes, they described the ideal girl

IGURE 15.3. The consequences of anorexia. Photographs of Karen Carpenter "before" and "after."

as having it "going on." This meant having what they had work for them: long nails, pretty eyes, big lips, nice thighs, whatever.

White adolescents tend to exhibit body-image dissatisfaction and abnormal concern about dieting and weight at about twice the rate of their black peers (Root, 1990). Older urban black women are significantly less likely to use extremely restrictive dieting practices than their white counterparts are (Thomas & James, 1988). However, a substantial percentage of these women did report fasting (25 percent), use of diuretics (11.9 percent) and laxatives (8.8 percent), and self-induced vomiting (2 percent) for weight control. Another study of Native-American women found that 24 percent were using purging as a means of weight control (Rosen et al., 1988).

It has been argued that the cultural context that equates beauty with whiteness "protects" minority women from eating disorders. These recent findings suggest, however, that cultural demands for thinness can extend beyond the original target group. It is also possible that prevailing stereotypes of the white, upper-middle-class victim may conspire against the early recognition of eating disorders in people of color (Root, 1990). If we do not look for a phenomenon, we are not likely to find it.

A Feminist Perspective

Obviously, some people are more susceptible to eating disorders than others. We have focused on social-risk factors rather than individual psychodynamic perspectives because it is important to keep individual behavior in cultural perspective. Why do people in some groups develop some symptoms much higher rate than others? This question is particularly important in sidering a disorder that appears to be increasingly common in recent year

This kind of refocusing of questions moves the problem away from ing the victim to issues of social and cultural change. Thus, we can ask why dards for women's attractiveness are under such tight social control and v society benefits from these standards. Feminist therapists argue that we c change a person's behavior in isolation from her situational context. And, sense, situational refers to political and economic as well as familial ci stances.

It is also important to retain a historical perspective in the area of eati orders. Anorexia is neither the first nor the last such disorder to be cu constructed. For example, from 1870 to 1920 a large number of America lescent girls were described as suffering from a disorder called *chlorosis* (berg, 1982). Victims were purported to be anemic but to suffer also "caprices and perversions" of the appetite, menstrual irregularities, and a sire for sleep and repose." No cause or cure was ever isolated. The "disease" appeared completely by 1930, probably because medical views about menst vulnerability had also declined and because chlorosis had become a social bility in terms of women's newfound views of themselves as responsible ma agers and nurturers.

Feminist therapy stresses that symptom selection does not occur in a cul tural vacuum. What is perceived as desirable and normative will influence how women and men behave. Culture also influences whether such behaviors are noticed and how they are labeled. It is important to ask who gains when a woman's behavior receives a "sick" label. What are the advantages of such a label to herself and others? And what do women gain when they acquire the ability to name their own experiences?

Agoraphobia

Agoraphobia is another psychological disorder more commonly found in women than in men. Based on an incidence rate of 6.3 per 1,000, more than a million women in the United States find their lives restricted by this phobia (Chambless & Goldstein, 1980). *Agoraphobia*—literally "fear of the marketplace"—is diagnosed when an individual shows generalized fear and avoidance of leaving a place of refuge (almost always the home) and entering the outside world. However, the degree of restriction varies widely. Affected individuals may fear crowds, bridges, tunnels, public places and conveyances, elevators, expressways, being distant from home, or being separated from a trusted companion. Many people with agoraphobia develop an extreme dependence on others to take care of them in situations that they perceive as dangerous.

Agoraphobia is considered to be the most common and serious phobic reaction seen by clinical practitioners. It has been linked with women's roles and is sometimes known as "housewife's disease." We will discuss it in some detail because it illustrates some of the ways people learn symptoms and how others around them can serve as complicitors in their symptomology.

The Intrapsychic View of Agoraphobia

Agoraphobic individuals have been described as passive and dependent people who lack the ability to express their feelings and needs. They label themselves as anxious rather than angry or sad (as they appear to others). They also rate themselves as more fearful of criticism, rejection, and disapproval than other phobic individuals, and they rate poorer on taking responsibility and making decisions (Chambliss & Goldstein, 1980).

These descriptions of agoraphobic women in terms of stereotypic feminine traits may be another example of blaming the victim. Extreme dependency is more acceptable for women in our culture. Other traits possessed by agoraphobic women such as fearfulness, indecision, and sensitivity to the criticism of oth ers are also exaggerations of traditional feminine stereotypes that bring som social rewards. They may, for example, cause less conflict than an overt reje tion of familial demands would. Agoraphobic behaviors place the blame for a marital difficulties within the woman. Because independence is so anxiety- voking for her, it may be easier for her to blame herself than to recognize culties with her marriage. Realistically, independence may be difficult be she may not have acquired the skills necessary to function autonomousl

The Social Reinforcement of Agoraphobia

Agoraphobia appears to be a learned response to stress. It often be a period of generalized anxiety that grows into a fear of panic attack fantasized consequences—a fear of fear. People with agoraphobia r the factors that make them anxious—seeing them as places or situ than people. Such nonadaptive attributional styles may be learne bers of their families. A high rate of phobic disorders has been re atives of agoraphobic individuals (Fodor, 1982).

Unlike some of the other disorders we have discussed, a re- quires the cooperation of others. The majority of people with ia are married women. As many as 60 percent state that they wou er to work outside the home if their symptoms permitted (Brehony, 198). However, only a small proportion of agoraphobic women do so. In severe cases, other family members must do all outside chores, such as shopping, driving, school visitation, and so on.

Despite (or because of) their wives' extreme dependence, husbands of agoraphobic women appear to find rewards in the relationship. Some recent research has found, for example, that men who are married to agoraphobic women are more satisfied with their marriages if their wives have traditional views about gender. The opposite is true in husbands with nonagoraphobic partners. The agoraphobic woman's inability to work outside the home and to achieve greater independence may contribute to her husband's marital satisfaction if the couple interprets her problem as evidence of her femininity (Hafner & Minge, 1989).

Since agoraphobia has been viewed primarily from a psychodynamic perspective, it is difficult to determine how much of women's behavior is due to physical as well as psychological constraints. Jane Ussher (1990) described her first encounter with an agoraphobic client in the following words:

> On my first clinical placement I saw a woman client, whom I shall call Helen, who was referred for agoraphobia. She experienced severe panic attacks upon leaving her home alone and could not travel any distance on the underground train. I was told that this was a "straightforward anxiety management case," and prepared to treat Helen with systematic desensitization, a form of behavior therapy, as instructed. Yet when evidence of physical and sexual abuse of Helen on the part of her husband emerged, I was informed that it was not relevant to the referred problem and should be ignored. . . . As Helen's husband would not attend for "couple therapy," and Helen did not spontaneously express any wish to leave the violent relationship, I was informed that the most positive outcome was to help her deal with the situation, conquer her fears, and that if she didn't like it, she wouldn't stay (Ussher, 1990, p. 56).

Most psychological therapy is designed to help change the individual. Beginning with Freud, such therapy has been more often used to reconcile the powerless to their circumstances rather than to assist them in creating social change. In the following section of this chapter, we will discuss the contributions of feminist theory, research, and practice in dealing with issues of personal and social change.

ISSUES IN TREATMENT

Sex Bias in Diagnosis: The Politics of Labeling

Treatment begins with diagnosis. However, as we discussed earlier, psychological diagnoses are not easy to make. Mental health practitioners are assisted in their diagnoses by a huge manual published by the American Psychiatric Association. This book, called the *Diagnostic and Statistical Manual of Mental Disorders* (DSM for short), contains a list of diagnostic categories, descriptions of each disorder, and criteria for their application. The clinical descriptions at the beginning of the chapter were taken from one of the recent versions of this manual.

The manual is periodically updated by a panel of experts—primarily white male psychiatrists. The controversy over the most recent editions, DSM-III-R and DSM-IV (American Psychiatric Association, 1987; 1994), illustrates the extent to which myths about women and femininity persist in traditional mental health circles. This persistence is of great concern to feminist practitioners because the DSM-III-R (and its successors) is used to determine which individuals are worthy of treatment and how they should be treated. DSM categories even determine whether government agencies or private insurance companies should pay for the therapist's services.

While the DSM-III-R was being revised, feminist therapists realized that several new categories were being considered for inclusion that had negative implications for women. Two of these categories were self-defeating personality disorder and late luteal phase dysphoric disorder. These correspond to what is popularly known as the masochistic personality and the premenstrual syndrome. Feminist objections to these diagnostic categories illustrate once again the political uses and consequences of the power to name.

Self-Defeating Personality Disorder

Feminist psychologists noted that the concept of masochism derives from psychoanalytic theory (Committee on Women in Psychology, 1985). It fails to take into account sociocultural variables that might yield similar behaviors in the absence of any personality disorder. Laura Brown (1986), for example, pointed out that victims of interpersonal violence have a high rate of psychiatric illness. Nevertheless, the researchers who conducted the field trial of more than 300 patients used in the development of the diagnosis of self-defeating personality disorder never questioned them about their past or current experiences of sexual, physical, or emotional abuse.

Personality traits are, moreover, considered to be enduring patterns of perceiving, relating to, and thinking about the environment and oneself. However, many of the behaviors associated with this diagnostic category decrease or disappear when the victimized individual is removed from the abusive context for as short a period as six months.

Ignoring a history of abuse and its behavioral consequences results in blaming the victim. Her personality may be seen as the source of the violence in her life rather than vice versa. Diagnosis of her behavior as pathological also illustrates the way double binds operate. Women are labeled as "sick" if they won't leave an abusive situation, although they are encouraged to keep their families together. They are blamed because they do not "look out for number one" although they are censured by the conservative press as selfish and foolish if they try to combine work and home life. A label such as masochistic personality allows both clinicians and society to blame women for their "failures" without requiring anyone to question the cultural context and its effects on psychological functioning (Brown, 1986).

Ignoring an abusive situation within the home can have devastating consequences. Sexual and physical abuse contribute to serious mental illness in women. For example, several recent studies of chronically psychotic women patients in mental institutions have indicated that a high proportion of those who appear to be irresponsive to treatment were the victims of childhood abuse. Childhood incest appears to be particularly likely to produce the most intractable symptomology (Beck & van der Kolk, 1987). The severity of hospitalized women's symptoms has also been linked with the amount of other sexual and physical abuse they had been exposed to as children (Bryer, Nelson, Miller, & Krol, 1987). These studies demonstrate how important it is for therapists to recognize and respond to the violence in an individual's home.

Late Luteal Phase Dysphoric Disorder

This disorder is very similar to the premenstrual syndrome we have already discussed. Here we will focus on another issue involving this diagnostic category. We will examine the question of what is wrong with naming a mental disorder in relation to the menstrual cycle.

There are a number of feminist answers to this question. First, this label establishes a mental disorder purportedly caused by a normal process unique to women. Although a number of examples of this kind of labeling occurred in the past, this diagnostic category is the first such example to occur in modern times.

The label adds another layer of taint to an already maligned physiological process. It targets women's biology as the source of their problems. Second, placing this diagnostic category in an official manual (even in an appendix entitled "Proposed Diagnostic Categories Needing Further Study") legitimizes a classification that has not been empirically validated. Research guided by the label may be directed away from the role of situational and social factors in the expression of symptoms. Finally, the label gives great importance to the menstrual cycle as an influence on behavior (Alagna & Hamilton, 1986).

What we look for determines what we find. Physiological terminology means that researchers look for physiological causes. Many studies have found no hormonal differences between women who experience large rather than small mood changes (Hamilton & Gallant, 1990). One of these negative studies has found, however, that the women who reported severe PMS were more likely to be married and to be working at home caring for small children (Sanders, Warner, Backstrom, & Bancroft, 1983). Many similar role and contextual effects might be found if more such studies were conducted.

Terminology can also affect women's perceptions of themselves. Jean Hamilton and Sheryl Gallant (1988), two prominent researchers in this field, offer an important statement about such connections:

> Women who report premenstrual changes may feel that a diagnosis will both legitimize their experiences and relieve them of responsibility for periodic gender-uncharacteristic behavior; that is, a biological rhythm can be seen as the cause of premenstrual feelings of anger or irritability which a woman finds unacceptable without such an attribution. Although this may seem to absolve women of responsibility for their actions in the short run and may elicit sympathy and compassion, it also reinforces the victim role, which may lead to feelings of powerlessness and may interfere with opportunities for psychotherapy directed at personal growth and self control (Hamilton & Gallant, 1988, p. 275).

To say that cyclic mood disorders may be socially constructed does not mean that women's experiences of premenstrual changes are not taken seriously by feminists. But their self-perceptions can be validated without being pathologized as a serious mental disorder.

Despite feminist objections, PMS has been incorporated into the new DSM-IV as premenstrual dysphoric disorder. It becomes even more important, therefore, to ask how diagnostic categories are determined. One feminist clinical psychologist's questions include:

> How does this construct figure in our accounts of otherwise unaccountable behavior? How is the boundary drawn between disorders on the one hand and crime, eccentricity, or alternative lifestyles on the other? Who is party to the negotiations that fix the boundaries, and who polices them? What kinds of claims-making activities surround the birth of new categories of disorders and the death of exhausted ones? (Marecek, 1993, p. 7).

You should also ask who gains by sex-biased diagnostic labels. Unfounded diagnoses do not help women, advance research, or make clinicians more empathetic. Labels can cause people to believe that a particular disorder *really* exists, but they do not make ambiguous data stronger (Alagna & Hamilton, 1986).

The Double Standard in Diagnostic Categories

While researchers are aware that vague diagnostic descriptions promote gender stereotyping and sex bias in diagnosis (Hamilton, Rothbart, & Dawes, 1986), other androcentric biases involving diagnostic categories have received less attention. The "experts" who construct these categories are predominantly powerful men with a psychodynamic perspective. The content of the DSM at any given time is the codified opinions of those in power (Brown, 1994).

Androcentric biases have led to a number of important omissions. The subjective experience of the victim has been ignored and, thus, the degree to which individuals feel able to leave an exploitative or abusive situation is overrated (Committee on Women in Psychology, 1985). The diagnostician may lack adequate information about life circumstances of individuals different from himself. Such ignorance can lead to race and class as well as sex biases. A psychodynamic orientation leads inevitably to the neglect of social context. This may result in pathologizing the individual without considering outside forces.

Androcentric biases induce presumptions that autonomy and individualism are healthier than dependency and concern with relationships. These categorizations may also be flawed. Cheryl Travis (1988b) has commented wittily on what could happen if we reversed our sex-biased definitions of dependency.

> Suppose dependency were defined as letting someone else choose one's underwear, clean one's clothing, cook one's meals, arrange details of one's vacation? Men who do not become competent in these spheres or exert energy in fulfilling these tasks are not perceived as dependent or having failed to separate. They are not thought to suffer psychologically or emotionally from the condition, nor perceived to be less developed as individuals. Rather men are thought to be exhibiting their independence of women and home by pursuing public activities (Travis, 1988b, p. 20).

In a similar vein, Paula Caplan (1991) has proposed a new diagnostic category called "delusional dominating personality disorder." This diagnostic category describes the psychopathology of men who conform to social norms for the "real man." Its behavioral criteria include the following:

> * The presence of any one of the following delusions: (a) the delusion of personal entitlement to the services of (1) any woman with whom one is personally associated, (2) females in general for males in general, (3) both of the above; (b) the delusion that women like to suffer and be ordered around; (c) the delusion that physical force is the best method of solving interpersonal problems; (d) the delusion that sexual and aggressive impulses are uncontrollable in (1) oneself, (2) males in general, (3) both of the above; (e) the delusion that pornography and erotica are identical. . . .
> * A pathological need to affirm one's social importance by displaying oneself in the company of females who meet any three of the following criteria: (a) are conventionally physically attractive; (b) are younger than oneself; (c) are shorter in stature than oneself; (d) weigh less than oneself; (e) appear to be lower on socioeconomic criteria than oneself; (f) are more submissive than oneself.
> * A distorted approach to sexuality, displaying itself in one or both of these ways: (a) a pathological need for flattery about one's sexual performance

and/or the size of one's genitalia; (b) an infantile tendency to equate large breasts on women with their sexual attractiveness.

* A tendency to feel inordinately threatened by women who fail to disguise their intelligence (Caplan, 1991, p. 173).

Caplan's new diagnostic category may or may not be taken seriously, but it demonstrates the extent to which social norms and individual pathology can be confused, as well as the effect values have on what is considered normative.

Sex Bias in Practitioner Attitudes

Some of the earliest studies on gender stereotypes found that clinical practitioners completely shared popular beliefs about the appropriate and normative characteristics of men and women (Broverman et al., 1972). More recent studies have found that clinical practitioners have become more willing to see human traits in less gender-biased ways. Nevertheless, clinicians still classify more stereotypically masculine than feminine characteristics as socially desirable. Differences between conceptions of a healthy female and a healthy adult whose sex was unspecified have also been found. But practitioners made no distinctions between healthy adults and healthy males (Phillips & Gilroy, 1985).

In a review of seventeen studies of gender stereotyping of mental health standards by therapists, Julia Sherman (1980) noted that only one showed no evidence of stereotyping. Male practitioners appeared to be more conservative than female practitioners in their attitudes toward women in five of ten studies surveyed. The evidence about sex-related differences among clinical practitioners is quite inconsistent and factors other than the clinician's sex may be more important in inducing gender biases. For example, clinicians of both sexes have been found to be more likely to view a female client more positively than a male with identical symptoms (Hansen & Reekie, 1990). They are also more likely to recommend more medication and less psychotherapy for elderly depressed female patients than for younger women or men of any age (Ford & Sbordone, 1980; Ray, McKinney, & Ford, 1987). These studies indicate that a double standard in beliefs about mental health continues to exist.

Sex Biases in Treatment: The Use of Medication

One alternative to psychotherapy is the use of what are known as psychotropic drugs—substances that alter mood, thinking, or behavior. Such drugs include tranquilizers, antidepressants, and sedatives that have a variety of generic and trade names (Valium, Librium, Elavil, Seconal, etc.). In the United States at the end of the 1970s, more than two-thirds of all prescriptions for psychotropic drugs each year were written for women. Women comprised 63 percent of those for whom tranquilizers were prescribed, 71 percent of those given stimulants, and 71 percent of those receiving antidepressants (Carmen, Russo, & Miller, 1981).

It may be helpful if we translate these percentages into actual numbers of prescriptions. Recent surveys indicate that women received 53 million prescriptions for psychotropic drugs versus 26 million for men (Travis, 1988b). This sex difference is not simply due to the fact that women go to the doctor more often than men. They receive such prescriptions at a higher rate (if 100 people visit a physician, approximately eight women versus six men will receive a prescription). And once women receive a prescription, there is a tendency for it to be continued over several years, whereas the pattern among men is to receive psychotropic drugs for more limited periods (Travis, 1988b).

No differences between men and women in the use of over-the-counter drugs have been found. Instead, women disproportionately use and abuse prescription drugs, which are stronger and which require the cooperation of a physician. Although great attention has been paid to the abuse of illicit drugs, more people use psychotropic drugs. In addition to being female, these people are more likely to be older, richer, and white than illicit drug users (Fidell, 1982).

A number of factors help to explain why women are likely to abuse psychotropic drugs. As you have just read, physicians are simply more likely to prescribe such medication to them than to men. Gender stereotypes among physicians lead them to perceive that women are likely to be depressed or to have anxiety reactions. Such stereotypes even carry over into the medications prescribed to women and men after life-threatening surgery. One recent study found, for example, that male patients were administered more pain medication after a coronary artery bypass and female patients were administered more sedatives (Calderone, 1990). These differences are consistent with the belief that women are more emotional than men and more apt to exaggerate complaints about pain.

Stereotypic beliefs are especially likely to affect behavior toward older women. The prescription rate for psychotropic drugs is quite similar for both sexes until age 45. After age 45, women have a substantially higher rate than men (Travis, 1988b). You may well ask what it is about women at age 40 and beyond that seems to require psychotropic drug prescriptions. Some answers to this question were given in Chapter 13.

Drug advertisements play a major role in supporting differential patterns of prescription use. The images they use support traditional gender stereotypes. An analysis of the contents of drug advertisements over a five-year period showed the following (Prather & Fidell, 1975):

1. There was a strong tendency to associate psychotropic drugs with female patients.
2. Nonpsychoactive drug advertisements usually showed a male patient (this combination is particularly insidious because it indicates that real illnesses are experienced by men while mental problems are suffered by women).
3. The symptoms listed for male and female users of psychotropic drugs were significantly different. Men were usually depicted as presenting specific and work-related symptoms, whereas women were shown to complain of diffuse anxiety, tension, and depression.

Current drug advertisements continue to stress the image of the troublesome woman. One such advertisement depicted a woman seated in a chair with her head and arms fading into the back and arms of the chair, while the caption asked, "Is this patient becoming a fixture in your office?" Advertisements also encourage the adaptation of women to traditional roles and responsibilities. For example, one advertisement illustrated a harassed housewife caged behind bars made of brooms and mops. The caption read, "You can't set her free, but you can make her feel less anxious." Another stated that the physician could help an entire family by tranquilizing the mother so that she would be able to cook and serve their meals. This caption read, "Treat one—six people benefit" (Travis, 1988b).

As early as 1971, Robert Seidenberg, a noted psychiatrist, pointed out that such advertisements can lead to false impressions (Seidenberg, 1971). They imply that difficulty with or reluctance to do housework may be a sign of mental illness. They suggest that it is medically sound to prescribe drugs to overcome possible resentment toward one's role in life, and they deflect attention from other alternatives for women.

Feminist therapists would consider many women's problems as structural rather than intrapsychic. However, most psychotropic drug prescriptions are written by general practitioners and internists—not psychologists (Fidell, 1982). Social changes are also harder to make than "advances" in drug therapy, although adequate child care, decent wages, or more responsive husbands might make many women less depressed.

Institutional Biases in the Treatment of Women and Men

Perceptions about gender-related differences in psychological disorders influence other aspects of treatment as well. Women's disorders may be characterized as "acting in" whereas men's disorders may be characterized as "acting out." There is a double standard in the way women and men are treated when they violate normative standards of acceptable behavior in these gender-typed ways. Women are more likely to be defined as mentally ill and are treated by clinical practitioners. Men are more likely to be seen as engaging in antisocial activities and are dealt with by the criminal justice system. Thus, they are not counted as suffering from psychological disorders. This kind of definitional difference helps make it appear that more women than men are mentally ill.

You might feel that it is better to be defined as ill than as a criminal. However, the standards of what is criminal behavior are clearer than definitions of mental instability (every society has, for example, a codified set of laws and penalties for breaking them). Definitions of criminality are applied to behavior, whereas mental illness is perceived as more internally based and less under the control of the patient. Psychological treatment, in contrast to a criminal's sentence, also has no time limits or criteria for termination. Our society's institutionalized responses to gender-typed deviance may, thus, contribute to social myths about women's greater weakness and instability.

GENDER AND THERAPY

The Feminist Critique of Traditional Treatment Methods

The use of drugs instead of psychotherapy and social change is probably the most negative aspect of a medical model of women's problems. The medical model has encouraged women to seek individual solutions to many problems that may not best be solved individually—or may not be responsive to individual remedies at all. It has discouraged women from finding more social or collective avenues of self-help. For people with less power—people whose emotional problems are most often rooted in social arrangements and practices that have severely restricted their life options—the medical model can be destructive. The belief that they can solve by themselves problems over which they have no control as individuals can have severely depressing results.

Powerless individuals are also more likely to be treated with drugs, electroshock, or medical hospitalization than with long-term individual psychotherapy (Greenspan, 1983). In Great Britain, for example, black women are more likely than white women to be diagnosed as having a chronic rather than an acute mental health problem and to be institutionalized for mental illness (Watson & Williams, 1992).

Psychologists generally view psychotherapy as a positive alternative to drugs or imprisonment for helping people cope with their problems. However, traditional theories of psychotherapy contain assumptions that are only marginally less destructive than physical "cures." For example, most such theories are psychodynamic in nature. This means that they assume that people's problems are "all in their heads"—that personal reality is mostly determined by unconscious forces in their minds. This belief is closely associated with a medical view of psychological disorders—that emotional problems can be cured in the same way as physical problems. A third assumption follows from the other two. "If the source of a person's emotional pain is a psychic disease or disorder, then only an expert in diagnosis and treatment is equipped to offer a cure" (Greenspan, 1983, p. 26).

Feminist therapists have charged that psychodynamic theories lead practitioners to make the fundamental attribution error (discussed in Chapter 5). The locus of causality is placed within individuals rather than in their circumstances. People are, therefore, viewed as ultimately responsible for their own discontent. Because of this perspective, traditional therapists are more likely to see pathology in normal behavior. This is especially true when they are evaluating people whose life circumstances are most different from their own. Women's coping strategies are particularly likely to be labeled as deviant when viewed from our society's androcentric perspective.

Traditional therapy can also be viewed as a form of social control. We have already discussed sex biases in diagnosis and treatment induced by the gender-stereotypic categories of DSM-III. Screening and diagnosis have political and economic elements that are particularly evident in the case of women (Chesler, 1972). For example, one study of women who had been hospitalized for mental disorders, released, and subsequently rehospitalized found that their prognosis depended partly on whether or not they could perform their household duties adequately (Angrist, Dinitz, Lefton, & Pasamanick, 1968). Husbands were found to be extremely tolerant of helpless dependent behavior in their wives as long as they continued to manage the household cleaning and cooking. The critical factor appeared to be whether the women acted in placid and acquiescent ways. Women who expressed their anger and refused to perform domestic services were typically returned to the hospital.

You may note the similarity between these results and those reported about agoraphobic women and their husbands. Husbands of agoraphobics reported themselves as happier than other husbands in the study despite their wives' extreme dependency. Drug advertisements discussed earlier in the chapter also propose chemical means to ensure domestic tranquility.

The most powerful feminist criticism of traditional psychotherapy is its focus on personal rather than social change. Women are often labeled as disordered when the true diagnosis should be an unjust society (Kaplan, 1983). As one feminist therapist has pointed out:

> As long as basic structural inequities of power exist in society, large numbers of women will manifest symptoms of this inequality. Working to correct social inequities is, in the long run, the only final cure for most forms of female emotional distress. Therapy can help people cope with certain intolerable social conditions, but it cannot improve those conditions unless it contributes to raising the consciousness of patients so that they will be less likely to tolerate them. On the one hand, this points to the necessity to demystify therapy so that people are no longer encouraged to believe that only individual psychological "treatment" can cure what ails them. On the other hand, this points to the by-and-large unexplored potential of therapy to be an instrument of social change (Greenspan, 1983, p. 36).

Greenspan argues that the ultimate goal of woman-oriented therapy is to help the female patient overcome the ways in which she colludes with her own oppression and thereby to help her more fully recognize her own power, both as an individual and as a member of a community of women.

Feminist therapists have criticized the process of therapy as well as its assumptions and goals. The myth of the detached and neutral expert has tended to cloud the fact that every therapist offers a world view to his or her clients—the terms by which they are to understand themselves and their world. As you have seen from the case of Dora early in this chapter, the therapist's choice of words, his choice of what to go after in therapy, what to analyze, what to stress and what to ignore, are all political acts laden with meaning. There is nothing the least bit neutral about this process (Greenspan, 1983).

Feminist Therapy

Consciousness-Raising (C-R) Groups

Feminist alternatives to traditional therapy began to emerge in the early 1970s. Many basic ideas were drawn from the ideology of the women's movement. One early development was the concept of consciousness raising based on the idea that an altered consciousness was necessary for social change. A key focus was that the problems experienced by women were social rather than individual in origin. One of the first things that women discovered in these groups was that the personal was political. They learned that their individual experiences of shame, dependency, and anger were felt by others. These experiences rested on shared conditions characterized by issues of dominance and power. Their sharing and analysis of personal experiences were a means for developing a class consciousness among women (Travis, 1988b). This class consciousness was perceived as a necessary vehicle for social change.

Consciousness raising was seen as a model for feminist therapy because it was not associated with the medical model; because it offered women an opportunity to share experiences without an expert therapist; and because C-R groups assumed that the environment plays a major role in the difficulties of individuals (Brodsky, 1973). C-R groups often provided positive changes for the women in them, including an altered world view, greater awareness of discrimination, positive changes in self-image, more self-acceptance, and increased awareness of anger (Kravetz, 1980).

Ironically, as more and more women who were not politically involved in the women's movement became members of consciousness-raising groups, their emphasis on societal change disappeared. Consciousness raising came to be seen as a form of group therapy and a means of personal change (Rosenthal, 1984). Like traditional psychotherapy, feminist therapy is also dependent on a set of values. These values developed in a particular historical context—the United States in the 1960s and 1970s (Rigby-Weinberg, 1986). As the historical context changed, personal growth came to be seen as more important than women's class status. This change was facilitated by the rather individualistic focus of even feminist therapy (Kahn & Yoder, 1989).

Some Principles of Feminist Therapy

A number of researchers have tried to list the principles of feminist therapy. Although these have evolved over time and continue to change, general agreement does exist about some basic principles. These include the fundamental idea that the personal is political. The client is helped to understand the role of society in shaping *all* individuals. She learns to validate her own experiences (She is not crazy!) and to explore her own values and attitudes. The emphasis is on change rather than adjustment (Gilbert, 1980).

It is particularly important for therapists to help women to validate their own perceptions of reality. Consider this case study (Hare-Mustin, 1991):

> A woman came home unexpectedly from work, found the door uncharacteristically locked, her husband only partially dressed, a woman leaving the bathroom straightening her clothing, and the bed sheets rumpled and stained with semen. Her husband denied that any sexual activity had taken place. The couple's relationship deteriorated. After three years of inconclusive therapy, the therapist invited a consultant, who asked each member of the couple to tell his or her own story about the event. The husband's story was quite vague and unconvincing, whereas the wife's was vivid and detailed. Each partner was asked to tell the other's story. The husband claimed he could not tell his wife's story because it was not true, but was persuaded to do so because he loved her.

The couple's subsequent relationship was much improved because the therapist had found a way to recognize the validity of the triggering event. In effect, the woman had been told that her reality did not exist and that she was "crazy."

This case bears a strong resemblance to the case of Dora, but with a much better outcome. Feminist therapists recognize that powerless individuals are often unheard.

Feminist therapists also agree on the fundamentally egalitarian nature of the therapeutic process. You may have noticed the shift from the word *patient* to the word *client* in our descriptions of feminist therapy. The client is encouraged to take a consumer attitude in seeking out psychological services and asking questions (Gilbert, 1980). The therapist is encouraged to disclose some aspects of her own life and to see the relationship as one between two adult women (Greenspan, 1986). This decrease in therapist distance helps to demystify the therapeutic process and to divest the client of her fantasies of rescue by another from her problems.

The empowering of clients is considered to be an ethical imperative by many feminist therapists. Some strategies used for empowering clients include:

1. Identifying how indirect forms of power are learned and how women and children are forced to develop covert ways of using power because overt means are either forbidden to them or too dangerous.
2. Affirming the client's ability to judge what is right for her, even in the face of disagreement.
3. Identifying internal and external costs and benefits both in terms of the client's experience of reality and present external realities.
4. Emphasizing the client's responsibility for her own behavior (Smith & Douglas, 1990).

Hannah Lerman and Natalie Porter (1990) present a set of ethical guidelines for practice, training, and research developed by the Feminist Therapy Institute. They focus on issues that have been found to be especially important in professional settings. As in any code of ethics, the well-being of clients is the guiding principle. The areas covered include cultural diversities and oppressions, power differentials and overlapping relationships between therapist and client, therapist accountability, and social change. These guidelines appear in Box 15.3, but you should remember that this is a living document and thus continually in a state of change.

The Difference between Nonsexist and Feminist Therapy

You might ask how feminist therapy differs from nonsexist therapy, which advocates the equal treatment of women and men. Feminist therapy incorporates the political values and philosophy of feminism in its therapeutic values and strategies (Brown, 1994). It may be considered revolutionary for psychology because it insists that internal change is not enough.

> We would question here the increasingly accepted notion that changes in inner experience constitute a positive outcome for women in therapy. Given the cultural and institutional prejudices against women, it is not enough that the woman client leave therapy with an increase in self-esteem, regardless of the nature and extent of behavior change. We question whether it can be considered a "successful" therapy when the client "adjusts" to the cultural, societal,

Box 15.3 Ethical Guidelines for Feminist Therapists

I. Cultural Diversities and Oppressions

A. A feminist therapist increases her accessibility to and for a wide range of clients from her own and other identified groups through flexible delivery of services. When appropriate, the feminist therapist assists clients in accessing other services.

B. A feminist therapist is aware of the meaning and impact of her own ethnic and cultural background, gender, class, and sexual orientation, and actively attempts to become knowledgeable about alternatives from sources other than her clients. The therapist's goal is to uncover and respect cultural experiential differences.

C. A feminist therapist evaluates her ongoing interactions with her clientele for any evidence of the therapist's biases or discriminatory attitudes and practice. The feminist therapist accepts responsibility for taking appropriate action to confront and change any interfering or oppressing biases she has.

II. Power Differentials

A. A feminist therapist acknowledges the inherent power differentials between client and therapist and models effective use of personal power. In using the power differential to the benefit of the client, she does not take control of power which rightfully belongs to her client.

B. A feminist therapist discloses information to the client which facilitates the therapeutic process. The therapist is responsible for using self-disclosure with purpose and discretion in the interests of the client.

C. A feminist therapist negotiates and renegotiates formal and/or informal contracts with clients in an ongoing mutual process.

D. A feminist therapist educates her clients regarding their rights as consumers of therapy, including procedures for resolving differences and filing grievances.

III. Overlapping Relationships

A. A feminist therapist recognizes the complexity and conflicting priorities inherent in multiple or overlapping relationships. The therapist accepts responsibility for monitoring such relationships to prevent potential abuse of or harm to the client.

B. A feminist therapist is actively involved in her community. As a result, she is especially sensitive about confidentiality. Recognizing that her client's concerns and general well-being are primary, she self-monitors both public and private statements and comments.

C. A feminist therapist does not engage in sexual intimacies or any overtly or covertly sexualized behavior with a client or former client.

IV. Therapist Accountability

A. A feminist therapist works only with those issues and clients within the realm of her competencies.

B. A feminist therapist recognizes her personal and professional needs and utilizes ongoing self-evaluation, peer support, consultation, supervision, continuing education, and/or personal therapy to evaluate, maintain, and improve her work with clients, her competencies, and her emotional well-being.

C. A feminist therapist continually reevaluates her training, theoretical background, and research to include developments in feminist knowledge. She integrates feminism into psychological theory, receives ongoing therapy training, and acknowledges the limits of her own competencies.

D. A feminist therapist engages in self-care activities in an ongoing manner. She acknowledges her own vulnerabilities and seeks to care for herself outside of the therapy setting. She models the ability and willingness to self-nuture in appropriate and self-empowering ways.

V. Social Change

A. A feminist therapist actively questions other therapeutic practices in her community that appear abusive to clients or therapists and, when possible, intervenes as early as appropriate or feasible or assists clients in intervening when it is facilitative to their growth.

B. A feminist therapist seeks multiple avenues for impacting change, including public education and advocacy within professional organizations, lobbying for legislative action, and other appropriate activities.

Source: Adapted from Lerman & Porter, "The contribution of feminism to ethics in psychotherapy." In H. Lerman and N. Porter (eds.), *Feminist Ethics in Psychotherapy*, pp. 5–13. 1990 Springer Publishing Company, Inc. New York 10012. Used by permission.

and familial contexts in which she lives without an awareness and understanding of their impact on her (Kaplan & Yasinski, 1980, p. 192).

> People without power, people who look around at the world and do not see themselves reflected in it, learn to feel marginal, unimportant. People for whom the social order shows contempt learn to hate themselves. Powerlessness breeds depression (Greenspan, 1983, p. 194).

These quotes show the extent to which internal power and external power or oppression and domination are seen as intermeshed by feminist therapists.

The Impact of Therapist Characteristics

Female versus Male Therapists

Although empirical studies do not clearly demonstrate the impact of therapists' sex on the outcome of therapy, we still tend to recommend that women select a woman therapist. First, if men need more experience to understand the social context of women's lives, how does one select the women they should practice on? Second, there is evidence that a greater number of similarities between client and therapist is associated with a more satisfactory therapeutic outcome (Lerman & Porter, 1990). Female therapists can provide role models of strong effective women for their clients (Gilbert, 1980; Greenspan, 1983). They have also been found to be better able to express feelings in interactions with clients than male therapists (Marecek & Johnson, 1980).

One of the most problematic aspects of therapy between a female client and male therapist is the possibility of sexual involvement between them. Although female–female relationships among therapists and clients have become increasingly visible in the past few years, sexual involvement is still overwhelmingly a problem of violations by male therapists with female clients (Bouhoutsos, Holroyd, Lerman, Forer, & Greenberg, 1983; Pope, 1994). The typical pattern is one in which sexual relations occur during therapy sessions while psychotherapy supposedly continues.

Such behavior totally violates the ethical code of the American Psychological Association. A therapist will be expelled from the organization if he is found to have engaged in sexual relationships with a client. It is considered to be a major abuse of the unequal power relationship between therapist and client.

Theoretical Orientation

We believe that feminist therapy is more beneficial to women than other forms of treatment. Most feminist therapists are defined by self-identification. At present, feminist therapists are more likely to be women than men although there is no theoretical reason a man cannot be a feminist therapist. Recently, some psychodynamic theorists have attempted to appropriate the label "feminist." While some traditional psychodynamic therapists can be helpful, there is a basic conflict between intrapsychic and feminist theory. Psychodynamic theories continue to locate the sources of a woman's distress within her. They also retain a fundamental power differential between the therapist and patient (Rigby-Weinberg, 1986).

Sexual Orientation

Lesbian clients may encounter dilemmas during psychotherapy when the therapist is heterosexual. Heterosexual therapists may have conscious or unconscious prejudices about a "homosexual lifestyle." They may also lack knowledge of lesbian communities. Rigby and Sophie (1990) have offered some questions designed to stimulate therapists' self-awareness.

1. Do I believe a heterosexual woman has a better chance at a happy life?
2. How do I respond to two women publicly showing affection in a manner that has obvious sexual overtones? How does this compare to the way I feel when a heterosexual couple shows similar public behavior?
3. How do I react when a female shows that she is sexually attracted to me?
4. Should a mother tell her children she is a lesbian? Why or why not?

You and your friends may want to answer these questions to explore your own level of awareness and/or discomfort about lesbians.

When both therapist and client are lesbian or bisexual, there is the possibility of sexual relationships between them. In such female–female relationships, the therapist is likely to terminate the therapy, refer the client elsewhere, and then enter a long-term relationship with her that frequently involves their living together. Such actions have great potential harm for the client and are unethical. True informed consent for any kind of sexual relationship is not possible, regardless of the client's expressed wish, because of the carryover from the unequal power of the therapist–client relationship (Lerman & Rigby, 1990). Despite these problems many lesbians feel it is important to have a lesbian therapist.

Race/Ethnicity

Issues of lifestyle differences between therapists and clients are particularly salient when they differ in race. The likelihood that any African-American woman will find a therapist who is also black, a woman, *and* a feminist is extremely small. APA's *Directory of Ethnic Minority Resources in Psychology* lists fewer than 300 black psychologists nationally. Fewer than 100 of these listed themselves as clinicians and, among these, fewer than ten people mentioned women's issues as a psychological interest (Childs, 1990). Therefore, a combination of white therapist–black client is most common, particularly in public health clinics and hospitals (Greene, 1986).

Most therapists have had little training in the treatment of patients of color. Psychodynamic therapists may be particularly insensitive about both race and gender issues. For example, one researcher found 78 percent of the 188 psychiatrists in her sample agreed with the statement that "The matriarchy structure of the black family contributes to identity problems for the black male" (Wilkinson, 1980).

As with sex, racial/ethnic similarity is probably a positive feature in therapeutic relationships. However, there is no empirical support for the position that black therapists are more effective than white therapists with African-American clients (Wilkinson, 1980). And, although anecdotal reports suggest that cultural similarity between clients and therapists is helpful, empirical studies of the consequences for Latina, Asian-American, and American-Indian women seem to be entirely lacking.

Therapy with Marginalized Populations

Groups that are marginalized and stigmatized in our society have special problems in therapeutic situations. These problems are primarily due to therapists' inability to "get inside the skin" of individuals whose life circumstances are very different from their own. We will review briefly some problems in therapy encountered by lesbians, poor women, African-American women, and Latinas.

Because lesbians are an invisible minority in current society, they have some unique problems. Dilemmas involving relationships are the most frequent reason lesbians enter therapy. The most commonly reported problems include where to meet other lesbians (besides bars); how the lack of "courtship and dating rituals" and the limitation of potential partners can lead to premature commitment; and how the tendency toward closeness and interdependence in lesbian love relationships makes separating difficult when the relationship ends (Rigby & Sophie, 1990). The first two problems are not intrapsychic ones at all but are caused by heterosexism. Therapists who are not aware of the societal context of lesbians may view these problems as issues involving personal identity rather than as social dilemmas.

Psychotherapy is based on the philosophical assumption that all members of society deserve life, liberty, and happiness. However, therapy is not equally available to all members of society. A user of therapy is more likely to be a middle-class person with discretionary income, as well as values that include being able to spend money on oneself rather than on family or children (Faunce, 1990).

Therapy is also not equally effective for all members of society. As we discussed earlier in the chapter for the case of Altamese Thomas, too much insight into a life that the client has no power to change may actually be harmful. For clients in poverty, the concern may not be so much how to express anger but whether or not to express it at all (Faunce, 1990). For women with little power, the expression of anger may have extremely negative consequences in terms of physical and social abuse (see Chapter 14).

Poor clients may also have a very different set of priorities than their middle-class therapists. The words of one participant in a black woman's support group illustrate the point:

> When I heard about this group I asked my therapist (a white woman) if I could attend. It seemed like all she was concerned about was the fact that I got raped. Hell! I know that was important, but that bastard got my last twenty-five dollars. That was all the money I had, till payday. I can deal with the rape later, but I won't have a job if I can't get back and forth to work (black rape victim, 1985, in Boyd, 1990, p. 156).

Therapists must be attentive to clients' material as well as personal needs. It is easy to confuse dire social circumstances with personal pathology. Some groups of women have been almost entirely ignored even by feminist psychologists. Pamela Reid's (1993) title for her presidential address to Division 35 focused sharply on this gap: "Poor women in psychological research: shut up and shut out." When researchers do examine neglected populations such as homeless women, they often find surprising results. For example, homeless women did not differ psychologically from a population of women from the same neighborhood who were not homeless (Jackson-Wilson & Borgers, 1993). Neither group of women had a high rate of psychological or physical disability. Instead, women in both groups were likely to be black and single and to have a higher than average number of children, an educational level of less than twelve years, and severely limited work histories. Social rather than intrapsychic variables appear to be the source of the homeless women's vulnerability. They had fewer sources of social support during a period of need.

White feminist therapists may have a particular problem in dealing with African-American women clients because they tend to see gender as the primary issue in the lives of all women, independent of their race, class, or color. They may be unaware of the powerful effect that being white has had on their own lives. As one feminist therapist of color has pointed out: "Many white feminist therapists forget that they were white long before they chose to become feminists or therapists. Being a feminist therapist does not negate the societal privilege that is inherent in being born white" (Boyd, 1990, p. 163).

White therapists' lack of awareness of the pervasive effects of racism can harm their black clients. For example, skin color variations within African-American families can be a source of conflict between family members. Beverly Greene (1992), an African-American therapist, has suggested that practitioners inquire about the skin color of family members, particularly those about whom there are intense feelings. Virginia Harris (1994) offers a vivid account of how intrafamily conflict may be driven by perceived color differences.

> When I was growing up, calling someone black was worse than calling them nigger. We sat on the porch steps, and in a terrible game of degradation, compared our colors. Who was the darkest? Who was "it"? I was, more times than not. I fought my sister and my brother because they called me black. I generally got beaten up in those fights, and then beaten up again by my light-skinned mother for my loud, violent, attention-getting behavior (Harris, 1994, p. 10).

"Colorism" (which is found among some Asian-American groups as well) is a consequence of the internalization of the dominant culture's standard of beauty. Until recently, however, it has gone unnamed and unrecognized.

Color is a salient and usually obvious characteristic. It often predicts where people will work, live, socialize, attend school, and receive health care, and how much money they may earn. Black women live in a culture that frequently reminds them of their skin color and the label of ugliness and inferiority that accompanies it. To ignore race is to fail to acknowledge the individual's complete experience (Greene, 1986).

There are many differences in the life experience of black and white women. For example, black women have always worked outside the home in greater numbers than white women. They continue to outnumber white women in lower-paid occupations. On the other hand, religious involvement has given them more satisfaction (Greene, 1986). The ability of black women to endure and survive oppressive social conditions has not left them unscarred. Survival has come at the cost of adaptation to high levels of stress and, not infrequently, moving from crisis to crisis with little respite (Greene, 1986).

African-American women are likely to enter therapy under much stress and to evince little trust in either the process or the therapist (Childs, 1990). Their expressions of anger and distrust may be seen as pathological when they are, in fact, justified by the reality of corrupt ghetto policemen or other authority figures who may abuse their power in the black community (Trotman, 1984).

Even highly successful African-American women may have problems resolving their high personal status with the low status of their collective community. They may come to feel that they have no kinship to important elements in their lives. If therapists deny the material reality of black existence, they will divorce these women from their history, leaving them isolated and alienated (McCombs, 1986). Thus, individual therapy for black women must acknowledge the collective experience of all African Americans.

Little has been written about problems of therapy with other ethnic minorities in American society. Many psychologists have replaced the "white-male middle-class college sophomore" with his sister (Brown, 1990). Feminist therapists have begun to recognize, however, that all women's lives are not the same. The rules for female behavior vary considerably from one culture to another. Groups differ, for example, on the distance women are allowed to go beyond the confines of their family, on what work is considered acceptable, and on how roles are distributed within the home (McGoldrick, Garcia-Preto, Hines, & Lee, 1989). The issues for various ethnic groups (such as Asian-American or Jewish-American women) are too varied to deal with in such a brief overview. To illustrate the importance of culture in the therapeutic practice, we will focus on issues involving Latina women.

In most Spanish-speaking countries, women learn how to be female in a man's world. They are taught to repress or sublimate their sexual drives and to be extremely modest while, at the same time, enhancing their sexual attractiveness in order to obtain a good husband. Traditionally, Latina women have been expected to be responsible for taking care of the home and children and for keeping the family together. They often feel obligated to sacrifice themselves for this goal, relying on other women within the extended family for support and strength. This sacrificial role is rewarded by the community; when they perform it well, women are admired (McGoldrick et al., 1989).

As might be expected from this pattern of extreme feminine socialization, rates of depression are high among some populations of Hispanic women. In Puerto Rico, for example, the rate of mild depression for women versus men is 4.75 to 1 (Canino, Rubio-Stipec, Shrout, Bravo, Strolberg, & Bird, 1987). The high rates of depression among Puerto Rican women remained even when age, marital status, employment, and health factors were controlled. These findings suggest that depression would be most relieved by social rather than personal change. The researchers suggested remediation through affirmative action, social legislation, and education through the mass media.

Just as cultural norms affect rates of depression in some Latina groups, they probably also determine other ways in which distress is expressed. A number of Latina psychologists have, for example, discussed the existence of a "Puerto

Rican syndrome" (Comas-Diaz, 1987; Ramos-McKay, Comas-Diaz, & Rivera, 1988) that includes hyperventilation, mutism, hyperkinesis, and violence. Julia Ramos-McKay and her associates have suggested that the syndrome is analogous to the hysterical "fits" observed in nineteenth-century American women (discussed earlier in this chapter). Like the earlier hysteria, these symptoms may represent an effort to resolve contradictions between the need to be soft, yielding, and submissive while, at the same time, fulfilling a strong maternal role requiring self-reliance and good managerial skills.

Such findings underline the point made repeatedly during this chapter that cultural forces create symptomology. Examination of culturally diverse populations helps us to see cultural construction in action. But we must also understand the life circumstances of diverse groups of women (and men) for their own sake so that we do not confuse individual pathology with social adaptations and culturally specific coping mechanisms.

ISSUES OF DIVERSITY

Feminist research on various ethnically diverse populations has increased in recent years (c.f. Landrine, 1995). There is great diversity among the groups categorized by the single label "Latina." For example, Cuban Americans have achieved higher levels of education and occupational attainment than individuals from other Latin-American countries. Puerto Ricans, Chicanas, and Cuban Americans also differ in terms of their acceptance of traditional values and gender roles (Ginorio, Gutierrez, Cauce, & Acosta, 1995).

A major factor that contributes to differences between various Latina populations is the conditions under which they immigrated to the United States (Espin, 1987; Ginorio, Gutierrez, Cauce, & Acosta, 1995). Immigration is probably more stressful to women than to men because women are considered to be responsible for maintaining family ties, ethnic traditions, etc. It is particularly stressful when migration has been forced by war or other forms of state-supported violence (Lykes, Brabeck, Ferns, & Radan, 1993). Some Asian-American populations (e.g., Vietnamese and Cambodians) have also been forced to immigrate by war (Root, 1995). And many Native-American groups have engaged in a kind of internal immigration because of the poverty and lack of opportunities available on their reservations (LaFromboise, Choney, James, & Running Wolf, 1995). Women in all these groups may show symptoms of multiple loss.

Many women from ethnic minority groups are unwilling to seek out mental health practitioners because they fear that such practitioners will not share their values and will denigrate important aspects of their culture. For example, religion and spirituality are often more important than they are in dominant secular society. Communality and the subordination of individual needs to group needs are also valued. Feminist concerns with the context of behavior can assist therapists in distinguishing between cultural practices and individual pathology.

It is important to recognize that although gender represents one way to organize social reality, it is not the only way to do so. Age, class, sexual orientation, ethnicity, and culture can also serve as organizing principles. They are all closely interwoven with gender. None of these categories is politically neutral or value-free. Each (separately and in combination) can serve as tools for oppression.

CONNECTING THEMES

1. Women's psychological disorders are more closely related to their status and roles (in other words, aspects of gender) than they are to sex. Emphasis on sex-related differences in psychological disorders is a consequence of lack of attention to the social context of people's lives.
2. Diagnostic categories are clear examples of the "power to name." Feminist critiques stress the need to question the economics and politics of diagnostic labels.
3. There are more issues involving diversity in clinical theory and practice than in most other parts of the study of women and gender. Power differentials between therapists and their clients continue to raise questions about the assumptions of therapy and whether therapy is beneficial under some circumstances.
4. Feminist therapy stresses social rather than personal change. Since therapy is an individual process, however, the contradiction between theory and practice is an ongoing problem for feminist therapists.

SUGGESTED READINGS

BROWN, LAURA and MARIA ROOT (Eds.) (1990). *Diversity and complexity in feminist therapy.* New York: Harrington Park Press. A book with a variety of sophisticated examinations of therapy issues involving differences among women.

GREENSPAN, MIRIAM (1983). *A new approach to women and therapy.* New York: McGraw-Hill. This candid and revealing analysis was written by a feminist psychotherapist. It not only provides information on how traditional psychotherapy fails women but also offers helpful suggestions about what they can do about it.

WORELL, JUDITH and PAM REMER (1992). *Feminist perspectives in therapy: An empowerment model for women.* New York: Wiley. A clearly written text for students interested in counseling psychology. It includes many helpful exercises as well as an excellent review of current feminist theory and practice.

Afterword

Now that you have completed this book (and probably a college course on women), we hope that you will think about what you have learned and your feelings during the learning process. This text is not the same as most of your other psychology books because its contents are more relevant to your daily life. One instructor who assigns this book, Judi Addelston, has described a trajectory through the course. See if the following description fits your learning experience.

> For the first three chapters, students perceive the psychology of women and gender as just another college course. They are skeptical about the amount of sexism described and argue with their instructors a lot. Chapter 4—images of women—gets them involved and angry. They become progressively angrier and more depressed as they read Chapters 5 through 8. Chapter 9—on sex, love, and romance—is another turning point. This chapter and the following four produce positive feelings and motivate students to examine the structures around them as they look to the future or reexamine their pasts. Chapters 14 and 15 induce both positive and negative emotions. Many students "come out" as survivors of various forms of violence and psychological disorders. They may find strong bonds with others who are also resisting the gendering process.

You may ask why we want you to experience this kind of emotional and intellectual roller coaster. Unfortunately, the realities of women's experience in our society are not entirely pleasant ones. Thus, the deconstruction of assumptions about women and gender is not entirely pleasant either. But knowledge is also empowering. We hope that you have learned the importance of the four themes that recur throughout this book:

- Gender is much more than just sex.
- We all have the power to name.
- Women are very diverse.
- Psychological research can contribute to social change.

We wrote this book in part because we believe that knowledge is a form of power. We are passing knowledge to you so that you can use it to become more effective agents of change. We believe that everyone has the ability and the responsibility to make the world a better place.

Change does not take place in a social vacuum. Equality between women and men cannot occur in the absence of social justice for other marginalized groups. Social change is slow. but as more members of formerly powerless groups gain power in society, they should make further changes in it. They will be able to do so, however, only if they continue to identify with the groups from which they emerged. People who understand the role of both the individual and the group appear to be most effective in creating social change.

You may not always be able to take action, but you can always ask the difficult questions. We want nothing to be sacred—including our own position. We have taken the view that there is no one unbiased, correct form of truth. Nevertheless, just because standpoints depend on current circumstances and are subject to change does not mean that we are free to abandon all our standards. Instead, we would argue that moral standards must be added to empirical ones. In this sense, morality means looking at questions such as "Who generates this knowledge?" "To whom will it be useful?" and "Useful for what?" These criteria may help us to decide what questions should be asked as well as to determine the value of the answers. In fact, a favorite saying of ours is "If they can get you to ask the wrong questions, they don't have to worry about the answers!" We hope this book helps you to keep asking the right questions.

References

Abrams, D., Sparkes, K., & Hogg, M. A. (1985). Gender salience and social identity: The impact of sex of siblings on educational and occupational aspirations. *British Journal of Educational Psychology, 55,* 224–232.

Abramson, P. E., Goldberg, P. A., Greenberg, J. H., & Abramson, L. M. (1977). The talking platypus phenomenon: Competency ratings as a function of sex and professional status. *Psychology of Women Quarterly, 2,* 114–124.

Achte, K. (1970). Menopause from the psychiatrist's point of view. *Acta Obstetrica et Gynecologica* (Suppl.), *1,* 3–17.

Adams, K. L., & Ware, N. C. (1989). Sexism and the English language: The linguistic implications of being a woman. In J. Freeman (Ed.), *Women: A feminist perspective* (4th ed.) (pp. 470–484). Mountain View, CA: Mayfield.

Adams, M. (1976). *Single blessedness.* New York: Basic Books.

Adelmann, P. K. (1993). Psychological well-being and homemaker versus retiree identity among older women. *Sex Roles, 29,* 195–212.

Adelmann, P. K., Antonucci, T. C., Crohan, S. E., & Coleman, L. M. (1989). Empty nest, cohort, and employment in the well-being of midlife women. *Sex Roles, 20,* 173–189.

Ader, D. N., & Johnson, S. B. (1994). Sample description, reporting and analysis of sex in psychological research: A look at APA and APA division journals in 1990. *American Psychologist, 49,* 216–218.

Adler, A. (1954). *Understanding human nature.* Greenwich, CT: Fawcett Premier.

Admissions Testing Program (1984). National college-bound seniors, 1984. Princeton, NJ: College Entrance Examination Board.

Adolph, M. A. (1993). The myth of the golden years: One older woman's perspective. In N. D. Davis, E. Cole, & E. D. Rothblum (Eds.), *Faces of women and aging.* Binghamton, NY: Harrington Park Press (pp. 55–66).

Ageton, S. S. (1983). *Sexual Assault among Adolescents.* Lexington, MA: D. C. Heath.

Affonso, D. D., & Mayberry, L. J. (1989). Common stressors reported by a group of childbearing American women. In P. N. Stern (Ed.), *Pregnancy and parenting* (pp. 41–55). New York: Hemisphere.

Aguilar, R. J., & Nightingale, N. N. (1994). The impact of specific battering experiences on the self-esteem of abused women. *Journal of Family Violence, 9,* 35–45.

Aida, Y., & Falbo, T. (1991). Relationships between marital satisfaction, resources, and power strategies. *Sex Roles, 24,* 43–56.

Aizenman, M., & Kelley, G. (1988). The incidence of violence and acquaintance rape in dating relationships among college men and women. *Journal of College Student Development, 29,* 305–311.

Alagna, S. W., & Hamilton, J. A. (1986). Science in the service of mythology: The psychopathologizing of menstruation. Paper presented at the meeting of the American Psychological Association, Washington, DC.

Alazarov-Por, N. (1983). Giftedness across cultures: A study of educational values. In B. Shore, S. Gagne, S. Tarievee, R. Tali, & R.

Tumbey (Eds.), *Face to face with giftedness.* New York: Nillian Books.

Albert, J. L. (1993, August 18). Who is getting abortions. *USA Today,* A11.

Aldous, J. (Ed.) (1982). *Two paychecks: Life in dual-earner families.* Beverly Hills, CA: Sage.

Alington, D. E., & Troll, L. E. (1984). Social change and equality: The roles of women and economics. In G. Baruch & J. Brooks-Gunn (Eds.), *Women in midlife.* (pp. 181–202) New York: Plenum Press.

Allan, J. S., Mayo, K., & Michel, Y. (1993). Body size values of White and Black women. *Research in Nursing and Health, 16,* 323–333.

Allen. I. L. (1984). Male sex roles and epithets for ethnic women in American slang. *Sex Roles, 11,* 43–50.

Allen, L. S., & Gorski, R. A. (1992). Sexual orientation and the size of the anterior commissure in the human brain. *Proceedings of the National Academy of Sciences, 89,* 7199–7202.

Allgood-Merten, B., & Stockard, J. (1991). Sex role identity and self-esteem: A comparison of children and adolescents. *Sex Roles, 25,* 129–139.

Allport, G. W. (1954). *The nature of prejudice.* Cambridge, MA: Addison-Wesley.

Almquist, E. M. (1979). Black women and the pursuit of equality. In J. Freeman (Ed.), *Women: A feminist perspective* (2nd ed.) (pp. 430–450). Palo Alto, CA: Mayfield.

Almquist, E. M. (1989). The experiences of minority women in the United States: Intersections of race, gender, and class. In J. Freeman (Ed.), *Women: A feminist perspective* (4th ed.) (pp. 414–445). Mountain View, CA: Mayfield.

Alper, T. G. (1974). Achievement motivation in college women: A now-you-see-it-now-you-don't phenomenon. *American Psychologist, 29,* 194–203.

Alpert, D., & Culbertson, A. (1987). Daily hassles and coping strategies of dual-earner and nondual-earner women. *Psychology of Women Quarterly, 11,* 359–366.

Altman, M. (1984). Everything they always wanted you to know. In C. S. Vance (Ed.) *Pleasure and danger: Exploring female sexuality* (pp. 115–130). Boston: Routledge & Kegan Paul.

Amaro, H. (1993). Reproductive choice in the age of AIDS: Policy and counselling issues. In C. Squire (Ed.), *Women and AIDS: Psychological perspectives* (pp. 20–41). London: Sage.

Amaro, H., Russo, N. F., & Johnson, J. (1987). Family and work predictors of psychological well-being among Hispanic women professionals. *Psychology of Women Quarterly, 11,* 523–532.

American Psychiatric Association (1987). *Diagnostic and statistical manual of mental disorders* (3rd ed.—revised). Washington, DC: American Psychiatric Association.

American Psychiatric Association (1994). *Diagnostic and statistical manual of mental disorders* (4th ed.). Washington, DC: American Psychiatric Association.

Amir, M. (1971). *Patterns of forcible rape.* Chicago, IL: University of Chicago Press.

Anderson, J.V. (1973). Psychological determinants. In R. B. Kundsin (Ed.), *Successful women in the sciences: An analysis of determinants.* New York: New York Academy of Sciences.

Angier, N. (1994, May 3). Male hormone molds women, too, in mind and body. *New York Times,* C1, 13.

Angrist, S., Dinitz, S., Lefton, M., & Pasamanick, B. (1968). *Women after treatment.* New York: Appleton-Century-Crofts.

Anson, O., Antonovsky, A., Sagy, S., & Adler, I. (1989). Family, gender, and attitudes toward retirement. *Sex Roles, 20,* 355–369.

Anson, O., Levenson, A., & Bonneh, D. Y. (1990). Gender and health on the kibbutz. *Sex Roles, 22,* 213–231.

Apfelbaum, E. (1993). Norwegian and French women in high leadership positions: The importance of cultural contexts upon gendered relations. *Psychology of Women Quarterly, 17,* 409–429.

Archer, D., Iritani, B., Kimes, D. D., & Barrios, M. (1983). Faceism: Five studies of sex differences in facial prominence. *Journal of Personality and Social Psychology, 45,* 725–735.

Arias, I., Samios, M., & O'Leary, K. D. (1987). Prevalence and correlates of physical aggression during courtship. *Journal of Interpersonal Violence, 2,* 82–90.

Arling, G. (1976a). The elderly widow and her family, neighbors, and friends. *Journal of Marriage and the Family, 38,* 757–768.

Arling, G. (1976b). Resistance to isolation among elderly widows. *International Journal of Aging and Human Development, 7,* 67–76.

Arms, S. (1973). *A season to be born.* New York: Harper & Row.

Arnold, F., & Kuo, E. C. (1984). The value of daughters and sons: A comparative study of the gender preferences of parents. *Journal of Comparative Family Studies, 15,* 299–318.

Asch, A., & Fine, M. (1988). Introduction: Beyond pedestals. In M. Fine & A. Asch (Eds.), *Women with disabilities: Essays in psychology, culture, and politics* (pp. 1–37). Philadelphia: Temple University Press.

Astin, A. W., King, M., & Richardson, B. T. (1980). *The American freshman: National norms for fall 1980.* Los Angeles: American Council on Education.

Astin, H. S. (1976). A profile of the women in continuing education. In H. Astin (Ed.), *Some action of her own: The adult woman and higher education.* Lexington, MA: Lexington.

Astin, H. S. (1984). The meaning of work in women's lives: A sociopsychological model of career choice and work behavior. *Counseling Psychologist, 12,* 117–126.

Atkinson, J., & Huston, T. L. (1984). Sex role orientation and division of labor early in marriage. *Journal of Personality and Social Psychology, 46,* 330–345.

Attie, I., & Brooks-Gunn, J. (1989). The development of eating problems in adolescent girls: A longitudinal study. *Developmental Psychology, 25,* 70–79.

Attorney's General's Commission on Pornography (1986). *Attorney General's Commission on Pornography: Final Report* (Vols. I and II). Washington, DC: U.S. Department of Justice.

Auerbach, J., Blum, L., Smith, V., & Williams, C. (1985). On Gilligan's In a different voice. *Feminist Studies, 11,* 149–161.

Baber, K. M., & Allen, K. R. (1992). *Women and families: Feminist reconstructions.* New York: Guilford.

Baenninger, M., & Newcombe, N. (1989). The role of experience in spatial test performance: A meta-analysis. *Sex Roles,* 20, 327–344.

Baker, S. W. (1980). Biological influences on human sex and gender. *Signs, 6,* 80–96.

Ballinger, S. (1990). Stress as a factor in lowered estrogen levels in the early postmenopause. In M. Flint, F. Kronenberg, & W. Utian (Eds.), *Multidisciplinary perspectives on menopause. Annals of the New York Academy of Sciences, 592,* 95–113.

Banaji, M. R., & Greenwald, A. G. (1994). Implicit stereotyping and prejudice. In M. P. Zanna & J. M. Olson (Eds.), *The psychology of prejudice* (pp. 55–76). Hillsdale, NJ: Erlbaum.

Banaji, M. R., Hardin, C., & Rothman, A. J. (1993). Implicit stereotyping in person judgment. *Journal of Personality and Social Psychology, 65,* 272–281.

Bandura, A. (1965). Influence of model's reinforcement contingencies on the acquisition of imitative responses. *Journal of Personality and Social Psychology, 1,* 589–595.

Bandura, A., & Huston, A. C. (1961). Identification as a process of incidental learning. *Journal of Abnormal and Social Psychology, 63,* 311–318.

Bandura, A., Ross, D., & Ross, S. A. (1963). A comparative test of the status envy, social power, and secondary reinforcement theories of identificatory learning. *Journal of Abnormal and Social Psychology, 67,* 527–534.

Bandura, A., & Walters, R. H. (1963). *Social learning and personality development.* New York: Holt, Rinehart & Winston.

Barak, A., Feldman, S., & Noy, A. (1991). Traditionality of children's interests as related to their parents' gender stereotypes and traditionality of occupations. *Sex Roles, 24,* 511–524.

Bardwell, J. R., Cochran, S. W., & Walker, S. (1986). Relationship of parental education, race, and gender to sex-role stereotyping in five-year-old kindergartners. *Sex Roles, 15,* 275–281.

Barnett, O. W., & Fagan, R. W. (1993). Alcohol use in male spouse abusers and their female partners. *Journal of Family Violence, 8,* 1–25.

Barnett, R. C., & Baruch, G. K. (1978). Women in the middle years: A critique of research and theory. *Psychology of Women Quarterly, 3,* 187–197.

Barnett, R. C., Marshall, N. L., Raudenbush, S. W., & Brennen, R. T. (1993). Gender and the relationship between job experiences and psychological distress: A study of dual-earner couples. *Journal of Personality and Social Psychology, 64,* 794–806.

Bart, P. (1970). Mother Portnoy's complaint. *Transaction, 8,* 69–74.

Bart, P. B. (1971). Sexism and social science: From the gilded cage to the iron cage, or, the perils of Pauline. *Journal of Marriage and the Family, 33,* 734–735.

Bart, P. B., & Grossman, M. (1978). Menopause. In M. T. Notman & C. C. Nadelson (Eds.), *The woman patient: Medical and psychological interfaces* (pp. 337–354). New York: Plenum.

Bar-Tal, D., & Saxe, L. (1976). Perceptions of similarly and dissimilarly attractive couples and individuals. *Journal of Personality and Social Psychology, 33,* 772–781.

Baruch, G. K. (1984). The psychological well-being of women in the middle years. In G. Baruch & J. Brooks-Gunn (Eds.), *Women in midlife* (pp. 161–180). New York: Plenum.

Baruch, G. K., Barnett R. C., & Rivers, C. (1983). *Lifeprints: New patterns of love and work for today's women.* New York: New American Library.

Basow, S. A., & Howe, K. G. (1980). Role model influence: Effects of sex and sex-role attitude in college students. *Psychology of Women Quarterly, 4,* 558–572.

Basow, S. A., & Kobrynowicz, D. (1993). What is she eating? The effects of meal size on impressions of a female eater. *Sex Roles, 28,* 335–344.

Bass, E., & Davis, L. (1988). *The courage to heal: A guide for women survivors of child sexual abuse.* New York: Harper and Row.

Bass, E., & Thornton, L. (1983). *I never told anyone: Writings by women survivors of child sexual abuse.* New York: Harper and Row.

Bassoff, E. S., & Glass, G. V. (1982). The relationship between sex roles and mental health: A meta-analysis of twenty-six studies. *Counseling Psychologist, 10,* 105–112.

Beasley, R., & Stoltenberg, C. D. (1992). Personality characteristics of male spouse abusers. *Professional Psychology: Research & Practice, 23,* 310–317.

Beatrice, J. (1985). A psychological comparison of heterosexuals, transvestites, preoperative transsexuals, and postoperative transsexuals. *Journal of Nervous and Mental Disease, 173,* 358–365.

Beavais, C., & Spence, J. T. (1987). Gender, prejudice, and categorization. *Sex Roles, 16,* 89–100.

Beck, A. T., Ward, C. H., Mendelson, M., Mock, J., & Erbaugh, J. (1961). An inventory for measuring depression. *Archives of General Psychiatry, 4,* 561–571.

Beck, J. C., & van der Kolk, B. (1987). Reports of childhood incest and current behavior of chronically hospitalized psychotic women. *American Journal of Psychiatry, 144,* 1474–1476.

Beck, R. W., & Beck, S. J. (1989). The incidence of extended households among middle-aged black and white women. *Journal of Family Issues, 10,* 147–168.

Becker, H. S. (1963). *Outsiders.* New York: Free Press.

Beckman, L. J., & Houser, B. B. (1982). The consequences of childlessness for the social-psychological well-being of older women. *Journal of Gerontology, 37,* 243–250.

Beckstein, D., Dahlin, M., & Wiley, D. (1986). Overview of sexuality education for young men. In C. H. Gregg and S. Renner (Eds.), *Sexuality educational strategy and resource guide: Programs for young men.* Washington, DC: Center for Population Options.

Beckwith, B. (1984). How magazines cover sex differences research. *Science for the People, 16,* 18–23.

Belk, S. S., Garcia-Falconi, R., Hernandez-Sanchez, J., & Snell, W. E. (1988). Avoidance strategy use in the intimate relationships of women and men from Mexico and the United States. *Psychology of Women Quarterly, 12,* 165–174.

Belknap, J. (1989). The sexual victimization of unmarried women by nonrelative acquaintances. In M. A. Pirog-Good & J. E. Stets (Eds.), *Violence in dating relationships: Emerging issues* (pp. 205–218). New York: Praeger.

Bell, I. P. (1989). The double standard: Age. In J. Freeman (Ed.), *Women: A feminist perspective* (4th ed.) (pp. 236–244). Mountain View, CA: Mayfield.

Bell-Scott, P., Guy-Sheftall, B., Royster, J. J., Sims-Wood, J., DeCosta-Willis, M., & Fultz, L. P. (Eds.) (1991). *Double stitch: Black women write about mothers and daughters.* New York: HarperCollins.

Bem, S. L. (1974). The measurement of psychological androgyny. *Journal of Consulting and Clinical Psychology, 42,* 155–162.

Bem, S. L. (1975). Sex role adaptability: One consequence of psychological androgyny. *Journal of Personality and Social Psychology, 31,* 634–643.

Bem, S. L. (1981). Gender schema theory: A cognitive account of sex typing. *Psychological Review, 88,* 354–364.

Bem, S. L. (1983). Gender schema theory and its implications for child development: Raising gender-aschematic children in a gender-schematic society. *Signs, 8,* 598–616.

Bem, S. L. (1985). Androgyny and gender schema theory: A conceptual and empirical integration. In T. B. Sonderegger (Ed.), *Nebraska Symposium on Motivation,* 1984 (Vol. 32, pp. 179–226). Lincoln: University of Nebraska Press.

Bem, S. L. (1987). Gender schema theory and the romantic tradition. In P. Shaver & C. Hendrick (Eds.), *Sex and gender* (pp. 251–271). Beverly Hills, CA: Sage.

Bem, S. L. (1989). Genital knowledge and gender constancy in preschool children. *Child Development, 60,* 649–662.

Bem, S. (1993). *The lenses of gender.* New Haven: Yale University Press.

Bem, S. L., & Bem, D. J. (1971). Training the woman to know her place: The power of a nonconscious ideology. In M. H. Garskof (Ed.), *Roles women play: Readings toward women's liberation* (pp. 84–96). Belmont, CA: Brooks Cole.

Bem, S. L., & Bem, D. J. (1973). Does sex-biased job advertising "aid and abet" sex discrimination? *Journal of Applied Social Psychology, 3,* 6–18.

Bem, S. L., & Lenney, E. (1976). Sex typing and the avoidance of cross-sex behavior. *Journal of Personality and Social Psychology, 33,* 48–54.

Bem, S. L., Martyna, W., & Watson, C. (1976). Sex typing and androgyny: Further explorations of the expressive domain. *Journal of Personality and Social Psychology, 34,* 1016–1023.

Bemis, K. M. (1978). Current approaches to etiology and treatment of anorexia nervosa. *Psychological Bulletin, 85,* 593–617.

Benbow, C. P. (1988). Sex differences in mathematical reasoning ability in intellectually talented preadolescents: Their nature, effects, and possible causes. *Behavioral and Brain Sciences, 11,* 169–132.

Benbow, C. P., & Stanley, J. C. (1980). Sex differences in mathematical ability: Fact or artifact? *Science, 210,* 1262–1264.

Beneke, T. (1982). *Men on rape.* New York: St. Martin's Press.

Benokraitis, N. V., & Feagin, J. R. (1986). *Modern sexism: Blatant, subtle, and covert discrimination.* Englewood Cliffs, NJ: Prentice-Hall.

Bequaert, L. (1976). *Single women alone and together.* Boston: Beacon.

Berardo, D. H., Shehen, C. L., & Leslie, G. R. (1987). A residue of tradition: Jobs, careers, and spouses' time in housework. *Journal of Marriage and the Family, 49,* 381–390.

Berenbaum, S. A., & Hines, M. (1992). Early androgens are related to childhood sex-typed toy preferences. *Psychological Science, 3,* 203–206.

Bergen, D. J., & Williams, J. E. (1991). Sex stereotypes in the United States revisited: 1972–1988. *Sex Roles, 24,* 413–423.

Berger, P. L., & Luckmann, T. (1966). *The social construction of reality: A treatise in the sociology of knowledge.* Garden City, NY: Doubleday.

Berger, R. M. (1990). Passing: Impact of the quality of same-sex couple relationships. *Social Work, 35,* 328–332.

Bergman, L. (1992). Dating violence among high school students. *Social Work,* 37, 21–27.

Berk, R. A. (1993). What the evidence shows: On the average, we can do no better than arrest. In R. J. Gelles & D. R. Loseke (Eds.), *Current controversies on family violence* (pp. 323–336). Newbury Park, CA: Sage.

Berman, P. W. (1980). Are women more responsive than men to the young? A review of developmental and situational variables. *Psychological Bulletin, 88,* 668–695.

Bermant, G., & Davidson, J. M. (1974). *Biological bases of sexual behavior.* New York: Harper & Row.

Bernal, M. E., Knight, G. P., Garja, C. E., Ocampo. K. A., & Cota, M. K. (1990). The development of ethnic identity in Mexican-American children. *Hispanic Journal of Behavioral Sciences, 12,* 3–24.

Bernard, J. (1972). *The future of marriage.* New York: World.

Bernard, J. (1974). *The future of motherhood.* New York: Penguin.

Bernard, J. (1981). The good provider role: Its rise and fall. *American Psychologist, 36,* 1–12.

Berryman-Fink, C., & Verderber, K. S. (1985). Attributions of the term feminist: A factor analytic development of a measuring instrument. *Psychology of Women Quarterly, 9,* 51–64.

Bersoff, D., & Crosby, F. (1984). Job satisfaction and family status. *Personality and Social Psychology Bulletin, 10,* 79–84.

Bethke, T. M. & DeJoy, D. M. (1993). An experimental study of factors influencing the acceptability of dating violence. *Journal of Interpersonal Violence,* 8, 36–51.

Betz, N. E., & Fitzgerald, L. E. (1987). *The career psychology of women.* New York: Academic Press.

Beutell, N. J., & Brenner, O. C. (1986). Sex differences in work values. *Journal of Vocational Behavior, 28,* 29–41.

Beyene, Y. (1989). *From menarche to menopause: Reproductive lives of peasant women in two cultures.* Albany: State University of New York Press.

Bianchi, S. M., & Spain, D. (1986). *American women in transition.* New York: Russell Sage Foundation.

Billingham, R. E. (1987). Courtship violence: The patterns of conflict resolution strategies across seven levels of emotional commitment. *Family Relations, 36,* 283–289.

Billingham, R. E., & Sack, A. R. (1986). Courtship violence and the interactive status of the relationship. *Journal of Adolescent Research, 1,* 315–325.

Billy, J. O., & Udry, J. R. (1985). The influence of male and female best friends on adolescent sexual behavior. *Adolescence, 20,* 21–32.

Birnbaum, J. A. (1975). Life patterns and self esteem in gifted family oriented and career committed women. In M. T. S. Mednick, S. S. Tangri, & L. W. Hoffman (Eds.), *Women and achievement* (pp. 396–419). Washington, DC: Hemisphere.

Birrell, S. J., & Cole, S. L. (1990). Double fault: Renee Richards and the construction and naturalization of difference. *Sociology of Sport Journal, 7,* 1–21.

Bishop, N. (1989). Abortion: The controversial choice. In J. Freeman (Ed.), *Women: A feminist perspective* (4th ed.) (pp. 45–56). Mountain View, CA: Mayfield.

Bjorkqvist, K. (1994). Sex differences in physical, verbal, and indirect aggression: A review of recent research. *Sex Roles, 30,* 177–188.

Black, S. M., & Hill, C. E. (1984). The psychological well-being of women in their middle years. *Psychology of Women Quarterly, 8,* 282–292.

Blair, S. L., & Lichter, D. T. (1991). Measuring the division of household labor: Gender segregation of housework among American couples. *Journal of Family Issues, 12,* 91–113.

Blakely, M. K. (1985). Is one woman's sexuality another woman's pornography? *Ms, 13,* 229–236.

Blanchard, R. (1985). Gender dysphoria and gender reorientation. In B. W. Steiner (Ed.), *Gender dysphoria: Development, research, management.* New York: Plenum.

Blanchard, R., Steiner, B. W., & Clemmensen, L. H. (1985). Gender dysphoria, gender reorientation, and the management of transsexualism. *Journal of Counseling and Clinical Psychology, 53,* 295–304.

Blechman, E. A. (1984). Women's behavior in a man's world: Sex differences in competence. In E. A. Blechman (Ed.), *Behavior modification with women.* (pp. 3–33). New York: Guilford Press.

Bleier, R. (Ed.) (1986). *Feminist approaches to science.* Elmsford, NY: Pergamon Press.

Bleier, R. (1988). Science and the construction of meanings in the neurosciences. In S. V. Rosser (Ed.), *Feminism within the science and health care professions: Overcoming resistance.* Elmsford, NY: Pergamon Press.

Block, J. H. (1973). Conceptions of sex role: Some cross-cultural and longitudinal perspectives. *American Psychologist, 28,* 512–526.

Block, J. H. (1976). Debatable conclusions about sex differences. *Contemporary Psychology, 21,* 517–522.

Block, J. H. (1983). Differential premises arising from differential socialization of the sexes: Some conjectures. *Child Development, 54,* 1335–1354.

Blood, R. O., & Wolfe, D. M. (1960). *Husbands and wives.* New York: Free Press.

Blum, R. W., & Resnick, M. D. (1982). Adolescent sexual decision-making: Contraception, pregnancy, abortion, and motherhood. *Pediatric Annals, 11,* 797–805.

Blumstein P., & Schwartz, P. (1983). *American couples.* New York: William Morrow.

Blumstein, P. W., & Schwartz, P. (1993). Bisexuality, Some social psychological issues. In L. D. Garnets & D. C. Kimmel (Eds.), *Psychological perspectives on lesbian and gay male experiences* (pp. 168–184). New York: Columbia University Press.

Boardman, S. K., Harrington, C. C., & Horowitz, S. V. (1987). Successful women: A psychological investigation of family class and education origins. In B. A. Gutek & L. Larwood (Eds.), *Women's career development* (pp. 66–85). Newbury Park, CA: Sage.

Bogal-Allbritten, R., & Allbritten, W. (1985). The hidden victims: Courtship violence among college students. *Journal of College Student Personnel, 19,* 201–204.

Bogal-Allbritten, R. B., & Allbritten, W. L. (1987). Availability of community services to student victims of courtship violence. *Response to the Victimization of Women and Children, 10,* 22–24.

Bograd, M. (1988). Feminist perspectives on wife abuse: An introduction. In K. Yllo and M. Bograd (Eds.), *Feminist perspectives on wife abuse,* (pp. 11–26). Berkeley, CA: Sage.

Bohmer, C. (1991). Acquaintance rape and the law. In A. Parrot & L. Bechhofer (Eds.), *Acquaintance rape: The hidden crime* (pp. 327–333). New York: John Wiley & Sons.

Boles, D. B. (1980). X-linkage of spatial ability: A critical review. *Child Development, 51,* 625–635.

Bolin, A. (1987). Transsexualism and the limits of traditional analysis. *American Behavioral Scientist, 31,* 41–65.

Bolz, B. (1987). Social security. In S. Martz (Ed.), *When I am an old woman I shall wear purple.* Watsonville, CA: Papier Mache Press.

Bond, S., & Cash, T. F. (1992) Black beauty: Skin color and body images among African-American college women. *Journal of Applied Social Psychology, 22,* 874–888.

Bonderant, B. (1994, March). Men's perceptions

of women's sexual interest: Sexuality or sexual aggression? Paper presented at Southeastern Psychological Association 40th Annual Meeting, New Orleans.

Bookwala, J., Frieze, I. H., Smith, C., & Ryan, K. (1992). Predictors of dating violence: A multivariate analysis. *Violence and Victims, 7,* 297–311.

Bordo, S. (1993). *Unbearable weight: Feminism, western culture and the body.* Berkeley, CA: University of California Press.

Bose, C. E. (1987). Dual spheres. In B. B. Hess & M. M. Ferree (Eds.), *Analyzing gender: A handbook of social science research* (pp. 267–285). Newbury Park, CA: Sage.

Boswell, S. L. (1979). Nice girls don't study mathematics: The perspective from elementary school. Presented at the meeting of the American Educational Research Association, San Francisco.

Boswell, S. L. (1985). The influence of sex-role stereotyping on women's attitudes and achievement in mathematics. In S. F. Chipman, L. R. Brush, & D. M. Wilson (Eds.), *Women and mathematics: Balancing the equation* (pp. 175–198). Hillsdale, NJ: Erlbaum.

Bouhoutsos, J., Holroyd J., Lerman, H., Forer, B. R., & Greenberg, M. (1983). Sexual intimacy between psychotherapists and patients. *Professional Psychology, Research and Practice, 14,* 185–196.

Boyd, B., & Wandersman, A. (1991). Predicting undergraduate condom use with the Fishbein and Ajzen and the Triandis attitude-behavior models: Implications for public health interventions. *Journal of Applied Social Psychology, 21,* 1810–1830.

Boyd, J. A. (1990). Ethnic and cultural diversity: Keys to power. In L. S. Brown & M. P. P. Root (Eds.), *Diversity and complexity in feminist therapy* (pp. 151–167). New York: Harrington Park Press.

Brabant, S., & Mooney, L. (1986). Sex role stereotyping in the Sunday comics: Ten years later. *Sex Roles, 14,* 141–148.

Bradbard, M. R., & Endsley, R. C. (1983). The effects of sex-typed labeling on preschool children's information-seeking and retention. *Sex Roles, 9,* 247–260.

Braden, A. (1986). Shoulder to shoulder. In J. B. Cole (Ed.), *All American women: Lines that divide, ties that bind* (pp. 74–80). New York: Macmillan.

Bradley, C. (1993). Women's power, children's labor. *Behavior Science Research, 27,* 70–96.

Brand, P. A., and Kidd, A. H. (1986). Frequency of physical aggression in heterosexual and female homosexual dyads. *Psychological Reports, 59,* 1307–1313.

Bransford, J. D., & Johnson, M. K. (1972). Contexual prerequisites for understanding: Some investigations of comprehension and recall. *Journal of Learning and Verbal Behavior, 11,* 717–726.

Breay, E., & Gentry, M. (1990, April). *Perceptions of a sexual double standard.* Paper presented at the meeting of the Eastern Psychological Association, Philadelphia, PA.

Breene, D. (1975). *The birth of a first child.* London: Tavistock.

Brehony, K. A. (1983). Women and agoraphobia: A case for the etiological significance of the feminine sex-role stereotype. In V. Franks & E. Rothblum (Eds.), *The stereotyping of women: Its effects on mental health* (pp. 112–128). New York: Springer.

Breines, W., & Gordon, L. (1983). The new scholarship on family violence. *Signs, 8,* 490–531.

Bremer, T. H., & Wittig, M. A. (1980). Fear of success: A personality trait or a response to occupational deviance and role overload? *Sex Roles, 6,* 27–46.

Bretl, D. J., & Cantor, J. (1988). The portrayal of men and women in U.S. television commercials: A recent content analysis and trends over 15 years. *Sex Roles, 18,* 595–609.

Bridges, J. S. (1993). Pink or blue: Gender-stereotypic perceptions of infants as conveyed by birth congratulations cards. *Psychology of Women Quarterly, 17,* 193–205.

Bridges, J. S., & Orza, A. M. (1992). The effects of employment role and motive for employment on the perceptions of mothers. *Sex Roles, 27,* 331–343.

Briere, J. (1987). Predicting self-reported likelihood of battering: Attitudes and childhood experience. *Journal of Research in Personality, 21,* 62–69.

Briere, J., & Lanktree, C. (1983). Sex-role related effects of sex bias in language. *Sex Roles, 9,* 625–632.

Briere, J., & Malamuth, N. M. (1983). Self-reported likelihood of sexually aggressive behavior: Attitudinal versus sexual explanations. *Journal of Research in Personality, 17,* 315–323.

Brinkerhoff, D. B., & Booth, A. (1984). Gender, dominance, and stress. *Journal of Social and Biological Structures, 7,* 159–177.

Brod, H. (1987). Cross-culture, cross-gender: Cultural marginality and gender transcendence. *American Behavioral Scientist, 31,* 5–11.

Broderick, C., & Smith, J. (1979). The general systems approach to the family. In W. R. Burr, R. Hill, F. I. Nye, & I. L. Reis (Eds.), *Contemporary theories about the family (Vol. 2)*. New York: Free Press.

Brodsky, A. (1973). The consciousness-raising group as a model for therapy with women. *Psychotherapy: Theory, Research, and Practice, 10*, 24–29.

Brody, E. (1981). "Women in the middle" and family help to older people. *Gerontologist, 21*, 471–485.

Brooks-Gunn, J. (1986). The relationship of maternal beliefs about sex typing to maternal and young children's behavior. *Sex Roles, 14*, 21–35.

Brooks-Gunn, J. (1987a). The impact of puberty and sexual activity upon the health and education of adolescent girls and boys. *Peabody Journal of Education, 64*, 88–112.

Brooks-Gunn, J. (1987b). Pubertal processes and girls' psychological adaptation. In R. M. Lerner & T. T. Foch (Eds.), *Biological-psychosocial interactions in early adolescence* (pp. 123–153). Hillsdale NJ: Erlbaum.

Brooks-Gunn, J. (1988). Antecedents and consequences of variations in girls' maturational timing. *Journal of Adolescent Health Care, 9*, 365–373.

Brooks-Gunn, J., Boyer, C. B., & Hein, K. (1988). Preventing HIV infections in children and adolescents: Behavioral research and intervention strategies. *American Psychologist, 43*, 958–964.

Brooks-Gunn, J., & Furstenberg, F. F., Jr. (1989). Adolescent sexual behavior. *American Psychologist, 44*, 249–257.

Brooks-Gunn, J., & Mathews, W. S. (1979). *He & she: How children develop their sex-role identity.* Englewood Cliffs, NJ: Prentice-Hall.

Brooks-Gunn, J., & Petersen, A. C. (1983a) (Eds.), *Girls at puberty: Biological and psychological perspectives.* New York: Plenum.

Brooks-Gunn, J., & Petersen, A. C. (1983b). The experience of menarche from a developmental perspective. In J. Brooks-Gunn & A. C. Petersen (Eds.), *Girls at puberty* (pp. 155–177). New York: Plenum.

Brooks-Gunn, J., & Ruble, D. N. (1983). Dysmenorrhea in adolescence. In S. Golub (Ed.), *Menarche* (pp. 251–261). Lexington, MA: Lexington Books.

Brooks-Gunn, J., Samelson, M., Warren, M. P., & Fox, R. (1986). Physical similarity of and disclosure of menarcheal status to friends: Effects of age and pubertal status. *Journal of Early Adolescence, 6*, 3–14.

Brooks-Gunn, J., & Warren, M. P. (1988). The psychological significance of secondary sexual characteristics in nine- to eleven-year-old girls. *Child Development, 59*, 1061–1069.

Brooks-Gunn, J., & Warren, M. P. (1989). Biological and social contributions to negative affect in young adolescent girls. *Child Development, 60*, 372–385.

Brooks-Gunn, J., & Zehayhevich (1989). Parent-daughter relationships in early adolescence: A developmental perspective. In K. Kreppner & R. Lerner (Eds.), *Family systems and life-span development.* Hillsdale, NJ: Erlbaum.

Broughton, J. M. (1983). Women's rationality and men's virtues: A critique of gender dualism in Gilligan's theory of moral development. *Social Research, 50*, 597–642.

Broverman, I. K., Vogel, S. R., Broverman, D. M., Clarkson, F. E., & Rosenkrantz, P. S. (1972). Sex-role stereotypes: A current appraisal. *Journal of Social Issues, 28*, 59–78.

Brown, B. A., Frankel, B. G., & Fennell, M. P. (1989). Hugs or shrugs: Parental and peer influence on continuity of involvement in sport by female adolescents. *Sex Roles, 20*, 397–409.

Brown, D. R., & Gary, L. E. (1985). Social support network differential among married and nonmarried black families. *Psychology of Women Quarterly, 9*, 229–241.

Brown, E. A. (1989, June 9). Happily ever after. *Christian Science Monitor*, p. 13.

Brown, J. D., & Campbell, K. (1986). Race and gender in music videos: The same beat but a different drummer. *Journal of Communication, 36*, 94–106.

Brown, J. K. (1982). A cross-cultural exploration of the end of the childbearing years. In A. M. Voda, M. Dinnerstein, & S. R. O'Donnell (Eds.), *Changing perspectives on menopause* (pp. 51–59). Austin: University of Texas Press.

Brown, L. M., & Gilligan, C. (1993). Meeting at the crossroads: Women's psychology and girls' development. *Feminism & Psychology, 3*, 11–35.

Brown, L. S. (1984). Finding new language: Getting beyond analytic verbal shorthand in feminist therapy. *Women and Therapy, 3*, 73–80.

Brown, L. S. (1986). Diagnosis and the Zeitgeist: The politics of masochism in the DSM-III-R. Paper presented at the meeting of the American Psychological Association, Washington, DC.

Brown, L. S. (1990). The meaning of a multicultural perspective for theory-building in feminist therapy. In L. S. Brown & M. P. P. Root (Eds.), *Diversity and complexity in feminist therapy* (pp. 1–21). New York: Harrington Park Press.

Brown, L. S. (1994). *Subversive dialogues: Theory in feminist therapy.* New York: Basic Books.

Brown, L. S., & Ballou, M. (Eds.) (1992). *Personality and psychopathology: Feminist reappraisals.* New York: Guilford.

Browne, A. (1993). Violence against women by male partners: Prevalence, outcomes, and policy implications. *American Psychologist, 48,* 1077–1087.

Browne, A., & Finkelhor, D. (1986). Impact of sexual abuse: A review of the research. *Psychological Bulletin, 99,* 66–77.

Browne A., & Williams, K. R. (1993). Gender, intimacy, and lethal violence: Trends from 1976 to 1987. *Gender & Society, 7,* 78–98.

Brownmiller, S. (1975). *Against our will: Men, women, and rape.* New York: Simon & Schuster.

Brumberg, J. J. (1982). Chlorotic girls, 1870–1920: A historical perspective on female adolescence. *Child Development, 53,* 1468–1477.

Bryant, B. K. (1985). The neighborhood walk: Sources of support in middle childhood. *Monographs of the Society for Research in Child Development, 50,* 11985.

Bryden, M. (1982). *Laterality: Functional asymmetry in the intact brain.* New York: Academic Press.

Bryer, J. B., Nelson, B. A., Miller, J. B., & Krol, P. A. (1987). Childhood sexual and physical abuse as factors in adult psychiatric illness. *American Journal of Psychiatry, 144,* 1426–1430.

Buhl, M. (1989, September/October). The feminist mystique. *In View,* p. 16.

Bumagin, V. E. (1982). Growing old female. *Journal of Psychiatric Treatment and Evaluation, 4,* 155–159.

Burch, B. (1987). Barriers to intimacy: Conflicts over power, dependency, and nurturing in lesbian relationships. In Boston Lesbian Psychologies Collective, *Lesbian psychologies: Explorations and challenges* (pp. 142–160). Urbana, IL: University of Illinois Press.

Burcky, W., Reuterman, N., & Kopsky, S. (1988). Dating violence among high school students. *School Counselor, 35,* 353–358.

Burgess, A. W., & Holmstrom, L. L. (1974). Rape trauma syndrome. *American Journal of Psychiatry, 131,* 981–986.

Burnett, S. A. (1986). Sex-related differences in spatial ability: Are they trivial? *American Psychologist, 41,* 1012–1014.

Burns, A., & Homel, R. (1989). Gender division of tasks by parents and their children. *Psychology of Women Quarterly, 13,* 113–125.

Burns, A. L., Mitchell, G., & Obradovich, S. (1989). Of sex roles and strollers: Female and male attention to toddlers at the zoo. *Sex Roles, 20,* 309–315.

Burns, J. (1992). Mad or just plain bad? Gender and the work of forensic clinical psychologists. In J. M. Ussher & P. Nicolson (Eds.), *Gender issues in clinical psychology* (pp. 106–128). London: Routledge.

Burt, M. (1980). Cultural myths and supports for rape. *Journal of Personality and Social Psychology, 38,* 217–230.

Busby, L. J. (1975, Autumn). Sex-role research on the mass media. *Journal of Communication,* 107–131.

Bush, T. L. (1990). The epidemiology of cardiovascular disease in postmenopausal women. In M. Flint, F. Kronenberg, & W. Utian (Eds.), *Multidisciplinary perspectives on menopause. Annals of the New York Academy of Sciences, 592,* 263–271.

Buss, D. M. (1989). Sex differences in human mate preferences: Evolutionary hypotheses tested in 37 cultures. *Behavioral and Brain Sciences, 12,* 1–49.

Buss, D. M., et al. (1990). International preferences in selecting mates: A study of 37 cultures. *Journal of Cross-Cultural Psychology, 21,* 5–47.

Bussey, K., & Bandura, A. (1984). Influence of gender constancy and social power on sex-linked modeling. *Journal of Personality and Social Psychology, 47,* 1292–1302.

Bussey, K., & Bandura, A. (1992). Self-regulatory mechanisms governing gender development. *Child Development, 63,* 1236–1250.

Butcher, J. E. (1989). Adolescent girls' sex role development: Relationship with sports participation, self-esteem, and age at menarche. *Sex Roles, 20,* 575–593.

Butler, D., & Geis, F. L. (1990). Nonverbal affect responses to male and female leaders: Implications for leadership evaluations. *Journal of Personality and Social Psychology, 58,* 48–59.

Butler, L. D., & Nolen-Hoeksema, S. (1994). Gender differences in responses to depressed mood in a college sample. *Sex Roles, 30,* 331–346.

Butler, R. N. (1980). Ageism: A foreword. *Journal of Social Issues, 36,* 8–11.

Buzawa, E. S., & Buzawa, C. G. (1993). The scientific is not conclusive: Arrest is no panacea. In R. J. Gelles & D. R. Loseke (Eds.), *Current controversies on family violence* (pp. 336–356). Newbury Park, CA: Sage.

Caldera, Y. M., Huston, A. C., & O'Brien, M. (1989). Social interactions and play patterns of parents and toddlers with feminine, masculine, and neutral toys. *Child Development, 60,* 70–76.

Calderone, K. L. (1990). The influence of gender on the frequency of pain and sedative medication administered to postoperative patients. *Sex Roles, 23,* 713–725.

Caldwell, M. A., & Peplau, L. A. (1984). The balance of power in lesbian relationships. *Sex Roles, 10,* 587–599.

Calof, D. (1987). *Treating adult survivors of incest and child abuse.* Workshop presented at The Family Network Symposium, Washington, DC.

Cameron E., Eisenberg, N., & Tryon, K. (1985). The relations between play and preschoolers' social behavior. *Sex Roles, 12,* 601–615.

Campbell, J. C., Miller, P., Cardwell, M. M., & Belknap, R. A. (1994). Relationship status of battered women over time. *Journal of Family Violence, 9,* 99–111.

Campbell, K. E., Kleim, D. M., & Olson, K. R. (1992). Conversational activity and interruptions among women and men. *Journal of Social Psychology, 132,* 419–421.

Canetto, S. S. (1992). Gender and suicide in the elderly. *Suicide and Life-Threatening Behavior, 22,* 80–97.

Canino, G. J., Rubio-Stipec, M., Shrout, P., Bravo, M., Stolberg R., & Bird, H. R. (1987). Sex differences and depression in Puerto Rico. *Psychology of Women Quarterly, 11,* 443–459.

Cann, A., & Garnett, A. K. (1984). Sex stereotype impacts on competence ratings by children. *Sex Roles, 11,* 333–343.

Canter, R. (1982). Achievement in women: Implications for equal employment opportunity policy. In B. A. Gutek (Ed.), *Sex role stereotyping and affirmative action policy* (pp. 9–64). Los Angeles: Institute of Industrial Relations, University of California.

Cantor, M. G. (1987). Popular culture and the portrayal of women: Content and control. In B. B. Hess & M. M. Ferree (Eds.), *Analyzing gender* (pp. 190–214). Newbury Park, CA: Sage.

Cantos, A. L., Neidig, P. H., & O'Leary, K. D. (1993). Men and women's attributions of blame for domestic violence. *Journal of Family Violence, 8,* 289–302.

Caplan, P. J. (1989). *Don't blame mother.* New York: Harper & Row.

Caplan, P. J. (1991). Delusional dominating personality disorder (DDPD). *Feminism & Psychology, 1,* 171–174.

Caplan, P. J., & Hall-McCorquodale, I. (1985). Mother-blaming in major clinical journals. *American Journal of Orthopsychiatry, 55,* 345–353.

Caplan, P. J., MacPherson, G. M., & Tobin, P. (1985). Do sex-related differences in spatial abilities exist? *American Psychologist, 40,* 786–799.

Cardell, M., Finn, S., & Marecek, J. (1981). Sex-role identity, sex-role behavior, and satisfaction in heterosexual, lesbian, and gay male couples. *Psychology of Women Quarterly, 5,* 488–494.

Carli, L. L. (1990). Gender, language, and influence. *Journal of Personality and Social Psychology, 59,* 941–951.

Carlson, B. (1987). Dating violence: A research review and comparison with spouse abuse. *Social Casework, 68,* 16–23.

Carlson, B. E., & Videka-Sherman, L. (1990). An empirical test of androgyny in the middle years: Evidence from a national survey. *Sex Roles, 23,* 305–324.

Carmen, E. H., Russo, N. F., & Miller, J. B. (1981). Women's inequality and women's mental health: An overview. *American Journal of Psychiatry, 138,* 1319–1330.

Carpenter, C. J., Huston, A. C., & Holt, W. (1986). Modification of pre-school sex-typed behaviors by participation in adult-structured activities. *Sex Roles, 14,* 603–615.

Carter, D. B. (1987). The roles of peers in sex role socialization. In D. B. Carter (Ed.), *Current conceptions of sex roles and sex typing: Theory and research* (pp. 101–121). New York: Praeger.

Carter, D. B., & McCloskey, L. A. (1984). Peers and the maintenance of sex-typed behavior: The development of children's conceptions of cross-gender behavior in their peers. *Social Cognition, 2,* 294–314.

Cash, T. F., Gillen, B., & Burns, D. S. (1977). Sexism and "beautyism" in personnel consultant decision making. *Journal of Applied Psychology, 62,* 301–310.

Cass, V. C. (1979). Homosexual identity formation: A theoretical model. *Journal of Homosexuality, 4,* 219–235.

Cate, C. A., Henton, J. M., Koval, J., Christopher, F. S., & Lloyd, S. (1982). Premarital abuse:

A social psychological perspective. *Journal of Family Issues, 3,* 79–90.

Cate, R., & Sugawara, A. I. (1986). Sex role orientation and dimensions of self-esteem among middle adolescents. *Sex Roles, 15,* 145–158.

Chacko, T. I. (1982). Women and equal employment opportunity: Some unintended effects. *Journal of Applied Psychology, 67,* 119–123.

Chaffin, R. J., & Winston, M. (1991). Conceptions of parenthood. *Journal of Applied Social Psychology, 21,* 1726–1757.

Chaikin, S., & Pliner, P. (1987). Women, but not men, are what they eat: The effect of meal size and gender on perceived femininity and masculinity. *Personality and Social Psychology Bulletin, 13,* 166–176.

Chambless, D. L., & Goldstein, A. J. (1980). Anxieties: Agoraphobia and hysteria. In A. M. Brodsky & R. Hare-Mustin (Eds.), *Woman and psychotherapy: An assessment of research and practice* (pp. 113–134). New York: Guilford Press.

Chan, C. S. (1993). Issues of identity development among Asian-American lesbians and gay men. In L. D. Garnets & D. C. Kimmel (Eds.), *Psychological perspectives on lesbian and gay male experiences* (pp. 376–388). New York: Columbia University Press.

Chandani, A. T., McKenna, K. T., & Maas, F. (1989). Attitudes of university students towards the sexuality of physically disabled people. *British Journal of Occupational Therapy, 52,* 233–236.

Chapkis, W. (1986). *Beauty secrets: Women and the politics of appearance.* Boston: South End Press.

Charlesworth, W. R., & Dzur, C. (1987). Gender comparisons of preschoolers' behavior and resource utilization in group problem-solving. *Child Development, 58,* 191–200.

Charlesworth, W. R., & LaFreniere, P. (1983). Dominance, friendship utilization and resource utilization in preschool children's groups. *Ethology and Sociobiology, 4,* 175–186.

Chavez, D. (1985). Perpetuation of gender inequality: A content analysis of comic strips. *Sex Roles, 13,* 93–102.

Check, J., & Malamuth, N. (1985). An empirical assessment of some feminist hypotheses about rape. *International Journal of Women's Studies, 8,* 414–423.

Check, J., & Maxwell, K. (1992, June). *Children's consumption of pornography and their attitudes regarding sexual violence.* Paper presented at the Canadian Psychological Association Meetings, Quebec.

Chehrazi, S. (1986). Female psychology. *Journal of the American Psychoanalytic Association, 34,* 111–162. Reprinted in M. R. Walsh (Ed.), *The psychology of women: Ongoing debates* (pp. 22–38). New Haven: Yale University Press.

Cherlin, A. J. (1981). *Marriage, divorce, remarriage.* Cambridge, MA: Harvard University Press.

Cherry, F., & Deaux, K. (1978). Fear of success versus fear of gender-inappropriate behavior. *Sex Roles, 4,* 97–101.

Chesler, P. (1972). *Women and madness.* New York: Doubleday.

Chi, J. G., Dooling, E. C., & Gilles, F. H. (1977). Gyral development of the human brain. *Annals of Neurology, 1,* 86–93.

Chicago, J. (1990, March). *The birth project.* Women's History Month Lecture, Trenton State College, Trenton, NJ.

Childs, E. K. (1990). Therapy, feminist ethics, and the community of color with particular emphasis on the treatment of black women. In H. Lerman & N. Porter (Eds.), *Feminist ethics in psychotherapy* (pp. 195–203). New York: Springer.

Chilman, C. S. (1983). *Adolescent sexuality in a changing American society* (2nd ed.). New York: John Wiley & Sons.

Chilman, C. S. (1987). Some psychosocial aspects of adolescent sexual and contraceptive behaviors in a changing American society. In B. A. Hamburg & J. B. Lancaster (Eds.), *School age pregnancy and parenthood* (pp. 191–217). New York: Aldine De Gruyter.

Chipman, S. F., Brush, L. R., & Wilson, D. M. (Eds.) (1985). *Women and mathematics: Balancing the equation.* Hillsdale, NJ: Erlbaum.

Chipman, S. F., & Thomas, V. G. (1985). Women's participation in mathematics: Outlining the problem. In S. F. Chipman, L. R. Brush, & D. M. Wilson (Eds.), *Women and mathematics: Balancing the equation* (pp. 1–24). Hillsdale, NJ: Erlbaum.

Chipman, S. F., & Wilson D. M. (1985). Understanding mathematics course enrollment and mathematics achievement: A synthesis of the research. In S. F. Chipman, L. R. Brush, & D. M. Wilson (Eds.), *Women and mathematics: Balancing the equation* (pp. 275–328). Hillsdale, NJ: Erlbaum.

Chodorow, N. (1978). *The reproduction of mothering.* Berkeley, CA: University of California Press.

Chodorow, N. (1979). Feminism and difference: Gender relation and difference in psychoanalytic perspective. *Socialist Review, 46,* 42–64.

Chow, E. N. (1987). The influence of sex-role identity and occupational attainment on the psychological well-being of Asian-American women. *Psychology of Women Quarterly, 11,* 69–82.

Chrisler, J. C., & Ghiz, L. (1993). Body image issues of older women. In N. D. Davis, E. Cole, & E. D. Rothblum (Eds.), *Faces of women and aging* (pp. 67–75). Binghamton, NY: Harrington Park Press.

Chrisler, J. C., Johnston, I. K., Champagne, N. M., & Preston, K. E. (1994). Menstrual joy: The construct and its consequences. *Psychology of Women Quarterly, 18,* 375–387.

Chrisler, J. C., Torrey, J. W., & Matthes, M. A. (1990). Brittle bones and sagging breasts, loss of femininity and loss of sanity: The media describe the menopause. In A. M. Voda & R. Conover (Eds.), *Proceedings of the eighth conference of the Society for Menstrual Cycle Research* (pp. 23–35). Salt Lake City: Society for Menstrual Cycle Research.

Chusmir, L. H. (1985). Motivation of managers: Is gender a factor? *Psychology of Women Quarterly, 9,* 153–160.

Ciancanelli, P., & Berch, B. (1987). Gender and the GNP. In B. B. Hess and M. M. Ferree (Eds.), *Analyzing gender: A handbook of social science research* (pp. 244–266). Newbury Park, CA: Sage.

Cleek, M. G., & Pearson, T. A. (1985). Perceived causes of divorce: An analysis of interrelationships. *Journal of Marriage and the Family, 47,* 179–183.

Clifton, L. (1980). *Two-headed woman.* Amherst, MA: University of Massachusetts Press.

Coates, D. L. (1987). Gender differences in the structure and support characteristics of black adolescents' social networks. *Sex Roles, 17,* 667–687.

Code, L. B. (1983). Responsibility and the epistemic community: Woman's place. *Social Research, 50,* 537–555.

Cohen, B. P., Berger, J., & Zelditch, M. (1972). Status conceptions and interactions: A case study of developing cumulative knowledge. In C. McClintock (Ed.), *Experimental social psychology.* New York: Holt, Rinehart, & Winston.

Cohen, C. E. (1981). Person categories and social perception: Testing some boundaries of the processing effects of prior knowledge. *Journal of Personality and Social Psychology, 40,* 441–452.

Cohen J. (1977). *Statistical power analysis for the behavioral sciences.* New York: Academic Press.

Colby, A., & Damon, W. (1983). Listening to a different voice: A review of Gilligan's In a different voice. *Merrill-Palmer Quarterly, 29,* 473–481.

Colen, S. (1986). "With respect and feelings": Voices of West Indian child care and domestic workers in New York City. In J. B. Cole (Ed.), *All American women: Lines that divide, ties that bind* (pp. 46–70). New York: Macmillan.

Coles, R. (1985). *Sex and the American teenager.* New York: Rolling Stone Press.

Collins, P. H. (1991). The meaning of motherhood in Black culture and Black mother-daughter relationships. In P. Bell-Scott, B. Guy-Sheftall, J. J. Royster, J. Sims-Wood, M. DiCosta-Willis, & L. P. Fultz (Eds.), *Double stitch: Black women write about mothers and daughters* (pp. 42–60). New York: HarperCollins.

Collins, P. H. (1993a). Pornography and Black women's bodies. In D. E. H. Russell (Ed.), *Making violence sexy: Feminist views on pornography* (pp. 97–104). New York: Teachers College Press.

Collins, P. H. (1993b). The sexual politics of Black womanhood. In P. B. Bart & E. G. Moran (Eds.), *Violence against women: The bloody footprints* (pp. 85–104). Newbury Park, CA: Sage.

Collins, S. K. (1988). Women at the top of women's fields: Social work, nursing, and education. In A. Statham, E. M. Miller, & H. O. Mauksch (Eds.), *The worth of women's work: A qualitative synthesis* (pp. 187–201). Albany, NY: State University of New York Press.

Comas-Diaz, L. (1987). Feminist therapy with mainland Puerto Rican women. *Psychology of Women Quarterly, 11,* 461–474.

Committee on Women in Psychology (1985, October). Statement on proposed diagnostic categories for DSM-III-R. *American Psychological Association,* Washington, DC.

Comstock, G. (1991). *Television and the American child.* San Diego: Academic Press.

Condon, J. (1987). Psychological and physical symptoms during pregnancy: A comparison of male and female expectant parents. *Journal of Infant and Reproductive Psychology, 5,* 207–220.

Condry, J. C., Jr., & Condry, S. M. (1976). Sex differences: A study of the eye of the beholder. *Child Development, 47,* 812–819.

Condry, J. C., Jr., & Ross, D. F. (1985). Sex and aggression: The influence of gender label on the perception of aggression in children. *Child Development, 56,* 225–233.

Condry, S. M., Condry, J. C., Jr., & Pogatshnik, L. W. (1983). Sex differences: A study of the ear of the beholder. *Sex Roles, 9,* 697–704.

Conner, J. M., Schackman, M., & Serbin, L. A. (1978). Sex-related differences in response to practice on a visual-spatial test and generalization to a related test. *Child Development, 49,* 24–29.

Conner, J. M., & Serbin, L. A. (1985). Visual-spatial skill: Is it important for mathematics? Can it be taught? In S. F. Chipman, L. R. Brush, & D. M. Wilson (Eds.), *Women and mathematics: Balancing the equation* (pp. 151–174). Hillsdale, NJ: Erlbaum.

Constantinople, A. (1973) Masculinity-femininity: An exception to a famous dictum? *Psychological Bulletin, 80,* 389–407.

Cook, E. P. (1985). *Psychological androgyny.* New York: Pergamon.

Cooper, V. W. (1985). Women in popular music: A quantitative analysis of feminine images over time. *Sex Roles, 13,* 499–506.

Cooperstock, R. (1980). Special problems of psychotropic drug use among women. *Canada's Mental Health, 28,* 3–5.

Cooperstock, R., & Lennard, H. L. (1979). Some social meanings of tranquilizer use. *Society of Health and Illness, 1,* 331–347.

Corbett, K. (1987). The role of sexuality and sex equity in the education of disabled women. *Peabody Journal of Education, 64,* 198–212.

Corley, M. C., & Mauksch, H. O. (1988). Registered nurses, gender, and commitment. In A. Statham, E. M. Miller, & H. O. Mauksch (Eds.), *The worth of women's work: A qualitative synthesis* (pp. 135–150). Albany, NY: State University of New York Press.

Costello, C., & Stone, A. J. (Eds.) (1994). *The American woman 1994–1995: Where we stand–Women and health.* New York: Norton.

Cota, A. A., & Dion, K. L. (1986). Salience of gender and sex composition of ad hoc groups: An experimental test of distinctiveness theory. *Journal of Personality and Social Psychology, 50,* 770–776.

Courtois, C. A. (1988). *Healing the incest wound: Adult survivors in therapy.* New York: W. W. Norton.

Covey, H. C. (1988). Historical terminology used to represent older people. *Gerontologist, 28,* 291–297.

Cowan, G. (1995). Black and White (and blue): Ethnicity and pornography. In H. Landrine (Ed.), *Bringing cultural diversity to feminist psychology: Theory, research, practice* (pp. 397–411). Washington, DC: American Psychological Association.

Cowan, G., & Campbell, R. R. (1994). Racism and sexism in interracial pornography: A content analysis. *Psychology of Women Quarterly, 18,* 323–338.

Cowan, G., & Hoffman, C. D. (1986). Gender stereotyping in young children: Evidence to support a concept-learning approach. *Sex Roles, 14,* 211–224.

Cowan, G., & O'Brien, M. (1990). Gender and survival vs. death in slasher films: A content analysis. *Sex Roles, 23,* 187–196.

Cowan, G., Warren, L. W., & Young, J. L. (1985). Medical perceptions of menopausal symptoms. *Psychology of Women Quarterly, 9,* 3–14.

Coward, R. T., & Dwyer, J. W. (1990). The association of gender, sibling network composition, and patterns of parent care by adult children. *Research on Aging, 12,* 158–181.

Cowen, J. R. (1993, October). Survey finds 70% of women rabbis sexually harassed. *Moment,* 34–37.

Cowen, R. (1991, March 9). Student researchers win top STS awards. *Science News,* pp. 139, 150.

Craig, R. S. (1992). The effect of television day part on gender portrayals in television commercials: A content analysis. *Sex Roles, 26,* 197–211.

Crawford, M. (1978). Evolution made me do it. *International Journal of Women's Studies, 1,* 533–543.

Crawford, M. (1978, November). Climbing the ivy-covered walls: How colleges deny tenure to women. *Ms.,* pp. 61–63, 91–94.

Crawford, M. (1981, August). Emmy Noether: She did Einstein's math. *Ms.,* pp. 86–89.

Crawford, M. (1982). In pursuit of the well-rounded life: Women scholars and the family. In M. Kehoe (Ed.), *Handbook for women scholars* (pp. 89–96). San Francisco: Americas Behavioral Research.

Crawford, M. (1988). Gender, age, and the social evaluation of assertion. *Behavior Modification, 12,* 549–564.

Crawford, M. (1989). Agreeing to differ: Feminist epistemologies and women's ways of knowing. In M. Crawford & M. Gentry

(Eds.), *Gender and thought* (pp. 128–145). New York: Springer Verlag.

Crawford, M. (1995). *Talking difference: On gender and language.* London: Sage.

Crawford, M., & Chaffin, R. (1986). The reader's construction of meaning: Cognitive research on gender and comprehension. In E. Flynn & P. Schweikart (Eds.), *Gender and reading: Essays on reader, text, and context* (pp. 3–30). Baltimore: Johns Hopkins.

Crawford, M., & English, L. (1984). Generic versus specific inclusion of women in language: Effects on recall. *Journal of Psycholinguistic Research, 13,* 373–381.

Crawford, M., Herrmann, D. J., Holdsworth, M., Randall, E., & Robbins, D. (1989). Gender and beliefs about memory. *British Journal of Psychology, 80,* 391–401.

Crawford, M., & MacLeod, M. (1990). Gender in the college classroom: An assessment of the "chilly climate" for women. *Sex Roles, 23,* 101–122.

Crawford, M., & Marecek, J. (1989). Psychology reconstructs the female. *Psychology of Women Quarterly, 13,* 147–166.

Crawford, M., & Stark, A. (unpublished manuscript). *The meaning of Ms: Social assimilation of a gender concept.*

Crawford, S. (1987). Lesbian families: Psychosocial stress and the family-building process. In Boston Lesbian Psychologies Collective, *Lesbian psychologies* (pp. 195–214). Urbana, IL: University of Illinois Press.

Crewdson, J. (1988). *By silence betrayed: Sexual abuse of children in America.* New York: Harper and Row.

Crews, D. (1987a). Diversity and evolution of behavioral controlling mechanisms. In D. Crews (Ed.), *Psychobiology of reproductive behavior: An evolutionary perspective* (pp. 89–119). Englewood Cliffs, NJ: Prentic-Hall.

Crews, D. (1987b). Functional associations in behavioral endocrinology. In J. M. Reinisch, L. A. Rosenblum, & S. A. Sanders (Eds.), *Masculinity/femininity: Basic perspectives* (pp. 83–106). New York: Oxford University Press.

Crittenden, D. (1995, January 25). Sisterhood vs. new-wave thought. *Wall Street Journal, 225,* A14.

Crocker, J., & McGraw, K. M. (1984). What's good for the goose is not good for the gander: Solo status as an obstacle to occupational achievement for males and females. *American Behavioral Scientist, 27,* 357–369.

Crocker, J., Voelkl, K., Testa, M., & Major, B. (1991). Social stigma: The affective consequences of attributional ambiguity. *Journal of Personality and Social Psychology, 60,* 218–228.

Crockett, L. J., & Petersen, A. C. (1987). Pubertal status and psychosocial development: Findings from the early adolescent study. In R. M. Lerner & T. T. Foch (Eds.), *Biological-psychosocial interactions in early adolescence* (pp. 173–188). Hillsdale, NJ: Erlbaum.

Croghan, R. (1991). First-time mothers' accounts of inequality in the division of labour. *Feminism & Psychology, 1,* 221–246.

Crohan, S. E., & Veroff, J. (1989). Dimensions of marital well-being among white and black newlyweds. *Journal of Marriage and the Family, 51,* 373–383.

Crosbie-Burnett, M., & Giles-Sims, J. (1991). Marital power in stepfather families: A test of normative-resource theory. *Journal of Family Psychology, 4,* 484–496.

Crosby, F. (1982). *Relative deprivation and working women.* New York: Oxford University Press.

Crosby, F. (1984). The denial of personal discrimination. *American Behavioral Scientist, 27,* 371–386.

Crosby, F. J. (1991). *Juggling: The unexpected advantages of balancing career and home for women and their families.* New York: Free Press.

Crosby, F. J. (1994, April 2,). *Gender, justice, and the meritocratic ideal.* Invited address at the meeting of the Southeastern Psychological Association, New Orleans.

Crosby, F. J., Clayton, S., Alksnis, O., & Hemker, K. (1986). Cognitive biases in the perception of discrimination: The importance of format. *Sex Roles, 14,* 637–646.

Crosby, F. J., Pufall, A., Snyder, R. C., O'Connell, M., & Whalen, P. (1989). The denial of personal disadvantage among you, me, and all the other ostriches. In M. Crawford and M. Gentry (Eds.), *Gender and thought: Psychological perspectives* (pp. 79–99). New York: Springer-Verlag.

Crovitz, E., & Hayes, L. (1979). A comparison of pregnant adolescents and non-pregnant sexually active peers. *Journal of the American Medical Women's Association, 34,* 102–104.

Crovitz, E., & Steinmann, A. (1980). A decade later: Black-white attitudes toward women's familial role. *Psychology of Women Quarterly, 5,* 171–176.

Culp, R. E., Cook, A. S., & Housley, P. C. (1983). A comparison of observed and reported adult-infant interactions: Effect of perceived sex. *Sex Roles, 9,* 475–479.

Cummings, N. (1992). Self-defense training for college women. *Journal of American College Health,* 40, 183–188.

Cusick, T. (1987). Sexism and early parenting: Cause and effect? *Peabody Journal of Education, 64,* 113–131.

Daley, D., & Gold, R. B. (1993). Public funding for contraceptive, sterilization, and abortion services, fiscal year 1992. *Family Planning Perspectives, 25,* 244–251.

Daly, M., & Wilson, M. (1983). *Sex, evolution, and behavior.* Boston: Williard Grant Press.

D'Amico, R. (1986). Authority in the workplace: Differences among mature women. In L. B. Shaw (Ed.), *Midlife women at work: A fifteen-year perspective.* Lexington, MA: D. C. Heath.

Dancer, L. S., & Gilbert, L. A. (1993). Spouses' family work participation and its relation to wives' occupational level. *Sex Roles, 28,* 127–145.

Danza, R. (1983). Menarche: Its effects on mother-daughter and father-daughter interactions. In S. Golub (Ed.), *Menarche* (pp. 99–105). Lexington, MA: Lexington Books.

Darnton, J. (1993, March 11). Tough abortion law provokes dismay in Poland. *New York Times,* A13.

Datan, N., Antonovsky, A., & Maoz, B. (1981). *A time to reap: The middle age of women in five Israeli subcultures.* Baltimore: Johns Hopkins Press.

Daubman, K. A., & Lehman, T. C. (1993). The effects of receiving help: Gender differences in motivation and performance. *Sex Roles, 28,* 693–707.

Davis, C. M., & Bauserman, R. (1993). Exposure to sexually explicit materials: An attitude change perspective. *Annual Review of Sex Research, 4,* 121–209.

Davis, D. M. (1990). Portrayal of women in prime-time network television: Some demographic characteristics. *Sex Roles, 23,* 325–332.

Davis, M., & Weitz, S. (1981). Sex differences in body movements and positions. In C. Mayo & N. Henley (Eds.), *Gender and nonverbal behavior* (pp. 81–92). New York: Springer-Verlag.

Dayhoff, S. A. (1983). Sexist language and person perception: Evaluation of candidates from newspaper articles. *Sex Roles, 9,* 527–539.

Deaux, K., (1984). From individual differences to social categories: Analysis of a decade's research on gender. *American Psychologist, 39,* 105–116.

Deaux, K., (1985). Sex and gender. *Annual Review of Psychology, 36,* 49–81.

Deaux, K. (1993). Commentary: Sorry, wrong number–A reply to Gentile's call. *Psychological Science, 4,* 125–126.

Deaux, K., & Emswiller, T. (1974). Explanations of successful performance on sex-linked tasks: What's skill for the male is luck for the female. *Journal of Personality and Social Psychology, 29,* 80–85.

Deaux, K., & Hanna, R. (1984). Courtship in the personals column: The influence of gender and sexual orientation. *Sex Roles, 11,* 363–375.

Deaux, K., & Kite, M. E. (1985). Gender stereotypes: Some thoughts on the cognitive organization of gender-related information. *Academic Psychology Bulletin, 7,* 123–144.

Deaux, K., Kite, M. E., & Lewis, L. L. (1985). Clustering and gender schemata: An uncertain link. *Personality and Social Psychology Bulletin, 11,* 387–397.

Deaux, K., & Lewis, L. L. (1984). The structure of gender stereotypes: Interrelationships among components and gender labels. *Journal of Personality and Social Psychology, 46,* 991–1004.

Deaux, K., & Major, B. (1987). Putting gender into context: An interactive model of gender-related behavior. *Psychological Review, 94,* 369–389.

Deaux, K., & Ullman, J. C. (1983). *Women of steel.* New York: Praeger.

Deaux, K., Winton, W., Crowley, M., & Lewis, L. L. (1985). Level of categorization and content of gender stereotypes. *Social Cognition, 3,* 145–167.

Dege, K., & Gretzinger, J. (1982). Attitudes of families toward menopause. In A. M. Voda, M. Dinnerstein, & S. R. O'Donnell (Eds.), *Changing perspectives on menopause* (pp. 60–69). Austin: University of Texas Press.

De Groot, S. C. (1980). Female and male returnees: Glimpses of two distinct populations. *Psychology of Women Quarterly, 5,* 358–361.

DeLamater, J., & MacCorquodale, P. (1979). *Premarital sexuality.* Madison: WI: University of Wisconsin Press.

Delaney, J., Lupton, M. J., & Toth, E. (1988). *The curse: A cultural history of menstruation* (rev. ed.). Urbana, IL: University of Illinois Press.

DeMaris, A. (1992). Male versus female initiation of aggression: The case of courtship violence. In E. C. Viano (Ed.), *Intimate violence: Interdisciplinary perspectives* (pp. 111–120). New York: Hemisphere Publishing Corp.

D'Emilio, J., & Freedman, E. B. (1988). *Intimate matters: A history of sexuality in America.* New York: Harper & Row.

Denmark, F. L. (1980). Psyche: From rocking the cradle to rocking the boat. *American Psychologist, 35,* 1057–1065.

Denmark, F. L., Russo, N. F., Frieze, I. H., & Sechzer, J. A. (1988). Guidelines for avoiding sexism in psychological research: A report of the ad hoc committee on nonsexist research. *American Psychologist, 43,* 582–585.

Deschamps, J-C. (1982). Social identity and relations of power between groups. In H. Tajfel (Ed.), *Social identity and intergroup relations.* Cambridge, England: Cambridge University Press.

Deutsch, F. M. (1990). Status, sex, and smiling: The effect of role on smiling in men and women. *Personality and Social Psychology Bulletin, 16,* 531–540.

Deutsch, F. M., LeBaron, D., & Fryer, M. M. (1987). What is in a smile? *Psychology of Women Quarterly, 11,* 341–351.

Deutsch, F. M., Zalenski, C. M., & Clark, M. E. (1986). Is there a double standard of aging? *Journal of Applied Social Psychology, 16,* 771–785.

Deutsch, H. (1944). *The psychology of women: A psychoanalytic interpretation.* New York: Grune & Stratton.

Devor, H. (1987). Gender blending females: Women and sometimes men. *American Behavioral Scientist, 31,* 12–40.

Devor, H. (1989). *Gender blending: Confronting the limits of duality.* Bloomington: University of Indiana Press.

Dew, M. A. (1985). The effect of attitudes on inferences of homosexuality and perceived physical attractiveness in women. *Sex Roles, 12,* 143–155.

Dew, M. A., Bromet, E. J., & Penkower, L. (1992). Mental health effects of job loss in women. *Psychological Science, 22,* 751–764.

Dew, M. A., Penkower, L., & Bromet, E. J. (1991). Effects of unemployment on mental health in the contemporary family. *Behavior Modification, 15,* 501–544.

Dewhurst, A. M., Moore, R. J., & Alfano, D. P. (1992). Aggression against women by men: Sexual and spousal assault. *Journal of Offender Rehabilitation, 18,* 39–47.

Diamond, M. A. (1965). A critical evaluation of the ontogeny of human sexual behavior. *Quarterly Review of Biology, 40,* 147–175.

Diamond, M. A. (1968). Genetic-endocrine interactions and human psychosexuality. In M. A. Diamond (Ed.), *Perspectives in reproduction and sexual behavior.* Bloomington: University of Indiana Press.

Diamond, M. A. (1982). Sexual identity, monozygotic twins reared in discordant sex roles and a BBC follow-up. *Archives of Sexual Behavior, 11,* 181–186.

Diamond, M. A. (1993). Some genetic considerations in the development of sexual orientation. In M. Haug, R. E. Whalen, C. Aron, & K. L. Olsen (Eds.), *The development of sex differences and similarities in behavior* (pp. 291–309). Dordrecht: Kluwer Publishing Company.

DiBlasio, F. A., & Benda, B. B. (1992). Gender differences in theories of adolescent sexual activity. *Sex Roles, 27,* 221–239.

Dickson, L. (1993). The future of marriage and family in Black America. *Journal of Black Studies, 23,* 472–491.

Di Leonardo, M. (1987). The female world of cards and holidays: Women, families, and the work of kinship. *Signs, 12,* 440–453.

Dion, K., & Dion, K. (1993). Individualistic and collectivistic perspectives on gender and the cultural context of love and intimacy. *Journal of Social Issues, 49,* 53–69.

Dion, K. K., Berscheid, E., & Walster, E. (1972). What is beautiful is good. *Journal of Personality and Social Psychology, 24,* 285–290.

Dion, K. L. (1975). Women's reaction to discrimination from members of the same or opposite sex. *Journal of Research in Personality, 9,* 292–306.

Dion, K. L. (1985). Sex, gender, and groups. In V. E. O'Leary, R. K. Unger, & B. S. Wallston (Eds.). *Women, gender, and social psychology* (pp. 293–347). Hillsdale, NJ: Erlbaum.

Dion, K. L. (1987). What's in a title? The Ms stereotype and images of women's titles of address. *Psychology of Women Quarterly, 11,* 21–36.

Dion, K. L., & Cota, A. A. (1991). The Ms. stereotype: Its domain and the role of explicitness in title preference. *Psychology of Women Quarterly, 15,* 403–410.

Dion, K. L., Earn, B. M., & Yee, P. H. N. (1978). The experience of being a victim of prejudice: An experimental approach. *International Journal of Psychology, 13,* 197–214.

DiPalma, L. M. (1994). Patterns of coping and characteristics of high-functioning incest survivors. *Archives of Psychiatric Nursing, 8(2),* 82–90.

Dobash, R. P., & Dobash, R. E. (1992). *Women, violence, and social change.* New York: Routledge.

Dodson, B. (1987). *Sex for one: The joy of self-loving.* New York: Crown.

Doherty, W. J., & Baldwin, C. (1985). Shifts and stability in locus of control during the 1970s: Divergence of the sexes. *Journal of Personality and Social Psychology, 48,* 1048–1053.

Dolan, E. M., & Lown, J. M. (1985). The remarried family: Challenges and opportunities. *Journal of Home Economics, 77,* 36–41.

Donnerstein, E. (1983). Public hearings on ordinances to add pornography as discrimination against women, Committee on Government Operations, City Council, Minneapolis, MN.

Dorans, N. J., & Livingston S. A. (1987). Male-female differences in SAT-verbal ability among students of high SAT-mathematic ability. *Journal of Educational Measurement, 24,* 65–71.

Doress, P. B., Siegal, D. L., & the Midlife and Old Women Book Project (1987). *Ourselves, growing older.* New York: Simon & Schuster.

Doress-Worters, P. B., & Siegal, D. L. (1994). *The new ourselves growing older.* New York: Simon & Schuster.

Dornbusch, S. M., Gross, R. T., Duncan, P. D., & Ritter, P. L. (1987). Stanford studies of adolescence using the national health examination survey. In R. M. Lerner & T. T. Foch (Eds.), *Biological-psychosocial interactions in early adolescence* (pp. 189–205). Hillsdale, NJ: Erlbaum.

Douglas, S. J. (1994). *Where the girls are: Growing up female with the mass media.* New York: Times Books/Random House.

Dovidio, J. F., Ellyson, S. L., Keating, C. F., Heltman, K., & Brown, C. E. (1988). The relationship of social power to visual displays of dominance between men and women. *Journal of Personality and Social Psychology, 54,* 233–242.

Dovidio, J. F., & Gaertner, S. L. (1981). The effects of race, status, and ability on helping behavior. *Social Psychology Quarterly, 44,* 192–203.

Dovidio, J. F., & Gaertner, S. L. (1983). The effects of sex, status, and ability on helping behavior. *Journal of Applied Social Psychology, 13,* 191–205.

Downs, A. C., & Harrison, S. K. (1985). Embarrassing age spots or just plain ugly? Physical attractiveness stereotyping as an instrument of sexism on American television commercials. *Sex Roles, 13,* 9–19.

Duncan, G. J., & Hoffman, S. D. (1991). A reconsideration of the economic consequences of marital dissolution. *Demography, 22,* 485.

Dunkle, J. H., & Francis, P. L. (1990). The role of facial masculinity/femininity in the attribution of homosexuality. *Sex Roles, 23,* 157–167.

Dunlop, E. (1968). Emotional imbalances in the premenopausal woman. *Psychosomatics, 9,* 44–47.

Dutton, D. (1988). *The domestic assault of women: Psychological and criminal justice perspectives,* Boston: Allyn and Bacon, 1988.

Dworkin, A. (1974). *Woman hating.* New York: E. P. Dutton.

Dworkin, A. (1987). *Intercourse.* New York: Free Press.

Dworkin, A., & MacKinnon, C. (1993). Questions and answers. In D. E. H. Russell (Ed.), *Making violence sexy: Feminist views on pornography* (pp. 78–96). New York: Teachers College Press.

Dwyer, C. A. (1979). The role of tests and their construction in producing apparent sex-related differences. In M. A. Wittig & A. C. Petersen (Eds.), *Sex-related differences in cognitive functioning: Developmental issues* (pp. 335–353). New York: Academic Press.

Eagly, A. H. (1983). Gender and social influence: A social psychological analysis. *American Psychologist, 38,* 971–981.

Eagly, A. H. (1987). *Sex differences in social behavior: A social role interpretation.* Hillsdale, NJ: Erlbaum.

Eagly, A. H., & Karau, S. J. (1991). Gender and the emergence of leaders: A meta-analysis. *Journal of Personality and Social Psychology, 60,* 685–710.

Eagly, A. H., Karau, S. J., & Makhijani, M. (1995). Gender and the effectiveness of leaders: A meta-analysis. *Psychological Bulletin, 117,* 125–145.

Eagly, A. H., & Mladinic, A. (1989). Gender stereotypes and attitudes toward women and men. *Personality and Social Psychology Bulletin, 15,* 543–558.

Eagly, A. H., Mladinic, A., & Otto, S. (1991). Are women evaluated more favorably than men? An analysis of attitudes, beliefs, and emotions. *Psychology of Women Quarterly, 15,* 203–216.

Eagly, A. H., & Steffen, V. J. (1984). Gender stereotypes stem from the distribution of women and men into social roles. *Journal of Personality and Social Psychology, 46,* 735–754.

Eagly, A. H., & Steffen, V. J. (1986). Gender stereotypes, occupational roles, and beliefs about part-time employees. *Psychology of Women Quarterly, 10,* 252–262.

Eagly, A. H., & Wood, W. (1982). Inferred sex differences in status as a determinant of gender stereotypes about social influence. *Journal of Personality and Social Psychology, 43,* 915–928.

Eagly, A. H., Wood, W., & Fishbaugh, L. (1981). Sex differences in conformity: Surveillance by the group as a determinant of male nonconformity. *Journal of Personality and Social Psychology, 40,* 384–394.

Eaton, W. O., vonBargen, D., & Keats, J. G. (1981). Gender understanding and dimensions of preschooler toy choice: Sex stereotypes versus activity level. *Canadian Journal of Behavioral Science, 13,* 203–209.

Eccles, J. S. (1989). Bringing young women to math and science. In M. Crawford and M. Gentry (Eds.), *Gender and thought: Psychological perspectives* (pp. 36–58). New York: Springer-Verlag.

Eccles, J. S. (1994). Understanding women's educational and occupational choices: Applying the Eccles et al. model of achievement-related choices. *Psychology of Women Quarterly, 18,* 585–610.

Eccles, J. S., Adler, T. F., Futterman, R., Goff, S. B., Kaczala, C. M., Meece, J. L., & Midgley, C. (1985). Self-perceptions, task perceptions, socializing influences, and the decision to enroll in mathematics. In S. F. Chipman, L. R. Brush, & D. M. Wilson (Eds.), *Women and mathematics: Balancing the equation* (pp. 95–122). Hillsdale, NJ: Erlbaum.

Eccles, J. S., & Jacobs, J. E. (1986). Social forces shape math attitudes and performance. *Signs, 11,* 367–389.

Eckes, T. (1994). Features of men, features of women: Assessing stereotypic beliefs about gender subtypes. *British Journal of Social Psychology, 33,* 107–123.

Edelson, M. S., & Omark, D. R. (1973). Dominance hierarchies in young children. *Social Science Information, 12,* 1.

Edman, C. D. (1983a). The climacteric. In H. J. Buchsbaum (Ed.), *The menopause* (pp. 23–33). New York: Springer-Verlag.

Edman, C. D. (1983b). Estrogen replacement therapy. In H. J. Buchsbaum (Ed.), *The menopause* (pp. 77–84). New York: Springer-Verlag.

Edwards, C. P., & Whiting, B. B. (1988). *Children of different worlds.* Cambridge, MA: Harvard University Press.

Ehrenreich, B., & English, D. (1979). *For her own good: 150 years of the experts' advice to women.* Garden City, NY: Anchor Books.

Ehrhardt, A. A., & Meyer-Bahlburg, H. F. L. (1981). Effects of prenatal sex hormones on gender-related behavior. *Science, 211,* 1312–1318.

Eichler, M. (1980). *The double standard: A feminist critique of feminist social science.* New York: St. Martin's Press.

Eichler, M. (1988). *Nonsexist research methods.* Boston: Allen & Unwin.

Eisenberg, N., Tryon, K., & Cameron, E. (1984). The relation of preschoolers' peer interaction to their sex-typed toy choices. *Child Development, 55,* 1044–1050.

Eldridge, N. S., & Gilbert, L. A. (1990). Correlates of relationship satisfaction in lesbian couples. *Psychology of Women Quarterly, 14,* 43–62.

Elkind, S. N. (1991, Winter). Letter to the editor. *Psychology of Women, 18,* 3.

Elliot, R. (1989). *Song of love.* New York: Harlequin.

Elliot, S. (1984). Pregnancy and after. In S. Rachman (Ed.), *Contributions to medical psychology 3* (pp. 93–116). New York: Pergamon Press.

Ellyson, S. L., Dovidio, J. F., & Brown, C. E. (1992). The look of power: Gender differences and similarities in visual dominance behavior. In C. L. Ridgeway (Ed.), *Gender, interaction, and inequality* (pp. 50–80). New York: Springer-Verlag.

Ellyson, S. L., Dovidio, J. F., & Fehr, B. J. (1981). Visual behavior and dominance in women and men. In C. Mayo & N. Henley (Eds.), *Gender and nonverbal behavior* (pp. 63–79). New York: Springer-Verlag.

Emmerich, W., & Shepard, K. (1984). Cognitive factors in the development of sex-typed preferences. *Sex Roles, 11,* 997–1007.

England, P. (1981). Assessing trends in occupational sex-segregation, 1900–1976. In I. Berg (Ed.), *Sociological perspectives on labor markets.* New York: Academic Press.

England, P., Kuhn, A., & Gardner, T. (1981). The ages of men and women in magazine advertisements. *Journalism Quarterly, 58,* 468–471.

England, P., & McCreary, L. (1987). Gender inequality in paid employment. In B. B. Hess and M. M. Ferree (Eds.), *Analyzing gender: A handbook of social science research* (pp. 286–320). Newbury Park, CA: Sage.

Erikson, E. H. (1963). *Childhood and society.* Canada: Norton.

Erikson, E. H. (1964). Inner and outer space: Reflections on womanhood. *Daedalus, 93,* 582–606.

Ernster, V. L. (1975). American menstrual expressions. *Sex Roles, 1,* 3–13.

Eron, L. D. (1980). Prescription for reduction of aggression. *American Psychologist, 35,* 244–252.

Espin, O. M. (1986). Cultural and historical influences on sexuality in Hispanic/Latin women. In J. Cole (Ed.), *All American women: Lines that divide, ties that bind* (pp. 272–284). New York: Free Press.

Espin, O. M. (1987a). Issues of identity in the psychology of Latina lesbians. In Boston Lesbian Psychologies Collective (Ed.), *Lesbian psychologies: Explorations and challenges* (pp. 35–55). Urbana: University of Illinois Press.

Espin, O. M. (1987b). Psychological impact of migration on Latinas: Implications of psychotherapeutic practice. *Psychology of Women Quarterly, 11,* 489–503.

Espin, O. M., & Gawelek, M. (1992). Women's diversity: Ethnicity, race, class, and gender in theories of feminist psychology. In L. S. Brown and M. Ballou (Eds.), *Personality and psychopathology: Feminist reappraisals* (pp. 88–110). New York: Guilford.

Etaugh, C. (1980). Effects of nonmaternal care on children: Research evidence and popular views. *American Psychologist, 35,* 309–319.

Etaugh, C., & Brown, B. (1975). Perceiving the causes of success and failure of male and female performers. *Developmental Psychology, 11,* 103.

Etaugh, C., & Liss, M. B. (1992). Home, school, and playroom: Training grounds for adult gender roles. *Sex Roles, 26,* 129–147.

Etter-Lewis, G. (1988). Power and social change: Images of Afro-American women in the print media. Paper presented at the annual meeting of the National Women's Studies Association, Minneapolis, MN.

Etzioni, A. (1969). *The semi-professions and their organization: Teachers, nurses, social workers.* New York: Free Press.

Faderman, L. (1981). *Surpassing the love of men: Romantic friendship and love between women from the Renaissance to the present.* New York: William Morrow.

Fagot, B. I. (1974). Sex differences in toddlers' behavior and parental reaction. *Developmental Psychology, 10,* 554–558.

Fagot, B. I. (1978). The influence of sex of child on parental reactions to toddler children. *Child Development, 49,* 459–465.

Fagot, B. I. (1985a). Beyond the reinforcement principle: Another step toward understanding sex role development. *Developmental Psychology, 21,* 1097–1104.

Fagot, B. I. (1985b). Changes in thinking about early sex role development. *Developmental Review, 5,* 83–98.

Fagot, B. I., & Leinbach, M. D. (1987). Socialization of sex roles within the family. In D. B. Carter (Ed.), *Current conceptions of sex roles and sex typing: Theory and research* (pp. 89–100). New York: Praeger.

Fagot, B. I., & Leinbach, M. D. (1989). The young child's gender schema: Environmental input, internal organization. *Child Development, 60,* 663–672.

Fairhurst, G. T., & Snavely, B. K. (1983). A test of the social isolation of male tokens. *Academy of Management Journal, 26,* 353–361.

Falbo, T., & Peplau, L. A. (1980). Power strategies in intimate relationships. *Journal of Personality and Social Psychology, 38,* 618–628.

Falk, P. J. (1993). Lesbian mothers: Psychosocial assumptions in family law. In L. D. Garnets & D. C. Kimmel (Eds.), *Psychological perspectives on lesbian and gay male experiences* (pp. 420–436). New York: Columbia University Press.

Faludi, S. (1991). *Backlash: The undeclared war against American women.* New York: Doubleday.

Farel, A. (1980). Effects of preferred maternal roles, maternal employment, and sociodemographic status on school adjustment and competence. *Child Development, 51,* 1179–1186.

Faulkner, A. O., & Heisel, M. A. (1987). Giving, receiving, and exchanging: Social transactions among inner-city black aged. In H. Strange & M. Teitelbaum (Eds.), *Aging and cultural diversity* (pp. 117–130). South Hadley, MA: Bergin & Garvin.

Faunce, P. S. (1990). Women in poverty: Ethical dimensions in therapy. In H. Lerman & N. Porter (Eds.), *Feminist ethics in psychotherapy* (pp. 185–194). New York: Springer.

Faust, M. G. (1983). Alternative constructions on adolescent growth. In J. Brooks-Gunn & A. C. Petersen (Eds.), *Girls at puberty* (pp. 105–125). New York: Plenum.

Fausto-Sterling, A. (1989). Life in the XY corral. *Women's Studies International Forum, 12,* 319–331.

Fausto-Sterling, A. (1992). *Myths of gender: Bio-*

logical theories about women and men (rev. ed.). New York: Basic Books.

Feather, N. T. (1985). Masculinity, femininity, self-esteem, and sub-clinical depression. *Sex Roles, 12,* 491–500.

Federal Bureau of Investigation (1985). *Uniform crime report.* Washington, DC: U.S. Department of Justice.

Federal Bureau of Investigation (1989). *Crime in the United States: Uniform crime reports.* Washington, DC: U.S. Department of Justice.

Feeney, J., Peterson, C., & Noller, P. (1994). Equality and marital satisfaction in the family life cycle. *Personal Relationships, 1,* 83–99.

Feild, H. S., & Beinen, L. B. (1980). *Jurors and rape: A study in psychology and law.* Lexington, MA: D. C. Heath.

Feingold, A. (1988). Cognitive gender differences are disappearing. *American Psychologist, 43,* 95–103.

Feingold, A. (1994). Gender differences in variability in intellectual abilities: A cross-cultural perspective. *Sex Roles, 30,* 81–92.

Feinman, S. (1981). Why is cross-sex-role behavior more approved for girls than for boys? A status characteristic approach. *Sex Roles, 7,* 289–300.

Feiring, C., & Lewis, M. (1987). The child's social network: Sex differences from three to six years. *Sex Roles, 17,* 621–636.

Feiring, C., & Lewis, M. (1991). The transition from middle childhood to early adolescence: Sex differences in the social network and perceived self-confidence. *Sex Roles, 24,* 489–509.

Feldman, R. S. (1994, May). Sexual harassment: The Navy reacts to the Tailhook scandal. Psychfax to McGraw-Hill.

Feldman-Summers, S., & Kiesler, S. J. (1974). Those who are number two try harder: The effects of sex on attributions of causality. *Journal of Personality and Social Psychology, 30,* 846–855.

Fenell, D. L. (1993). Characteristics of long-term first marriages. *Journal of Mental Health Counseling, 15,* 446–460.

Fernberger, S. W. (1948). Persistence of stereotypes concerning sex differences. *Journal of Abnormal and Social Psychology, 43,* 97–101.

Ferree, M. M. (1987). She works hard for a living: Gender and class on the job. In B. B. Hess & M. M. Ferree (Eds.), *Analyzing gender: A handbook of social science research* (pp. 322–347). Newbury Park, CA: Sage.

Fidell, L. S. (1970). Empirical verification of sex discrimination in hiring practices in psychology. *American Psychologist, 25,* 1094–1098.

Fidell, L. S. (1982). Gender and drug use and abuse. In I. Al-Issa (Ed.), *Gender and psychopathology* (pp. 221–236). New York: Academic Press.

Field, T., Widmayer, S., Stoller, S., & de Cubes, M. (1986). School-age parenthood in different ethnic groups and family constellations: Effect on infant development. In B. A. Hamburg & J. B. Lancaster (Eds.), *School age pregnancy and parenthood* (pp. 263–272). New York: Aldine De Gruyter.

Fine, M. (1983–1984). Coping with rape: Critical perspectives on consciousness. *Imagination, Cognition, and Personality, 3,* 249–267.

Fine, M. (1985). Reflections on a feminist psychology of women: Paradoxes and prospects. *Psychology of Women Quarterly, 9,* 167–183.

Fine, M. (1988). Sexuality, schooling, and adolescent females: The missing discourse of desire. *Harvard Educational Review, 58,* 29–53.

Fine, M., & Asch, A. (1981). Disabled women: Sexism without the pedestal. *Journal of Sociology and Social Welfare, 8,* 233–248.

Fine, M., & Asch, A. (1988). *Women with disabilities: Essays in psychology, culture, and politics.* Philadelphia: Temple University Press.

Fine, M., & Gordon, S. M. (1989). Feminist transformations of/despite psychology. In M. Crawford & M. Gentry (Eds.), *Gender and thought* (pp. 146–174). New York: Springer-Verlag.

Fine, M., & Macpherson, P. (1992). Over dinner: Feminism and adolescent female bodies. In M. Fine (Ed.), *Disruptive voices: The possibilities of feminist research* (pp. 175–203). Ann Arbor: University of Michigan Press.

Fine, M., & Zane, N. (1988). Bein' wrapped too tight: When low income women drop out of high school. In L. Weis (Ed.), *Dropouts in schools: Issues, dilemmas, solutions.* Albany: SUNY Press.

Finkel, J. S., & Hanson, F. J. (1992). Correlates of retrospective marital satisfaction in long-lived marriages: A social constructivist approach. *Family Therapy, 19,* 1–16.

Finkelhor, D. (1979). *Sexually victimized children.* New York: Free Press.

Finkelhor, D. (1980). Risk factors in the sexual victimization of children. *Child Abuse and Neglect, 4,* 265–273.

Finkelhor, D. (1983). Common features of family abuse. In D. Finkelhor, R. J. Gelles, G. T.

Hotaling, & M. A. Straus (Eds.), *The dark side of families* (pp. 17–18). Beverly Hills: Sage.

Finkelhor, D. (1984). *Child sexual abuse: New theory and research.* New York: Free Press.

Finkelhor, D., & Hotaling, G. T. (1984). Sexual abuse in the national incidence study of child abuse and neglect: An appraisal. *Child Abuse and Neglect, 8,* 23–32.

Finkelhor, D., Hotaling, G., Lewis, I. A., & Smith, C. (1990). Sexual abuse in a national survey of adult men and women: Prevalence, characteristics, and risk factors. *Child Abuse and Neglect, 14,* 533–542.

Finlay, B., & Scheltema, K. (1991). The relation of gender and sexual orientation to measures of masculinity, femininity, and androgyny: A further analysis. *Journal of Homosexuality, 21,* 71–85.

Fischer, J. L., & Narus, L. R. (1981). Sex-role development in late adolescence and adulthood. *Sex Roles, 7,* 97–106.

Fisher, J. D., Nadler, A., & Whitcher-Alagna, S. (1982). Recipient reactions to aid. *Psychological Bulletin, 91,* 27–54.

Fisher, W., Byrne, D., & White, L. (1983). Emotional barriers to contraception. In D. Byrne & W. Fisher (Eds.), *Adolescents, sex, and contraception* (pp. 207–239). Hillsdale, NJ: Erlbaum.

Fiske, A. P., Haslam, N., & Fiske, S. T. (1991). Confusing one person with another: What errors reveal about the elementary forms of social relations. *Journal of Personality and Social Psychology, 60,* 656–674.

Fiske, S. T. (1993). Controlling other people: The impact of power on stereotyping. *American Psychologist, 48,* 621–628.

Fiske, S. T., Bersoff, D. N., Borgida, E., Deaux, K., & Heilman, M. E. (1991). Social science research on trial: Use of sex stereotyping research in Price Waterhouse v. Hopkins. *American Psychologist, 46,* 1049–1060.

Fiske, S. T., & Stevens, L. E. (1993). What's so special about sex? Gender stereotyping and discrimination. In S. Oskamp & M. Constanzo (Eds.), *Gender issues in contemporary society* (pp. 173–196). Newbury Park, CA: Sage.

Fitzgerald, L. F. (1993). Sexual harassment: Violence against women in the workplace. *American Psychologist, 48,* 1070–1076.

Fitzgerald, L. F., & Betz, N. E. (1983). Issues in the vocational psychology of women. In W. B. Walsh & S. H. Osipow (Eds.), *Handbook of vocational psychology,* Vol. 1. Hillsdale, NJ: Erlbaum.

Fivush, R. (1989). Exploring sex differences in the emotional content of mother-child conversations about the past. *Sex Roles, 20,* 675–691.

Flanders, L. (1992). Mothers and other soldiers: The media's "woman warrior." *Extra,* Special Issue, p. 23.

Fleming, J. (1978). Fear of success, achievement-related motives and behaviors in Black college women. *Journal of Personality, 46,* 694–716.

Fling, S., and Manosevitz, M. (1972). Sex typing in nursery school children's play interests. *Developmental Psychology, 7,* 146–152.

Flint, M. (1975). The menopause: Reward or punishment? *Psychosomatics, 16,* 161–163.

Flint, M., & Samil, R. S. (1990). Cultural and subcultural meanings of the menopause. In M. Flint, F. Kronenberg, & W. Utian (Eds.), Multidisciplinary perspectives on menopause. *Annals of the New York Academy of Sciences, 592,* 134–155.

Foa, E. B., Olasov, B., and Steketee, G. S. (1987). *Treatment of rape victims.* Paper presented at the conference, State of the Art in Sexual Assault, Charleston, SC.

Fodor, I. G. (1982). Gender and phobia. In I. Al-Issa (Ed.), *Gender and psychopathology* (pp. 179–197). New York: Academic Press.

Fodor, I. G., & Rothblum, E. D. (1984). Strategies for dealing with sex-role stereotypes. In C. M. Brody (Ed.), *Women therapists working with women: New theory and process of feminist therapy* (pp. 86–95). New York: Springer.

Follingstad, D. R., Rutledge, L. L., McNeill-Hawkins, K., & Polek, D. S. (1992). Factors related to physical violence in dating relationships. In E. C. Viano (Ed.), *Intimate violence: Interdisciplinary perspectives* (pp. 121–135). New York: Hemisphere.

Ford, C. V., & Sbordone, R. J. (1980). Attitudes of psychiatrists toward elderly patients. *American Journal of Psychiatry, 137,* 571–575.

Ford, M. R., & Lowery, C. R. (1986). Gender differences in moral reasoning: A comparison of the use of justice and care orientations. *Journal of Personality and Social Psychology, 50,* 777–783.

Fordham, S. (1993). "Those loud black girls": (Black) women, silence, and gender "passing" in the academy. *Anthropology and Education Quarterly, 24,* 3–32.

Foreit, K. G., Agor, A. T., Byers, J., Larue, J., Lokey, H., Palazzini, M., Patterson, M., & Smith, L. (1980). Sex bias in the newspaper treatment of male-centered and femalecentered news stories. *Sex Roles, 6,* 475–480.

Forisha, B. L. (1978). *Sex roles and personal awareness.* Morristown, NJ: General Learning Press.

Forward, J. R., & Williams, J. R. (1970). Internal-external control and black militancy. *Journal of Social Issues, 26,* 75–92.

Foschi, M., & Freeman, S. (1991). Inferior performance, standards, and influence in same-sex dyads. *Canadian Journal of Behavioral Sciences, 23,* 99–113.

Foucault, M. (1978). *The history of sexuality.* New York: Pantheon.

Fowers, B. J. (1991). His and her marriages: A multivariate study of gender and marital satisfaction. *Sex Roles, 24,* 209–221.

Fox, G. L. (1981). The family's role in adolescent sexual behavior. In T. Ooms (Ed.), *Teenage pregnancy in a family context.* Philadelphia: Temple University Press.

Frable, D. E. S., & Bem, S. L. (1985). If you're gender-schematic, all members of the opposite sex look alike. *Journal of Personality and Social Psychology, 49,* 459–468.

Frank, A. (1952). *Anne Frank: The diary of a young girl.* Garden City, NY: Doubleday.

Frank, E., Anderson, C., & Rubenstein, D. (1978). Frequency of sexual dysfunction in "normal" couples. *New England Journal of Medicine, 299,* 111–115.

Frank, R. E., & Greenberg, M. G. (1980). *The public's use of television: Who watches and why.* Beverly Hills, CA: Sage.

Franks, V. (1986). Sex stereotyping and the diagnosis of psychopathology. In D. Howard (Ed.), *The dynamics of feminist therapy* (pp. 219–232). New York: Haworth Press.

Franz, C. E., & Stewart, A. J. (Eds.) (1994). *Women creating lives: Identities, resilience, and resistance.* Boulder, CO: Westview.

Frasher, R. S., Nurss, J. R., & Brogan, D. R. (1980). Children's toy preferences revisited: Implications for early childhood education. *Child Care Quarterly, 9,* 26–31.

Freedman, R. (1986). *Beauty bound.* Lexington, MA: D. C. Heath.

Freud, S. (1933/1965). *New introductory lectures on psychoanalysis.* New York: Norton.

Freud, S. (1948). *Some psychological consequences of the anatomical distinction between the sexes.* In *Collected papers* (Vol. V, pp. 186–197). London: Hogarth.

Freud, S. (1966). In James Strachey (Ed. and Trans.), *New introductory lectures on psychoanalysis.* New York: Norton.

Frey, C., & Hoppe-Graff, S. (1994). Serious and playful aggression in Brazilian girls and boys. *Sex Roles, 30,* 249–268.

Friday, N. (1973). *My secret garden: Women's sexual fantasies.* New York: Simon & Schuster.

Friedman, A., & Pines, A. M. (1992). Increase in Arab women's perceived power in the second half of life. *Sex Roles, 26,* 1–9.

Friedman, H., & Zebrowitz, L. A. (1992). The contribution of typical sex differences in facial maturity to sex role stereotypes. *Personality and Social Psychology Bulletin, 18,* 430–438.

Frieze, I. H. (1979). Perceptions of battered wives. In I. H. Frieze, D. Bar-Tal, & S. Carroll (Eds.), *New approaches to social problems* (pp. 79–108). San Francisco: Jossey-Bass.

Frisch, R. E. (1983a). Fatness, menarche, and fertility. In S. Golub (Ed.), *Menarche: The transition from girl to woman* (pp. 5–20). Lexington, MA: Lexington Books.

Frisch, R. E. (1983b). Fatness, puberty, and fertility: The effects of nutrition and physical training on menarche and ovulation. In J. Brooks-Gunn & A. C. Petersen (Eds.), *Girls at puberty* (pp. 29–49). New York: Plenum.

Furby, L. (1979). Individualistic bias in studies of locus of control. In A. R. Buss (Ed.), *Psychology in social context* (pp. 169–190). New York: Irvington.

Furnham, A., & Bitar, N. (1993). The stereotyped portrayal of men and women in British television advertisements. *Sex Roles, 29,* 297–310.

Furnham, A., & Singh, A. (1986). Memory for information about sex differences. *Sex Roles, 15,* 479–486.

Furstenberg, F. F., Jr., Brooks-Gunn, J., & Chase-Lansdale, L. (1989). Teenaged pregnancy and childbearing. *American Psychologist, 44,* 313–320.

Furstenberg, F. F., Jr., Herceg-Baron, R., Shea, J., & Webb, D. (1986). Family communication and contraceptive use among sexually active adolescents. In B. A. Hamburg & J. B. Lancaster (Eds.), *School age pregnancy and parenthood* (pp. 219–243). New York: Aldine De Gruyter.

Furstenberg, F. F., Jr., Moore, K. A., & Peterson, J. L. (1986). Sex education and sexual experience among adolescents. *American Journal of Public Health, 75,* 1221–1222.

Furumoto, L. (1979). Mary Whiton Calkins (1863–1930): Fourteenth president of the American Psychological Association. *Journal of the History of the Behavioral Sciences, 15,* 346–356.

Gagnon, J. H. (1983). Age at menarche and sexual conduct in adolescence and young adulthood. In S. Golub (Ed.), *Menarche* (pp.

175–185). Lexington, MA: Lexington Books.

Gagnon, J. H., & Simon, W. (1973). *Sexual conduct: The social sources of human sexuality.* Chicago: Aldine.

Gaiter, D. (1994, March 8). The gender divide: Black women's gains in corporate America outstrip Black men's. *Wall Street Journal, 223,* 1.

Galambos, N. L., Petersen, A. C., Richards, M., & Gitelson, I. B. (1985). The Attitudes toward Women Scale for Adolescents (AWSA): A study of reliability and validity. *Sex Roles, 13,* 343–356.

Galanis, C. M. B., & Jones, E. E. (1986). When stigma confronts stigma: Some conditions enhancing a victim's tolerance of other victims. *Personality and Social Psychology Bulletin,* 12, 169–177.

Galler, R. (1984). The myth of the perfect body. In C. S. Vance (Ed.), *Pleasure and danger: Exploring female sexuality* (pp. 165–172). Boston: Routledge & Kegan Paul.

Galligan, R. F., & Terry, D. J. (1993). Romantic ideals, fear of negative implications, and the practice of safe sex. *Journal of Applied Social Psychology, 23,* 1685–1711.

Gama, E. P. (1985). Achievement motivation of women: Effects of achievement and affiliation arousal. *Psychology of Women Quarterly, 9,* 89–104.

Gannon, L. R. (1985). *Menstrual disorders and menopause: Biological, psychological and cultural research.* New York: Praeger.

Gannon, L. R., & Ekstrom, B. (1993). Attitudes toward menopause: The influence of sociocultural paradigms. *Psychology of Women Quarterly, 17,* 275–288.

Gannon, L. R., Luchetta, T., Rhodes, K., Pardie, L., & Segrist, D. (1992). Sex bias in psychological research: Progress or complacency? *American Psychologist, 47,* 389–396.

Garcia, N., Kennedy, C., Pearlman, S. F., & Perez, J. (1987). The impact of race and culture differences: Challenges to intimacy in lesbian relationships. In Boston Lesbian Psychologies Collective (Ed.), *Lesbian psychologies: Explorations and challenges* (pp. 161–174). Urbana: University of Illinois.

Garland, A. W. (1988). *Women activists: Challenging the abuse of power.* New York: Feminist Press.

Garland, H., Hale, K. F., & Burnson, M. (1982). Attributions for the success and failure of female managers: A replication and extension. *Psychology of Women Quarterly, 7,* 155–162.

Garn, S. M. (1966). Body size and its implications. In L. W. Hoffman & M. L. Hoffman (Eds.), *Review of Child Development Research,* Vol. 2., New York: Russell Sage.

Garner, D. M., Garfinkel, P. E., Schwartz, D., & Thompson, M. (1980). Cultural expectations of thinness in women. *Psychological Reports, 47,* 483–491.

Gaskill, L. R. (1991). Same-sex and cross-sex mentoring of female proteges: A comparative analysis. *Career Development Quarterly, 40,* 48–63.

Gastil, J. (1990). Generic pronouns and sexist language: The oxymoronic character of masculine generics. *Sex Roles, 23,* 629–643.

Gauna-Trujillo, B., & Higgins, P. G. (1989). Sexual intercourse and pregnancy. In P. N. Stern (Ed.), *Pregnancy and parenting* (pp. 31–40). New York: Hemisphere.

Gayford, J. J. (1975). Wife-battering: A preliminary survey of 100 cases. *British Medical Journal, 1,* 194–197.

Geis, F. L., Boston, M. B., & Hoffman, N. (1985). Sex of authority role models and achievements by men and women: Leadership performance and recognition. *Journal of Personality and Social Psychology, 49,* 636–653.

Geis, F. L., Brown, V., Jennings, J., & Corrado-Taylor, D. (1984). Sex vs. status in sex-associated stereotypes. *Sex Roles, 11,* 771–785.

Geis, F. L., Brown, V., Jennings, J., & Porter, N. (1984). TV commercials as achievement scripts for women. *Sex Roles, 10,* 513–525.

Gelles, R. J. (1988). Violence and pregnancy: Are pregnant women at greater risk of abuse? *Journal of Marriage and the Family, 50,* 841–847.

Gelles, R. J., & Straus, M. A. (1988). *Intimate violence: The definitive study of the causes and consequences of abuse in the American family.* New York: Simon & Schuster.

Gelwick, B. P. (1984, September). Lifestyles of six professional women engaged in college student development careers. *Journal of College Student Personnel,* 418–429.

Gentile, D. A. (1993). Just what are sex and gender, anyway?: A call for a new terminological standard. *Psychological Science, 4,* 120–122.

Gentry, M. (1989). Introduction: Feminist perspectives on gender and thought: Paradox and potential. In M. Crawford & M. Gentry (Eds.), *Gender and thought* (pp. 1–16). New York: Springer-Verlag.

Geraghty, C. (1991). *Women and soap opera: A*

study of prime-time soaps. Cambridge, England: Polity Press.

Gergen, M. M. (1990). Finished at 40: Women's development within the patriarchy. *Psychology of Women Quarterly, 14,* 471–493.

Gerike, A. E. (1990). On gray hair and oppressed brains. *Journal of Women & Aging, 1,* 35–46.

Gerson, M. (1980). The lure of motherhood. *Psychology of Women Quarterly, 5,* 207–218.

Gerstel, N. (1988). Divorce, gender, and social integration. *Gender & Society, 2,* 343–367.

Gervasio, A. H., & Crawford, M. (1989). Social evaluations of assertiveness: A critique and speech act reformulation. *Psychology of Women Quarterly, 13,* 1–26.

Geschwind, N., & Behan, P. (1982). Left-handedness: Association with immune disease, migraine, and developmental learning disorder. *Proceedings of National Academy of Sciences, 79,* 5097–5100.

Giacomini, M., Rozee-Koker, P., & Pepitone-Arreola-Rockwell, F. (1986). Gender bias in human anatomy textbook illustrations. *Psychology of Women Quarterly, 10,* 413–419.

Gibber, J. R. (1981). Infant-directed behaviors in male and female rhesus monkeys. Unpublished doctoral dissertation. Department of Psychology, University of Wisconsin–Madison.

Gibbons, J. L., Stiles, D. A., & Shkodriani, G. M. (1991). Adolescents' attitudes toward family and gender roles: An international comparison. *Sex Roles, 25,* 625–643.

Giddings, P. (1984). *When and where I enter: The impact of black women on race and sex in America.* New York: Morrow.

Gidycz, C. A., Coble, C. N., Latham, L., & Layman, M. J. (1992). Relation of a sexual assault experience on adulthood to prior victimization experiences: A prospective analysis. *Psychology of Women Quarterly, 7,* 151–168.

Gieve, K. (1989). *Balancing acts: On being a mother.* London: Virago.

Gilbert, D. T., & Hixon, G. (1991). The trouble of thinking: Activating and application of stereotypic beliefs. *Journal of Personality and Social Psychology, 60,* 509–517.

Gilbert, L. A. (1980). Feminist therapy. In A. M. Brodsky & R. Hare-Mustin (Eds.), *Women and psychotherapy: An assessment of research and practice* (pp. 245–265). New York: Guilford Press.

Gilbert, L. A. (1987). What makes dual-career marriages tick? ERIC Document Reproduction Service No. ED 289 135.

Gilbert, L. A. (1993). *Two careers/One family: The promise of gender equality.* London: Sage.

Gilbert, L. A. (1994). Reclaiming and returning gender to context: Examples from studies of heterosexual dual-earner families. *Psychology of Women Quarterly, 18,* 539–558.

Gilbert, L. A., Galessich, J. M., & Evans, S. L. (1983). Sex of faculty role model and students' self-perceptions of competency. *Sex Roles, 9,* 597–607.

Gilbert, L. A., & Rossman, K. M. (1992). Gender and the mentoring process for women: Implications for professional development. *Professional Psychology: Research and Practice, 23,* 233–238.

Gilbert, S. M., & Gubar, S. (1978). *The madwoman in the attic.* New Haven: Yale University Press.

Gillen, B. (1981). Physical attractiveness: A determinant of two types of goodness. *Personality and Social Psychology Bulletin, 7,* 277–281.

Gilligan, C. (1982). *In a different voice.* Cambridge, MA: Harvard University Press.

Gillman, R. D. (1968). The dreams of pregnant women and maternal adaptation. *American Journal of Orthopsychiatry, 38,* 688–692.

Gilmore, D. D. (1990). *Mankind in the making: Cultural concepts of masculinity.* New Haven: Yale University Press.

Ginorio, A., Gutierrez, L., Cauce, A. M., & Acosta, M. (1995). Psychological issues for Latinas. In H. Landrine (Ed.), *Bringing cultural diversity to feminist psychology* (pp. 241–263). Washington, DC: American Psychological Association.

Glenn, N. D., & McLanahan, S. (1981). The effects of offspring on the psychological wellbeing of older adults. *Journal of Marriage and the Family, 43,* 409–421.

Goffman, E. (1963). *Stigma.* Englewood Cliffs, NJ: Prentice-Hall.

Gold, A. R., & St. Ange, M. C. (1974). Development of sex role stereotypes in Black and White elementary school girls. *Developmental Psychology, 10,* 461.

Goldberg, P. A. (1968). Are women prejudiced against women? *Transaction, 5,* 28–30.

Goldberg, P. A. (1974). Prejudice toward women: Some personality correlates. *International Journal of Group Tensions, 4,* 53–63.

Goldberg-Ambrose, C. (1992). Unfinished business in rape law reform. *Journal of Social Issues, 48,* 173–186.

Golden, C. (1987). Diversity and variability in women's sexual identities. In Boston Lesbian Psychologies Collective (Eds.), *Lesbian psychologies* (pp. 18–34). Urbana: University of Illinois Press.

Goldfoot, D. A., & Neff, D. A. (1987). Assessment of behavioral sex differences in social contexts: Perspectives from primatology. In J. M. Reinisch et al. (Eds.), *Masculinity/femininity: Basic perspectives.* New York: Oxford University Press.

Golding, J. M. (1988). Gender differences in depressive symptoms: Statistical considerations. *Psychology of Women Quarterly, 12,* 61–74.

Goldman, K. (1993, August 23). Sexy Sony ad riles a network of women. *Wall Street Journal,* B5.

Goldman, R., & Goldman, J. (1982). *Children's sexual thinking.* London: Routledge & Kegan Paul.

Goldman, W., & Lewis, P. (1977). Beautiful is good: Evidence that the physically attractive are more socially skillful. *Journal of Experimental Social Psychology, 13,* 125–130.

Goldstein, D. (1983). Spouse abuse. In A. Goldstein (Ed.), *Prevention and Control of Aggression* (pp. 37–65). New York: Pergamon Press.

Goldstein, E. (1979). Effect of same-sex and cross-sex role models on the subsequent academic productivity of scholars. *American Psychologist, 34,* 407–410.

Goleman, D. (1989, April 11). Subtle and intriguing differences found in the brain anatomy of men and women. *New York Times,* pp. 15, 20.

Golombok, S., & Fivush, R. (1994). *Gender development.* New York: Cambridge University Press.

Goodchilds, J. D., Zellman, G. L., Johnson, P. B., & Giarrusso, R. (1988). Adolescents and their perceptions of sexual interactions. In A. W. Burgess (Ed.), *Rape and sexual assault,* Vol. II (pp. 245-270). New York: Garland.

Goodman, M. J. (1982). A critique of menopause research. In A. M. Voda, M. Dinnerstein, & S. R. O'Donnell (Eds.), *Changing perspectives on menopause* (pp. 273–288). Austin: University of Texas Press.

Goodman, M. J., Stewart, C. J., & Gilbert, F., Jr. (1977). Patterns of menopause: A study of certain medical and physiological variables among Caucasian and Japanese women living in Hawaii. *Journal of Gerontology, 32,* 291–298.

Gordon, C. (1968). Self-conceptions: Configurations of content. In C. Gordon & K. Gergen (Eds.), *The self in social interaction.* New York: Wiley.

Gordon, J. W., & Ruddle, F. H. (1981). Mammalian gonadal determination and gametogenesis. *Science, 211,* 1265–1271.

Gordon, L. (1988). *Heroes of their own lives: The politics and history of family violence.* New York: Penguin.

Gordon, R. R., & Gordon, K. K. (1967). Factors in postpartum emotional adjustment. *American Journal of Orthopsychiatry, 37,* 359–360.

Gorski, R. A. (1987). Sex differences in the rodent brain: Their nature and origin. In J. M. Reinisch et al. (Eds.), *Masculinity/femininity: Basic perspectives* (pp. 37–67). New York: Oxford University Press.

Gottman, J. M., & Parker, J. G. (Eds.) (1987). *Conversations of friends: Speculations in affective development.* New York: Cambridge University Press.

Gough, K. (1984). The origin of the family. In J. Freeman (Ed.), *Women: A feminist perspective* (3rd ed., pp. 83–99). Palo Alto, CA: Mayfield.

Gould, L. (1972). X: A fabulous child's story. *Ms.,* 1, 74–76; 105–106.

Gould, S. J. (1980). *The panda's thumb.* New York: Norton,

Gould, S. J. (1981). *The mismeasure of man.* New York: Norton.

Gove, W. R. (1972). The relationship between sex roles, marital status, and mental illness. *Social Forces, 51,* 34–44.

Gove, W. R., & Shin, H-C. (1989). The psychological well-being of divorced and widowed men and women: An empirical analysis. *Journal of Family Issues, 10,* 122–144.

Goy, R. W. (1970). Early hormonal influences on the development of sexual and sex-related behavior. In F. O. Schmitt (Ed.), *The neurosciences: Second study program.* New York: Rockefeller University Press.

Grady, K. E. (1977, April). The belief in sex differences. Paper presented at the meeting of the Eastern Psychological Association, Boston.

Grady, K. E. (1979). Androgyny reconsidered. In J. H. Williams (Ed.), *Psychology of women: Selected readings* (pp. 172–177). New York: Norton.

Grady, K. E. (1981). Sex bias in research design. *Psychology of Women Quarterly, 5,* 628–636.

Graham, A. (1975). The making of a nonsexist dictionary. In B. Thorne & N. Henley (Eds.), *Language and sex: Difference and dominance.* Rowley, MA: Newbury House.

Grainger, P. (1984). One hour mama. In C. S. Vance (Ed.), *Pleasure and danger: Exploring female sexuality* (pp. 415–416). Boston: Routledge & Kegan Paul.

Grambs, J. D. (1989). *Women over forty: Visions and realities.* New York: Springer.

Gravenkemper, S. A., & Paludi, M. A. (1983).

Fear of success revisited: Introducing an ambiguous cue. *Sex Roles, 9,* 897–900.

Gray, J. D. (1983). The married professional woman: An examination of her role conflicts and coping strategies. *Psychology of Women Quarterly, 7,* 235–243.

Grayson, D. A. (1987). Emerging equity issues related to homosexuality in education. *Peabody Journal of Education, 64,* 132–145.

Green, R. (1974). *Sexual identity conflict in children and adults.* New York: Basic Books.

Green, R., Williams, K., & Goodman, M. (1982). Ninety-nine "tomboys" and "non-tomboys": Behavioral contrasts and demographic similarities. *Archives of Sexual Behavior, 11,* 247–266.

Greene, A. L., & Adams-Price, C. (1990). Adolescents' secondary attachments to celebrity figures. *Sex Roles, 23,* 325–347.

Greene, B. A. (1986). When the therapist is white and the patient is black: Considerations for psychotherapy in the feminist heterosexual and lesbian communities. In D. Howard (Ed.), *The dynamics of feminist therapy* (pp. 41–65). New York: Haworth Press.

Greene, B. A. (1990). Sturdy bridges: The role of African-American mothers in the socialization of African-American children. In J. P. Knowles & E. Cole (Eds.), *Motherhood: A feminist perspective* (pp. 205–225). New York: Haworth.

Greene, B. A. (1992). Still here: A perspective on psychotherapy with African American women. In J. C. Chrisler & D. Howard (Eds.), *New directions in feminist psychology: Practice, theory, and research* (pp. 13–25). New York: Springer.

Greenglass, E. R., & Burke, R. J. (1988). Work and family precursors of burnout in teachers: Sex differences. *Sex Roles, 18,* 215–229.

Greenspan, M. (1983). *A new approach to women and therapy.* New York: McGraw-Hill.

Greenspan, M. (1986). Should therapists be personal? Self-disclosure and therapeutic distance in feminist therapy. In D. Howard (Ed.), *The dynamics of feminist therapy* (pp. 5–17). New York: Haworth Press.

Greenwood-Audant, L. M. (1984). The internalization of powerlessness: A case study of the displaced homemaker. In J. Freeman (Ed.), *Women: A feminist perspective* (3rd ed., pp. 264–281). New York: Mayfield.

Griffin, S. (1971). Rape: The all-American crime. *Ramparts, 10,* 26–35.

Grimm, D. E. (1987). Toward a theory of gender: Transsexualism, gender, sexuality, and relationships. *American Behavioral Scientist, 31,* 66–85.

Griscom, J. L. (1992). Women and power: Definition, dualism, and difference. *Psychology of Women Quarterly, 16,* 389–414.

Groth, A. N., & Birnbaum, H. J. (1979). *Men who rape: The psychology of the offender.* New York: Plenum Press.

Gruber, J. E., & Bjorn, L. (1982). Blue-collar blues: The sexual harassment of women autoworkers. *Work and Occupations, 9,* 271–298.

Guinn, S., & Russell, L. G. (1987). Personnel decisions and the dual-earner couple. *Employment Relations Today, 14,* 83–90.

Gutek, B. A. (1985). *Sex and the workplace.* San Francisco: Jossey-Bass.

Gutek, B. A. (1989). Relocation, family, and the bottom line: Results from the Division 35 survey. *Psychology of Women Quarterly, 16,* 5–7.

Gutek, B. A., & Larwood, L. (Eds.) (1987). *Women's career development.* Newbury Park, CA: Sage.

Gutek, B. A., Repetti, R. L., & Silver, D. L. (1988). Nonwork roles and stress at work. In C. L. Cooper & R. Payne (Eds.), *Causes, coping, and consequences of stress at work* (pp. 141–174). New York: Wiley.

Guthrie, R. V. (1976). *Even the rat was white: A historical view of psychology.* New York: Harper & Row.

Gwartney-Gibbs, P. A., Stockard, J., & Brohmer, S. (1983). Learning courtship violence: The influence of parents, peers and personal experiences. *Family Relations, 36,* 276–282.

Haaken, J. (1988). Field dependence research: A historical analysis of a psychological construct. *Signs, 13,* 311–330.

Haavind, H. (1983). Love and power in marriage. In H. Holter (Ed.), *Patriarchy in a welfare society* (pp. 136–167.) Oxford, England: Oxford University Press.

Haddock, G., & Zanna, M. P. (1994). Preferring "housewives" to "feminists": Categorization and the favorability of attitudes toward women. *Psychology of Women Quarterly, 18,* 25–52.

Hafner, R. J., & Minge, P. J. (1989). Sex role stereotyping in women with agoraphobia and their husbands. *Sex Roles, 20,* 705–711.

Hagan, J. L. & Davis, L. V. (1992). Working with women: Building a policy and practice agenda. *Social Work, 37,* 495–502.

Hagestad, G. O. (1987). Able elderly in the family context: Changes, chances, and challenges. *Gerontologist, 27,* 417–422.

Hale, G., Duckworth, J., Zimostrad, S., and Nicholas, D. (1988). Abusive Partners:

MMPI profiles of male batterers. *Journal of Mental Health Counseling, 10* (4), 214–224.

Hall, D. T. (1972). A model of coping with role conflict: The role behavior of college educated women. *Administrative Science Quarterly, 17,* 471–489.

Hall, J. A. (1985). *Nonverbal sex differences: Communication accuracy and expressive style.* Baltimore: Johns Hopkins University Press.

Hall, J. A., & Halberstadt, A. G. (1986). Smiling and gazing. In J. S. Hyde and M. C. Linn (Eds.), *The psychology of gender: Advances through meta-analysis* (pp. 136–158). Baltimore: Johns Hopkins University Press.

Hall, M. (1994, March 31). Feds, states clash on abortion. *USA Today,* A3.

Hall, N. L. (1984). *The true story of a single mother.* Boston: South End Press.

Halpern, D. F. (1986). *Sex differences in cognitive abilities.* Hillsdale, NJ: Erlbaum.

Halpern, D. F. (1992). *Sex differences in cognitive abilities* (2nd ed.). Hillsdale, NJ: Erlbaum.

Hamberger, L. K., Saunders, D. G., & Hovey, M. (1992). The prevalence of domestic violence in community practice and rate of physician inquiry. *Family Medicine, 24* (4), 283–287.

Hamburg, B. A. (1986). Subsets of adolescent mothers: Developmental, biomedical, and psychosocial issues. In B. A. Hamburg & J. B. Lancaster (Eds.), *School age pregnancy and parenthood* (pp. 115–145). New York: Aldine De Gruyter.

Hamer, D. H., Hu, S., Magnuson, V., Hu, N., & Pattatucci, A. M. L. (1993). A linkage between DNA markers in the X chromosome and male sexual orientation. *Science, 261,* 321–327.

Hamilton, J. A., & Gallant (Alagna), S. J. (1988). On a premenstrual psychiatric diagnosis: What's in a name? *Professional Psychology: Research and Practice, 19,* 271–278.

Hamilton, J. A., & Gallant, S. J. (1990). Problematic aspects of diagnosing premenstrual phase dysphoria: Recommendations for psychological research and practice. *Professional Psychology: Research and Practice, 21,* 60–68.

Hamilton, L. H., Brooks-Gunn, J., Warren, M. P., & Hamilton, W. G. (1987, December). The impact of thinness and dieting on the professional ballet dancer. *Journal of Medical Problems of Performing Artists,* 117–122.

Hamilton, M. C. (1988). Masculine generics and misperceptions of AIDS risk. *Journal of Applied Social Psychology, 18,* 1222–1240.

Hamilton, M. C. (1991). Masculine bias in the attribution of personhood: People = male, male = people. *Psychology of Women Quarterly, 15,* 393–402.

Hamilton, M. C., & Henley, N. M. (1982, March). Detrimental consequences of generic masculine usage: Effects on the reader/hearer's cognitions. Paper presented at the meeting of the Western Psychological Association, Sacramento, CA.

Hamilton, M. C., & Henley, N. M. (1986). Sex bias in language: Effects on the reader/hearer's cognitions. Unpublished paper cited in Henley (1989).

Hamilton, S., Rothbart, M., & Dawes, R. M. (1986). Sex bias, diagnosis, and DSM-III. *Sex Roles, 15,* 269–274.

Hammen, C. L., & Peters, S. D. (1977). Differential responses to male and female depressive reactions. *Journal of Abnormal Psychology, 85,* 994–1001.

Hammen, C. L., & Peters, S. D. (1978). Interpersonal consequences of depression: Responses to men and women enacting a depressed role. *Journal of Abnormal Psychology, 87,* 322–332.

Hammer, M. (1970). Preference for a male child: Cultural factor. *Journal of Individual Psychology, 26,* 54–56.

Hammond, J. A., & Mahoney, C. W. (1983). Reward-cost balancing among women coalminers. *Sex Roles, 9,* 17–29.

Hansen, F. J., & Reekie, L. (1990). Sex differences in clinical judgments of male and female therapists. *Sex Roles, 23,* 51–64.

Hanson, K. A., & Gidycz, C. A. (1993). An evaluation of a sexual assault prevention program. *Journal of Consulting and Clinical Psychology, 61,* 1046–1052.

Harding, S. (1986). *The science question in feminism.* Ithaca, NY: Cornell University Press.

Harding, S. (Ed.) (1987). *Feminism and methodology.* Bloomington: Indiana University Press.

Hardon, A. (1992). Norplant: Conflicting views on its safety and acceptability. In H. B. Holmes (Ed.), *Issues in reproductive technology.* New York: Garland.

Hare-Mustin, R. T. (1983). An appraisal of the relationship between women and psychotherapy: 80 years after the case of Dora. *American Psychologist, 38,* 593–601.

Hare-Mustin, R. T. (1991). Sex, lies, and headaches: The problem is power. In T. J. Goodrich (Ed.), *Women and power: Perspectives for therapy* (pp. 63–85). New York: W. W. Norton.

Hare-Mustin, R. T., & Marecek, J. (1988). The meaning of difference: Gender theory, postmodernism, and psychology. *American Psychologist, 43,* 455–464.

Hare-Mustin, R. T., & Marecek, J. (Eds.) (1990). *Making a difference: Psychology and the construction of gender.* New Haven: Yale University Press.

Harlan, S. L., & O'Farrell, B. (1982). After the pioneers: Prospects for women in nontraditional blue-collar jobs. *Work and Occupations, 9,* 363–386.

Harlow, H. (1971). *Learning to love.* New York: Albion.

Harris, B. J. (1984). The power of the past: History and the psychology of women. In M. Lewin (Ed.), *In the shadow of the past* (pp. 1–5). New York: Columbia University Press.

Harris, M. B. (1990). Is love seen as different for the obese? *Journal of Applied Social Psychology, 20,* 1209–1224.

Harris, M. B., Begay, C., & Page, P. (1989). Activities, family relationships and feelings about aging in a multicultural elderly sample. *International Journal of Aging and Human Development, 29,* 103–117.

Harris, V. R. (1994). Prison of color. In E. Featherston (Ed.), *Skin deep: Women writing on color, culture, and identity* (pp. 8–15). Freedom, CA: The Crossing Press.

Harrison, A. A., & Saeed, L. (1977). Let's make a deal: An analysis of revelations and stipulations in lonely hearts advertisements. *Journal of Personality and Social Psychology, 35,* 257–264.

Harrison, A. O., & Minor, J. H. (1978). Interrole conflict, coping strategies, and satisfaction among black working wives. *Journal of Marriage and the Family, 40,* 799–805.

Hart, B. (1986). Lesbian battering: An examination. In K. Loebel (Ed.), *Naming the violence* (pp. 173–189). Seattle, WA: Seal.

Hartl, D. L. (1983). *Human genetics.* New York: Harper & Row.

Hartzler, K., & Franco, J. N. (1985). Ethnicity, division of household tasks and equity in marital roles: A comparison of Anglo and Mexican American couples. *Hispanic Journal of Behavioral Sciences, 7,* 333–344.

Haslett, B. J., Geis, F. L., & Carter, M. R. (1992). *The organizational woman: Power and paradox.* Norwood, NJ: Ablex.

Hatch, L. R. (1990). Gender and work at midlife and beyond. *Generations, 14,* 48–52.

Hatch, L. R. (1995). Gray clouds and silver linings: Women's resources in later life. In J. Freeman (Ed.), *Women: A feminist perspective* (5th ed., pp. 182–196). Mountain View, CA: Mayfield Publishing Co.

Hatton, B. J. (1994, March). The experiences of African American lesbians: Family, community, and intimate relationships. Poster presented at the Southeastern Psychological Association Convention. New Orleans, LA.

Haug, M., Whalen, R. E., Aron, C., & Olsen, K. L. (Eds.) (1993). *The development of sex differences and similarities in behavior.* Dordrecht: Kluwer Publishing Company.

Hayes, C. D. (Ed.) (1987). *Risking the future: Adolescent sexuality, pregnancy, and childbearing.* Washington, DC: National Academy Press.

Healy, S. (1986). Growing to be an old woman: Aging and ageism. In J. Alexander, D. Berrow, L. Domitrovich, M. Donnelly, & C. McLean (Eds.), *Women and aging* (pp. 58–62). Corvallis, OR: Calyx.

Healy, S. (1993). Confronting ageism: A must for mental health. In N. D. Davis, E. Cole, & E. D. Rothblum (Eds.), *Faces of women and aging* (pp. 41–54). Binghamton, NY: Harrington Park Press.

Heckman, N. A., Bryson, R., & Bryson, J. B. (1977). Problems of professional couples: A content analysis. *Journal of Marriage and the Family, 39,* 323–330.

Hedges, L. V., & Becker, B. J. (1986). Statistical methods in the meta-analysis of research on gender differences. In J. G. Hyde & M. C. Linn (Eds.), *The psychology of gender: Advances through meta-analysis* (pp. 14–50). Baltimore: Johns Hopkins.

Hedlund, R. D., Freeman, P. K., Hamm, K. E., & Stein, R. M. (1979). The electability of women candidates: The effects of sex role stereotypes. *Journal of Politics, 41,* 513–524.

Heilbrun, C. (1973). *Toward a recognition of androgyny.* New York: Knopf.

Heilman, M. E., Block, C. J., Martell, R. F., & Simon, M. C. (1989). Has anything changed? Current characterizations of men, women, and managers. *Journal of Applied Psychology, 74,* 935–942.

Heilman, M. E., Simon, M. C., & Repper, D. P. (1987). Intentionally favored, unintentionally harmed? Impact of sex-based preferential selection on self-perceptions and self-evaluations. *Journal of Applied Psychology, 72,* 62–68.

Heilman, M. E., & Stopeck, M. H. (1985). Attractiveness and corporate success: Differential causal attributions for males and females. *Journal of Applied Psychology, 70,* 379–388.

Helmreich, R. L., & Spence, J. T. (1978). The work and family orientation questionnaire:

An objective instrument to assess components of achievement motivation and attitudes towards family and career. *JSAS Catalog of Selected Documents in Psychology, 8,* 35.

Helmreich, R. L., Spence, J. T., & Gibson, R. H. (1982). Sex-role attitudes: 1972–1980. *Personality and Social Psychology Bulletin, 8,* 656–662.

Helmreich, R. L., Spence, J. T., & Holahan, C. K. (1979). Psychological androgyny and sex role flexibility: A test of two hypotheses. *Journal of Personality and Social Psychology, 37,* 1631–1644.

Helson, R. M. (1978). Creativity in women. In J. Sherman & F. Denmark (Eds.), *Psychology of women: Future directions of research* (pp. 553–604). New York: Psychological Dimensions.

Hemmer, J. D., & Kleiber, D. A. (1981). Tomboys and sissies: Androgynous children? *Sex Roles, 7,* 1205–1211.

Henley, N. M. (1977). *Body politics: Power, sex, and nonverbal communication.* Englewood Cliffs, NJ: Prentice-Hall.

Henley, N. (1985). Psychology and gender. *Signs, 11,* 101–119.

Henley, N. M. (1989). Molehill or mountain? What we do know and don't know about sex bias in language. In M. Crawford & M. Gentry (Eds.), *Gender and thought* (pp. 59–78). New York: Springer-Verlag.

Henley, N. M., & Freeman, J. (1989). The sexual politics of interpersonal behavior. In J. Freeman (Ed.), *Women: A feminist perspective* (4th ed., pp. 457–469). Mountainview, CA: Mayfield.

Henley, N. M., & Pincus, F. (1978). Interrelationship of sexist, racist, and antihomosexual attitudes. *Psychological Reports, 42,* 83–90.

Henton, J., Cate, R., Koval, J., Lloyd, S., & Christopher, S. (1983). Romance and violence in dating relationships. *Journal of Family Issues, 4,* 467–482.

Hepburn, C. (1985). Memory for the frequency of sex-typed versus neutral behaviors: Implications for the maintenance of sex stereotypes. *Sex Roles, 12,* 771–776.

Herdt, G. H., & Davidson, J. (1988). The Sambra "Turnim-man": Sociocultural and clinical aspects of gender formation in male pseudohermaphrodites with 5 alpha-reductase deficiency in Papua New Guinea. *Archives of Sexual Behavior, 17,* 33–56.

Herek, G. M. (1987). Religious orientation and prejudice: A comparison of racial and sexual attitudes. *Personality and Social Psychology Bulletin, 13,* 34–44.

Herek, G. M. (1993). The context of antigay violence: Notes on cultural and psychological heterosexism. In L. D. Garnets & D. C. Kimmel (Eds.), *Psychological perspectives on lesbian and gale male experiences* (pp. 89–108). New York: Columbia University Press.

Herman, A. (1988). Foreward. In A. Statham, E. M. Miller, & H. O. Mauksch (Eds.), *The worth of a women's work: A qualitative synthesis* (pp. ix–xi). Albany, NY: State University of New York Press.

Herman, J. & Hirschman, L. (1977). Father-daughter incest. *Signs, 2,* 735–756.

Herman, J., & Hirschman, L. (1981). Families at risk for father-daughter incest. *American Journal of Psychiatry, 138,* 967–970.

Herrmann, D. J., Crawford, M., & Holdsworth, M. (1992). Gender-linked differences in everyday memory performance. *British Journal of Psychology, 82,* 221–231.

Hernandez, D. G. (1994). Good and the bad about women's news in newspapers. *Editor and Publisher,* May 21, pp. 17, 41.

Herrenkohl, R., Herrenkohl, L., & Toedter, L. (1983). Perspective on the intergenerational transmission of abuse. In D. Finkelhor, R. J. Gelles, G. T. Hotaling, & M. A. Straus (Eds), *The dark side of families* (pp. 305–316). Beverly Hills, CA: Sage.

Herzog, D. B., Norman, D. K., Gordon, C., & Pepose, M. (1984). Sexual conflict and eating disorders in 27 males. *American Journal of Psychiatry, 141,* 989–990.

Hess, B. B. (1990). Gender and aging: The demographic parameters. *Generations, 14,* 12–15.

Hesse-Biber, S. (1989). Eating patterns and disorders in a college population: Are college women's eating problems a new phenomenon? *Sex Roles, 20,* 71–89.

Hetherington, E. M. (1965). A developmental study of the effects of sex of the dominant parent on sex-role preference, identification, and imitation in children. *Journal of Personality and Social Psychology, 2,* 188–194.

Hetherington, E. M., & Parke, R. D. (1975). *Child Psychology: A Contemporary Viewpoint.* New York: McGraw-Hill.

Heywood, S. (1989). *Fantasy lover.* Ontario, Canada: Harlequin.

Hill, J. P. (1988). Adapting to menarche: Familial control and conflict. In M. R. Gunnar & W. A. Collins (Eds.), *Development during the transition to adolescence. Minnesota symposia on child development* (Vol. 21, pp. 43–77). Hillsdale, NJ: Erlbaum.

Hill, J. P., & Holmbeck, G. N. (1987). Familial adaptation to biological change during adolescence. In R. M. Lerner & T. T. Foch (Eds.), *Biological-psychosocial interactions in early adolescence* (pp. 207–223). Hillsdale, NJ: Erlbaum.

Hill, J. P., & Lynch, M. E. (1983). The intensification of gender-related role expectations during early adolescence. In J. Brooks-Gunn & A. C. Petersen (Eds.), *Girls at puberty* (pp. 201–228). New York: Plenum.

Hill, M. (1987). Child-rearing attitudes of black lesbian mothers. In Boston Lesbian Psychologies Collective (Eds.), *Lesbian psychologies* (pp. 215–225). Urbana: University of Illinois Press.

Hillier, L., & Foddy, M. (1993). The role of observer attitudes in judgments of blame in cases of wife assault. *Sex Roles, 29,* 629–644.

Hite, S. (1976). *The Hite report.* New York: Macmillan.

Hite, S. (1987). *The Hite report: Women and love; a cultural revolution in progress.* New York: Knopf.

Hochschild, A. R. (1978). *The unexpected community: Portrait of an old-age subculture.* Berkeley, CA: University of California Press.

Hochschild, A. R. (1987, November 15). Why can't a man be more like a woman? *New York Times Book Review,* pp. 3, 32.

Hochschild, A. R. (1989). *The second shift: Working parents and the revolution at home.* New York: Viking.

Hoecker, K. S., & White, J. W. (in press). Rape-related post-traumatic stress disorder. In Miller, D. J. (Ed.), *Handbook of Post-Traumatic Stress Disorders.* New York: Plenum.

Hoffman, C., & Hurst, N. (1990). Gender stereotypes: Perceptions or rationalization? *Journal of Personality and Social Psychology, 58,* 197–208.

Hoffman, L. W. (1974). Effects of maternal employment on the child—a review of the research. *Development Psychology, 10,* 204–228.

Hoffnung, M. (1989). Motherhood: Contemporary conflict for women. In J. Freeman (Ed.), *Women: A feminist perspective* (4th ed., pp. 157–175). Mountain View, CA: Mayfield.

Holland, D., & Skinner, D. (1987). Prestige and intimacy: The cultural models behind Americans' talk about gender types. In D. Holland & N. Quinn (Eds.), *Cultural models in language and thought* (pp. 78–111). Cambridge, England: Cambridge University Press.

Hollander, N. (1987). *Never take your cat to a salad bar.* New York: Random House.

Hollander, N. (1994). Sylvia. *Hysteria, 6,* 26.

Hollin, C. R. (1987). Sex roles in adolescence. In D. J. Hargreaves & A. M. Colley (Eds.), *The psychology of sex roles* (pp. 176–197). New York: Hemisphere.

Hollingworth, H. L. (1990). *Leta Stetter Hollingworth: A biography.* Bolton, MA: Anker.

Hollingworth, L. S. (1916). Social devices for impelling women to bear and rear children. *American Journal of Sociology, 22,* 19–29.

Holtzworth-Munroe, A. (1988). Causal attributions in marital violence: Theoretical and methodological issues. *Clinical Psychology Review, 8,* (3), 331–344.

Holtzworth-Munroe, A., & Hutchinson, G. (1993). Attributing negative intent to wife behavior: The attributions of maritally violent versus nonviolent men. *Journal of Abnormal Psychology, 102,* 206–211.

hooks, b. (1984). *Feminist theory: From margin to center.* Boston: South End Press.

hooks, b. (1989). *Talking back: Thinking feminist, thinking black.* Boston: South End Press.

hooks, b. (1994). Gangsta culture–sexism and misogyny, who will take the rap. In b. hooks (Ed.), *Outlaw culture: Resisting representations* (pp. 115–123). New York: Routledge.

Hooper, C. (1992). *Mothers surviving child sexual abuse.* New York: Routledge.

Hopkins, J., Marcus, M., & Campbell, S. B. (1984). Postpartum depression: A critical review. *Psychological Bulletin, 95,* 498–515.

Horgan, D. (1983). The pregnant woman's place and where to find it. *Sex Roles, 9,* 333–339.

Horner, M. S. (1972). Toward an understanding of achievement-related conflicts in women. *Journal of Social Issues, 28,* 157–176.

Horney, K. (1926). The flight from womanhood. *International Journal of Psychoanalysis, 7,* 324–339.

Horney, K. (1966). *New ways in psychoanalysis.* New York: Norton.

Hort, B., Leinbach, M., & Fagot, B. (1991). Is there a coherence among the cognitive components of gender acquisition? *Sex Roles, 24,* 195–207.

Horwitz, A. V. (1982). Sex-role expectations, power, and psychological distress. *Sex Roles, 8,* 607–623.

Hossain, Z., & Roopmarine, J. L. (1993). Division of household labor and child care in dual-earner African-American families with infants. *Sex Roles, 29,* 571–584.

Houseknecht, S. K. (1979). Timing of the decision to remain voluntarily childless: Evidence for continuous socialization. *Psychology of Women Quarterly, 4,* 81–86.

Houser, B., & Garvey, C. (1985). Factors that affect nontraditional vocational enrollment among women. *Psychology of Women Quarterly, 9,* 105–118.

Howe, K. G. (1989). Telling our mothers' story: Changing daughters' perceptions of their mothers in a women's studies course. In R. K. Unger (Ed.), *Representations: Social constructions of gender* (pp. 45–60). Amityville, NY: Baywood.

Howe, L. K. (1977). *Pink collar workers.* New York: Putnam.

Howell, M., & Pugliesi, K. (1988). Husbands who harm: Predicting spousal violence by men. *Journal of Family Violence, 3(1),* 15–27.

Hrdy, S. B. (1988, April). Daughters or sons. *Natural History,* 64–82.

Hughey, M. J., McElin, T. W., & Young, T. (1978). Maternal and fetal outcome of Lamaze-prepared patients. *Obstetrics and Gynecology, 51,* 643–647.

Hunt, M. (1974). *Sexual behavior in the 1970s.* Chicago: Playboy Press.

Hunter, G. T. (1974). Pediatrician. In R. B. Kundsin (Ed.), *Women and success: The anatomy of achievement* (pp. 58–61). New York: Morrow.

Hunter, M. S. (1990). Psychological and somatic experience of the menopause: A prospective study. *Psychosomatic Medicine, 52,* 357–367.

Hurlbert, D. F., & Whittaker, K. E. (1991). The role of masturbation in marital and sexual satisfaction: A comparative study of female masturbators and nonmasturbators. *Journal of Sex Education and Therapy, 17,* 272–282.

Hurtig, A. L., & Rosenthal, I. M. (1987). Psychological findings in early treated cases of female pseudohermaphroditism caused by virilizing congenital adrenal hyperplasia. *Archives of Sexual Behavior, 16,* 209–223.

Huston, A. C. (1983). Sex-typing. In P. H. Mussen (Ed.), *Handbook of child psychology* (Vol. 4; 4th ed., pp. 387–467). New York: Wiley.

Hyde, J. S. (1981). How large are cognitive gender differences? *American Psychologist, 36,* 892–910.

Hyde, J. S. (1984). How large are gender differences in aggression? A developmental meta-analysis. *Developmental Psychology, 20,* 722–736.

Hyde, J. S. (1990). *Understanding human sexuality* (4th ed.). New York: McGraw-Hill.

Hyde, J. S. Fennema, E., & Lamon, S. J. (1990). Gender differences in mathematics performance: A meta-analysis. *Psychological Bulletin, 107,* 139–155.

Hyde, J., Fennema, E., Ryan, M., Frost, L., & Hopp, C. (1990). Gender comparisons of mathematics attitudes and affects: A meta-analysis. *Psychology of Women Quarterly, 14,* 299–324.

Hyde, J. S., & Linn, M. C. (Eds.) (1986). *The psychology of gender: Advances through meta-analysis.* Baltimore: Johns Hopkins.

Hyde, J. S., & Linn, M. C. (1988). Gender differences in verbal ability: A meta-analysis. *Psychological Bulletin, 104,* 53–69.

Hyde, J. S., Rosenberg, B. G., & Behrman, J. (1977). "Tomboyism." *Psychology of Women Quarterly, 2,* 73–75.

Idle, T., Wood, E., & Desmarais, S. (1993). Gender role socialization in toy play situations: Mothers and fathers with their sons and daughters. *Sex Roles, 28,* 679–691.

Ihinger-Tallman, M., & Pasley, K. (1987). *Remarriage.* Beverly Hills, CA: Sage.

Imperato-McGinley, J., & Peterson, R. E. (1976). Male pseudohermaphrodism: The complexities of male phenotypic development. *American Journal of Medicine, 61,* 251–272.

Imperato-McGinley, J., Peterson, R. E., Gautier, T., & Sturla, E. (1979). Androgens and the evolution of male-gender identity among male pseudohermaphrodites with 5 alpha-reductase deficiency. *New England Journal of Medicine, 300,* 1233–1237.

Isaacs, M. B. (1981). Sex role stereotyping and the evaluation of the performance of women: Changing trends. *Psychology of Women Quarterly, 6,* 187–195.

Izraeli, D. N. (1983). Sex effects or structural effects? An empirical test of Kanter's theory of proportions. *Social Forces, 62,* 153–165.

Izraeli, D. N. (1993). "They have eyes and see not"–gender politics in the Diaspora Museum. *Psychology of Women Quarterly, 17,* 515–523.

Jacklin, C. N. (1981). Methodological issues in the study of sex-related differences. *Developmental Review, 1,* 266–273.

Jackson, L. A., Sullivan, L. A., & Rostker, R. (1988). Gender, gender role, and body image. *Sex Roles, 19,* 429–443.

Jackson, M. (1987). "Facts of life" or the eroticization of women's oppression? Sexology and the social construction of heterosexuality. In P. Caplan (Ed.), *The cultural construction of sexuality* (pp. 52–71). London: Tavistock.

Jackson, T. L. (1991). A university athletic department's rape and assault experiences. *Journal of College Student Development, 32,* 77–78.

Jackson-Wilson, A. G., & Borgers, S. B. (1993). Disaffiliation revisited: A comparison of homeless and nonhomeless women's perception of family of origin and social supports. *Sex Roles, 28,* 361–377.

Jacobs, J. A. (1992). Women's entry into management: Trends in earnings, authority, and values among salaried managers. Special issue: Process and outcome: Perspectives on the distribution of rewards in organizations. *Administrative Science Quarterly, 37,* 282–301.

Jacobs, J. A., & Powell, B. (1985). Occupational prestige: A sex-neutral concept? *Sex Roles, 12,* 1061–1071.

Jacobson, M. B., Antonelli, J., Winning, P. U., & Opeil, D. (1977). Women as authority figures: The use and nonuse of authority. *Sex Roles, 3,* 365–375.

Jaffe, P. G., Suderman, M., Reitzel, D., & Killip, S. M. (1992). An evaluation of a secondary school primary prevention program on violence in intimate relationships. *Violence and Victims, 7,* 129–146.

Janda, L. H., O'Grady, K. E., & Capps, C. F. (1978). Fear of success in males and females in sex-linked occupations. *Sex Roles, 4,* 43–50.

Jenkins, R. (1985). *Sex differences in psychiatric morbidity.* Cambridge, England: Cambridge University Press Psychological Medicine Monograph, suppl. 7.

Jensen, S. (1991, January/February). Pornography does make women sex objects. *Utne Reader,* p. 13.

John, B. A., & Sussman, L. E. (1984–1985). Initiative-taking as a determinant of role-reciprocal organization. *Imagination, Cognition, and Personality, 4,* 277–291.

Johnson, C. L., & Johnson, F. A. (1977). Attitudes toward parenting in dual-career families. *American Journal of Psychiatry, 134,* 391–395.

Johnson, E. S. (1984). Sex differences in problem solving. *Psychological Bulletin, 76,* 1359–1371.

Johnson, P. (1974, May). Social power and sex role stereotypes. Paper presented at the meeting of the Western Psychological Association, San Francisco.

Johnson, P. (1976). Women and power: Toward a theory of effectiveness. *Journal of Social Issues, 32,* 99–110.

Johnston, L., & Hewstone, M. (1992). Cognitive models of stereotype change: Subtyping and the perceived typicality of disconfirming group members. *Journal of Experimental Social Psychology, 28,* 260–286.

Jordan, J. V., Kaplan, A. G., Miller, J. B., Stiver, I. P., & Surrey, J. L. (1991). *Women's growth in connection.* New York: Guilford.

Jorgensen, S. R., & Alexander, S. J. (1983). Research on adolescent pregnancy-risk: Implications for sex education programs. *Theory into Practice, 22,* 125–133.

Josefowitz, N. (1983). Impressions from an office. *Is this where I was going?* New York: Warner Books.

Joseph, G., & Lewis, J. (1981). *Common differences: Conflicts in black and white feminist perspectives.* Boston: South End Press.

Joseph, G. I. (1991). Black mothers and daughters: Traditional and new perspectives. In P. Bell-Scott, B. Guy-Sheftall, J. J. Royster, J. Sims-Wood, M. DiCosta-Willis, & L. P. Fultz (Eds.), *Double stitch: Black women write about mothers and daughters* (pp. 94–106). New York: HarperCollins.

Jost, J. T., & Banaji, M. R. (1994). The role of stereotyping in system-justification and the production of false consciousness. *British Journal of Social Psychology, 33,* 1–27.

Jung, C. G. (1953). Anima and animus. In *Two essays on analytical psychology: Collected works of C. G. Jung,* Vol. 7 (pp 186–209). New York: Bollinger Foundation.

Jung, C. G. (1971). *The portable Jung* (J. Campbell, Ed.). New York: Viking.

Jutras, S., & Veilleux, F. (1991). Gender roles and care giving to the elderly: An empirical study. *Sex Roles, 25,* 1–18.

Kagan, J. (1958). The concept of identification. *Psychological Review, 65,* 296–305.

Kahn, A. S., & Jean, P. J. (1983). Integration and elimination or separation and redefinition: The future of the psychology of women. *Signs, 8,* 659–670.

Kahn, A. S., & Yoder, J. D. (1989). The psychology of women and conservatism: Rediscovering social change. *Psychology of Women Quarterly, 13,* 417–432.

Kahn, J., Smith, K., & Roberts, E. (1984). *Familial communication and adolescent sexual behavior.* Final Report to the Office of Adolescent Pregnancy Programs. Cambridge, MA: American Institutes for Research. Cited in J. Brooks-Gunn & F. F. Furstenberg, Jr. (1989).

Kaiser, K. (1990). Cross-cultural perspectives on menopause. In M. Flint, F. Kronenberg, & W. Utian (Eds.), *Multidisciplinary perspectives on menopause. Annals of the New York Academy of Science, 592,* 430–432.

Kanekar, S., & Seksaria, V. (1993). Acquaintance versus stranger rape: Testing the ambiguity reduction hypothesis. *European Journal of Social Psychology, 23,* 485–494.

Kanter, R. M. (1977). *Men and women of the corporation.* New York: Basic Books.

Kaplan, A. G., & Bean, J. P. (1976). *Beyond sex-role stereotypes: Readings toward a psychology of androgyny.* Boston: Little, Brown.

Kaplan, A. G., & Sedney, M. A. (1980). *Psychology and sex roles: An androgynous perspective.* Boston: Little, Brown.

Kaplan, A. G., & Surrey, J. L. (1984). The relational self in women: Developmental theory and public policy. In L. E. Walker (Ed.), *Women and mental health policy* (pp. 79–94). Beverly Hills, CA: Sage.

Kaplan, A. G., & Yasinski, L. (1980). Psychodynamic perspectives. In A. M. Brodsky & R. Hare-Mustin (Eds.), *Women and psychotherapy: An assessment of research and practice* (pp. 191–215). New York: Guilford Press.

Kaplan, B. J. (1986). A psychobiological review of depression during pregnancy. *Psychology of Women Quarterly, 10,* 35–38.

Kaplan, M. (1983). A woman's view of DSM-III. *American Psychologist, 39,* 786–792.

Kaplan, M. M. (1992). *Mothers' images of motherhood.* New York: Routledge.

Karabenick, S. A., & Knapp, J. R. (1988). Effects of computer privacy on help-seeking. *Journal of Applied Social Psychology, 18,* 461–472.

Karbon, M., Fabes, R. A., Carlo, G., & Martin, C. L. (1992). Preschoolers' beliefs about sex and age differences in emotionality. *Sex Roles, 27,* 377–390.

Katz, B. L. (1991). The psychological impact of stranger versus nonstranger rape on victims' recovery. In A. Parrot & L. Bechhofer, (Eds.), *Acquaintance rape: The hidden crime* (pp. 251–269). New York: Wiley.

Katz, D. (1987). Sex discrimination in hiring: The influence of organizational climate and need for approval on decision making behavior. *Psychology of Women Quarterly, 11,* 11–20.

Katz, P. A. (1986). Modification of children's gender-stereotypical behavior: General issues and research considerations. *Sex Roles, 14,* 591–602.

Katz, P. A., & Boswell, S. (1986). Flexibility and traditionality in children's gender roles. *Genetic, Social, & General Psychology Monographs, 112,* 103–147.

Kaufert, P. L. (1990). Methodological issues in menopause research. In M. Flint, F. Kronenberg, & W. Utian (Eds.), *Multidisciplinary perspectives on menopause. Annals of the New York Academy of Sciences, 592,* 114–122.

Kaufert, P. L., & Gilbert, P. (1986). Women, menopause, and medicalization. *Culture, Medicine & Psychiatry, 10,* 7–21.

Kaufman, G. (Ed.) (1991). *In stitches.* Bloomington: Indiana University Press.

Keating, C. F. (1985). Gender and the physiognomy of dominance and attractiveness. *Social Psychology Quarterly, 48,* 61–70.

Kellerman, J. (1974). Sex role stereotypes and attitudes toward parental blame for the psychological problems of children. *Journal of Consulting and Clinical Psychology, 42,* 153–154.

Kelley, H. H., Cunningham, J. D., Grisham, J. A., Lefebvre, L. M., Sink, C. R., & Yablon, G. (1978). Sex differences in comments made during conflict within close heterosexual pairs. *Sex Roles, 4,* 473–491.

Kelly, D., & Sanchez, S. (1994, May 17). Judge: Vassar used female stereotype to deny tenure. *USA Today,* A1.

Kennedy, C. W., & Camden, C. (1983). Interruptions and nonverbal gender differences. *Journal of Nonverbal Behavior, 8,* 91–108.

Kennell, J., Klaus, M., McGrath, S., Robertson, S., Hinkley, C. (1991). Continuous emotional support during labor in a US hospital. *Journal of the American Medical Association, 265,* 2197–2201.

Kessler, S. J. (1990). The medical construction of gender: Case management of intersexed infants. *Signs, 16,* 3–26.

Kessler, S. J., & McKenna, W. (1978). *Gender: An ethnomethodological approach.* New York: Wiley.

Kiesler, S., Sproull, L., & Eccles, J. S. (1985). Pool halls, chips, and war games: Women in the culture of computing. *Psychology of Women Quarterly, 9,* 451–462.

Kilpatrick, D., & Best, C. L. (1990, April). Sexual assault victims: Data from a random national probability sample. Paper presented at symposium conducted at the meeting of the Southeastern Psychological Association, Atlanta.

Kilpatrick, D. G., Best, C. L., Veronen, L. J., Amick, A. E., Villeponteaux, L. A., & Ruff, G. A. (1985). Mental health correlates of criminal victimization: A random community survey. *Journal of Consulting and Clinical Psychology, 53,* 866–873.

Kilpatrick, D. G., Edmunds, C. N., Seymour, A., & Boyle, J. (1992). *Rape in America: A report to the nation.* Charleston, SC: Crime Victims Research and Treatment Center.

Kim, E. H. (1986). With silk wings: Asian American women at work. In J. B. Cole (Ed.), *All American women: Lines that divide, ties that bind* (pp. 95–100). New York: Macmillan.

Kim, P. K., & Johnson, D. P. (1984). Sexism and ruralism: A reality for clinical social workers in community mental health centers. *Journal of Social Service Research, 8,* 61–70.

Kimball, M. (1988, November 5). Personal communication.

Kimmel, D. C. (1988). Ageism, psychology, and public policy. *American Psychologist, 43,* 175–178.

Kimmel, E. B. (1989). The experience of feminism. *Psychology of Women Quarterly, 13,* 133–146.

Kincaid-Ehlers, E. (1982). Bad maps for an unknown region: Menopause from a literary perspective. In A. M. Voda, M. Dinnerstein, & S. R. O'Donnell (Eds.), *Changing perspectives on menopause* (pp. 24–38). Austin: University of Texas Press.

King, S. (1974). *Carrie.* New York: Doubleday.

Kinsey, A. C., Pomeroy, W. B., & Martin, C. E. (1948). *Sexual behavior in the human male.* Philadelphia: Saunders.

Kinsey, A. C., Pomeroy, W. B., Martin, C. E., & Gebhard, P. H. (1953). *Sexual behavior in the human female.* Philadelphia: Saunders.

Kinzer, S. (1993, May 29). German court restricts abortion, angering feminists and the East. *New York Times,* A1.

Kirchmeyer, C. (1993). Nonwork-to-work spillover: A more balanced view of the experiences and coping of professional women and men. *Sex Roles, 28,* 531–552.

Kirkpatrick, C. (1936). The construction of a belief pattern scale for measuring attitudes toward feminism. *Journal of Social Psychology, 7,* 421–437.

Kirkpatrick, M., Smith, C., & Roy, R. (1981). Lesbian mothers and their children: A comparative survey. *American Journal of Orthopsychiatry, 51,* 545–551.

Kishor, S. (1993). "May God give sons to all": Gender and child mortality in India. *American Sociological Review, 58,* 247–265.

Kite, M. E., & Deaux, K. (1987). Gender belief systems: Homosexuality and the implicit inversion theory. *Psychology of Women Quarterly, 11,* 83–96.

Kite, M. E., Deaux, K., & Miele, M. (1991). Stereotypes of young and old: Does age outweigh gender? *Psychology and Aging, 6,* 19–27.

Kitzinger, C. (1987). *The social construction of lesbianism.* London: Sage.

Kitzinger, S. (1983). *Women's experience of sex.* London: Dorling Kindersley.

Kocel, K. M. (1977). Cognitive abilities: Handedness, familial sinistrality, and sex. *Annals of the New York Academy of Sciences, 299,* 233–243.

Koch, L. (1990). The fairy tale as a model for women's experience of in vitro fertilization. In H. B. Holmes (Ed.), *Issues in reproductive technology I* (pp. 303–320). New York: Garland.

Koff, E. (1983). Through the looking glass of menarche: What the adolescent girl sees. In S. Golub (Ed.), *Menarche* (pp. 77–86). Lexington, MA: Lexington Books.

Koff, E., Rierdan, J., & Jacobson, S. (1981). The personal and interpersonal significance of menarche. *Journal of the American Academy of Child Psychiatry, 20,* 148–158.

Koff, E., Rierdan, J., & Silverstone, E. (1978). Changes in representation of body image as a function of menarcheal status. *Developmental Psychology, 14,* 635–642.

Kohlberg, L. (1966). A cognitive-developmental analysis of children's sex role concepts and attitudes. In E. E. Maccoby (Ed.), *The development of sex differences* (pp. 82–173). Stanford, CA: Stanford University Press.

Kohlberg, L. (1981). *The philosophy of moral development: Essays on moral development,* Vols. I & II. San Francisco: Harper & Row.

Kolata, G. (1983). Math genius may have hormonal basis. *Science, 222,* 1312.

Kolata, G. (1992, February 12). Track federation urges end to gene test for femaleness. *New York Times.*

Kollock, P., Blumstein, P., & Schwartz, P. (1985). Sex and power in interaction: Conversational privileges and duties. *American Sociological Review, 50,* 34–46.

Konner, M. (1983). *The tangled wing: Biological constraints on the human spirit.* New York: Harper Colophon Books.

Kortenhaus, C. M., & Demarest, J. (1993). Gender role stereotyping in children's literature: An update. *Sex Roles, 28,* 219–232.

Koslow, R. E. (1987). Sex-related differences and visual-spatial mental imagery as factors affecting symbolic motor skill acquisition. *Sex Roles, 17,* 521–528.

Koss, M. P. (1985). The hidden rape victim: Personality, attitudinal, and situational characteristics. *Psychology of Women Quarterly, 9,* 193–212.

Koss, M. P. (1988). Hidden rape: Sexual aggression and victimization in a national sample of students in higher education. In A. W. Burgess (Ed.), *Rape and sexual assault, Vol. II* (pp. 3–25). New York: Garland.

Koss, M. P. (1990). The women's mental health research agenda: Violence against women. *American Psychologist, 45*, 374–380.

Koss, M. P. (1992). The underdetection of rape: Methodological choices influence incidence estimates. *Journal of Social Issues, 48*, 61–75.

Koss, M. P., & Burkhart, B. R. (1989). A conceptual analysis of rape victimization. *Psychology of Women Quarterly, 13*, 27–40.

Koss, M. P., & Dinero, T. E. (1989). Discriminant analysis of risk factors for sexual victimization among a national sample of college women. *Journal of Consulting and Clinical Psychology, 52*, 1–9.

Koss, M. P., & Gaines, J. A. (1993). The prediction of sexual aggression by alcohol use, athletic participation, and fraternity affiliation. *Journal of Interpersonal Violence, 8*, 94–108.

Koss, M. P., Gidycz, C. A., & Wisniewski, N. (1987). The scope of rape: Incidence and prevalence of sexual aggression and victimization in a national sample of higher education students. *Journal of Consulting and Clinical Psychology, 55*, 162–170.

Koss, M. P., Goodman, L., Fitzgerald, L., Russo, N., Keita, G., & Browne, A. (1994). *No safe haven*. Washington, DC: American Psychological Association.

Kowalski, R. M. (1992). Nonverbal behaviors and perceptions of sexual intentions: Effects of sexual connotativeness, verbal response, and rape outcome. *Basic and Applied Social Psychology, 13*, 427–445.

Kozlowski, J. (1993). Women, film, and the midlife Sophie's choice: Sink or Sousatzka? In J. C. Callahan (Ed.), *Menopause: A midlife passage*, (pp. 3–22). Bloomington: University of Indiana Press.

Kramarae, C., & Treichler, P. A. (1985). *A feminist dictionary*. Boston: Pandora.

Kravetz, D. (1980). Consciousness-raising and self-help. In A. M. Brodsky & R. Hare-Mustin (Eds.), *Women and psychotherapy* (pp. 267–283). New York: Guilford.

Krieger, S. (1982). Lesbian identity and community: Recent social science literature. *Signs, 8*, 91–108.

Krishnan, V. (1987). Preference for sex of children: A multivariate analysis. *Journal of Biosocial Science, 18*, 367–376.

Kronenberg, F. (1990). Hot flashes: Epidemiology and physiology. In M. Flint, F. Kronenberg, & W. Utian (Eds.), *Multidisciplinary perspectives on menopause. Annals of New York Academy of Sciences, 592*, 52–86.

Kropp, J. J., & Halverson, C. F. (1983). Preschool children's preferences and recall for stereotyped versus nonstereotyped stories. *Sex Roles, 9*, 261–272.

Kuebli, J., & Fivush, R. (1992). Gender differences in parent-child conversations about past emotions. *Sex Roles, 27*, 683–698.

Kuhl, A. (1984). Personality traits of abused women: Masochism myth refuted. *Victimology: An International Journal, 2*, 450–463.

Kurdek, L. A. (1988). Perceived social support in gays and lesbians in cohabitating couples. *Journal of Personality and Social Psychology, 54*, 504–509.

Kurdek, L. A. (1993). The allocation of household labor in gay, lesbian, and heterosexual married couples. *Journal of Social Issues, 49*, 127–139.

Kutner, N. G., & Brogan, D. (1974). An investigation of sex-related slang vocabulary and sex-role orientation among male and female university students. *Journal of Marriage and the Family, 36*, 474–484.

Lackey, P. N. (1989). Adults' attitudes about assignments of household chores to male and female children. *Sex Roles, 20*, 271–281.

LaFrance, M. (1992). Gender and interruptions: Individual infraction or violation of the social order? *Psychology of Women Quarterly, 16*, 497–512.

La Freniere, P., Strayer, F. F., & Gauthier, R. (1984). The emergence of same-sex affiliative preferences among preschool peers: A developmental/ethological perspective. *Child Development, 55*, 1958–1965.

LaFromboise, T. D., Choney, S. B., James, A., & Running Wolf, P. (1995). American Indian women and psychology. In H. Landrine (Ed.), *Bringing cultural diversity to feminist psychology* (pp. 191–239). Washington, DC: American Psychological Association.

Lakoff, G. (1987). *Women, fire, and dangerous things*. Chicago: University of Chicago Press.

Lakoff, R. (1975). *Language and woman's place*. New York: Harper & Row.

Lakoff, R. (1990). *Talking power: The politics of language*. New York: Basic Books.

Lamb, M. E. (Ed.) (1976). *The role of the father in child development*. New York: Wiley.

Landa, A. (1990). No accident: The voices of voluntarily childless women–An essay on the social construction of fertility choices.

In J. P. Knowles & E. Cole (Eds.), *Motherhood: A feminist perspective* (pp. 139–158). New York: Haworth.

Landrine, H. (1985). Race x class stereotypes of women. *Sex Roles, 13,* 65–75.

Landrine, H. (1987). On the politics of madness: A preliminary analysis of the relationship between social roles and psychopathology. *Psychological Monographs, 113* (3), 341–406.

Landrine, H. (1988). Depression and stereotypes of women: Preliminary empirical analyses of the gender-role hypothesis. *Sex Roles, 19,* 527–541.

Landrine, H. (1989). The politics of personality disorder. *Psychology of Women Quarterly, 13,* 325–339.

Landrine, H. (Ed.) (1995). *Bringing cultural diversity to feminist psychology.* Washington, DC: American Psychological Association.

Landrine, H., Klonoff, E. A., & Brown-Collins, A. (1992). Cultural diversity and methodology in feminist psychology: Critique, proposal, empirical example. *Psychology of Women Quarterly, 16,* 145–163.

Lane, K. E., & Gwartney-Gibbs, P. A. (1985). Violence in the context of dating and sex. *Journal of Family Issues, 6,* 45–59.

Laner, M. R. (1979). Growing older female: Heterosexual and homosexual. *Journal of Homosexuality, 4,* 267–275.

Laner, M. R. (1983). Courtship abuse and aggression: Contextual aspects. *Sociological Spectrum, 3,* 69–83.

Laner, M. R. (1989). Competition and combativeness in courtship: Reports from women. *Journal of Family Violence,* 4, 181–195.

Laner, M. R., & Thompson, J. (1982). Abuse and aggression in courting couples. *Deviant Behavior, 3,* 229–244.

LaPlante, M. N., McCormick, N., & Brannigan, G. G. (1980). Living the sexual script: College students' views of influence in sexual encounters. *Journal of Sex Research, 16,* 338–355.

Laqueur, T. (1990). *Making sex: Body and gender from the Greeks to Freud.* Cambridge, MA: Harvard University Press.

Larkin, J., & Popaleni, K. (1994). Heterosexual courtship violence and sexual harassment: The private and public control of young women. *Feminism & Psychology, 4,* 213–227.

Larwood, L., Szwajkowski, E., & Rose, S. (1988). Sex and race discrimination resulting from manager-client relationships: Applying the rational bias theory of managerial discrimination. *Sex Roles, 18,* 9–30.

Lauerman, J. (1990, January-February). The time machine. *Harvard Magazine,* 43–46.

Laws, J. L., & Schwartz, P. (1977). *Sexual scripts.* Hinsdale, IL: Dryden.

Laws, S. (1983). The sexual politics of premenstrual tension. *Women's Studies International Forum, 6,* 19–31.

Leaper, C. (1991). Influences and involvement in children's discourse: Age, gender, and partner effects. *Child Development, 62,* 797–811.

Lee, G. R. (1988). Marital intimacy among older persons: The spouse as confidant. *Journal of Family Issues, 9,* 273–284.

Lees, S. (1993). *Sugar and spice: Sexuality and adolescent girls.* London: Penguin.

Leffler, A., Gillespie, D. L., & Conaty, J. C. (1982). The effects of status differentiation on nonverbal behavior. *Social Psychology Quarterly, 45,* 153–161.

LeGuin, U. K. (1974). *The dispossessed.* New York: Harper & Row.

Leidholdt, D. (1981, March 15). Where pornography meets fascism. *WIN Magazine,* 18–22.

Leidholdt, D., & Russell, D. E. H. (Eds.) (1989). *No safe place for women: Feminists on pornography.* Oxford: Pergamon Books.

Leinbach, M. D., & Fagot, B. I. (1991). Attractiveness in young children: Sex-differentiated reactions of adults. *Sex Roles, 25,* 269–284.

Lembright, M. F., & Riemer, J. W. (1982). Women truckers' problems and the impact of sponsorship. *Work and Occupations, 9,* 457–474.

Lemkau, J. P. (1979). Personality and background characteristics of women in male-dominated occupations: A review. *Psychology of Women Quarterly, 4,* 221–240.

Lemkau, J. P. (1983). Women in male-dominated professions: Distinguishing personality and background characteristics. *Psychology of Women Quarterly, 8,* 144–165.

Lemkau, J. P. (1988). Emotional sequelae of abortion: Implications for clinical practice. *Psychology of Women Quarterly, 12,* 461–472.

Lenney, E., Mitchell, L., & Browning, C. (1983). The effect of clear evaluation criteria on sex bias in judgments of performance. *Psychology of Women Quarterly, 7,* 313–328.

Lennon, M. C. (1987). Is menopause depressing? An investigation of three perspectives. *Sex Roles, 17,* 1–16.

Lerman, H. (1986). From Freud to feminist personality theory: Getting there from here. *Psychology of Women Quarterly, 10,* 1–18.

Lerman, H., & Porter, N. (1990). The contribution of feminism to ethics in psychotherapy. In H. Lerman & N. Porter (Eds.), *Fem-*

inist ethics in psychotherapy (pp. 5–13). New York: Springer.

Lerman, H., & Rigby, D. N. (1990). Boundary violations: Misuse of the power of the therapist. In H. Lerman & N. Porter (Eds.), *Feminist ethics in psychotherapy* (pp. 51–59). New York: Springer.

Lerner, R. M., Lerner, J. V., & Tubman, J. T. (1989). Organismic and contextual bases of development in adolescence: A developmental contextual view. In G. R. Adams, R. Montemayor, & T. P. Gullotta (Eds.), *The biology of adolescent behavior and development* (pp. 11–37). Newbury Park, CA: Sage.

LeVay, S. (1991). A difference in hypothalamic structure between heterosexual and homosexual men. *Science, 253,* 1034–1037.

Levenson, R. W., Carstensen, L. L., & Gottman, J. M. (1993). Long-term marriage: Age, gender, and satisfaction. *Psychology and Aging, 8,* 301–313.

Levine, M. P., & Leonard, R. (1984). Discrimination against lesbians in the work force. *Signs, 4,* 700–710.

Levinger, G. (1964). Task and social behavior in marriage. *Sociometry, 27,* 433–448.

Levinson, R. M. (1975). Sex discrimination and employment practices: An experiment with unconventional job inquiries. *Social Problems, 22,* 533–542.

Levy, E. (1990). Stage, sex, and suffering: Images of women in American films. *Empirical-Studies-of-the-Arts, 8,* 53–76.

Lewin, M., & Tragos, L. M. (1987). Has the feminist movement influenced sex role attitudes? A reassessment after a quarter century. *Sex Roles, 16,* 125–135.

Lewis, C. (1987). Early sex-role socialization. In D. J. Hargreaves & A. M. Colley (Eds.), *The psychology of sex roles* (pp. 95–117). New York: Hemisphere.

Lewis, M. (1972). Parents and children: Sex role development. *The School Review, 80,* 229–240.

Lewis, S. (1979). *Sunday's women: Lesbian life today.* Boston: Beacon.

Lewittes, H. J. (1988). Just being friendly means a lot: Women, friendship, and aging. *Women & Health, 14,* 139–159.

L'Hommedieu, T. (1984). *The divorce experiences of working and middle class women.* Ann Arbor: UMI Research Press.

Liang, J. (1982). Sex differences in life satisfaction among the elderly. *Journal of Gerontology, 37,* 100–108.

Lie, G., & Gentlewarrior, S. (1991). Intimate violence in lesbian relationships: Discussion of survey findings and practice implications. *Journal of Social Service Research, 15,* 41–59.

Lieblich, A. (1985). Sex differences in intelligence test performance of Jewish and Arab school children in Israel. In M. P. Safir, M. S. Mednick, D. Izraeli, & J. Bernard (Eds.), *Women's worlds: From the new scholarship.* New York: Praeger.

Lieblich, A., & Friedman, G. (1985). Attitudes toward male and female homosexuality and sex-role stereotypes in Israeli and American students. *Sex Roles, 12,* 561–570.

Lifschitz, S. (1983). Male and female careers: Sex-role and occupational stereotypes among high school students. *Sex Roles, 9,* 725–735.

Lindemalm, G., Korlin, D., & Uddenberg, N. (1986). Long-term follow-up of "sex change" in 13 male-to-female transsexuals. *Archives of Sexual Behavior, 15,* 187–210.

Linimon, D., Barron, W. L., & Falbo, T. (1984). Gender differences in perception of leadership. *Sex Roles, 11,* 1075–1089.

Linn, M. C. (1986). Meta-analysis of studies of gender differences: Implications and future directions. In J. S. Hyde & M. C. Linn (Eds.), *The psychology of gender: Advances through meta-analysis* (pp. 210–231). Baltimore: Johns Hopkins.

Linn, M. C., & Petersen, A. C. (1985). Emergence and characterization of sex difference in spatial ability: A meta-analysis. *Child Development, 56,* 1479–1498.

Linn, M. C., & Petersen, A. C. (1986). A meta-analysis of gender differences in spatial ability: Implications for mathematics and science achievement. In J. S. Hyde & M. C. Linn (Eds.), *The psychology of gender: Advances through meta-analysis* (pp. 67–101). Baltimore: Johns Hopkins.

Linsky, A., & Straus, M. (1986). *Social Stress in the United States.* Dover, MA: Auburn House.

Lipman-Blumen, J., & Leavitt, H. J. (1976). Vicarious and direct achievement patterns in adulthood. *The Counseling Psychologist, 6,* 26–31.

Lippard, L. (1986). Elizabeth Layton. In J. Alexander, D. Berrow, L. Domitrovich, M. Donnelly, & C. McLean (Eds.), *Woman and aging* (pp. 148–151). Corvallis, OR: Calyx.

Lippman, W. (1922). *Public opinion.* New York: Harcourt.

Liss, M. B. (Ed.) (1983). *Social and cognitive skills: Sex roles and children's play.* New York: Academic Press.

Locher, P. Unger, R. K., Sociedade, P., & Wahl, J. (1993). At first glance: Accessibility of the physical attractiveness stereotype. *Sex Roles, 28,* 729–743.

Lock, M. (1986). Ambiguities of aging: Japanese experience and perceptions of menopause. *Culture, Medicine, and Psychiatry, 10,* 23–46.

Lock, M., & Kaufert, P. (1988). Cultural construction of the menopausal syndrome: The Japanese case. *Maturitas, 10,* 317–332.

Lockheed, M. E. (1985). Sex and social influence: A meta-analysis guided by theory. In J. Berger & M. Zeldich (Eds.), *Status, relations, and rewards.* San Francisco: Jossey-Bass.

Lockheed, M. E. (1986). Reshaping the social order: The case of gender segregation. *Sex Roles, 14,* 617–628.

Locksley, A., & Colten, M. E. (1979). Psychological androgyny: A case of mistaken identity? *Journal of Personality and Social Psychology, 37,* 1017–1031.

Lofland, J. (1969). *Deviance and identity.* Englewood Cliffs, NJ: Prentice-Hall.

Logothetis, M. L. (1991). Women's decisions about estrogen replacement therapy. *Western Journal of Nursing Research, 13,* 458–474.

Logothetis, M. L. (1993). Disease or development: Women's perceptions of menopause and the need for hormone replacement therapy. In J. C. Callahan (Ed.), *Menopause: A midlife passage* (pp. 123–135). Bloomington: University of Indiana Press.

Loiacano, D. K. (1993). Gay identity issues among Black Americans: Racism, homophobia, and the need for validation. In L. D. Garnets & D. C. Kimmel (Eds.), *Psychological perspectives on lesbian and gay male experiences* (pp. 364–375). New York: Columbia University Press.

Long, J., & Porter, K. L. (1984). Multiple roles of midlife women. In G. Baruch & J. Brooks-Gunn (Eds.), *Women in midlife* (pp. 109–159). New York: Plenum Press.

Long-Scott, E., & Southworth, J. (1992) Norplant: Birth control or control of poor women? *Extra,* Special issue, 17–18.

Longino, H. (1980). What is pornography? In L. Lederer (Ed.), *Take back the night: Women on pornography.* New York: William Morrow.

Lont, C. M. (1990). The roles assigned to females and males in non-music radio programming. *Sex Roles, 22,* 661–668.

Looft, W. R. (1971). Sex differences in the expression of vocational aspirations by elementary school children. *Developmental Psychology, 5,* 366–372.

Lopez, N. (1987). *Hispanic teenage pregnancy: Overview and implications.* Washington, DC: National Council of La Raza. Reported in Cusick (1987).

LoPiccolo, J., & Stock, W. E. (1986). Treatment of sexual dysfunction. *Journal of Consulting and Clinical Psychology, 54,* 158–167.

Lorber, J. (1986). Dismantling Noah's Ark. *Sex Roles, 14,* 567–580.

Lorber, J. (1993a). Believing is seeing: Biology as ideology. *Gender & Society, 7,* 568–581.

Lorber, J. (1993b). *Paradoxes of gender.* New Haven: Yale University Press.

Lord, C. G., & Saenz, D. S. (1985). Memory deficits and memory surfeits: Differential cognitive consequences of tokenism for tokens and observers. *Journal of Personality and Social Psychology, 49,* 918–926.

Lorenzi-Cioldi, F. (1993). They all look alike, but so do we . . . sometimes: Perceptions of in-group and out-group homogeneity as a function of sex and context. *British Journal of Social Psychology, 32,* 111–124.

Lott, B. (1978). Behavioral concordance with sex role ideology related to play areas, creativity, and parental sex-typing of children. *Journal of Personality and Social Psychology, 36,* 1087–1100.

Lott, B. (1981). A feminist critique of androgyny: Toward the elimination of gender attributions for learned behavior. In C. Mayo & N. M. Henley (Eds.), *Gender and nonverbal behavior* (pp. 171–180). New York: Springer-Verlag.

Lott, B. (1985). The devaluation of women's competence. *Journal of Social Issues, 41,* 43–60.

Lott, B. (1986). *Women's lives: Themes and variations in gender learning.* Monterey, CA: Brooks-Cole.

Lott, B. (1987). Sexist discrimination as distancing behavior: I. A laboratory demonstration. *Psychology of Women Quarterly, 11,* 47–58.

Lovelace, L. (1980). *Ordeal.* New York: Berkeley Books.

Lovelace, L. (1986). *Out of Bondage.* Secaucus, NJ: Lyle Stuart.

Low, M. D. (1983). The perimenopausal woman in literature. In H. J. Buchsbaum (Ed.), *The menopause* (pp. 205–213). New York: Springer-Verlag.

Lowe, R., & Wittig, M. A. (Eds.) (1989). Achieving pay equity through comparable worth. Special issue of the *Journal of Social Issues, 45.*

Luebke, B. F. (1989). Out of focus: Images of women and men in newspaper photographs. *Sex Roles, 20,* 121–133.

Lundberg-Love, P., & Geffner, R. (1989). Date

rape: Prevalence, risk factors, and a proposed model. In M. A. Pirog-Good & J. E. Stets (Eds.), *Violence in dating relationships* (pp. 169–184). New York: Praeger.

Lykes, M. B. (1985, June). Gender and individualistic vs. collectivist bases for notions about the self. *Journal of Personality, 53,* 356–383.

Lykes, M. B., Brabeck, M. M., Ferns, T., & Radan, A. (1993). Human rights and mental health among Latin American women in situations of state-sponsored violence: Bibliographic resources. *Psychology of Women Quarterly, 17,* 525–544.

Lytton, H., & Romney, D. M. (1991). Parents' differential socialization of boys and girls: A meta-analysis. *Psychological Bulletin, 109,* 267–296.

Maccoby, E. E. (1980). *Social development: Psychological growth and the parent-child relationship.* New York: Harcourt Brace Jovanovich.

Maccoby, E. E. (1988). Gender as a social category. *Developmental Psychology, 24,* 755–765.

Maccoby, E. E., & Jacklin, C. (1974). *The psychology of sex differences.* Stanford, CA: Stanford University Press.

Maccoby, E. E., & Jacklin, C. N. (1987). Gender segregation in childhood. In E. H. Reese (Ed.), *Advances in child development.* New York: Academic Press.

Macdonald, B., & Rich, C. (1983). *Look me in the eye: Old women, aging and ageism.* San Francisco: Spinsters Ink.

MacFarlane, A. (1977). *The psychology of childbirth.* Cambridge, MA: Harvard University Press.

MacKinnon, C. (1979). *Sexual harassment of working women.* New Haven: Yale University Press.

MacLusky, N. J., & Naftolin, F. (1981). Sexual differentiation of the central nervous system. *Science, 211,* 1294–1303.

MacPherson, K. I. (1985). Osteoporosis and menopause: A feminist analysis of the social construction of a syndrome. *Advances in Nursing Science, 7,* 11–22.

MacPherson, K. I. (1993). The false promises of hormone replacement therapy and current dilemmas. In J. C. Callahan (Ed.), *Menopause: A midlife passage* (pp. 145–159). Bloomington: University of Indiana Press.

Maddi, S. R. (1989). *Personality theories: A comparative analysis* (5th ed.). Chicago: Dorsey.

Maddux, H. C. (1975). *Menstruation.* New Canaan, CT: Tobey.

Magnusson, D., Strattin, H., & Allen, V. L. (1985). Biological maturation and social development: A longitudinal study of some adjustment processes from mid-adolescence to adulthood. *Journal of Youth and Adolescence, 14,* 267–283.

Major, B. (1994). From social inequality to personal entitlement: The role of social comparisons, legitimacy appraisals, and group membership. In M. P. Zanna (Ed.), *Advances in experimental social psychology,* Vol. 26 (pp. 293–355). New York: Academic Press.

Major, B., Cozzarelli, C., Testa, M., & Mueller, P. (1992). Male partners' appraisals of undesired pregnancy and abortion: Implications for women's adjustment to abortion. *Journal of Applied Social Psychology, 22,* 599–614.

Major, B., & Deaux, K. (1982). Individual differences in justice behavior. In J. Greenberg & R. L. Cohen (Eds.), *Equity and justice in social behavior.* New York: Academic Press.

Major, B., McFarlin, D. B., & Gagnon, D. (1984). Overworked and underpaid: On the nature of gender differences in personal entitlement. *Journal of Personality and Social Psychology, 47,* 1399–1412.

Makepeace, J. (1981). Courtship violence among college students. *Family Relations, 30,* 97–102.

Makepeace, J. M. (1984). The severity of courtship violence injuries and individual precautionary measures. Paper presented at the Second National Family Violence Research Conference, University of New Hampshire, Durham, NH.

Makepeace, J. M. (1986). Gender differences in courtship violence victimization. *Family Relations, 35,* 383–388.

Makepeace, J. M. (1987). Social factor and victim-offender differences in courtship violence. *Family Relations, 36,* 87–91.

Makepeace, J. (1989). Dating, living together, and courtship violence. In M. A. Pirog-Good & J. E. Stets (Eds.), *Violence in dating relationships* (pp. 94–107). New York: Praeger.

Makosky, V. P. (1989). Comments on the mommy track. *Division 35 Newsletter, 16,* 7–8.

Malamuth, N. (1981). Rape proclivity among males. *Journal of Social Issues, 37,* 138–157.

Malamuth, N. (1985). Testimony to the Attorney General's Commission on Pornography hearings, Houston. Unpublished transcript.

Malamuth, N. M., & Brown, L. M. (1994). Sexually aggressive men's perceptions of women's communications: Testing three explanations. *Journal of Personality and Social Psychology, 67*, 699–712.

Malamuth, N. M., Sockloskie, R., Koss, M. P., & Tanaka, J. (1991). The characteristics of aggressors against women: Testing a model using a national sample of college students. *Journal of Consulting and Clinical Psychology, 59*, 670–681.

Malamuth, N. M., & Thornhill, N. W. (1994). Hostile masculinity, sexual aggression, and gender-biased domineeringness in conversations. *Aggressive Behavior, 20*, 185–194.

Malo, C. (1994). Ex-partner, family, friends, and other relationships: Their role within the social network of long-term single mothers. *Journal of Applied Social Psychology, 24*, 60–81.

Maltz, D. N., & Borker, R. A. (1983). A cultural approach to male-female miscommunication. In J. A. Gumperz (Ed.), *Language and social identity* (pp. 196–216). New York: Cambridge University Press.

Mansfield, P. K., Koch, P. B., Henderson, J., Vicary, J. R., Kohn, M., & Young, E. W. (1991). The job climate for women in traditionally male blue-collar occupations. *Sex Roles, 25*, 63–79.

Mantecon, V. H. (1993). Where are the archetypes? Searching for symbols of women's midlife passage. In N. D. Davis, E. Cole, & E. D. Rothblum (Eds.), *Faces of women and aging* (pp. 77–88). Binghamton, NY: Harrington Park Press.

Marecek, J. (1983, March). Identity and individualism in feminist psychology. Paper presented at the Penn Women's Studies Conference, Philadelphia.

Marecek, J. (1986, March). Sexual development and girls' self-esteem. Paper presented at the Seminar on girls: Promoting self-esteem, sponsored by the Girls' Coalition of Southeastern Pennsylvania, Swarthmore, PA.

Marecek, J. (1989). Introduction to special issue: Theory and method in feminist psychology. *Psychology of Women Quarterly, 13*, 367–378.

Marecek, J. (1990, August). Discussion. In R. T. Hare-Mustin & J. Marecek (co-chairs), The construction of gender in psychology. Symposium conducted at the American Psychology Association, Boston.

Marecek, J. (1993). Silences, gaps, and anxious rhetoric: Gender in abnormal psychology textbooks. *Journal of Theoretical and Philosophical Psychology, 13*, 602–611.

Marecek, J., & Johnson, M. (1980). Gender and the process of therapy. In A. M. Brodsky & R. Hare-Mustin (Eds.), *Women and psychotherapy* (pp. 67–93). New York: Guilford Press.

Margolin, L. (1989). Gender and the prerogatives of dating and marriage: An experimental assessment of a sample of college students. *Sex Roles, 20*, 91–102.

Markides, K. S. (Ed.) (1989). *Aging and health: Perspectives on gender, race, ethnicity, and class.* Newbury Park, CA: Sage.

Markson, E. W., & Taylor, C. A. (1993). Real versus reel world: Older women and the Academy Awards. In N. D. Davis, E. Cole, & E. D. Rothblum (Eds.), *Faces of women and aging* (pp. 157–172). Binghamton, NY: Harrington Park Press.

Markus, H., Crane, M., Bernstein, S., & Siladi, M. (1982). Self-schemas and gender. *Journal of Personality and Social Psychology, 42*, 38–50.

Martin, C. L. (1989). Children's use of gender-related information in making social judgments. *Developmental Psychology, 25*, 80–88.

Martin, C. L. (1990). Attitudes and expectations about children with nontraditional and traditional gender roles. *Sex Roles, 22*, 151–165.

Martin, C. L., & Little, J. K. (1990). The relation of gender understanding to children's sex-typed preferences and gender stereotypes. *Child Development, 61*, 1427–1439.

Martin, E. (1987). *The woman in the body: A cultural analysis of reproduction.* Boston: Beacon Press.

Martin, S. E. (1988). Think like a man, work like a dog, and act like a lady: Occupational dilemmas of policewomen. In A. Statham, E. M. Miller, & H. O. Mauksch (Eds.), *The worth of women's work: A qualitative synthesis* (pp. 205–224). Albany, NY: State University of New York Press.

Mason, D. O., & Lu, Y. (1988). Attitudes toward women's familial roles: Changes in the United States, 1977–1985. *Gender & Society, 2*, 39–57.

Masters, W. H., & Johnson, V. (1966). *Human sexual response.* Boston: Little, Brown.

Masters, W. H., & Johnson, V. (1979). *Homosexuality in perspective.* Boston: Little, Brown.

Mathews, W. S. (1977). Sex-role perception, portrayal, and preference in the fantasy play of young children. *Resources in Education*, August, Document No. ED 136949.

Matlin, M. W., & Matkoski, K. M. (1985). Gen-

der-stereotyping of cognitive abilities. Paper presented at the annual meeting of the Eastern Psychological Association, Boston.

Matthews, W. J. (1984). Violence in college students. *College Student Journal, 18*, 150–158.

Mauldin, T., & Meeks, C. B. (1990). Sex differences in children's time use. *Sex Roles, 22*, 537–554.

Mayall, A., & Russell, D. E. H. (1993). Racism in pornography. In D. E. H. Russell (Ed.), *Making violence sexy: Feminist views on pornography* (pp. 167–178). New York: Teachers College Press.

Maypole, D. E. (1986). Sexual harassment of social workers at work: Injustice within? *Social Work, 31*, 29–34.

Maypole, D. E., & Skaine, R. (1983). Sexual harassment in the workplace. *Social Work, 28*, 385–390.

Mays, V. M., & Cochran, S. D. (1988). Issues in the perception of AIDS risk and risk reduction activities by black and Hispanic/Latina women. *American Psychologist, 43*, 949–957.

Mazzella, C., Durkin, K., Cerini, E., & Buralli, P. (1992). Sex role stereotyping in Australian television advertisements. *Sex Roles, 26*, 243–259.

McAdoo, H. P. (1980). Black mothers and the extended family support network. In L. Rodgers-Rose (Ed.), *The black woman* (pp. 125–144). Beverly Hills, CA: Sage.

McCaulay, M., Mintz, L., & Glenn, A. A. (1988). Body image, self-esteem, and depression-proneness: Closing the gender gap. *Sex Roles, 18*, 381–391.

McClelland, D. C. (1964). Wanted: A new self-image for women. In R. J. Lifton (Ed.), *The woman in America.* Boston: Beacon Press.

McClelland, D. C., Atkinson, J. W., Clark, R. A., & Lowell, E. L. (1953). *The achievement motive.* Englewood Cliffs, NJ: Prentice-Hall.

McCloskey, L. A., & Coleman, L. M. (1992). Difference without dominance: Children's talk in mixed- and same-sex dyads. *Sex Roles, 27*, 241–257.

McCombs, H. G. (1986). The application of an individual/collective model to the psychology of black women. In D. Howard (Ed.), *The dynamics of feminist therapy* (pp. 67–80). New York: Haworth Press.

McConaghy, M. J. (1979). Gender permanence and the genital basis of gender: Stages in the development of gender identity. *Child Development, 50*, 1223–1226.

McCormick, N. B. (1979). Come-ons and put-offs: Unmarried students' strategies for having and avoiding sexual intercourse. *Psychology of Women Quarterly, 4*, 194–211.

McCormick, N. B., & Jesser, C. J. (1983). The courtship game: Power in the sexual encounter. In E. R. Allgeier & N. B. McCormick (Eds.), *Changing boundaries: Gender roles and sexual behavior* (pp. 64–86). Palo Alto, CA: Mayfield.

McCormick, N. B., & Jones, M. A. (1989). Gender differences in nonverbal flirtation. *Journal of Sex Education and Therapy, 15*, 271–282.

McEwen, B. S. (1981). Neural gonadal steroid actions. *Science, 211*, 1303–1311.

McFarlane, J., Parker, B., Soeken, K., & Bullock, L. (1992). Assessing for abuse during pregnancy: Severity and frequency of injuries associated with entry into prenatal care. *JAMA, 267 (23)*, 3176–3178.

McFarlane, J. M., & Williams, T. M. (1994). Placing premenstrual syndrome in perspective. *Psychology of Women Quarterly, 18*, 339–373.

McGee, M. G. (1979). Human spatial abilities: Psychometric studies and environmental, genetic, hormonal, and neurological influences. *Psychological Bulletin, 86*, 889–918.

McGloshen, T. H., & O'Bryant, S. L. (1988). The psychological well-being of older, recent widows. *Psychology of Women Quarterly, 12*, 99–116.

McGoldrick, M., Garcia-Preto, N., Hines, P. M., & Lee, E. (1989). Ethnicity and women. In M. McGoldrick, C. M. Anderson, & F. Walsh (Eds.), *Women in families: A framework of feminist theory* (pp. 169–199). New York: Norton.

McGrath, E., Keita, G. P., Strickland, B. R., & Russo, N. F. (1990). *Women and depression: Risk factors and treatment issues.* Washington, DC: American Psychological Association.

McGrath, J. E., (1986). Continuity and change: Time, method, and the study of social issues. *Journal of Social Issues, 42*, 5–19.

McGuire, J. (1988). Gender stereotypes of parents with two-year-olds and beliefs about gender differences in behavior. *Sex Roles, 19*, 233–240.

McGuire, W. J., McGuire, C. V., & Winton, W. (1979). Effects of household sex composition on the salience of one's gender in the spontaneous self-concept. *Journal of Experimental Social Psychology, 15*, 77–90.

McGuire, W. J. & Padawer-Singer, A. (1976). Trait salience in the spontaneous self-concept. *Journal of Personality and Social Psychology, 33*, 743–754.

McHugh, M. D., Koeske, R. D., & Frieze, I. H. (1986). Issues to consider in conducting nonsexist psychological research: A guide for researchers. *American Psychologist, 41,* 879–890.

McKay, J., Pyke, S. W., & Goranson, R. (1984). Whatever happened to inner space? A failure to replicate. *International Journal of Women's Studies, 7,* 387–396.

McKenna, W., & Kessler, S. J. (1977). Experimental design as a source of sex bias in social psychology. *Sex Roles, 3,* 117–128.

McLaurin, P. (1989). From Beulah to Clair Huxtable, you've come a long way girl, or have you: The black woman and television. Paper presented at the meeting of the International Communications Association.

McPherson, K. S., & Spretino, S. K. (1983). Androgyny and sex-typing: Differences in beliefs regarding gender polarity in ratings of ideal men and women. *Sex Roles, 9,* 441–451.

Mednick, M. T. S. (1989). On the politics of psychological constructs: Stop the bandwagon, I want to get off. *American Psychologist, 44,* 1118–1123.

Meece, J. L., Parsons, J. E., Kaczala, C. M., Goff, S. B., & Futterman, R. (1982). Sex differences in math achievement: Toward a model of academic choice. *Psychological Bulletin, 91,* 324–348.

Mellin, L. M., Scully, S., & Irwin, C. E. (1986, October 28). Disordered eating characteristics in preadolescent girls. Paper presented at the American Dietetic Annual Meeting, Las Vegas. Cited in Hesse-Biber (1989).

Mercer, R. T. (1986). *First-time motherhood.* New York: Springer.

Mercer, R. T. (1990). *Parents at risk.* New York: Springer.

Messenger, J. C. (1969). *Inis Beag, isle of Ireland.* New York: Holt, Rinehart, & Winston.

Messick, D. M., & Mackie, D. M. (1989). Intergroup relations. *Annual Review of Psychology, 40,* 45–82.

Messner, M. A. (1994). Ah, ya throw like a girl! In M. A. Messner & D. F. Sabo (Eds.), *Sex, violence, and power in sports: Rethinking masculinity* (pp. 28–32). Freedom, CA: The Crossing Press.

Messner, M. A., Duncan, M. C., & Jensen, K. (1993). Separating the men from the girls: The gendered language of televised sports. *Gender & Society, 7,* 121–137.

Miller, C. L. (1987). Qualitative differences among gender-stereotyped toys: Implications for cognitive and social development in girls and boys. *Sex Roles, 16,* 473–488.

Miller, C. T. (1986). Categorization and stereotypes about men and women. *Personality and Social Psychology Bulletin, 12,* 502–512.

Miller, J. B. (1984a). Culture and the development of everyday social explanation. *Journal of Personality and Social Psychology, 46,* 961–978.

Miller, J. B. (1984b). *The development of women's sense of self (Work in Progress Papers No. 84-01).* Wellesley, MA: Wellesley College, The Stone Center.

Miller, J. B. (1986). *Toward a new psychology of women* (2nd ed.). Boston: Beacon Press.

Miller, M., Moen, P., & Dempster-McClain, D. (1991). Motherhood, multiple roles, and maternal well-being: Women of the 1950s. *Gender & Society, 5,* 565–582.

Miller, T. W. (1974). Male attitudes toward women's rights as a function of their level of self esteem. *International Journal of Group Tensions, 4,* 35–44.

Mills, C. S., & Granoff, B. J. (1992). Date and acquaintance rape among a sample of college students. *Social Work, 37,* 504–509.

Mirowsky, J., & Ross, K. E. (1987). Belief in innate sex roles: Sex stratification versus interpersonal influence in marriage. *Journal of Marriage and the Family, 49,* 527–540.

Mischel, W. (1966). A social learning view of sex differences in behavior. In E. Maccoby (Ed.), *The development of sex differences.* Stanford, CA: Stanford University Press.

Mischel, W. (1968). *Personality and assessment.* New York: Wiley.

Mischel, W. (1970). Sex-typing and socialization. In P. H. Mussen (Ed.), *Carmichael's manual of child psychology* (pp. 3–72). New York: Wiley.

Mischel, W. (1984). Convergences and challenges in the search for consistency. *American Psychologist, 39,* 351–364.

Mischel, W., & Grusec, J. (1966). Determinants of the rehearsal and transmission of neutral and aversive behaviors. *Journals of Personality and Social Psychology, 3,* 197–205.

Mitchell, G., Obradovich, S., Herring, F., Tromborg, C., & Burns, A. L. (1992). Reproducing gender in public places: Adults' attention to toddlers in three public locales. *Sex Roles, 26,* 323–330.

Mitchell, V., & Helson, R. (1990). Women's prime in life: Is it the 50's? *Psychology of Women Quarterly, 14,* 451–470.

Mittwoch, U. (1973). *Genetics of sex differentiation.* New York: Academic Press.

Miura, I. (1987). The relationship of computer self-efficacy expectations to computer interest and course enrollment in college. *Sex Roles, 16,* 303–312.

Modleski, T. (1980). The disappearing act: A study of Harlequin romances. *Signs, 5,* 435–448.

Moffat, M. (1989). *Coming of age in New Jersey.* New Brunswick, NJ: Rutgers University Press.

Moller, L. C., Hymel, S., & Rubin, K. H. (1992). Sex typing in play and popularity in middle childhood. *Sex Roles, 26,* 331–353.

Molm, L. D. (1986). Gender, power, and legitimation: A test of three theories. *American Journal of Sociology, 91,* 1356–1386.

Molm, L. D., & Hedley, M. (1992). Gender, power, and social exchange. In C. L. Ridgeway (Ed.), *Gender, interaction, and inequality* (pp. 1–28). New York: Springer-Verlag.

Monahan, L., Kuhn, D., & Shaver, P. (1974). Intrapsychic versus cultural explanations of the fear of success motive. *Journal of Personality and Social Psychology, 29,* 60–64.

Money, J. (1955). Hermaphroditism, gender and precocity in hyperandrenocorticism: Psychological findings. *Bulletin of Johns Hopkins Hospital, 96,* 253–264.

Money, J. (1974). Prenatal hormones and postnatal socialization in gender identity differentiation. In J. K. Cole & R. Dienstbier (Eds.), *Nebraska Symposium on Motivation 1973,* Lincoln: University of Nebraska Press.

Money, J. (1987a). Propaedeutics of diecious G-I/R: Theoretical foundations for understanding dimorphic gender-identity role. In J. M. Reinisch, L. A. Rosenblum, & S. A. Sanders (Eds.), *Masculinity/femininity: Basic perspectives* (pp. 13–28). New York: Oxford University Press.

Money, J. (1987b). Sin, sickness, or status? Homosexual gender identity and psychoneuroendocrinology. *American Psychologist, 42,* 384–399.

Money, J., & Ehrhardt, A. (1972). *Man and woman, boy and girl.* Baltimore: Johns Hopkins University Press.

Money, J., & Mathews, D. (1982). Prenatal exposure to virilizing progestins: An adult follow-up study on 12 young women. *Archives of Sexual Behavior, 11,* 73–83.

Montemayor, R., & Hanson, E. A. (1985). A naturalistic view of conflict between adolescents and their parents and siblings. *Journal of Early Adolescence, 3,* 83–103.

Montgomery, R. J. V., & Kamo, Y. (1989). Parent care by sons and daughters. In J. A. Mancini (Ed.), *Aging parents and adult children* (pp. 213–230). Lexington, MA: Heath.

Mooney, L., & Brabant, S. (1987). Two martinis and a rested woman: "Liberation" in the Sunday comics. *Sex Roles, 17,* 409–420.

Moore, T. E., Griffiths, K., & Payne, B. (1987). Gender, attitudes toward women and the appreciation of sexist humor. *Sex Roles, 16,* 521–531.

Morawski, J. G. (1987). The troubled quest for masculinity, femininity, and androgyny. In P. Shaver and C. Hendrick (Eds.), *Sex and gender* (pp. 44–69). Beverly Hills, CA: Sage.

Morgan, L. A. (1989). Economic well-being following marital termination: A comparison of widowed and divorced women. *Journal of Family Issues, 10,* 86–101.

Morgan, L. A. (1991). *After marriage ends: Economic consequences for midlife women.* London: Sage.

Mori, D. L., Chaikin, S., & Pliner, P. (1987). "Eating lightly" and the self-presentation of femininity. *Journal of Personality and Social Psychology, 53,* 240–254.

Morokoff, P. J. (1983). Toward the elimination of rape: A conceptualization of sexual aggression against women. In A. P. Goldstein, *Prevention and Control of Aggression* (pp. 101–144). New York: Pergamon Press.

Morokoff, P. (1990, August). Women's sexuality: Expression of self vs. social construction. In C. Travis (chair), The social construction of women's sexuality. Symposium presented at the meeting of the American Psychological Association, Boston.

Morris, J. (1974). *Conundrum.* New York: Harcourt Brace Jovanovich.

Moulton, J. M., Robinson, G. M., & Elias, C. (1978). Sex bias in language use: Neutral pronouns that aren't. *American Psychologist, 33,* 1032–1036.

Moynihan, D. P. (1965). *The Negro family: The case for national action.* Washington, DC: U.S. Department of Labor.

Muehlenhard, C. L., & Hollabough, L. C. (1988). Do women sometimes say no when they mean yes? The prevalence and correlates of women's token resistance to sex. *Journal of Personality and Social Psychology, 54,* 872–879.

Muehlenhard, C. L., & Linton, M. A. (1987). Date rape and sexual aggression in dating situations: Incidence and risk factors. *Journal of Counseling Psychology, 34,* 186–196.

Muehlenhard, C. L., & McCoy, M. L. (1991).

Double standard/double bind: The sexual double standard and women's communication about sex. *Psychology of Women Quarterly, 15,* 447–461.

Muehlenhard, C. L., & Scardino, T. J. (1985). What will he think? Men's impressions of women who initiate dates and achieve academically. *Journal of Counseling Psychology, 32,* 560–569.

Mullen, P. E. (1993). Child sexual abuse and adult mental health: The development of disorder. *Journal of Interpersonal Violence, 8,* 429.

Mundy-Castle, A., Wilson, D., Sibanda, P., & Sibanda, J. (1989). Cognitive effects of LOGO among black and white Zimbabwean girls and boys. *International Journal of Psychology, 24,* 539–546.

Munroe, R. H., Shimmin, H. S., & Munroe, R. L. (1984). Gender understanding and sex role preference in four cultures. *Developmental Psychology, 20,* 673–682.

Munter, C. (1984). Fat and the fantasy of perfection. In C. S. Vance (Ed.), *Pleasure and danger: Exploring female sexuality* (pp. 225–231). Boston: Routledge & Kegan Paul.

Murstein, B. I. (1986). *Paths to marriage.* Beverly Hills, CA: Sage.

Mussen, P. H. (1969). Early sex-role development. In D. A. Goslin (Ed.), *Handbook of socialization theory and research.* Chicago: Rand McNally.

Mussen, P. H., & Rutherford, E. (1963). Parent-child relations and parental personality in relation to young children's sex-role preferences. *Child Development, 34,* 589–607.

Myers, D. G. (1986). *Psychology.* New York: Worth.

Nacoste, R. W., & Lehman, D. (1987). Procedural stigma. *Representative Research in Social Psychology, 17,* 25–38.

Nadler, A., & Fisher, J. D. (1986). The role of threat to self-esteem and perceived control in recipient reaction to help: Theory development and empirical validation. In L. Berkowitz (Ed.), *Advances in Experimental Social Psychology,* Vol. 19. New York: Academic Press.

Nails, D. (1983). Social-scientific sexism: Gilligan's mismeasure of man. *Social Research, 50,* 643–664.

Naples, N. A. (1992). Activist mothering: Cross-generational continuity in the community work of women from low-income urban neighborhoods. Special issue: Race, class, and gender. *Gender & Society, 6,* 441–463.

Nash, S. C. (1975). The relationship among sex-role stereotyping, sex-role preference and the sex difference in spatial visualization. *Sex Roles, 1,* 15–32.

National Committee on Pay Equity (1994). *Newsnotes, 15,* 1–13.

Needleman, R., & Nelson, A. (1988). Policy implications: The worth of women's work. In A. Statham, E. M. Miller, & H. O. Mauksch (Eds.), *The worth of women's work: A qualitative synthesis* (pp. 293–307). Albany, NY: State University of New York Press.

Nelson, H. L. (1992). Scrutinizing surrogacy. In H. B. Holmes (Ed.), *Issues in reproductive technology* (pp. 297–302). New York: Garland.

Nettles, S. M., & Scott-Jones, D. (1987). The role of sexuality and sex equity in the education of minority adolescents. *Peabody Journal of Education, 64,* 183–197.

Neuberg, S. L., Smith, D. M., Hoffman, J. C., & Russell, F. J. (1994). When we observe stigmatized and "normal" individuals interacting: Stigma by association. *Personality and Social Psychology Bulletin, 20,* 196–209.

Neugarten, B., Wood, V., Kraines, R., & Loomis, B. (1963). Women's attitudes towards the menopause. *Vita Humana, 6,* 140–151.

Nevid, J. S. (1984). Sex differences in factors of romantic attraction. *Sex Roles, 11,* 401–411.

Newcombe, N., Bandura, M., & Taylor, D. G. (1984). Sex differences in spatial ability and spatial activities. *Sex Roles, 9,* 377–386.

Newson, J., & Newson, E. (1987). Family and sex roles in middle childhood. In D. J. Hargreaves & A. M. Colley (Eds.), *The psychology of sex roles* (pp. 142–158). New York: Hemisphere.

Newton, N. (1970). The effect of psychological environment on childbirth: Combined cross-cultural and experimental approach. *Journal of Cross-Cultural Psychology, 1,* 85–90.

Nichter, M., & Vuckovic, N. (1994). Fat talk: Body image among adolescent girls. In N. Sault (Ed.), *Many mirrors: Body image and social relations* (pp. 109–131). New Brunswick, NJ: Rutgers University Press.

Nicolson, P. (1986). Developing a feminist approach to depression following childbirth. In S. Wilkinson (Ed.), *Feminist social psychology* (pp. 135–150). Milton Keynes: Open University Press.

Nicolson, P. (1990). A brief report of women's expectations of men's behavior in the transition to parenthood: Contradictions and conflicts for counselling psychology practice. Special Issue: Sexual and marital counselling: Perspectives on theory, research and practice. *Counselling Psychology Quarterly, 3,* 353–361.

Nicolson, P. (1993). Motherhood and women's lives. In D. Richardson & V. Robinson (Eds.), *Thinking feminist: Key concepts in women's studies* (pp. 201–224). New York: Guilford.

Nieva, V. F. (1982). Equity for women at work: Models for change. In B. A. Gutek (Ed.), *Sex role stereotyping and affirmative action policy* (pp. 185–227). Los Angeles: Institute of Industrial Relations, University of California.

Nieva, V. F., & Gutek, B. A. (1981). *Women and work: A psychological perspective.* New York: Praeger.

Nigro, G. N., Hill, D. E., Gelbein, M. E., & Clark, C. L. (1988). Changes in the facial prominence of women and men over the last decade. *Psychology of Women Quarterly, 12,* 225–235.

Noble, B. P. (1993, April 18). Worthy child-care pay scales. *New York Times, 25.*

Noble, B. P. (1994, February 6). Old age is no place for sissies. *New York Times,* F29.

Norton, A. J., & Moorman, J. E. (1987). Current trends in marriage and divorce among American women. *Journal of Marriage and the Family, 49,* 3–14.

NOW (1983). *The myth of equality.* (Available from NOW Legal Defense Fund, 132 W. 43rd St., New York, NY 10036.)

Nyquist, L., Slivken, K., Spence, J. T., & Helmreich, R. L. (1985). Household responsibilities in middle-class couples: The contribution of demographic and personality variables. *Sex Roles, 12,* 15–34.

Oakley, A. (1974). *The sociology of housework.* New York: Pantheon.

Oakley, A. (1986). *Telling the truth about Jerusalem.* London: Blackwell.

Oakley, A. (1992). Social support in pregnancy: Methodology and findings of a 1-year follow-up study. *Journal of Reproductive and Infant Psychology, 10,* 219–231.

O'Brien, M., & Huston, A. C. (1985a). Development of sex-typed play in toddlers. *Developmental Psychology, 21,* 866–871.

O'Brien, M., & Huston, A. C. (1985b). Activity level and sex stereotyped toy choice in toddler boys and girls. *Journal of Genetic Psychology, 146,* 527–534.

O'Bryant, S. L. (1988). Sex-differentiated assistance in older widows' support systems. *Sex Roles, 19,* 91–106.

O'Connell, A. N., & Russo, N. F. (Eds.) (1980). Eminent women in psychology: Models of achievement, Special issue. *Psychology of Women Quarterly, 5.*

O'Connell, J. C. (1983). Children of working mothers: What the research tells us. *Young Children, 38,* 62–70.

O'Farrell, B., & Harlan, S. L. (1982). Craftworkers and clerks: The effect of male coworker hostility on women's satisfaction with nontraditional jobs. *Social Problems, 29,* 252–265.

Office of Civil Rights (1980). *Fall enrollment and compliance report of institutions of higher education.* Washington, DC: U.S. Department of Education.

Ogletree, R. J. (1993). Sexual coercion experience and help-seeking behavior of college women. *Journal of American College Health, 41,* 149–153.

O'Heron, C., & Orlofsky, J. (1990). Stereotypic and nonstereotypic sex role trait and behavior orientations, gender identity, and psychological adjustment. *Journal of Personality and Social Psychology, 58,* 134–143.

O'Keefe, E. S. C., & Hyde, J. S. (1983). The development of occupational sex-role stereotypes: The effects of gender stability and age. *Sex Roles, 9,* 481–492.

O'Keeffe, N. K., Brockopp, K., & Chew, E. (1986). Teen dating violence. *Social Work, 31,* 465–468.

O'Laughlin, M. A. (1983). Responsibility and moral maturity in the control of fertility–or, a woman's place is in the wrong. *Social Research, 50,* 556–575.

Olday, D., & Wesley, B. (1983). Premarital courtship violence: A summary report. Moorehead State University, Moorehead, KY. Unpublished.

O'Leary, V. E., & Hammack, B. (1975). Sex role orientations and achievement context as determinants of the motive to avoid success. *Sex Roles, 1,* 225–234.

Oliver, M. B., & Hyde, J. S. (1993). Gender differences in sexuality: A meta-analysis. *Psychological Bulletin, 114,* 29–51.

Oliver, S. J., & Toner, B. B. (1990). The influence of gender role typing on the expression of depressive symptoms. *Sex Roles, 22,* 775–790.

Olsen, N. J., & Willemson, E. W. (1978). Fear of success–fact or artifact? *Journal of Psychology, 98,* 65–70.

O'Neil, J., Egan, J., Owen, S., & Murry, V. (1993). The Gender Role Journey Measure: Scale development and psychometric evaluation. *Sex Roles, 28,* 167–185.

Orlinsky, D. E., & Howard, K. I. (1980). Gender and psychotherapeutic outcome. In A. M. Brodsky & R. Hare-Mustin (Eds.), *Women and psychotherapy* (pp. 3–34). New York: Guilford Press.

Ostrove, J. M., & Stewart, A. J. (1994). Meanings and uses of marginal identities: Social class at Radcliffe in the 1960s. In C. E. Franz & A. J. Stewart (Eds.), *Women creating lives: Identities, resilience, and resistance* (pp. 289–307). Boulder, CO: Westview.

O'Sullivan, C. S. (1991). Acquaintance gang rape on campus. In A. Parrot & L. Bechhofer (Eds.), *Acquaintance rape: The hidden crime* (pp. 140–156). New York: Wiley.

Padavic, I. (1991). Attractions of male blue-collar jobs for Black and White women: Economic need, exposure, and attitudes. *Social Science Quarterly, 72,* 33–49.

Padesky, C. A., & Hammen, C. L. (1981). Sex differences in depressive symptom expression and help-seeking among college students. *Sex Roles, 7,* 309–320.

Padgett, D. (1988). Aging minority women: Issues in research and health policy. *Women & Health, 14,* 213–225.

Paige, K. E. (1971). Effects of oral contraceptives on affective fluctuations associated with the menstrual cycle. *Psychosomatic Medicine, 33,* 515–537.

Paige, K. E., & Paige, J. M. (1981). *The politics of reproductive ritual.* Berkeley: University of California Press.

Paludi, M. A., (1979). Horner revisited: How successful must Ann and John be before fear of success sets in? *Psychological Reports, 44,* 1319–1322.

Paludi, M. A. (1984). Psychometric properties and underlying assumptions of four objective measures of fear of success. *Sex Roles, 10,* 765–781.

Paludi, M. A., & Bauer, W. D. (1983). Goldberg revisited: What's in an author's name? *Sex Roles, 9,* 387–390.

Paludi, M. A., & Fankell-Hauser, J. (1986). An idiographic approach to the study of women's achievement striving. *Psychology of Women Quarterly, 10,* 89–100.

Paludi, M. A., & Strayer, L. A. (1985). What's in an author's name? Differential evaluations of performance as a function of author's name. *Sex Roles, 10,* 353–361.

Papanek, H. (1973). Men, women, and work: Reflections on the two-person career. *American Journal of Sociology, 78,* 852–870.

Parke, R. D. (1976). Family interaction in the newborn period: Some findings, some observations, and some unresolved issues. In K. Riegel & J. Meacham (Eds.), *The developing individual in a changing world,* Vol. 2. The Hague: Mouton.

Parker, S., Nichter, M., Nichter, M., Vuckovic, N., Sims, C., & Ritenbaugh, C. (1995). Body image and weight concerns among African American and White adolescent females: Differences which make a difference. *Human Organization, 54,* 103–114.

Parlee, M. B. (1975). Review essay: Psychology. *Signs, 1,* 119–138.

Parlee, M. B. (1979). Psychology and women. *Signs, 5,* 121–133.

Parlee, M. B. (1981). Appropriate control groups in feminist research. *Psychology of Women Quarterly, 5,* 637–644.

Parlee, M. B. (1985). Psychology of women in the 80s: Promising problems. *International Journal of Women's Studies, 8,* 193–204.

Parlee, M. B. (1989, March). The science and politics of PMS research. Paper presented at the meeting of the Association for Women in Psychology, Newport, RI.

Parlee, M. B. (1990). Integrating biological and social scientific research on menopause. In M. Flint, F. Kronenberg, & W. Utian (Eds.), *Multidisciplinary perspectives on menopause. Annals of the New York Academy of Sciences, 592,* 379–389.

Parrot, A. (1991a). Institutional response: How can acquaintance rape be prevented? In A. Parrot & L. Bechhofer (Eds.), *Acquaintance rape: The hidden crime* (pp. 335–367). New York: Wiley.

Parrot, A. (1991b). Recommendations for college policies and procedures to deal with acquaintance rape. In A. Parrot & L. Bechhofer (Eds.), *Acquaintance rape: The hidden crime* (pp. 368–380). New York: Wiley.

Parsons, T., & Bales, R. F. (1955). *Family, socialization, and interaction process.* Glencoe, IL: Free Press.

Patterson, E. T., & Hale, E. S. (1985). Making sure: Integrating menstrual care practices into activities of daily living. *Advances in Nursing Science, 7,* 18–31.

Payne, B., & Whittington, F. (1976). Older women: An examination of popular stereotypes and research evidence. *Social Problems, 23,* 488–504.

Pearlman, S. F. (1993). Late mid-life astonishment: Disruptions to identity and self-esteem. In N. D. Davis, E. Cole, & E. D. Rothblum (Eds.), *Faces of women and aging* (pp. 1–12). Binghamton, NY: Harrington Park Press.

Pedersen, P., & Thomas, C. D. (1992). Prevalence and correlates of dating violence in a Canadian university sample. *Canadian Journal of Behavioural Science, 24,* 490–501.

Peirce, K. (1990). A feminist theoretical perspective on the socialization of teenage girls through Seventeen Magazine. *Sex Roles, 23,* 491–500.

Peirce, K. (1993). Socialization of teenage girls through teen-magazine fiction: The making of a new woman or an old lady? *Sex Roles, 29,* 59–68.

Pelligrini, A. D., & Perlmutter, J. C. (1989). Classroom contextual effects on children's play. *Developmental Psychology, 25,* 289–296.

Pence, E., & Shepard, M. (1988). Integrating feminist theory and practice: The challenge of the battered women's movement. In K. Yllo & M. Bograd (Eds.), *Feminist perspectives on wife abuse* (pp. 11–26). Berkeley, CA: Sage.

Peplau, L. A. (1976). Impact of fear of success and sex-role attitudes on women's competitive achievement. *Journal of Personality and Social Psychology, 34,* 561–568.

Peplau, L. A. (1983). Roles and gender. In H. H. Kelley et al. (Eds.), *Close relationships.* New York: W. H. Freeman.

Peplau, L. A., & Campbell, S. M. (1989). The balance of power in dating and marriage. In J. Freeman (Ed.), *Women: A feminist perspective* (4th ed.) (pp. 121–137). Mountain View, CA: Mayfield.

Peplau, L. A., & Cochran, S. D. (1980). Sex differences in values concerning love relationships. Paper presented at American Psychological Association, cited in Peplau, L. A., & Gordon, S. L. (1983). The intimate relationships of lesbians and gay men. In E. R. Allgeier & N. B. McCormick (Eds.), *Changing boundaries: Gender roles and sexual behavior* (pp. 226–244). Palo Alto, CA: Mayfield.

Peplau, L. A., & Cochran, S. D. (1990). A relationship perspective on homosexuality. In D. P. McWhirter, S. A. Sanders, & J. M. Reinisch (Eds.), *Homosexuality/heterosexuality: The Kinsey scales and current research* (pp. 226–244). New York: Oxford University Press.

Peplau, L. A., & Conrad, E. (1989). Beyond nonsexist research: The perils of feminist methods in psychology. *Psychology of Women Quarterly, 13,* 379–400.

Peplau, L. A., & Gordon, S. L. (1983). The intimate relationships of lesbians and gay men. In E. R. Allgeier & N. B. McCormick (Eds.), *Changing boundaries: Gender roles and sexual behavior* (pp. 226–244). Palo Alto, CA: Mayfield.

Peplau, L. A., & Gordon, S. L. (1985). Women and men in love: Gender differences in close heterosexual relationships. In V. E. O'Leary, R. K. Unger, & B. S. Wallston (Eds.), *Women, gender, and social psychology* (pp. 257–292). Hillsdale, NJ: Erlbaum.

Perlmutter, E., & Bart, P. B. (1982). Changing news of "The Change": A critical review and suggestions for an attributional approach. In A. M. Voda, M. Dinnerstein, & S. R. O'Donnell (Eds.), *Changing perspectives on menopause* (pp. 185–199). Austin: University of Texas Press.

Perry, D. G., & Bussey, K. (1979). The social learning theory of sex differences: Imitation is alive and well. *Journal of Personality and Social Psychology, 37,* 1699–1712.

Perry, D. G., Perry, L. C., & Weiss, R. J. (1989). Sex differences in the consequences that children anticipate for aggression. *Developmental Psychology, 25,* 312–319.

Perry, D. G., White, A. J., & Perry, L. C. (1984). Does early sex-typing result from children's attempts to match their behavior to sex role stereotypes? *Child Development, 55,* 2114–2121.

Perry, W. G. (1970). *Forms of intellectual and ethical development in the college years.* New York: Holt, Rinehart, & Winston.

Perun, P. J., & Bielby, D. D. (1981). Towards a model of female occupational behavior: A human development approach. *Psychology of Women Quarterly, 6,* 234–252.

Peters, D. K., & Cantrell, P. J. (1993). Gender roles and role conflict in feminist lesbian and heterosexual women. *Sex Roles, 28,* 379–392.

Petersen, A. C. (1980). Biopsychosocial processes in the development of sex-related differences. In J. E. Parsons (Ed.), *The psychobiology of sex differences and sex roles* (pp. 31–55). Washington, DC: Hemisphere.

Petersen, A. C. (1983). Menarche: Meaning of measures and measuring meaning. In S. Golub (Ed.), *Menarche: The transition from girl to woman* (pp. 63–76). Lexington, MA: Lexington Books.

Petersen, A. C. (1987). The nature of biological-psychosocial interactions: The sample case of early adolescence. In R. M. Lerner & T. T. Foch (Eds.), *Biological-psychosocial interactions in early adolescence* (pp. 35–61). Hillsdale, NJ: Erlbaum.

Peterson, E. (1974). Consumer specialist. In R. B. Kundsin (Ed.), *Women and success: The anatomy of achievement* (pp. 78–80). New York: William Morrow.

Peterson, R. E., Imperato-McGinley, J., Gautier, T., & Sturla, E. (1977). Male pseudohermaphrodism due to steroid 5 alpha-reductase deficiency. *American Journal of Medicine, 62,* 170–191.

Phares, E. J. (1984). *Introduction to personality* (2nd ed.). Glenview, IL: Scott, Foresman.

Phares, V., & Compas, B. E. (1993). Fathers and developmental psychotherapy. *Current Directions in Psychological Science, 2,* 162.

Phillips, R. D., & Gilroy, F. D. (1985). Sex-role stereotypes and clinical judgments of mental health: The Brovermans' findings reexamined. *Sex Roles, 12,* 179–193.

Philpps-Yonas, S. (1980). Teenage pregnancy and motherhood: A review of the literature. *American Journal of Orthopsychiatry, 50,* 403–431.

Phoenix, A., Woollett, A., & Lloyd, E. (Eds.) (1991). *Motherhood: Meanings, practices, and ideologies.* London: Sage.

Piercy, M. (1976). The homely war. In *Living in the open* (pp. 60–61). New York: Knopf.

Piercy, M. (1982). Rape poem. In *Circles on the water.* New York: Knopf.

Pietromonaco, P. R., Manis, J., & Frohart-Lane, K. (1986). Psychological consequences of multiple social roles. *Psychology of Women Quarterly, 10,* 373–382.

Piliavin, J. A., & Unger, R. K. (1985). The helpful but helpless female: Myth or reality? In V. E. O'Leary, R. K. Unger, & B. S. Wallston (Eds.), *Women, gender, and social psychology* (pp. 149–190). Hillsdale, NY: Erlbaum.

Pleck, J. H. (1975). Masculinity-femininity: Current and alternate paradigms. *Sex Roles, 1,* 161–178.

Pleck, J. H. (1977). The work-family role system. *Social Problems, 24,* 417–427.

Pleck, J. H. (1983). Husbands' paid work and family roles: Current research issues. In H. Z. Lopata & J. H. Pleck (Eds.), *Research in the interweave of social roles: Jobs and families,* Vol. 3 (pp. 251–333). Greenwich, CT: JAI.

Pleck, J. H. (1984). Men's family work: Three perspectives and some new data. In P. Voydanoff (Ed.), *Work and family: Changing roles of men and women* (pp. 89–103). Palo Alto, CA: Mayfield.

Pleck, J. H. (1987). Dual-career families: A comment. *Counseling Psychologist, 15,* 131–133.

Pleck, J. H., Sonenstein, F. L., & Ku, L. C. (1991). Adolescent males' condom use: Relationships between perceived cost-benefits and consistency. *Journal of Marriage and the Family, 53,* 733–746.

Pleck, J. H., Sonenstein, F. L., & Ku, L. C. (1994). Attitudes toward male roles among adolescent males: A discriminant validity analysis. *Sex Roles, 30,* 481–501.

Plumb, P., & Cowan, G. (1984). A developmental study of destereotyping and androgynous activity preferences of tomboys, nontomboys, and males. *Sex Roles, 10,* 703–712.

Polakow, V. (1993). *Lives on the edge: Single mothers and their children in the other America.* Chicago: University of Chicago Press.

Polansky, E. (1975–1976). Take him home, Mrs. Smith. *Healthright,* Vol. II, No. 2.

Pollack, S. (1990). Lesbian parents: Claiming our visibility. In J. P. Knowles & E. Cole (Eds.), *Motherhood: A feminist perspective* (pp. 181–194). New York: Haworth.

Pomerleau, A., Bloduc, D., Malcuit, G., & Cossette, L. (1990). Pink or blue: Environmental gender stereotypes in the first two years of life. *Sex Roles, 22,* 359–367.

Ponse, B. (1978). *Identities in the lesbian world.* Westport, CT: Greenwood Press.

Poole, D. A., & Tapley, A. E. (1988). Sex roles, social roles, and clinical judgments of mental health. *Sex Roles, 19,* 265–272.

Pooler, W. S. (1991). Sex of child preferences among college students. *Sex Roles, 25,* 569–576.

Pope, K. (1994). *Sexual involvement with therapists: Patient assessment, subsequent treatment, forensics.* Washington, DC: American Psychological Association.

Popenoe, D. (1987). Beyond the nuclear family: A statistical portrait of the changing family in Sweden. *Journal of Marriage and the Family, 49,* 173–183.

Porter, N., & Geis, F. (1981). Women and nonverbal leadership cues: When seeing is not believing. In C. Mayo & N. Henley (Eds.), *Gender and nonverbal behavior* (pp. 39–61). New York: Springer-Verlag.

Porter, N., Geis, F. L., Cooper, E., & Newman, E. (1985). Androgyny and leadership in mixed sex groups. *Journal of Personality and Social Psychology, 49,* 808–823.

Porter, N., Geis, F. L., & Jennings (Walstedt), J. (1983). Are women invisible as leaders? *Sex Roles, 9,* 1035–1049.

Poulton, K. (1986). "Though not occasioned." In J. Alexander, D. Berrow, L. Domitrovich, M. Donnelly, & C. McLean (Eds.), *Women and aging.* Corvallis, OR: Calyx.

Pour-El, M. B. (1974). Mathematician. In R. B. Kundsin (Ed.), *Women and success: The anatomy of achievement* (pp. 36–37). New York: William Morrow.

Powell, A. D., & Kahn, A. S. (1995). Racial differences in women's desire to be thin. *International Journal of Eating Disorders, 17,* 191–195.

Power, T. (1981). Sex typing in infancy: The role

of the father. *Infant Mental Health Journal, 2,* 226–240.

Powlishta, K. K., Serbin, L. A, & Moller, L. C. (1993). The stability of individual differences in gender typing: Implications for understanding gender segregation. *Sex Roles, 29,* 723–737.

Prather, J. E., & Fidell, L. S. (1975). Sex differences in the content and style of medical advertisements. *Social Science and Medicine, 9,* 23–26.

Press, M. (1988). Sex and sex roles: What are we really telling kids? *Equal Play, 7*(1), 9–10.

Price, S. J., & McKenry, P. C. (1988). *Divorce.* Beverly Hills, CA: Sage.

Price-Bonham, S., & Skeen, P. (1982). Black and white fathers' attitudes toward children's sex roles. *Psychological Reports, 50,* 1187–1190.

Public Interest Directorate of the American Psychological Association (1987). Follow-up report to oral presentation of December 2, 1987. Psychological sequelae of abortion.

Pugh, M. D., & Wahrman, R. (1983). Neutralizing sexism in mixed-sex groups: Do women have to be better than men? *American Journal of Sociology, 88,* 746–762.

Puig, A. (1984). Predomestic strife: A growing college counseling concern. *Journal of College Student Personnel, 25,* 268–269.

Purcell, P., & Stewart, L. (1990). Dick and Jane in 1989. *Sex Roles, 22,* 177–185.

Purdy, L. M. (1992). Another look at contract pregnancy. In H. B. Holmes (Ed.), *Issues in reproductive technology* (pp. 303–320). New York: Garland.

Purifoy, F. E., & Koopmans, L. H. (1980). Androstenedione, T and free T concentrations in women of various occupations. *Social Biology, 26,* 179–188.

Radloff, L. (1975). Sex differences in depression: The effects of occupation and marital status. *Sex Roles, 1,* 249–265.

Radlove, S. (1983). Sexual response and gender roles. In E. R. Allgeier & N. B. McCormick (Eds.), *Changing boundaries: Gender roles and sexual behavior* (pp. 87–105). Palo Alto, CA: Mayfield.

Radway, J. A. (1984). *Reading the romance: Women, patriarchy, and popular literature.* Chapel Hill, NC: University of North Carolina Press.

Raines, R. S., Hechtman, S. B., & Rosenthal, R. (1990). Nonverbal behavior and gender as determinants of physical attractiveness. *Journal of Nonverbal Behavior, 14,* 253–267.

Ramos-McKay, J., Comas-Diaz, L., & Rivera, L. (1988). Puerto Ricans. In L. Comas-Diaz & E. E. H. Griffith (Eds.), *Clinical guidelines in cross-cultural mental health* (pp. 204–232). New York: Wiley.

Rand, L. M., & Miller, A. L. (1972). A developmental cross-sectioning of women's career and marriage attitudes and life plans. *Journal of Vocational Behavior, 2,* 317–331.

Rapaport, K. R., & Posey, C. D. (1991). Sexually coercive college males. In A. Parrot & L. Bechhofer (Eds.), *Hidden rape: Sexual assault among acquaintances, friends, and intimates* (pp. 217–228). New York: Wiley.

Ray, D. C., McKinney, K. A., & Ford, C. V. (1987). Ageism in psychiatrists: Associations with gender, certification, and theoretical orientation. *The Gerontologist, 27,* 82–86.

Raymond, J. G. (1979). *The transsexual empire: The making of the she-male.* Boston: Beacon Press.

Raymond, J. G. (1993). *Women as wombs: Reproductive technologies and the battle over women's freedom.* New York: HarperCollins.

Rebecca, M., Hefner, R., & Oleshansky, B. (1976). A model of sex-role transcendence. *Journal of Social Issues, 32,* 197–206.

Reid, P. T. (1982). Socialization of black female children. In P. W. Berman & E. R. Ramey (Eds.), *Women: A developmental perspective.* Washington, DC: NIH Publication No. 82-2298.

Reid, P. T. (1993). Poor women in psychological research: Shut up and shut out. *Psychology of Women Quarterly, 17,* 133–150.

Reid, P. T., & Kelly, E. (1994). Research on women of color: From ignorance to awareness. *Psychology of Women Quarterly, 18,* 477–486.

Reid, P. T., Tate, C. C., & Berman, P. W. (1989). Preschool children's self-presentations in situations with infants: Effects of sex and race. *Child Development, 60,* 710–714.

Reid, P. T., & Trotter, K. H. (1993). Children's self-presentations with infants: Gender and ethnic comparisons. *Sex Roles, 29,* 171–181.

Reiff, P. (1966). *The triumph of the therapeutic: Uses of faith after Freud.* New York: Harper & Row.

Reilly, M. E., & Lynch, J. M. (1990). Power-sharing in lesbian partnerships. *Journal of Homosexuality, 19,* 1–30.

Reineke, M. J. (1989). *Out of order: A critical perspective on women in religion.* In J. Freedman (Ed.), Women: A feminist perspective (4th ed., pp. 395–414). Mountain View, CA: Mayfield.

Reitz, R. (1981). *Menopause: A positive approach.* London: Unwin.

Renzetti, C. (1992). *Violent betrayal: Partner abuse in lesbian relationships.* Newbury Park, CA: Sage.

Reuterman, N. A., & Burcky, W. D. (1989). Dating violence in high school: A profile of the victims. *Psychology: A Journal of Human Behavior, 26,* 1–9.

Rheingold, H. L., & Cook, K. V. (1975). The contents of boys' and girls' rooms as an index of parents' behavior. *Child Development, 46,* 459–463.

Rhoades, J. M. (1989). Social support and the transition to the maternal role. In P. N. Stern (Ed.), *Pregnancy and parenting* (pp. 131–142). New York: Hemisphere.

Rice, F. P. (1984). *The adolescent: Development, relations, and culture.* Boston: Allyn & Bacon.

Rice, J. (1994). Reconsidering research on divorce, family life cycle, and the meaning of family. *Psychology of Women Quarterly, 18,* 559–584.

Rich, A. (1975). Dialogue. In *Poems selected and new, 1950–1974* (p. 195). New York: Norton.

Rich, A. (1976). *Of woman born: Motherhood as experience and institution.* New York: Norton.

Rich, A. (1980). Compulsory heterosexuality and lesbian existence. *Signs, 5,* 631–660.

Rich, M. K., & Cash, T. F. (1993). The American image of beauty: Media representations of hair color for four decades. *Sex Roles, 29,* 113–124.

Richards, M., Bernal, J., & Brackbill, Y. (1975). Early behavioral differences: Gender or circumcision? *Developmental Psychobiology, 9,* 89–95.

Richardson, D., & Hammock, G. (1990). The role of alcohol in acquaintance rape. In A. Parrot & L. Bechhofer (Eds.), *Acquaintance rape: The hidden crime* (pp. 83–95). New York: Wiley.

Richardson, D. C., Bernstein, S., & Taylor, S. P. (1979). The effect of situational contingencies on female retaliative behavior. *Journal of Personality and Social Psychology, 37,* 2044–2048.

Rierdan, J. (1983). Variations in the experience of menarche as a function of preparedness. In S. Golub (Ed.), *Menarche* (pp. 119–125). Lexington, MA: Lexington Books.

Rigby, D. N., & Sophie, J. (1990). Ethical issues and client sexual preference. In H. Lerman & N. Porter (Eds.), *Feminist ethics in psychotherapy* (pp. 165–175). New York: Springer.

Rigby-Weinberg, D. N. (1986). A future direction for radical feminist therapy. In D. Howard (Ed.), *The dynamics of feminist therapy* (pp. 191–205). New York: The Haworth Press.

Riley, S., & Wrench, D. (1985). Mentoring among women lawyers. *Journal of Applied Social Psychology, 15,* 374–386.

Risman, B. J. (1987). Intimate relationships from a microstructural perspective: Men who mother. *Gender & Society, 1,* 6–32.

Rix, S. E. (Ed.) (1990). *The American woman 1990–91: A status report.* New York: Norton.

Robinson, C. C., & Morris, J. T. (1986). The gender-stereotyped nature of Christmas toys received by 36-, 48-, and 60-month-old children: A comparison between nonrequested and requested toys. *Sex Roles, 15,* 21–32.

Rodeheaver, D. (1990). Labor market progeria. *Generations, 14,* 53–58.

Rodin, J., & Langer, E. (1980). Aging labels: The decline of control and the fall of self-esteem. *Journal of Social Issues, 36,* 12–19.

Rodin, J., Silverstein, L. R., Striegel-Moore, R. H. (1984). Women and weight: A normative discontent. In T. B. Sonderegger (Ed.), *Psychology and gender: Nebraska Symposium on Motivation, 1984* (pp. 267–307). Lincoln: University of Nebraska Press.

Roesler, T. A., & McKenzie, N. (1994). Effects of childhood trauma on psychological functioning in adults sexually abused as children. *The Journal of Nervous and Mental Disease, 182,* 145–150.

Roff, L. L., & Klemmack, D. L. (1986). Norms for employed daughters' and sons' behavior toward frail older parents. *Sex Roles, 14,* 363–368.

Rollins, B., & Feldman, H. (1970). Marital satisfaction over the family life cycle. *Journal of Marriage and the Family, 36,* 271–282.

Romero, G. J., Castro, F. G., Cervantes, R. C. (1988). Latinas without work: Family, occupational and economic stress following unemployment. *Psychology of Women Quarterly, 12,* 281–298.

Roopnarine, J. L. (1984). Sex-typed socialization in mixed-age preschool classrooms. *Child Development, 55,* 1078–1084.

Roopnarine, J. L. (1986). Mothers' and fathers' behaviors toward the toy play of their infant sons and daughters. *Sex Roles, 14,* 59–68.

Root, M. P. P. (1990). Disordered eating in women of color. *Sex Roles, 22,* 525–536.

Root, M. P. P. (1995). The psychology of Asian women. In H. Landrine (Ed.), *Bringing cul-*

tural diversity to feminist psychology: Theory, research, practice (pp. 265–301). Washington, DC: American Psychological Association.

Roscoe, B., & Benaske, N. (1985). Courtship violence experienced by abused wives: Similarities in patterns of abuse. *Family Relations, 34*, 419–424.

Roscoe, B., & Kelsey, T. (1986). Dating violence among high school students. *Psychology, 23*, 53–59.

Rose, S., & Frieze, I. H. (1989). Young singles' scripts for a first date. *Gender & Society, 3*, 258–268.

Rosen, L. W., Shafer, C. L., Dummer, G. M., Cross, L. K., Deuman, G. W., & Malmberg, S. R. (1988). Prevalence of pathogenic weight-control behaviors among Native American women and girls. *International Journal of Eating Disorders, 7*, 807–811.

Rosenbaum, A., & O'Leary, D. (1981). Marital violence: Characteristics of abusive couples. *Journal of Consulting and Clinical Psychology, 49*, 63–71.

Rosenbaum, M. (1979). The changing body image of the adolescent girl. In M. Sugar (Ed.), *Female adolescent development*. New York: Bruner/Mazel.

Rosenberg, F. R., & Simmons, R. G. (1975). Sex differences in the self-concept during adolescence. *Sex Roles, 1*, 147–160.

Rosenberg, J., Perlstadt, H., & Phillips, W. R. (1993). Now that we are here: Discrimination, disparagement, and harassment at work and the experience of women lawyers. *Gender & Society, 7*, 415–433.

Rosenberg, R. (1982). *Beyond separate spheres: Intellectual roots of modern feminism*. New Haven: Yale University Press.

Rosenthal, N. B. (1984). Consciousness raising: From revolution to reevaluation. *Psychology of Women Quarterly, 8*, 309–326.

Rosenwasser, S. M., Gonzales, M. H., & Adams, V. (1985). Perceptions of a housespouse: The effects of sex, economic productivity, and subject background variables. *Psychology of Women Quarterly, 9*, 258–264.

Rosenwasser, S. M., & Patterson, W. (1984–1985). Nontraditional males: Men with primary childcare/household responsibilities. *Psychology and Human Development, 1*, 101–111.

Ross, L., Anderson, D. R., & Wisocki, P. A. (1982). Television viewing and adult sex-role attitudes. *Sex Roles, 8*, 589–592.

Rosser, P. (1992). *The SAT gender gap: ETS responds: A research update*. Washington, DC: Center for Women Policy Studies.

Rosser, P., with the staff of the National Center for Fair and Open Testing (1987). *Sex bias in college admissions tests: Why women lose out* (2nd ed.). Cambridge, MA: National Center for Fair and Open Testing.

Roth, S., Dye, E., & Lebowitz, L. (1988). Group therapy for sexual-assault victims. *Psychotherapy, 25*, 82–93.

Roth, S., & Lebowitz, L. (1988). The experience of sexual trauma. *Journal of Traumatic Stress, 1*, 79–107.

Roth, S., Wayland, K., & Woolsey, M. (1990). Victimization history and victim-assailant relationship as factors in recovery from sexual assault. *Journal of Traumatic Stress, 3*, 169–180.

Rothblum, E. D. (1983). Sex-role stereotypes and depression in women. In V. Franks & E. D. Rothblum (Eds.), *The stereotyping of women: Its effects on mental health* (pp. 83–111). New York: Springer.

Rothman, B. K. (1988). *The tentative pregnancy: Prenatal diagnosis and the future of motherhood*. London: Unwin Hyman.

Rousso, H. (1988). Daughters with disabilities: Defective women or minority women? In M. Fine & A. Asch (Eds.), *Women with disabilities: Essays in psychology, culture,and politics* (pp. 139–171). Philadelphia: Temple University Press.

Rubin, G. (1984). Thinking sex: Notes for a radical theory of the politics of sexuality. In C. S. Vance (Ed.), *Pleasure and danger: Exploring female sexuality* (pp. 267–319). Boston: Routledge & Kegan Paul.

Rubin, R. T., Reinisch, J. M., & Haskett, R. F. (1981). Postnatal gonadal steroid effects on human behavior. *Science, 211*, 1318–1324.

Ruble, D. N., Balaban, T., & Cooper, J. (1981). Gender constancy and the effects of sex-typed televised toy commercials. *Child Development, 52*, 667–673.

Ruble, D. N., Fleming, A. S., Hackel, L. S., & Stangor, C. (1988). Changes in the marital relationship during the transition to first time motherhood: Effects of violated expectations concerning division of household labor. *Journal of Personality and Social Psychology, 85*, 78–87.

Ruble, T. L. (1983). Sex stereotypes: Issues of change in the 1970s. *Sex Roles, 9*, 397–402.

Ruddick, S., & Daniels, P. (Eds.) (1977). *Working it out*. New York: Pantheon Books.

Ruggiero, J. A., & Weston, L. C. (1985). Work options for women in women's magazines: The medium *and* the message. *Sex Roles, 12*, 535–547.

Russell, D. E. H. (1976). Introduction. In D. Martin, *Battered wives* (p. ix). San Francisco, Volcano Press.

Russell, D. E. H. (1982). *Rape in marriage.* New York: Macmillan.

Russell, D. E. H. (1983). The incidence and prevalence of intrafamilial and extrafamilial sexual abuse of female children. *Child Abuse and Neglect, 7,* 133–146.

Russell, D. E. H. (1984a). The prevalence and seriousness of incestuous abuse: Stepfathers vs. biological fathers. *Child Abuse and Neglect, 8,* 15–22.

Russell, D. E. H. (1984b). *Sexual exploitation: Rape, child sexual abuse, and workplace harassment.* Beverly Hills, CA: Sage.

Russell, D. E. H. (1986). *The secret trauma: Incest in the lives of girls and women.* New York: Basic Books.

Russell, D. E. H. (1988). Pornography and rape: A causal model. *Political Psychology, 2,* 41–73.

Russell, D. E. H. (Ed.) (1993). *Making violence sexy: Feminist views on pornography.* New York: Teachers College Press.

Russell, G. W., Horn, V. E., & Huddle, M. J. (1988). Male responses to female aggression. *Social Behavior and Personality, 16,* 51–57.

Russell, M., Lipov, E., Phillips, N., & White, B. (1989, Spring). Psychological profiles of violent and nonviolent maritally distressed couples. *Psychotherapy, 26,* 81–87.

Russett, C. E. (1989). *Sexual science: The Victorian construction of womanhood.* Cambridge, MA: Harvard University Press.

Russo, N. F. (1979). Overview: Sex roles, fertility, and the motherhood mandate. *Psychology of Women Quarterly, 4,* 7–15.

Russo, N. F. (1985). *A women's mental health agenda.* Washington, DC: American Psychological Association.

Russo, N. F., & Denmark, F. L. (1984). Women, psychology, and public policy: Selected issues. *American Psychologist, 39,* 1161–1165.

Rust, P. C. (1993). Neutralizing the political threat of the marginal woman: Lesbians' beliefs about bisexual women. *Journal of Sex Research, 30,* 214–228.

Ruth, S. (1990). *Issues in feminism.* Mountain View, CA: Mayfield.

Ryan, W. (1971). *Blaming the victim.* New York: Random House.

Sadker, M., & Sadker, D. (1994). *Failing at fairness: How America's schools cheat girls.* New York: Scribner.

Safir, M. P. (1986). The effects of nature or of nurture on sex differences in intellectual functioning: Israeli findings. *Sex Roles, 14,* 581–590.

Safran, C. (1976, November). What men do to women on the job: A shocking look at sexual harassment. *Redbook,* pp. 148–149, 217–218, 220, 222, 224.

Sagrestano, L. M. (1992). Power strategies in interpersonal relationships: The effects of expertise and gender. *Psychology of Women Quarterly, 16,* 481–495.

Samelson, F. (1978). From "race psychology" to "studies in prejudice": Some observations on the thematic reversals in social psychology. *Journal of the History of the Behavioral Sciences, 14,* 265–278.

Sanchez, L. (1993). Women's power and the gendered division of domestic labor in the Third World. *Gender & Society, 7,* 434–459.

Sanday, P. R. (1981). The socio-cultural context of rape: A cross-cultural study. *Journal of Social Issues, 37,* 4, 5–27.

Sanders, D., Warner, P., Backstrom, T., & Bancroft, J. (1983). Mood, sexuality, hormones, and the menstrual cycle. *Psychosomatic Research, 45,* 487–501.

Sanders, G. S., & Schmidt, T. (1980). Behavioral discrimination against women. *Personality and Social Psychology Bulletin, 6,* 484–488.

Sanger, S. P., & Alker, H. A. (1972). Dimensions of internal-external locus of control and the women's liberation movement. *Journal of Social Issues, 28,* 115–129.

Sangren, P. S. (1983). Female gender in Chinese religious symbols: Kuan Yin, Ma Tsu, and the "Eternal Mother." *Signs, 9,* 4–25.

Santee, R. T., & Jackson, S. E. (1982). Identity implications of conformity: Sex differences in normative and attributional judgments. *Social Psychology Quarterly, 45,* 121–125.

Sapiro, V. (1994). *Women in American society: An introduction to women's studies* (3rd ed.). Mountain View, CA: Mayfield.

Sarantakos, S. (1991). Cohabitation revisited: Paths of change among cohabiting and noncohabiting couples. *Australian Journal of Marriage and Family, 12,* 144–155.

Saunders, D. (1988). Wife abuse, husband, or mutual combat?: A feminist perspective on the empirical findings. In K. Yllo and M. Bograd (Eds.), *Feminist perspectives on wife abuse* (pp. 90–113). Berkeley, CA: Sage.

Saunders, R. M., & Naus, P. J. (1993). The impact of social content and audience factors on responses to sexually explicit videos. *Journal of Sex Education & Therapy, 19,* 117–130.

Scanzoni, L., & Scanzoni, J. (1976). *Men, women, and change: A sociology of marriage and the family.* New York: McGraw-Hill.

Scarborough, E., & Furumoto, L. (1987). *Untold lives: The first generation of American women psychologists*. New York: Columbia University Press.

Scarr, S., Phillips, D., & McCartney, K. (1990). Facts, fantasies and the future of child care in the United States. *Psychological Science, 1*, 26–35.

Schafer, A. T., & Gray, M. W. (1981). Sex and mathematics. *Science, 211*, 231.

Schilit, R., Lie., G., & Montagne, M. (1990). Substance use as a correlate of violence in intimate lesbian relationships. *Journal of Homosexuality, 19*, 51–65.

Schlesinger, B. (1982). Lasting marriages in the 1980's. *Conciliation Courts Review, 20*, 43–49.

Schlossberg, N. K. (1984). The midlife woman as student. In G. Baruch & J. Brooks-Gunn (Eds.), *Women in midlife* (pp. 315–339). New York: Plenum Press.

Schneider, M. S. (1986). The relationships of cohabiting lesbian and heterosexual couples: A comparison. *Psychology of Women Quarterly, 10*, 234–239.

Schoen, R., & Kluege, J. R. (1988). The widening gap in black and white marriage rates: The impact of population composition and differential marriage propensities. *American Sociological Review, 53*, 895–907.

Schoen, R., & Wooldredge, J. (1989). Marriage choices in North Carolina and Virginia, 1969–71 and 1979–81. *Journal of Marriage and Family, 51*, 465–481.

Schofield, J. (1982). *Black and white in school*. New York: Praeger.

Schooler, C., Miller, J., Miller, K., & Richtand, C. N. (1984). Work for the household: Its nature and consequences for husbands and wives. *American Journal of Sociology, 90*, 97–124.

Schulman, G. I., & Hoskins, M. (1986). Perceiving the male versus the female face. *Psychology of Women Quarterly, 10*, 141–154.

Schulman, M. (1979). *A survey of spousal violence against women in Kentucky*. Washington, DC: U.S. Department of Justice, Law Enforcement Assistance Administration.

Schultz, M. R. (1975). The semantic derogation of women. In B. Thorne & N. Henley (Eds.), *Language and sex: Difference and dominance* (pp. 64–73). Rowley, MA: Newbury House.

Schur, E. M. (1983). *Labeling women deviant: Gender, stigma, and social control*. New York: Random House.

Schutte, N. S., Malouff, J. M., Post-Gorden, J. C., & Rodasta, A. L. (1988). Effects of playing videogames on children's aggressive and other behaviors. *Journal of Applied Social Psychology, 18*, 454–460.

Schwartz, F. N. (1989). Management women and the new facts of life. *Harvard Business Review, 89*, 65–76.

Schwartz, I. (1993). Affective reactions of American and Swedish women to their first premarital coitus: A cross-cultural comparison. *Journal of Sex Research, 30*, 18–26.

Schwartz, L. A., & Markham, W. T. (1985). Sex stereotyping in children's toy advertisements. *Sex Roles, 12*, 157–170.

Schwartz, M. D. (1989). Asking the right questions: Battered wives are not all passive. *Sociological Viewpoints, 5*, 46–61.

Schwartz, P. (1994). *Peer marriage*. New York: Free Press.

Seagoe, M. V. (1975). *Terman and the gifted*. Los Altos, CA: William Kaufmann.

Searles, P., & Berger, R. J. (1987). The current status of rape reform legislation: An examination of state statutes. *Women's Rights Law Reporter, 10*, 25–43.

Sears, D. O., (1986). College sophomores in the laboratory: Influences of a narrow data base on social psychology's view of human nature. *Journal of Personality and Social Psychology, 51*, 515–530.

Sedney, M. A. (1987). Development of androgyny: Parental influences. *Psychology of Women Quarterly, 11*, 311–326.

Sedney, M. A. (1989). Conceptual and methodological sources of controversies about androgyny. In R. K. Unger (Ed.), *Representations: Social constructions of gender* (pp. 126–144). Amityville, NY: Baywood.

Segel, E. (1986). "As the twig is bent . . .": Gender and childhood reading. In E. Flynn & P. Schweikart (Eds.), *Gender and reading: Essays on readers, texts, and contexts* (pp. 165–186). Baltimore: Johns Hopkins.

Seidenberg, R. (1971). Advertising and abuse of drugs. *New England Journal of Medicine, 284*, 789–790.

Selkow, P. (1984). *Assessing sex bias in testing: A review of the issues and evaluations of 74 psychological and educational tests*. Westport, CT: Greenwood.

Sen, A. (1990, December 20). More than one hundred million women are missing. *New York Review of Books*.

Serbin, L. A., & Conner, J. M. (1979). Sex-typing of children's play preferences and patterns of cognitive performance. *Journal of Genetic Psychology, 134*, 315–316.

Serbin, L. A., & Sprafkin, C. (1986). The salience of gender and the process of sex-typing in three- to seven-year-old children. *Child Development, 57,* 1188–1199.

Serbin, L. A., Sprafkin, C., Elman, M., & Doyle, A. B. (1984). The development of sex differentiated patterns of social influence. *Canadian Journal of Social Science, 14,* 350–363.

Settin, J. M. (1982). Clinical judgment in geropsychology practice. *Psychotherapy: Theory, Research, and Practice, 19,* 397–404.

Severne, L. (1982). Psychosocial aspects of the menopause. In A. M. Voda, M. Dinnerstein, & S. R. O'Donnell (Eds.), *Changing perspectives on menopause* (pp. 239–247). Austin: University of Texas Press.

Shachar, S. A., & Gilbert, L. A. (1983). Working lesbians: Role conflicts and coping strategies. *Psychology of Women Quarterly, 7,* 244–256.

Shaffer, J. W. (1963). Masculinity-femininity and other personality traits in gonadal aplasia (Turner's Syndrome). In H. G. Beigel (Ed.), *Advances in sex research.* New York: Harper & Row.

Shakin, M., Shakin, D., & Sternglanz, S. H. (1985). Infant clothing: Sex labeling for strangers. *Sex Roles, 12,* 955–963.

Shamir, B. (1986). Unemployment and household division of labor. *Journal of Marriage and the Family, 48,* 195–206.

Shange, N. (1978). With no immediate cause. In *Nappy edges* (pp. 114–117). New York: St. Martin's Press.

Shankar, A. (1994). Mamawoman. In D. Taylor (Ed.), *Feminist parenting: Struggles, triumphs, and comic interludes* (pp. 63–65). Freedom, CA: Crossing Press.

Shapiro, J. P. (1979). "Fear of success" imagery as a reaction to sex-role inappropriate behavior. *Journal of Personality Assessment, 43,* 33–38.

Sharp, C., & Post, R. (1980). Evaluation of male and female applicants for sex-congruent and sex-incongruent jobs. *Sex Roles, 6,* 391–401.

Sharps, M., Welton, A., & Price, J. (1992, August 17). Spatial cognition and gender: Task-related determinants of performance. Poster presented at the annual meeting of the American Psychological Association, Washington, DC.

Shea, C. (1994). "Gender gap" on examinations shrank again this year. *Chronicle of Higher Education, 41,* A54.

Sheehy, G. (1974). *Passages: Predictable crises of adult life.* New York: Dutton.

Shepelak, N. J., Ogden, D., & Tobin-Bennett, D. (1984). The influence of gender labels on the sex typing of imaginary occupations. *Sex Roles, 11,* 983–996.

Sherif, C. W. (1976). *Orientation in social psychology.* New York: Harper & Row.

Sherif, C. W. (1979). Bias in psychology. In J. A. Sherman & E. T. Beck (Eds.), *The prisms of sex: Essays in the sociology of knowledge* (pp. 93–133). Madison: University of Wisconsin Press.

Sherif, C. W. (1982). Needed studies in the concept of gender identity. *Psychology of Women Quarterly, 6,* 375–398.

Sherif, M., & Sherif, C. W. (1969). *Social psychology.* New York: Harper & Row.

Sheriffs, A. C., & McKee, J. P. (1957). Qualitative aspects of beliefs about men and women. *Journal of Personality, 25,* 451–467.

Sherman, J. A. (1967). Problem of sex differences in space perception and aspects of intellectual functioning. *Psychological Review, 74,* 290–299.

Sherman, J. A. (1980). Therapist attitudes and sex-role stereotyping. In A. M. Brodsky & R. Hare-Mustin (Eds.), *Women and psychotherapy* (pp. 35–66). New York: Guilford Press.

Sherman, J. A. (1982). Continuing in mathematics: A longitudinal study of the attitudes of high school girls. *Psychology of Women Quarterly, 7,* 132–140.

Sherman, J. A. (1983). Factors predicting girls' and boys' enrollment in college preparatory mathematics. *Psychology of Women Quarterly, 7,* 272–281.

Sherman, J. A., & Fennema, E. (1978). Distribution of spatial visualization and mathematical problem solving scores: A test of Stafford's X-linked hypothesis. *Psychology of Women Quarterly, 3,* 157–167.

Sherman, J. A., Koufacos, C., & Kenworthy, J. (1978). Therapists: Their attitudes and information about women. *Psychology of Women Quarterly, 2,* 299–313.

Shields, S. A., (1975). Functionalism, Darwinism, and the psychology of women: A study in social myth. *American Psychologist, 30,* 739–754.

Shields, S. A. (1982). The variability hypothesis: The history of a biological model of sex difference in intelligence. *Signs, 7,* 769–797.

Shields, S. A., Steinke, P., & Koster, B. A. (1995). The double bind of caregiving: Representation of gendered emotion in American advice literature. *Sex Roles, 33,* 718.

Shipman, G. (1971). The psychodynamics of sex education. In R. E. Muuss (Ed.), *Adolescent behavior and society: A book of readings.* New York: Random House.

Shorter, E. (1982). *A history of women's bodies.* New York: Basic Books.

Shotland, R. L. (1989). A model of the causes of date rape in developing and close relationships. In C. Hendrick (Ed.), *Close relationships* (pp. 247–270). Newbury Park, CA: Sage.

Shotland, R. L., & Goodstein, L. (1992). Sexual precedence reduces the perceived legitimacy of sexual refusal: An examination of attributions concerning date rape and consensual sex. *Personality and Social Psychology Bulletin, 18,* 756–764.

Shotland, R. L., & Straw, M. (1976). Bystander response to an assault: When a man attacks a woman. *Journal of Personality and Social Psychology, 34,* 5, 990–999.

Showalter, E. (1987). *The female malady: Women, madness, and English culture, 1830–1980.* New York: Pantheon Books.

Shuster, R. (1987). Sexuality as a continuum: The bisexual identity. In Boston Lesbian Psychologies Collective (Eds.), *Lesbian psychologies* (pp. 56–71). Urbana: University of Illinois Press.

Siegel, R. J. (1983). Accumulated inequalities: Problems in long-term marriages. *Women and Therapy, 2,* 171–178.

Siegel, R. J. (1993). Between midlife and old age: Never too old to learn. In N. D. Davis, E. Cole, & E. D. Rothblum (Eds.), *Faces of women and aging* (pp. 173–185). Binghamton, NY: Harrington Park Press.

Sigelman, C. K., Thomas, D. B., Sigelman, L., & Ribich, F. D. (1986). Gender, physical attractiveness and electability: An experimental investigation of voter biases. *Journal of Applied Social Psychology, 16,* 229–248.

Sigelman, L, & Sigelman, C. K. (1982). Sexism, racism, and ageism in voting behavior: An experimental analysis. *Social Psychology Quarterly, 45,* 263–269.

Sigelman, L., & Welch, S. (1984). Race, gender, and opinion toward black and female presidential candidates. *Public Opinion Quarterly, 48,* 467–475.

Signorella, M. L., & Jamison, W. (1986). Masculinity, femininity, androgyny, and cognitive performance: A meta-analysis. *Psychological Bulletin, 100,* 207–228.

Signorielli, N. (1989). Television and conceptions about sex roles: Maintaining conventionality and the status quo. *Sex Roles, 21,* 341–360.

Signorielli, N., & Lears, M. (1992). Children, television, and conceptions about chores: Attitudes and behaviors. *Sex Roles, 27,* 157–170.

Silberstein, L. R., Striegel-Moore, R. H., Timko, C., & Rodin, J. (1988). Behavioral and psychological implications of body dissatisfaction: Do men and women differ? *Sex Roles, 19,* 219–232.

Silverman, P. R. (1981). *Helping women cope with grief.* Beverly Hills, CA: Sage.

Silverstein, B., Perdue, L., Peterson, B., & Kelly, E. (1986). The role of the mass media in promoting a thin standard of bodily attractiveness for women. *Sex Roles, 14,* 519–532.

Silverstein, B., Peterson, B., & Perdue, L. (1986). Some correlates of the thin standard of bodily attractiveness for women. *International Journal of Eating Disorders, 5,* 895–905.

Silverstein, L. B., (1991). Transforming the debate about child care and maternal employment. *American Psychologist, 46,* 1025–1032.

Simmons, R. G., & Blyth, D. A. (1987). *Moving into adolescence: The impact of pubertal change and school context.* New York: Aldine De Gruyter.

Simmons, R. G., Blyth, D. A., Van Cleave, E. F., & Bush, D. M. (1979). Entry into early adolescence: The impact of school structure, puberty, and early dating on self esteem. *American Sociological Review, 44,* 948–967.

Simmons, R. G., Burgeson, R., & Reef, M. J. (1988). In M. R. Gunnar & W. A. Collins (Eds.), *Development during the transition to adolescence* (pp. 123–150). Hillsdale, NJ: Erlbaum.

Simmons, R. G., & Rosenberg, F. R. (1975). Sex, sex-roles, and self-image. *Journal of Youth and Adolescence, 4,* 229–258.

Simon, B. L. (1987). *Never-married women.* Philadelphia: Temple University Press.

Singer, J. M., & Stake, J. E. (1986). Mathematics and self-esteem: Implications for women's career choices. *Psychology of Women Quarterly, 10,* 339–351.

Sinnott, J. D. (1984). Older men, older women: Are their perceived roles similar? *Sex Roles, 10,* 847–856.

Skrypnek, B. J., & Snyder, M. (1982). On the self-perpetuating nature of stereotypes about women and men. *Journal of Experimental Social Psychology, 18,* 277–291.

Slaby, R. G., & Guerra, N. G. (1988). Cognitive mediators of aggression in adolescent offenders: I. Assessment. *Developmental Psychology, 24,* 580–588.

Sleek, S. (1994, August). APA amicus brief affects outcome of Va. court case. *American Psychological Association Monitor*, 8.

Smetana, J. G. (1988). Concepts of self and social convention: Adolescents' and parents' reasoning about hypothetical and actual family conflicts. In M. Gunnar & W. A. Collins (Eds.), *Development during the transition to adolescence: Minnesota symposia on child psychology*, Vol. 21. (pp. 79–119). Hillsdale, NJ: Erlbaum.

Smetana, J. G., & Letourneau, J. (1984). Development of gender constancy and children's sex-typed free-play behavior. *Developmental Psychology*, *20*, 691–696.

Smith, A. J., & Douglas, M. A. (1990). Empowerment as an ethical imperative. In H. Lerman & N. Porter (Eds.), *Feminist ethics in psychotherapy* (pp. 43–50). New York: Springer.

Smith, B. (1943). *A tree grows in Brooklyn*. New York: Harper & Row.

Smith, E. A. (1989). A biosocial model of adolescent sexual behavior. In G. R. Adams, R. Montemayor, & T. P. Gullotta (Eds.), *Advances in adolescent development* (pp. 143–167). Newbury Park, CA: Sage.

Smith, J. (1991). Conceiving selves: A case study of changing identities during the transition to motherhood. *Journal of Language and Social Psychology*, *10*, 225–243.

Smith, J. I. (1987). Islam. In A. Sharma (Ed.), *Women in world religions*. Albany: State University of New York Press.

Smith, P. A., & Midlarsky, E. (1985). Empirically derived conceptions of femaleness and maleness: A current view. *Sex Roles*, *12*, 313–328.

Smith, P. K. (1987). Exploration, play and social development in boys and girls. In D. J. Hargreaves & A. M. Colley (Eds.), *The psychology of sex roles* (pp. 118–141). New York: Hemisphere.

Smith-Lovin, L., & Brody, C. (1989). Interruptions in group discussions: The effects of gender and group composition. *American Sociological Review*, *54*, 425–435.

Smith-Rosenberg, C. (1975). The female world of love and ritual: Relations between women in nineteenth-century America. *Signs*, *1*, 1–30.

Smith-Rosenberg, C. (1985). *Disorderly conduct: Visions of gender in Victorian America*. New York: Oxford University Press.

Snavely, B. K., & Fairhurst, G. T. (1984). The male nursing student as a token. *Research in Nursing and Health*, *7*, 287–294.

Snizek, W. E., & Neil, C. C. (1992). Job characteristics, gender stereotypes, and perceived gender discrimination in the workplace. *Organization Studies*, *13*, 403–427.

Snodgrass, S. E. (1985). Women's intuition: The effect of subordinate role on interpersonal sensitivity. *Journal of Personality and Social Psychology*, *49*, 146–155.

Snodgrass, S. E. (1992). Further effects of role versus gender on interpersonal sensitivity. *Journal of Personality and Social Psychology*, *62*, 154–158.

Snow, J. T., & Harris, M. B. (1985). Maintenance of weight loss: Demographic, behav-ioral, and attitudinal correlates. *The Journal of Obesity and Weight Regulation*, *4*, 234–255.

Snow, J. T., & Harris, M. B. (1986). An analysis of weight and diet content in five women's interest magazines. *The Journal of Obesity and Weight Regulation*, *5*, 194–214.

Snow, J. T., & Harris, M. B. (1989). Disordered eating in Southwestern Pueblo Indians and Hispanics. *Journal of Adolescence*, *12*, 329–336.

Snow, M. E., Jacklin, C. N., & Maccoby, E. E. (1983). Sex-of-child differences in father-child interaction at one year of age. *Child Development*, *54*, 227–232.

Snyder, M., & Swann, W. B., Jr. (1978a). Behavioral confirmation in social interaction: From social perception to social reality. *Journal of Experimental Social Psychology*, *14*, 148–162.

Snyder, M., & Swann, W. B., Jr. (1978b). Hypothesis-testing processes in social interaction. *Journal of Personality and Social Psychology*, *36*, 1202–1212.

Snyder, M., Tanke, E. D., & Berscheid, E. (1977). Social perception and interpersonal behavior: On the self-fulfilling nature of social stereotypes. *Journal of Personality and Social Psychology*, *35*, 656–666.

Snyder, M., & Uranowitz, S. W. (1978). Reconstructing the past: Some cognitive consequences of person perception. *Journal of Personality and Social Psychology*, *36*, 941–950.

Sohoni, N. K. (1994). Where are the girls? *Ms.*, *5* (#1), 96.

Soley, L. C., & Kurzbard, G. (1986). Sex in advertising: A comparison of 1964 and 1984 magazine advertisements. *Journal of Advertising*, *15*, 46–64.

Sommers-Flanagan, R., Sommers-Flanagan, J., & Davis, B. (1993). What's happening on music television? A gender-role content analysis. *Sex Roles*, *28*, 745–753.

Sontag, S. (1979). The double standard of aging. In J. H. Williams (Ed.), *Psychology of women:*

Selected readings (pp. 462–478). New York: Norton.

Sorensen, A., & McLanahan, S. (1987). Married women's economic dependency, 1940–1980. *American Journal of Sociology, 93,* 659–687.

Sorenson, S. B., & Siegel, J. M. (1992). Gender, ethnicity, and sexual assault: Findings from the Los Angeles epidemiological catchment area study. *Journal of Social Issues, 48,* 93–104.

Spanier, G. B. (1983). Married and unmarried cohabitation in the United States: 1980. *Journal of Marriage and the Family, 45,* 277–288.

Spence, J. T. (1991). Do the BSRI and PAQ measure the same or different concepts? *Psychology of Women Quarterly, 15,* 141–165.

Spence, J. T., Deaux, K., & Helmreich, R. L. (1985). Sex roles in contemporary American society. In G. Lindzey & E. Aronson (Eds.), *The handbook of social psychology* (3rd ed.) (pp. 149–178). New York: Random House.

Spence, J. T., & Helmreich, R. L. (1978). *Masculinity and femininity.* Austin: University of Texas Press.

Spence, J. T., & Helmreich, R. L. (1980). Masculine instrumentality and feminine expressiveness: Their relationships with sex role attitudes and behaviors. *Psychology of Women Quarterly, 5,* 147–163.

Spence, J. T., & Helmreich, R. L. (1981). Androgyny versus gender schema: A comment on Bem's gender schema theory. *Psychological Review, 88,* 365–368.

Spence, J. T., & Helmreich, R. L. (1983). Achievement-related motives and behaviors. In J. T. Spence (Ed.), *Achievement and achievement motives.* San Francisco: Freeman.

Spence, J. T., & Sawin, L. L. (1985). Images of masculinity and femininity. In V. E. O'Leary, R. K. Unger, & B. S. Wallston (Eds.), *Women, gender, and social psychology* (pp. 35–66). Hillsdale, NJ: Erlbaum.

Spencer, D. A. (1988). Public schoolteaching: A suitable job for a woman. In A. Statham, E. M. Miller, & H. O. Mauksch (Eds.), *The worth of women's work: A qualitative synthesis* (pp. 167–186). Albany: State University of New York Press.

Sprecher, S. (1985). Sex differences in bases of power in dating relationships. *Sex Roles, 12,* 449–462.

Spurlock, J. (1984). Black women in the middle years. In G. Baruch & J. Brooks-Gunn (Eds.), *Women in midlife* (pp. 245–260). New York: Plenum Press.

Stack, C. B. (1986). The culture of gender: Women and men of color. *Signs, 11,* 321–324.

Stacy, R. D., Prisbell, M., & Tollefsrud, K. (1992). A comparison of attitudes among college students toward sexual violence committed by strangers and by acquaintances: A research report. *Journal of Sex Education and Therapy, 18,* 257–263.

Stake, J., & Lauer, M. L. (1987). The consequences of being overweight: A controlled study of gender differences. *Sex Roles, 17,* 31–47.

Stallard, K., Ehrenreich, B., & Sklar, H. (1983). *Poverty in the American dream: Women and children first.* Boston: South End Press.

Stangor, C., Lynch, L., Duan, C., & Glass, B. (1992). Categorization of individuals on the basis of multiple social features. *Journal of Personality and Social Psychology, 62,* 207–218.

Stanley, J. P. (1977). Paradigmatic woman: The prostitute. In D. L. Shores & C. P. Hines (Eds.), *Papers in language variation* (pp. 303–321). University of Alabama: University of Alabama Press.

Stark, E., Flitcraft, A., & Frazier, W. (1979). Medicine and patriarchal violence: The social construction of a private event. *International Journal of Health Services, 9,* 461–493.

Statham, A., Miller, E. M., & Mauksch, H. O. (Eds.) (1988). *The worth of women's work: A qualitative synthesis.* Albany: State University of New York Press.

Stead, B. A., & Zinkhan, G. M. (1986). Service priority in department stores: The effect of customer gender and sex. *Sex Roles, 15,* 601–611.

Steele, B. F. (1986). Notes on the lasting effects of early child abuse throughout the life cycle. *Child Abuse and Neglect, 10,* 283–291.

Steil, J. M. (1983). Marriage: An unequal partnership. In B. B. Wolman & G. Stricker (Eds.), *Handbook of family and marital therapy* (pp. 49–60). New York: Plenum Press.

Steil, J. M. (1989). Marital relationships and mental health: The psychic costs of inequality. In J. Freeman (Ed.), *Women: A feminist perspective* 4th ed. (pp. 138–140). Mountain View, CA: Mayfield.

Steil, J. M. (1994). Supermoms and second shifts: Marital inequality in the 90's. In J. Freeman (Ed.), *Women: A feminist perspective* (5th ed.) (pp. 149–161). Mountain View, CA: Mayfield.

Steil, J. M., & Hillman, J. L. (1993). The perceived value of direct and indirect influence strategies: A cross-cultural comparison. *Psychology of Women Quarterly, 17,* 457–462.

Steil, J. M., & Turetsky, B. A. (1987a). Marital influence levels and symptomatology among wives. In F. Crosby (Ed.), *Spouse, parent, worker: On gender and multiple roles* (pp. 74–90). New Haven, CT: Yale University Press.

Steil, J. M., & Turetsky, B. A. (1987b). Is equal better? The relationship between marital equality and psychological symptomatology. In S. Oskamp (Ed.), *Family processes and problems: Social psychological aspects* (pp. 73–97). Beverly Hills, CA: Sage.

Steil, J. M., & Weltman, K. (1991). Marital inequality: The importance of resources, personal attributes, and social norms on career valuing and the allocation of domestic responsibilities. *Sex Roles, 24,* 161–179.

Steinberg, L. (1981). Transformations in family relations at puberty. *Developmental Psychology, 17,* 833–840.

Steinberg, L., & Silverberg, S. B. (1987). Influences on marital satisfaction during the middle stages of the family life cycle. *Journal of Marriage and the Family, 49,* 751–760.

Steinem, G. (1983). *Outrageous acts and everyday rebellions.* New York: New American Library.

Steinmetz, S. (1977–1978). The battered husband syndrome. *Victimology: An International Journal, 2,* 499–509.

Stern, M., & Karraker, K. H. (1989). Sex stereotyping of infants: A review of gender labeling studies. *Sex Roles, 20,* 501–522.

Sternglanz, S. H., & Serbin, L. A. (1974). Sex-role stereotyping in children's television programs. *Developmental Psychology, 10,* 710–715.

Stevens, G., & Gardner, S. (1987). But can she command a ship? Acceptance of women by peers at the Coast Guard Academy. *Sex Roles, 16,* 181–188.

Stewart. A. J. (1980). Personality and situation in the prediction of women's life patterns. *Psychology of Women Quarterly, 5,* 195–206.

Stewart, A. J. (1994a). The Women's Movement and women's lives: Linking individual development and social events. In A. Leiblich & R. Josselson (Eds.), *Exploring identity and gender: The narrative study of lives* (pp. 230–250). London: Sage.

Stewart, A. J. (1994b). Toward a feminist strategy for studying women's lives. In C. E. Franz & A. J. Stewart (Eds.), *Women creating lives: Identities, resilience, and resistance* (pp. 11–36). Boulder, CO: Westview Press.

Stewart, A. J., & Gold-Steinberg, S. (1990). Midlife women's political consciousness: Case studies of psychosocial development and political commitment. *Psychology of Women Quarterly, 14,* 543–566.

Stewart, A. J., & Healy, J. (1989). Linking individual development and social changes. *American Psychologist, 44,* 30–42.

Stewart, A. J., & Lykes, M. B. (1985). *Gender and personality.* Durham, NC: Duke University Press.

Stiles, D., Gibbons, J. L., Hardardottir, S., & Schnellman, J. (1987). The ideal man or woman as described by young adolescents in Iceland and the United States. *Sex Roles, 17,* 313–320.

Stimpson, C. R. (1982). The fallacy of bodily reductionism. In A. M. Voda, M. Dinnerstein, & S. R. O'Donnell (Eds.), *Changing perspectives on menopause* (pp. 265–272). Austin: University of Texas Press.

Stimpson, C. R. (1986). *Women's studies in the United States.* New York: Ford Foundation.

Stoltenberg, J. (1989). *Refusing to be a man: Essays on sex and justice.* New York: Penguin Books.

Stoltzman, S. M. (1986). Menstrual attitudes, beliefs, and symptom experience of adolescent females, their peers, and their mothers. *Health Care for Women International, 7,* 97–114.

Stoneman, Z., Brody, G. H., & MacKinnon, C. (1984). Naturalistic observations of children's activities and roles while playing with their siblings and friends. *Child Development, 55,* 617–627.

Storms, M. D., Stivers, M. L., Lambers, S. M., & Hill, C. A. (1981). Sexual scripts for women. *Sex Roles, 7,* 699–707.

Stout, H. (1988, January 24). The economics of the minimum wage: Propping up payments at the bottom. *New York Times,* F4.

Straus, M. (1977–1978). Wife beating: How common and why? *Victimology: An International Journal, 2,* 443–458.

Straus, M. A., (1978). Family patterns and child abuse in a nationally representative American sample. Paper presented at the Second International Congress of Child Abuse and Neglect, London.

Straus, M. A. (1993). Physical assaults by wives: A major social problem. In R. J. Gelles and D. R. Loseke (Eds.), *Current controversies on family violence* (pp. 67–87). Newbury Park, CA: Sage.

Straus, M., & Gelles, R. (1986). Societal change in family violence from 1975 to 1985 as revealed by two national surveys. *Journal of Marriage and the Family, 48,* 465–479.

Straus, M. A., & Gelles, R. J. (1990). *Physical violence in American families: Risk factors and adaptations to violence in 8,145 families*. New Brunswick, NJ: Transaction.

Straus, M., Gelles, R., & Steinmetz, S. (1980). *Behind closed doors: Violence in the American family*. New York: Anchor Press.

Stricker, L., Rock, D., & Burton, N. (1992). *Sex differences in SAT predictions of college grades*. New York: The College Board.

Striegel-Moore, R. H., Silberstein, L. R., & Rodin, J. (1986). Toward an understanding of the risk factors in bulimia. *American Psychologist, 41*, 246–263.

Strommen, E. F. (1993). "You're a what?": Family member reactions to the disclosure of homosexuality. In L. D. Garnets & D. C. Kimmel (Eds.), *Psychological perspectives on lesbian and gay male experiences* (pp. 248–266). New York: Columbia University Press.

Stueve, A., & O'Donnell, L. (1984). The daughter of aging parents. In G. Baruch & J. Brooks-Gunn (Eds.), *Women in midlife* (pp. 203–225). New York: Plenum Press.

Sugarman, D. B., & Hotaling, G. T. (1989). Dating violence: Prevalence, context, and risk markers. In M. A. Pirog-Good & J. E. Stets (Eds.), *Violence in dating relationships* (pp. 3–32). New York: Praeger.

Suh, M. (1990, September/October). Lesbian battery. *Ms.*

Summit, R. (1983). The child sexual abuse accommodation syndrome. *Child Abuse and Neglect, 7*, 177–193.

Sutherland, E., & Veroff, J. (1985). Achievement motivation and sex roles. In V. E. O'Leary, R. K. Unger, & B. S. Wallston (Eds.), *Women, gender, and social psychology* (pp. 101–128). Hillsdale, NJ: Erlbaum.

Sutherland, S., & Scherl, D. J. (1970). Patterns of response among victims of rape. *American Journal of Orthopsychiatry, 40*, 503–505.

Swaab, D. F., & Hofman, M. A. (1990). An enlarged suprachiasmatic nucleus in homosexual men. *Brain Research, 537*, 141–148.

Swarz, N., Wagner, D., Bannert, M., & Mathes, L. (1987). Cognitive accessibility of sex role concepts and attitudes toward political participation: The impact of sexist advertisements. *Sex Roles, 17*, 593–601.

Swinson, A. P. (1994, October 14). Man shot his family, police say. *Greensboro News and Record*, p. B1.

Tajfel, H. (1984). Intergroup relations, social myths, and social justice in social psychology. In H. Tajfel (Ed.), *The social dimension*. Cambridge, England: Cambridge University Press.

Tannen, D. (1994). *Talking from nine to five*. New York: William Morrow.

Tanner, J. M. (1978). *Fetus into man*. Cambridge, MA: Harvard University Press.

Tashakkori, A. (1993). Gender, ethnicity, and the structure of self-esteem: An attitude theory approach. *Journal of Social Psychology, 133*, 479–488.

Taylor, M. C., & Hall, J. A. (1982). Psychological androgyny: Theories, methods, and conclusions. *Psychological Bulletin, 92*, 347–366.

Taylor, S. E. (1983). Adjustment to threatening events: A theory of cognitive adaptation. *American Psychologist, 38*, 1161–1173.

Taylor, S. E., & Falcone, H. (1982). Cognitive bases of stereotyping: The relationship between categorization and prejudice. *Personality and Social Psychology Bulletin, 8*, 426–432.

Taylor, S. E., Fiske, S. T., Etcoff, N. L., & Ruderman, A. J. (1978). Categorical and contextual bases of person memory and stereotyping. *Journal of Personality and Social Psychology, 36*, 778–793.

Taylor, S. E., & Langer, E. J. (1977). Pregnancy: A social stigma? *Sex Roles, 3*, 27–35.

Teachman, J. D., & Polenko, K. A. (1990). Cohabitation and marital stability in the United States. *Social Forces, 69*, 207–220.

Teitelbaum, P. (1989). Feminist theory and standardized testing. In A. M. Jaggar & S. Bordo (Eds.), *Gender/body/knowledge* (pp. 324–335). New Brunswick, NJ: Rutgers University Press.

Telch, C., & Lindquist, C. (1984, Summer). Violent versus nonviolent couples: A comparison of patterns. *Psychotherapy, 21*, 242–248.

Teri, L. (1982). Effects of sex and sex-role style on clinical judgment. *Sex Roles, 8*, 639–649.

Terman, L. M., & Oden, M. H. (1959). *Genetic studies of genius. V. The gifted group at midlife: Thirty-five years' follow-up of the superior child*. Stanford, CA: Stanford University Press.

Tevlin, H. E., & Leiblum, S. R. (1983). Sex-role stereotypes and female sexual dysfunction. In V. Franks & E. D. Rothblum (Eds.), *Stereotyping of women: Its effects on mental health* (pp. 129–148). New York: Springer.

Thibault, J. W., & Kelley, H. H. (1959). *The social psychology of groups*. New York: Wiley.

Thoits, P. A. (1987). Negotiating roles. In F. J. Crosby (Ed.), *Spouse, parent, worker: On gender and multiple roles* (pp. 11–22). New Haven: Yale University Press.

Thomas, V. G., & James, M. D. (1988). Body

image, dieting tendencies, and sex role traits in urban black women. *Sex Roles, 18*, 523–529.

Thompson, C. (1964). *On women*. New York: New American Library.

Thompson, E. H. (1991). The maleness of violence in dating relationships: An appraisal of stereotypes. *Sex Roles, 24*, 261–278.

Thompson, S. (1986). Pregnancy on purpose. *Village Voice, 31*(51), 31–37. Cited in Cusick (1987). Sexism and early parenting: Cause and effect? *Peabody Journal of Education, 64*, 113–131.

Thompson, S. K. (1975). Gender labels and early sex role development. *Child Development, 46*, 339–347.

Thornberry, O. T., Wilson, R. W., & Golden, P. (1986). Health promotion and disease prevention provisional data from the National Health Interview Survey: United States, January-June, 1985. *Vital and Health Statistics of the National Center for Health Statistics, 119*, 1–16.

Thorne, B. (1986). Girls and boys together, but mostly apart. In W. W. Hartup and Z. Rubin (Eds.), *Relationships and development* (pp. 167–184). Hillsdale, NJ: Erlbaum.

Thorne, B. (1993). *Gender play: Girls and boys in school*. New Brunswick, NJ: Rutgers University Press.

Thorne, B., & Luria, Z. (1986). Sexuality and gender in children's daily worlds. *Social Problems, 33*, 176–190.

Tiefer, L. (1988). A feminist perspective on sexology and sexuality. In M. Gergen (Ed.), *Feminist thought and the structure of knowledge* (pp. 16–26). New York: New York University Press.

Tiefer, L. (1989, August). Feminist transformations of sexology. In M. Crawford (chair), Feminist psychological science: Frameworks, strengths, visions, and a few examples. Symposium conducted at meeting of the American Psychological Association, New Orleans, LA.

Tiefer, L. (1991). Commentary on the status of sex research: Feminism, sexuality and sexology. *Journal of Psychology and Human Sexuality, 4*, 5–42.

Tilby, P. J., & Kalin, R. (1980). Effects of sex-role deviant lifestyles in otherwise normal persons on the perception of maladjustment. *Sex Roles, 6*, 581–592.

Tobach, E. (1994). Comment made at the meeting of the Eastern Psychological Association, Providence, RI, April 16.

Tobin-Richards, M. H., Boxer, A. M., & Petersen, A. C. (1983). The psychological significance of pubertal change: Sex differences in perceptions of self during early adolescence. In J. Brooks-Gunn & A. C. Petersen (Eds.), *Girls at puberty* (pp. 127–154). New York: Plenum Press.

Todd, J., Friedman, A., & Kariuki, P. W. (1990). Women growing stronger with age: The effect of status in the United States and Kenya. *Psychology of Women Quarterly, 14*, 567–577.

Tolman, R. M. (1989). The development of a measure of psychological maltreatment of women by their male partners. *Violence and Victims, 4*, 159–177.

Tontodonato, P., & Crew, B. K. (1992). Dating violence, social learning theory, and gender: A multivariate analysis. *Violence and Victims, 7*, 3–14.

Tracy, D. M. (1987). Toys, spatial ability, and science and mathematics achievement: Are they related? *Sex Roles, 17*, 115–138.

Travis, C. B. (1988a). *Women and health psychology: Biomedical issues*. Hillsdale, NJ: Erlbaum.

Travis, C. B. (1988b). *Women and health psychology: Mental health issues*. Hillsdale, NJ: Erlbaum.

Travis, C. (1990, August). *The social construction of women's sexuality*. Paper presented at the meeting of the American Psychological Association, Boston, MA.

Travis, C. B., & Seipp, P. H. (1978). An examination of secondary reinforcement, operant conditioning, and status envy hypotheses in relation to sex role ideology. *Sex Roles, 4*, 525–538.

Treadway, C. R., Kane, F. J., Jarrahi-Zadeh, A., & Lipton, M. A. (1969). A psycho-endocrine study of pregnancy and puerperium. *American Journal of Psychiatry, 125*, 1380–1386.

Trends in Education, APA education directorate news (1995). 2, 2–3.

Trent, K. & South, S. J. (1989). Structural determinants of the divorce rate: A cross-societal analysis. *Journal of Marriage and the Family, 51*, 391–404.

Tronick, E. Z., & Cohn, J. F. (1989). Infant-mother face-to-face interaction: Age and gender differences in coordination and the occurrence of miscoordination. *Child Development, 60*, 85–92.

Tronto, J. C. (1987). Beyond gender difference to a theory of care. *Signs, 12*, 644–663.

Trotman, F. K., (1984). Psychotherapy of black women and the dual effects of racism and sexism. In C. M. Brody (Ed.), *Women thera-*

pists working with women: New theory and process of feminist therapy (pp. 96–108). New York: Springer.

Tuchman, G. (1978). Introduction: The symbolic annihilation of women by the mass media. In G. Tuchman, A. K. Daniels, & J. Benet (Eds.), *Hearth and home: Images of women in the mass media* (pp. 3–38). New York: Oxford University Press.

Tulloch, M. I., & Tulloch, J. C. (1992). Attitudes to domestic violence: School students' responses to a television drama. *Australian Journal of Marriage and Family, 13*, 62–69.

Turk, J. L., & Bell, N. W. (1972). Measuring power in families. *Journal of Marriage and the Family, 34*, 215–223.

Udry, J. R., Billy, J. O. G., Morris, N. M., Groff, T. R., & Raj, M. H. (1985). Serum androgenic hormones motivate sexual behavior in boys. *Fertility and Sterility, 43*, 90–94.

Udry, J. R., Talbert, L., Morris, N. M. (1986). Biosocial foundations for adolescent female sexuality. *Demography, 23*, 217–230.

Unger, R. K. (1976). Male is greater than female: The socialization of status inequality. *The Counseling Psychologist, 6*, 2–9.

Unger, R. K. (1978). The politics of gender: A review of relevant literature. In J. Sherman & F. Denmark (Eds.), *Psychology of women: Future directions of research* (pp. 463–517). New York: Psychological Dimensions.

Unger. R. K. (1979a). *Female and male: Psychological perspectives*. New York: Harper & Row.

Unger, R. K. (1979b). Toward a redefinition of sex and gender. *American Psychologist, 34*, 1085–1094.

Unger, R. K. (1981). Sex as a social reality: Field and laboratory research. *Psychology of Women Quarterly, 5*, 645–653.

Unger, R. K. (1983). Through the looking glass: No Wonderland yet! (The reciprocal relationship between methodology and models of reality.) *Psychology of Women Quarterly, 8*, 9–32.

Unger, R. K. (1984–1985). Explorations in feminist ideology: Surprising consistencies and unexamined conflicts. *Imagination, Cognition, and Personality, 4*, 395–403.

Unger, R. K. (1988). Psychological, feminist, and personal epistemology. In M. M. Gergen (Ed.), *Feminist thought and the structure of knowledge* (pp. 124–141). New York: New York University Press.

Unger, R. K. (Ed.) (1989). *Representations: Social constructions of gender*. Amityville, NY: Baywood.

Unger, R. K., (1990). Imperfect reflections of reality: Psychology and the construction of gender. In R. Hare-Mustin & J. Marecek (Eds.), *Making a difference: Representations of gender in psychology* (pp. 102–149). New Haven: Yale University Press.

Unger, R. K. (1992). Will the real sex difference please stand up? *Feminism & Psychology, 2*, 231–238.

Unger, R. K., & Crawford, M. (1989). Methods and values in decisions about gender differences (Review of Alice H. Eagly, *Sex differences in social behavior: A social role interpretation.*) *Contemporary Psychology, 34*, 122–123.

Unger, R., & Crawford, M. (1993). Commentary: Sex and gender–The troubled relationship between terms and concepts. *Psychological Science, 4*, 122–124.

Unger, R. K., Draper, R. D., & Pendergrass, M. L. (1986). Personal epistemology and personal experience. *Journal of Social Issues, 42*, 67–79.

Unger, R. K., Hilderbrand, M., & Madar, T. (1982). Physical attractiveness and assumptions about social deviance: Some sex by sex comparisons. *Personality and Social Psychology Bulletin, 8*, 293–301.

Unger, R. K., & Saundra (1993). Sexism: An integratory perspective. In F. L. Denmark & M. Paludi (Eds.), *Psychology of women: A handbook of issues and theories* (pp. 141–188). Westport, CT: Greenwood Press.

Unger, R. K., & Sussman, L. E. (1986). "I and thou": Another barrier to societal change? *Sex Roles, 14*, 629–636.

United Nations (1991a). *The world's women 1970–1990: Trends and statistics*. New York: United Nations.

United Nations (1991b). *Women: Challenges to the year 2000*. New York: United Nations.

U.S. Bureau of the Census (1989). *A statistical abstract of the United States*. Washington, DC: Government Printing Office.

U.S. Department of Labor (1977). *Dictionary of occupational titles*. Washington, DC: U.S. Government Printing Office.

U.S. Department of Labor, Woman's Bureau (1993, December). *Facts on Working Women* (No. 93-5). Washington, DC.

Urberg, K. A. (1982). The development of the concepts of masculinity and femininity in young children. *Sex Roles, 6*, 659–668.

Ussher, J. (1989). *The psychology of the female body*. London: Routledge.

Ussher, J. (1990). Choosing psychology or not throwing the baby out with the bathwater.

In E. Burman (Ed.), *Feminists and psychological practice* (pp. 47–61). London: Sage.

Vance, B. K., & Green, V. (1984). Lesbian identities: An examination of sexual behavior and sex role attribution as related to age of initial same-sex sexual encounter. *Psychology of Women Quarterly, 8,* 293–307.

Vance, C. S. (1984a). Pleasure and danger: Toward a politics of sexuality. In C. S. Vance (Ed.), *Pleasure and danger: Exploring female sexuality* (pp. 1–27). Boston: Routledge and Kegan Paul.

Vance, C. S. (Ed.) (1984b). *Pleasure and danger: Exploring female sexuality.* Boston: Routledge and Kegan Paul.

Vance, E. B., & Wagner, N. N. (1976). Written descriptions of orgasm: A study of sex differences. *Archives of Sexual Behavior, 5,* 87–98.

Vandenberg, S. G., & Kuse, A. R. (1979). Spatial ability: A critical review of the sex-linked major-gene hypothesis. In M. A. Wittig & A. C. Petersen (Eds.), *Sex-related differences in cognitive functioning: Developmental issues* (pp. 67–95). New York: Academic Press.

Vanek, J. (1984). Housewives as workers. In P. Voydanoff (Ed.), *Work and family: Changing roles of men and women* (pp. 89–103). Palo Alto, CA: Mayfield.

Verhovek, S. H. (1990, March 4). Girls win 51.3% in Regents Series. *New York Times,* p. 23.

Vernon, J. A., Williams, J. A., Jr., Phillips, T., & Wilson, J. (1991). Media stereotyping: A comparison of the way elderly women and men are portrayed on prime-time television. *Journal of Women & Aging, 2,* 55–68.

Veroff, J., Wilcox, S., & Atkinson, J. W. (1953). The achievement motive in high school and college age women. *Journal of Abnormal and Social Psychology, 43,* 108–119.

Vida, V. (Ed.) (1978). *Our right to love: A lesbian resource book.* Englewood Cliffs, NJ: Prentice-Hall.

Vobejda, B. (1994, June 16). Abortion rate slowing in U.S., study concludes. *Washington Post,* p. A13.

Voda, A. M. (1982). Menopausal hot flash. In A. M. Voda, M. Dinnerstein, & S. R. O'Donnell (Eds.), *Changing perspectives on menopause* (pp. 136–159). Austin: University of Texas Press.

Vogel, S. R., Broverman, I. K., Broverman, D. M., Clarkson, F. E., & Rosenkrantz, P. S. (1970). Maternal employment and perception of sex roles among college students. *Developmental Psychology, 3,* 384–391.

von Baeyer, C. L., Sherk, D. L., & Zanna, M. P. (1981). Impression management in the job interview: When the female applicant meets the male (chauvinist) interviewer. *Personality and Social Psychology Bulletin, 7,* 45–51.

Vredenburg, K., Krames, L., & Flett, G. L. (1986). Sex differences in the clinical expression of depression. *Sex Roles, 14,* 37–49.

Wahrman, R., & Pugh, M. D. (1972). Competence and conformity: Another look at Hollander's study. *Sociometry, 35,* 376–386.

Wahrman, R., & Pugh, M. D. (1974). Sex, nonconformity, and influence. *Sociometry, 37,* 137–147.

Walker, L. (1979). *The battered woman.* New York: Harper and Row.

Walker, L. (1983). Victimology and the psychological perspectives of battered women. *Victimology: An International Journal, 8,* 82–104.

Walker, L. (1984). *The battered woman syndrome.* New York: Springer.

Walker, L. (1989). Psychology and violence against women. *American Psychologist, 44,* 695–702.

Walker, L. (1993). The battered woman syndrome is a psychological consequence of abuse. In R. J. Gelles & D. R. Loseke (Eds.), *Current controversies on family violence* (pp. 133–153). Newbury Park, CA: Sage.

Walker, L. J. (1984). Sex differences in the development of moral reasoning: A critical review. *Child Development, 55,* 667–691.

Walker, L. J. (1986). Experiential and cognitive sources of moral development in adulthood. *Human Development, 29,* 113–124.

Wallston, B. S., & Grady, K. E. (1985). Integrating the feminist critique and the crisis in social psychology: Another look at research methods. In V. E. O'Leary, R. K. Unger, & B. S. Wallston (Eds.), *Women, gender and social psychology* (pp. 7–34). Hillsdale, NJ: Erlbaum.

Wallston, B. S., & O'Leary, V. E. (1981). Sex makes a difference: Differential perceptions of women and men. In L. Wheeler (Ed.), *Review of personality and social psychology,* Vol. 2 (pp. 9–41). Beverly Hills, CA: Sage.

Walsh, M. R. (1985). The psychology of women course: A continuing catalyst for change. *Teaching of Psychology, 12,* 198–203.

Walsh, M. R. (1987). *The psychology of women: Ongoing debates.* New Haven: Yale University Press.

Walum, L. R. (1974). The changing door ceremony: Notes on the operation of sex roles in everyday life. *Urban Life and Culture, 2,* 506–515.

Ware, M. C., & Stuck, M. F. (1985). Sex-role messages vis-a-vis microcomputer use: A look at the pictures. *Sex Roles, 13,* 205–214.

Warren, M. P. (1983). Physical and biological aspects of puberty. In J. Brooks-Gunn & A. C. Petersen (Eds.), *Girls at puberty* (pp. 3–28). New York: Plenum Press.

Warshaw, R. (1988). *I never called it rape: The Ms. report on recognizing, fighting and surviving date and acquaintance rape.* New York: Harper & Row.

Waterman, C., Dawson, L., & Bologna, M. (1989). Sexual coercion in gay and lesbian relationships: Predictors and implications for support services. *Journal of Sex Research, 26,* 118–124.

Watson, G., & Williams, J. (1992). Feminist practices in therapy. In J. M. Ussher & P. Nicolson (Eds.), *Gender issues in clinical psychology* (pp. 212–236). London: Routledge.

Watterson, B. (1991). *Scientific progress goes "boink".* New York: Andrews and McMeel.

Weaver, J. B., Masland, J. L., & Zillman, D. (1984). Effect of erotica on young men's aesthetic perception of their female sexual partners. *Perceptual Motor Skills, 58,* 929–930.

Webb, T. E., & VanDevere, C. A. (1985). Sex differences in the development of depression: A developmental interaction effect. *Sex Roles, 12,* 91–95.

Weidiger, P. (1975). *Menstruation and menopause.* New York: Knopf.

Weimann, G. (1985). Sex differences in dealing with bureaucracy. *Sex Roles, 12,* 777–790.

Weinraub, B. (1994, September 18). Meryl Streep's peculiar career. *New York Times Magazine,* 42–45.

Weinraub, M., Clemens, L. P., Sockloff, A., Ethridge, T., Gracely, E., & Myers, B. (1984). The development of sex role stereotypes in the third year: Relationships to gender labeling, gender identity, sex-typed toy preference, and family characteristics. *Child Development, 55,* 1493–1503.

Weisstein, N. (1968). *Kinder, Kirche, Kuche as scientific law: Psychology constructs the female.* Boston: New England Free Press.

Weitz, R., & Gordon, L. (1993). Images of black women among Anglo students. *Sex Roles, 28,* 19–34.

Weitzman, L. (1985). *The divorce revolution.* New York: Free Press.

Weitzman, L. J. (1979). *Sex role socialization.* Palo Alto, CA: Mayfield.

Weitzman, N., Birns, B., & Friend, R. (1985). Traditional and nontraditional mothers' communication with their daughters and sons. *Child Development, 56,* 894–898.

Werner, P. D., & LaRussa, G. W. (1985). Persistence and change in sex-role stereotypes. *Sex Roles, 12,* 1089–1100.

Wertz, D. C. (1992). How parents of affected children view selective abortion. In H. B. Holmes (Ed.), *Issues in reproductive technology* (pp. 161–189). New York: Garland.

West, C., & Zimmerman, D. H. (1987). Doing gender. *Gender & Society, 1,* 125–151.

Westney, O. E., Jenkins, R. R., & Benjamin, C. A. (1983). Sociosexual development of preadolescents. In J. Brooks-Gunn & A. C. Petersen (Eds.), *Girls at puberty* (pp. 273–300). New York: Plenum Press.

Westoff, C. F., Potter, R. G., Jr., & Sagi, P. C. (1963). *The third child.* Princeton, NJ: Princeton University Press.

Weston, P. J., & Mednick, M. T. S. (1970). Race, social class, and the motive to avoid success in women. *Journal of Cross-Cultural Psychology, 1,* 283–291.

Whisnant, L., Brett, E., & Zegans, L. (1975). Implicit messages concerning menstruation in commercial educational materials prepared for young adolescent girls. *American Journal of Psychiatry, 132,* 815–820.

Whitbourne, S. (1986). *The me I know: A study of adult identity.* New York: Springer-Verlag.

White, J. M. (1987). Premarital cohabitation and marital stability in Canada. *Journal of Marriage and the Family, 49,* 641–647.

White, J. W., & Humphrey, J. A. (1990a, June). Assaultive stress; and its consequences for the victim's mental health and use of intoxicants. Paper presented at the Third International Conference on Social Stress Research. Regent's College, London, England.

White, J. W., & Humphrey, J. A. (1990b, March). A theoretical model of sexual assault: An empirical test. Paper presented at Symposium on Sexual Assault: Research, Treatment, and Education. Southeastern Psychological Association Meeting, Atlanta, GA.

White, J. W., & Humphrey, J. A. (1991). Young people's attitudes toward rape. In A. Parrot & L. Bechhofer (Eds.), *Acquaintance rape: The hidden crime* (pp. 43–56). New York: Wiley.

White, J. W., & Humphrey, J. A. (1992, August). Predictors of repeated victimization. Paper presented at the meeting of the American Psychological Association.

White, J. W., & Humphrey, J. A. (1994a, March).

The relationship between perceived justification for forced sexual intercourse and self-reported sexual aggression. Paper presented at Southeastern Psychological Association, New Orleans.

White, J. W., & Humphrey, J. A. (1994b, July). Alcohol/drug use and sexual aggression: Distal and proximal influences. Paper presented at XI World Meeting: International Society for Research on Aggression. Delray Beach, FL.

White, J. W., & Koss, M. P. (1991). Courtship violence: Incidence in a national sample of higher education students. *Violence and Victims, 6,* 247–256.

White, J. W., & Koss, M. P. (1993). Adolescent sexual aggression within heterosexual relationships: Prevalence, characteristics, and causes. In H. E. Barbarbee, W. L. Marshall, & D. R. Laws (Eds.), *The juvenile sexual offender* (pp. 182–202). New York: Guilford.

White, J. W., Koss, M. P., & Kissling, G. (1991, June). Gender differences in structural models of courtship violence. Poster presented at American Psychological Society, Washington, DC.

White, J. W., & Kowalski, R. M. (1994). Deconstructing the myth of the nonaggressive woman: A feminist analysis. *Psychology of Women Quarterly, 18,* 477–498.

White, J. W., & Roufail, M. (1989). Gender and influence strategies of first choice and last resort. *Psychology of Women Quarterly, 13,* 175–189.

Whiting, B. B., & Edwards, C. P. (1973). A cross-cultural analysis of sex differences in the behavior of children aged three through eleven. *Journal of Social Psychology, 91,* 171–188.

Whitley, B. E., Jr. (1983). Sex-role orientation and self-esteem: A critical meta-analytic review. *Journal of Personality and Social Psychology, 44,* 765–785.

Whitley, B. E., Jr. (1985). Sex-role orientation and psychological well-being: Two meta-analyses. *Sex Roles, 12,* 207–225.

Whitley, B. E., Jr. (1987). The relationship of sex-role orientation to heterosexuals' attitudes toward homosexuals. *Sex Roles, 17,* 103–113.

Wiest, W. M. (1977). Semantic differential profiles of orgasm and other experiences among men and women. *Sex Roles, 3,* 399–403.

Wikan, U. (1977). Man becomes woman: Transsexualism in Oman as a key to gender roles. *Man, 12,* 304–319.

Wilder, D. A. (1986). Social categorization: Implications for creation and reduction of intergroup bias. In L. Berkowitz (Ed.), *Advances in experimental social psychology,* Vol. 19. Orlando, FL: Academic Press.

Wiley, M. G., & Eskilson, A. (1982). Coping in the corporation: Sex role constraints. *Journal of Applied Social Psychology, 12,* 1–11.

Wilkinson, D. Y. (1980). Minority women: Social-cultural issues. In A. M. Brodsky & R. Hare-Mustin (Eds.), *Women and psychotherapy* (pp. 285–304). New York: Guilford.

Williams, J. E., & Best, D. L. (1990). *Measuring sex stereotypes: A multination study.* Newbury Park, CA: Sage.

Williams, L. R. (1983). Beliefs and attitudes of young girls regarding menstruation. In S. Golub (Ed.), *Menarche* (pp. 139–148). Lexington, MA: Lexington Books.

Williams, L. S. (1992). Biology or society? Parenthood motivation in a sample of Canadian women seeking in vitro fertilization. In H. B. Holmes (Ed.), *Issues in reproductive technology* (pp. 261–274). New York: Garland.

Williams, N. (1990). *The Mexican American family: Tradition and change.* New York: General Hall.

Williams, W. L. (1986). *The spirit and the flesh: Sexual diversity in American Indian culture.* Boston: Beacon Press.

Williams, W. L. (1987). Women, men, and others: Beyond ethnocentrism in gender theory. *American Behavioral Scientist, 31,* 135–141.

Willis, S. L., & Schaie, K. W. (1988). Gender differences in spatial ability in old age: Longitudinal and intervention findings. *Sex Roles, 18,* 189–204.

Wilson, B. J., Linz, D., Donnerstein, E., & Stipp, H. (1992). The impact of social issue television programming on attitudes toward rape. *Human Communication Research, 19,* 179–208.

Wilson, E., & Ng, S. H. (1988). Sex bias in visual images evoked by generics: A New Zealand study. *Sex Roles, 18,* 159–168.

Wilson, J. D., George, F. W., & Griffin, J. E. (1981). The hormonal control of sexual development. *Science, 211,* 1278–1284.

Wine, J. D. (1981). From defect to competence models. In J. D. Wine & M. D. Smye (Eds.), *Social competence* (pp. 3–35). New York: Guilford.

Wine, J. D., Moses, B., & Smye, M. D. (1980). Female superiority in sex difference competence comparisons: A review of the literature. In C. Stark-Adamec (Ed.), *Sex roles: Origins, influences, and implications for women*. Montreal: Eden.

Witkin, H. A. (1949). The nature and importance of individual differences in perception. *Journal of Personality, 18*, 145–170.

Witkin, H. A. (1967). A cognitive-style approach to cross-cultural research. *International Journal of Psychology, 2*, 233–250.

Witkin, H. A., Dyk, R. B., Faterson, H. F., Goodenough, D. R., & Karp, S. A. (1962). *Psychological differentiation: Studies of development*. New York: Wiley.

Witkin, H. A., Mednick, S. A., Schulsinger, F., Bakkestrom, E., Christiansen, K. O., Goodenough, D. R., Hirschhorn, K., Lundsteen, C., Owen, D. R., Philip, J., Rubin, D. B., & Stocking, M. (1976). Criminality in XXY and XYY men. *Science, 193*, 547–555.

Wittig, M. A. (1985). Metatheoretical dilemmas in the psychology of gender. *American Psychologist, 40*, 800–811.

Wolman, C., & Frank, H. (1975). The solo woman in a professional peer group. *American Journal of Orthopsychiatry, 45*, 164–171.

Women's Programs Office (1991). *Graduate faculty interested in psychology of women*. Washington, DC: American Psychological Association.

Wood, A. D., & McHugh, M. C. (1994). Woman battering: The response of the clergy. *Pastoral Psychology, 42*, 185–196.

Wood, W., & Karten, S, J. (1986). Sex differences in interactive style as a product of perceived sex differences in competence. *Journal of Personality and Social Psychology, 50*, 341–347.

Wood, W., & Rhodes, N. (1992). Sex differences in interaction style in task groups. In C. L. Ridgeway (Ed.), *Gender, interaction, and inequality* (pp. 97–121). New York: Springer-Verlag.

Woods, N. F., Dery, G. K, & Most, A. (1983). Recollections of menarche, current menstrual attitudes, and perimenstrual symptoms. In S. Golub (Ed.), *Menarche: The transition from girl to woman* (pp. 87–97). Lexington, MA: Lexington Books.

Wooley, H. T. (1910). Psychological literature: A review of the recent literature on the psychology of sex. *Psychological Bulletin, 7*, 335–342.

Wooley, S. C,, & Wooley, O. W. (1980). Eating disorders: Anorexia and obesity. In A. M. Brodsky & R. Hare-Mustin (Eds.), *Women and psychotherapy* (pp. 135–158). New York: Guilford.

Woollett, A., White, D., & Lyon, L. (1982). Fathers' involvement with their infants: The role of holding. In N. Beail & J. McGuire (Eds.), *Fathers: Psychological perspectives*. London: Junction.

Worell, J. (1981). Lifespan sex roles: Development, continuity, and change. In R. N. Lerner & N. A. Busch-Rossnagel (Eds.), *Individuals as producers of their development* (pp. 313–346). New York: Academic Press.

Worell, J. (1988). Women's satisfaction in close relationships. *Clinical Psychology Review, 8*, 477–498.

Worell, J., & Remer, P. (1992). *Feminist perspectives in therapy: An empowerment model for women*. New York: Wiley.

Worell, J., & Robinson, D. (1994). Reinventing analogue methods for research with women. *Psychology of Women Quarterly, 18*, 463–476.

Workman, J. E., & Johnson, K. K. P. (1991). The role of cosmetics in attributions about sexual harassment. *Sex Roles, 24*, 759–769.

World Wire (1993, December 21). China proposed eugenics law. *Wall Street Journal*, A6.

Worth, D. M., Matthews, P. A., & Coleman, W. R. (1990). Sex role, group affiliation, family background, and courtship violence in college students. *Journal of College Student Development, 31*, 250–254.

Wyatt, G. E. (1985). The sexual abuse of Afro-American and White-American women in childhood. *Child Abuse and Neglect, 9*, 507–519.

Wyatt, G. (1991). Sociocultural context of African American and White American women's rape. *Journal of Social Issues, 48*, 77–92.

Wyatt, G. E., Guthrie, G., & Notgrass, C. M. (1992). Differential effects of women's child sexual abuse and subsequent sexual revictimization. *Journal of Consulting and Clinical Psychology, 60*, 167–173.

Wyatt, G. E., & Riederle, M. H. (1994). Reconceptualizing issues that affect women's sexual decision-making and sexual functioning. *Psychology of Women Quarterly, 18*, 611–626.

Wynn, R. L., & Fletcher, C. (1987). Sex role development and early educational experiences. In D. B. Carter (Ed.), *Current conceptions of sex roles and sex typing: Theory and research* (pp. 79–88). New York: Praeger.

Yarkin, K. L., Town, J. P., Wallston, B. S. (1982). Blacks and women must try harder: Stimulus persons' race and sex and attributions of causality. *Personality and Social Psychology Bulletin, 8*, 21–30.

Yee, B. W. K. (1990). Gender and family issues in minority groups. *Generations, 14*, 39–42.

Yllo, K., & Bograd, M. (Eds.) (1988). *Feminist perspectives on wife abuse*. Beverly Hills, CA: Sage.

Yoder, J. D. (1985). An academic woman as a token: A case study. *Journal of Social Issues, 41*, 61–72.

Yoder, J. D., Adams, J., Grove, S., & Priest, R. F. (1985). To teach is to learn: Overcoming tokenism with mentors. *Psychology of Women Quarterly, 9*, 119–132.

Yoder, J. D., Crumpton, P. L., & Zipp, J. F. (1989). The power of numbers in influencing hiring decisions. *Gender & Society, 3*, 269–276.

Yoder, J. D., & Kahn, A. S. (1992). Toward a feminist understanding of women and power. *Psychology of Women Quarterly, 16*, 381–388.

Yoder, J. D., & Sinnett, L. M. (1985). Is it all in the numbers? A case study of tokenism. *Psychology of Women Quarterly, 9*, 413–418.

Zahaykevich, M., Sirey, J. A., & Brooks-Gunn, J. (Unpublished). Mother-daughter individuation during early adolescence. Cited in J. Brooks-Gunn & M. Zahaykevich (1988).

Zander, A., & Van Egmond, E. (1958). Relationship of intelligence and social power to the interpersonal behavior of children. *Journal of Educational Psychology, 49*, 257–268.

Zanna, M. P., & Pack, S. J. (1975). On the self-fulfilling nature of apparent sex differences in behavior. *Journal of Experimental Social Psychology, 11*, 583–591.

Zelnik, M., Kantner, J. F., & Ford, K. (1981). *Sex and pregnancy in adolescence*. Beverly Hills, CA: Sage.

Zelnik, M., & Shah, F. K. (1983). First intercourse among young Americans. *Family Planning Perspectives, 15*, 64–70.

Zevy, L., with Cavallaro, S. A. (1987). Invisibility, fantasy, and intimacy: Princess Charming is not a prince. In Boston Lesbian Psychologists Collective (Eds.), *Lesbian psychologies: Explorations and challenges* (pp. 83–94). Urbana: University of Illinois Press.

Zillmann, D., & Bryant, J. (1986). Shifting preferences in pornography consumption. *Communications Research, 13*, 560–578.

Zimmerman, M. K. (1987). The women's health movement: A critique of medical enterprise and the position of women. In B. B. Hess & M. M. Ferree (Eds.), *Analyzing gender* (pp. 442–472). Newbury Park, CA: Sage.

Zinkhan, G. M., & Stoiadin, L. F. (1984). Impact of sex role stereotypes on service priority in department stores. *Journal of Applied Psychology, 69*, 691–693.

Zita, J. N. (1993). Heresy in the female body: The rhetoric of menopause. In J. C. Callahan (Ed.), *Menopause: A midlife passage* (pp. 59–78). Bloomington: University of Indiana Press.

Zuckerman, M., & Kieffer, S. C. (1994). Race differences in faceism: Does facial prominence imply dominance? *Journal of Personality and Social Psychology, 66*, 86–92.

Permissions Acknowledgments

Permission to reprint is gratefully acknowledged for the following:

Page 43: From Lawrence Kohlberg, "A cognitive developmental analysis of children's sex role concepts and attitudes." In E.E. Maccoby (Ed.), *The Development of Sex Differences*, pp. 82-173. © 1966 Stanford University Press. Reprinted by permission.

Page 88: Reprinted with permission of Scribner, a Division of Simon & Schuster, Inc. from *Failing at Fairness* by Myra and David Sadker. Copyright © 1994 Myra and David Sadker.

Page 146: From *Women: A Feminist Perspective*, 4th ed., by Jo Freeman, edited by permission of Mayfield Publishing Company. Copyright © 1989 by Mayfield Publishing Company.

Page 197: From Stephen Jay Gould, *The Mismeasure of Man*, pp. 104-105. Copyright © 1981 W.W. Norton & Company. Reprinted by permission.

Page 213: From Diamond, "Sexual identity, monozygotic twins reared in discordant sex roles and a BBC follow-up," *Archives of Sexual Behavior, 11:* 183. Copyright © 1982 Plenum Publishing Corporation. Reprinted by permission.

Pages 222-223: From the book *He & She: How Children Develop Their Sex-Role Identity*, by Jeanne Brooks-Gunn and Wendy Schempp Matthews © 1979. Reprinted by permission of Prentice Hall.

Page 251: From M. A. Messner, "Ah, ya throw like a girl!" In M.A. Messner and D.F. Sabo (Eds.), *Sex, Violence and Power in Sports: Rethinking Masculinity*, pages 29-30. The Crossing Press, Freedom, CA, 1994. Reprinted by permission of Michael A. Mesner.

Page 271: From Delaney et al., *The Curse: A Cultural History of Menstruation* (rev. ed.), p. 126. 1988 University of Illinois Press. Reprinted by permission.

Page 272: Excerpt from *A Tree Grows in Brooklyn* by Betty Smith. Copyright 1943, 1947 by Betty Smith. Copyright renewed 1971 by Betty Smith (Finch). Reprinted by permission of HarperCollins Publishers, Inc.

Page 273: From *The Woman in the Body* by Emily Martin © 1987, 1992 by Emily Martin. Reprinted by permission of Beacon Press.

Page 285: From Larkin and Popaleni, "Heterosexual courtship violence and sexual harrassment: The private and public control of young women," *Feminism and Psychology, 4,* 220. Copyright © 1994, by permission of Sage Publications, Ltd.

Page 288: From K. Peirce, "Socialization of teenage girls through teen-magazine fiction: The making of a new woman or an old lady" *Sex Roles, 29:* 64. Copyright © 1993 Plenum Publishing Corporation. Reprinted by permission.

Page 291: From bell hooks, *Talking Back: Thinking Feminist, Thinking Black*, page 149. Copyright © 1989 South End Press. Reprinted by permission.

Page 293: From Zevy, "Invisibility, fantasy and intimacy: Princess Charming is not a prince. In Boston Lesbian Psychologists Collective (Eds.), *Lesbian Psychologies: Explorations and Challenges*, pages 85-87. 1987 University of Illinois Press. Reprinted with permission.

Pages 302-303: Reprinted by permission of Curtis Brown Ltd. Copyright © 1980 by University of Massachusetts Press. First appeared in two-headed woman. Published by University of Massachusetts Press.

Page 324: From Michael Moffatt, *Coming of Age in New Jersey*, copyright © 1989 by Rutgers, The State University. Reprinted by permission of Rutgers University Press.
Page 337: From Kitzinger, *The Social Construction of Lesbianism*, pp. 99, 110, 113. Copyright 1987, by permission of Sage Publications Ltd.
Page 422-424: From Katherine Gieve (Ed.), *Balancing Acts: On Being a Mother*. 1989 Virago Press Ltd. Reprinted by permission of Katherine Gieve.
Pages 449-450: From Barbara A. Gutek, *Sex and the Workplace: The Impact of Sexual Behavior and Harassment on Women, Men, and Organizations*, pp. 80, 82, 89. Copyright 1985 by Jossey-Bass, Inc. Publishers. Reprinted by permission.
Page 458: From Hunter, "Pediatrician," in R.B. Kundsin (Ed.), *Women and Success: The Anatomy of Achievement*, pp. 58-61. 1974. Morrow.
Pages 499-500: From Doress-Worters, Paula B., and Diana Laskin Siegal in cooperation with the Boston Women's Health Book Collective. *The New Ourselves, Getting Older: Women Aging with Knowledge and Power*. New York: Simon and Schuster, 1994. Reprinted by permission of Diana Laskin Siegal and Paula D. Doress-Worters.
Page 514: From "With no immediate cause." In *Nappy Edges* by Ntozake Shange, St. Martin's Press, Inc., New York. Copyright © 1972, 1974, 1975, 1976, 1977, 1978 by Ntozake Shange.
Pages 561-562: From John and Sussman, "Initiative taking as a determinant of role reciprocal organization." *Representations: Social Constructions of Gender*, edited by Rhoda Unger. Copyright © 1989 Baywood Publishing Company, Inc. Reprinted with permission.
Page 586: From Smith and Douglas, "Empowerment as an ethical imperative." In H. Lerman and N. Porter (eds.), *Feminist Ethics in Psychotherapy*, pp. 43-50. 1990 Springer Publishing Company, Inc., New York 10012. Used by permission.

Photo Credits

Page 34: Elizabeth Crews/The Image Works; p. 39: Kathy Sloane; p. 44: Elizabeth Crews/Stock, Boston; p. 56: J. Fossett/The Image Works; p. 63: David Longstreet/AP Wide World; p. 89: John Coletti/Stock, Boston; p. 102: (bottom left), Patrick Watson/The Image Works; (bottom right), Rhoda Sidney/The Image Works; (top right), Bob Daemmrich/The ImageWorks; (top left) Kerbs/Monkmeyer; p. 114: John Iacono/Sports Illustrated; p. 115: Jeff Vinnick/Reuters/Bettman; p. 120: Time, Inc. © 1993, reprinted by permission; p. 128: Courtesy of MGM; p. 133: Bruce Young/New York Times Pictures; p. 138: Reuters; p. 147: Porter and Geis, 1981; p. 150: Globe Photos/AK; p. 165: (bottom), AP/Wide World Photos; (top), John Duricka/AP/Wide World Photos; p. 177: Barbara Hansen; p. 184: © 1995 Newsweek, Inc. All rights reserved. Reprinted by permission. Photo by Doug Levere; p. 187: Frank O'Connell/New York Times; p. 194: Penny Gentieu © 1992 Newsweek, Inc. All rights reserved. Reprinted by permission; p. 217: Holly DeVor; p. 227: Dr. M. Kahn/UNICEF; p. 244: © 1990 Newsweek, Inc. All rights reserved. Reprinted by permission; p. 259: Sam Ogden, Reprinted with permission from Science, Volume 260, April 16, 1993, and Sam Ogden; p. 277: (left), William Stevens/Gamma-Liaison; (right), Capital Features/The Image Works; p. 287: Anne Manning; p. 309: Archives of the History of American Psychology; p. 405: Suzanne Arms/The Image Works; p. 410: Photo by Michele Maier; p. 422: Steve Jacobs/Albany *Times-Union*; p. 436: Spencer Grant/Stock, Boston; p. 503: © 1990 Newsweek, Inc. All rights reserved. Reprinted by permission; p. 510: Elizabeth Layton; p. 519: © 1994 Donna Ferrato/DOMESTIC ABUSE AWARENESS PROJECT, NYC from the book "Living With the Enemy" (Aperture); p. 534: Michael Sulik/The Image Works; p. 545: Alan Carey/The Image Works; p. 570: Barbara Hansen; p. 573: (left), UPI/Bettman; (right), Bonnie Schiffman/Onyx.

Author Index

Abrams, D., 255
Abramson, P. E., 442–443
Achte, K., 488
Adams, K. L., 21, 322
Adams, M., 369
Adelmann, P. K., 497, 499
Ader, D. N., 13
Adler, A., 32
Adolph, M. A., 476
Affonso, D. D., 405
Aguilar, R. J., 547
Aida, Y., 359
Aizenman, M., 535
Alagna, S., 578
Alazorov-Por, N., 96
Albert, J. L., 393
Aldous, J., 353
Alington, D. E., 507
Allan, J. S., 320
Allen, I. L., 124
Allen, L. S., 193
Allgood-Merten, B., 282
Allport, G. W., 144
Almquist, E. M., 416, 418, 434
Alper, T. G., 455
Alpert, D., 464
Altman, M., 328, 330, 334
Amaro, H., 395, 460, 464
American Psychiatric Association, 576
Amir, M., 536
Anderson, J. V., 255
Angier, N., 187, 190
Angrist, S., 583
Anson, O., 492, 498
Apfelbaum, E., 170, 179, 451

Note: Because of space considerations, only the names of first authors are listed in this index. Second authors are listed only if they are also first authors of other articles. Page numbers in italics indicate figures; page numbers followed by t indicate tables.

Archer, D., 121, 137
Arms, S., 404, *405*
Arnold, F., 226
Asch, A., 163
Astin, A. W., 349
Astin, H. S., 427, 459
Attie, I., 277, 278, 290
Attorney General's Commission on Pornography, 517, 520
Auerbach, J., 49

Baber, K. M., 392, 397, 398, 428, 429, 445, 469
Baenninger, M., 84
Baker, S. W., 201
Ballinger, S., 483
Banaji, M. R., 142, 151, 152
Bandura, A., 37, 41, 42, 60
Barak, A., 235
Bardwell, J. R., 250, 256
Barnett, O. W., 546
Barnett, R. C., 477, 495, 498
Bart, P. B., 13, 484, 488, 489, 490, 491t, 496
Bar-Tal, D., 317
Baruch, G. K., 389, 391, 430, 431, 432, 439, 464, 504, 505
Basow, S. A., 448, 570
Bass, E., 523, 526, 527
Basset, B., *112*
Bassoff, E. S., 53
Beasley, R., 546
Beatrice, J., 216
Beck, J. C., 577
Beck, R. W., 502
Becker, H. S., 164
Beckman, L. J., 498
Beckstein, D., 295
Beckwith, B., 98
Belk, S. S., 341
Belknap, J., 537
Bell, I. P., 474, 476, 477
Bem, S. L., 24, 45, 51, 52, 53, 55, 57, 58, 59, 60, 76, 125, 139, 252, 352, 440
Bemis, K. M., 572
Benbow, C. P., 85, 90, 91
Beneke, T., 519
Benokraitis, N. V., 166
Bentley, *425*
Bequaert, L., 368, 369
Berardo, D. H., 355
Berebaum, S. A., 207
Bergen, D. J., 140
Berger, P. L., 21
Berger, R. M., 365
Bergman, L., 529
Berk, R. A., 550
Berman, P. W., 240
Bermant, G., 185
Bernal, M. E., 60
Bernard, J., 349, 357, 358, 384, 386, 387, 463, 464
Berryman-Fink, C., 9
Bersoff, D., 464
Bethke, T. M., 528
Betz, N. E., 434, 435, 437, 438, 439, 440, 444, 452, 453, 458t, 460, 464, 466
Beutell, N. J., 452
Beyene, Y., 480
Bianchi, S. M., 347, 348, 350, 366, *366*, 368, 371, *371*, 375
Billingham, R. E., 527, 528
Birrell, S. J., 205
Bishop, N., 392, 393, 394
Bjorkqvist, K., 245
Black, S. M., 497, 498
Blair, S. L., 428
Blakely, M. K., 517
Blanchard, R., 215, 216
Blechman, E. A., 559
Bleier, Ruth, 76, 77, 198, 199
Block, J. H., 41, 55, 74, 247
Blood, R. O., 354
Blum, R. W., 292
Blumstein, P. W., 333, 347, 350, 353, 354, 355, 356, 361, 363, 364, 365, 367, 376, *377*, 379
Boardman, S. K., 459
Bogal-Allbritten, R., 532

Bograd, M., 342, 543, 544
Bohmer, C., 540
Bolen, J. S., *103*
Bolin, A., 218
Bolz, B., 509
Bond, S., 320
Bondurant, B., 513, 538
Bookwala, J., 530
Bordo, S., 279
Bose, C. E., 434
Boswell, S. L., 86, 89, 90
Bouhoutsos, J., 588
Boyd, B., 329
Boyd, J. A., 590, 591
Brabant, S., 112
Bradbard, M. R., 237
Braden, A., 460, 461
Bradley, C., 255
Brand, P. A., 543, 544
Bransford, J. D., 58, 59
Breay, E., 324
Breene, D., 408
Brehony, K. A., 575
Breines, W., 526
Bremer, T. H., 455
Bretl, D. J., 116
Bridges, J. S., 228, 465
Briere, J., 126, 520, 544
Brinkerhoff, D. B., 170
Broca, P.-P., 197
Brod, H., 220
Brodsky, A., 585
Brody, E., 502
Brooks-Gunn, J., 223, 225, 235, 263, 264, 265, 268, 274, 275, 276t, 278, 281, 282, 283, 284, 286, 289, 290, 295, 296, 297, *298,* 300
Broughton, J. M., 49
Broverman, I. K., 107, 580
Brown, B. A., 254
Brown, D. R., 501, 506
Brown, E. A., 312
Brown, J. D., 119
Brown, J. K., 490
Brown, L. S., 37, 65, 555, 565, 577, 579, 586, 592
Brown, L. M., 284
Browne, A., 526, 544, 545
Brownmiller, Susan, 534
Brumberg, J. J., 574
Bryant, B. K., 83, 238
Bryden, M. P., 198
Bryer, J. B., 577
Buhl, M., 9
Bumagin, V. E., 477
Burcky, W., 529
Burnett, S. A., 79
Burns, A., 247, 255
Burns, J., 568
Busby, L. J., 111
Bush, T. L., 482
Buss, D. M., 137, 348
Bussey, K., 42, 60
Butcher, J. E., 289
Butler, D., 161
Butler, L. D., 564
Butler, R. N., 473
Buzawa, E. S., 550

Caldera, Y. M., 233
Calderone, K. L., 581
Caldwell, M. A., 341, 364
Calof, D., 525
Cameron, E., 238
Campbell, J. C., 547
Campbell, K. E., 160
Canetto, S. S., 506
Canino, G. J., 592
Canter, R., 454
Cantor, M. G., 120
Cantos, A. L., 547, 548
Caplan, P. J., 79, 198, 424, 426, 579–580
Cardell, M., 364
Carli, L. L., 161
Carlson, B. E., 494
Carmen, E. H., 580
Carpenter, C. Jan, 256
Carter, D. B., 251
Cash, T. F., 121, 320, 442
Cass, V. C., 60, 336
Cate, C. A., 528
Cate, R., 289
Chacko, T. I., 179
Chaffin, R. J., 385
Chaikin, S., 570
Chambless, D. L., 559, 574, 575
Chan, C. S., 339
Chandani, A. T., 321
Chapkis, W., 321
Charlesworth, W. R., 242
Chavez, D., 112
Check, J., 517, 518, 519
Chehrazi, S., 33
Cherlin, A. J., 375, 378
Cherry, F., 455
Chesler, P., 556, 583
Chi, J. G., 199
Chicago, J., 408, *410*
Childs, E. K., 589, 592
Chilman, C. S., 291, 295, 296, 297
Chipman, S. F., 85, 87, 88, 91
Chodorow, N., 39, 388
Chow, E. N., 460
Chrisler, J. C., 475, 479, 565
Chusmir, L. H., 454
Ciancanelli, P., 430, 435
Cleek, M. G., 372, *372*
Clifton, L., 302, 303, 330
Coates, D. L., 286
Code, L. B., 48
Cohen, B. P., 158
Cohen, C. E., 152
Colby, A., 49
Colen, S., 465
Coles, R., 313, 323
Collins, P. H., 119, 416, 418, 419, 437, 456, 518
Comas-Diaz, L., 592, 593
Committee on Women in Psychology, 577, 579
Comstock, G., 115
Condon, J., 402
Condry, J. C., Jr., 230
Condry, S. M., 230
Conner, J. M., 84, 85
Constantinople, A., 50
Cook, E. P., 49, 51, 53
Cooper, V. W., 124
Corbett, K., 321
Corley, M. C., 437
Costello, C., 370, 376
Cota, A. A., 156
Courtois, C. A., 522, 524
Covey, H. C., 472, 473t
Cowan, G., 119, 136, 254, 288, 289, 483, 518
Coward, R. T., 501
Cowen, J. R., 95, 450
Craig, R. S., 116
Crawford, M., 2–3, 15, 17, 22, 24, 57, 59, 60, 76, 82, 90, 126, 448, 455, 463
Crawford, S., 419, 420
Crewdson, J., 527
Crews, J., 186, 188
Crittenden, D., 10
Crocker, J., 167, 180
Crockett, L. J., 277, 278
Croghan, R., 401
Crohan, S. E., 368
Crosbie-Burnett, M., 378
Crosby, F. J., 178, 179, 380, 445, 451, 463, 464
Crovitz, E., 292, 351
Culp, R. E., 232
Cummings, N., 541
Cusick, T., 292, 293, 295, 299

Daley, D., 394
D'Amico, R., 435
Dancer, L. S., 428
Danza, R., 283
Darnton, J., 394
Datan, N., 492, 493
Daubman, K. A., 176
Davis, C. M., 518
Davis, D. M., 116
Davis, M., 160
Dayhoff, S. A., 115
Deaux, K., 5, 21, 72, 108, 110, 110t, 131, 135, 316, 441–442, 455, 460, 461, 462
Dege, K., 490
De Groot, S. C., 507
DeLamater, J., 323
Delaney, J., 269, 271, 275

DeMaris, A., 530
D'Emilio, J., 306–307, 332, 521
Denmark, F. L., 12, 14, 15, 170
Deschamps, J-C., 156
Deutsch, F. M., 130, 172, 473
Deutsch, H., 32
Devor, H., 216
Dew, M. A., 130, 439
Dewhurst, A. M., 547
Di Leonardo, M., 432
Diamond, M. A., 186, 193, 201, 212, 213
DiBlasio, F. A., 291
Dickson, L., 347, 348
Dion, K. L., 127, 156, 167, 180, 314
Dion, K. K., 129, 154
DiPalma, L. M., 526
Dobash, R. P., 549
Dodson, B., 311
Doherty, W. J., 180
Dolan, E. M., 378
Donat, P. L. N., 513
Donnelly, L., *374*
Donnerstein, E., 520
Dorans. N. J., 85
Doress, P. B., 481, 483, 487, 499, 500, 504, 505, 507
Doress-Worters, P. B., 481
Dornbusch, S. M., 279, 282
Douglas, S. J., 8, 9, 10, 234
Dovidio, J. F., 159, 175, 175t
Downs. A. C., 116
Duncan, G. J., 376
Dunkle, J. H., 131
Dunlop, E., 488
Dutton, D., 545, 546, 550
Dworkin, A., 234, 330, 520
Dwyer, C. A., 87

Eagly, A. H., 75, 131, 132, 140, 169, 170, 171, 172, 173, 176
Eaton, W. O., 234
Eccles, J. S., 19, 73, 78, 87, 88, 89, 91, *92*, 95, 98, 453, 459
Eckes, T., 109
Edelson, M. S., 242
Edman, C. D., 475, 481, 482, 483, 486
Edwards, C. P., 239
Ehrenreich, B., 567, 568
Ehrhardt, A. A., 196, 206, 208, 215
Eichler, M., 15, 215
Eisenberg, N., 238
Eldridge, N. S., 364
Elkind, S. N., 396
Elliot, R., 326
Elliot, S., 565
Ellyson, S. N., 159, 161, 162
Emmerich, W., 250
England, P., 116, 435, 437, 438, 451
Erikson, E. H., 32
Ernster, V. L., 273
Eron, L. D., 243

Espin, O. M., 60, 314, 315, 321, 323, 338, 593
Etaugh, C., 234, 247, 442, 465
Etter-Lewis, G., 112

Faderman, L., 332
Fagot, B. I., 45, 46, 229, 231, 232, 235, 239
Falbo, T., 341, 359
Falk, P. J., 420, 421
Faludi, S., 9, 389
Farel, A., 465
Faulkner, A. O., 494, 495
Faunce, P. S., 590
Faust, M. G., 276
Fausto-Sterling, A., 190, 193, 196
Feather, N. T., 564
Federal Bureau of Investigation, 533, 545
Feeney, J., 358
Feingold, A., 79, 85, 93, 96, 98
Feinman, S., 250
Feiring, C., 83, 238, 239, 279
Feldman, R. S., 449
Feldman-Summers, S., 442
Fenell, D. L., 360, 360t
Fernberger, S. W., 106
Ferrato, D., *545*
Ferree, M. M., 428, 440, 452, 456, 461, 462
Fidell, L. S., 444, 581, 582
Field, T., 299
Fine, M., 2, 97, 163, 280, 283, 291, 292, 293, 294, 300, 321, 329, 330, 561, 562
Finkel, J. S., 358
Finkelhor, D., 522, 524, 525, 544
Finlay, B., 53
Fischer, J. L., 509
Fisher, J. D., 176
Fisher, W., 291
Fiske, A. P., 148
Fiske, S. T., 106, 133, 134, 142, 148, 151
Fitzgerald, L. F., 444, 449, 450, 462
Fivush, R., 230, 250
Flanders, L., 386
Flint, M., 480
Foa, E. B., 515
Fodor, I. G., 559t, 575
Follingstad, D. R., 530
Ford, C. V., 580
Ford, M. R., 49
Fordham, S., 285
Foreit, K. G., 113
Forisha, B. L., 50, 56
Forward, J. R., 181
Foschi, M., 168
Foucalt, M., 303
Fowers, B. J., 358
Frable, D. E. S., 59
Frank, A., 52, 273
Frank, E., 327

Franks, V., 558
Franz, C. E., 65
Frasher, R. S., 234
Freedman, R., 317, 319, 320
Freud, S., 31, 383
Frey, C., 245
Friday, N., 330
Friedman, A., 491
Friedman, H., 131
Frieze, I. H., 16, 305t, 548
Frisch, R. E., 266, 267
Furby, L., 180
Furnham, A., 118
Furstenberg, F. F., Jr., 291, 296, 297, 298, 299

Gagnon, J. H., 294, 304
Gaiter, D., 457
Galambos, N. L., 287, 288
Galanis, C. M. B., 139
Galler, R., 321
Galligan, R. F., 329
Gama, E. P., 454
Gannon, L. R., 13, 479, 480, 481, 488, 489
Garcia, N., 365
Garland, A. W., 511
Garland, H., 442
Garn, S. M., 202
Garner, D. M., 319
Gaskill, L. R., 449
Gastil, J., 125
Gauna-Trujillo, B., 403
Gayford, J. J., 532
Geis, F. L., 122, 134, 161, 169, *169*, 172
Gelles, R. J., 543, 546
Gelwick, B. P., 450
Gentile, D. A., 21
Gentry, M., 27
Geraghty, C., 116
Gergen, M. M., 496
Gerike, A. E., 475
Gerson, M., 391
Gerstel, N., 373
Gervasio, A. H., 468
Geschwind, N., 199
Giacomini, M., 127
Gibber, J. R., 195
Gibbons, J. L., 287
Giddings, P., 418
Gidycz, C. A., 536
Gieve, K., 422
Gilbert, D. T., 142
Gilbert, L. A., 379, 428, 448, 449, 463, 464, 585, 586, 588
Gilbert, S. M., 554
Gillen, B., 130
Gilligan, C., 46, 47, 65, 284
Gillman, R. D., 226
Gilmore, D. D., 103

Ginorio, A., 593
Glenn, N. D., 498
Goffman, Erving, 163
Gold, A. R., 256
Goldberg, A. C., 540
Goldberg, P. A., 138, 442
Golden, C., 333, 335, 336
Goldfoot, D. A., 195, 196
Golding, J. M., 564
Goldman, K., 116
Goldman, W., 154
Goldstein, D., 547
Goleman, D., 199
Golombok, S., 250
Goodchilds, J. D., 533, 537
Goodman, M. J., 480, 485
Gordon, C., 155, 156
Gordon, J. W., 188
Gordon, L., 549
Gordon, R. R., 226
Gottman, J. M., 242
Gough, K., 347
Gould, L. 72, 252, 253
Gould, S. J., 76, 197
Gove, W. R., 358, 373, 506
Goy, R. W., 195
Grady, K. E., 1–2, 72, 148
Graham, A., 124
Grambs, J. D., 477, 493, 494, 499, 508, 509, 510
Gravenkemper, S. A., 456
Gray, J. D., 463
Grayson, D. A., 294
Green, R., 218
Greene, A. L., 281
Greene, B. A., 418, 589, 591, 592
Greenglass, E. R., 465
Greenspan, M., 583, 584, 586, 588
Greenwood-Audant, L. M., 373
Griffin, S., 551, 552
Grimm, D. E., 215
Griscom, J. L., 157
Groth, A. N., 517
Gruber, J. E., 450, 462
Guinn, S., 380
Gutek, B. A., 355, 443, 449, 450, 464
Guthrie, Robert V., 4
Gwartney-Gibbs, P. A., 530

Haaken, J., 80
Haavind, H., 380
Haddock, G., 140–141
Hafner, R. J., 575
Hagan, J. L., 544
Hagestad, G. O., 493, 494
Hale, G., 546–547
Hall, J. A., 53, 160, 172
Hall, M., 394
Hall, N. L., 402
Halpern, D., 78, 79, 80, *80*, 85, 98
Hamberger, L. K., 545
Hamburg, B. A., 291
Hamer, D. H., 193
Hamilton, Jean A., 578
Hamilton, L. H., 279
Hamilton, M. C., 126
Hamilton, M. C., 125, 126
Hamilton, S., 579
Hammen, C. L., 563
Hammer, M., 225
Hammond, J. A., 460, 461
Hamod, K., 258
Hansen, F. J., 580
Hanson, K. A., 541
Harding, S., 76
Hardon, A., 392
Hare-Mustin, R. T., 2, 12, 49, 560, 585
Harlan, S. L., 460
Harlow, H., 73
Harris, B. J., 3
Harris, M. B., 494, 501, 569, 570, 572
Harris, V. R., 591
Harrison, A. A., 314, 315
Harrison, A. O., 464
Hart, B., 544
Hartl, D. L., 201, 202, 206
Hartzler, K., 429
Haslett, B. J., 470
Hatch, L. R., 474
Hatton, B. J., 339
Haug, M., 192
Hayes, C. D., 290, 291, 296, 297
Healey, S., 472, 474
Healy, S., 478
Heckman, N. A., 463
Hedges, L. V., 75
Hedlund, R. D., 170
Heilbrun, C., 51
Heilman, M. E., 134, 152, 179
Helmreich, R. L., 52, 140, 454
Helson, R. M., 257, 497, 508
Hemmer, J. D., 254
Henley, N. M., 21, 125, 139, 146, 158, 174, 467
Herdt, G. H., 211
Herek, G. M., 139, 334
Herman, A., 466
Hernandez, D. G., 113
Herrmann, D. J., 82
Herzog, D. B., 572
Hess, B. B., 499
Hesse-Biber, S., 571
Hetherington, E. M., 42, 231
Heywood, S., 346
Hill, J. P., 282, 283, 284
Hill, M., 420
Hillier, L., 544
Hilts, E., 357
Hite, S., 309, 310, 311, 324, 325, 330
Hochschild, A. R., 351, 429, 509
Hoecker, K. S., 539
Hoffman, C., 135
Hoffman, L. W., 466
Hoffnung, M., 386
Holland, D., 316
Hollander, N., 306, 313, 318, 430
Hollin, C. R., 263
Hollingworth, L. S., 388–389, 390
Holtzworth-Munroe, A., 547, 548
hooks, bell, 6, 291–292
Hooper, C., 425
Hopkins, J., 414
Horner, Matina S., 454
Horney, K., 32
Hort, B. L., 60, 248, 250
Hossain, Z., 429
Houseknecht, S. K., 391
Houser, B., 461
Howard, Greg, *440*
Howe, K. G., 426, 448
Howe, L. K., 440
Howell, M., 546
Hrdy, S. B., 226
Hunt, M., 310
Hunter, G. T., 458
Hunter, M. S., 483
Hurlbert, D. F., 311
Hurtig, A. L., 208, 214
Huston, A. C., 42, 229, 233, 252, 256
Hyde, J. S., 45, 75, 76, 77, 85, 88, 90, 91, 93, 97, 98, 250, 254, 306, 307, 310, 327, 329, 334, 411, 412

Idle, T., 238
Ihinger-Tallman, M., 377, 378
Imperato-McGinley, J., 209, 210
Isaacs, M. B., 444
Izraeli, D. N., 137, 167

Jacklin, C. N., 41, 72, 73, 74, 78, 93, 94, 230, 239
Jackson, L. A., 319
Jackson, M., 308, 330
Jackson, T. L., 536
Jacobs, J. A., 456
Jacobson, M. B., 162
Jaffe, P. G., 532
Janda, L. H., 455
Jenkins, R., 565
Jensen, S., 518
John, B. A., 148, 149
Johnson, C. L., 463
Johnson, E. S., 99
Johnson, P., 161
Johnston, L., 142
Jordan, J. V., 64, 65
Jorgensen, S. R., 292
Josefowitz, N., 443
Joseph, G. I., 283, 303, 314, 330, 332, 339, 388
Jost, J. T., 151
Jung, C. S., 33, 51
Jutras, S., 501

Kagan, T., 40
Kahn, A. S., 2, 23, 282, 585
Kahn, J., 295
Kaiser, K., 490
Kanekar, S., 539
Kanter, R. M., 432, 433, 437, 440, 446, 448, 452, 459
Kaplan, A., 65
Kaplan, A. G., 51, 52, 53, 588
Kaplan, B. J., 404
Kaplan, M., 556, 584
Kaplan, M. M., 388
Karabenick, S. A., 176
Karbon, M., 230
Katz, B. L., 538
Katz, D., 445
Katz, P. A., 250, 257
Kaufert, P. L., 480, 485
Kaufman, G., *309*, *362*
Kelley, H. H., 340
Kelly, D., 444
Kennedy, C. W., 160
Kennell, J., 413
Kessler, S. J., 218, 252
Kiesler, S., 84, 245
Kilpatrick, D., 515, 522–523, 539
Kim, E. H., 434, 437
Kim, P. K., 439
Kimball, M., 78
Kimmel, D. C., 472, 473, 474
Kimmel, E. B., 26
Kincaid-Ehlers, E., 475, 476
King, S., 272–273
Kinsey, A. C., 306, 307, 308, 310, 335
Kinzer, S., 394
Kirchmeyer, C., 465
Kirkpatrick, C., 106
Kishor, S., 227
Kite, M. E., 130, 135, 472
Kitzinger, C., 332, 333, 335, 337, 338
Kitzinger, S., 403
Kocel, K. M., 198
Koch, L., 398
Koff, E., 267, *267*, 268, 269, 281
Kohlberg, L., 42, 43, 47, *50*
Kolata, G., 199, 205
Kollock, P., 162
Konner, M., 185
Kortenhaus, C. M., 235
Koslow, R. E., 85
Koss, M. P., 515, 532, 535–536, 537, 539, 549
Kowalski, R. M., 538
Kozachenko, K., 483, 484
Kozlowski, J., 475
Kramarae, C., 5
Kravetz, D., 585
Krieger, S., 381
Krishnan, V., 226
Kronenberg, F., 480
Kropp, J. J., 250
Kuebli, J., 230
Kuhl, A., 547
Kurdek, L. A., 363, 365
Kutner, N. G., 124

La Freniere, P., 238
Lackey, P. N., 255
LaFramboise, T. D., 593
LaFrance, M., 160
Lakoff, G., 384, 385
Lakoff, R., 124
Lakoff, R., 560, 561
Lamb, M. E., 42
Landa, A., 391
Landrine, H., 53, 135, 136, 556, 593
Laner, M. R., 477, 530, 531
LaPlante, M. N., 324
Laqueur, T., 187
Larkin, J., 285–286
Larwood, L., 445
Lauerman, J., 227–228
Laws, J. L., 304
Laws, S., 565, 568
Leaper, C., 241
Lee, G. R., 359
Lees, S., 286
Leffler, A., 159
LeGuin, U. K., 409
Leidholdt, D., 517, 518
Leinbach, M. D., 230
Lembright, M. F., 462
Lemkau, J. P., 395, 396, 457
Lenney, E., 444
Lennon, M. C., 483
Lerman, H., 29, 35, 36, 37, 586, 587, 588, 589
Lerner, R. M., 286
LeVay, S., 193
Levenson, R. W., 360
Levine, M. P., 445, 450
Levinger, G., 349
Levinson, R. M., 444
Levy, E., 116, 118t
Lewin, M., 287
Lewis, C., 228
Lewis, M., 229
Lewis, S., 334, 335
Lewittes, H. J., 509
L'Hommedieu, T., 375
Lie, G., 543, 544
Lieblich, A., 96
Lindemalm, G., 216
Linimon, D., 170
Linn, M. C., 75–77, 79, 91
Lipman-Blumen, J., 433
Lippmann, W., 106
Liss, M. B., 232
Locher, P., 111
Lock, M., 480, 485
Lockheed, M. E., 243, 256
Locksley, A., 53
Lofland, J., 181
Logothetis, M. L., 484, 487, 489
Loiacano, D. K., 339
Long, J., 496, 497, 498, 500, 506
Long-Scott, E., 392
Lont, C. M., 288
Looft, W. R., 451
Lopez, N., 293, 298–299
LoPiccolo, J., 311
Lorber, J., 113, 114, 205, 386, 416, 428, 435, 437, 446, 447, 448, 462, 468, 469
Lorenzi-Cioldi, F., 151
Lott, B., 54, 55, 158, 159t, 254, 443
Lovelace, L. (Marchiano), 517
Low, M. D., 475
Lowe, R., 468
Luebke, B. F., 115
Lykes, M. B., 65, 593
Lytton, H., 229

McAdoo, H. P., 501
McCaulay, M., 569
McClelland, D. C., 80, 453
McCloskey, L. A., 241
Maccoby, E. E., 41, 43, 72, 74, 78, 93, 94, 230, 236, 237t, 239, 243
McCombs, H. G., 592
McConaghy, M. J., 252
McCormick, N. B., 332, 340
Macdonald, B., 511
McEwen, B. S., 187
MacFarlane, A., 410, 411, 412
McFarlane, J., 543
McFarlane, J. M., 565
McGee, M. G., 78
McGloshen, T. H., 506
McGoldrick, M., 256, 592
McGrath, E., 564
McGrath, J. E., 24
McGuire, J., 156, 229
McHugh, M. D., 16, 544
McKay, J., 32
MacKinnon, C., 450
MacLusky, N. J., 192
MacPherson, K. I., 482, 486
Maddi, S. R., 28
Maddux, H. C., 273
Magnusson, D., 278
Mahlstedt, D., 542
Major, B., 179, 180, 396, 451
Makepeace, J. M., 531
Makosky, V. P., 468
Malamuth, N. M., 519, 520, 537
Malo, C., 416
Maltz, D. N., 243
Mansfield, P. K., 462
Mantecon, V. H., 476
Marchiano, L. (Lovelace), 517
Marecek, J., 2, 12, 15, 49, 329, 364, 578, 588
Margolin, L., 324
Markides, K. S., 472
Markson, E. W., 475
Markus, H., 57

Martin, C. L., 247, 251
Martin, E., 273, 274, 280, 480, 487, 488
Martin, S. E., 460, 462
Mason, D. O., 380
Masters, W. H., 307, 310, 328, 335, 403
Mathews, W. S., 236
Matlin, M. W., 93
Mauldin, T., 246
Mayall, A., 519
Maypole, D. E., 450
Mays, V. M., 300
Mazzella, C., 118
Meece, J. L., 78
Mellin, L. M., 572
Mercer, R. T., 414, 419
Messick, D. M., 151
Messner, M. A., 113, 251
Miller, C. L., 84t
Miller, C. T., 437
Miller, J. B., 62–63, 64, 65, 580
Miller, M., 464
Miller, T. W., 138
Mills, C. S., 536
Mirowsky, J., 349
Mischel, W., 37, 40, 42, 54
Mitchell, G., 230
Mitchell, V., 497, 508
Mittwoch, U., 190
Miura, I., 88
Modleski, T., 312
Moffat, M., 313, 322, 323, 324, 327
Moller, L. C., 250
Molm, L. D., 157
Monahan, L., 455
Money, J., 186, 202, 208, 209, 211, 212, 213, 332
Montemayor, R., 283
Montgomery, R. J. V., 501
Mooney, L., 112
Moore, T. E., 139
Morawski, J. G., 54, 55, 60
Morgan, L. A., 376, 506
Mori, D. L., 570
Morokoff, P. J., 327, 328, 521
Morris, J., 214, 215
Mosher, C., 305, 306
Moulton, J. M., 125
Moynihan, D. P., 418
Muehlenhard, C. L., 325, 340, 342
Mullen, P. E., 526
Mundy-Castle, A., 85
Munroe, R. H., 247
Munter, C., 319
Murstein, B. I., 367, 368
Mussen, P. H., 40, 42
Myers, D. G., 68

Nacoste, R. W., 179
Nadler, A., 176
NAEP, 85
Nails, D., 49
Naples, N. A., 419
Nash, S. C., 83
National Committee on Pay Equity, *436*, 437, 438, *438*, *439*
Needleman, R., 435, 437
Nelson, H. L., 398
Nettles, S. M., 295, 298
Neuberg, S. L., 166
Nevid, J. S., 314, 315, 316t
New York City Department of Consumer Affairs, 127t
New York Times, *187*, 500
Newcombe, N., 82
Newson, J., 245, 254
Newton, N., 411
Nichter, M., 572
Nicolson, P., 401, 407
Nieva, V. F., 435, 437, 438, 439, 440, 442, 444, 448, 452, 459, 464, 465, 467
Nigro, G. N., 122
Noble, B. P., 437, 499
Norton, A. J., 347, 371, 375

Oakley, A., 386, 408, 428, 565
O'Brien, M., 232, 233
O'Bryant, S. L., 501, 502, 504
O'Connell, A. N., 448
O'Connell, J. C., 465
O'Farrell, B., 461, 462
Ogletree, R. J., 539
O'Heron, C., 53
O'Keefe, E. S. C., 250
O'Keeffe, N. K., 528, 529
O'Laughlin, M. A., 49
Olday, D., 531
Oliver, M. B., 310, 327
Oliver, S. J., 563
Olsen, N. J., 455
O'Neil, J., 60
Ostrove, J. M., 60
O'Sullivan, C. S., 536

Padavic, I., 461
Padesky, C. A., 563
Padgett, D., 474, 494
Paige, K. E., 264, 290, 403
Paludi, M., 442, 455–456
Papanek, H., 432
Parke, R. D., 228, 229
Parker, S., 572
Parlee, M. B., 1, 3, 13, 15, 72, 97, 491, 565
Parsons, T., 431
Patterson, E. T., 274
Payne, B., 472
Pearlman, S. F., 477
Pederson, P., 528
Peirce, K., 288
Pellegrini, A. D., 236
Pence, E., 550
Peplau, L. A., 15, 16, 17, 313, 314, 340, 341, 346, 349, 350, 359, 361, 362, 363, 364, 365
Perlmutter, E., 490
Perry, D. G., 42, 233, 243
Perun, P. J., 434
Peters, D. K., 464
Petersen, A. C., 79, 91, 268, 271, 277, 278, 281, 286
Peterson, E., 456
Peterson, R. E., 209
Phares, E. J., 28
Phares, V., 425
Phillips, R. D., 580
Philpps-Yonas, S., 296
Phoenix, A., 389
Piercy, M., 303, 514
Pietromonaco, P. R., 464
Piliavin, J. A., 174
Pleck, J. H., 55, 287, 296, 353, 462
Plumb, P., 254, 288
Polakow, V., 415, 416
Polansky, E., 504
Pollack, S., 420, 421
Pomerleau, A., 231, 232
Ponse, B., 336
Pooler, W. S., 226
Pope, K., 588
Popenoe, N., 367, 376
Porter, N., 160, 168, 586–588
Poulton, K., 471
Pour-El, M. B., 446
Powell, A. D., 282
Power, T., 228
Powlishta, K. K., 236, 238
Prather, J. E., 581
Press, M., 292
Price, S. J., 371, 372, 373, 374, 375, 376
Price-Bonham, S., 256
Public Interest Directorate, 396
Pugh, M. D., 168
Purcell, P., 235
Purdy, L. M., 398
Purifoy, F. E., 196

Radicalesbians, 333
Radloff, L., 564
Radlove, S., 304, 327, 328
Radway, J. A., 312
Raines, R. S., 122
Ramos-McKay, J., 593
Rand, L. M., 434
Rapaport, K. R., 519
Ray, D. C., 580
Raymond, J., 215
Raymond, J. G., 397, 398
Rebecca, M., 55
Reid, P. T., 13, 14, 240, 256, 299, 590–591
Reiff, P., 37
Reilly, M. E., 364
Reineke, M. J., 104

Reitz, R., 487
Renzetti, C., 544
Reuben, D., 334
Reuterman, N. A., 531
Rheingold, H. L., 232
Rhoades, J. M., 401
Rice, F. F., 527
Rice, J., 377
Rich, A., 36, 333, 389, 402, 406, 408, 410, 425
Rich, M. K., 121
Richards, M., 228
Richardson, D. C., 177, 537
Rierdan, J., 271
Rigby, D. N., 589, 590
Rigby-Weinberg, D. N., 585, 588
Riley, S., 448
Risman, B. J., 388
Rix, S. E., 457t
Robinson, C. C., 233
Rodeheaver, D., 478
Rodin, J., 473, 569
Roesler, T. A., 526
Roff, L. L., 501
Rollins, B., 358
Romero, G. J., 439
Roopnarine, J. L., 233, 238
Root, M. P. P., 119, 558, 573, 593
Roscoe, B., 531, 532
Rose, S., 305t
Rosen, L. W., 573
Rosenberg, F. R., 282
Rosenberg, J., 450
Rosenberg, R., 4, 5
Rosenthal, N. B., 585
Rosenwasser, S. M., 431
Ross, L., 123
Rosser, P., 86, 93, 99
Roth, S., 524, 539
Rothblum, E. D., 558, 562
Rothman, B. K., 397
Rousso, H., 322
Rubin, G., 303
Rubin, R. T., 196, 210, 211
Ruble, D. N., 250, 358, 401, 402
Ruble, T. L., 140, 141t
Ruddick, S., 258
Ruggiero, J. A., 120
Russell, D. E. H., 342, 517, 521, 522, 524
Russell, M., 546, 547
Russett, E., 76
Russo, N. F., 12, 388, 437, 448, 460, 464, 515, 580
Rust, P. C., 333, 336
Ruth, S., 408
Ryan, W., 467

Sadker, M., 19, 38, 86, 87, 88, *88*, 453
Safir, M. P., 96
Sagrestano, L. M., 162
Sanchez, L., 429
Sanders, D., 578
Sanders, G. S., 173
Sanger, S. P., 181
Sangren, P. S., 104
Santee, R. T., 173
Sapiro, V., 234, 415, 416, 462
Sarantakos, S., 376
Saunders, D., 543
Saunders, R. M., 517
Scanzoni, L., 350, 379
Scarborough, E., 4, 22, 23
Scarr, S., 465, 466, *467*
Schafer, A. T., 90–91
Schilit, R., 544
Schlesinger, B., 358, 360, 360t
Schlossberg, N. K., 507
Schneider, M. S., 364
Schoen, R., 350
Schofield, J., 239
Schulman, G. I., 130
Schulman, M., 545–546
Schultz, M. R., 123
Schur, E. M., 163
Schutte, N. S., 243
Schwartz, F. N., 468
Schwartz, I., 326
Schwartz, L. A., 234
Schwartz, M. D., 547
Schwartz, P., 350, 351, 352, 377, 379, 381
Seagoe, M. V., 441
Searles, P., 540
Sears, D. O., 13
Sedney, M. A., 54, 56
Segel, E., 99
Seidenberg, R., 582
Selkow, P., 86–87
Sen, A., 227
Serbin, L. A., 83, 118, 119, 236, 238, 242
Settin, J. M., 473
Severne, L., 489
Shachar, S. A., 464
Shaffer, J. W., 202
Shakin, M., 231
Shange, N., 514
Shankar, A., 417–418
Shapiro, J. P., 455
Shapiro, L., *11*
Sharp, C., 445
Sharps, M., 82
Shea, C., 86
Sheehy, G., 495
Sherif, C. W., 1, 4, 15, 24, 147
Sheriffs, A. C., 106, 139
Sherman, J. A., 80, 84, 88, 91, 580
Shields, S. A., 4, 76, 77, 98, 197, 425
Shipman, G., 267
Shorter, E., 411
Shotland, R. L., 537, 538
Showalter, E., 554–555, 566, 567
Shuster, R., 333, 334, 337
Siegel, R. J., 360, 507
Sigelman, C. K., 170
Sigelman, L., 170
Signorielli, N., 116, 122, 245, 250
Silberstein, L. R., 571
Silverstein, B., 318, 319
Silverstein, L. B., 465, 466
Simmons, R. G., 278, 280, 282, 283, 285, 286
Simon, B. L., 368, 369, 370
Singer, J. M., 89
Sinnott, J. D., 509
Skrypnek, B. J., 154
Slaby, R. G., 243
Sleek, S., 421
Smetana, J. G., 250
Smith, B., 272
Smith, E. A., 291, 294
Smith, J. I., 104
Smith, J., 407
Smith, P. A., 136
Smith, P. K., 248, 249
Smith-Lovin, L., 160
Smith-Rosenberg, C., 332, 566, 567
Snavely, B. K., 447
Snizek, W. E., 444
Snodgrass, S. E., 172
Snow, J. T., 569, 572
Snow, M. E., 230
Snyder, M., 152, 153, 154, 180
Sohoni, N. K., 226
Sommers-Flanagan, R., 119
Sontag, S., 474
Sorensen, S. B., 535
Sorenson, A., 350
Spanier, G. B., 366
Spence, J. T., 51, 52–53, 54, 60, 108, 139, 454
Sprecher, S., 340
Spurlock, J., 501, 506
Stacy, R. D., 539
Stake, J., 319
Stall, S., 568
Stangor, C., 148
Stanley, J. P., 322
Stark, E., 545
Statham, A., 465
Stead, B. A., 173
Steele, B. F., 521
Steil, J. M., 162, 351, 354, 356, 358, 359, 364, 380, 381, 549
Steinberg, L., 284, 358
Steinem, G., 22
Stern, M., 232
Sternglanz, S. H., 118, 119
Stevens, G., 456
Stevens, M., 258
Stewart, A. J., 61, 62, 65, 511
Stiles, D., 314, 315
Stimpson, C. R., 258
Stoltenberg, J., 7
Stoltzman, S. M., 274
Storms, M. D., 130
Straus, M., 545

Straus, M. A., 543, 545, 546
Stricker, L., 86
Striegel-Moore, R. H., 569, 572
Strommen, E. F., 419
Stueve, A., 501, 502, 504, 505
Sugarman, D. B., 531
Suh, Mary, 544
Summit, R., 524
Sutherland, E., 454
Swaab, D. F., 193
Swarz, N., 168
Swinson, A. P., 544

Tajfel, H., 156, 178
Tannen, D., 317
Tashakkori, A., 281
Taylor, D., 417–418
Taylor, M. C., 52, 53, 540
Taylor, S. E., 151, 406
Teachman, J. D., 368
Teitelbaum, P., 87, 97
Terman, L., 441
Tevlin, H. E., 325, 327, 328
Thibault, J. W., 355
Thoits, P. A., 380, 381
Thomas, V. G., 573
Thompson, E. H., 531
Thompson, S., 299
Thompson, S. K., 45, 247
Thornberry, O. T., 279
Thorne, B., 239, 240, 241, 242, 243, 245, 275
Tiefer, L., 15, 308
Tobach, E., 211
Tobin-Richards, M. H., 277, 278
Todd, J., 491, 498
Tolman, R. M., 543
Tontodanato, P., 530
Tracy, D. M., 83
Travis, C. B., 42, 64, 157, 303, 479, 486, 579, 580, 581, 582, 585
Treadway, C. R., 403, 414
Trends in Education, 4, 23
Trent, K., 371
Tronick, E. Z., 229
Tronto, J. C., 49
Trotman, F. K., 592
Tuchman, G., 123
Tulloch, M. I., 550
Turk, J. L., 354

Udry, J. R., 294, 295
Unger, R. K., 4, 14, 15, 16, 17, 18, 21, 24, 25, 53, 69, 72, 75, 77, 98, 111, 130, 131, 147, 157, 158, 179, 181, 198, 200, 243, 252, 255, 257, 316, 369, 389, 391, 453, 455, 492, 558
United Nations, 226, 347, 349, 394, 434, 435
Urberg, K. A., 250
U.S. Bureau of the Census, 411
U.S. Department of Labor, 544
Ussher, J., 318, 323, 384, 399, 402, 403, 405, 406, 407, 483, 487, 565, 575–576

Vance, B. K., 293
Vance, C. S., 303, 331, 552
Vance, E. B., 309
Vanek, J., 428, 429, 430
Verhovek, S. H., 86
Vernon, J. A., 475
Veroff, J., 454
Vida, V., 330
Vobejda, B., 394
von Baeyer, C. L., 153
Vredenburg, K., 563

Wahrman, R., 166
Walker, L., 49, 545, 546, 547, 548–549
Wallston, B. S., 13, 14, 111, 152, 442
Walsh, M. R., 66, 455
Walum, L. R., 174
Ware, M. C., 128
Warren, M. P., 266
Warshaw, R., 542
Waterman, C., 544
Watson, G., 583
Weaver, J. B., 518
Webb, T. E., 563
Weidiger, P., 268
Weinraub, B., 474
Weinraub, M., 247
Weisstein, N., 2, 258
Weitz, R., 135
Weitzman, L., 373, 374, 375, 376
Weitzman, L. J., 458, 459
Weitzman, N., 235
Werner, P. D., 139
Wertz, D. C., 397
West, C., 146
Westney, O. E., 295
Westoff, C. F., 226
Weston, P. J., 456
Whisnant, L., 269
Whitbourne, S., 428, 429, 430
White, J. W., 162, 513, 528, 530, 531, 535, 536, 537, 538
Whiting, B. B., 255
Whitley, B. E., 53, 139, 563, 564
Wiest, W. M., 309
Wikan, U., 219
Wilder, D. A., 148
Wiley, M. G., 162
Wilkinson, D. Y., 589
Williams, J. E., 104, 105, 137, 140
Williams, L. R., 274
Williams, L. S., 397, 398
Williams, N., 429
Williams, W. L., 219
Willis, S. L., 85
Wilson, B. J., 542–543
Wilson, E., 125
Wilson, J. D., 190, 192
Wine, J. D., 94
Witkin, H. A., 79, 80, 202
Wittig, M. A., 455, 468
Wolman, C., 164, 166
Women's Programs Office, 3
Wood, A. D., 544
Wood, W., 168
Woods, N. F., 268
Wooley, H. T., 4
Wooley, S. C., 569, 570
Woollett, A., 228
Worell, J., 51, 342, 343, 562
Workman, J. E., 289
World Wire, 395
Worth, D. M., 531
Wyatt, G. E., 318, 523, 535, 536
Wynn, R. L., 237

Yarkin, K. L., 152, 442
Yee, B. W. K., 494
Yllo, K., 342
Yoder, J. D., 23, 445, 447, 448, 449

Zanna, M. P., 140–141, 153
Zelnick, M., 294, 295, 296
Zevy, L., 293, 294
Zillman, D., 518
Zimmerman, M. K., 484, 485
Zinkhan, G. M., 173
Zita, J. N., 479
Zuckerman, M., 122

Subject Index

Abortion
mandatory, 394–395
psychological effects, 395–396
reproductive freedom, 392–395
selective, 397
sex-selective, 226, 227–228
Abortion dilemma, 47–49
Absences, in language, 322
Academic performance, 278–279
Achieved status, 157, 159
Achievement, midlife, 507–508
Achievement motivation, 453–454
Acquaintance rape, 532–543
Acquaintance rapists, 536–537
Activism among older women, 509–512, *510*
Actor-observer difference, 132, 134
Addams, Jane, 567
Adler, Alfred, 32, 36
Adolescence
AIDS and, 299–300
contraceptive use and, 296–299
distinguished from puberty, 263
gender inequality, 287–289, 288t
psychological changes, 289–290
Adolescent sexuality
antecedents of, 294–295
demographics of, 290–291
negative attitudes toward, 291–294, 318
physical maturation and, 290
Advertisements
breast development and, 275
contraceptive use and, 297–298
gender stereotypes, 116–118, *117*
impact of sexism in, 122, 127t
personal. *See* Personal ads
for sanitary products, 271
Advice manuals, 342
Affective traits, 107
Affiliative responses, 238

Note: Page numbers in italics indicate figures; page numbers followed by t indicate tables.

African-American adolescents
contraceptive use by, 299, 300
eating disorders and, 572–573
effects of peer culture on, 286
gender roles and, 287
pressure for sexual activity, 294–295
self-esteem of, 281–282
African-American culture, ideals of love in, 314
African-American women
active grandmothering, 500–501
aging and, 494
caregiving and, 502
depicted in pornography, 518
feminist therapy and, 591–592
lesbianism among, 338–339
marriage rate of, 346, 348
matriarchal myth, 416, 418–419
pregnancy and, 407–408
professional success of, 460
in professions, 456–457
standards of beauty for, 319–321
widowhood and, 506
Age
adjustment to widowhood and, 505
in difference research, 74
divorce rates and, 371
at marriage, 348, 371
social invisibility and, 477
Ageism, 473
in media, 474–475, *476*
sexism and, 473–474, 512
Agency, 131, 132
Aggression, 194
courtship violence. *See* Courtship violence
gender-related differences, 530
as social control, 176–177, *177*
socialization of, 243, *244*, 245
XYY males and, 203
Aging, 471–512
active feminism, 509–512, *510*
double standard of, 116, *117*
menopause, 478–492
Aging *(Cont.)*:
psychological well-being and, 508–509
role transitions and, 492–508
social context of, 472–478
Agoraphobia, 558, 574–576, 584
AIDS, 299–300, 300, 328–329
Alcohol use, 535, 537, 546
All-girls' schools, 457
All-male groups, rape and, 536
Ambiguous situations, discrimination and, 444
Ambivalence
about menarche, 268
about pregnancy, 405
about sexuality, 322–324
toward aging, 472, *473*
American Association of Retired Persons, 511
American Medical Association, 392
American Psychiatric Association, 322–323
American Psychological Association (APA), 22, 133, 257, 355, 396, 445, 449, 476, 515, 564, 588
Division of Psychology of Women, 3, 5, 16, 449
Androcentric bias, 155
in diagnostic categories, 579
in gender development, 66
personality development theories, 29
Androcentrism, 2
criticisms of, 17–18
in standardized tests, 97
Androgen(s), 190, 196
Androgen insensitivity, 208–209
Androgenital syndrome, 206–208, *207*
Androgynous personality, *50*, 51–53
evaluation of theory, 53–55
Anorexia nervosa, 558, 566, 568–572, *573*
Anti-feminist backlash, 6–10, *8*, *11*
Art
childbirth in, 408–409, *410*
motherhood in, 390
women and madness in, 554–555

Ascribed characteristics, 158
Ascribed status, 157–158
Asian cultures
  ideals of love in, 314
  preference for sons in, 226
  standards of beauty and, 320–321
Asian women, pornography and, 518
Asian-American women, 339, 460
Assertiveness, 170
Association for Women in Psychology (AWP), 3
Attentiveness, stereotyping and, 143
Attributional biases, 152–153, 441
Attributions
  differential labeling, 567–568
  in gender-differentiated socialization, 229–231
Atypical behavior, 142
Authority, abuse of, 523, 533
Autonomy, 65, 369–370

Bad Mother myth, 424
Battered woman's syndrome, 549
Beauty. *See* Physical attractiveness
Behavior shaping, 38
Behavioral confirmation, 153–155
Behavioral flexibility, 51–53
Behaviorism, 37–38
Berdache, 219
Bias(es)
  in research, 12, 13, 73, 76, 77, 353, 466, 488, 490
  stereotyping and, 106, 143
Biological determinism, 184, 194–196
  depression and, 565
  hormones and, 195–196
  hot flashes, 479–480
  menopause and, 478–479, 491–492
  PMS and, 577–578
  popularity of, 193
  prenatal hormones, 195
  "reproductive syndromes," 566
  social factors in, 195
Biological differences, 30–32
Biological influences
  adolescent sexuality, 294
  mathematics abilities, 90–91, *92*
"Biologizing" differences, 99
Biology, 183–220, *184*
  cross-rearing and, 212–214
  cultural influences and, 218–220
  definitions of sex, 185–188
  developmental anomalies, 200–211
  gender identity change, 214–218
  influence of brain, 197–200
  prenatal development, 188–193
Birth announcements, 228
"Birthday party effect," 239
Bisexuality
  definitions of, 333–334
  identity development, 337
  research on, 334–335
Black, Barbara Aronstein, 508
Blue-collar occupations, 457t, 460–462
Blume, Judy, 268
Body fat, 265–267, *266*
Body image
  anorexia and, 573
  distorted perceptions of, 319
  effects of maturation on, 281
  gender identity and, 214, 216, *217*, 218
  menarche and, 268–269, *270*
  during pregnancy, 403–404
  puberty and, 276–277, *277*, 289–290
  in sexual scripts, 327
Body maturation
  during puberty, 274–277
  sexual activity and, 295
  timing of, 278–279
Body-ism, 121–122
Bottoms, Sharon, 420
Boundary maintenance, 163–171
  deviance and, 163–164, *165*, 166–167
  group dynamics and, 167–169, *169*
  leadership, 169–170, *171*
  legitimacy, 170–171
  social mechanisms for, 241–242
  stigma and, 163
  "token woman" and, 167
Brain
  differences in, 197, 199–200
  neural laterality, 198
Brain-size hypothesis, 76, 77
Breast development, 264, *265*, 275, 276t
British Psychological Society, 3
Bulimia, 571
Bullying, 245
Burnout, 465
Bush, Barbara, 10, 432
"Butch" stereotype, 334

Caesarean births, 411–412
Calkins, Mary, 22–23
Career
  lesbian couples and, 363
  limited options for, 451
  marriage and, 355, 356–357
Caregiver roles, 499–501, 501–505
Caretaker, self-development and, 33–34, *34*
Carpenter, Karen, *579*
Categorical bias, 180–181
Categorical reward, 179
Central nervous system, 192–193, *194*
Child sexual abuse, 535
  See also Incest
Child support, 375–376, 416
Childbirth, 408–414
  family-centered, 412–413
  medicalized, 410–412
  postpartum depression, 413–414
  social construction of, 408–410, *410*
Childhood, 222–260
  early school years, 238–245
  equated with women, 124
  infants and toddlers, 229–236
  middle school, 245–260, *246*
  newborns, 228
  nursery school, 236–238
  prenatal preferences, 225–226
Childlessness, 359, 389, 391
Children
  divorce and, 375–376
  motherhood mandate, 388–389, 390
  paid work and, 465–466, *467*
  reasons for having, 387–388
  reproductive freedom, 391–396
Chivalry, 551
Chlorosis, 574
Chodorow, Nancy, 33–35, *34*, 36, 66
Chromosomal anomalies, 201–205
  Turner's syndrome, 201–203
  XYY and XXY males, 203–204
Chromosomes, 188–190, *189*, 204–205
Civil Rights Act of 1964, 443
Clients, 586, 588, 589
Clinical symptoms, 557
Clinton, Hillary R., 10, *165*, 432
Cloning, 186
Clothing, 231–232
Cognitive abilities
  mathematics performance, 85–91
  similarities in, 94–95
  spatial abilities, 79–80, *80–82*, 82–85, 84t
  verbal, *82*, 92–94
Cognitive categories, 108–111, 110t, 384–385
Cognitive developmental theory
  evaluations of, 44–46, 48–49
  moral thinking and, 46–48
  stage theory, 42–44, *44*
Cognitive maturity, 45–46
Cognitive schema, 57–60
Cognitive strategies, 150–153
Cohabitation
  breakup of, 376, *377*
  marital choices and, 368
  POSSLQs, 365–366
  relationship characteristics, 367–368
  trends in, *366*, 366–367
Cohort effects, 61–62, 493–494
"Colorism," 591
Comic strips, 111–113, *112*
Coming out, 335
Commitment, equality and, 379
Communication, 342–343

Communication skills, 94
Communion stereotypes, 131–132
Comparison groups, 13
Compliance, 173
Computers, 245–256, *246*
  spatial skills and, 83, 85
  stereotypes of users, 128, *128*
Condoms, 300, 329
Conformity, 173
  importance to boys, 250–251
  pressure for, 224, 233–234, 389
Confounding variables, 73
Congenital adrenal hyperplasia (CAH), 206–208, *207*
Consciousness-raising groups, 584–585
Contraception
  by adolescents, 291, 292, 296
  factors in rejection of, 296–297
  parental communication and, 297
  reproductive freedom and, 392
  role of media in, 297–298
  unmarried childbearing and, *298*, 298–299
Contract motherhood, 398–399
Control
  during childbirth, 413
  contraception and, 296
  courtship violence and, 527
  loss during pregnancy, 405
Cooperative child rearing, 416, 418
Coping strategies
  deviance and, 164, *165*, 166, 583
  of incest survivors, 526
  multiple roles and, 465
  therapy and, 561–562
Coronary heart disease, 482–483
"Corporate husbands," 433–434
Corporate wives, 432
Corpus callosum, 199, 200
Courtship violence
  consequences of, 531–532
  defining, 527–528
  frequency of, 528–529
  inflicting and sustaining, 529–531
  occurrence of, 531
  prevention of, 532
Cox, Ida, 330
Crawford, Mary, 25–26
Cross-gender activities, 237–238, 255
Cross-sex chasing, 241–242
Cross-sex rearing, 212–214
Cultural feminism, 5
Cultural messages, 60–61
Cultural norms, depression and, 592–593
Cultural scripts, 312–313
Culture
  adolescent sexuality and, 295
  fear of success and, 455
  feminist therapy and, 589–590
  gender identity and, 218–220
  gender ideology, 181
Culture *(Cont.)*:
  gender typing and, 255–256
  mate preferences and, 348–349
  norms shaped by, 343
  personality and, 60
  sex differentiation and, 210–211
  sexuality shaped by, 303–304
  stereotyping and, 137, *138*
Custody disputes, lesbian parents and, 420–421

Date rape, 342
Dating pressures, 282
Dating scripts, violence and, 516
Dating violence, 342
Debasement, in language, 123, 124
Decision making, factors in, 459
Deference confrontations, 174
Degradation, in pornography, 517
Dehumanization, in pornography, 518
"Delusional dominating personality disorder," 579–580
Depression, 558, 562–566
  blaming women for, 564–566
  courtship violence and, 530
  postpartum, 413–414
  pregnancy and, 403–404
  retirement and, 499
  roles, power and, 562–564
Derogatory language, 124
Descriptors, 108
Desirability, 315–317, 316t
Deutsch, Helene, 32–33
Devaluation
  of characteristic traits, 282
  of housework, 429–431
  by language, 21
  of women's role, 45
  of work performance, 442–443
Deviance
  attractiveness and, 129–130
  cultural stereotypes of, 455
  in groups, 164, *165*, 166–167
  positive effects, 257–260, *259*
  power to define, 163–164, 181
Diagnosis, 556–557
Diagnostic and Statistical Manual (DSM), 522, 571, 576
Difference research, 71–75
  individual studies in, 71–73
  methodological flaws in, 72
  summarizing studies in, 74–75
  values and ideology in, 76–78
Differential Aptitude Test (DAT), 79, 93
Differential earnings, 437–439, *438–440*
Differential reinforcement, 239–240
Differential treatment by parents, 224
Differential weight standards, 569, *571*
Diffuse status characteristics, 158
Dihydrotestosterone, 190
Direct action, *63*, 64
Direct observation, 307, 308
Disabled women, 321–322
Disconfirmation, 142–143
Discrimination, 21, *133*, 133–134
  in hiring and promotion, 443–445
  informal, 443, 444
  weight and, 569–571, *571*
Disinformation, 126–127
Displaced homemakers, 373–374
Dispositional attributions, 132
Dispositional traits, 154
Diversity
  cognitive developmental theory, 45
  feminist personality theory, 30
  psychoanalytic theory, 35–36
  social learning theory, 40–41
  social organization and, 23–24
Divorce
  consequences of, 373–376
  correlates of, 371–373, 372t
  following remarriage, 378
  nonmarital breakups, 376, *377*
  rates of, 370–371, *371*
  research biases, 377
"Doing gender," 145–182
  boundary maintenance, 163–171
  internalizing norms, 178–181
  power, 157–158
  social behaviors, 171–178
  as social category, *147*, 147–156
  status differences, 158–162
  in workplace, 441–451
Dominance
  face-ism and, 122
  nonverbal cues to, 160–161
  self-categorization and, 155–156
  social influence and, 242–243
  tokenism and, 167
  in traditional marriage, 354–355
Dominance behavior, 242
Dominance hierarchy, 151
Dominant groups, 63–64, 76
Domination, 537, 550, 551
"Dora" case, 560, 561, 584
Double binds, 134, 161, 289
  mental illness and, 559–560
Double standard(s), 323–324, 325, 343–344
  of aging, 474
  diagnostic categories, 579–580
  for sexuality, 295
  for tokenism, 446–447
  wife abuse and, 552
Drug advertisements, 581–582, 584

Drugs, 411, 537, 580–582
Dual-career couples, 359–360
Dual-earner families, 355–356

Early dating, 294
Eating disorders, 319, 568–574
  demographics of, 572–573
  differential standards, 569, *571*
  discrimination and, 569–570, *570*
  feminist perspective of, 573–574
  as pathology, 570–572, *573*
  racial differences in, 279–280
Economic dependence
  in marriage, 350–351
  motherhood mystique, 386
  wife abuse and, 543–544
Economic disadvantages
  divorce and, 374–375, 376
  empty nest and, 498
  for lesbian mothers, 419
  of retirement, 499
  woman-headed households, 415
Education
  gender inequity in, 87–88, *88*
  menopause and, 489–490
  motherhood and, 390
Egalitarian marriage, 352, 379–381
Egalitarian relationships
  cohabitation, 367–368
  of lesbian couples, 365
Electra complex, 31, 32
Emotions, 230, 422–423
Empty nest syndrome, 489, 496–498
Empty-nest stage, 358
Encoding processes, 151
Endometrial cancer, 486
Environment
  cognitive skills and, 95
  gender typing and, 231–234
  mathematics abilities and, 90–91
Equal Rights Amendment, 10
Equality, commitment and, 379
Erikson, Erik, 32, 36, 495
Erotica, 517
Estrogen, 190, 192, 479, 481
Estrogen replacement, 482, 486–487
Ethical guidelines for feminist therapists, 586, 587
Ethnic diversity, 593–594
Ethnic minority women
  "invisibility" of, 111–112
  marriage statistics on, 347
  paid employment of, 434, 434t
  scarcity of research on, 13–14
Ethnicity
  aging and, 494–495
  derogatory language and, 124
  in feminist therapy, 589–590
  gender typing and, 256
Ethnicity *(Cont.)*:
  professional success, 459–460
  widowhood and, 506
Exclusion, in language, 124, 125
Expectations of success, 459
Experimental methods, 15–16
Expert power, 161, 162
External genitalia, 188, *189, 191,* 192
External locus of control, 180
Externality of categories, 148
Extinction, in behaviorism, 37
Extramarital sex, 324
Extrinsic rewards, 452

Fable of Baby X, 252, 253
Face-ism, 121–122, 137
Failure attributions, 441–442, 443
Faking orgasm, 328
False memory syndrome, 522
Families, forms of, 399, 400
Family roles, 435, 437
Family values, incest and, 525
Family-centered childbirth, 412–413
Fantasy play, 236
"Fat spurt," 265–267, *266*
Father-invisibility, 425
Fathers, 283, 401, 458
Fear of success, 454–456
"Female disorders," 566–568
Feminine socialization, 292, 592
Femininity, wife abuse and, 551
Feminism
  activism of older women, 511–512
  backlash against, 6–10
  egalitarian marriage and, 380
  gender-related differences, 69
  marriage statistics and, 347–348
  meanings of, 5–6
  motherhood mandate and, 389
  personality research and, 66
  pro-choice perspectives of, 392
Feminist personality theory, 29–30
Feminist researchers, 80
Feminist therapists, 98, 555
  eating disorders and, 574
  female *versus* male, 588
  race/ethnicity of, 589–590
  sexual orientation of, 589
  theoretical orientation of, 588
Feminist therapy
  consciousness raising, 584–585
  ethical guidelines for, 586, 587
  impact of therapist in, 588–590
  marginalized populations, 590–593
  nonsexist therapy and, 586, 588
  principles of, 585–586
  traditional methods and, 582–584
Feminist Therapy Institute, 586
Feminist values in research, 15–17
Ferraro, Geraldine, 113
Fertility, end of, 492
Fetal "rights," 397
Field, Sally, 474
Field independence, 14, 79–80
Field sensitivity, 14, 80
"File drawer problem," 72, 74
Financial security, 439–440
First-date scripts, 304, 305t
5-alpha-reductase deficiency, *207,* 209–211
Fonda, Jane, 474
Foreplay, 328
Fraternities, 542
Freud, S., 30–32, 35, 36, 560, 561
Friendship networks, 350, 508–509
Full-time homemakers, 359
Fundamental attribution error, 152–153, 583

Galton, Sir Francis, 76
Gang rape, 536
"Gay gene," 193, *194*
Gender
  as classification system, 18–19
  concepts related to, 20–21
  cultural ideology about, 181
  distinguished from sex, 18
  marital expectations and, 349
  social construction of, 260
  social interaction and, 19–20
Gender constancy, 43, 248–249, *249*
Gender development, 50–51
Gender equality, 287–289, 288t
Gender identity, 28–29
  body image, 214, 216, *217,* 218
  changing, 210–211, 214–218
  cross-sex rearing and, 212–214
  cultural constructions, 218–220
  cultural influences, 218–220
  social pressures and, 218
Gender intensification, 282–283
Gender labels, 247
Gender norms, 178–181
Gender roles, 20, 43, *44*
Gender schema, 247
Gender schema theory, 57–60
Gender segregation
  aggression and, 243, *244,* 245
  group dynamics of, 240–241
  maintaining boundaries, 241–242
  reinforcement of, 239–240
  social dominance and, 242–243
  social networks, 238–239
  "unlearning" behaviors and, 240
Gender stability, 248
Gender stereotypes. *See* Stereotypes
Gender typing, 29, 49–60, *50*
  androgynous personality and, *50,* 51–55
  in child's environment, 231–234
  as cognitive schema, 57–60
  in gender schema theory, 57–58
  in gender-role transcendence, 55–57, *56*

Gender typing *(Cont.)*:
resistance to, 253–257
social learning theory and, 37–40, *39*, 41
in stories and books, 234–235
transcending, 55–60
Gender understanding
cognitions, 247–250, *248–249*
genital knowledge and, 252
impact of stereotypes, 250
stereotyping among boys, 250–251
Gender-differentiated socialization, 224–225, 229–231
Gender-neutral behavior, 238
Gender-related differences, 21
about parenting, 385
in aging, 495
in cognitive abilities, 78–94
conformity and, 173
defining, 69–71, *70*, *71*
in helping behavior, 173–174
implications of, 94–97
measuring, 71–75
moral reasoning and, 49
in nonverbal behaviors, 158–160, 159t
in power, 305t, 339–340
in psychological disorders, 558–562
research values/ideology, 76–78
in romantic love, *313*, 313–314
social consequences of, 97–99
Gender-role transcendence, 55–60
Gender-schema theory, 57–60, 317
Gender-specific "cultures," 260
Gender-stereotyped jobs, 444
Gender-stereotypic differences, 563
Gender-typed behavior, 38–39, *39*
Gender-typing, 20
"Generic he," 21, 125–126
Gifted children, 441
Gilligan, Carol, 46–49, 66
Gilman, Charlotte Perkins, 567
Gingrich, Newt, 9, 10
Ginsburg, Ruth Bader, 113
Glass ceiling, 435
Gonadotropins, 264
Gonads, 186, 188, *189*, 290
Grainger, Porter, 330, 331
Grandma Moses, 507–508
Grandmothers, 499–501
Gray Panthers, 511
Greek goddesses, 103t, 103–104
Group differences, 136–137, *138*
Group dynamics, 167–169, *169*, 240–241
Group pressure, 173
Growth spurt, 264
Guevedoce, 210

Hanks, Tom, 474
Harding, Tonya, 114, *115*
Health, 328–329, 369, 481–482
Helping behavior, 173–176, 175t, 230
Helplessness, 161
depression and, 176
incest and, 523
socialization into, 230–231
of wife abuse victims, 547, 549
Hepburn, Katherine, 475
Heterosexism, 333, 334
effect on lesbian couples, 365
feminist therapy and, 590
job discrimination and, 445
in work environment, 464
Heterosexual relationships, 339–341
power in, 305t, 339–340
Hierarchical relationships, 174–176, 175t
Hill, Anita, *63*, 64, 449, 450
Hiring and promotion, 443–445
Hollingworth, Leta Stetter, 4, 23, 77, 388–389, 390, *390*
Homicide, 545
Homophobia, 294, 420
Homosexuality, 193, *194*, 293–294
Homosexuals, 130–131, 307
Hopkins, Ann, *133*, 133–134
Hopkins v. *Price-Waterhouse* (1989), *132*, 132–133, *133*, 133–134
Hormonal anomalies, 205–211
Hormonal changes, 403, 414
Hormones, 186–187, *187*, 188, *189*, 190, *191*, 192
effects on behavior, 195–196
Horney, Karen, 32, 35, 36
Hostility, 286, *287*
Hot flashes, 479–480
Household duties, 246–247, 429
mental illness and, 583
shared by lesbian couples, 363
sharing, 428–429
"Housewife's disease." *See* Agoraphobia
Housewives, 428–431
Housework, 359, 428–431
depicted in comic strips, 112
in dual-career marriage, 355
value of, 429–431
Humor, 149–150, *150*
Hyde Amendment (1976), 393–394
Hypothalamus, 193
Hypothesis testing, error in, 72
Hysteria, 566, 593

Identification, 39–40, 43
Identity changes, 407–408, 422
Idiosyncratic beliefs, 106–107
Images, 101, *102*, 103
of aging, 472–473, 473t, 475–477
appearance and, 317
cross-cultural perspective, 104–105
in language, 123–124
mothers and motherhood, 384–386
pictorial, 115–119, *117*, 118t

Images *(Cont.)*:
religious, 103t, 103–104
stereotypical. *See* Stereotypes
Imitation, 38–39, *39*, 41–42
Immaturity, femininity and, 108
Immigration, effects of, 593
In vitro fertilization, 397–398
Incest, 521–527
characteristics of, 523
consequences of, 525–526
defining, 521
frequency of, 522–523
perpetrators of, 524
protection from, 527
self-defeating personality disorder and, 577
victims of, 524–525
Income, power and, 355–356
Indirect aggressive strategies, 245
Indirect power, 161
Indirect power strategies, 161, 162, 340–341
Individual-deficit model of achievement, 467–468
Infertility technology, 397–398
Influence strategies, 340–341
Influence styles, 242–243
Informal adoption, 416, 418
Informal discrimination, 443, 444
Informational power, 161
Inner space, 32
Institutional biases, 582
Instrumental orientation, 453, 461
Instrumentality, 107, 245–260, *246*
Intelligence measures, 78
Interdependence, 143
Intergroup power, 468
Internal accessory organs, 188, *189*
Internalization of behavior, 154, 259
International Childbirth Education Association, 412–413
Interruptions, 160
Intersexuality. *See* Pseudohermaphrodism
Intrinsic rewards, 452
Invisible work roles. *See* Unpaid work
Ito, Midori, 114

Jacobi, Mary Putman, 4, 23
James, Alice, 567
Job discrimination. *See* Discrimination
Job sectors for women, 438–439
Jung, Carl, 33

Kingston, Maxine Hong, 321
Klinefelter's syndrome, 203, 204, 205

Kohlberg, Lawrence, 42–49, *44*
Kuhn, Maggie, 508, 511

Labeling
  attributional pattern, 567–568
  negative connotations, 123–124
  of sexual assault, 533, 534–535
  of sexual orientation, 336–337
Labels, power of, 343
Lamaze method, 412
Landers, Ann, 391
Language
  about menopause, 487–488
  generic "he," 125–126
  images in, 123–124
  sexist, 126–127
  sexuality and, 322–323
  as source of power, 21–23
  stereotypes of aging, 473, 473t
Language-processing disorders, 93–94
Late luteal phase dysphoric disorder, 576, 577–578
Lateralization of brain, 198
Latina women
  aging and, 494
  contraceptive use, 298–299, 300
  depicted in pornography, 518
  ethnic diversity of, 593
  feminist therapy for, 592–593
  ideals of love and, 314–315
  lesbianism among, 338
  standards of beauty and, 321
  teenage birthrate, 293
Laws and statutes
  divorce and, 374–375
  on marriage, 346–347
  motherhood and, 390
  against rape, 540
Layton, Elizabeth, 510, *510*
Leadership, 169–170, *171*
Lee, Spike, 321
Left-handedness, 198, 199
Legitimacy, 171–172
Legitimate power, 161
LeGuin, Ursula, 150
Lesbian couples
  breakup of, 376, *377*
  egalitarian relationships, 381
  leisure activities of, 363–364
  loss of life-partner, 506–507
  as parents, 399, 419–421
  power in, 364
  relationship characteristics, 363–364
  relationship dynamics, 341
  research limitations, 365
  satisfaction of, 364–365
  stereotypes about, 361
  surveys of, 361–363
Lesbianism
  among teenage girls, 293–294
  developing identity, 335–339
  research on, 334–335
  social history of, 332–334
  stereotypes of, 334
Lesbians
  aging and, 476–477
  feminist therapy and, 589, 590
  job discrimination and, 445
  relationship abuse and, 544
  role conflict of, 464
  sexual harassment of, 450
Levinson, Daniel, 495
Liberal feminism, 5
Life patterns, 564
Lifelong marriages, 360t, 360–361, *362*
Lilith, 104
"Linking," 241
Long-term relationships, 345–381
  cohabitation, 365–368
  divorce and separation, 370–377
  equality and commitment, 378–381
  inequality of, 381
  lesbian couples, 361–365
  marriage, 346–361
  never-married women, 368–370
  remarriage, 377–378
Lordosis, 192
Loss of significant other, 505–507

Machismo, 315
Madonna/whore dichotomy, 323, 343
Magazines, 119–121
  female images in, 288, 288t, 317
  messages about weight in, 318
  sex surveys in, 307
Male(s)
  adjustment to divorce, 373
  evaluation of behavior of, 19–20
  gender stereotyping, 250–251
  as norm, 44, 46–47, 66–67
  preference for, 225–226
  romantic love and, 313
Male bonding, 240–241
"Male" professions, 456–457, 457t
Male-only research studies, 13
"Mamawoman" (Shankar), 417–418
Mandatory contraception, 392, 393
Marchiano, Linda, 517
Marianismo, 315
Marital violence. *See* Violence
Marriage
  biases in research on, 353
  inequality of roles, 401
  as institution, 346–347
  "marriage gradient," 349–350
  patterns of, 347–348
  power in, 353–357
  previous cohabitation and, 368
  satisfaction in, *357*, 357–361
  spouse choices, 348–349
Marriage *(Cont.):*
  varieties of, 350–352
Marriage gradient, 349–350, 369
"Masculine" traits, 458t, 458–459
Masculinity model of adjustment, 53, 563–564
Masculinity-femininity test, 49–50
Masochism, 31, 32
Masochistic personality, 576
Masturbation, 307, 310–311
Mathematics, 85–91, 452–453
Matriarchal myth, 416, 418–419
Mead, Margaret, 305, 408
Media
  ageism in, 474–475, *476*
  comic strips, 111–113, *112*
  contraception, 297–298
  descriptions of menopause, 479
  gender-related differences, 91, *92*, *98*
  images of adolescents, 288, 288t
  images of women in, 1–3
  magazines and fiction, 119–121
  messages about weight in, 318
  news media, 113–115, *114*, *115*
  overweight women and, 569
  pictorial images in, 115–119, *117*, 118t
  on sex differentiation, 193
  sex surveys in, 307
  sexism in, 122–123, 127t, 168–169, 474–475, *476*
  sports images, 113–114, *114*, *115*
  treatment of divorce, 370
  treatment of feminism, 8–9
Medicaid, 393–394
Medical interests, PMS and, 565
Medical models
  of childbirth, 410–412
  of pregnancy, 399
  of psychological disorders, 558
Medicalization
  of childbirth, 410–412
  of menopause, 483–486, *485*
Men as feminists, 6, 7
Menarche, 264, 267
  significance of, 267–269, *270*
  as taboo subject, 269, 271
  treatment in literature, 272–273
Menopausal syndrome, 485–486, 565
Menopause, 476, 478–492
  alternative views of, 488–489
  biological determinism, 479–480
  estrogen replacement, 486–487
  health risks of, 481–483
  language about, 487–488
  meaning of, 491–492
  medicalization of, 483–486, *485*
  power and status, 490–491, 491t
  social meaning of, 478–479
  transitions in, 489–490
Menstruation
  negative expectations about, 274

Menstruation *(Cont.):*
race and, 280
reactions to, 273–274
as taboo subject, 269, 271
treatment in literature, 272–273
Mental-rotation tasks, 79
Mentors, 448–449
Meta-analysis, 75, 79, 90
Metaphors, negative, 123–124
Methodological biases, 488
Methodology, 15–16, 108
Midlife, meanings of, 477–478
Midlife transitions
caregiver roles, 499–505
cultural context of, 492–495
nature of, 495–498
retirement, 498–499, *500*
Miscommunication, 538
Mitchell, Silas Weir, 567
Mixed-sex interactions, 161–162
Modeling, 38–39, *39*
Moderator variables, 75
Modern marriage, 351, 352
Modified double standard, 323–324
"Mommy track," 468
Monetary rewards, 179–180
Montague, Helen, 77
Mood changes of pregnancy, 403
Moore, Demi, 407
Moral development, 46–48
Moral reasoning, 46, 48
Morris, Jan (James), 214
Morrison, Toni, 321
Mother(s)
African-American, 416, 418–419
definition of, 384–385
differential treatment of children, 235–236
lesbian, 419–421
participation in sports and, 254
Mother-blaming, 424–425
Mother-child relationship, 423
Mother-daughter relationship, 283, 525
Motherhood, 383–426
aging women and, 475
childbirth, 408–414
decision to have child, 387–399
images of, 384–386
obstacles to, 421, 424
realities of, 415–424
responsibility and blame, 424–425, *425*
societal emphasis on, 497
transition to, 399, 401–408
Motherhood mandate, 388–389, 390, 426
Motherhood mystique, 385–386, *386, 387*, 401, 426
Mothering, 35
Mother-son conflict, 283–284
Mounting behavior, 192
Movies, 289, 370

MTV, 116–117, 119
Music videos, sexuality in, 119

Naming
control and, 555
deviance and, 163–164, 181
of sexual parts, 318
as source of power, 21–23
spatial abilities and, 82
of women in sports, 113
Narcissism, 31, 32
National Black Women's Health Project, 392
National Merit tests, 86
Natural childbirth, 412–413
Negative assessments
of coping strategies, 418
of female sexuality, 322–323
of lesbian mothers, 419
of never-married women, 368–369
of nonmaternal care, 465
of women's bodies, 318, 319
Negative characterizations
of aging, 472
of menopause, 479, 487–488, 489
as response to success, 454–455
Negotiation, 380
Neurasthenia, 566
Never-married women, 368–370, 381
News media, 113–115, *114, 115*
Noether, Emmy, 90
Nonconformity. *See* Deviance
Nonsexist language, 22
Nonsexist research
question formulation in, 12–13
research design, 12, 13–14
results of, 12, 14–15
statistical techniques, 12, 14
Nonsexist therapy, 586, 588
Nontraditional occupations, 457t, 460–462
Nonverbal behaviors, 158–160, 159t
Non-Western societies, menopause in, 490–491, 491t
Norm(s)
deference confrontations, 174
male as, 44, 46–47, 66–67
for psychometric tests, 79
white middle class, 23, 24, 418
Normative beliefs, 168
Norplant implantation, 392, 393
Nuclear family, 36
Nursery school, 236–238
Nurturance, 194, 195

Observational learning, 39, 40, 42
Occupations
depictions of, 112, 116, 118t
stereotyping, 108, 111, 131–132, *133*, 133–134
O'Connor, Sandra Day, 113
O'Dell, Scott, 99
Oedipal complex, 31

"Off time" role behavior, 496
"Old-boy network," 448
Older Women's League (OWL), 511
Organizational backlash, 447
Orgasm, 308–310, 328, 403
Osteoporosis, 481–482
Ovaries, 190, 192
Overgeneralization, 72–73

Paid employment, 434t, 434–441
children and, 465–466, *467*
of cohabiting couples, 367
differential earnings, 437–439, *438–440*
divorce rates and, 371
economic benefits of, 466
in egalitarian marriage, 379–381
family roles and, 435, 437, 462–466
marital equality and, 355–357
marriage and, 351, 353
motherhood and, 401
segregation and stratification, 434–435, *436*
social policy and, 466–469
unemployment and underemployment, 439–441
Parent-child incest, 524
Parent-child relationships, 42, 283–284
Parents
adolescent contraception, 297
aggression by, 530, 531
differential treatment by, 224, 229, 235–236
disabled child and, 321–322
gender typing and, 254–255
gender-stereotyped toys and, 233
mathematics performance and, 89
professional success, 457–458
Passivity
in Freudian theory, 31, 32
romantic ideal and, 324
in sexual scripts, 328
teenage pregnancy and, 292
wife abuse and, 552
Patriarchal society, 551–552
Peer influences, violence and, 531
Peer pressures, 286, *287*, 295
Peers, 225, 239–240
Penis envy, 31, 32
Perceptions of reality, 585–586
Perceptions of women, 168
Perfect Mother myth, 424
Permanence of categories, 148
Permissible play space, 83
Personal ads, 315–316
Personal change, 584
Personal entitlement, 171–172, 178–180

Personal fulfillment, 337
Personal prejudices, 444–445
Personality, 28
  childlessness and, 391
  cognitive development and, 42–49
  life patterns and, 62
  midlife achievement and, 507
  psychoanalytic theories, 30–37
  social influences on, 61
  social learning theory, 37–42
  status and, 172
Physical abuse, 517, 543
Physical aggression, 528–529, 531
Physical appearance, 108, 113, 131, 282, 477–478
Physical attractiveness, 129–130, 315–322
  in advertising, 116–118, *117*
  caring about, 317–318, *318*
  desirability and, 315–317, 316t
  disabled women and, 321–322
  evaluations of, 285–286
  gender identity and, 218
  in magazines and fiction, 121
  minority women and, 319–321
  self-fulfilling prophecies, 154
  sex reassignment and, 214
  sexuality and, 315–322
  testicular-feminization syndrome, 209
  weight standards, 318–319, *320*
Physical exercise, osteoporosis and, 481
Physical maturity, 289
Physical restraint, 523
Piaget, Jean, 42
Pink-collar employment, 440
Plain, Belva, 508
Play activities, 234, 236, 237t
Political activism, 7, *510*, 510–511
Political cartoonists, 7, *8*
Political consciousness, 584–585
Poor and working-class women
  controlling, 120–121
  feminist therapy for, 590–591
  as head of household, 415
  menopause and, 485
  pregnancy and, 407–408
  scarcity of research on, 14
"Pop psych" books, 342–343
Pornography, 516, 517
  effects of, *518*, 518–520
  racist images in, 119
  social implications of, 520–521
POSSLQs. *See* Cohabitation
Post-abortion counseling, 396
Postconventional moral reasoning, 46, 48
"Postfeminist" era, 8–9
Postpartum depression, 413–414, 565
Posttraumatic stress disorder (PTSD), 515, 526, 539, 549
Poverty, older women and, 508
Power
  adjustment to marriage and, 359
  beauty as, 316–317
  depression in women and, 562–563
  devalued role of women and, 45
  effect on personality, *63*, 63–65
  failure to achieve and, 468
  in feminist therapy, 586, 588
  images of, 118–119
  in marriage, 353–357
  mental illness and, 555
  patterns of violence and, 516
  in relationships, 305t, 339–340, 341, 364, 378–379, 381
  sexual harassment and, 450
  slang vocabulary and, 124
  stereotyping and, 106, 142–143
  therapy based on, 560–562
Power and status
  in menopause, 490–491, 491t, 493
  sex education and, 300
  as social influences, *63*, 63–65
Preconventional moral reasoning, 46, 47–48
Pregnancy, 399, 401–408
  body image during, 403–404
  sexual scripts and, 328, 329
  sexuality and, 402–403
  social reactions to, 406
Premenstrual syndrome (PMS), 565, 568, 576
Prenatal development
  chromosomal sex, 188–190
  genital sex, *189*, *191*, 192
  gonadal and hormonal sex, 190, *191*, 192
  nervous system, 192–193, *194*
Prenatal hormones, 195
Prepared childbirth, 412–413
Prescriptive stereotypes, 129
Priming, 141–142
Procedural stigma, 179
Professions
  achievement in, 456–460
  nontraditional, 457t, 460–462
Progesterone, 206
Protection from abuse, 527
Pseudohermaphrodism, 205–206, *207*
Psychoanalytic theories
  evaluation of, 35–37
  feminist perspective, 33–35, *34*
  Freudian, 30–32
  negative views of women in, 35
Psychodynamic theories, 588
Psychological abuse, 543
Psychological adjustment, 358–360, 373–374, *374*
Psychological androgyny, *50*, 51–55
Psychological consequences
  of acquaintance rape, 538–540
  of incest, 525–526
Psychological consequences (*Cont.*):
  of sexual harassment, 450
  of wife abuse, 548–549
Psychological disorders, 554–594
  depression, 562–566
  diversity issues, 593–594
  gender-specificity, 259, 558–562
  problems of diagnosis, 556–557
  social construction of, 566–568
  symptomology, 568–576
  therapy for, 582–593
  treatment issues, 576–582
Psychological research, 24–25, 477
Psychological treatment
  diagnosis, 576–580
  institutional biases in, 582
  practitioner attitudes, 580
  use of medication, 580–582
Psychological well-being
  aging and, 508–509
  childlessness and, 391
  of children, 425–526
  financial security and, 439–440
  at middle age, 492–493
  multiple roles and, 464–465
  of older women, 408–409
Psychology, racism/sexism in, 4–5
Psychology of women
  backlash against feminism, 6–10
  diversity of women and, 23–24
  emergence as field of study, 1–4
  feminist perspectives in, 5–6
  gender distinctions, 18–21
  history of, 4–5
  language and naming in, 21–23
  methods and values in, 11–17
  nonsexist research in, 12–15
  social change and, 24–25
Psychology of Women Division (APA), 3, 5, 16, 449
Psychoneurotic disorders, 483
Psychotropic drugs, 580–582, 582–583
Puberty, 261–263
  body maturation, 274–279
  defined, 263–267
  impact of, 280–286
  menarche, 267–274
  race and class effects, 279–280
Publication bias, 14–15, 72
"Puerto Rican syndrome," 592–593
Punishments, 37, 43–44

Question formulation, 12–13

Race
  adolescent sexuality and, 295
  aging and, 494–495
  cohabitation trends, 366, 368
  contraceptive use and, 291
  economic dependency and, 351

Race (*Cont.):*
face-ism and, 122
in feminist therapy, 489
incest and, 523
menopause and, 485
motherhood and, 416, 418–419
parent-child relationships, 283
professional success, 459–460
puberty and, 279–280
sexual behavior and, 290–291
standards of beauty and, 319–321
status and, 175t, 175–176
in stereotyping, 135–137, 143
weight standards and, 320
woman-headed households and, 415
Racism
effects of, 591
in pornography, 518
in psychology, 4–5
Radical feminism, 6, 337
Radio, 288–289
Rape fantasies, 519
Rape prevention programs, 541–542
Rape trauma syndrome, 540
Rationality, 282
Reality, 106, 585–586
Referent power, 161
Regents scholarships, 86
Reinforcements, 37, 38, 43–44
Reiter, Ashley Melia, 95
Relational roles, 431–432, 495–496
Relationship characteristics
cohabitation, 367–368
of lesbian couples, 363–364
ratings of, 315, 316t
Relationship dynamics
courtship violence, 342, 528
heterosexual, 339–341
lesbian, 341
"pop psych" manuals on, 342–343
Relationship skills, 342–343
Religion, 103t, 103–104, 307, 339, 346–347, 390
Remarriage, 377–378, 474
Repressed memories, 522
Reproductive freedom, 391–396
Reproductive function, depression and, 564–566
Reproductive technology, 396–399
Research
feminist values in, 15–17
limitations on, 365
on menopause, 488, 490
Research design, 12, 13–14, 71–73
"Rest cure," 567
Retirement, 498–499, *500*
Retrospective research, 459, 461
Revaluing women, 65–66
Richards, René, 214–215
Risher, Mary Jo, 421
Roe v. *Wade* (1973), 393
Role(s)
status and, 171–172
Role(s) *(Cont.):*
stereotyping by, 114–115, *128*, 128–129
Role behaviors, 108–109
Role conflict, 463–464
Role models, 257, 447–448
for achievement, 457–458
employed mothers as, 466
Role overload, 463, 464
Role transitions, 492–508
Romance novels, 119–121, 312–313, 326
Romantic love, 312–315
cultural differences, 314–315
as cultural script, 312–313
experience of, *313*, 313–314
lesbianism and, 337
Rough-and-tumble play, 194, 195, 236, 237t

SAGE (Senior Action in a Gay Environment), 511
Same-sex activity, 336
Same-sex parent, 41–42
Same-sex playmates, 238
Sapir, Edward, 21
Satisfaction
of caregiving role, 505
changes in, 357–358
housework and, 431
of lesbian couples, 364–365
in nontraditional work, 461
in second marriages, 378
sexual harassment and, 450
Schema(s), 57, 304
Schema theory, 57
Schematic processing, 58, 59
Schlafly, Phyllis, 9–10
Scholastic Aptitude Test, 86, 93
School(s)
classroom dominance, 87–88, *88*
effects of transitions, 285
gender segregation in, 238–245
gender typing and, 256–257
Scripts, 304, 305t, 324–325
Selective abortion, 397
Selective attention, 151
Selective interpretation, 152
Selective recall, 151–152
Self, sense of, 33–34, *34*
Self-actualization, 55–56
Self-categorization, 155–156
Self-confidence, 52, 88–89, *89*
Self-defeating personality disorder, 576, 577
Self-defense, from wife abuse, 543
Self-esteem
androgynous personality and, 53
body image and, 319
depression and, 563–564
effects of help-seeking on, 176
effects of puberty on, 281–282
images of women and, 101, 103
Self-esteem *(Cont.):*
retirement and, 499
of wife abuse victims, 547
Self-fulfilling prophecies, 82–83, 153–155, 162
Self-identity, 139
Self-improvement programs, 467
Self-perceptions, 181
Self-presentation, 153
Self-selected samples, 465
Seneca Falls Declaration (1848), 3
Separateness, 34–35
Service components of women's work, 435, *436*, 437
Sex
biological determinants, 185–188
distinguished from gender, 18
gender typing and, 66
self-categorization and, 155–156
as social category, *147*, 147–156
status variables, 175t, 175–176
in stereotyping, 136
Sex bias
in diagnoses, 576–580
in drugs prescribed, 580–582
in psychology of women, 2
in testing, 86–87
in therapist attitudes, 580
Sex differentiation
chromosomal anomalies, 201–205
hormonal anomalies, 205–211
Sex education, 318, 329
failures of, 291
power and status issues, 300
teenage pregnancy and, 292–293
Sex manuals, 328, 330, 334
Sex reassignment, 212–214
Sex research, 304–308, *306*, *309*
Sex segregation, 434–435, *436*
Sex stratification, 435
Sex-biased diagnostic labels, 578
"Sex-inappropriate" success, 455
Sexism, 20–21
ageism and, 473–474, 512
caregiving and, 501
in media, 474–475, *476*
status norms and, 177–178
Sexist language, 125–127
Sex-reassignment surgery, 215–216
Sex-role labels, 164, *165*, 166
Sex-selective abortion, 226, 227–228
Sexual aggression, 533, 537
Sexual arousal, 520
Sexual assault
defining, 532–534
frequency of, 534–535
likelihood of, 537–538
perpetrators of, 536–537
prevention of, 540–543
psychological impact of, 538–540

Sexual assault *(Cont.):*
  rape and, 532–543
  risk factors for, 535–536
Sexual desire, 291–292, 402–403
Sexual dimorphism, 186, 263–264
Sexual dysfunction, 327–328
Sexual fantasies, 310, 311
Sexual harassment, 449–451, 461–462
Sexual intercourse, 326–327, 403
Sexual involvement of client and therapist, 588, 589
Sexual orientation, 193, *194*
  of feminist therapists, 589
  personal views of, 337–338
  psychoanalytic theory and, 36
  stereotypes, 130–131
Sexual scripts, 304, 305t, 327–328
Sexuality
  ambivalence about, 322–324
  cultural influences on, 303–304
  desire and pleasure, 324–332
  of disabled women, 321–322
  feminine socialization and, 292
  images of, 119, *120*
  masturbation, 310–311
  men as feminists and, 7
  orgasm, 308–310
  physical attractiveness, 315–322
  pregnancy and, 402–403
  romantic love, 312–315
  social construction of, 329–330
  social contests of, 308–332
  studies of, 304–308, *306*
Sexually transmitted diseases, 328–329
Shell shock, 567
Silencing, 284–285, 329–330
Situational attributions, 132, 154
Size, as status cue, 202–203
Sleep deprivation, 414
Soap operas, 116, 297
Social attributions
  gender and, 132, 134–135
  occupation and, 131–132, *133*, 133–134
  physical attractiveness, 129–130
  sexual orientation, 130–131
Social behaviors, 171–178
Social boundaries, 441
Social categories, *147*, 147–156, 182
Social change, 6, 24–25
Social class
  caregiving and, 501–502
  gender typing and, 255–256, 260
  incest and, 525
  marital expectations and, 349
  menopause and, 489–490
  in stereotyping, 135, 136
  widowhood and, 506
  wife abuse and, 546
Social construction
  of childbirth, 408–410, *410*
  of cyclic mood disorders, 578
  of deviance, 164
  of "female disorders," 566–568
  of gender, 260
  of mental illness, 555, 559–560
  of sexuality, 329–330
Social context
  of aging, 472–478
  in feminist research, 16–17, 23
  gender-related differences, 178
  of menopause, 491–492
  of research, 304–308, *306*
  of wife abuse, 551–552
Social control
  aggression as, 176–177, *177*
  gender and, 146
  by psychotherapy, 583–584
  of weight, 570
Social deviance. *See* Deviance
Social dominance, 148–149, 242–243
Social exchange theory, 355, 356
Social individuality, 65
Social influence(s)
  cultural diversity, 60–61
  dominance and, 242–243
  interaction with traits, 62–63
  on personality, 62
  power and status, *63*, 63–65
  revaluing women and, 65–66
  in social learning theory, 40
Social interaction, 19–20
Social invisibility of older women, 477
Social labels, 252
Social learning theory, 37–42, *39*
Social mechanisms, 241–242
Social myths, 178
Social networks, school, 238–239
Social norms
  adolescent sexuality, 294–295
  against childlessness, 389
  on marriage, 346–347
Social organization, 111
Social policy, 98–99, 466–469
Social position, 49, 99
Social power, 157
  gender and, 161–162
  See also Power
Social reactions to tokens, 446–447
Social rejection, 455
Social roles, 83, 132
"Social Security" (Bolz), 509
Social status
  effect on personality, *63*, 63–65
  sense of self and, 67
  weight standards and, 320
  See also Status
Socialized differences, 451, 452–453
Spatial abilities, 79–80, *80–82*, 82–85, 84t, 198
Spatial-perception tasks, 79
Spatial-visualization tasks, 79
Speck, Richard, 204
Speech disorders, 93–94
Speech production, 94
Speech styles, 241
Sports
  images in, 113–114, *114*, *115*
  self-esteem and, 289
  spatial-skills components of, 83
  tomboyism and, 254
Spouse
  abuse of, 543–544
  choices of, 348–349
Stage theory, 42–44, *44*, 336
Standardized tests, 86–87, 96, 97
Statistical inference, 72
Statistical significance, 14, 70–71
Status, 157
  in gender segregation, 243
  gender stereotyping and, 250–251
  nonverbal cues to, 160–161
  self-categorization and, 155–156
  size as cue to, 202–203
  social behaviors and, 171–178
Status cues, 202–203, 441
Status norm violation, 177–178
Steinem, Gloria, 9
Stereotypes, 20, 105
  about personality, 29
  of aging, 472–473
  "butch" lesbians, 334
  characteristics of, 106
  as cognitive categories, 108–111, 110t
  defined, 106–107
  diagnostic labels and, 556–557
  of disabled women, 321
  of gender-related psychological disorders, 558–559, 559t
  impact on children, 250
  of lesbian couples, 361
  math performance and, 89–90
  measuring, 107–108
  in media, 111–123
  of motherhood, 384–385
  of never-married women, 368–369
  in paid employment, 437
  persistence of, 139–144
  in sexual scripts, 324–325
  social attributions and, 129–132, 134–135
  as social demands, 127–129, *128*
Stereotyping
  agoraphobia and, 575
  of feminists, 8–9
  in gender-differentiated socialization, 229
  group differences, 136–137, *138*
  individual differences, 138–139
  by language, 21
  in psychology of women, 2
  stimulus variables in, 135–136
  of toys, 232–234, *233*
Stigma, 163, 179

Stigmatization
divorce and breakups, 376, 377
of overweight, 569
subordination and, 163–164
Stimulus variables, 135–136
Stress(es)
agoraphobia and, 575
of caregiving role, *504*, 504–505
during divorce, 373
Stress response, 549
Structural-level model of achievement, 468
"Studs," 323–324
Submission, wife abuse and, 551
Subordinates, 63–64, 172
Subordination
internalized by women, 20
in paid employment, 435, 437
psychological consequences, 64
self-categorization and, 155–156
stigmatization and, 163–164
Subtypes, 108–109, 144
Subtyping, 140–141, 142
Success
achievement motivation, 453–454
attributions for, 441–442, 443
fear of, 454–456
Superego, 31
Support networks, 508–509
Supreme Court, 393, 394, 520
Surveys
of lesbian couples, 361–363
of sexual behavior, 305–307, 308, 309
on violence, 516
Symbolic annihilation, 123, 127t, 137, *138*

Talking platypus phenomenon, 442–443
Task Force on Women and Depression (APA), 564
Teasing, 241, 275
Teenage pregnancy, 262
contraceptive use and, *298*, 298–299
feminine socialization and, 292
Television
ads for sanitary products, 271
gender stereotypes in, 250
sexism in, 122–123, 127t
treatment of divorce, 370
violence on, 243, 245
Tentative language, 161
Testability, 30, 36, 41, 45–46
Testes, *189*, 190
Testicular-feminization syndrome, 208–209
Testing, sex bias in, 86–87
Testosterone, 190, 199
Thematic Apperception Test (TAT), 453, 455
Therapists, sex bias of, 580
Thomas, Altamese, 561–562, 590
Thomas, Clarence, 449
Token resistance, 325
Tokenism, 167, 446–447, 457t, 460–461
Tomboyism, 253–254
"Touch privilege," 174
Toys
gender-typed, 83, 84t, 232–234, *233*
influence on behaviors, 257
preferences in, 236–238
Traditional marriage, 350–351, *351*
divorce and, 373–374
male dominance in, 354–355
Traditional script, 305t, 339–340
Transsexualism, 212, 214–216
Transvestites, 215
Truth, Sojourner, 407–408, 416
Turner's syndrome, 201–203
"Turnim-man," 219
Two-person career, 432–433, *433*

Underemployment, 439, 440–441
Unemployment, 439–440, 546
Unger, Rhoda, 25–26
"Unlearning" behaviors, 240
Unpaid work, 428–434
benefits and costs, 433–434
housewives, 428–431
relational work, 431–432
two-person career, 432–433, *433*
U.S. politics, 169–170

Value of males, 224, 250
Value of women, 6, 429–431, 439
Value orientations, 50, 52
Values
effect on research, 17
work roles and, 452
Variability hypothesis, 76
Verbal abilities, *82*, 92–94
Verbal aggression, 245, 528–529, 531
Verbal persuasion, 242
Victim blaming, 152–153
in agoraphobia, 575
in failure to achieve, 467–468
in mental illness, 559
for poverty, 416
in wife abuse, 551–552
Violence, 513–553, 515t
acquaintance rape, 532–543
during courtship, 527–532
courtship and marital, 531–532
incest, 521–527
pornography, 516, 517–521
self-defeating personality disorder and, 577
Violence *(Cont.):*
statistics on, 516
on television, 243, 245
wife abuse, 543–550, *545*
Virgin goddesses, 104
Visual dominance, 161, 162
Vulnerability of displaced homemakers, 433

Weakness, influence strategies and, 340–341
Weight
attitudes toward, 279
prejudice and, 569–570, *570*
pubertal changes, 275–277, *277*
standards of, 318–319, *320*
West, Rebecca, 5
Westinghouse National Science Talent Search, 95
Wharton, Edith, 567
Whorf, Benjamin, 21
Whorfian hypothesis, 21, 322–323
Widowhood, 505–506
Wife abuse
consequences of, 548–549
frequency of, 544–546
perpetrators of, 546–547
prevention of, 549–550
spouse abuse and, 543–544
victims of, 547–548
Woman-headed households, 415–416
Womb envy, 32, 35
Women's movement, 61–62
"Women's professions," 440, 456
Wooley, Helen Thompson, 4
Woolf, Virginia, 567
Work and family roles
balancing, 463–464
benefits of, 464–465
children and, 465–466, *467*
combining, 462–466
midlife changes in, 495–496
Workplace sexism
attributions, 441–442
devaluing performance, 442–443
discrimination and, 443–445
mentors and role models, 447–449
sexual harassment, 449–451
social reactions, 446–447
Workplace social structure, 452

Xanith, 219
XYY and XXY males, 203–204